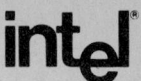

OEM SYSTEMS HANDBOOK

1986

About Our Cover:
The design on our front cover has been created with the purpose of demonstrating to the reader that Intel is a technology leader in developing boards and systems that aid the OEM systems designer. Our MULTIBUS® I and II boards provide the building blocks of open systems architecture that are the key to flexibility that Intel provides to the design engineer for development of MULTIBUS® systems architecture.

Intel Corporation makes no warranty for the use of its products and assumes no responsibility for any errors which may appear in this document nor does it make a commitment to update the information contained herein.

Intel retains all rights to make changes to these specifications at any time, without notice.

Contact your local sales office to obtain the latest specifications before placing your order.

The following are trademarks of Intel Corporation and may only be used to identify Intel Products:

Above, BITBUS, COMMputer, CREDIT, Data Pipeline, GENIUS, i, $\overset{\triangle}{\text{i}}$, ICE, iCEL, iCS, iDBP, iDIS, I²ICE, iLBX, i_m, iMDDX,, iMMX, Insite, Intel, int$_e$l, int$_e$lBOS, Intelevision, int$_e$ligent Identifier, int$_e$ligent Programming, Intellec, Intellink, iOSP, iPDS, iPSC, iRMX, iSBC, iSBX, iSDM, iSXM, KEPROM, Library Manager, MAP-NET, MCS, Megachassis, MICROMAINFRAME, MULTIBUS, MULTICHANNEL, MULTIMODULE, ONCE, OpenNET, PC-BUBBLE, Plug-A-Bubble, PROMPT, Promware, QUEST, QueX, Quick-Pulse Programming, Ripplemode, RMX/80, RUPI, Seamless, SLD, UPI, and VLSiCEL, and the combination of ICE, iCS, iRMX, iSBC, iSBX, MCS, or UPI and a numerical suffix, 4-SITE.

MDS is an ordering code only and is not used as a product name or trademark. MDS® is a registered trademark of Mohawk Data Sciences Corporation.

*MULTIBUS is a patented Intel bus.

Additional copies of this manual or other Intel literature may be obtained from:

Intel Corporation
Literature Distribution
Mail Stop SC6-59
3065 Bowers Avenue
Santa Clara, CA 95051

©INTEL CORPORATION 1985

Table of Contents

CHAPTER 1
MULTIBUS I Architecture
DATA SHEETS
- MULTIBUS System Bus... 1-1
- MULTICHANNEL I/O Bus... 1-11
- iLBX Execution Bus.. 1-21
- iSBX I/O Expansion Bus.. 1-29

APPLICATION NOTES
- AP-28A Intel MULTIBUS Interfacing... 1-39

CHAPTER 2
Single Board Computers
DATA SHEETS
- iSBC 80/10B Single Board Computer... 2-1
- iSBC 80/20-4 Single Board Computer.. 2-8
- iSBC 80/24A Single Board Computer... 2-15
- iSBC 80/30 Single Board Computer.. 2-24
- iSBC 86/05A Single Board Computer... 2-32
- iSBC 86/14 and iSBC 86/30 Single Board Computer............................... 2-42
- iSBC 86/35 Single Board Computer.. 2-50
- iSBC 88/25 Single Board Computer.. 2-60
- iSBC 88/40A Measurement and Control Computer.................................. 2-68
- iSBC 186/03A Single Board Computer.. 2-76
- iSBC 286/10A Single Board Computer.. 2-87
- iSBC 286/12 Single Board Computer... 2-97
- iSBC 386/20 Single Board Computer Starter Kit................................. 2-108

APPLICATION NOTES
- AP-114 Using the iSBC 88/40 Measurement and Control Computer in PID Applications................ 2-115

ARTICLE REPRINTS
- AR-229 Enchanced μC Boards Strengthen Factory and Office Controllers.......................... 2-137
- AR-267 Choosing a Bus For Control... 2-144
- AR-268 Standard Buses Capture Fancy of Most OEM's............................. 2-150

BENCHMARKS
- AR-387 Benchmarking UNIX Systems.. 2-155

RELIABILITY REPORTS
- RR-53 iSBC 86/XX Single Board Computers and iSBC 304 MULTIMODULE Board Reliability............ 2-170

CHAPTER 3
High Speed Math Boards
DATA SHEETS
- iSBC 337A MULTIMODULE Numeric Data Processor.................................. 3-1
- iSBX 331 Fixed/Floating Point Math MULTIMODULE Board.......................... 3-9

CHAPTER 4
Memory Expansion Boards
DATA SHEETS
- iBCK 10-1 and iBCK 10-4 Intel Bubble Cassette System Production Kit........... 4-1
- iBCK 12 Intel Bubble Cassette Prototype Kit................................... 4-5

Table of Contents

CHAPTER 4 (Continued)
Memory Expansion Boards
DATA SHEETS
iPCB 76 Bubble Memory Expansion... 4-7
iSBC 012B Ram Memory Board.. 4-10
iSBC 012C ECC Ram Boards... 4-12
iSBC 012CX, 010CX, and 020CX iLBX Ram Boards.................................. 4-16
iSBC 012EX, 010EX, 020EX, 040EX High Performance Ram Boards.................. 4-21
iSBC 028A/056A Ram Memory Boards.. 4-25
iSBC 254S Bubble Memory Board... 4-28
iSBC 264 Magnetic Bubble Memory Board... 4-31
iSBC 300 32K Byte Ram Expansion Module.. 4-35
iSBC 300A 32K Byte Ram MULTIMODULE Board...................................... 4-44
iSBC 301 4K Byte MULTIMODULE Board.. 4-39
iSBC 302 8K Byte MULTIMODULE Ram.. 4-42
iSBC 304 128K Byte Ram MULTIMODULE Board...................................... 4-44
iSBC 307 128K Byte Ram MULTIMODULE Board with Parity.......................... 4-47
iSBC 314 512K Byte Ram MULTIMODULE Board...................................... 4-50
iSBC 340 16K Byte EPROM Expansion Module...................................... 4-35
iSBC 341 28-Pin MULTIMODULE EPROM... 4-54
iSBC 428 Universal Site Memory Expansion Board................................ 4-56
iSBC 464 641K Byte EPROM Expansion Board...................................... 4-60
iSBX 251 and 251C Bubble Memory MULTIMODULE Board............................. 4-63
iSBX 258 Interface MULTIMODULE For Intel Bubble Cassette System............... 4-68

RELIABILITY REPORTS
RR-54 Series C/CX Memory Board Reliability.................................... 4-72

CHAPTER 5
Peripheral Controllers
DATA SHEETS
iSBC 208 Flexible Diskette Controller... 5-1
iSBC 214 Peripheral Controller Subsystem...................................... 5-5
iSBC 215 Generic Winchester Controller.. 5-8
iSBC 220 SMD Disk Controller.. 5-13
iSBC 226 High Performance SMD Controller...................................... 5-17
iSBX 217C 1/4-inch Tape Drive Interface MULTIMODULE Board..................... 5-20
iSBX 218A Flexible Disk Controller.. 5-24

CHAPTER 6
Graphics
DATA SHEETS
iSBC 186/78A Intelligent Video Graphics Subsystem............................. 6-1
iSBX 270 Alpha-Numeric Display Controller..................................... 6-10
iSBX 275 Video Graphics Controller.. 6-14
iVDI 720 Graphics Virtual Device Interpreter.................................. 6-18

CHAPTER 7
Digital and Analog I/O Expansion
DATA SHEETS
iSBC 517 Combination I/O Expansion Boards..................................... 7-1
iSBC 519 Programmable I/O Expansion Boards.................................... 7-5

Table of Contents

CHAPTER 7 (Continued)
Digital and Analog I/O Expansion
DATA SHEETS
- iSBC 556 Optically Isolated I/O Board 7-9
- iSBC 569 Intelligent Digital Controller 7-11
- iSBX 311 Analog Input MULTIMODULE Board 7-16
- iSBX 328 Analog Output MULTIMODULE Board 7-20
- iSBX 350 Parallel I/O MULTIMODULE Board 7-24
- iSBX 351 Serial I/O MULTIMODULE Board 7-28
- iSBX 352 Bit Serial Communications MULTIMODULE Board 7-34
- iSBX 354 Dual Channel Serial I/O MULTIMODULE Board 7-40
- iSBX 488 GPIB MULTIMODULE Board 7-45

APPLICATION NOTES
- AP-96 Designing iSBX MULTIMODULE Boards 7-49

CHAPTER 8
Communication Controllers
DATA SHEETS
- iDCM 911-1 INTELLINK ETHERNET Cluster Module 8-1
- iSBC 88/45 Advanced Communications Computer 8-3
- iSBC 186/51 Communicating Computer 8-12
- iSBC 188/48 Advanced Communications Controller 8-25
- iSBC 188/56 Advanced Communicating Computer 8-35
- iSBC 534 Four Channel Communications Expansion Board 8-44
- iSBC 544 Intelligent Communications Controller 8-48
- iSBC 550 Ethernet Communications Controller 8-55
- iSBC 552/iSXM 552 Ethernet Communication Engine Products 8-59
- iSBC 554 MAP Communication Engine 8-68
- iSBC 561, SOEMI (Serial OEM Interface) Controller board 8-75
- iSBC 570, 576, 577 Intel Speech Transaction Family 8-80
- iSBC 570 Speech Transaction Development Kit 8-85
- iSBC 576 Speech Transaction Board 8-88
- iSBC 577 Speech Transaction Recognition Chip Set 8-93
- iSBC 580 MULTICHANNEL Bus to iLBX Bus Interface 8-94
- iSBC 589 Intelligent DMA Controller 8-98

CHAPTER 9
Communication Software
- iNA 960 Network Software 9-1
- iRMX Networking Software 9-13
- XENIX Networking Software 9-19

CHAPTER 10
System Packaging and Power Supplies
DATA SHEETS
- iCS 80 Industrial Chassis Kit 10-1
- iSBC 604/614 Modular Cardcage Assemblies 10-6
- iSBC 608/618 Cardcage 10-8
- iSBC 640 Power Supply 10-12
- iSBC 660 Chassis 10-14
- iSBC 661 System Chassis 10-17

Table of Contents

CHAPTER 10 (Continued)
System Packaging and Power Supplies
DATA SHEETS
iSBC 665 System Chassis.. 10-21
iSYP 384 System Chassis.. 10-23

CHAPTER 11
BITBUS Architecture
DATA SHEETS
Introduction 11-1
8044 BITBUS Enhanced Microcontroller..................................... 11-5
iRCB 44/10 BITBUS Digital I/O Remote Controller Board.................. 11-26
iRCB 44/20 Analog I/O Remote Controller Board.......................... 11-36
iSBX 344 BITBUS Intelligent MULTIMODULE Board......................... 11-37
APPLICATION NOTES
AP-224 BITBUS Interconnect: From Flight Simulation To
  Process Control.. 11-46
AP-251 Development and Support of BITBUS NETWORKS
  Using The Intel Personal Development System........................... 11-54
ARTICLE REPRINTS
AR-347 BITBUS Promises to Standarize Control............................ 11-78
AR-351 Intel's BITBUS Microcontroller Interconnect — A Modern
  Method of Robot Communication... 11-84
AR-358 Serial Bus Simplifies Distributed Control........................ 11-91
RELIABILITY REPORTS
RR-57 iSBX 344 BITBUS Controller MULTIMODULE Board And
  iRCB 44/10 BITBUS Remote Controller Reliability....................... 11-96

CHAPTER 12
Distributed Control Software
DATA SHEETS
iDCX 51 Distributed Control Executive................................... 12-1
iDCX 96 Distributed Control Executive................................... 12-8
iRMX 510 iDCM Support Package... 12-16
ARTICLE REPRINTS
AR-410 Real-time Executive Juggles Multicontrol Systems
  Like A Pro.. 12-20

CHAPTER 13
Integrated Microcomputer Systems
FACT SHEETS
System 310 Microcomputer System... 13-1
System 380 Microcomputer System... 13-6
310 AP XENIX Systems.. 13-12
311 Peripheral Expansion Sub-system..................................... 13-14
APEX Advanced Processor Extension Series................................ 13-16
DATA SHEETS
iSXM Series Systems Extension Modules................................... 13-18
RELIABILITY REPORTS
System 310 Reliability... 13-20

Table of Contents

CHAPTER 14
System Software
DATA SHEETS
- iRMX 86 Operating System ... 14-1
- iRMX 286 Operating System ... 14-20
- iSDM 86 System Debug Monitor ... 14-40
- iSDM 286 System Debug Monitor ... 14-45
FACT SHEETS
- iDIS Database Information System ... 14-49
- iRMX Language ... 14-51
- iRMX Operating System ... 14-56
- iRMX 286/386 Software System ... 14-62
- OpenNET Product Family XENIX Networking Software ... 14-64
- XENIX*Languages ... 14-69
- XENIX* 3.0 Operating System ... 14-73
- XENIX* 286 Application Development Software ... 14-79

CHAPTER 15
MULTIBUS II Architecture
DATA SHEETS
- MULTIBUS II iLBX II Local Bus Extension ... 15-1
- MULTIBUS II iPSB Parallel System Bus ... 15-7
- MULTIBUS II iSSB Serial System Bus ... 15-20
ARTICLE REPRINTS
- AR-350 Message Passing Supports Multiple Processor Design ... 15-23
- AR-356 Multiprocessor Bus is Ready To Meet 32-Bit Applications of The Future ... 15-30

CHAPTER 16
MULTIBUS II Products
DATA SHEETS
- iRMX 86 MULTIBUS II Support Package ... 16-1
- iSBC 186/224 High Performance MultiPeripheral Controller ... 16-4
- iSBC 286/100 MULTIBUS II Single Board Computer ... 16-8
- iSBC 386/100 PP and MEM 2xx ... 16-16
- iSBC MEM/312, 310, 320, 340 Cache-based MULTIBUS II Ram Boards ... 16-22
- iSBC-PKG/606, iSBC PKG/609 MULTIBUS II Cardcage Assemblies ... 16-26
- iSBC-PKG/902, iSBC PKG/903 MULTIBUS II iLBX II Backplane ... 16-30
- iSBC CSM/001 Central Services Module ... 16-33
- iSBC LNK/001 MULTIBUS II to MULTIBUS I Link ... 16-38
FACT SHEETS
- iSYP/500-PP MULTIBUS II System Chassis ... 16-43
- MULTIBUS II Starter System ... 16-45
APPLICATION NOTES
- AP-256 MULTIBUS II Interfacing Using the BAC and MIC ... 16-47
ARTICLE REPRINTS
- AR-411 MULTIBUS II Products Exploit Advanced Bus Features ... 16-99

CHAPTER 17
Service and Support
- Open Systems Maintenance Agreement Service ... 17-1

Table of Contents

CHAPTER 17 (Continued)
Service and Support
- Software Support Contract 17-5
- Training Workshop 17-11
- iMBX 100/110/120/130 MULTIBUS Exchange Hardware
  Subscription Service 17-15
- INSITE User's Program Library 17-17
- iRUG Description 17-21

Alphanumeric Index

APEX Advanced Processor Extension Series	13-16
iBCK 10-1 Intel Bubble Cassette System Production Kit	4-1
iBCK 10-4 Intel Bubble Cassette System Production Kit	4-1
iBCK 12 Intel Bubble Cassette Prototype Kit	4-5
iCS Industrial Chassis Kit	10-1
iDCM 911-1 INTELLINK™ ETHERNET™ Cluster Module	8-1
iDCX 51 Distributed Control Executive	12-1
iDCX 96 Distributed Control Executive	12-8
iDIS Database Information System	14-49
iLBX Execution Bus	1-21
iNA 960 Network Software	9-1
iPCB-76 Bubble Memory Expansion	4-7
iRCB 44/10 BITBUS Digital I/O Remote Controlled Board	11-26
iRCB 44/20 Analog I/O Remote Controller Board	11-36
iRMX Language	14-51
iRMX Networking Software	9-13
iRMX Operating System	14-56
iRMX 86 MULTIBUS II Support Package	16-1
iRMX 86 Operating System	14-1
iRMX 286 Operating System	14-20
iRMX 286/386 Software System	14-62
iRMX 510 iDCM Support Package	12-16
iSBC CSM/001 Central Services Module	16-33
iSBC LNK/001 MULTIBUS II to MULTIBUS I Link	16-38
iSBC MEM/312, 310, 320, 340, Cache-based MULTIBUS II Ram Boards	16-22
iSBC pkg 606/609 MULTIBUS II Cardcage Assemblies	16-26
iSBC pkg 902/iSBC pkg 903 MULTIBUS II iLBX Backplane	16-30
iSBC 010CX iLBX Ram Board	4-16
iSBC 010EX High Performance Ram Board	4-21
iSBC 012B Ram Memory Board	4-10
iSBC 012C ECC Ram Board	4-12
iSBC 012CX iLBX Ram Board	4-16
iSBC 012EX High Performance Ram Board	4-21
iSBC 020CX iLBX Ram Board	4-16
iSBC 020EX High Performance Ram Board	4-21
iSBC 028A Ram Memory Board	4-25
iSBC 028CX iLBX Ram Board	4-16
iSBC 040EX High Performance Ram Board	4-21
iSBC 056A ECC Ram Board	4-25
iSBC 80/10B Single Board Computer	2-1
iSBC 80/20-4 Single Board Computer	2-8
iSBC 80/24A Single Board Computer	2-15
iSBC 80/30 Single Board Computer	2-24
iSBC 86/05A Single Board Computer	2-32
iSBC 86/14 Single Board Computer	2-42
iSBC 86/30 Single Board Computer	2-42
iSBC 86/35 Single Board Computer	2-50
iSBC 88/25 Single Board Computer	2-60
iSBC 88/40A Measurement and Control Computer	2-68
iSBC 88/45 Advanced Data Communications Processor Board (3-Channel)	8-3
iSBC 186/03A Single Board Computer	2-76

Alphanumeric Index

iSBC 186/51 Communicating Computer	8-12
iSBC 186/78A Intelligent Video Graphics Subsystem	6-1
iSBC 186/224 High Performance MultiPeripheral Controller	16-4
iSBC 188/48 Advanced Communications Computer (8-Channel)	8-25
iSBC 188/56 Advanced Communicating Computer	8-35
iSBC 208 Flexible Diskette Controller	5-1
iSBC 214 Peripheral Controller Subsystem	5-5
iSBC 215 Generic Winchester Controller	5-8
iSBC 220 SMD Disk Controller	5-13
iSBC 226 High Performance SMD Controller	5-17
iSBC 254S Bubble Memory Board	4-28
iSBC 264 Magnetic Bubble Memory Board	4-31
iSBC 286/10A Single Board Computer	2-87
iSBC 286/12 Single Board Computer	2-97
iSBC 286/100 MULTIBUS Single Board Computer	16-8
iSBC 300 32K Byte Ram Expansion Module	4-35
iSBC 300A 32K Byte Ram MULTIMODULE board	4-44
iSBC 301 4K Byte MULTIMODULE Board	4-39
iSBC 302 8K Byte MULTIMODULE Ram	4-42
iSBC 304 128K Byte Ram MULTIMODULE Board	4-44
iSBC 307 128K Byte Ram MULTIMODULE Board with Parity	4-47
iSBC 314 512K Byte RAM MULTIMODULE Board	4-50
iSBC 337A MULTIMODULE Numeric Data Processor	3-1
iSBC 340 16K Byte EPROM Expansion Module	4-35
iSBC 341 28-Pin MULTIMODULE EPROM	4-54
iSBC 386/20 Single Board Computer Starter Kit	2-108
iSBC 386/100 PP and MEM 2XX	16-16
iSBC 428 Universal Site Memory Expansion board	4-56
iSBC 464 641K Byte EPROM Expansion Board	4-60
iSBC 517 Combination I/O Expansion Boards	7-1
iSBC 519 Programmable I/O Expansion Boards	7-5
iSBC 534 Four Channel Communication Expansion Board	8-44
iSBC 544 Intelligent Communication Controller (4-Channel)	8-48
iSBC 550 Ethernet Communications Controller	8-55
iSBC 552 Ethernet Communications Engine Product	8-59
iSBC 554 MAP Communication Engine	8-68
iSBC 556 Optically Isolated I/O Board	7-9
iSBC 561 SOEMI (Serial OEM Interface) Controller Board	8-75
iSBC 569 Intelligent Digital Controller	7-11
iSBC 570, 576, 577 Intel Speech Transaction Family	8-80
iSBC 570 Speech Transaction Development Set	8-85
iSBC 576 Speech Transaction Board	8-88
iSBC 577 Speech Transaction Recognition Chip Set	8-93
iSBC 580 MULTICHANNEL Bus To iLBX Bus Interface	8-94
iSBC 589 Intelligent DMA Controller	8-98
iSBC 604 Modular Cardcage Assembly	10-6
iSBC 608 Cardcage	10-8
iSBC 614 Modular Cardcage Assembly	10-6
iSCB 618 Cardcage	10-8
iSBC 640 Power Supply	10-12
iSBC 660 System Chassis	10-14

Alphanumeric Index

iSBC 661 System Chassis.. 10-17
iSBC 665 System Chassis.. 10-21
iSBX I/O Expansion Bus... 1-29
iSBX 217C 1/4-inch Tape Drive Interface MULTIMODULE Board................... 5-20
iSBX 218A Flexible Disk Controller... 5-24
iSBX 251 Bubble Memory Board... 4-63
iSBX 251C Bubble Memory Board.. 4-63
iSBX 258 Interface MULTIMODULE for Intel Bubble Cassette System............ 4-68
iSBX 270 Alpha-Numeric Display Controller.................................. 6-10
iSBX 275 Video Graphics Controller... 6-14
iSBX 311 Analog Input MULTIMODULE Board.................................... 7-16
iSBX 328 Analog Output MULTIMODULE Expansion Board......................... 7-20
iSBX 331 Fixed/Floating Point Math MULTIMODULE Board....................... 3-9
iSBX 350 Parallel I/O MULTIMODULE Board.................................... 7-24
iSBX 351 Serial I/O Bubble Memory MULTIMODULE Board........................ 4-63
iSBX 251C Bubble Memory MULTIMODULE Board.................................. 4-63
iSBX 352 Bit Serial Communications MULTIMODULE Board....................... 7-34
iSBX 354 Dual Channel Serial I/O MULTIMODULE Board......................... 7-40
iSBX 488 GPIB MULTIMODULE Board.. 7-45
iSDM 86 System Debug Monitor... 14-40
iSDM 286 iAPX 286 System Debug Monitor..................................... 14-45
iSYP 384 System Chassis.. 10-23
iSYP/500-PP MULTIBUS II System Chassis..................................... 16-43
iSXM 552 Ethernet Communications Engine Product............................ 8-59
iVDI 720 Graphics Virtual Device Interpreter............................... 6-18
iXSM Series Extension Modules.. 13-18
MULTIBUS System Bus.. 1-1
MULTIBUS II iLBX II Local Bus Expansion.................................... 15-1
MULTIBUS II iPSB Parallel System Bus....................................... 15-7
MULTIBUS II iSSB Serial System Bus... 15-20
MULTIBUS II Starter System... 16-45
MULTICHANNEL I/O Bus... 1-11
OpenNET Product Family XENIX Networking Software........................... 14-64
System 310 Microcomputer System.. 13-1
System 380 Microcomputer Systems... 13-6
XENIX Languages.. 14-69
XENIX Networking Software.. 9-19
XENIX 286 Application Development Software................................. 14-79
XENIX 3.0 Operating System... 14-73
310 AP XENIX Systems... 13-12
311 Peripheral Expansion Sub-System.. 13-14
8044 BITBUS Enhanced Microcontroller....................................... 11-5

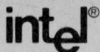

CUSTOMER SUPPORT

CUSTOMER SUPPORT

Customer Support is Intel's complete support service that provides Intel customers with Customer Training, Software Support and Hardware Support.

After a customer purchases any system hardware or software product, service and support become major factors in determining whether that product will continue to meet a customer's expectations. Such support requires an international support organization and a breadth of programs to meet a variety of customer needs. Intel's extensive customer support includes factory repair services as well as worldwide field service offices providing hardware repair services, software support services and customer training classes.

HARDWARE SUPPORT

Hardware Support Services provides maintenance on Intel supported products at board and system level. Both field and factory services are offered. Services include several types of field maintenance agreements, installation and warranty services, hourly contracted services (factory return for repair) and specially negotiated support agreements for system integrators and large volume end-users having unique service requirements. For more information contact your local Intel Sales Office.

SOFTWARE SUPPORT

Software Support Service provides maintenance on software packages via software support contracts which include subscription services, information phone support, and updates. Consulting services can be arranged for on-site assistance at the customer's location for both short-term and long-term needs. For complex products such as NDS II or I²ICE, orientation/installation packages are available through membership in Insite User's Library, where customer-submitted programs are catalogued and made available for a minimum fee to members. For more information contact your local Intel Sales Office.

CUSTOMER TRAINING

Customer Training provides workshops at customer sites (by agreement) and on a regularly scheduled basis at Intel's facilities. Intel offers a breadth of workshops on microprocessors, operating systems and programming languages, etc. For more information on these classes contact the Training Center nearest you.

TRAINING CENTER LOCATIONS

To obtain a complete catalog of our workshops, call the nearest Training Center in your area.

Boston	(617) 692-1000	London	(0793) 696-000
Chicago	(312) 310-5700	Munich	(089) 5389-1
San Francisco	(415) 940-7800	Paris	(01) 687-22-21
Washington, D.C.	(301) 474-2878	Stockholm	(468) 734-01-00
Israel	(972) 349-491-099	Milan	39-2-82-44-071
Tokyo	03-437-6611	Benelux (Rotterdam)	(10) 21-23-77
Osaka (Call Tokyo)	03-437-6611	Copenhagen	(1) 198-033
Toronto, Canada	(416) 675-2105	Hong Kong	5-215311-7

MULTIBUS® I Architecture 1

MULTIBUS® SYSTEM BUS

- **IEEE 796 industry standard system bus**
- **Supports multiple processor systems with multi-master bus structure**
- **8-bit, 16-bit, and 32-bit devices share the same MULTIBUS® system resources**
- **Foundation of Intel's Total System Architecture: MULTIBUS,® iLBX,™ MULTICHANNEL™, BITBUS™ and iSBX™ buses**
- **16 Mbyte addressing capability**
- **Bus bandwidth of up to 10 megabytes per second**
- **Supported by a complete family of single board computers, memory, digital and analog I/O, peripheral controllers, graphics and speech recognition, packaging and software**
- **Supported by over 200 vendors providing over 2000 compatible products**

The MULTIBUS® System bus is one of a family of standard bus structures resident within Intel's total system architecture. The MULTIBUS interface is a general purpose system bus structure containing all the necessary signal lines to allow various system components to interact with one another. This device interaction is built upon the master-slave concept. The "handshaking" between master and slave devices allows modules of different speeds to use the MULTIBUS interface and allows data rates of up to 5 million transfers per second. The MULTIBUS system bus can support multiple master devices (16) on a 18 inch backplane and can directly address up to 16 megabytes of memory. As a non-proprietary, standard system bus, the MULTIBUS interface has become the most prominent 8/16-bit microcomputer system bus in the industry with over 200 vendors supplying over 2000 MULTIBUS compatible products. Its success as the industry standard has been reinforced by adoption of the MULTIBUS specification by the Institute of Electrical and Electronic Engineers—(IEEE 796 System Backplane Bus). MULTIBUS-based systems have been designed into applications, such as, industrial automation and control, office systems and word processing, graphics systems and CAD/CAM, telecommunications systems and distributed processing.

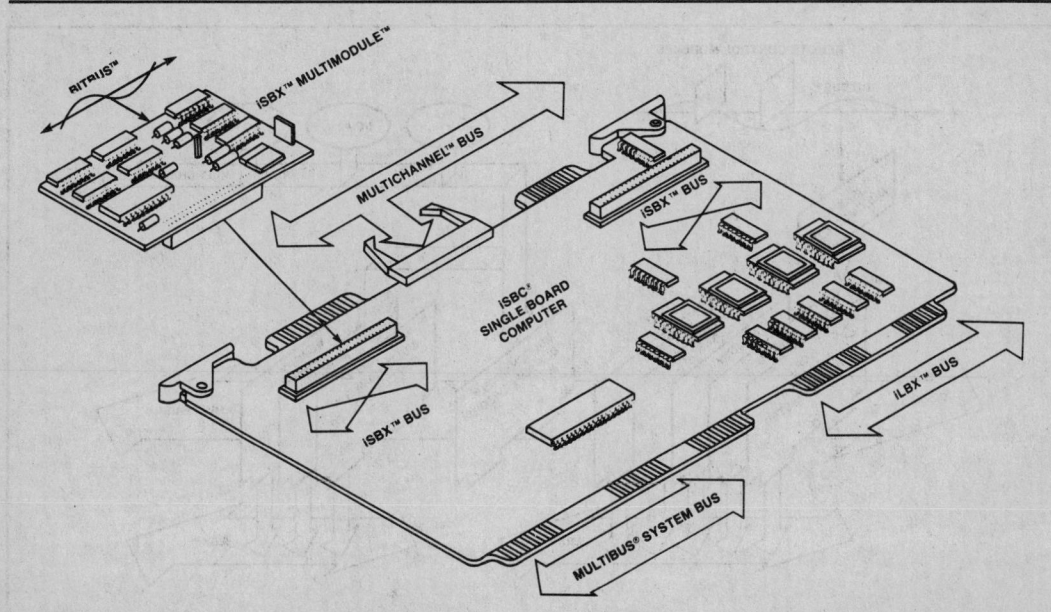

MULTIBUS® SYSTEM BUS

FUNCTIONAL DESCRIPTION

Architectural Overview

The MULTIBUS® system bus is the physical framework and the conceptual foundation of Intel's total system architecture. It is a general purpose system bus used in conjunction with the single board computer concept to provide a flexible mechanism for inter-module processing, control and communication. The MULTIBUS interface supports modular CPU, memory and I/O expansion in flexible, cost effective microcomputer system configurations. These configurations implement single board computers and expansion modules in a multiple processor approach to enhance system performance. This enhanced performance is achieved through partitioning of overall system functions into tasks that each of several processors can handle individually. When new system functions are added (peripherals) more processing power can be applied to handle them without impacting existing processor tasks.

Structural Features

The MULTIBUS interface is an asynchronous, multiprocessing system bus designed to perform 8-bit and 16-bit transfers between single board computers, memory and I/O expansion boards. Its interface structure consists of 24 address lines, 16 data lines, 12 control lines, 9 interrupt lines, and 6 bus exchange lines. These signal lines are implemented on single board computers and a mating backplane in the form of two edge connectors resident on 6.75" × 12.00" form factor PC boards. The primary 86-pin P1 connector contains all MULTIBUS signal lines except the four address extension lines. The auxiliary 60-pin P2 connector contains the four MULTIBUS address extension lines, and reserves the remaining 56 pins for implementing the iLBX™ Execution Bus into the MULTIBUS system architecture.

Bus Elements

The MULTIBUS system bus supports three device categories: 1) Master, 2) Slave, 3) Intelligent Slave.

A bus master device is any module which has the ability to control the bus. This ability is not limited to only one master device. The MULTIBUS interface is capable of supporting multiple masters on the same system through bus exchange logic. Once access has been acquired by a master device, it has a period of exclusive control to affect data transfers through a generation of command signals, address signals and memory or I/O addresses.

A bus slave device is a module that decodes the address lines on the MULTIBUS and acts upon the command signals from the bus masters. Slave devices are not capable of controlling the MULTIBUS interface.

The intelligent slave has the same bus interface attributes as the slave device but also incorporates an on-

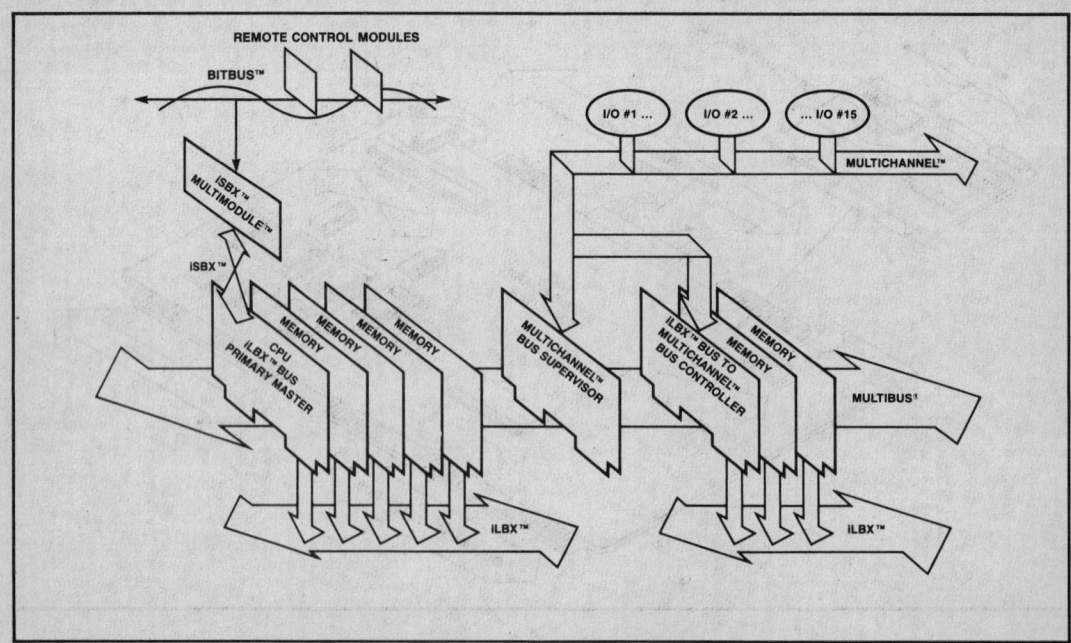

Figure 1. MULTIBUS® System Architecture

MULTIBUS® SYSTEM BUS

board microprocessor to control on-board memory and I/O tasks. This combination of on-board processor, memory and I/O allow the intelligent slave to complete on-board operations without MULTIBUS access.

Bus Interface/Signal Line Descriptions

The MULTIBUS system bus signal lines are grouped into five classes based on the functions they perform: 1) control lines, 2) address and inhibit lines, 3) data lines, 4) interrupt lines, 5) bus exchange lines. Figure 2 shows the implementation of these signal lines.

The MULTIBUS control lines are broken down into five sub-groups: clock signals (2), commands (4), acknowledge (1), initialize (1), and lock (1). The two clock signals provide for the generation of a master clock for the system and the synchronization of bus arbitration logic. The four command lines are the communications links between the bus masters and bus slaves, specifying types of operations to be performed such as reads or writes from memory or I/O. The transfer acknowledge line is the slave's acknowledgement that a requested action of the master is complete. The initialize signal is generated to reset the entire system to a known state. The lock signal is used by an active bus master to lock dual-ported for mutual exclusion.

The address and inhibit lines are made up of 24 address lines, two inhibit lines, and one byte control line. The 24 address lines are signal lines used to carry the address of the memory location or the I/O device that is being referenced. These 24 lines allow a maximum of 16 million bytes of memory to be accessed. When addressing an I/O device, sixteen address lines are used to address a maximum of 64 thousand devices. The two inhibit lines are used to allow different types of memory (RAM, ROM, etc.) having the same memory address to be accessed in a preferred priority arrangement. The byte control line is used to select the upper byte of a 16-bit word in systems incorporating 16-bit memory and I/O modules.

The MULTIBUS interface supports sixteen bi-directional data lines to transmit or receive information to or from a memory location or an I/O port.

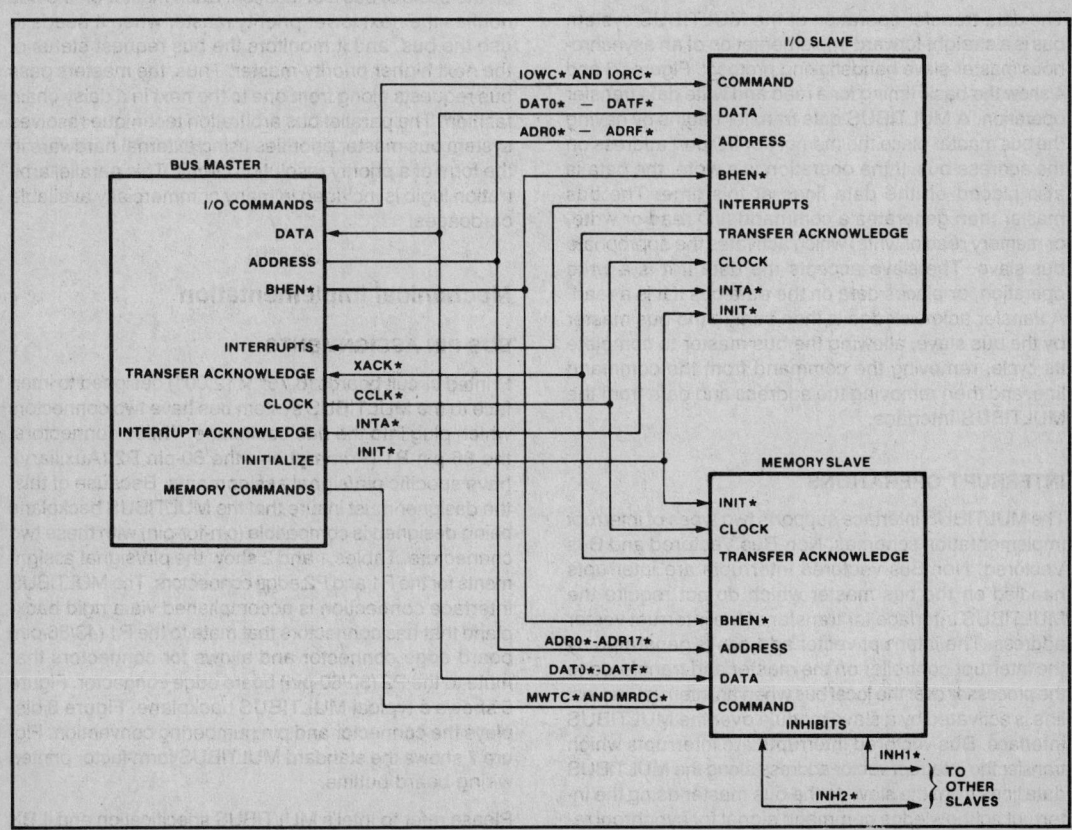

Figure 2. MULTIBUS® Interface Signal Lines

MULTIBUS® SYSTEM BUS

The MULTIBUS interrupt lines consist of eight interrupt request lines and one interrupt acknowledge line. Interrupts are requested by activating one of the eight interrupt request lines. The interrupt acknowledge signal is generated by the bus master when an interrupt request is received. It effectively freezes interrupt status and requests the placement of the interrupt vector address onto the data lines. There are six bus exchange lines that support two bus arbitration schemes on the MULTIBUS system bus. A bus master gains control of the bus through the manipulation of these signals. The bus request, bus priority, bus busy, and bus clock signals provide for a slot dependent priority scheme to resolve bus master contention on the MULTIBUS interface. Use of the common bus request signal line can save arbitration time by providing for a higher priority path to gain control of the system bus.

Bus Operation Protocol

DATA TRANSFER OPERATION

The data transfer operation of the MULTIBUS system bus is a straight-forward implementation of an asynchronous master-slave handshaking protocol. Figures 3 and 4 show the basic timing for a read and write data transfer operation. A MULTIBUS data transfer begins by having the bus master place the memory or I/O port address on the address bus. If the operation is a write, the data is also placed on the data lines at this time. The bus master then generates a command (I/O read or write, or memory read or write) which activates the appropriate bus slave. The slave accepts the data if it is a write operation, or places data on the data bus if it is a read. A transfer acknowledge is then sent to the bus master by the bus slave, allowing the bus master to complete its cycle, removing the command from the command line, and then removing the address and data from the MULTIBUS interface.

INTERRUPT OPERATIONS

The MULTIBUS interface supports two types of interrupt implementation schemes, Non-Bus Vectored and Bus Vectored. Non-Bus vectored interrupts are interrupts handled on the bus master which do not require the MULTIBUS interface for transfer of the interrupt vector address. The interrupt vector address is generated by the interrupt controller on the master and transfered to the processor over the local bus when an interrupt request line is activated by a slave module over the MULTIBUS interface. Bus vectored interrupts are interrupts which transfer the interrupt vector address along the MULTIBUS data lines from the slave to the bus master using the interrupt acknowledge command signal for synchronization. When an interrupt request occurs, the interrupt control logic on the bus master interrupts the processor, generating an interrupt acknowledge command that freezes the interrupt logic on the bus for priority resolution and locks the MULTIBUS system bus. After the bus master selects the highest priority active interrupt request lines, a set of interrupt sequences allow the bus slave to put its interrupt vector address on the data lines. This address is used as a pointer to interrupt the service routine.

BUS EXCHANGE TECHNIQUES

The MULTIBUS system bus can accommodate several bus masters on the same system, each one taking control of the bus as it needs to affect data transfers. The bus masters request bus control through a bus exchange sequence.

The MULTIBUS interface provides for two bus exchange priority techniques: a serial technique and a parallel technique. In a serially arbitrated MULTIBUS system, requests for system bus access are ordered by priority on the basis of bus slot location. Each master on the bus notifies the next lower priority master when it needs to use the bus, and it monitors the bus request status of the next higher priority-master. Thus, the masters pass bus requests along from one to the next in a daisy chain fashion. The parallel bus arbitration technique resolves system bus master priorities using external hardware in the form of a priority resolution circuit. This parallel arbitration logic is included in many commercially available cardcages.

Mechanical Implementation

BUS PIN ASSIGNMENTS

Printed circuit boards (6.75″ × 12.00″) designed to interface to the MULTIBUS system bus have two connectors which plug into the bus backplane. These connectors, the 86-pin P1 (Primary) and the 60-pin P2 (Auxiliary), have specific pin/signal assignments. Because of this, the designer must insure that the MULTIBUS backplane being designed is compatible (pin-for-pin) with these two connectors. Tables 1 and 2 show the pin/signal assignments for the P1 and P2 edge connectors. The MULTIBUS interface connection is accomplished via a rigid backplane that has connectors that mate to the P1 (43/86-pin) board edge connector and allows for connectors that mate to the P2 (30/60-pin) board edge connector. Figure 5 shows a typical MULTIBUS backplane. Figure 6 displays the connector and pin numbering convention. Figure 7 shows the standard MULTIBUS form-factor printed wiring board outline.

Please refer to Intel's MULTIBUS specification and iLBX bus specification for more detailed information.

MULTIBUS® SYSTEM BUS

Table 1. MULTIBUS® Pin/Signal Assignment — (P1)

	Pin	(Component Side)		Pin	(Circuit Side)	
		Mnemonic	Description		Mnemonic	Description
Power Supplies	1	GND	Signal GND	2	GND	Signal GND
	3	+5V	+5Vdc	4	+5V	+5Vdc
	5	+5V	+5Vdc	6	+5V	+5Vdc
	7	+12V	+12Vdc	8	+12V	+12Vdc
	9		Reserved, bussed	10		Reserved, bussed
	11	GND	Signal GND	12	GND	Signal GND
Bus Controls	13	BCLK*	Bus Clock	14	INIT*	Initialize
	15	BPRN*	Bus Pri. In	16	BPRO*	Bus Pri. Out
	17	BUSY*	Bus Busy	18	BREQ*	Bus Request
	19	MRDC*	Mem Read Cmd	20	MWTC*	Mem Write Cmd
	21	IORC*	I/O Read Cmd	22	IOWC*	I/O Write Cmd
	23	XACK*	XFER Acknowledge	24	INH1*	Inhibit 1 (disable RAM)
Bus Controls and Address	25	LOCK*	Lock	26	INH2*	Inhibit 2 (disable PROM or ROM)
	27	BHEN*	Byte High Enable	28	AD10*	
	29	CBRQ*	Common Bus Request	30	AD11*	Address
	31	CCLK*	Constant Clk	32	AD12*	Bus
	33	INTA*	Intr Acknowledge	34	AD13*	
Interrupts	35	INT6*	Parallel	36	INT7*	Parallel
	37	INT4*	Interrupt	38	INT5*	Interrupt
	39	INT2*	Requests	40	INT3*	Requests
	41	INT0*		42	INT1*	
Address	43	ADRE*		44	ADRF*	
	45	ADRC*		46	ADRD*	
	47	ADRA*	Address	48	ADRB*	Address
	49	ADR8*	Bus	50	ADR9*	Bus
	51	ADR6*		52	ADR7*	
	53	ADR4*		54	ADR5*	
	55	ADR2*		56	ADR3*	
	57	ADR0*		58	ADR1*	
Data	59	DATE*		60	DATF*	
	61	DATC*		62	DATD*	
	63	DATA*	Data	64	DATB*	Data
	65	DAT8*	Bus	66	DAT9*	Bus
	67	DAT6*		68	DAT7*	
	69	DAT4*		70	DAT5*	
	71	DAT2*		72	DAT3*	
	73	DAT0*		74	DAT1*	
Power Supplies	75	GND	Signal GND	76	GND	Signal GND
	77		Reserved, bussed	78		Reserved, bussed
	79	−12V	−12Vdc	80	−12V	−12Vdc
	81	+5V	+5Vdc	82	+5V	+5Vdc
	83	+5V	+5Vdc	84	+5V	+5Vdc
	85	GND	Signal GND	86	GND	Signal GND

All Reserved pins are reserved for future use and should not be used if upwards compatibility is desired.

*Note: The Reserved MULTIBUS P2 connector pin/signal assignments are contained in Intel's iLBX Bus Specification.

MULTIBUS® SYSTEM BUS

Table 2. MULTIBUS® Pin/Signal Assignment — (P2)

	Pin	(Component Side) Mnemonic	(Component Side) Description	Pin	(Circuit Side) Mnemonic	(Circuit Side) Description
	1		Reserved	2		Reserved
	3		Reserved	4		Reserved
	5		Reserved	6		Reserved
	7		Reserved	8		Reserved
	9		Reserved	10		Reserved
	11		Reserved	12		Reserved
	13		Reserved	14		Reserved
	15		Reserved	16		Reserved
	17		Reserved	18		Reserved
	19		Reserved	20		Reserved
	21		Reserved	22		Reserved
	23		Reserved	24		Reserved
	25		Reserved	26		Reserved
	27		Reserved	28		Reserved
	29		Reserved	30		Reserved
	31		Reserved	32		Reserved
	33		Reserved	34		Reserved
	35		Reserved	36		Reserved
	37		Reserved	38		Reserved
	39		Reserved	40		Reserved
	41		Reserved	42		Reserved
	43		Reserved	44		Reserved
	45		Reserved	46		Reserved
	47		Reserved	48		Reserved
	49		Reserved	50		Reserved
	51		Reserved	52		Reserved
	53		Reserved	54		Reserved
Address	55	ADR16*	Address Bus	56	ADR17*	Address Bus
	57	ADR14*		58	ADR15*	
	59		Reserved, Bussed	60		Reserved, Bussed

All Reserved Pins are reserved for future use and should not be used if upwards compatibility is desired.

*Note: The Reserved MULTIBUS P2 connector pin/signal assignments are contained in Intel's iLBX Bus Specification.

SPECIFICATION

Word Size
Data — 8 and 16-bit

Memory Addressing
24-bits — 16 megabyte – direct access

I/O Addressing
16-bits — 64 Kbytes

Maximum Bus Backplane Length
18 inches

Bus Devices Supported
16 total devices — (Master, Slave, Intelligent Slave)

Bus Bandwidth
10 megabytes/sec — 16-bit

5 megabytes/sec — 8-bit

Bus Exchange Cycle
200 nsec – Best Case; 300 nsec – Worst Case (assuming no bus master is currently active on the bus.)

MULTIBUS® SYSTEM BUS

Electrical Characteristics

BUS POWER SUPPLY SPECIFICATIONS

Table 3.

Parameter	Standard[1]			
	Ground	+5	+12	−12
Mnemonic	GND	+5V	+12V	−12V
Bus Pins	P1-1,2,11,12, 75,76,85,86	P1-3,4,5,6, 81,82,83, 84	P1-7,8	P1-79,80
Tolerance	Ref.	±1%	±1%	±1%
Combined Line & Load Reg	Ref.	0.1%	0.1%	0.1%
Ripple (Peak to Peak)	Ref.	50 mV	50 mV	50 mV
Transient Response (50% Load Change)		100 µs	100 µs	100 µs

[1] Point of measurement is at connection point between motherboard and power supply. At any card edge connector a degradation of 2% maximum (e.g. voltage tolerance ±2%) is allowed.

BUS TIMING

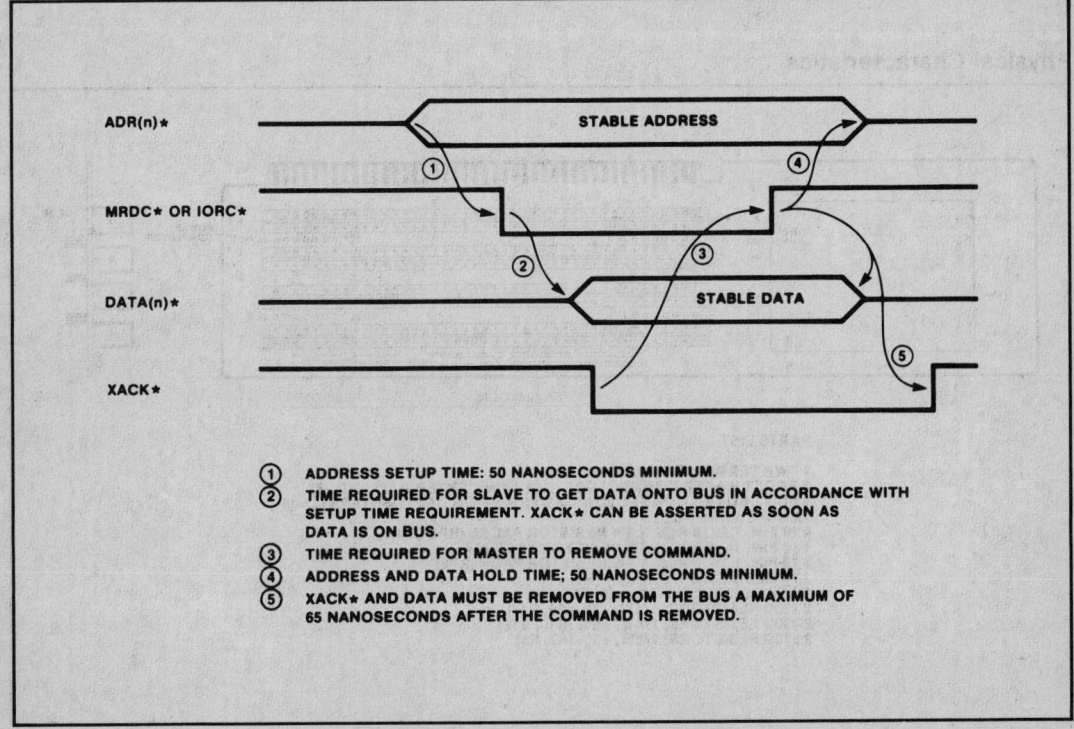

① ADDRESS SETUP TIME: 50 NANOSECONDS MINIMUM.
② TIME REQUIRED FOR SLAVE TO GET DATA ONTO BUS IN ACCORDANCE WITH SETUP TIME REQUIREMENT. XACK★ CAN BE ASSERTED AS SOON AS DATA IS ON BUS.
③ TIME REQUIRED FOR MASTER TO REMOVE COMMAND.
④ ADDRESS AND DATA HOLD TIME; 50 NANOSECONDS MINIMUM.
⑤ XACK★ AND DATA MUST BE REMOVED FROM THE BUS A MAXIMUM OF 65 NANOSECONDS AFTER THE COMMAND IS REMOVED.

Figure 3. Memory or I/O Read Timing

MULTIBUS® SYSTEM BUS

BUS TIMING (Con't)

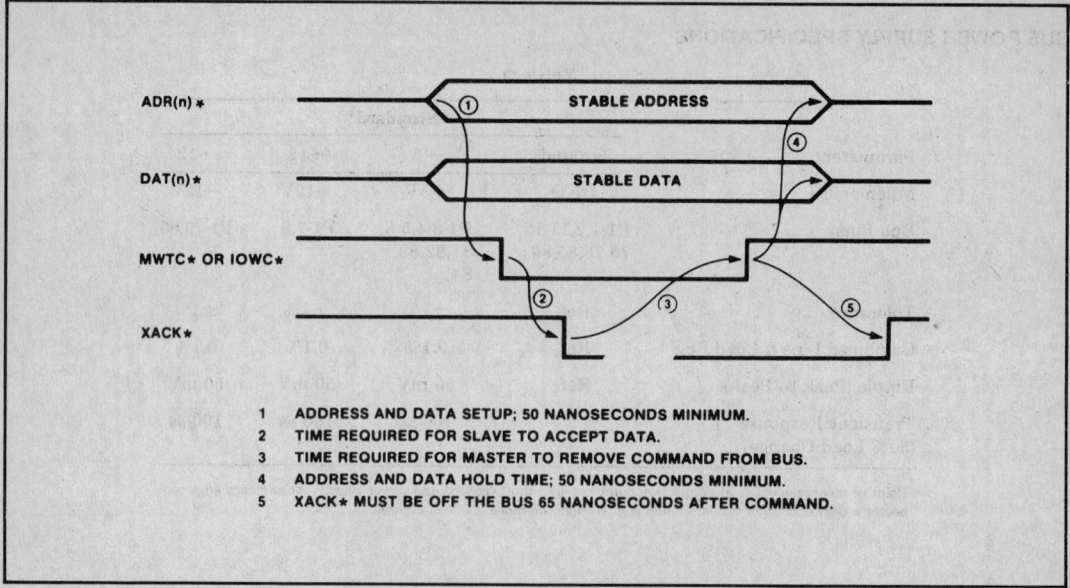

Figure 4. Memory or I/O Write Timing

Physical Characteristics

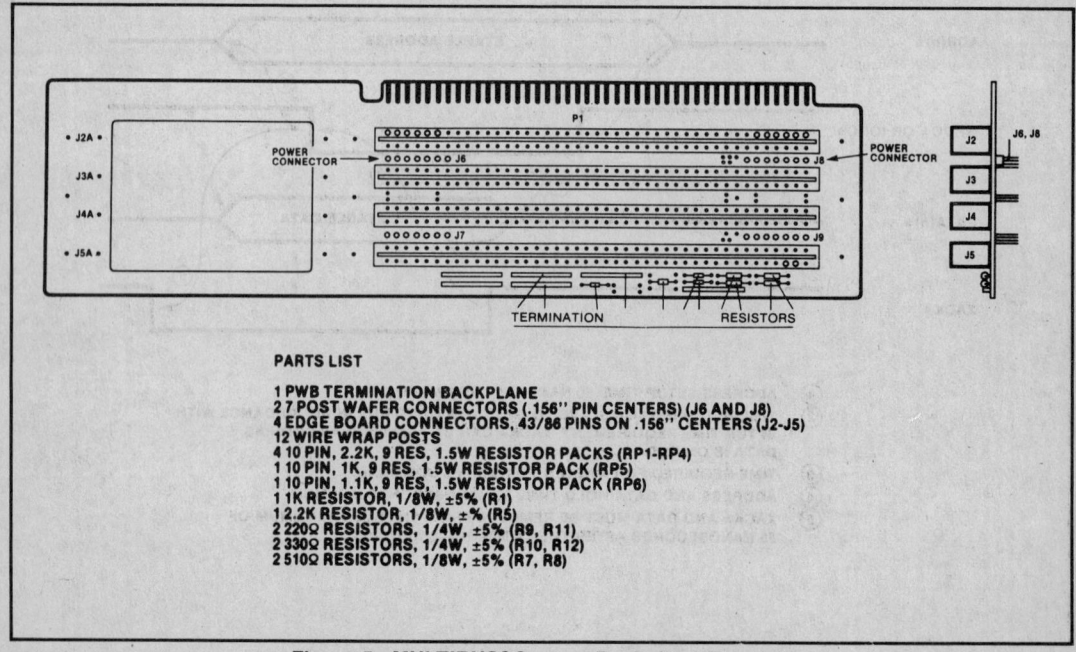

Figure 5. MULTIBUS® System Backplane Example

MULTIBUS® SYSTEM BUS

PHYSICAL CHARACTERISTICS (Con't)

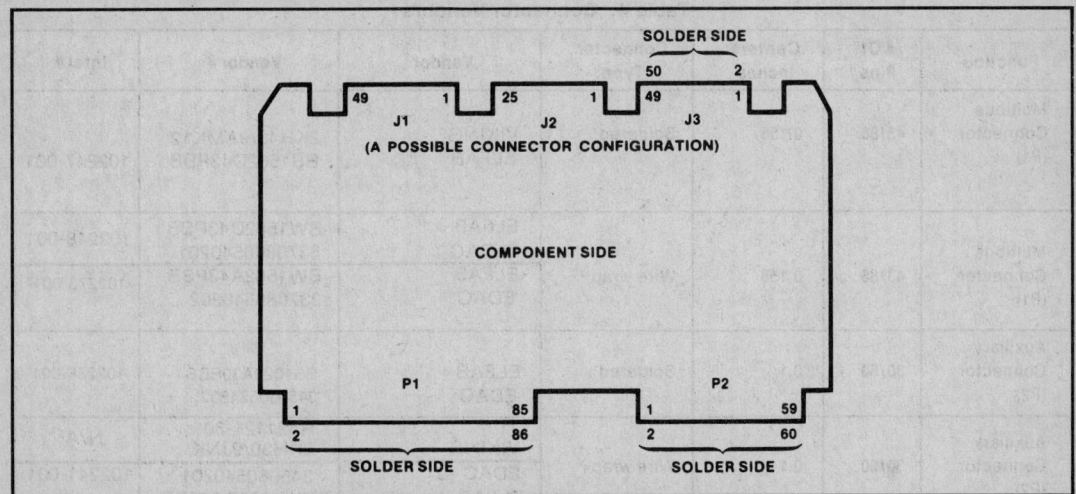

Figure 6. Connector and Pin Numbering

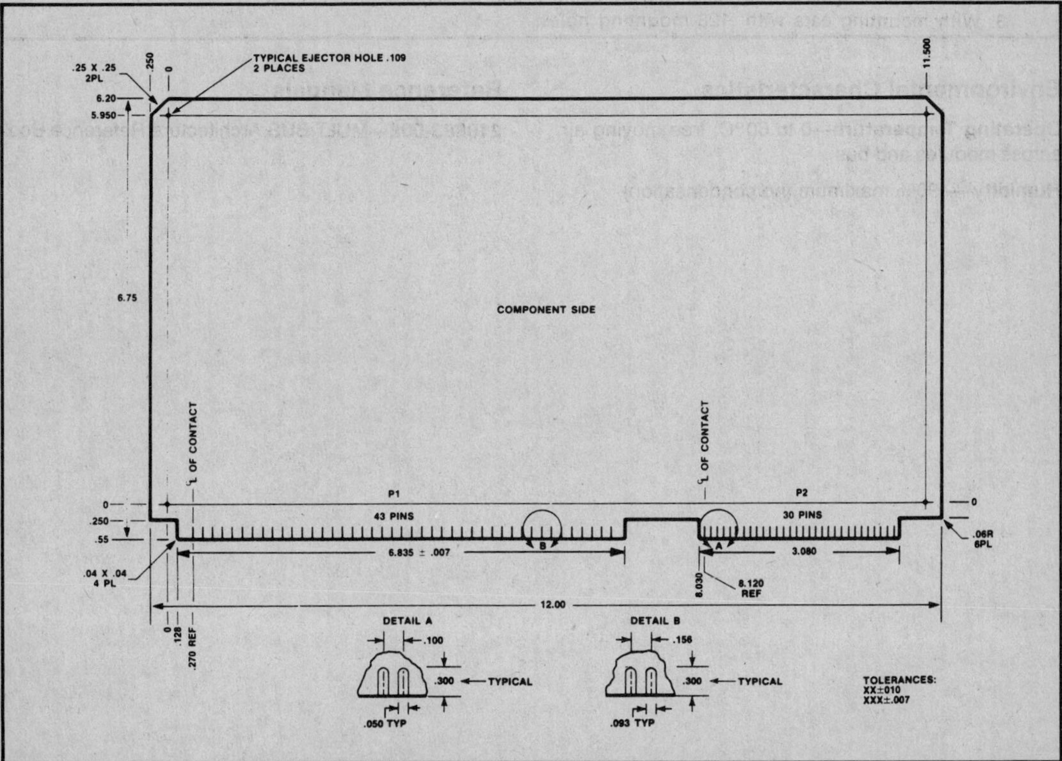

Figure 7. Standard Printed Wiring Board Outline

1-9

MULTIBUS® SYSTEM BUS

Backplane Connectors

Table 4. Connector Vendors

Function	# Of Pins	Centers Inches	Connector Type	Vendor	Vendor #	Intel #
Multibus Connector (P1)	43/86	0.156	Soldered[1]	VIKING ELFAB	2KH43/9AMK12 BS1562D43PBB	102247-001
Multibus Connector (P1)	43/86	0.156	Wire wrap[2]	ELFAB ELDAC ELFAB EDAC	BW1562D43PBB 3370860540201 BW1562A43PBB 337086540202	102248-001 102273-001[3]
Auxiliary Connector (P2)	30/60	0.1	Soldered[1]	ELFAB EDAC	BS1020A30PBB 345060524802	102238-001
Auxiliary Connector (P2)	30/60	0.1	Wire wrap[2]	TI VIKING EDAC ELFAB	H421121-30 3KH30/9JNK 345060540201 BW1020D30PBB	N/A[3] 102241-001

Notes:
1. Connector heights are not guaranteed to conform to Intel packaging equipment.
2. Wirewrap pin lengths are not guaranteed to conform to Intel packaging equipment.
3. With mounting ears with .128 mounting holes.

Environmental Characteristics

Operating Temperature—0 to 60°C; free moving air across modules and bus

Humidity — 90% maximum (no condensation)

Reference Manuals

210883-002—MULTIBUS Architecture Reference Book

MULTICHANNEL™ I/O BUS

- **High speed 8- or 16-bit block transfers between memory and/or I/O**
- **Transfer rates up to 8 megabytes/sec.**
- **Full speed operation at distances of up to 15 meters.**
- **Supports Supervisor, Controller, or basic Talker/Listener capabilities**
- **Off-loads burst mode I/O activities from host CPU**
- **Up to 16 devices may be interfaced to the bus.**
- **16 megabytes of memory and 16 megabytes of I/O are addressable on each device**

The MULTICHANNEL™ I/O Bus is one of a family of standard bus structures resident within Intel's total system architecture. The MULTICHANNEL bus is a general purpose, high-speed I/O bus capable of significantly increasing system performance by providing a separate data path for DMA I/O activities. By isolating I/O transfers from the system bus, the MULTICHANNEL bus off-loads I/O activity from the host CPU, reduces the probability of bus saturation on the system bus, and reduces contention between I/O and data processing activities on the system bus. The MULTICHANNEL bus can support up to 16 devices at distances up to 15 meters with a maximum burst throughput of 8 megabytes per second. These 16 devices are classified in a manner similar to the IEEE 488 bus concept: Supervisors, Controllers, or Talker and Listeners. As a non-proprietary, standardized I/O bus, the MULTICHANNEL bus is a cost-effective DMA interface ideal for applications such as computer graphics, specialized peripheral control, automatic test equipment, video camera image processing, data acquisition, and high-speed MULTIBUS® system-to-system communication.

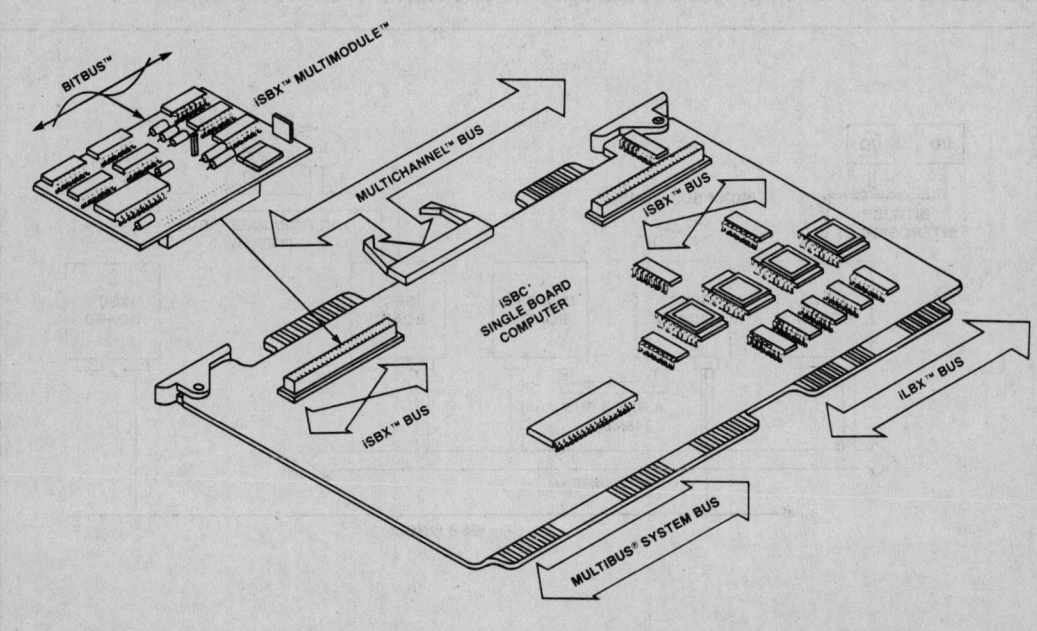

MULTICHANNEL™ I/O BUS

FUNCTIONAL DESCRIPTION

Architectural Overview

The MULTICHANNEL bus is the standard high speed I/O interface to MULTIBUS-based systems. Its general purpose design and high performance (8 MB/sec) augment the overall system design by improving I/O interface flexibility and system throughput. The flexibility is realized by using an easy-to-use public standard interface that can support up to sixteen 8-bit or 16-bit devices at up to 15 meters. This structure allows the MULTICHANNEL bus to provide easy I/O system expansion, effective box-to-box communication, and a growth path capable of supporting new generations of high-performance I/O devices. The MULTICHANNEL bus increases system throughput by providing a high-performance data path for efficient movement of large amounts of data.

Structural Features

MULTICHANNEL™ BUS CONFIGURATION

The MULTICHANNEL bus is a multiplexed, asynchronous block transfer, 16-bit I/O bus designed to handle 8-bit and 16-bit transfers between peripherals and single board computers. Its structure (pictured in Figure 2) consists of 16 address/data lines, 6 control lines, 2 interrupt lines, plus parity and reset. These signal lines are implemented as either a 60 conductor flat ribbon cable or a twisted-pair cable spanning a distance of up to 15 meters. A 30/60-pin 3M® connector is recommended for device connection to the MULTICHANNEL bus. The male connectors are installed on each MULTICHANNEL device and the female connectors are mounted on the cable. To insure system integrity, the MULTICHANNEL cable is terminated at both ends.

BUS ELEMENTS

Three device types — the Basic device, the bus Controller device, and the bus Supervisor device — each provide a different level of capability. The Basic Talker/Listener device has lowest capability, responding only to data transfer requests issued by a Supervisor or Controller. The bus Controller device has higher capability than a Basic Talker/Listener on the bus. It can respond to data transfer requests, control data transfers, and can program other MULTICHANNEL devices under direction from a bus Supervisor. Operating at the highest capability is the bus Supervisor device. It provides major control and management of the MULTICHANNEL bus. The bus Supervisor resolves and grants MULTICHANNEL bus priority, monitors bus status, handles interrupts, and controls the reset line, in addition to performing all bus Controller functions.

3M is a registered trademark of 3M Corporation.

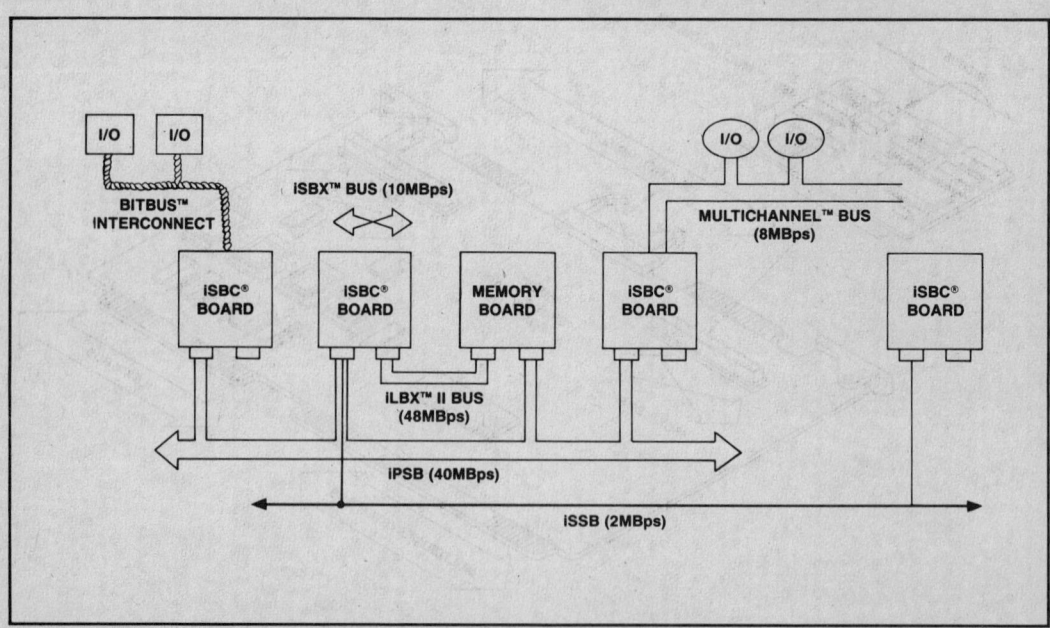

Figure 1. MULTIBUS® System Architecture

MULTICHANNEL™ I/O BUS

MULTICHANNEL bus devices are functionally flexible, creating overlaps between types of bus functions and types of bus devices performing those functions. These devices perform functions in various states of operation: master, slave, talker, listener. When a device is controlling the command/action lines, it is in the master state, and both the bus Supervisor and the bus Controller can operate in this state, although not simultaneously. The slave state indicates a device that can monitor the command/action lines. Only Controllers and Basic Talker/Listeners operate as slaves. All three device types can operate in the talker state or the listener state, but not all at the same time. A Talker is any device selected by the bus master which is writing data to the bus. A Listener is any selected device which is reading data from the bus.

BUS INTERFACE/SIGNAL LINE DESCRIPTIONS

The MULTICHANNEL bus signal lines are grouped into five classes based on the functions they perform: address/data, control, interrupt, parity, and reset. The 16 address/data lines are multiplexed by a control line to act either as 16 unidirectional address lines or 16 bidirectional data lines. When used as address lines, they transmit the device address to all devices attached to the MULTICHANNEL bus. When used as bidirectional data lines, they transmit and receive data to or from MULTICHANNEL devices. The six control lines determine the overall operation of the bus from specifying the type of data transfer to providing the handshake for data transfers between MULTICHANNEL devices. Two interrupt lines are supplied to initiate and terminate data transfers, and to indicate device failures, memory failures, or parity errors. A parity line and a reset line provide support for a parity option and system reset capability whenever required.

BUS PIN ASSIGNMENTS

For proper MULTICHANNEL implementation, a 60 conductor (twisted pair or flat) cable using a 30/60 pin 3M connector, is used for device connection to the bus. Figure 3 is an outline drawing of the MULTICHANNEL bus connector which also shows the pin numbering. The MULTICHANNEL bus connector signal pin assignments are listed in Table 1. Cable termination is implemented at both cable ends to insure proper system integrity over a 15-meter cable. Figure 4 is a schematic of the cable termination circuits. A cable termination module could be created that would then be connected to the cable end via a 30/60 pin connector.

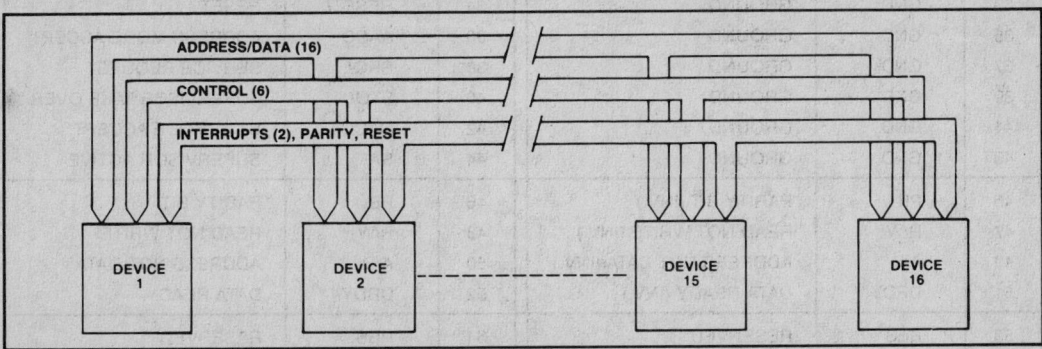

Figure 2. Block Diagram of MULTICHANNEL™ Bus Structure

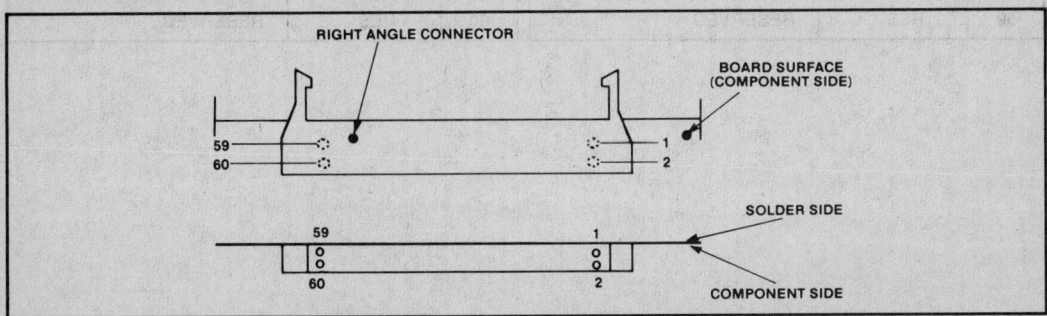

Figure 3. Connector Example

MULTICHANNEL™ I/O BUS

Table 1. MULTICHANNEL™ Bus Pin Assignments

Lower Row			Upper Row		
Pin	Mnemonic	Signal Name	Pin	Mnemonic	Signal Name
1	GND	GROUND	2	AD0/	ADDRESS DATA LINE 0
3	GND	GROUND	4	AD1/	ADDRESS DATA LINE 1
5	GND	GROUND	6	AD2/	ADDRESS DATA LINE 2
7	GND	GROUND	8	AD3/	ADDRESS DATA LINE 3
9	GND	GROUND	10	AD4/	ADDRESS DATA LINE 4
11	GND	GROUND	12	AD5/	ADDRESS DATA LINE 5
13	GND	GROUND	14	AD6/	ADDRESS DATA LINE 6
15	GND	GROUND	16	AD7/	ADDRESS DATA LINE 7
17	GND	GROUND	18	AD8/	ADDRESS DATA LINE 8
19	GND	GROUND	20	AD9/	ADDRESS DATA LINE 9
21	GND	GROUND	22	ADA/	ADDRESS DATA LINE 10
23	GND	GROUND	24	ADB/	ADDRESS DATA LINE 11
25	GND	GROUND	26	ADC/	ADDRESS DATA LINE 12
27	GND	GROUND	28	ADD/	ADDRESS DATA LINE 13
29	GND	GROUND	30	ADE/	ADDRESS DATA LINE 14
31	GND	GROUND	32	ADF/	ADDRESS DATA LINE 15
33	GND	GROUND	34	RESET/	RESET
35	GND	GROUND	36	AACC	ADDRESS MODE ACCEPT
37	GND	GROUND	38	SRQ/	SERVICE REQUEST
39	GND	GROUND	40	STO/	SUPERVISOR TAKE OVER
41	GND	GROUND	42	DACC/	DATA MODE ACCEPT
43	GND	GROUND	44	SA/	SUPERVISOR ACTIVE
45	PB*/	PARITY BIT (INV.)	46	PB/	PARITY BIT
47	R/W/	READ NOT WRITE (INV.)	48	R/W	READ NOT WRITE
49	A/D/	ADDRESS NOT DATA (INV.)	50	A/D	ADDRESS NOT DATA
51	DRDY*/	DATA READY (INV.)	52	DRDY/	DATA READY
53	RES	RESERVED	54	RES	RESERVED
55	RES	RESERVED	56	RES	RESERVED
57	RES	RESERVED	58	RES	RESERVED
59	RES	RESERVED	60	RES	RESERVED

MULTICHANNEL™ I/O BUS

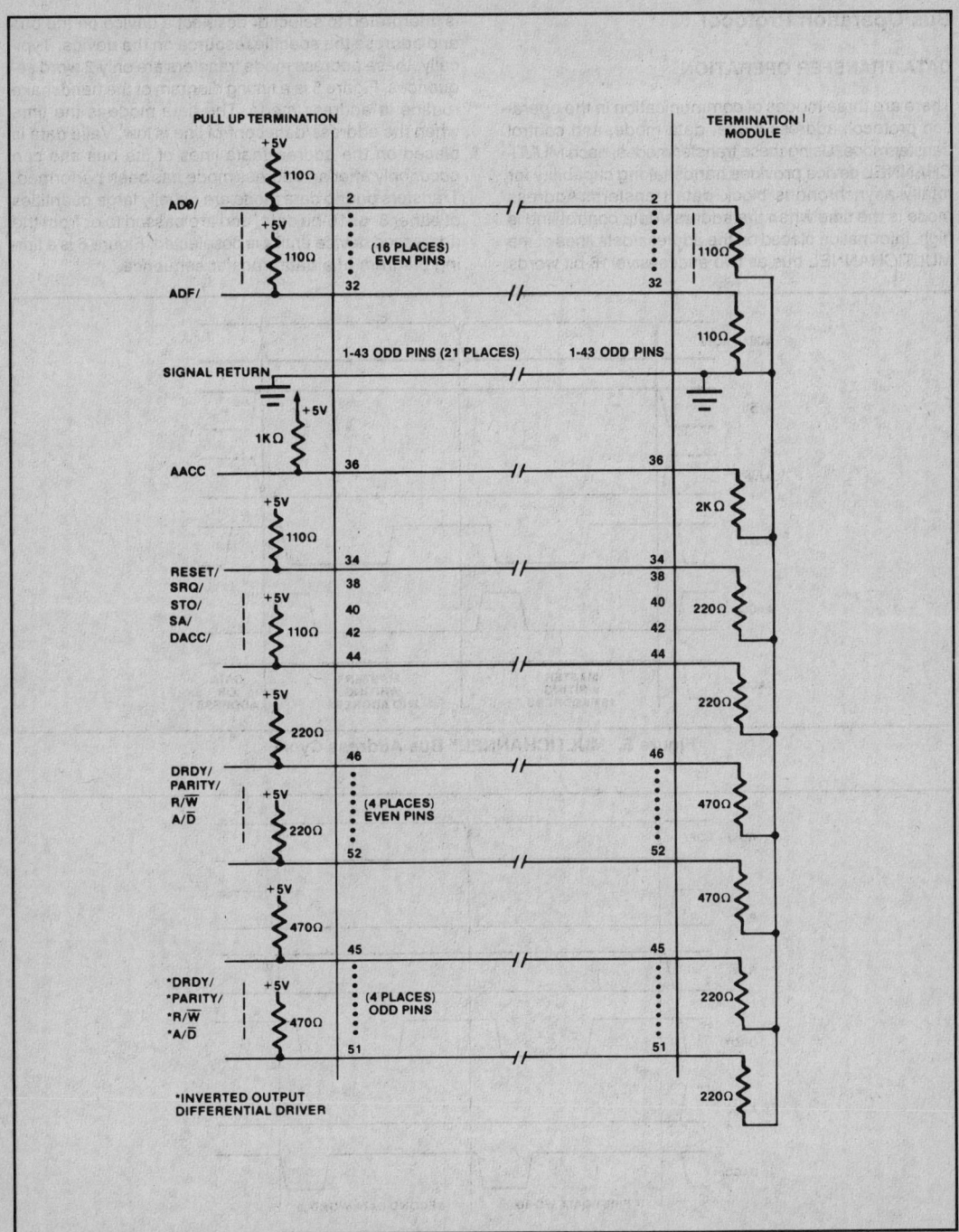

Figure 4. Bus Termination Schematic

MULTICHANNEL™ I/O BUS

Bus Operation Protocol

DATA TRANSFER OPERATION

There are three modes of communication in the operation protocol: address mode, data mode, and control transfer mode. Using these transfer modes, each MULTICHANNEL device provides handshaking capability for totally asynchronous block data transfers. Address mode is the time when the address/data control line is high. Information placed on the address/data lines of the MULTICHANNEL bus as two successive 16-bit words is interpreted to select or deselect a device on the bus and address the specific resource on the device. Typically, these address mode transfers are only 2 word sequences. Figure 5 is a timing diagram of the handshake routine in address mode. The data mode is the time when the address/data control line is low. Valid data is placed on the address/data lines of the bus and can occur only after an address mode has been performed. Transfers during data mode are usually large quantities of either 8- or 16-bit data, and are passed to or from the addressed device until it is deselected. Figure 6 is a timing diagram of a data transfer sequence.

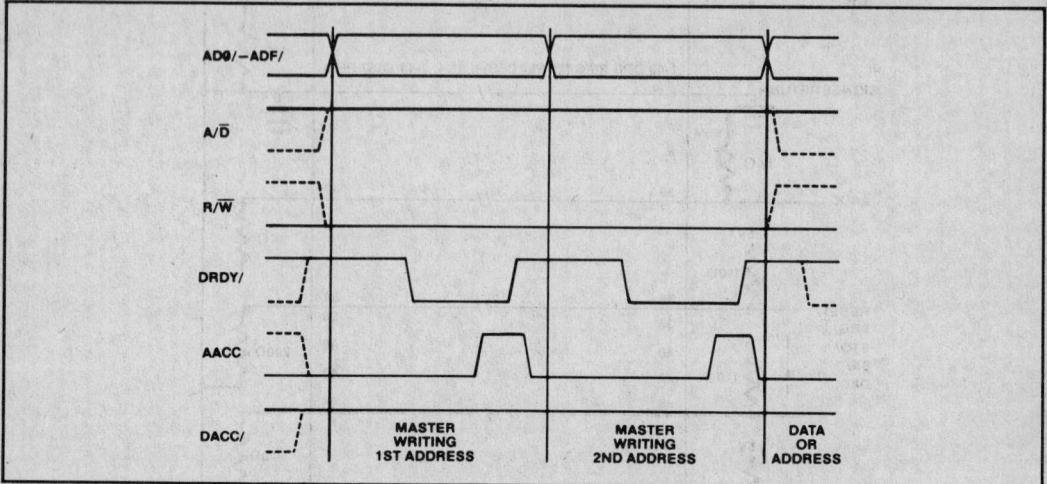

Figure 5. MULTICHANNEL™ Bus Address Cycle

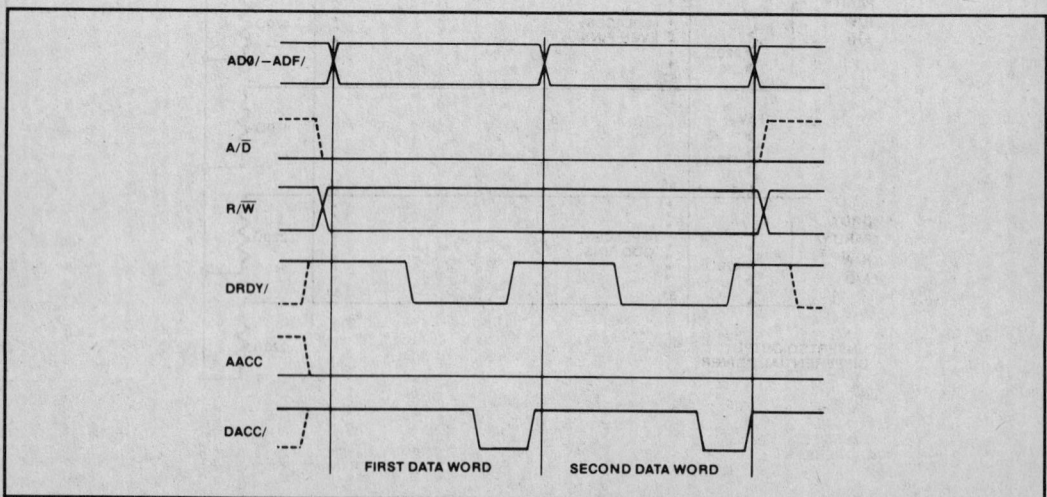

Figure 6. MULTICHANNEL™ Bus Data Transfer Sequence

MULTICHANNEL™ I/O BUS

Control transfer mode is the time when the bus Supervisor selects the bus Controller and programs its registers with required information. Once programmed, a bus Controller may select a device and originate a data transfer operation.

The operational sequences of these transfer modes are similar in handling read and write operations to and from the 16 megabytes of memory and the 16 megabytes of registers addressable on each MULTICHANNEL device.

A typical transfer sequence begins when the master sends a two-word address sequence to select a MULTICHANNEL device and specify address, direction and resource (memory vs. I/O) of the data transfer. Following device selection, the Talker proceeds to send the data as a continuous 8 or 16-bit data word stream until the block data move is complete. The master terminates the transfer by issuing another two-word address sequence for device deselection.

The transfer sequence described is identical for both memory and register type transfers. The master controls similar read and write operations between devices, and the address select and deselect sequences use the same address format. Figure 7 contains the MULTICHANNEL bus address format.

DEVICE REGISTER DEFINITION

Of the 16 megabytes of register space per device, the first 16 registers are pre-defined to provide a standard register area common to all devices. The remaining registers are user definable. Table 2 lists the 16 defined registers along with their function. The use of this register concept allows for standard interface between all MULTICHANNEL devices. Please refer to the MULTICHANNEL Bus Specification for more detailed information.

Table 2. MULTICHANNEL™ Device Register Definitions

Register Number	Definition	Mode
0	STO Flag/Status	Read Only
1	SRQ Flag/Status	Read Only
2	SRQ Mask	Write Only
3	Device Command	Write Only
4	Device Parameter	Write Only
5	Data Address 1	Read or Write
6	Data Address 2	Read or Write
7	Block Length 1	Read or Write
8	Block Length 2	Read or Write
9	Error Address 1	Read Only
10	Error Address 2	Read Only
11	Address Extension	Write Only
12-15	Reserved	
16-16 Mbyte	User Defined	Read or Write

BUS INTERRUPT HANDLING

The MULTICHANNEL bus Supervisor, being responsible for bus access and control, monitors the two bus interrupt lines. The Supervisor Take-Over interrupt (STO) is used to inform the bus Supervisor that a device wants to return control of the bus to the Supervisor or that an error has occurred. The Service Request Interrupt (SRQ) is used by devices which do not have control of the bus, but require service from the bus Supervisor. To locate a device transmitting a bus interrupt, the bus Supervisor

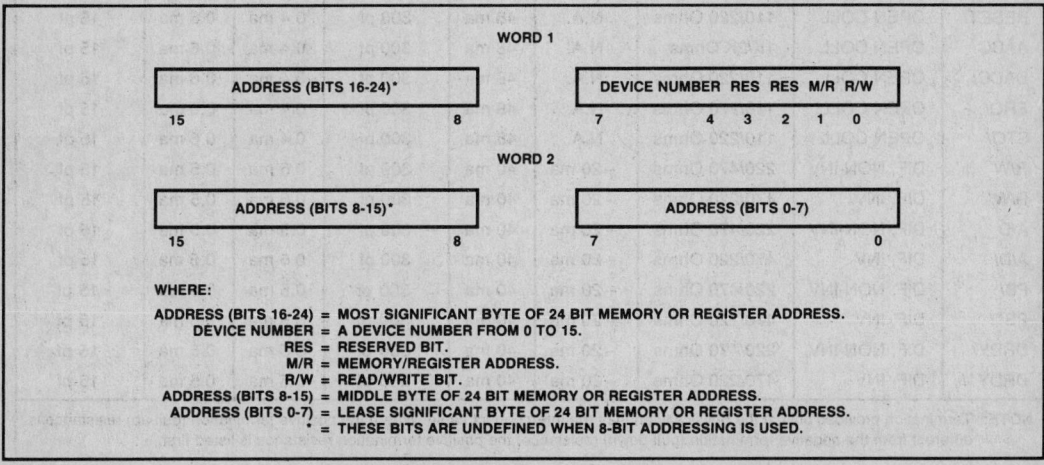

Figure 7. MULTICHANNEL™ Bus Address Format

MULTICHANNEL™ I/O BUS

polls each device attached to the bus by reading the appropriate register of each device and testing for a non-zero value.

PARITY AND RESET

Parity operation on the MULTICHANNEL bus is provided, but is not required. The bus Supervisor selects between parity mode and non-parity mode depending upon system requirements. If parity mode is selected all Talkers must generate odd parity. All active Listeners monitor the parity line and generate an STO interrupt signal if there is a parity error.

A reset function is also supported by the MULTICHANNEL bus, and is controlled by the bus Supervisor to bring the bus to a known state. It is used to reset all devices after power-up, and when required to gain control of the bus.

SPECIFICATIONS

Word Size

Data — 8, 16-bit

Memory Addressing

24-bits — 16 megabyte – direct access – automatic incrementing

Register Addressing

24-bits — 16 megabyte – direct access

Electrical Characteristics

DC SPECIFICATIONS

Maximum Bus Length

15 meters (50 feet)

Bus Devices Supported

16 total devices — (Supervisor, Controller, and Talker/Listener)

Bus Bandwidth (at 15 meters)

8 megabytes/sec. — 16-bit

4 megabytes/sec. — 8-bit

Table 3. DC Specifications

Signal Name	Driver Type	Termination (see Note)	Min. Driver Requirements			Max. Receiver Requirements		
			High	Low	Load Cap	High	Low	Load Cap
AD15-0/	TRI-STATE	110 Ohms	– 5 ma	48 ma	300 pf	0.2 ma	0.8 ma	15 pf
SA/	OPEN COLL	110/220 Ohms	N.A.	48 ma	300 pf	0.4 ma	0.6 ma	15 pf
RESET/	OPEN COLL	110/220 Ohms	N.A.	48 ma	300 pf	0.4 ma	0.6 ma	15 pf
AACC	OPEN COLL	1K/2K Ohms	N.A.	48 ma	300 pf	0.4 ma	0.6 ma	15 pf
DACC/	OPEN COLL	110/220 Ohms	N.A.	48 ma	300 pf	0.4 ma	0.6 ma	15 pf
SRQ/	OPEN COLL	110/220 Ohms	N.A.	48 ma	300 pf	0.4 ma	0.6 ma	15 pf
STO/	OPEN COLL	110/220 Ohms	N.A.	48 ma	300 pf	0.4 ma	0.6 ma	15 pf
R/W	DIF, NON-INV	220/470 Ohms	– 20 ma	40 ma	300 pf	0.5 ma	0.5 ma	15 pf
R/W/	DIF, INV	470/220 Ohms	– 20 ma	40 ma	300 pf	0.5 ma	0.5 ma	15 pf
A/D	DIF, NON-INV	220/470 Ohms	– 20 ma	40 ma	300 pf	0.5 ma	0.5 ma	15 pf
A/D/	DIF, INV	470/220 Ohms	– 20 ma	40 ma	300 pf	0.5 ma	0.5 ma	15 pf
PB/	DIF, NON-INV	220/470 Ohms	– 20 ma	40 ma	300 pf	0.5 ma	0.5 ma	15 pf
PB*/	DIF, INV	470/220 Ohms	– 20 ma	40 ma	300 pf	0.5 ma	0.5 ma	15 pf
DRDY/	DIF, NON-INV	220/470 Ohms	– 20 ma	40 ma	300 pf	0.5 ma	0.5 ma	15 pf
DRDY*/	DIF, INV	470/220 Ohms	– 20 ma	40 ma	300 pf	0.5 ma	0.5 ma	15 pf

NOTE: Termination provided only at the physically ends of the interconnect cable. Where the positive termination (pull-up) resistance is different from the negative termination (pull-down) resistance, the positive termination resistance is listed first.

MULTICHANNEL™ I/O BUS

MULTICHANNEL bus devices are functionally flexible, creating overlaps between types of bus functions and types of bus devices performing those functions. These devices perform functions in various states of operation: master, slave, talker, listener. When a device is controlling the command/action lines, it is in the master state, and both the bus Supervisor and the bus Controller can operate in this state, although not simultaneously. The slave state indicates a device that can monitor the command/action lines. Only Controllers and Basic Talker/Listeners operate as slaves. All three device types can operate in the talker state or the listener state, but not all at the same time. A Talker is any device selected by the bus master which is writing data to the bus. A Listener is any selected device which is reading data from the bus.

BUS INTERFACE/SIGNAL LINE DESCRIPTIONS

The MULTICHANNEL bus signal lines are grouped into five classes based on the functions they perform: address/data, control, interrupt, parity, and reset. The 16 address/data lines are multiplexed by a control line to act either as 16 unidirectional address lines or 16 bidirectional data lines. When used as address lines, they transmit the device address to all devices attached to the MULTICHANNEL bus. When used as bidirectional data lines, they transmit and receive data to or from MULTICHANNEL devices. The six control lines determine the overall operation of the bus from specifying the type of data transfer to providing the handshake for data transfers between MULTICHANNEL devices. Two interrupt lines are supplied to initiate and terminate data transfers, and to indicate device failures, memory failures, or parity errors. A parity line and a reset line provide support for a parity option and system reset capability whenever required.

BUS PIN ASSIGNMENTS

For proper MULTICHANNEL implementation, a 60 conductor (twisted pair or flat) cable using a 30/60 pin 3M connector, is used for device connection to the bus. Figure 3 is an outline drawing of the iSBC® MULTICHANNEL connector which also shows the pin numbering. The MULTICHANNEL bus connector signal pin assignments are listed in Table 1. Cable termination is implemented at both cable ends to insure proper system integrity over a 15-meter cable. Figure 4 is a schematic of the cable termination circuits. A cable termination module could be created that would then be connected to the cable end via a 30/60 pin connector.

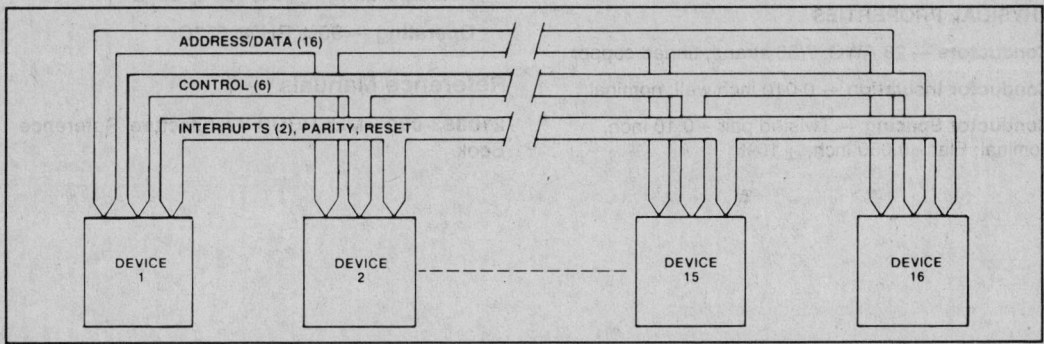

Figure 2. Block Diagram of MULTICHANNEL™ Bus Structure

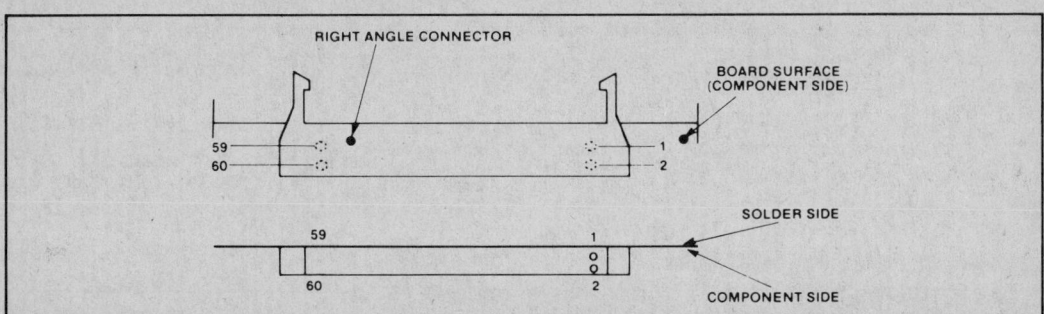

Figure 3. Connector Example

MULTICHANNEL™ I/O BUS

Cables and Connectors

Table 3. Cable and Receptacle Vendors

MULTICHANNEL™ Bus Compatible Cable			
Vendor	Ribbon Type	Vendor No.	Conductor
Belden	Plain Flat	9L28060	60
Belden	Twisted-Pair	9V28060	60
Belden	Insulated Flat	9L28260	60
Spectrastrip	Plain Flat	455-240-60	60
Spectrastrip	Twisted-Pair	455-248-60	60
Spectrastrip	Insulated Flat	151-2830-060	60

MULTICHANNEL™ Bus Compatible Receptacles			
Vendor	Type	Vendor No.	Pins
Berg	Male	65823-103	60
Berg	Female	65949-960	60
3M	Male	3372-1302	60
3M	Female	3334-6000	60

PHYSICAL PROPERTIES

Conductors — 28 AWG, 7/36 strand, tinned copper

Conductor Insulation — 0.010 inch wall, nominal

Conductor Spacing — Twisted pair – 0.10 inch, nominal; Flat – 0.050 inch, ±10%

Cable Thickness — Flat – 0.042 inch, nominal

Temperature Rating — 80°C

ELECTRICAL PROPERTIES

Impedance (nominal) — 105 ohms ±10%

Propagation Velocity (nominal) — 1.7 ns/ft

Capacitance (nominal) — 22 pf/ft

INSULATION REQUIREMENTS

Voltage Rating (minimum) — 100 Vdc

Insulation Resistance (minimum) — 1×10^{10} ohms

Environmental Characteristics

Temperature:
(inlet air) at 200 LFM airflow over boards

Non-operating — −40 to +70°C

Operating — 0 to 55°C

Humidity:

Non-Operating — 95% RH @ 55°C

Operating — 90% RH @ 55°C

Reference Manuals

210883-002—MULTIBUS Architecture Reference Book

iLBX™ EXECUTION BUS

- **High bus bandwidth**
  — 9.5 Mbytes/sec. for 8-bit transfers
  — 19 Mbytes/sec. for 16-bit transfers
- **16 Mbyte addressing range**
- **8 and 16-bit data transfers**
- **Supports up to 5 iLBX™ compatible devices per bus**
- **Primary and secondary master bus exchange capabilities**
- **Standard 60-pin MULTIBUS® P2 connector**

The iLBX™ Execution Bus is one of a family of standard bus structures resident within Intel's total system architecture. The Local Bus Extension (iLBX) Bus is a dedicated execution bus capable of significantly increasing system performance by extending the processor board's on-board local bus to off-board resources. This extension provides for arbitration-free, direct access to high-performance memory. Acting as a "virtual" iSBC®, up to 16 megabytes of processor addressable memory can be accessed over the iLBX bus and appear as though it were resident on the processor board. The iLBX Bus preserves advantages in performance and architecture of on-board memory, while allowing memory configurations larger than possible on a single board computer. High throughput and independence from MULTIBUS® activities make the iLBX bus an ideal solution for "working store" type program memory and data processing applications requiring large amounts of high performance memory. Such applications include graphics systems, robotics, process control, office systems, and CAD/CAM.

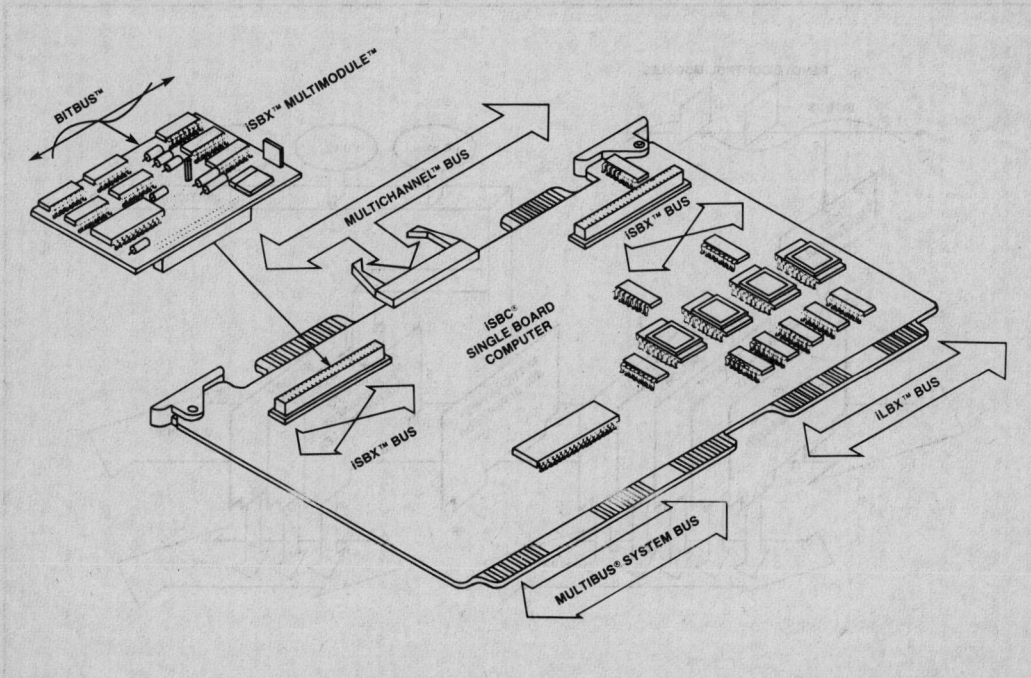

iLBX™ EXECUTION BUS

FUNCTIONAL DESCRIPTION

Architectural Overview

The iLBX bus is an architectural solution for supporting large amounts of high performance memory. It is the first structure that allows the CPU board selection to be decoupled from the on-board memory requirement, and still maximizes the processor's performance potential. It eliminates the processor's need to access its off-board memory resources solely over the MULTIBUS system bus. Architectural consistency with the single board computer approach including iLBX memory can be maintained by dual port access of memory resources between the iLBX bus and the MULTIBUS system bus. This allows for global access by other processors and I/O devices while still providing high speed local CPU operations. This sub-system created by the iLBX bus of a single board computer and a maximum of 4 memory cards can be perceived architecturally as a "virtual single board computer". The implementation of iLBX bus "virtual modules" makes it possible to create functional modules with a new level of flexibility and performance in implementing a wide range of memory capabilities. With future needs in mind, the iLBX bus has the capability of accessing a full 16 megabytes of memory.

Structural Features

The iLBX bus uses a non-multiplexed 16-bit configuration capable of 8 and 16-bit transfers. Used in conjunction with the MULTIBUS interface, the iLBX bus resides on the MULTIBUS form factor P2 connector and supercedes the MULTIBUS interface definitions for the P2 signals. The iLBX bus uses the standard 60-pin MULTIBUS P2 connector and occupies 56 of the P2 connector pins with 16 data lines, 24 address lines plus control, command access, and parity signals. The four MULTIBUS address extension lines on the MULTIBUS/iLBX P2 connector retain the standard MULTIBUS interface definition.

Bus Elements

The iLBX bus supports three distinct device categories: 1) Primary Master, 2) Secondary Master, 3) Slave. These three device types may be combined to create several iLBX local busses ranging (in size) from a minimum of two to a maximum of five devices per iLBX bus. There is only one Primary Master in any given implementation of iLBX bus, and its presence is required along with the attachment of at least one Slave device. To provide alternate access over an iLBX bus, one optional Sec-

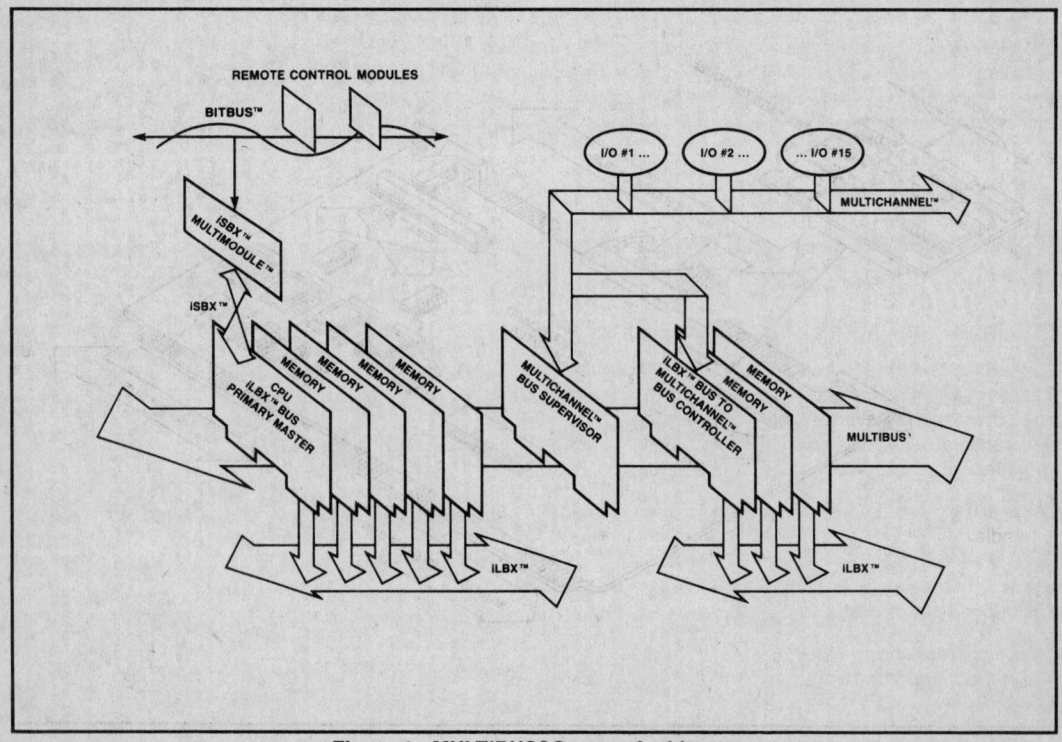

Figure 1. MULTIBUS® System Architecture

iLBX™ EXECUTION BUS

ondary Master may be incorporated to create a "two-master" local bus subsystem. By limiting the iLBX bus to two masters (a Primary and a Secondary), bus arbitration is reduced to a simple request and acknowledge process, with privileged use of the bus maintained by the Primary Master, and limited access granted to the Secondary Master when needed.

The Primary Master executes the role of iLBX bus "supervisor" by controlling the general operation of the bus and managing Secondary Master accesses to the Slave memory resources.

The Secondary Master Device is an option providing alternate access to the Slave resources on the iLBX bus. Secondary master devices are typically DMA driven. This feature is provided for implementation flexibility when occasional DMA transfers in and out of iLBX memory resources can optimize the overall system performance. The Secondary Master essentially duplicates the Primary Master's data transfer capability, but must rely on the Primary Master to grant access. Once access is granted, the Secondary Master controls the bus, and drives all signal lines until the operation is complete and control is passed back to the Primary Master.

The Slave devices contain the memory resources used by the Primary Master and the optional Secondary Master. Each iLBX implementation can contain a maximum of four Slave devices. Using 64K RAM technology on four slave devices with ECC can provide for over 2 megabytes of "on-board" high performance memory. With 256K RAM chips, each iLBX bus could contain slave devices with memory totalling 8 megabytes. As memory technology increases, the iLBX bus is designed to incorporate it in rapid fashion because it is capable of directly accessing a full 16 megabytes of memory on its high-performance Slave devices.

Bus Interface/Signal Line Descriptions

The iLBX bus interface is divided into four functional classes of signal lines: address and data lines, control lines, command lines, and bus access lines. The 40 address and data lines defined by the iLBX Bus Specification consist of 16 data lines and 24 address lines.

There are 16 bi-directional data lines exclusively used to handle 8-bit and 16-bit data transfers between the active bus master and the selected slave device. The iLBX bus uses these data lines for all data transfers, and are driven by tri-state drivers.

The 24 address lines on the iLBX bus provide the ability to directly address 16 megabytes of memory. These single-direction address lines are exclusively driven by the active bus master. The iLBX bus master uses them to select a specific slave device. Three control lines specify the type of data transfer between master and slave devices, while the three command lines initiate, control, and terminate the transfer. There are also three bus access lines used to transfer bus control between master devices.

Bus Pin Assignments

The iLBX bus uses the standard 60-pin MULTIBUS P2 connector. The physical location of each pin assignment and its corresponding function is listed in Table 1.The four MULTIBUS address extension lines (pins 55-58 on the P2 connector) retain the standard MULTIBUS interface functions.

Bus Operation Protocol

The operation protocol for the iLBX bus is a straightforward set of procedures consisting of three basic operations: bus control access, write data to memory, read data from memory. These operations use asynchronous protocol with positive acknowledgment.

Bus Access

The iLBX bus is shared by at most two masters; one Primary Master and one optional Secondary Master, each providing an alternate access path to iLBX bus memory resources. The mechanism for obtaining bus access is a simple request and acknowledge process communicated between masters. Each master is a bus controller of similar capabilities, responsible for data transfer operations between devices, but the Primary Master has the added responsibility of controlling iLBX bus accesses.

The Primary Master has default control of the iLBX bus. If the Secondary Master needs access to the bus, it must initiate a request and wait for acknowledgment from the Primary Master. The choice of when to surrender control of the bus rests with the Primary Master, but if no data transfer is in progress, the Primary Master normally relinquishes control immediately to the Secondary Master.

Data Transfer Operation

The iLBX bus supports two types of data transfer operations: write data to memory and read data from memory. These data transfer operations facilitate the passing of information between the active bus master and the selected slave device. The operation of these two transfer types is very similar; the only differences being the direction of the data transfer and the device driving the data lines.

For either type of data transfer, the active bus master first initiates the transfer operation by placing the memory address on the address lines (AB23-AB0) and a con-

iLBX™ EXECUTION BUS

trol configuration on the control lines to select the slave device. Once the slave device is selected, the type of data transfer becomes the key factor. With the write operation, the active master maintains control of the data lines and provides valid data within the specified time. Upon accepting a data element, the slave sends a receipt acknowledgment signal to the master which completes the data transfer operation.

With the read operation, the slave device drives the data lines and places valid data on the data lines before sampling by the active master. The slave acknowledges the master to signal the end of the data transfer, and the master completes the operation.

The iLBX Bus Specification includes provisions for both optimized and non-optimized data transfers. Optimized

Table 1. iLBX™ Bus Pin Assignments, P2 Edge Connector

Component Side			Solder Side		
16-Bit Pin	Mnemonic	Signal Name	16-Bit Pin	Mnemonic	Signal Name
1	DB0	DATA LINE 0	2	DB1	DATA LINE 1
3	DB2	DATA LINE 2	4	DB3	DATA LINE 3
5	DB4	DATA LINE 4	6	DB5	DATA LINE 5
7	DB6	DATA LINE 6	8	DB7	DATA LINE 7
9	GND	GROUND	10	DB8	DATA LINE 8
11	DB9	DATA LINE 9	12	DB10	DATA LINE 10
13	DB11	DATA LINE 11	14	DB12	DATA LINE 12
15	DB13	DATA LINE 13	16	DB14	DATA LINE 14
17	DB15	DATA LINE 15	18	GND	GROUND
19	AB0	ADDRESS LINE 0	20	AB1	ADDRESS LINE 1
21	AB2	ADDRESS LINE 2	22	AB3	ADDRESS LINE 3
23	AB4	ADDRESS LINE 4	24	AB5	ADDRESS LINE 5
25	AB6	ADDRESS LINE 6	26	AB7	ADDRESS LINE 7
27	GND	GROUND	28	AB8	ADDRESS LINE 8
29	AB9	ADDRESS LINE 9	30	AB10	ADDRESS LINE 10
31	AB11	ADDRESS LINE 11	32	AB12	ADDRESS LINE 12
33	AB13	ADDRESS LINE 13	34	AB14	ADDRESS LINE 14
35	AB15	ADDRESS LINE 15	36	GND	GROUND
37	AB16	ADDRESS LINE 16	38	AB17	ADDRESS LINE 17
39	AB18	ADDRESS LINE 18	40	AB19	ADDRESS LINE 19
41	AB20	ADDRESS LINE 20	42	AB21	ADDRESS LINE 21
43	AB22	ADDRESS LINE 22	44	AB23	ADDRESS LINE 23
45	GND	GROUND	46	ACK*	SLAVE ACKNOWLEDGE
47	BHEN	BYTE HIGH ENABLE	48	R/W̄	READ NOT WRITE
49	ASTB*	ADDRESS STROBE	50	DSTB*	DATA STROBE
51	SMRQ*	SECONDARY MASTER REQUEST	52	SMACK*	SECONDARY MASTER ACKNOWLEDGE
53	LOCK*	ACCESS LOCK	54	GND	GROUND
55	ADR22*	MULTIBUS® ADDRESS EXTENSION LINE 22	56	ADR23*	MULTIBUS® ADDRESS EXTENSION LINE 23
57	ADR20*	MULTIBUS® ADDRESS EXTENSION LINE 20	58	ADR21*	MULTIBUS® ADDRESS EXTENSION LINE 21
59	RES	RESERVED	60	TPAR*	TRANSFER PARITY

iLBX™ EXECUTION BUS

operation uses pipelining and signal overlapping techniques to manage the data transfer timing relationships between the active bus master and the selected slave. The use of signal overlapping requires that every device attached to the iLBX bus provide a means for varying the timing of the slave request and acknowledge signals. The non-optimized operation uses fixed signal sequences, instead of signal overlapping, to assure a valid data transfer, and a device does not need a variable request or acknowledge to read data-valid timing on the iLBX bus. Please refer to the iLBX Bus Specification for detailed descriptions of these transfer operations.

Mechanical Implementation

Because the iLBX bus uses the P2 connector of the MULTIBUS form factor, the iLBX bus "shares" a MULTIBUS chassis with the MULTIBUS backplane system bus in the system design. The iLBX mechanical specifications are synonymous with the MULTIBUS specifications for board-to-board spacing, board thickness, component lead length, and component height above the board. The iLBX bus interconnection can use either flexible ribbon cable or a rigid backplane. The iLBX bus interconnect maximum length is limited to 10 cm (approximately 4 inches); that is sufficient to span 5 card slots across two connected chassis. Figure 2 shows an iLBX bus cable assembly.

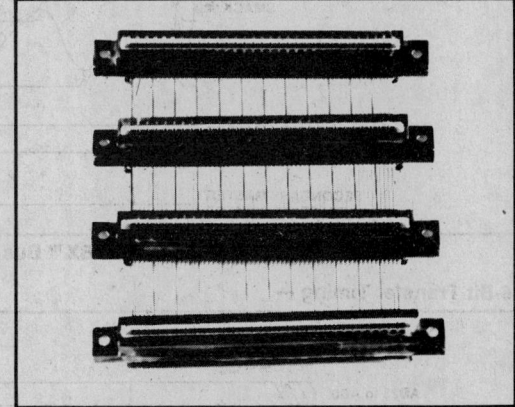

Figure 2. Typical iLBX™ Bus Interface Cable Assembly

SPECIFICATIONS

Word Size

Data — 8 and 16-bit

Memory Addressing

24-bits – 16 megabyte – direct access

Bus Bandwidth

9.5 megabytes/sec — 8-bit

19 megabytes/sec — 16-bit

Electrical Characteristics

DC SPECIFICATIONS

Table 2. DC Specifications

Signal Name	Driver Type	Termination (to +5 Vdc) At Master	Min. Driver Requirements			Max. Receiver Requirements		
			High	Low	Load Cap.	High	Low	Load Cap.
DB15-0	TRI-STATE	10K Ohms	0.6 ma	9 ma	75 pf	0.15 ma	2 ma	18 pf
TPAR*	TRI-STATE	10K Ohms	0.6 ma	9 ma	75 pf	0.15 ma	2 ma	18 pf
AB23-0	TRI-STATE	None	0.4 ma	20 ma	120 pf	0.10 ma	5 ma	30 pf
R/W	TRI-STATE	None	0.2 ma	8 ma	75 pf	0.05 ma	2 ma	18 pf
BHEN	TRI-STATE	None	0.2 ma	8 ma	75 pf	0.05 ma	2 ma	18 pf
LOCK*	TRI-STATE	None	0.2 ma	8 ma	75 pf	0.05 ma	2 ma	18 pf
SMRQ*	TTL	10K Ohms	0.05 ma	2 ma	20 pf	0.05 ma	2 ma	18 pf
SMACK*	TTL	None	0.05 ma	2 ma	20 pf	0.05 ma	2 ma	18 pf
†ASTB*	TRI-STATE	10K Ohms	0.2 ma	9 ma	75 pf	0.05 ma	2 ma	18 pf
†DSTB*	TRI-STATE	10K Ohms	0.2 ma	9 ma	75 pf	0.05 ma	2 ma	18 pf
ACK*	OPEN COLL.	330 Ohms	N.A.	20 ma	45 pf	0.05 ma	2 ma	18 pf

†At slave, additional series RC termination to GND (100 ohm, 10 pf)

iLBX™ EXECUTION BUS

BUS TIMING

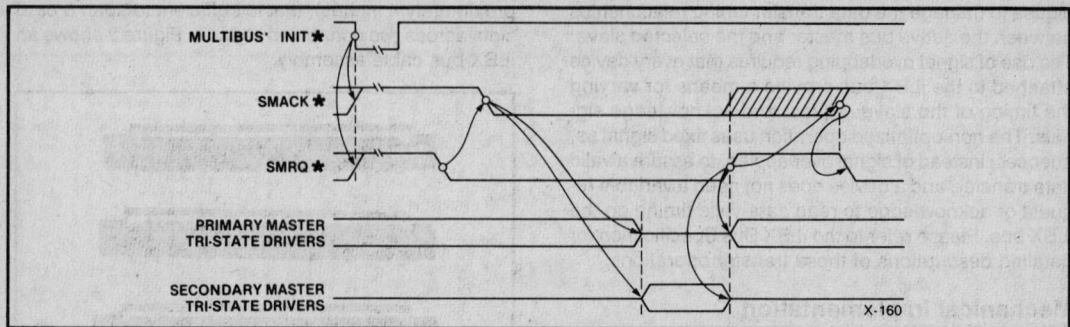

Figure 3. iLBX™ Bus Granting Timing Chart

16-Bit Transfer Timing —

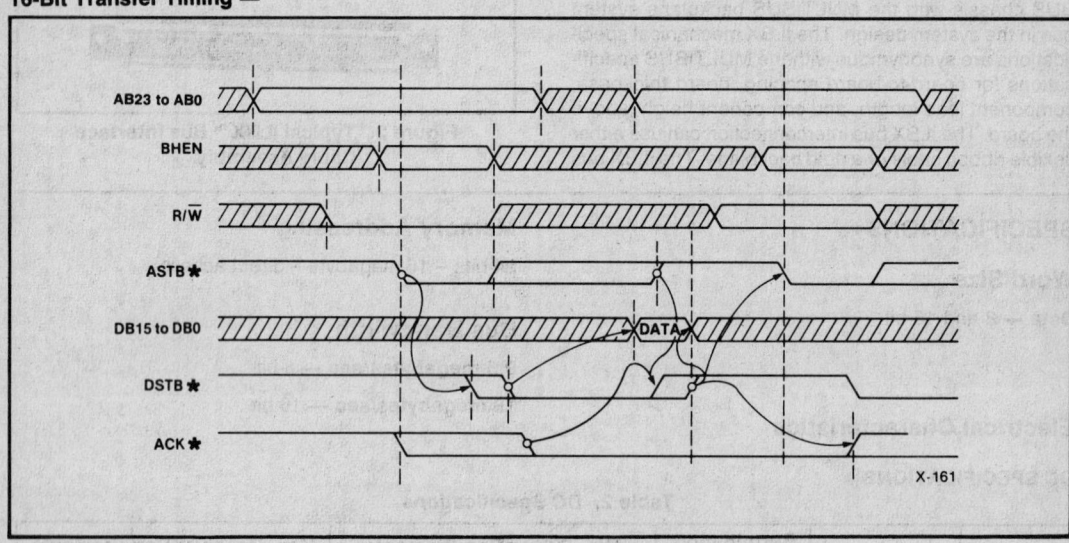

Figure 4. Write Data-To-Memory

1-26

iLBX™ EXECUTION BUS

BUS TIMING
16-Bit Transfer Timing (Con't.) —

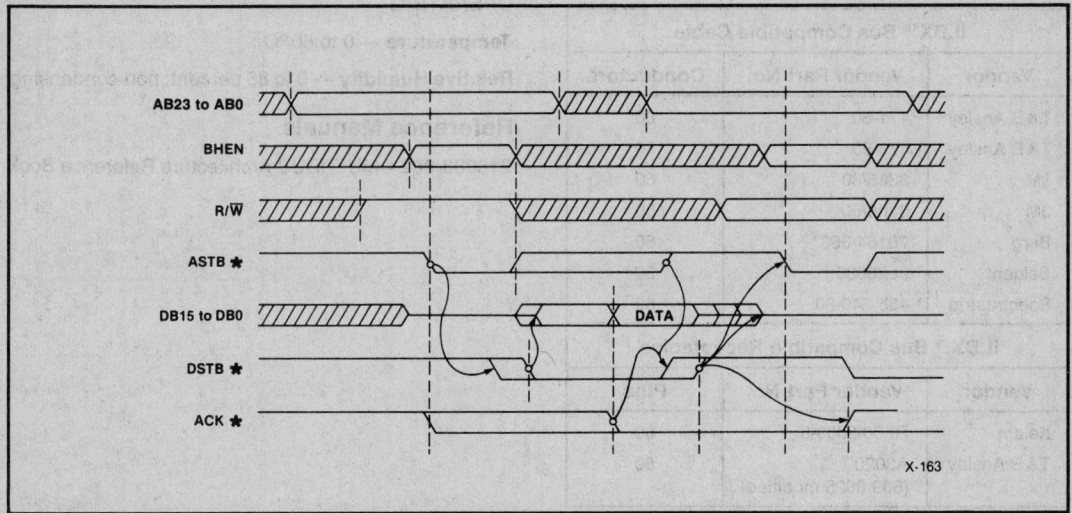

Figure 5. Read Data-From-Memory

Physical Characteristics

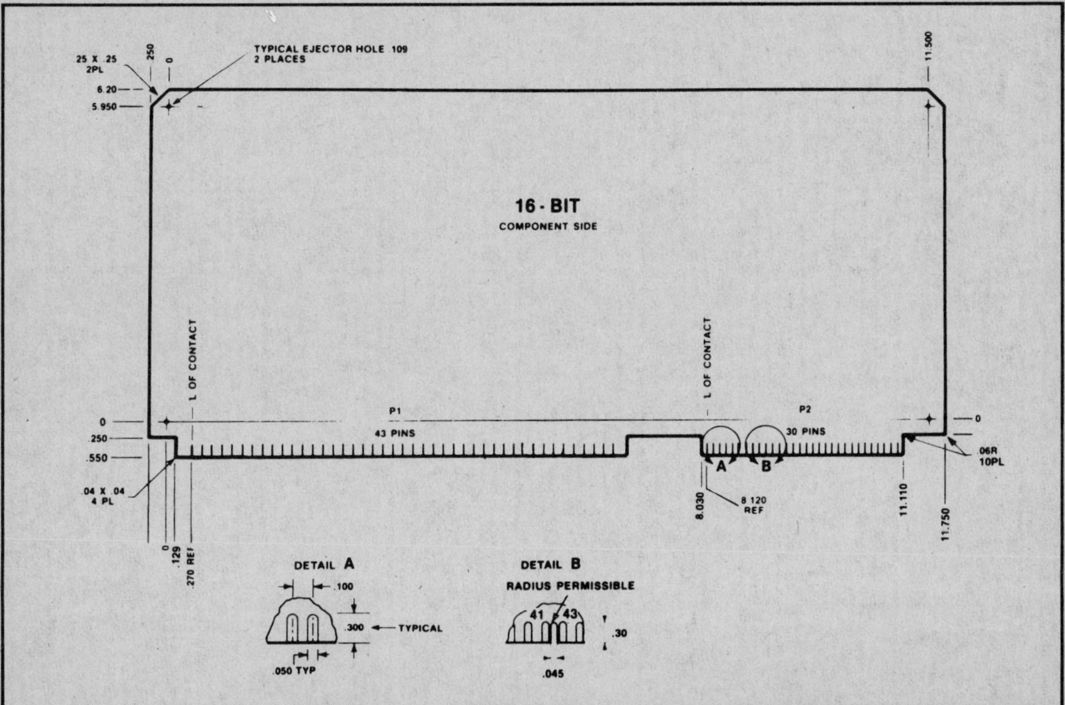

Figure 6. iLBX™ Bus Standard Printed Circuit Board Outline

iLBX™ EXECUTION BUS

Cables and Connectors

Table 3. Cable and Receptacle Vendors

iLBX™ Bus Compatible Cable		
Vendor	Vendor Part No.	Conductors
T&B Ansley	171-60	60
T&B Ansley	173-60	60
3M	3365/60	60
3M	3306/60	60
Berg	76164-060	60
Belden	9L28060	60
Spectrastrip	455-240-60	60

iLBX™ Bus Compatible Receptacles		
Vendor	Vendor Part No.	Pins
Kelam	RF30-2803-5	60
T&B Ansley	A3020 (609-6025 modified)	60

Environmental Characteristics

OPERATING

Temperature — 0 to 60°C

Relative Humidity — 0 to 85 percent; non-condensing

Reference Manuals

210883-002—MULTIBUS Architecture Reference Book

iSBX™ I/O EXPANSION BUS

- **IEEE P959 industry standard I/O expansion bus**
- **Provides on-board expansion of system resources**
- **Small iSBX™ MULTIMODULE™ boards plug directly into iSBC® boards**
- **Supports compatible 8- and 16-bit data transfer operations**
- **Part of Intel's Total System Architecture: MULTIBUS,® iLBX,™ MULTICHANNEL,™ and iSBX™**
- **Low-cost "vehicle" to incorporate the latest VLSI technology into iSBC®-based systems**
- **Provides increased functional capability and high performance**
- **Supported by a complete line of iSBC® base boards and iSBX™ MULTIMODULE™ boards, providing analog and digital I/O, high-speed math, serial and parallel I/O, video graphics, and peripheral controllers**

The iSBX™ I/O Expansion Bus is one of a family of standard bus structures resident within Intel's total system architecture. The iSBX bus is a modular, I/O expansion bus capable of increasing a single board computer's functional capability and overall performance by providing a structure to attach small iSBX MULTIMODULE™ boards to iSBC® base boards. It provides for rapid incorporation of new VLSI into iSBC MULTIBUS® systems, reducing the threat of system obsolescence. The iSBX bus offers users new economics in design by allowing both system size and system cost to be kept at minimum. As a result, the system design achieves maximum on-board performance while allowing the MULTIBUS interface to be used for other system activities. The iSBX bus enables users to add-on capability to a system as the application demands it by providing off-the-shelf standard MULTIMODULE boards in the areas of graphics controllers, advanced mathematics functions, parallel and serial I/O, disk and tape peripheral controllers, and magnetic bubble memory. A full line of MULTIBUS boards and iSBX MULTIMODULE boards are available from Intel and other third party sources in the industry.

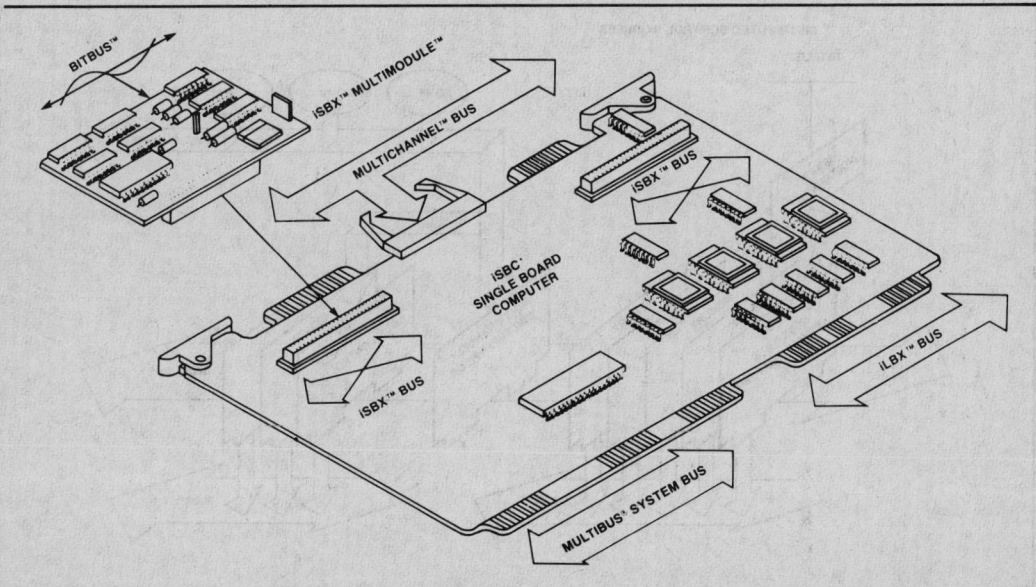

MARCH, 1985
ORDER NUMBER: 280055-002

iSBX™ I/O EXPANSION BUS

FUNCTIONAL DESCRIPTION

Bus Elements

The iSBX™ MULTIMODULE™ system is made up of two basic elements: base boards and iSBX MULTIMODULE boards. In an iSBX system, the role of the base board is simple. It decodes I/O addresses and generates the chip selects for the iSBX MULTIMODULE boards.

The iSBX bus supports two classes of base boards, those with direct memory access (DMA) support and those without. Base boards with DMA support have DMA controllers that work in conjunction with an iSBX MULTIMODULE board (with DMA capability) to perform direct I/O to memory or memory to I/O operations. Base boards without DMA support use a subset of the iSBX bus and simply do not use the DMA feature of the iSBX MULTIMODULE board.

The iSBX MULTIMODULE boards are small, specialized, I/O mapped boards which plug into base boards. The iSBX boards connect to the iSBX bus connector and convert iSBX bus signals to a defined I/O interface.

Bus Interface/Signal Line Descriptions

The iSBX bus interface can be grouped into six functional classes: control lines, address and chip select lines, data lines, interrupt lines, option lines, and power lines. The iSBX bus provides nine control lines that define the communications protocol between base board and iSBX MULTIMODULE boards. These control lines are used to manage the general operation of the bus by specifying the type of transfer, the coordination of the transfer, and the overall state of the transfer between devices. The five address and chip select signal lines are used in conjunction with the commmand lines to establish the I/O port address being accessed, effectively selecting the proper iSBX MULTIMODULE. The data lines on the iSBX bus can number 8 or 16, and are used to transmit or receive information to or from the iSBX MULTIMODULE ports. Two interrupt lines are provided to make interrupt requests possible from the iSBX board to the base board. Two option lines are reserved on the bus for unique user requirements, while several power lines provide +5 and ±12 volts to the iSBX boards.

Bus Pin Assignments

The iSBX bus uses widely available, reliable connectors that are available in 18/36 pin for 8-bit devices and 22/44 pin for 16-bit devices. The male iSBX connector is attached to the iSBX MULTIMODULE board and the female iSBX connector is attached to the base board. Figure 2 shows the dimensions and pin numbering of the 18/36 pin iSBX connector, while Figure 3 does the same for the 22/44 pin iSBX connector. A unique scheme allows the 16-bit female connector to support 8 or 16-bit male MULTIMODULE boards. Table 1 lists the signal/pin assignments for the bus.

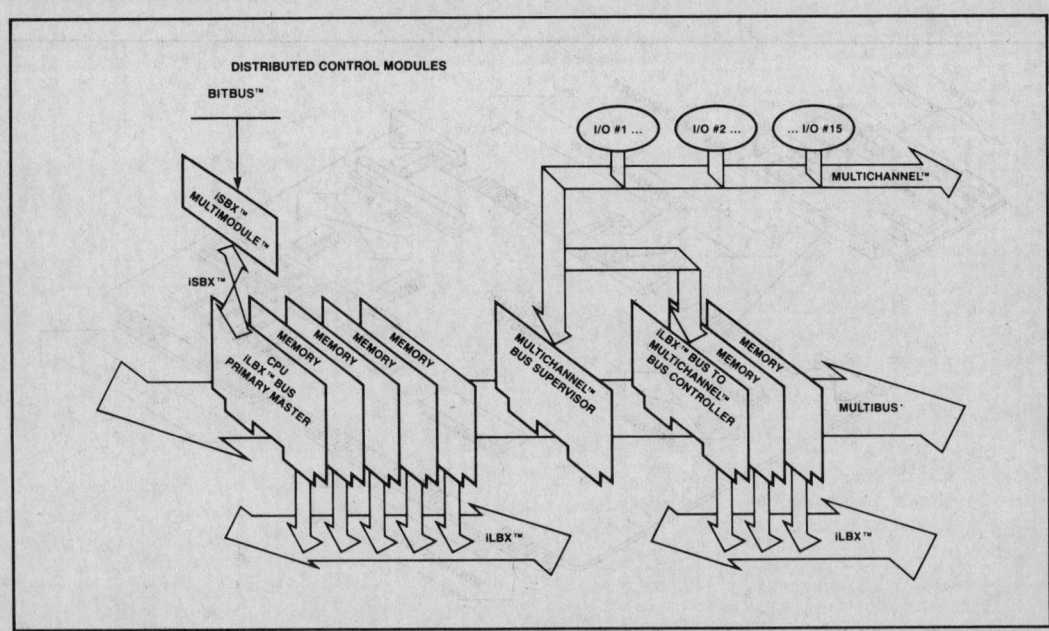

Figure 1. MULTIBUS® System Architecture

iSBX™ I/O EXPANSION BUS

Table 1. iSBX™ Signal/Pin Assignments

Pin[1]	Mnemonic	Description	Pin[1]	Mnemonic	Description
43	MD8	MDATA Bit 8	44	MD9	MDATA Bit 9
41	MDA	MDATA Bit A	42	MDB	MDATA Bit F
39	MDC	MDATA Bit C	40	MDD	MDATA Bit D
37	MDE	MDATA Bit E	38	MDF	MDATA Bit F
35	GND	Signal Gnd	36	+5V	+5 Volts
33	MD0	MDATA Bit 0	34	MDRQT	M DMA Request
31	MD1	MDATA Bit 1	32	MDACK/	M DMA Acknowledge
29	MD2	MDATA Bit 2	30	OPT0	Option 0
27	MD3	MDATA Bit 3	28	OPT1	Option 1
25	MD4	MDATA Bit 4	26	TDMA	Terminate DMA
23	MD5	MDATA Bit 5	24		Reserved
21	MD6	MDATA Bit 6	22	MCS0/	M Chip Select 0
19	MD7	MDATA Bit 7	20	MCS1/	M Chip Select 1
17	GND	Signal Gnd	18	+5V	+5 Volts
15	IORD/	I/O Read Cmd	16	MWAIT/	M Wait
13	IOWRT/	I/O Write Cmd	14	MINTR0	M Interrupt 0
11	MA0	M Address 0	12	MINTR1	M Interrupt 1
9	MA1	M Address 1	10		Reserved
7	MA2	M Address 2	8	MPST/	iSBX Multimodule Board Present
5	RESET	Reset	6	MCLK	M Clock
3	GND	Signal Gnd	4	+5V	+5 Volts
1	+12V	+12 Volts	2	-12V	-12 Volts

Notes:
1. Pins 37-44 are used only on 8/16-bit systems
2. All undefined pins are reserved for future use.

Bus Operation Protocol

COMMAND OPERATION

The iSBX bus supports two types of transfer operations between iSBX elements: I/O Read and I/O Write. An iSBX board can respond to these I/O transfers using either full speed mode or extended mode.

For a full speed I/O Read (Figure 4) the base board generates a valid I/O address and a valid chip select for the iSBX MULTIMODULE board. After set-up, the base board activates the I/O Read line causing the iSBX board to generate valid data from the addressed I/O port. The base board then reads the data and removes the read command, address, and chip select. The full speed I/O Write (Figure 5) operation is similar to the I/O Read except that the base board generates valid data on the lines and keeps the write command line active for the specified a hold time.

The extended Read operation (Figure 6) is used by iSBX MULTIMODULE boards that aren't configured to meet full speed specifications. It's operation is similar to full speed mode, but must use a wait signal to ensure proper

iSBX™ I/O EXPANSION BUS

data transfer. The base board begins the operation by generating a valid I/O address and chip select. After set-up, the base board activates the Read line causing the iSBX board to generate a Wait signal. This causes the CPU on the base board to go into a wait state. When the iSBX board has placed valid Read data on the data lines, the MULTIMODULE board will remove the Wait signal and release the base board CPU to read the data and deactivate the command, address, and chip select. The extended Write operation (Figure 7) is similar to the extended Read except that the Wait signal is generated after the base board places valid Write data on the data lines. The iSBX board removes the Wait signal when the write pulse width requirements are satisfied, and the base board can then remove the write command after the hold time is met.

DMA OPERATION

An iSBX MULTIMODULE system can support DMA when the base board has a DMA controller and the iSBX MULTI-MODULE board can support DMA mode. Burst mode DMA is fully supported, but for clarity and simplicity, only a single DMA transfer for an 8-bit base board is discussed.

A DMA cycle (Figure 8) is initiated by the iSBX board when it activates the DMA request line going to the DMA controller on the base board. When the DMA controller gains control of the base board bus, it acknowledges back to the iSBX board and activates an I/O or Memory Read. The DMA controller then activates an I/O or Memory Write respectively. The iSBX board removes the DMA request during the cycle to allow completion of the DMA cycle. Once the write operation is complete, the DMA controller is free to deactivate the write and read command lines after a data hold time.

INTERRUPT OPERATION

The iSBX MULTIMODULE board on the iSBX bus can support interrupt operations over its interrupt lines. The iSBX board initiates an interrupt by activating one of its two interrupt lines which connect to the base board. The CPU processes the interrupt and executes the interrupt service routine. The interrupt service routine signals the iSBX MULTIMODULE board to remove the interrupt, and then returns control to the main line program when the service routine is completed.

Please refer to the Intel iSBX Bus Specification for more detailed information on its operation and implementation.

SPECIFICATIONS

Word Size

Data — 8, 16-bit

Power Supply Specifications

Table 3.

Minimum (volts)	Nominal (volts)	Maximum (volts)	Maximum (current)*
+4.75	+5.0	+5.25	3.0A
+11.4	+12	+12.6	1.0A
−12.6	−12	−11.4	1.0A
—	GND	—	3.0A

*Per iSBX Multimodule board mounted on base board.

Port Assignments

Table 2. iSBX™ MULTIMODULE™ Base Board Port Assignments

iSBX™ Connector Number	Chip Select	8-Bit Base Board Address	16-Bit Base Board Address (8-bit mode)	16-Bit Base Board Address (16-bit mode)
iSBX™ 1	MCS0/ MCS1/	F0-F7 F8-FF	0A0-0AF 0B0-0BF	0A0, 2, 4, 6, 8, A, C, E 0A1, 3, 5, 7, 9, B, D, F
iSBX™ 2	MCS0/ MCS1/	C0-C7 C8-CF	080-08F 090-09F	080, 2, 4, 6, 8, A, C, E 081, 3, 5, 7, 9, B, D, F
iSBX™ 3	MCS0/ MCS1/	B0-B7 B8-BF	060-06F 060-06F	060, 2, 4, 6, 8, A, C, E 061, 3, 5, 7, 9, B, D, F

iSBX™ I/O EXPANSION BUS

DC Specifications

Table 4. iSBX™ MULTIMODULE™ Board I/O DC Specifications

Output[1]

Bus Signal Name	Type[2] Drive	I_{OL} Max −Min (mA)	@ Volts (V_{OL} Max)	I_{OH} Max −Min (µA)	@ Volts (V_{OH} Min)	C_O (Min) (pf)
MD0-MDF	TRI	1.6	0.5	−200	2.4	130
MINTR0-1	TTL	2.0	0.5	−100	2.4	40
MDRQT	TTL	1.6	0.5	−50	2.4	40
MWAIT/	TTL	1.6	0.5	−50	2.4	40
OPT1-2	TTL	1.6	0.5	−50	2.4	40
MPST/	TTL	Note 3				

Input[1]

Bus Signal Name	Type[2] Receiver	I_{IL} Max (mA)	@ V_{IN} MAX (volts) Test Cond.	I_{IH} Max (µA)	@ V_{IN} MAX (volts) Test Cond.	C_I Max (pf)
MD0-MDF	TRI	−0.5	0.4	70	2.4	40
MA0-MA2	TTL	−0.5	0.4	70	2.4	40
MCS0/-MCS1/	TTL	−4.0	0.4	100	2.4	40
MRESET	TTL	−2.1	0.4	100	2.4	40
MDACK/	TTL	−1.0	0.4	100	2.4	40
IORD/ IOWRT/	TTL	−1.0	0.4	100	2.4	40
MCLK	TTL	−2.0	0.4	100	2.4	40
OPT1-OPT2	TTL	−2.0	0.4	100	2.4	40

NOTES:
1. Per iSBX MULTIMODULE I/O board.
2. TTL = standard totem pole output. TRI = Three-state.
3. iSBX MULTIMODULE board must connect this signal to ground.

All Inputs: Max V_{IL} = 0.8V
Min V_{IH} = 2.0V

iSBX™ I/O EXPANSION BUS

Connectors

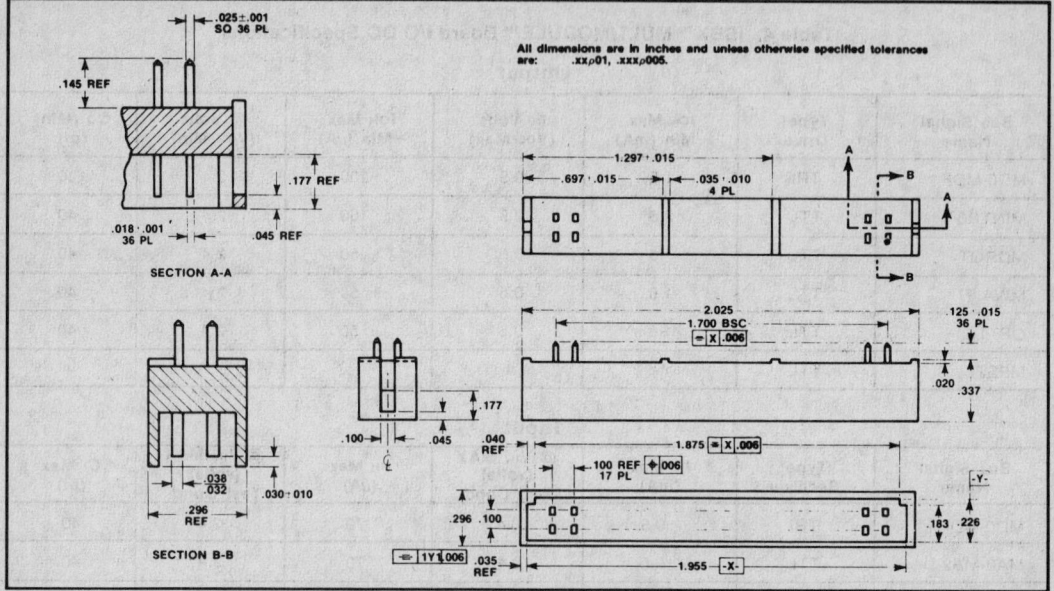

Figure 2. 18/36 Pin iSBX™ Connector

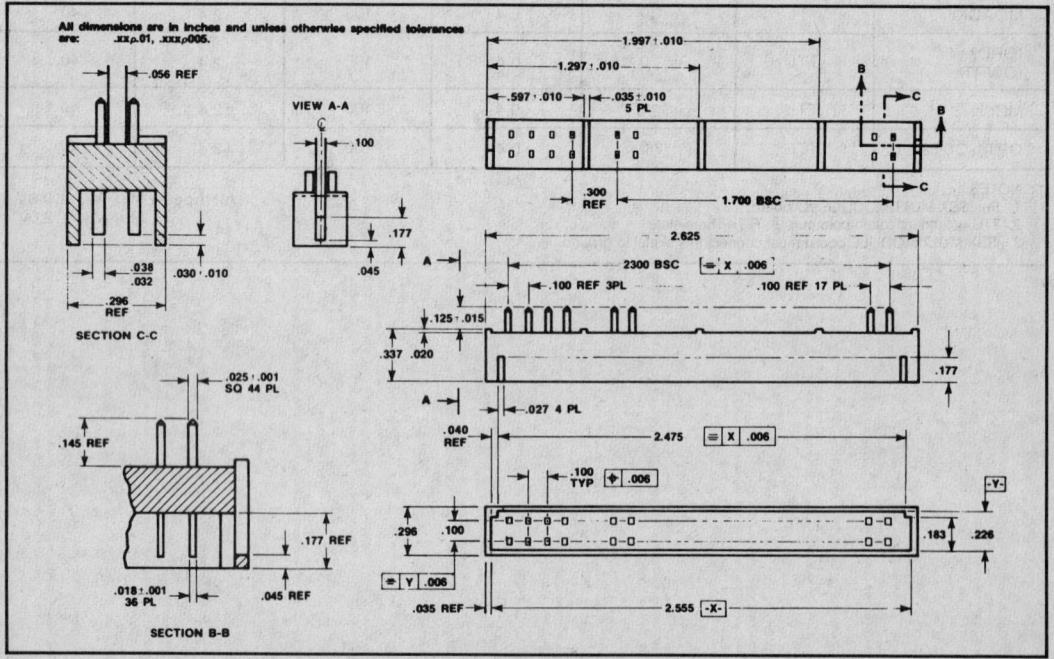

Figure 3. 22/44 Pin iSBX™ Connector

iSBX™ I/O EXPANSION BUS

Bus Timing Diagrams

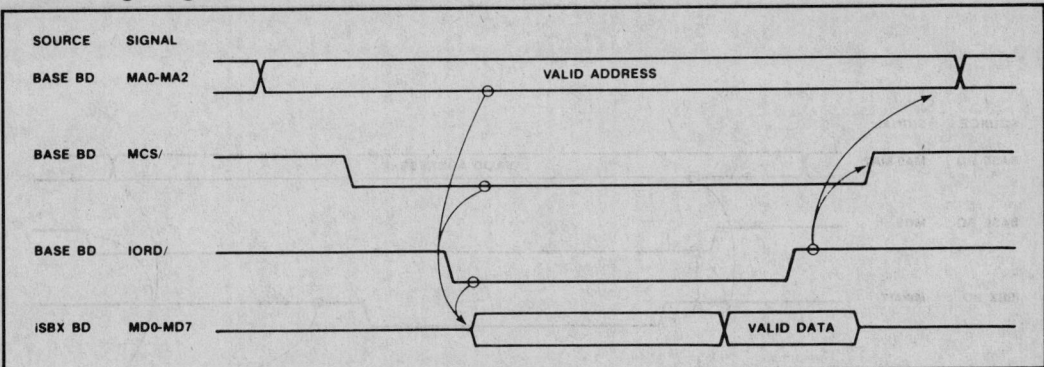

Figure 4. iSBX™ MULTIMODULE™ Read, Full Speed

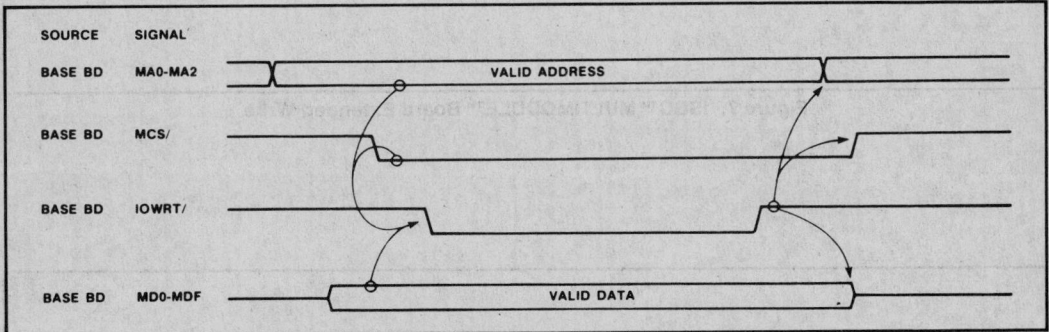

Figure 5. iSBX™ MULTIMODULE™ Board Write, Full Speed

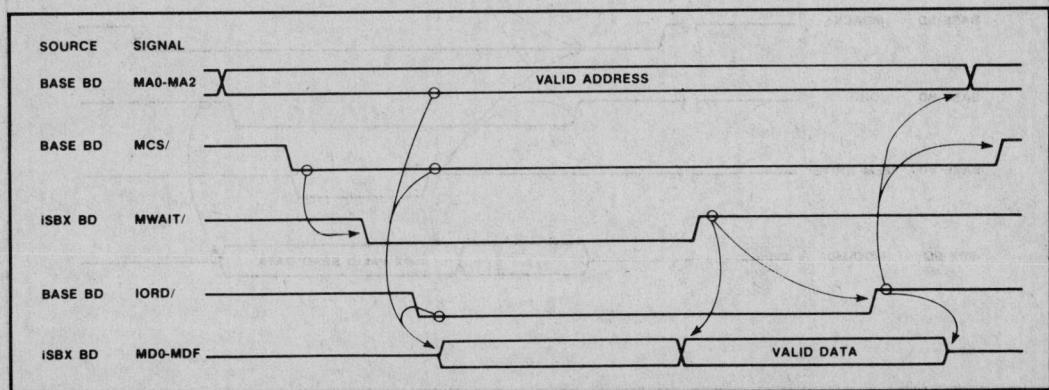

Figure 6. iSBX™ MULTIMODULE™ Board Extended Read

iSBX™ I/O EXPANSION BUS

Bus Timing Diagram (Con't)

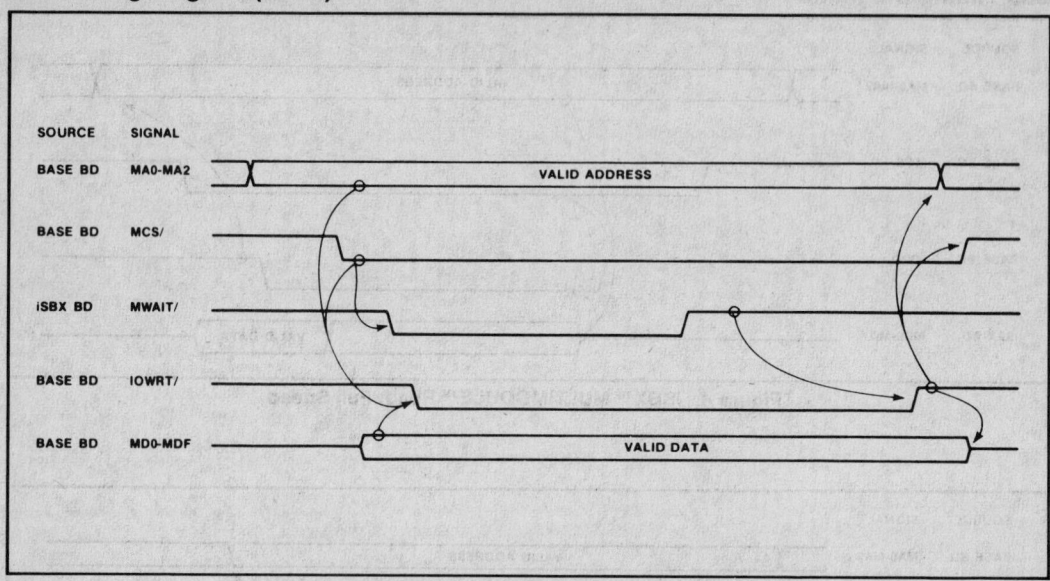

Figure 7. iSBC™ MULTIMODULE™ Board Extended Write

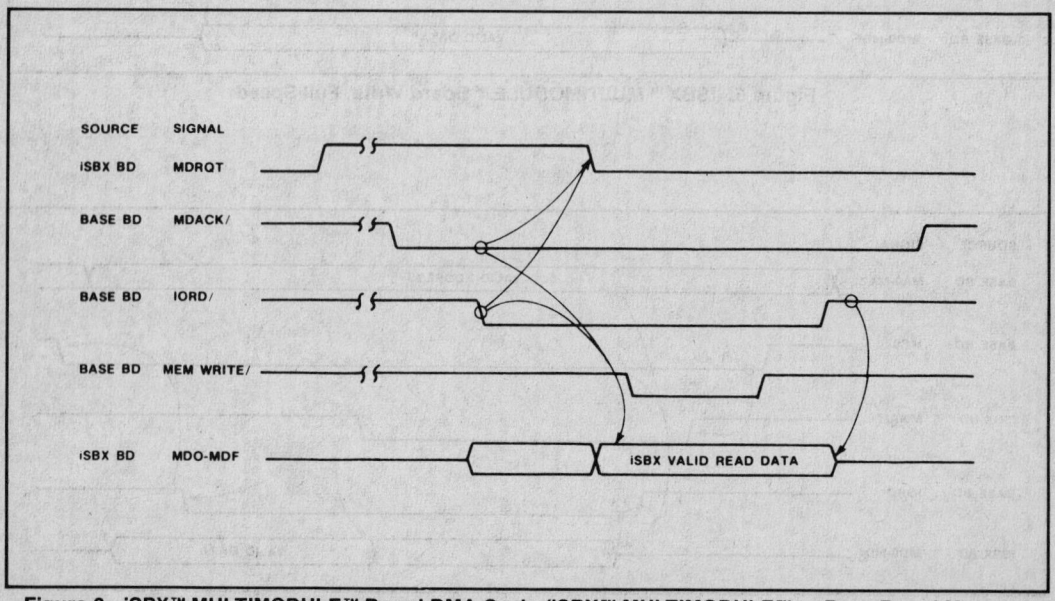

Figure 8. iSBX™ MULTIMODULE™ Board DMA Cycle (iSBX™ MULTIMODULE™ to Base Board Memory)

iSBX™ I/O EXPANSION BUS

Board Outlines

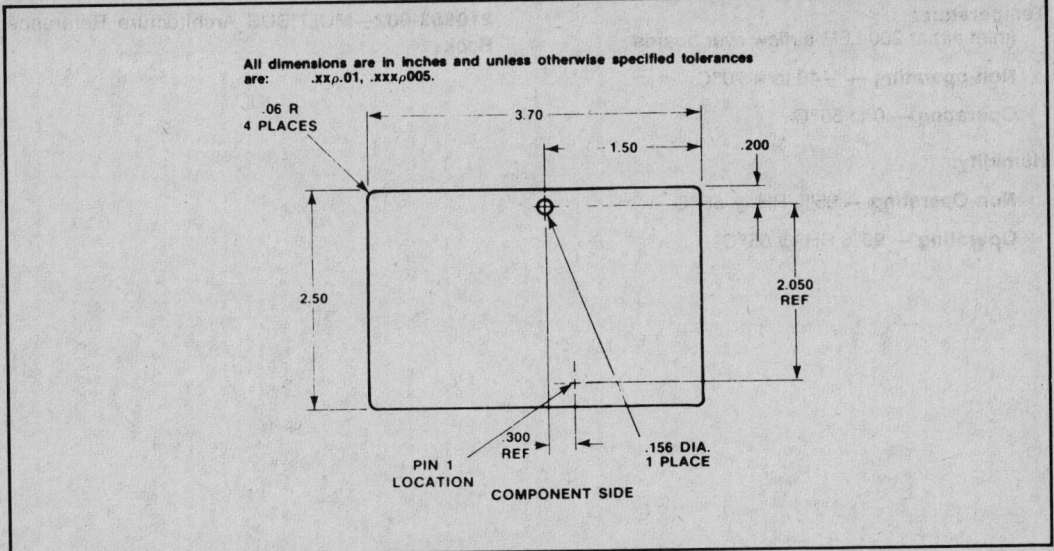

Figure 9. iSBX™ Board Outline

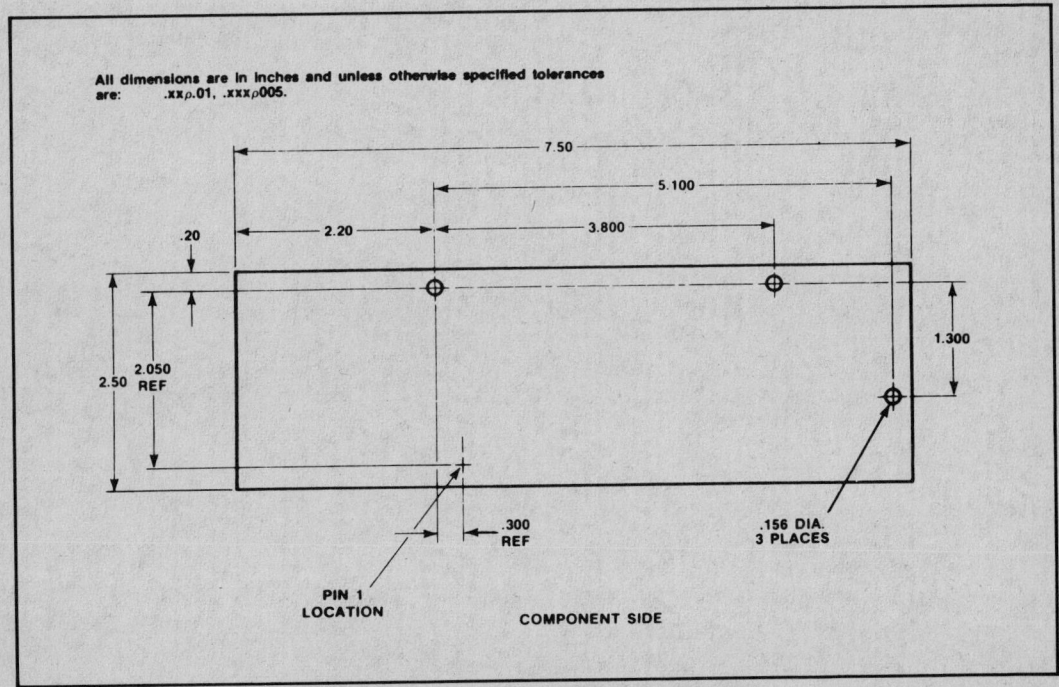

Figure 10. Double Wide iSBX™ Board Outline

iSBX™ I/O EXPANSION BUS

Environmental Characteristics

Temperature:
(inlet air) at 200 LFM airflow over boards

Non-operating — −40 to +70°C

Operating — 0 to 55°C

Humidity:

Non-Operating — 95% RH @ 55°C

Operating — 90% RH @ 55°C

Reference Manuals

210883-002—MULTIBUS Architecture Reference Book

APPLICATION NOTE

AP-28A

January, 1983

Intel MULTIBUS® Interfacing

Joe Barthmaier

© INTEL CORPORATION 1980, 1982, 1983

Order Number: 210895-001

AP-28A

I. INTRODUCTION

A significant measure of the power and flexibility of the Intel OEM Computer Product Line can be attributed to the design of the Intel MULTIBUS system bus. The bus structure provides a common element for communication between a wide variety of system modules which include: Single Board Computers, memory, digital, and analog I/O expansion boards, and peripheral controllers.

The purpose of this application note is to help you develop a working knowledge of the Intel MULTIBUS specification. This knowledge is essential for configuring a system containing multiple modules. Another purpose is to provide you with the information necessary to design a bus interface for a slave module. One of the tools that will be used to achieve this goal is the complete description of a MULTIBUS slave design example. Other portions of this application note provide an in depth examination of the bus signals, operating characteristics, and bus interface circuits.

This application note was originally written in 1977. Since 1977, the MULTIBUS specification has been significantly expanded to cover operation with both 8 and 16-bit system modules and with an auxiliary power bus. This application note now contains information on these new MULTIBUS specification features.

In addition, a detailed MULTIBUS specification has also been published which provides the user with further information concerning MULTIBUS interfacing. The MULTIBUS specification and other useful documents are listed in the overleaf of this note under Related Intel Publications.

II. MULTIBUS® SYSTEM BUS DESCRIPTION

Overview

The Intel MULTIBUS signal lines can be grouped in the following categories: 20 address lines, 16 bidirectional data lines, 8 multilevel interrupt lines, and several bus control, timing and power supply lines. The address and data lines are driven by three-state devices, while the interrupt and some other control lines are open-collector driven.

Modules that use the MULTIBUS system bus have a master-slave relationship. A bus master module can drive the command and address lines: it can control the bus. A Single Board Computer is an example of a bus master. A bus slave cannot control the bus. Memory and I/O expansion boards are examples of bus slaves. The MULTIBUS architecture provides for both 8 and 16-bit bus masters and slaves.

Notice that a system may have a number of bus masters. Bus arbitration results when more than one master requests control of the bus at the same time. A bus clock is usually provided by one of the bus masters and may be derived independently from the processor clock. The bus clock provides a timing reference for resolving bus contention among multiple requests from bus masters. For example, a processor and a DMA (direct memory access) module may both request control of the bus. This feature allows different speed masters to share resources on the same bus. Actual transfers via the bus, however, proceed asynchronously with respect to the bus clock. Thus, the transfer speed is dependent on the transmitting and receiving devices only. The bus design prevents slow master modules from being handicapped in their attempts to gain control of the bus, but does not restrict the speed at which faster modules can transfer data via the same bus. Once a bus request is granted, single or multiple read/write transfers can proceed. The most obvious applications for the master-slave capabilities of the bus are multiprocessor configurations and high-speed direct-memory-access (DMA) operations. However, the master-slave capabilities of the bus are by no means limited to these two applications.

MULTIBUS® Signal Descriptions

This section defines the signal lines that comprise the Intel MULTIBUS system bus. These signals are contained on either the P1 or P2 connector of boards compatible with the MULTIBUS specification. The P1 signal lines contain the address, data, bus control, bus exchange, interrupt and power supply lines. The P2 signal lines contain the optional auxiliary signal lines. Most signals on the bus are active-low. For example, a low level on a control signal on the bus indicates active, while a low level on an address or data signal on the bus represents logic "1" value.

NOTE

In this application note, a signal will be designated active-low by placing a slash (/) after the mnemonic for the signal.

Appendix A contains a pin assignment list of the following signals:

AP-28A

MULTIBUS P1 Signal Lines —

Initialization Signal Line

INIT/

Initialization signal; resets the entire system to a known internal state. INIT/ may be driven by one of the bus masters or by an external source such as a front panel reset switch.

Address and Inhibit Lines

ADR0/ - ADR13/

20 address lines; used to transmit the address of the memory location or I/O port to be accessed. The lines are labeled ADR0/ through ADR9/, ADRA/ through ADRF/ and ADR10/ through ADR13/. ADR13/ is the most significant bit. 8-bit masters use 16 address lines (ADR0/ - ADRF/) for memory addressing and 8 address lines (ADR0/ - ADR7/) for I/O port selection. 16-bit masters use all twenty address lines for memory addressing and 12 address lines (ADR0/ - ADRB/) for I/O port selection. Thus, 8-bit masters may address 64K bytes of memory and 256 I/O devices while 16-bit masters may address 1 megabyte of memory and 4096 I/O devices. (The 8086 CPU actually permits 16 address bits to be used to specify I/O devices, the MULTIBUS specification, however, states that only the low order 12 address bits can be used to specify I/O ports.) In a 16-bit system, the ADR0/ line is used to indicate whether a low (even) byte or a high (odd) byte of memory or I/O space is being accessed in a word oriented memory or I/O device.

BHEN/

Byte High Enable; the address control line which is used to specify that data will be transferred on the high byte (DAT8/ - DATF/) of the MULTIBUS data lines. With current iSBC boards, this signal effectively specifies that a word (two byte) transfer is to be performed. This signal is used only in systems which incorporate sixteen bit memory or I/O modules.

INH1/

Inhibit RAM signal; prevents RAM memory devices from responding to the memory address on the system address bus. INH1/ effectively allows ROM memory devices to override RAM devices when ROM and RAM memory are assigned the same memory addresses. INH1/ may also be used to allow memory mapped I/O devices to override RAM memory.

INH2/

Inhibit ROM signal; prevents ROM memory devices from responding to the memory address on the system address bus. INH2/ effectively allows auxiliary ROM (e.g., a bootstrap program) to override ROM devices when ROM and auxiliary ROM memory are assigned the same memory addresses. INH2/ may also be used to allow memory mapped I/O devices to override ROM memory.

Data Lines

DAT0/ - DATF/

16 bidirectional data lines; used to transmit or receive information to or from a memory location or I/O port. DATF/ being the most significant bit. In 8-bit systems, only lines DAT0/ - DAT7/ are used (DAT7/ being the most significant bit). In 16-bit systems, either 8 or 16 lines may be used for data transmission.

Bus Priority Resolution Lines

BCLK/

Bus clock; the negative edge (high to low) of BCLK/ is used to synchronize bus priority resolution circuits. BCLK/ is asynchronous to the CPU clock. It has a 100 ns minimum period and a 35% to 65% duty cycle. BCLK/ may be slowed, stopped, or single stepped for debugging.

CCLK/

Constant clock; a bus signal which provides a clock signal of constant frequency for unspecified general use by modules on the system bus. CCLK/ has a minimum period of 100 ns and a 35% to 65% duty cycle.

BPRN/

Bus priority in signal; indicates to a particular master module that no higher priority module is requesting use of the system bus. BPRN/ is synchronized with BCLK/. This signal is not bused on the backplane.

BPRO/

Bus priority out signal; used with serial (daisy chain) bus priority resolution schemes. BPRO/ is passed to the BPRN/ input of the master module with the next lower bus priority. BPRO/ is synchronized with BCLK/. This signal is not bused on the backplane.

BUSY/

Bus busy signal; an open collector line driven by the bus master currently in control to indicate that the bus is currently in use. BUSY/ prevents all other master modules from gaining control of the bus. BUSY/ is synchronized with BCLK/.

BREQ/

Bus request signal; used with a parallel bus priority network to indicate that a particular master module requires use of the bus for one or more data transfers. BREQ/ is synchronized with BCLK/. This signal is not bused on the backplane.

CBRQ/

Common bus request; an open-collector line which is driven by all potential bus masters and is used to inform the current bus master that another master wishes to use the bus. If CBRQ/ is high, it indicates to the bus master that no other master is requesting the bus, and therefore, the present bus master can retain the bus. This saves the bus exchange overhead for the current master.

Information Transfer Protocol Lines

A bus master provides separate read/write command signals for memory and I/O devices: MRDC/, MWTC/, IORC/ and IOWC/, as explained below. When a read/write command is active, the address signals must be stabilized at all slaves on the bus. For this reason, the protocol requires that a bus master must issue address signals (and data signals for a write operation) at least 50 ns ahead of issuing a read/write command to the bus, initiating the data transfer. The bus master must keep address signals unchanged until at least 50 ns after the read/write command is turned off, terminating the data transfer.

A bus slave must provide an acknowledge signal to the bus master in response to a read or write command signal.

MRDC/

Memory read command; indicates that the address of a memory location has been placed on the system address lines and specifies that the contents (8 or 16 bits) of the addressed location are to be read and placed on the system data bus. MRDC/ is asynchronous with respect to BCLK/.

MWTC/

Memory write command; indicates that the address of a memory location has been placed on the system address lines and that data (8 or 16 bits) has been placed on the system data bus. MWTC/ specifies that the data is to be written into the addressed memory location. MWTC/ is asynchronous with respect to BCLK/.

IORC/

I/O read command; indicates that the address of an input port has been placed on the system address bus and that the data (8 or 16 bits) at that input port is to be read and placed on the system data bus. IORC/ is asynchronous with respect to BCLK/.

IOWC/

I/O write command; indicates that the address of an output port has been placed on the system address bus and that the contents of the system data bus (8 or 16 bits) are to be output to the address port. IOWC/ is asynchronous with respect to BCLK/.

XACK/

Transfer acknowledge signal; the required response of a slave board which indicates that the specified read/write operation has been completed. That is, data has been placed on, or accepted from, the system data bus lines. XACK/ is asynchronous with respect to BCLK/.

Asynchronous Interrupt Lines

INT0/ - INT7/

8 Multi-level, parallel interrupt request lines;

used with a parallel interrupt resolution network. INT0/ has the highest priority, while INT7/ has lowest priority. Interrupt lines should be driven with open collector drivers.

INTA/

Interrupt acknowledge; an interrupt acknowledge line (INTA/), driven by the bus master, requests the transfer of interrupt information onto the bus from slave priority interrupt controllers (8259s or 8259As). The specific information timed onto the bus depends upon the implementation of the interrupt scheme. In general, the leading edge of INTA/ indicates that the address bus is active while the trailing edge indicates that data is present on the data lines.

MULTIBUS P2 Signal Lines — The signals contained on the MULTIBUS P2 auxiliary connector are used primarily by optional power back-up circuitry for memory protection. P2 signals are not bused on the backplane, and therefore, require a separate connector for each board using the P2 signals. Present iSBC boards have a slot in the card edge and should be used with a keyed P2 edge connector. Use of the P2 signal lines is optional.

ACLO

AC Low; this signal generated by the power supply goes high when the AC line voltage drops below a certain voltage (e.g., 103v AC in 115v AC line voltage systems) indicating D.C. power will fail in 3 msec. ACLO goes low when all D.C. voltages return to approximately 95% of the regulated value. This line must be pulled up by the optional standby power source, if one is used.

PFIN/

Power fail interrupt; this signal interrupts the processor when a power failure occurs, it is driven by external power fail circuitry.

PFSN/

Power fail sense; this line is the output of a latch which indicates that a power failure has occurred. It is reset by PFSR/. The power fail sense latch is part of external power fail circuitry and must be powered by the standby power source.

PFSR/

Power fail sense reset; this line is used to reset the power fail sense latch (PFSN/).

MPRO/

Memory protect; prevents memory operation during period of uncertain DC power, by inhibiting memory requests. MPRO/ is driven by external power fail circuitry.

ALE

Address latch enable; generated by the CPU (8085 or 8086) to provide an auxiliary address latch.

HALT/

Halt; indicates that the master CPU is halted.

AUX RESET/

Auxiliary Reset; this externally generated signal initiates a power-up sequence.

WAIT/

Bus master wait state; this signal indicates that the processor is in a wait state.

Reserved — Several P1 and P2 connector bus pins are unused. However, they should be regarded as reserved for dedicated use in future Intel products.

Power Supplies — The power supply bus pins are detailed in Appendix A which contains the pin assignment of signals on the MULTIBUS backplane.

It is the designer's responsibility to provide adequate bulk decoupling on the board to avoid current surges on the power supply lines. It is also recommended that you provide high frequency decoupling for the logic on your board. Values of 22uF for +5v and +12v pins and 10uF for −5v and −12v pins are typical on iSBC boards.

Operating Characteristics

Beyond the definition of the MULTIBUS signals themselves, it is important to examine the operating characteristics of the bus. The AC requirements outline the timing of the bus signals and in particular, define the relationships between the various bus signals. On the other hand, the DC requirements specify the bus driver characteristics, maximum bus loading per board, and the pull-up/down resistors.

The AC requirements are best presented by a discussion of the relevant timing diagrams. Appendix B contains a list of the MULTIBUS timing specifications. The following sections will discuss data transfers, inhibit operations, interrupt operations, MULTIBUS multi-master operation and power fail considerations.

Data Transfers — Data transfers on the MULTIBUS system bus occur with a maximum bandwidth of 5 MHz for single or multiple read/write transfers. Due to bus arbitration and memory access time, a typical maximum transfer rate is often on the order of 2 MHz.

Read Data

Figure 1 shows the read operation AC timing diagram. The address must be stable (t_{AS}) for a minimum of 50 ns before command (IORC/ or MRDC/). This time is typically used by the bus interface to decode the address and thus provide the required device selects. The device selects establish the data paths on the user system in anticipation of the strobe signal (command) which will follow. The minimum command pulse width is 100 ns. The address must remain stable for at least 50 ns following the command (t_{AH}). Valid data should not be driven onto the bus prior to command, and must not be removed until the command is cleared. The XACK/ signal, which is a response indicating the specified read/write operation has been completed, must coincide or follow both the read access and valid data (t_{DXL}). XACK/ must be held until the command is cleared (t_{XAH}).

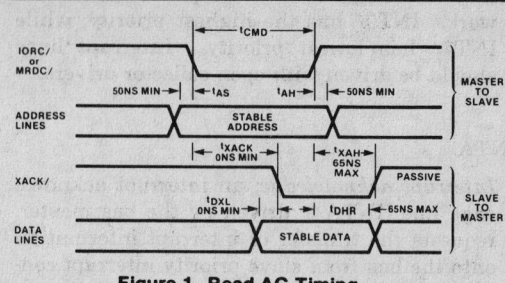

Figure 1. Read AC Timing

Write Data

The write operation AC timing diagram is shown in Figure 2. During a write data transfer, valid data must be presented simultaneously with a stable address. Thus, the write data setup time (t_{DS}) has the same requirement as the address setup time (t_{AS}). The requirement for stable data both before and after command (IOWC/ or MWTC/) enables the bus interface circuitry to latch data on either the leading or trailing edge of command.

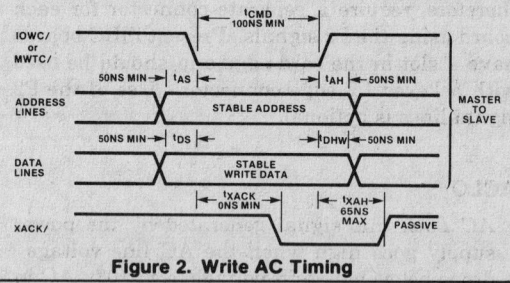

Figure 2. Write AC Timing

Data Byte Swapping in 16-bit Systems

A 16-bit master may transfer data on the MULTIBUS data lines using 8-bit or 16-bit paths depending on whether a byte or word (2 byte) operation has been specified. (A word transfer specified with an odd I/O or memory address will actually be executed as two single byte transfers.) An 8-bit master may only perform byte transfers on the MULTIBUS data lines DAT0/ - DAT7/.

In order to maintain compatibility with older 8-bit masters and slaves, a byte swapping buffer is included in all new 16-bit masters and 16-bit slaves. In the iSBC product line, all byte transfers will take place on the low 8 data lines DAT0/ - DAT7/. Figure 3 contains a example of 8/16-bit data driver logic for 16-bit master and slave systems. In the 8/16-bit system, there are three sets of buffers; the lower byte buffer which accesses DAT0/ - DAT7/, the upper byte buffer which accesses DAT8/ - DATF/, and the swap byte buffer which accesses the MULTIBUS data lines DAT0/ - DAT7/ and transfers the data to/from the on-board data bus lines D8 - DF.

Figure 4 summarizes the 8 and 16-bit data paths used for three types of MULTIBUS transfers. Two signals control the data transfers.

Byte High Enable (BHEN/) active indicates that the bus is operating in sixteen bit mode, and Address Bit 0 (ADR0/) defines an even or odd byte transfer address.

On the first type of transfer, BHEN/ is inactive, and ADR0/ is inactive indicating the transfer of an even eight bit byte. The transfer takes place across data lines DAT0/ - DAT7/.

On the second type of transfer, BHEN/ is inactive, and ADR0/ is active indicating the transfer of a high (odd) byte. On this type of transfer, the odd (high) byte is transferred through the Swap Byte Buffer to DAT0/ - DAT7/. This makes eight bit and sixteen bit systems compatible.

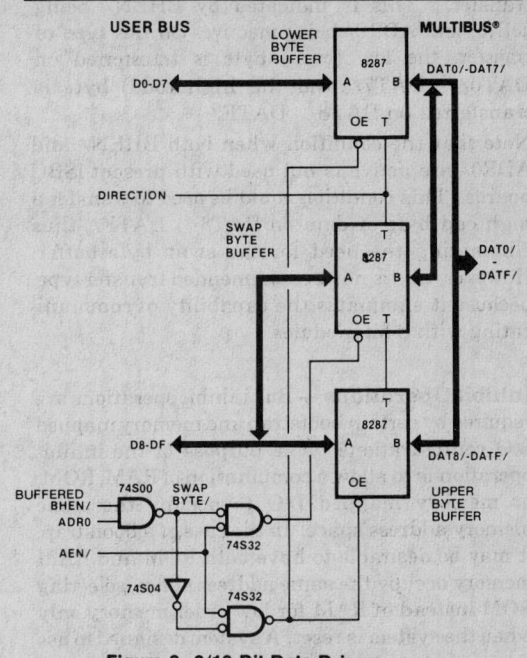

Figure 3. 8/16-Bit Data Drivers

16-BIT DEVICE	MULTIBUS®	BHEN/	ADR0/	MULTIBUS® TRANSFER DATA PATH	DEVICE BYTE TRANSFERRED
LOW, EVEN BYTES → DAT0/ - DAT7/ ; HIGH, ODD BYTES → DAT8/ - DATF/		H	H	8-BIT, DAT0/ - DAT7/	EVEN
LOW, EVEN BYTES → DAT0/ - DAT7/ ; HIGH, ODD BYTES → DAT8/ - DATF/		H	L	8-BIT, DAT0/ - DAT7/	ODD
LOW, EVEN BYTES → DAT0/ - DAT7/ ; HIGH, ODD BYTES → DAT8/ - DATF/		L	H	16-BIT, DAT0/ - DATF/	EVEN AND ODD

Figure 4. 8/16-Bit Device Transfer Operation

The third type of transfer is a 16 bit (word) transfer. This is indicated by BHEN/ being active, and ADR0/ being inactive. On this type of transfer, the low (even) byte is transferred on DAT0/ - DAT7/ and the high (odd) byte is transferred on DAT8/ - DATF/.

Note that the condition when both BHEN/ and ADR0/ are active is not used with present iSBC boards. This condition could be used to transfer a high odd byte of data on DAT8/ - DATF/, thus eliminating the need for the swap byte buffer. However, this is not a recommended transfer type, because it eliminates the capability of communicating with 8-bit modules.

Inhibit Operations — Bus inhibit operations are required by certain bootstrap and memory mapped I/O configurations. The purpose of the inhibit operation is to allow a combination of RAM, ROM, or memory mapped I/O to occupy the same memory address space. In the case of a bootstrap, it may be desirable to have both ROM and RAM memory occupy the same address space, selecting ROM instead of RAM for low order memory only when the system is reset. A system designed to use memory mapped I/O, which has actual memory occupying the memory mapped I/O address space, may need to inhibit RAM or ROM memory to perform its functions.

There are two essential requirements for a successful inhibit operation. The first is that the inhibit signal must be asserted as soon as possible, within a maximum of 100 ns (t_{CI}), after stable address. The second requirement for a successful inhibit operation is that the acknowledge must be delayed (t_{XACKB}) to allow the inhibited slave to terminate any irreversible timing operations initiated by detection of a valid command prior to its inhibit.

This situation may arise because a command can be asserted within 50 ns after stable address (t_{AS}) and yet inhibit is not required until 100 ns (t_{ID}) after stable address. The acknowledge delay time (t_{XACKB}) is a function of the cycle time of the inhibited slave memory. Inhibiting the iSBC 016 RAM board, for example, requires a minimum of 1.5 usec. Less time is typically needed to inhibit other memory modules. For example, the iSBC 104 board requires 475 ns.

Figure 5 depicts a situation in which both RAM

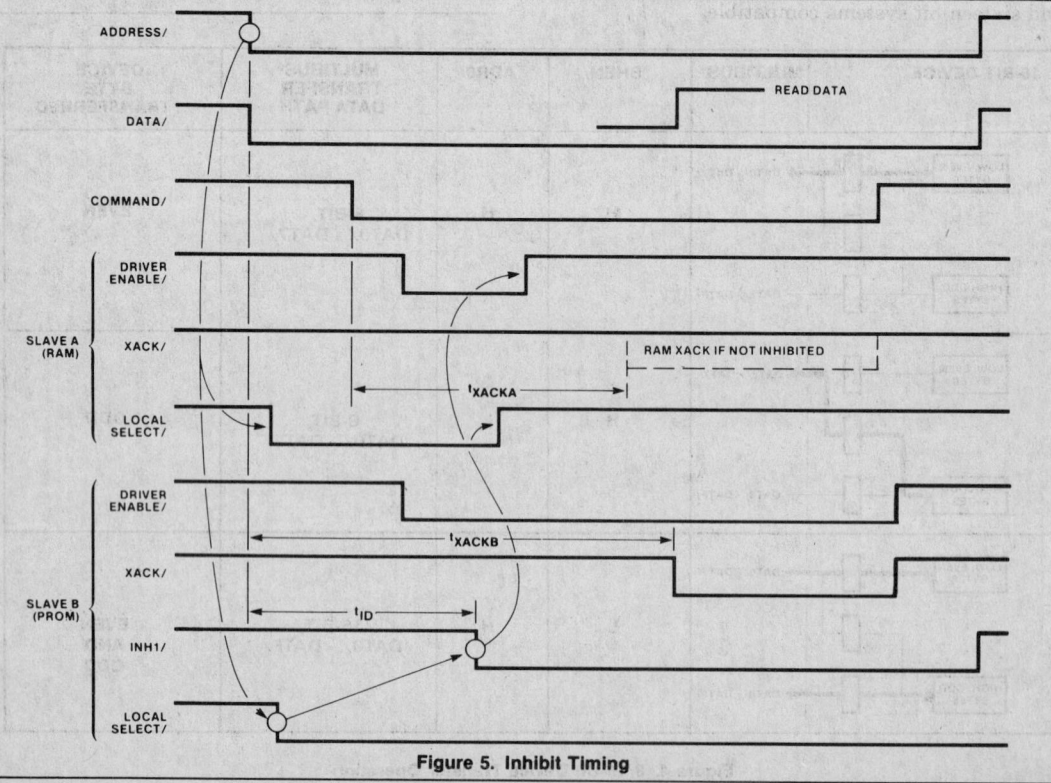

Figure 5. Inhibit Timing

AP-28A

and PROM memory have the same memory addresses. In this case, PROM inhibits RAM, producing the effect of PROM overriding RAM. After address is stable, local selects are generated for both the PROM and the RAM. The PROM local select produces the INH1/ signal which then removes the RAM local select and its driver enable. Because the slave RAM has been inhibited after it had already begun its cycle, the PROM XACK/ must be delayed (t_{XACKB}) until after the latest possible acknowledgement from the RAM (t_{XACKA}).

Interrupt Operations — The MULTIBUS interrupt lines INT0/ - INT7/ are used by a MULTIBUS master to receive interrupts from bus slaves, other bus masters or external logic such as power fail logic. A bus master may also contain internal interrupt sources which do not require the bus interrupt lines to interrupt the master. There are two interrupt implementation schemes used by bus interrupts, Non Bus Vectored Interrupts and Bus Vectored Interrupts. Non Bus Vectored Interrupts do not convey interrupt vector address information on the bus. Bus Vectored Interrupts are interrupts from slave Priority Interrupt Controllers (PICs) which do convey interrupt vector address information on the bus.

Non Bus Vectored Interrupts

Non Bus Vectored Interrupts are those interrupts whose interrupt vector address is generated by the bus master and do not require the MULTIBUS address lines for transfer of the interrupt vector address. The interrupt vector address is generated by the interrupt controller on the master and transferred to the processor over the local bus. The source of the interrupt can be on the master module or on other bus modules, in which case the bus modules use the MULTIBUS interrupt request lines (INT0/ - INT7/) to generate their interrupt requests to the bus master. When an interrupt request line is activated, the bus master performs it own interrupt operation and processes the interrupt. Figure 6 shows an example of Non Bus Vectored Interrupt implementation.

Bus Vectored Interrupts

Bus Vectored Interrupts (Figure 7) are those interrupts which transfer the interrupt vector address along the MULTIBUS address lines from the slave to the bus master using the INTA/ command signal for synchronization.

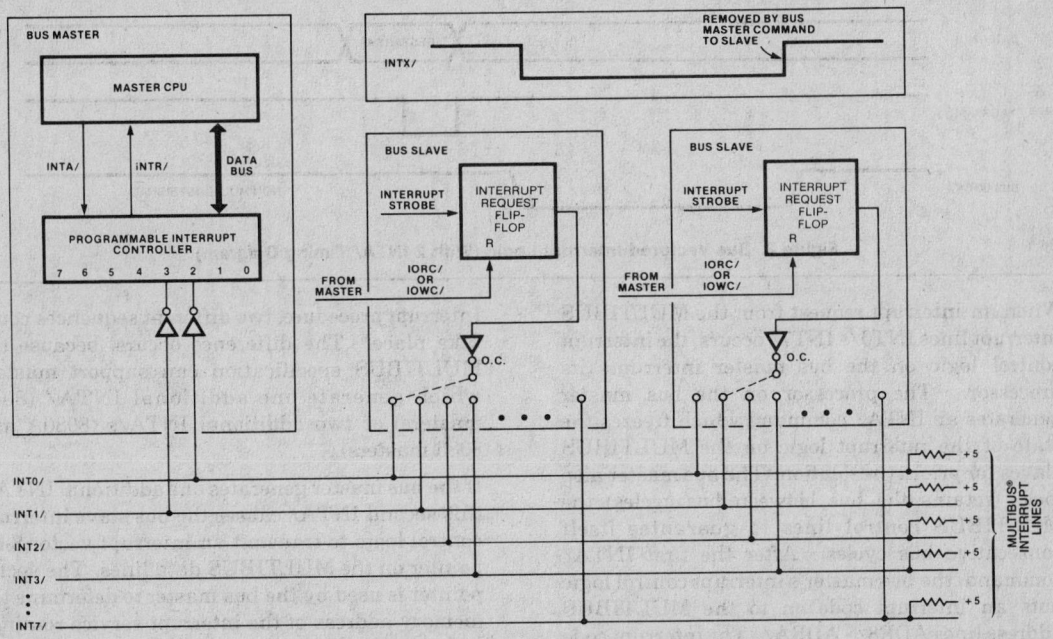

Figure 6. Non Bus Vectored Interrupt Implementation

AP-28A

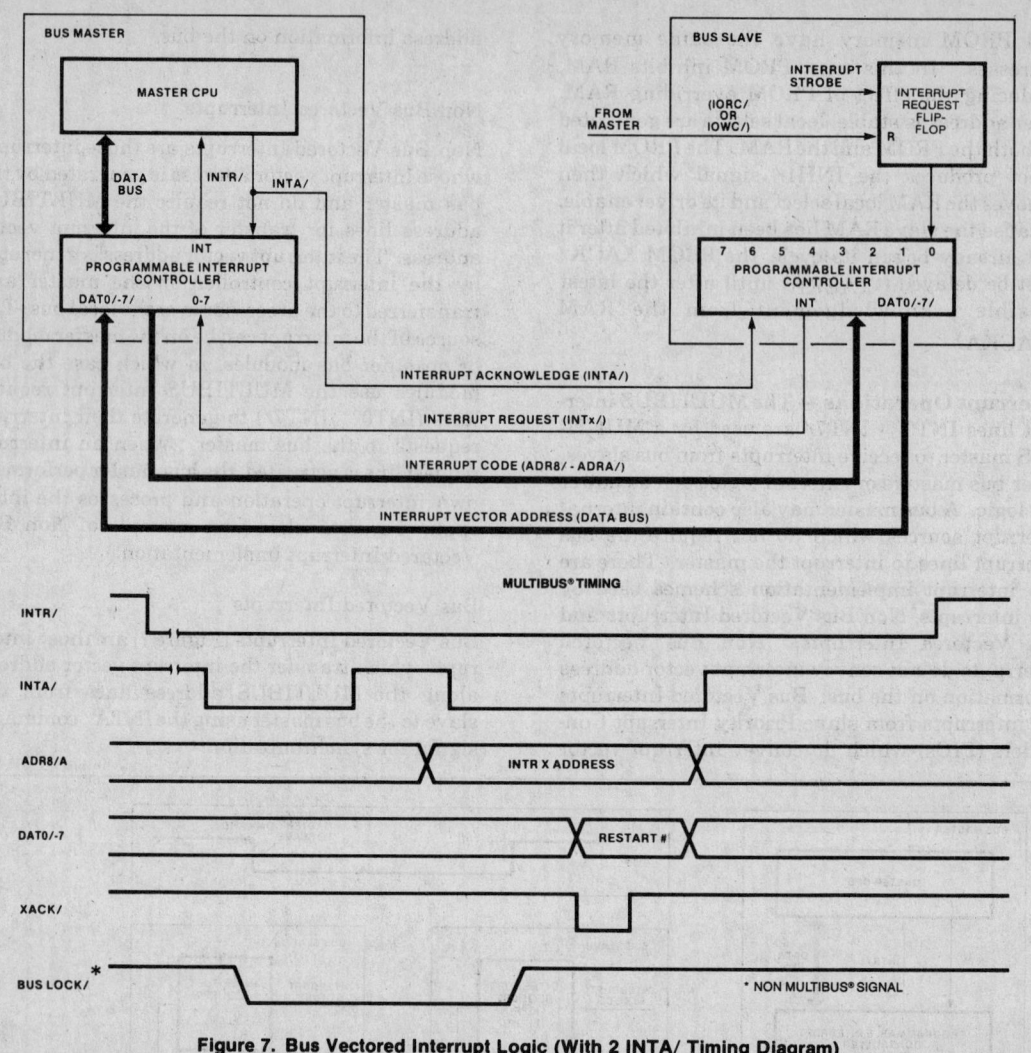

Figure 7. Bus Vectored Interrupt Logic (With 2 INTA/ Timing Diagram)

When an interrupt request from the MULTIBUS interrupt lines INT0/ - INT7/ occurs, the interrupt control logic on the bus master interrupts its processor. The processor on the bus master generates an INTA/ command which freezes the state of the interrupt logic on the MULTIBUS slaves for priority resolution. The bus master also locks (retains the bus between bus cycles) the MULTIBUS control lines to guarantee itself consecutive bus cycles. After the first INTA/ command, the bus master's interrupt control logic puts an interrupt code on to the MULTIBUS address lines ADR8/ - ADRA/. The interrupt code is the address of the highest priority active interrupt request line. At this point in the Bus Vectored Interrupt procedure, two different sequences could take place. The difference occurs, because the MULTIBUS specification can support masters which generate one additional INTA/ (8086 masters) or two additional INTA/s (8080A and 8085 masters).

If the bus master generates one additional INTA/, this second INTA/ causes the bus slave interrupt control logic to transmit an interrupt vector 8-bit pointer on the MULTIBUS data lines. The vector pointer is used by the bus master to determine the memory address of the interrupt service routine.

If the bus master generates two additional INTA/s, these two INTA/ commands allow the

1-48

bus slave to put a two byte interrupt vector address on to the MULTIBUS data lines (one byte for each INTA/). The interrupt vector address is used by the bus master to service the interrupt.

The MULTIBUS specification provides for only one type of Bus Vectored Interrupt operation in a given system. Slave boards which have an 8259 interrupt controller are only capable of 3 INTA/ operation (2 additional INTA/s after the first INTA/). Slave boards with the 8259A interrupt controller are capable of either 2 INTA/ or 3 INTA/ operation. All slave boards in a given system must operate in the same way (2 INTA/s or 3 INTA/s) if Bus Vectored Interrupts are to be used. However, the MULTIBUS specification does provide for Bus Vectored Interrupts and Non Bus Vectored Interrupts in the same system.

MULTIBUS® Multi-Master Operation — The MULTIBUS system bus can accommodate several bus masters on the same system, each one taking control of the bus as it needs to affect data transfers. The bus masters request bus control through a bus exchange sequence.

Two bus exchange priority resolution techniques are discussed, a serial technique and a parallel technique. Figures 8 and 9 illustrate these two techniques. The bus exchange operation discussed later is the same for both techniques.

Serial Priority Technique

Serial priority resolution is accomplished with a daisy chain technique (see Figure 8). The priority input (BPRN/) of the highest priority master is tied to ground. The priority output (BPRO/) of the highest priority master is then connected to the priority input (BPRN/) of the next lower priority master, and so on. Any master generating a bus request will set its BPRO/ signal high to the next lower priority master. Any master seeing a high signal on its BPRN/ line will sets its BPRO/ line high, thus passing down priority information to lower priority masters. In this implementation, the bus request line (BREQ/) is not used outside of the individual masters. A limited number of masters can be accommodated by this technique, due to gate delays through the daisy chain. Using the current Intel MULTIBUS controller chip on the master boards up to 3 masters may be accommodated if a BCLK/ period of 100 ns is used. If more bus masters are required, either BCLK/ must be slowed or a parallel priority technique used.

Parallel Priority Technique

In the parallel priority technique, the priority is resolved in a priority resolution circuit in which the highest priority BREQ/ input is encoded with a priority encoder chip (74148). This coded value is then decoded with a priority decoder chip (74S138) to activate the appropriate BPRN/ line. The BPRO/ lines are not used in the parallel priority scheme. However, since the MULTIBUS backplane contains a trace from the BPRN/ signal of one card slot to the BPRO/ signal of the adjacent lower card slot, the BPRO/ must be disconnected from the bus on the board or the backplane trace must be cut. A practical limit of sixteen masters can be accommodated using the parallel priority technique due to physical bus length limitations. Figure 9 contains the schematic for a typical parallel resolution network. Note that the parallel priority resolution network must be externally supplied.

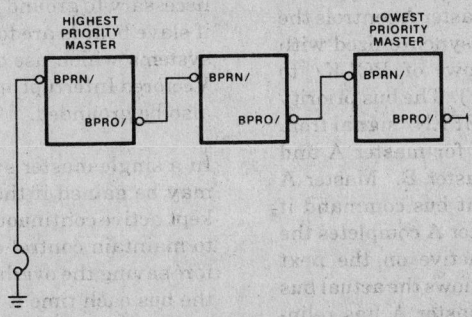

Figure 8. Serial Priority Technique

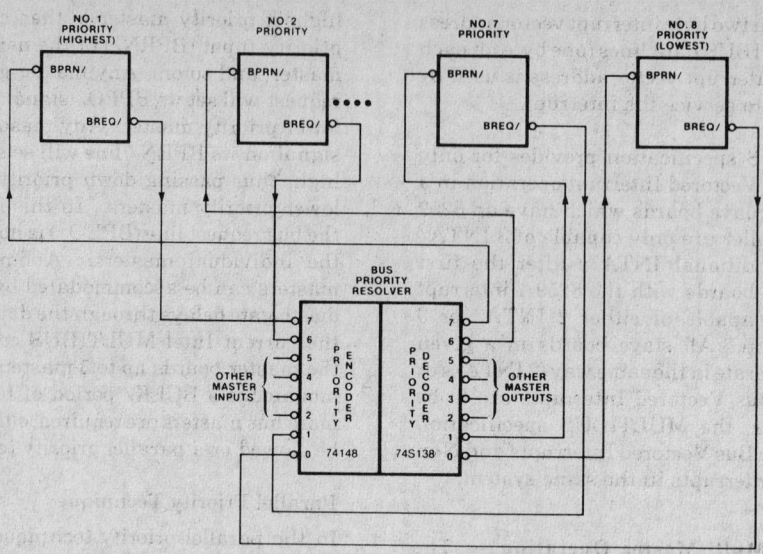

Figure 9. Parallel Priority Technique

MULTIBUS® Exchange Operation — A timing diagram for the MULTIBUS exchange operation is shown in Figure 10. This implementation example uses a parallel resolution scheme, however, the timing would be basically the same for the serial resolution scheme.

In this example, master A has been assigned a lower priority than master B. The bus exchange occurs because master B generates a bus request during a time when master A has control of the bus.

The exchange process begins when master B requires the bus to access some resource such as an I/O or memory module while master A controls the bus. This internal request is synchronized with the trailing edge (high to low) of BCLK/ to generate a bus request (BREQ/). The bus priority resolution circuit changes the BPRN/ signal from active (low) to inactive (high) for master A and from inactive to active for master B. Master A must first complete the current bus command if one is in operation. After master A completes the command, it sets BUSY/ inactive on the next trailing edge of BCLK/. This allows the actual bus exchange to occur, because master A has relinquished control of the bus, and master B has been granted its BPRN/. During this time, the drivers for master A are disabled. Master B must take control of the bus with the next trailing edge of BCLK/ to complete the bus exchange. Master B takes control by activating BUSY/ and enabling its drivers.

It is possible for master A to retain control of the bus and prevent master B from getting control. Master A activates the Bus Override (or Bus Lock) signal which keeps BUSY/ active allowing control of the bus to stay with master A. This guarantees a master consecutive bus cycles for software or hardware functions which require exclusive, continuous access to the bus.

Note that in systems with only a single master it is necessary to ground the BPRN/ pin of the master, if slave boards are to be accessed. In single board systems which use a CPU board capable of Bus Vectored Interrupt operation, the BPRN/ pin must also be grounded.

In a single master system bus transfer efficiency may be gained if the BUS OVERRIDE signal is kept active continuously. This permits the master to maintain control of the bus at all times, therefore saving the overhead of the master reacquiring the bus each time it is needed.

The CBRQ/ line may be used by a master in control of the bus to determine if another master

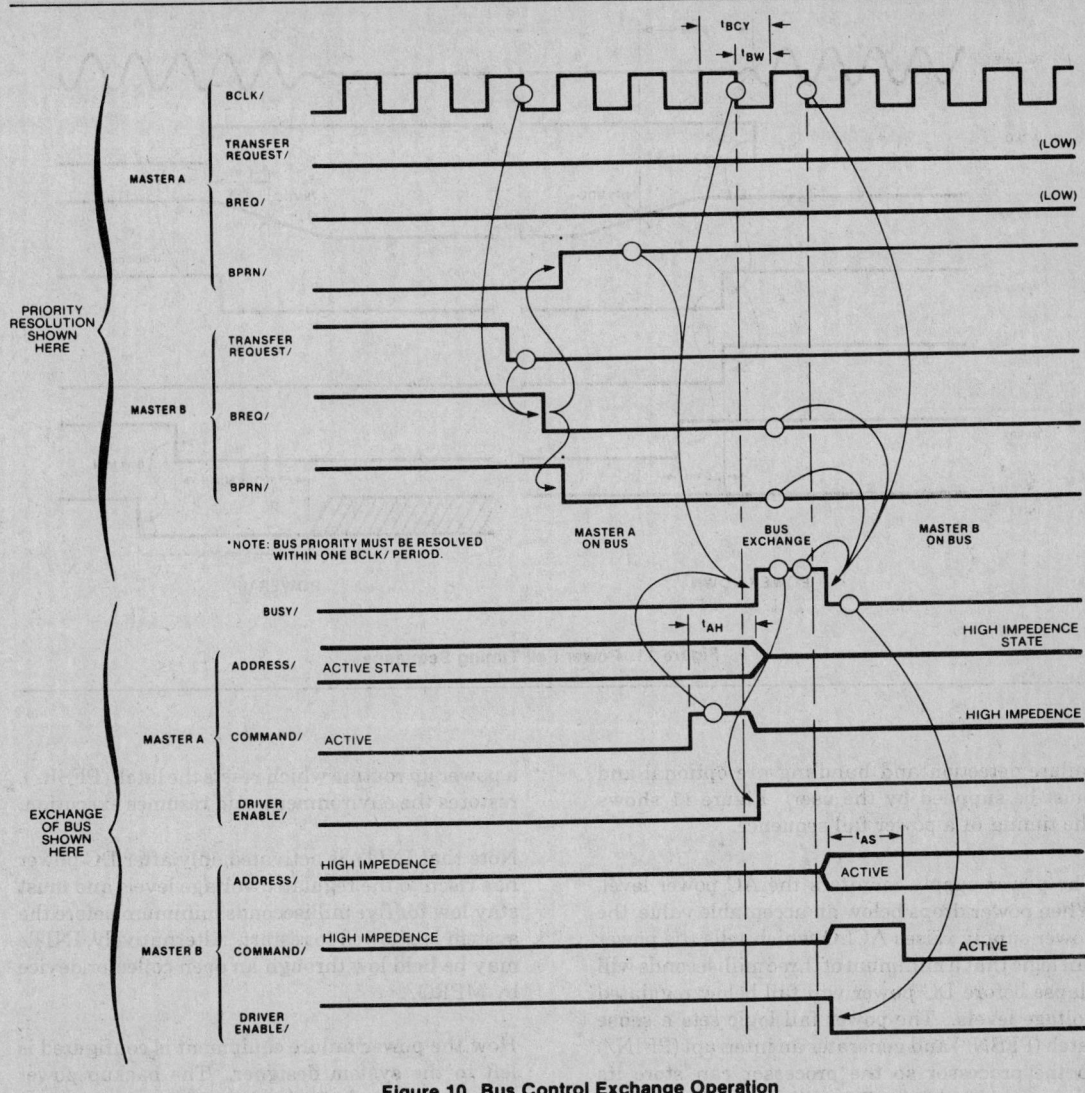

Figure 10. Bus Control Exchange Operation

requires the bus. If a master currently in control of the bus sees the CBRQ/ line inactive, it will maintain control of the bus between adjacent bus accesses. Therefore, when a bus access is required, the master saves the overhead of reacquiring the bus. If a current bus master sees the CBRQ/ line active, it will then relinquish control of the bus after the current bus access and will contend for the bus with the other master(s) requiring the bus. The relative priorities of the masters will determine which master receives the bus.

Note that except for the BUS OVERRIDE state, no single master may keep exclusive control of the bus. This is true because it is impossible for the CPU on a master to require continuous access to the bus. Other lower priority masters will always be able to gain access to the bus between accesses of a higher priority master.

Power Fail Considerations — The MULTIBUS P2 connector signals provide a means of handling power failures. The circuits required for power

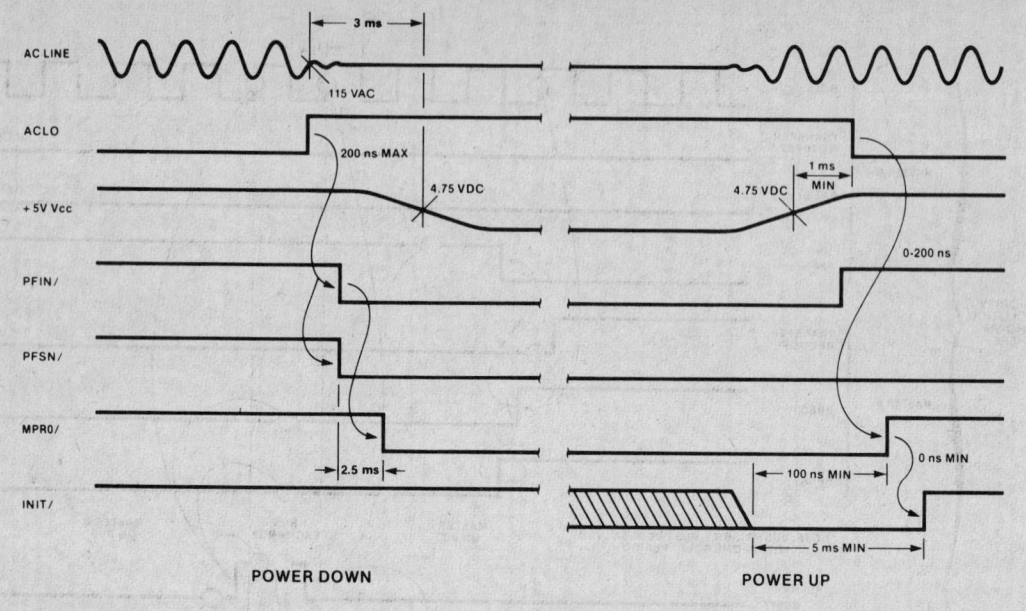

Figure 11. Power Fail Timing Sequence

failure detection and handling are optional and must be supplied by the user. Figure 11 shows the timing of a power fail sequence.

The power supply monitors the AC power level. When power drops below an acceptable value, the power supply raises ACLO which tells the power fail logic that a minimum of three milliseconds will elapse before DC power will fall below regulated voltage levels. The power fail logic sets a sense latch (PFSN/) and generates an interrupt (PFIN/) to the processor so the processor can store its environment. After a 2.5 millisecond timeout, the memory protect signal (MPRO/) is asserted by the power fail logic preventing any memory activity. As power falls, the memory goes on standby power. Note that the power fail logic must be powered from the standby source.

As the AC line revives, the logic voltage level is monitored by the power supply. After power has been at its operating level for one millisecond minimum, the power supply sets the signal ACLO low, beginning the restart sequence. First, the memory protect line (MPRO/) then the initialize line (INIT/) become inactive. The bus master now starts running. The bus master checks the power fail latch (PFSN/) and, if it finds it set, branches to a power up routine which resets the latch (PFSR/), restores the environment, and resumes execution.

Note that INIT/ is activated only after DC power has risen to the regulated voltage levels and must stay low for five milliseconds minimum before the system is allowed to restart. Alternatively, INIT/ may be held low through an open collector device by MPRO/.

How the power failure equipment is configured is left to the system designer. The backup power source may be batteries located on the memory boards or more elaborate facilities located off-board. The location of the power fail logic determines which MULTIBUS power fail lines are used. Pins on the P2 connector have been specified for the power failure functions for use as needed.

To further clarify the location and use of the power fail circuitry, an example of a typical power fail system block diagram is shown in Figure 12. A single board computer and a slave memory board are contained in the system. It is desired to power the memory circuit elements of the memory board from auxiliary power. The single board computer will remain on the main power supply. To accomplish this, user supplied power fail logic and

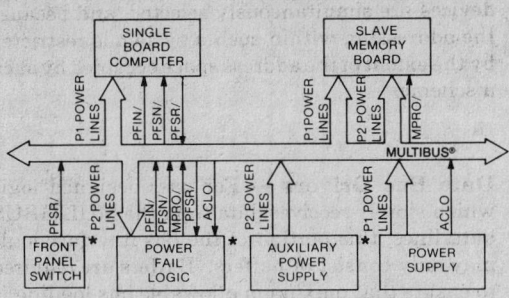

Figure 12. Typical Power Fail System Block Diagram

*USER SUPPLIED

an auxiliary power supply have been included in the system.

The single board computer is powered from the P1 power lines and accesses the P2 signal lines PFIN/, PFSN/ and PFSR/ (only the P2 signal lines used by a particular functional block are shown on the block diagram). The PFSR/ line is driven from two sources: a front panel switch and the single board computer. The front panel switch is used during normal power-up to reset the power fail sense latch. The single board computer uses the PFSR/ line to reset the latch during a power-up sequence after a power failure. Current single board computers must access the PFSN/ and PFSR/ signals either directly with dedicated circuitry and a P2 pin connection or through the parallel I/O lines with a cable connection from the parallel I/O connector to the P2 connector.

The slave memory board uses both the P1 and P2 power lines, the P2 power lines are used (at all times) to power the memory circuit elements and other support circuits, the P1 power lines power all other circuitry. In addition, the MPRO/ line is input and used to sense when memory contents should be protected.

The power fail logic contains the power fail sense latch, and uses the PFSR/ and ACLO lines for inputs and the PFIN/ PFSN/, and MPRO/ lines for outputs. The power fail logic must be powered by the P2 power lines.

DC Requirements — The drive and load characteristics of the bus signals are listed in Appendix C. The physical locations of the drivers and loads, as well as the terminating resistor value for each bus line, are also specified. Appendix D contains the MULTIBUS power specifications.

MULTIBUS® Slave Interface Circuit Elements

There are three basic elements of a slave bus interface: address decoders, bus drivers, and control signal logic. This section discusses each of these elements in general terms. A description of a detailed implementation of a slave interface is presented in a later section of this application note.

Address Decoding — This logic decodes the appropriate MULTIBUS address bits into RAM requests, ROM requests, or I/O selects. Care must be taken in the design of the address decode logic to ensure flexibility in the selection of base address assignments. Without this flexibility, restrictions may be placed upon various system configurations. Ideally, switches and jumper connections should be associated with the decode logic to permit field modification of base address assignments.

The initial step in designing the address decode portion of a MULTIBUS interface is to determine the required number of unique address locations. This decision is influenced by the fact that address decoding is usually done in two stages. The first stage decodes the base address, producing an enable for the second stage which generates the actual device selects for the user logic. A convenient implementation of this two stage decoding scheme utilizes a pair of decoders driven by the high order bits of the address for the first stage and a second decoder for the low order bits of the address bus. This technique forces the number of unique address locations to be a power of two, based at the address decoded by the first stage. Consider the scheme illustrated in Figure 13.

As shown in Figure 13, the address bits A_4 - A_B are used to produce switch selected outputs of the first stage of decoding. The 1 out of 8 binary decoders have been used. The top decoder decodes address lines A_4 - A_7, and the bottom decoder decodes address lines A_8 - A_B. If only address lines A_0 - A_7 are being used for device selection, as in the case of I/O port selection in 8-bit systems, the bottom decoder may be disabled by setting switch S2 to the ground position. Address lines A_7 and A_B drive enable inputs E2 or E3 of the decoders. The address lines A_0 - A_3 enter the second stage address decoder to produce 8 user device selects. The second stage decoder must first be enabled by an address that corresponds to the switch-selected base address.

Address decoding must be completed before the arrival of a command. Since the command may become active within 50 ns after stable address, the decode logic should be kept simple with a minimal number of layers of logic. Furthermore, the timing is extremely critical in systems which make use of the inhibit lines.

A linear or unary select scheme in which no binary encoding of device address (e.g., address bit A_0 selects device 0, address bit A_1 selects device 1, etc.) is performed is not recommended because the scheme offers no protection in case multiple devices are simultaneously selected, and because the addressing within such a system is restricted by the extent of the address space occupied by such a scheme.

Data Bus Drivers — For user designed logic which simply receives data from the MULTIBUS data lines, this portion of the bus interface logic may only consist of buffers. Buffers are required to ensure that maximum allowable bus loading is not exceeded by the user logic.

In systems where the user designed logic must place data onto the MULTIBUS data lines, three-state drivers are required. These drivers should be enabled only when a memory read command (MRDC/) or an I/O read command (IORC/) is present and the module has been addressed.

When both the read and write functions are required, parallel bidirectional bus drivers (e.g., Intel 8226, 8287, etc.) are used. A note of caution must be included for the designer who uses this type of device. A problem may arise if data hold time requirements must be satisfied for user logic following write operations. When bus commands are used to directly produce both the chip select for the bidirectional bus driver and a strobe to a latch in the user logic, removal of that signal may not provide the user's latch with adequate data hold time. Depending on the specifics of the user logic, this problem may be solved by permanently enabling the data buffer's receiver circuits and controlling only the direction of the buffers.

Control Signal Logic — The control signal logic consists of the circuits that forward the I/O and memory read/write commands to their respective destinations, provide the bus with a transfer acknowledge response, and drive the system interrupt lines.

Bus Command Lines

The MULTIBUS information transfer protocol lines (MRDC/, MWTC/, IORD/. and IOWC/) should be buffered by devices with very high speed switching. Because the bus DC requirements specify that each board may load these lines with 2.0 mA, Schottky devices are recommended. LS devices are not recommended due to their poor noise immunity. The commands should be gated

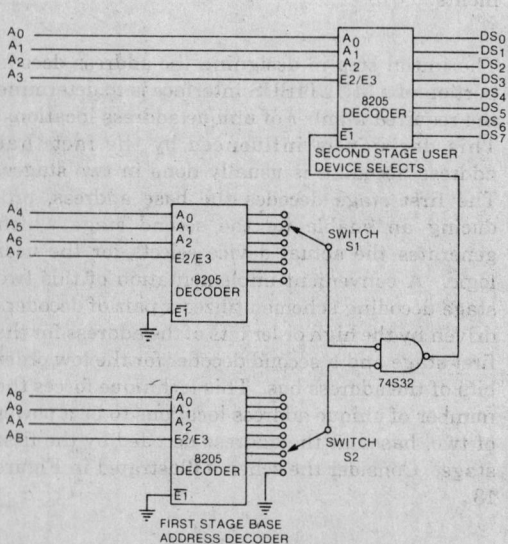

Figure 13. Two Stage Decoding Scheme

with a signal indicating the base address has been decoded to generate read and write strobes for the user logic.

Transfer Acknowledge Generation

The user interface transfer acknowledge generation logic provides a transfer acknowledge response, XACK/, to notify the bus master that write data provided by the bus master has been accepted or that read data it has requested is available on the MULTIBUS data lines. XACK/ allows the bus master to conclude its current instruction.

Since XACK/ timing requirements depend on both the CPU of the bus master and characteristics of the user logic, a circuit is needed which will provide a range of easily modified acknowledge responses.

The transfer acknowledge signals must be driven by three-state drivers which are enabled when the bus interface is addressed and a command is present.

Interrupt Signal Lines

The asynchronous interrupt lines must be driven by open collector devices with a minimum drive of 16 mA.

In a typical Non Bus Vectored Interrupt system, logic must be provided to assert and latch-up an interrupt signal. In addition to driving the MULTIBUS interrupt lines, the latched interrupt signal would be read by an I/O operation such as reading the module's status. The interrupt signal would be cleared by writing to the status register.

III. MULTIBUS® SLAVE DESIGN EXAMPLE

A MULTIBUS slave design example has been included in this application note to reinforce the theory previously discussed. The design example is of general purpose I/O slave interface. This design example could easily be modified to be used as a slave memory interface by buffering the address signals and using the appropriate MULTIBUS memory commands. In addition, to help the reader better understand an application for an I/O slave interface, two Intel 8255A Parallel Peripheral Interface (PPI) devices are shown connected to the slave interface.

The design example is shown in both 8/16-bit version and an 8-bit version. The 8/16-bit version is an I/O interface which will permit a 16-bit master to perform 8 or 16 bit data transfers. 8-bit masters may also use the 8/16-bit version of the design example to perform 8-bit data transfers.

The 8-bit version of the design example may be used by both 8 or 16-bit masters, but will only perform 8-bit data transfers. It does not contain the circuitry required to perform 16-bit data transfers.

Both the 8/16-bit version and the 8-bit version of the design example were implemented on an iSBC 905 prototype board. The schematics for each of the examples are given in Appendices F and G.

Functional/Programming Characteristics

This section describes the organization of the slave interface from two points of view, the functional point of view and the programming characteristics. First, the principal functions performed by the hardware are identified and the general data flow is illustrated. This point of view is intended as an introduction to the detailed description provided in the next section; Theory of Operation. In the second point of view, the information needed by a programmer to access the slave is summarized.

Functional Description — The function of this I/O slave is to provide the bus interface logic for general purpose I/O functions and for two Intel 8255A Parallel Peripheral Interface (PPI) devices. Eight device selects (port addresses) are available for general purpose I/O functions. One of these device select lines is used to read and reset the state of an interrupt status flip-flop, the other seven device selects are unused in this design. An additional eight I/O device port addresses are used by the two 8255A devices; four I/O port addresses per 8255A (three I/O port address for the three parallel ports A, B, and C and the fourth I/O port address for the device control register).

Figure 14 contains a functional block diagram of the slave design example. This block diagram shows the fundamental circuit elements of a bus slave: bidirectional data bus drivers/receivers, address decoding logic and bus control logic. Also shown is the address decoding logic for the low order four bits, the interrupt logic which is selected by this decoding logic, and the two 8255A devices.

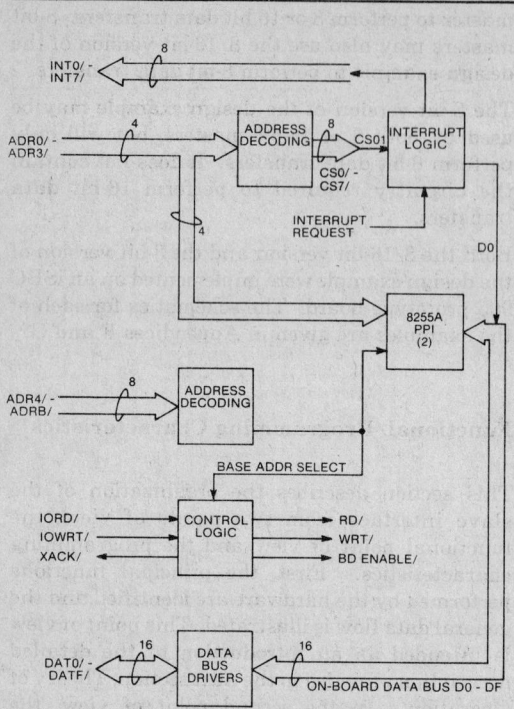

Figure 14. MULTIBUS® Slave Design Example Functional Block Diagram

Programming Characteristics — The slave design example provides 16 I/O port addresses which may be accessed by user software. The base address of the 16 contiguous port addresses is selected by wire wrap connections on the prototype board. The wire wrap connections specify address bits ADR4/ - ADRB/. They allow the selection of a base address on any 16 byte boundary. Twelve address bits (ADR0/ - ADRB/) are used since 16-bit (8086 based) masters use 12 bits to specify I/O port addresses. If an 8 bit (8080 or 8085 based) master is used with this slave board, the high order address bits (ADR8/ - ADRB/) must not be used by the decoding circuits; a wire wrap jumper position (ground position) is provided for this.

The 16 I/O port addresses are divided into two groups of 8 port addresses by decoding address line ADR3/. Port addresses XX0 - XX7 are used for general I/O functions (XX indicates any hexidecimal digit combination). Port address XX0 is used for accessing the interrupt status flip-flop and port addresses XX1 - XX7 are not used in this example. Port addresses XX8 - XXF are used for accessing the PPIs. If port addresses XX8 - XXF are selected, then ADR0/ is used to specify which of two PPIs are selected. If the address is even (XX8, XXA, XXC, or XXE) then one PPI is selected. If the address is odd (XX9, XXB, XXD, or XXF), then the other PPI is selected. ADR1/ and ADR2/ are connected directly to the PPIs. Table 1 summarizes the I/O port addresses of the slave design example. Note that if a 16-bit master is used, it is possible to access the slave in a byte or word mode. If word access is used with port address XX8, XXA, XXC, or XXE, then 16 bit transfers will occur between the PPIs and the master. These 16 bit transfers occur because an even address has been specified and the MULTIBUS BHEN/ signal indicates that a 16-bit transfer is requested.

Theory of Operation

In the preceding section, each of the slave design example functional blocks was identified and briefly explained. This section explains how these functions are implemented. For detailed circuit information, refer to the schematics in Appendices F and G. The schematic in Appendix F is on a foldout page so that the following text may easily be related to the schematic.

The discussion of the theory of operation is divided into five segments, each of which discusses a different function performed by the MULTIBUS slave design example. The five segments are:

1. Bus address decoding
2. Data buffers
3. Control signals
4. Interrupt logic
5. PPI operation

Each of these topics are discussed with regard to the 8/16-bit version of the design example; followed by a discussion of the circuit elements which are required by the 8-bit version of the interface.

Bus Address Decoding — Bus address decoding is performed by two 8205 1 out of 8 binary decoders. One decoder (A3) decodes address bits ADR8/ - ADRB/ and the second decoder (A2) decodes address bits ADR4/ - ADR7/. The base address

Table 1
SLAVE DESIGN EXAMPLE PORT ADDRESSES

I/O PORT ADDRESS	READ	WRITE
BYTE ACCESS		
XX0	Bit 0 = Interrupt Status	Reset Interrupt Status
XX1 - XX7	Unused	Unused
XX8	Parallel Port A, Even PPI	Parallel Port A, Even PPI
XX9	Parallel Port A, Odd PPI	Parallel Port A, Odd PPI
XXA	Parallel Port B, Even PPI	Parallel Port B, Even PPI
XXB	Parallel Port B, Odd PPI	Parallel Port B, Odd PPI
XXC	Parallel Port C, Even PPI	Parallel Port C, Even PPI
XXD	Parallel Port C, Odd PPI	Parallel Port C, Odd PPI
XXE	Illegal Condition	Control, Even PPI
XXF	Illegal Condition	Control, Odd PPI
WORD ACCESS		
XX0	Bit 0 = Interrupt Status	Reset Interrupt Status
XX2 - XX6	Unused	Unused
XX8	Parallel Port A, Even and Odd PPIs	Parallel Port A, Even and Odd PPIs
XXA	Parallel Port B, Even and Odd PPIs	Parallel Port B, Even and Odd PPIs
XXC	Parallel Port C, Even and Odd PPIs	Parallel Port C, Even and Odd PPIs
XXE	Illegal Condition	Control, Even and Odd PPIs

XX = Any hex digits, assigned by jumpers; XX defines the base address.

selected is determined by the position of wire wrap jumpers. The outputs of the two decoders are ANDed together to form the BASE ADR SELECT/ signal. This signal specifies the base address for a group of 16 I/O ports. Using the wire wrap jumper positions shown in the schematic, a base address of E3 has been selected. Therefore, this MULTIBUS slave board will respond to I/O port addresses in the E30 - E3F range.

If this slave board is to be used with 8-bit MULTIBUS masters, the high order address bits must not be decoded. Therefore, the wire wrap jumper which selects the output of decoder A3 must be placed in the top (ground) position (pin 10 of gate A9 to ground).

The low order 4 address lines (ADR0/ - ADR3/) are buffered and inverted using 74LS04 inverters. These address lines are input to an 8205 for decoding a chip select for the interrupt logic; the address lines are also used directly by the PPIs. LS-Series logic is required for buffering to meet the MULTIBUS specification for I_{IL} (low level input current). S-Series or standard series logic will not meet this specification.

Address decoder A4 is used to decode addresses E30 - E37. The CS0/ output of this decoder is used to select the interrupt logic, thus I/O port address E30 is used to read and reset the interrupt latch. The remaining outputs from decoder A4 (CS1/ - CS7/) are not used in this example. They would normally be used to select other functions in a slave board with more capability. Note that in the schematic shown in Appendix G for the 8-bit version of this slave design example, the high order (ADR8/ - ADRB/) address decoder is not included and the BHEN/ signal is not used.

Data Buffers — Intel 8287 8-bit parallel bi-directional bus drivers are used for the MULTIBUS data lines DAT0/ - DATF/. In the 8/16-bit version of the slave board, three 8287 drivers are used.

When an 8-bit data transfer is requested, either driver A5, which is connected to on-board data lines D0 - D7, or driver A6, which is connected to on-board data lines D8 - DF, is used. If a byte transfer is requested from an even address, driver A5 will be selected. If a byte transfer from an odd address is requested, driver A6 will be selected. All byte transfers take place on MULTIBUS data lines DAT0/ - DAT7/. When a word (16-bit) transfer is requested from an even address, drivers A5 and A7 will be used. Note that if a user program requests a word transfer from an odd address, 16-bit masters in the iSBC product line will actually perform two byte transfer requests.

The logic which determines the chip selection (8287 input signal OE, output enable) signals for the bus drivers uses the low order address bit (ADR0/) and the buffered Byte High Enable signal (BHENBL/). Note that the MULTIBUS signal BHEN/ has been buffered with an 74LS04 inverter. This is done to meet the bus address line loading specification. The SWAP BYTE/ signal which is generated is qualified by the BD ENBL/ signal and used to select the bus drivers.

The steering pin for the 8287 drivers is labelled T (transmit) and is driven by the signal RD. When an input (read) request is active or when neither a read or write command is being serviced, the direction of data transfer of the 8287 will be set for B to A.

The 8287 drivers are set to point IN (direction B to A) when no MULTIBUS I/O transfer command is being serviced for two reasons. First, if the driver were pointed OUT (direction A to B) and a write command occured, it would be necessary to turn the buffers IN and set the OE (output enable) signal active before the data could be transferred to the on-board bus. A possibility of a "buffer-fight" could occur in some designs if the OE signal permitted an 8287 to drive the MULTIBUS data lines momentarily before the steering signal could switch the direction of the 8287. In this case, both the MULTIBUS master and the slave would be driving the data lines; this is not recommended. (In this particular design, the steering signal will always stabilize before the OE signal becomes active.)

The second reason the driver is pointing IN when no command is present is due to the "data valid after WRITE" requirements of the 8255As. The 8255A requires that data remain on its data lines for 30 ns after the WRITE command ($\overline{WR}$ at the 8255A) is removed. This requirement will be met if the direction of the 8287 drivers is not switched when the MULTIBUS IOWC/ signal is removed (WRT/ could have been used to steer the 8287 instead of RD); and if the capacitance of the on-board data bus lines is sufficient to hold the data values on the bus after the 8287 OE signal and the 8255A PPI WRT/ signal go inactive. The on-board data bus may easily be designed such that the capacitance of the lines is sufficient to meet the 30 ns data hold time requirement. In addition, the current leakage of all devices connected to the on-board bus must be kept small to meet the 30 ns data hold time requirement.

The 8-bit version of this design example uses only one 8287 instead of the three required by the 8/16-bit version. The logic required to control the swap byte buffer is also not necessary. The chip select signal used for the 8287 is the BD ENBL/ signal.

Control Signals — The MULTIBUS control signals used by this slave design example are IORC/, IOWC/, and XACK/. IORC/ and IOWC/ are qualified by the BASE ADR SELECT/ signal to form the signals RD and WRT. RD and WRT are used to drive the interrupt logic, the PPI logic and the XACK/ (transfer acknowledge) logic.

For the XACK/ logic RD and WRT are ORed to form the BD ENBL/ signal which is inverted and used to drive the CLEAR pin of a shift register. When the slave board is not being accessed, the CLEAR pin of the shift register will be low (BD ENBL/ is high). This causes the shift register to remain cleared and all outputs of the shift register will be low. When the slave board is accessed, the CLEAR pin will be high, and the A and B inputs (which are high) will be clocked to the output pins by CCLK/. To select a delay for the XACK/ signal, a jumper must be installed from one of the shift register output pins to the 8089 tri-state driver. Each of the shift register output pins select an integer multiple of CCLK/ periods for the signal delay. Since the CCLK/ signal is asynchronous, the actual delay selected may only be specified with a tolerance of one CCLK/ period. In this example a delay of 3 - 4 CCLK/ periods was selected; with a CCLK/ period of 100 ns, the XACK/ delay would occur somewhere within the range of 300 - 400 ns from the time when the CLEAR signal goes high.

The control signal logic used in the 8-bit version of the slave design example is identical to the logic used in the 8/16-bit version.

AP-28A

Interrupt Logic — The interrupt logic uses a 74S74 flip-flop to latch an asynchronous interrupt request from some external logic. The Q output of the INTERRUPT REQUEST LATCH is output through an open collector gate to one of the MULTIBUS interrupt lines. The state of the INTERRUPT REQUEST LATCH is transferred to the INTERRUPT STATUS LATCH when a read command is performed on I/O port BASE ADDRESS+0 (E30 for the jumper configuration shown). The Q output of INTERRUPT STATUS LATCH is used to drive data line D0 of the on-board data bus by using an 8089 tri-state driver. If a user program performs an INPUT from I/O port E30, data bit 0 will be set to 1 if the INTERRUPT REQUEST LATCH is set.

The purpose of INTERRUPT STATUS LATCH is to minimize the possibility of the asynchronous interrupt occuring while the interrupt status is being read by a bus master. If the latch was not included in the design and an asynchronous interrupt did occur while a bus master is reading MULTIBUS data line DAT0/, a data buffer on the master could go into a meta-stable state. By adding the extra latch, which is clocked by the IORD/ command for I/O port E30, the possibility of data line DAT0/ changing during a bus master read operation is eliminated.

The INTERRUPT REQUEST LATCH is cleared when a user program performs an OUTPUT to I/O port E30.

This interrupt structure assumes that several interrupt sources may exist on the same MULTIBUS interrupt line (for example, INT3/). When the MULTIBUS master gets interrupted, it must poll the possible sources of the interrupt received and after determining the source of the interrupt, it must clear the INTERRUPT REQUEST LATCH for that particular interrupt source.

The interrupt logic for the 8-bit version of the design example is identical to the interrupt logic of the 8/16-bit version of the design example.

PPI Operation — Two 8255A Parallel Peripheral Interface (PPI) devices are shown interfaced to the slave design example logic. One PPI is connected to the on-board data bus lines D0 - D7 and is addressed with the even I/O port addresses E38, E3A, E3C, and E3E. The second PPI is connected to data bus lines D8 - DF and is addressed with the odd I/O port addresses E39, E3B, E3D, and E3F. The even or odd I/O port selection is controlled by using the ADR0 address line in the chip select term of the PPIs. In addition, the odd PPI (A11) is selected when the BHENBL term is high. This occurs when the MULTIBUS signal BHEN/ is low indicating that a word (16-bit) I/O instruction is being executed. When a word I/O instruction is executed, both PPIs will perform the I/O operation specified.

The specifications of the 8255A device state that the address lines A0 and A1 and the chip select lines must be stable before the $\overline{RD}$ or $\overline{WR}$ lines are activated. The MULTIBUS specification address set-up time of 50 ns and the short gate propagation delays in this design assure that the address lines are stable before $\overline{RD}$ or $\overline{WR}$ are active.

The data hold requirements of the 8255A were discussed in a previous section. The 8255A specification states that data will be stable on the data bus lines a maximum of 250 ns after a READ command. This specification was used to select the delay for the XACK/ signal.

The PPI operation for the 8-bit version of the design example is slightly different than that used for the 8/16-bit version. The chip select signal for the bottom PPI does not use the BHENBL term since 16-bit data transfers are not possible with an 8-bit I/O slave board. Also, the chip select and address signals have been swapped so the top PPI occupies I/O address range X8 - XB, and the bottom PPI occupies I/O address range XC - XF (X is the base address of the 8-bit version). This swapping of the address lines was not necessary; however, it was thought to be more convenient to access the PPIs in two groups of 4 contiguous I/O port addresses.

IV. SUMMARY

This application note has shown the structure of the Intel MULTIBUS system bus. The structure supports a wide range of system modules from the Intel OEM Microcomputer Systems product line that can be extended with the addition of user designed modules. Because the user designed modules are no doubt unique to particular applications, a goal of this application note has been to describe in detail the singular common element - the bus interface. Material has also been presented to assist the systems designer to understanding the bus functions so that successful systems integration can be achieved.

Appendix

Contents

APPENDIX A — MULTIBUS® PIN ASSIGNMENTS 2-103

APPENDIX B — BUS TIMING SPECIFICATIONS 2-105

APPENDIX C — BUS DRIVERS, RECEIVERS, AND TERMINATIONS 2-107

APPENDIX D — BUS POWER SUPPLY SPECIFICATIONS 2-108

APPENDIX E — MECHANICAL SPECIFICATIONS 2-109

APPENDIX F — MULTIBUS® SLAVE DESIGN EXAMPLE SCHEMATIC 8/16-BIT VERSION 2-110

APPENDIX G — MULTIBUS® SLAVE DESIGN EXAMPLE SCHEMATIC 8-BIT VERSION 2-112

APPENDIX A
PIN ASSIGNMENT OF BUS SIGNALS ON MULTIBUS® BOARD P1 CONNECTOR

	\multicolumn{3}{c}{(COMPONENT SIDE)}	\multicolumn{3}{c}{(CIRCUIT SIDE)}
	PIN	MNEMONIC	DESCRIPTION	PIN	MNEMONIC	DESCRIPTION
POWER SUPPLIES	1	GND	Signal GND	2	GND	Signal GND
	3	+5V	+5Vdc	4	+5V	+5Vdc
	5	+5V	+5Vdc	6	+5V	+5Vdc
	7	+12V	+12Vdc	8	+12V	+12Vdc
	9	−5V	−5Vdc	10	−5V	−5Vdc
	11	GND	Signal GND	12	GND	Signal GND
BUS CONTROLS	13	BCLK/	Bus Clock	14	INIT/	Initialize
	15	BPRN/	Bus Pri. In	16	BPRO/	Bus Pri. Out
	17	BUSY/	Bus Busy	18	BREQ/	Bus Request
	19	MRDC/	Mem Read Cmd	20	MWTC/	Mem Write Cmd
	21	IORC/	I/O Read Cmd	22	IOWC/	I/O Write Cmd
	23	XACK/	XFER Acknowledge	24	INH1/	Inhibit 1 disable RAM
BUS CONTROLS AND ADDRESS	25		Reserved	26	INH2/	Inhibit 2 disable PROM or ROM
	27	BHEN/	Byte High Enable	28	AD10/	
	29	CBRQ/	Common Bus Request	30	AD11/	Address
	31	CCLK/	Constant Clk	32	AD12/	Bus
	33	INTA/	Intr Acknowledge	34	AD13/	
INTERRUPTS	35	INT6/	Parallel	36	INT7/	Parallel
	37	INT4/	Interrupt	38	INT5/	Interrupt
	39	INT2/	Requests	40	INT3/	Requests
	41	INT0/		42	INT1/	
ADDRESS	43	ADRE/		44	ADRF/	
	45	ADRC/		46	ADRD/	
	47	ADRA/	Address	48	ADRB/	Address
	49	ADR8/	Bus	50	ADR9/	Bus
	51	ADR6/		52	ADR7/	
	53	ADR4/		54	ADR5/	
	55	ADR2/		56	ADR3/	
	57	ADR0/		58	ADR1/	
DATA	59	DATE/		60	DATF/	
	61	DATC/		62	DATD/	
	63	DATA/	Data	64	DATB/	Data
	65	DAT8/	Bus	66	DAT9/	Bus
	67	DAT6/		68	DAT7/	
	69	DAT4/		70	DAT5/	
	71	DAT2/		72	DAT3/	
	73	DAT0/		74	DAT1/	
POWER SUPPLIES	75	GND	Signal GND	76	GND	Signal GND
	77		Reserved	78		Reserved
	79	−12V	−12Vdc	80	−12V	−12Vdc
	81	+5V	+5Vdc	82	+5V	+5Vdc
	83	+5V	+5Vdc	84	+5V	+5Vdc
	85	GND	Signal GND	86	GND	Signal GND

All Mnemonics © Intel Corporation 1978

AP-28A

APPENDIX A (Continued)
P2 CONNECTOR PIN ASSIGNMENT OF OPTIONAL BUS SIGNALS

	(COMPONENT SIDE)			(CIRCUIT SIDE)	
PIN	MNEMONIC	DESCRIPTION	PIN	MNEMONIC	DESCRIPTION
1	GND	Signal GND	2	GND	Signal GND
3	5 VB	+5V Battery	4	5 VB	+5V Battery
5		Reserved	6	VCCPP	+5V Pulsed Power
7	−5 VB	−5V Battery	8	−5 VB	−5V Battery
9		Reserved	10		Reserved
11	12 VB	+12V Battery	12	12 VB	+12V Battery
13	PFSR/	Power Fail Sense Reset	14		Reserved
15	−12 VB	−12V Battery	16	−12 VB	−12V Battery
17	PFSN/	Power Fail Sense	18	ACLO	AC Low
19	PFIN/	Power Fail Interrupt	20	MPRO/	Memory Protect
21	GND	Signal GND	22	GND	Signal GND
23	+15V	+15V	24	+15V	+15V
25	−15V	−15V	26	−15V	−15V
27	PAR1/	Parity 1	28	HALT/	Bus Master HALT
29	PAR2/	Parity 2	30	WAIT/	Bus Master WAIT STATE
31			32	ALE	Bus Master ALE
33			34		Reserved
35			36		Reserved
37			38	AUX RESET/	Reset switch
39			40		
41			42		
43		Reserved	44		
45			46		
47			48		
49			50		Reserved
51			52		
53			54		
55			56		
57			58		
59			60		

Notes:
1. PFIN, on slave modules, if possible, should have the option of connecting to INT0/ on P1.
2. All undefined pins are reserved for future use.

All Mnemonics © Intel Corporation 1978

APPENDIX B
BUS TIMING SPECIFICATIONS SUMMARY

Parameter	Description	Minimum	Maximum	Units
t_{BCY}	Bus Clock Period	100	D.C.	ns
t_{BW}	Bus Clock Width	$0.35\, t_{BCY}$	$0.65\, t_{BCY}$ (Not Restricted)	
t_{SKEW}	BCLK/skew		3	ns
t_{PD}	Standard Bus Propagation Delay		3	
t_{AS}	Address Set-Up Time (at Slave Board)	50		ns
t_{DS}	Write Data Set Up Time	50		ns
t_{AH}	Address Hold Time	50		ns
t_{DHW}	Write Data Hold Time	50		ns
t_{DXL}	Read Data Set Up Time To XACK	0		ns
t_{DHR}	Read Data Hold Time	0	65	ns
t_{XAH}	Acknowledge Hold Time	0	65	ns
t_{XACK}	Acknowledge Time	0	8	μs
t_{CMD}	Command Pulse Width	100	9.5	ns
t_{ID}	Inhibit Delay	0	100 (Recommend < 100 ns)	ns
t_{XACKA}	Acknowledge Time of of an Inhibited Slave	t_{IAD} + 50 ns	1500	
t_{XACKB}	Acknowledge Time of an Inhibiting Slave	1.5	8	μs
t_{IAD}	Acknowledge Disable from Inhibit (An internal parameter on an inhibited slave; used to determine t_{XACKA} Min.)	0	100 (arbitrary)	ns
t_{AIZ}	Address to Inhibits High Delay		100	ns
t_{INTA}	INTA/ Width	250		ns
t_{CSEP}	Command Separation	100		ns

APPENDIX B (Continued)
BUS TIMING SPECIFICATIONS SUMMARY

Parameter	Description	Minimum	Maximum	Units
t_{BREQL}	↓BCLK/ to BREQ/ Low Delay	0	35	ns
t_{BREQH}	↓BCLK/ to BREQ/ High Delay	0	35	ns
t_{BPRNS}	BPRN/ to ↓BCLK/ Setup Time	22		ns
t_{BUSY}	BUSY/ delay from ↓BCLK/	0	70	ns
t_{BUSYS}	BUSY/ to ↓BCLK/ Setup Time	25		ns
t_{BPRO}	↓BCLK/ to BPRO/ (CLK to Priority Out)	0	40	ns
t_{BPRNO}	BPRN/ to BPRO/ (Priority In to Out)	0	30	ns
t_{CBRO}	↓BCLK/ to CBRQ/ (CLK to Common Bus Request)	0	60	ns
t_{CBRQS}	CBRQ/ to ↓BCLK/ Setup Time	35		ns
t_{XCD}	XACK↑ to Command↑ Delay	0	1500	ns
t_{BSYO}	CBRQ/↓ and BUSY/↑ to BUSY/↓	—	12	μs
t_{CCY}	C-clock Period	100	110	ns
t_{CW}	C-clock Width	0.35 t_{CCY}	0.65 t_{CCY}	ns
t_{INIT}	INIT/ Width	5		ms
t_{INITS}	INIT/ to MPRO/ Setup Time	100		ns
t_{PBD}	Power Backup Logic Delay	0	200	ns
t_{PFINW}	PFIN/ Width	2.5		ms
t_{MPRO}	MPRO/ Delay	2.0	2.5	ms
t_{ACLOW}	ACLO/ Width	3.0		ms
t_{PFSRW}	PFSR/ Width	100		ns
t_{TOUT}	Timeout Delay	5	∞ (D.C.)	ms
t_{DCH}	D.C. Power Supply Hold from ALCO/	3.0		ms
t_{DCS}	D.C. Power Supply Setup to ACLO/	5		ms

APPENDIX C
BUS DRIVERS, RECEIVERS, AND TERMINATIONS

Bus Signals	Driver 1,3					Receiver 2,3				Termination			
	Location	Type	I_{OL} Min$_{ma}$	I_{OH} Min$_{\mu a}$	C_O Max$_{pf}$	Location	I_{IL} Max$_{ma}$	I_{IH} Max$_{\mu a}$	C_I Max$_{pf}$	Location	Type	R	Units
DAT0/→DATF/ (16 lines)	Masters and Slaves	TRI	16	-2000	300	Masters and Slaves	-0.8	125	18	1 place	Pullup	2.2	KΩ
ADR0/-ADRB/, BHEN/ (21 lines)	Masters	TRI	16	-2000	300	Slaves	-0.8	125	18	1 place	Pullup	2.2	KΩ
MRDC/,MWTC/	Masters	TRI	32	-2000	300	Slaves (Memory; memory-mapped I/O)	-2	125	18	1 place	Pullup	1	KΩ
IORC/,IOWC/	Masters	TRI	32	-2000	300	Slaves (I/O)	-2	125	18	1 place	Pullup	1	KΩ
XACK/	Slaves	TRI	32	-2000	300	Masters	-2	125	18	1 place	Pullup	510	Ω
INH1/,INH2/	Inhibiting Slaves	OC	16	—	300	Inhibited Slaves (RAM, PROM, ROM, Memory-Mapped I/O)	-2	50	18	1 place	Pullup	1	KΩ
BCLK/	1 place (Master us)	TTL	48	-3000	300	Master	-2	125	18	Motherboard	To +5V To GND	220 330	Ω Ω
BREQ/	Each Master	TTL	5	-200	60	Central Priority Module	2	50	18	Central Priority Module (not req)	Pullup	1	KΩ
BPRO/	Each Master	TTL	5	-200	60	Next Master in Serial Priority Chain at its BPRN/	-1.6	50	18	(not req)			
BPRN/	Parallel: Central Priority Module Serial:Prev Masters BPRO/	TTL	5	-200	300	Master	-4	100		(not req)			
BUSY/, CBRQ	All Masters	O.C.	20	—	300	All Masters	-2	50	18	1 place	Pullup	1	KΩ
INIT/	Master.	O.C.	32	—	300	All	-2	50	18	1 place	Pullup	2.2	KΩ
CCLK/	1 place	TTL	48	-3000	300	Any	-2	125	18	Motherboard	To +5V To GND	220 330	Ω Ω
INTA/	Masters	TRI	32	-2000	300	Slaves (Interrupting I/O)	-2	125	18	1 place	Pullup	1	KΩ
INT0/→INT7/ (8 lines)	Slaves	O.C.	16	—	300	Masters	-1.6	40	18	1 place	Pullup	1	KΩ
PFSR/	User's Fron Panel?	TTL	16	-400	300	Slaves, Masters	-1.6	40	18	1 place	Pullup	1	KΩ
PFSN/	Power Back Up Unit	TTL	16	-400	300	Masters	-1.6	40	18	1 place	Pullup	1	KΩ
ACLO	Power Supply	O.C.	16	-400	300	Slaves, Masters	-1.6	40	18	1 place	Pullup	1	KΩ
PFIN/	Power Back-Up Unit	O.C.	16	-400	300	Masters	-1.6	40	18	1 place	Pullup	1	KΩ
MPRO/	Power Back-Up Unit	TTL	16	-400	300	Slaves Masters	-1.6	40	18	1 place	Pullup	1	KΩ

AP-28A

APPENDIX C (Continued)
BUS DRIVERS, RECEIVERS, AND TERMINATIONS

Bus Signals	Driver 1,3					Receiver 2,3				Termination			
	Location	Type	I_{OL} Min$_{ma}$	I_{OH} Min$_{\mu a}$	C_O Max$_{pf}$	Location	I_{IL} Max$_{ma}$	I_{IH} Max$_{\mu a}$	C_I Max$_{pf}$	Location	Type	R	Units
Aux Reset/	User's Front Panel?	Switch to GND (Note 5)	—	—	—	Masters	−2	50	18	None			

Notes:
1. Driver Requirements
   - I_{OH} = High Output Current Drive
   - I_{OL} = Low Output Current Drive
   - C_O = Capacitance Drive Capability
   - TRI = 3-State Drive
   - O.C. = Open Collector Driver
   - TTL = Totem-pole Driver
2. Receiver Requirements
   - I_{IH} = High Input Current Load
   - I_{IL} = Low Input Current Load
   - C_I = Capacitive Load
3. TTL low state must be ≥ −0.5v but ≤ 0.8v at the receivers
   TTL high state must be ≥ 2.0v but ≤ 5.5v at the receivers
4. For the iSBC 80/10 and the iSBC 80/10A use only a 1K pull-up resistor to +5v for BCLK/ and CCLK/ termination.
5. Recommend a 47Ω resistor in series with switch.

APPENDIX D
BUS POWER SPECIFICATIONS

	Standard (P1)				Optional (P2)					
					Analog Power		Battery Power Backup			
	Ground	+5	+12	−12	+15	−15	+5	+12	−12	−5
Mnemonic	GND	+5V	+12V	−12V	+15V	−15V	+5B	+12B	−12B	−5B
Bus Pins	P1 + 1,2, 11,12, 75,76 85,86	P1 + 3,4, 5,6,81, 82,83, 84	P1 + 7,8	P1 + 79, 80	P2 + 23, 24	P2 + 25, 26	P2 + 3,4, 5,6	P2 + 11, 12	P2 + 15, 16	P2 − 7,8
Nominal Output	Ref.	+5.0V	+12.0V	−12.0V	+15.0V	−15.0V	+5.0V	+12.0V	−12.0V	−5.0V
Tolerance from Nominal[1]	Ref.	±5%	±5%	±5%	±3%	±3%	±5%	±5%	±5%	±5%
Ripple (Pk-Pk)[2]	Ref.	50 mV	50 mV	50 mV	10 mV	10 mV	50 mV	50 mV	50 mV	50 mV
Transient Response Time[3]		500 μs	500 μs	500 μs	100 μs	100 μs	500 μs	500 μs	500 μs	500 μs
Transient Deviation[4]		±10%	±10%	±10%	±10%	±10%	±10%	±10%	±10%	±10%

NOTES:
1. Tolerance is worst case, including initial voltage setting line and load effects of power source, temperature drift, and any additional steady state influences.
2. As measured over any bandwidth not to exceed 0 to 500 kHz.
3. As measured from the start of a load change to the time an output recovers within ±0.1% of final voltage.
4. Measured as the peak deviation from the initial voltage.

APPENDIX E
MECHANICAL SPECIFICATIONS

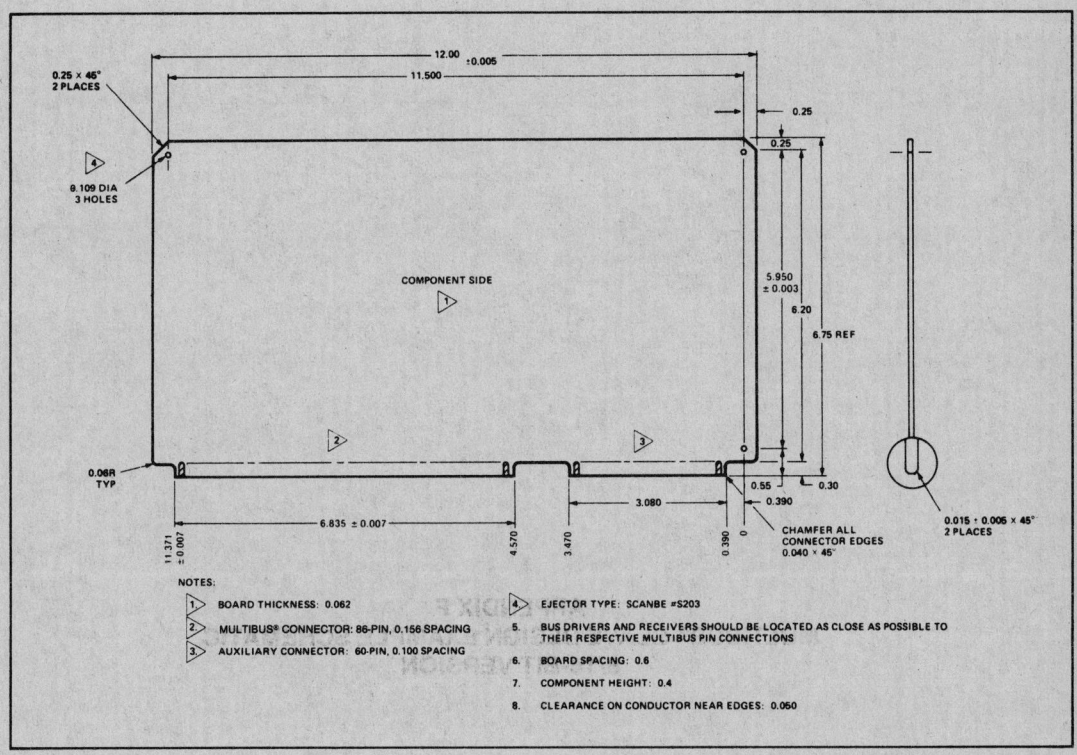

APPENDIX F
MULTIBUS® SLAVE DESIGN EXAMPLE SCHEMATIC
8/16-BIT VERSION

AP-28A
APPENDIX F

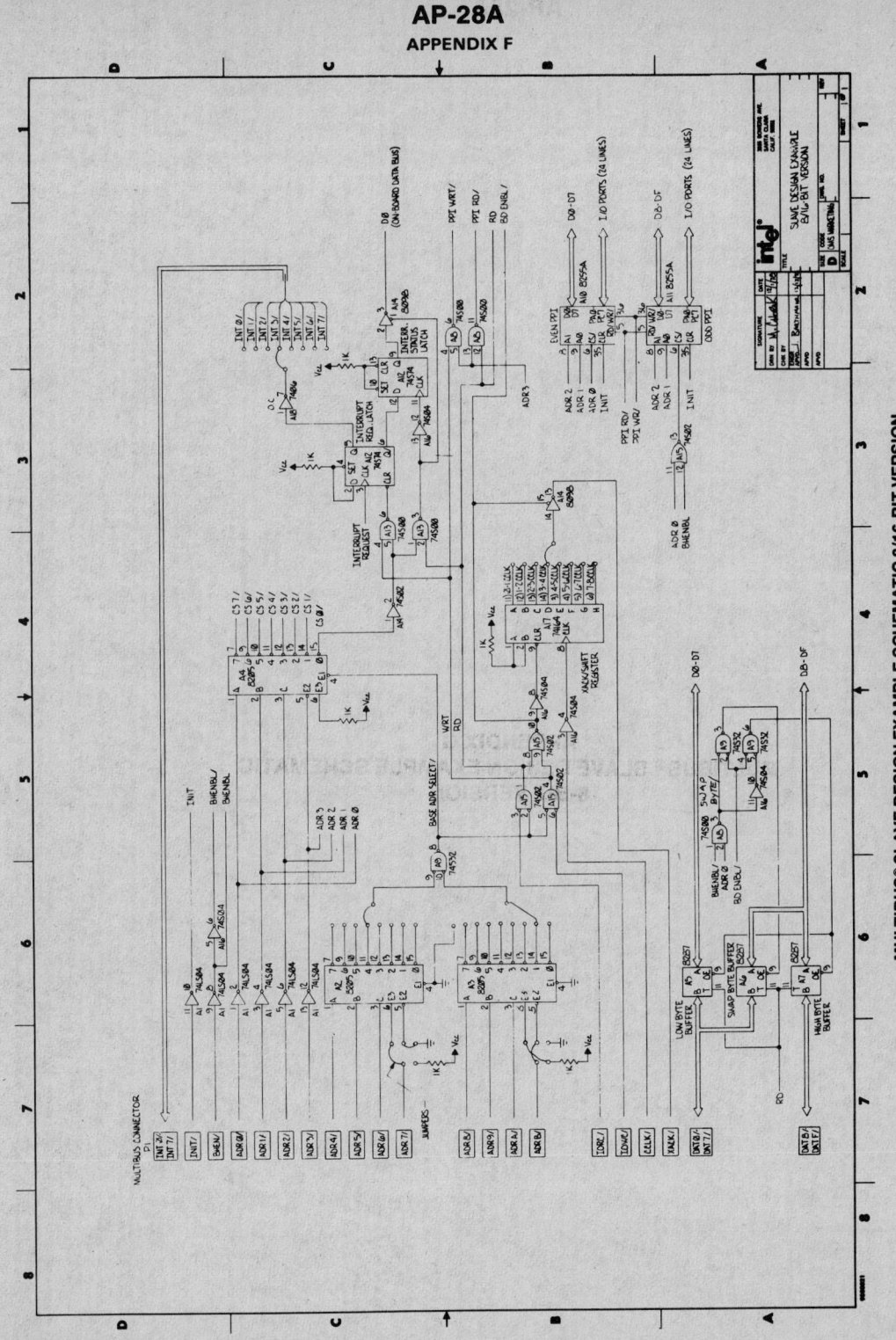

MULTIBUS® SLAVE DESIGN EXAMPLE SCHEMATIC 8/16-BIT VERSION

AP-28A

**APPENDIX G
MULTIBUS® SLAVE DESIGN EXAMPLE SCHEMATIC
8-BIT VERSION**

AP-28A

APPENDIX G

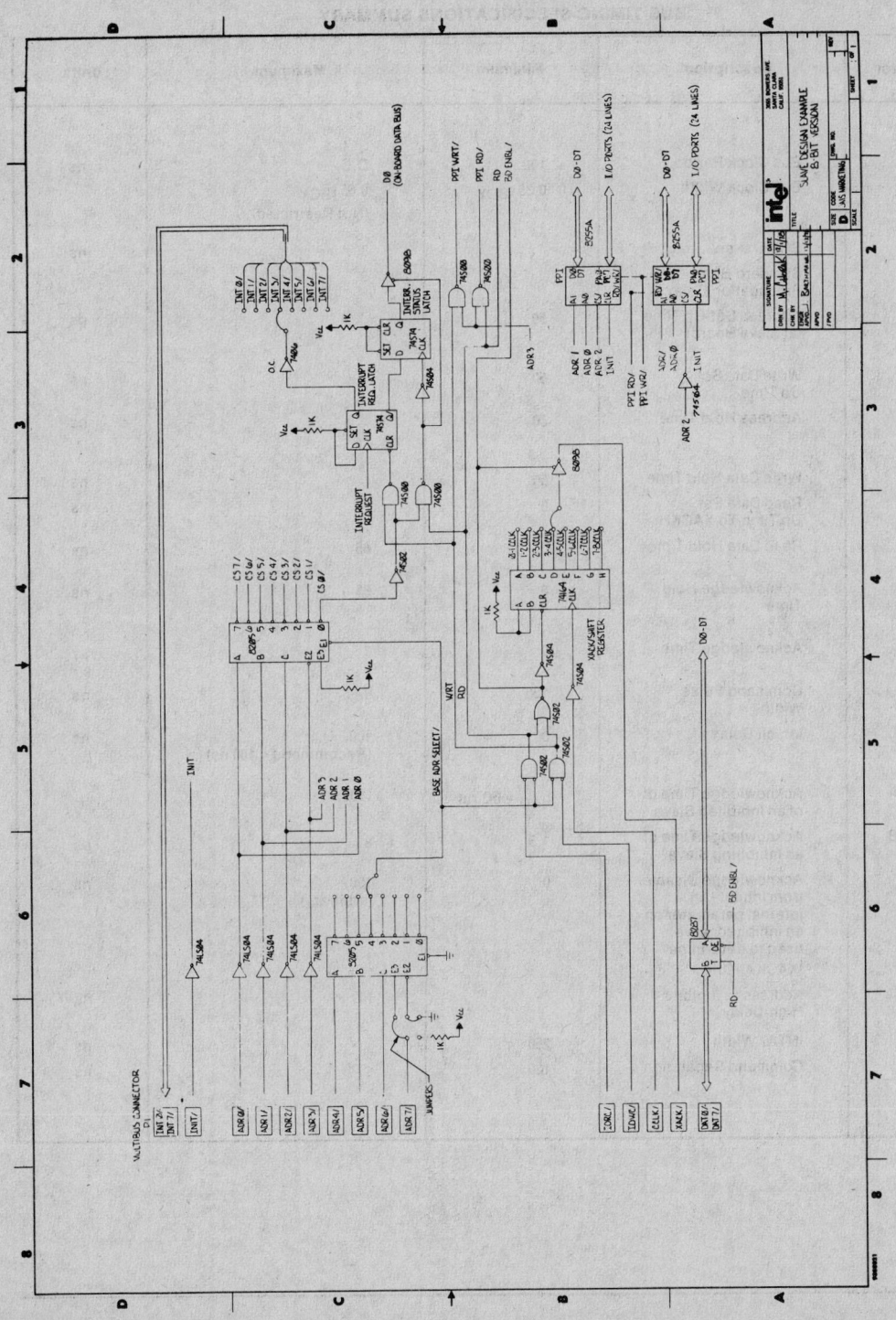

MULTIBUS® SLAVE DESIGN EXAMPLE SCHEMATIC 8-BIT VERSION

APPENDIX B
BUS TIMING SPECIFICATIONS SUMMARY

Parameter	Description	Minimum	Maximum	Units
t_{BCY}	Bus Clock Period	100	D.C.	ns
t_{BW}	Bus Clock Width	$0.35\, t_{BCY}$	$0.65\, t_{BCY}$ (Not Restricted)	
t_{SKEW}	BCLK/skew		3	ns
t_{PD}	Standard Bus Propagation Delay		3	
t_{AS}	Address Set-Up Time (at Slave Board)	50		ns
t_{DS}	Write Data Set Up Time	50		ns
t_{AH}	Address Hold Time	50		
t_{DHW}	Write Data Hold Time	50		ns
t_{DXL}	Read Data Set Up Time To XACK	0		ns
t_{DHR}	Read Data Hold Time	0	65	ns
t_{XAH}	Acknowledge Hold Time	0	65	ns
t_{XACK}	Acknowledge Time	0	8	μs
t_{CMD}	Command Pulse Width	100	9.5	ns
t_{ID}	Inhibit Delay	0	100 (Recommend < 100 ns)	ns
t_{XACKA}	Acknowledge Time of of an Inhibited Slave	$t_{IAD} + 50$ ns	1500	
t_{XACKB}	Acknowledge Time of an Inhibiting Slave	1.5	8	μs
t_{IAD}	Acknowledge Disable from Inhibit (An internal parameter on an inhibited slave; used to determine t_{XACKA} Min.)	0	100 (arbitrary)	ns
t_{AIZ}	Address to Inhibits High Delay		100	ns
t_{INTA}	INTA/ Width	250		ns
t_{CSEP}	Command Separation	100		ns

AP-28A

APPENDIX B (Continued)
BUS TIMING SPECIFICATIONS SUMMARY

Parameter	Description	Minimum	Maximum	Units
t_{BREQL}	↓BCLK/ to BREQ/ Low Delay	0	35	ns
t_{BREQH}	↓BCLK/ to BREQ/ High Delay	0	35	ns
t_{BPRNS}	BPRN/ to ↓BCLK/ Setup Time	22		ns
t_{BUSY}	BUSY/ delay from ↓BCLK/	0	70	ns
t_{BUSYS}	BUSY/ to ↓BCLK/ Setup Time	25		ns
t_{BPRO}	↓BCLK/ to BPRO/ (CLK to Priority Out)	0	40	ns
t_{BPRNO}	BPRN/ to BPRO/ (Priority In to Out)	0	30	ns
t_{CBRO}	↓BCLK/ to CBRQ/ (CLK to Common Bus Request)	0	60	ns
t_{CBRQS}	CBRQ/ to ↓BCLK/ Setup Time	35		ns
t_{XCD}	XACK↓ to Command↑ Delay	0	1500	ns
t_{BSYO}	CBRQ/↓ and BUSY/↓ to BUSY/↑	—	12	μs
t_{CCY}	C-clock Period	100	110	ns
t_{CW}	C-clock Width	0.35 t_{CCY}	0.65 t_{CCY}	ns
t_{INIT}	INIT/ Width	5		ms
t_{INITS}	INIT/ to MPRO/ Setup Time	100		ns
t_{PBD}	Power Backup Logic Delay	0	200	ns
t_{PFINW}	PFIN/ Width	2.5		ms
t_{MPRO}	MPRO/ Delay	2.0	2.5	ms
t_{ACLOW}	ACLO/ Width	3.0		ms
t_{PFSRW}	PFSR/ Width	100		ns
t_{TOUT}	Timeout Delay	5	∞ (D.C.)	ms
t_{DCH}	D.C. Power Supply Hold from ALCO/	3.0		ms
t_{DCS}	D.C. Power Supply Setup to ACLO/	5		ms

AP-28A

APPENDIX C
BUS DRIVERS, RECEIVERS, AND TERMINATIONS

Bus Signals	Driver 1,3					Receiver 2,3				Termination			
	Location	Type	I_{OL} Min$_{ma}$	I_{OH} Min$_{\mu a}$	C_O Max$_{pf}$	Location	I_{IL} Max$_{ma}$	I_{IH} Max$_{\mu a}$	C_I Max$_{pf}$	Location	Type	R	Units
DAT0/→DATF/ (16 lines)	Masters and Slaves	TRI	16	−2000	300	Masters and Slaves	−0.8	125	18	1 place	Pullup	2.2	KΩ
ADR0/-ADRB/, BHEN/ (21 lines)	Masters	TRI	16	−2000	300	Slaves	−0.8	125	18	1 place	Pullup	2.2	KΩ
MRDC/,MWTC/	Masters	TRI	32	−2000	300	Slaves (Memory; memory-mapped I/O)	−2	125	18	1 place	Pullup	1	KΩ
IORC/,IOWC/	Masters	TRI	32	−2000	300	Slaves (I/O)	−2	125	18	1 place	Pullup	1	KΩ
XACK/	Slaves	TRI	32	−2000	300	Masters	−2	125	18	1 place	Pullup	510	Ω
INH1/,INH2/	Inhibiting Slaves	OC	16	—	300	Inhibited Slaves (RAM, PROM, ROM, Memory-Mapped I/O)	−2	50	18	1 place	Pullup	1	KΩ
BCLK/	1 place (Master us)	TTL	48	−3000	300	Master	−2	125	18	Motherboard	To +5V To GND	220 330	Ω Ω
BREQ/	Each Master	TTL	5	−200	60	Central Priority Module	2	50	18	Central Priority Module (not req)	Pullup	1	KΩ
BPRO/	Each Master	TTL	5	−200	60	Next Master in Serial Priority Chain at its BPRN/	−1.6	50	18	(not req)			
BPRN/	Parallel: Central Priority Module Serial:Prev Masters BPRO/	TTL	5	−200	300	Master	−4	100		(not req)			
BUSY/, CBRQ	All Masters	O.C.	20	—	300	All Masters	−2	50	18	1 place	Pullup	1	KΩ
INIT/	Master.	O.C.	32	—	300	All	−2	50	18	1 place	Pullup	2.2	KΩ
CCLK/	1 place	TTL	48	−3000	300	Any	−2	125	18	Motherboard	To +5V To GND	220 330	Ω Ω
INTA/	Masters	TRI	32	−2000	300	Slaves (Interrupting I/O)	−2	125	18	1 place	Pullup	1	KΩ
INT0/→INT7/ (8 lines)	Slaves	O.C.	16	—	300	Masters	−1.6	40	18	1 place	Pullup	1	KΩ
PFSR/	User's Fron Panel?	TTL	16	−400	300	Slaves, Masters	−1.6	40	18	1 place	Pullup	1	KΩ
PFSN/	Power Back Up Unit	TTL	16	−400	300	Masters	−1.6	40	18	1 place	Pullup	1	KΩ
ACLO	Power Supply	O.C.	16	−400	300	Slaves, Masters	−1.6	40	18	1 place	Pullup	1	KΩ
PFIN/	Power Back-Up Unit	O.C.	16	−400	300	Masters	−1.6	40	18	1 place	Pullup	1	KΩ
MPRO/	Power Back-Up Unit	TTL	16	−400	300	Slaves Masters	−1.6	40	18	1 place	Pullup	1	KΩ

APPENDIX C (Continued)
BUS DRIVERS, RECEIVERS, AND TERMINATIONS

Bus Signals	Driver 1,3						Receiver 2,3				Termination			
	Location	Type	I_{OL} Min_{ma}	I_{OH} $Min_{\mu a}$	C_O Max_{pf}		Location	I_{IL} Max_{ma}	I_{IH} $Max_{\mu a}$	C_I Max_{pf}	Location	Type	R	Units
Aux Reset/	User's Front Panel?	Switch to GND (Note 5)	—	—	—		Masters	−2	50	18	None			

Notes:
1. Driver Requirements

    I_{OH} = High Output Current Drive
    I_{OL} = Low Output Current Drive
    C_O = Capacitance Drive Capability
    TRI = 3-State Drive
    O.C. = Open Collector Driver
    TTL = Totem-pole Driver

2. Receiver Requirements

    I_{IH} = High Input Current Load
    I_{IL} = Low Input Current Load
    C_I = Capacitive Load

3. TTL low state must be $\geq$ −0.5v but $\leq$ 0.8v at the receivers
   TTL high state must be $\geq$ 2.0v but $\leq$ 5.5v at the receivers
4. For the iSBC 80/10 and the iSBC 80/10A use only a 1K pull-up resistor to +5v for BCLK/ and CCLK/ termination.
5. Recommend a 47Ω resistor in series with switch.

APPENDIX D
BUS POWER SPECIFICATIONS

	Standard (P1)				Optional (P2)					
					Analog Power		Battery Power Backup			
	Ground	+5	+12	−12	+15	−15	+5	+12	−12	−5
Mnemonic	GND	+5V	+12V	−12V	+15V	−15V	+5B	+12B	−12B	−5B
Bus Pins	P1 + 1,2, 11,12, 75,76 85,86	P1 + 3,4, 5,6,81, 82,83, 84	P1 + 7,8	P1 + 79, 80	P2 + 23, 24	P2 + 25, 26	P2 + 3,4, 5,6	P2 + 11, 12	P2 + 15, 16	P2 − 7,8
Nominal Output	Ref.	+5.0V	+12.0V	−12.0V	+15.0V	−15.0V	+5.0V	+12.0V	−12.0V	−5.0V
Tolerance from Nominal[1]	Ref.	±5%	±5%	±5%	±3%	±3%	±5%	±5%	±5%	±5%
Ripple (Pk−Pk)[2]	Ref.	50 mV	50 mV	50 mV	10 mV	10 mV	50 mV	50 mV	50 mV	50 mV
Transient Response Time[3]		500 μs	500 μs	500 μs	100 μs	100 μs	500 μs	500 μs	500 μs	500 μs
Transient Deviation[4]		±10%	±10%	±10%	±10%	±10%	±10%	±10%	±10%	±10%

NOTES:
1. Tolerance is worst case, including initial voltage setting line and load effects of power source, temperature drift, and any additional steady state influences.
2. As measured over any bandwidth not to exceed 0 to 500 kHz.
3. As measured from the start of a load change to the time an output recovers within ±0.1% of final voltage.
4. Measured as the peak deviation from the initial voltage.

AP-28A

APPENDIX E
MECHANICAL SPECIFICATIONS

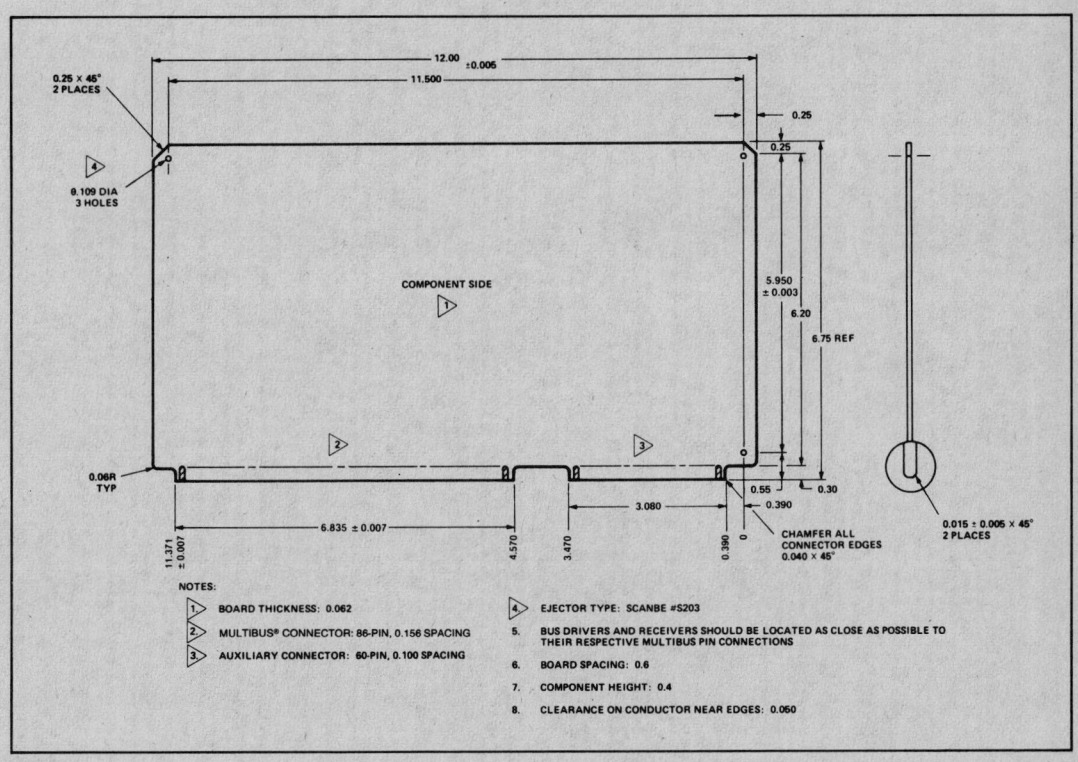

Single Board Computers   2

iSBC® 80/10B
SINGLE BOARD COMPUTER

- 8080A CPU used as central processing unit
- One iSBX™ bus connector for iSBX™ MULTIMODULE™ board expansion
- 1K byte of read/write memory with sockets for expansion up to 4K bytes
- Sockets for up to 16K bytes of read only memory
- 48 programmable parallel I/O lines with sockets for interchangeable line drivers and terminators
- Programmable synchronous/asynchronous communications interface with selectable RS232C or teletypewriter compatibility
- Single level interrupt with 11 interrupt sources
- Auxiliary power bus and power-fail interrupt control logic for RAM battery backup
- 1.04 millisecond interval timer
- Limited master MULTIBUS® interface

The Intel® iSBC 80/10B board is a member of Intel's complete line of OEM microcomputer systems which take full advantage of Intel's LSI technology to provide economical, self-contained computer-based solutions for OEM applications. The iSBC 80/10B board is a complete computer system on a single 6.75 x 12.00-inch printed circuit card. The CPU, system clock, iSBX bus interface, read/write memory, read only memory sockets, I/O ports and drivers, serial communications interface, bus control logic, and drivers all reside on the board.

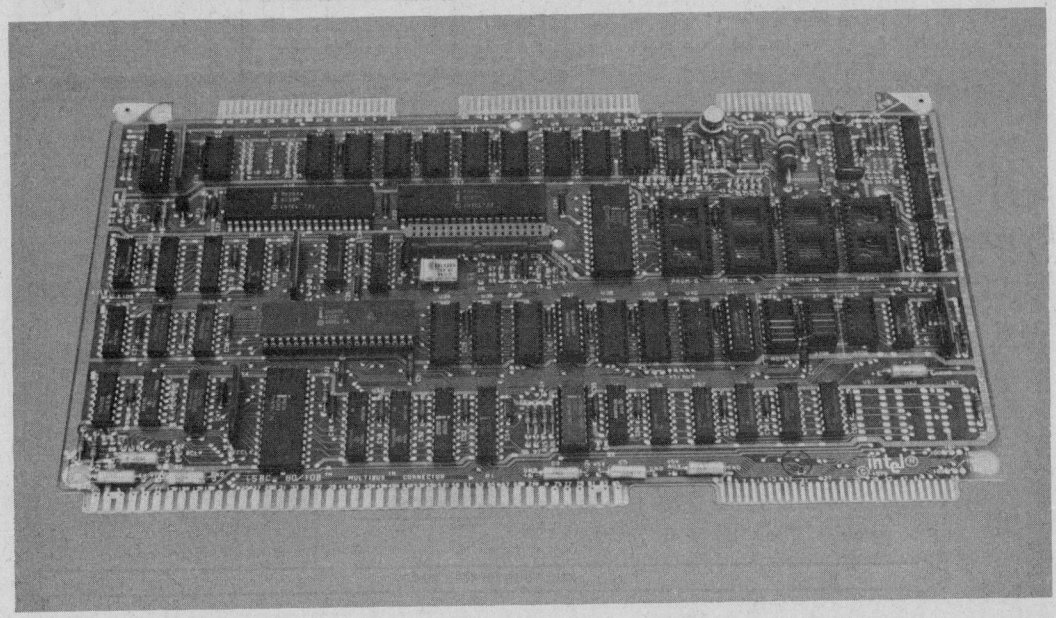

October, 1984
AFN-01688B

iSBC® 80/10B

FUNCTIONAL DESCRIPTION

Intel's powerful 8-bit n-channel MOS 8080A CPU, fabricated on a single LSI chip, is the central processor for the iSBC 80/10B board. The 8080A contains six 8-bit general purpose registers and an accumulator. The six general purpose registers may be addressed individually or in pairs, providing both single and double precision operators. A block diagram of iSBC 80/10B board functional components is shown in Figure 1.

iSBX™ Bus MULTIMODULE™ Board Expansion

The new iSBX bus interface brings an entirely new dimension to system design offering incremental on-board expansion with small iSBX boards. One iSBX bus connector interface is provided to accomplish plug-in expansion with any iSBX MULTIMODULE board. iSBX boards are available to provide expansion equivalent to the I/O available on the iSBC 80/10B board or the user may configure entirely new functionality such as math directly on-board. The iSBX 350 programmable I/O MULTIMODULE board provides 24 I/O lines using an 8255A programmable peripheral interface. Therefore, the iSBX 350 module together with the iSBC 80/10B board may offer 72 lines of programmable I/O. Alternately, a serial port may be added using the iSBX 351 serial I/O multimodule board or math may be configured on-board with the iSBX 332 floating point math MULTIMODULE board.

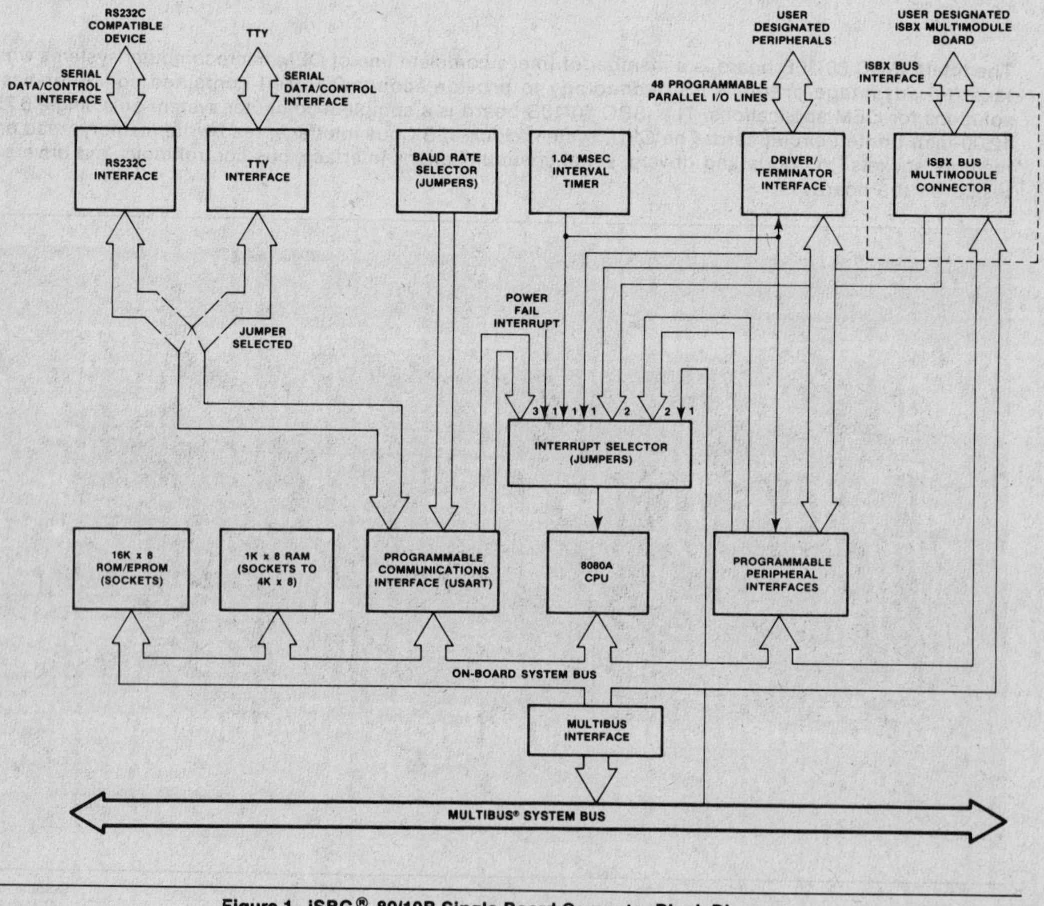

Figure 1. iSBC® 80/10B Single Board Computer Block Diagram

iSBC® 80/10B

The iSBX board is a logical extension of the on-board programmable I/O and is accessed by the iSBC 80/10B single board computer as common I/O port locations. The iSBX board is coupled directly to the 8080A CPU and therefore becomes an integral element of the iSBC 80/10B single board computer providing optimum performance.

Memory Addressing

The 8080A has a 16-bit program counter which allows direct addressing of up to 64K bytes of memory. An external stack, located within any portion of read/write memory, may be used as a last-in/first-out storage area for the contents of the program counter, flags, accumulator, and all of the six general purpose registers. A 16-bit stack pointer controls the addressing of this external stack. This stack provides subroutine nesting bounded only by memory size.

Memory Capacity

The iSBC 80/10B board contains 1K bytes of read/write static memory. In addition, sockets for up to 4K bytes of RAM memory are provided on board. Read/write memory may be added in 1K byte increments using two 1K x 4 Intel 2114A-5 static RAMs. All on-board RAM read and write operations are performed at maximum processor speed. Sockets for up to 16K bytes of nonvolatile read-only-memory are provided on the board. Read-only-memory may be added in 1K byte increments up to 4K bytes (using Intel 2708 or 2758); in 2K byte increments up to 8K bytes (using Intel 2716); or in 4K byte increments up to 16K bytes (using Intel 2732). All on-board ROM or EPROM read operations are performed at maximum processor speed.

Parallel I/O Interface

The iSBC 80/10B board contains 48 programmable parallel I/O lines implemented using two Intel 8255A programmable peripheral interfaces. The system software is used to configure the I/O lines in any combination of unidirectional input/output, and bidirectional ports indicated in Table 1. Therefore, the I/O interface may be customized to meet specific peripheral requirements. In order to take full advantage of the large number of possible I/O configurations, sockets are provided for interchangeable I/O line drivers and terminators. Hence, the flexibility of the I/O interface is further enhanced by the capability of selecting the appropriate combination of optional line drivers and terminators to provide the required sink current, polarity, and drive/termination characteristics for each application. The 48 programmable I/O lines and signal ground lines are brought out to two 50-pin edge connectors that mate with flat cable or round cable.

Serial I/O Interface

A programmable communications interface using the Intel® 8251A Universal Synchronous/Asynchronous Receiver/Transmitter (USART) is contained on the board. A jumper selectable baud rate generator provides the USART with all common communications frequencies. The USART can be

Table 1. Input/Output Port Modes of Operation

Port	Lines (qty)	Mode of Operation					
		Unidirectional				Bidirectional	Control
		Input		Output			
		Unlatched	Latched & Strobed	Latched	Latched & Strobed		
1	8	X	X	X	X	X	
2	8	X	X	X	X		
3	8	X		X			X[1]
4	8	X		X			
5	8	X		X			
6	4	X		X			
	4	X		X			

Notes

Port 3 must be used as a control port when either port 1 or port 2 are used as a latched and strobed input or a latched and strobed output port or port 1 is used as a bidirectional port.

programmed by the system software to select the desired synchronous or asynchronous serial data transmission technique (including IBM Bi-Sync). The mode of operation (i.e., synchronous or asynchronous), data format, control character format and parity are all under program control. The 8251A provides full duplex, double-buffered transmit and receive capability. Parity, overrun, and framing error detection are all incorporated in the USART. The inclusion of jumper selectable TTY or RS232C compatible interfaces on the board, in conjunction with the USART, provides a direct interface to teletypes, CRTs, RS232C compatible cassettes, and asynchronous and synchronous modems. The RS232C or TTY command lines, serial data lines, and signal ground lines are brought out to a 26-pin edge connector that mates with RS232C compatible flat or round cable.

Interrupt Capability

Interrupt requests may originate from 11 sources. Two jumper selectable interrupt requests can be automatically generated by the programmable peripheral interface when a byte of information is ready to be transferred to the CPU (i.e., input buffer is full) or a byte of information has been transferred to a peripheral device (i.e., output buffer is empty). Three jumper selectable interrupt requests can be automatically generated by the USART when a character is ready to be transferred to the CPU (i.e., receive channel buffer is full), a character is ready to be transmitted (i.e., the USART is ready to accept a character from the CPU), or when the transmitter is empty (i.e., the USART has no character to transmit). These five interrupt request lines are all maskable under program control. Two interrupt request lines may be interfaced directly to user designated peripheral devices; one via the MULTIBUS system bus and the other via the I/O edge connector. One jumper selectable interrupt request may be interfaced to the power-fail interrupt control logic. One jumper selectable interrupt request may originated from the interval timer. Two general purpose interrupt requests are jumper selectable from the iSBX interface. These two signals permit a user installed MULTIMODULE board to interrupt the 8080A CPU. The eleven interrupt request lines share a single CPU interrupt level. When an interrupt request is recognized, a restart instruction (RESTART 7) is generated. The processor responds by suspending program execution and executing a user defined interrupt service routine originating at location 38_{16}.

Power-Fail Control

A power-fail interrupt may be detected through the AC-low signal generated by the power supply. This signal may be configured to interrupt the 8080A CPU to initiate an orderly power down instruction sequence.

Interval Timer

A 1.04 millisecond timer is available for interval interrupts or as a clock output to the parallel I/O connector. The timer output is jumper selectable to the programmable parallel interface, the parallel I/O connector (J1), or directly to the 8080A CPU.

MULTIBUS® System Expansion Capabilities

Memory and I/O capacity may be expanded and additional functions added using Intel MULTIBUS™ system compatible expansion boards. Memory may be expanded to 65,536 bytes by adding user specified combinations of RAM boards, EPROM boards, or combination boards. Input/output capacity may be increased by adding digital I/O and analog I/O expansion boards. In addition, the iSBC 80/10B board performs as a limited bus master in that it must occupy the lowest priority when used with other MULTIBUS masters. The bus master may take control of the MULTIBUS system bus by halting the iSBC 80/10B board program execution. Mass storage capability may be achieved by adding single density diskette, double density diskette, or hard disk controllers. Modular expandable backplanes and cardcages are available to support multiboard systems.

System Development Capability

The development cycle of iSBC 80/10B-based products may be significantly reduced using Intel's system development tools available today. For those not requiring hardware emulation capability, Intel provides a new low cost microcomputer development system. The iPDS, Personal Development System, provides low cost system development for the iSBC 80/10B board, while at the same time providing personal computer capability for the engineer. The Intellec Series II family of compatible microcomputer development systems provides a range of capability from a low cost disk-based edit debug workstation to a high performance, fully compatible hard-disk-based software development system. A unique in-circuit emulator (ICE-80) option provides the capability of developing and debugging software directly on the iSBC 80/10B.

Programming Capability

PL/M-80 — Intel's high level programming language, PL/M, is also available as a resident Intellec microcomputer development system option. PL/M provides the capability to program in a natural, algorithmic language and eliminates the need to manage register usage or allocate memory. PL/M programs can be written in a much shorter time than assembly language programs for a given application.

FORTRAN-80 — For applications requiring computational and formatted I/O capabilities, the ANSI 77 standard high level FORTRAN-80 programming language is available as a resident option of the Intellec system. The FORTRAN compiler produces relocatable object code that may be easily linked with PL/M or assembly language program modules. In addition, the iSBC 801 FORTRAN-80 run-time package is a complete, ready-to-use set of linkable object modules which are fully compatible with iRMX 80 systems. The modules, when combined with the FORTRAN-80 coded application, provide the appropriate interfaces to the disk file and terminal I/O of iRMX 80, and to the iSBC 310A Math Unit for applications requiring high speed math.

BASIC-80 — A high level language interpreter is available with extended disk capabilities which operates under the iRMX 80 Real-Time Multitasking Executive and translates BASIC-80 source programs into an internally executable form. This language interpreter, provided as a set of linkable object modules, is ideally suited to the OEM who requires a pass through programming language. The BASIC-80 programs may be created, stored, and interpreted on the iSBC 80 based systems using the iSBC 802 BASIC-80 Configurable iRMX 80 Disk-Based Interpreter. The iSBC 802 Interpreter has a complete ready-to-use set of linkable object modules which are fully compatible with Intel's iRMX 80 Real-Time Multitasking Executive Software. The modules provide interfaces to disk file and terminal I/O, software floating point, or interface to other routines provided by the user.

SPECIFICATIONS

Word Size
Instruction — 8, 16, or 24 bits
Data — 8 bits

Cycle Time
Basic Instruction Cycle — 1.95 μsec
Note
Basic instruction cycle is defined as the fastest instruction (i.e., four clock cycles).

Memory Addressing
On-Board ROM/EPROM
 0-0FFF using 2708, 2758
 0-1FFF using 2716
 0-3FFF using 2732

On-Board RAM
 3C00-3FFF with no RAM expansion
 3000-3FFF with 2114A-5 expansion
Note
All RAM configurations are automatically moved up to a base address of 4XXX when configuring EPROM for 2732.

Memory Capacity
On-Board ROM/EPROM
 16K bytes (sockets only)

On-Board RAM
 1K byte with user expansion in 1K increments to 4K bytes using Intel 2114A-5 RAMs

Off-Board Expansion
 Up to 64K bytes using user specified combinations of RAM, ROM, and EPROM.

I/O Addressing
On-Board Programmable I/O

Device	I/O Address
8255A No. 1	
Port A	E4
Port B	E5
Port C	E6
Control	E7
8255A No. 2	
Port A	E8
Port B	E9
Port C	EA
Control	EB
8251A	
Data	EC
Control	ED
iSBX Multimodule	
MCS0	F0-F7
MCS1	F8-FF

iSBC® 80/10B

I/O Capacity
Parallel — 48 programmable lines
Serial — 1 transmit, 1 receive
MULTIMODULE — 1 iSBX Bus MULTIMODULE Board

Serial Baud Rates

Frequency (kHz) (Jumper Selectable)	Baud Rate (Hz)	
	Synchronous	Asynchronous (Program Selectable)
		÷ 16 ÷ 64
307.2	—	19200 4800
153.6	—	9600 2400
76.8	—	4800 1200
38.4	38400	2400 600
19.2	19200	1200 300
9.6	9600	600 150
6.98	6980	— 110
4.8	4800	300 75

Serial Communications Characteristics
Synchronous — 5-8 bit characters; internal or external character synchronization; automatic sync insertion

Asynchronous — 5-8 bit characters; break character generation; 1, 1½, or 2 stop bits; false start bit detectors

Interrupts
Single-level with on-board logic that automatically vectors the processor to location 38H using a restart instruction (RESTART7). Interrupt requests may originate from user specified I/O (2); the programmable peripheral interface (2); the iSBX MULTIMODULE board (2); the programmable communications interface (3); the power fail interrupt (1); or the interval timer (1).

Interfaces
MULTIBUS — All signals TTL compatible

iSBX Bus — All signals TTL compatible

Parallel I/O — All signals TTL compatible

Serial I/O — RS232C or a 20 mil current loop TTY interface (jumper selectable)

Interrupt Requests — All TTL compatible (active-low)

Clocks
System Clock — 2.048 MHz ± 0.1%
Interval Timer — 1.042 msec ± 0.1% (959.5 HZ)

Connectors

Interface	Double-Sided Pins (qty)	Centers (in.)	Mating Connectors
MULTIBUS System	86	0.156	Viking 2KH43/9AMK12 Wire-wrap
iSBX Bus	36	0.1	iSBX 960-5
Parallel I/O (2)	50	0.1	3M 3415-000 Flat
Serial I/O	26	0.1	AMP 87194-6 Flat

Physical Characteristics
Width — 12.00 in. (30.48 cm)
Height — 6.75 in. (17.15 cm)
Depth — 0.05 in. (1.27 cm)
Weight — 14 oz. (397.3 gm)

Electrical Characteristics
DC Power Requirements

Voltage	Without EPROM[1]	With 2708 EPROM[2]	With 2758, 2716, or 2732 EPROM[3]	Power Down Requirements (RAM and Support Circuit)
$V_{CC} = +5V \pm 5\%$	$I_{CC}^{4} = 2.0A$	3.1 A	3.46 A	84 mA + 140 mA/K (2114A-5)
$V_{DD} = +12V \pm 5\%$	$I_{DD} = 150$ mA	400 mA	150 mA	Not Required
$V_{BB} = -5V \pm 5\%$	$I_{BB} = 2$ mA	200 mA	2 mA	Not Required
$V_{AA} = -12V \pm 5\%$	$I_{AA} = 175$ mA	175 mA	175 mA	Not Required

NOTES:
1. Does not include power required for optional ROM/EPROM, I/O drivers, or I/O terminators.
2. With four Intel 2708 EPROMS and 220Ω/330Ω for terminators, installed for 48 input lines. All terminator inputs low.
3. Same as #2 except with four 2758s, 2716s, or 2732s installed.
4. I_{CC} shown without RAM supply current. For 2114A-5 add 140 mA per K byte to a maximum of 560 mA.

iSBC® 80/10B

Line Drivers and Terminators

I/O Drivers — The following line drivers and terminators are all compatible with the I/O driver sockets on the iSBC 80/10B Board:

Driver	Characteristic	Sink Current (mA)
7438	I,OC	48
7437	I	48
7432	NI	16
7426	I,OC	16
7409	NI,OC	16
7408	NI	16
7403	I,OC	16
7400	I	16

Note
I - inverting, NI - non-inverting, OC - open collector.

Port 1 has 25 nA totem pole drivers and 1 kΩ terminators.

I/O Terminators — 220Ω/330Ω divider or 1 kΩ pull up.

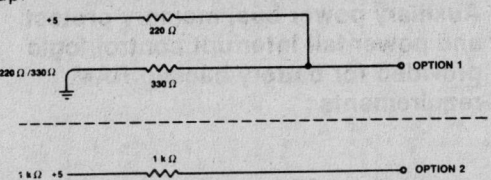

MULTIBUS® Drivers

Function	Characteristic	Sink Current (mA)
Data	Tri-State	25
Address	Tri-State	25
Commands	Tri-State	25

Environmental Characteristics
Operating Temperature — 0°C to 55°C

Equipment Supplied
iSBC 80/10B Single Board Computer
iSBC 80/10B Schematics

Reference Manual
9803119-01 — iSBC 80/10B Single Board Computer Hardware Reference Manual (NOT SUPPLIED).

Manuals may be ordered from any Intel sales representative, distributor office or from Intel Literature Department, 3065 Bowers Avenue, Santa Clara, California 95051.

ORDERING INFORMATION

Part Number	Description
SBC 80/10B	Single Board Computer

iSBC® 80/20-4
SINGLE BOARD COMPUTER

- 8080A CPU used as central processor
- 4K bytes of static read/write memory
- Sockets for up to 8K bytes of erasable reprogrammable or masked read only memory
- 48 programmable parallel I/O lines with sockets for interchangeable line drivers and terminators
- Programmable synchronous/asynchronous RS232C compatible serial interface with fully software selectable baud rate generation
- Full MULTIBUS® control logic allowing up to 16 masters to share system bus
- Two programmable 16-bit BCD and binary timers
- Eight-level programmable interrupt control
- Compatible with optional memory and I/O expansion boards
- Auxiliary power bus, memory protect, and power-fail interrupt control logic provided for battery backup RAM requirements

The iSBC 80/20-4 Single Board Computer is a member of Intel's complete line of OEM computer systems which take full advantage of Intel's LSI technology to provide economical, self-contained computer-based solutions for OEM applications. Each iSBC 80/20-4 is a complete computer system on a single 6.75 × 12.00-inch printed circuit card. The CPU, system clock, read/write memory, nonvolatile read only memory, I/O ports and drivers, serial communications interface, priority interrupt logic, two programmable timers, MULTIBUS control logic, and bus expansion drivers all reside on each board.

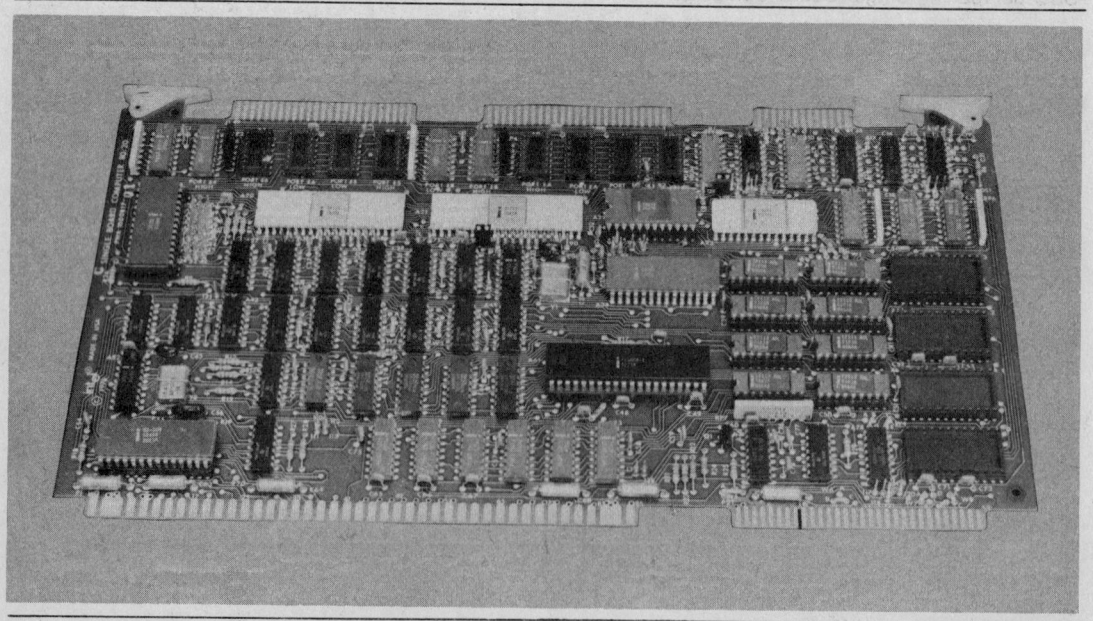

October, 1984
AFN-01499B

iSBC® 80/20-4

FUNCTIONAL DESCRIPTION

Intel's powerful 8-bit n-channel MOS 8080A CPU, fabricated on a single LSI chip, is the central processor for the iSBC 80/20-4. The 8080A contains six 8-bit general purpose registers and an accumulator. The six general purpose registers may be addressed individually or in pairs, providing both single and double precision operators. Minimum instruction execution time is 1.86 microseconds. A block diagram of iSBC 80/20-4 functional components is shown in Figure 1.

Memory Addressing

The 8080A has a 16-bit program counter which allows direct addressing of up to 65,536 bytes of memory. An external stack, located within any portion of read/write memory, may be used as a last-in/first-out storage area for the contents of the program counter, flags, accumulator, and all of the six general purpose registers. A 16-bit stack pointer controls the addressing of this external stack. This stack provides subroutine nesting bounded only by memory size.

Memory Capacity

The iSBC 80/20-4 contains 4K bytes of static read/write memory using Intel low power static RAMs. All on-board RAM read and write operations are performed at maximum processor speed. Power for on-board RAM memory is provided on an auxiliary power bus, and memory protect logic is included for battery backup RAM requirements. Sockets for up to 8K bytes of nonvolatile read only memory are provided on the board. Read only memory may be added in 1K-byte increments using Intel 2708 erasable and electrically reprogrammable ROMs (EPROMs), or read only memory may be added in 2K-byte increments using Intel 2716 EPROMs. All on-board ROM read operations are performed at maximum processor speed.

Parallel I/O Interface

The iSBC 80/20-4 contains 48 programmable parallel I/O lines implemented using two Intel 8255 programmable peripheral interfaces. The system software is used to configure the I/O lines in any combination of the unidirectional input/output, and bidirectional ports indicated in Table 1. Therefore, the I/O interface may be customized to meet specified peripheral requirements. In order to take full advantage of the large number of possible I/O configurations, sockets are provided for interchangeable I/O line drivers and terminators. Hence, the flexibility of the I/O interface is further enhanced by the capability of selecting the appropriate combination of optional line drivers and terminators to provide the required sink current, polarity, and drive/termination characteristics for each application. The 48 programmable I/O lines and signal ground lines are brought out to two 50-pin edge connectors that mate with flat, woven, or round cable.

Serial I/O Interface

A programmable communications interface using Intel's 8251 Universal Synchronous/Asynchronous Receiver/Transmitter (USART) is contained on the iSBC

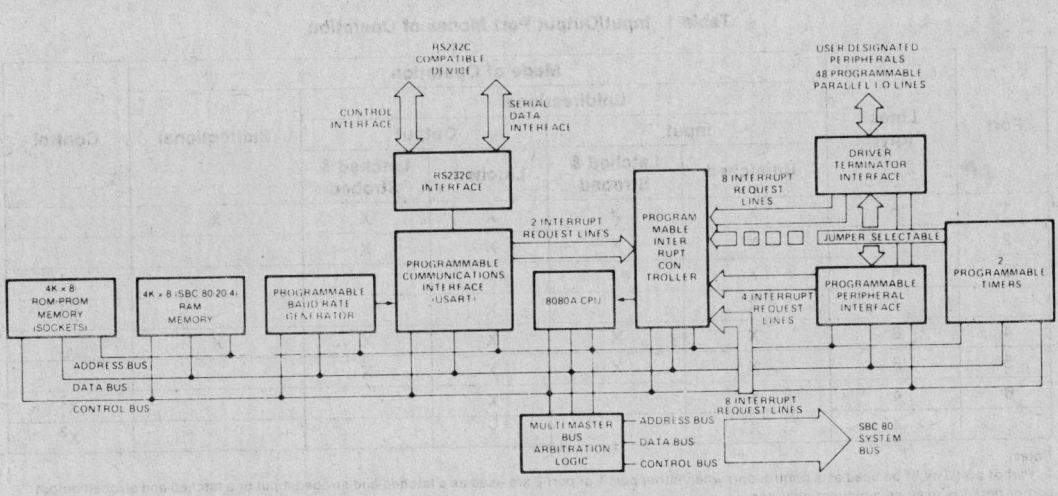

Figure 1. iSBC® 80/20 and iSBC® 80/20-4 Block Diagram Showing Functional Components

iSBC® 80/20-4

80/20-4 board. A software selectable baud rate generator provides the USART with all common communications frequencies. The USART can be programmed by the system software to select the desired asynchronous or synchronous serial data transmission technique (including IBM Bi-Sync). The mode of operation (i.e., synchronous or asynchronous), data format, control character parity, and baud rate are all under program control. The 8251 provides full duplex, double-buffered transmit and receive capability. Parity, overrun, and framing error detection are all incorporated in the USART. The RS232C compatible interface on each board, in conjunction with the USART, provides a direct interface to RS232C compatible terminals, cassettes, and asynchronous and synchronous modems. The RS232C command lines, serial data lines, and signal ground line are brought out to a 26-pin edge connector that mates with RS232C compatible flat or round cable.

Multimaster Capability

The iSBC 80/20-4 is a full computer on a single board with resources capable of supporting the majority of OEM system requirements. For those applications requiring additional processing capacity and the benefits of multiprocessing (i.e., several CPUs and/or controllers logically share system tasks with communication over the system bus), the iSBC 80/20-4 provides full MULTIBUS arbitration control logic. This control logic allows up to three iSBC 80/20-4 or high speed controllers to share the system bus in serial (daisy chain) priority fashion, and up to 16 masters may share the system bus with the addition of an external priority network. Once bus control is attained, a bus bandwidth of up to 5M bytes/sec may be achieved.

The bus controller provides its own clock which is derived independently from the processor clock. This allows different speed controllers to share resources on the same bus, and transfers via the bus proceed asynchronously. Thus, transfer speed is dependent on transmitting and receiving devices only. This design prevents slow master modules from being handicapped in their attempts to gain control of the bus, but does not restrict the speed at which faster modules can transfer data via the same bus. Once a bus request is granted, single or multiple read/write transfers can proceed at a maximum rate of 5 million data words per second. The most obvious applications for the master-slave capabilities of the bus are multiprocessor configurations, high speed direct-memory-access (DMA) operations and high speed peripheral control, but are by no means limited to these three.

Programmable Timers

The iSBC 80/20-4 board provides three fully programmable and independent BCD and binary 16-bit interval timers/event counters utilizing an Intel 8253 Programmable Interval Timer. Two of these timers/counters are available to the systems designer to generate accurate time intervals under software control. Routing of these counters is jumper selectable. Each may be independently routed to the programmable interrupt controller, the I/O line drivers and terminators, or outputs from the 8255 programmable peripheral interfaces. The third interval timer in the 8253 provides the programmable baud

Table 1. Input/Output Port Modes of Operation

Port	Lines (qty)	Mode of Operation				Bidirectional	Control
		Unidirectional					
		Input		Output			
		Unlatched	Latched & Strobed	Latched	Latched & Strobed		
1	8	X	X	X	X	X	
2	8	X	X	X	X		
3	4	X		X			X[1]
	4	X		X			X[1]
4	8	X	X	X	X	X	
5	8	X	X	X	X		
6	4	X		X			X[2]
	4	X		X			X[2]

Notes
1. Part of port 3 must be used as a control port when either port 1 or port 2 are used as a latched and strobed input or a latched and strobed output port or port 1 is used as a bidirectional port.
2. Part of port 6 must be used as a control port when either port 4 or port 5 are used as a latched and strobed input or a latched and strobed output port or port 4 is used as a bidirectional port.

iSBC® 80/20-4

rate generator for the iSBC 80/20-4 RS232C USART serial port. In utilizing the iSBC 80/20-4, the systems designer simply configures, via software, each timer independently to meet system requirements. Whenever a given time delay or count is needed, software commands to the programmable timers/event counters select the desired function. Seven functions are available, as shown in Table 2. The contents of each counter may be read at any time during system operation with simple read operations for event counting applications, and special commands are included so that the contents of each counter can be used "on the fly".

Table 2. Programmable Timer Functions

Function	Operation
Interrupt on terminal count	When terminal count is reached, an interrupt request is generated. This function is extremely useful for generation of real-time clocks.
Programmable one-shot	Output goes low upon receipt of an external trigger edge or software command and returns high when terminal count is reached. This function is retriggerable.
Rate generator	Divide by N counter. The output will go low for one input clock cycle, and the period from one low-going pulse to the next is N times the input clock period.
Square-wave rate generator	Output will remain high until one-half the count has been completed, and go low for the other half of the count.
Software triggered strobe	Output remains high until software loads count (N). N counts after count is loaded, output goes low for one input clock period.
Hardware triggered strobe	Output goes low for one clock period N counts after rising edge on counter trigger input. The counter is retriggerable.
Event counter	On a jumper selectable basis, the clock input becomes an input from the external system. CPU may read the number of events occurring after the counting "window" has been enabled or an interrupt may be generated after N events occur in the system.

Interrupt Capability

Operation and Priority Assignments — An Intel 8259 Programmable Interrupt Controller (PIC) provides vectoring for eight interrupt levels. As shown in Table 3, a selection of four priority processing modes is available to the systems designer so that the manner in which requests are processed may be configured to match system requirements. Operating mode and priority assignments may be reconfigured dynamically via software at any time during system operation. The PIC accepts interrupt requests from the programmable parallel and serial I/O interfaces, the programmable timers, the system bus, or directly from peripheral equipment. The PIC then determines which of the incoming requests is of the highest priority, determines whether this request is of higher priority than the level currently being serviced, and if appropriate, issues an interrupt to the CPU. Any combination of interrupt levels may be masked through storage via software, of a single byte to the interrupt register of the PIC.

Table 3. Programmable Interrupt Modes

Mode	Operation
Fully nested	Interrupt request line priorities fixed at 0 as highest, 7 as lowest.
Auto-rotating	Equal priority. Each level, after receiving service, becomes the lowest priority level until the next interrupt occurs.
Specific priority	System software assigns lowest priority level. Priority of all other levels based in sequence numerically on this assignment.
Polled	System software examines priority-encoded system interrupt status via interrupt status register.

Interrupt Addressing — The PIC generates a unique memory address for each interrupt level. These addresses are equally spaced at intervals of 4 or 8 (software selectable) bytes. This 32- or 64-byte block may be located to begin at any 32- or 64-byte boundary in the 65,536-byte memory space. A single 8080 jump instruction at each of these addressed then provides linkage to locate each interrupt service routine independently anywhere in memory.

Interrupt Request Generation — Interrupt requests may originate from 26 sources. Four jumper selectable interrupt requets can be automatically generated by the programmable peripheral interface when a byte of information is ready to be transferred to the CPU (i.e., input buffer is full) or a byte of information has been transferred to a peripheral device (i.e., output buffer is empty). Two jumper selectable interrupt requests can be automatically generated by the USART when a character is ready to be transfer to the CPU (i.e., receive channel buffer is full), or a character is ready to be transmitted (i.e., transmit channel data buffer is empty). A jumper selectable request can be generated by each of the programmable timers. Nine additional interrupt request lines are available to the user for direct interface to user designated peripheral devices via the system bus, and eight interrupt request lines may be jumper routed directly from peripherals via the parallel I/O driver/terminator section.

Power-Fail Control — Control logic is also included for generation of a power-fail interrupt which works in conjunction with the AC-low signal from iSBC 635 Power Supply or equivalent.

iSBC® 80/20-4

Expansion Capabilities

Memory and I/O capacity may be expanded and additional functions added using Intel MULTIBUS compatible expansion boards. High speed integer and floating-point arithmetic capabilities may be added by using the iSBC 310A High Speed Mathematics Unit. Memory may be expanded to 65,536 bytes by adding user specified combinations of RAM boards, EPROM boards, or combination boards. Input/output capacity may be increased by adding digital I/O and analog I/O expansion boards. Mass storage capability may be achieved by adding single or double density diskette controllers as subsystems. Modular expandable backplanes and cardcages are available to support multiboard systems.

System Development Capability

The development cycle of iSBC 80/20-4-based products may be significantly reduced using Intel's system development tools available today. For those not requiring hardware emulation capability, Intel provides a new low cost microcomputer development system. The iPDS, Personal Development System, provides low cost system development for the iSBC 80/20-4 board, while at the same time providing personal computer capability for the engineer. The Intellec Series II family of compatible microcomputer development systems provides a range of capability from a low cost disk-based edit debug workstation to a high performance, fully compatible hard-disk-based software development system. A unique in-circuit emulator (ICE-80) option provides the capability of developing and debugging software directly on the iSBC 80/20-4 board.

Programming Capability

PL/M-80 — Intel's high level programming language, PL/M, is also available as a resident Intellec microcomputer development system option. PL/M provides the capability to program in a natural, algorithmic language and eliminates the need to manage register usage or allocate memory. PL/M programs can be written in a much shorter time than assembly langauge programs for a given application.

FORTRAN-80 — For applications requiring computational and formatted I/O capabilities, the high level FORTRAN-80 programming language is also available as a resident option of the Intellec system. The FORTRAN compiler produces relocatable object code that may be easily linked with PL/M or assembly language program modules. This gives the user a wide flexibility in developing software.

BASIC-80 — A high level language interpreter with extended disk capabilities which operates under the RMX/80 Real-Time Multi-Tasking Executive and translates BASIC-80 source programs into an internally executable form. This language interpreter, provided as a set of linkable object modules, is ideally suited to the OEM who requires a pass through programming language. The BASIC-80 programs may be created, stored and interpreted on the iSBC 80 based system. The BASIC-80 language has a rich complement of statements, functions, and commands to program applications requiring a full range of 1) string manipulation and disk I/O for data processing, 2) single and double precision floating point and array handling for numeric analysis, or 3) port I/O with mask operations controlled through bit-wise Boolean logical operators.

SPECIFICATIONS

Word Size

Instruction — 8, 16, or 24 bits
Data — 8 bits

Cycle Time

Basic Instruction Cycle — 1.86 µs

Note
Basic instruction cycle is defined as the fastest instruction (i.e., four clock cycles).

Memory Addressing

On-Board ROM/EPROM — 0–0FFF (2708) or 0–1FFF (2716)

On-Board RAM — 4K bytes ending on a 16K boundary (e.g., 3FFF$_H$, 7FFF$_H$, BFFF$_H$, . . . FFFF$_H$)

Memory Capacity

On-Board ROM/EPROM — 8K bytes (sockets only)

On-Board RAM — 4K bytes

Off-Board Expansion — Up to 65,536 bytes in user specified RAM, ROM, and EPROM

Note
ROM/EPROM may be added in 1K or 2K-byte increments.

I/O Addressing

On-Board Programmable I/O (see Table 1)

Port	8255 No. 1			8255 No. 2			8255 No. 1 Control	8255 No. 2 Control	USART Data	USART Control
	1	2	3	4	5	6				
Address	E4	E5	E6	E8	E9	EA	E7	EB	EC	ED

iSBC® 80/20-4

I/O Capacity

Parallel — 48 programmable lines (see Table 1)

Note
Expansion to 504 input and 504 output lines can be accomplished using optional I/O boards.

Serial Communications Characteristics

Synchronous — 5-8 bit characters; internal or external character synchronization; automatic sync insertion

Asynchronous — 5-8 bit characters; break character generation; 1, 1½, or 2 stop bits; false start bit detection

Baud Rates

Frequency (kHz) (Software Selectable)	Baud Rate (Hz)		
	Synchronous	Asynchronous	
		÷ 16	÷ 64
153.6	—	9600	2400
76.8	—	4800	1200
38.4	38400	2400	600
19.2	19200	1200	300
9.6	9600	600	150
4.8	4800	300	75
2.4	2400	150	—
1.76	1760	110	—

Note
Frequency selected by I/O write of appropriate 16-bit frequency factor to baud rate register.

Register Address (hex notation, I/O address space)
DE Baud rate register

Note
Baud rate factor (16 bits) is loaded as two sequential output operations to same address (DE_H).

Interrupts

Register Addresses (hex notation, I/O address space)
DA Interrupt request register
DA In-service register
DB Mask register
DA Command register
DB Block address register
DA Status (polling register)

Note
Several registers have the same physical address; sequence of access and one data bit of control word determine which register will respond.

Timers

Register Addresses (hex notation, I/O address space)
DF Control register
DC Timer 1
DD Timer 2

Note
Timer counts loaded as two sequential output operations to same address, as given.

Input Frequencies

Reference	Event Rate
1.0752 MHz ± 10% (0.930 µs period, nominal)	1.1 MHz max

Note
Maximum rate for external events in event counter function.

Output Frequencies/Timing Intervals

Function	Single Timer/Counter		Dual Timer/Counter (Two Timers Cascaded)	
	Min	Max	Min	Max
Real-time interrupt	1.86 µs	60.948 ms	3.72 µs	1.109 hr
Programmable one-shot	1.86 µs	60.948 ms	3.72 µs	1.109 hr
Rate generator	16.407 Hz	537.61 kHz	0.00025 Hz	268.81 kHz
Square-wave rate generator	16.407 Hz	537.61 kHz	0.00025 Hz	268.31 kHz
Software triggered strobe	1.86 µs	60.948 ms	3.72 µs	1.109 hr
Hardware triggered strobe	1.86 µs	60.948 ms	3.72 µs	1.109 hr

Interfaces

Bus — All signals TTL compatible
Parallel I/O — All signals TTL compatible
Interrupt Requests — All TTL compatible
Timer — All signals TTL compatible
Serial I/O — RS232C compatible, data set configuration

System Clock (8080A CPU)

2.1504 MHz ± 0.1%

Auxiliary Power

An auxiliary power bus is provided to allow separate power to RAM for systems requiring battery backup of read/write memory. Selection of this auxiliary RAM power bus is made via jumpers on the board.

Memory Protect

An active-low TTL compatible memory protect signal is brought out on the auxiliary connector which, when asserted, disables read/write access to RAM memory on the board. This input is provided for the protection of RAM contents during system power-down sequences.

Connectors

Interface	Double-Sided Pins (qty)	Centers (in.)	Mating Connectors*
MULTIBUS System Bus	86	0.156	ELFAB BS1562043PBB Viking 2KH43/9AMK12 Soldered PCB Mount EDAC 337086540201 ELFAB BW1562D43PBB EDAC 337086540202 ELFAB BW1562A43PBB Wire Wrap
Auxiliary Bus	60	0.100	EDAC 345060524802 ELFAB BS1020A30PBB EDAC 345060540201 ELFAB BW1020D30PBB Wire Wrap
Parallel I/O (2)	50	0.100	3M 3415-001 Flat Crimp GTE Sylvania 6AD01251A1DD Soldered
Serial I/O	26	0.100	AMP 15837151 EDAC 345026520202 PCB Soldered 3M 3462-0001 AMP 88373-5 Flat Crimp

*Note: Connectors compatible with those listed may also be used.

iSBC® 80/20-4

Line Drivers and Terminators

I/O Drivers — The following line drivers are all compatible with the I/O driver sockets on the iSBC 80/20-4.

Driver	Characteristic	Sink Current (mA)
7438	I,OC	48
7437	I	48
7432	NI	16
7426	I,OC	16
7409	NI,OC	16
7408	NI	16
7403	I,OC	16
7400	I	16

Note
I = inverting; NI = non-inverting; OC = open collector.

Ports 1 and 4 have 20 mA totem-pole bidirectional drivers and 1 kΩ terminators.

I/O Terminators — 220Ω/330Ω divider or 1 kΩ pull-up

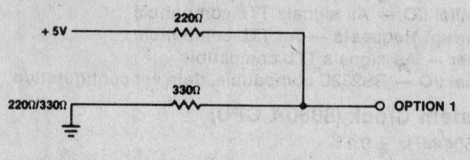

Bus Drivers

Driver	Characteristic	Sink Current (mA)
Data	Tri-state	50
Address	Tri-state	50
Commands	Tri-state	32

Physical Characteristics

Width — 12.00 in. (30.48 cm)
Height — 6.75 in. (17.15 cm)
Depth — 0.50 in. (1.26 cm)
Weight — 14 oz (397.6 gm)

Electrical Characteristics

DC Power Requirements

Voltage (±5%)	Without PROM[1] (max)	With 4K PROM[2] (max)	With iSBC 530[3] (max)	RAM Only[4] (max)	With 8K PROM[5] (max)
V_{CC} = +5V	I_{CC} = 4.0A	4.9A	4.9A	1.1A	5.2A
V_{DD} = +12V	I_{DD} = 90 mA	350 mA	450 mA	—	90 mA
V_{BB} = −5V	I_{BB} = 2 mA	180 mA	180 mA	—	2 mA
V_{AA} = −12V	I_{AA} = 20 mA	20 mA	120 mA	—	20 mA

Notes
1. Does not include power required for optional PROM, I/O drivers, and I/O terminators.
2. With four 2708 EPROMs and 220Ω/330Ω input terminators installed for 32 I/O lines, all terminator inputs low.
3. With four 2708 EPROMs, 220Ω/330Ω input terminators installed for 32 I/O lines, all terminator inputs low, and iSBC 530 Teletypewriter Adapter drawing power from serial port connector.
4. RAM chips powered via auxiliary power bus.
5. With four 8716 EPROMs and eight 220Ω/330Ω input terminators installed, all terminator inputs low.

Environmental Characteristics

Operating Temperature — 0°C to 55°CC

Reference Manual

9800317D — iSBC 80/20-5 Hardware Reference Manual (NOT SUPPLIED)

Reference manuals are shipped with each product only if designated SUPPLIED (see above). Manuals may be ordered from any Intel sales representative, distributor office or from Intel Literature Department, 3065 Bowers Avenue, Santa Clara, California 95051.

ORDERING INFORMATION

Part Number	Description
SBC 80/20-4	Single Board Computer with 4K bytes RAM

iSBC® 80/24A
SINGLE BOARD COMPUTER

- Upward compatible with iSBC® 80/20-4 Single Board Computer
- 8085A-2 CPU operating at 4.8 or 2.4 MHz
- Two iSBX™ bus connectors for iSBX™ MULTIMODULE™ board expansion
- 8K bytes of static read/write memory
- Sockets for up to 32K bytes of read only memory
- 48 programmable parallel I/O lines with sockets for interchangeable line drivers and terminators
- Programmable synchronous/asynchronous RS232C compatible serial interface with software selectable baud rates
- Full MULTIBUS® control logic for multi-master configurations and system expansion
- Two programmable 16-bit BCD or binary timers/event counters
- 12 levels of programmable interrupt control
- Auxiliary power bus, memory protect, and power-fail interrupt control logic provided for battery backup RAM requirements

The Intel® 80/24A Single Board Computer is a member of Intel's complete line of OEM microcomputer systems which take full advantage of Intel's LSI technology to provide economical, self-contained computer-based solutions for OEM applications. The iSBC 80/24A board is a complete computer system on a single 6.7 × 12.00-inch printed circuit card. The CPU, system clock, iSBX bus interface, read/write memory, read only memory sockets, I/O ports and drivers, serial communications interface, priority interrupt logic, and programmable timers all reside on the board. Full MULTIBUS interface logic is included to offer compatibility with the Intel OEM Microcomputer Systems family of Single Board Computers, expansion memory options, digital and analog I/O expansion boards, and peripheral and communications controllers.

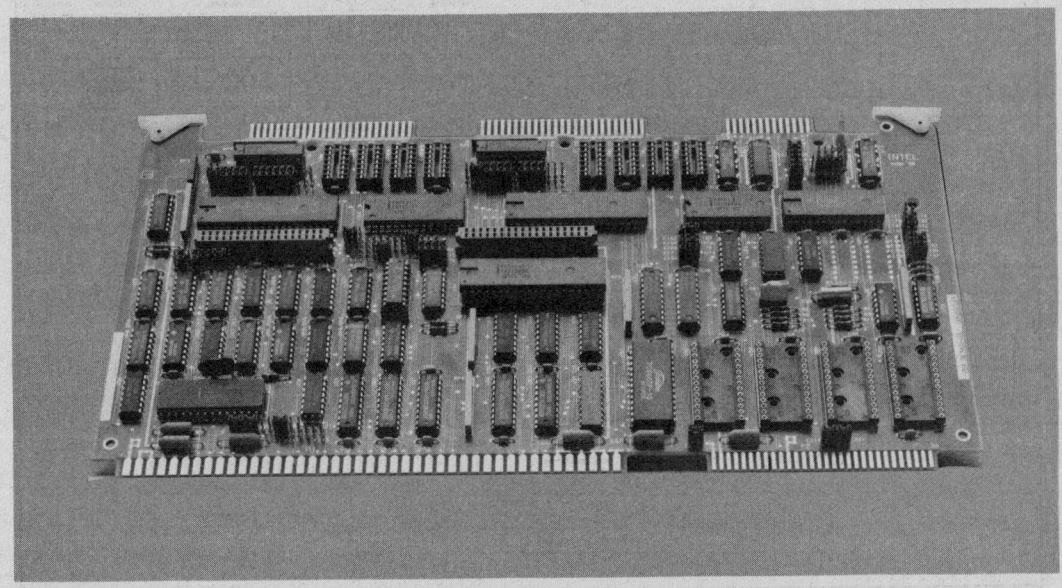

Intel Corporation assumes no responsibility for the use of any circuitry other than circuitry embodied in an Intel product. No other circuit patent licenses are implied. Information contained herein supersedes previously published specifications on these devices from Intel.

© INTEL CORPORATION, 1985

APRIL, 1985
ORDER NUMBER: 142927-003

iSBC® 80/24A BOARD

FUNCTIONAL DESCRIPTION

Central Processing Unit

Intel's powerful 8-bit N-channel 8085A-2 CPU fabricated on a single LSI chip, is the central processor for the iSBC 80/24A board operating at either 4.8 or 2.4 MHz (jumper selectable). The 8085A-2 CPU is directly software compatible with the Intel 8080A CPU. The 8085A-2 contains six 8-bit general purpose registers and an accumulator. The six general purpose registers may be addressed individually or in pairs, providing single and double precision operators. Minimum instruction execution time is 826 nanoseconds. A block diagram of the iSBC 80/24A functional components is shown in Figure 1.

MULTIMODULE™ Board Expansion

The iSBX bus interface brings designers incremental on-board expansion at minimal cost. Two iSBX bus MULTIMODULE connectors are provided for plug-in expansion of any iSBX MULTIMODULE board. The iSBX MULTIMODULE concept provides the ability to adapt quickly to new technology, the economy of buying only what is needed, and the ready availability of a spectrum of functions for greater application potential. iSBX boards are available to provide expansion equivalent to the I/O available on the iSBC 80/24A board or the user may configure entirely new functionality, such as math, directly on board. The iSBX 350 Parallel I/O MULTIMODULE board provides 24 I/O lines using an 8255A Programmable Peripheral Interface. Therefore two iSBX 350 modules together with the iSBC 80/24A board may offer 96 lines of programmable I/O. Alternately, a serial port may be added using the iSBX 351 Serial I/O MULTIMODULE board and math may be configured on-board with the iSBX 331 Fixed/Floating Point Math MULTIMODULE board. Future iSBX products are also planned. The iSBX MULTIMODULE board is a logical extension of the on-board programmable I/O and is accessed by the iSBC 80/24A single board computer as common I/O port locations. The iSBX board is coupled directly to the 8085A-2 CPU and therefore becomes an integral element of the iSBC 80/24A single board computer providing optimum performance. All MULTIMODULE boards offer incremental expansion, optimum performance, and minimal cost.

Memory Addressing

The 8085A-2 has a 16-bit program counter which allows direct addressing of up to 64K bytes of memory. An external stack, located within any portion of read/write memory, may be used as a last-in/first-out storage area for the contents of the program counter, flags, accumulator, and all of the six general purpose registers. A 16-bit stack pointer controls the addressing of this external stack. This stack provides subroutine nesting bounded only by memory size.

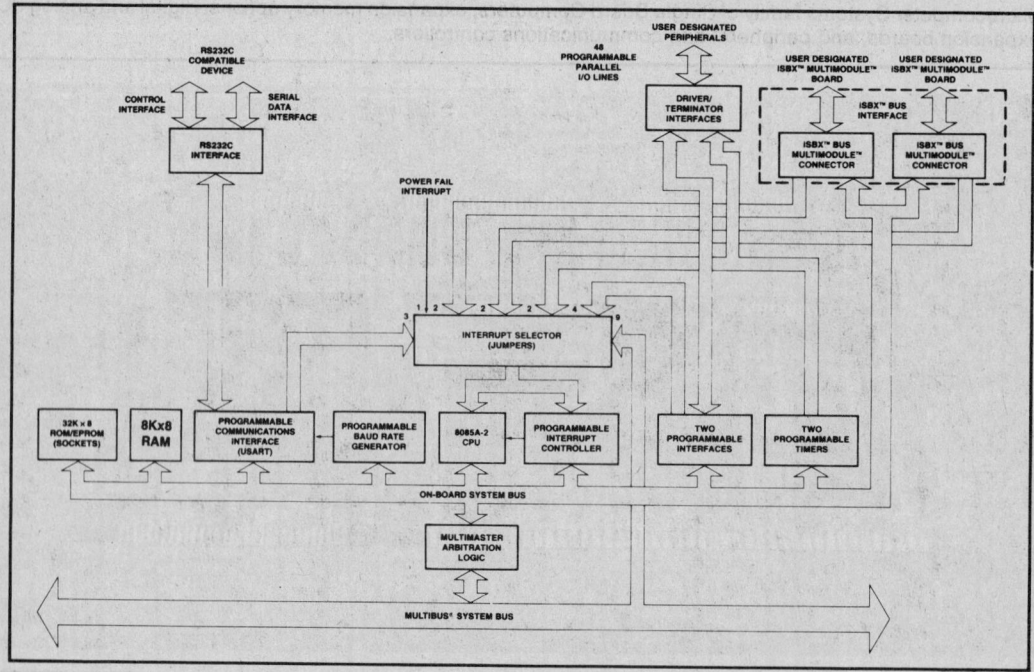

Figure 1. iSBC® 80/24A Single Board Computer Block Diagram

iSBC® 80/24A BOARD

Memory Capacity

The iSBC 80/24A board contains 8K bytes of static read/write memory using an 8K × 8 SRAMs. All RAM read and write operations are performed at maximum processor speed. Power for the on-board RAM may be provided on an auxiliary power bus, and memory protect logic is included for RAM battery backup requirements.

Four sockets are provided for up to 32K bytes of nonvolatile read only memory on the iSBC 80/24A board. EPROM may be added as shown with white-out and 2732A.

Parallel I/O Interface

The iSBC 80/24A board contains 48 programmable parallel I/O lines implemented using two Intel 8255A Programmable Peripheral Interfaces. The system software is used to configure the I/O lines in any combination of unidirectional input/output and bidirectional ports as indicated in Table 1. Therefore, the I/O interface may be customized to meet specific peripheral requirements. In order to take full advantage of the large number of possible I/O configurations, sockets are provided for interchangeable I/O line drivers and terminators. Hence, the flexibility of the I/O interface is further enhanced by the capability of selecting the appropriate combination of optional line drivers and terminators to provide the required sink current, polarity, and drive/termination characteristics for each application. The 48 programmable I/O lines and signal ground lines are brought out to two 50-pin edge connectors that mate with flat, woven, or round cables.

Serial I/O Interface

A programmable communications interface using the Intel 8251A Universal Synchronous/Asynchronous Receiver/Transmitter (USART) is contained on the iSBC 80/24A board. A software selectable baud rate generator provides the USART with all common communication frequencies. The USART can be programmed by the system software to select the desired asynchronous or synchronous serial data transmission technique (including IBM Bi-Sync). The mode of operation (i.e. synchronous or asynchronous), data format, control character format, parity, and baud rate are all under program control. The 8251A provides full duplex, double buffered transmit and receive capability. Parity, overrun, and framing error detection are all incorporated in the USART. The RS232C compatible interface, in conjunction with the USART, provides a direct interface to RS232C compatible terminals, cassettes, and asynchronous and synchronous modems. The RS232C command lines, serial data lines, and signal ground line are brought out to a 26-pin edge connector that mates with RS232C compatible flat or round cable.

Multimaster Capability

The iSBC 80/24A board is a full computer on a single board with resources capable of supporting a large variety of OEM system requirements. For those appli-

Table 1. Input/Output Port Modes of Operation

Port	Lines (qty)	Mode of Operation					
		Unidirectional				Bidirectional	Control
		Input		Output			
		Unlatched	Latched & Strobed	Latched	Latched & Strobed		
1	8	X	X	X	X	X	
2	8	X	X	X	X		
3	4	X		X			X[1]
	4	X		X			X[1]
4	8	X	X	X	X	X	
5	8	X	X	X	X		
6	4	X		X			X[2]
	4	X		X			X[2]

NOTES:
1. Part of port 3 must be used as a control port when either port 1 or port 2 are used as a latched and strobed input or a latched and strobed output port or port 1 is used as a bidirectional port.
2. Part of port 6 must be used as a control port when either port 4 or port 5 are used as a latched and strobed input or a latched and strobed output port or port 4 is used as a bidirectional port.

iSBC® 80/24A BOARD

cations requiring additional processing capacity and the benefits of multiprocessing (i.e. several CPUs and/or controllers logically sharing system tasks through communication over the system bus), the iSBC 80/24A board provides full MULTIBUS arbitration control logic. This control logic allows up to three iSBC 80/24A boards or other bus masters to share the system bus in serial (daisy chain) priority fashion, and up to 16 masters to share the MULTIBUS system bus with the addition of an external priority network. The MULTIBUS arbitration logic operates synchronously with a MULTIBUS clock (provided by the iSBC 80/24A board or optionally connected directly to the MULTIBUS clock) while data is transferred via a handshake between the master and slave modules. This allows different speed controllers to share resources on the same bus since transfers via the bus proceed asynchronously. Thus, transfer speed is dependent on transmitting and receiving devices only. This design provides slow master modules from being handicapped in their attempts to gain control of the bus, but does not restrict the speed at which faster modules can transfer data via the same bus. The most obvious applications for the master-slave capabilities of the bus are multiprocessor configurations, high speed direct memory access (DMA) operations, and high speed peripheral control, but are by no means limited to these three.

Programmable Timers

The iSBC 80/24A board provides three independent, fully programmable 16-bit interval timers/event counters utilizing the Intel 8254 Programmable Interval Timer. Each counter is capable of operating in either BCD or binary modes. Two of these timers/counters are available to the systems designer to generate accurate time intervals under software control. Routing for the outputs and gate/trigger inputs of two of these counters is jumper selectable. The outputs may be independently routed to the 8259A Programmable Interrupt Controller, to the I/O line drivers associated with the 8255A Programmable Peripheral Interface, or may be routed as inputs to the 8255A chip. The gate/trigger inputs may be routed to I/O terminators associated with the 8255A or as output connections from the 8255A. The third interval timer in the 8254 provides the programmable baud rate generator for the RS232C USART serial port. In utilizing the iSBC 80/24A board, the systems designer simply configures, via software, each timer independently to meet system requirements. Whenever a given time delay or count is needed, software commands to the programmable timers/event counters select the desired function. Seven functions are available, as shown in Table 2. The contents of each counter may be read at any time during system operation with simple read operations for event counting applications, and special commands are included so that the contents of each counter can be read "on the fly".

Table 2. Programmable Timer Functions

Function	Operation
Interrupt on terminal count	When terminal count is reached, an interrupt request is generated. This function is extremely useful for generation of real-time clocks.
Programmable one-shot	Output goes low upon receipt of an external trigger edge or software command and returns high when terminal count is reached. This function is retriggerable.
Rate generator	Divide by N counter. The output will go low for one input clock cycle, and the period from one low-going pulse to the next is N times the input clock period.
Square-wave rate generator	Output will remain high until one-half the count has been completed, and go low for the other half of the count.
Software triggered strobe	Output remains high until software loads count (N). N counts after count is loaded, output goes low for one input clock period.
Hardware triggered strobe	Output goes low for one clock period N counts after rising edge on counter trigger input. The counter is retriggerable.
Event counter	On a jumper selectable basis, the clock input becomes an input from the external system. CPU may read the number of events occurring after the counting "window" has been enabled or an interrupt may be generated after N events occur in the system.

Interrupt Capability

The iSBC 80/24A board provides vectoring for 12 interrupt levels. Four of these levels are handled directly by the interrupt processing capability of the 8085A-2 CPU and represent the four highest priority interrupts of the iSBC 80/24A board. Requests are routed to the 8085A-2 interrupt inputs – TRAP, RST 7.5, RST 6.5, and RST 5.5 (in decreasing order of priority), each of which generates a call instruction to a unique address (TRAP: 24H; RST 7.5: 3CH; RST 6.5: 34H; and RST 5.5: 2CH). An 8085A-2 JMP instruction at each of these addresses then provides linkage to interrupt service routines located independently anywhere in memory. All interrupt inputs with the exception of the trap interrupt may be masked via software. The trap interrupt should be used for conditions such as power-down sequences which require immediate attention by the 8085A-2 CPU. The Intel 8259A Programmable Interrupt Controller (PIC) provides vectoring for the next eight interrupt levels. As shown in Table 3, a

iSBC® 80/24A BOARD

selection of four priority processing modes is available to the systems designer for use in designing request processing configurations to match system requirements. Operating mode and priority assignments may be reconfigured dynamically via software at any time during system operation. The PIC accepts interrupt requests from the programmable parallel and serial I/O interfaces, the programmable timers, the system bus, iSBX bus, or directly from peripheral equipment. The PIC then determines which of the incoming requests is of the highest priority, determines whether this request is of higher priority than the level currently being serviced, and, if appropriate, issues an interrupt to the CPU. Any combination of interrupt levels may be masked, via software, by storing a single byte in the interrupt mask register of the PIC. The PIC generates a unique memory address for each interrupt level. These addresses are equally spaced at intervals of 4 or 8 (software selectable) bytes. This 32 or 64-byte block may be located to begin at any 32 or 64-byte boundary in the 65,536-byte memory space. A single 8085A-2 JMP instruction at each of these addresses then provides linkage to locate each interrupt service routine independently anywhere in memory.

Table 3. Programmable Interrupt Modes

Mode	Operation
Fully nested	Interrupt request line priorities fixed at 0 as highest, 7 as lowest.
Autorotating	Equal priority. Each level, after receiving service, becomes the lowest priority level until next interrupt occurs.
Specific priority	System software assigns lowest priority level. Priority of all other levels based in sequence numerically on this assignment.
Polled	System software examines priority-encoded system interrupt status via interrupt status register.

Interrupt Request Generation

Interrupt requests may originate from 23 sources. Two jumper selectable interrupt requests can be generated by each iSBX MULTIMODULE board. Two jumper selectable interrupt requests can be automatically generated by each programmable peripheral interface when a byte of information is ready to be transferred to the CPU (i.e., input buffer is full) or a byte of information has been transferred to a peripheral device (i.e., output buffer is empty). Three jumper selectable interrupt requests can be automatically generated by the USART when a character is ready to be transferred to the CPU (i.e., receiver channel buffer is full), a character is ready to be transmitted (i.e., the USART is ready to accept a character from the CPU), or when the transmitter is empty (i.e., the USART has no

character to transmit). A jumper selectable request can be generated by each of the programmable timers. Nine interrupt request lines are available to the user for direct interface to user designated peripheral devices via the MULTIBUS system bus. A power-fail signal can also be selected as an interrupt source.

Power-Fail Control

A power-fail interrupt may be detected through the AC-low signal generated by the power supply. This signal may be configured to interrupt the 8085A-2 CPU to initiate an orderly power down instruction sequence.

MULTIBUS® System Expansion Capabilities

Memory and I/O capacity may be expanded and additional functions added using Intel MULTIBUS system compatible expansion boards. Memory may be expanded to 65,536 bytes by adding user specified combinations of RAM boards, EPROM boards, or combination boards. Input/output capacity may be increased by adding digital I/O and analog I/O expansion boards. Mass storage capability may be achieved by adding single or double density diskette or hard disk controllers as subsystems. Expanded communication needs can be handled by communication controllers. Modular expandable backplanes and card cages are available to support multiboard systems.

System Development Capability

The development cycle of iSBC 80/24A-based products may be significantly reduced using Intel's system development tools available today. For those not requiring hardware emulation capability, Intel provides a new low cost microcomputer development system. The iPDS, Personal Development System, provides low cost system development for iSBC 80/24A board, while at the same time providing personal computer capability for the engineer. The Intellec Series II family of compatible microcomputer development systems provides a range of capability from a low cost disk-based edit debug workstation to a high performance, fully compatible hard-disk-based software development system. A unique in-circuit emulator (ICE-85A) option provides the capability of developing and debugging software directly on the iSBC 80/24A board.

Programming Capability

PL/M-80—Intel's high level system programming language, PL/M, is also available as a resident Intellec microcomputer development system option. PL/M provides the capability to program in a natural, algorithmic language and eliminates the need to manage register usage or allocate memory. PL/M programs can be written in a much shorter time than assembly language programs.

iSBC® 80/24A BOARD

FORTRAN-80—For applications requiring computational and formatted I/O capabilities, the ANSI 77 standard high level FORTRAN-80 programming language is available as a resident option of the Intellec system. The FORTRAN compiler produces relocatable object code that may be easily linked with PL/M or assembly language program modules. In addition, the iSBC 801 FORTRAN-80 Run-Time Package is a complete, ready-to-use set of linkable object modules which are fully compatible with iRMX 80 systems. The modules, when combined with the FORTRAN-80 coded application, provide the appropriate interfaces to the disk file and terminal I/O of iRMX 80 Operating System.

BASIC-80—A high level language interpreter is available with extended disk capabilities which operates under the iRMX 80 Real-Time Multitasking Executive and translates BASIC-80 source programs into an internally executable form. This language interpreter, provided as a set of linkable object modules, is ideally suited to the OEM who requires a pass through programming language. The BASIC-80 programs may be created, stored, and interpreted on the iSBC 80-based systems using the iSBC 802 BASIC-80 Configurable iRMX 80 Disk-Based Interpreter. The iSBC 802 Interpreter has a complete ready-to-use set of linkable object modules which are fully compatible with Intel's iRMX 80 Real-Time Multitasking Executive Software. The modules provide interfaces to disk file and terminal I/O, software floating point, or interface to other routines by the user.

SPECIFICATIONS

Word Size

Instruction—8, 16, or 24 bits
Data—8 bits

Cycle Time

BASIC INSTRUCTION CYCLE

826 nsec (4.84 MHz operating frequency)
1.65 μsec (2.42 MHz operating frequency)

NOTE:
Basic instruction cycle is defined as the fastest instruction (i.e., four clock cycles).

Memory Addressing

ON-BOARD EPROM

0-0FFF using 2708, 2758 (1 wait state)
0-1FFF using 2716 (1 wait state)
0-3FFF using 2732 (1 wait state)
 using 2732A (no wait states)
0-7FFF using 2764A (no wait states)

ON-BOARD RAM

E000-FFFF

NOTE:
Default configuration—may be reconfigured to top end of any 16K boundary.

Memory Capacity

ON-BOARD EPROM

32K bytes (sockets only)

May be added in 1K (using 2708 or 2758), 2K (using 2716), 4K (using Intel 2732A), or 8K (using Intel 2764A) byte increments.

ON-BOARD RAM

8K bytes

OFF-BOARD EXPANSION

Up to 64K bytes using user specified combinations of RAM, ROM, and EPROM.

Up to 128K bytes using bank select control via I/O port and 2 jumper options.

May be disabled using PROM ENABLE via I/O port and jumper option, resulting in off-board RAM overlay capability.

I/O Addressing

ON-BOARD PROGRAMMABLE I/O

Device	I/O Address
8255A No. 1	
Port A	E4
Port B	E5
Port C	E6
Control	E7
8255A No. 2	
Port A	E8
Port B	E9
Port C	EA
Control	EB
8251A	
Data	EC, EE
Control	ED, EF
iSBX MULTIMODULE J5	
MCS0	C0-C7
MCS1	C8-CF
iSBX MULTIMODULE J6	
MCS0	F0-F7
MCS1	F8-FF

iSBC® 80/24A BOARD

I/O Capacity

Parallel—48 programmable lines

Serial—1 transmit, 1 receive, 1 SID, 1 SOD

iSBX™ MULTIMODULE™—2 iSBX MULTIMODULE Boards

Serial Communications Characteristics

Synchronous—5-8 bit characters; internal or external character synchronization; automatic sync insertion

Asynchronous—5-8 bit characters; break character generation; 1, 1½, or 2 stop bits; false start bit detectors

Baud Rates

Output Frequency in kHz	Baud Rate (Hz)	
	Synchronous	Asynchronous
		÷16 ÷64
153.6	—	9600 2400
76.8	—	4800 1200
38.4	38400	2400 600
19.2	19200	1200 300
9.6	9600	600 150
4.8	4800	300 75
2.4	2400	150 —
1.76	1760	110 —

NOTE:
Frequency selected by I/O write of appropriate 16-bit frequency factor to baud rate register.

Register Address (hex notation, I/O address space)

DE Baud rate register

NOTE:
Baud rate factor (16 bits) is loaded as two sequential output operations to same address (DE_H).

Interrupts

Addresses for 8259A Registers (hex notation, I/O address space)

DA or D8	Interrupt request register
DA or D8	In-service register
DB or D9	Mask register
DA or D8	Command register
DB or D9	Block address register
DA or D8	Status (polling register)

NOTE:
Several registers have the same physical address; sequence of access and one data bit of control word determine which register will respond.

Interrupt levels routed to 8085A-2 CPU automatically vector the processor to unique memory locations:

Interrupt Input	Memory Address	Priority	Type
TRAP	24	Highest	Non-maskable
RST 7.5	3C	↓	Maskable
RST 6.5	34		Maskable
RST 5.5	2C	Lowest	Maskable

Timers

Register Addresses (hex notation, I/O address space)

DF	Control register
DC	Timer 0
DD	Timer 1
DE	Timer 2

NOTE:
Timer counts loaded as two sequential output operations to same address as given.

Input Frequencies

Reference: 1.0752 MHz ±0.1% (0.930 μsec period, nominal)

Event Rate: 1.1 MHz max.

Output Frequencies/Timing Intervals

Function	Single Timer/Counter		Dual Timer/Counter (Two Timers Cascaded)	
	Min.	Max.	Min.	Max.
Real-Time Interrupt	1.86 μsec	60.948 msec	3.72 μsec	1.109 hrs
Programmable One-Shot	1.86 μsec	60.948 msec	3.72 μsec	1.109 hrs
Rate Generator	16.407 Hz	537.61 kHz	0.00025 Hz	268.81 kHz
Square-Wave Rate Generator	16.407 Hz	537.61 kHz	0.00025 Hz	268.81 kHz
Software Triggered Strobe	1.86 μsec	60.948 msec	3.72 μsec	1.109 hrs
Hardware Triggered Strobe	1.86 μsec	60.948 msec	3.72 μsec	1.109 hrs

NOTE:
Input frequency to timers is 1.0752 MHz (default configuration).

Interfaces

MULTIBUS®—All signals TTL compatible

iSBX™ Bus—All signals TTL compatible

Parallel I/O—All signals TTL compatible

iSBC® 80/24A BOARD

Serial I/O—RS232C compatible, configurable as a data set or data terminal

Timer—All signals TTL compatible

Interrupt Requests—All TTL compatible

System Clock (8085A-2 CPU)

4.84 or 2.42 MHz ±0.1% (jumper selectable)

Auxiliary Power

An auxiliary power bus is provided to allow separate power to RAM for systems requiring battery backup of read/write memory. Selection of this auxiliary RAM power bus is made via jumpers on the board.

Connectors

Interface	Double-Sided Pins (qty)	Centers (in.)	Mating Connectors*
MULTIBUS System Bus	86	0.156	ELFAB BS1562043PBB Viking 2KH43/9AMK12 Soldered PCB Mount EDAC 337086540201 ELFAB BW1562D43PBB EDAC 337086540202 ELFAB BW1562A43PBB Wire Wrap
Auxiliary Bus	60	0.100	EDAC 345060524802 ELFAB BS1020A30PBB EDAC 345060540201 ELFAB BW1020D30PBB Wire Wrap
iSBX Bus (2)	36	0.100	iSBX 960-5
Parallel I/O (2)	50	0.100	3M 3415-001 Flat Crimp GTE Sylvania 6AD01251A1DD Soldered
Serial I/O	26	0.100	AMP 15837151 EDAC 345026520202 PCB Soldered 3M 3462-0001 AMP 88373-5 Flat Crimp

*Note: Connectors compatible with those listed may also be used.

Memory Protect

An active-low TTL compatible memory protect signal is brought out on the auxiliary connector which, when asserted, disables read/write access to RAM memory on the board. This input is provided for the protection of RAM contents during system power-down sequences.

Line Drivers and Terminators

I/O Drivers—The following line drivers and terminators are all compatible with the I/O driver sockets on the iSBC 80/24A Board:

Driver	Characteristic	Sink Current (mA)
7438	I, OC	48
7437	I	48
7432	NI	16
7426	I, OC	16
7409	NI, OC	16
7408	NI	16
7403	I, OC	16
7400	I	16

NOTE:
I = inverting; NI = non-inverting; OC = open collector.

Ports E4 and E8 have 32 mA totem-pole drivers and 1K terminators.

I/O Terminators—220Ω/330Ω divider of 1 kΩ pullup

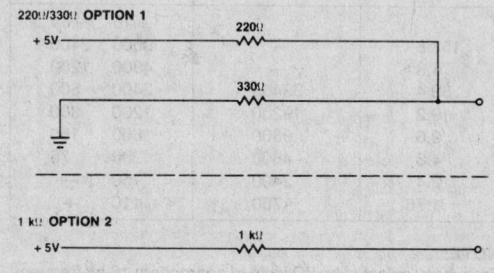

Bus Drivers

Function	Characteristic	Sink Current (mA)
Data	Tri-State	32
Address	Tri-State	32
Commands	Tri-State	32

Physical Characteristics

Width—12.00 in. (30.48 cm)

Height—6.75 in. (17.15 cm)

Depth—0.50 in. (1.27 cm)

Weight—12.64 oz. (354 gm)

iSBC® 80/24A BOARD

Electrical Characteristics

DC POWER REQUIREMENTS

Configuration	Current Requirements			
	$V_{CC} = +5V$ ±5% (max)	$V_{DD} = +12V$ ±5% (max)	$V_{BB} = -5V$ ±5% (max)	$V_{AA} = -12V$ ±5% (max)
Without EPROM[1]	2.66A	40 mA	—	20 mA
RAM Only[2]	.01A	—	—	—
With iSBC 530[3]	2.66A	140 mA	—	120 mA
With 4K EPROM[4] (using 2708)	3.28A	300 mA	180 mA	20 mA
With 4K EPROM[4] (using 2758)	3.44A	40 mA	—	20 mA
With 8K EPROM[4] (using 2716)	3.44A	40 mA	—	20 mA
With 16K EPROM[4] (using 2732A)	3.46A	40 mA	—	20 mA
With 32K EPROM[4] (using 2764A)	3.42A	40 mA	—	20 mA

NOTES:
1. Does not include power for optional EPROM, I/O drivers, and I/O terminators.
2. RAM chips powered via auxiliary power bus.
3. Does not include power for optional EPROM, I/O drivers, and I/O terminators. Power for iSBC 530 Adapter is supplied via serial port connector.
4. Includes power required for four EPROM chips, and I/O terminators installed for 16 I/O lines; all terminator inputs low.

Environmental Characteristics

Operating Temperature—0°C to 55°C

Reference Manual

148437-001–iSBC 80/24A Single Board Computer Hardware Reference Manual (NOT SUPPLIED)

Manuals may be ordered from any Intel sales representative, distributor office or from Intel Literature Department, 3065 Bowers Avenue, Santa Clara, California 95051.

ORDERING INFORMATION

Part Number   Description
SBC 80/24A   Single Board Computer

iSBC® 80/30
SINGLE BOARD COMPUTER

- 8085A CPU used as central processing unit
- 16K bytes of dual port dynamic read/write memory with on-board refresh
- Sockets for up to 8K bytes of read only memory
- Sockets for 8041A/8741A Universal Peripheral Interface and interchangeable line drivers and line terminators
- 24 programmable parallel I/O lines with sockets for interchangeable line drivers and terminators
- Programmable synchronous/asynchronous RS232C compatible serial interface with fully software selectable baud rate generation
- Full MULTIBUS® control logic allowing up to 16 masters to share the system
- 12 levels of programmable interrupt control
- Two programmable 16-bit BCD or binary counters
- Auxiliary power bus, memory protect, and power-fail interrupt control logic for RAM battery backup
- Compatible with optional iSBC® 80 CPU, memory, and I/O expansion boards

The iSBC 80/30 Single Board Computer is a member of Intel's complete line of OEM computer systems which take full advantage of Intel's LSI technology to provide economical self-contained computer-based solutions for OEM applications. The iSBC 80/30 is a complete computer system on a single 6.75 × 12.00-inch printed circuit card. The CPU, system clock, read/write memory, nonvolatile read only memory, universal peripheral interface capability, I/O ports and drivers, serial communications interface, priority interrupt logic, programmable timers, MULTIBUS control logic, and bus expansion drivers all reside on the board.

iSBC® 80/30

FUNCTIONAL DESCRIPTION

Central Processing Unit

Intel's powerful 8-bit n-channel 8085A CPU, fabricated on a single LSI chip, is the central processor for the iSBC 80/30. The 8085A CPU is directly software compatible with the Intel 8080A CPU. The 8085A contains six 8-bit general purpose registers and an accumulator. The six general purpose registers may be addressed individually or in pairs, providing both single and double precision operators. The minimum instruction execution time is 1.45 microseconds. The 8085A CPU has a 16-bit program counter. An external stack, located within any portion of iSBC 80/30 read/write memory, may be used as a last-in/first-out storage area for the contents of the program counter, flags, accumulator, and all of the six general purpose registers. A 16-bit stack pointer controls the addressing of this external stack. This stack provides subroutine nesting bounded only by memory size.

Bus Structure

The iSBC 80/30 has an internal bus for all on-board memory and I/O operations and a system bus (i.e., the MULTIBUS) for all external memory and I/O operations. Hence, local (on-board) operations do not tie up the system bus, and allow true parallel processing when several bus masters (i.e., DMA devices, other single board computers) are used in a multimaster scheme. A block diagram of the iSBC 80/30 functional components is shown in Figure 1.

RAM Capacity

The iSBC 80/30 contains 16K bytes of dynamic read/write memory using Intel 2117 RAMs. All RAM read and write operations are performed at maximum processor speed. Power for the on-board RAM may be provided on an auxiliary power bus, and memory protect logic is included for RAM battery backup requirements. The iSBC 80/30 contains a dual port controller, which provides dual port capability for the on-board RAM memory. RAM accesses may occur from either the iSBC 80/30 or from any other bus master interfaced via the

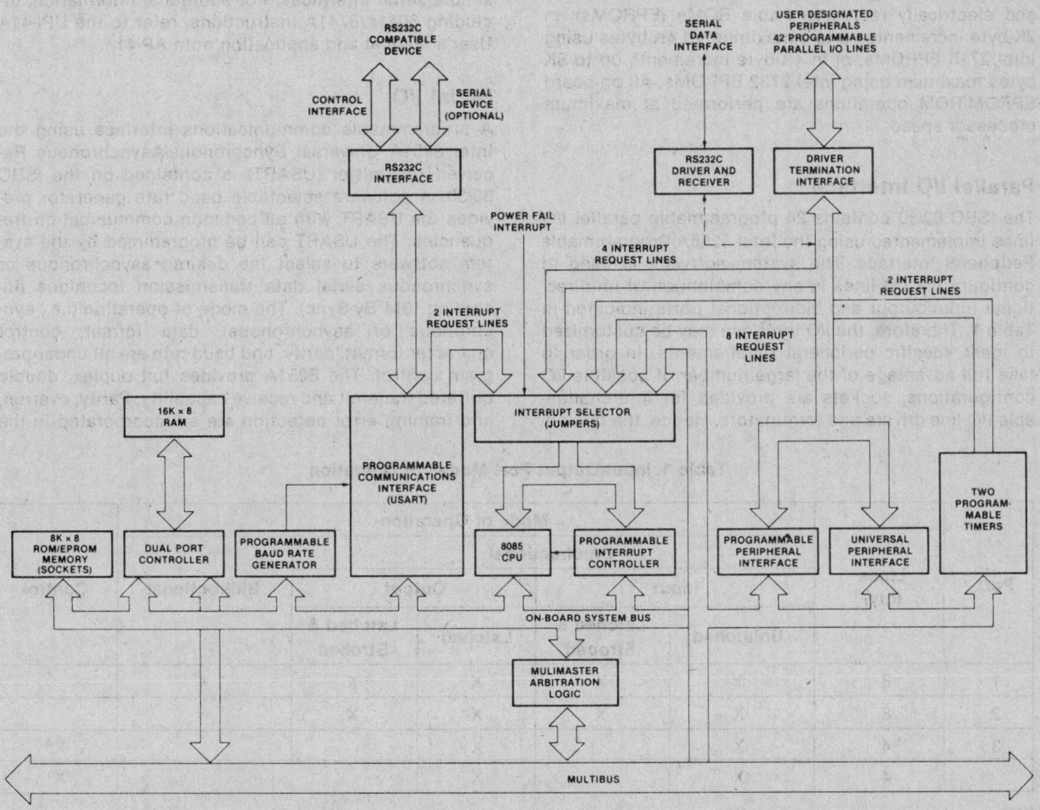

Figure 1. iSBC® 80/30 Single Board Computer Block Diagram

2-25

AFN-00263B

iSBC® 80/30

MULTIBUS. Since on-board RAM accesses do not require the MULTIBUS, the bus is available for any other concurrent operations (e.g., DMA data transfers) requiring the use of the MULTIBUS. Dynamic RAM refresh is accomplished automatically by the iSBC 80/30 for accesses originating from either the CPU or via the MULTIBUS. Memory space assignment can be selected independently for on-board and MULTIBUS RAM accesses. The on-board RAM, as seen by the 8085A CPU, may be placed anywhere within the 0- to 64K-address space. The iSBC 80/30 provides extended addressing jumpers to allow the on-board RAM to reside within a one megabyte address space when accessed via the MULTIBUS. In addition, jumper options are provided which allow the user to reserve 8K- and 16K-byte segments of on-board RAM for use by the 8085A CPU only. This reserved RAM space is not accessible via the MULTIBUS and does not occupy any system address space.

EPROM/ROM Capacity

Sockets for up to 8K bytes of nonvolatile read only memory are provided on the iSBC 80/30 board. Read only memory may be added in 1K-byte increments up to a maximum of 2K bytes using Intel 2708 or 2758 erasable and electrically reprogrammable ROMs (EPROMs); in 2K-byte increments up to a maximum of 4K bytes using Intel 2716 EPROMs; or in 4K-byte increments up to 8K bytes maximum using Intel 2732 EPROMs. All on-board EPROM/ROM operations are performed at maximum processor speed.

Parallel I/O Interface

The iSBC 80/30 contains 24 programmable parallel I/O lines implemented using the Intel 8255A Programmable Peripheral Interface. The system software is used to configure the I/O lines in any combination of unidirectional input/output and bidirectional ports indicated in Table 1. Therefore, the I/O interface may be customized to meet specific peripheral requirements. In order to take full advantage of the large number of possible I/O configurations, sockets are provided for interchangeable I/O line drivers and terminators. Hence, the flexibility of the I/O interface is further enhanced by the capability of selecting the appropriate combination of optional line drivers and terminators to provide the required sink current, polarity, and drive/termination characteristics for each application. The 24 programmable I/O lines and signal ground lines are brought out to a 50-pin edge connector that mates with flat, woven, or round cable.

Universal Peripheral Interface (UPI)

The iSBC 80/30 provides sockets for a user supplied Intel 8041A/8741A Universal Peripheral Interface (UPI) chip and the associated line drivers and terminators for the UPI's I/O ports. The 8041A/8741A is a single chip microcomputer containing a CPU, 1K bytes of ROM (8041A) or EPROM (8741A), 64 bytes of RAM, 18 programmable I/O lines, and an 8-bit timer. Special interface registers included in the chip allow the 8041A to function as a slave processor to the iSBC 80/30's 8085A CPU. The UPI allows the user to specify algorithms for controlling user peripherals directly in the chip, thereby relieving the 8085A for other system functions. The iSBC 80/30 provides an RS232C driver and an RS232C receiver for optional connection to the 8041A/8741A in applications where the UPI is programmed to handle simple serial interfaces. For additional information, including 8041A/8741A instructions, refer to the UPI-41A User's Manual and application note AP-41.

Serial I/O

A programmable communications interface using the Intel 8251A Universal Synchronous/Asynchronous Receiver/Transmitter (USART) is contained on the iSBC 80/30. A software selectable baud rate generator provides the USART with all common communication frequencies. The USART can be programmed by the system software to select the desired asynchronous or synchronous serial data transmission technique (including IBM By-Sync). The mode of operation (i.e., synchronous or asynchronous), data format, control character format, parity, and baud rate are all under program control. The 8251A provides full duplex, double buffered transmit and receive capability. Parity, overrun, and framing error detection are all incorporated in the

Table 1. Input/Output Port Modes of Operation

Port	Lines (qty)	Mode of Operation					Control
		Unidirectional				Bidirectional	
		Input		Output			
		Unlatched	Latched & Strobed	Latched	Latched & Strobed		
1	8	X	X	X	X	X	
2	8	X	X	X	X		
3	4	X		X			X[1]
	4	X		X			X[1]

Note
1. Part of port 3 must be used as a control port when either port 1 or port 2 are used as a latched and strobed input or a latched and strobed output port or port 1 is used as a bidirectional port.

iSBC® 80/30

USART. The RS232C compatible interface on each board, in conjunction with the USART, provides a direct interface to RS232C compatible terminals, cassettes, and asynchronous and synchronous modems. The RS232C command lines, serial data lines, and signal ground line are brought out to a 26-pin edge connector that mates with RS232C compatible flat or round cable.

Multimaster Capability

The iSBC 80/30 is a full computer on a single board with resources capable of supporting a great variety of OEM system requirements. For those applications requiring additional processing capacity and the benefits of multiprocessing (i.e., several CPUs and/or controllers logically sharing system tasks through communication over the system bus), the iSBC 80/30 provides full MULTIBUS arbitration control logic. This control logic allows up to three iSBC 80/30's or other bus masters to share the system bus in serial (daisy chain) priority fashion, and up to 16 masters to share the MULTIBUS with the addition of an external priority network. The MULTIBUS arbitration logic operates synchronously with a MULTIBUS clock (provided by the iSBC 80/30 or optionally connected directly to the MULTIBUS clock) while data is transferred via a handshake between the master and slave modules. This allows different speed controllers to share resources on the same bus, and transfers via the bus proceed asynchronously. Thus, transfer speed is dependent on transmitting and receiving devices only. This design prevents slow master modules from being handicapped in their attempts to gain control of the bus, but does not restrict the speed at which faster modules can transfer data via the same bus. The most obvious applications for the master-slave capabilities of the bus are multiprocessor configurations, high speed direct memory access (DMA) operations, and high speed peripheral control, but are by no means limited to these three.

Programmable Timers

The iSBC 80/30 provides three independent, fully programmable 16-bit interval timers/event counters utilizing the Intel 8253 Programmable Interval Timer. Each counter is capable of operating in either BCD or binary modes. Two of these timers/counters are available to the systems designer to generate accurate time intervals under software control. Routing for the outputs and gate/trigger inputs of two of these counters is jumper selectable. The outputs may be independently routed to the 8259A Programmable Interrupt Controller, to the I/O line drivers associated with the 8255A Programmable Peripheral Interface, and to the 8041A/8741A Universal Programmable Interface, or may be routed as inputs to the 8255A and 8041A/8741A chips. The gate/trigger inputs may be routed to I/O terminators associated with the 8255A or as output connections from the 8255A. The third interval timer in the 8253 provides the programmable baud rate generator for the iSBC 80/30 RS232C USART serial port. In utilizing the iSBC 80/30, the systems designer simply configures, via software, each timer independently to meet system requirements.

Whenever a given time delay or count is needed, software commands to the programmable timers/event counters select the desired function. Seven functions are available, as shown in Table 2. The contents of each counter may be read at any time during system operation with simple read operations for event counting applications, and special commands are included so that the contents of each counter can be read "on the fly".

Table 2. Programmable Timer Functions

Function	Operation
Interrupt on terminal count	When terminal count is reached, an interrupt request is generated. This function is extremely useful for generation of real-time clocks.
Programmable one-shot	Output goes low upon receipt of an external trigger edge or software command and returns high when terminal count is reached. This function is retriggerable.
Rate generator	Divide by N counter. The output will go low for one input clock cycle, and the period from one low-going pulse to the next is N times the input clock period.
Square-wave rate generator	Output will remain high until one-half the count has been completed, and go low for the other half of the count.
Software triggered strobe	Output remains high until software loads count (N). N counts after count is loaded, output goes low for one input clock period.
Hardware triggered strobe	Output goes low for one clock period N counts after rising edge on counter trigger input. The counter is retriggerable.
Event counter	On a jumper selectable basis, the clock input becomes an input from the external system. CPU may read the number of events occurring after the counting "window" has been enabled or an interrupt may be generated after N events occur in the system.

Interrupt Capability

The iSBC 80/30 provides vectoring for 12 interrupt levels. Four of these levels are handled directly by the interrupt processing capability of the 8085A CPU and represent the four highest priority interrupts of the iSBC 80/30. Requests are routed to the 8085A interrupt inputs, TRAP, RST 7.5, RST 6.5, and RST 5.5 (in decreasing order of priority) and each input generates a unique memory address (TRAP: 24H; RST 7.5: 3CH; RST 6.5: 34H; and RST 5.5: 2CH). An 8085A jump instruction at each of these addresses then provides linkage to interrupt service routines located independently anywhere in memory. All interrupt inputs with the exception of the trap interrupt may be masked via software. The trap interrupt should be used for conditions such as power-down sequences which require immediate attention by the 8085A CPU. The Intel 8259A Programmable Interrupt Controller (PIC) provides vectoring for the next eight interrupt levels. As shown in Table 3, a selection of four priority processing modes is available to the systems designer for use in designing request processing configurations to match system requirements. Operating mode and priority assignments may be reconfigured dynamically via software at any time during system operation. The PIC accepts interrupt requests from the programmable parallel and serial I/O interfaces, the programmable timers, the system bus, or directly from peripheral equipment. The PIC then determines which of the incoming requests is of the highest priority, determines whether this request is of higher priority than the level currently being serviced, and, if appropriate, issues an interrupt to the CPU. Any combination of interrupt levels may be masked, via software, by storing a single byte in the interrupt mask register of the PIC. The PIC generates a unique memory address for each interrupt level. These addresses are equally spaced at intervals of 4 or 8 (software selectable) bytes. This 32- or 64-byte block may be located to begin at any 32- or 64-byte boundary in the 65,536-byte memory space. A single 8085A jump instruction at each of these addresses then provides linkage to locate each interrupt service routine independently anywhere in memory.

Table 3. Programmable Interrupt Modes

Mode	Operation
Fully nested	Interrupt request line priorities fixed at 0 as highest, 7 as lowest.
Auto-rotating	Equal priority. Each level, after receiving service, becomes the lowest priority level until next interrupt occurs.
Specific priority	System software assigns lowest priority level. Priority of all other levels based in sequence numerically on this assignment.
Polled	System software examines priority-encoded system interrupt status via interrupt status register.

Interrupt Request Generation — Interrupt requests may originate from 18 sources. Two jumper selectable interrupt requests can be automatically generated by the programmable peripheral interface when a byte of information is ready to be transferred to the CPU (i.e., input buffer is full) or a byte of information has been transferred to a peripheral device (i.e., output buffer is empty). Two jumper selectable interrupt requests can be automatically generated by the USART when a character is ready to be transferred to the CPU (i.e., receive channel buffer is full), or a character is ready to be transmitted (i.e., transmit channel data buffer is empty). A jumper selectable request can be generated by each of the programmable timers and by the universal peripheral interface, eight additional interrupt request lines are available to the user for direct interface to user designated peripheral devices via the system bus, and two interrupt request lines may be jumper routed directly from peripherals via the parallel I/O driver/terminator section.

Power-Fail Control

Control logic is also included to accept a power-fail interrupt in conjunction with the AC-low signal from the iSBC 635 Power Supply or equivalent.

Expansion Capabilities

Memory and I/O capacity may be expanded and additional functions added by using Intel MULTIBUS compatible expansion boards. High speed integer and floating point arithmetic capabilities may be added by using the iSBC 310A High Speed Mathematics Unit. Memory may be expanded to 65,536 bytes by adding user specified combinations of RAM boards, EPROM boards, or combination boards. Input/output capacity may be increased by adding digital I/O and analog I/O expansion boards. Mass storage capability may be achieved by adding single or double density diskette controllers as subsystems. Modular expandable backplanes and card-cages are available to support multi-board systems.

System Development Capability

The development cycle of iSBC 80/30-based products may be significantly reduced using Intel's system development tools available today. For those not requiring hardware emulation capability, Intel provides a new low cost microcomputer development system. The iPDS, Personal Development System, provides low cost system development for the iSBC 80/30 board, while at the same time providing personal computer capability for the engineer. The Intellec Series II family of compatible microcomputer development systems provides a range of capability from a low cost disk-based edit debug workstation to a high performance, fully compatible hard-disk-based software development system. A unique in-circuit emulator (ICE-85A) option provides the capability of developing and debugging software directly on the iSBC 80/30 board.

Programming Capability

PL/M-80 — Intel's high level programming language, PL/M, is also available as a resident Intellec microcomputer development system option. PL/M provides the capability to program in a natural, algorithmic language and eliminates the need to manage register usage or

allocate memory. PL/M programs can be written in a much shorter time than assembly language programs for a given application.

FORTRAN-80 — For applications requiring computational and formatted I/O capabilities, the high level FORTRAN-80 programming language is also available as a resident option of the intellec system. FORTRAN-80 meets and exceeds the ANS FORTRAN 77 subset language specification. The FORTRAN-80 compiler produces relocatable object code that may be easily linked with other FORTRAN-80, PL/M, or assembly language program modules. This gives the user wide flexibility in developing software by using the best software tool for a particular functional module within the user's application.

BASIC-80 — A high level language interpreter with extended disk capabilities which operates under the iRMX 80 Real-Time Multi-tasking Executive and translates BASIC-80 source programs into an internally executable form. This language interpreter, provided as a set of linkable object modules, is ideally suited to the OEM who requires a pass thru programming language. The BASIC-80 programs may be created, stored and interpreted on the iSBC 80-based system. The BASIC-80 language has a rich complement of statements, functions, and commands to program applications requiring a full range of 1) string manipulation and disk I/O for data processing, 2) single and double precision floating point and array handling for numeric analysis, or 3) port I/O with mask operations controlled through bit-wise Boolean logical operators.

SPECIFICATIONS

Word Size
Instruction — 8, 16, or 24 bits
Data — 8 bits

Cycle Time
Basic Instruction Cycle — 1.45 μs

Note
Basic instruction cycle is defined as the fastest instruction (i.e., four clock cycles).

Memory Addressing
On-Board ROM/EPROM — 0-07FF (using 2708 or 2758 EPROMs); 0-0FFF (using 2716 EPROMs); 0-1FFF (using 2716 EPROMs; 0-1FFF (using 2732 EPROMs).

On-Board RAM — 16K bytes of dual port RAM starting on a 16K boundary. One or two 8K-byte segments may be reserved for CPU use only.

Memory Capacity
On-Board Read Only Memory — 8K bytes (sockets only)
On-Board RAM — 16K bytes
Off-Board Expansion — Up to 65,536 bytes in user specified combinations of RAM, ROM, and EPROM

Note
Read only memory may be added in 1K, 2K, or 4K-byte increments.

I/O Addressing
On-Board Programmable I/O (see Table 1)

Port	8255A				8041A/8741A		USART	
	1	2	3	Control	Data	Control	Data	Control
Address	E8	E9	EA	EB	E4 or E6	E5 or E7	EC	ED

I/O Capacity
Parallel — 42 programmable lines using one 8255A (24 I/O lines) and an optional 8041A/8741A (18 I/O lines)
Serial — 2 programmable lines using one 8251A and an optional 8041A/8741A programmed for serial operation

Note:
For additional information on the 8041A/8741A refer to the UPI-41 User's Manual (Publication 9800504).

Serial Communications Characteristics
Synchronous — 5—8 bit characters; internal or external character synchronization; automatic sync insertion.
Asynchronous — 5—8 bit characters; break character generation; 1, 1½, or 2 stop bits; false start bit detection.

Baud Rates

Frequency (kHz)	Baud Rate (Hz)	
(Software Selectable)	Synchronous	Asynchronous
		÷ 16 ÷ 64
153.6	—	9600 2400
76.8	—	4800 1200
38.4	38400	2400 600
19.2	19200	1200 300
9.6	9600	600 150
4.8	4800	300 75
2.4	2400	150 —
1.76	1760	110 —

Note
Frequency selected by I/O write of appropriate 16-bit frequency factor to baud rate register (8253 Timer 2).

Interrupts
Addresses for 8259A Registers (Hex notation, I/O address space)

DA   Interrupt request register
DA   In-service register
DB   Mask register
DA   Command register
DB   Block address register
DA   Status (polling register)

Note
Several registers have the same physical address; sequence of access and one data bit of control word determine which register will respond.

Interrupt Levels routed to 8085A CPU automatically vector the processor to unique memory locations:

Interrupt Input	Memory Address	Priority	Type
TRAP	24	Highest	Non-maskable
RST 7.5	3C	↕	Maskable
RST 6.5	34		Maskable
RST 5.5	2C	Lowest	Maskable

iSBC® 80/30

Timers

Register Addresses (Hex notation, I/O address space)
DF Control register
DC Timer 0
DD Timer 1
DE Timer 2

Note
Timer counts loaded as two sequential output operations to same address, as given.

Input Frequencies
Reference: 2.46 MHz ± 0.1% (0.041 μs period, nominal); 1.23 MHz ± 0.1% (0.81 μs period, nominal); or 153.60 kHz ± 0.1% (6.51 μs period nominal).

Note
Above frequencies are user selectable

Event Rate: 2.46 MHz max

Note
Maximum rate for external events in event counter function.

Output Frequencies/Timing Intervals

Function	Single Timer/Counter		Dual Timer/Counter (Two Timers Cascaded)	
	Min	Max	Min	Max
Real-time interrupt	1.63 μs	427.1 ms	3.26 μs	466.50 min
Programmable one-shot	1.63 μs	427.1 ms	3.26 μs	466.50 min
Rate generator	2.342 Hz	613.5 kHz	0.000036 Hz	306.8 kHz
Square-wave rate generator	2.342 Hz	613.5 kHz	0.000036 Hz	306.8 kHz
Software triggered strobe	1.63 μs	427.1 ms	3.26 μs	466.50 min
Hardware triggered strobe	1.63 μs	427.1 ms	3.26 μs	466.50 min

Interfaces
MULTIBUS — All signals TTL compatible
Parallel I/O — All signals TTL compatible
Interrupt Requests — All TTL compatible
Timer — All signals TTL compatible
Serial I/O — RS232C compatible, data set configuration

System Clock (8085A CPU)
2.76 MHz ± 0.1%

Auxiliary Power
An auxiliary power bus is provided to allow separate power to RAM for systems requiring battery backup of read/write memory. Selection of this auxiliary RAM power bus is made via jumpers on the board.

Connectors

Interface	Pins (qty)	Centers (in.)	Mating Connectors
Bus	86	0.156	Viking 2KH43/9AMK12
Parallel I/O	50	0.1	3M 3415-000
Serial I/O	26	0.1	3M 3462-000

Memory Protect
An active-low TTL compatible memory protect signal is brought out on the auxiliary connector which, when asserted, disables read/write access to RAM memory on the board. This input is provided for the protection of RAM contents during system power-down sequences.

Line Drivers and Terminators

I/O Drivers — The following line drivers are all compatible with the I/O driver sockets on the iSBC 80/30.

Driver	Characteristic	Sink Current (mA)
7438	I,OC	48
7437	I	48
7432	NI	16
7426	I,OC	16
7409	NI,OC	16
7408	NI	16
7403	I,OC	16
7400	I	16

Note
I = inverting; NI = non-inverting; OC = open collector

Port 1 of the 8255A has 20 mA totem-pole bidirectional drivers and 1 kΩ terminators.

I/O Terminators — 220Ω/330Ω divider or 1 kΩ pullup

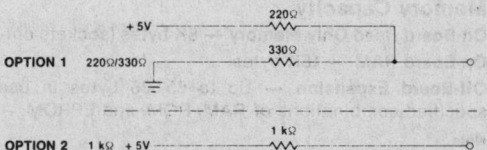

Bus Drivers

Function	Characteristic	Sink Current (mA)
Data	Tri-state	50
Address	Tri-state	50
Commands	Tri-state	32

Physical Characteristics
Width — 12.00 in. (30.48 cm)
Height — 6.75 in. (17.15 cm)
Depth — 0.50 in. (1.27 cm)
Weight — 18 oz. (509.6 gm)

iSBC® 80/30

Electrical Characteristics
DC Power Requirements

Configuration	Current Requirements			
	$V_{CC} = +5V$ ±5%(max)	$V_{DD} = +12V$ ±5%(max)	$V_{BB} = -5V$ ±5%(max)	$V_{AA} = -12V$ ±5%(max)
Without EPROM[1]	$I_{CC} = 3.5A$	$I_{DD} = 220$ mA	$I_{BB} = -$	$I_{AA} = 50$ mA
With 8041/8741[2]	3.6A	220 mA	—	50 mA
RAM only[3]	350 mA	20 mA	2.5 mA	—
With iSBC 530[4]	3.5A	320 mA	—	150 mA
With 2K EPROM[5] (using 8708)	4.4A	350 mA	95 mA	40 mA
With 2K EPROM[5] (using 2758)	4.6A	220 mA	—	50 mA
With 4K EPROM[5] (using 2716)	4.6A	220 mA	—	50 mA
With 8K EPROM[5] (using 2332)	4.6A	220 mA	—	50 mA

Notes

1. Does not include power required for optional EPROM/ROM, 8041/8741A I/O drivers, and I/O terminators.
2. Does not include power required for optional EPROM/ROM, I/O drivers and I/O terminators.
3. RAM chips powered via auxiliary power bus
4. Does not include power required for optional EPROM/ROM, 8041/8741A I/O drivers, and I/O terminators. Power for iSBC 530 is supplied through the serial port connector.
5. Includes power required for two EPROM/ROM chips, 8041A/8741A and 220Ω/330Ω input terminators installed for 34 I/O lines; all terminator inputs low.

Environmental Characteristics
Operating Temperature — 0°C to 55°C

Reference Manual

9800611B — iSBC 80/30 Single Board Computer Hardware Reference Manual (NOT SUPPLIED)

Reference manuals are shipped with each product only if designated SUPPLIED (see above). Manuals may be ordered from any Intel sales representative, distributor office or from Intel Literature Department, 3065 Bowers Avenue, Santa Clara, California 95051.

ORDERING INFORMATION

Part Number	Description
SBC 80/30	Single Board Computer with 16K bytes RAM

iSBC® 86/05A
SINGLE BOARD COMPUTER

- iAPX 86/10 (8086-2) Microprocessor with 5 or 8 MHz CPU clock
- Software compatible with iAPX 86/88/186/286 based 16-bit Single Board Computers
- Optional iAPX 86/20 Numeric Data Processor with iSBC® 337 A MULTIMODULE™ Processor
- 8K bytes of static RAM; expandable on-board to 16K bytes
- Sockets for up to 256K bytes of JEDEC 24/28-pin standard memory devices; expandable on-board to 512K bytes
- Two iSBX™ bus connectors
- Programmable synchronous/asynchronous RS232C compatible serial interface with software selectable baud rate
- 24 programmable parallel I/O lines
- Two programmable 16-bit BCD or binary timers/event counters
- 9 levels of vectored interrupt control, expandable to 65 levels
- MULTIBUS® bus interface for multimaster configurations and system expansion
- Supported by a complete family of single board computers, memory, digital and analog I/O, peripheral controllers, packaging and software

The iSBC® 86/05A Single Board Computer is a member of Intel's complete line of OEM microcomputer systems which take full advantage of Intel's technology to provide economical, self-contained, computer-based solutions for OEM applications. The iSBC 86/05A board is a complete computer system on a single 6.75 × 12.00 in. printed circuit card. The CPU, system clock, read/write memory, nonvolatile read only memory, I/O ports and drivers, serial communications interface, priority interrupt logic and programmable timers, all reside on the board. The large control storage capacity makes the iSBC 86/05A board ideally suited for control-oriented applications such as process control, instrumentation, industrial automation, and many others.

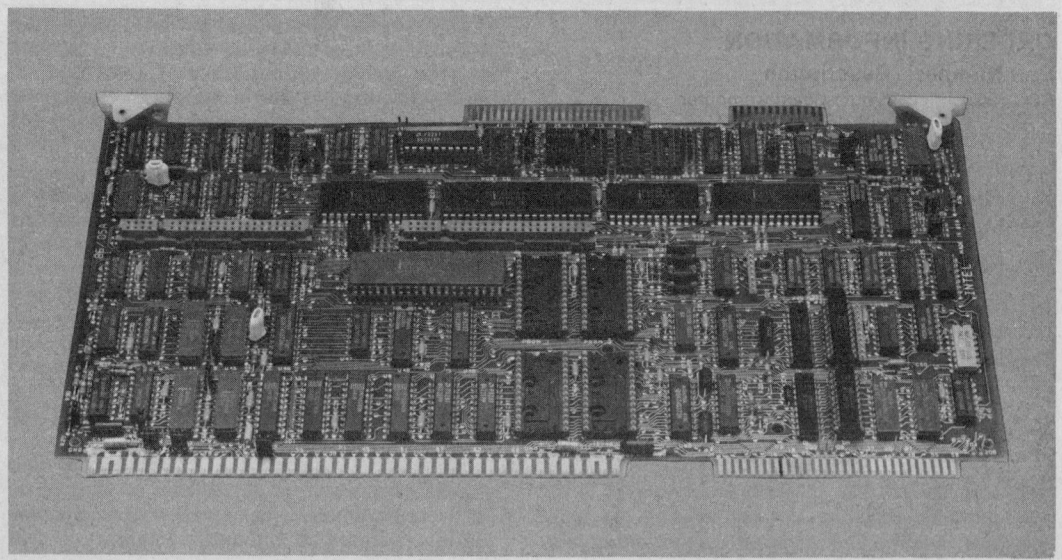

Intel Corporation assumes no responsibility for the use of any circuitry other than circuitry embodied in an Intel product. No other patent licenses are implied. Information contained herein supersedes previously published specifications on these devices from Intel.

• INTEL CORPORATION, 1985

MARCH 1985
ORDER NUMBER: 143325-002

iSBC® 86/05A Single Board Computer

FUNCTIONAL DESCRIPTION
Central Processing Unit

The central processor for the iSBC® 86/05A board is Intel's iAPX 86/10 (8086-2) CPU. A clock rate of 8 MHz is supported with a jumper selectable option of 5 MHz. The CPU architecture includes four 16-bit byte addressable data registers, two 16-bit memory base pointer registers and two 16-bit index registers. All are accessed by a total of 24 operand addressing modes for comprehensive memory addressing and for support of the data structures required for today's structured, high level languages as well as assembly language.

Instruction Set

The 8086 instruction repertoire includes variable length instruction format (including double operand instructions), 8-bit and 16-bit signed and unsigned arithmetic operators for binary, BCD and unpacked ASCII data, and iterative word and byte string manipulation functions.

For enhanced numerics processing capability, the iSBC 337A MULTIMODULE Numeric Data Processor extends the iAPX 86/10 architecture and data set. Over 60 numeric instructions offer arithmetic, trigonometric, transcendental, logarithmic and exponential instructions. Supported data types include 16, 32, and 64-bit integer, and 32 and 64-bit floating point, 18-digit packed BCD and 80-bit temporary.

Architectural Features

A 6-byte instruction queue provides pre-fetching of sequential instructions and can reduce the 740 nsec minimum instruction cycle to 250 nsec for queued instructions. The stack-oriented architecture readily supports modular programming by facilitating fast, simple, inter-module communication, and other programming constructs needed for asynchronous real-time systems. The memory expansion capabilities offer a 1 megabyte addressing range. The dynamic relocation scheme allows ease in segmentation of pure procedure and data for efficient memory utilization. Four segment registers (code, stack, data, extra) contain program loaded offset values which are used to map 16-bit addresses to 20-bit addresses. Each register maps 64K bytes at a time with activation of a specific register controlled explicitly by program control and selected implicity by specific functions and instructions. All Intel languages support the extended memory capability, relieving the programmer of managing the megabyte memory space yet allowing explicit control when necessary.

Memory Configuration

The iSBC 86/05A microcomputer contains 8K bytes of high-speed 8K x 4 bit static RAM on-board. In addition, the above on-board RAM may be expanded to 16K bytes with the iSBC 302 MULTIMODULE RAM option which mounts on the iSBC 86/05A board. All on-board RAM is accessed by the 8086-2 CPU with no wait states, yielding a memory cycle time of 500 nsec.

The iSBC 86/05A board also has four 28-pin, 8-bit wide (byte-wide) sockets, configured to accept JEDEC 24/28-pin standard memory devices. Up to 256K bytes of EPROM are supported in 64K-byte increments with Intel 27512 EPROMs. The iSBC 86/05A board also supports 2K x 8, 4K x 8, 8K x 8, 16K x 8 and 32K x 8 EPROM memory devices. These sites also support 2K x 8 and 8K x 8 byte-wide static RAM (SRAM) devices and iRAM devices, yielding up to 32K bytes of SRAM in 8K byte increments on the baseboard.

With the addition of the iSBC 341 MULTIMODULE EPROM option, the on-board capacity for these devices is doubled, providing up to 512K bytes of EPROM and 64K bytes of byte-wide SRAM capacity on-board.

Parallel I/O Interface

The iSBC 86/05A Single Board Computer contains 24 programmable parallel I/O lines implemented using the Intel 8255A Programmable Peripheral Interface. The system software is used to configure the I/O lines in any combination of unidirectional input/output and bidirectional ports indicated in Table 1. In order to take advantage of the large number of possible I/O configurations, sockets are provided for interchangeable I/O line drivers and terminators, allowing the selection of the appropriate combination of optional line drivers and terminators with the required drive/termination characteristics. The 24 programmable I/O lines and signal ground lines are brought out to a 50-pin edge connector.

Serial I/O

A programmable communications interface using the Intel 8251A Universal Synchronous/ Asynchronous Receiver/Transmitter (USART) is contained on the iSBC 86/05A board. A software selectable baud rate generator provides the USART with all common communication frequencies. The mode of operation (i.e., synchronous or asynchronous), data format, control character format, parity, and baud rate are all under program control. The 8251A provides full duplex, double buffered transmit and receive capability. Parity, overrun, and framing error detection are all incorporated in the USART. The RS232C compat-

iSBC® 86/05A Single Board Computer

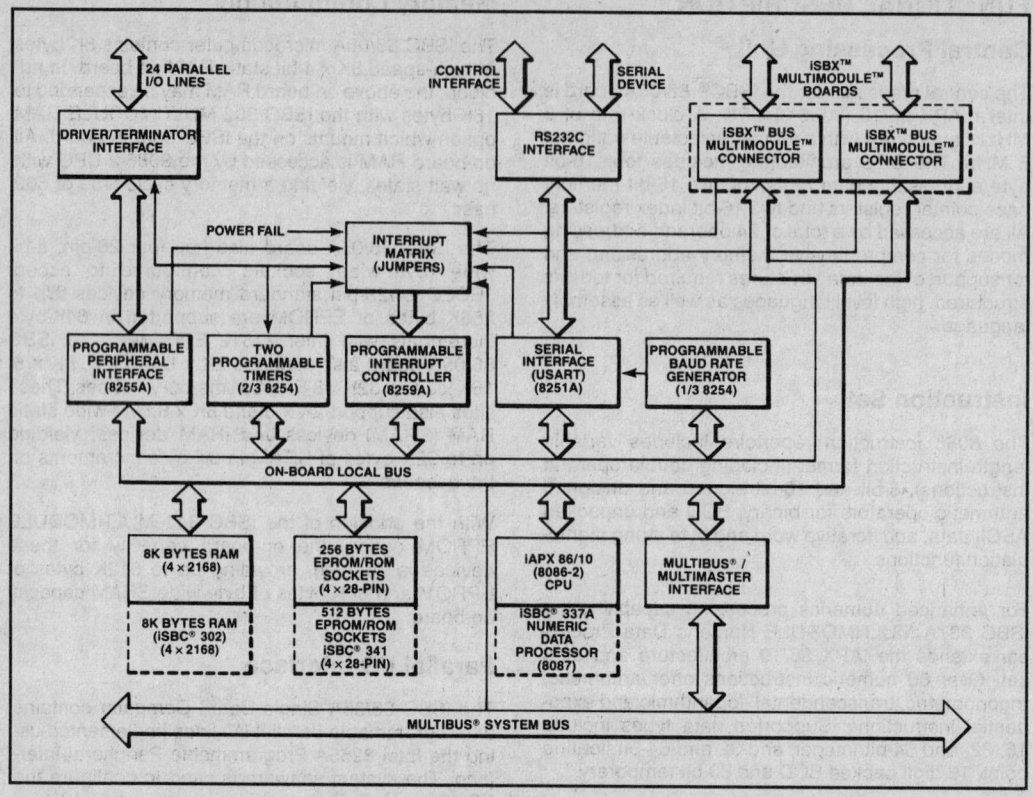

Figure 1. iSBC® 86/05A Block Diagram

ible interface in conjunction with the USART, provides a direct interface to RS232C compatible terminals, cassettes, and asynchronous/ synchronous modems. The RS232C command lines, serial data lines and signal ground line are brought out to a 26-pin edge connector.

Programmable Timers

The iSBC 86/05A board provides three independent, fully programmable 16-bit interval timers/event counters utilizing the Intel 8254 Programmable Interval Timer. Each counter is capable of operating in either BCD or binary modes. Two of these timers/counters are available to the systems designer to generate accurate time intervals under software control. Routing for the outputs and gate/trigger inputs of two of these counters is jumper selectable. The outputs may be independently routed to the 8259A Programmable Interrupt Controller and to the I/O terminators associated with the 8255A to allow external devices or an 8255A port to gate the timer or to count external events. The third interval timer in the 8254 provides the programmable baud rate generator for the iSBC 86/05A board RS232C USART serial port. The system software configures each timer independently to select the desired function. Seven functions are available as shown in Table 2. The contents of each counter may be read at any time during system operation.

iSBX™ MULTIMODULE™ On-Board Expansion

Two 8/16-bit iSBX MULTIMODULE connectors are provided on the iSBC 86/05A microcomputer. Through these connectors, additional on-board I/O and memory functions may be added. iSBX MULTIMODULE boards support functions such as additional parallel and serial I/O, analog I/O, mass storage device controllers (e.g., cassettes and floppy disks), BITBUS™ controllers, bubble memory, and other custom interfaces to meet specific needs. By mounting directly on the single board

2-34

143325-002

iSBC® 86/05A Single Board Computer

Table 1. Input/Output Port Modes of Operation

Port	Lines (qty)	Unidirectional				Bidirectional	Control
		Input		Output			
		Latched	Latched & Strobed	Latched	Latched & Strobed		
1	8	X	X	X	X	X	
2	8	X	X	X	X		
3	4	X		X			X[1]
	4	X		X			X[1]

NOTE:
1. Part of port 3 must be used as a control port when either port 1 or port 2 are used as a latched and strobed input or a latched and strobed output port or port 1 is used as a bidirectional port.

Table 2. Programmable Timer Functions

Function	Operation
Interrupt on terminal count	When terminal count is reached, an interrupt request is generated. This function is extremely useful for generation of real-time clocks.
Programmable one-shot	Output goes low upon receipt of an external trigger edge or software command and returns high when terminal count is reached. This function is retriggerable.
Rate generator	Divide by N counter. The output will go low for one input clock cycle, and the period from one low going pulse to the next is N times the input clock period.
Square-wave rate generator	Output will remain high until one-half the count has been completed, and go low for the other half of the count.
Software triggered strobe	Output remains high until software loads count (N). N counts after count is loaded, output goes low for one input clock period.
Hardware triggered strobe	Output goes low for one clock period N counts after rising edge counter trigger input. The counter is retriggerable.
Event counter	On a jumper selectable basis, the clock input becomes an input from the external system. CPU may read the number of events occurring after the counter "window" has been enabled or an interrupt may be generated after N events occur in the system.

computer, less interface logic, less power, simpler packaging, higher performance, and lower cost result when compared to other alternatives such as MULTIBUS form factor compatible boards. The iSBX connectors on the iSBC 86/05A board provide all signals necessary to interface to the local on-board bus, including 16 data lines for maximum data transfer rates. iSBX MULTIMODULE boards designed with 8-bit data paths and using the 8-bit iSBX connector are also supported on the iSBC 86/05A microcomputer. A broad range of iSBX MULTIMODULE options are available in this family from Intel. Custom iSBX modules may also be designed for use on the iSBC 86/05A board. An iSBX bus interface specification is available from Intel.

iSBC® 86/05A Single Board Computer

MULTIBUS® SYSTEM BUS AND MULTIMASTER CAPABILITIES

Overview

The MULTIBUS system bus (IEEE 796) is Intel's industry standard microcomputer bus structure. Both 8 and 16-bit single board computers are supported on the MULTIBUS structure with 24 address and 16 data lines. In its simplest application, the MULTIBUS system bus allows expansion of functions already contained on a single board computer (e.g., memory and digital I/O). However, the MULTIBUS structure also allows very powerful distributed processing configurations with multiple processors and intelligent slave I/O, and peripheral boards capable of solving the most demanding microcomputer applications. The MULTIBUS system bus is supported with a broad array of board level products, LSI interface components, detailed published specifications and application notes.

Expansion Capabilities

Memory and I/O capacity may be expanded and additional functions added using Intel MULTIBUS compatible expansion boards. Memory may be expanded by adding user specified combinations of RAM boards, EPROM boards, or combination boards. Input/output capacity may be added with digital I/O and analog I/O expansion boards. Mass storage capability may be achieved by adding single or double density diskette controllers, or hard disk controllers.

Multimaster Capabilities

For those applications requiring additional processing capacity and the benefits of multiprocessing (i.e., several CPUs and/or controllers logically sharing system tasks through communication of the system bus), the iSBC 86/05A board provides full MULTIBUS arbitration control logic. This control logic allows up to three iSBC 86/05A boards or other bus masters to share the system bus using a serial (daisy chain) priority scheme and allows up to 16 masters to share the MULTIBUS system bus with an external parallel priority decoder. In addition to the multiprocessing configurations made possible with multimaster capability, it also provides a very efficient mechanism for all forms of DMA (Direct Memory Access) transfers.

Interrupt Capability

The iSBC 86/05A board provides 9 vectored interrupt levels. The highest level is the NMI (Non-Maskable Interrupt) line which is directly tied to the 8086 CPU. This interrupt is typically used for signaling catastrophic events (e.g., power failure). The Intel 8259A Programmable Interrupt Controller (PIC) provides control and vectoring for the next eight interrupt levels. As shown in Table 3, a selection of four priority processing modes is available for use in designing request processing configurations to match system requirements for efficient interrupt servicing with minimal latencies. Operating mode and priority assignments may be reconfigured dynamically via software at any time during system operation. The PIC accepts interrupt requests from all on-board I/O resources and from the MULTIBUS system bus. The PIC then resolves requests according to the selected mode and, if appropriate, issues an interrupt to the CPU. Any combination of interrupt levels may be masked via software, by storing a single byte in the interrupt mask register of the PIC. In systems requiring additonal interrupt levels, slave 8259A PICs may be interfaced via the MULTIBUS system bus, to generate additional vector addresses, yielding a total of 65 unique interrupt levels.

Interrupt Request Generation

Interrupt requests to be serviced by the iSBC 86/05A board may originate from 24 sources. Table 4 includes a list of devices and functions supported by interrupts. All interrupt signals are brought to the interrupt jumper matrix where any combination of interrupt sources may be strapped to the desired interrupt request level on the 8259A PIC or the NMI input to the CPU directly.

Power-Fail Control and Auxiliary Power

Control logic is also included, to accept a power-fail interrupt in conjunction with a power-supply having AC-low signal generation capabilities, to initiate an orderly shut down of the system in the event of a power failure. Additionally, an active-low TTL compatible memory protect signal is brought out on the auxiliary connector which, when asserted, disables read/write access to RAM for systems requiring battery backup of read/write memory. Selection of this auxiliary RAM power bus is made via jumpers on the board.

iSBC® 86/05A Single Board Computer

Table 3. Programmable Interrupt Modes

Mode	Operation
Fully nested	Interrupt request line priorities fixed at 0 as highest, 7 as lowest.
Auto-rotating	Equal priority. Each level, after receiving service, becomes the lowest priority level until next interrupt occurs.
Specific priority	System software assigns lowest priority level. Priority of all other levels based in sequence numerically on this assignment.
Polled	System software examines priority-encoded system interrupt status via interrupt status register.

System Development Environment

Development support for the iSBC 86/05A board is offered on the Series II, Series III and Series IV Microcomputer Development Systems, as well as the iRMX™ 86 Operating System Development environment. Cross development support of 8085 based

Table 4. Interrupt Request Sources

Device	Function	Number of Interrupts
MULTIBUS bus interface	Requests from MULTIBUS resident peripherals or other CPU boards	8; may be expanded to 64 with slave 8259A PICs on MULTIBUS boards
8255A Programmable Peripheral Interface	Signals input buffer full or output buffer empty; also BUS INTR OUT general purpose interrupt from driver/terminator sockets	3
8251A USART	Transmit buffer empty and receive buffer full	2
8254 Timers	Timer 0, 1 outputs; function determined by timer mode	2
iSBX connectors	Function determined by iSBX MULTIMODULE board	4 (2 per iSBX connector)
Bus fail safe timer	Indicates addressed MULTIBUS resident device has not responded to command within 6-10 msec	1
Power fail interrupt	Indicates AC power is not within tolerance	1
Power line clock	Source of 120 Hz signal from power supply	1
External interrupt	General purpose interrupt from auxiliary (P2) connector on backplane	1
iSBC 337A MULTIMODULE Numeric Data Processor	Indicates error or exception condition	1

iSBC® 86/05A Single Board Computer

designs is provided by the Series II, languages offered are Assembler and PLM-86. In Series III, IV, and iRMX 86 operating system development environments languages offered are Assembler, PLM-86, C, Fortran and Pascal. A powerful software debugger, PSCOPE, is also offered on all development systems. PSCOPE provides Software Trace Execution, defineable breakpoints and user defined/executable debugging procedures.

In-Circuit Emulator

The I²ICE™/ICE™-86A In-Circuit Emulators provide the necessary link between the software development environment provided by the Intellec system and the "target" iSBC 86/05A board, the I²ICE/ICE-86A In-Circuit Emulator provides a sophisticated command set to assist in debugging software and final integration of the user hardware and software.

iSDM™ 86 System Debug Monitor

The Intel iSDM 86 System Debug Monitor package contains the necessary hardware, software, cables, EPROMs and documentation required to interface, through a serial or parallel connection, an iSBC 86/05A target system to an MDS 800, Series II, Series III, or Series IV Intellec® Microcomputer Development System for execution and interactive debugging of applications software on the target system. The Monitor can: load programs into the target system; execute the programs instruction by instruction or at full speed; set breakpoints; and examine/modify CPU registers, memory content, and other crucial environmental details. Additional custom commands can be built using the Command Extension Interface (CEI).

Software Support

The iRMX 86 operating system provides users with a powerful set of system building blocks for developing many different real-time applications. Key iRMX 86 operating system features include multitasking, multiprogramming, interrupt management, device independence, file protection and control, interactive debugging, plus interfaces to many Intel and non-Intel developed hardware and software products.

The iRMX 86 operating system is highly modular and configurable, and includes a sophicasted file management, I/O system, and powerful human interface. The iRMX 86 operating system is also easily customized and extended by the user to match unique requirements.

SPECIFICATIONS

Word Size

Instruction — 8, 16, 24, or 32 bits
Data — 8, 16 bits

System Clock

5.00 MHz or 8.00 MHz ± 0.1% (jumper selectable)

Basic Instruction Cycle

At 8 MHz — 750 nsec
— 250 nsec (assumes instruction in the queue)
At 5 mhz — 1.2 sec
— 400 nsec (assumes instruction in the queue)

Note:

Basic instruction cycle is defined as the fastest instruction time (i.e., two clock cycles).

Memory Cycle Time

500 ns cycle time (no wait states requires a memory component access time of 250 ns or less).
RAM - 500 nsec
EPROM - Jumper selectable from 500 nsec to 875 nsec

iSBC® 86/05A Single Board Computer

Memory Capacity/Addressing

JEDEC 24/28 PIN SITES		
Device	Total Capacity	Address Range
2K × 8	8K bytes	FE000-FFFFF$_H$
4K × 8	16K bytes	FC000-FFFFF$_H$
8K × 8	32K bytes	F8000-FFFFF$_H$
16K × 8	64K bytes	F0000-FFFFF$_H$
32K × 8	128K bytes	E0000-FFFFF$_H$
64K × 8	256K bytes	C0000-FFFFF$_H$

With iSBC® 341 MULTIMODULE™ EPROM/SRAM		
Device	Total Capacity	Address Range
2K × 8	16K bytes	FC000-FFFFF$_H$
4K × 8	32K bytes	F8000-FFFFF$_H$
8K × 8	64K bytes	F0000-FFFFF$_H$
16K × 8	128K bytes	E0000-FFFFF$_H$
32K × 8	256K bytes	C0000-FFFFF$_H$
64K × 8	512K bytes	80000-FFFFF$_H$

NOTE:
iSBC 86/05A EPROM sockets support JEDEC 24/28-pin standard EPROMs and RAMs.

ON-BOARD STATIC RAM

8K bytes — 0-1FFF$_H$
16K bytes — 0-3FFF$_H$ (with iSBC 302 MULTIMODULE Board)

I/O CAPACITY

PARALLEL — 24 programmable lines using one 8255A.

SERIAL — 1 programmable line using one 8251A

iSBX MULTIMODULE — 2 iSBX single wide MULTIMODULE board or 1 iSBX double-wide MULTIMODULE board.

SERIAL COMMUNICATIONS CHARACTERISTICS

SYNCHRONOUS — 5-8 bit characters; internal or external character synchronization; automatic sync insertion.

ASYNCHRONOUS — 5-8 bit characters; break character generation; 1, 1-1/2, or 2 stop bits; false start bit detection.

Baud Rates

Frequency (kHz) (Software Selectable)	Baud Rate (Hz)	
	Synchronous	Asynchronous
		+16 +64
153.6	—	9600 2400
76.8	—	4800 1200
38.4	38400	2400 600
19.2	19200	1200 300
9.6	9600	600 150
4.8	4800	300 75
2.4	2400	150 —
1.76	1760	110 —

NOTE:
1. Frequency selected by I/O write of appropriate 16-bit frequency factor to baud rate register (8254 Timer 2).

TIMERS

Input Frequencies

Reference: 2.46 MHz ± 0.1% (0.041 sec period, nominal); or 153.60 KHz ± 0.1% (6.51 sec period, nominal)

Note: Above frequencies are user selectable

Event Rate: 2.46 MHz max

Output Frequencies/Timing Intervals

Function	Single Timer/Counter		Dual Timer/Counter (Two Timers Cascaded)	
	Min	Max	Min	Max
Real-time Interrupt	1.63 μs	427.1 ms	3.26 s	466.50 min
Programmable one-shot	1.63 μs	427.1 ms	3.26 s	466.50 min
Rate generator	2.342 Hz	613.5 kHz	0.000036 Hz	306.8 kHz
Square-wave rate generator	2.342 Hz	613.5 kHz	0.000036 Hz	306.8 kHz
Software triggered strobe	1.63 μs	427.1 ms	3.26 s	466.50 min
Hardware triggered strobe	1.63 μs	427.1 ms	3.26 s	466.50 min
Event counter	—	2.46 MHz	—	—

iSBC® 86/05A Single Board Computer

INTERFACES

MULTIBUS Bus — All signals TTL compatible
iSBX BUS Bus — All signals TTL compatible
PARALLEL I/O — All signals TTL compatible
SERIAL I/O — RS232C compatible, configurable as a data set or data terminal
TIMER — All signals TTL compatible
INTERRUPT REQUESTS — All TTL compatible

Connectors

Interface	Double-Sided Pins (qty)	Centers (in.)	Mating Connectors
MULTIBUS System	86	0.156	Viking Wire Wrap
iSBX Bus			
8-Bit Data	36	0.1	iSBX 960-5
16-Bit Data	44	0.1	iSBX 961-5
Parallel I/O (2)	50	0.1	3M Flat or T1 Pins
Serial I/O	26	0.1	3M Flat or AMP Flat

LINE DRIVERS AND TERMINATORS

I/O Drivers

The following line drivers are all compatible with the I/O driver sockets on the iSBC 86/05A board.

Driver	Characteristic	Sink Current (mA)
7438	I,OC	48
7437	I	48
7432	NI	16
7426	I,OC	16
7409	NI,OC	16
7408	NI	16
7403	I,OC	16
7400	I	16

NOTES:
I = inverting; NI = non-inverting; OC = open collector.

Port 1 of the 8255A has 20 mA totem-pole bidirectional drivers and 1 K terminators.

I/O Terminators

220/330 divider or 1K pullup

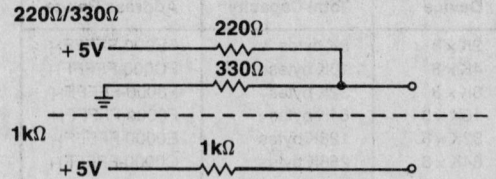

MULTIBUS® DRIVERS

Function	Characteristic	Sink Current (mA)
Data	Tri-State	50
Address	Tri-State	50
Commands	Tri-State	32
Bus Control	Open Collector	20

Physical Characteristics

Width — 12.00 in. (30.48 cm)
Height — 6.75 in. (17.15 cm)
Depth — 0.70 in. (1.78 cm)
Weight — 14 oz (388 gm)

ELECTRICAL CHARACTERISTICS

DC Power Requirements

Configuration	Current Requirements (All Voltages ±5%)		
	+5V	+12V	−12V
Without EPROM[1]	4.7A	25 mA	23 mA
RAM only[2]	120 mA		
With 8K EPROM[3] (using 2716)	5.0A	25 mA	23 mA
With 16K EPROM[3] (using 2732)	4.9A	25 mA	23 mA
With 32K EPROM[3] (using 2764)	4.9A	25 mA	23 mA

iSBC® 86/05A Single Board Computer

NOTES:
1. Does not include power for optional ROM/EPROM, I/O drivers, and I/O terminators.
2. RAM chips powered via auxiliary power bus in power-down mode.
3. Includes power required for 4 ROM/EPROM chips, and I/O terminators installed for 16 I/O lines; all terminator inputs low.

ENVIRONMENTAL CHARACTERISTICS

OPERATING TEMPERATURE — 0°C to 55°C

RELATIVE HUMIDITY — to 90% (without condensation)

REFERENCE MANUAL

Order no.- 147162-001 — *iSBC 86/05A Hardware Reference Manual* (NOT SUPPLIED)

Manuals may be ordered from any Intel sales representative, distributor office or from Intel Literature Department, 3065 Bowers Avenue, Santa Clara, California 95051.

ORDER INFORMATION

PART NUMBER	DESCRIPTION
SBC 86/05A	16-bit Single Board Computer with 8K bytes RAM

iSBC® 86/14 and iSBC® 86/30 SINGLE BOARD COMPUTERS

- iAPX 86/10 (8086-2) Microprocessor with 5 or 8 MHz CPU clock
- Fully software compatible with iSBC® 86/12A Single Board Computer
- Optional iAPX 86/20 Numeric Data Processor with iSBC® 337A MULTIMODULE™ processor
- 32K/128K bytes of dual-port read/write memory expandable on-board to 256K bytes with on-board refresh
- Sockets for up to 64K bytes of JEDEC 24/28-pin standard memory devices
- Two iSBX™ bus connectors
- 24 programmable parallel I/O lines
- Programmable synchronous/asynchronous RS232C compatible serial interface with software selectable baud rates
- Two programmable 16-bit BCD or binary timers/event counters
- 9 Levels of vectored interrupt control, expandable to 65 levels
- MULTIBUS® interface for multimaster configurations and system expansion
- Supported by a complete family of single board computers, memory, digital and analog I/O, peripheral controllers, packaging and software

The iSBC 86/14 and iSBC 86/30 Single Board Computers are members of Intel's complete line of OEM microcomputer systems which take full advantage of Intel's technology to provide economical, self-contained, computer-based solutions for OEM applications. Each board is a complete computer system on a single 6.75 × 12.00-in. printed circuit card distinguished by RAM memory content with 32K bytes and 128K bytes provided in the iSBC 86/14 and iSBC 86/30 board, respectively. The CPU, system clock, read/write memory, nonvolatile read only memory, I/O ports and drivers, serial communications interface, priority interrupt logic and programmable timers, all reside on the boards.

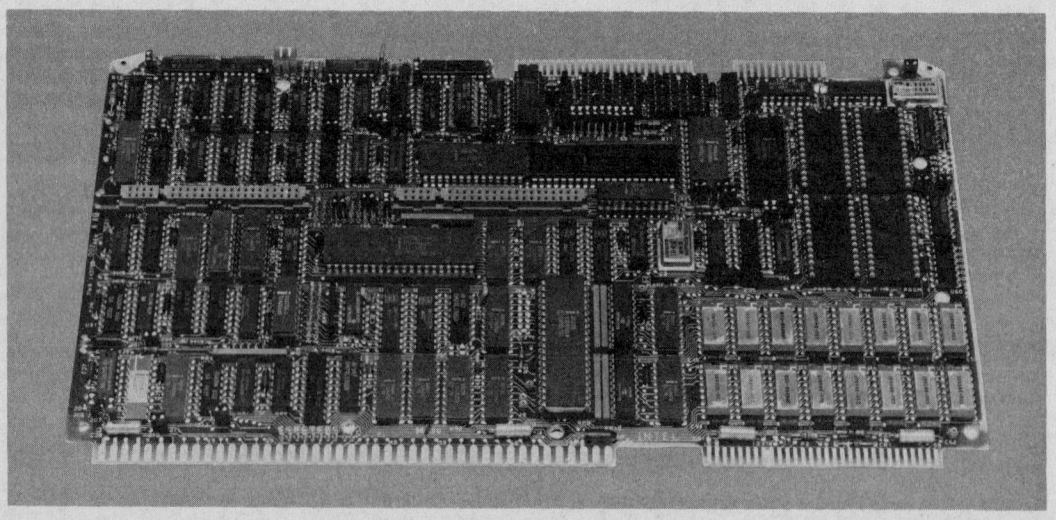

The following are trademarks of Intel Corporation and may be used only to describe Intel products: CREDIT, Index, Intel, Insite, Intellec, Library Manager, Megachassis, Micromap, MULTIBUS, PROMPT, UPI, μScope, Promware, MCS, ICE, iRMX, iSBC, iSBX, MULTIMODULE and iCS. Intel Corporation assumes no responsibility for the use of any circuitry other than circuitry embodied in an Intel product. No other circuit patent licenses are implied.

© INTEL CORPORATION, 1981

iSBC® 86/14 and iSBC® 86/30

FUNCTIONAL DESCRIPTION

Central Processing Unit

The central processor for the iSBC 86/XX[1] boards is Intel's iAPX 86/10 (8086-2) CPU. A clock rate of 8 MHz is supported with a jumper selectable option of 5 MHz. The CPU architecture includes four 16-bit byte addressable data registers, two 16-bit memory base pointer registers and two 16-bit index registers, all accessed by a total of 24 operand addressing modes for comprehensive memory addressing and for support of the data structures required for today's structured, high level languages as well as assembly language.

[1] iSBC 86/XX designates both the iSBC 86/14 and iSBC 86/30 CPU boards.

Instruction Set

The 8086 instruction repertoire includes variable length instruction format (including double operand instructions), 8-bit and 16-bit signed and unsigned arithmetic operators for binary, BCD and unpacked ASCII data, and iterative word and byte string manipulation functions.

For enhanced numerics processing capability, the iSBC 337A MULTIMODULE Numeric Data Processor extends the iAPX 86/10 architecture and data set. Over 60 numeric instructions offer arithmetic, trigonometric, transcendental, logarithmic and exponential instructions. Supported data types include 16-, 32-, and 64-bit integer, and 32- and 64-bit floating point, 18-digit packed BCD and 80-bit temporary.

Architectural Features

A 6-byte instruction queue provides pre-fetching of sequential instructions and can reduce the 750 nsec minimum instruction cycle to 250 nsec for queued instructions. The stack-oriented architecture readily supports modular programming by facilitating fast, simple, inter-module communication, and other programming constructs needed for asynchronous real-time systems. The memory expansion capabilities offer a 1 megabyte addressing range. The dynamic relocation scheme allows ease in segmentation of pure procedure and data for efficient memory utilization. Four segment registers (code, stack, data, extra) contain program loaded offset values which are used to map 16-bit addresses to 20-bit addresses. Each register maps 64K bytes at a time and activation of a specific register is controlled explicitly by program control and is also selected implicitly by specific functions and instructions.

RAM Capabilities

The iSBC 86/14 and iSBC 86/30 microcomputers contain 32K bytes and 128K bytes of dual-port dynamic RAM, respectively. In addition, on-board

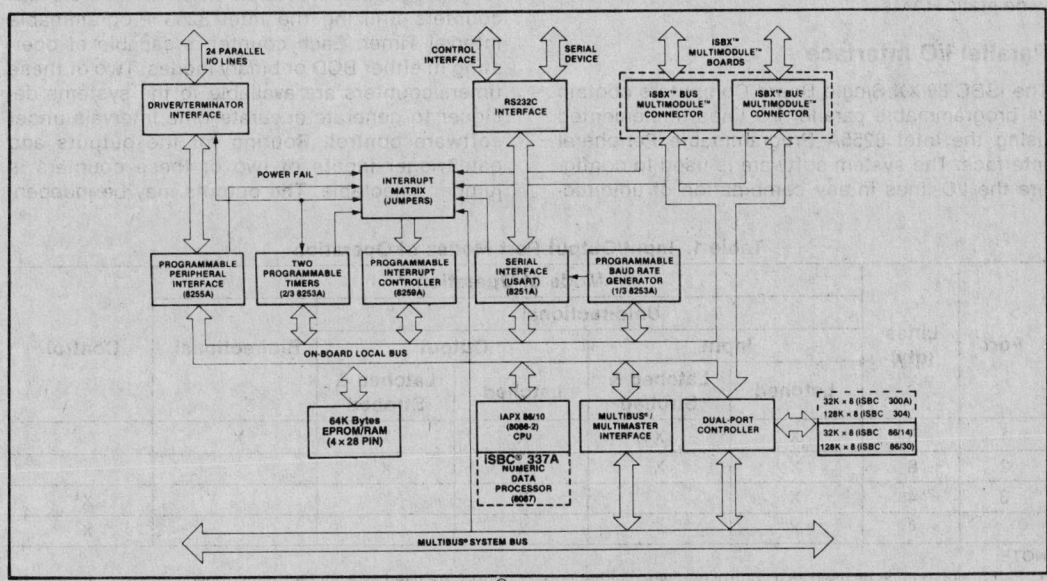

Figure 1. iSBC® 86/XX Block Diagram

iSBC® 86/14 and iSBC® 86/30

RAM may be doubled on each microcomputer by optionally adding RAM MULTIMODULE boards. The on-board RAM may be expanded to 256K bytes with the iSBC 304 MULTIMODULE Board mounted onto the iSBC 86/30 board. Likewise, the iSBC 86/14 microcomputer may be expanded to 64K bytes with the iSBC 300A MULTIMODULE option. The dual-port controller allows access to the on-board RAM (including RAM MULTIMODULE options) from the iSBC 86/XX boards and from any other MULTIBUS master via the system bus. Segments of on-board RAM may be configured as a private resource, protected from MULTIBUS system access. The amount of memory allocated as a private resource may be configured in increments of 25% of the total on-board memory ranging from 0% to 100% (optional RAM MULTIMODULE boards double the increment size). These features allow the multiprocessor systems to establish local memory for each processor and shared system memory configurations where the total system memory size (including local on-board memory) can exceed one megabyte without addressing conflicts.

EPROM Capabilities

Four 28-pin sockets are provided for the use of Intel 2716s, 2732As, 2764s, 27128s, and their respective ROMs. When using 27128s, the on-board EPROM capacity is 64K bytes. Other JEDEC standard pinout devices are also supported, including byte-wide static RAMs.

Parallel I/O Interface

The iSBC 86/XX Single Board Computers contain 24 programmable parallel I/O lines implemented using the Intel 8255A Programmable Peripheral Interface. The system software is used to configure the I/O lines in any combination of unidirectional input/output and bidirectional ports indicated in Table 1. In order to take advantage of the large number of possible I/O configurations, sockets are provided for interchangeable I/O line drivers and terminators, allowing the selection of the appropriate combination of optional line drivers and terminators with the required drive/termination characteristics. The 24 programmable I/O lines and signal ground lines are brought out to a 50-pin edge connector.

Serial I/O

A programmable communications interface using the Intel 8251A Universal Synchronous/Asynchronous Receiver/Transmitter (USART) is contained on the iSBC 86/XX boards. A software selectable baud rate generator provides the USART with all common communication frequencies. The mode of operation (i.e., synchronous or asynchronous), data format, control character format, parity, and baud rate are all under program control. The 8251A provides full duplex, double buffered transmit and receive capability. Parity, overrun, and framing error detection are all incorporated in the USART. The RS232C command lines, serial data lines and signal ground line are brought out to a 26-pin edge connector.

Programmable Timers

The iSBC 86/XX boards provide three independent, fully programmable 16-bit interval timers/event counters utilizing the Intel 8253 Programmable Interval Timer. Each counter is capable of operating in either BCD or binary modes. Two of these timers/counters are available to the systems designer to generate accurate time intervals under software control. Routing for the outputs and gate/trigger inputs of two of these counters is jumper selectable. The outputs may be indepen-

Table 1. Input/Output Port Modes of Operation

Port	Lines (qty)	Mode of Operation				Bidirectional	Control
		Unidirectional					
		Input		Output			
		Latched	Latched & Strobed	Latched	Latched & Strobed		
1	8	X	X	X	X	X	
2	8	X	X	X	X		
3	4	X		X			X[1]
	4	X		X			X[1]

NOTE:
1. Part of port 3 must be used as a control port when either port 1 or port 2 are used as a latched and strobed input or a latched and strobed output port or port 1 is used as a bidirectional port.

iSBC® 86/14 and iSBC® 86/30

dently routed to the 8259A Programmable Interrupt Controller and to the I/O terminators associated with the 8255A to allow external devices or an 8255A port to gate the timer or to count external events. The third interval timer in the 8253 provides the programmable baud rate generator for the iSBC 86/XX boards' RS232C USART serial port. The system software configures each timer independently to select the desired function. Seven functions are available as shown in Table 2. The contents of each counter may be read at any time during system operation.

Table 2. Programmable Timer Functions

Function	Operation
Interrupt on terminal count	When terminal count is reached, an interrupt request is generated. This function is extremely useful for generation of real-time clocks.
Programmable one-shot	Output goes low upon receipt of an external trigger edge or software command and returns high when terminal count is reached. This function is retriggerable.
Rate generator	Divide by N counter. The output will go low for one input clock cycle, and the period from one low going pulse to the next is N times the input clock period.
Square-wave rate generator	Output will remain high until one-half the count has been completed, and go low for the other half of the count.
Software triggered strobe	Output remains high until software loads count (N). N counts after count is loaded, output goes low for one input clock period.
Hardware triggered strobe	Output goes low for one clock period N counts after rising edge counter trigger input. The counter is retriggerable.
Event counter	On a jumper selectable basis, the clock input becomes an input from the external system. CPU may read the number of events occurring after the counter "window" has been enabled or an interrupt may be generated after N events occur in the system.

iSBX™ MULTIMODULE™ On-Board Expansion

Two 8/16-bit iSBX MULTIMODULE connectors are provided on the iSBC 86/XX microcomputers. Through these connectors, additional on-board I/O functions may be added. iSBX MULTIMODULE boards optimally support functions provided by VLSI peripheral components such as additional parallel and serial I/O, analog I/O, small mass storage device controllers (e.g., cassettes and floppy disks), and other custom interfaces to meet specific needs. By mounting directly on the single board computer, less interface logic, less power, simpler packaging, higher performance, and lower cost result when compared to other alternatives such as MULTIBUS form factor compatible boards. The iSBX connectors on the iSBC 86/XX boards provide all signals necessary to interface to the local on-board bus, including 16 data lines for maximum data transfer rates. iSBX MULTIMODULE boards designed with 8-bit data paths and using the 8-bit iSBX connector are also supported on the iSBC 86/XX microcomputers. A broad range of iSBX MULTIMODULE options are available in this family from Intel. Custom iSBX modules may also be designed for use on the iSBC 86/XX boards. An iSBX bus interface specification and iSBX connectors are available from Intel.

MULTIBUS® SYSTEM BUS AND MULTIMASTER CAPABILITIES

Overview

The MULTIBUS system bus is Intel's industry standard microcomputer bus structure. Both 8 and 16-bit single board computers are supported on the MULTIBUS structure with 24 address and 16 data lines. In its simplest application, the MULTIBUS system bus allows expansion of functions already contained on a single board computer (e.g., memory and digital I/O). However, the MULTIBUS structure also allows very powerful distributed processing configurations with multiple processors and intelligent slave I/O, and peripheral boards capable of solving the most demanding microcomputer applications. The MULTIBUS system bus is supported with a broad array of board level products, LSI interface components, detailed published specifications and application notes.

Expansion Capabilities

Memory and I/O capacity may be expanded and additional functions added using Intel MULTIBUS compatible expansion boards. Memory may be expanded by adding user specified combinations of RAM boards, EPROM boards, or combination boards. On-board EPROM capacity may be expanded to 128K by user reprogramming of a PAL device to support 27256 EPROM devices. Input/output capacity may be added with digital I/O and analog I/O expansion boards. Mass storage capability may be achieved by adding single or double density diskette controllers, or hard disk controllers. Modular expandable backplanes and cardcages are available to support multiboard systems.

Multimaster Capabilities

For those applications requiring additional processing capacity and the benefits of multiprocessing (i.e., several CPUs and/or controllers logically sharing system tasks through communication of the system bus), the iSBC 86/XX boards provide full MULTIBUS arbitration control logic. This control logic allows up to three iSBC 86/XX boards or other bus masters, including iSBC 80 family MULTIBUS compatible 8-bit single board computers to share the system bus using a serial (daisy chain) priority scheme and allows up to 16 masters to share the MULTIBUS system bus with an external parallel priority decoder. In addition to the multiprocessing configurations made possible with multimaster capability, it also provides a very efficient mechanism for all forms of DMA (Direct Memory Access) transfers.

Interrupt Capability

The iSBC 86/XX boards provide 9 vectored interrupt levels. The highest level is the NMI (Non-Maskable Interrupt) line which is directly tied to the 8086 CPU. This interrupt is typically used for signaling catastrophic events (e.g., power failure). The Intel 8259A Programmable Interrupt Controller (PIC) provides control and vectoring for the next eight interrupt levels. As shown in Table 3, a selection of four priority processing modes is available for use in designing request processing configurations to match system requirements for efficient interrupt servicing with minimal latencies. Operating mode and priority assignments may be reconfigured dynamically via software at any time

Table 3. Programmable Interrupt Modes

Mode	Operation
Fully nested	Interrupt request line priorities fixed at 0 as highest, 7 as lowest.
Auto-rotating	Equal priority. Each level, after receiving service, becomes the lowest priority level until next interrupt occurs.
Specific priority	System software assigns lowest priority level. Priority of all other levels based in sequence numerically on this assignment.
Polled	System software examines priority-encoded system interrupt status via interrupt status register.

during system operation. The PIC accepts interrupt requests from all on-board I/O resources and from the MULTIBUS system bus. The PIC then resolves requests according to the selected mode and, if appropriate, issues an interrupt to the CPU. Any combination of interrupt levels may be masked via software, by storing a single byte in the interrupt mask register of the PIC. In systems requiring additional interrupt levels, slave 8259A PICs may be interfaced via the MULTIBUS system bus, to generate additional vector addresses, yielding a total of 65 unique interrupt levels.

Interrupt Request Generation

Interrupt requests to be serviced by the iSBC 86/XX boards may originate from 28 sources. Table 4 includes a list of devices and functions supported by interrupts. All interrupt signals are brought to the interrupt jumper matrix where any combination of interrupt sources may be strapped to the desired interrupt request level on the 8259A PIC or the NMI input to the CPU directly.

Power-Fail Control and Auxiliary Power

Control logic is also included to accept a power-fail interrupt in conjunction with the AC-low signal from the iSBC 635 and iSBC 640 Power Supply or equivalent, to initiate an orderly shut down of the system in the event of a power failure. Additionally, an active-low TTL compatible memory protect signal is brought out on the auxiliary connector which, when asserted, disables read/write access to RAM memory on the board. This input is provided for the protection of RAM contents during system power-down sequences. An auxiliary power bus is also provided to allow separate power to RAM for systems requiring battery backup of read/write memory. Selection of this auxiliary RAM power bus is made via jumpers on the board.

System Development Capabilities

The development cycle of iSBC 86/XX products can be significantly reduced and simplified by using either the System 86/310 or the Intellec Series Microcomputer Development Systems. The Assembler, Locating Linker, Library Manager, Text Editor and System Monitor are all supported by the ISIS-II disk-based operating system. To facilitate conversion of 8080A/8085A assembly language programs to run on the iSBC 86/XX boards, CONV-86 is available under the ISIS-II operating system.

iSBC® 86/14 and iSBC® 86/30

IN-CIRCUIT EMULATOR

The Intellec ICE-86 In-Circuit Emulator provides the necessary link between the software development environment provided by the Intellec system and the "target" iSBC 86/XX execution system. In addition to providing the mechanism for loading executable code and data into the iSBC 86/XX boards, the ICE-86 In-Circuit Emulator provides a sophisticated command set to assist in debugging software and final integration of the user hardware and software.

PL/M-86

Intel's system's implementation language, PL/M-86, is standard in the System 86/310 and is also available as an Intellec Microcomputer Development System option. PL/M-86 provides the capability to program in algorithmic language and eliminates the need to manage register usage or allocate memory while still allowing explicit control of the system's resources when needed. FORTRAN 86 and PASCAL 86 are also available on Intellec or 86/310 systems.

Run-Time Support

Intel also offers two run-time support packages; iRMX 88 Realtime Multitasking Executive and the iRMX 86 Operating System. The iRMX 88 executive is a simple, highly configurable and efficient foundation for small, high performance applications. Its multitasking structure establishes a solid foundation for modular system design and provides task scheduling and management, intertask communication and synchronization, and interrupt servicing for a variety of peripheral devices. Other configurable options include terminal handlers, disk file system, debuggers and other utilities. The iRMX 86 Operating System is a high functional operating system with a very rich set of features and options based on an object-oriented architecture. In addition to being modular and configurable, functions beyond the nucleus include a sophisticated file management and I/O system, and powerful human interface. Both packages are easily customized and extended by the user to match unique requirements.

Table 4. Interrupt Request Sources

Device	Function	Number of Interrupts
MULTIBUS® interface	Requests from MULTIBUS® resident peripherals or other CPU boards	8; may be expanded to 64 with slave 8259A PICs on MULTIBUS® boards
8255A Programmable Peripheral Interface	Signals input buffer full or output buffer empty; also BUS INTR OUT general purpose interrupt from driver/terminator sockets	3
8251A USART	Transmit buffer empty and receive buffer full	2
8253 Timers	Timer 0, 1 outputs; function determined by timer mode	2
iSBX™ connectors	Function determined by iSBX™ MULTIMODULE™ board	4 (2 per iSBX™ connector)
Bus fail safe timer	Indicates addressed MULTIBUS® resident device has not responded to command within 6 msec	1
Power fail interrupt	Indicates AC power is not within tolerance	1
Power line clock	Source of 120 Hz signal from power supply	1
External interrupt	General purpose interrupt from auxiliary (P2) connector on backplane	1
iSBC™ 337A MULTIMODULE™ Numeric Data Processor	Indicates error or exception condition	1
Parity error	Indicates on-board RAM parity error from iSBC™ 303 parity MULTIMODULE™ board (iSBC™ 86/14 option)	1
Edge-level conversion	Converts edge triggered interrupt request to level interrupt	1
OR-gate matrix	Outputs of OR-gates on-board for multiple interrupts	2

iSBC® 86/14 and iSBC® 86/30

SPECIFICATIONS

Word Size
INSTRUCTION — 8, 16, 24, or 32 bits
DATA — 8, 16 bits

System Clock
5.00 MHz or 8.00 MHz ± 0.1% (jumper selectable)

Cycle Time
BASIC INSTRUCTION CYCLE
8 MHz — 750 ns
  — 250 ns (assumes instruction in the queue)
5 MHz — 1.2 μsec
  — 400 ns (assumes instruction in the queue)

NOTE: Basic instruction cycle is defined as the fastest instruction time (i.e., two clock cycles).

Memory Cycle Time
RAM — 750 ns
EPROM — Jumper selectable from 500 ns to 875 ns

Memory Capacity/Addressing
ON-BOARD EPROM

Device	Total Capacity	Address Range
2716	8K bytes	FE000–FFFFF$_H$
2732A	16K bytes	FC000–FFFFF$_H$
2764	32K bytes	F8000–FFFFF$_H$
27128	64K bytes	F0000–FFFFF$_H$

NOTE: iSBC 86/XX EPROM sockets support JEDEC 24/28-pin standard EPROMs and RAMs. Total EPROM capacity may be increased to 128 bytes by the user reprogramming an on-board PAL.

ON-BOARD RAM

Board	Total Capacity	Address Range
iSBC 86/14	32K bytes	0–07FFF$_H$
iSBC 86/30	128K bytes	0–1FFFF$_H$

WITH MULTIMODULE™ RAM

Board	Total Capacity	Address Range
iSBC 300A (with iSBC 86/14)	64K bytes	0–0FFFF$_H$
iSBC 304 (with iSBC 86/30)	256K bytes	0–3FFFF$_H$

I/O Capacity
PARALLEL — 24 programmable lines using one 8255A.
SERIAL — 1 programmable line using one 8251A
iSBX™ MULTIMODULE™ — 2 iSBX boards

Serial Communications Characteristics
SYNCHRONOUS — 5–8 bit characters; internal or external character synchronization; automatic sync insertion

ASYNCHRONOUS — 5–8 bit characters; break character generation; 1, 1½, or 2 stop bits; false start bit detection

BAUD RATES

Frequency (kHz) (Software Selectable)	Baud Rate (Hz)	
	Synchronous	Asynchronous
		÷16 ÷64
153.6	—	9600 2400
76.8	—	4800 1200
38.4	38400	2400 600
19.2	19200	1200 300
9.6	9600	600 150
4.8	4800	300 75
2.4	2400	150 —
1.76	1760	110 —

NOTE: Frequency selected by I/O write of appropriate 16-bit frequency factor to baud rate register (8253 Timer 2).

Timers
INPUT FREQUENCIES
Reference: 2.46 MHz ± 0.1% (0.041 μsec period, nominal); or 153.60 kHz ± 0.1% (6.51 μsec period, nominal)

NOTE: Above frequencies are user selectable.

Event Rate: 2.46 MHz max

OUTPUT FREQUENCIES/TIMING INTERVALS

Function	Single Timer/Counter		Dual Timer/Counter (Cascaded)	
	Min	Max	Min	Max
Real-time Interrupt	1.63 μs	427.1 ms	3.26s	466.50 min
Programmable one-shot	1.63 μs	427.1 ms	3.26s	466.50 min
Rate generator	2.342 Hz	613.5 kHz	0.000036 Hz	306.8 kHz
Square-wave rate generator	2.342 Hz	613.5 kHz	0.000036 Hz	306.8 kHz
Software triggered strobe	1.63 μs	427.1 ms	3.26s	466.50 min
Hardware triggered strobe	1.63 μs	427.1 ms	3.26s	466.50 min
Event counter	—	2.46 MHz	—	—

Interfaces
MULTIBUS® — All signals TTL compatible
iSBX™ BUS — All signals TTL compatible
PARALLEL I/O — All signals TTL compatible
SERIAL I/O — RS232C compatible, configurable as a data set or data terminal

iSBC® 86/14 and iSBC® 86/30

TIMER — All signals TTL compatible
INTERRUPT REQUESTS — All TTL compatible

Connectors

Interface	Double-Sided Pins	Centers (in.)	Mating Connectors
MULTIBUS® System	86	0.156	Viking 3KH43/9AMK12 Wire Wrap
iSBX™ Bus 8-Bit Data	36	0.1	iSBX 960-5
Parallel I/O (2)	50	0.1	3M 3415-000 Flat or TI H312125 Pins
Serial I/O	26	0.1	3M 3462-0001 Flat or AMP 88106-1 Flat

Line Drivers and Terminators

I/O DRIVERS — The following line drivers are all compatible with the I/O driver sockets on the iSBC 86/05 board

Driver	Characteristic	Sink Current (mA)
7438	I,OC	48
7437	I	48
7432	NI	16
7426	I,OC	16
7409	NI,OC	16
7408	NI	16
7403	I,OC	16
7400	I	16

NOTE: I = inverting; NI = non-inverting; OC = open collector.

Port 1 of the 8255A has 20 mA totem-pole bidirectional drivers and 1 kΩ terminators

I/O TERMINATORS — 220Ω/330Ω divider or 1 kΩ pullup

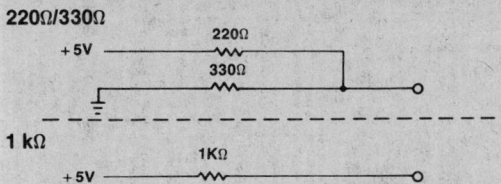

MULTIBUS® Drivers

Function	Characteristic	Sink Current (mA)
Data	Tri-State	32
Address	Tri-State	32
Commands	Tri-State	32
Bus Control	Open Collector	20

Physical Characteristics
WIDTH — 12.00 in. (30.48 cm)
HEIGHT — 6.75 in. (17.15 cm)
DEPTH — 0.70 in. (1.78 cm)
WEIGHT — 14 oz (388 gm)

Environmental Characteristics
OPERATING TEMPERATURE — 0°C to 55°C
RELATIVE HUMIDITY — to 90% (without condensation)

Electrical Characteristics
DC POWER REQUIREMENTS

Configuration	Current Requirements (All Voltages ±5%)		
	+5V	+12V	−12V
Without EPROM[1]	5.1A	25 mA	23 mA
RAM only[2]	600 mA	—	—
With 8K EPROM[3] (using 2716)	5.4A	25 mA	23 mA
With 16K EPROM[3] (using 2732A)	5.5A	25 mA	23 mA
With 32K EPROM[3] (using 2764)	5.6A	25 mA	23 mA

NOTES:
1. Does not include power for optional ROM/EPROM, I/O drivers, and I/O terminators.
2. RAM chips powered via auxiliary power bus in power-down mode.
3. Includes power required for 4 ROM/EPROM chips, and I/O terminators installed for 16 I/O lines; all terminator inputs low.

Environmental Characteristics
OPERATING TEMPERATURE — 0°C to 55°C
RELATIVE HUMIDITY — to 90% (without condensation)

Reference Manual
144044-001 — iSBC 86/14 and iSBC 86/30 Hardware Reference Manual (NOT SUPPLIED)

Manuals may be ordered from any Intel sales representative, distributor office or from Intel Literature Department, 3065 Bowers Avenue, Santa Clara, California 95051.

ORDERING INFORMATION

Part Number	Description
SBC 86/14	Single Board Computer
SBC 86/30	Single Board Computer

iSBC® 86/35
SINGLE BOARD COMPUTER

- iAPX 86/10 (8086-2) Microprocessor with 5 or 8 MHz CPU clock
- Optional iAPX 86/20 Numeric Data Processor with iSBC® 337A MULTIMODULE™ processor
- Upward compatible with iSBC 86/30 Single Board Computer
- 512K bytes of dual-port read/write memory expandable on-board to 640K or 1M bytes
- Sockets for up to 128K bytes of JEDEC 24/28-pin standard memory devices
- Two iSBX™ bus connectors
- 24 programmable parallel I/O lines
- Programmable synchronous/asynchronous RS232C compatible serial interface with software selectable baud rates
- Three programmable 16-bit BCD or binary timers/event counters
- 9 levels of vectored interrupt control, expandable off board to 65 levels
- MULTIBUS® interface for multimaster configurations and system expansion
- Supported by a complete family of single board computers, memory, digital and analog I/O, peripheral controllers, packaging and software

The iSBC 86/35 Single Board Computer is a member of Intel's complete line of OEM microcomputer systems that take full advantage of Intel's technology to provide economical, self-contained, computer-based solutions for OEM applications. The board is a complete computer system containing the CPU, system clock, dual port read/write memory, nonvolatile read only memory, I/O ports and drivers, serial communications interface, priority interrupt logic and programmable timers, all on a single 6.75 x 12.00 in. printed circuit card. The iSBC 86/35 board is distinguished by its large RAM content of 512K bytes which is expandable on-board to 1 megabyte; the direct addressing capability of the 8086-2 CPU. The large, on-board memory resource combined with the iAPX 86/10 microprocessor provides high-level system performance ideal for applications, such as robotics, process control, medical instrumentation, office systems, and business data processing.

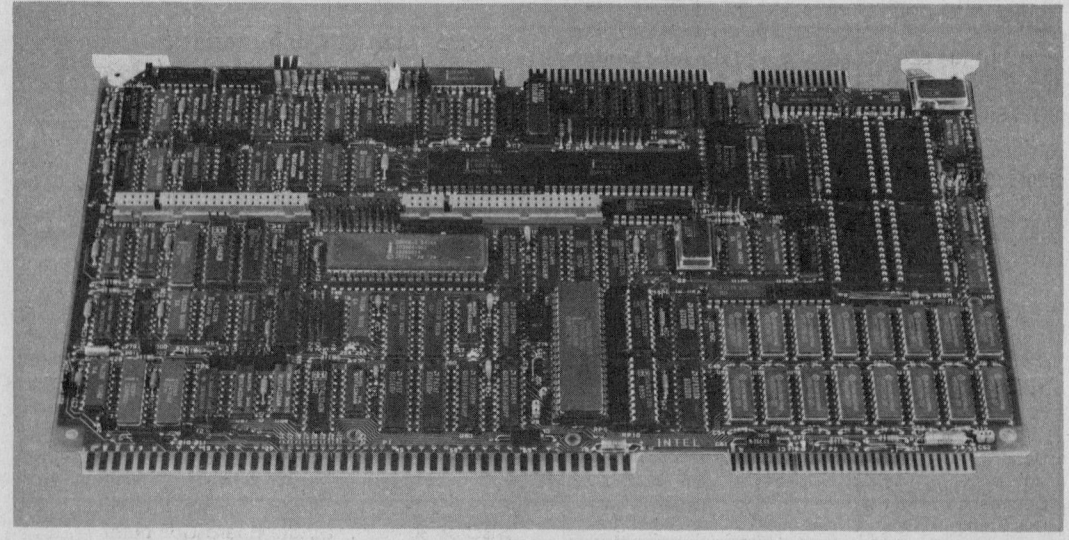

The following are trademarks of Intel Corporation and may be used only to describe Intel products: Intel, MULTIBUS, UPI, ICE, iRMX, iSBC, iSBX, MULTIMODULE, iSDM and ICS. Intel Corporation assumes no responsibility for the use of any circuitry other than circuitry embodied in an Intel product. No other circuit patent licenses are implied.
© INTEL CORPORATION, 1984

October 1985
ORDER NUMBER: 210219-003

iSBC® 86/35 Single Board Computer

FUNCTIONAL DESCRIPTION

Overview

The iSBC 86/35 board combines the power of the industry standard 8086 CPU with up to a megabyte page of board resident, dual ported system memory to improve the systems overall performance. By placing the direct memory addressing capability of the iAPX 86/10 CPU on board, MULTIBUS® access to system memory can be eliminated, significantly improving system throughput. Intel's incorporation of 256K bit DRAM technology, parallel and serial I/O, iSBX™ connectors, and interrupt control capabilities make this high performance single board computer system a reality.

Central Processing Unit

The central processor for the iSBC 86/35 board is Intel's iAPX 86/10 (8086-2) CPU. A clock rate of 8 MHz is supported with a jumper selectable option for 5 MHz. The CPU architecture includes four 16-bit byte addressable data registers, two 16-bit index registers, all accessed by a total of 24 operand addressing modes for comprehensive memory addressing and for support of the data structures required for today's structured, high level languages as well as assembly language.

Instruction Set

The 8086 instruction repertoire includes variable length instruction format (including double operand instructions), 8-bit and 16-bit signed and unsigned arithmetic operators for binary, BCD and unpacked ASCII data, and iterative word and byte string manipulation functions.

For enhanced 5 or 8 MHz numerics processing capability, the iSBC 337A MULTIMODULE Numeric Data Processor extends the iAPX 86/10 architecture and data set. Over 60 numeric instructions offer arithmetic, trigonometric, transcendental, logarithmic and exponential instructions. Supported data types include 16-, 32-, and 64-bit integer, and 32- and 64-bit floating point, 18-digit packed BCD and 80-bit temporary.

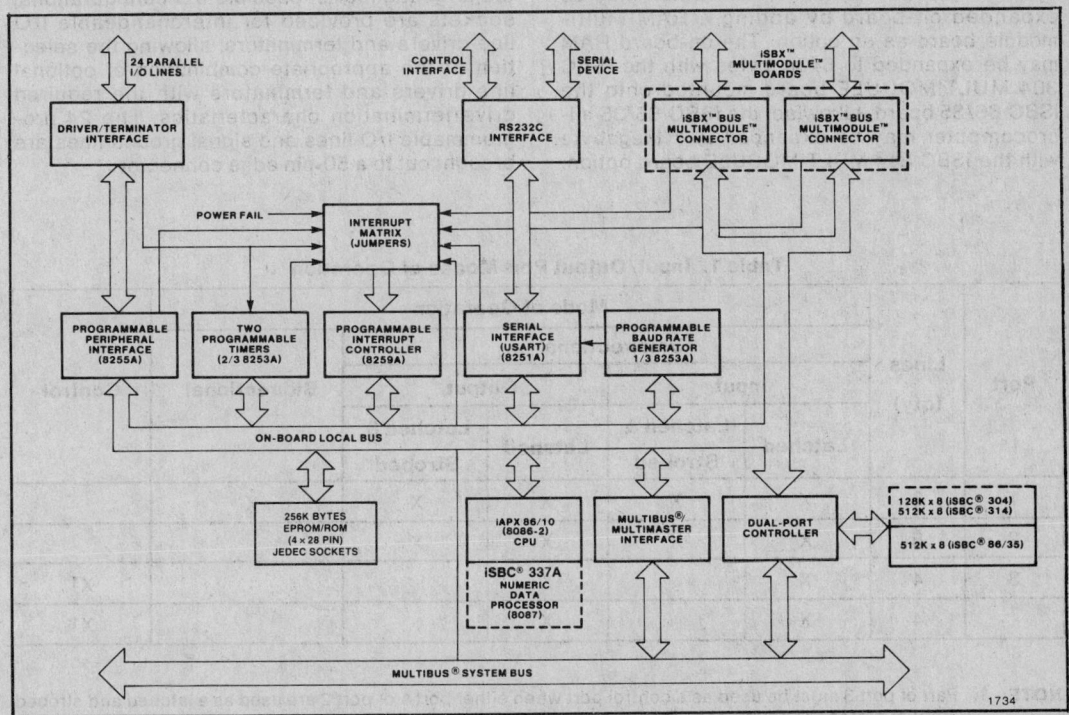

Figure 1. iSBC® 86/35 Block Diagram

iSBC® 86/35 Single Board Computer

Architectural Features

A 6-byte instruction queue provides pre-fetching of sequential instructions and can reduce the 750 nsec minimum instruction cycle to 250 nsec for queued instructions. The stack-oriented architecture readily supports modular programming by facilitating fast, simple, inter-modular communication, and other programming constructs needed for asynchronous real-time systems. The memory expansion capabilities offer a 1 megabyte addressing range. The dynamic relocation scheme allows ease in segmentation of pure procedure and data for efficient memory utilization. Four segment registers (code, stack, data, extra) contain program loaded offset values which are used to map 16-bit addresses to 20-bit addresses. Each register maps 64K bytes at a time and activation of a specific register is controlled explicitly by program control and is also selected implicitly by specific functions and instructions.

RAM Capabilities

The iSBC 86/35 microcomputer contains 512K bytes of dual-port dynamic RAM which may be expanded on-board by adding a RAM Multimodule board as an option. The on-board RAM may be expanded to 640K bytes with the iSBC 304 MULTIMODULE board mounted onto the iSBC 86/35 board. Likewise, the iSBC 86/35 microcomputer may be expanded to 1 Megabyte with the iSBC 314 MULTIMODULE board option.

The dual-port controller allows access to the on-board RAM (including RAM MULTIMODULE board options) from the iSBC 86/35 board and from any other MULTIBUS master via the system bus. Segments of on-board RAM may be configured as a private resource, protected from MULTIBUS system access.

EPROM Capabilities

Four 28-pin JEDEC sockets are provided for the use of Intel 2764, 27128, 27256, 27512, EPROMS and their respective ROMs. When using 27512, the on-board EPROM capacity is 256K bytes. Other JEDEC standard pinout devices are also supported, including byte-wide static RAMs.

Parallel I/O Interface

The iSBC 86/35 Single Board Computer contains 24 programmable parallel I/O lines implemented using the Intel 8255A Programmable Peripheral Interface. The system software is used to configure the I/O lines in any combination of unidirectional input/output and bidirectional ports indicated in Table 1. In order to take advantage of the large number of possible I/O configurations, sockets are provided for interchangeable I/O line drivers and terminators, allowing the selection of the appropriate combination of optional line drivers and terminators with the required drive/termination characteristics. The 24 programmable I/O lines and signal ground lines are brought out to a 50-pin edge connector.

Table 1. Input/Output Port Modes of Operation

Port	Lines (qty)	Mode of Operation				Bidirectional	Control
		Unidirectional					
		Input		Output			
		Latched	Latched & Strobed	Latched	Latched & Strobed		
1	8	X	X	X	X	X	
2	8	X	X	X	X		
3	4	X		X			X[1]
	4	X		X			X[1]

NOTE: 1. Part of port 3 must be used as a control port when either port 1 or port 2 are used as a latched and strobed input or a latched and strobed output port or port 1 is used as a bidirectional port.

iSBC® 86/35 Single Board Computer

Serial I/O

A programmable communications interface using the Intel 8251A Universal Synchronous/Asynchronous Receiver/Transmitter (USART) is contained on the iSBC 86/35 board. A software selectable baud rate generator provides the USART with all common communication frequencies. The mode of operation (i.e., synchronous or asynchronous), data format, control character format, parity, and baud rate are all under program control. The 8251A provides full duplex, double buffered transmit and receive capability. Parity, overrun, and framing error detection are all incorporated in the USART. The RS232C command lines, serial data lines and signal ground line are brought out to a 26-pin edge connector.

Programmable Timers

The iSBC 86/35 board provides three independent, fully programmable 16-bit interval timers/event counters utilizing the Intel 8253 Programmable Interval Timer. Each counter is capable of operating in either BCD or binary modes. Two of these timers/counters are available to the systems designer to generate accurate time intervals under software control. Routing for the outputs and gate/trigger inputs of two of these counters is jumper selectable. The outputs may be independently routed to the 8259A Programmable Interrupt Controller and to the I/O terminators associated with the 8255A to allow external devices or an 8255A port to gate the timer or to count external events. The third interval timer in the 8253 provides the programmable baud rate generator for the iSBC 86/35 board's RS232C USART serial port. The system software configures each timer independently to select the desired function. Seven functions are available as shown in Table 2. The contents of each counter may be read at any time during system operation.

iSBX™ MULTIMODULE™ On-Board Expansion

Two 8/16-bit iSBX MULTIMODULE connectors are provided on the iSBC 86/35 microcomputer. Through these connectors, additional on-board I/O functions may be added. iSBX MULTIMODULE boards optimally support functions provided by VLSI peripheral components such as additional parallel and serial I/O, analog I/O, small mass storage device controllers (e.g., cassettes and floppy disks), and other custom

Table 2. Programmable Timer Functions

Function	Operation
Interrupt on terminal count	When terminal count is reached, an interrupt request is generated. This function is extremely useful for generation of real-time clocks.
Programmable one-shot	Output goes low upon receipt of an external trigger edge or software command and returns high when terminal count is reached. This function is retriggerable.
Rate generator	Divide by N counter. The output will go low for one input clock cycle, and the period from one low going pulse to the next is N times the input clock period.
Square-wave rate generator	Output will remain high until one-half the count has been completed, and go low for the other half of the count.
Software triggered strobe	Output remains high until software loads count (N). N counts after count is loaded, output goes low for one input clock period.
Hardware triggered strobe	Output goes low for one clock period N counts after rising edge counter trigger input. The counter is retriggerable.
Event counter	On a jumper selectable basis, the clock input becomes an input from the external system. CPU may read the number of events occurring after the conter "window" has been enabled or an interrupt may be generated after N events occur in the system.

iSBC® 86/35 Single Board Computer

interfaces to meet specific needs. By mounting directly on the single board computer, less interface logic, less power, simpler packaging, higher performance, and lower cost result when compared to other alternatives such as MULTIBUS form factor compatible boards. The iSBX connectors on the iSBC 86/35 board provides all signals necessary to interface to the local on-board bus, including 16 data lines for maximum data transfer rates. iSBX MULTIMODULE boards designed with 8-bit data paths and using the 8-bit iSBX connector are also supported on the iSBC 86/35 microcomputer. A broad range of iSBX MULTIMODULE options are available in this family from Intel. Custom iSBX modules may also be designed for use on the iSBC 86/35 board. An iSBX bus interface specification and iSBX connectors are available from Intel.

MULTIBUS® System Bus Capabilities

Overview

The MULTIBUS system bus is Intel's industry standard (IEEE 796) microcomputer bus structure. Both 8- and 16-bit single board computers are supported on the MULTIBUS structure with 24 address and 16 data lines. In its simplest application, the MULTIBUS system bus allows expansion of functions already contained on a single board computer (e.g., memory and digital I/O). However, the MULTIBUS structure also allows very powerful distributed processing configurations with multiple processors and intelligent slave I/O, and peripheral boards capable of solving the most demanding microcomputer applications. The MULTIBUS system bus is supported with a broad array of board level products, LSI interface components, detailed published specifications and application notes. Please refer to the MULTIBUS Handbook (order number 210883) for more detailed information.

Multimaster Capabilities

For those applications requiring additional processing capacity and the benefits of multiprocessing (i.e. several CPUs and/or controllers logically sharing system tasks through communication on the system bus), the iSBC 86/35 board provides full MULTIBUS arbitration control logic. This control logic allows both serial (daisy chain) and parallel priority schemes. The serial scheme allows up to three iSBC 86/35 boards/bus masters to share the MULTIBUS system bus; while up to 16 masters may be connected using the parallel scheme and external decode logic.

Interrupt Capability

The iSBC 86/35 board provides 9 vectored interrupt levels. The highest level is the NMI (Non-Maskable Interrupt) line which is directly tied to the 8086-2 CPU. This interrupt is typically used for signaling catastrophic events (e.g., power failure). The Intel 8259A Programmable Interrupt Controller (PIC) provides control and vectoring for the next eight interrupt levels. As shown in Table 3, a selection of four priority processing modes is available for use in designing request processing configurations to match system requirements for efficient interrupt servicing with minimal latencies. Operating mode and priority assignments may be reconfigured dynamically via software at any time during system operation. The PIC accepts interrupt requests from all on-board I/O resources and from the MULTIBUS system bus. The PIC then resolves requests according to the selected mode and, if appropriate, issues an interrupt to the CPU. Any combination of interrupt levels may be masked via software, by storing a single byte in the interrupt mask register of the PIC. In systems requiring additional interrupt levels, slave 8259A PICs may be interfaced via the MULTIBUS system bus, to generate additional vector addresses, yielding a total of 65 unique interrupt levels.

Table 3. Programmable Interrupt Modes

Mode	Operation
Fully nested	Interrupt request line priorities fixed at 0 as highest, 7 as lowest.
Auto-rotating	Equal priority. Each level, after receiving service, becomes the lowest priority level until next interrupt occurs.
Specific priority	System software assigns lowest priority level. Priority of all other levels based in sequence numerically on this assignment.
Polled	System software examines priority-encoded system interrupt status via interrupt status register.

iSBC® 86/35 Single Board Computer

Interrupt Request Generation

Interrupt requests to be serviced by the iSBC 86/35 board may originate from 28 sources. Table 4 includes a list of devices and functions supported by interrupts. All interrupt signals are brought to the interrupt jumper matrix where any combination of interrupt sources may be strapped to the desired interrupt request level on the 8259A PIC or the NMI input to the CPU directly.

Power-Fail Control and Auxiliary Power

Control logic is included to accept a power-fail interrupt in conjunction with the AC-low signal from the Power Supply to initiate an orderly shut down of the system in the event of a power failure. Additionally, an active-low TTL compatible memory protect signal is brought out on the auxiliary connector which, when asserted, disables read/write access to RAM memory on the board. This input is provided for the protection of RAM contents during system power-down

Table 4. Interrupt Request Sources

Device	Function	Number of Interrupts
MULTIBUS® interface	Requests from MULTIBUS® resident peripherals or other CPU boards	8; may be expanded to 64 with slave 8259A PICs on MULTIBUS® boards
8255A Programmable Peripheral Interface	Signals input buffer full or output buffer empty; also BUS INTR OUT general purpose interrupt from driver/terminator sockets	3
8251A USART	Transmit buffer empty and receive buffer full	2
8253 Timers	Timer 0, 1 outputs; function determined by timer mode	2
iSBX™ connectors	Function determined by iSBX™ MULTIMODULE™ board	4 (2 per iSBX™ connector)
Bus fail safe timer	Indicates addressed MULTIBUS® resident device has not responded to command within 6 msec	1
Power fail interrupt	Indicates AC power is not within tolerance	1
Power line clock	Source of 120 Hz signal from power supply	1
External interrupt	General purpose interrupt from auxiliary (P2) connector on backplane	1
iSBC® 337 MULTIMODULE™ Numeric Data Processor	Indicates error or exception condition	1
Edge-level conversion	Converts edge triggered interrupt request to level interrupt	1
OR-gate matrix	Outputs of OR-gates on-board for multiple interrupts	2

iSBC® 86/35 Single Board Computer

sequences. An auxiliary power bus is also provided to allow separate power to RAM for systems requiring battery backup of read/write memory. Selection of this auxiliary RAM power bus is made via jumpers on the board.

System Development Capabilities

The development cycle of iSBC 86/35 products can be significantly reduced and simplified by using either the System 86/330 or the Intellec® Series Microcomputer Development Systems. The Assembler, Locating Linker, Library Manager, Text Editor and System Monitor are all supported by the ISIS-II disk-based operating system.

IN-CIRCUIT EMULATOR

The Intellec ICE™-86A In-Circuit Emulator provides the necessary link between the software development environment provided by the Intellec system and the "target" iSBC 86/35 execution system. In addition to providing the mechanism for loading executable code and data into the iSBC 86/35 board, the ICE-86A In-Circuit Emulator provides a sophisticated command set to assist in debugging software and final integration of the user hardware and software.

Software Support

Real time support for the iSBC 86/35 board is provided by the iRMX 86 operating system. The iRMX 86 Operating System is a highly functional operating system with a rich set of features and options based on an object-oriented architecture. In addition to being modular and configurable, functions beyond the nucleus include a sophisticated file management and I/O system, and powerful human interface. Both packages are easily customized and extended by the user to match unique requirements.

Interactive multi-user support will be provided by the Xenix* operating system. Xenix is a compatible derivative of Unix**, System III.

Language support for the iSBC 86/35 board includes Intels ASM 86, PL/M 86, and PASCAL, and FORTRAN, as well as many third party 8086 languages. Programs developed in these languages can be downloaded from an Intel Series II, or Series III development system to the iSBC 86/35 board via the iSDM™ 86 system debug monitor. The iSDM 86 monitor also provides on-target, interactive system debug capability including breakpoint and memory examination features. The monitor supports iSBC/iAPX 86, 88, 186, and 188 based applications.

* is a trademark of Microsoft Corp.
** is a trademark of Bell Labs.

SPECIFICATIONS

Word Size

INSTRUCTION — 8, 16, 24, or 32 bits

DATA — 8, 16 bits

System Clock

5 MHz or 8 MHz ± 0.1% (jumper selectable)

Cycle Time

BASIC INSTRUCTION CYCLE

8 MHz — 250 ns (assumes instruction in the queue)

5 MHz — 400 ns (assumes instruction in the queue)

NOTE: Basic instruction cycle is defined as the fastest instruction time (i.e., two clock cycles). Jumper selectable for 1 wait-state on-board memory access.

Memory Capacity/Addressing

ON-BOARD EPROM

Device	Total Capacity	Address Range
2764	32K bytes	F8000-FFFFF$_H$
27128	64K bytes	F0000-FFFFF$_H$
27256	128K bytes	E0000-FFFFF$_H$
27512	256K bytes	D0000-FFFFF$_H$

ON-BOARD RAM

Board	Total Capacity	Address Range
iSBC 86/35	512K bytes	0-7FFFF$_H$

WITH MULTIMODULE™ RAM

Board	Total Capacity	Address Range
iSBC 304	640K bytes	8-9 FFFF$_H$
iSBC 314	1M bytes	8-FFFFF$_H$

iSBC® 86/35 Single Board Computer

I/O Capacity

PARALLEL — 24 programmable lines using one 8255A.

SERIAL — 1 programmable line using one 8251A

iSBX™ MULTIMODULE™ — 2 iSBX boards

Serial Communications Characteristics

SYNCHRONOUS — 5-8 bit characters; internal or external character synchronization; automatic sync insertion

ASYNCHRONOUS — 5-8 bit characters; break character generation; 1, 1½, or 2 stop bits; false start bit detection

BAUD RATES

Frequency (kHz) (Software Selectable)	Baud Rate (Hz)	
	Synchronous	Asynchronous
		÷16 ÷64
153.6	—	9600 2400
76.8	—	4800 1200
38.4	38400	2400 600
19.2	19200	1200 300
9.6	9600	600 150
4.8	4800	300 75
2.4	2400	150 —
1.76	1760	110 —

NOTE: Frequency selected by I/O write of appropriate 16-bit frequency factor to baud rate register (8253 Timer 2).

Timers

INPUT FREQUENCIES

Reference: 2.46 MHz ±0.1% (0.041 µsec period, nominal); or 153.60 kHz ±0.1% (6.51 µsec period, nominal).

NOTE: Above frequencies are user selectable.

Event Rate: 2.46 MHz max

OUTPUT FREQUENCIES/TIMING INTERVALS

Function	Single Timer/Counter		Dual Timer/Counter (Cascaded)	
	Min	Max	Min	Max
Real-time Interrupt	1.63 µs	427.1 ms	3.26s	466.50 min
Programmable one-shot	1.63 µs	427.1 ms	3.26s	466.50 min
Rate generator	2.342 Hz	613.5 kHz	0.000036 Hz	306.8 kHz
Square-wave rate generator	2.342 Hz	613.5 kHz	0.000036 Hz	306.8 kHz
Software triggered strobe	1.63 µs	427.1 ms	3.26s	466.50 min
Hardware triggered strobe	1.63 µs	427.1 ms	3.26s	466.50 min
Event counter	—	2.46 MHz	—	—

Interfaces

MULTIBUS® — All signals TTL compatible
iSBX™ BUS — All signals TTL compatible
PARALLEL I/O — All signals TTL compatible
SERIAL I/O — RS232C compatible, configurable as a data set or data terminal
TIMER — All signals TTL compatible
INTERRUPT REQUESTS — All TTL compatible

Connectors

Interface	Double-Sided Pins	(in.)	Connectors
MULTIBUS® System	86	0.156	Viking 3KH43/9AMK12 Wire Wrap
iSBX™ Bus 8-Bit Data 16-Bit Data	36 44	0.1 0.1	Viking 000292-0001 000293-0001
Parallel I/O (2)	50	0.1	3M3415-000 Flat or TI H312125 Pins
Serial I/O	26	0.1	3M 3462-0001 Flat or AMP 88106-1 Flat

2-57

210219-003

iSBC® 86/35 Single Board Computer

Line Drivers and Terminators

I/O DRIVERS — The following line drivers are all compatible with the I/O driver sockets on the iSBC 86/05 board

Driver	Characteristic	Sink Current (mA)
7438	I,OC	48
7437	I	48
7432	NI	16
7426	I,OC	16
7409	NI,OC	16
7408	NI	16
7403	I,OC	16
7400	I	16

NOTE: I = inverting; NI = non-inverting; OC = open collector.

Port 1 of the 8255A has 20 mA totem-pole bi-directional drives and 1 kΩ terminators

I/O TERMINATORS — 220Ω/330Ω divider or 1 kΩ pullup

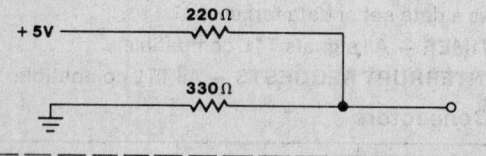

(OPTION 1) 220Ω/330Ω

(OPTION 2) 1 kΩ

MULTIBUS® Drivers

Function	Characteristic	Sink Current (mA)
Data	Tri-State	32
Address	Tri-State	32
Commands	Tri-State	32
Bus Control	Open Collector	20

Physical Characteristics

WIDTH — 12.00 in. (30.48 cm)
HEIGHT — 6.75 in. (17.15 cm)
DEPTH — 0.70 in. (1.78 cm)
WEIGHT — 14 oz. (388 gm)

Electrical Characteristics

DC POWER REQUIREMENTS

Configuration	Current Requirements (All Voltages ±5%)		
	+5V	+12V	−12V
Without EPROM[1]	5.1A	25 mA	23 mA
RAM only[2]	600 mA	—	—
With 32K EPROM[3] (using 2764)	5.6A	25 mA	23 mA
With 64K EPROM (using 27128)	5.7A	25 mA	23 mA
With 128K EPROM (using 27256)	5.8A	25 mA	23 mA

NOTES:
1. Does not include power for optional ROM/EPROM, I/O drivers, and I/O terminators.
2. RAM chips powered via auxiliary power bus in power-down mode.
3. Includes power required for 4 ROM/EPROM chips, and I/O terminators installed for 16 I/O lines; all terminator inputs low.

Environmental Characteristics

OPERATING TEMPERATURE — 0°C to 55°C @ 200 linear feet per minute (LFM) air velocity
RELATIVE HUMIDITY — to 90% (without condensation)

Reference Manual

146245-002 — iSBC 86/35 Hardware Reference Manual (NOT SUPPLIED)

Manuals may be ordered from any Intel sales representative, distributor office of from Intel Literature Department, 3065 Bowers Avenue, Santa Clara, California 95051.

iSBC® 86/35 Single Board Computer

ORDERING INFORMATION

Part Number	Description
SBC 86/35	Single Board Computer

iSBC® 88/25
SINGLE BOARD COMPUTER

- 8-bit 8088 Microprocessor operating at 5 MHz
- One megabyte addressing range
- Two iSBX™ bus connectors
- Optional Numeric Data Processor with iSBC® 337 MULTIMODULE™ Processor
- 4K bytes of static RAM; expandable on-board to 16K bytes
- Sockets for up to 64K bytes of JEDEC 24/28-pin standard memory devices; expandable on-board to 128K bytes
- Programmable synchronous/asynchronous RS232C compatible serial interface with software selectable baud rates
- 24 programmable parallel I/O lines
- Two programmable 16-bit BCD or binary timers/event counters
- 9 Levels of vectored interrupt control, expandable to 65 levels
- MULTIBUS® interface for multimaster configurations and system expansion
- Development support with Intel's iPDS, low cost Personal Development System, and EMV-88 Emulator

The iSBC 88/25 Single Board Computer is a member of Intel's complete line of OEM microcomputer systems which take full advantage of Intel's technology to provide economical, self-contained, computer-based solutions for OEM applications. The iSBC 88/25 board is a complete computer system on a single 6.75 × 12.00-in. printed circuit card. The CPU, system clock, read/write memory, nonvolatile read only memory, I/O ports and drivers, serial communications interface, priority interrupt logic and programmable timers, all reside on the board. The large control storage capacity makes the iSBC 88/25 board ideally suited for control-oriented applications such as process control, instrumentation, industrial automation, and many others.

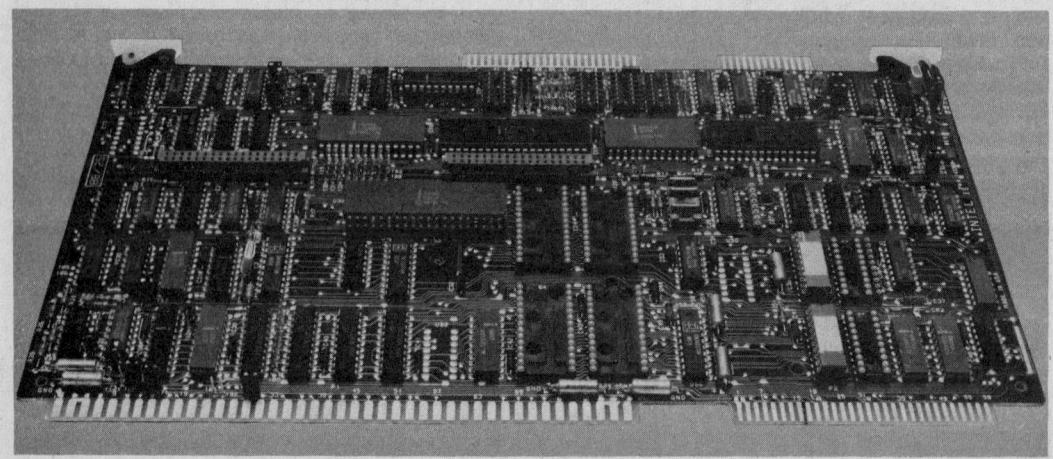

The following are trademarks of Intel Corporation and may be used only to describe Intel products: CREDIT, Index, Intel, Insite, Intellec, Library Manager, Megachassis, Micromap, MULTIBUS, PROMPT, UPI, μScope, Promware, MCS, ICE, iRMX, iSBC, iSBX, MULTIMODULE and iCS. Intel Corporation assumes no responsibility for the use of any circuitry other than circuitry embodied in an Intel product. No other circuit patent licenses are implied.
© INTEL CORPORATION, 1981

October, 1984
Order Number: 143847-002

iSBC® 88/25

FUNCTIONAL DESCRIPTION

Central Processing Unit

The central processor for the iSBC 88/25 board is Intel's 8088 CPU operating at 5 MHz. The CPU architecture includes four 16-bit byte addressable data registers, two 16-bit memory base pointer registers and two 16-bit index registers, all accessed by a total of 24 operand addressing modes for comprehensive memory addressing and for support of the data structures required for today's structured, high level languages, as well as assembly language.

Instruction Set

The 8088 instruction repertoire includes variable length instruction format (including double operand instructions), 8-bit and 16-bit signed and unsigned arithmetic operators for binary, BCD and unpacked ASCII data, and iterative word and byte string manipulation functions.

For enhanced numerics processing capability, the iSBC 337 MULTIMODULE Numeric Data Processor extends the architecture and data set. Over 60 numeric instructions offer arithmetic, trigonometric, transcendental, logarithmic and exponential instructions. Supported data types include 16, 32, and 64-bit integer, and 32 and 64-bit floating point, 18-digit packed BCD and 80-bit temporary.

Architectural Features

A 4-byte instruction queue provides pre-fetching of sequential instructions and can reduce the 750 nsec minimum instruction cycle to 250 nsec for queued instructions. The stack-oriented architecture readily supports modular programming by facilitating fast, simple, inter-module communication, and other programming constructs needed for asynchronous real-time systems. The memory expansion capabilities offer a 1 megabyte addressing range. The dynamic relocation scheme allows ease in segmentation of pure procedure and data for efficient memory utilization. Four segment registers (code, stack, data, extra) contain program loaded offset values which are used to map 16-bit addresses to 20-bit addresses. Each register maps 64K bytes at a time and activation of a specific register is controlled explicitly by program control and is also selected implicitly by specific functions and instructions. All Intel® languages support the extended memory capability, relieving the programmer of managing the megabyte memory space, yet allowing explicit control when necessary.

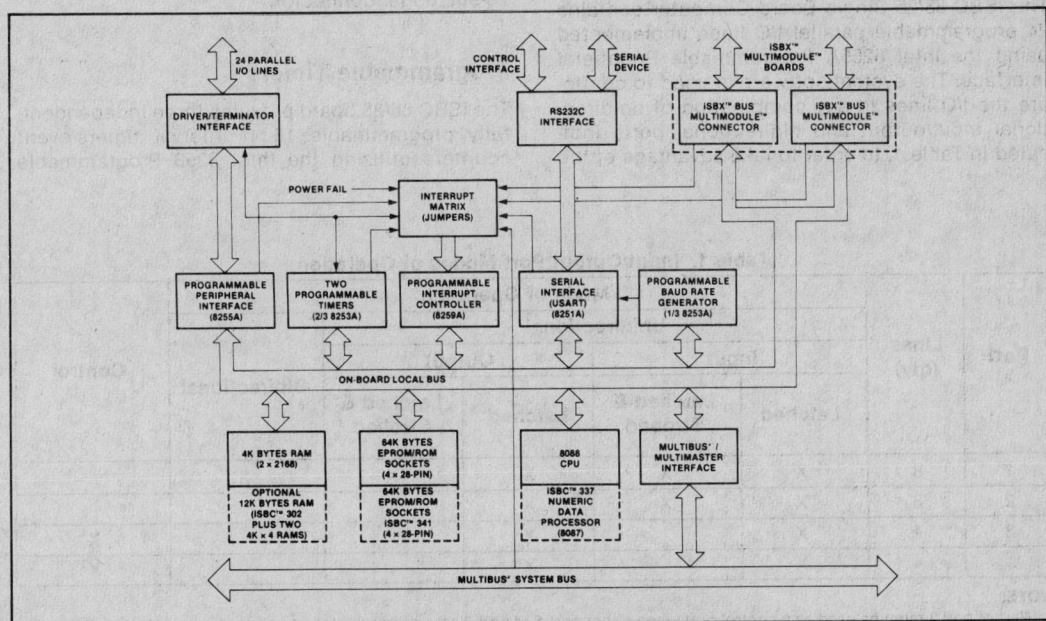

Figure 1. iSBC ® 88/25 Block Diagram

iSBC® 88/25

Memory Configuration

The iSBC 88/25 microcomputer contains 4K bytes of high-speed static RAM on-board. In addition, the on-board RAM may be expanded to 12K bytes via the iSBC 302 8K byte RAM module which mounts on the iSBC 88/25 board and then to 16K bytes by adding two 4K × 4 RAM devices in sockets on the iSBC 302 module. All on-board RAM is accessed by the 8088 CPU with no wait states, yielding a memory cycle time of 800 nsec.

In addition to the on-board RAM, the iSBC 88/25 board has four 28-pin sockets, configured to accept JEDEC 24/28-pin standard memory devices. Up to 64K bytes of EPROM are supported in 16K-byte increments with Intel 27128 EPROMs. The iSBC 88/25 board is also compatible with the 2716, 2732, and 2764 EPROMs allowing a capacity of 8K, 16K, and 32K bytes, respectively. Other JEDEC standard pinout devices are also supported, including byte-wide static and integrated RAMs.

With the addition of the iSBC 341 MULTIMODULE EPROM option, the on-board capacity for these devices is doubled, providing up to 128K bytes of EPROM capacity on-board.

Parallel I/O Interface

The iSBC 88/25 Single Board Computer contains 24 programmable parallel I/O lines implemented using the Intel 8255A Programmable Peripheral Interface. The system software is used to configure the I/O lines in any combination of unidirectional input/output and bidirectional ports indicated in Table 1. In order to take advantage of the large number of possible I/O configurations, sockets are provided for interchangeable I/O line drivers and terminators, allowing the selection of the appropriate combination of optional line drivers and terminators with the required drive/termination characteristics. The 24 programmable I/O lines and signal ground lines are brought out to a 50-pin edge connector.

Serial I/O

A programmable communications interface using the Intel 8251A Universal Synchronous/Asynchronous Receiver/Transmitter (USART) is contained on the iSBC 88/25 board. A software selectable baud rate generator provides the USART with all common communication frequencies. The mode of operation (i.e., synchronous or asynchronous), data format, control character format, parity, and baud rate are all under program control. The 8251A provides full duplex, double buffered transmit and receive capability. Parity, overrun, and framing error detection are all incorporated in the USART. The RS232C compatible interface on each board, in conjunction with the USART, provides a direct interface to RS232C compatible terminals, cassettes, and asynchronous and synchronous modems. The RS232C command lines, serial data lines and signal ground line are brought out to a 26-pin edge connector.

Programmable Timers

The iSBC 88/25 board provides three independent, fully programmable 16-bit interval timers/event counters utilizing the Intel 8253 Programmable

Table 1. Input/Output Port Modes of Operation

Port	Lines (qty)	Unidirectional				Bidirectional	Control
		Input		Output			
		Latched	Latched & Strobed	Latched	Latched & Strobed		
1	8	X	X	X	X	X	
2	8	X	X	X	X		
3	4	X		X			X[1]
	4	X		X			X[1]

NOTE:
1. Part of port 3 must be used as a control port when either port 1 or port 2 are used as a latched and strobed input or a latched and strobed output port or port 1 is used as a bidirectional port.

iSBC® 88/25

Interval Timer. Each counter is capable of operating in either BCD or binary modes. Two of these timers/counters are available to the systems designer to generate accurate time intervals under software control. Routing for the outputs and gate/trigger inputs of two of these counters is jumper selectable. The outputs may be independently routed to the 8259A Programmable Interrupt Controller and to the I/O terminators associated with the 8255A to allow external devices or an 8255A port to gate the timer or to count external events. The third interval timer in the 8253 provides the programmable baud rate generator for the iSBC 88/25 board RS232C USART serial port. The system software configures each timer independently to select the desired function. Seven functions are available as shown in Table 2. The contents of each counter may be read at any time during system operation.

Table 2. Programmable Timer Functions

Function	Operation
Interrupt on terminal count	When terminal count is reached, an interrupt request is generated. This function is extremely useful for generation of real-time clocks.
Programmable one-shot	Output goes low upon receipt of an external trigger edge or software command and returns high when terminal count is reached. This function is retriggerable.
Rate generator	Divide by N counter. The output will go low for one input clock cycle, and the period from one low going pulse to the next is N times the input clock period.
Square-wave rate generator	Output will remain high until one-half the count has been completed, and go low for the other half of the count.
Software triggered strobe	Output remains high until software loads count (N). N counts after count is loaded, output goes low for one input clock period.
Hardware triggered strobe	Output goes low for one clock period N counts after rising edge counter trigger input. The counter is retriggerable.
Event counter	On a jumper selectable basis, the clock input becomes an input from the external system. CPU may read the number of events occurring after the counter "window" has been enabled or an interrupt may be generated after N events occur in the system.

iSBX™ MULTIMODULE™ On-Board Expansion

Two 8-bit iSBX MULTIMODULE connectors are provided on the iSBC 88/25 microcomputer. Through these connectors, additional on-board I/O functions may be added. iSBX MULTIMODULES optimally support functions provided by VLSI peripheral components such as additional parallel and serial I/O, analog I/O, small mass storage device controllers (e.g., cassettes and floppy disks), and other custom interfaces to meet specific needs. By mounting directly on the single board computer, less interface logic, less power, simpler packaging, higher performance, and lower cost result when compared to other alternatives such as MULTIBUS form factor compatible boards. The iSBX connectors on the iSBC 88/25 provide all signals necessary to interface to the local on-board bus. A broad range of iSBX MULTIMODULE options are available in this family from Intel. Custom iSBX modules may also be designed for use on the iSBC 88/25 board. An iSBX bus interface specification and iSBX connectors are available from Intel.

MULTIBUS® SYSTEM BUS AND MULTIMASTER CAPABILITIES

Overview

The MULTIBUS system bus is Intel's industry standard microcomputer bus structure. Both 8 and 16-bit single board computers are supported on the MULTIBUS structure with 24 address and 16 data lines. In its simplest application, the MULTIBUS system bus allows expansion of functions already contained on a single board computer (e.g., memory and digital I/O). However, the MULTIBUS structure also allows very powerful distributed processing configurations with multiple processors and intelligent slave I/O, and peripheral boards capable of solving the most demanding microcomputer applications. The MULTIBUS system bus is supported with a broad array of board level products, LSI interface components, detailed published specifications and application notes.

Expansion Capabilities

Memory and I/O capacity may be expanded and additional functions added using Intel MULTIBUS compatible expansion boards. Memory may be expanded by adding user specified combinations of RAM boards, EPROM boards, or combination boards. Input/output capacity may be added with digital I/O and analog I/O expansion boards. Mass storage capability may be achieved by adding single or double density diskette controllers, or hard disk controllers. Modular expandable backplanes and cardcages are available to support multiboard systems.

Multimaster Capabilities

For those applications requiring additional processing capacity and the benefits of multiprocessing (i.e., several CPUs and/or controllers logically sharing system tasks through communication of the system bus), the iSBC 88/25 board provides full MULTIBUS arbitration control logic. This control logic allows up to three iSBC 88/25 boards or other bus masters, including iSBC 80 and iSBC 86 family MULTIBUS compatible single board computers to share the system bus using a serial (daisy chain) priority scheme and allows up to 16 masters to share the MULTIBUS system bus with an external parallel priority decoder. In addition to the multiprocessing configurations made possible with multimaster capability, it also provides a very efficient mechanism for all forms of DMA (Direct Memory Access) transfers.

Interrupt Capability

The iSBC 88/25 board provides 9 vectored interrupt levels. The highest level is the NMI (Non-Maskable Interrupt) line which is directly tied to the 8088 CPU. This interrupt is typically used for signaling catastrophic events (e.g., power failure). The Intel 8259A Programmable Interrupt Controller (PIC) provides control and vectoring for the next eight interrupt levels. As shown in Table 3, a selection of four priority processing modes is available for use in designing request processing configurations to match system requirements for efficient interrupt servicing with minimal latencies. Operating mode and priority assignments may be reconfigured dynamically via software at any time during system operation. The PIC accepts interrupt requests from all on-board I/O resources and from the MULTIBUS system bus. The PIC then resolves requests according to the selected mode and, if appropriate, issues an interrupt to the CPU. Any combination of interrupt levels may be masked via software, by storing a single byte in the interrupt mask register of the PIC. In systems requiring additional interrupt levels, slave 8259A PICs may be interfaced via the MULTIBUS system bus, to generate additional vector addresses, yielding a total of 65 unique interrupt levels.

Table 3. Programmable Interrupt Modes

Mode	Operation
Fully nested	Interrupt request line priorities fixed at 0 as highest, 7 as lowest.
Auto-rotating	Equal priority. Each level, after receiving service, becomes the lowest priority level until next interrupt occurs.
Specific priority	System software assigns lowest priority level. Priority of all other levels based in sequence numerically on this assignment.
Polled	System software examines priority-encoded system interrupt status via interrupt status register.

Interrupt Request Generation

Interrupt requests to be serviced by the iSBC 88/25 board may originate from 24 sources. Table 4 includes a list of devices and functions supported by interrupts. All interrupt signals are brought to the interrupt jumper matrix where any combination of interrupt sources may be strapped to the desired interrupt request level on the 8259A PIC or the NMI input to the CPU directly.

Power-Fail Control and Auxiliary Power

Control logic is also included to accept a power-fail interrupt in conjunction with the AC-low signal from the iSBC 635 and iSBC 640 Power Supply or equivalent, to initiate an orderly shut down of the system in the event of a power failure. Additionally, an active-low TTL compatible memory protect signal is brought out on the auxiliary connector which, when asserted, disables read/write access to RAM memory on the board. This input is provided for the protection of RAM contents during system power-down sequences. An auxiliary power bus is also provided to allow separate power to RAM for systems requiring battery back-up of read/write memory. Selection of this auxiliary RAM power bus is made via jumpers on the board.

System Development Capabilities

The development cycle of iSBC 88/25 products can be significantly reduced and simplified by using the Intellec Series Microcomputer Development Systems. The Assembler, Locating Linker, Library Manager, Text Editor and System Monitor

iSBC® 88/25

are all supported by the ISIS-II disk-based operating system. To facilitate conversion of 8080A/8085A assembly language programs to run on the iSBC 88/25 board, CONV-86 is available under the ISIS-II operating system. The iSBC 88/25 board is also supported by Intel's iPDS, Personal Development System. This system provides low cost development support while at the same time providing personal computer capability for the engineer.

IN-CIRCUIT EMULATOR

The ICE-88 In-Circuit Emulator provides the necessary link between the software development environment provided by the Intellec system and the "target" iSBC 88/25 execution system. In addition to providing the mechanism for loading executable code and data into the iSBC 88/25 board, the ICE-88 In-Circuit Emulator provides a sophisticated command set to assist in debugging software and final integration of the user hardware and software. The EMV-88 Emulator, designed for 8088-based product support on the iPDS, provides for a complete development solution at low cost.

PL/M-86

Intel's system's implementation language, PL/M-86, is also available as an Intellec Microcomputer Development System option. PL/M-86 provides the capability to program in algorithmic language and eliminates the need to manage register usage or allocate memory while still allowing explicit control of the system's resources when needed.

Run-Time Support

Intel also offers two run-time support packages; iRMX 88 Realtime Multitasking Executive and the iRMX 86 Operating System. iRMX 88 is a simple, highly configurable and efficient foundation for small, high performance applications. Its multitasking structure establishes a solid foundation for modular system design and provides task scheduling and management, intertask communication and synchronization, and interrupt servicing for a variety of peripheral devices. Other configurable options include terminal handlers, disk file system, debuggers and other utilities. iRMX 86 is a high functional operating system with a very rich set of features and options based on an object-oriented architecture. In addition to being modular and configurable, functions beyond the nucleus include a sophisticated file management and I/O system, and powerful human interface. Both packages are easily customized and extended by the user to match unique requirements.

Table 4. Interrupt Request Sources

Device	Function	Number of Interrupts
MULTIBUS interface	Requests from MULTIBUS resident peripherals or other CPU boards	8; may be expanded to 64 with slave 8259A PIC's on MULTIBUS boards
8255A Programmable Peripheral Interface	Signals input buffer full or output buffer empty; also BUS INTR OUT general purpose interrupt from driver/terminator sockets	3
8251A USART	Transmit buffer empty and receive buffer full	2
8253 Timers	Timer 0, 1 outputs; function determined by timer mode	2
iSBX connectors	Function determined by iSBX MULTIMODULE board	4 (2 per iSBX connector)
Bus fail safe timer	Indicates addressed MULTIBUS resident device has not responded to command within 6 msec	1
Power fail interrupt	Indicates AC power is not within tolerance	1
Power line clock	Source of 120 Hz signal from power supply	1
External interrupt	General purpose interrupt from parallel port J1 connector	1
iSBC 337 MULTIMODULE Numeric Data Processor	Indicates error or exception condition	1

iSBC® 88/25

SPECIFICATIONS

Word Size
INSTRUCTION — 8, 16, 24, or 32 bits
DATA — 8 bits

System Clock
5.00 MHz or 4.17 MHz ± 0.1% (jumper selectable)
NOTE: 4.17 MHz required with the optional iSBC 337 module.

Cycle Time
BASIC INSTRUCTION CYCLE
At 5 MHz — 1.2 µsec
— 400 nsec (assumes instruction in the queue)

NOTES: Basic instruction cycle is defined as the fastest instruction time (i.e., two clock cycles).

Memory Cycle Time
RAM — 800 nsec (no wait states)
EPROM — Jumper selectable from 800 nsec to 1400 nsec

Memory Capacity/Addressing
ON-BOARD EPROM

Device	Total Capacity	Address Range
2716	8K bytes	FE000-FFFFF$_H$
2732	16K bytes	FC000-FFFFF$_H$
2764	32K bytes	F8000-FFFFF$_H$
27128	64K bytes	F0000-FFFFF$_H$

WITH iSBC 341 MULTIMODULE EPROM

Device	Total Capacity	Address Range
2716	16K bytes	FC000-FFFFF$_H$
2732	32K bytes	F8000-FFFFF$_H$
2764	64K bytes	F0000-FFFFF$_H$
27128	128K bytes	E0000-FFFFF$_H$

NOTES: iSBC 88/25 EPROM sockets support JEDEC 24/28-pin standard EPROMs and RAMs (2 sockets); iSBC 341 sockets also support E^{2}PROMs.

ON-BOARD RAM
4K bytes — 0-0FFF$_H$

WITH iSBC 302 MULTIMODULE RAM
12K bytes — 0-2FFF$_H$

WITH iSBC 302 MULTIMODULE BOARD AND TWO 4K × 4 RAM CHIPS
16K bytes — 0-3FFF$_H$

I/O Capacity
PARALLEL — 24 programmable lines using one 8255A
SERIAL — 1 programmable line using one 8251A
iSBX MULTIMODULE — 2 iSBX MULTIMODULE boards

Serial Communications Characteristics
SYNCHRONOUS — 5-8 bit characters; internal or external character synchronization; automatic sync insertion

ASYNCHRONOUS — 5-8 bit characters; break character generation; 1, 1½, or 2 stop bits; false start bit detection

BAUD RATES

Frequency (kHz) (Software Selectable)	Baud Rate (Hz)	
	Synchronous	Asynchronous
		÷16 ÷64
153.6	—	9600 2400
76.8	—	4800 1200
38.4	38400	2400 600
19.2	19200	1200 300
9.6	9600	600 150
4.8	4800	300 75
2.4	2400	150 —
1.76	1760	110 —

NOTES:
Frequency selected by I/O write of appropriate 16-bit frequency factor to baud rate register (8253 Timer 2).

Timers
INPUT FREQUENCIES
Reference: 2.458 MHz ± 0.1% (406.9 nsec period, nominal); or 1.229 MHz ± 0.1% (813.8 nsec period, nominal); or 153.6 kHz ± 0.1% (6.510 µsec period, nominal)

NOTES:
Above frequencies are user selectable.

Event Rate: 2.46 MHz max

OUTPUT FREQUENCIES/TIMING INTERVALS

Function	Single Timer/Counter		Dual Timer/Counter (Two Timers Cascaded)	
	Min	Max	Min	Max
Real-time Interrupt	1.63 µs	427.1 ms	3.26s	466.50 min
Programmable one-shot	1.63 µs	427.1 ms	3.26s	466.50 min
Rate generator	2.342 Hz	613.5 kHz	0.000036 Hz	306.8 kHz
Square-wave rate generator	2.342 Hz	613.5 kHz	0.000036 Hz	306.8 kHz
Software triggered strobe	1.63 µs	427.1 ms	3.26s	466.50 min
Hardware triggered strobe	1.63 µs	427.1 ms	3.26s	466.50 min
Event counter	—	2.46 MHz	—	—

iSBC® 88/25

Interfaces

MULTIBUS — All signals TTL compatible
iSBX BUS — All signals TTL compatible
PARALLEL I/O — All signals TTL compatible
SERIAL I/O — RS232C compatible, configurable as a data set or data terminal
TIMER — All signals TTL compatible
INTERRUPT REQUESTS — All TTL compatible

Connectors

Interface	Double-Sided Pins (qty)	Centers (in.)	Mating Connectors
MULTIBUS System	86	0.156	Viking 3KH43/9AMK12 Wire Wrap
iSBX Bus 8-Bit Data	36	0.1	iSBX 960-5
Parallel I/O (2)	50	0.1	3M 3415-000 Flat or TI H312125 Pins
Serial I/O	26	0.1	3M 3462-0001 Flat or AMP 88106-1 Flat

Line Drivers and Terminators

I/O DRIVERS — The following line drivers are all compatible with the I/O driver sockets on the iSBC 88/25 board

Driver	Characteristic	Sink Current (mA)
7438	I,OC	48
7437	I	48
7432	NI	16
7426	I,OC	16
7409	NI,OC	16
7408	NI	16
7403	I,OC	16
7400	I	16

NOTES:
I = inverting; NI = non-inverting; OC = open collector.

Port 1 of the 8255A has 32 mA totem-pole bidirectional drivers and 10 kΩ terminators

I/O TERMINATORS — 220Ω/330Ω divider or 1 kΩ pullup

220Ω/330Ω Option 1.

1 kΩ Option 2.

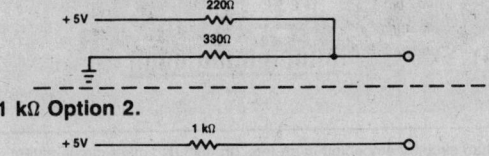

MULTIBUS Drivers

Function	Characteristic	Sink Current (mA)
Data	Tri-State	32
Address	Tri-State	24
Commands	Tri-State	32
Bus Control	Open Collector	20

Physical Characteristics

WIDTH — 12.00 in. (30.48 cm)
HEIGHT — 6.75 in. (17.15 cm)
DEPTH — 0.70 in. (1.78 cm)
WEIGHT — 14 oz (388 gm)

Electrical Characteristics

DC POWER REQUIREMENTS

Configuration	Current Requirements (All Voltages ±5%)		
	+5V	+12V	−12V
Without EPROM[1]	3.8A	25 mA	23 mA
RAM only[2]	104 mA		
With 8K EPROM[3] (using 2716)	4.3A	25 mA	23 mA
With 16K EPROM[3] (using 2732)	4.4A	25 mA	23 mA
With 32K EPROM[3] (using 2764)	4.4A	25 mA	23 mA

NOTES:
1. Does not include power for optional ROM/EPROM, I/O drivers, and I/O terminators.
2. RAM chips powered via auxiliary power bus in power-down mode. Does not include power for optional RAM.
3. Includes power required for 4 ROM/EPROM chips, and I/O terminators installed for 16 I/O lines; all terminator inputs low.

Environmental Characteristics

OPERATING TEMPERATURE — 0°C to 55°C
RELATIVE HUMIDITY — to 90% (without condensation)

Reference Manual

143825-001 — iSBC 88/25 Hardware Reference Manual (NOT SUPPLIED)

Manuals may be ordered from any Intel sales representative, distributor office or from Intel Literature Department, 3065 Bowers Avenue, Santa Clara, California 95051.

ORDERING INFORMATION

Part Number	Description
SBC 88/25	8-bit Single Board Computer with 4K bytes RAM

2-67

143847-002

iSBC® 88/40A
MEASUREMENT AND CONTROL COMPUTER

- High performance 4.8/6.67 MHz 8088 8-bit HMOS processor
- 12-bit kHz analog-to-digital converter with programmable gain control
- 16-bit differential/32 single-ended analog input channels
- Three iSBX™ MULTIMODULE™ connectors for analog, digital, and other I/O expansion
- 4K bytes static RAM, expandable via iSBC 301 MULTIMODULE RAM to 8K bytes (1K byte dual-ported)
- Four EPROM/E² PROM sockets for up to 64K bytes, expandable to 128K bytes with iSBC 341 expansion MULTIMODULE
- MULTIBUS® Intelligent Slave or Multimaster

The Intel iSBC 88/40A Measurement and Control Computer is a member of Intel's large family of Single Board Computers that takes full advantage of Intel's VLSI technology to provide an economical self-contained computer based solution for applications in the areas of process control and data acquisition. The on-board 8088 processor with its powerful instruction set allows users of the iSBC 88/40A board to update process loops as much as 5-10 times faster than previously possible with other 8-bit microprocessors. For example, the high performance iSBC 88/40A can concurrently process and update 16 control loops in less than 200 milliseconds using a traditional PID (Proportional-Integral-Derivative) control algorithm. The iSBC 88/40A board consists of a 16 differential/32 single ended channel analog multiplexer with input protected circuits, A/D converter, programmable central processing unit, dual port and private RAM, read only memory sockets, interrupt logic, 24 channels of parallel I/O, three programmable timers and MULTIBUS® control logic on a single 6.75 by 12.00-inch printed circuit card. The iSBC 88/40A board is capable of functioning by itself in a stand-alone system or as a multimaster or intelligent slave in a large MULTIBUS system.

Intel Corporation assumes no responsibility for the use of any circuitry other than circuitry embodied in an Intel product. No other circuit patent licenses are implied. Information contained herein supersedes previously published specifications on these devices from Intel.

iSBC® 88/40A BOARD

FUNCTIONAL DESCRIPTION

Three Modes of Operation
The iSBC 88/40A Measurement and Control Computer (MACC) is capable of operating in one of three modes: stand-alone controller, bus multimaster or intelligent slave. A block diagram of the iSBC 88/40A Measurement and Control Computer is shown in Figure 1.

Stand-Alone Controller
The iSBC 88/40A Measurement and Control Computer may function as a stand-alone single board controller with CPU, memory and I/O elements on a single board. The on-board 4K bytes of RAM and up to 64K bytes of read only memory, as well as the analog-to-digital converter and programmable parallel I/O lines allow significant control and monitoring capabilities from a single board.

Bus Multimaster
In this mode of operation the iSBC 88/40A board may interface and control a wide variety of iSBC memory and I/O boards or even with additional iSBC 88/40 boards or other single board computer masters or intelligent slaves.

Intelligent Slave
The iSBC 88/40A board can perform as an intelligent slave to any Intel 8 or 16-bit MULTIBUS master CPU by not only offloading the master of the analog data collection, but it can also do a significant amount of pre-processing and decision-making on its own. The distribution of processing tasks to intelligent slaves frees the system master to do other system functions. the Dual port RAM with flag bytes for signaling allows the iSBC 88/40A board to process and store data without MULTIBUS memory or bus contention.

Central Processing Unit
The central processor unit for the iSBC 88/40A board is a powerful 8-bit HMOS 8088 microprocessor. By moving on-board jumpers, the user can select either a 4.8 or 6.67 MHz CPU clock rate. The iSBC 88/40A board can also run at 8 MHz by changing the CPU clock oscillator to a 24 MHz unit. For 8 MHz operation, the iSBC 88/40A board should either be the only MULTIBUS master in the system or be an intelligent slave that never directly accesses the MULTIBUS interface.

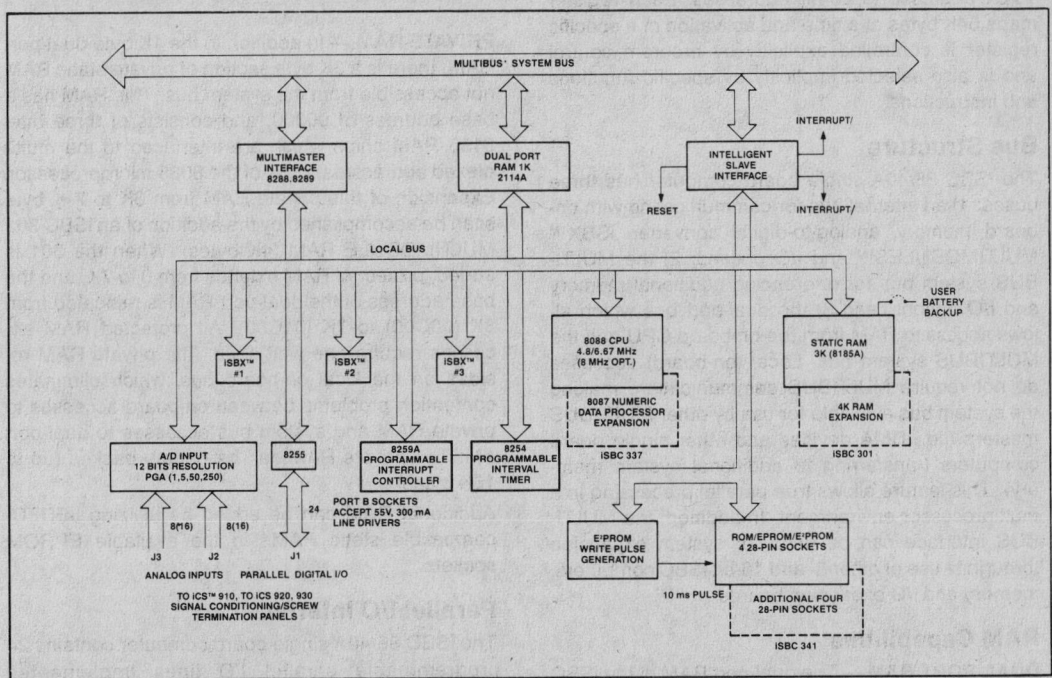

Figure 1. iSBC® 88/40A Measurement and Control Computer Block Diagram

iSBC® 88/40A BOARD

INSTRUCTION SET — The 8088 instruction repertoire includes variable length instruction format (including double operand instructions), 8-bit and 16-bit signed and unsigned arithmetic operators for binary, BCD and unpacked ASCII data, and iterative word and byte string manipulation functions. the instruction set of the 8088 is a superset of the 8080A/8085A family and with available software tools, programs written for the 8080A/8085A can be easily converted and run on the 8088 processor. Programs can also be run that are implemented on the 8088 with little or no modification.

ARCHITECTURAL FEATURES — A 4-byte instruction queue provides pre-fetching of sequential instructions and can reduce the 1.04 msec minimum instruction cycle to 417 nsec (at 4.8 MHz clock rate) for queued instructions. The stack oriented architecture facilitates nested subroutines and co-routines, reentrant code and powerful interrupt handling. The memory expansion capabilities offer a 1 megabyte addressing range. The capabilities offer a 1 megabyte addressing range. The dynamic relocation scheme allows ease in segmentation of pure procedure and data for efficient memory utilization. Four segment registers (code, stack, data, extra) contain program loaded offset values which are used to map 16-bit addresse to 20-bit addresses. Each register maps 64K bytes at a time and activation of a specific register is controlled explicitly by program control and is also selected implicitly by specific functions and instructions.

Bus Structure

The iSBC 88/40A single board computer has three buses: 1) an internal bus for communicating with on-board memory, analog-to-digital converter, iSBX™ MULTIMODULES™ and I/O options; 2) the MULTIBUS system bus for referencing additional memory and I/O options, and 3) the dual-port bus which allows access to RAM from the on-board CPU and the MULTIBUS system bus. Local (on-board) accesses do not require MULTIBUS communication, making the system bus available for use by other MULTIBUS masters (i.e., DMA devices and other single board computers transferring to additional system memory). This feature allows true parallel processing in a multiprocessor environment. In addition, the MULTIBUS interface can be used for system expansion through te use of other 8- and 16-bit iSBC computers, memory and I/O expansion boards.

RAM Capabilities

DUAL-PORT RAM — The dual-port RAM of the iSBC 88/40A board consists of 1K bytes of static RAM, implemented with Intel 2114A chips. The on-board base address of this RAM is 00C00 (3K) normally; it is relocated to 01C00 (7K) when the iSBC 301 MULTIMODULE RAM is added to the protected RAM. The MULTIBUS port base address of the dual-port RAM can be jumpered to any 1K byte boundaryin the 1M byte address space. The dual-port RAM can be accessed in a byte-wide fashion from the MULTIBUS system bus. When accessed from the MULTIBUS system bus, the dual-port RAM decode logic will generate INH1/ (Inhibit RAM) to allow dual-port RAM to overlay other system RAM. The dual-port control logic is designed to favor an on-board RAM access. If the dual-port is not currently performing a memory cycle for the MULTIBUS system port, only one wait state will be required. The on-board port may require more than one wait state if the dual-port RAM was busy when the on-board cycle was requested. The LOCK prefix facility of the iAPX 88/10 assembly language will disallow system bus accesses to the dual-port RAM. In addition, the on-board port to the dual-port RAM can be locked by other compatible MULTIBUS masters, which allows true symmetric semaphore operation. When the board is functioning in the master mode, the LOCK prefix will additionally disable other masters from obtaining the system bus.

PRIVATE RAM — In addition to the 1K byte dual-port RAM, there is a 3K byte section of private static RAM not accessible from the system bus. This RAM has a base address of 00000, and consists of three Intel 8185 RAM chips which are interfaced to the multiplexed address/data bus of the 8088 microprocessor. Expansion of this private RAM from 3K to 7 K byte scan be accomplished by the addition of an iSBC 301 MULTIMODULE RAM (4K bytes). When the 301 is added, protected RAM extends from 0 to 7K, and the base address of the dual-port RAM is relocated from 3K (00C00) to 7K (01C00). All protected RAM accesses require one wait state. The private RAM resides on the local on-board bus, which eliminates contention problems between on-board accesses to private RAM and system bus accesses to dual-port AM. The private RAM can be battery backed (up to 16K bytes).

Additional RAM can be added by utilizing JEDEC-compatible static RAMs in the available EPROM sockets.

Parallel I/O Interface

The iSBC 88/40A single board computer contains 24 programmable parallel I/O lines implemented using the Intel 8255A Programmable Peripheral In-

iSBC® 88/40A BOARD

terface. The system software is used to configure the I/O lines in any combination of unidirectional input/output and bidirectional ports indicated in Table 1. There the I/O interface may be customized to meet specific peripheral requirements. In order to take full advantage of the large number of possible I/O configurations, sockets are provided for interchangeable I/O line drivers and terminators. Port 2 can also accept TTL compatible peripheral drives, such as 75461/462, 75471/472, etc. These are open collector, high voltage drivers (up to 55 volts) which can sink 300 mA. Hence, the flexibility of the I/O interface is further enhanced by the capability of selecting the appropriate combination of optional line drivers and terminators to provide the required sink current, polarity, and drive/termination characteristics for each application. The 24 programmable I/O lines and signal ground lines are brought out to a 50-pin edge connector that mates with flat, woven, or round cable. This edge connector is also compatible with the Intel iCS™ 920 Digital I/O and iCS 930 AC Signal Conditioning/Termination Panels, for field wiring, optical isolation and high power (up to 3 amp) power drive.

EPROM Capabilities

Four (4) 28-pin sockets are provided for the use of Intel 2716s, 2732s, 2764s, 27128s, future JEDEC-compatible 128K and 256K bit EPROMs and their respective ROMs. When using 27128s the on-board EPROM capacity is 64K bytes. Read only memory expansion is available through the use of the iSBC 341 EPROM/ROM memory expansion MULTIMODULE. When the iSBC 341 is used an additional four (4) EPROM sockets are made available, for a total iSBC 88/40A board capacity of 128K bytes EPROM with Intel 27128s.

E²PROM Capabilities

The four 28-pin sockets can also accommodate Intel 2817A or 2816A E²PROMs, for dynamic storage of control loop setpoints, conversion parameters, or other data (or programs) that change periodically but must be kept in nonvolatile storage.

Timing Logic

The iSBC 88/40A board provides an 8254-2 Programmable Interval Timer, which contains three independent, programmable 16-bit timers/event counters. All three of these counters are available to generate time intervals or event counts under software control. The outputs of the three counters may be independently routed to the interrupt matrix. The inputs and outputs of timers 0 and 1 can be connected to parallel I/O lines on the J1 connector, where they replace 8255A port C lines. The third counter is also used for timing E²PROM write operations.

Interrupt Capability

The iSBC 88/40A board provides 9 vectored interrupt levels. The highest level is NMI (Nonmaskable Interrupt) line which is directly tied to the 8088 CPU. This interrupt cannot be inhibited by software and is typically used for signalling catastrophic events (i.e., power failure). On servicing this interrupt, program control will be implicitly transferred through location 00008_H. The Intel 8259A Programmable Interrupt Controller (PIC) provides vectoring for the next eight interrupt levels. As shown in Table 2, a selection of four priority processing modes is available to the designer to match system requirements. Operating

Table 1. Input/Output Port Modes of Operation

Port	Lines (qty)	Mode of Operation					Control
		Unidirectional				Bidirectional	
		Input		Output			
		Latched	Latched & Strobed	Latched	Latched & Strobed		
1	8	X	X	X	X	X	
2	8	X	X	X	X		
3	4	X		X			X[1]
	4	X		X			X[1]

NOTE:
1. Part of port 3 must be used as a control port when either port 1 or port 2 are used as a latched and strobed input or a latched and strobed output port or port 1 is used as a bidirectional port.

mode and priority assignments may be reconfigured dynamically via software at any time during system operation. The PCI accepts interrupt requests from the programmable parallel and/or iSBX interfaces, the programmable timers, the system bus, or directly from peripheral equipment. The PIC then determines which of the incoming requests is of the highest priority than the level currently being serviced, and, if appropriate, issues an interrupt to the CPU. Any combination of interrupt levels may be masked, via software, by storing a single byte in the interrupt make register of the PIC. The PIC generates a unique memory address for each interrupt level. These addresses are equally spaced at 4-byte intervals. This 32-byte lock may begin at any 32-byte boundary in the lowest 1K bytes of memory, and contains unique instruction pointers and code segment offset values (for expanded memory operation) for each interrupt level. After acknowledging an interrupt and obtaining advice identifier byte from the 8259A PIC, the CPU will store its status flags on the stack and execute an indirect CALL instruction through the vector location (derived from the device identifier) to the interrupt service routine.

*NOTE: The first 32 vector locations are reserved by Intel for dedicated vectors. Users who wish to maintain compatibility with present and future Intel products should not use these locations for user-defined vector addresses.

Table 2. Programmable Interrupt Modes

Mode	Operation
Fully nested	Interrupt request line priorities fixed at 0 as highest, 7 as lowest.
Auto-rotating	Equal priority. Each level, after receiving service, becomes the lowest priority level until next interrupt occurs.
Specific priority	System software assigns lowest priority level. Priority of all other levels based in sequence numerically on this assignment.
Polled	System software examines priority-encoded system interrupt status via interrupt status register.

INTERRUPT REQUEST GENERATION — Interrupt requests may originate from 26 sources. Two jumper selectable interrupt requests can be automatically generated by the programmable peripheral interface when a byte of information is ready to be transferred to the CPU (i.e., input buffer is full) or a byte of information has been transferred to a peripheral device (i.e., output buffer is empty). A jumper selectable request can be generated by each of the programmable timers. An additional interrupt request line may be jumpered directly from the parallel I/O driver terminator section. Eight prioritized interrupt request lines allow the iSBC 88/40A board to recognize and service interrupts originating from peripheral boards interfaced via the MULTIBUS system bus. The fail safe timer can be selected as an interrupt source. Also, interrupts are provided from the iSBX connectors (6), end-of-conversion, PFIN and from the power line clock.

Power-Fail Control

Control logic is also included to accept a power-fail interrupt in conjunction with the AC-low signal from the iSBC 635, iSBC 640, and iCS 645 Power Supply or equivalent.

iSBX™ MULTIMODULE™ Expansion Capabilities

Three iSBX MULTIMODULE connectors are provided on the iSBC 88/40A board. Up to three (3) single wide MULTIMODULE or one (1) double wide and one (1) single wide iSBX MULTIMODULE can be added to the iSBC 88/40A board. A wide variety of peripheral controllers, analog and digital expansion options are available. For more information on specific iSBX MULTIMODULES consult the Intel OEM Microcomputer System Configuration Guide.

Processing Expansion Capabilities

The addition of a iSBC 337 Multimodule Numeric Data Processor offers high performance integer and floating point math functions to users of the iSBC 88/40A board. The iSBC 337 incorporates the Intel 8087 and because of the MULTIMODULE implementation, it allows on-board expansion directly on the iSBC 88/40A board, eliminating the need for additional boards or floating point requirements.

MULTIBUS® Expansion

Memory and I/O capacity may be expanded further and additional functions added using Intel MULTIBUS compatible expansion boards. Memory may be expanded by adding user specified combinations of RAM boards, EPROM boards, or memory combination boards. Input/output capacity may be increased by adding digital I/O and analog I/O MULTIBUS expansion boards. Mass storage capability may be acheived by adding single or double density diskette controllers, or hard disk con-

iSBC® 88/40A BOARD

trollers either through the use of expansion boards and iSBX MULTIMODULES. Modular expandable backplanes and cardcages are available to support multiboard systems.

NOTE: Certain system restrictions may be incurred by the inclusion of some of the iSBC 80 family options in an iSBC 88/40 system. Consult the Intel OEM Microcomputer System Configuration Guide for specific data.

Analog Input Section

The analog section of the iSBC 88/40A board receives all control signals through the local bus to initiate channel selection, gain selection, sample and hold operation, and analog-to-digital conversion. See Figure 2.

INPUT CAPACITY — 32 separate analog signals may be randomly or sequentially sampled in single-ended mode with the 32 input multiplexers and a common ground. For noiser environments, differential input mode can be configured to achieve 16 separate differential signal inputs, or 32 pseudo differential inputs.

RESOLUTION — The analog section provides 12-bit resolution with a successive approximation analog-to-digital converter. For bipolar operation (−5 to +5 or −10 to +10 volts) it provides 11 bits plus sign.

SPEED — The A-to-D converter conversion speed is 50 µs (20 kHz samples per second). Combined with the programming interface, maximum throughput via the local bus and into memory will be 55 microseconds per sample, or 18 kHz samples per second, for a single channel, a random channel, or a sequential channel scan at a gain of 1, 5 ms at a gain of 5,250 ms at a gain of 50, and 20 ms at a gain of 250. A-to-D conversion is initiated via a programmed command from the 8088 central processor. Interrupt on end-of-conversion is a standard feature to ease programming and timing constraints.

ACCURACY — High quality components are used to achieve 12 bits resolution and accuracy of 0.035% full scale range ± ½ LSB at gain = 1. Offset is adjustable under program control to obtain a nominal ± 0.024% FSR ± ½ LSB accuracy at any fixed temperature between 0°C and 60°C (gain = 1). See specifications for other gain accuracies.

GAIN — To allow sampling of millivolt level signals such as strain gauges and thermocouples, gain is made configurable via user program commands up to 250× (20 millivolts full scale input range). User can select gain ranges of 1 (5V), 5 (1V), 50 (100 mV), 250 (20 mV) to match his application.

OPERATIONAL DESCRIPTION — The iSBC 88/40A single board computer addresses the analog-to-digital converter by executing IN or OUT instructions to the port address. Analog-to-digital conversions can be programmed in either of two modes: 1) start conversion and poll for end-of-conversion (EOC), or 2) start conversion and wait for interrupt at end of conversion. When the conversion is complete as signaled by one of the above techniques, INput instructions read two bytes (low and high bytes) containing the 12-bit data word as shown on the following page.

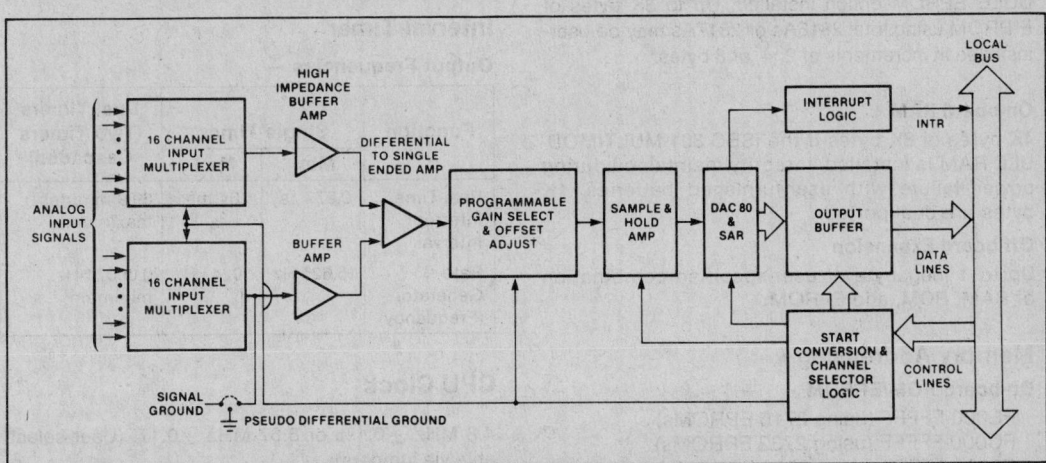

Figure 2. iSBC® 88/40 Analog Input Section

iSBC® 88/40A BOARD

Output Command — Select input channel and start conversion.

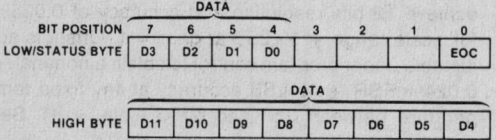

Input Data — Read converted data (low byte) or Read converted data (high byte).

BIT POSITION	7	6	5	4	3	2	1	0
LOW/STATUS BYTE	D3	D2	D1	D0				EOC

				DATA				
HIGH BYTE	D11	D10	D9	D8	D7	D6	D5	D4

Offset Correction — At higher gains ($\times 50$, $\times 250$) the voltage offset tempco in the A/D circuitry can sometimes cause unacceptable inaccuracies. To correct for this offset, one channel can be dedicated to be used as a reference standard. This channel can be read from the program to determine the amount of offset. The reading from this channel will then be subtracted from all other channel readings, in effect eliminating the offset tempco.

System Software Development

The development cycle of the iSBC 88/40 board may be significantly reduced using an Intel Intellec Microcomputer Development System and Intel's FORTRAN, PASCAL, or PL/M 86/88 Software packages.

SPECIFICATIONS

Word Size

Instruction — 8, 16, or 32 bits
Data — 8 bits

Instruction Cycle Time (minimum)

Instruction	8088 Clock Rate			Number of Clock Cycles
	4.8 MHz	6.67 MHz	8.0 MHz	
In Queue	417 ns	300 ns	250 ns	2
Not in Queue	1.04 μs	750 ns	625 ns	5

Memory Capacity

On-board ROM/EPROM/E²PROM

Up to 64K bytes; user installed in 2K, 4K, 8K or 16K byte increments or up to 128K if iSBC 341 MULTIMODULE EPROM option installed. Up to 8K bytes of E²PROM using Intel 2816As or 2817As may be user-installed in increments of 2, 4, or 8 bytes.

On-board RAM

4K bytes or 8K bytes if the iSBC 301 MULTIMODULE RAM is installed. Integrity maintained during power failure with user-furnished batteries. 1K bytes are dual-ported.

Off-board Expansion

Up to 1 megabyte of user-specified combination of RAM, ROM, and EPROM.

Memory Addressing

On-board ROM/EPROM
  FE000-FFFFF (using 2716 EPROMs)
  FC000-FFFFF (using 2732 EPROMs)
  F8000-FFFFF (using 2764 EPROMs)
  F0000-FFFFF (using 27128 EPROMs)

On-board ROM/EPROM (With iSBC 341 MULTIMODULE EPROM option installed)
  FC000-FFFFF (using 2716 EPROMs)
  F8000-FFFFF (using 2732 EPROMs)
  F0000-FFFFF (using 2764 EPROMs)
  E0000-FFFFF (using 27128 EPROMs)

On-board RAM (CPU Access)
  00000-00FFF
  00000-01FFF (if iSBC 301 MULTIMODULE RAM option installed)

On-board RAM

Jumpers allow 1K bytes of RAM to act as slave RAM for access by another bus master. Addressing may be set within any 1K boundary in the 1-megabyte system address space.

Slave RAM Access

Average; 350 nanoseconds

Interval Timer

Output Frequencies —

Function	Single Timer		Dual Timers (Two Timers Cascaded)
	Min.	Max.	
Real-Time Interrupt Interval	0.977 μs	64 ms	69.9 minutes maximum
Rate Generator (Frequency)	15.625 Hz	1024 kHz	0.00024 Hz minimum

CPU Clock

4.8 MHz $\pm 0.1\%$ or 6.67 MHz ± 0.17. (User selectable via jumpers);

8.0 MHz (with user installed 24 MHz oscillator)

iSBC® 88/40A BOARD

I/O Addressing
All communications to parallel I/O ports, iSBX bus, A/D port, timers, and interrupt controller are via read and write commands from the on-board 8088 CPU.

Interface Compatability
Parallel I/O — 24 programmable lines (8 lines per port); one port includes a bidirectional bus driver. IC sockets are included for user installation of line drivers and/or I/O terminators and/or peripheral drivers as required for interface ports.

iSBX Bus Connectors — Three iSBX bus connectors are provided. These connectors accept 8-bit iSBX MULTIMODULE boards. One set of the three iSBX MULTIMODULE connectors will accept a double wide iSBX MULTIMODULE board.

Interrupts
8088 CPU includes a non-maskable interrupt (NMI). NMI interrupt is provided for catastrophic events such as power failure. The on-board 8259A PIC provides 8-bit identifier of interrupting device to CPU. CPU multiplies identifier by four to derive vector address. Jumpers select interrupts from 26 sources without necessity of external hardware. PIC may be programmed to accommodate edge-sensitive or level-sensitive inputs.

Analog Input
16 differential (bipolar operation) or 32 single-ended (unipolar operation).
Full Scale Voltage Range — -5 to $+5$ volts (bipolar), 0 to $+5$ volts (unipolar).
NOTE: Ranges of 0 to 10V and ± 10V achievable with externally supplied ± 15V power.
Gain — Program selectable for gain of 1, 5, 50, or 250.
Resolution — 12 bits (11 bits plus sign for ± 5, ± 10 volts).
Accuracy — Including noise and dynamic errors

Gain	25°C
1	± .035% FSR*
5	± .06% FSR*
50	± .07% FSR*
250	± .12% FSR*

*NOTE: FSR = Full Scale Range ± ½ LSB. Figures are in percent of full scale reading. At any fixed temperature between 0°C and 60°C, the accuracy is adjustable to ± 0.05% of full scale.

Gain TC (at gain = 1) — 30 PPM (typical), 56 PPM (max) per degree centigrade, 40 PPM at other gains.

Offset TC — (in % of FSR/°C)	Gain	Offset TC (typical)
	1	0.0018%
	5	0.0036%
	50	0.024%
	250	0.12%

Sample and Hold-sample Time — 15 µs
Aperature-hold Aperature Time — 120 ns
Input Overvoltage Protection — 30 volts
Input Impedance — 20 megohms (min.)
Conversion Speed — 50 µs (max.) at gain = 1
Common Mode Rejection Ratio — 60 dB (min.)

Physical Characteristics
Width — 30.48 cm (12.00 in.)
Length — 17.15 cm (6.75 in.)
Height — 1.78 cm (0.7 in.)
2.82 cm (1.13 in.) with iSBC Memory Expansion, MULTIMODULES, iSBX Numeric Data Processor or iSBX MULTIMODULES.

Electrical Requirements
Power Requirements

Voltage	Current	
	Max.	Typ
+5v	5.5A	4A
+5v Aux	150 ma	100 ma
+12v	120 ma	80 ma
−12v	40 ma	30 ma

NOTES:
1. The current requirement includes one worst case (active-standby) EPROM current.
2. If +5V Aux is supplied by the iSBC 88/40A board, the total +5V current is the sum of the +5V and the +5V Aux.

Environmental Requirements
Operating Temperature — 0° to 60° with 6CFM min. air flow across board
Relative Humidity — to 90% without condensation

Equipment Supplied
iSBC 88/40A Measurement and Control Computer Schematic diagram

Reference Manuals
147049-001 — SBC 88/40A Measurement and Control Computer Hardware Reference Manual (Order Separately).

Manuals may be ordered from an Intel sales representative, distributor office or from Intel Literature Department, 3065 Bowers Avenue, Santa Clara, California 95051.

ORDERING INFORMATION

Part Number	Description
SBC 88/40A	Measurement and Control Computer

iSBC® 186/03A
SINGLE BOARD COMPUTER

- 8.0 MHz iAPX 80186 microprocessor with optional 8087 Numeric Data Processor.
- Eight (expandable to 12) JEDEC 28-pin sites
- Six programmable timers and 27 levels of vectored interrupt control
- MULTIBUS® interface for system expansion and multimaster configuration
- 24 programmable I/O lines configurable as a SCSI interface, Centronics interface or general purpose I/O
- Two iSBX™ bus interface connectors for low cost I/O expansion
- iLBX™ (Local Bus Extension) interface for high-speed memory expansion
- Two programmable serial interfaces; one RS 232C, the other RS 232C or RS 422 compatible

The iSBC 186/03A Single Board Computer is a member of Intel's complete line of microcomputer modules and systems that take advantage of Intel's VLSI technology to provide economical, off-the-shelf, computer-based solutions for OEM applications. The board is a complete microcomputer system on a 7.05 x 12.0 inch printed circuit card. The CPU, system clock, memory, sockets, I/O ports and drivers, serial communications interface, priority interrupt logic and programmable timers, all reside on the board.

The iSBC 186/03A board incorporates the iAPX 186 CPU and SCSI interface on one board. The extensive use of high integration VLSI has produced a high-performance single-board system. For large memory applications, the iLBX local bus expansion maintains this high performance.

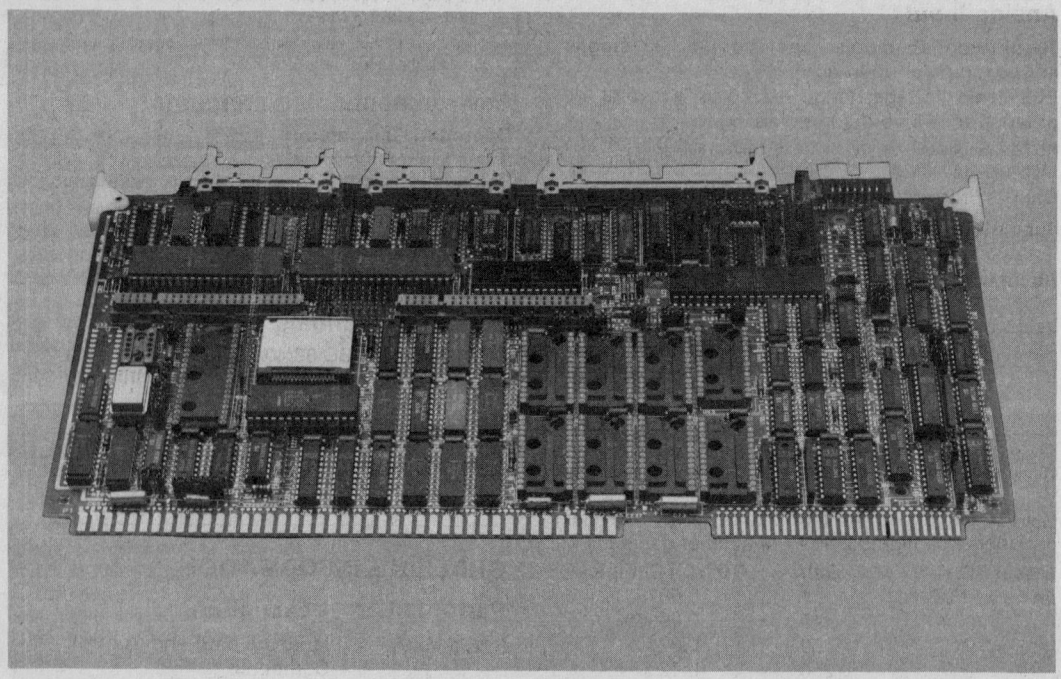

Intel Corporation assumes no responsibility for the use of any circuitry other than circuitry embodied in an Intel product. No other circuit patent licenses are implied. Information contained herein supersedes previously published specifications on these devices from Intel.

© INTEL CORPORATION, 1985   AUGUST, 1985   ORDER NUMBER: 230988-003

iSBC® 186/03A BOARD

OVERVIEW

Operating Environment

The iSBC 186/03A single board computer features have been designed to meet the needs of numerous microcomputer applications. Typical applications include:

- Multiprocessing single board computer
- BITBUS™ master controller
- Stand-alone single board system

MULTIPROCESSING SINGLE BOARD COMPUTER

High-performance systems often need to divide system functions among multiple processors. A multiprocessing single board computer distributes an applications processing load over multiple processors that communicate over a system bus. Since these applications use the system bus for inter-processor communication, it is required that each processor has local execution memory.

The iSBC 186/03A board supports loosely coupled multiprocessing (where each processor performs a specific function) through its MULTIBUS compatible architecture. The IEEE 796 system bus facilitates processor to processor communication, while the iLBX bus makes high-speed data and execution memory available to each CPU as shown in Figure 1. This architecture allows multiple processors to run in parallel enabling very high-performance applications.

BITBUS™ MASTER CONTROLLER

The BITBUS interconnect environment is a high performance low-cost microcontroller interconnect technology for distributed control of intelligent industrial machines such as robots and process controllers. The BITBUS interconnect is a special purpose serial bus which is ideally suited for the fast transmission of short messages between the microcontroller nodes in a modularly distributed system.

The iSBC 186/03A board can be implemented as the MULTIBUS-based master controller CPU which monitors, processes and updates the control status of the distributed system. The iSBX 344 board is used to interface the iSBC 186/03A board to the BITBUS interconnect. Actual message transfer over the iSBX bus can be accomplished by either software polling by the CPU or by using the on-chip 80186 DMA hardware instead of the CPU. Using DMA, the CPU is only required to start the DMA process and then poll for the completion of the message transfer, thus dramatically improving the data transmission rate and master control processor efficiency. The maximum transfer rates over the iSBX bus for the iSBC 186/03A board are about 900 messages/second in polled mode and 2500 messages/second in DMA mode. An 8 MHz iSBC 186/03A board in DMA mode is 3 times as fast as a typical 5 MHz iSBC 86/30 board running in polled mode. The iSBC 186/03A board in DMA mode provides the highest performance/price solution for BITBUS message transmission out of all of Intel's complete line of 16-bit CPU modules.

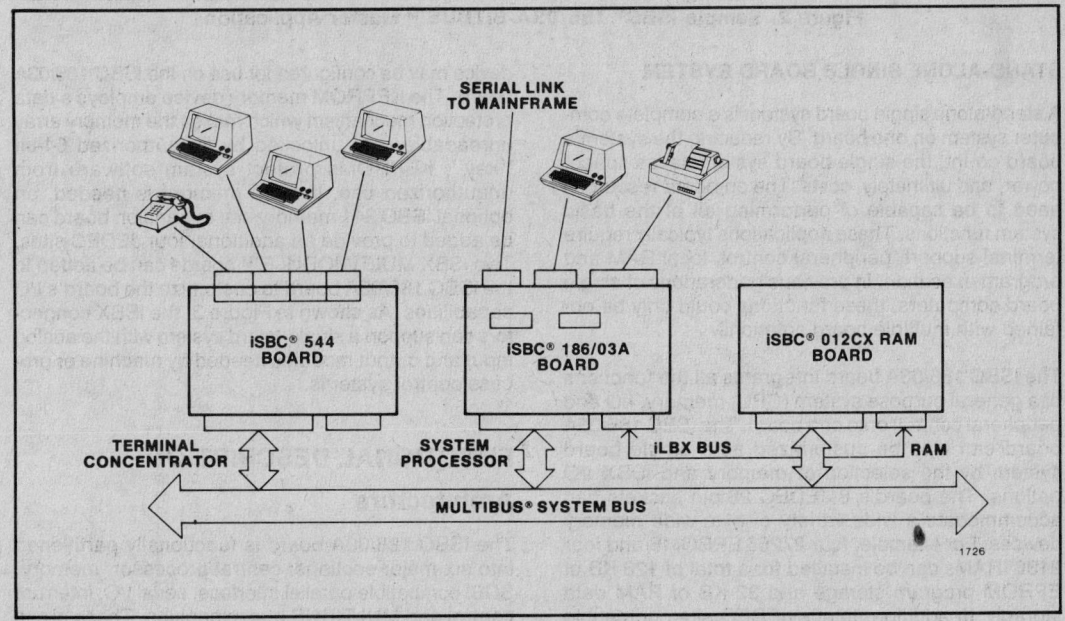

Figure 1. A Multiprocessing Single Board Computer Application

intel
iSBC® 186/03A BOARD

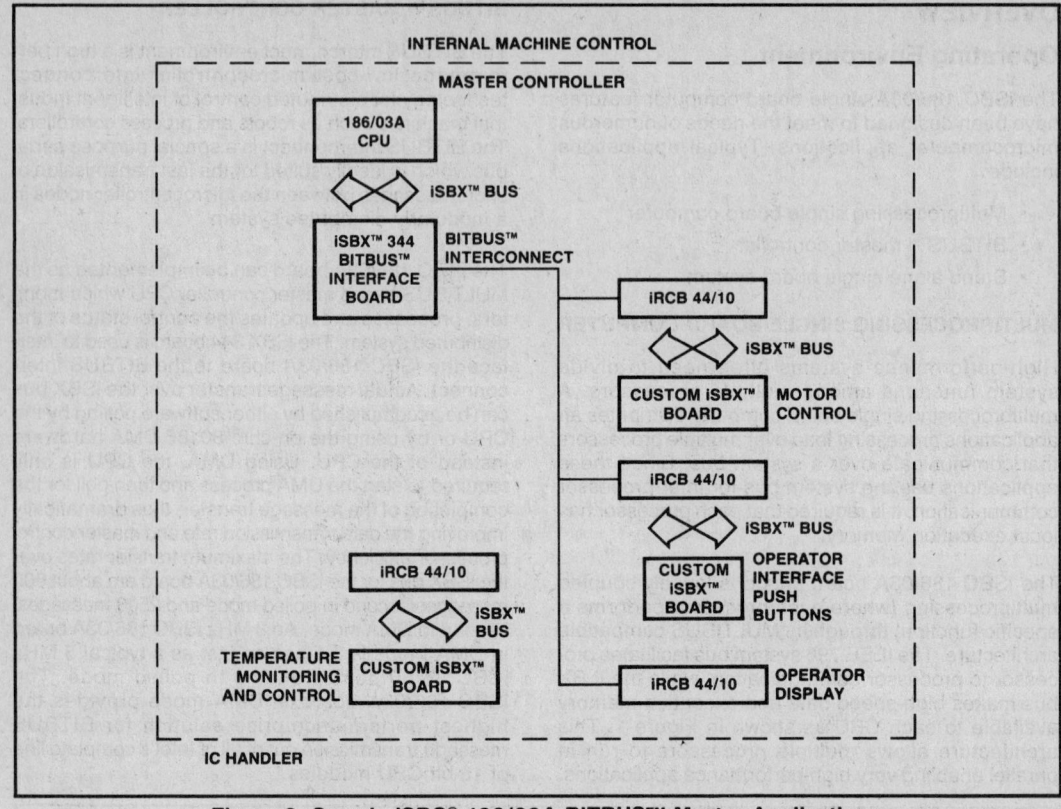

Figure 2. Sample iSBC® 186/03A BITBUS™ Master Application

STAND-ALONE SINGLE BOARD SYSTEM

A stand-alone single board system is a complete computer system on one board. By reducing the system's board count, the single board system saves space, power, and ultimately, costs. The on-board resources need to be capable of performing all of the basic system functions. These applications typically require terminal support, peripheral control, local RAM and program execution. In previous generations of single board computers, these functions could only be obtained with multiple board solutions.

The iSBC 186/03A board integrates all the functions of a general purpose system (CPU, memory, I/O and peripheral control) onto one board. The iSBC 186/03A board can also be customized as a single board system by the selection of memory and iSBX I/O options. The board's 8 JEDEC 28-pin sockets can accommodate a wide variety of byte-wide memory devices. For example, four 27256 EPROMS and four 2186 IRAMs can be installed for a total of 128 KB of EPROM program storage and 32 KB of RAM data storage. In addition, Intel's JEDEC site compatible 27916 KEPROM™ (Keyed Access EPROM) memory device may be configured for use on the iSBC 186/03A board. The KEPROM memory device employs a data protection mechanism which makes the memory array unreadable until unlocked by an authorized 64-bit "key". KEPROMs protect system software from unauthorized use. If more memory is needed, an optional iSBC 341 memory site expansion board can be added to provide an additional four JEDEC sites. Two iSBX MULTIMODULE™ boards can be added to the iSBC 186/03A board to customize the board's I/O capabilities. As shown in Figure 3, the iSBX connectors can support a single-board system with the analog input and output modules needed by machine or process control systems.

FUNCTIONAL DESCRIPTION
Architecture

The iSBC 186/03A board is functionally partitioned into six major sections: central processor, memory, SCSI compatible parallel interface, serial I/O, interrupt control and MULTIBUS bus expansion. These areas are illustrated in Figure 4.

iSBC® 186/03A BOARD

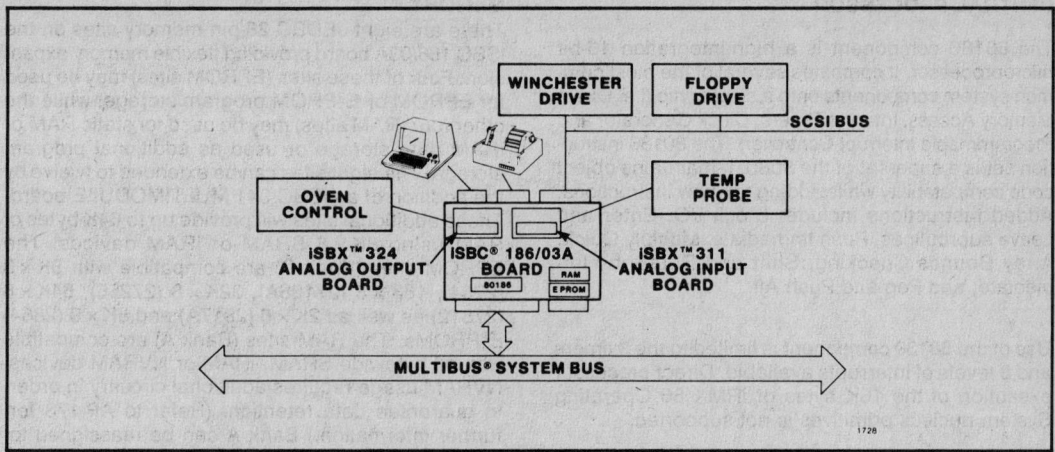

Figure 3. A Stand-alone Single Board System Application

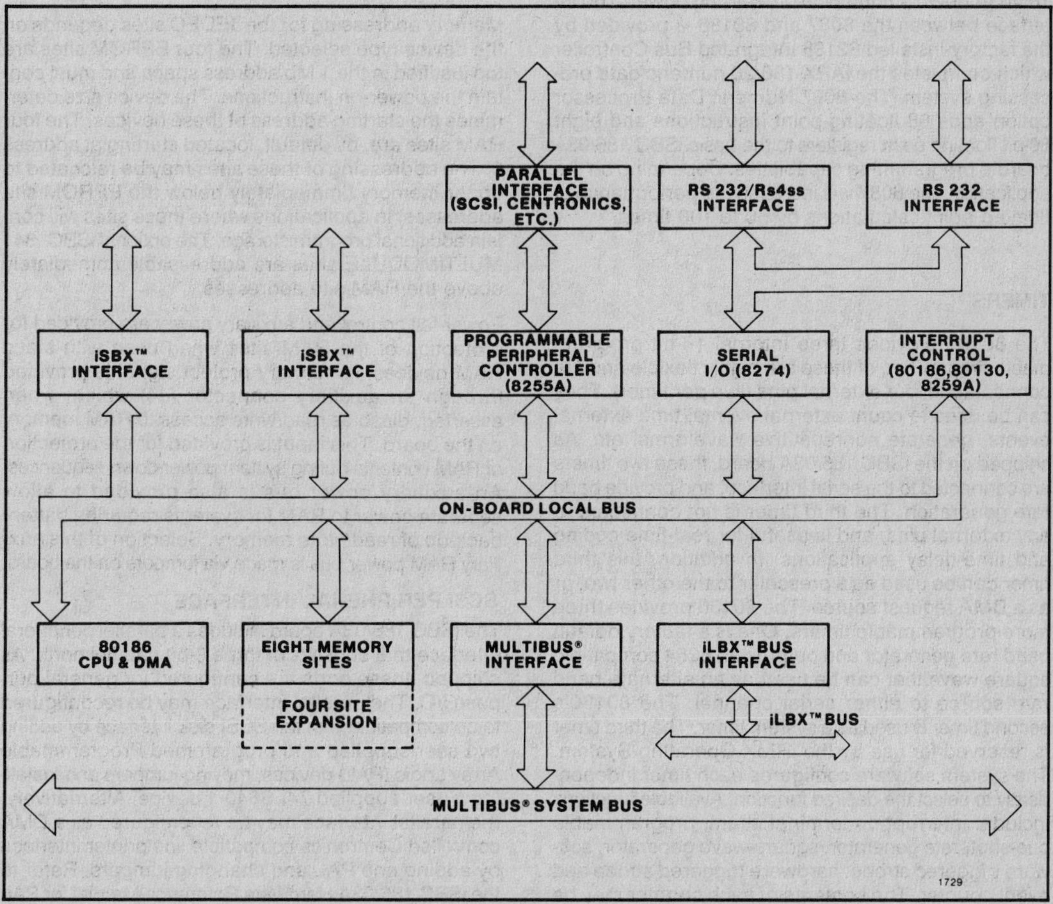

Figure 4. iSBC® 186/03A Board Block Diagram

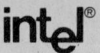

iSBC® 186/03A BOARD

CENTRAL PROCESSOR

The 80186 component is a high-integration 16-bit microprocessor. It combines several of the most common system components onto a single chip (i.e. Direct Memory Access, Interval Timers, Clock Generator and Programmable Interrupt Controller). The 80186 instruction set is a superset of the 8086. It maintains object code compatability while adding ten new instructions. Added instructions include: Block I/O, Enter and Leave subroutines, Push Immediate, Multiply Quick, Array Bounds Checking, Shift and Rotate by Immediate, and Pop and Push All.

Use of the 80130 component is limited to the 3 timers and 8 levels of interrupts available. Direct processor execution of the 16K bytes of iRMX 86 Operating System nucleus primitives is not supported.

An optional 8087 Numeric Data Processor may be installed by the user to dramatically improve the 186/03A board's numerical processing power. The interface between the 8087 and 80186 is provided by the factory-installed 82188 Integrated Bus Controller which completes the iAPX 186/20 numeric data processing system. The 8087 Numeric Data Processor option adds 68 floating-point instructions and eight 80-bit floating point registers to the basic iSBC 186/03A board's programming capabilities. Depending on the application, the 8087 will increase the performance of floating point calculations by 50 to 100 times.

TIMERS

The 80186 provides three internal 16-bit programmable timers. Two of these are highly flexible and are connected to four external pins (two per timer). They can be used to count external events, time external events, generate nonrepetitive waveforms, etc. As shipped on the iSBC 186/03A board, these two timers are connected to the serial interface, and provide baud rate generation. The third timer is not connected to any external pins, and is useful for real-time coding and time-delay applications. In addition, this third timer can be used as a prescaler to the other two, or as a DMA request source. The 80130 provides three more programmable timers. One is a factory default baud rate generator and outputs an 8254 compatible square wave that can be used as an alternate baud rate source to either serial channel. The 80130's second timer is used as a system timer. The third timer is reserved for use by the iRMX Operating System. The system software configures each timer independently to select the desired function. Available functions include: interrupt on terminal count, programmable one-shot, rate generator, square-wave generator, software triggered strobe, hardware triggered strobe and event counter. The contents of each counter may be read at any time during system operation.

MEMORY

There are eight JEDEC 28-pin memory sites on the iSBC 186/03A board providing flexible memory expansion. Four of these sites (EPROM sites) may be used for EPROM or E^2PROM program storage, while the other four (RAM sites) may be used for static RAM or iRAM data storage or used as additional program storage. The eight sites can be extended to twelve by the addition of an iSBC 341 MULTIMODULE board. These additional sites will provide up to 64K bytes of RAM using $8K \times 8$ SRAM or iRAM devices. The EPROM sites (Bank B) are compatible with $8K \times 8$ (2764), $16K \times 8$ (27128A), $32K \times 8$ (27256), $64K \times 8$ (27512) as well as $2K \times 8$ (2817A) and $8K \times 8$ (2864) E^2PROMs. The RAM sites (Bank A) are compatible with all bytewide SRAM, iRAM or NVRAM devices. NVRAM usage requires additional circuitry in order to guarantee data retention. (Refer to AP-173 for further information.) Bank A can be reassigned to upper memory just below the assigned memory space for Bank B to support additional EPROM or E^2PROMs.

Memory addressing for the JEDEC sites depends on the device type selected. The four EPROM sites are top justified in the 1 Mb address space and must contain the power-on instructions. The device size determines the starting address of these devices. The four RAM sites are, by default, located starting at address 0. The addressing of these sites may be relocated to upper memory (immediately below the EPROM site addresses) in applications where these sites will contain additional program storage. The optional iSBC 341 MULTIMODULE sites are addressable immediately above the RAM site addresses.

Power-fail control and auxiliary power are provided for protection of the RAM sites when used with static RAM devices. A memory protect signal is provided through an auxiliary connector (J4) which, when asserted, disables read/write access to RAM memory on the board. This input is provided for the protection of RAM contents during system power-down sequences. An auxiliary power bus is also provided to allow separate power to RAM for systems requiring battery back-up of read/write memory. Selection of this auxiliary RAM power bus is made via jumpers on the board.

SCSI PERIPHERAL INTERFACE

The iSBC 186/03A board includes a parallel peripheral interface that consists of three 8-bit parallel ports. As shipped, these ports are configured for general purpose I/O. The parallel interface may be reconfigured to be compatible with the SCSI disk interface by adding two user-supplied and programmed Programmable Array Logic (PAL) devices, moving jumpers and installing a user-supplied 74LS640-1 device. Alternatively, the parallel interface may be reconfigured as a DMA controlled Centronics compatible line printer interface by adding one PAL and changing jumpers. Refer to the iSBC 186/03A Hardware Reference Manual for PAL equations and a detailed implementation procedure.

iSBC® 186/03A BOARD

The SCSI (Small Computer Systems Interface) interface allows up to 8 mass storage peripherals such as Winchester disk drives, floppy disk drives and tape drives to be connected directly to the iSBC 186/03A board. Intel's iSBC 186/03A board utilizes a single initiator, single target implementation of the SCSI bus specification. Bus arbitration and deselect/reselect SCSI features are not supported. Single host, multiple target configurations can be used. However, the iSBC 186/03A board will stay connected to one target until the transaction is completed before switching to the second target. The iSBC 186/03A board's SCSI interface implements a 5 megabit/second transfer rate. A sample SCSI application is shown in Figure 5. Intel tested iSBC 186/03A board compatible SCSI controllers include Adaptek 4500, DTC 1410, Iomega Alpha 10, Shugart 1601 and 1610, Vermont Research 8103 and Xebec 1410.

The Centronics interface requires very little software overhead since a PAL device is used to provide neccesary handshake timing. Interrupts are generated for printer fault conditions and a DMA request is issued for every character. The interface supports Centronics type printers compatible with models 702 or 737.

SERIAL I/O

The iSBC 186/03A Single Board Computer contains two programmable communications interfaces using the Intel 8274 Multi-Protocol Serial Controller (MPSC). Two 80186 timer outputs are used as software selectable baud rate generators capable of supplying the serial channels with common communications frequencies. An 80130 baud rate timer may be jumpered to either serial port to provide higher frequency baud rates. The mode of operation (i.e., asynchronous, byte synchronous or bisynchronous protocols), data format, control character format, parity, and baud rate are all under program control. The 8274 provides full duplex, double buffered transmit and receive capability. Parity, overrun, and framing error detection are all incorporated in the MPSC. The iSBC 186/03A board supports operation in the polled, interrupt and DMA driven interfaces though jumper options. The default configuration is with channel A as RS422A/RS449, channel B as RS232C. Channel A can optionally be configured to support RS232C. Both channels are default configured as data set (DCE). Channel A can be reconfigured as data terminal (DTE) for connection to a modem-type device.

INTERRUPT CONTROL

The iSBC 186/03A board provides 27 on-board vectored interrupt levels to service interrupts generated from 33 possible sources.

The interrupts are serviced by four programmable interrupt controllers (PICs): one in the 80186 component, one in the 80130 component, one in the 8259A com-

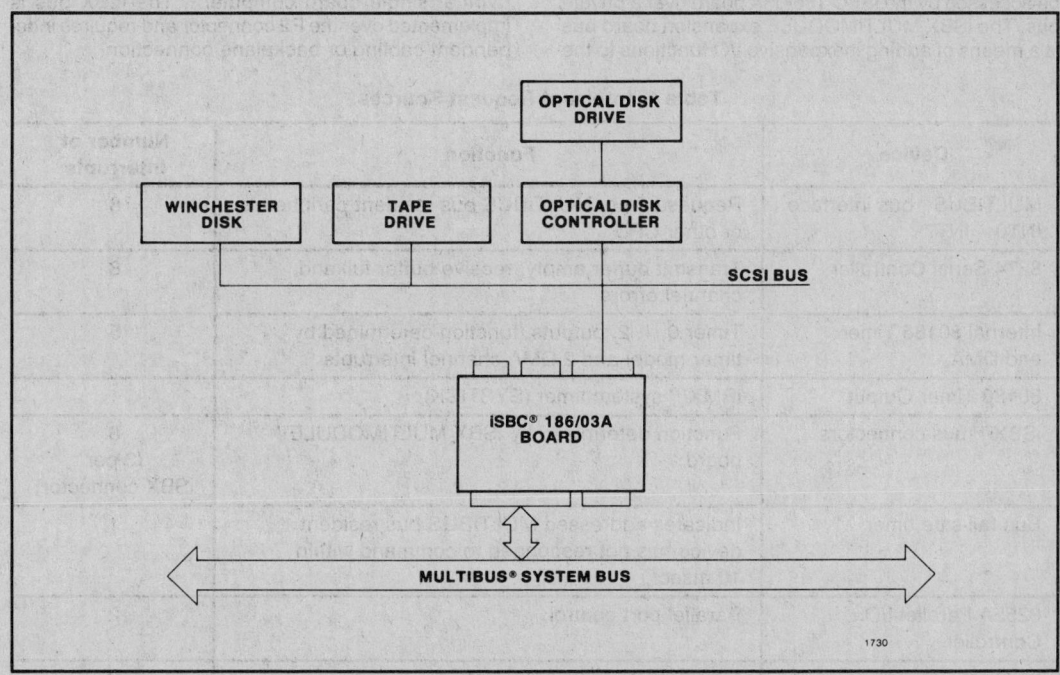

Figure 5. Sample SCSI Application

ponent and one in the 8274 component. The 80186, 8259A and 8274 PICs act as slaves to the 80130 master PIC. The highest priority interrupt is the Non-Maskable Interrupt (NMI) line which is tied directly to the 80186 CPU. This interrupt is typically used to signal catastrophic events (e.g. power failure). The PICs provide prioritization and vectoring for the other 26 interrupt requests from on-board I/O resources and from the MULTIBUS system bus. The PICs then resolve the requests according to the programmable priority resolution mode, and if appropriate, issue an interrupt to the CPU.

Table 1 contains a list of devices and functions capable of generating interrupts. These interrupt sources are jumper configurable to the desired interrupt request level.

Expansion

OVERVIEW

The iSBC 186/03A board architecture includes three bus structures: the MULTIBUS system bus, the iLBX local bus expansion and the iSBX MULTIMODULE expansion bus as shown in Figure 6. Each bus structure is optimized to satisfy particular system requirements. The system bus provides a basis for general system design including memory and I/O expansion as well as multiprocessing support. The iLBX bus allows large amounts of high performance memory to be accessed by the iSBC 186/03A board over a private bus. The iSBX MULTIMODULE expansion board bus is a means of adding inexpensive I/O functions to the iSBC 186/03A board. Each of these three bus structures are implemented on the iSBC 186/03A board providing a flexible system architecture solution.

MULTIBUS® SYSTEM BUS – IEEE 796

The MULTIBUS system bus is an industry standard (IEEE 796) microcomputer bus structure. Both 8- and 16-bit single board computers are supported on the IEEE 796 structure with 20 or 24 address and 16 data lines. In its simplest application, the system bus allows expansion of functions already contained on a single board computer (e.g., memory and I/O). However, the IEEE 796 bus also allows very powerful distributed processing configurations with multiple processors and intelligent slave, I/O and peripheral boards capable of solving the most demanding microcomputer applications. The MULTIBUS system bus is supported with a broad array of board-level products, LSI interface components, detailed published specifications and application notes.

iLBX™ BUS — LOCAL BUS EXTENSION

The iSBC 186/03A board provides a local bus extension (iLBX) interface. This standard extension allows on-board memory performance with physically off-board memory. The combination of a CPU board and iLBX memory boards is architecturally equivalent to a single board computer and thus can be called a "virtual single board computer". The iLBX bus is implemented over the P2 connector and requires independent cabling or backplane connection.

Table 1. Interrupt Request Sources

Device	Function	Number of Interrupts
MULTIBUS® bus interface INT0 – INT7	Requests from MULTIBUS bus resident peripherals or other CPU	8
8274 Serial Controller	Transmit buffer empty, receive buffer full and channel errors	8
Internal 80186 Timer and DMA	Timer 0, 1, 2, outputs (function determined by timer mode) and 2 DMA channel interrupts	5
80130 Timer Output	iRMX™ system timer (SYSTICK)	1
iSBX™ bus connectors	Function determined by iSBX MULTIMODULE™ board	6 (3 per iSBX connector)
Bus fail-safe timer	Indicates addressed MULTIBUS bus resident device has not responded to command within 10 msec	1
8255A Parallel I/O Controller	Parallel port control	2
J4 Connector	External/Power-fail interrupts	2

iSBC® 186/03A BOARD

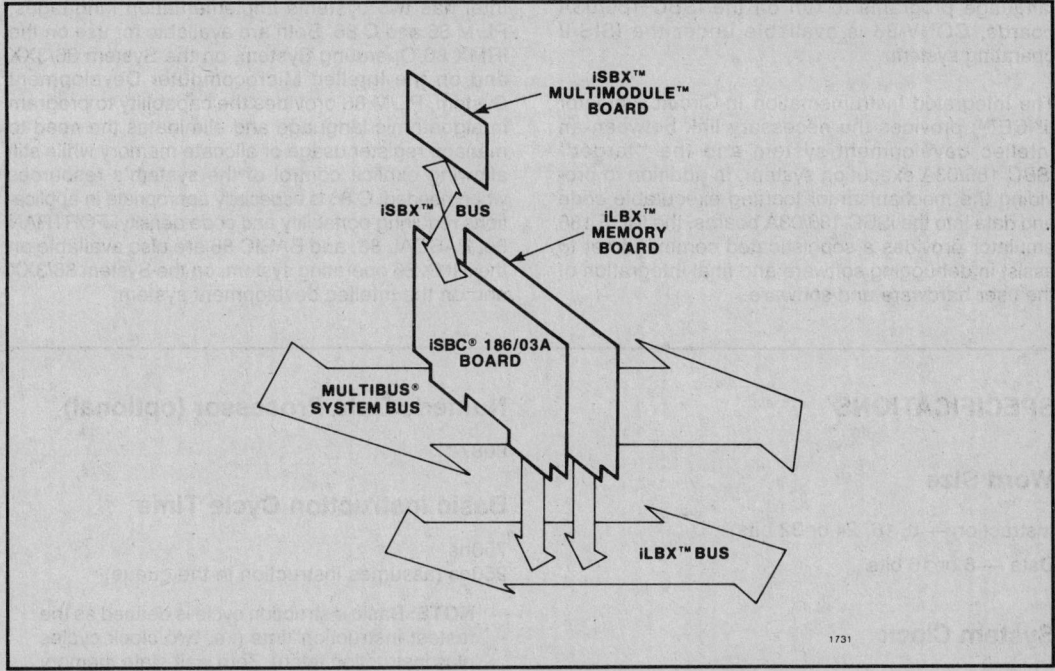

Figure 6. iSBC® 186/03A Board System Architecture

iSBX™ BUS MULTIMODULE™ ON-BOARD EXPANSION

Two iSBX MULTIMODULE board connectors are provided on the iSBC 186/03A microcomputer board. Through these connectors, additional on-board I/O functions may be added. iSBX MULTIMODULE boards optimally support functions provided by VLSI peripheral components such as additional parallel and serial I/O, analog I/O, and graphics control. The iSBX bus connectors on the iSBC 186/03A board provide all signals necessary to interface to the local on-board bus, including 16 data lines for maximum data transfer rates. MULTIMODULE boards designed with 8-bit data paths and using the 8-bit iSBX connector are also supported on the iSBC 186/03A board. A broad range of iSBX MULTIMODULE options are available from Intel. Custom iSBX bus modules may also be designed. An iSBX bus interface specification is available from Intel.

OPERATING SYSTEM SUPPORT

Intel's iRMX 86 Operating System is a highly functional operating system with a very rich set of features and options based on an object-oriented architecture. In addition to being modular and configurable, functions include a sophisticated file management and I/O system, and a powerful human interface. The iRMX 86 Release 6 Operating System can be used with the iSBC 186/03A board to generate application code for iRMX 86 based systems.

NOTE: Intel does not support the direct processor execution of the 16K bytes of the iRMX 86 Operating System nucleus primitives from the 80130 component.

DEVELOPMENT ENVIRONMENT

Intel offers numerous tools to aid in the development of iSBC 186/03A board applications. These include on-target development, full development systems, in-circuit emulators and programming languages. Some of the features of each are described below.

Using the iRMX 86 Release 6 Operating System, software development can be performed directly on the iSBC 186/03A board. This on-target development is the most economical way to develop iSBC 186/03A board based projects.

The development cycle of iSBC 186/03A board products can be significantly reduced and simplified by using either the System 86/3XX (iRMX 86-based) or the Intellec® Series Microcomputer Development Systems. The Assembler, Locating Linker, Library Manager, Text Editor and System Monitor are all supported by the ISIS-II disk-based operating system. To facilitate conversion of 8080A/8085A assembly

iSBC® 186/03A BOARD

language programs to run on the iSBC 186/03A boards, CONV-86 is available under the ISIS-II operating system.

The Integrated Instrumentation In-Circuit Emulator (I²ICE™) provides the necessary link between an Intellec development system and the "target" iSBC 186/03A execution system. In addition to providing the mechanism for loading executable code and data into the iSBC 186/03A boards, the I²ICE 186 emulator provides a sophisticated command set to assist in debugging software and final integration of the user hardware and software.

Intel has two systems implementation languages, PL/M 86 and C 86. Both are available for use on the iRMX 86 Operating System, on the System 86/3XX and on the Intellec Microcomputer Development System. PL/M 86 provides the capability to program in algorithmic language and eliminates the need to manage register usage or allocate memory while still allowing explicit control of the system's resources when needed. C 86 is especially appropriate in applications requiring portability and code density. FORTRAN 86, PASCAL 86, and BASIC 86 are also available on the iRMX 86 operating system, on the System 86/3XX and on the Intellec development system.

SPECIFICATIONS

Word Size

Instruction — 8, 16, 24 or 32 bits
Data — 8 or 16 bits

System Clock

8.0 MHz

Numeric Data Processor (optional)

8087-1

Basic Instruction Cycle Time

750ns
250ns (assumes instruction in the queue)

NOTE: Basic instruction cycle is defined as the fastest instruction time (i.e. two clock cycles plus instruction fetch). Zero wait-state memory is assumed.

MEMORY RESPONSE TIMES

Device Type	Max Access Time (from chip enable)	Min Cycle Time
EPROM Memory Sites		
0 wait states	245ns	318ns
1 wait state	370ns	443ns
RAM Memory Sites		
with SRAMs or EPROMS		
0 wait states	197ns	318ns
1 wait state	322ns	443ns
with 2186 IRAMs		
1 wait state	261ns	443ns
2 wait states	386ns	568ns

Note: The number of wait states inserted is jumper selected depending on memory device specifications.

iSBC® 186/03A BOARD

MEMORY CAPACITY/ADDRESSING

Four EPROM Sites

Device	Capacity	Address Range
2764 EPROM	32Kb	$F8000_H$—$FFFFF_H$
27128 EPROM	64Kb	$F0000_H$—$FFFFF_H$
27256 EPROM	128Kb	$E0000_H$—$FFFFF_H$
27512 EPROM	256Kb	$C0000_H$—$FFFFF_H$

Four RAM Sites

Device	Capacity	Address Range
2K SRAM	8Kb	0—$01FFF_H$
8K SRAM	32Kb	0—$07FFF_H$
32K SRAM	128Kb	0—$1FFFF_H$
2186 RAM	32Kb	0—$07FFF_H$
2817A E^{2}PROM	8Kb	$F0000_H$—$F7FFF_H$*
2764 EPROM	32Kb	$F0000_H$—$F7FFF_H$ (below EPROM sites)
27128 EPROM	64Kb	$E0000_H$—$EFFFF_H$ (below EPROM sites)
27256 EPROM	128Kb	$C0000_H$—$DFFFF_H$ (below EPROM sites)

Four iSBC® 341 Expansion Sites

Device	Capacity	Address Range
2K SRAM	8Kb	02000_H—$03FFF_H$
8K SRAM	32Kb	08000_H—$0FFFF_H$
32K SRAM	128Kb	10000_H—$1FFFF_H$
2186 RAM	32Kb	08000_H—$0FFFF_H$
2817A E^{2}PROM	8Kb	02000_H—$03FFF_H$**

NOTE: All on-board memory is local to the CPU (ie. not dual-ported)

*Must use 8K x 8 decode option, there are four copies of the E^{2}PROM in the 8K x 8 address area.

**(may be mixed with 2K x 8 SRAM)

Serial Communications Characteristics

Synchronous — 5-8 bit characters, internal or external character synchronization; automatic sync insertion; break character generation

Asynchronous — 5-8 bit characters; 1, ½, or 2 stop bit; false start bit detection.

Common Baud Rates

Using 80186 Timers:	Using 80130 Timer:
500K	750K
125K	500K
64K	125K
48K	64K
19.2K	48K
9600	19.2K
4800	9600
2400	4800
1200	2400
600	1200
300	600
150	300
110*	150
75*	110*
	75*

*Asynchronous use only

NOTE: Frequency selected by I/O write of appropriate 16-bit frequency factor to baud rate register of 80186 or 80130 timers.

Timer Input Frequency

80186 Reference: 2.0 MHz ± 0.1%
80130 Reference: 8.0 MHz ± 0.1%

Interface Compliance

MULTIBUS — IEEE 796 compliance: Master D16 M24 116 VO EL

iSBX Bus — Two 8/16 bit iSBX bus connectors allow use of up to 2 single-wide modules or 1 single-wide and 1 double-wide module. Intel iSBX bus compliance: D16/16 DMA

iLBX Bus — Intel iLBX bus compliance: PM D16

Serial I/O — Channel A: Configurable as RS 422A or RS 232C compatible, configurable as a data set or data terminal
Channel B: RS 232C compatable, configured as data set

Parallel I/O — SCSI (ANSI — X3T9, 2/82-s) compatible or Centronics 702 or 737 compatible (requires user supplied PALs and 74LS640-1)

iSBC® 186/03A BOARD

CONNECTORS

Interface	Double-sided Pins	Mating Connectors
MULTIBUS System	86 (P1)	Viking 3KH43/9AMK12 Wire Wrap
	60 (P2)	Viking 3KH30/9JNK
iSBX Bus 8-Bit Data	36	Viking 000292-0001
16-Bit Data	44	Viking 000293-0001
Serial I/O	26	3M 3452-0001 Flat AMP88106-1 Flat
iLBX Bus	60	Kelam RF30-2853-542
Parallel Interface	50	3M 3425-6000 3M 3425-6050 w/strain Ansley 609-5001M

PHYSICAL CHARACTERISTICS

Width — 12.00 in. (30.48 cm)

Length — 7.05 (17.90 cm)

Height — 0.50 in. (1.78 cm)

Weight — 13 ounces

ENVIRONMENTAL CHARACTERISTICS

Operating Temperature — 0°C to 60°C at 6 CFM airflow over the board.

Relative Humidity — to 90% (without condensation)

ELECTRICAL CHARACTERISTICS

The maximum power required per voltage is shown below. These numbers do not include the power required by the optional memory devices, SCSI PALs, battery back-up or expansion modules.

Voltage (volts)	Max. Current (amps)	Max Power (watts)
+5	5.4	27
+12	.04	.48
−12	.04	.48

ORDERING INFORMATION

Part Number   **Description**
SBC 186/03A   186-based single board computer

REFERENCE MANUAL

iSBC® 186/03A Single Board Computer Hardware Reference Manual — Order Number 148060

iSBC® 286/10A
SINGLE BOARD COMPUTER

- 8 MHz 80286 microprocessor
- Optional 80287 Numeric Data Processor
- iLBX™ interface for iLBX memory board expansion
- 0 wait-state synchronous interface to EX memory expansion boards
- Eight JEDEC 28-pin sites for optional SRAM/iRAM/EPROM/E²PROM components
- Optional expansion to sixteen JEDEC 28-pin sites with two iSBC® 341 boards
- Maximum on-board memory capacity 384 KB, expandable to 640 KB
- Two iSBX™ bus interface connectors for I/O expansion
- 16 levels of vectored interrupt control
- Centronics-compatible parallel I/O printer interface
- Two programmable multiprotocol synchronous/asynchronous serial interfaces; one RS232C, the other RS232C or RS422/449 compatible
- MULTIBUS® interface for multimaster configurations and system expansion

The iSBC® 286/10A Single Board Computer is a member of Intel's complete line of microcomputer modules and systems which take advantage of Intel's VLSI technology to provide economical, off-the-shelf, computer-based solutions for OEM applications. The board is a complete microcomputer system on a 6.75 x 12.0 inch printed circuit card. The CPU, system clock, memory sockets, I/O ports and drivers, serial communications interface, priority interrupt logic and programmable timers all reside on the board. The iSBC 286/10A board offers both a standard iLBX interface for high-speed memory access to Intel's series of iLBX memory boards and a new, 0 wait-state, synchronous interface for use with Intel's EX series of memory boards. The iSBC 286/10A Single Board Computer is fully compatible with its predecessor, the iSBC 286/10 board, and can be used in applications originally designed for the earlier model. In some cases, software timing loops may need to be adjusted to accommodate the faster CPU clock rate.

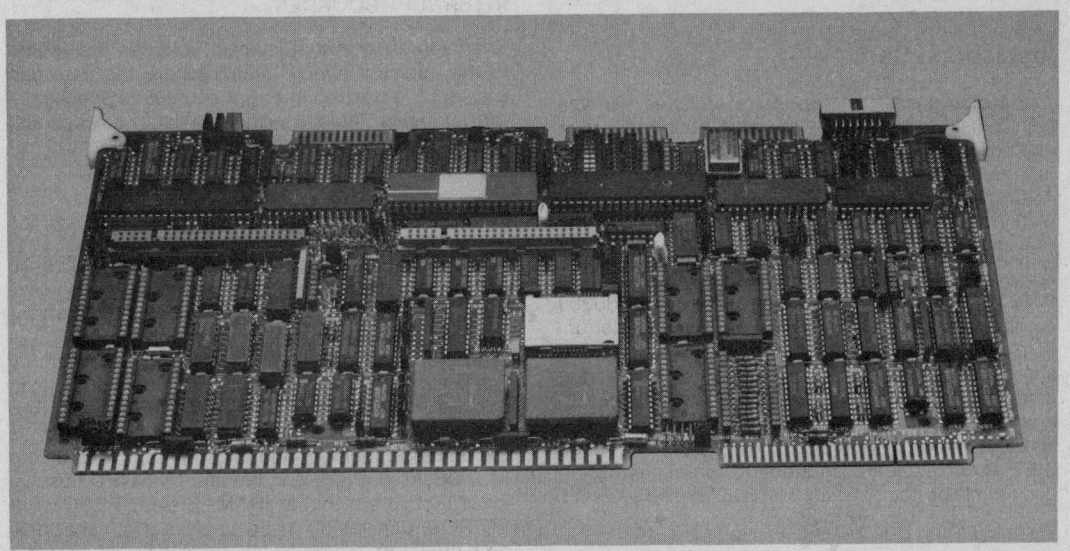

Intel Corporation assumes no responsibility for the use of any circuitry other than circuitry embodied in an Intel product. No other circuit patent licenses are implied. Information contained herein supersedes previously published specifications on these devices from Intel.

© Intel Corporation, 1985

MAY 1985
Order Number: 280079-003

iSBC® 286/10A Single Board Computer

FUNCTIONAL DESCRIPTION

Overview

The iSBC 286/10A board utilizes the powerful iAPX 286 CPU within the MULTIBUS® system architecture, enhanced by the industry standard iLBX bus and a new, 0 wait-state, synchronous memory interface, to provide a high performance 16-bit solution. This board also includes on-board interrupt, memory and I/O features facilitating a complete single board computer system. The iSBC 286/10A board is designed to be fully compatible with the iSBC 286/10 board, and only minor changes to software timing loops may be required.

Central Processing Unit

The central processor for the iSBC 286/10A board is the 80286 CPU operating at a 8.0 MHz clock rate. The 80286 CPU is upwardly compatible with Intel's iAPX 88 and iAPX 86 CPUs. The 80286 CPU runs iAPX 88 and 86 code at substantially higher speeds due to it's parallel chip architecture. In addition, the 80286 CPU provides on chip memory management and protection and virtual memory addressing of up to 1 gigabyte per task. Numeric processing power may be enhanced with the optional 80287 numerics processor. The clock rates for the 80286 and the 80287 are independent with the 80287 rate jumper selectable at either 5.3 or 8.0 MHz.

Instruction Set

The 80286 instruction repertoire includes variable length instruction format (including double operand instructions), 8-bit and 16-bit signed and unsigned arithmetic operators for binary, BCD and unpacked ASCII data, and iterative word and byte string manipulation functions.

For enhanced numerics processing capability, the 80287 Numeric Data Processor extends the 80286 architecture and data set. Over 60 numeric instructions offer arithmetic, trigonometric, transcendental, logarithmic and exponential instructions. Supported data types include 16-, 32-, and 64-bit integer, 32- and 64-bit floating point, 18-digit packed BCD and 80-bit temporary. The 80287 meets the proposed IEEE P754 standard for numeric data processing and maintains compatibility with 8087-based systems.

Architectural Features

The iAPX 86, 88, 186, and 286 microprocessor family contains the same basic set of registers, instructions, and addressing modes. The 80286 processor is upward compatible with the 8086, 8088, and 80186 CPUs.

The 80286 operates in two modes: iAPX 86 real address mode, and protected virtual address mode. In iAPX 86 real address mode, programs use real address with up to one megabyte of address space. Programs use virtual addresses in protected virtual address mode, also called protected mode. In protected mode, the 80286 CPU automatically maps 1 gigabyte of virtual addresses per task into a 16 megabyte real address space. This mode also provides memory protection to isolate the operating system and ensure privacy of each task's programs and data. Both modes provide the same base instruction set, registers, and addressing modes.

VECTORED INTERRUPT CONTROL

Incoming interrupts are handled by two on-board 8259A programmable interrupt controllers and by the 80286's NMI line. Interrupts originating from up to 16 sources are prioritized and then sent to the CPU as a vector address. Further interrupt capability is available through bus vectored interrupts where slave 8259 interrupt controllers are resident on separate iSBC boards and are then cascaded into the on-board interrupt control.

INTERRUPT SOURCES

Twenty-three potential interrupt sources are routed to the interrupt jumper matrix where the user can connect the desired interrupt sources to specific interrupt levels. Table 1 includes a list of devices and functions supported by interrupts.

MEMORY CAPABILITIES

There are a total of eight 28-pin JEDEC sites on board. Four sites are for local memory and can contain up to 256K bytes of EPROM devices. By replacing an address PAL component with a reprogrammed device (user supplied), local memory range can be expanded to 512 KB. Instructions to do this are included in the iSBC 286/10A Hardware Reference Manual. The four other sites are known as the dual-port memory and may be addressed by the MULTIBUS interface and the on-board CPU bus. Up to 128K bytes of either iRAM, SRAM, EPROM, or E^2PROM can reside in these sites. Both the local and dual-port memory can be expanded to eight sites by using two iSBC 341 JEDEC expansion modules. In this way, smaller size memory devices can be used up to the 512KB (local) and 128KB (dual-port) memory capacities.

iSBC® 286/10A Single Board Computer

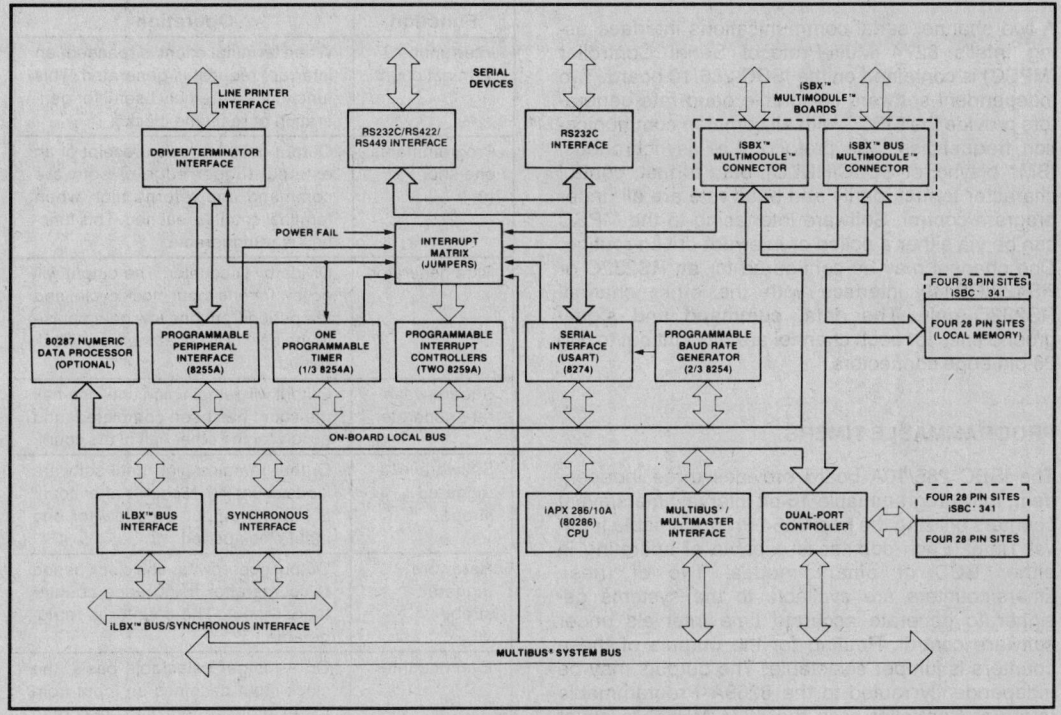

Figure 1. iSBC® 286/10A Block Diagram

Table 1. Interrupt Request Sources

Device	Function	Number of Interrupts
MULTIBUS® interface	Requests from MULTIBUS® resident peripherals or other CPU boards	8*
8259A programmable interrupt controller	8 level vectored interrupt request cascaded to master 8259A	1
8274 serial controller	8 level vectored interrupt request cascaded to master 8259A	1
8255A line printer interface	Signals output buffer empty	1
8254 timers	Timer 0, 1 outputs; function determined by timer mode	2
iSBX™ connectors	Function determined by iSBX™ MULTIMODULE™ board	4 (2 per iSBX™ connector)
Bus fail safe timer	Indicates addressed MULTIBUS® resident device has not responded to command within 6 msec	1
Power fail interrupt	Indicates AC power is not within tolerance	1
External interrupt	General purpose interrupt from auxiliary connector, commonly used as front panel interrupt	1
On-board logic	Conditioned interrupt source from edge sense latch, inverter, or OR gate	3

*May be expanded to 56 with slave 8259A PICs on MULTIBUS® boards

iSBC® 286/10A Single Board Computer

SERIAL I/O

A two channel serial communications interface using Intel's 8274 Multi-Protocol Serial Controller (MPSC) is contained on the iSBC 286/10 board. Two independent software selectable baud rate generators provide the MPSC with all common communication frequencies. The protocol (i.e. asynchronous, IBM* bisync, or SDLC/HDLC), data format, control character format, parity and baud rate are all under program control. Software interfacing to the MPSC can be via either a polled or interrupt driven routine. One channel may be configured for an RS232C or RS422/RS449 interface with the other channel RS232C only. The data, command and signal ground lines for each channel are brought out to two 26-pin edge connectors.

PROGRAMMABLE TIMERS

The iSBC 286/10A board provides three independent, fully programmable 16-bit interval timers/event counters utilizing the Intel 8254 Programmable Interval Timer. Each counter is capable of operating in either BCD or binary modes. Two of these timers/counters are available to the systems designer to generate accurate time intervals under software control. Routing for the outputs of these counters is jumper selectable. The outputs may be independently routed to the 8259A Programmable Interrupt Controller or to the 8274 MPSC to count external events or provide baud rate generation. The third interval timer in the 8254 is dedicated to providing a clock for the programmable baud rate generator in the iSBC 286/10A board's MPSC serial controller. The system software configures each timer independently to select the desired function. Seven functions are available as shown in Table 2. The contents of each counter may be read at any time during system operation.

LINE PRINTER INTERFACE

An 8255A Programmable Peripheral Interface (PPI) provides a line printer interface, several on-board functions, and four non-dedicated input bits. Drivers are provided for a complete Centronics compatible line printer interface. The on-baord functions implemented with the PPI are power fail sense, override, NMI mask, non-volatile RAM enable, clear timeout interrupt, LED 0 and 1, clear edge sense flop, MULTIBUS interrupt, and serial channel A loopback. The PPI's I/O lines are divided into three eight bit ports: A, B, and C. Four non-dedicated input bits allow the state of four user-configured jumper connections to be input. The PPI must be programmed for

*IBM is a registered trademark of International Business Machines

Table 2. Programmable Timer Functions

Function	Operation
Interrupt on terminal count	When terminal count is reached, an interrupt request is generated. This function is extremely useful for generation of real-time clocks.
Programmable one-shot	Output goes low upon receipt of an external trigger edge or software command and returns high when terminal count is reached. This function is retriggerable.
Rate generator	Divide by N counter. The output will go low for one input clock cycle, and the period from one low going pulse to the next is N times the input clock period.
Square-wave rate generator	Output will remain high until one-half the count has been completed, and go low for the other half of the count.
Software triggered strobe	Output remains high until software loads count (N). N counts after count is loaded, output goes low for one input clock period.
Hardware triggered strobe	Output goes low for one clock period N counts after rising edge counter trigger input. The counter is retrigerable.
Event counter	On a jumper selectable basis, the clock input becomes an input from the external system. CPU may read the number of events occurring after the counter "window" has been enabled or an interrupt may be generated after N events occur in the system.

mode 0 with ports A and C used as outputs and port B as input. A 16-bit write to Port B is used to set the iSBC 286/10A board into 24-bit address mode. The parallel port assignment is shown in Table 3.

MULTIBUS® SYSTEM ARCHITECTURE

Overview

The MULTIBUS system architecture includes three bus structures: the system bus, the local bus extension and the MULTIMODULE expansion bus as shown in Figure 2. Each bus structure is optimized to satisfy particular system requirements. The system bus provides a basis for general system design including memory and I/O expansion as well as multiprocessing support. The local bus extension allows large amounts of high performance memory to be accessed from a CPU board over a private bus. The MULTIMODULE extension bus is a means of adding inexpensive I/O functions to a base CPU

iSBC® 286/10A Single Board Computer

Table 3. Parallel Port Bit Assignment

Port A — Output	
Bit	Function
0	Line Printer Data Bit 0
1	Line Printer Data Bit 1
2	Line Printer Data Bit 2
3	Line Printer Data Bit 3
4	Line Printer Data Bit 4
5	Line Printer Data Bit 5
6	Line Printer Data Bit 6
7	Line Printer Data Bit 7
Port B — Input	
Bit	Function
0	General Purpose Input 0
1	General Purpose Input 1
2	General Purpose Input 2
3	General Purpose Input 3
4	Line Printer ACK/ (Active Low)
5	Power Fail Sense/ (Active Low)
6	Line Printer Error (Active Hi)
7	Line Printer Busy (Active Hi)
Port C — Output	
Bit	Function
0	Line Printer Data Strobe (Active Hi)
1	Override/ (Active Low)
2	NMI Mask (0 = NMI Enabled)
3	Non-Volatile RAM Enable; Clear Timeout Interrupt/
4	LED 0 (1 = On); Clear Edge Sense Flop/
5	MULTIBUS* Interrupt (1 = Active)
6	Serial CHA Loopback (0 = Online, 1 = Loopback)
7	LED 1 (1 = 0n); Clear Line Printer Ack Flop/

board. Each of these three bus structures are implemented on the iSBC 286/10A board providing a total system architecture solution.

SYSTEM BUS — IEEE 796

The MULTIBUS system bus is Intel's industry standard, IEEE 796, microcomputer bus structure. Both 8- and 16-bit single board computers are supported on the IEEE 796 structure with 24 address and 16 data lines. In its simplest application, the system bus allows expansion of functions already contained on a single board computer (e.g., memory and digital I/O). However, the IEEE 796 bus also allows very powerful distributed processing configurations using multiple processors, I/O boards, and peripheral boards. The MULTIBUS system bus is supported with a broad array of board level products. VLSI interface components, detailed published specifications and application notes.

SYSTEM BUS — EXPANSION CAPABILITIES

Memory and I/O capacity may be expanded and additional functions added using Intel MULTIBUS compatible expansion boards. Memory may be expanded by adding user specified combinations of RAM boards, EPROM boards, bubble memory boards, or combination boards. Input/output capacity may be added with digital I/O and analog I/O expansion boards. Mass storage capability may be achieved by adding single or double density diskette controllers, or hard disk controllers. Modular expandable backplanes and cardcages are available to support multiboard systems.

SYSTEM BUS — MULTIMASTER CAPABILITIES

For those applications requiring additional processing capacity and the benefits of multiprocessing (i.e., several CPUs and/or controllers logically sharing system tasks through communication of the system bus), the iSBC 286/10A board provides full system bus arbitration control logic. This control logic allows up to three iSBC 286/10A board or other bus masters, including the iSBC 80 board family of MULTIBUS compatible 8-bit single board computers to share the system bus using a serial (daisy chain) priority scheme and allows up to 16 masters to share the MULTIBUS system bus with an external parallel priority decoder. In addition to multiprocessing configuration made possible with multimaster capability, it also provides a very efficient mechanism for all forms of DMA (Direct Memory Access) transfers.

HIGH SPEED OFF-BOARD MEMORY

The iSBC 286/10A board can access off-board memory either over the MULTIBUS (P1) interface, or over the P2 interface as shown in figure 3. Memory transfers over the P2 interface are faster because the CPU board doesn't have to contend for access to the MULTIBUS interface.

Using the P2 interface, the iSBC 286/10A board can be configured to operate with either a standard iLBX interface or with a high-performance, synchronous interface.

The iSBC 286/10A board as supplied is configured to operate with an iLBX interface, and is compatible with Intel's CX series of memory expansion boards interface which are available in sizes ranging from 512 K bytes up to 2 M bytes. Memory expansion

iSBC® 286/10A Single Board Computer

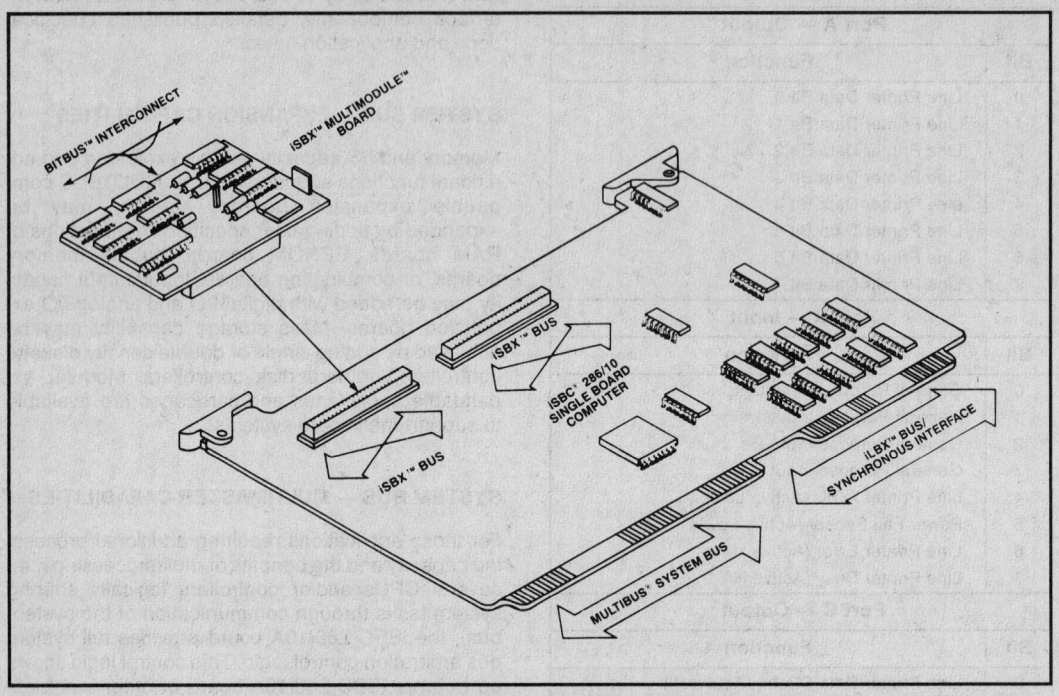

Figure 2. MULTIBUS® System Architecture

boards from other manufacturers that meet the iLBX bus standard may also be used. CPU to memory access time is usually 1 or more wait-states depending on the speed of the memory used.

By moving several jumpers on the board, the iSBC 286/10A single board computer may be reconfigured for a synchronous, P2 interface. This high-performance interface is designed to connect to Intel's new EX series of memory expansion boards to yield a CPU to memory access time of 0 wait-states for all types of memory accesses. The EX memory expansion boards are available in sizes ranging from 512 K bytes up to 4 M bytes.

A total of four memory board can be placed on the iLBX or synchronous interface bus. With 4 M byte memory boards, this results in a total of 16 M bytes on the memory expansion bus.

iSBX™ BUS MULTIMODULE™ ON-BOARD EXPANSION

Two 8/16-bit iSBX™ MULTIMODULE connectors are provided on the iSBC 286/10A microcomputer board. Through these connectors, additional on-board I/O functions may be added. iSBX MULTIMODULEs optimally support functions provided by VLSI peripheral components such as additional parallel and serial I/O, analog I/O, small mass storage device controllers (e.g., bubble cassettes and floppy disks), and other custom interfaces to meet specific needs. By mounting directly on the single board computer, less interface logic, less power, simpler packaging, higher performance, and lower cost result when compared to other alternatives such as MULTIBUS Board form factor compatible boards. The iSBX interface connectors on the iSBC 286/10A provide all signals necessary to interface to the local on-board bus, including 16 data lines for maximum data transfer rates. iSBX MULTIMODULE boards designed with 8-bit data paths and using the 8-bit iSBX connector are also supported on the iSBC 286/10A microcomputer board. A broad range of iSBX MULTIMODULE options are available from Intel. Custom iSBX modules may also be designed. An iSBX bus interface specification and iSBX connectors are available from Intel.

Software Support

Software support from Intel includes the iRMX 86, iRMX 286, and XENIX* operating systems, assem-

*XENIX is a trademark of MICROSOFT Inc.

iSBC® 286/10A Single Board Computer

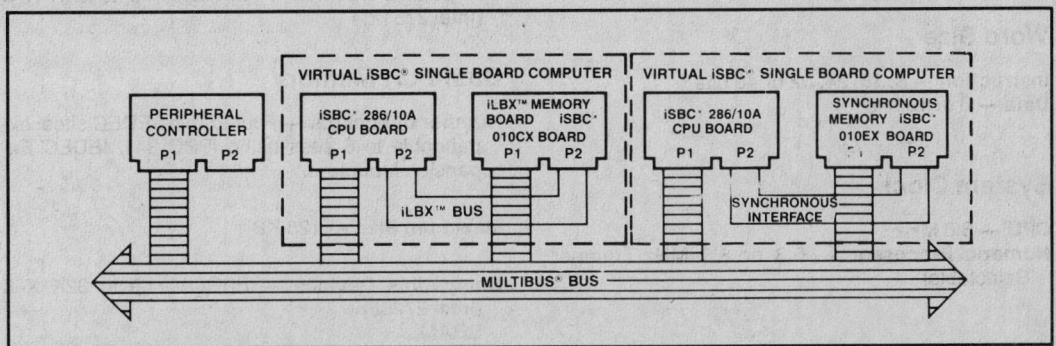

Figure 3. MULTIBUS® /iLBX™/Synchronous Interface Configurations

bly and high level languages, development ststems, in-circuit emulators, and various other hardware and software tools.

For those applications needing a real-time, multitasking operating system, Intel offers the iRMX 86 Release 6 and iRMX 286 Release 1 operating systems. The iRMX operating systems are particularly well suited for industrial or commercial applications where the processor is simultaneously controlling multiple, real-time, interrupt intensive processes. Typical applications include machine and process control, data aquisition, signal processing, front-end processing, and digital PABX control. The iRMX operating systems employ a highly configurable, modular structure that allows easy system configuration and expansion.

The iRMX 86 Release 6 operating system enables the iSBC 286/10A board to address up to 1MB of memory in real address mode. Using the iRMX 286 operating system, this address range is extended to 16MB in native mode. The iRMX 286 operating system also allows the user to take advantage of the hardware traps built into the iAPX 286 processor that provide expanded debug capabilities and increased code reliability.

Applications software written for earlier releases of the iRMX 86 Operating System is upwardly compatible through Release 6. Furthermore, application code written for the iRMX 86 operating system can be compiled using 286 compilers to run under the iRMX 286 operating system. Application code will require only minor changes.

Assembly and many high level languages are supported by the iRMX operating systems and Intellec® Series III and Series IV development systems. Language support for the iSBC 286/10A board in real address board includes Intel's ASM 86, PL/M 86, PASCAL 86, FORTRAN 86, and C86, as well as many third party 8086 languages. Language support for native address mode include ASM 286, PL/M 286, PASCAL 286 and FORTRAN 286. Programs developed in these languages can be downloaded from an Intel Series III or IV Development System to the iSBC 286/10A board via the iSDM™ 286 System Debug Monitor. The iSDM 286 monitor also provides on-target program debugging support including breakpoint and memory examination features.

Intel also offers the XENIX operating system which is designed for those applications needing an interactive, multiple user system. Typical applications include small business systems, software development/engineering workstations, distributed data processing, communications, and graphics.

Intel's XENIX operating system is a fully licensed derivative of UNIX*, enhanced by Intel to provide device driver support for Intel board and component products plus other features that yield greater flexibility, increased reliability, and easier configurability. Intel's XENIX operating system has been optimized for use with the 80286 microprocessor and supports such features as on-chip memory management and protection which provide ease of portability and higher performance.

Applications software can be written in either Intel's FORTRAN, COBOL, or BASIC languages using a XENIX based, Intel 286/310 or 286/380 system, or by using an Intel iDIS™ Database Information System. The user can also select from a wide variety of existing third party languages and applications software.

*UNIX is a trademark of BELL Labs.

iSBC® 286/10A Single Board Computer

SPECIFICATIONS

Word Size

Instruction — 8, 16, 24, 32 or 40 bits
Data — 8 or 16 bits

System Clock

CPU — 8.0 MHz
Numeric Processor — 5.3 or 8.0 MHz (Jumper Selectable)

Cycle Time

Basic Instruction — 8.0 MHz — 375 ns; 250 ns (assumes instruction in queue)

NOTE: Basic instruction cycle is defined as the fastest instruction time (i.e. two clock cycles)

Local Memory

Number of sockets — Four 28-pin JEDEC sites, expandable to 8 sites using iSBC 341 JEDEC Expansion Module

Maximum Size — 256 KB (as shipped) expandable to 512 KB by installing a reprogrammed Primary Address Decode PAL device.

NOTE: Reprogrammed PAL is user supplied. Instructions for programming the PAL device are in the iSBC 286/10A Hardware Reference Manual. The iSBC 341 module must be installed for the 512 KB configuration.

Compatible Devices — EPROM, up to 64K X 8 (Intel 27512)

Dual-Port Memory

Number of sockets — Four 28-pin JEDEC sites, expandable to 8 sites using iSBC 341 JEDEC Expansion Module

Maximum Size — 128 KB

Compatible Devices — EPROM, up to 32K X 8 (Intel 27256)
SRAM
iRAM, up to 8K × 8 (Intel 2186)
E²PROM, up to 2K × 8 (Intel 2817A)

Off-Board Physical Memory

Operating System	Address Mode	Size
iRMX 86 Rlse. 6	Real	1 MB
iRMX 286 Rlse. 1	Native	16 MB
XENIX Rlse. 3	Native	16 MB

I/O Capability

Parallel — Line printer interface, on-board functions, and four non-dedicated input bits

Serial — Two programmable channels using one 8274 device

Timers — Three programmable timers using one 8254 device

Expansion — Two 8/16-bit iSBX MULTIMODULE connectors

BAUD RATES

Frequency (kHz) (Software Selectable) Reference: 1.23 MHz	Baud Rate (Hz)				
	Synchronous	Asynchronous			
	÷1	÷1	÷16	÷32	÷64
615.	615,000	615,000	38,400	19,200	9,600
307.	307,000	307,000	19,200	9,600	4,800
154.	154,000	154,000	9,600	4,800	2,400
76.8	76,800	76,800	4,800	2,400	1,200
56.0	56,000	—	—	—	—
38.4	38,400	38,400	2,400	1,200	600
19.2	19,200	19,200	1,200	600	300
9.6	9,600	9,600	600	300	150
4.8	4,800	4,800	300	150	75
2.4	2,400	2,400	150	75	—
1.2	1,200	1,200	75	—	—
0.6	600	600	—	—	—

Serial Communications Characteristics

Synchronous — 5-8 bit characters; internal or HDLC/SDLC character synchronization; automatic sync insertion; even or odd parity

Asynchronous — 5-8 bit characters; break character generation; 1, 1-1/2, or 2 stop bits; false start bit detection; even or odd parity

Interrupt Capacity

Potential Interrupt Sources — 23, 20, jumper selectable

Interrupt Levels — 16 vectored requests using two 8259As and the 80286's NMI line.

Timers

Input Frequencies — 1.23 MHz ± 0.1% or 3.00 MHz ± 0.1% (Jumper Selectable)

OUTPUT FREQUENCIES/TIMING INTERVALS

Function	Single Timer/Counter		Dual Timer/Counter (two timers cascaded)	
	Min	Max	Min	Max
Real-time interrupt	667 ns	53.3 ms	1.33 μs	58.2 min
Programmable one-shot	667 ns	53.3 ms	1.33 μs	58.2 min
Rate generator	18.8 Hz	1.50 MHz	0.000286 Hz	750 kHz
Square-wave rate generator	18.8 Hz	1.50 MHz	0.000286 Hz	750 kHz
Software triggered strobe	667 ns	53.3 ms	1.33 μs	58.2 min
Hardware triggered strobe	667 ns	53.3 ms	1.33 μs	58.2 min
Event counter	—	8.0 MHz	—	—

CONNECTORS

Interface	Double-Sided Pins (qty.)	Centers (in.)	Mating Connectors
MULTIBUS System	86	0.156	Viking 3KH43/9AMK12 Wire Wrap
iSBX Bus — 8-Bit Data	36	0.1	iSBX 960-5
16-Bit Data	44	0.1	iSBX 961-5
iLBX BUS/ Synchronous Interface	60	0.1	Kelam RF30-2803-5 or T&B Ansley A3020 (609-6026 modified)
Parallel I/O	26	0.1	3M 3462-0001 Flat or AMP 88106-1 Flat
Serial I/O	26	0.1	3M 3462-0001 Flat or AMP 88106-1 Flat

INTERFACES

MULTIBUS Bus — All signals TTL compatible

iSBX Bus — All signals TTL compatible

iLBX Bus — All signals TTL compatible

Synchronous Interface — All signals TTL compatible

Serial I/O — Channel A: RS232C/RS422/RS449 compatible, DCE or DTE; Channel B; RS232C compatible, DCE only

NOTE: User supplied 34487 line driver and SIP termination rresistor need to be installed forr RS422/RS449 operation.

Timer — All signals TTL compatible

Interrupt Requests — All TTL compatible

iSBC® 286/10A Single Board Computer

MULTIBUS® DRIVERS

Function	Characteristic	Sink Current (mA)
Data	Tri-State	16
Address	Tri-State	16
Commands	Tri-State	32
Bus Control	Open Collector	20

iLBX™ DRIVERS

Function	Characteristic	Sink Current (mA)
Data	Tri-State	9
Address	Tri-State	20
Commands	Tri-State	8
Bus Control	TTL	8

Physical Characteristics

Width — 12.00 in. (30.48 cm)

Height — 6.75 in. (17.15 cm)

Depth — 0.4 in. (1.0 cm)

Minimum Slot Spacing — 0.6 in. (1.5 cm)

Weight — 14 oz. (397 gm)

Electrical Characteristics

DC Power Requirements — +5V, 7.0A; ±12V, 50mA (serial I/O)

NOTE: Does not include power for optional EPROM, E²PROM, or RAM memory devices, or installed MULTIMODULE boards

Environmental Characteristics

Operating Temperature — 0°C to 60°C with 7 CFM airflow across board

Relative Humidity — to 90% (without condensation)

Reference Manual

147532-001 *iSBC® 286/10A Hardware Reference Manual* (order sepeartely)

ORDERING INFORMATION

Part Number	Description
SBC 286/10A	Single Board Computer

iSBC® 286/12
SINGLE BOARD COMPUTER

- 8 MHz 80286 microprocessor
- Two JEDEC 28-pin sites for up to 128K bytes of local EPROM memory, expandable to 256K bytes using an iSBC® 341 Expansion Module
- 1 megabyte, 0 wait-state, dual-port, parity memory
- Supports user installed 80287 Numeric Data Processor and 82258 Advanced DMA Controller devices
- Two iSBX™ bus interface connectors for I/O expansion
- Synchronous high-speed interface for 0 wait-state read/write to EX memory expansion boards
- iLBX™ interface for iLBX™ memory board expansion
- 16 levels of vectored interrupt control
- Centronics-compatible parallel I/O printer interface
- Two programmable multiprotocol synchronous/asynchronous serial interfaces; one RS232C, the other RS232C or RS422/449 compatible

The iSBC 286/12 Single Board Computer is a member of Intel's high performance family of 16-bit microcomputers. The board features an 80286 microprocessor running at 8 MHz together with 1 megabyte of dual-ported, 0 wait-state, parity memory. These features make the iSBC 286/12 Board the ideal single board solution for applications requiring high performance and up to 1 megabyte of memory. For those applications needing more memory, up to four memory expansion boards may be connected to the iSBC 286/12 Board over its P2 interface. The P2 interface supports both standard iLBX memory boards and Intel's new EX series of synchronous, 0 wait-state, memory boards that provide up to 16 megabytes of system memory. The iSBC 286/12 Board also features two sockets for user installed 80287 Numeric Data Processor and 82258 Advanced Direct Memory Access Controller devices. These components further increase board performance by off-loading time intensive tasks from the 80286 microprocessor. The iSBC 286/12 CPU Board is a true single-board solution that also includes two serial I/O channels, one parallel line printer channel, local memory, interrupt controllers and programmable timers all on one board.

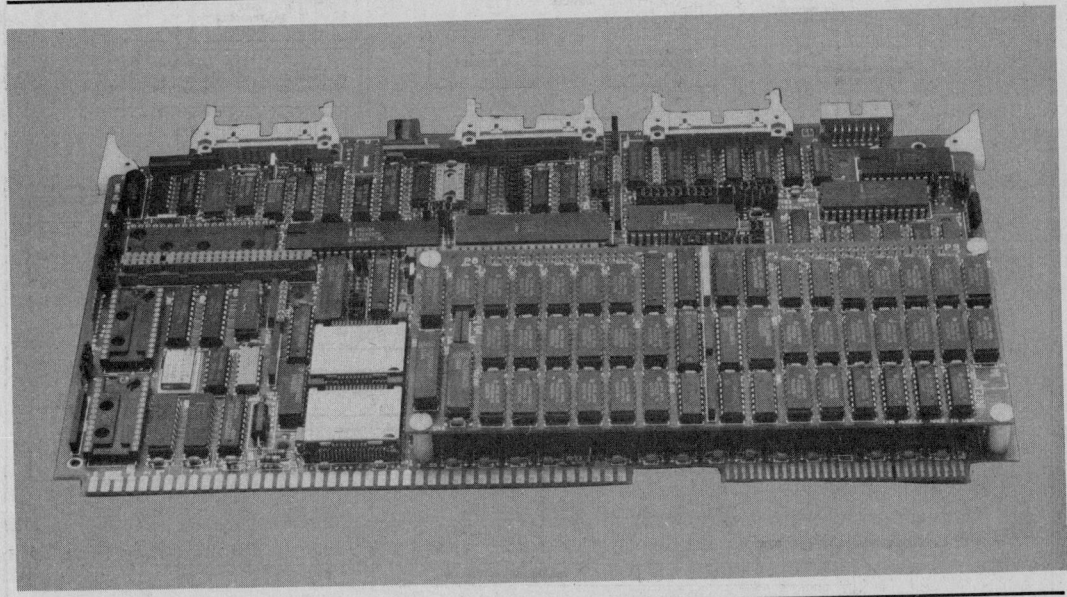

Intel Corporation assumes no responsibility for the use of any circuitry other than circuitry embodied in an Intel product. No other circuit patent licenses are implied. Information contained herein supersedes previously published specifications on these devices from Intel.

© INTEL CORPORATION, 1985

JULY, 1985
ORDER NUMBER: 280147-001

iSBC® 286/12 BOARD

FUNCTIONAL DESCRIPTION

Overview

The iSBC 286/12 Board utilizes the powerful iAPX 286 CPU within the MULTIBUS® system architecture, enhanced by the industry standard iLBX bus and a new, 0 wait-state, synchronous memory interface, to provide a high-performance 16-bit solution. This board features 1 megabyte of dual-port, 0 wait-state, parity memory plus interrupt, memory and I/O features facilitating a complete single-board computer system. The iSBC 286/12 Board can be used in many applications originally designed for Intel's other 16-bit microcomputers. Only minor changes to the system hardware or applications software may be required to match the application to the iSBC 286/12 Board. These changes may include adjusting software timing loops, changing the (jumper) default configuration of the board, and using pin and socket I/O connectors in place of edge connectors.

Central Processing Unit

The central processor for the iSBC 286/12 Board is the 80286 CPU operating at an 8.0 MHz clock rate. The 80286 CPU is upwardly compatible with Intel's iAPX 88 and iAPX 86 CPUs. The 80286 CPU runs iAPX 88 and 86 code at substantially higher speeds due to its parallel architecture. In addition, the 80286 CPU provides on-chip memory management and protection and virtual memory addressing of up to 1 gigabyte per task. Processing speed and efficiency may be further enhanced by installing an 80287 numerics co-processor and an 82258 ADMA controller. The clock rates for the 80286 and the 80287 are independent with the 80287 rate jumper selectable at either 5.3 or 8.0 MHz.

Instruction Set

The 80286 instruction repertoire includes variable length instruction format (including double operand instructions), 8-bit and 16-bit signed and unsigned arithmetic operators for binary, BCD and unpacked ASCII data, and iterative word and byte string manipulation functions.

Numeric Data Processor

For enhanced numerics processing capability, the 80287 Numeric Data Processor extends the 80286 architecture and data set. Over 60 numeric instructions offer arithmetic, trigonometric, transcendental, logarithmic and exponential instructions. Supported data types include 16-, 32-, and 64-bit integer, 32- and 64-bit floating point, 18-digit packed BCD and 80-bit temporary. The 80287 meets the proposed IEEE P754 standard for numeric data processing and maintains compatibility with 8087-based systems.

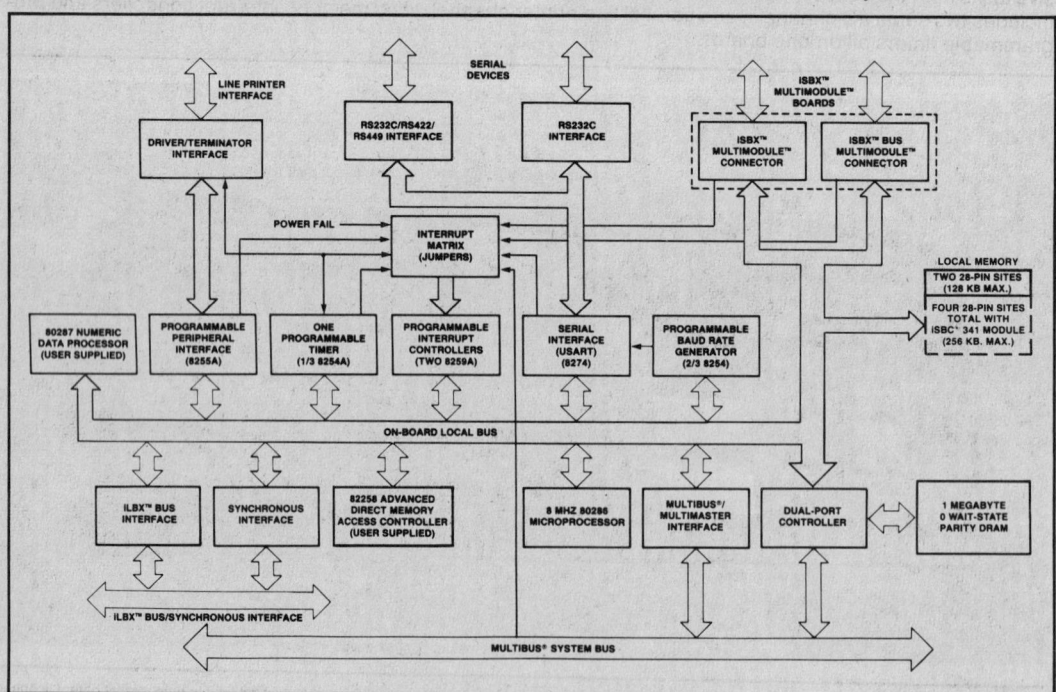

Figure 1. iSBC® 286/12 Block Diagram

iSBC® 286/12 BOARD

Advanced DMA Controller

For those applications which require frequent moving of large blocks of data, the user may install an Intel 82258, 4 channel, advanced DMA (ADMA) controller to further increase system performance. The ADMA Controller supports DMA requests from the 8274 USART (2 channels) and the iSBX interfaces on the board (1 per interface). The ADMA can also perform data transfers over the on board CPU bus, the MULTIBUS (P1) interface, and the iLBX/synchronous (P2) interface. With this arrangement, the device can rapidly move blocks of data between the iSBC 286/12 Board and iSBX MULTIMODULE™ Boards installed on the baseboard, between the iSBC 286/12 Board and other boards installed in the system, or between any other memory/controller/I/O boards installed in the system.

ARCHITECTURAL FEATURES

The iAPX 86, 88, 186, and 286 microprocessor family contains the same basic set of registers, instructions, and addressing modes. The 80286 processor is upward compatible with the 8086, 8088, and 80186 CPUs.

The 80286 operates in two modes: iAPX 86 real address mode, and protected virtual address mode. In iAPX 86 real address mode, programs use real address with up to one megabyte of address space. Programs use virtual addresses in protected virtual address mode, also called protected mode. In protected mode, the 80286 CPU automatically maps 1 gigabyte of virtual addresses per task into a 16 megabyte real address space. This mode also provides memory protection to isolate the operating system and ensure privacy of each task's programs and data. Both modes provide the same base instruction set, registers, and addressing modes.

Vectored Interrupt Control

Incoming interrupts are handled by two on-board 8259A programmable interrupt controllers (PIC) and by the 80286's NMI line. Interrupts originating from up to 15 sources are prioritized and then sent to the CPU. The 8259 devices support both polled and vectored mode of operation. Further interrupt capability is available through bus vectored interrupts where slave 8259 interrupt controllers resident on separate iSBC Boards supply an interrupt vector to the on-board CPU.

Interrupt Sources

Twenty-six potential interrupt sources are routed to the slave PIC device and to the interrupt jumper matrix where the user can connect the desired interrupt sources to specific interrupt levels. Table 1 includes a list of devices and functions supported by interrupts.

Memory Capabilities

DUAL-PORT MEMORY

The iSBC 286/12 Board features 1 megabyte of 0 wait-state, parity memory installed on the board. This memory, which is implemented using 256K DRAMs

Table 1. Interrupt Request Sources

Device	Function	Number of Interrupts
MULTIBUS interface	Requests from MULTIBUS resident peripherals or other CPU boards	8*
8259A programmable interrupt controller	8 level vectored interrupt request from slave 8259A	1
8274 serial controller	6 internal interrupt requests directed to master 8259A	1
8255A line printer interface	Signals output buffer empty. Directed to slave PIC.	1
8254 timers	Timer 0, 1 outputs; function determined by timer mode	2
iSBX connectors	Function determined by iSBX MULTIMODULE board. Directed to slave PIC.	2 per iSBX connector
Bus fail safe timer	Indicates addressed MULTIBUS resident device has not responded to command within 10 msec	1
Power fail interrupt	Indicates AC power is not within tolerance (from power supply)	1
ADMA interrupt	Common interrupt for 4 DMA channels	1
Parity Interrupt	Parity error indicator from memory module	1
On-board logic	Conditioned interrupt source from edge sense latch, inverter, or OR gate	3
Bus request error	Indicates CPU was unable to access the MULTIBUS interface	1
External interrupt	Supports system front panel reset switch	1

*May be expanded to 56 with slave 8259A PICs on MULTIBUS® boards.

iSBC® 286/12 BOARD

installed on a daughter board, is dual-ported to the on-board CPU bus and the MULTIBUS (P1) interface. For those applications requiring more memory, the iSBC 286/12 Board also features an iLBX and synchronous memory interface to increase physical memory capacity to 16 megabytes.

LOCAL MEMORY

Two, 28-pin sites are provided for installing up to 128KB of EPROM firmware.

By installing an iSBC 341 EPROM expansion module, local memory can be increased to four sites to support up to 256KB of EPROM. Local memory access time is selectable at one, two, or three wait-states and is a function of the speed of the devices used.

Serial I/O

A two-channel serial communications interface using Intel's 8274 Multi-Protocol Serial Controller (MPSC) is contained on the iSBC 286/12 Board. Two independent software selectable baud rate generators (²/₃ of the 8254 timer) provide the MPSC with all common communication frequencies. The protocol (i.e. asynchronous, bisync, or SDLC/HDLC), data format, control character format, parity and baud rate are all under program control. Software interfacing to the MPSC can be via either a polled or interrupt driven routine. Channel A may be configured for an RS232C or RS422/RS449 interface; channel B is set for RS232C operation only. DMA operation for channel A is available if the optional 82258 (ADMA) is installed. The data, clock, control, and signal ground lines for each channel are brought out to two 26-pin, pin and socket connectors.

Programmable Timers

The iSBC 286/12 Board provides three independent, fully programmable 16-bit interval timers/event counters utilizing the Intel 8254 Programmable Interval Timer. Each counter is capable of operating in either BCD or binary modes. Two of these timers/counters are available to the systems designer to generate accurate time intervals under software control. Routing for the outputs of these counters is jumper selectable. The outputs may be independently routed to the 8259A Programmable Interrupt Controller or to the 8274 MPSC to count external events or provide baud rate generation. The third interval timer in the 8254 is dedicated to providing a clock for the programmable baud rate generator in the iSBC 286/12 Board's MPSC serial controller. The system software configures each timer independently to select the desired function. Seven functions are available as shown in Table 2. The contents of each counter may be read at any time during system operation.

Table 2. Programmable Timer Functions

Function	Operation
Interrupt on terminal count	When terminal count is reached, an interrupt request is generated. This function is extremely useful for generation of real-time clocks.
Programmable one-shot	Output goes low upon receipt of an external trigger edge or software command and returns high when terminal count is reached. This function is retriggerable.
Rate generator	Divide by N counter. The output will go low for one input clock cycle, and the period from one low going pulse to the next is N times the input clock period.
Square-wave rate generator	Output will remain high until one-half the count has been completed, and go low for the other half of the count.
Software triggered strobe	Output remains high until software loads count (N). N counts after count is loaded, output goes low for one input clock period.
Hardware triggered strobe	Output goes low for one clock period N counts after rising edge counter trigger input. The counter is retriggerable.
Event counter	On a jumper selectable basis, the clock input becomes an input from the external system. CPU may read the number of events occurring after the counter "window" has been enabled or an interrupt may be generated after N events occur in the system.

Line Printer Interface/Board ID

An 8255A Programmable Peripheral Interface (PPI) provides a Centronics compatible line printer interface, several on-board functions, and four non-dedicated input bits. Drivers are provided for a complete Centronics compatible line printer interface. The on-board functions implemented with the PPI are Power Fail Sense, Lock Override, NMI Mask, Clear Timeout Interrupt, LED 1 and 4, Clear Edge Sense flop, and MULTIBUS interface directed interrupts (2). The PPI's I/O lines are divided into three eight bit ports: A, B, and C. The PPI must be programmed for mode 0 with ports A and C used as outputs and port B as input. A 16-bit write to Port B is used to set the iSBC 286/12 Board into 24 bit address mode.

Three jumpers on the iSBC 286/12 Board let the software determine, by examining bits 0, 1, and 2 of port B, the board type (iSBC 286/10A Board or iSBC 286/12 Board), and the presence of hardware options

iSBC® 286/12 BOARD

(82258 ADMA and 80287 Numeric Data Processor devices) installed on the board. The parallel port assignment is shown in Table 3.

Table 3. Parallel Port Bit Assignment

Bit	Port A — Output Function
0	Line Printer Data Bit 0
1	Line Printer Data Bit 1
2	Line Printer Data Bit 2
3	Line Printer Data Bit 3
4	Line Printer Data Bit 4
5	Line Printer Data Bit 5
6	Line Printer Data Bit 6
7	Line Printer Data Bit 7

Bit	Port B — Input Function
0	Board ID Bit 0
1	Board ID Bit 1
2	Board ID Bit 2
3	LPT Interrupt (Active High)
4	Line Printer ACK/ (Active Low)
5	Power Fail Sense/ (Active Low)
6	Line Printer Error (Active High)
7	Line Printer Busy (Active High)

Bit	Port C — Output Function
0	Line Printer Data Strobe (Active High)
1	Override/ (0 = lock asserted)
2	NMI Mask (0 = NMI Enabled)
3	Clear Timeout Interrupt (Active High)
4	LED 0 (1 = On); Clear Edge Sense Flop/
5	MULTIBUS Interrupt 1 (Active High)
6	MULTIBUS Interrupt 2 (Active High)
7	LED 1 (1 = On); Clear Line Printer ACK Flop/ (Active High)

Soft Reset

The soft reset feature allows the 80286 microprocessor to return to Real Address Mode operation from PVAM under software control. The system reset line (INIT*) and the dual-port memory are not affected, and all I/O context is preserved. The soft reset is activated by a byte write to I/O location 00E0H. To distinguish the soft reset from a true system initialization reset, a flag is provided. Another flag is provided that indicates whether the iSBC 286/12 Board hardware (not the 80286 device) is currently configured for PVAM or Real Address Mode.

MULTIBUS® SYSTEM ARCHITECTURE

Overview

The MULTIBUS system architecture includes three bus structures: the system bus, the local bus extension and the iSBX MULTIMODULE expansion bus as shown in Figure 2. Each bus structure is optimized to satisfy particular system requirements. The system bus provides a basis for general system design including memory and I/O expansion as well as multiprocessing support. The local bus extension allows large amounts of high performance memory to be accessed from a CPU board over a private bus. The MULTIMODULE extension bus is a means of adding inexpensive I/O functions to a base CPU board. Each of these three bus structures are implemented on the iSBC 286/12 Board providing a total system architecture solution.

System Bus — IEEE 796

The MULTIBUS system bus is Intel's industry standard, IEEE 796, microcomputer bus structure. Both 8- and 16-bit single board computers are supported on the IEEE 796 structure with 24 address and 16 data lines. In its simplest application, the system bus allows expansion of functions already contained on a single board computer (e.g., memory and digital I/O). However, the IEEE 796 bus also allows very powerful distributed processing configurations using multiple processors, I/O boards, and peripheral boards. The MULTIBUS system bus is supported with a broad array of board level products. VLSI interface components, detailed published specifications and application notes.

System Bus — Expansion Capabilities

Memory and I/O capacity may be expanded and additional functions added using Intel MULTIBUS compatible expansion boards. Memory may be expanded by adding user specified combinations of RAM boards, EPROM boards, bubble memory boards, or combination boards. Input/output capacity may be added with digital I/O and analog I/O expansion boards. Mass storage capability may be achieved by adding single or double density diskette controllers, or hard disk controllers. Modular expandable backplanes and card-cages are available to support multiboard systems.

System Bus — Multimaster Capabilities

For those applications requiring additional processing capacity and the benefits of multiprocessing (i.e., several CPUs and/or controllers logically sharing system tasks through communication of the system bus), the iSBC 286/12 Board provides full system bus arbitration control logic. This control logic allows up to three other bus masters, including the iSBC 80 Board family of MULTIBUS compatible 8-bit single

iSBC® 286/12 BOARD

board computers to share the system bus using a serial (daisy chain) priority scheme and allows up to 16 masters to share the MULTIBUS system bus with an external parallel priority decoder. In addition to multiprocessing configuration made possible with multimaster capability, it also provides a very efficient mechanism for all forms of DMA (Direct Memory Access) transfers.

High Speed Off-Board Memory

The iSBC 286/12 Board can access off-board memory either over the MULTIBUS (P1) interface, or over the P2 interface as shown in Figure 3. Memory transfers over the P2 interface are faster because the CPU board doesn't have to arbitrate for access to the MULTIBUS interface.

Using the P2 interface, the iSBC 286/12 Board can be configured to operate with either a standard iLBX interface or with a high-performance, synchronous interface.

The iSBC 286/12 Board as supplied is configured to operate with a synchronous, P2 interface. This high-performance interface is designed to connect to Intel's new EX series of memory expansion boards to yield a CPU to memory read/write time of 0 wait-states. The EX memory expansion boards are available in sizes ranging from 512K bytes up to 4M bytes.

By moving several jumpers on the board, the iSBC 286/12 Single Board Computer may be reconfigured for an iLBX interface, and is compatible with Intel's CX series of memory expansion boards which are

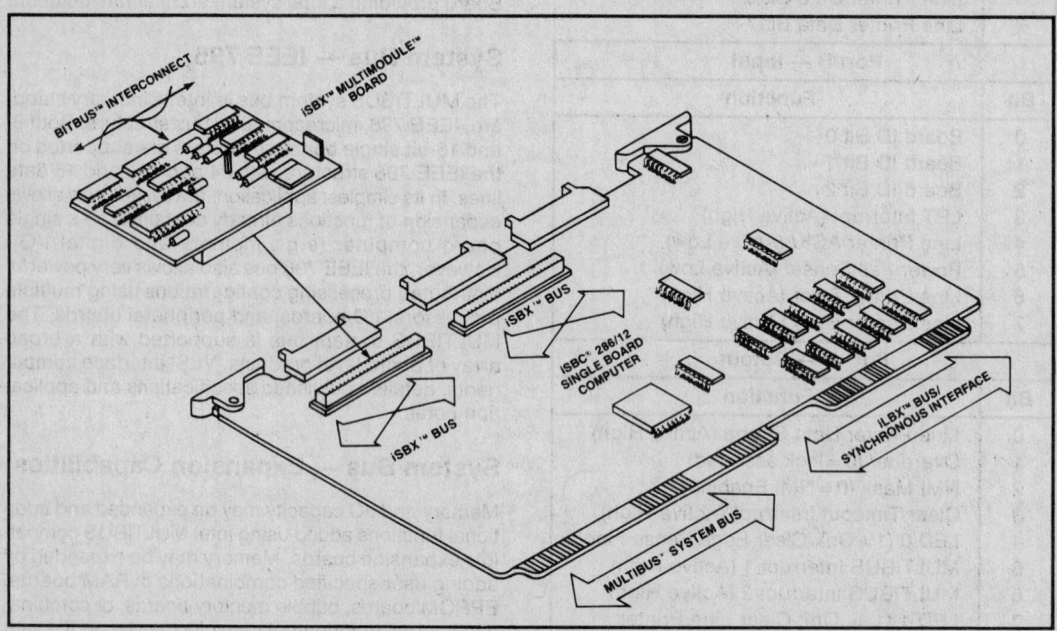

Figure 2. MULTIBUS® System Architecture

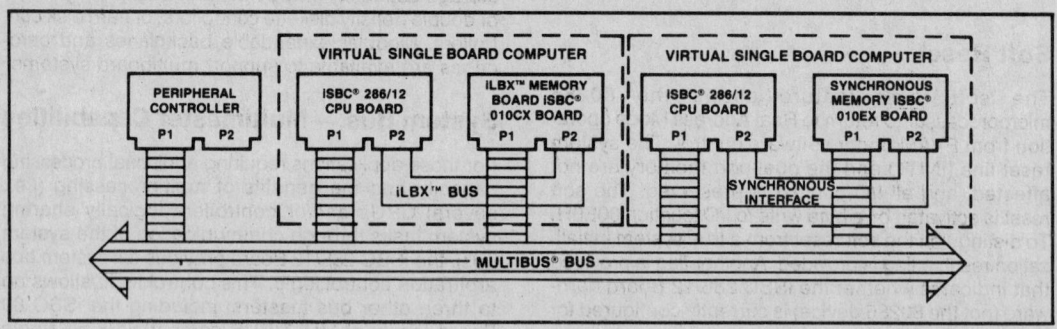

Figure 3. MULTIBUS®/iLBX™/Synchronous Interface Configurations

2-102

280147-001

available in sizes ranging from 512K bytes up to 2M bytes. Memory expansion boards from other manufacturers that meet the iLBX standard may also be used. CPU to memory access time is usually 1 or more wait-states depending on the speed of the memory used.

A total of four memory boards can be placed on the iLBX or synchronous interface bus. With 4M byte memory boards, this results in a total of 16M bytes on the memory expansion bus.

iSBX™ Bus MULTIMODULE™ On-Board Expansion

Two 8-, 16-bit iSBX MULTIMODULE connectors are provided on the iSBC 286/12 Board. Through these connectors, additional on-board I/O functions may be added. The iSBX MULTIMODULE Boards optimally support functions provided by VLSI peripheral components such as additional parallel and serial I/O, analog I/O, small mass storage device controllers (e.g., floppy disks), and other custom interfaces to meet specific needs. By mounting directly on the single board computer, less interface logic, less power, simpler packaging, higher performance, and lower cost result when compared to other alternatives such as MULTIBUS Board form factor compatible boards. The iSBX interface connectors on the iSBC 286/12 Board provide all signals necessary to interface to the local on-board bus, including 16 data lines for maximum data transfer rates. The iSBX MULTIMODULE Boards designed with 8-bit data paths and using the 8-bit iSBX connector are also supported on the iSBC 286/12 microcomputer board. A broad range of iSBX MULTIMODULE Board options are available from Intel. Custom iSBX modules may also be designed. An iSBX bus interface specification is available from Intel.

SOFTWARE SUPPORT

Software support from Intel includes the iRMX 86, iRMX 286, and XENIX* Operating Systems, assembly and high level languages, development systems, in-circuit emulators, and various other hardware and software tools.

For those applications needing a real time, multitasking operating system, Intel offers the iRMX 86 Release 6 and iRMX 286 Release 1 Operating Systems. The iRMX operating systems are particularly well suited for industrial or commercial applications where the processor is simultaneously controlling multiple, real time, interrupt-intensive processes. Typical applications include machine and process control, data acquisition, signal processing, front-end processing, and digital PABX control. The iRMX operating systems employ a highly configurable, modular structure that allows easy system configuration and expansion.

The iRMX 86 Release 6 Operating System enables the iSBC 286/12 Board to address up to 1 MB of memory in real address mode. Using the iRMX 286 Operating System, this address range is extended to 16 MB in native mode. The iRMX 286 Operating System also allows the user to take advantage of the hardware traps built into the iAPX 286 processor that provide expanded debug capabilities and increased code reliability.

Applications software written for earlier releases of the iRMX 86 Operating System is upwardly compatible through Release 6. Furthermore, application code written for the iRMX 86 Operating System can be compiled using 286 compilers to run under the iRMX 286 Operating System. Application code will require only minor changes.

Assembly and many high level languages are supported by the iRMX Operating Systems and Intellec® Series III and Series IV development systems. Language support for the iSBC 286/12 Board in real address board includes Intel's ASM 86, PL/M 86, PASCAL 86, FORTRAN 86, and C86, as well as many third party 8086 languages. Language support for native address mode include ASM 286, PL/M 286, PASCAL 286 and FORTRAN 286. Programs developed in these languages can be downloaded from an Intel Series III or IV Development System to the iSBC 286/12 Board via the iSDM™ 286 System Debug Monitor. The iSDM 286 monitor also provides on-target program debugging support including breakpoint and memory examination features.

Intel also offers the XENIX operating system which is designed for those applications needing an interactive, multiple user system. Typical applications include small business systems, software development/engineering workstations, distributed data processing, communications, and graphics.

Intel's XENIX operating system is a fully licensed derivative of UNIX*, enhanced by Intel to provide device driver support for Intel board and component products plus other features that yield greater flexibility, increased reliability, and easier configurability. Intel's XENIX operating system has been optimized for use with the 80286 microprocessor and supports such features as on-chip memory management and protection which provide ease of portability and higher performance.

Applications software can be written in either Intel's FORTRAN, COBOL, or BASIC languages using a XENIX based, Intel 286/310 or 286/380 system, or by using an Intel iDIS™ Database Information System. The user can also select from a wide variety of existing third party languages and applications software.

* XENIX is a registered trademark of Microsoft Corp.

* UNIX is a trademark of Bell Laboratories

iSBC® 286/12 BOARD

SPECIFICATIONS

Word Size

Instruction — 8, 16, 24, 32 or 40 bits

Data — 8 or 16 bits

System Clock

CPU — 8.0 MHz

Numeric Processor — 5.3 or 8.0 MHz (Jumper Selectable)

Cycle Time

Basic Instruction — 8.0 MHz - 250 ns (assumes instruction in queue)

NOTE: Basic instruction cycle is defined as the fastest instruction time (i.e. two clock cycles)

Dual-Port Memory

1 megabyte, 0 wait-state, parity DRAM dual-ported to the on-board CPU bus and the MULTIBUS interface.

Local Memory

Number of sockets — Two 28-pin JEDEC sites, expandable to 4 sites using iSBC 341 JEDEC Expansion Module

Maximum Size — 128 KB expandable to 256 KB by installing an iSBC 341 EPROM Expansion Module. Memory size is set by jumpers on the iSBC 286/12 Board.

Compatible Devices — EPROM, up to 64K × 8 (Intel 27512)

Memory Map

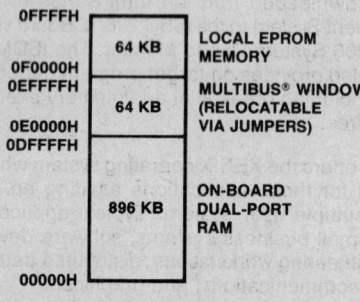

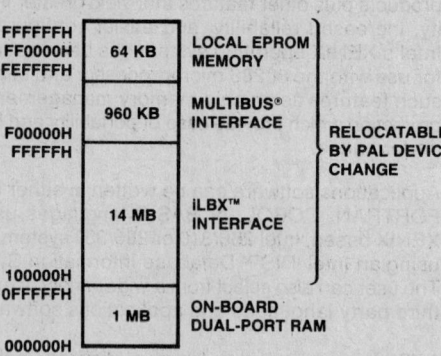

2-104

280147-001

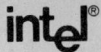

iSBC® 286/12 BOARD

Off-Board Physical Memory

Operating System	Address Mode	Size
iRMX 86 Rise 6 O.S.	Real	1 MB
iRMX 286 Rise 1 O.S.	Native	16 MB
XENIX Rise 3 O.S.	Native	16 MB

Socket provided for Intel 82258, 4 channel, advanced DMA controller. Data transfer rate = 4 MB per second (two cycle transfer mode, memory to memory); 2.67 MB per second (16-bit iSBX I/O to dual-port memory).

I/O Capability

Parallel — Line printer interface, on-board functions, and 3-bit board installed options code

Serial — Two programmable channels using one 8274 device

Timers — Three programmable timers using one 8254 device

Expansion — Two 8/16-bit iSBX MULTIMODULE connectors

Interrupt Capacity

26 Interrupt Sources, 15 jumper selectable

Interrupt Levels — 16 vectored requests using two 8259A devices and the 80286 microprocessor's NMI line.

Serial Communications Characteristics

Synchronous — 5-8 bit characters; internal or HDLC/SDLC character synchronization; automatic sync insertion; even or odd parity

Asynchronous — 5-8 bit characters; break character generation; 1, 1½, or 2 stop bits; false start bit detection; even or odd parity

BAUD RATES

Frequency (kHz) (Software Selectable)	Baud Rate (Hz)				
	Synchronous	Asynchronous			
Reference: 1.23 MHz	÷1	÷1	÷16	÷32	÷64
615.0	615,000	615,000	38,400	19,200	9,600
307.0	307,000	307,000	19,200	9,600	4,800
154.0	154,000	154,000	9,600	4,800	2,400
76.8	76,800	76,800	4,800	2,400	1,200
56.0	56,000	—	—	—	—
38.4	38,400	38,400	2,400	1,200	600
19.2	19,200	19,200	1,200	600	300
9.6	9,600	9,600	600	300	150
4.8	4,800	4,800	300	150	75
2.4	2,400	2,400	150	75	—
1.2	1,200	1,200	75	—	—
0.6	600	600	—	—	—

Timers

Input Frequencies — 1.23 MHz ± 0.1% or 4.00 MHz ± 0.1% (Jumper Selectable)

OUTPUT FREQUENCIES/TIMING INTERVALS

Function	Single Timer/Counter		Dual Timer/Counter (two timers cascaded)	
	Min	Max	Min	Max
Real-time interrupt	500 ns	53.3 ms	1.0 µs	58.2 min
Programmable one-shot	500 ns	53.3 ms	1.0 µs	58.2 min
Rate generator	18.8 Hz	2.0 MHz	0.000286 Hz	750 kHz
Square-wave rate generator	18.8 Hz	2.0 MHz	0.000286 Hz	750 kHz
Software triggered strobe	500 ns	53.3 ms	1.0 µs	58.2 min
Hardware triggered strobe	500 ns	53.3 ms	1.0 µs	58.2 min
Event counter	—	8.0 MHz	—	—

iSBC® 286/12 BOARD

Interfaces

MULTIBUS Bus — All signals TTL compatible

iSBX Bus — All signals TTL compatible

iLBX Bus — All signals TTL compatible

Synchronous Interface — All signals TTL compatible

Serial I/O — Channel A: RS232C/RS422/RS449 compatible, DCE or DTE;
Channel B: RS232C compatible, DCE

NOTE: For RS422/RS449 operation, user supplied line drivers and resistor terminators must be installed.

Timer — All signals TTL compatible

Interrupt Requests — All TTL compatible

MULTIBUS® DRIVERS

Function	Type	Sink Current (ma)
Data	Tri-State	64
Address	Tri-State	24
Commands	Tri-State	32
Bus Control	Open Collector	16/32

iLBX™ DRIVERS

Function	Type	Sink Current (ma)
Data	Tri-State	64
Address	Tri-State	24
Commands	Tri-State	24
Bus Control	TTL	24

PHYSICAL CHARACTERISTICS

Width — 12.00 in. (30,48 cm)

Height — 7.05 in. (18,00 cm)

Depth — 0.88 in. (2,24 cm)
1.16 in. (2,95 cm) with iSBX MULTIMODULE board installed

Recommended Slot Spacing (without iSBX MULTIMODULE) — 1.2 in. (3,0 cm)

Weight — 26 oz. (731 gm)

ELECTRICAL CHARACTERISTICS

DC Power Requirements

Maximum — +5V, 8.7A; ±12V, 35mA (for serial I/O)
Typical   — +5V, 5.7A; ±12V, 20mA

NOTE: Power requirements are for the default configuration. Does not include power for optional EPROM, 80287 or 82258 devices, or installed iSBX MULTIMODULE boards

ENVIRONMENTAL CHARACTERISTICS

Operating Temperature — 0°C to 60°C with 8 CFM airflow across board (default configuration)

Relative Humidity — to 90% (without condensation)

REFERENCE MANUAL

147533-001   iSBC 286/12 Hardware Reference Manual (order separately)

Mating Connectors (or Equivalent Part)

Function	# of Pins	Centers (in)	Connector Type	Vendor	Vendor Part No.
iSBX Bus Connector 16-bit (J5, J6)	44	0.1	Soldered	Viking	000293-0001
I/O Connectors (J1-J3)	26	0.1	Flat Crimp	3M	3399-6026
Front Panel Connector (J4)	14	0.5	Flat Crimp	3M	3385-6014
iLBX/Synch. Interface Edge Connector (P2)	60	0.1	Flat Crimp	KEL-AM T & B Ansley	RF30-2803-5 A3020

iSBC® 286/12 BOARD

ORDERING INFORMATION

Part Number	Description
SBC 286/12	Single Board Computer
C80287-3	Numeric Processor Ext., 5 MHz
D80287-8	Numeric Processor Ext., 8 MHz
R82258-8	ADMA Coprocessor, 8 MHz

280147-001

PRELIMINARY

iSBC® 386/20
SINGLE BOARD COMPUTER
STARTER KIT

- Starter Kit includes iSBC® 386/20P CPU board, 2MB Memory Board, and Monitor software
- High performance 32-bit processor system using the 80386 microprocessor
- High speed numerics coprocessor
- Cache memory provides 0 wait-state memory reads
- High speed 32-bit memory interface
- iSBX™ interface supports I/O expansion using iSBX MULTIMODULE™ boards
- 128 KB of EPROM local memory
- MULTIBUS® interface for multimaster configurations and system expansion

The Starter Kit includes an iSBC® 386/20P CPU board, a 2 megabyte memory board, monitor software, interconnecting cables, and documentation. This kit allows the board or system level designer to quickly assemble an 80386-based MULTIBUS I System and evaluate the iSBC 386/20P board and 80386 microprocessor. All of the hardware pieces are provided, preconfigured to speed start-up time.

The iSBC 386/20P Single Board Computer, included in the kit, is Intel's highest performance MULTIBUS I CPU board. The iSBC 386/20P board features an 80386 32-bit microprocessor, a 16 kilobyte cache memory, and a high speed, dual-port memory interface that supports up to 2 megabytes of physical memory. The board also features a math coprocessor to offload the CPU and greatly enhance system performance in floating point, math-intensive applications. To take advantage of the 80386 32-bit architecture, all data transfers between the microprocessor and the dual-port memory are 32 bits wide.

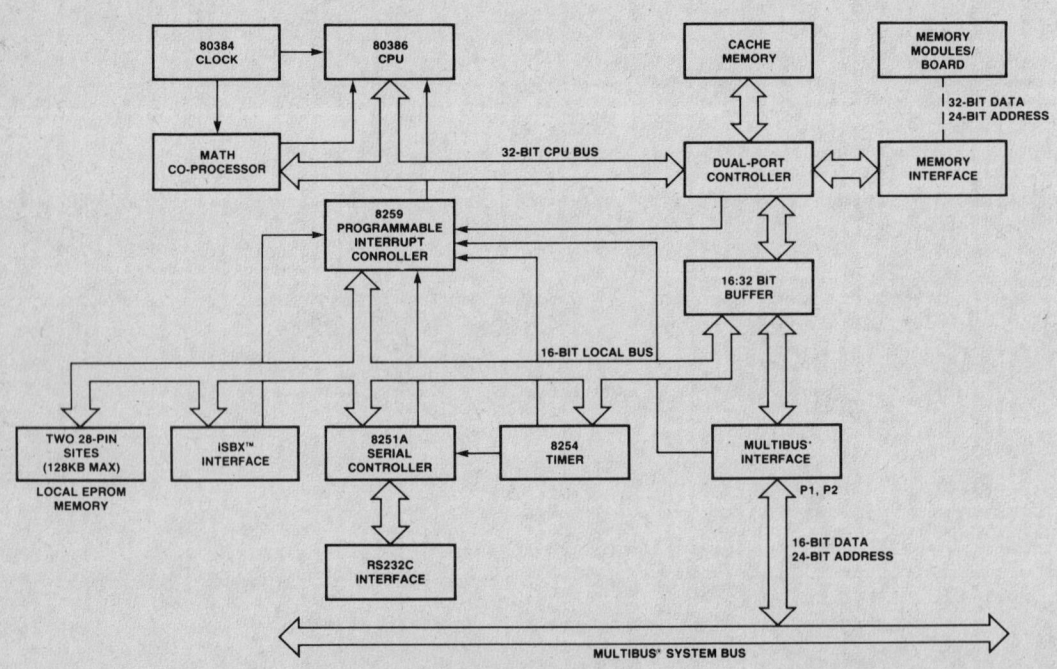

Intel Corporation assumes no responsibility for the use of any circuitry other than circuitry embodied in an Intel product. No other circuit patent licenses are implied. Information contained herein supersedes previously published specifications on these devices from Intel. Specifications to change without notice.

© INTEL CORPORATION, 1985

AUGUST, 1985
ORDER NUMBER: 280161-001

iSBC® 386/20 SBC STARTER KIT

PRELIMINARY

FUNCTIONAL DESCRIPTION

Overview—iSBC® 386/20 Starter Kit

The iSBC 386/20 Starter Kit is a set of hardware and software products designed to allow the user to evaluate the iSBC 386/20P CPU board and the 80386 microprocessor. The kit includes an iSBC 386/20P CPU board, an iSBC 402P 2 megabyte memory board, monitor software, memory and RS232C (9-pin) ribbon cables, and user documentation. All hardware and software is preconfigured to reduce start-up time.

The monitor software is designed to work with a host system, and includes host diskette software, and target EPROM firmware installed on the iSBC 386/20P board. Five basic functions are provided:

- Read and write to all memory locations and processor registers
- Execute code—Go and Single Step
- Insert software breakpoints
- Disassemble code into 386 assembly language mnemonics
- Download user programs

Overview—iSBC® 386/20P CPU Board

The iSBC 386/20P board is Intel's first 32-bit MULTIBUS I single board computer using the 80386 microprocessor. The board employs a dual-bus structure: a 32-bit CPU bus for data transfers between the CPU and memory; and a 16-bit bus for data transfers over the MULTIBUS, iSBX, local memory, and 8-bit I/O interfaces. In this manner, the board takes advantage of the 80386 CPU's 32-bit wide data bus while maintaining full compatibility with the MULTIBUS interface and iSBX MULTIMODULE boards.

The iSBC 386/20P board can be used in many applications originally designed for Intel's other 16-bit microcomputers, such as the iSBC 286/10A and iSBC 286/12, 8 MHz, 80286-based, single board computers. In this way, performance can be easily upgraded without requiring major hardware or software changes.

The iSBC 386/20P CPU board, which is the starter kit, is an early release version of the iSBC 386/20 production board.

Central Processor Unit

The heart of the iSBC 386/20P board is an 80386 microprocessor. This device utilizes address pipelining, a high speed execution unit, and on-chip memory management/protection to provide the highest level of system performance. The 80386 microprocessor also features an Address Translation Unit that supports up to 64 terabytes of virtual memory.

The 80386 CPU is upwardly compatible with Intel's 8088, 8086, 80186, and 80286 CPUs. Application software written for these other 8 and 16 bit microprocessor families can be easily recompiled to run on the 80386 microprocessor.

The 80386 microprocessor resides on the 32-bit wide CPU bus which interconnects the CPU with the math coprocessor and dual-port memory. This arrangement tightly couples the CPU to the memory to form a high performance processor/memory "engine". Separate 16-bit buses couple the CPU and dual-port memory to the MULTIBUS and iSBX interfaces, local EPROM memory, and other on-board I/O resources. With this arrangement, the iSBC 386/20P board can take full advantage of the 80386 microprocessor's 32-bit architecture while maintaining full compatibility with the MULTIBUS and iSBX interfaces.

Instruction Set

The 80386 instruction set includes variable length instruction format (including double operand instructions), 8-, 16-, and 32-bit signed and unsigned arithmetic operators for binary, BCD and unpacked ASCII data, and iterative word and byte string manipulation functions. All existing instructions have been extended to support 32-bit addresses and operands. New bit manipulation and other instructions have been added for extra flexibility in designing complex software.

Numeric Data Processor

For enhanced numerics processing capability, the iSBC 386/20 Starter Kit includes an 80287-based math module which is installed on the iSBC 386/20P board. Over 60 numeric instructions offer arithmetic, trigonometric, transcendental, logarithmic and exponential instructions. Supported data types include 16-, 32-, and 64-bit integer, 32- and 64-bit floating point, 18-digit packed BCD and 80-bit temporary. The numeric data processor meets the proposed IEEE P754 standard for numeric data processing and maintains compatibility with 80287 and 8087-based systems. Data transfers to/from the on-board CPU bus are 16-bits wide. On future iSBC 386/20 boards, this module will be replaced by an 80387 numeric coprocessor. This device will provide higher performance through a 32-bit data path to the CPU bus and added numeric instructions.

Architectural Features

The 8086, 8088, 80186, 80188, 80286, and 80386 microprocessor family contains the same basic sets of registers, instructions, and addressing modes. The

iSBC® 386/20 SBC STARTER KIT

PRELIMINARY

80386 processor is upward compatible with the 8086, 8088, 80186, and 80286 CPUs.

The 80386 operates in two modes: protected virtual address mode, and iAPX 86 real address mode. In protected virtual address mode (also called protected mode), programs use virtual addresses. In this mode, the 80386 CPU automatically maps one gigabyte of virtual addresses per task into a 16 megabyte real address space. This mode also provides memory protection to isolate the operating system and ensure privacy of each task's programs and data. In iAPX 86 real address mode, programs use real address with up to one megabyte of address space. Both modes provide the same base instruction set, registers, and addressing modes.

Interrupt Control

Incoming interrupts are handled by two on-board 8259A programmable interrupt controllers and by the 80386's NMI line. Eighteen potential interrupt sources are routed to the programmable controllers and the interrupt jumper matrix. Using this jumper matrix, the user can connect the desired interrupt sources to specific interrupt levels. Interrupts originating from up to 15 sources are then prioritized and sent to the CPU. Table 1 includes a list of devices and functions supported by interrupts.

Memory Capabilities

The iSBC 386/20P board supports both EPROM local memory located on board and DRAM dual-port memory which connects to the iSBC 386/20P board. The dual-port memory is supported by a high speed on-board cache memory.

DUAL-PORT MEMORY INTERFACE

The iSBC 386/20P pre production board supports a high-speed, 32-bit memory interface that connects to the iSBC 402P 2 megabyte memory expansion board using a pair of ribbon cables supplied in the kit. The iSBC 402P board is a standard MULTIBUS I formfactor board. Production iSBC 386/20 CPU boards will use low-profile memory modules that plug directly onto the iSBC 386/20 board. The modules use surface mount technology devices and will be available in 1, 2, 4, and 8 megabyte sizes. Two modules may be used together to provide up to 16 MB of system memory. The iSBC 386/20 board automatically determines the size of dual-port memory installed. Neither the memory expansion board nor the modules need to be jumper configured for starting/ending address locations. Both the board and modules support byte-parity error detection and have 32-bit wide data paths to the 80386 CPU and 16-bit wide data path, to the MULTIBUS interface.

CACHE MEMORY

A 16KB cache memory on the iSBC 386/20P board supports the 80386 microprocessor, and provides 0 wait-state reads for data and program code resident in the cache memory. The cache memory is updated whenever data is written into the dual-port memory or when the CPU executes a read cycle and the data or program code is not already present in cache memory. This process is controlled by the cache replacement algorithm.

The cache memory supports 4K entries, with each entry comprised of a 32-bit data field and an 8-bit tag cache field. The tag field is used to determine which actual memory word currently resides in a cache entry. The cache memory size and effective replacement

Table 1. Interrupt Request Sources

Device	Function	Number of Interrupts
MULTIBUS® Interface	Requests from MULTIBUS resident peripherals or other CPU boards	8
8251A Serial Controller	Indicates status of transmit and receive buffers of Ring Indicator lead of the RS232C interface	3
8254 Timers	Timer 0, 1 outputs; function determined by timer mode	2
iSBX Connector	Function determined by iSBX MULTIMODULE board	2
Bus Timeout	Indicates addressed MULTIBUS or iSBX resident device has not responded to command within 10 msec	1
Power Fail Interrupt	Indicates AC power is not within tolerance. Signal generated by system power supply	1
Parity Interrupt	Indicates on-board or MULTIBUS® parity error	1

iSBC® 386/20 SBC STARTER KIT

algorithm are designed to optimize both the probability of cache "hits" and local bus utilization.

LOCAL MEMORY

The local memory consists of two 28-pin JEDEC sites that support EPROM devices, and are intended for boot-up and system diagnostic/monitor routines. Maximum local memory capacity is 128 KB using high capacity Intel 27512 EPROM devices. The iSBC 386/20P board provided in the starter kit includes two EPROM devices which are programmed with monitor software.

The local memory resides at the upper end of the 80386 device's memory space for both real and protected mode operation. Local memory access time is selectable at from three to six wait-states and is a function of the speed of the device used.

Programmable Timer

Three 16-bit, programmable interval timer/counters are provided using an 8254 device, with one timer dedicated to the serial port for use as a baud rate generator. The other two timers can be used to generate accurate time intervals under software control or to count external events and raise an interrupt to the CPU when a certain count is reached. Seven timer/counter modes are available as listed in Table 2. Each counter is capable of operating in either BCD or binary modes. The contents of each counter may be read at any time during system operation.

Serial I/O

The iSBC 386/20P board includes one RS232C serial channel, which is configured as an asynchronous, DTE interface. Data rates up to 9600 baud may be selected. The serial channel can connect either to a host system to use the monitor software provided in the starter kit, or to a standalone terminal for field diagnostic support. For standalone use, unhosted monitor software needs to be programmed by the user into the local EPROM memory. The physical interface is a 10-pin ribbon-style connector located on the front edge of the board. Included in the starter kit is a 10-pin to 25-pin "D"-type connector ribbon cable assembly.

iSBX™ Interface

For iSBX MULTIMODULE support, the iSBC 386/20P CPU board provides a 16-bit iSBX connector which may be configured for use with either 8- or 16-bit, single or double-wide iSBX MULTIMODULE boards. Using the iSBX interface, a wide variety of specialized I/O functions can be easily and inexpensively added to the iSBC 386/20P board.

Table 2. Programmable Timer Functions

Function	Operation
Interrupt on terminal count	When terminal count is reached, an interrupt request is generated. This function is extremely useful for generation of real-time clocks.
Programmable one-shot	Output goes low upon receipt of an external trigger edge or software command and returns high when terminal count is reached. This function is retriggerable.
Rate generator	Divide by N counter. The output will go low for one input clock cycle, and the period from one low going pulse to the next is N times the input clock period.
Square-wave rate generator	Output will remain high until one-half the count has been completed, and go low for the other half of the count.
Software triggered strobe	Output remains high until software loads count (N). N counts after count is loaded, output goes low for one input clock period.
Hardware triggered strobe	Output goes low for one clock period N counts after rising edge counter trigger input. The counter is retriggerable.
Event counter	On a jumper selectable basis, the clock input becomes an input from the external system. CPU may read the number of events occurring after the counter "window" has been enabled or an interrupt may be generated after N events occur in the system.

Reset Functions

The iSBC 386/20P board is designed to accept an AUX (auxilliary) reset signal via the board's P2 interface. In this way, system designs which require front panel reset switches are supported. The iSBC 386/20P board uses the AUX reset signal to reset all on-board logic (excluding DRAM refresh circuitry) and to generate an INIT (initialize) reset signal over the MULTIBUS interface to reset other boards in the system. The iSBC 386/20P board will also respond to an INIT Reset Signal generated by another board in the system.

LED Status Indicators

Mounted on the top edge of the iSBC 386/20P board are four LED indicators which indicate the operating status of the board and system. One indicator is used to show that an on-board parity error or a MULTIBUS bus parity error has occurred. A second LED indicates that a MULTIBUS or iSBX bus access timeout has occurred. The third LED is triggered by the start of an 80386 bus cycle and will go off if the 80386 CPU stops executing bus cycles. The fourth LED can be set under program control to illuminate by writing to a specific I/O location.

MULTIBUS® SYSTEM ARCHITECTURE

Overview

The MULTIBUS system architecture includes three bus structures: the system bus, the local bus extension and the iSBX MULTIMODULE expansion bus. Each bus structure is optimized to satisfy particular system requirements. The system bus provides a basis for general system design including memory and I/O expansion as well as multiprocessing support. The MULTIBUS System architecture also includes the iLBX™ memory interface which is not supported by the iSBC 386/20P board.

System Bus—IEEE 796

The MULTIBUS system bus is Intel's industry standard, IEEE 796, microcomputer bus structure. Both 8- and 16-bit single board computers are supported on the IEEE 796 structure with 24 address and 16 data lines. In its simplest application, the system bus allows expansion of functions already contained on a single board computer (e.g., memory and digital I/O). However, the IEEE 796 bus also allows very powerful distributed processing configurations using multiple processors, I/O boards, and peripheral boards. The MULTIBUS system bus is supported with a broad array of board level products, VLSI interface components, detailed published specifications and application notes.

System Bus—Expansion Capabilities

Memory and I/O capacity may be expanded and additional functions added using Intel MULTIBUS compatible expansion boards. Memory may be expanded by adding user specified combinations of EPROM boards, DRAM boards, or bubble memory boards. Input/output capacity may be added with digital I/O and analog I/O expansion boards. Mass storage capability may be achieved by adding single or double density diskette controllers, or hard disk controllers. Modular expandable backplanes and cardcages are available to support multiboard systems.

System Bus—Multimaster Capabilities

For those applications requiring additional processing capacity and the benefits of multiprocessing (i.e., several CPUs and/or controllers logically sharing system tasks through communication over the system bus), the iSBC 386/20P board provides full system bus arbitration control logic. This control logic allows up to three iSBC 386/20P boards or other bus masters to share the system bus using a serial (daisy chain) priority scheme. By using an external parallel priority decoder, this may be extended to 16 bus masters. In addition to multiprocessing, the multimaster capability also provides a very efficient mechanism for all forms of DMA (Direct Memory Access) transfers.

iSBX™ Bus MULTIMODULE® On-Board Expansion

One 8-, 16-bit iSBX MULTIMODULE connector is provided on the iSBC 386/20P microcomputer board. Through this connector, additional on-board I/O functions may be added. The iSBX MULTIMODULE boards optimally support functions provided by VLSI peripheral components such as additional parallel and serial I/O, analog I/O, small mass storage device controllers (e.g., floppy disks), BITBUS™ Control, and other custom interfaces to meet specific needs. By mounting directly on the single board computer, less interface logic, less power, simpler packaging, higher performance, and lower cost result when compared to other alternatives such as MULTIBUS form factor compatible boards. The iSBX interface connector on the iSBC 386/20P board provides all the signals necessary to interface to the local on-board bus, including 16 data lines. The iSBX MULTIMODULE boards designed with 8-bit data paths and using the 8-bit iSBX connector are also supported on the iSBC 386/20P microcomputer board. A broad range of iSBX MULTIMODULE options are available from Intel. Custom iSBX modules may also be designed. An iSBX bus interface specification is available from Intel.

SOFTWARE SUPPORT

Operating Systems

Both the iRMX™ 286/386 Release 2 Operating System and the XENIX* Operating System will support the iSBC 386/20P CPU board.

The iRMX 286/386 software is a part of the iRMX 286 Release 2 Operating System designed to manage and extend the resources of iSBC single board computers and other 80386 based microcomputers. The iRMX 286/386 software is a real-time multi-tasking and multiprogramming software system capable of executing all the configurable layers of the iRMX 286 operating system on the 80386 microprocessor and the iSBC 386/20 single board computer.

For multiple user, interactive systems, Intel will offer the XENIX Operating System which is fully compatible with current Intel XENIX products.

*XENIX is a trademark of Microsoft Corporation

iSBC® 386/20 SBC STARTER KIT

PRELIMINARY

LANGUAGES AND TOOLS

Intel will be offering several languages supported by the iRMX and XENIX operating systems. For the iRMX 286/386 Software System, this will include ASM 286, Pascal 286, PL/M 286, C 286, and FORTRAN 286. For the XENIX Operating System, languages will include ASM 386, C 386, PL/M 386, and FORTRAN 386. Software development tools will include PSCOPE Monitor 386, PSCOPE 286 Program Debugger, and an ICE™ 386 in-circuit emulator.

System Compatibility

The iSBC 386/20P Single Board Computer is complemented by a wide range of MULTIBUS hardware and software products from over 200 manufacturers worldwide. This enables the designer to easily and quickly incorporate the iSBC 386/20P board into his system design to satisfy a wide range of high performance applications.

Applications which use other 16-bit MULTIBUS single board computers (such as Intel's iSBC 286/10A and iSBC 286/12 8 MHz, 80286 based single board computers) can be easily upgraded to use the iSBC 386/20P board. Only minor changes to hardware and systems software (for speed and I/O configuration dependent code) may be required.

SPECIFICATIONS

Word Size
Instruction—8, 16, 24, 32 or 40 bits
Data—8, 16, 32 bits

System Clock
CPU—12/16 MHz
Numeric Processor—80287 module—8 MHz

Dual-Port Memory
Capacity—One memory expansion board
Maximum Physical Memory—
  4 Megabytes (protected mode)
  1 Megabyte (real mode)
Compatible DRAM Memory—
  iSBC 402P 2 Megabyte parity memory board (supplied with starter kit)

Local Memory
Number of sockets—Two 28-pin JEDEC Sites
Maximum size—128KB with 27512 EPROM (supplied with starter kit) 64KB with 27256 EPROM

I/O Capability
Serial Channel
  Type—One RS232C DTE Asynchronous channel using an 8251A device.
  Max speed—9600 baud
  Leads supported—TD, RD, RTS, CTS, DSR, DTR, RI, CD, SG
  Connector Type—10 pin ribbon
Expansion—One 8/16-bit iSBX interface connector for single or double wide iSBX MULTIMODULE board.

Timers
Quantity—Two programmable timers using one 8274 device.
Input Frequency—1.23 MHz ± 0.1%

Interfaces
MULTIBUS Bus—All signals TTL compatible
iSBX Bus—All signals TTL compatible
Serial I/O—RS232C, DTE
Timer—All signals TTL compatible
Interrupt Requests—All TTL compatible

MULTIBUS® DRIVERS

Function	Type	Sink Current (ma)
Data	Tri-State	64
Address	Tri-State	24
Commands	Tri-State	32
Bus Control	Open Collector	16/32

OUTPUT FREQUENCIES/TIMING INTERVALS

Function	Single Timer/Counter		Dual Timer/Counter (two timers cascaded)	
	Min	Max	Min	Max
Real-time interrupt	667 ns	53.3 ms	1.33 μs	58.2 min
Programmable one-shot	667 ns	53.3 ms	1.33 μs	58.2 min
Rate generator	18.8 Hz	1.50 MHz	0.000286 Hz	750 kHz
Square-wave rate generator	18.8 Hz	1.50 MHz	0.000286 Hz	750 kHz
Software triggered strobe	667 ns	53.3 ms	1.33 μs	58.2 min
Hardware triggered strobe	667 ns	53.3 ms	1.33 μs	58.2 min
Event counter	—	8.0 MHz	—	—

iSBC® 386/20 SBC STARTER KIT

PRELIMINARY

Mating Connectors

Function	# of Pins	Centers (in)	Connector Type	Vendor*	Vendor Part* Number
iSBX Bus Connector	44	0.1	Soldered	Viking	000293-0001
I/O Connector	10	0.1	Flat Crimp	3M	3399-6010
Front Panel Connector	14	0.5	Flat Crimp	3M	3385-6014
P2 Interface Edge Connector	60	0.1	Flat Crimp	KEL-AM T&B Ansley	RF30-2803-5 A3020

*Or equivalent

Physical Characteristics

DIMENSIONS:

iSBC 386/20P CPU Board—
    Width—12.00 in. (30.48 cm)
    Height—8.75 in. (22.22 cm)

iSBC 402P Memory Board—
    Width—12.00 in. (30.48 cm)
    Height—6.75 in. (17.15 cm)

RECOMMENDED MINIMUM CARDCAGE SLOT SPACING:

iSBC 386/20P CPU Board—1.2 in. (3.0 cm)
    (with or without iSBX MULTIMODULE)
iSBC 402P Memory Board—0.8 in. (2.0 cm)

APPROXIMATE WEIGHT:

iSBC 386/20P CPU Board—26 oz. (731 gm)
iSBC 402P Memory Board—18 oz. (510 gm)

DC Power Requirements

Board	Voltage	Current (Approx.)
iSBC 386/20 CPU Board*	+5V	11A (max) 9A (typ)
	±12V	35mA (max) 20mA (typ)
iSBC 402P Memory Board	+5V	5.5A (max) 3.9A (typ)

*Includes power for local EPROM Memory

ORDERING INFORMATION

Part Number	Description
SBC38620SPKG	iSBC 386/20 Starter Kit

Supplied: iSBC 386/20P CPU board, iSBC 402P 2MB parity memory board, set of CPU/Memory ribbon cable assemblies, 10-pin to 25-pin RS232C cable, monitor EPROM firmware, monitor host software on 5¼" diskette, user documentation.

intel

APPLICATION NOTE

AP-114

October 1981

Using the iSBC® 88/40 Measurement and Control Computer in PID Applications

Peter Andersen
OMS Applications Engineering

Order Number: 210263-001

2-115

AP-114

INTRODUCTION

During the past twenty years, the automated process control industry has matured significantly. This is due to the introduction of the digital computer as an element of the control system. At the beginning of this period, the use of the digital computer was limited to a supervisory status in which the actual control was performed by various combinations of relay, analog, and pneumatic systems. Today, systems are off-the-shelf digital hardware and software to perform all the control applications. Indeed, the use of the hardware/software combination has opened entirely new areas of control applications.

The significant increase in computer capabilities and the corresponding reduction in size has been accompanied by a substantial drop in cost. This has led to a strong incentive for users to employ computers in totally new application areas which have resulted from this change in economics. Twenty years ago, few computer control projects were initiated and those which were could only be justified economically in terms of control systems which controlled upwards of 100 loops. Today, a microcomputer system can be justified for a small process which contains as few as 3 or 4 control loops.

Today, the control system engineer's decision is not so much an economic justification of a digital process as it is a choice of whether to use a single or a multiple microcomputer based design.

The trend toward the use of digital technology in the control world has been driven, in part, by the products which have been introduced into the marketplace by Intel Corporation. A recently announced product, the iSBC 88/40 Measurement and Control Computer, is intended to further simplify the implementation of digital technologies into varied control applications and is the subject of this application note. Its architecture is well suited for both single microcomputer and multicomputing environments. The board is also easily adapted to a wide variety of input/output configurations through on-board facilities and iSBX MULTIMODULE expansion boards.

Generalized Computer Application Areas

Those applications in which computers are finding acceptance can generally be broken down into two broad areas. The first involves the acquisition and manipulation of process data by the computer, and is sometimes referred to as being a class of passive applications. The second, known as active systems, also involves the manipulation of the process itself. The systems in the latter class also provide various degrees of passive data manipulation.

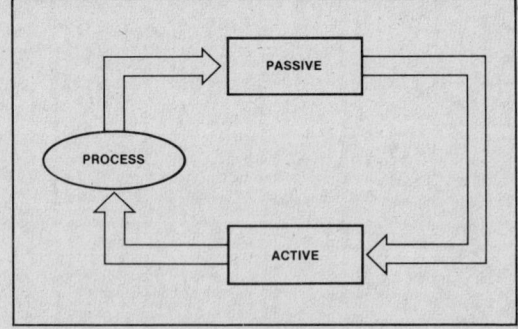

Figure 2. Classes of Computer Applications

Figure 1. The iSBC® 88/40 Measurement and Control Computer

At first glance, the area of passive computer applications seems to have little or nothing to do with process control; however, many computer design projects are being split into two phases. One phase is to characterize the process and the second is concerned with the actual control system. Many designs never move from phase one and are used as data acquisition systems.

The majority of passive systems involve measuring physical parameters of the process application. Examples are the measurement of pressure, temperature, flow, force, and level. Most transducers associated with these physical parameters provide an analog signal which is proportional to the physical property being sensed. Thus, the ability to measure analog voltages is a requirement of process control systems, both active and passive.

The iSBC 88/40 Measurement and Control Computer is ideally suited for these classes of systems because of the board's built-in analog to digital conversion circuitry. Each input channel (there are 16 differential or 32 single-ended channels on the board) has its own programmable gain which can be software selected to provide full scale inputs ranging from 20 millivolts to 10 volts. The board is thus compatible with most commonly available transducer elements. Examples of typical interface drivers are given in later sections of this application note.

Active applications must interact with the control system in order to manage the process. This normally involves the activation and movement of a mechanical element which is incorporated into the process loop. An amplifier and transducer are required to convert the electrical output of the controller into mechanical energy. The majority of these activators are electro-pneumatic, requiring both an electrical control signal (usually 4-20 milliamps) from the controller and an air supply for its internal pneumatic amplifier. Less common, but still in substantial numbers, are activators which use either a frequency input control signal or stepping motors.

Again, the iSBC 88/40 Measurement and Control Computer provides features designed to allow easy interface to various control actuators. For those actuators using digital frequencies or stepping motors, the board has a parallel output capability to drive up to 24 digital lines. Pulse output signals can be routed from programmable timers/counters (to generate a variety of pulse type outputs) to the external I/O devices. Analog actuators can be driven using the iSBX 328 Analog Output MULTIMODULE Board. This board connects to the measurement and control computer using one of the three iSBX connectors on the iSBC 88/40 board. Each iSBX 328 board can generate up to 8 analog output signals, each of which can function in either a voltage or current (4-20 milliamps) output mode.

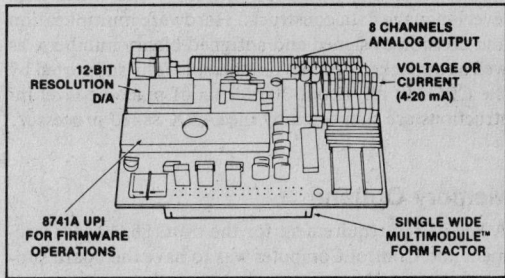

Figure 3. iSBX™ 328 Analog Output MULTIMODULE™ Board

Computer Processing Capabilities

The key to the rapid growth of digital computers in process control has been the flexibility offered by the software. The same hardware can be used in widely varying applications by allowing customization through software programmming. To be successful in the process control marketplace, a digital computer system must be designed in a manner which optimizes the hardware/software relationships. The iSBC 88/40 Measurement and Control Computer does this well.

A powerful instruction set is mandatory if operations are to be efficiently performed by the processor. An instruction set optimized to perform business operations will perform poorly in an industrial process application. The processor used on the iSBC 88/40 board is the Intel iAPX 88/10 microprocessor. This third generation microprocesor is suitable for a wide spectrum of applications. The large application domain is made possible by the processor's dual operating modes and built-in multiprocessing features. The iAPX 88/10 microprocessor is from four to six times more powerful than the 8080A microprocessor.

The high performance of the iAPX 88/10 microprocessor is realized by combining an internal data path with a pipelined architecture that allows instructions to be prefetched during spare bus cycles. Also contributing to performance is a compact instruction format that enables more instructions to be fetched in a given amount of time.

Software for high-performance iAPX 88/10 processors need not be written in assembly language (although it certainly can be). The CPU is designed to provide direct hardware support for programs written in high level languages such as Intel's PL/M-86. Because most high level languages store variables in memory, the instruc-

AP-114

tion set supports direct operation on memory operands, including operands on the stack. The hardware addressing modes provide efficient implementations of based variables, arrays, arrays of structures and other high level language data constructs. Hardware multiplication and division of signed and unsigned binary numbers, as well as unpacked decimal numbers, is fully supported by the CPU. In all, about 300 forms of machine level instructions are supported by the iAPX 88/10 processor.

Memory Options

A key design requirement for the iSBC 88/40 Measurement and Control Computer was to have the board support a variety of memory types and capacities. The result is a product which can easily be configured to meet a wide range of process control application requirements.

Program storage support for small to very large applications is obtained through the board's ability to include EPROM storage capacities ranging up to 64K bytes. Maximum standard storage capacity is from 8K bytes (using 2716 EPROM devices) to 32K bytes (using the 2764 EPROM). An optional EPROM expansion MULTIMODULE board can be mounted onto the iSBC 88/40 board to double the memory storage capacities.

Variables used in an application are usually stored in RAM memory. A standard on-board RAM capacitiy of 4K bytes is included on the measurement and control computer. In order to efficiently support multi-computer system design, 1K bytes of this memory is dual-ported. Dual-porting introduces a three bus system architecture to system design. An on-board local bus creates a data path between the iAPX 88/10 CPU and its local RAM. Data paths to RAM located on other iSBC boards are provided by the facilities of the MULTIBUS system bus. Finally, a third bus provides a gateway into the local RAM by other MULTIBUS single board computers or bus masters. If additional RAM is required, a small MULTIMODULE RAM expansion board can be attached to the iSBC 88/40 board to add 4K bytes of random access memory.

Even more flexibility can be gained by using unneeded EPROM memory sockets. Because JEDEC standard 24/28 pin sockets have been used, byte wide RAM modules can be inserted into areas of the EPROM memory space. The use of this RAM can considerably enhance the design of certain applications. The board capabilities are such that it is not necessary to have all devices residing in the EPROM sockets be of the same type or size.

Many process control applications require the use of non-volatile memory for the storage of parameter lists and system setpoints. Provision has been made on the iSBC 88/40 Measurement and Control Computer to fully support Intel's new 2816 Electrically Eraseable and Programmable Read Only Memory (E^2PROM). This device gives the user 2K bytes of memory. Depending on the application, up to eight devices (16K bytes) can be used on the iSBC 88/40 board. The board includes all required voltages and wave-shaping circuits to fully support the use of the 2816. A byte of 2816 memory can be programmed in 16 milliseconds. A subsequent section of this application note contains a comprehensive discussion of the operation of the board with the 2816.

Arithmetic Functions

Using computers as an element in a control system leads to extensive arithmetic and mathematical functions. To be effective and attractive to the designer, a computer board must provide a wide range of mathematical capabilities. The iSBC 88/40 Measurement and Control Computer easily meets these needs with varying capabilities for hardware and software functions.

Many applications are adequately handled using the hardware add/subtract and multiply/divide instructions of the on-board iAPX 88/10 processor. Functions needing integer arithmetic of varying precisions are easily programmed using this facility. In some cases, more complex operations may require the use of software libraries to gain the required mathematical functions. The speed and instruction set of the CPU, in conjunction with PL/M-86 statements, make programmers comfortable with these operations.

As processes become more involved and their control algorithms more complex, the need for the processor to support more precise numbers becomes important. The additional precision is usually obtained through the use of a floating point representation. Intel supplies several tools which simplify the implementation of systems requiring floating point operations. Complete support for the floating point numbers is provided as an integral part of the PL/M-86 compiler. Thus, variables can be specified as real numbers. The compiler will perform all numerical operations on these numbers in the floating point format. The data formats of all Intel floating point support conform to the proposed IEEE Floating Point Standard, insuring highly accurate results.

An important feature of the iAPX 88/10 processor is its ability to use a co-processor. The Intel 8087 is mounted on the iSBC 337 MULTIMODULE Numeric Data Processor to provide arithmetic and logical instruction extensions to the 8086 and 8088 CPU's. The instruction set consists of arithmetic, transcendental, logical, trigonometric, and exponential instructions which can all operate on seven different data types. In many cases, the use of this MULTIMODULE board results in two orders of magnitude performance enhancement over a software solution. This board is the subject of a subsequent section of this application note.

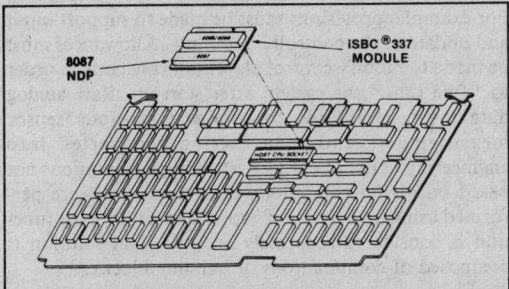

Figure 4. iSBC® 337 MULTIMODULE™ Numeric Data Processor

APPLICATION EXAMPLE

The features of the iSBC 88/40 Measurement and Control Computer can best be shown through an example. This application note describes the classical control system application of an agitated heating tank. Figure 5 shows the prominent features of this process control applications. The process consists of a storage vessel, a temperature sensor which measures the temperature of the fluid leaving the vessel, and a steam coil whose steam flow is regulated by a proportional valve. A motor drives an agitator to insure the temperature of the tank remains homogeneous.

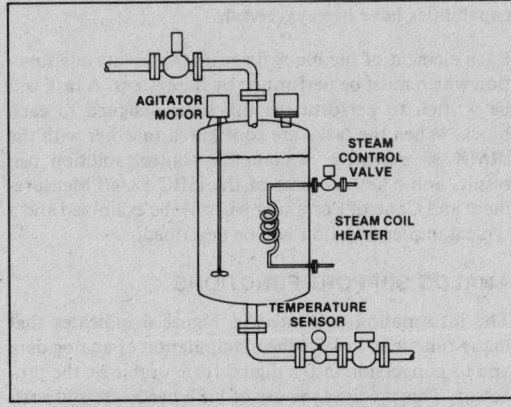

Figure 5. An Agitated Heating Tank

The passive portion of the application involves measuring the actual temperature of the fluid as it leaves the tank (and thus the temperature of all the fluid in the tank). If a control system is to be constructed which will control the temperature, an algorithm must be implemented which will provide control of the steam valve based upon the actual and the desired temperatures. This is the active portion of the application.

The control algorithm selected to control the tank temperature must be capable of compensating for disturbances created by a variety of conditions. For example, the temperature can be affected by changes in steam temperature, input temperature of the fluid, output flow rate, ambient temperature, and the flow rate of steam through the steam coil. Our control system will have control of only one of the variables and will only monitor the output temperature. To gain a degree of stability under these conditions, a feedback control algorithm is required. Alternatively, a system could be implemented using a feed-forward control algorithm. Unfortunately, the latter technique would require extensive instrumentation of all possible variables which could cause a disturbance. A feedback control system can take corrective action regardless of the source of a disturbance. Its chief drawback is that no corrective action is taken until an error is actually detected and, if not "tuned" correctly, some oscillations can occur.

Classical Controller Approaches

Before proceeding with a discussion of how a control system can be implemented using single board computers, a short discussion of classical control system theory is in order. This material will provide a background into the control algorithms which will be used as a basis for the digital control solution which will be developed.

The classical controller for feedback systems uses the "three mode" or PID (Proportional, Integral, Derivative) algorithm. In this system, the control output signal is a function of the error (the difference between the setpoint and the measured system variable). A specific application will use some combination of one, two, or all three terms making up the control statement.

Before continuing with the implementation of the control algorithm on the iSBC 88/40 Measurement and Control Computer, the various terms of the equation will be reviewed.

For Proportional control, the controller output is given by the equation:

$$m(t) = b + k_0 e(t) \qquad (eq.\ 1)$$

where $m(t)$ is the output signal, b is an adjustable bias value, k_0 is a gain constant, and $e(t)$ is the measured error signal. Proportional control systems are normally not used by themselves since corrections can not be made until an appreciable error has been detected. In addition, they tend to introduce oscillations into the system if the gain is set too large. Another disadvantage of proportional only systems is their inability to maintain a control element at some point (other than at its zero point using the bias term) in the absence of an error signal.

The second term in the PID solution is the Integral. The result of this term is to eliminate steady-state error or offset. The elimination of the offset is an important control objective; thus, the integral control term is widely used in conjunction with the proportional control element. The equation for the integral term is:

$$m(t) = (1/k_1) \int e(t)dt \qquad (eq.\ 2)$$

where k_1 is the integral or reset time.

The Derivative term in the algorithm is used to provide an output which is a function of the rate of change in the error signal. It anticipates the future behavior of the system and improves the dynamic response to the controlled variable by decreasing the process response time. The format for the derivative term is:

$$m(t) = k_2(de/dt) \qquad (eq.\ 3)$$

where k_2 is a constant representing the derivative time expressed in seconds or minutes. Because the output of the term is zero for a constant error, derivative control is never used alone in a control system. Instead, it is always used in conjunction with proportional and integral control. The derivative term is seldom used in flow controllers because derivative control tends to amplify "noise" which is picked up in the flow measurement, leading to an unstable control system. In addition, systems which have very large time delays do not benefit from the use of this term.

Implementation Using Digital Techniques

With an exposure to the fundamental concepts of control theory complete, the development of a solution using the iSBC 88/40 Measurement and Control Computer can proceed. A modular "top-down" approach will be used in this application note. The general requirements will be defined and "black boxes" will be developed to meet these requirements. Finally, the individual pieces will be combined to form a complete solution to the agitated tank control problem.

An effective control algorithm must deal not only with the mathematical solution of the control equation, but must also provide tests on limits and error conditions.

As this application note will show, the iSBC 88/40 Measurement and Control Computer is easily able to support these additional requirements.

Additional supporting functions are also needed to effectively implement a complete control system solution. For example, provisions must be made to support input and update of the controller setpoints. Allowances must be made to modify control algorithm constants in order to "fine tune" the system after start-up. Raw analog data must be filtered to eliminate spurious sensor measurements and then must be converted into engineering units. In earlier system implementations not based on digital computers, these functions were performed using a "black box" approach. Here, each function is considered separately and the final solution is composed of combinations of building blocks.

Digital technology offers a simple analogy to this approach. Because application design is performed with software, a "black box" design is available for use with microcomputers. The black box corresponds to a software "task" and the system is integrated into a functional unit using a real time operating system. The iRMX 88 Real Time Executive provides all the tools needed by the software designer to implement his required functions for the application. This application note will show how the iRMX 88 executive can be used to simplify the design and to provide significant features in a process design example.

Figure 6 shows a block diagram of the operations needed to implement the control of one loop for the agitated heating tank. An attribute of using digital microcomputers is that additional loops can be run using the same hardware and software until the I/O or processing capabilities have been exceeded.

Each element of the block diagram represents one function which must be performed by the system. A task will be written to perform the functions assigned to each block. When the tasks are configured together with the iRMX 88 executive, a complete control solution will result. Some key features of the iSBC 88/40 Measurement and Control Computer will now be examined and a typical implementation will be described.

ANALOG SUPPORT FUNCTIONS

The information presented in Figure 6 indicates that many functions involve the manipulation of analog data and its conversion into a digital form usable by the processor. This involves the use of both hardware and software. This section of the application note demonstrates how the iSBC 88/40 board features can be applied to the solution of the analog portions of the system implementation. Both software programming concepts and hardware support products are examined.

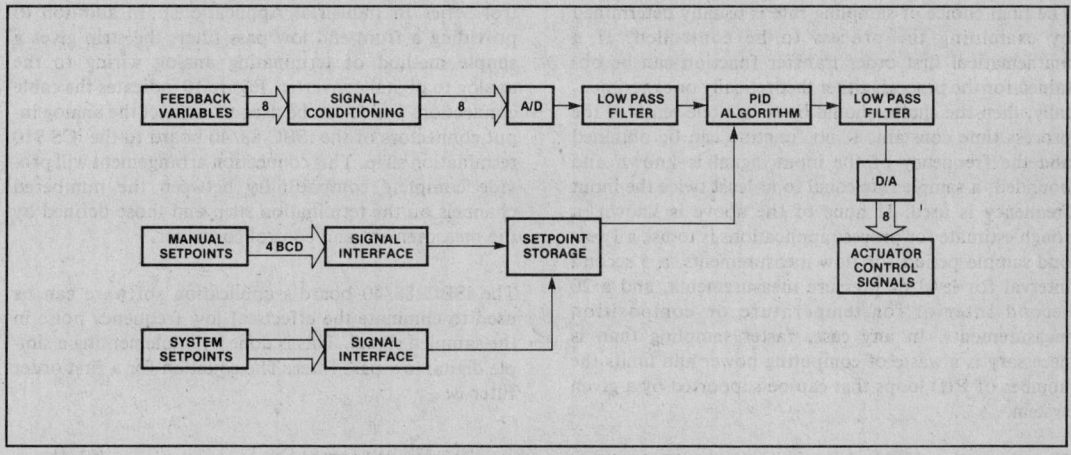

Figure 6. Control System Block Diagram

A digital computer performs most of the control system operations using software. Data is sampled from the process sensor and converted to an equivalent digital format. Subsequent operations use the digital form of the data. Unfortunately, this requirement for operating on sampled data, rather than continuous actual data, can lead to errors if the system is not properly implemented. Care must be taken to minimize errors when the original signal is digitized. Figure 7 shows how the digital signal may look when an analog signal is sampled using an analog to digital converter. A glance at the figure indicates that the error can be minimized by taking samples at shorter time intervals so that the staircase more closely resembles the original signal. Indeed, this is true, but what sample rate is best for a particular input signal?

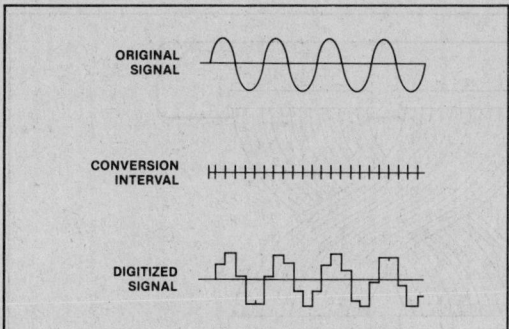

Figure 7. Analog Signal Digitization

A rule for digital control system designers is that the sample must be performed more than twice each period of the original analog signal. Thus, the sampling period must be less than one half the period of the sinusoidal frequency component which must be digitized. Even this method does not, in itself, assure an accurate measurement. Figure 8 shows the effects of the aliasing phenomenon on a high frequency signal. Aliasing converts the high frequency components into fictitious low frequency signals in the sampled results. Before data obtained from a digital system can be used, the unwanted signals must be filtered from the original sensor signal.

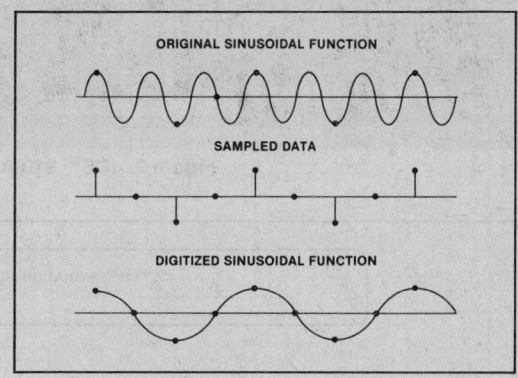

Figure 8. High Frequency Aliasing Error

Two approaches can be considered for filtering the data. One is the creation of an analog low pass filter and the second is the implementation of a digital filter. Unfortunately, a digital filter cannot remove aliasing error and is normally used to provide filtering of very low frequency oscillations. Analog filtering provides effective removal of unwanted frequencies but is expensive when attempting to gain sharp cut-off frequencies. A combination of the two technologies results in an ideal situation when used with digital controllers such as the iSBC 88/40 Measurement and Control Computer.

The final choice of sampling rate is usually determined by examining the process to be controlled. If a mathematical first order transfer function can be obtained for the process, either theoretically or experimentally, then the choice should be to use one tenth of the process time constant. If no function can be obtained and the frequency of the input signal is known and bounded, a sample rate equal to at least twice the input frequency is used. If none of the above is known, a rough estimate for process applications is to use a 1 second sample period for flow measurements, a 5 second interval for level or pressure measurements, and a 20 second interval for temperature or composition measurements. In any case, faster sampling than is necessary is a waste of computing power and limits the number of PID loops that can be supported by a given system.

The elimination of high frequency noise in systems using Intel's control products is best accomplished using the iCS 910 Analog Termination Strip. This strip has provision for the installation of a single pole RC low pass filter (details on the use of this strip in industrial control applications can be found in AP-52, Using Intel's Control Series In Industrial Applications). In addition to providing a front-end low pass filter, the strip gives a simple method of terminating analog wiring to the analog to digital converter. Figure 10 indicates the cable connections which can be used to connect the analog input connectors of the iSBC 88/40 board to the iCS 910 termination strip. This connection arrangement will provide complete compatibility between the numbered channels on the termination strip and those defined by the measurement and control computer.

The iSBC 88/40 board's application software can be used to eliminate the effects of low frequency noise in the sampled signal. This is done by implementing a simple digital low pass filter. The equation for a first order filter is:

$$Sf = a(Sm) + (1-a)\,(Sf') \qquad (eq.\ 4)$$

where Sf represents the filtered output, a is a function of the cutoff frequency, Sm is the measured sample, and Sf' is the last filtered output result. If additional poles are required, the equations can be cascaded as required.

Figure 9. iCS™ 910 Analog Termination Strip

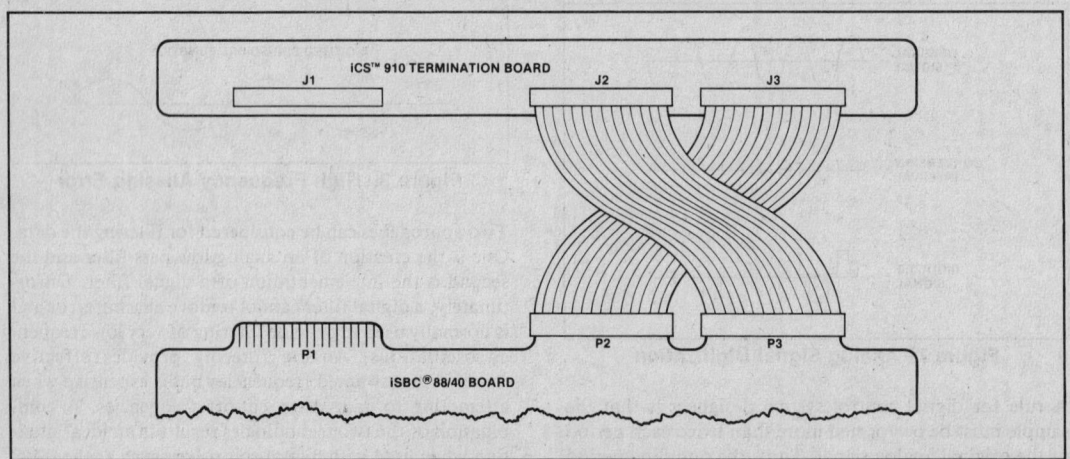

Figure 10. Termination Board Interconnects

AP-114

The implementation of this filter using Intel's PL/M-86 high level language is straightforward. A simple procedure can be written in which the measured value, the last filter output value, and the value for a are passed with the call. The procedure returns the new filtered value. The code for such a procedure is shown in Figure 11. Note that the computation is performed in steps to prevent any stack overflows from occurring when real numbers are used. This should be done whenever the algebraic equation exceeds eight terms. The 8087 stack used in internal operations can overflow when more than eight operations are nested together. Breaking the equation into smaller steps can prevent any overflow errors from occurring.

```
1        Analog$filter$module: Do;
2    1   Analog$filter:
         Procedure (present$value, last$output, cutoff) real public;
3    2   Declare (present$value, last$output, cutoff) pointer;

4    2   Declare New$signal based present$value real;
5    2   Declare Old$filter based last$output real;
6    2   Declare Alpha based cutoff real;

7    2   Declare New$filter real;

8    2   Declare temp1 real;
9    2   Declare temp2 real;
10   2   Declare temp3 real;
11   2   Declare One real data (1.0);

12   2   temp1 = Alpha * New$signal;
13   2   temp2 = One - Alpha;
14   2   temp3 = temp2 * Old$filter;
15   2   New$filter = temp1 + temp3;
16   2   Return New$filter;

17   2   end Analog$filter;
18   2   end Analog$filter$module;
```

Figure 11. Low Pass Filter Algorithm

Before data can be sent to the filter, it must be converted into floating point format and then into engineering units. The conversion into engineering units can involve a complex algorithm if the raw data is non-linear. The design of future systems can be simplified if the programmer generates procedures which are general enough to cover the majority of cases found in his application environment. The following example shows how the iSBC 88/40 board can be programmed to provide the linearization and conversion for the general case.

LINEARIZATION FUNCTIONS

The program developed for this application example uses an interpolation technique. A table look-up enables a program to be written which will support both linear and non-linear analog sensors. The number of entries in the table is a function of the desired resolution and of the non-linearity. For example, linear functions needing only scaling and offset (y = ax + b) require only two table entries. A separate table is maintained for each sensor channel. The program is written to support a maximum of 256 entries per channel which should provide at least 0.1 percent accuracy for all but the most non-linear applications.

Each table entry consists of a raw value and a corresponding real engineering unit value expressed in floating point format. The linearization program's declaration of such a table is shown in Figure 12. The application software must determine the bracket or location of the terms in the table which lie above and below the raw input value. The algorithm to find the bracket in the table which corresponds to the raw data input can be programmed as shown in Figure 13. Once the bracket has been found, the actual engineering value can be calculated and passed back to the calling program. The code for performing the interpolation calculation might look like that shown in Figure 14. Data for the tables can be determined from known characteristics of the sensor or a program can be written which allows the user to enter known points into the table dynamically during calibration. In this application note, an assumption is made that the data has been entered into the table from known characteristics rather than actual calibration.

```
6    2   Declare (table based table$pointer) (255) structure (
                 x word,
                 y real );
```

Figure 12. Declaration of Table

```
10   2         Do while table (n).x < raw$value;
11   3           n = n + 1;
               /* special case, above table */
12   3         If n > table$entries
                 then do;
14   4           eu = table(n - 1).y;
15   4           return eu;
16   4         end;
17   3         end;

               /* special case, below table */
18   2         If n = 0
                 then do;
20   3           eu = table(n).y;
21   3           return eu;
22   3         end;
```

Figure 13. Bracketing Algorithm

2-123

AFN-02015A

```
                    /* interpolate engineering units */
     23   2    dx = float(int(table(n).x − table(n − 1).x));
     24   2    dy = table(n).y − table(n − 1).y;
     25   2    dr = float(int(raw$value − table(n − 1).x));
     26   2    eu = dr * dy;
     27   2    eu = eu / dx;
     28   2    eu = eu + table(n − 1).y;
```

Figure 14. Interpolation Algorithm

One final component of the analog design which is required is the creation of software which will actually interface with the analog to digital converter and transform data from the analog world into a digital domain. Again, a program should be developed which is general enough to handle a wide variety of applications. It should be compatible with both the on-board A/D sections and with the iSBC 311 Analog Input MULTIMODULE Board, which may be installed for analog expansion.

The interface with the analog portions of the boards is easily handled using software. The ADC can be commanded to select the desired analog channel and begin a conversion by sending the appropriate byte containing the channel and gain bits to a port corresponding to the ADC. When using the on-board converter, the iSBC 88/40 board user should send the command byte to port 0D8 hex. The actual selection of the desired channel and the conversion takes only 50 microseconds, so little is gained by using an interrupt instead of status testing to detect the end of conversion. The status bit is tested by reading the input status port (0D8 hex for the on-board converter). When the conversion is complete, the bit will have a value of 0.

Certain multiplexer components used in the ADC require that a delay time be added to the basic 50 microseconds for the channel to settle after a new gain setting has been selected before reading the sample and hold converter. The amount of delay is a function of the gain and varies from 0 (gain = 1) to 30 milliseconds (gain = 250). The analog driver software must take this settle time into account. Figure 15 shows the required settle times for the various gain settings. The delay is easily implemented using the facilities of the iRMX 88 nucleus. While the system is waiting for the settling time, other tasks can use the processor to execute their code. Figure 16 provides an example of a program which gets data from the analog to digital converter for a selected channel and gain. The iRMX 88 request for a time delay is implemented using the call to RQWAIT specifying the desired delay. In the example, the system delay increment is assumed to be 5 milliseconds, so the required number of delay increments is specified as 6 in order to wait for 30 milliseconds at high gains. Note that, for gains of one, the delay is skipped. After the required delay has elapsed, the converter is again activated using another output to its command port. This output must again include the channel and gain information.

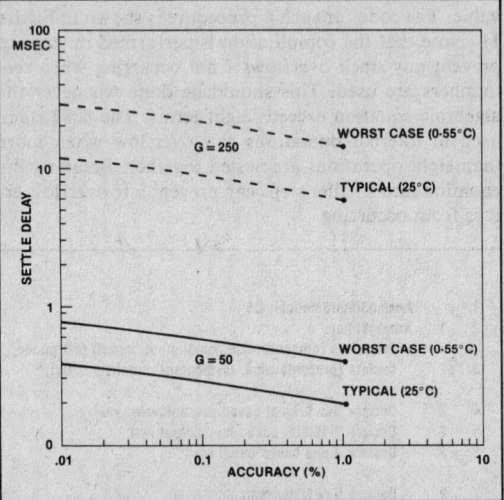

Figure 15. Analog Settle Times

```
                    /* select mux channel */
     14   2    output(port$adr) = channel or gain;
     15   2    if gain < 40h
                   then do;
                    /* settling delay for high gains */
     17   3        msg$ptr = rqwait(.timeout, 6);
     18   3        output(port$adr) = channel or gain;
     19   3    end;
                    /* wait for end of conversion */
     20   2    do while (input(port$adr) and 01h) > 0; end;

                    /* get adc data */
     22   2    low$raw$data = input(port$adr) and 0f0h;
     23   2    high$raw$data = input(port$adr + 1);
     24   2    raw$data = shl(high$raw$data, 8) or low$raw$data;
```

Figure 16. Analog Input Routine

A workable analog driver must provide more than just the ability to get data from a specified channel. At a minimum, the zero offset induced by the temperature of the circuitry must be removed from the raw data. In some cases, an additional correction is required to compensate for gain error induced by temperature. However, the effect of the latter is small and can usually be ignored.

Provisions are included on the iSBC 88/40 Measurement and Control Computer to simplify the task of providing a zero offset correction. Wire-wrap stakes are mounted on the board to facilitate grounding one of the input channels. In the differential mode of operation, channel 15 represents the zero reference offset voltage. If a data channel has the offset subtracted from it, the result will be a value which is compensated for offset drift and which is highly accurate over a wide range of board temperatures. Figure 17 shows the software which can be used to collect data from a channel and which will deliver a zero compensated value to a calling program. In Figure 17, note that the values are converted to an offset binary representation to be compatible with the standard output of the analog to digital circuitry.

```
        2     zero$data = get$channel (gain, ref$chan, port$adr);

              /* get data channel */
  35    2     raw$data = get$channel (gain, channel, port$adr);

              /* support negative offset */
  36    2     if zero$data > raw$data
              then do;
  38    3        raw$data = zero$data − raw$data;
  39    3        raw$data = 8000h − raw$data;
  40    3     end;
  41    2     else do;
  42    3        raw$data = raw$data − zero$data;
  43    3        raw$data = raw$data + 8000h;
  44    3     end;
```

Figure 17. Zero Compensation Procedure

The analog input driver required for the application can now be constructed using the software building blocks which have been created. Generally, the input data will consist of either thermocouple inputs or non-temperature sensitive inputs. The driver must be able to support both by providing a selective cold junction compensation correction for those channels which are designated as thermocouples.

The problem is illustrated in Figure 18. The voltage which represents the temperature of the thermocouple consists of the sum of the actual thermocouple voltage plus the voltage which is generated by the thermocouple junctions created where the wiring is terminated. The error introduced by the termination must be removed before a junction temperature can be calculated. If the thermo/voltage characteristics of the termination junction are known, the induced error can be subtracted and the temperature of the thermocouple can be calculated.

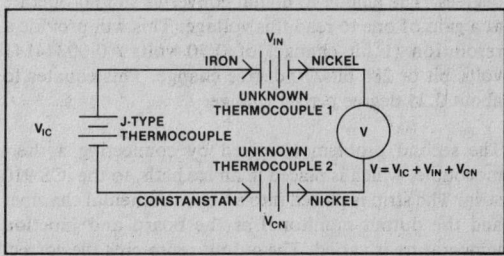

Figure 18. Thermocouple Cold Junction Error

Two things must be known for the correction voltage to become available. First, the actual temperature of the junction board must be known. Second, the electrical characteristics of the junction with respect to temperature must be defined. With this data available, the correction voltage can be obtained using the linearization program which has been created as an analog building block.

The first problem is solved by installing a temperature sensing circuit onto the iCS 910 Analog Termination Strip. Figure 19 shows such a circuit which can be used to provide an extremely accurate measurement of the board and terminator temperature. Note that the circuit is installed onto the termination board using the mounting locations originally designed for the installation of a low pass filter. The output of the temperature sensing is

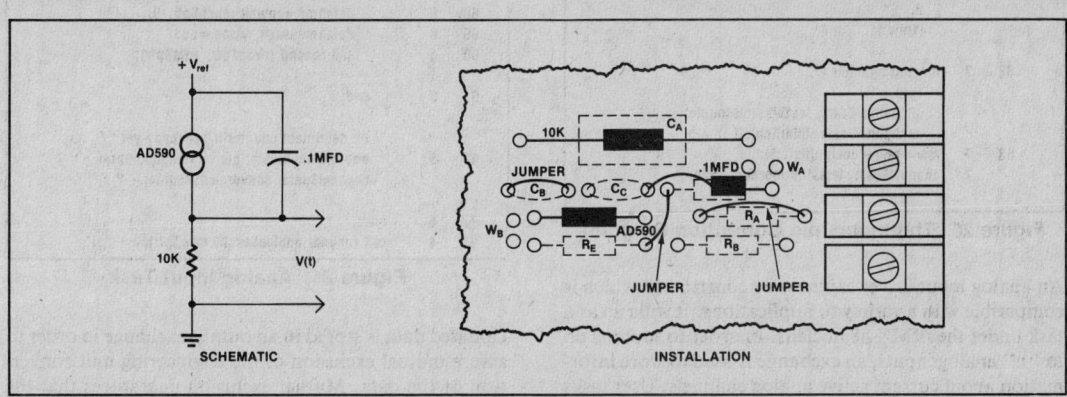

Figure 19. iCS™ 910 Board Sensing Circuit

AP-114

related only to the temperature of the sensor device which provides a current of 1 microamp per degree Kelvin through the 10K resistor. The temperature is related to the voltage by the equation:

$$V = (273 + T) / 100 \qquad (eq. 5)$$

Thus, the voltage read from the termination strip as the temperature varies from 0 to 70 degrees Centigrade will vary from 2.73 volts at 0 degrees to 3.43 volts at 70 degrees. The analog to digital converter should operate at a gain of one to read this voltage. This will provide a resolution (1 bit change) of 0.70 volts / 0.00244141 volts/bit or 286 bits/70 degree change. This equates to about 0.25 degree per bit change.

The second problem is solved by connecting a thermocouple, which is placed in an ice bath, to the iCS 910 strip. The strip is placed into an environmental chamber and the output monitored as the board and junction temperature is varied. The output represents the correction required at each temperature. Tests made for this application note indicated that the error was essentially linear over the board range from 0 to 70 degrees Centigrade. The correction voltage was found to vary linearly from minus 0.102 millivolt at 0 degrees to 3.578 millivolts at 70 degrees. This data was placed into a linearization table to give an offset correction for a measured temperature of the board. Figure 20 shows the table and the code required to correct the raw temperature value from thermocouple inputs.

```
            /* get thermocouple reference junction temp */
60   7   j$raw = analog$to$digital$conversion (
             gain$one,
             13,
             channel$data, port$number );

61   7   tc = analog$linearization (
             @cold$junction$table,
             2,
             j$raw );

62   7   tc = analog$filter (
             @tc,
             @channel$data, last$thermocouple,
             @channel$data, filter$cutoff );

63   7   raw = raw + unsign(fix(tc));
     7   channel$data, last$thermocouple = tc;
```

Figure 20. Thermocouple Correction Program

An analog input driver can now be constructed which is compatible with a variety of applications. It will run as a task under the iRMX 88 nucleus. In order to support up to "n" analog inputs, an exchange is used to store information about current active analog channels. User tasks requiring analog facilities send a request to the analog exchange indicating the parameters of the desired channel. Because an exchange has a FIFO storage capacity for messages, each active channel is sampled by the task in turn, then placed back onto the exchange. A unique message is used to indicate the beginning of the channel requests. Figure 21 provides a partial listing of the code used to make up the analog input task.

```
57   3   msg$ptr = rqwait (.timeout, 2);

58   3   last$channel = false;

59   3   do while last$channel = false;

60   4     msg$ptr = rqwait (.analog$exch, 0);
61   4     if channel$data, type = null$type
             then last$channel = true;
63   4     else do;
                  /* test for conversion time request */
64   5        if channel$data, conversion$counter = 0
                  then do;
                  /* get raw data from adc */
74   6           raw = analog$to$digital$conversion (
                     gain,
                     channel$number,
                     port$number );

                  /* perform engineering unit conversion */
83   6           eu = analog$linearization (
                     table$pointer,
                     number$of$entries,
                     raw );

                  /* filter the data */
84   6           eu = analog$filter (
                     @eu,
                     @channel$data, last$value,
                     @filter$cutoff );

85   6           channel$data, last$value = eu;

86   6           channel$data, conversion$counter
                     = conversion$interval;

87   6           exch$ptr = channel$data, output$exchange$ptr;
88   6           data$ptr = rqwait (exch$ptr, 0);
89   6           data$message, value = eu;
90   6           call rqsend (exch$ptr, data$ptr);

91   6        end;
                  /* decriment counter if not ready yet */
92   5        else channel$data, conversion$counter =
                     channel$data, conversion$counter - 1;

93   5     end;
94   4   call rqsend(.analgo$exch, msg$ptr);
```

Figure 21. Analog Input Task

Updated data is stored in an output exchange in order to assure mutual exclusion of the engineering unit conversion of the data. Mutual exclusion guarantees that the data cannot be read by another task while it is being up-

2-126

AFN-02015A

dated (during the updating process, multiple bytes of data must be changed; until all are modified, the number cannot be considered valid). The exchange mechanism of iRMX executives supports the movement of messages (this might be compared to a letter in a mailbox). If the data is stored as a message in an exchange, it is available to the first user requesting it. While that user has the message (letter), it is not available to anyone else. When he is finished with it, he will return it to the exchange so that other users may operate upon the data. Note that the sample interval of each channel is selected by the requesting task so that optimum processor efficiency can be obtained.

Certain parameters used by the analog input task must be retained even if the system power is shut off for an extended period of time. These parameters are used to provide the task with unique information such as the channel and port address, the desired gain, the conversion interval and the linearization and engineering conversion data. On the other hand, some information used by the task can be easily created dynamically and does not require the use of non-volatile storage. Examples of the latter category include addresses of the storage exchanges and addresses of the various messages.

The use of E^2PROM on the iSBC 88/40 Measurement and Control Computer provides the mechanism for the storage of those parameters which must be occasionally modified. Figure 22 shows a possible technique for passing the analog input task its required information and pointers to the non-volatile data. Intel's PL/M-86 provides a convenient mechanism for referencing variables whose physical location is passed as a parameter. This is the BASED VARIABLE. A declaration is made which indicates the location of the variable containing the address of the data. For example:

　　Declare CONSTANT$POINTER pointer;
　　Declare CONSTANT based
　　　　CONSTANT$POINTER real;

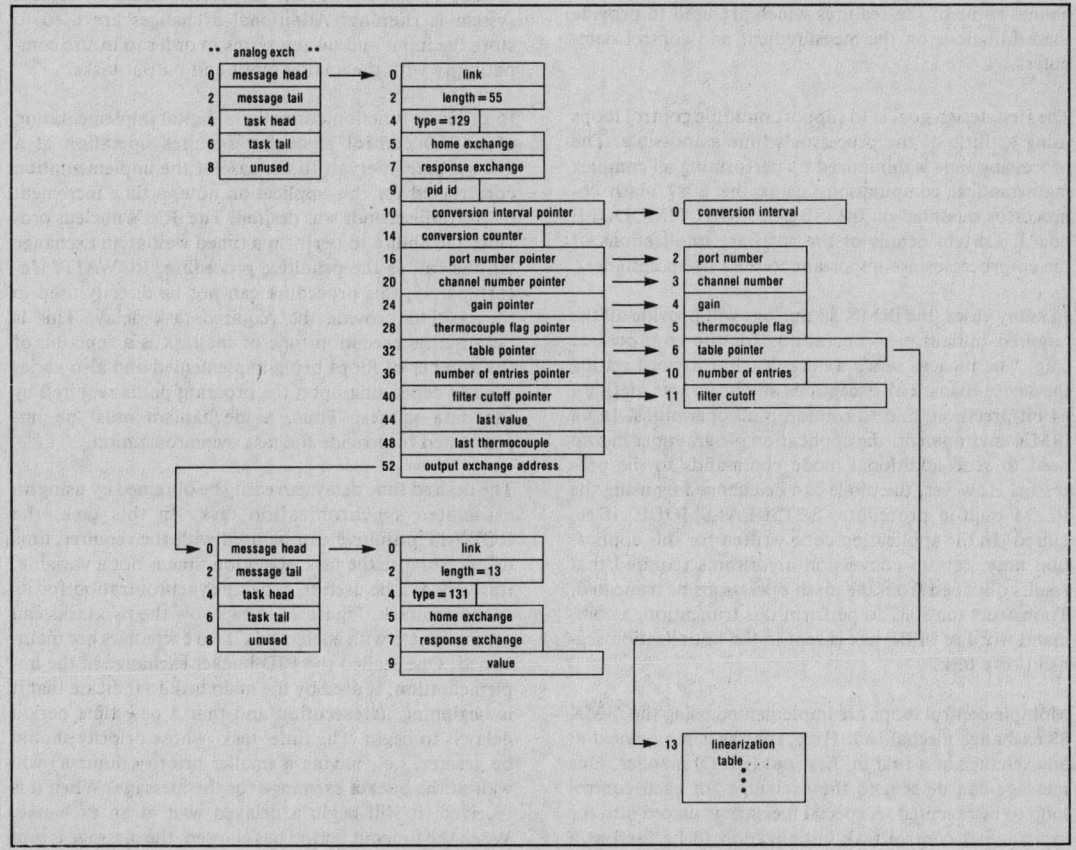

Figure 22. Analog Input Data Structures

AP-114

The CONSTANT$POINTER contains the address of the constant which is to be used in the calculations. Any program reference to CONSTANT will cause the processor to use the real number stored in the address pointed to by CONSTANT$POINTER.

This technique allows a message to contain pointers to E^2PROM constants which can be used by the task in performing its functions. Indeed, multiple levels of based variables can be used as shown in Figure 22.

CONTROL ALGORITHM

The implementation of a control algorithm on the iSBC 88/40 computer involves more than just implementing the PID equation. To become truly cost effective, multiple loops must be supported by the board and error checking/correction must be included. As with the analog input functions, system control parameters must be maintained in non-volatile memory. Finally, the system must be capable of operating in real time with a minimum of required processor time. This section examines some of the features which are used to provide these functions on the measurement and control computer.

The first design goal is to support multiple control loops using as little of the processor's time as possible. The processing time is minimized by performing all complex mathematical computations using the 8087 math coprocessor mounted on the iSBC 337 MULTIMODULE board. Certain details of the software implications of the co-processor are important to the system designer.

In many cases, the iRMX 88 nucleus will provide all the required initialization operations for the co-processor chip. The nucleus sends a default control word setting the device to mask all exceptions and interrupts, define a 64 bit precision, and to round up all operations. In an iRMX environment, the application programmer has no need to send additional mode commands to the processor. However, the mode can be changed by using the PL/M built-in procedure, SET$REAL$MODE, if required. In the application code written for this application note, certain conversion algorithms required that results obtained from the math operations be truncated. To instruct the 8087 to perform this truncation, a command word of 0FBF hex is sent in the initialization segment of a task.

Multiple control loops are implemented using the iRMX 88 exchange mechanism. Here, messages are queued at an exchange in a first in, first out (FIFO) manner. One message can be sent to the exchange for each control loop to be executed. A special message is placed into the exchange at control task initialization to be used as a pointer to the end of the queue. Each time the control task is to run, it will read messages sequentially from the exchange until it encounters its end of queue message. Each message corresponds to one control loop's specifications and is returned to the exchange when the loop has been completed. A separate control interface task manages the control loop activation by sending a message containing the necessary parameters to the control exchange. This technique allows the interface task to also remove a control task by taking the appropriate message from the exchange when parameter modifications or control loop deletion is requested.

Each message at the control exchange (in the application example, this exchange is called PID$EXCH) contains pointers to various other exchanges or data structures. The relationships of these structures is shown in Figure 23. Note that some system parameters should be stored in non-volatile E^2PROM memory. System constants are stored in an exchange pointed to by the primary control message. An exchange is used here so that the system can provide mutual exclusion of the data if it is required to modify one or more of the parameters while the control system is running. Additional exchanges are used to store the input and output terms in order to insure compatibility with the analog input and output tasks.

In order to function correctly, a digital implementation of a PID control algorithm requires operation at a known time interval. In the case of the implementation constructed for this application note, a time increment of 100 milliseconds was desired. The iRMX nucleus provides the ability to perform a timed wait at an exchange via the call to the primitive procedure, RQWAIT. Unfortunately, this procedure can not be directly used in the task to provide the required task delay. This is because the execution time of the task is a function of the number of loops being implemented and also varies slightly depending upon the program paths required by the data values. Thus, a mechanism must be implemented to provide the task synchronization.

The desired time delay can easily be obtained by using an associated synchronization task. In this task, the RQWAIT primitive can be used with the required time delay. Because the task execution time is not a variable, this task can be used to provide synchronization for its supported task. Figure 24 shows how the two tasks can communicate with each other. Two exchanges are maintained. One, called the PID bucket exchange in the implementation, is used by the main task to indicate that it is beginning its execution and that a new time period delay is to begin. The timer task (whose priority should be greater, i.e., having a smaller priority number) will wait at the bucket exchange for the message. When it is received, it will begin a delayed wait at an exchange. When the timeout period has elapsed, the message is sent to a second exchange (in the figure, this exchange is called the PID trigger exchange). The main task, after completing the servicing of all operational PID control loops, will wait at the trigger exchange for a message from the timer task. In the case of the application example, the message will arrive 100 milliseconds after the task began its last update of the control loops.

When iRMX 88 timed wait operations are implemented on the iSBC 88/40 Measurement and Control Computer, timer 0 of the on-board 8253 programmable interval timer must be used. A wire wrap jumper must be installed to vector the output of the timer to one of the interrupts of the 8259A programmable interrupt controller chip.

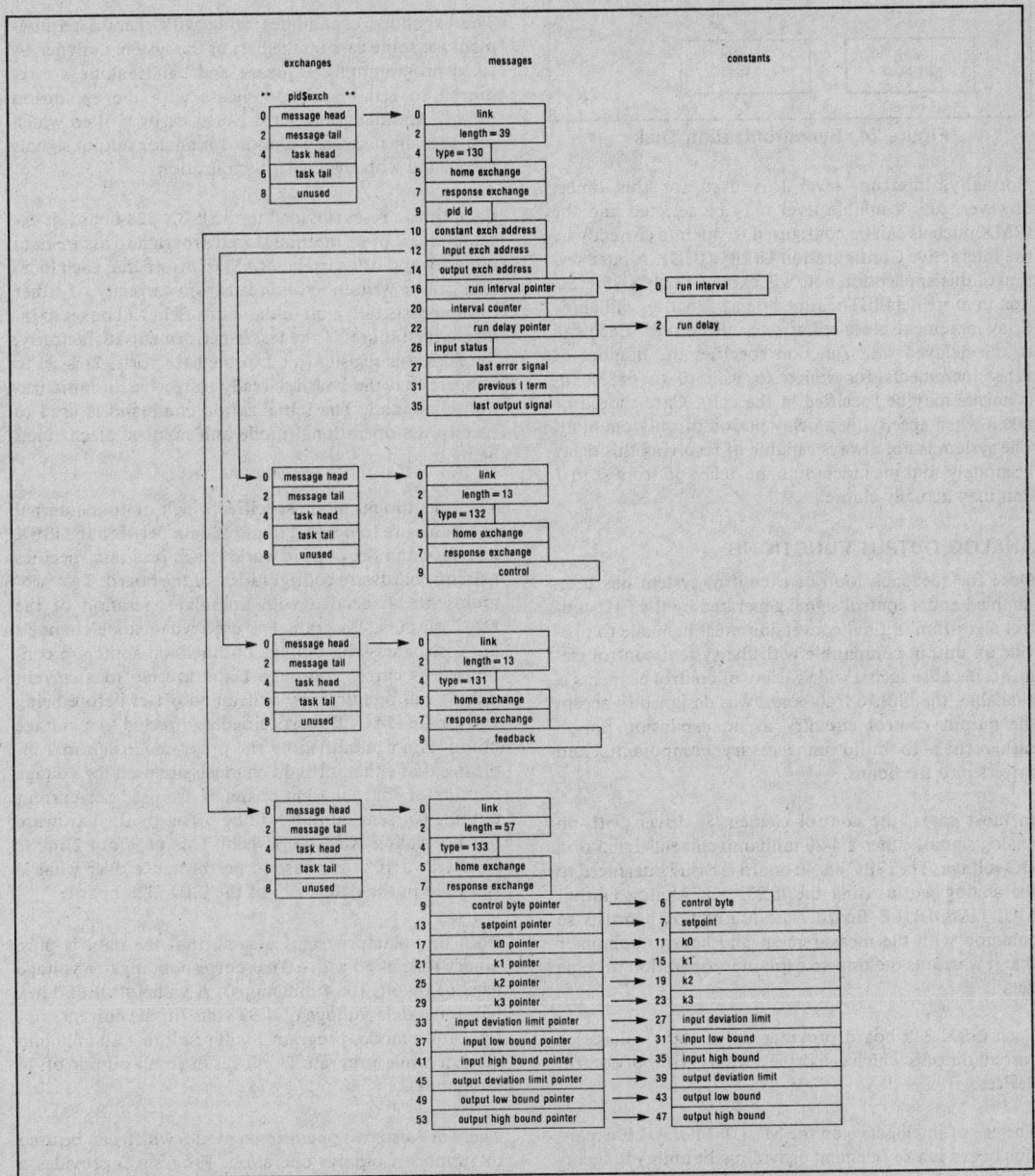

Figure 23. Control Structure Relationships

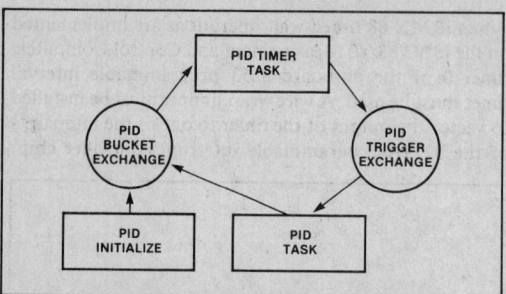

Figure 24. Synchronization Task

Normally, interrupt level 1 is used for this timer; however, any available level may be selected and the iRMX nucleus can be configured to operate correctly by the Interactive Configuration Utility (ICU). A later section of this application note will explain the ICU interaction in more detail. The timed delay function will allow delay increments as small as one millisecond. Each call to the delayed wait function specifies the number of delay increments for which to wait (0 to 65535 increments may be specified in the call). Care should be taken when specifying a delay period of only one unit. The system is not always capable of resolving this delay accurately and an indeterminant delay of from 0 to 1 unit may actually elapse.

ANALOG OUTPUT FUNCTIONS

Once the feedback loop of a control system has been sampled and a control signal generated by the PID control algorithm, a final conversion must be made to provide an output compatible with the system control element. Because such a wide variety of control elements is available, the iSBC 88/40 board was designed to accept the output control circuitry as an expansion option rather than to build unnecessary components and drivers into the board.

In most cases, the control element is driven with an analog signal, either a 4-20 milliamp current signal or a DC voltage. The iSBC 88/40 board is easily interfaced to the analog world using the iSBX 328 Analog Output MULTIMODULE Board. The use of this board is so common with the measurement and control computer that it warrants the time to explain its operation in some detail.

Each iSBX 328 board provides up to eight voltage or current outputs which can drive a wide variety of control devices.

The use of intelligence on the MULTIMODULE expansion board is a key element providing the ability to incorporate eight channels in a very small physical area. The capabilities of the intelligence allow the board to provide significant enhancements to the basic operational characteristics of the host iSBC 88/40 board. One example is the ability to perform diagnostics of the analog output module upon command from the 8088 processor on the host measurement and control board.

The expanded capabilities bring with them a requirement for some care on the part of the system designer. A fixed programming sequence and handshaking are required to reliably communicate with the expansion board. An analog output driver is easily written which provides the necessary support for analog output signals associated with the control application.

Each time a reset is issued to the iSBX 328 board, it executes a test of its internal stored program to assure data integrity and of its usable RAM to insure that each location can be written to and read from correctly. If either of these tests fail, a bit in the status field will be set to indicate the failure. If the test is performed satisfactorily, the F0 status register (bit 2 of the base port + 2) is set to indicate that the board is ready to receive an initialization command. The initialization command is used to specify the operational mode and number of channels being used.

The operational mode specifies which of four internal programs are to be used to move data between the iSBX interface and the outside world. Each program specifies a unique hardware configuration of the board. Two programs are associated with unipolar operation of the DAC outputs. Program 1 is used when some channels are associated with voltage outputs and some are configured as current outputs. Data directed to a current output will be internally scaled and offset before being sent to the DAC. Data specified as directed to a voltage output is not modified by the program. Program 2 indicates that either all eight channels are used for voltage outputs or that all eight channels are used for current output. Current outputs will be offset by the hardware but no scaling is accomplished. This program 2 mode results in a 10% increase in performance over what is specified in the data sheet of the iSBX 328 board.

Both unipolar programs assume that the data is pure binary formatted with a 0 hex corresponding to a voltage level of 0 volts (or 4 milliamps). A value of 0FFF0 hex will generate a voltage of 4.99 volts (in the current configuration mode, program 1 will result in a 20 milliamp current while program 2 will result in an output of 24 milliamps).

There are also two operational modes which can be used to support a bipolar operation. Program 2 provides a direct hardware support capability for those cases where all outputs are either configured as entirely voltage or entirely current outputs. No adjustments are made to the data prior to being sent to the DAC. The data format used for both bipolar modes is the offset binary representation of a number. Negative numbers are represented by the values 0 (-32752) to 8000 hex (0). Positive numbers range from 8000 hex (0) to 0FFF0 hex ($+32752$). Channels defined as current outputs have no legal negative output values.

Finally, program 4 is used to support bipolar operations where the outputs are mixed between current and voltage. The program does not alter data destined to voltage channels but does offset and scale data for channels designated as current outputs.

Once the device has been initialized, subsequent data transfers are all through the data transfer port located at the base address of the board's MULTIMODULE socket. Before each write to the device, the driver software must check the IBF bit (bit 1) of the status to verify that the input buffer is not full. An additional bit is used to specify to the host processor which data byte (high or low) is next to be passed. The low order bits of the low data byte specify which channel the data is for and also what configuration (voltage or current) corresponds to that channel.

Like the analog input task, the application driver for the analog output can be an iRMX 88 task using exchanges and messages for data transfer. In the example implemented for this application note, an exchange, DAC$EXCH, was dedicated to the control of the task. It contains messages which specify the output port, channel used, and output mode (current or voltage). The task runs at a twenty millisecond time interval and updates each channel as indicated by the control messages. The location of the exchange used to store the output data is also specified by the control message. The use of this exchange mechanism provides mutual exclusion of the output data.

The external connections to the iSBX 328 analog output board can be made using the Intel iCS 910 Analog Termination Strip. When used in this mode, the analog outputs are available on the terminal strips originally designated as analog input channels. Figure 25 shows how the interconnect cable can be used to install the termination panel to the board.

E²PROM FUNCTIONS

Several references have been made to the advantages gained by using E²PROM 2816 devices on the iSBC 88/40 board for the storage of non-volatile variables. Many configurations mixing E²PROM devices with combinations of EPROM, ROM, and/or byte wide RAM are possible. Support is provided for the installation of one, two, four, or eight (using the iSBC 341 MULTIMODULE EPROM board) 2816 devices. Complete E²PROM write capability is provided on the board. The Intel supplied hardware for this support includes a switching power supply and wave-shaping circuitry. Only minimal user programming overhead is required by the application program.

The on-board wave-shaping circuitry provides a 2816 compatible programming pulse of approximately 16 milliseconds duration. In order to generate this pulse, use is made of the on-board 8253 programmable interval timer. Wirewrap jumper posts are provided to route the timer output to the pulse generator. The gate to the timer is connected using an additional jumper to the memory decode logic to signal a write request to a 2816 device. User software must be provided to program the 8253 for the generation of a 14 millisecond pulse. This code is most easily located in the initialization portion of one of the application tasks associated with writing data into

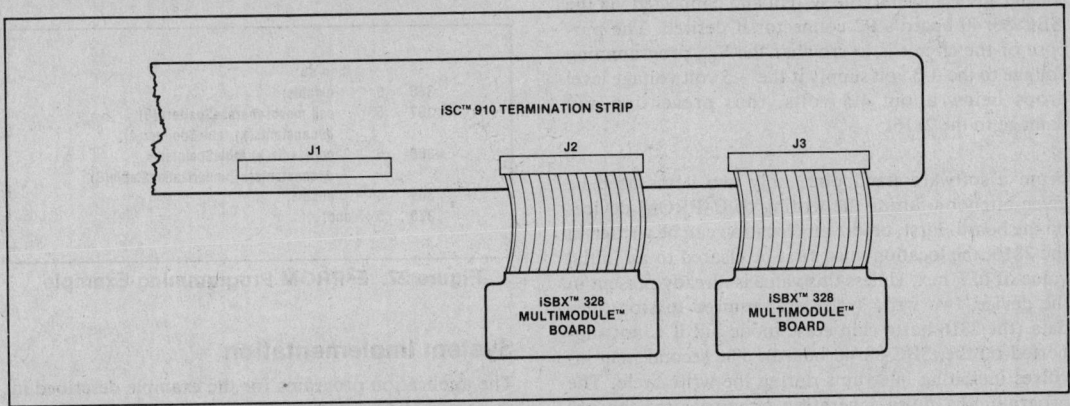

Figure 25. Analog Output Terminations

the devices. Only three lines of PL/M-86 code are required to perform the initialization. The application example includes the code:

```
output(0D6H) = 0B2H;
    /* timer 2 to mode 2 */
output(0D4H) = 000H;
    /* most significant byte */
output(0D4H) = 038H;
    /* least significant byte */
```

The hardware will now generate the appropriate programming pulses to write into the 2816 each time data is written into an address occupied by the device. When the EPROM size is larger than 2K bytes size of the 2816, the system will create a duplicate image of the 2K block as many times as is required to fill the size specified for the EPROM. For example, if 2732A EPROM devices are used and one 2816 is installed at a base location of 0F8000 hex, one image of the E^2PROM data will occupy the memory from 0F8000 hex to 0F87FF hex while a second image will be seen from 0F8800 hex to 0F8FFF hex. Reads or writes to either image will access the same data and either may be used.

The user must consider the possibility of system power failures and their impact when designing systems which use the iSBC 88/40 board's E^2PROM capabilities. This is especially true in systems whose power supply for the +5 volt source is protected by a crowbar circuit. The on-board switching power supply which generates the high voltage programming pulse operates at very low input voltages and its RC time constant will provide significant voltage levels even if the +5 volt input supply is abruptly removed. The presence of a programming voltage in the absence of a +5 volt supply to a 2816 can cause irreversible damage to the E^2PROM chip. The potential for this condition during a write cycle must be considered by the designer. Figure 26 shows a circuit which can be added to the system and connected via the iSBC 88/40 board's P2 connector if desired. The purpose of the circuit is to crowbar the V_{pp} programming voltage to the +5 volt supply if the +5 volt voltage level drops below about 4.5 volts, thus preventing any damage to the 2816.

From a software standpoint, only two items need be given attention during the writing of E^2PROM devices on the board. First, before any location can be written in the 2816, the location must first be cleared to an initial value of 0FF hex. Unless this value is already present in the device, two write cycles are required to store new data (the 2816 has a chip erase mode but it is not supported on the iSBC 88/40 board). The second item involves inhibiting interrupts during the write cycle. The programming pulse generation circuitry uses the on-board timeout circuitry, so the timeout interrupt, if used, must be masked off prior to beginning the write cycle (this implies that the hardware for the timeout acknowledge must be installed to all the circuitry to become a part of the pulse generator). In an iRMX 88 environment using timed waits, the interval timer must also be masked off during the write cycle. If these interrupts are not masked off, the processor can respond to an interrupt and begin modifying its internal registers which point to the memory. This will result in incorrect programming of the E^2PROM device. An example of the code which might be used to program a 2816 is shown in Figure 27. The programmer should keep in mind that, during the programming of the 2816, the iAPX 88/10 processor is in a wait state and cannot process any instructions. Thus, for each byte written, approximately 36 milliseconds must elapse before processing can again begin (18 milliseconds for the clearing of the byte and another 18 for the data write). If timed waits are being performed, an error will be introduced into the system. Some critical applications may need to take this into account.

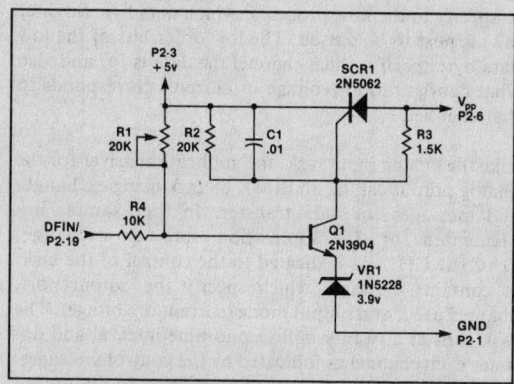

Figure 26. E^2PROM Crowbar Protection

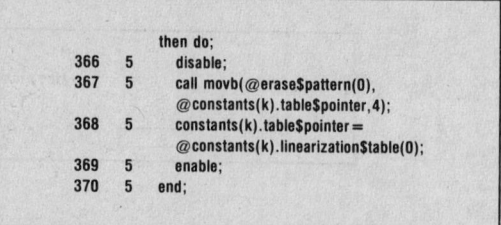

Figure 27. E^2PROM Programming Example

System Implementation

The application programs for the example described in this application note have been implemented using Version 1.1 of the iRMX 88 executive. The use of the Interactive Configuration Utility (ICU88) considerably reduces the effort required to bring a system on line by providing a question and answer session with the programmer. The output of the ICU consists of a system configuration module and a submit file which provides most of the required LINK and LOCATE commands.

In the application, a system time wait increment of 5 milliseconds was chosen. Figure 28 shows the dialogue required to implement the timed wait feature using the board with the output of channel 0 (from the 8253 programmable interval timer) connected to interrupt level 2. Note that the system time unit of 6140 corresponds to a 5 millisecond increment.

```
INTERRUPTS: Y
    8259A PORT: C0H
    8259 INTERVAL: 2
    INTERRUPT SERVICE ROUTINE VECTOR BASE: 56
    TIMED WAITS: YES
        TIMER LEVEL: 2
        8253 PORT: D0H
        SYSTEM TIME UNIT: 6140
```

Figure 28. ICU Timed Wait Dialogue

Additional entries into the ICU define the system tasks and their associated exchanges. The desired locations of the RAM and EPROM are specified and the configuration modules created. The location of the E^2PROM module is specified in one of the user created modules as a public pointer which is initialized with the base address of the device. An example might be:

```
e2prom$module: do;
    declare e2prom$pointer pointer public
    data (0f8000h);
end e2prom$module;
```

All references to the data structures in the 2816 are by means of a based variable or structure.

Before executing the submit file for a ROM based system, it is necessary to edit the LOCATE command to include the BOOTSTRAP request. This will assure that the locator places a long jump at the reset vector location when the system is executed out of EPROM. Execution of the LOCATE facility will generate a warning 38 which should be ignored. The corrected LOCATE code is shown in Figure 29.

```
ISIS-II MCS-86 LOCATER, V1.3 INVOKED BY:
LOC86 :F1:ADCINP.LNK TO :F1:ADCINP    MAP
    PRINT(:F1:ADCINP.MP2)&
    BOOTSTRAP ORDER(CLASSES(DATA,STACK,CODE))&
    ADDRESSES(CLASSES(CODE(0FC000H), DATA(000400H)))
    WARNING 38: SEGMENT WITH MEMORY ATTRIBUTE NOT PLACED
    HIGHEST IN MEMORY SEGMENT: MEMORY
```

Figure 29. LOCATE Modification

The total control system for the application example can now be assembled using the hardware and software discussed in this note. The same "black box" approach used in hardware designs can be extended to include both software and hardware implementations. Figure 30 shows the complete solution to the control of up to eight agitated heating tanks.

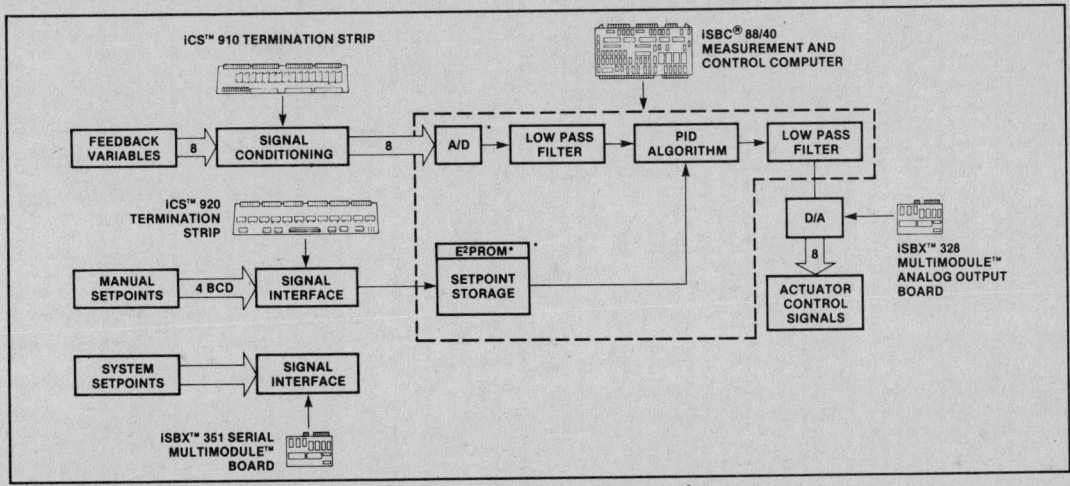

Figure 30. System Implementation

AP-114

CONCLUSIONS

The purpose of this application note is to illustrate how the Intel iSBC 88/40 Measurement and Control Computer can be used to solve a complex control application. This has been done in Intel's lab and the results obtained from operating the board indicate that the system performance is sufficient to support the operation of eight loops each 100 milliseconds. Observed operation of the analog input and engineering unit conversion task indicated a 4 millisecond per channel execution time. The actual PID code required only 5 milliseconds per loop to execute.

The ease of implementation and fast execution time for multiple complex loops is a result of many Intel product features. For example, the use of the iRMX 88 Real Time Executive provided fast, small, and easy-to-use multitasking real time software for use on the single board computer. The iSBC 337 MULTIMODULE Numeric Data Processor Board enabled the use of high accuracy, easy-to-use floating point calculations without taking excessive execution time. If desired, a fixed point integer math algorithm could have been substituted for the floating point without changing the system performance appreciably. The iSBX 328 Analog Output MULTIMODULE Board provided low cost customization of the base board to support a variety of controllers and actuators.

Finally, the use of the Intel 2816 E^2PROM provided the non-volatile storage for system setpoints and constants which is required in a control situation.

Above all, the iSBC 88/40 Measurement and Control Computer provided a platform and execution vehicle for mounting and operation of the various ancillary features. Its iAPX 88/10 processor, memory and MULTIMODULE expansion sockets provided the flexibility to easily customize the board to a particular application environment.

APPENDIX A

AP-114

APPLICATION CODE AVAILABILITY

The programs which were used to construct the application example are available from Intel through Insite. Insite, Intel's Software Index and Technology Exchange, is a collection of programs, subroutines, procedures and macros written by users of Intel's 8008, 8080, 8085, 8086, 8088, and 8048 microcomputers. Information on how to join Insite and obtain the source code can be obtained from your local Intel sales office or distributor, or by writing to:

North America

Intel Corporation
User's Library 6-5000
Microcomputer Systems
3065 Bowers Avenue
Santa Clara, California 95051

Europe

Intel International Corp. S.A.
User's Library
Rue du Moulin a Papier 51
Boite 1
B-1160 Brussels, Belgium

Orient

Intel Japan K.K.
User's Library
Flowerhill-Shinmachi, East Bldg.
1-23-9 Shinmachi, Setagaya-ku
Tokyo 154, Japan

ARTICLE REPRINT

AR-229

July 1982

Enhanced μC Boards Strengthen Factory and Office Controllers

Gary Sawyer
Scott Tetrick
Don Peterson
Electronic Design

"Reprinted with permission from *Electronic Design*, Volume 30, Number 15; copyright Hayden Publishing Company, Inc., 1982."

Order Number: 210825-001

New single-board computers sport dramatic advances in density and speed. The upshot: much more capable factory and office controllers.

Enhanced µC boards strengthen factory and office controllers

Designers of control and computer systems for the factory or office should be aware of the updated performance capabilities of the latest breed of single-board microcomputers. Faster microprocessors with wider word lengths are joining with denser, faster static memories to effect even finer control of time-critical operations. Yet the new crop maintains bus and software compatibility with earlier designs, needs fewer power supplies, and remarkably, charges no penalty for the extra work. In some cases, costs will dip.

Using such boards as the iSBC 86/XX family, designers can trade in 8 bits for 16 (see "A Bridge from 8- to 16-bit Processing"), 5-MHz operation for 8, older memory sockets for standard 28-pin JEDEC EPROM sockets. In addition, plug-on modules offer low-cost expansion. That adds up to double the EPROM capacity with no redesign and to quadruple the RAM capacity.

Moreover, the iSBX 86/XX boards support the full IEEE-796 Multibus specification—including 16-Mbyte addressing features (send and receive) and the use of the lock feature (Fig. 1). Four additional address lines on the Multibus can be used to address memories larger than 1 Mbyte. The lock function increases system speed—by preventing arbitration delays—and serves in semaphore signaling applications (for more particulars, see "Meet the Family").

In a multiprocessing system, individual processors must have a method of synchronization and mutual exclusion. A semaphore is the most common software method for providing these functions. Figure 2 shows an example of the semaphore concept and the need for dual locking. Assuming as in the figure that the system consists of two processors and a disk-controller board, only one processor can access the mass-storage controller at any given time. A global memory byte indicates whether the disk-controller board is in use—a 1 indicates not busy; a 0, busy.

When a request is made for a disk file, the requesting processor must check the global byte to determine whether the controller is busy. Although the process appears simple, there could be pitfalls (Fig. 3a). The hardware must allow the processors to read the semaphore bit without the intervening write cycle, to prevent deadlocking.

Earlier boards needed global memory, not dual porting, to support semaphores easily. They relied on Multibus arbitration to prevent deadlock, but that required an additional memory. Moreover, the boards required much more hardware and software to ensure proper operation. With the introducton of the IEEE-796 Multibus specification, a lock line added to the system bus allows a much simpler implementation of semaphores in a dual-port memory (Fig. 3b).

The on-board processor can prevent access to the dual port, and system accesses can lock the local processor out of the dual port. Both functions must be implemented to ensure the integrity of the semaphore byte. Figure 4 shows the arbitration scheme for a dual port.

Other board enhancements include Schmitt-trigger inputs on all critical Multibus command lines, which improves noise immunity. Pull-up resistors on all input lines allow for easy testing. The new board layouts minimize the length of the Multibus signal lines, reducing the line's susceptibility to crosstalk pickup. These improvements result in a mean time between failures (MTBF) that is 50% greater than that of comparable first-generation boards.

Most measures of a computer board's processing power are summed up in one specification, the clock

Gary Sawyer, Product Manager
Scott Tetrick, Product Engineer
Don Peterson, Marketing Engineer
Intel Corp.
5200 N.E. Elam Young Pkwy.
Hillsboro, Ore. 97123

Enhanced single-board control

rate. With an 8-MHz 8086-2 microprocessor on board, processing speeds up 60% over 5-MHz operation.

Because of increased processing speed, on-board circuitry must be upgraded to handle higher data and instruction rates. Thus, some control functions are implemented with programmable logic arrays (PLAs). These high-speed devices not only replace dedicated chips, but also allow logic operations to be performed at clock rates exceeding 10 MHz.

Stepping up the speed

To accommodate the demand for greater data handling, RAM access time is 750 ns, compared with 1000 ns in earlier single-board computers. An additional benefit of faster access time is the capacity for dual-port access. With this feature, dual-port RAMs can be accessed from the Multibus in 500 ns when locked and 800 ns when unlocked. High-speed, dual-port access permits interprocessor communications to occur at a much faster rate.

Since each iSBC board contains a different RAM storage capacity, speed performance is linked closely to a board's memory capacity. As Fig. 5 shows, numbers on the vertical scale indicate increasing performance for a given storage capacity.

The timing/storage performance graphs of Fig. 5 have been determined by making certain assumptions about system operation. First, it is assumed that the system has no Multibus contention for the global memory as is the case in a single-master system. Also, all memory is accessed constantly, independent of on- or off-board optimization. For example, because of delays encountered in acquiring the Multibus, data rates plunge (in the iSBC 86/05) if more processors are added to a system.

The expanded memory space—320 kbytes—can serve either for enhanced multiprocessing or for the storage of large amounts of application code. The new design prevents performance-reducing arbitration delays in multiple-processor system operation. Proper partitioning of the system memory allows code accesses from the on-board memory. Since code fetching operations occupy most of the system-bus bandwidth, execution from local memory greatly accelerates system throughput.

At home in factory or office

Two key application areas—and their diverse requirements—stand out for single-board computers. One area includes machine and process control, instrumentation, and specialized data acquisition. Here, high-performance single-board computers are required to have extensive EPROM capacity to provide sufficient program storage without relying on mass storage.

The other area covers communications systems, small-business computers, and word and data processing. Single-board computers in office-of-the-

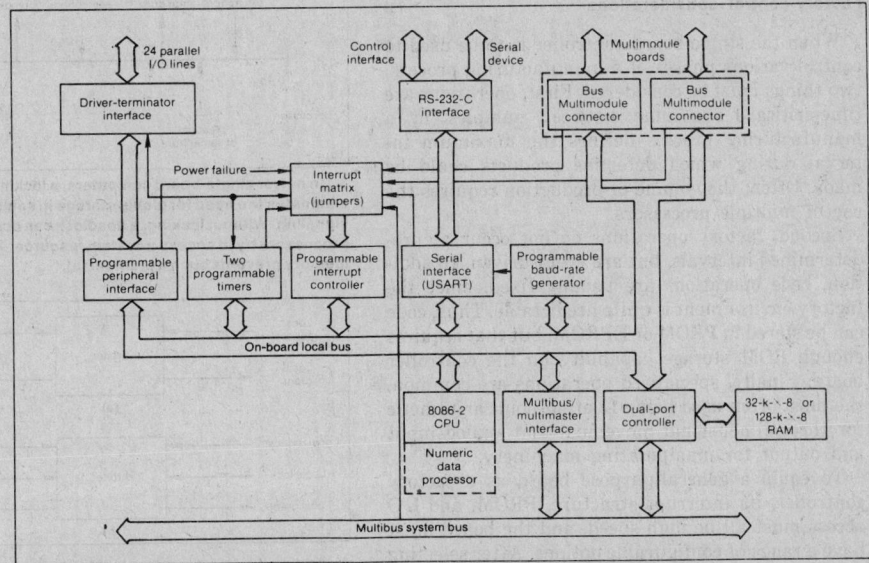

1. Advances in digital LSI and VLSI have expanded the capabilities of single-board computers. The result is more speed and more memory, yet compatibility with earlier versions.

future applications are generally RAM-intensive, with programs downloaded from a disk. A small amount of EPROM serves to bootstrap the system RAM at power-up. Mass storage is used to hold the large data bases required, but the computer board must support an I/O terminal for the human interface. Typically, word-processing systems require a high-performance CPU, a large RAM capacity, an interface for mass storage, a CRT terminal, and a printer.

For RAM-intensive applications, a 128-kbyte RAM module fits on board. An on-board serial I/O port and 24 programmable I/O lines provide the interface with the CRT display and printer. With the inclusion of the iSBX bus on the board, low-cost I/O expansion is possible. Also, the iSBX 218 single- or double-density, single- or double-sided floppy-disk controller allows the entire system to fit on a single board. Moreover, even with those components on the board, there is room for a mathematics module. So the same basic system can serve as a high-performance small-business computer.

In high-speed communications applications, a high-end single-board controller outfitted with an iSBX module offers an interface capable of handling processing needs well into the future. Since the iSBX module communicates directly with the CPU over the iSBX bus, Multibus contention does not pose a problem. Another benefit of the bus-module approach: reduced size and power consumption.

Factory-control considerations

When the single-board controller is to be used to control various phases of a manufacturing process, two things must be considered. First, operations are time-critical. The time between samples in a manufacturing process defines the maximum interval during which defective products could be made. Often, the volume of production requires the use of multiple processors.

Second, factory operations do not occur at predetermined intervals, but are event-driven. In addition, code operations are usually fixed, since the factory environment is quite predictable. Thus, code can be stored in PROM or EPROM, but that requires enough ROM storage capability on the controller board. Finally, specialized operations are common, the most often used being floating-point arithmetic for three-dimensional movement and analog input and output for manipulating machinery.

To equip a general-purpose board as a factory controller, its interrupt structure, PROM, and I/O access must all be high-speed, and the board must have a range of configurable options. After selecting a board, the designer should determine his maximum interrupt-speed requirement by measuring two

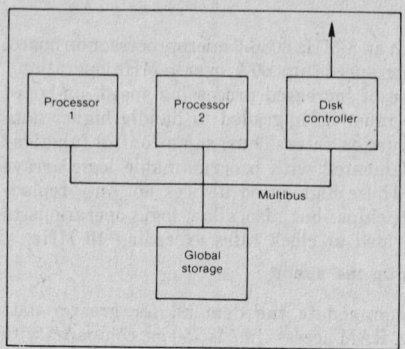

2. Semaphore signaling is a method of synchronizing the operation of processors in a multiprocessing system. In an earlier single-board system (shown here), global storage provides the control signal for indicating the status of the disk controller—busy or not busy.

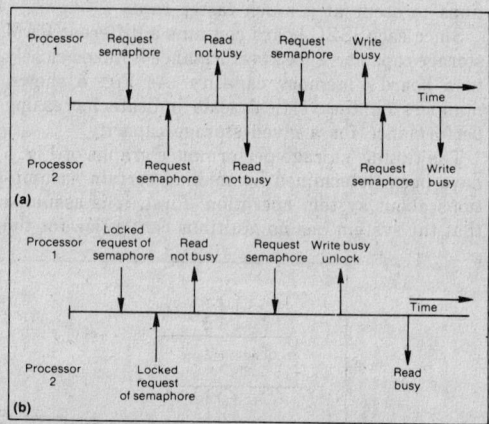

3. In newer single-board computers, a locking feature eliminates the need for global storage in semaphore signaling. Without locking, a deadlock can occur (a) when two processors try to access a system resource. The dual-port memory prevents such a problem (b).

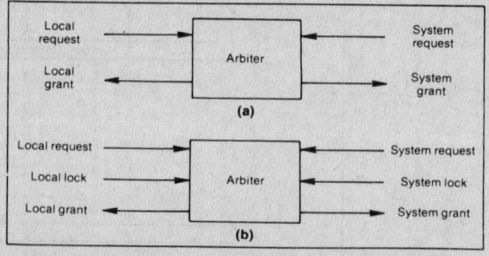

4. Adding dual-port memory locking to computer boards inhibits arbitration until the locked operation is completed (a). Earlier boards relied on global storage (b).

Enhanced single-board control

things: the interrupt delay time, or the maximum time allowed from an interrupt request until the interrupt service routine instructions are executed, and the maximum number of interrupts that may need servicing in a given period.

To compute interrupt delay, both hardware and software must be considered. For example, hardware on the board controls the processor's acknowledgment of the interrupt request. The board's 8086 processor retrieves the address of the interrupt-service routine from the interrupt vector table, which is stored in an on-board RAM. Interrupt-service routines often store all registers on the stack before the servicing of an interrupting device begins. The total delay time is computed as follows:

INT to 8259A to INTR at 8086	350 ns
INTA service time (16 8086 clocks)	2000 ns (hardware)
8086 INT vector computation (56 clocks)	7000 ns (processor)
Storage of nine 8086 registers (103 clocks)	12,875 ns (software)
Total interrupt delay time	22,225 ns

The interrupt frequency depends on the interrupt delay time, the execution time of the interrupt-service routine, and the time to restore program execution. Time spent executing the service routine is highly device-dependent, but the return to program execution can be computed as follows:

Retrieval of nine 8086 registers (90 clocks)	11,250 ns (software)
Interrupt return of 8086 (30 clocks)	3750 ns (processor)
Code fetch of next instruction (four clocks)	500 ns (hardware)
Total return time	15,500 ns

Interrupt frequencies for the iSBC 86/14—assuming several I/O service routines—are 24,600 per second for sending a character to a CRT, 24,600/s for receiving a character from the CRT, and 22,000/s for clock interrupts.

The access times of current EPROMs range from 200 to 1000 ns. For slower devices, wait states (an integer number of processor clock times) are added to the access time. At an 8-MHz processing frequency, a 200-ns EPROM operates with zero wait states. The most critical time, access time from a chip

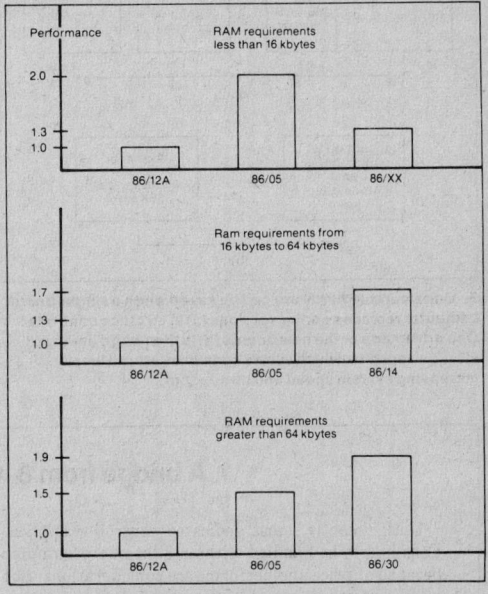

5. The random-access-memory performance of single-board computers is related to the amount of storage a board provides. The latest boards are designed to work most efficiently with storage capacities of 16 to 256 kbytes.

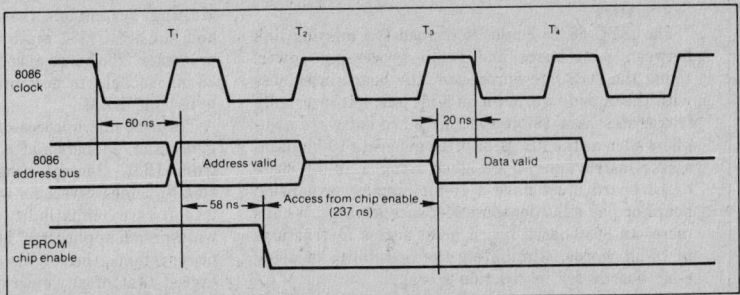

6. Factory controllers execute most of the system code from EPROMs. With a high-speed EPROM, valid data appears on the Multibus about 300 ns after valid addresses are applied.

enable, is 200 ns. The timing relationships for accessing an EPROM are shown in Fig. 6.

From a system standpoint, all peripheral components can be accessed in about 300 ns after a command. At a clock rate of 5 MHz, that forces one wait state; at 8 MHz, two wait states. A variety of devices interfaces with the iSBX bus, permitting custom configurations of a single-board controller for factory applications. Two analog modules, one for input and one for output, can monitor or control plant equipment. For expansion of digital inputs or outputs, a parallel I/O module can be added.

Whereas interrupt response time is a critical parameter in a factory environment, other considerations become critical in an office environment. One of those is throughput, the number of tasks a worker can perform. As a result, office controllers must provide the user with fast response time. In addition, since office controllers usually perform a wide variety of tasks, execution is mainly from RAM, not ROM. Moreover, because most tasks are dynamic, large mass-storage devices are needed. Programs are loaded from mass storage into the processor's memory and executed. In addition, most programs are in a high-level language (for word processing and other office tasks), which requires considerable hardware and software support.

As with factory controllers, configurable systems are important in the office environment, since special applications will require additional hardware. Word processors, for example, are generally linked via a serial communications line to a central processor, or mass-storage device, and the link must be a high-speed one to minimize response time.

To meet office system requirements, computer boards should have the following features: an operating system having a human interface (keyboard), a program loader and configurable peripheral support for mass storage, communications controllers and high-level languages; a maximum-size RAM with minimum access-time devices for program support;

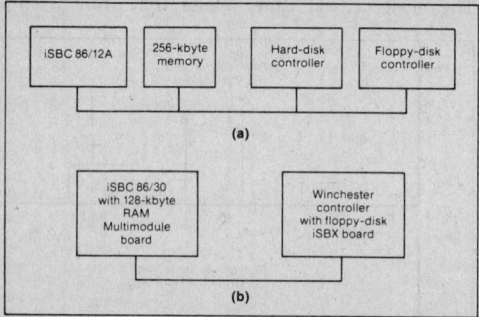

7. **Considerable hardware can be saved when a single-board computer replaces earlier versions (a) in an office controller. One advantage of the new boards (b) is their large on-board storage capacity, which allows code to be stored locally, increasing system speed and throughput.**

A bridge from 8- to 16-bit processing

Until recently, most dedicated controller applications had to be handled with an 8-bit microcomputer because of price and performance considerations. But with performance and software needs on the rise, designers are faced with moving up to 16-bit devices to obtain the necessary computing power. When the move up happens, however, hardware and software compatibility considerations often get the short end of the stick.

The iSBC 88/25 could be termed the missing link between 8-bit buses and 16-bit processing power. Using the 8088 microprocessor, the board interfaces with the outside world on an 8-bit bus, but internally it operates as a 16-bit system. Since software compilers such as the PL/M-86 often generate 16-bit data-access instructions, a designer using a 16-bit 8086-based board must have a 16-bit memory expansion board or pay a burdensome software penalty. What's more, an 8086-based board must access instructions in 16-bit words, eliminating the possibility of using 8-bit boards for instruction storage.

The iSBC 88/25 automatically breaks all 16-bit words into 8-bit bytes on the Multibus. Therefore, independently of software, the hardware converts all accesses to 8-bit bytes transparently to the user. This gives the board the dual advantage of being fully compatible with all 8-bit hardware devices and 16-bit software. To retain compatibility with Intel standards, the board is designed to interface with the Multibus system bus, the iSBX bus, memory modules, and the iSBC 337 math module and numeric data processor. The board also contains JEDEC-compatible 28-pin sockets to accommodate EPROM and static byte-wide RAM.

The 8088 microprocessor is being used in the second generation of personal computers, such as the one from IBM. Several other personal-computer and small-business systems will also use the 8088. With its software compatibility with the 8086 processor and widespread application in personal and small-business systems, the software repertoire of the 8088 will exceed that of any microprocessor.

and hardware support for both mass storage and communications.

Office controllers call for lots of RAM, and a board with a capacity of up to 256 kbytes is suitable. A dynamic RAM controller handles the automatic refreshing and generates the proper timing for the row and column addresses. PLA devices send commands to the controller to initiate the RAM access.

The differences between early and updated office controllers are shown in Fig. 7. Additional memory expansion on the Multibus is necessary to meet system requirements. The floppy-disk controller

---

Meet the family

Progress in semiconductor density and speed translates into more functions and greater throughput in the latest breed of single-board computers. Another, more subtle, benefit accrues: board-level controllers can be made to fit within a wide range of performance and cost slots, resulting in greater freedom of design choice.

Thus whereas one board, the iSBC 86/05, provides high-speed, low-cost compatibility with earlier units, two other boards, the iSBC 86/14 and iSBC 86/30, drop into the high-performance end of system integration. Both controller boards are memory-intensive: the former is available with 32 kbytes of RAM, expandable to 64 kbytes; the latter starts with 128 kbytes of RAM and can be expanded to 256 kbytes. Large storage capacity is backed up by 8-MHz processing rates and iSBX-bus support.

Since all 16-bit single-board controllers are software-compatible, both present and future controller systems can be upgraded with minimal extra investment. Once established and proven in prior designs, bus and software standards reduce hardware conversion costs.

Since iSBC 86/XX boards constitute a family, hardware and software are interchangeable throughout. For example, the earlier iSBC 86/12A is compatible with the ICE 86, the in-circuit emulator for debugging hardware and software, and with the iSBC 337, the multimodule numeric data processor for high-speed mathematics.

For external interfacing, the 86/12A offers three connections: a serial port, a parallel port, and the Multibus interface. All these connections are available with at least the same user options. Since the connector pinouts stay the same, all single-board controllers are plug-compatible.

---

board alone must be implemented with a full size Multibus board. Using newer boards not only reduces system size, but also improves performance. The large on-board memory stores enough program information to allow operation that is 100% faster than first-generation boards. □

The iRMX 86 operating system standard, together with its application software, dictates that all single-board controllers have the same memory-access capability and I/O resources. To ensure compatibility between the earlier and the newer boards, the new iSBC 86/14 is designed with the same memory capabilities as the iSBC 86/12A for on- and off-board access to memory. In addition, the iSBC 86/30, with its 128 kbytes of RAM, further extends the system's capabilities. I/O controllers are contained on iSBC 86/XX boards in the same default configuration as on iSBC 86/12A boards. Thus, the software—like the hardware—is plug-compatible, virtually eliminating the need for additional software expense when upgrading a system.

If a system's RAM requirements are under 16 kbytes, an iSBC 86/05 supported by a high-speed 8-kbyte RAM Multimodule board (iSBC 302), offers better performance than either an 86/12A or any newer board. For factory applications, the 86/05 offers twice the EPROM capacity of the 86/14 or 30 board. But as RAM requirements grow past 16 kbytes, the 86/05 becomes less desirable because the additional memory required must be accessed from the Multibus. Data accesses from the bus occur at a much slower rate than those from the on-board memory.

For midrange RAM storage applications—16 to 64 kbytes—there is the iSBC 86/14 and a 32-kbyte RAM Multimodule board (iSBC 300A). The 86/30 runs as fast as the 86/14, but for RAM requirements exceeding 64 kbytes, the 86/30 continues to access its internal memory, providing faster operation. Moreover, an expanded memory space—a total of 320 kbytes consisting of 256 kbytes of RAM and 64 kbytes of EPROM—make the 86/30 the performance leader in large system applications.

intel®

ARTICLE REPRINT

AR-267

April 1983

Choosing a Bus for Control

John Beaston
OEM Modules Operation
MULTIBUS® Architect

"Reprinted with permission from Instruments & Control Systems, March 1983 issue."

Choosing a bus for control

Which system bus is best for your application? Both business and technical factors should be considered when making a selection.

John Beaston
Multibus Architect
Intel Corporation
Hillsboro, OR 97123

Last month's installment of our "Bus boards for control" series provided a broad overview of bus-based systems, including a look at their features, advantages and disadvantages. This second installment describes the business and technical factors that must be considered when selecting a bus for your application from the dozens available.

• • • • •

The importance of selecting the best bus for your application can't be overemphasized. This is true whether you're working for an OEM or are building a one-of-a-kind product for internal use. The choice you make can impact such important areas as system performance, the engineering time needed for system configuration (which affects time-to-market for OEM's), and the ability to enhance the system in the future.

To help you with this critical decision, this article looks at both the business issues and technical aspects that should be considered when choosing a bus. It uses six of the more popular buses available to make example comparisons.

These include Multibus, VME, Versabus, STD, S-100, and the Q-bus.

Business factors

Because many of the buses have similar technical capabilities, business factors often sway the final decision in bus selection. The most important of these are described in the material that follows. (Table 1 compares business factors for the six buses mentioned earlier.)

Public specification

Choosing a bus with publicly available specifications can provide some measure of compatibility among the board products supplied by different vendors. Unless all board designers use the same spec, compatibility is a hit-or-miss proposition.

Controlling body

Having a public spec, however, does not guarantee compatibility. Public specs can change with time. There-

Table 1: Business factors for various buses

	Multibus	VME	Versabus	STD	S-100	Q-bus
Public spec	Yes	Yes	Yes	Yes	Yes	Yes
Controlling body	IEEE 796	Motorola, Signetics, Mostek	Motorola IEEE P970*	IEEE P961	IEEE 696	DEC
Multiple vendors	150	21	10	75	100	10
Second sources	Yes				Yes	
VLSI support	Yes	Yes	Yes			Yes
Processors	8080, 8085, 8086, 80186, 80188, 80286, Z80, Z8000, 68000, 16032, 6800, 6100, NCS800, 6802, 6808	68000, 80186, 16032	68000	8085, 8088, 6800, Z80	8080, 8085, 8088, 80186, 80286, Z80 6800, 68000, 16032	LSI-11

*Pending

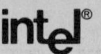

fore, to prevent incompatibility and give bus users confidence, any changes made should receive an impartial review by a single controlling body.

A single point of control is critical. For example, until it was adopted by the IEEE, the S-100 bus had no control at all, let alone from a single point. Stores of incompatible S-100 boards are well-known. Now, with IEEE control and standardization, compatibility should be assured, at least for new products.

Multiple vendors

No one manufacturer can serve all the needs of the bus board marketplace. And the best bus specification in the world doesn't mean a thing if the type of board you need isn't available. In general, the number of products available on a given bus is proportional to the number of vendors supporting it. Thus, selecting a bus with strong multiple vendor support can be to your advantage.

Second sources

Some bus manufacturers are second sourcing the more popular boards. This helps assure board availability, and can also mean competitive pricing.

Processor independence

One issue that can affect future system enhancements is processor independence. Some buses are specific for a particular microprocessor family or type of processor. This can lock you into a processor family or type even though technology advancements offer better solutions. A bus which supports many processors lets you choose the best processor for your application without having to throw away your investment in the bus.

VLSI support

The final business issue is VLSI (very large scale integration) support for the bus. Some manufacturers have reduced the interface to the buses they support to a handful of VLSI devices. Having these available can greatly simplify the job of building a board, and can improve its performance and functionality by freeing up more board real estate for useful functions. It can also make off-the-shelf boards less expensive.

Technical factors

Let's turn now to a look at the technical factors in bus selection. Areas to be discussed include: address range, data width, bandwidth, interrupts, multiple bus masters, arbitration, mutual exclusion, board size, connector type, and I/O module bus. (Table 2 compares these factors for the six buses mentioned earlier.)

Address range

A system's memory requirements tend to go up as its capabilities and performance requirements increase. Therefore, you should choose a bus which supports an address space at least as large as the highest level processor you expect to use on it. This is generally a good idea even though at first, you might only be using a small portion of the address space. It will allow for later expansion.

On buses which specify expanded or optional address ranges, be very careful when selecting board products. Be sure the product decodes all of the address range you need. For example, if you use a 24-bit address range and buy a memory board which decodes only 20 bits, you'll find its address space is duplicated every 1 Mbyte on your 16 Mbyte space—which can be very inconvenient. Some buses, like VME and Versabus, have a way around this.

Data width

A processor presents a certain number of external data pins to the outside world and the bus you select should match this. While it is possible to put a 16-bit processor on a 8-bit wide bus and have the bus do two transfers each time the processor requests 16 bits, it's slow, clumsy, and complicated.

Bandwidth

Table 2 gives the maximum theoretical bandwidth for each bus at various data widths. Note that, with two exceptions, the bandwidths for any given data width are within about 20% of each other. This is because all the buses dis-

Table 2: Technical factors for various buses

	Multibus	VME	Versabus	STD	S-100	Q-bus
Address width	24	16, 24, 32	16, 24, 32	16	16 standard 24 expanded	16 standard 22 expanded
Data width	8 | 16	8 | 16 | 32	8 | 16 | 32	8	8 | 16	8 | 16
Bandwidth (Mbytes/s)	5 | 10	6 | 12 | 24	6 | 12 | 24	1	6 | 12	0.8 | 1.6
Interrupt lines	8	7	7	2	10	4
Interrupt ack	Polled	Daisy-chain	Daisy-chain	Daisy-chain	Polled	Daisy-chain
Mutual exclusion	Bus lock	RMW+bus lock	RMW+bus lock	None	Bus lock	None
Arbitration	Serial or parallel	Serial or parallel with daisy-chain	Parallel with daisy-chain	Serial	Parallel	Serial
MECHANICAL						
Form factor	6.75x12	6.3x9.2	9.25x14.5	4.5x6.5	5.1x10	5.25x8.9
Area (in.²)	81	58	134	29	51	47
Connector size	86/60	96/96	140/120	56	100	36/36
Connector type	Edge	DIN	Edge	Edge	Edge	Edge

cussed in this article use an asynchronous bus protocol with roughly the same timing. The only exceptions are the STD and Q-bus, which have relaxed timing specs.

The bandwidth figures given in Table 2 ignore bus arbitration delays and assume zero memory access times. But memory access times constitute over half the time of a typical bus transfer. They reduce the available bandwidth by more than 50%, and make the comparison come out even closer. Only the STD and Q-bus are restrained by their bus timing. The others are at the mercy of their memory boards. If you're looking for maximum performance, pick the bus that enables you to buy the fastest memory boards.

Interrupts

Systems are usually divided along functional lines. For example, a control system might be partitioned into analog I/O, digital I/O, and operator console functional modules. These modules could all be physically located on the same board and controlled by a single processor, or each module might be on a different board with individual control processors. However they're arranged, the modules must communicate.

The traditional method is with interrupts. Ideally, each module would have its own interrupt line, and each line would have a different priority, as shown in Fig. 1. Since often there are too many modules for this to be practical, bus designs are the result of a compromise. They allow the modules to share the interrupt lines, leaving it up to the interrupted device to figure out the source of the interrupt.

There are two main ways of doing this: software polling and daisy-chained acknowledge.

In software polling (Fig. 2), the interrupted module polls, or asks, each of the modules on the applicable interrupt request line. The module which generated the interrupt replies when polled.

Daisy-chained acknowledge (Fig. 3) is a hardware method. An interrupt acknowledge signal is passed down a line daisy-chained between all modules on the shared interrupt line. Modules not signalling the interrupt let the acknowledge signal pass on down the daisy-chain. Once the signal arrives at the interrupting module, the module captures it and places an identifying code on the data bus. The interupted module then reads this code to figure out the source.

It's hard to say whether one method is better than the other. Polling, being software based, is very flexible and easy to debug, but tends to be slower than a hardware method. Daisy-chaining is fast but makes the priorities of modules sharing an interrupt line depend on their positions.

If there are fewer modules than the number of interrupt lines, neither method offers an advantage.

Multiple bus masters

If there is one characteristic which tells if a bus is suitable for mid-to-high end systems, it is its support of multiple bus masters. Such support greatly enhances the architectural flexibility of the bus.

Simple buses like the STD and Q-buses support only one bus master in addition to the main processor. This usually must be a direct memory access (DMA) device. Typically, both masters can't operate at the same time. If the DMA device is active, the main processor suspends operation temporarily even though it might be using only on-board private resources. Once the DMA device is done with the bus, the main processor resumes operation. This nonconcurrency generally restricts these buses to low-to-mid range performance systems.

The remaining buses support multiple bus masters in the true sense of the term. On these buses, it's possible to have many processors sharing the bus. Usually the processors operate with their on-board resources while sharing a common global pool of memory and/or I/O.

Multiple-master buses give you a lot of flexibility in system architecture. A simple system might use a single main processor board with a dumb analog I/O board. Or you could increase the system's throughput by replacing the dumb I/O board with an intelligent board containing its

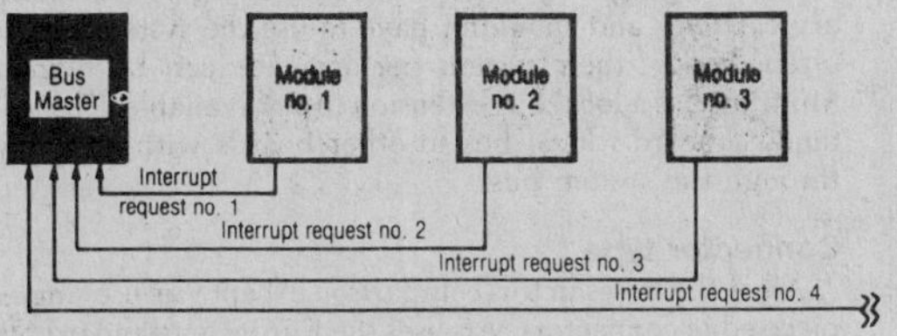

Fig. 1 (left, top): If there are more interrupt request lines than interrupting modules, the sources of the interrupts are obvious.

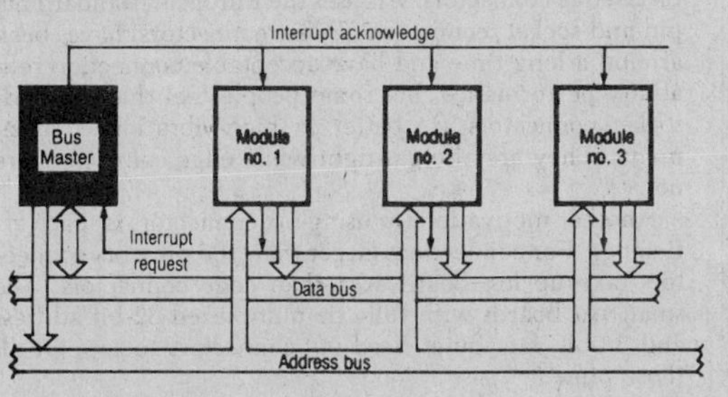

Fig. 2 (left, bottom): When modules must share interrupt request lines, there must be some way to find the source of an interrupt. In software polling, the bus master asks each module in turn if it is the source.

Fig. 3 (below): In daisy-chained acknowledge, the module which caused the interrupt captures the acknowledge signal to indicate that it is the source. Priority then depends upon position on the bus.

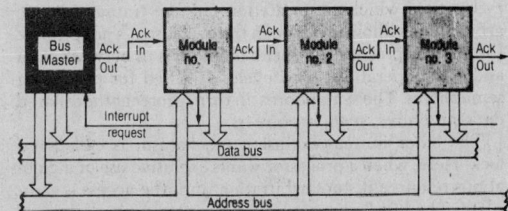

BUS BOARDS FOR CONTROL SERIES 2

own dedicated processor. This intelligent board would operate in parallel with the main processor. The support of multiple masters lets a bus span a tremendous cost/performance range.

Arbitration

All of the buses mentioned only allow one bus master at any one time. Since several masters might want the bus at the same time, arbitration is needed to resolve the conflict and figure out which one gets the bus and which one has to wait.

This can be done with either serial or parallel methods. In parallel arbitration, each bus master (or group of masters in those buses with daisy-chained arbitration) generates a bus request, which goes to a central arbitration module. This module then resolves any simultaneous requests based upon a priority algorithm and returns a grant to use the bus to the winning master. In a purely parallel scheme, there are as many separate request and grant lines as there are masters. However, buses like VME and Versabus allow bus masters to share common request lines. The grant for each request line is then daisy-chained to determine which of the masters gets the bus.

All parallel arbitration schemes require external arbitration logic. Sometimes this logic is placed on the backplane, other times it's included on a processor board, and still other times a separate board is used. How it's done is an implementation detail that you should be aware of when you choose board products for your selected bus.

To save the cost of parallel arbitration for simpler systems, the Multibus uses a serial arbitration scheme. This requires no external logic but can only support three bus masters, which is often enough. VME can also do serial arbitration, with up to 20 masters.

Mutual exclusion

Systems which share common resources, such as a shared memory pool or a peripheral, need some way to prevent conflict. One popular method is to set a bit in memory called a semaphore to indicate that the resource is in use. A processor wanting to use the resource will read the semaphore; if it is not set, the processor will set it and use the resource.

But there can be a problem. After the bit is read, and before it can be set, another processor can read it, find it cleared, and try to set it. To avoid this problem, buses may use mutual exclusion.

The various buses provide mutual exclusion in different ways. VME and Versabus use read-modify-write (RMW) bus cycles. These are read and write cycles to the same memory location, which are treated as one bus transaction. No arbitration is allowed between the cycles so it's not possible for another processor to sneak on the bus in between read and write operations. RMW cycles are used for protecting semaphores. The semaphores, in turn, protect other shared data structures, such as pointers.

The other mutual exclusion mechanism is called bus lock. Here, when a processor wants exclusive use of a global bus resource it stops arbitration until the access is complete. The bus lock can cover more than just a read and write cycle. It could apply over many bus cycles if so desired.

It is also useful with dual-ported memory. It can inhibit access from any port of a multi-ported resource so that even though a local processor is using its local bus, it cannot violate mutual exclusion.

Board size

Perhaps the most important factor in determining the type of systems a bus supports is its form. Smaller boards are very modular. They allow you to get exactly what you need with few excess or unused functions. On the other hand, they may have lower performance. Since each function usually has its own board, and its own bus interface, more real estate goes to interfacing to the bus. Larger boards can have more functions per board, so the percentage of area devoted to the bus is lower. This leaves more room for extra functions.

The problem with larger boards is finding ones with the right mix of functions. Unused functions waste real estate, power, and money. Supporters of the larger boards (Multibus and Versabus) have recognized this problem and have developed I/O module bus structures as extensions to the primary system bus. We'll discuss these extensions shortly.

The other tradeoff on board size is performance. Many of the boards use a local bus. This is an on-board bus which the processor can use without disturbing the main system bus. These local buses tend to have very high performance, since the distances are short and arbitration is usually not required. It's good to maximize the time a processor spends on its local bus since it raises its overall performance. No matter how fast the system bus may be, the local bus is always faster.

In general, smaller boards have less room for local bus resources. This is particularly true for memory. Once the processor exceeds the amount of local memory, it must use the system bus and suffer the delays of arbitration and multiple logic gates. Larger boards have larger local memory capacity and shouldn't have to use the system bus as often; hence, their system performance can be higher. Multibus has a local bus extension (iLBX) available. This extends a board's local bus to other boards without going through the system bus.

Connector type

All of the buses in this comparison except VME use single-piece edge connectors. VME uses the European standard DIN pin-and-socket connector. Edge connectors have been around a long time and have acceptable connection reliability performance, but some people feel that pin-and-socket connectors are better in high-vibration environments. They are also gas-tight while edge connectors are not.

Another motivation for using DIN connectors is space efficiency. For connections larger than 100 pins, DIN connectors take up less board area than edge connectors. The small VME boards with fully demultiplexed 32-bit address and 32-bit data buses need DIN connectors to support all those pins.

Table 3: Comparison of I/O module buses

I/O Modular Bus	iSBX	I/O Channel
Companion system bus	Multibus	Versabus VME
Public spec	Yes	Yes
Controlling body	IEEE P959	Motorola
Multiple vendors	10	2
Address width	5	12
Data width	8 | 16	8
Bandwidth (mByte/sec)	5 | 10	2
DMA support	Yes	
I/O connection type	Daughter board	Separate cable or backplane

The other major differences are cost and current capacity. Pin-and-socket connectors are more expensive than edge connectors, and they handle less current than edge connector fingers (1 to 1.5 A per pin connection vs 1 to 5 A per edge connector finger). This means that buses using pin-and-socket connectors need to use more pins to supply power.

I/O module bus

As mentioned earlier, the supporters of the larger boards have developed specialized I/O buses to improve their modularity. Multibus uses the iSBX I/O Expansion Bus and VME/Versabus have the I/O Channel. Table 3 gives a comparison of these buses.

While the goals are similar, the methods are different. The I/O Channel uses a separate ribbon cable or backplane, and can extend up to twelve feet from the host system. Up to 16 slave devices can be connected, transferring data over an 8-bit wide path.

The iSBX is a small daughter board which plugs directly into a host Multibus board, and each daughter board handles one kind of I/O. Both 8 and 16-bit data transfers are possible.

A final word

With this information you should be able to make a more informed choice of a bus for your application. Just remember that there are a lot of buses available, not just the six discussed here. And there may be more than one which will suit a particular application. ■

The author, John Beaston, will be available to answer any questions you may have about this article. Mr. Beaston can be reached at (503) 681-8080 during normal business hours.

intel

ARTICLE REPRINT

AR-268

April 1983

"Standard Buses Capture Fancy of Most OEM's"

"Building Blocks for Micros"

Mitchell York
Michael Azzara
Computer Systems News

Copyright © 1983 by CMP Publications, Inc., 111 East Shore Road, Manhasset, N.Y. Reprinted with permission from "Computer Systems News."

Intel Corporation, 1983
Order Number: 230727-001

Standard Buses Capture Fancy Of Most OEMs

By Mitchell York

Before OEMs or systems builders can choose a single-board computer around which to configure a multiboard system, they must first decide on a system bus.

It used to be they simply designed proprietary buses. But the evolution of board-level computers and standard bus architectures that began in the mid-1970s has changed all that: OEMs and systems houses now perceive the use of standard buses and bus-compatible board-level components as a way to reduce costs and lay the groundwork for the integration of future technological advances. The days of the proprietary bus are numbered, industry executives agree.

Several standard buses are now fighting for market share, with Intel Corp.'s Multibus leading the pack with more than half the 16-bit segment and one-third to one-half of the 8-bit market, according to managing analyst David Aronovitz of research house Gnostic Concepts Inc. Pro-Log Corp.'s STD bus is another major contender in the 8-bit arena, he said.

And both are bracing for stiff competition from a more recent offering sponsored by a coalition of semiconductor manufacturers led by Motorola Inc. The coalition's VME bus is compatible with 8-, 16-, and 32-bit architectures.

Additional competition is provided in the 8-bit market by the S-100 bus developed by MITS Inc. and in the 16-bit market by Digital Equipment Corp.'s Q-Bus. The proprietary bus is still an option, but industry experts are betting against it.

Many OEMs and systems builders are looking to standard buses to reduce engineering overhead and help position them to expand and modify their systems when new technologies become available. Those two factors — economics and technological advances — are the driving forces behind the mounting attention being focused on standard buses, according to industry executives.

"The technology has moved to a point where the user can integrate the baseline of his system onto a single-board computer," said Gary Sawyer, board products marketing manager for Intel's OEM Modules Group. "But we have very few customers out there who use a single-board solution. The primary advantage (of a single-board computer) is more content on a single board, so that as an OEM configures a system on his bus, he has a simpler configuration to perform. And that's why the bus question becomes so important," Sawyer said.

"The market, now that it has reached an adolescence, is maturing to a point where customers have to consider what bus they're deciding on first, and where that bus can take them in the future. Then they can evaluate the vendors and the products that are available.

While many OEMs still stand by proprietary buses, there are growing indications that the economics of the OEM business will not allow them to resist standardization for long. "There are still companies out there that are emphatically clinging to dedicated systems architectures for mini and microcomputers," said Ray Burkley, president of Astraea Computer Corp., Sunnyvale, Calif., which is marketing a VME bus-compatible single-board computer. "They are the ones that will end up getting hurt in the long run, because all the other reasons germane to using (standard) buses make sense."

"I think a proprietary bus is a definite tactical error," said Gnostic's Aronovitz. "It locks you out of the market, it forces you to design everything in-house, and it delays your entry into the marketplace, he said.

Standard Advantage

One reason for moving to standard architecture is that it is becoming prohibitive to design systems starting from the chip level, some OEMs said, unless the number of systems needed is high and unless the technology is likely to remain constant for a long time.

Observers say there is a proliferation of systems builders making small quantities of systems aimed at profitable vertical markets. Because these OEMs do not enjoy economies of scale and cannot afford to build from scratch, they are increasingly turning to standard architectures. In addition, with semiconductor and microprocessor technology moving so rapidly, it is likely that systems will have increasingly shorter marketing life cycles, thus further fueling the standard bus movement.

If systems builders are thinking about standard buses, vendors cannot be far behind. Aronovitz reports that there are 300 vendors in the board-level market and all have aligned their products with one or more of the standard buses.

The attention standard buses are receiving cannot help but grow exponentially in the coming years, industry executives say, because of backing from such powerhouse companies as Intel, DEC, and Motorola. Those companies and several others are helping create vast secondary markets to supply bus-compatible products geared for the systems builder. And the more products put out on the market for OEMs, the more OEMs are likely to use them and the buses they are made for, according to observers.

While OEMs and their suppliers may differ about which bus is best, there seems to be widespread agreement on the need to seriously address systems building starting at the board level and employing some standardized bus. It's a simple question of speed, according to Jeff Gorin, product manager of Motorola's MOS Integrated Circuits Group.

Faster Integration

"The fundamental advantage of modular product implementations using boards with common bus interfaces is that the systems integrator is going to be able to accomplish system integration faster — assuming he can find board-level components — by plugging together existing, documented boards rather than starting from scratch from chips," said Gorin.

Speed of product entry was the key factor that led Control Automation Inc., a Princeton, N.J.-based maker of factory automation equipment, to adopt an industry-standard bus. The company, which makes industrial robots and vision processors, was concerned with cutting down its engineering time and ramping up production, said director of electronic development Abe Abramovich.

Control Automation accordingly decided to build its robots with boards compatible with Multibus. "We came up to speed in our product development cycle more rapidly by buying off-the-shelf computer boards with all the functionality we require. By not having to design circuitry, we were able to apply our energy where it was really required — value-added interfaces."

The time savings that standard buses yield can be enormous, said Astraea's Burkley. Standard buses, with the myriad off-the-shelf board-level products available, allow an OEM to get to market from six to 18 months sooner than if the systems builder were to design his own proprietary bus and boards, Burkley said. "It's a make-buy decision. Do you want to take 30 months to develop a proprietary product, or buy at the board level, add software, and be in the marketplace?"

Once the decision is made to build with standard boards that are compatible with standard buses, the issue becomes which bus to use. Several have emerged as leaders because they have won acceptance from components manufacturers who intend to create an array of products for systems builders.

One of the latest buses to achieve a growing degree of recognition is the VME bus. Motorola, Signetics Corp., Mostek Corp. and Thomson-EFCIS last year all threw their weight behind VME, and now an IEEE committee chaired by Signetics' engineering manager Michael Clader has been formed to draft a standard.

Proponents of VME, which is specially designed for use with the 68000 chip, say its main attribute is its ability to support 8-, 16-, and 32-bit microprocessors. This is important to OEMs that want to design 16-bit systems now that will work in the 32-bit environment when the technology is available.

"The VME bus is the only bus architecture that really allows us to build things today for both 16- and 32-bit," Burkley said. "It's our intention to build 32-bit supermini-computers. A lot of LSI components we need aren't there today, so we selected a bus architecture that will allow us to grow from the present 16-bit capability to 32-bit.

"We'll start building board-level products now that we can sell and which will generate feedback as well as profits. When full 32-bit capability is available, we'll only have to add a couple of boards to do the upgrade."

VME is also cited by systems integrators as more expandable than several other major bus options. "It gave me more real estate. That was critical to me," said Roger Vass, president of Victory Computer Systems Inc., San Jose, Calif. With VME, he said, Victory can achieve the cost efficiency of single-board computer design without sacrificing system expandability.

"VME has architectural aspects that are directly coincident with my marketing strategy," Vass continued, "I am going into the fault-tolerant, multiple-CPU, transaction processing market within a year." VME's speed is essential to succeeding in Victory's targeted markets, Vass said. "I need that kind of bus speed in order to execute fault-tolerant systems. I got it."

What Victory also got by adopting VME, Vass said, is a bus architecture that has been endorsed by major semiconductor houses, which gives it market credibility. "And it's a new bus. From a marketing standpoint, it's attractive because it's new."

VME is frequently compared to Intel's well-established Multibus. VME supporters maintain that Multibus can not fully support microprocessors as powerful as the 68000. Multibus enthusiasts counter by noting the constant stream of upgrades that have been made in the bus since its introduction to the OEM market in 1976.

Sawyer noted that even though Multibus was originally conceived as a bus that would address the 8-bit market, it has been adapted for 16-bit. "There have been six improvements made in Multibus to adapt to new VLSI. We are at the forefront of yet another evolution of Multibus to adapt it to our 80286 microprocessor."

LBX Refinement

The latest Multibus refinement is LBX — Local Bus Extension — which the company said allows a microprocessor to address up to 16 Mbytes of local system memory at very high speeds. LBX, Intel said, supports a data transfer rate of 9.5 Mbytes per second for 8-bit data and 19 Mbytes per second for 16-bit data. Intel said six single-board computer manufacturers have notified them of plans to develop products based on LBX.

It is just this kind of secondary market support that is crucial to the success of a bus, according to industry executives. There are now 165 suppliers of more than 1000 Multibus-compatible products, according to Fred Mazenac, president of Ironoak Co., the La Jolla, Calif.-based publisher of the *Multibus Buyers Guide.*

Motivating Factor

"Very clearly, one of the most important motivating factors in users selecting a bus is the number of vendors and products available for that particular bus," said Mazenac, who is now involved in assembling a Multibus manufacturers association.

Intel said the market last year for single-board computers was $375 million, about one-half of which was Multibus-compatible. By 1985, Intel said, revenues are expected to grow to $800 million, and Multibus is expected to retain its approximate 50 percent market share.

Sawyer said another boon to Multibus is its endorsement by the IEEE, which recently declared it a standard. With a firm, unchangeable standard in place, more vendors are expected to develop Multibus-compatible products, Sawyer said.

While Multibus is being used for a broad range of applications, Pro-Log's STD bus is geared primarily for industrial uses. Companies that build products compatible with the STD bus, also known as Standard bus, note that its small card size makes it attractive for single-board systems vendors that focus on industrial applications.

Dick Thomas, director for product development for Pro-Log, said STD "has an I/O intensity rather than a number-crunching intensity," which makes it better for control purposes than for data processing.

Thomas said the main advantage of STD is its price competitiveness. STD-based products are less expensive than Multibus-based products, but also less versatile. "What tends to happen (with the large Multibus card) is that people use it up and put a lot of things on the board just because there is a lot of room. It can be overkill.

"If you need what's on a Multibus card, like two I/O channels, it probably becomes more cost-effective. But that rarely happens, and that's where our advantage is. STD allows you to modularize to specific functions. Consequently there is a big price advantage," Thomas said.

While STD hasn't made its way into many office systems because of its data processing limitations, the older S-100 bus is most often used in small business systems. S-100, developed in 1975 for the Altair home computer, "is very flexible and modular," said Mark Garetz, president of CompuPro Systems, Oakland Airport, Calif.

CompuPro works with S-100, Garetz said, because it can be used with almost any processor. "It's not that hard to put various processors on it; it's not that processor specific."

Garetz said the cost/performance ratio of the S-100 "is unequaled by any of the other bus structures." Equivalent products based on Multibus can cost three to four times as much as S-100 products, he said.

AR-268

Building Blocks For Micros

As Systems Get Smaller, The Role Of Single-Board Computers Gets Bigger

By Michael Azzara

On the most basic level, a single-board computer is just what the name implies: the essential components of a computer system — a CPU, memory, and at least one I/O channel — on a single printed-circuit board. But the widespread assumption that it's a single board that constitutes a computer system is usually wrong.

So what's right? Single-board computer vendors agree that their products are malleable; they can be used alone in some applications, while in others they must be tied with additional boards to make a working system.

The fact is that use of single-board computers is pervasive in the microcomputer industry: Such boards are the building blocks of most modern microcomputer systems. The majority are manufactured from scratch by high-volume general-purpose hardware vendors, but more and more systems houses and OEMs in narrower vertical markets are buying single-board computers, usually from one of the approximately half-dozen semiconductor houses that analysts estimate control about 98 percent of the board-level products market.

The phrase single-board computer was coined by Intel Corp. in 1976 and has become virtually a generic term for microprocessor-based CPU boards. Many single-board computer vendors, however, point out that the term is somewhat misleading, since most of their OEMs actually include more than one board in their final products. But they agree nonetheless that there are important advantages to cramming the essential components of a system onto a single board rather than using three, four, or more boards strung together to make a computer system.

The primary benefits they cite are increases in performance and decreases in both cost and physical size, not necessarily in that order — and not all vendors agree on the relative importance of each.

On the flip side of the coin, single-board computers are a cost-effective solution for OEMs in only a narrow range of volumes. In very low-volume applications, an OEM may find a packaged system to be a better buy, while high-volume applications may call for an OEM to turn to component-level integration. Most of the applications that fall in that range are technical in nature, such as controlling scientific instruments or industrial machines.

Within that volume range — usually anywhere up to 1000 units during the life of a system — the advantages far outweigh the disadvantages, vendors say.

Performance is improved over multiboard systems because execution speed and reliability both increase when more work is performed within the confines of one board, rather than through communications on a system bus. Cost goes down because using one board to perform functions that once required three or more saves on board expenses. And because the final system can be made smaller than multiboard systems, doors are opened to applications that previously required smaller systems than could be built.

Besides those technical advantages, many vendors point out that buying single-board computers allows OEMs to concentrate their efforts on their own expertise in a particular applications area, rather than expending engineering talent to duplicate electronics that are already available in standard packages.

There are also the obvious benefits derived by the OEMs whose applications can be handled by one stand-alone single-board computer. These applications tend to be in the area of industrial automation and process control, such as the control of medical and scientific instruments.

All single-board computers, however, are not sold to OEMs. In fact, the market in 1982 was evenly split between the captive and OEM segments, according to managing analyst David Aronovitz of Gnostic Concepts Inc. He said, however, that he expects the captive percentage to grow as board manufacturers like Intel and Mostek Corp. begin selling more of their own systems. Adding to the captive segment are companies like NCR Corp., which makes boards for itself but doesn't sell in the OEM market.

Aronovitz said Intel shipped approximately 30,000 16-bit single-board computers in 1982 — about one-third to one-half of the 16-bit market. Specific figures for 8-bit single-board computers weren't available, but Aronovitz said volumes are much higher — in the hundreds of thousands.

In the OEM segment, most single-board computers are sold through the major electronics distributors such as Avnet Inc. and Schweber Electronics Inc. Smaller vendors sell through manufacturers representatives, Aronovitz said.

But despite their increasing popularity, single-board computers aren't a panacea. Before buying such a board, OEMs must consider several factors, primarily the questions of application and volume. OEMs must first consider whether the application is suited to a single-board solution. If it is, the OEM must then determine whether the solution promises to sell in volumes that fall into the range that makes board-level integration cost-effective.

How long it will take to bring a product to market must also be taken into account. If an OEM must react quickly to a closing market window, single-board computers provide a faster answer than in-house design, and buying packaged systems is a solution that's faster still.

"There are economies of scale at the various levels of integration," said Gary Sawyer, board products marketing manager for Intel's OEM Modules Operation. "Components are the lowest cost, highest risk, and take the longest time to (bring a product to) market. At the other end are systems where the OEM's value-added is software. They're the highest cost, lowest risk, and take the least time to market.

"At the board level, we're right in the middle," Sawyer said. "Primarily, we're talking about a board crammed with technology, about 81 inches square, that goes into a laboratory or factory environment," he said. About 80 percent of Intel's single-board computers are used in those types of technical applications, while applications for the remainder are varied.

Sawyer said microprocessors are pervasive in the desktop computer area, but because the volumes for those applications are enormous, manufacturers primarily use components and design their own boards.

More Than One

Sawyer admitted that despite the name single-board computer, most OEMs use more than one board.

"But there is a great benefit to solving your problems within the confines of a single board and using your bus as a system resource. You move questions and answers across the system, on the bus, but keep real hard work off the bus. When you have hundreds of thousands of bytes of memory in a single-board computer and can do the work on such a localized basis, your performance benefits are enormous," Sawyer said.

"Another thing is that with several boards, you have to continually go back and forth through the bus to fetch instructions, move memory, etc. What you want to do, in my view, is localize those functions and maintain that precious system bus activity for system-kind of functions, like communications between the CPU and disk drives or CRTs. You don't want to use that bus to move bits and bytes around like that," concluded Sawyer.

Even as single-board computer vendors tout their latest semiconductor advances, waiting offstage is the next major step in the miniaturization process — single-chip computers.

Semiconductor houses are already selling what they call microcontrollers — chips that include not only a microprocessor, but nonvolatile memory and I/O capability as well — in large volumes for simple control applications. Industry observers believe it's just a matter of time before chip makers are able to squeeze enough sophistication into a silicon wafer to make it indistinguishable from current single-board computers.

"That's the new wave," said Rod Zwonitzer, system products marketing manager for Mostek Corp. "Taking what you have on a single board and shrinking it onto a chip. This technology is a continually shrinking thing."

Existing microcontrollers, with most software embedded in ROM, are used to control predetermined functions in peripheral devices such as disk drives, CRTs, printers and keyboards, according to Graham Alcott, Intel Corp.'s microcontroller products marketing manager.

They are also used in much higher volumes in consumer products such as televisions, telephones, automobiles and microwave ovens.

Extremely Small

Because of their extremely small size and price, microcontrollers can cost-effectively replace mechanical and electromechanical devices in those applications, said Joseph Baranowski, assistant marketing manager of Intel's microcontroller operation.

And because those are such high-volume applications, microcontroller production is high. According to a recent Dataquest Inc. market report, U.S. semiconductor houses shipped approximately 50 million microcontroller chips in the third quarter of 1982, Baranowski said. He added that Intel will not even entertain orders for fewer than 1000 pieces.

Intel's Latest

Intel's latest device, the 8096, packs in a 16-bit CPU, 8k bytes of ROM, 256 bytes of RAM, and multiple I/O channels, including eight analog-to-digital converters, he said.

The analog communications capability is an important aspect of microcontrollers, since it enables them to control the functions of devices in a realtime environment, Alcott said.

Compared with Intel's first single-board computer, the 8010, which was based on the 8-bit 8080 microprocessor chip, the 8096 single-chip computer provides double the memory and more than double the performance, according to Baranowski.

"A lot of what we're now doing on single chips were actually board-level products less than five years ago," he said.

Future Trend

"The trend in the future is that microcontrollers will continue to be a dominant way people design," said Baranowski.

"The typical office of the future will have numerous disks, keyboards, printers, all with one or more microcontrollers, and there will likely be only one microprocessor acting as CPU for the whole system," he said.

Besides Intel and Mostek, prominent microcontroller manufacturers in the United States include Motorola Inc. and Zilog Inc.

ARTICLE REPRINT

AR-387

May 1985

Benchmarking UNIX Systems

By
David F. Hinnant

"Reprinted with permission from the August, 1984 issue of BYTE Magazine.
Copyright © by McGraw-Hill, Inc.; New York 10020. All rights reserved."

Order Number: 231534-001

UNIX is a trademark of Bell Laboratories

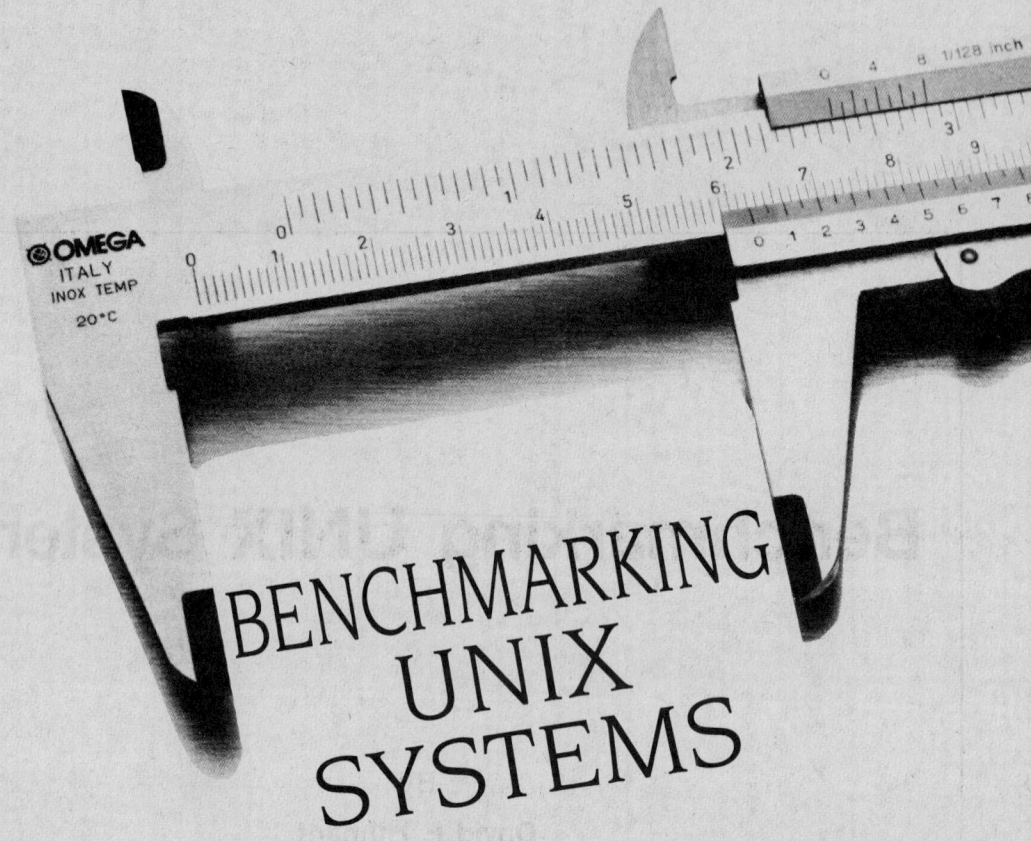

BENCHMARKING UNIX SYSTEMS

UNIX *performance on microcomputers and minicomputers*

BY DAVID F. HINNANT

WITH THE ADVENT of inexpensive but powerful 16- and 32-bit microprocessors, the multiuser, multitasking UNIX operating system is available on many new microcomputers. Because UNIX is becoming a standard multiuser operating system, this article presents benchmarks for several microcomputer UNIX implementations and shows how they perform when compared to minicomputer versions of UNIX.

Almost every week, new versions of UNIX for popular microcomputers or new UNIX-based microcomputers are being announced. They come from everyone from AT&T (UNIX was developed at Bell Laboratories) and IBM down to previously unknown companies who license UNIX from AT&T and then implement, or port it for new hardware configurations. For some UNIX implementations on microcomputers, you need additional hardware (at least a hard-disk system for the megabytes of utilities and programs

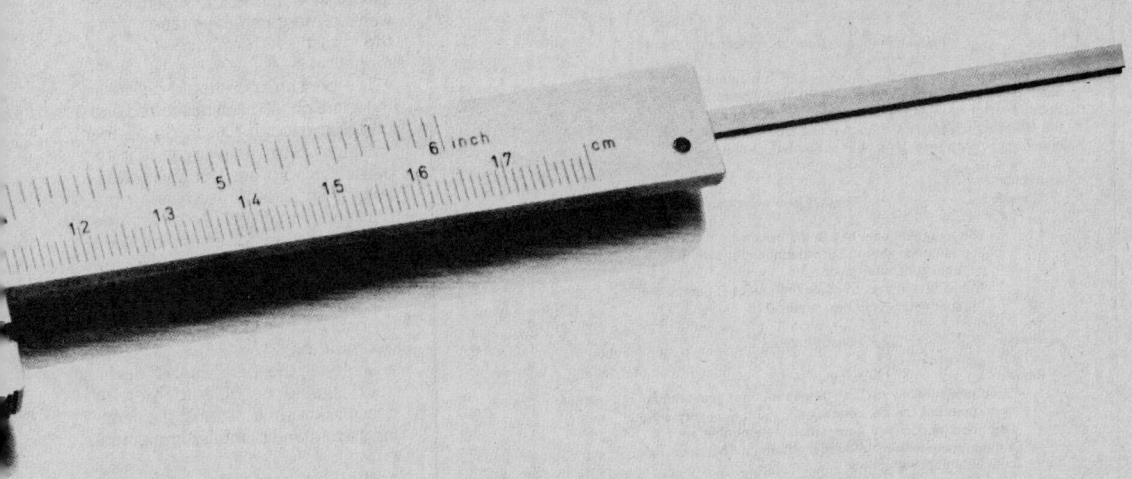

that come with UNIX), while some implementations run by just inserting a disk and booting up the run-time operating system.

Quite a few releases of UNIX software are also available, including Version 6, Version 7, System III, and System V (AT&T's new standard) from Bell Labs; the 4.1 BSD and 4.2 BSD UNIX extensions from the University of California, Berkeley; XENIX, an enhanced UNIX Version 7 from Microsoft; VENIX, a finely tuned UNIX with real-time capabilities; Uniplus+, an enhanced UNIX System III from Unisoft; also, many systems claim to be "UNIX-like." Do all these UNIX implementations look and work alike? What do you look for in determining which is the better UNIX-based machine? Some will be faster than others because of hardware constraints, but how can you tell if you're getting the best system for your operating conditions? That's usually the bottom line. Enter the UNIX benchmarks.

Just what is a benchmark? For our purposes, a benchmark is a set of instructions that measures how well the hardware and software of a computer system perform together. Benchmarks can either exercise singular, specific functions of a compiler or operating system (e.g., function-call overhead or system-call overhead) or they can test the general peformance of the machine by exercising a number of operations (e.g., looping, searching, etc). In both cases, these timings are compared to results on other machines.

Benchmarking an operating system is much more complex than benchmarking a compiler. However, since UNIX and its language compilers are written in the high-level language C, compiler implementation is just as important, as we will see. What should an operating-system benchmark do?

The purist approach tests only well-defined individual functions of the operating system (e.d., pipe implementation, disk throughput, system-call overhead and context switching). This is difficult to do, as any program that exercises one particular operating-system function inadvertently includes statements that are not related to the function under scrutiny. We must reconcile ourselves to a benchmark that includes as little superfluous code as possible. Since this unwanted overhead varies from program to program, in most cases, the execution-time results cannot be manipulated in an arithmetic fashion to produce true timings of a particular operating-system function. They can, however, be compared to timings on other machines.

The practical approach tests overall system performance by performing many typical functions (e.g., sorts; compilations; and creating, listing, and deleting files) but in a controlled fashion. Again, these timings are compared with timings on other UNIX machines.

Both approaches have merit, and examples of both will be presented here.

SOME BENCHMARK GUIDELINES

Let's develop some guidelines for benchmarking operating systems in general and apply them specifically to UNIX. In order to benchmark any operating system, as many environmental variables as possible should be eliminated:

- The benchmarks should be run in a multiuser environment so that any normal operating-system overhead (e.g., context switching between processes and other operating-system housekeeping) is taken into account. (Most UNIX implementations offer a single-user mode as well as a multi-user mode).
- The benchmarks should be taken more than once and averaged to compensate for any system-level background processes that repeatedly sleep awhile and work awhile. (A good UNIX example is the routine update that wakes up ever 30 seconds and, among other things, flushes buffers and in-core tables to disk.)
- The benchmarks should be performed while the system is otherwise idle so that the timings are as true as possible. On microcomputers, even one additional user can distort benchmark results significantly; depending, of course, on what is being done.
- All available optimizations should be used. Implementations that take advantage of the hardware con-

(continued)

David Hinnant (2017 Hunterfield Lane, Raleigh, NC 27609) holds a B.S. degree in physics and is a UNIX systems programmer with ITT Telecom in Raleigh. He is coauthor of a book on UNIX microcomputers soon to be published by Robert J. Brady Co. His UNIX UUCP address is ...ucbvax!devax!ittvax!ittral!hinnant. Machine-readable copies of the benchmark suite are available upon request to the UUCP address. Benchmark results from UNIX systems not mentioned in this article are welcome.

PHOTOGRAPHED BY PAUL AVIS

Listing 1: *The UNIX pipe benchmark.*

```
/*
 *
 *                UNIX Operating System Implementation Test #1
 *
 *   This program evaluates pipe efficiency and implementation.
 *   Since pipes are commonly used in UNIX, pipe performance is often a
 *   decisive factor in overall system performance, and says a lot about
 *   the UNIX implementation. Here we test pipe implementation by
 *   cramming 0.5 MB through a pipe as fast as possible.
 *
 *   Instructions:
 *       Compile by:              cc -O -s -o pipes pipes.c
 *
 *              The -O option says to use the optimizer.
 *              The -s option says to strip the namelist from the
 *                 object file after linking.
 *              The -o option says to place the object file in the file
 *                 specified by the next argument.
 *
 *       Time by:                 /bin/time pipes
 *
 *       Results:
 *              Since pipes usually use the disk as a buffer, real time is
 *              important, but can be misleading if the disk is very slow.
 *              Of greater importance here is the 'system' time, as it is
 *              a direct measurement of kernel efficiency. The 'user' time
 *              is of little importance.
 *
 */

#define BLOCKS 1024

        /* the buffer */
char buffer[512];
        /* file descriptor for pipe */
int fid[2];

main()
{
            /* want to test pipe implementation: not arithmetic */
        register int i;
            /* initialize the pipe */
        pipe(fid);
            /* fork the child process */
        if ( fork() ) {
            /* parent process writes to pipe in 512 byte chunks */
            for (i = 0; i < BLOCKS; i++)
                if (write(fid[1], buffer, 512) < 0)
                    /* if there is a problem, say so */
                    printf("Error in writing: i=%d\n", i);
            /* close the pipe when we're done */
            if (close(fid[1]) != 0)
                printf("Error in parent closing\n");
        }
        else {
            /* close, since we aren't writing */
            if (close(fid[1]) != 0)
                printf("Error in child closing\n");
            /* child process reads the pipe until EOF */
            for (;;)
                if (read(fid[0], buffer, 512) == 0) {
                    break;
                }
        }
}
```

set of benchmarks to aid the consumer in determining which hardware/software implementation gives the most performance for the money.

• The benchmarks should be *exactly* the same on all machines tested and portable enough to run on all the machines. Some may argue that if a particular software option is available, it should be used as an optimization is used (a binary-tree search function, for example). Keep in mind that extensions are not optimizations. Although the distinction can become cloudy, an extension is probably not used as routinely as an optimization.

• Some of the benchmarks developed should be able to exercise specific, known functions of operating-system and compiler implementation.

• The benchmarks developed should also contain tests of overall performance by simulating typical user activities. This should include executing background processes concurrently with foreground processes (if possible) to see how the system responds under a multitasking load.

• The benchmark timings should be made using a consistent and accurate method. A stopwatch just won't do. Fortunately, UNIX has a standard timing mechanism that reports elapsed (real) and processor times used by a process. The processor time is further divided into user and system times.

User time is the amount of time the process spent executing nonprivileged instructions (e.g., arithmetic calculations, sorting, searching, calling user-level functions, etc.).

System time is the time the process spent executing privileged (kernel) commands (i.e., system calls) plus some system-level overhead (e.g. context switching between processes).

The elapsed time is just that. And it is often not the sum of the user and system times. The majority of the missing time is spent waiting for I/O (input/output) operations to complete, waiting for a signal from another process, sleeping, or swapped out on disk while another program is running. It is unfortunate that in some implementations of UNIX the elapsed time reported by this timing mechanism is given only to the second. Thus, the sum of the system and user times can on occasion be greater

figuration are generally better to begin with. If a compiler option for object-code optimization is available, it should be used. If the hardware can support fast (register in the case of C) variables, they should be used. In the benchmarks discussed here, all variables that can be of the register type will be declared as such. In reality, the number of registers available for use by register variables varies widely because of hardware differences between microprocessors. Remember, our goal here is not to develop benchmarks that determine which UNIX machine is the best under a given set of requirements but to develop a general

Table 1: The results of UNIX benchmarks for some common microcomputers and minicomputers. The table is sorted on the fastest execution (real) time for the shell benchmark in listing 6a.

System			Time in Seconds							
			1. Pipe			2. System Call			3. Function Call	
No.	Machine	Version	real	user	sys	real	user	sys	real	
1	VAX-11/780	4.1 BSD	3.2	0.1	1.2	4.8	1.4	4.0	1.0	
2	Masscomp	Sys III+	5.7	0.0	2.8	6.3	0.4	5.8	0.9	
3	Sun-2/120	4.2 BSD	7.6	0.1	3.7	6.8	1.1	5.6	0.8	
4	VAX-11/750	4.1 BSD	4.6	0.2	2.1	7.0	0.9	6.2	1.7	
5	PDP-11/70	2.8 BSD	8.1	0.0	3.4	8.0	0.2	7.5	1.0	
6	Altos 986	XENIX	6.0	0.1	2.8	11.0	0.8	10.3	0.4	
7	IBM PC XT	PC/IX	16.6	0.1	7.6	39.8	2.9	35.6	4.7	
8	PDP-11/23	VENIX	30.0	0.1	9.5	24.0	3.2	20.4	3.3	
9	IBM PC XT %	VENIX/86	18.0	0.1	7.3	20.5	2.3	17.8	2.8	
10	SCI-1000 ~	Sys III+	9.3	0.0	3.1	26.2	0.7	24.2	1.2	
11	Omnibyte	Idris •8:	32.0	0.1	30.4	21.3	2.5	18.4	1.7	
12	TRS-80 16B	XENIX	8.0	0.1	3.4	15.0	1.5	12.7	1.4	
13	PDP-11/23	V7	23.0	0.1	10.7	36.5	0.9	33.7	3.6	
14	DEC Pro/350	VENIX	26.0	0.5	13.8	33.3	5.8	26.5	3.5	
15	Apple Lisa	Sys III+	8.1	0.0	3.0	10.5	0.2	9.1	1.3	

System			Time in Seconds												
			4. Sieve			5a. Disk Write	5b. Disk Read	6a. Shell			7. Loop				
No.	Machine	Version	real	user	sys	real	real	real	user	sys	real	user	sys		
1	VAX-11/780	4.1 BSD	1.7	1.5	0.1	2.0	8.0	3.3	0.3	1.3	2.6	2.5	0.1		
2	Masscomp	Sys III+	2.8	2.5	0.1	1.7	—	3.5	0.4	1.4	6.6	6.3	0.1		
3	Sun-2/120	4.2 BSD	5.1	2.8	0.4	1.8	4.9	3.5	0.3	2.0	7.4	7.0	0.1		
4	VAX-11/750	4.1 BSD	2.4	2.7	0.1	3.0	8.0	3.8	0.4	1.5	5.1	4.9	0.1		
5	PDP-11/70	2.8 BSD	2.3	1.6	0.1	4.0	9.5	4.0	0.2	1.7	7.9	7.1	0.2		
6	Altos 986	XENIX	3.3	3.0	0.0	3.5	7.3	7.0	0.4	1.6	13.3	13.0	0.1		
7	IBM PC XT	PC/IX	8.2	7.8	0.3	11.6	20.7	8.5	1.1	3.2	32.2	31.5	0.3		
8	PDP-11/23	VENIX •	5.5	5.1	0.1	8.0	33.7	12.0	0.7	4.8	26.0	25.2	0.1		
9	IBM PC XT %	VENIX/86	9.0	8.2	0.3	7.0	25.6	13.0	0.8	4.2	32.7	31.4	0.3		
10	SCI-1000 ~	Sys III+	4.4	3.6	0.1	4.3	9.1	13.6	0.5	1.9	14.5	13.6	0.2		
11	Omnibyte	Idris •8:	7.0	5.4	0.4	12.3	$	17.6	0.3	16.1	17.0	16.1	0.4		
12	TRS-80 16B	XENIX	6.0	4.8	0.3	8.0	22.0	18.0	0.4	2.6	14.0	12.5	0.5		
13	PDP-11/23	V7	5.8	5.3	0.1	22.0	32.7	20.4	0.8	8.5	27.4	25.9	0.3		
14	DEC Pro/350	VENIX	6.3	5.1	0.1	7.7	28.0	27.0	0.8	4.7	26.7	25.3	0.1		
15	Apple Lisa	Sys III+	6.1	5.3	0.1	20.8	44.5	37.6	0.4	3.2	14.0	12.0	0.2		

+ Indicates UNIX System III plus some Berkeley enhancements.
• The benchmark in listing 1 had to be modified slightly to run under Idris 2.1, perhaps explaining the large times that resulted.
$ Idris 2.1 is a Version 6-based UNIX system, and hence did not have the **rand()** system call. Thus, the benchmark could not be run.
— Unfortunately, this time was not available at the time of publication.
~ The SCI-1000 benchmarked was a preproduction 80186 system with debugging code in the kernel and compiler.
% For some reason, the C compiler optimizer caused the operating system to crash, so these results are with nonoptimized benchmarks.

System Configuration:
1 — 4-megabyte RAM, two 256-megabyte disk drives
2 — 2-megabyte RAM, one 50-megabyte disk drive
3 — 2-megabyte RAM, one 42-megabyte disk drive
4 — 2-megabyte RAM, one 121-megabyte disk drive
5 — 1.5-megabyte RAM, 400 megabytes of disk drives
6 — 1-megabyte RAM, one 40-megabyte disk drive
7 — 512K-byte RAM, one 10-megabyte disk drive
8 — 256K-byte RAM, two 5-megabyte disk drives
9 — 512K-byte RAM, one 40-megabyte disk drive
10 — 640K-byte RAM, one 10-megabyte disk drive
11 — 384K-byte RAM, one 20-megabyte disk drive
12 — 384K-byte RAM, one 15-megabyte disk drive
13 — 256K-byte RAM, two 10-megabyte disk drives
14 — 256K-byte RAM, one 5-megabyte disk drive
15 — 1-megabyte RAM, one 5-megabyte disk drive

than the elapsed time.

This mechanism is the **time** command, which is invoked explicitly by

/bin/time *filename*

where *filename* is the program to be timed. Under UNIX, *filename* can be either an object file or a text file of shell commands. Of course, some overhead is in the **time** command itself, since it has to start *filename* executing, but it is small and can be neglected because all our benchmarks will be timed this way. The results are compared to other UNIX machines timed in the same manner.

THE UNIX BENCHMARK SUITE

How can we apply these guidelines to the UNIX operating system and its most important language, the C compiler? What should we test? That question can be answered by answering the question, "What does UNIX do most often?"

UNIX has a number of unique and powerful features that are used quite heavily. If implemented efficiently, these features can make slow hardware seem fast. If implemented poorly, they can make even the most elegant hardware seem archaic. UNIX benchmarks should concentrate on some critical areas.

UNIX was developed on a small machine with limited memory and is disk intensive by its very nature. Therefore, we should test features of UNIX that use the disk.

The user interface to the UNIX system is called the shell (several common varieties exist). Since all requests made by the user are processed by the shell, it should be tested extensively.

The UNIX pipe qualifies on all the above criteria. A pipe is an I/O channel that is written into by one program and read by another. Pipes are used by a number of UNIX utilities, the shell in particular. Pipes are also often buffered on disk. A UNIX benchmark using a pipe is given in listing 1. The program creates a child process to read the pipe using the **fork()** system call and then crams 0.5 megabyte through the pipe. What do the results tell us? The two times of interest are the system and elapsed times. The system time, for all practical purposes, is a measurement of how long it took to set up and perform the piping. It thus is a direct measurement of pipe efficiency. The elapsed time is of interest because it helps give a good measurement of how slow the disk is. Elapsed time minus system time minus user time is essentially the disk-overhead time. Since microcomputers usually don't have the fastest disks, this is an important measurement for them. User time by itself is of little importance.

So you can get some idea of the time required to execute this and other benchmarks discussed in this article, table I shows the timings for some common minicomputers and microcomputers running UNIX. These times are average times on an otherwise idle system, as per the guidelines established above.

In the pipe benchmark, we measured the time it took to perform certain system calls (**fork()**, **read()**, **write()**, etc.) that were related to pipe implementation. The time to perform just one system call can be divided into several components:

1. The time required for the user-program system-call library interface to set up and execute a trap (an SVC to IBM 370 users) to the kernel so that privileged instructions can be executed. When this happens, the registers needed by the processor (stack pointers, program counter, etc.) to run the user program are saved so that they can be restored after the system call is complete.
2. The time the processor is performing the desired function.
3. The time required for the user-program registers to be restored and control transferred so that the user program can resume computation with the result from the system call in hand.
4. The time used when a context switch between processes is required.

It would be nice to measure 1, 3, and 4, since they can be considered the majority of the overhead in making a system call. The program in listing 2 does just that. It does nothing but repeatedly (25,000 times) query the operating system concerning its process identity with the **getpid()** system call. This information is kept in an in-core process table, so access is extremely fast and actual computation very small, as long as no other processes are competing for the processor. (See the need for an idle system?) Since we're interested in measuring overhead, and the program doesn't do much other than system calls, the elapsed time is important here. System time should be close to the elapsed time, and user time should be very small. Both are insignificant. Again, the results of this benchmark are shown in table 1.

Now that we've benchmarked system-call overhead, the overhead involved in an ordinary user function call and return naturally follows. This benchmark may initially seem superficial but consider that it is compiler implementation that to a large degree determines object-code efficiency, and the same compiler (C in our case) is probably used to compile the operating-system kernel. If so, it *should* be considered when evaluating the operating system. It should also be noted that an inefficient compiler can nullify any speed gained by structured-programming techniques. Benchmarking compilers is a topic by itself and will be left alone here. Let's just measure function-call overhead and consider it representative of compiler efficiency.

It is possible to determine the overhead involved in a function call in a number of ways. The method used here is believed to be more accurate than others. Since our comparison is two-way, two programs should be written: one that uses a function to achieve a goal and one that does not. The two programs, however, should perform the same task. After these programs are run, the user-execution time from the program not using the function is subtracted from the user-execution time of the program that does. This difference is the function-call overhead involved. This number can be divided by the number of times the call was made to arrive at a seconds-per-call overhead value, which can be enlightening when compared from system to system. An example of how this is done is shown in listing 3. Even though the program could have been made simpler by not passing a value to the function **empty()**, in real life all functions return at least one value, whether examined or not, and most functions pass at least one value (which is overhead, really). Using the C preprocessor, it is possible to write two distinct programs in one text file, depending on how the text file is compiled. The program in listing 3 is either compiled with **-DEMPTY** to generate the empty function program or with **-DASSIGN** to generate the program that doesn't use a function but achieves the same goal.

As mentioned above, the user time, not the real time, is used in the calculation. This is because the real time is accurate only to the second, whereas the user time is accurate to the tenth. And, since we're generating a nonrelative numerical result, where virtually no system time is used, the measurement with the greater precision is needed.

Let's turn our attention to the C compiler. When most people think of compiler benchmarks, they think of the Sieve of Eratosthenes, which tests compiler efficiency and processor throughput quite well. It's an excellent test for looping, testing, and incrementing. The program in listing 4 is a slightly modified copy of the Sieve presented in the January 1983 BYTE (page 283). Since we're not using a stopwatch, all unnec-

BENCHMARKING

essary I/O has been removed. Also, by the guidelines established above, register declarations have been added. The time to be interested in here is the elapsed time. The user time should be about the same as the elapsed time, while the system time should be quite small.

We briefly touched on disk performance with the pipes test, but disk performance deserves a more in-depth evaluation. UNIX provides methods for both sequential and random-access files, and both should be tested. Listings 5a and 5b are benchmarks that test random-access disk implementation. The program in listing 5a creates, opens, and writes a 256- by 512-byte file. The number of blocks manipulated is specified by a **#define** statement and can easily be changed if it is too large for a small microcomputer implementation. The program in listing 5b randomly reads the file created in listing 5a and removes it afterward.

While sequential access should be tested, it is not presented here since disk access is by and large random access. It should be easy to derive a sequential-access test from the random-access program given in listings 5a and 5b. Since the file created by benchmark 5a is relatively large, it's doubtful that it could be stored on one large, contiguous chunk of disk. More than likely, it will be segmented into several pieces, depending upon how full the filesystem is. Most efficient UNIX (and UNIX-like) implementations segment a physical disk into more than one logical disk partition. Each partition is called a filesystem. When the filesystem is created, all disk blocks are contiguous. As the filesystem is used more and more, it becomes more splintered with many small chunks of contiguous space.

Since we would like to run the bench-
(continued)

Listing 2: *The system-call benchmark.*

```
/*
 *
 *              UNIX Operating System Implementation Test #2
 *
 * This program compounds the kernel overhead involved in executing
 * a system call. Making a system call involves a 'trap' to kernel
 * or supervisor mode, performing the desired function, and returning.
 * Context switching is, when it occurs, also overhead. The getpid()
 * system call is used because all it does is look in an in-core table
 * for the numeric process id.
 *
 * Instructions:
 *    Compile by:              cc -O -s -o scall scall.c
 *
 *        The -O option says to use the optimizer.
 *        The -s option says to strip the namelist from the
 *              object file after linking.
 *        The -o option says to place the object file in the file
 *              specified by the next argument.
 *
 *    Time by:                 /bin/time scall
 *
 *    Results:
 *        Since we're testing system overhead, the elapsed time is of
 *              interest here.
 *
 */

#define TIMES  25000

main()
{
              /* take advantage of the hardware */
        register int i;
        for (i = 0; i < TIMES; i++)
                getpid();

}
```

BENCHMARKING

marks under normal operating conditions, benchmark 5 should be executed in a filesystem that is used regularly. Several UNIX implementations place the directory /tmp in a filesystem of its own, since /tmp is used frequently under normal conditions. In any case, this benchmark should be run in an active filesystem in order to give a more realistic result as to what the response time under a real user load would be. This benchmark, of course, is extremely disk dependent, but that's what we're testing. As implied, the elapsed time is important here because the time spent waiting for I/O completion is not charged to either user or system time.

One of the things programmers do best is compile programs, and the compiler is a good operating-system exerciser because of it. The command to compile a C program under UNIX is cc. This command is actually a small C program that invokes the C preprocessor, the compiler proper, the assembler, and the linker in succession. To time the compilation process, just place /bin/time in front of the cc command line. Naturally, the C compiler is disk intensive, and with today's fast microprocessors, the disk is often the bottleneck in compilation throughput.

Something needs to be said about the size of the object files that the compiler leaves us with. It can be found by direct examination that the size of the object files compiled on comparable microcomputers can vary by an order of magnitude. In early UNIX days, when memory address space was limited, the loader didn't include a lot of unused code in the object file when it resolved all function references. With today's microcomputers having more memory than minicomputers of a few years ago, some implementations include unnecessary system-call hooks that are never referenced in the program. A good way to test this is to compile the following program:

```
main ()
{
}
```

which is the shortest C program possible. To tell how much memory the object file will use when loaded into memory, look at the size of the object file with the UNIX size command. Size reports the size of the text, data, and bss segments. The text segment is composed of program instructions. The data segment contains initialized program data. The bss segment contains uninitialized program data. The total size is usually given in both decimal and/or octal or hexadecimal. Another command of interest is nm, which will list the symbol table (NaMelist) of an object file. Some of the library modules loaded will be present in any program, and with good reason (__exit, __environ, __cleanup, __main, and crt0.o, for example). Some are pure excess (malloc.o, isatty.o, write.o, and stty.o, for example) and usually result from one library func-

---

Listing 3: *The user function-call benchmark.*

```
/*
 *
 *               UNIX Operating System Implementation Test #3
 *
 * This program enables precise arithmetic calculations of user function
 * overhead by subtracting the execution user time when compiled without
 * using a function from execution user time using a function.
 *
 * Instructions:
 *     Compile by:
 *                           cc -O -DEMPTY -s -o fcalle fcall.c
 *         and
 *                           cc -O -DASSIGN -s -o fcalla fcall.c
 *
 *         The -O option says to use the optimizer.
 *         The -D option specifies C preprocessor action.
 *         The -s option says to strip the namelist from the
 *             object file after linking.
 *         The -o option says to place the object file in the file
 *             specified by the next argument.
 *
 *     Time by:             /bin/time fcalle
 *         and
 *                          /bin/time fcalla
 *
 *     Results:
 *         Since the user time is more accurate than the real time,
 *         and since system time effectively does not contribute to
 *         the real time number, we can use the difference between
 *         the user times in seconds as an accurate numerical account
 *         of function call overhead.
 */

#define TIMES .50000

main()
          /* The first way of doing things — use a function call */
#ifdef EMPTY
{
          register unsigned int i, j;
          for (i=0; i < TIMES; i++)
                   j = empty(i);
}

          /* the empty function */
empty(k)
register unsigned int k;
{
          return(k);
}
#endif
#ifdef ASSIGN
          /* The second way of doing things — without a function call */
{
          register unsigned int i, j;
          for (i = 0; i < TIMES; i++)
                   j = i;
}
#endif
```

tion referencing another in a larger module, creating a cascade effect. The compactness of the code generated says something about the efficiency and implementation of the compiler and loader.

We've covered most of the more frequently used aspects of UNIX individually up to now. Let's develop some tests for the UNIX system interface, the shell. The best way to test this is by having a shell program do what users normally do when they sit down at the keyboard.

A good general UNIX benchmark is the shell script, or program, in listing 6a. This program, named **tst.sh**, invokes several commonly used UNIX commands and exercises disk access with them. This program was originally written for use in evaluating UNIX microcomputers at the '83 USENIX (an association of UNIX users) conference. In retrospect, it should have contained some commands to run concurrently in the background, such as the compilation of one of the C benchmarks described above. This benchmark makes use of the shell's I/O redirection and indirection (indirection being the ability to take input from the current input stream instead of a file) to sort, save on disk, manipulate, and ultimately remove from disk a list of English words. The utilities used (**sort**, which sorts; **od**, which gives an octal listing; **grep**, which does pattern matching; **tee**, which makes a disk copy of the input given it; **wc**, which counts words, lines, and characters; and **rm**, which removes disk files) are all standard UNIX tools. The shell variable $$ is the current numerical process ID and is used to make unique filenames. The shell benchmark is run with the command **/bin/time /bin/sh tst.sh**. Execution times for even this simple benchmark varied widely, as shown in table 1.

A few words should be said about determining how many users a small multiuser system can support. With small multiuser systems, accurately simulating real user load is more important than with large multiuser systems because of the limited amount of memory, disk, and processor resources. You can simulate a real user load in several ways, but the only true way is to have someone at another terminal executing the same program you are at the same time. Why can't a process running in the background simulate a real user load? Because background processes usually run with a lower priority. Additionally, some multiuser microcomputer implementations limit the amount of memory an individual user can use at one time, even if no other user is on the system! What's more, some implementations impose an incredibly small limit on the number of files you can have open or the number of processes you can have running at any one time, again regardless of the number of other users or processes on the system. Watch out for these systems.

Since we're mainly concerned with microcomputer implementations, where there may or may not be additional terminals, and since we want portable benchmarks that can be run on any

(continued)

Listing 4: *The Sieve of Eratosthenes benchmark.*

```
/*
 *           UNIX Operating System Implementation Test #4
 *
 * No benchmark suite would be complete without the ever-popular
 * sieve benchmark. It is a good test of compiler efficiency and
 * CPU throughput. Below is a sieve benchmark as presented in the
 * January 1983 issue of BYTE, with some minor changes: Register
 * declarations have been added, and some unnecessary (from our
 * standpoint) printf() statements removed.
 *
 * Instructions:
 *     Compile by:                cc -O -s -o sieve sieve.c
 *
 *              The -O option says to use the optimizer.
 *              The -s option says to strip the namelist from the
 *                  object file after linking.
 *              The -o option says to place the object file in the file
 *                  specified by the next argument.
 *
 *     Time by:                   /bin/time sieve
 *
 *     Results:
 *         In the past, the elapsed time has been used, since most
 *         operating systems can measure real time. Actually, user
 *         time is a better value.
 *
 */

/* Eratosthenes Sieve Prime Number program in C */
#define TRUE    1
#define FALSE   0
#define SIZE    8190

char flags[SIZE + 1];

main() {
    register int i, prime, k, count, iter;
/*  printf("10 iterations\n"); */                   /* We don't need this */
    for (iter = 1; iter <= 10; iter++) {            /* do program 10 times */
        count = 0;                                  /* prime counter */
        for (i = 0; i <= SIZE; i++)
            flags[i] = TRUE;                        /* set all flags TRUE */
        for (i = 0; i <= SIZE; i++) {
            if (flags[i]) {
                prime = i + i + 3;                  /* found a prime */
/*              printf("\n%d", prime); */           /* twice index + 3 */
                                                    /* Nor this */
                for (k = i + prime; k <= SIZE; k += prime)
                    flags[k] = FALSE;               /* kill all multiples */
                count++;                            /* primes found */
            }
        }
    }
/*  printf("\n%d primes.", count); */               /* primes found on 10th pass */
}
```

BENCHMARKING

UNIX system no matter how small, our only recourse is to benchmark a varying number of background processes (i.e., a multitasking benchmark) and assume that the results can be extrapolated to a multiuser environment. Even if the benchmark is used to help decide which single-user system to buy, evaluating background-process performance is beneficial since the ability to have many background processes is a strong point of UNIX.

Using the shell benchmark in listing 6a as a starting point, we can invoke that script in the background a number of times to see how long it takes to execute one, two, three, four, five, and even six of these identical background processes. The shell script in listing 6b does just that. Contained in a file called **multi.sh**, it executes the shell test found in listing 6a in the background a number of times. The number of background processes created is determined by the number of command-line parameters given the shell script. The actual values of the command-line parameters are not important, it's the quantity of positional parameters that the shell script uses. Although any character would do as a positional parameter, for readability it is convenient to use the characters "1," "2," "3," etc. as those parameters. The benchmark is run as shown in table 2.

The shell statement **wait** causes the shell script to pause until all background processes have terminated. Invoking **tst.sh** more than six times may not be possible (depending upon your operating system) if a "per-user process limit" is defined.

Table 3 shows the results from the multitasking shell benchmark given in listing 6b for a variety of UNIX-based systems. The table is sorted on the fastest elapsed time for six background processes. Remember, this benchmark does not measure how many users the system will support but is rather a measure of how many processes the system will support comfortably.

By plotting the number of invocations versus execution time, you can graph how a multitasking load varies with response time. See figure 1 for a plot of the results of table 3 in this manner. With fast disks the graph should be linear, with a change in slope when there are more processes than can remain concurrently in memory.

Listing 5a: A *benchmark to create and write a disk file.*

```
/*
 *
 *            UNIX Operating System Implementation Test #5a
 *
 * This portion of the disk throughput benchmark creates and writes
 * a 512x256 byte file. Since UNIX is so disk intensive, it is important
 * to have some general idea of how fast (or slow) disk operations are.
 *
 * Instructions:
 *      Compile by:             cc -O -s -o dwrite dwrite.c
 *
 *            The -O option says to use the optimizer.
 *            The -s option says to strip the namelist from the
 *               object file after linking.
 *            The -o option says to place the object file in the file
 *               specified by the next argument.
 *
 *      Time By:                /bin/time dwrite
 *
 *      Results:
 *            The time to observe is the elapsed time, as we are trying to
 *            gauge disk throughput.
 */

#include <stdio.h>

#define BLOCKS 256

main()
{
                /* the buffer for writing */
        char buffer[512];
                /* the filename */
        char *filename = "a__large__file";
                /* a counter to keep up with the blocks written */
        register int i;
                /* file descriptor for the disk file */
        int fildes;
                /* create the file */
        if ((fildes = creat(filename, 0640)) < 0) {
                printf("Cannot create file\n");
                exit(1);
        } else {
                close(fildes);
                        /* open the file for writing */
                if ((fildes = open(filename, 1)) < 0) {
                        printf("Cannot open file\n");
                        exit(1);
                }
        }
        for (i = 0; i < BLOCKS; i++)
                /* write the file, one block at a time */
                if (write(fildes, buffer, 512) < 0) {
                        printf("Error writing block %d\n", i);
                        exit(1);
                }
                /* close the file now that we're done */
        close(fildes);
}
```

Listing 5b: A *benchmark to randomly read the disk file created by listing 5a.*

```
/*
 *
 *            UNIX Operating System Implementation Test #5b
 *
 * This portion of the benchmark opens and reads a 256x512 byte
 * file. This benchmark uses a random instead of sequential access
 * read, since the majority of disk access is random. Due to differences
```

(continued)

BENCHMARKING

- in the rand() routine between UNIX versions, you need to determine if
- the rand() on the machine to be tested generates numbers in the range
- $0 - 2^{15}$ or in the range $0 - 2^{31}$, and compile the benchmark accordingly.
-
- Instructions:
- Compile By: cc -DSIXTEEN -O -s -o dread dread.c
-                  for machines with rand() in the range $0 - 2^{15}$
-
-                  cc -DTHIRTYTWO -O -s -o dread dread.c
-                  for machines with rand() in the range $0 - 2^{31}$
-
-   The -O option says to use the optimizer.
-   The -s option says to strip the namelist from the
-       object file after linking.
-   The -o option says to place the object file in the file
-       specified by the next argument.
-
- Time By: /bin/time dread
-
- Results:
-   The time to observe is the elapsed time, as we are trying to
-   gauge disk throughput.
-
*/

```c
#include <stdio.h>

#define BLOCKS 256

long lseek();

main()
{
                /* the buffer for writing */
        char buffer[512];
                /* the filename */
        char *filename = "a__large__file";
                /* a counter counting blocks read */
        register int i;
                /* the file descriptor */
        int fildes;
                /* offset to seek into file */
        long int offset;

                /* open the file */
        if ((fildes = open(filename, 0)) < 0) {
                printf("Cannot find '%s'. Run 'dwrite' first.\n", filename);
                exit(1);
        }

        for (i = 0; i < BLOCKS; i++) {
                /* pick a byte, any byte */
#ifdef SIXTEEN
                offset = (long)rand() * 4L;
#endif
#ifdef THIRTYTWO
                offset = (long)rand() / 16384L;
#endif
                /* seek to it */
                if (lseek(fildes, offset, 0) < 0L) {
                        printf("Lseek to %ld failed i=%d\n", offset, i);
                        exit(1);
                }
                /* read a block, starting with the current byte */
                if (read(fildes, buffer, 512) < 0) {
                        printf("Error reading block at byte %ld\n", offset);
                        exit(1);
                }
        }
                /* get rid of the file */
        unlink(filename);
}
```

A short benchmark that tests incrementing and looping is shown in listing 7. It originally appeared on UNIX USENET news (article megatest.186) in February 1983. This little benchmark tests long integer arithmetic (increment and test) and is totally processor bound. It is a lot like the functional benchmarks shown earlier; it tests long integer arithmetic but does little else. It could be improved by multiplying by 2, dividing by 2, adding 2, and then subtracting 1 to better test long integer arithmetic functions. The benchmark is presented here in its original form because I had already tested a number of machines with that particular version. See the results in table 1.

RESULTS

A lot has happened in the last nine months during which this article was written. Several UNIX implementations now exist for the IBM PC. Microcomputer UNIX systems continue to infiltrate the business environment, and the UNIX application-software market seems to be developing at a good pace. Both DEC and IBM have embraced UNIX as an alternative to their own proprietary operating systems, which lends legitimacy to the claim that UNIX is an industry-standard operating system. There does not yet seem to be a clear winner in the UNIX microcomputer marketplace though several vendors are in the forefront of the cost/performance ratio contest.

Judging from the systems I've seen, the best performance comes from the Altos 586. It has less memory and fewer I/O ports than the Altos 986 but is otherwise identical. For about $10,000, you get an excellent multiuser UNIX system (512K-byte RAM, 40-megabyte [formatted] Winchester, and six serial ports) that under moderate load approaches DEC VAX performance for most tasks that a user would normally invoke. Some may argue that if the operating system isn't spelled U-N-I-X, it isn't real UNIX. That's just not the case. Altos XENIX *is* Version 7 UNIX with some useful extensions, including a screen-oriented editor, record and file locking, and semaphores. Although AT&T no longer markets Version 7 UNIX, it is well established in the marketplace and will be around for quite a while.

(continued)

BENCHMARKING

The Sun-2/120 and Masscomp computers *are* VAX-class machines, but their cost is beyond the reach of most prospective microcomputer owners. They both offer superb graphics and excellent response time under loading.

The TRS-80 16B is a usable multiuser microcomputer system, but its response time is hindered by the relatively slow internal 15-megabyte Winchester. Thus, depending upon the applications run, it may not be desirable for more than a two-user load.

The SCI-1000 system benchmarked is still under development, and the times reported here should not be taken as gospel. This system, with an 80186 chip, has the potential for better performance than the Altos 586 at less cost and offers System III UNIX.

IBM's UNIX, PC/IX, was not developed in house. It is a System III port with added features (a **vi**-like full-screen editor) done by Interactive Systems Corporation. It is a complete, usable single-user implementation that does what can be done with the 8088. It's interesting to note that both IBM PC (16-/8-bit 8088) implementations performed better than did the old reliable 16-bit F-11 chip used in the PDP-11/23 and DEC Professional.

The Omnibyte OB68K with Idris was one of the first UNIX work-alike systems around. As such, the implementation is not the de facto Version 7 standard. I understand that a new version of Idris is coming out (to borrow a phrase from Jerry Pournelle) Real Soon Now for the Omnibyte that increases performance substantially.

The VENIX implementations on the DEC Professional and IBM PC perform adequately but seem to have a problem with multiple background processes. Although it makes sense to limit the number of processes a user may have on a multiuser minicomputer, it doesn't make much sense to impose those

---

Listing 6a: *A general-purpose shell benchmark. The shell script shown is contained in a file called* **tst.sh** *and is invoked by* **/bin/time /bin/sh tst.sh**.

```
sort >sort.$$ <</*EOF
Now
is
the
time
for
all
good
men
to
come
to
the
aid
of
their
country
/*EOF
od sort.$$ | sort -n +1 > od.$$
grep the sort.$$ | tee grep.$$ | wc > wc.$$
rm sort.$$ grep.$$ od.$$ wc.$$
```

Listing 6b: *A multitasking benchmark with a variable number of background processes. This shell script is contained in a file called* **multi.sh**. *The number of concurrent processes created is determined by the number of command-line parameters, such as* **/bin/time /bin/sh multi.sh 1 2 3**.

```
for i
do
        echo $i
        /bin/sh tst.sh &
done
wait
```

BENCHMARKING

limits on a microcomputer that will probably never be used by more than one person. What's more, no message is given the user when the number of processes reaches the per-user process limit. Instead, quite literally, nothing happens. Granted that the multitasking benchmark is a little esoteric, it is the only way to simulate a multiuser/multitasking load short of having multiple users and is a good measure of how efficiently or inefficiently competing background processes are handled.

And then there's Apple's Lisa. Due to disk I/O limitations, Lisa's in a class by herself when it comes to disk-intensive tasks, as can be easily seen from figure 1. This exemplifies my claim that disk I/O is the single most limiting factor in overall response time and system throughput. If Apple could improve the disk throughput for Lisa to the same as an Altos, Lisa would rival the Altos in the best-value category, not to mention the possibility of excellent graphics.

It should be noted that some of the systems above that were implied to be single-user are really multiuser, but the response time is such that they would not be usable in a multiuser environment. This is the case with such computers as the IBM PC, DEC Professional, and Apple Lisa.

CONCLUSIONS

Some words of caution: a few microcomputer systems that claim to be
(continued)

Table 2: *The shell benchmark run sequence.*

```
/bin/time /bin/sh multi.sh 1
/bin/time /bin/sh multi.sh 1 2
/bin/time /bin/sh multi.sh 1 2 3
/bin/time /bin/sh multi.sh 1 2 3 4
/bin/time /bin/sh multi.sh 1 2 3 4 5
/bin/time /bin/sh multi.sh 1 2 3 4 5 6
```

Table 3: *Results for the multitasking UNIX benchmark in listing 6b with a variable number of background processes. The data are the elapsed (real) times for the benchmark to complete. The table is sorted on the fastest execution times with six background processes (the last column) where possible.*

	System		Elapsed (Real) Time in Seconds					
			Number of Concurrent Processes					
No.	Machine	UNIX Version	1	2	3	4	5	6
1	VAX-11/780	4.1 BSD	4.3	5.5	7.8	9.0	11.0	13.8
2	VAX-11/750	4.1 BSD	4.3	5.5	8.8	10.3	13.3	15.0
3	PDP-11/70	2.8 BSD	5.0	7.8	9.3	11.8	14.3	16.7
4	Masscomp	Sys III +	4.2	5.5	9.1	11.8	14.5	17.8
5	Sun-2/120	4.2 BSD	3.6	6.2	8.7	11.8	14.4	18.0
6	Altos 986	XENIX	6.3	7.3	9.3	19.3	27.2	36.0
7	TRS-80 16B	XENIX	20.0	24.5	33.0	56.5	1:10.5	1:39.3
8	SCI-1000	Sys III +	15.1	28.6	51.8	1:17.4	1:34.8	1:57.2
9	PDP-11/23	V7	22.3	37.3	52.3	1:14.8	1:31.0	2:05.0
10	IBM PC XT	PC/IX	10.6	23.4	42.8	1:14.1	1:24.2	2:10.7
11	Apple Lisa	Sys III +	38.1	1:14.8	1:54.5	2:34.2	3:14.6	3:48.6
12	PDP-11/23	VENIX	14.0	32.8	—	—	—	—
13	IBM PC XT	VENIX/86	15.0	23.5	39.0	—	—	—
14	DEC Pro/350	VENIX	26.0	41.0	1:22.3	—	—	—
15	Omnibyte	Idris 1.2(•)	—	—	—	—	—	—

+ Indicates UNIX System III plus some Berkeley enhancements.
− Indicates a benchmark that would not complete.
• The Idris shell command **wait** did not appear to function properly, and thus the benchmark could not be run.

BENCHMARKING

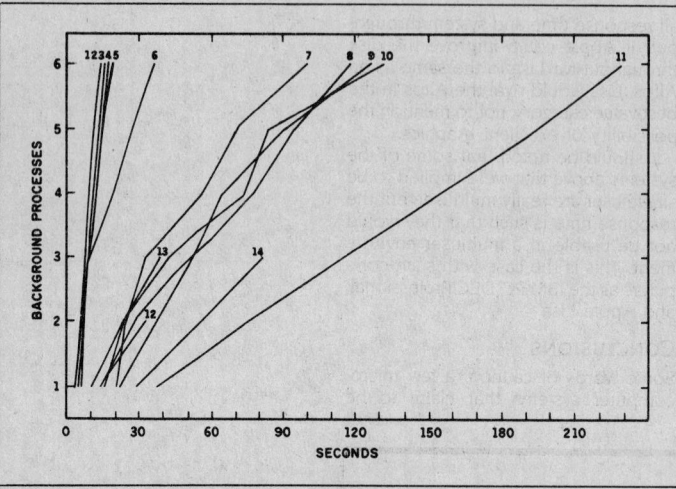

Figure 1: *A graph of the multitasking benchmark data in table 2 with the number of background processes versus elapsed time for each computer. The numbers at the top of each line correspond to the computers as listed in table 3. It is interesting to note the cluster of high-performance systems on the left-hand side and the cluster of other systems on the right.*

Listing 7: *A simple benchmark to test incrementing and looping.*

```
/*
 *          UNIX Operating System Implementation Test #7
 *
 * This program tests long integer incrementation. It is
 * taken from USENET news article "megatest.186".
 *
 * Instructions:
 *    Compile by:            cc -O -s -o loop loop.c
 *
 *          The -O option says to use the optimizer.
 *          The -s option says to strip the namelist from the
 *              object file after linking.
 *          The -o option says to place the object file in the file
 *              specified by the next argument.
 *
 *    Time by:               /bin/time loop
 *
 *    Results:
 *          Although not very significant, it does say something about the
 *          speed of the processor, since the compiler would hopefully
 *          compile the "i++" as an INCR instruction and not an ADD
 *          instruction. The benchmark is presented here for historical
 *          reasons.
 *
 */
main()
{
    long i;
    for (i = 0; i < 1000000; i++)
        ;
    printf("Done\n");
}
```

multiuser and UNIX-like do not swap. That is, they cannot swap a process out to disk and bring in another user's process. A system that cannot swap is neither truly multiuser nor UNIX-like. When a process runs out of primary memory in these systems, it dies. These implementations are substantially cheaper than most others, so be suspicious of low-cost UNIX-like systems.

As mentioned earlier, some systems implement a relatively low predefined limit on the amount of memory or number of processes one user can have, regardless of other system activity (or inactivity). Once this limit is exceeded, activity grinds to a halt, as a deadlock has been reached. Each blocked process (blocked in the sense that it is waiting for resources before it can continue) is waiting for the other to terminate before it can continue. If you plan to be an active user on a small multiuser system in a single-user environment, look out for this. The multitasking benchmark in listing 6b will usually bring any problems to light.

Knowledgeable 4.1 BSD and 4.2 BSD users should beware of systems that claim to have Berkeley enhancements. This means that the Berkeley version of some UNIX commands have been added. For example, most so-called Berkeley-enhanced systems include the **termcap** (terminal capability) database, **more** (a utility that prints files one screen at a time), and a version of **ls** (a utility to list the files in a directory) that lists files across, rather than down the screen. Don't expect to find the **newtty** driver and the job-control facilities of real Berkeley UNIX systems.

If you're considering a UNIX microcomputer, remember that response doesn't always vary linearly with load (even on large UNIX systems). This is due to several factors, most notably available real memory and disk-access speed. If you plan to add a user or two later, test the prospective system now. Find out if the hardware can support additional memory and/or faster disks.

The benchmarks presented here try not to be blind to what users do at the keyboard (not all users execute programs similar to the Sieve of Eratosthenes), but they do try to evaluate operating-system features that are routinely used. By explaining how benchmarks should be developed, this article

BENCHMARKING

Benchmark the specific kinds of things you will be doing as well as overall performance.

has tried to dispel the myth that all benchmarks do is see how fast a machine can crunch numbers (e.g., the Whetstone benchmark has not been mentioned).

Of course, benchmark results are not the only means to judge microcomputers. Clear and sufficient documentation, a solid customer base, and good product-support history are also important. If you do perform benchmarks on systems you are considering purchasing, try to benchmark the specific kinds of things you will be doing as well as overall performance in case your needs change. This sounds incredibly obvious, but many people have been disappointed by systems purchased yesterday that don't meet their needs today. ■

REFERENCES
1. Gilbreath, Jim, and Gary Gilbreath. "Eratosthenes Revisited: Once More through the Sieve." BYTE, January 1983, page 283.
2. Lions, J. "A Commentary on the UNIX Operating System." 1977.
3. Peterson, J., and A. Silberschatz. *Operating System Concepts*. Reading, MA: Addison-Wesley, 1983.
4. UNIX *Programmer's Manual*, 7th ed., Virtual VAX-11 Version, volumes 1 and 2c. Berkeley, CA: University of California, Department of Electrical Engineering and Computer Science, June 1981.
5. UNIX *Programmer's Manual*, 7th ed., volumes 1, 2a, and 2b. Murray Hill, NJ: Bell Telephone Laboratories, January 1979.

ACKNOWLEDGMENTS
Thanks to Ellen Mendelson and Walt Kennedy of the Durham and Raleigh Radio Shacks for access to the TRS-80 Model 16. Thanks to David Holloman of Keystone Systems Inc. of Raleigh for access to the Altos 586. Thanks to Michael Smith of East Carolina University for running the Idris benchmarks. Special thanks to the North Carolina Educational Computing Service for allowing me access to most of the remaining machines listed in table 1.

intel

RELIABILITY REPORT

RR-53

August 1984

iSBC® 86/XX Single Board Computers and iSBC® 304 MULTIMODULE™ Board Reliability

CLEONE HAWKINSON
OREGON SYSTEMS QUALITY AND RELIABILITY

©1984, INTEL CORPORATION

Order Number: 280065-001

RR-53

Reliability Report: iSBC® 86/XX SINGLE BOARD COMPUTERS AND iSBC® 304 MULTIMODULE™ BOARD

RELIABILITY: THE ABILITY OF A PRODUCT TO CONSISTENTLY OPERATE, FAILURE-FREE, IN THE ENVIRONMENT FOR WHICH IT WAS DESIGNED FOR A SPECIFIED AMOUNT OF TIME

SUMMARY

This report describes the iSBC® 86/14, 86/30, and 86/35 Intel Single Board Computers and the iSBC 304 MULTIMODULE™ board and presents the results of these products' reliability evaluations. This report also reviews Intel's standard component and board Quality Assurance and Reliability qualification program.

The products described in this report have passed a series of reliability tests that include accelerated life and environmental tests (vibration, humidity, temperature, voltage margin, and circuit timing analysis). The evaluations of the iSBC 86/14, 86/30, and 304 boards were conducted at the same time. The reliability evaluation of the iSBC 86/35, an upgrade of the iSBC 86/30, was recently completed. A summary of the Mean Time Between Failures (MTBF) data is below, demonstrating the established reliability of these iSBC products. Detailed test results are presented in the text.

iSBC Board	MTBF 55°C (in hours)	Confidence Level
86/14	21,000	60%
86/30	16,500	60%
86/35	22,500	60%
304	14,500	60%

DESCRIPTION OF THE iSBC® 86/XX SINGLE BOARD COMPUTERS

The iSBC 86/14, 86/30, and 86/35 Single Board Computers (hereafter, the iSBC 86/XX) are economical, self-contained, computer-based solutions for OEM applications. Each board is a complete computer system on a single printed circuit card. The CPU, system clock, read/write memory, nonvolatile read only memory, I/O ports and drivers, serial communications interface, priority interrupt logic and programmable timers all reside on the boards.

Figure 1. iSBC® 86/30 Single Board Computer

The iSBC 86/XX boards have several important features:

- iAPX (8086-2) Central Processing Unit
- Expandable RAM
- Four 28-Pin EPROM Sockets
- Two 16-Bit iSBX™ Connectors
- MULTIBUS® Compatibility

Central Processing Unit: The central processor for the iSBC 86/XX boards is Intel's iAPX 86/10 (8086-2) microprocessor. This CPU has a clock rate of 8 MHz or jumper selectable option of 5 MHz. The CPU architecture is designed for both structured, high-level languages and assembly language.

Expandable RAM: The size of expandable RAM is the major distinction between the iSBC 86/XX boards (Table 1). On-board RAM may be doubled by adding a RAM MULTIMODULE™ board. The iSBC 300A MULTIMODULE option expands the capabilities of the iSBC 86/14 board from 32K-bytes to 64K-bytes. The iSBC 304 MULTIMODULE board expands the capabilities of both the iSBC 86/30 and 86/35 boards. The 86/30 expands from 128K-bytes to 256K-bytes; the 86/35 from 512K-bytes to 640K-bytes. Further, the 86/35 may be expanded to 1 MB using the iSBC 314 MULTIMODULE board.

EPROM Sockets: Four 28-pin sockets support Intel EPROMs (2716, 2732A, 2764, 27128, 27256, and 27512) and their respective ROMs. Other JEDEC standard pinout devices are also supported, including byte-wide static RAMs.

iSBX Connectors: Two 16-bit iSBX connectors allow add-on versatility. For example, the iSBX 218 flexible diskette controller, the iSBX 488 interface, and the iSBX 275 color graphics options are available.

MULTIBUS® Compatibility: The iSBC 86/XX boards are MULTIBUS compatible. As an industry bus standard IEEE 796, MULTIBUS provides the physical framework and conceptual foundation of Intel's open system architecture. For single board computers, the MULTIBUS system bus allows expansion of on-board functions, such as memory and digital I/O capacity. Figure 2 is a block diagram of the iSBC 86/XX, illustrating the MULTIBUS interface.

DESCRIPTION OF THE iSBC® 304 MULTIMODULE™ BOARD

The iSBC 304 module provides 128K-bytes of on-board RAM to the iSBC 86/30 and 86/35 boards. The module expands the memory configuration on-board, eliminating the need to access additional memory via the MULTIBUS system bus. This increases system throughput and has a low power requirement. The iSBC 304 module contains dynamic RAM devices and sockets for the Intel 8203 dynamic RAM controller and memory interface latches. The relationship of the MULTIMODULE board to the host board is illustrated in Figure 3.

BOARD PRODUCT QUALITY ASSURANCE

The quality and reliability of products like the iSBC 86/XX boards are a function of the quality of components used, the care taken in board design and fabrication, and the extent of testing performed on the product before shipment. An examination of each of these functions will provide an understanding of the Intel Quality Assurance program for microcomputer board products.

Component Quality Assurance

Standard Intel Component Quality Assurance processing and 100% screening are applied to all Intel manufactured components before they are assembled on the boards. Once a component has been qualified as reliable and transferred to board-level manufacturing, complete process controls ensure the continuation of high quality.

Table 1. iSBC® 86/XX RAM Capacity

iSBC® Board	DRAM Devices	On-board RAM	On-board RAM expands to
86/14	16K-bit 2118	32K-bytes	64KB (with iSBC 300A)
86/30	64K-bit 2164	128K-bytes	256KB (with iSBC 304)
86/35	256K-bit 21256	512K-bytes	640KB (with iSBC 304) 1MB (with iSBC 314)

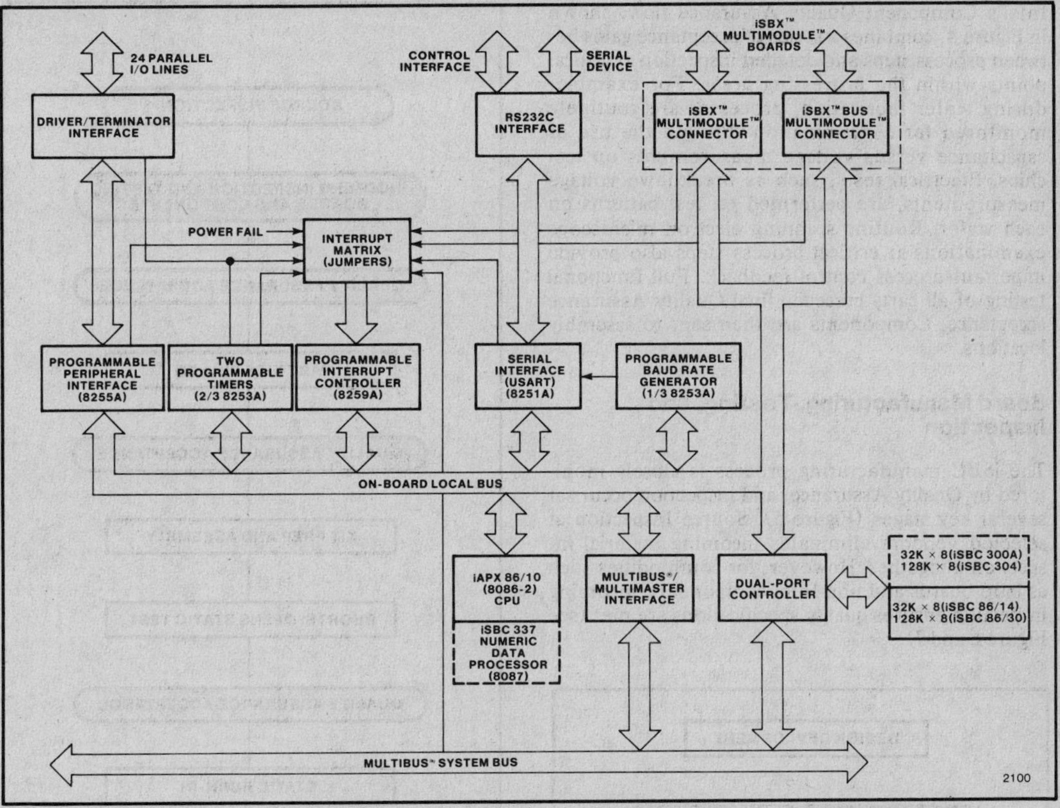

Figure 2. iSBC® 86/XX Block Diagram

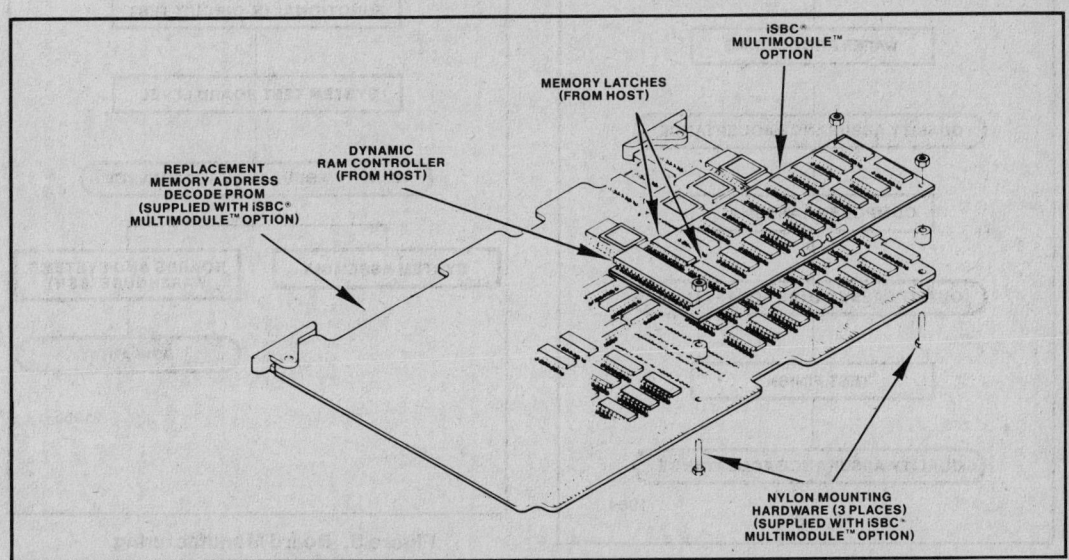

Figure 3. Installation of MULTIMODULE™ Board onto the Host Board

RR-53

Intel's Component Quality Assurance flow, shown in Figure 4, combines a series of acceptance gates between process steps and detailed inspection at critical points within the processing areas. For example, during wafer fabrication, processes are routinely monitored for contamination through the use of capacitance versus voltage measurements on test chips. Electrical tests, such as breakdown voltage measurements, are performed on test patterns on each wafer. Routine scanning electron microscope examinations at critical process steps also provide important process control feedback. Full functional testing of all parts precedes final Quality Assurance acceptance. Components are then sent to assembly locations.

Board Manufacturing, Testing, and Inspection

The iSBC manufacturing process is closely monitored by Quality Assurance, and inspection occurs at several key stages (Figure 5). Source Inspection at selected vendors eliminates incoming material inspection altogether. However, for commodities such as bare boards and non-Intel components, incoming inspection ensures quality specifications are met (see Figure 6 and 7).

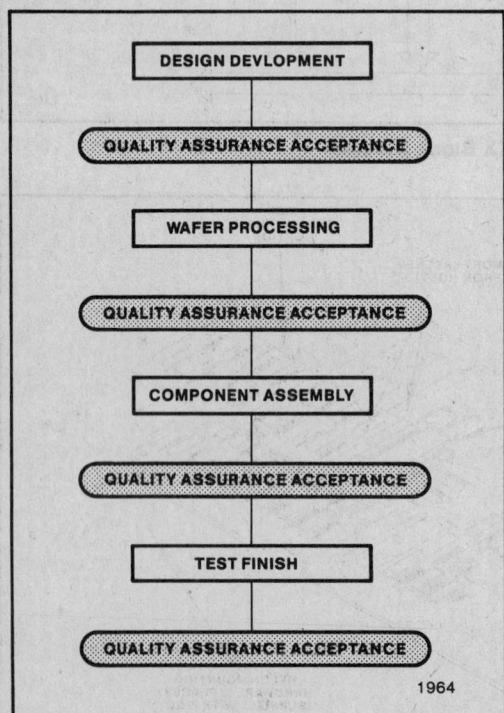

Figure 4. Component Quality Assurance Flow

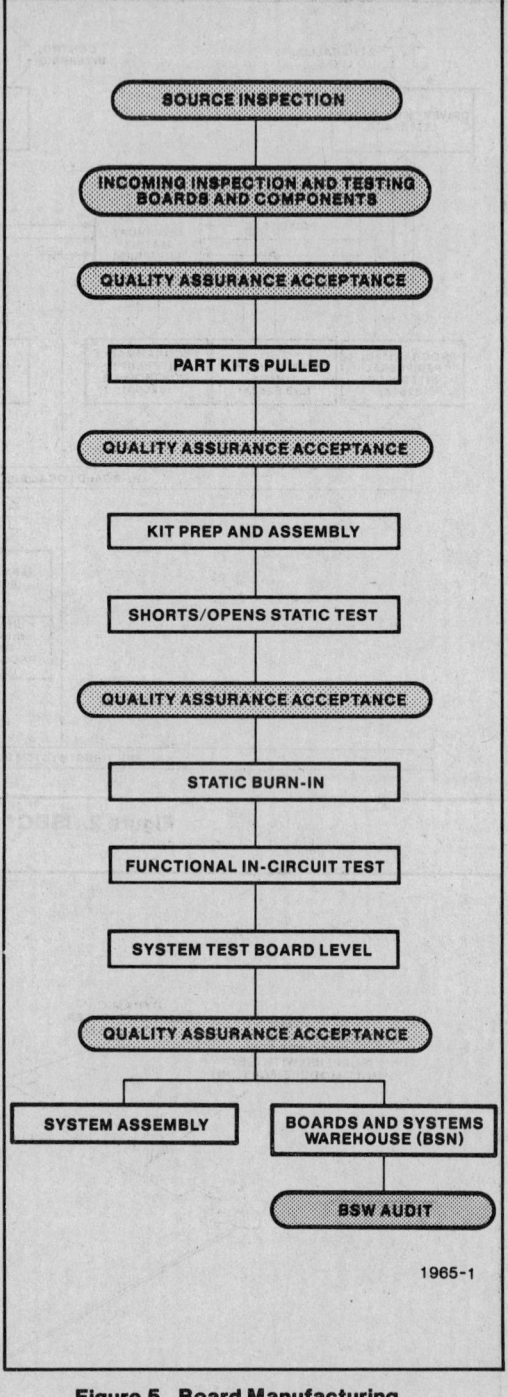

Figure 5. Board Manufacturing, Testing, and Inspection

Figure 6. Bare Board Validator

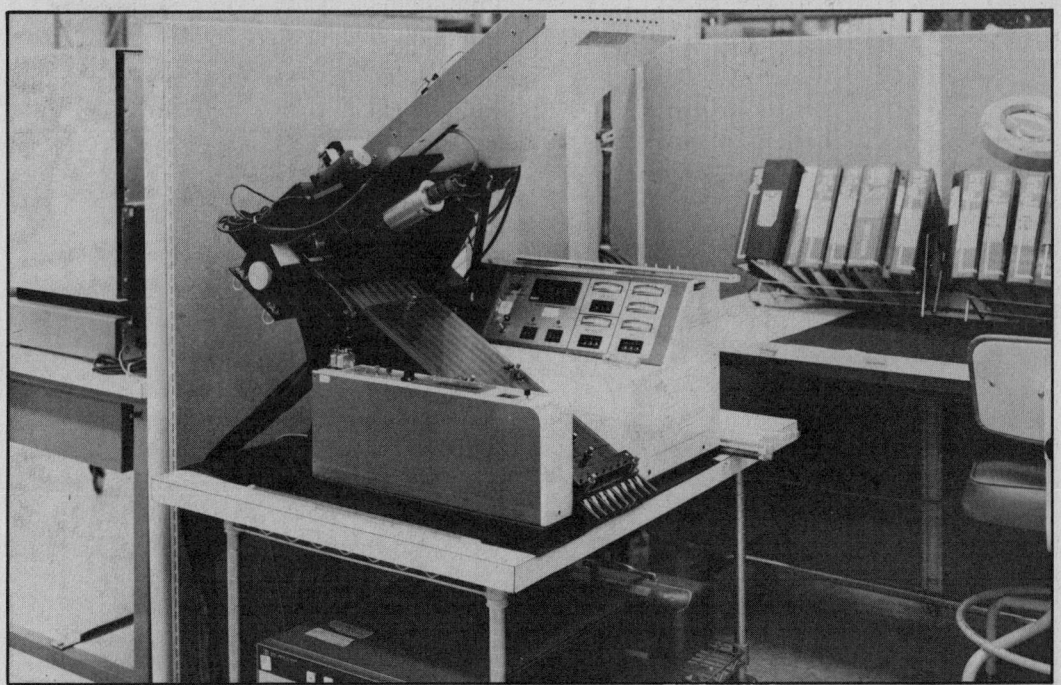

Figure 7. Integrated Circuit Tester

After Incoming Inspection and test, components for an assembly "kit" are pulled together and readied for the assembly operation. Each kit is visually inspected and components are assembled onto the bare board.

Without tiring, machines do repetitive, precision jobs increasing productivity and ensuring consistent quality. Programmed Dual In-line Package (DIP) auto-insertion equipment installs integrated circuits on to bare boards (Figure 8). Next, the axial lead inserter is programmed to install capacitors, diodes, and resistors. After automatic stake pin insertion, a three-station robot (Figure 9) puts low profile jumper plugs in place. Finally, a machine masks the areas of the boards which do not need to be soldered.

Parts unsuitable for automatic assembly are manually assembled onto the board. The board is then inspected for accuracy prior to wave solder and for soldering defects after wave solder.

Intel is proud of its wave solder process control. The post solder cleaning process includes detergent and rinse baths monitored and controlled for concentration, temperature, and contamination. Boards are selected at random and then checked under a microscope to ensure compliance to wave solder process and cleanliness standards.

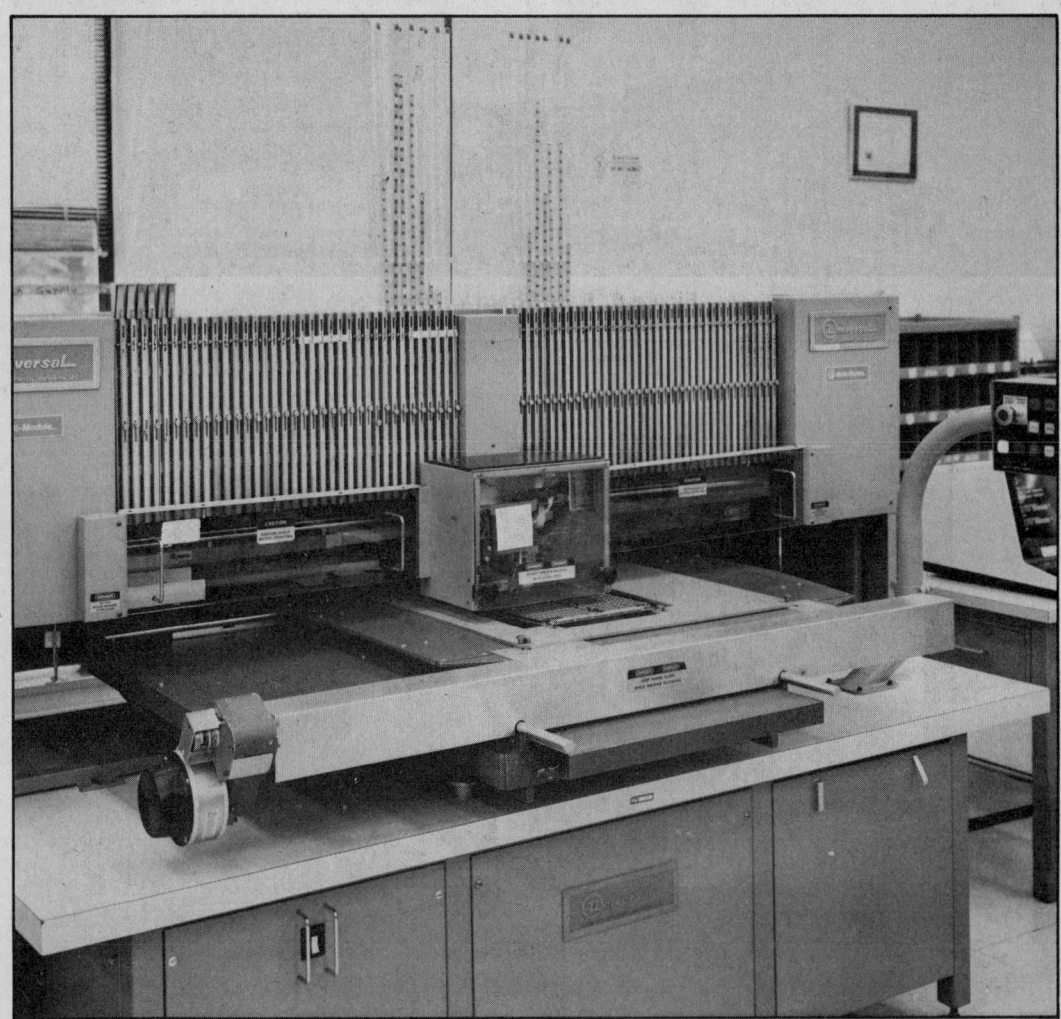

Figure 8. Dual In-line Package Auto-Insertion Equipment

Figure 9. Robot

Two other process checks are in place. Boards are sample tested in an Omegameter (Figure 10), which measures ionic contamination. Further, one board per lot is placed in the Thermotron steady-state environmental chamber at elevated temperature (70°C) and humidity (85% RH) for 96 hours. The board is then checked under a microscope for contamination corrosion. In the rare event any deviation occurs, the Quality Assurance Inspector stops the process until compliance is restored.

In touch-up and second assembly, such items as connectors and process sensitive components are added to a board. As the final phase of assembly, a board is tested for "shorts" and "opens" on the Teradyne L529 Automatic Test Equipment. Final assembly inspection verifies the boards are acceptable for test.

The next stage is static burn-in at elevated temperature and voltage margins (70°C, +6% VDC). Burn-in eliminates temperature- and voltage-related "infant mortality" failures that occur early in the life of a product. All boards are burned-in for six hours in ovens (Figure 11).

intel® RR-53

Figure 10. Omegameter: Wave Solder Process Control

Figure 11. Board Burn-in Ovens

The boards are then tested on a Teradyne L125/L135 In-Circuit Tester (Figure 12). This system has a "test the tester" feature that verifies all test points are functioning before actual boards are tested. A special "bed of nails" vacuum fixture ensures that all critical board test points may be accessed by the test system. Any components that fail are replaced, and the boards are retested on the Teradyne system.

Next, boards are functionally tested at System Test Board Level (STBL). For these tests a set of monitor and diagnostic EPROMs are installed. The board is placed in a General Purpose Test Fixture (GPTF) shown in Figure 13. This is a three-phased test. The first test sequence is performed at room temperature and nominal voltage. The second phase is at elevated temperature (70°C) and voltage (+6% VDC). The final phase is at 70°C and −6% VDC. The STBL program verifies the board's performance throughout these sequences by testing the CPU, I/O interface, and MULTIBUS interface in a multiprocessing environment.

After test, the boards are inspected to ensure that they comply with required quality standards. Boards passing this final screening are then released by Quality Assurance for use in an Intel system product or sent to packaging.

After packaging, a board is sent to the Boards and Systems Warehouse (BSW) to await shipment to the customer. Quality Assurance conducts monthly finished goods audits on randomly selected products in the BSW. This audit reviews documentation, tests for compliance to environmental specifications (temperature, humidity, vibration), and confirms functional performance over time. This finished goods audit is a final in-house monitor of the quality that reaches the customer. Results are reported back to the factory.

Product performance in the field is also tracked. Results are monitored on a computerized data system, and feedback is used to ensure corrective actions when required. This rigorous testing, tracking, and

Figure 12. Teradyne Tester

corrective action system ensures Intel's product specifications and the customer's quality and reliability expectations are met.

BOARD PRODUCT RELIABILITY

The Life Curve

Three categories of failures can occur during product life:

- Infant Mortality
- Random
- Wear Out

Each category has a distinct distribution when failure frequency is plotted against time. When the three distributions are combined, the resulting failure rate/time distribution produces a characteristic curve known as a "bathtub" curve. The three distributions and the combined bathtub curve are represented in Figure 14.

The boundaries between the categories are less precise than they appear because the failure categories have overlapping distributions. For example, Infant Mortality failures may extend into the Random failure category, but at a very low level. Wear Out failures may, in fact, occasionally occur before the expected Wear Out period.

The Infant Mortality area of the curve shows failures caused by manufacturing defects in the components and boards. These are "quality failures," and their frequency decreases with time. Infant Mortality for boards depends on the quality and test history of the components used in manufacturing and is eliminated by burn-in.

Random failures occur during the "useful life" of the product between Infant Mortality and Wear Out. These failures are primarily a function of temperature and circuit complexity. The early phase of the Random failure period is identified during burn-in. As the failure pattern becomes random, it approaches a low constant value (flat distribution).

Wear Out failures are primarily due to mechanical wear or chemical degradation resulting in lack of conformance to specifications. Statistically, Wear Out will not happen until many thousands of hours have elapsed for VLSI-based products.

Mean Time Between Failures and Confidence Levels

In reliability evaluation, mean time between failures (MTBF) is the average time in hours expected to elapse between failures. The point estimate

Figure 13. General Purpose Test Fixture

of the MTBF is calculated by dividing the total test operating hours for a sample of system products by the total number of failures during the test period. The demonstrated value at a specific confidence level is calculated using the Chi-Square probability distribution[1]. The confidence level defines the probability that the true MTBF of the product exceeds the demonstrated MTBF value. For board testing the required minimum confidence level defined in the reliability test is 60%. This means that the true product MTBF will be higher than the demonstrated MTBF, 60% of the time.

As the ratio of operating test hours to the true MTBF increases, the confidence that the true MTBF exceeds the specified lower limit also increases. For example, to demonstrate an MTBF of 5000 hours with a confidence level of 60% takes 10,000 hours of operation with one failure. To demonstrate the same MTBF at a 90% confidence level requires 19,500 hours. The values of MTBF for boards are normally at the 60% confidence level when the product is qualified for full production. Higher confidence level is attained as data are accumulated from the accelerated life test.

[1]See Reference 1

RELIABILITY QUALIFICATION

Reliability qualification serves at least three important functions:
- Provides reliability feedback to product design
- Demonstrates the MTBF and verifies product fitness
- Checks the manufacturing process

First, reliability evaluation serves as a feedback mechanism for product design. Lessons learned from building one product can be used to improve the design of new products. Second, the evaluation demonstrates the MTBF of a product. Also, a wide range of reliability tests verify that the product performs to specification in the intended environment. This information helps customers to evaluate Intel systems, and helps Intel anticipate customers' product support requirements. Finally, it serves as a manufacturing process check. When failures attributed to the manufacturing process occur, they can be quickly identified as exceptions and corrective actions can be implemented. Information gathered from reliability evaluation helps in each of these areas, allowing Intel to produce the most reliable products possible.

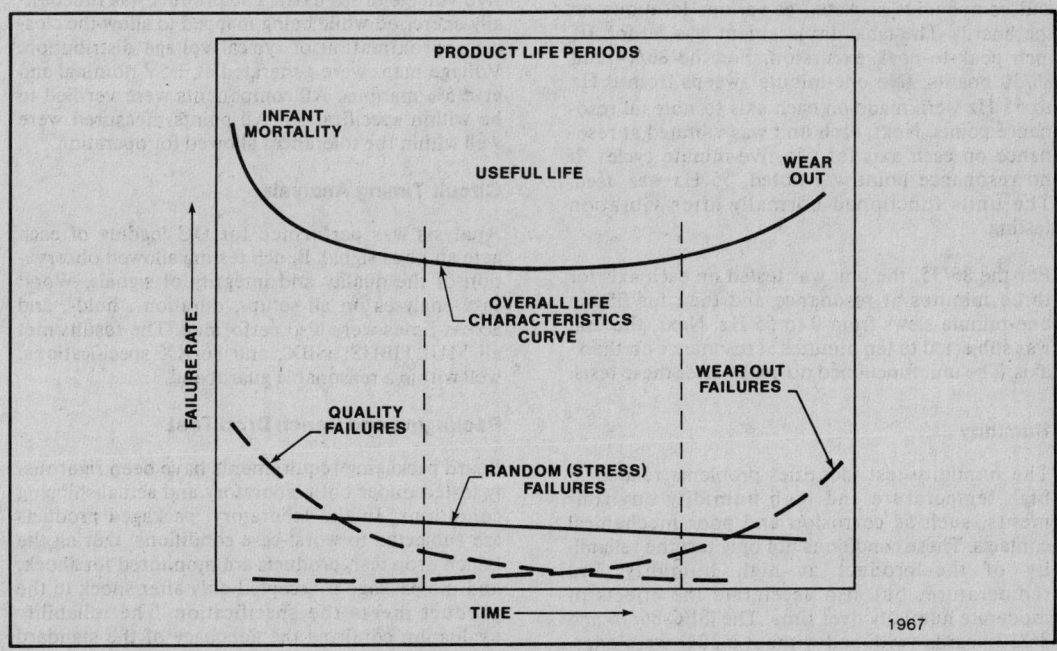

Figure 14. Reliability Life Curve

RR-53

Intel's System Quality and Reliability Department performed a multiphased reliability qualification on the iSBC 86/XX and iSBC 304 products that included environmental and reliability testing.

Environmental Testing

A series of environmental tests were performed on the iSBC 86/XX and iSBC 304 boards. Some of the test criteria for the 86/35, an upgrade of the 86/30, vary slightly from the earlier product evaluations. All test criteria are described in Table 2.

The reliability evaluation is designed to ensure these boards will perform under the physical conditions found in a commercial or light industrial environment. Special test software was used for the evaluation. In addition to the standard commands, special commands were used for an extended RAM test, an interrupt test, a timer test, and a parallel port test. The test fixture consisted of the units under test, an iSBC 604 backplane, and an iSBC 640 linear power supply. The airflow rate during all tests was 200 LFM (linear feet per minute), ensuring proper cooling.

Vibration

Vibration testing identifies mechanically related problems a product could sustain under normal conditions. The areas of concern were the jumpers and components socketed at various locations on the boards. The table displacement was set for .01 inch peak-to-peak excursion. For the 86/14 and 86/30 boards, five one-minute sweeps from 0 Hz to 55 Hz were made on each axis to note all resonance points. Next, each unit was vibrated at resonance on each axis for two five-minute cycles. If no resonance point was noted, 55 Hz was used. The units functioned normally after vibration testing.

For the 86/35, the unit was tested on each axis for three minutes at resonance and then for fifteen one-minute slews from 0 to 55 Hz. Next, the unit was subjected to ten minutes at resonance on the x-axis. The unit functioned normally after these tests.

Humidity

The humidity test identifies problems related to high temperature and high humidity environments, such as corrosion and poor mechanical contacts. These conditions not only test the reliability of the product at high humidity and temperature, but also accelerate the effects of moderate humidity over time. The iSBC 86/14 and 86/30 boards (with and without a 304) were exercised at 90% relative humidity (non-condensing)

and 70°C for 48 hours with no failures. The iSBC 86/35 board was subjected to 85% relative humidity at 65°C for 72 hours with no failures.

Temperature Tests and Mapping

The boards were tested at two temperature ranges: 0°C to 60°C (functional) and −40°C to 70°C (non-functional). No failures occurred; the boards functioned normally. Temperature test details for each product are given in Table 2.

Temperature maps identify potential "hot spots" and are made for each board. Temperatures were measured on selected components representing all areas of the board. The temperature maps for the 86/14 and 86/30 were made at 25°C and repeated at 55°C ambient. The temperature maps for the 86/35 were made at 25°C and 70°C. All areas were well below the allowed maximum temperature rise above ambient.

DC Voltage Margins and Voltage Mapping

All combinations of extreme power supply settings for the ±5 and ±12 voltage supplies at ±10% nominal voltage were tested over the specified temperature range (0°C to 70°C). No failures occurred.

Voltage mapping measures the voltage potential at various points on the board and ensures no excessive voltage drops exist. The product was functionally exercised while being mapped to allow the closest approximation of typical voltage distribution. Voltage maps were generated at +5V nominal and at ±5% margins. All components were verified to be within specification. All points measured were well within the tolerances allowed for operation.

Circuit Timing Analysis

Analysis was performed for DC loading of each gate and bus signal. Bench testing allowed observation of the quality and integrity of signals. Worst case analyses on all setup-, duration-, hold-, and access-times were also performed. The results met all MULTIBUS, iSBX, and 86/XX specifications, well within a reasonable guardband.

Packaging and Bench Drop Test

Board packaging requirements have been rigorously tested under both laboratory and actual shipping conditions. In the laboratory, packaged products are subjected to worst-case conditions. During the bench drop test, products are monitored for shock, and the package is accepted only after shock to the product meets the specification. The reliability evaluation confirms the adequacy of the standard packaging.

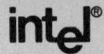

RR-53

Table 2. Environmental Qualification Data

THIS INFORMATION, BASED ON SMALL SAMPLES, IS INTERNAL QUALIFICATION TEST DATA GATHERED UNDER CONDITIONS THAT EXCEED SPECIFICATIONS AND SHOULD NOT BE CONFUSED WITH WARRANTED SPECIFICATIONS. ALL CONFIGURATIONS TESTED PASSED ALL TESTS.

Product	Sample	Test	Description
		VIBRATION	
86/14	1	Passed	0-55 Hz x,y,z axes .01″ PTP displacement with one 5-minute sweep; two 5-minute dwells at resonance or 55 Hz.
86/30	1	Passed	
86/35	1	Passed	0-55Hz x,y,z axes 3 minutes at resonance; 15 1-minute slews; x axis one 10-minute dwell at resonance
		HUMIDITY	
86/14	1	Passed	Functional:
86/30	1	Passed	90% RH (non-condensing)
304	1	Passed	70°C for 48 hours
86/35	1	Passed	85% RH (non-condensing) 65°C for 72 hours
		TEMPERATURE	
86/14	1	Passed	Functional: two hours each at 0°, 20°, 40°, 60°C
86/30	1	Passed	Non-functional: −40°C to +70°C
304	1	Passed	
86/35	1	Passed	Functional: Cycled 4 times in 8 hours between 0°- 55°C. Non-functional: −40°C to +70°C
		TEMPERATURE MAP	
86/14	1	Passed	38 IC test points: 25°C, 55°C Maximum temperature rise allowed 20° above ambient Maximum delta: 25°C / 55°C; 40.7°C / 68.4°C; 35.3°C / 65.7°C
86/30	1	Passed	
86/35	1	Passed	Test points at: 55°C, 70°C Maximum delta: 70.7°C, 85.2°C
		DC VOLTAGE MARGINS	
86/14	1	Passed	0°C to 70°C; ±5, ±12 voltage supplies at ±10% nominal voltage for four hours
86/30	1	Passed	
304	1	Passed	
86/35	1	Passed	
		CIRCUIT TIMING ANALYSIS	
86/14	1	Passed	Bench testing performed to observe quality and integrity of each signal. Worst-case setup-, duration-, hold-, and access-times. Met all specifications well within guardbands
86/30	1	Passed	
304	1	Passed	
86/35	1	Passed	

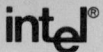

Reliability Test Evaluation

The reliability evaluations of the iSBC 86/XX and 304 products easily surpassed the minimum calculated MTBFs required for full production. Although the MTBF is demonstrated at 70°C, an MTBF at 55°C can be derived from the test data. The elevated temperature of 70°C during the evaluation provides an accelerated life factor of 2.16 above the 55°C level, based on the Arrhenius equation[1]. The derived point estimate failure rate is calculated by dividing the number of failures by the number of operating hours. When no failures occurred, one failure was assumed. The test results are reported separately (Table 3) and are discussed below.

iSBC® 86/14 Board

The 86/14 board easily met the minimum specified qualification requirement of 11,039 hours MTBF at 55°C. Twenty iSBC 86/14 units accumulated 18,714 total operating hours with no failures. This results in a derived 21,000 hour MTBF at 55°C at 60% confidence level, an 8200 hour derived MTBF at 90% confidence level, and a 6250 hour derived MTBF at 95% confidence level. The derived point estimate failure rate is 5.3% per thousand hours, assuming one failure.

[1]See Reference 2

iSBC® 86/30 Board

The 86/30 board surpassed the minimum specified requirement of 10,499 hours MTBF at 55°C. Twenty iSBC 86/30 units accumulated 53,130 total operating hours with two failures. One failure was due to a defective RAM device; the second was a resettable soft error. At 55°C the derived MTBF at 60% confidence level is 16,500 hours. At 90% confidence level the derived MTBF is 9900 hours. At 95% confidence level the derived MTBF is 8600 hours. The derived point estimate failure rate is 3.8% per thousand hours.

iSBC® 86/35 Board

The 86/35 board easily surpassed the minimum specified requirement of 7,923 hours MTBF at 55°C. Twenty iSBC 86/35 units accumulated 21,000 total operating hours with no failures. This results in a 22,500 hour derived MTBF at 55°C at 60% confidence level, a 9000 hour derived MTBF at 90% confidence level, and a 7500 hour derived MTBF at 95% confidence level. The derived point estimate failure rate is 4.8% per thousand hours, assuming one failure.

iSBC® 304 MULTIMODULE™ Board

The iSBC 304 MULTIMODULE board qualified with the 86/30 evaluation with a point estimate of 29,518 total operating hours. Twenty iSBC 304 units

Table 3. Summary of Reliability Test Results

iSBC Board (n)	Operating Hours	Failures	Failure Rate/1000[1]	MTBF 55°C (hours)	Confidence Level
86/14 (n=20)	18,714	0	5.3%	21,000 8,200 6,250	60% 90% 95%
86/30 (n=20)	53,130	2[2]	3.8%	16,500 9,900 8,600	60% 90% 95%
86/35 (n=20)	21,000	0	4.8%	22,500 9,000 7,000	60% 90% 95%
304 (n=20)	29,518	1[3]	3.4%	14,500 7,500 6,250	60% 90% 95%

[1]Failure Rate = 1/MTBF
[2]86/30 Failures: 1 defective RAM device; 1 resettable soft error
[3]304 Failure: 1 defective RAM device

were run with one failure, a defective RAM device. This results in a 14,500 hour derived MTBF at 55°C at 60% confidence level, 7500 hour derived MTBF at 90% confidence level, and a 6250 hour derived MTBF at 95% confidence level. The derived point estimate failure rate is 3.4% per thousand hours.

CONCLUSION

This report has reviewed Intel's Quality Assurance and Reliability program and presented information on the reliability evaluation of the iSBC 86/XX and 304 products. These evaluations demonstrate the high reliability of each of these products. These boards clearly surpass the performance requirements Intel established.

REFERENCES

1. *Reliability Mathematics: Fundamentals; Practices; and Procedures,* B. L. Amstadler, 1971. McGraw-Hill, Inc.

2. *Semiconductor Device Reliability and the Arrhenius Model,* National Semiconductor Reliability Report G-11, January 1977.

High Speed Math Boards 3

iSBC® 337A and iSBC® 337 MULTIMODULE™ NUMERIC DATA PROCESSOR

- **High speed fixed and floating point functions for 8 or 5 MHz iSBC® 86, 88, and iAPX 86, 88 systems**

- **Extends host CPU instruction set with arithmetic, logarithmic, transcendental and trigonometric instructions**

- **MULTIMODULE™ option containing 8087 Numeric Data Processor**

- **Up to 80X performance improvement in Whetstone benchmarks over 8MHz iAPX-86/10 performance**

- **Supports seven data types including single and double precision integer and floating point**

- **Software support through ASM 86/88 Assembly Language and High Level Languages**

- **Fully supported in the multi-tasking environment of the iRMX™ 86 Operating System**

The Intel iSBC® 337A/337 MULTIMODULE™ Numeric Data Processor offers high performance numerics support for iSBC 86 and iSBC 88 Single Board Computer users, for applications including simulation, instrument automation, graphics, signal processing and business systems. The coprocessor interface between the 8087 and the host CPU provides a simple means of extending the instruction set with over 60 additional numeric instructions supporting six additional data types. The MULTIMODULE implementation allows the iSBC 337A module to be used on all iSBC 86 and iAPX 88 board designs.

The coprocessor interface between the 8087 Numeric Data Processor and the host CPU provides a simple means of extending the instruction set with over 60 additional numeric instructions supporting seven data types. The MULTIMODULE implementation allows the iSBC 337A/337 module to be used on all iSBC 86/88'' single board computers and can be added as an option to custom iAPX board designs.

The following are trademarks of Intel Corporation and may be used only to describe Intel products: Index, Intel, MULTIBUS, RMX, iRMX, UPI, ICE iSBC, iSBX, MULTIMODULE, iAPX and iCS. Intel Corporation assumes no responsibility for the use of any circuitry other than circuitry embodied in an Intel product. No other circuit patent licenses are implied.

©INTEL CORPORATION, 1984

iSBC® 337A and iSBC® 337 Module

OVERVIEW

The iSBC 337A/337 MULTIMODULE Numeric Data Processor (also called NDP) provides arithmetic and logical instruction extensions to the 86/88 of the iAPX 86/88 families. The instruction set consists of arithmetic, transcendental, logical, trigonometric and exponential instructions which can all operate on seven different data types. The data types are 16, 32, and 64 bit integer, 32 and 64 bit floating point, 18 digit packed BCD and 80 bit temporary.

Coprocessor Interface

The coprocessor interface between the host CPU and the iSBC 337A/337 processor provides easy to use and high performance math processing. Installation of the iSBC 337A/337 processor is simply a matter of removing the host CPU from its socket, installing the iSBC 337A/337 processor into the host's CPU socket, and reinstalling the host CPU chip into the socket provided for it on the iSBC 337A/337 processor (see Figure 1).

All synchronization and timing signals are provided via the coprocessor interface with the host CPU. The two processors also share a common address/data bus. (See Figure 2). The NDP component is capable of recognizing and executing NDP numeric instructions as they are fetched by the host CPU. This interface allows concurrent processing by the host CPU and the NDP. It also allows NDP and host CPU instructions to be intermixed in any fashion to provide the maximum overlapped operation and the highest aggregate performance.

High Performance and Accuracy

The 80-bit wide internal registers and data paths contribute significantly to high performance and minimize the execution time difference between single and double precision floating point formats. This 80-bit architecture provides very high resolution and accuracy.

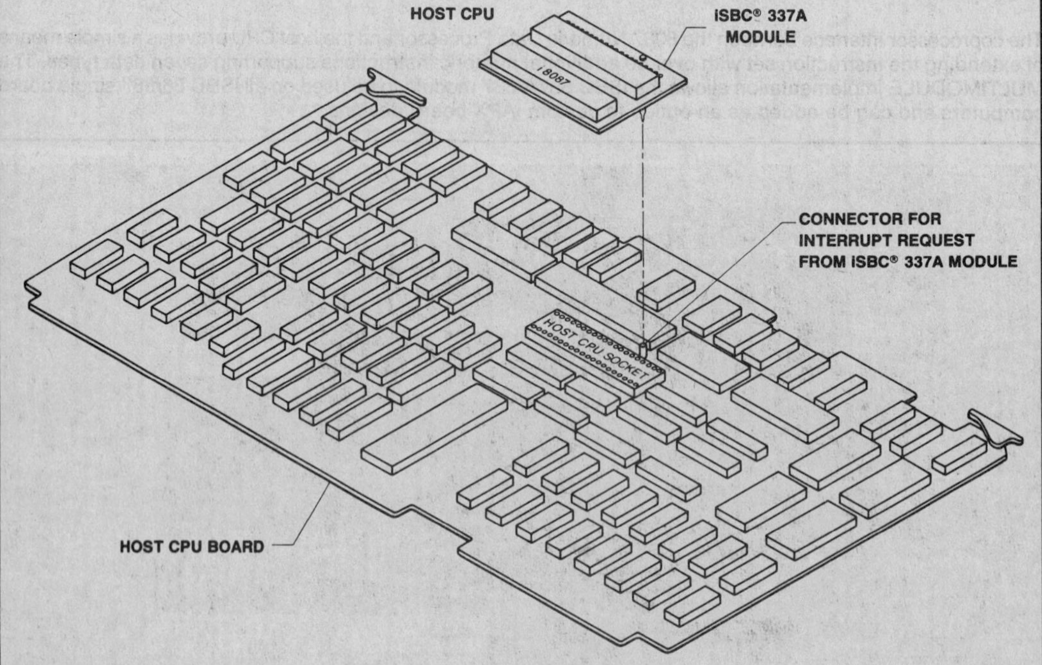

Figure 1. iSBC® 337A Module Installation

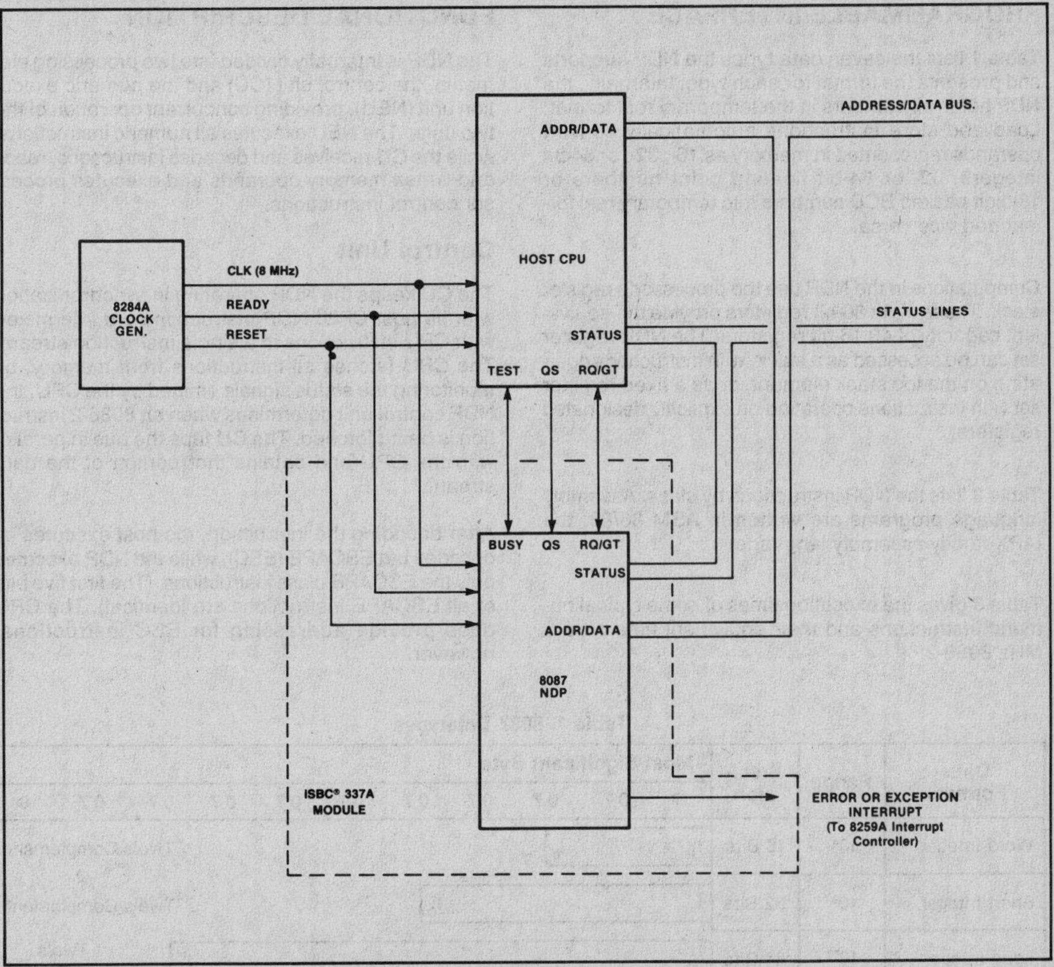

iSBC® 337A and iSBC® 337 Module

Figure 2. iSBC® 337A System Configuration

This precision is complemented by extensive exception detection and handling. Six different types of exceptions can be reported and handled by the NDP. The user also has control over internal precision, infinity control and rounding control.

SYSTEM CONFIGURATION

As a coprocessor to the Host CPU, the NDP is wired in parallel with the CPU as shown in Figure 2. The CPU's status and queue status lines enable the NDP to monitor and decode instructions in synchronization with the CPU and without any CPU overhead. Once started, the NDP can process in parallel with and independent of the host CPU. For resynchronization, the NDP's BUSY signal informs the CPU that the NDP is executing an instruction and the CPU WAIT instruction tests this signal to insure that the NDP is ready to execute subsequent instructions.

The NDP can interrupt the CPU when it detects an error or exception. The interrupt request line is routed to the CPU through an 8259A Programmable Interrupt Controller. This interrupt request signal is brought down from the iSBC 337A/337 module to the single board computer through a single pin connector (see Figure 1). The signal is then routed to the interrupt matrix for jumper connection to the 8259A Interrupt Controller. Other iAPX designs may use a similar arrangement, or by masking off the CPU "READ" pin from the iSBC 337A/337 socket, provisions are made to allow the now vacated pin of the host's CPU socket to be used to bring down the interrupt request signal for connection to the base board and then to the 8259A. Another alternative is to use a wire to establish this connection.

iSBC® 337A and iSBC® 337 Module

PROGRAMMABLE INTERFACE

Table 1 lists the seven data types the NDP supports and presents the format for each type. Internally, the NDP holds all numbers in the temporary real format. Load and store instructions automatically convert operands represented in memory as 16-, 32-, or 64-bit integers, 32- or 64-bit floating point numbers or 18-digit packed BCD numbers into temporary real format and vice versa.

Computations in the NDP use the processor's register stack. These eight 80-bit registers provide the equivalent capacity of 40 16-bit registers. The NDP register set can be accessed as a stack, with instructions operating on the top stack element, or as a fixed register set with instructions operating on explicitly designated registers.

Table 2 lists the NDP instructions by class. Assembly language programs are written in ASM 86/88, the iAPX family assembly language.

Table 3 gives the execution times of some typical numeric instructions and their equivalent time on a 8 MHz 8086-2.

FUNCTIONAL DESCRIPTION

The NDP is internally divided into two processing elements, the control unit (CU) and the numeric execution unit (NEU), providing concurrent operation of the two units. The NEU executes all numeric instructions, while the CU receives and decodes instructions, reads and writes memory operands and executes processor control instructions.

Control Unit

The CU keeps the NDP operating in synchronization with its host CPU. NDP instructions are intermixed with CPU instructions in a single instruction stream. The CPU fetches all instructions from memory; by monitoring the status signals emitted by the CPU, the NDP control unit determines when an 8086-2 instruction is being fetched. The CU taps the bus in parallel with the CPU and obtains that portion of the data stream.

After decoding the instruction, the host executes all opcodes but ESCAPE (ESC), while the NDP executes only the ESCAPE class instructions. (The first five bits of all ESCAPE instructions are identical). The CPU does provide addressing for ESC instructions, however.

Table 1. 8087 Datatypes

Data Formats	Range	Precision	Most Significant Byte		
Word Integer	10^4	16 Bits	I_{15} ... I_0		Two's Complement
Short Integer	10^9	32 Bits	I_{31} ... I_0		Two's Complement
Long Integer	10^{19}	64 Bits	I_{63} ... I_0		Two's Complement
Packed BCD	10^{18}	18 Digits	S — D_{17} D_{16} ... D_1 D_0		
Short Real	$10^{\pm 38}$	24 Bits	S E_7 E_0 F_1 ... F_{23}		F_0 Implicit
Long Real	$10^{\pm 308}$	53 Bits	S E_{10} E_0 F_1 ... F_{52}		F_0 Implicit
Temporary Real	$10^{\pm 4932}$	64 Bits	S E_{14} E_0 F_0 ... F_{63}		

Note:
Integer: I Sign: S Packed BCD: $(-1)^S(D_{17}...D_0)$ Bias = 127 for Short Real
Fraction: F BCD Digit (4 Bits): D Real: $(-1)^S(2^{E-BIAS})(F_0 F_1 ...)$ 1023 for Long Real
Exponent: E 16i383 for Temp Real

Table 2. 8087 Instruction Set

Data Transfer Instructions

Real Transfers
- FLD — Load real
- FST — Store real
- FSTP — Store real and pop
- FXCH — Exchange registers

Integer Transfers
- FILD — Integer load
- FIST — Integer store
- FISTP — Integer store and pop

Packed Decimal Transfers
- FBLD — Packed decimal (BCD) load
- FBSTP — Packed decimal (BCD) store and pop

Comparison Instructions
- FCOM — Compare real
- FCOMP — Compare real and pop
- FCOMPP — Compare real and pop twice
- FICOM — Integer compare
- FICOMP — Integer compare and pop
- FTST — Test
- FXAM — Examine

Transcendental Instructions
- FPTAN — Partial tangent
- FPATAN — Partial arctangent
- F2XM1 — $2^X - 1$
- FYL2X — $Y \cdot \log_2 X$
- FYL2XP1 — $Y \cdot \log_2(X + 1)$

Arithmetic Instructions

Addition
- FADD — Add real
- FADDP — Add real and pop
- FIADD — Integer add

Subtraction
- FSUB — Subtract real
- FSUBP — Subtract real and pop
- FISUB — Integer subtract
- FSUBR — Subtract real reversed
- FSUBRP — Subtract real reversed and pop
- FISUBR — Integer subtract reversed

Multiplication
- FMUL — Multiply real
- FMULP — Multiply real and pop
- FIMUL — Integer multiply

Division
- FDIV — Divide real
- FDIVP — Divide real and pop
- FIDIV — Integer divide
- FDIVR — Divide real reversed
- FDIVRP — Divide real reversed and pop
- FIDIVR — Integer divide reversed

Other Operations
- FSQRT — Square root
- FSCALE — Scale
- FPREM — Partial reminder
- FRNDINT — Round to integer
- FXTRACT — Extract exponent and significand
- FABS — Absolute value
- FCHS — Change sign

Processor Control Instructions

- FINIT/FNINIT — Initialize processor
- FDISI/FNDISI — Disable interrupts
- FENI/FNENI — Enable interrupts
- FLDCW — Load control word
- FSTCW/FNSTCW — Store control word
- FSTSW/FNSTSW — Store status word
- FCLEX/FNCLEX — Clear exceptions
- FSTENV/FNSTENV — Store environment
- FLDENV — Load environment
- FSAVE/FNSAVE — Save state
- FRSTOR — Restore state
- FINCSTP — Increment stack pointer
- FDECSTP — Decrement stack pointer
- FFREE — Free register
- FNOP — No operation
- FWAIT — CPU wait

Table 3. Execution Time for Selected 8087 Actual and Emulated Instructions

Floating Point Instruction	Approximate Execution Time (microseconds)		
	8087 (5 MHz Clock)	8086 Emulation	8087 (8 MHz Clock)
Add/Subtract Magnitude	14/18	1,600	9/11
Multiply (single precision)	19	1,600	12
Multiply (extended precision)	27	2,100	17
Divide	39	3,200	24
Compare	9	1,300	6
Load (double precision)	10	1,700	6
Store (double precision)	21	1,200	13
Square Root	36	19,600	23
Tangent	90	13,000	56
Exponentiation	100	17,100	63

iSBC® 337A and iSBC® 337 Module

An NDP instruction either will not reference memory, will require loading one or more operands from memory into the NDP, or will require storing one or more operands from the NDP into memory. In the first case, a non-memory reference escape is used to start NDP operation. In the last two cases, the CU makes use of a "dummy read" cycle initiated by the CPU, in which the CPU calculates the operand address and initiates a bus cycle, but does not capture the data. Instead, the CU captures and saves the address which the CPU places on the bus. If the instruction is a load, the CU additionally captures the data word when it becomes available on the local data bus. If data required is longer than one word, the CU immediately obtains the bus from the CPU using the request/grant protocol and reads the rest of the information in consecutive bus cycles. In a store operation, the CU captures and saves the store address as in a load, and ignores the data word that follows in the "dummy read" cycle. When the NDP is ready to perform the store, the CU obtains the bus from the CPU and writes the operand starting at the specified address.

Numeric Execution Unit

The NEU executes all instructions that involve the register stack. These include arithmetic, logical, transcendental, constant and data transfer instructions. The data path in the NEU is 80 bits wide (64 fraction bits, 15 exponent bits and a sign bit) which allows internal operand transfers to be performed at very high speeds.

When the NEU begins executing an instruction, it activates the NDP BUSY signal. This signal is used in conjunction with the CPU WAIT instruction to resynchronize both processors when the NEU has completed its current instruction.

Register Set

The NDP register set is shown in Figure 3. Each of the eight data registers in the NDP's register stack is 80 bits wide and is divided into "fields" corresponding to the NDP's temporary real data type. The register set may be addressed as a push down stack, through a top of stack pointer or any register may be addressed explicitly relative to the top of stack.

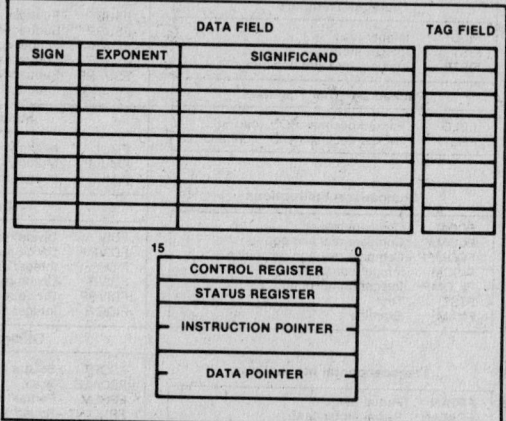

Figure 3. 8087 Register Set

Status Word

The status word shown in Figure 4 reflects the overall state of the NDP; it may be stored in memory and then inspected by CPU code. The status word is a 16-bit register divided into fields as shown in Figure 4. The busy bit (bit 15) indicates whether the NEU is executing an instruction (B = 1) or is idle (B = 0). Several

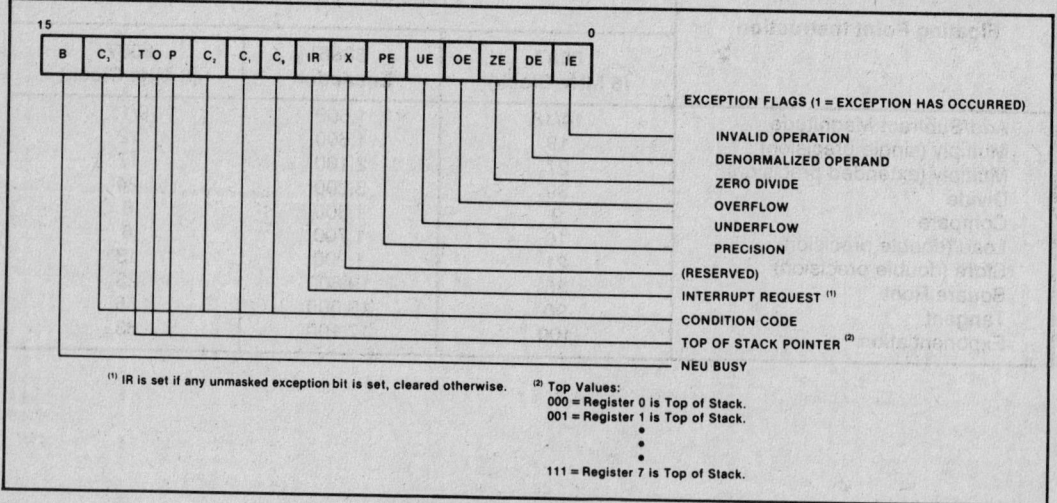

Figure 4. 8087 Status Word

3-6

instructions which store and manipulate the status word are executed exclusively by the CU, and these do not set the busy bit themselves.

The four numeric condition code bits (C_0-C_3) are similar to the flags in a CPU: various instructions update these bits to reflect the outcome of NDP operations.

Bits 13-11 of the status word point to the NDP register that is the current top-of-stack (TOP).

Bit 7 is the interrupt request bit. This bit is set if any unmasked exception bit is set and cleared otherwise.

Bits 5-0 are set to indicate that the NEU has detected an exception while executing an instruction.

Tag Word

The tag word marks the content of each register as shown in Figure 5. The principal function of the tag word is to optimize the NDP's performance. The tag word can be used, however, to interpret the contents of NDP registers.

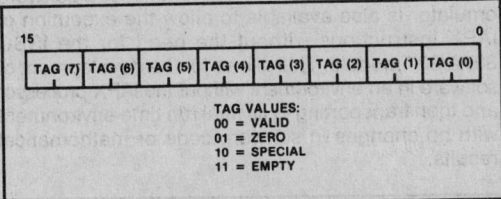

Figure 5. 8087 Tag Word

Instruction and Data Pointers

The instruction and data pointers (see Figure 6) are provided for user-written error handlers. Whenever the NDP executes an NEU instruction, the CU saves the instruction address, the operand address (if present) and the instruction opcode. The NDP can then store this data in memory.

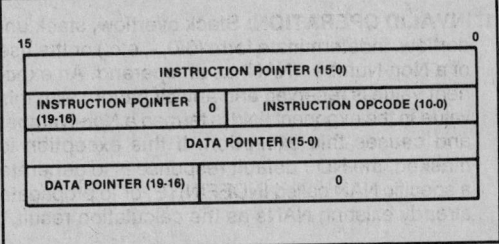

Figure 6. 8087 Instruction and Data Pointers

Control Word

The NDP provides several processing options which are selected by loading a word from memory into the control word. Figure 7 shows the format and encoding of the fields in the control word.

Exception Handling

The NDP detects six different exception conditions that can occur during instruction execution. Any or all exceptions will cause an interrupt if unmasked and interrupts are enabled.

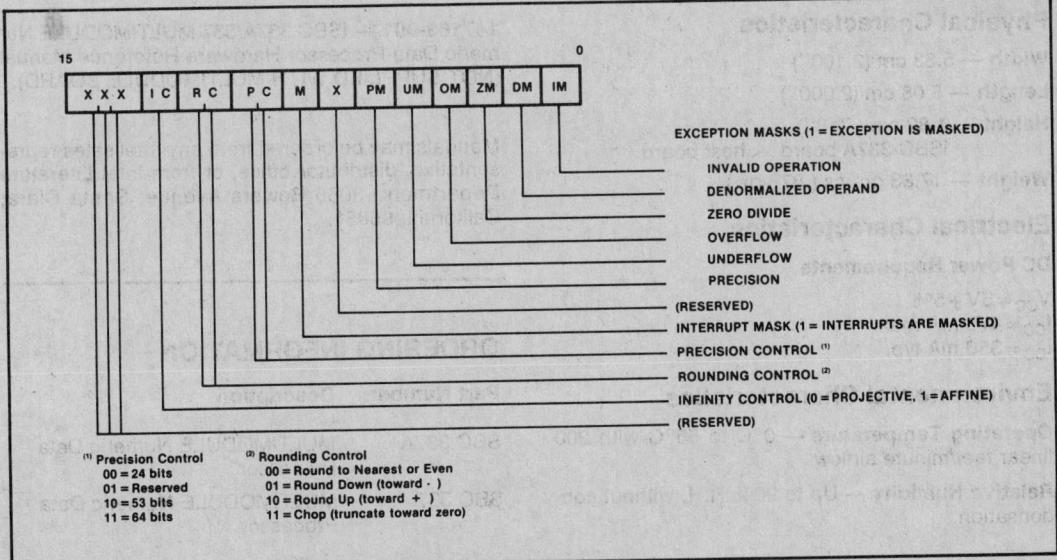

Figure 7. 8087 Control Word

iSBC® 337A and iSBC® 337 Module

If interrupts are disabled, the NDP will simply suspend execution until the host clears the exception. If a specific exception class is masked and that exception occurs however, the NDP will post the exception in the status register and perform an on-chip default exception handling procedure, thereby allowing processing to continue. The exceptions that the NDP detects are the following:

1. **INVALID OPERATION:** Stack overflow, stack underflow, indeterminate form (0/0, -, etc.) or the use of a Non-Number (NAN) as an operand. An exponent value is reserved and any bit pattern with this value in the exponent field is termed a Non-Number and causes this exception. If this exception is masked, the NDP default response is to generate a specific NAN called INDEFINITE, or to propagate already existing NANs as the calculation result.

2. **OVERFLOW:** The result is too large in magnitude to fit the specified format. The NDP will generate the code for infinity if this exception is masked.

3. **ZERO DIVISOR:** The divisor is zero while the dividend is a non-infinite, non-zero number. Again, the NDP will generate the code for infinity if this exception is masked.

4. **UNDERFLOW:** The result is non-zero but too small in magnitude to fit in the specified format. If this exception is masked the NDP will denormalize (shift right) the fraction until the exponent is in range. This process is called gradual underflow.

5. **DENORMALIZED OPERAND:** At least one of the operands or the result is denormalized; it has the smallest exponent but a non-zero significand. Normal processing continues if this exception is masked off.

6. **INEXACT RESULT:** If the true result is not exactly representable in the specified format, the result is rounded according to the rounding mode, and this flag is set. If this exception is masked, processing will simply continue.

SOFTWARE SUPPORT

The iSBC 337A/337 module is supported by the following Intel software products: iRMX™ 86 Operating System, iRMX 88 Real-time Multi-tasking Executive, ASM 86/88 Assembly language, PL/M 86/88 Systems Implementation Languages, Pascal 86/88, Fortran 86/88 along with iRMX Development Utilities Package. In addition to the instructions provided in the languages to support the additional math functions, a software emulator is also available to allow the execution of iAPX instructions without the need for the iSBC 337A/337 module. This allows for the development of software in an environment without the iAPX processor and then transporting to its final run time environment with no changes in software code or mathematical results.

SPECIFICATIONS

Physical Characteristics

Width — 5.33 cm (2.100'')
Length — 5.08 cm (2.000'')
Height — 1.82 cm (.718'')
  iSBC 337A board + host board
Weight — 17.33 grams (.576 oz.)

Electrical Characteristics

DC Power Requirements

$V_{CC} = 5V \pm 5\%$
$I_{CC} = 475$ mA max.
$I_{CC} = 350$ mA typ.

Environmental Characteristics

Operating Temperature — 0°C to 55°C with 200 linear feet/minute airflow
Relative Humidity — Up to 90% R.H. without condensation.

Reference Manual

147163-001 — iSBC 337A/337 MULTIMODULE Numeric Data Processor Hardware Reference Manual (NOT SUPPLIED WITH MULTIMODULE BOARD).

Manuals may be ordered from any Intel sales representative, distributor office, or from Intel Literature Department, 3065 Bowers Avenue, Santa Clara, California, 95051.

ORDERING INFORMATION

Part Number	Description
SBC 337A	MULTIMODULE Numeric Data Processor
SBC 337	MULTIMODULE Numeric Data Processor

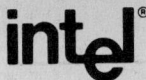

iSBX™ 331
FIXED/FLOATING POINT MATH
MULTIMODULE BOARD

- **iSBX™ bus compatible high speed fixed/floating point math expansion**
- **4 MHz operation**
- **Fixed point single and double precision (16/32-bit)**
- **Floating point double precision (32-bit)**
- **Binary data formats**
- **Add, subtract, multiply and divide**
- **Trignometric and inverse trigonometric functions**
- **Square root, log, and exponential functions**
- **Float-to-fixed and fixed-to-float conversions**
- **End of operation interrupt**
- **Software reset control**
- **Low power requirements**
- **iSBX™ bus on-board expansion eliminates MULTIBUS® system bus latency and increases system throughput**

The Intel® iSBX 331 Fixed/Floating Point Math MULTIMODULE Board is a member of Intel's new line of iSBX bus compatible MULTIMODULE products. The iSBX MULTIMODULE board plugs directly into any iSBX bus compatible host board offering low cost incremental on-board expansion. As a result, any iSBX bus compatible host board may be expanded to perform high speed math computations, affording up to a 40× improvement in speed compared to software math. The iSBX 331 module performs single/double (16/32-bit) precision fixed point plus double (32-bit) precision floating point arithmetic operations. In addition, the module performs transcendental, data manipulation, and fixed to float/float to fixed point conversion operations. The command operations run entirely independent of the host board permitting efficient concurrent processing. The iSBX board is closely coupled to the host board through the iSBX bus, and as such, offers maximum on-board performance and frees MULTIBUS system traffic for other system resources. Incremental power dissipation is minimal requiring only 2.73 watts.

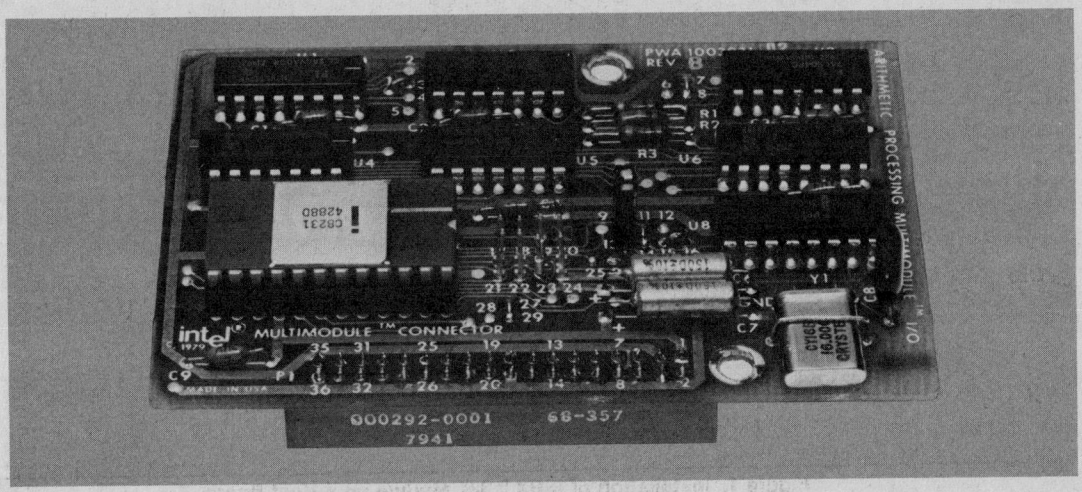

iSBX™ 331

FUNCTIONAL DESCRIPTION

The iSBX 331 module uses the Intel 8231 Arithmetic Processing Unit (APU) to accomplish high speed (4 MHz) math operation. The system software may communicate with the iSBX 331 module across the iSBX bus using I/O read/write commands. All transfers, including operand, result, status, and command information, take place over an 8-bit bidirectional data bus. Operands are pushed onto an internal stack and commands are issued to perform operations on the data. Results are then available from the stack. A status byte may be read to monitor execution completion and the nature of the result (zero, sign, or errors). In addition, control logic is included on the iSBX 331 module to facilitate single instruction software reset control.

Command Functions

The iSBX 331 module commands fall into three categories: double precision floating point, single precision fixed point, and double precision fixed point (see Table 1). There are four arithmetic operations that can be performed in either fixed or floating point numbers: add, subtract, multiply, and divide. These operations require two operands. The 8231 assumes these operands are located in the internal stack as Top of Stack (TOS) and Next on Stack (NOS). The result will always be returned to TOS. There are four types of transcendental operations that can be performed in floating point numbers: trigonometric functions, logarithms, exponentials, and square roots. The results of these operations will be returned to TOS. There are four types of data manipulation operations that can be performed in either fixed or floating point numbers: sign change of TOS, exchange of TOS and NOS and copying or popping operands onto or off of TOS. Fixed to floating point conversion can be performed on floating point instructions and floating point to fixed point conversion can be performed on fixed point instructions.

The execution times of the commands are shown in Table 2.

Interrupt Requests

There is one interrupt line from the APU that may generate an interrupt request to the host: END (MINTRI). The END interrupt line is active upon command completion. The END signal is cleared by a reset or status register read.

Installation

The iSBX 331 module plugs directly into the female iSBX connector on the host board. The module is then secured at one additional point with nylon hardware to insure the mechanical security of the assembly (see Figures 1 and 2).

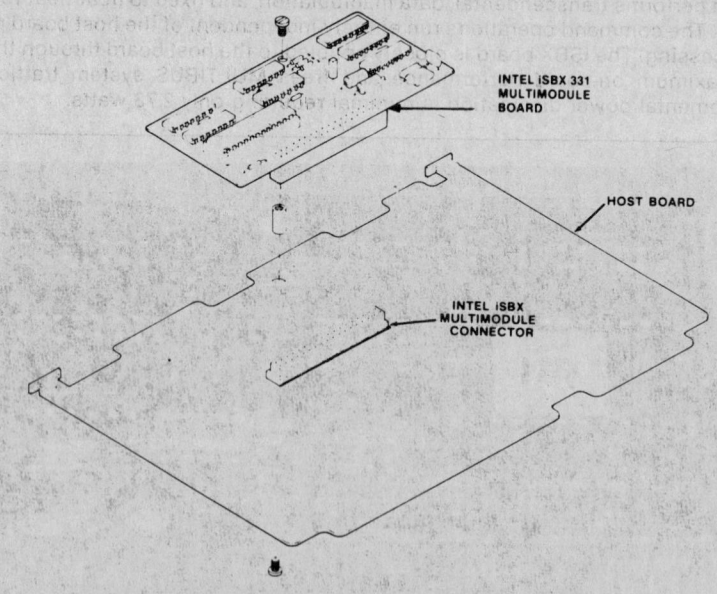

Figure 1. Installation of ISBX™ 331 Module on a Host Board

iSBX™ 331

Table 1. Command Summary

Double Precision Floating Point Instructions (32-Bit)

Instruction	Description	Hex Code	Stack Contents After Execution[1] A B C D	Status Flags Affected[3]
ACOS	Inverse Cosine of A	0 6	R U U U	S, Z, E
ASIN	Inverse Sine of A	0 5	R U U U	S, Z, E
ATAN	Inverse Tangent of A	0 7	R B U U	S, Z
CHSF	Sign Change of A	1 5	R B C D	S, Z
COS	Cosine of A (radians)	0 3	R B U U	S, Z
EXP	e^A Function	0 A	R B U U	S, Z, E
FADD	Add A and B	1 0	R C D U	S, Z, E
FDIV	Divide B by A	1 3	R C D U	S, Z, E
FLTD	32-Bit Fixed to Floating Point Conversion	1 C	R B C U	S, Z
FLTS	16-Bit Fixed to Floating Point Conversion	1 D	R B C U	S, Z
FMUL	Multiply A and B	1 2	R C D U	S, Z, E
FSUB	Subtract A from B	1 1	R C D U	S, Z, E
LOG	Common Logarithm (base 10) of A	0 8	R B U U	S, Z, E
LN	Natural Logarithm of A	0 9	R B U U	S, Z, E
POPF	Stack Pop	1 8	B C D A	S, Z
PTOF	Stack Push	1 7	A A B C	S, Z
PUPI	Push π onto Stack	1 A	R A B C	S, Z
PWR	B^A Power Function	0 B	R C U U	S, Z, E
SIN	Sine of A (radians)	0 2	R B U U	S, Z
SQRT	Square Root of A	0 1	R B C U	S, Z, E
TAN	Tangent of A (radians)	0 4	R B U U	S, Z, E
XCHF	Exchange A and B	1 9	B A C D	S, Z

Double Precision Fixed Point Instructions (32-Bit)

Instruction	Description	Hex Code	Stack Contents After Execution[1] A B C D	Status Flags Affected[3]
CHSD	Sign Change of A	3 4	R B C D	S, Z, O
DADD	Add A and B	2 C	R C D A	S, Z, C, E
DDIV	Divide B by A	2 F	R C D U	S, Z, E
DMUL	Multiply A and B (R = lower 32 bits)	2 E	R C D U	S, Z, O
DMUU	Multiply A and B (R = upper 32 bits)	3 6	R C D U	S, Z, O
DSUB	Subtract A from B	2 D	R C D A	S, Z, C, O
FIXD	Floating to Fixed Point Conversion	1 E	R B C U	S, Z, O
POPD	Stack Pop	3 8	B C D A	S, Z
PTOD	Stack Push	3 7	A A B C	S, Z
XCHD	Exchange A and B	3 9	B A C D	S, Z

3-11

iSBX™ 331

Table 1. Command Summary (continued)

Single Precision Fixed Point Instructions (16-Bit)

Instruction	Description	Hex Code		Stack Contents After Execution[2] A_U A_L B_U B_L C_U C_L D_U D_L	Status Flags Affected[3]
CHSS	Change Sign of A_U	7	4	R A_L B_U B_L C_U C_L D_U D_L	S, Z, O
FIXS	Floating to Fixed Point Conversion	1	F	R B_U B_L C_U C_L U U U	S, Z, O
POPS	Stack Pop	7	8	A_L B_U B_L C_U C_L D_U D_L A_U	S, Z
PTOS	Stack Push	7	7	A_U A_U A_L B_U B_L C_U C_L D_U	S, Z
SADD	Add A_U and A_L	6	C	R B_U B_L C_U C_L D_U D_L A_U	S, Z, C, E
SDIV	Divide A_L by A_U	6	F	R B_U B_L C_U C_L D_U D_L U	S, Z, E
SMUL	Multiply A_L by A_U (R = lower 16 bits)	6	E	R B_U B_L C_U C_L D_U D_L U	S, Z, E
SMUU	Multiply A_L by A_U (R = upper 16 bits)	7	6	R B_U B_L C_U C_L D_U D_L U	S, Z, E
SSUB	Subtract A_U from A_L	6	D	R B_U B_L C_U C_L D_U D_L A_U	S, Z, C, E
XCHS	Exchange A_U and A_L	7	9	A_L A_U B_U B_L C_U C_L D_U D_L	S, Z
NOP	No Operation	0	0	A_U A_L B_U B_L C_U C_L D_U D_L	

NOTES:
1. The stack initially is composed of four 32-bit numbers (A, B, C, D). A is equivalent to Top Of Stack (TOS) and B is Next On Stack (NOS). Upon completion of a command the stack is composed of: the result (R); undefined (U); or the initial contents (A, B, C, or D).
2. The stack initially is composed of eight 16-bit numbers (A_U, A_L, B_U, B_L, C_U, C_L, D_U, D_L). A_U is the TOS and A_L is NOS. Upon completion of a command the stack is composed of: the result (R); undefined (U); or the initial contents (A_U, A_L, B_U, B_L,...).
3. Nomenclature: Sign (S); Zero (Z); Overflow (O); Carry (C); Error Code Field (E).

Table 2. Command Execution Times

Command Mnemonic	μSeconds	Command Mnemonic	μSeconds
SADD	4.25	ASIN	1917
SSUB	7.5	ACOS	1933.5
SMUL	21–23.5	ATAN	1501.5
SMUU	20–24.5	LOG	1118.5–1783
SDIV	21–23.5	LN	1074.5–1739
DADD	5.25	EXP	948.5–1219.5
DSUB	9.5	PWR	2072.5–3008
DMUL	48.5–52.5	NOP	1
DMUU	45.5–54.5	CHSS	5.75
DDIV	52	CHSD	6.75
FIXS	23–54	CHSF	4.5
FIXD	25–86.5	PTOS	4
FLTS	24.5–46.5	PTOD	5
FLTD	24.5–94.5	PTOF	5
FADD	13.5–92	POPS	2.5
FSUB	17.5–92.5	POPD	3
FMUL	36.5–42	POPF	3
FDIV	38.5–46	XCHS	4.5
SQRT	200	XCHD	6.5
SIN	1116	XCHF	6.5
COS	1029.5	PUPI	4
TAN	1438.5		

NOTE: Assumes 4 MHz operation.

iSBX™ 331

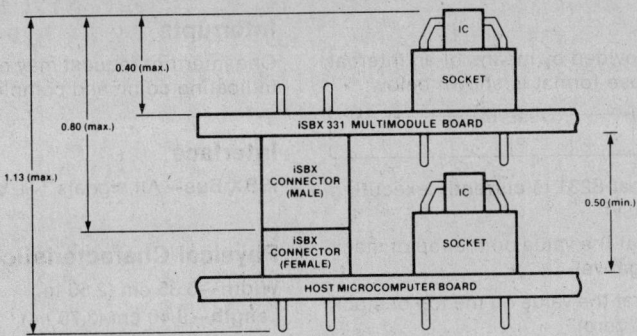

Figure 2. iSBX 331 MULTIMODULE Board Mounting Clearances (inches)

SPECIFICATIONS

Word Size
Data—8 bits.

On-Board Clock Rate
4.0 MHz ± 0.1%.

I/O Addressing

Function	Type of Operation	iSBX Connector Port Address
Data Transfer	Read or Write	X0, X2, X4, or X6
Command Transfer	Write	X1, X3, X5, or X7
Status Transfer	Read	X1, X3, X5, or X7
Reset	Write	X8 through XF

NOTE:
The port addresses are determined on the host iSBC microcomputer. Refer to the Hardware Reference Manual for your host iSBC microcomputer to determine the first digit (X) of the connector port addresses.

Arithmetic Functions
See Table 1.

Data Formats

Single Precision Fixed Point (16 bits)

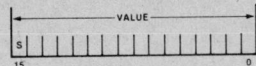

Bit 15: S = Sign of the operand. Positive values are represented by a sign bit of zero (S = 0). Negative values are represented by the two's complement of the corresponding positive value with a sign bit equal to 1 (S = 1).

Bits 0–14: Values in the range from −32,768 to +32,767.

Double Precision Fixed Point (32 bits)

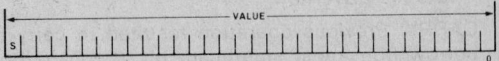

Bit 31: S = Sign of operand. Positive values are represented by a sign of zero (S = 0). Negative values are represented by the two's complement of the corresponding positive value with a sign bit equal to 1 (S = 1).

Bits 0–30: Values in the range from −2,147,483,648 to +2,147,483,647.

Double Precision Floating Point (32 bits)

Bit 31: MS = Sign of the mantissa. 1 represents negative and 0 represents positive.

Bits 24–30: ES = the exponent expressed as a two's complement 7-bit value having a range of −64 to +63.

Bits 0–23: The mantissa is expressed as a 24-bit (fractional) value. The 8231 APU requires that floating point data be represented by a fractional mantissa value between 0.5 and 1 multiplied by 2 raised to an appropriate power (exponent). This is expressed as follows:

$$\text{Value} = \text{mantissa} \times 2^{\text{exponent}}$$

iSBX™ 331

Device Status

Device status is provided by means of an internal status register whose format is shown below:

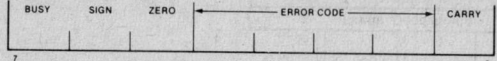

BUSY: Indicates that 8231 is currently executing a command (1 = Busy)

SIGN: Indicates that the value on the top of stack is negative (1 = Negative)

ZERO: Indicates that the value on the top of stack is zero (1 = Value is zero)

ERROR CODE: This field contains an indication of the validity of the result of the last operation. The error codes are:

0000 —	No error
1000 —	Divide by zero
0100 —	Square root or log of negative number
1100 —	Argument of inverse sine, cosine, or e^x too large
XX10 —	Underflow
XX01 —	Overflow

CARRY: Previous operation resulted in carry or borrow from most significant bit. (1 = Carry/Borrow, 0 = No Carry/No Borrow.)

If the BUSY bit in the status register is a one, the other status bits are not defined; if zero, indicating not busy, the operation is complete and the other status bits are defined as given above.

Access Time

Read—1900 ns (max.)
Write—1900 ns (max.)

NOTE:
Actual transfer speed is dependent upon the cycle time of the host microcomputer. The listed times assume no operation in progress. If an operation is executing when an access is attempted, the command execution time must be added to the above times for all accesses except status read.

Interrupts

One interrupt request may originate from the APU indicating command completion (END).

Interface

iSBX Bus—All signals TTL compatible

Physical Characteristics

Width—6.35 cm (2.50 in.)
Length—9.40 cm (3.70 in.)
Height*—2.04 cm (0.80 in.) iSBX 331 Board
—2.86 cm (1.13 in.) iSBX 331 Board + Host Board
Weight—51 gm (1.79 oz)

*See Figure 2.

Electrical Characteristics

DC Power Requirements
$V_{CC} = +5V \pm 5\%$ $I_{CC} = 365$ mA max.
$V_{DD} = +12V \pm 5\%$ $I_{DD} = 75$ mA max.

Environmental

Operating Temperature—0°C to 55°C

Free moving air across the base board and iSBX board.

Reference Manual

142668-01—iSBX 331 Floating Point Math MULTIMODULE Board (NOT SUPPLIED)

Reference manuals may be ordered from any Intel sales representative, distributor office or from Intel Literature Department, 3065 Bowers Avenue, Santa Clara, California 95051.

ORDERING INFORMATION

Part Number	Description
SBX 331	Fixed/Floating Point Math MULTIMODULE Board

3-14

Memory Expansion Boards 4

iBCK 10-1 and iBCK 10-4
INTEL BUBBLE CASSETTE SYSTEM PRODUCTION KIT

- iBCK 10-1 0-65°C
  iBCK 10-4 10-50°C
  At 20% Average Duty Cycle
- 128 KBytes of Non-Volatile Bubble Memory Per Cassette
- Simple Interface: Complete iSBX™ Compatibility optional using iSBX™ iBC Interface MULTIMODULE™
- Performance:
  —Average Access Time: 48 msec
  —Burst Data Rate: 12.5 KBytes/Sec
- High Reliability Under Harsh Environments
- 2 Cassette to Holder Keying Options
- Power Fail Data Protection
- Operates under Standard +5 and +12Vdc Power Supplies
- Bubble Detector Switching Saves Power
- Write Protect Mode

The Intel iBCK 10-1 and iBCK 10-4 Bubble Memory Cassette Systems are fully assembled and tested removeable nonvolatile storage systems based on the Intel 7110A one megabit bubble memory and support components. Each iBCK 10-1 and iBCK 10-4 comes with one iBCH 110 Bubble Cassette Holder and one iBC 128-1 or iBC 128-4 bubble cassette. Extra bubble cassettes are available separately. The 128 KByte bubble cassettes are completely interchangeable from one 128 KByte bubble cassette holder to any other; the operating temperature range of the system is determined by the bubble cassette used. Cassette-to-holder keying is accomplished using grooves on the front bezel of the cassette holder which must match those on the bottom of the cassette to allow entry of the cassette. A sliding tab on the cassette places the bubble memory in the write protected mode.

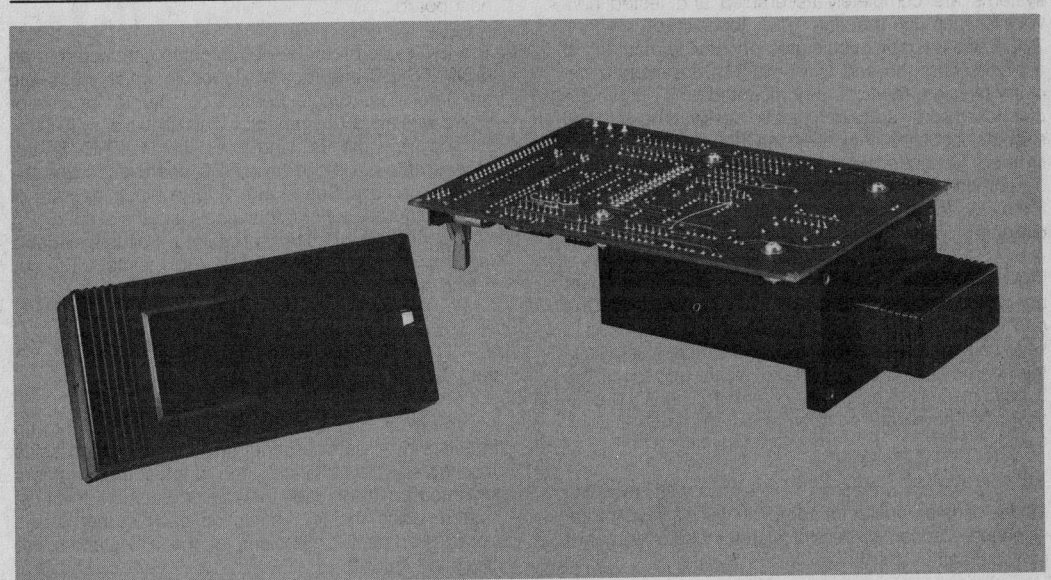

Intel Corporation Assumes No Responsibility for the Use of Any Circuitry Other Than Circuitry Embodied in an Intel Product. No Other Circuit Patent Licenses are Implied.
© INTEL CORPORATION, 1984

APRIL 1985
ORDER NUMBER: 231084-002

iBCK 10-1 and iBCK 10-4

The Intel Bubble Cassette System offers OEM systems designers a rugged, reliable high performance alternative to disk and tape drives. The iBC system will function reliably in the hot, dusty, humid environments where tapes and disks will not. And because of its solid state memory technology and simple packaging, it can operate through high levels of shock and vibration. The system has only one mechanical or moving part, the cassette-to-holder connector. This is an industry-standard AMP D-type pin connector finished with AMP's Duragold and rated at 10,000 insertions for the male half (mounted in the holder) and 5000 insertions for the female half (mounted in the cassette).

The iBCK 10-1 and iBCK 10-4 bubble cassette systems may be designed into Intel SBC-based systems using the optional iSBX 258 iBC Interface Multimodule. The iBC system may also be designed into any user designed microprocessor board. The bubble memory support circuitry and ribbon cable connector on the bubble cassette holder board provide the user with a simple interface to the bubble memory.

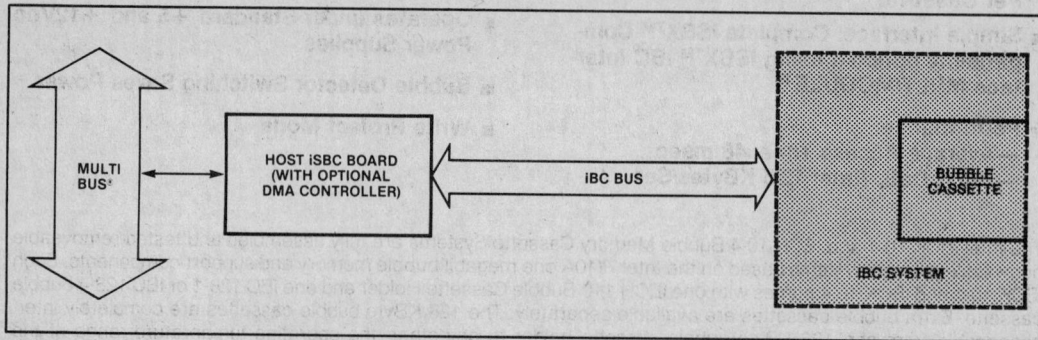

Figure 1. Block Diagram of MULTIBUS® iBC Configuration

FUNCTIONAL DESCRIPTION

The iBCK 10-1 and iBCK 10-4 bubble memory cassette systems are completely assembled and tested non-volatile memory systems. They consist of an Intel 7110A one megabit bubble memory device mounted in a plastic cassette and all of the 7110A's support circuitry plus interface circuitry mounted on a printed circuit board screwed onto a plastic cassette holder. The support circuitry includes the Intel 7220 Bubble Memory Controller (BMC) through which the host processor communicates with the bubble memory. See Figure 1 for a system and bubble memory block diagram.

The BMC provides a convenient 8 bit bi-directional data bus which requires only two port or I/O addresses. One port is used to transfer data while the other is used to send commands or view operational status. A set of sixteen commands are available to initiate and monitor a bubble memory data transfer (refer to the 7220 data sheet for more detailed information on the BMC commands).

The iBC system provides the designer with three I/O modes of data transfer for complete flexibility. I/O mode selection is accomplished through the use of on-board jumpers and user software:

1. Polled
2. Interrupt-driven mode
3. Direct Memory Access (DMA) mode

DMA mode requires the use of a DMA controller on the host board.

The iBC system can be ribbon cable connected to an iSBX 258 iBC Interface Multimodule which plugs into any Intel iSBC Single Board Computer or processor board with an iSBX connector. This allows easy iSBX interface from the iBC and frees the MULTIBUS® for other traffic while the host iSBC board accesses the bubble memory. See Figure 2 for a block diagram of this configuration. For ribbon cable lengths of up to 18", no signal drive circuitry is required. For longer cable lengths, sufficient drive circuitry to maintain iBC bus timing specifications must be used.

MOUNTING TECHNIQUE

As shown in Figure 3, the iBC holder screws into an opening in an outside panel of the host system using four screws. Additionally, the printed circuit board mounted on the holder may be screwed to the host system using the four holes on each corner of the board. Pertinent dimensions of the iBC system are given in Figure 3.

iBCK 10-1 and iBCK 10-4

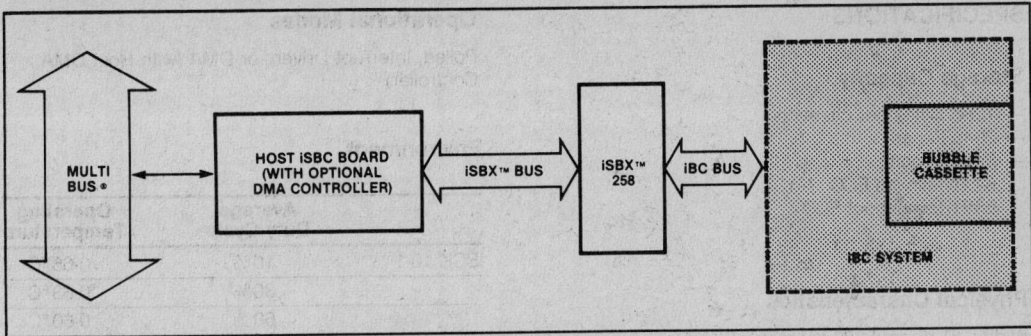

Figure 2. MULTIMODULE™ Mounting

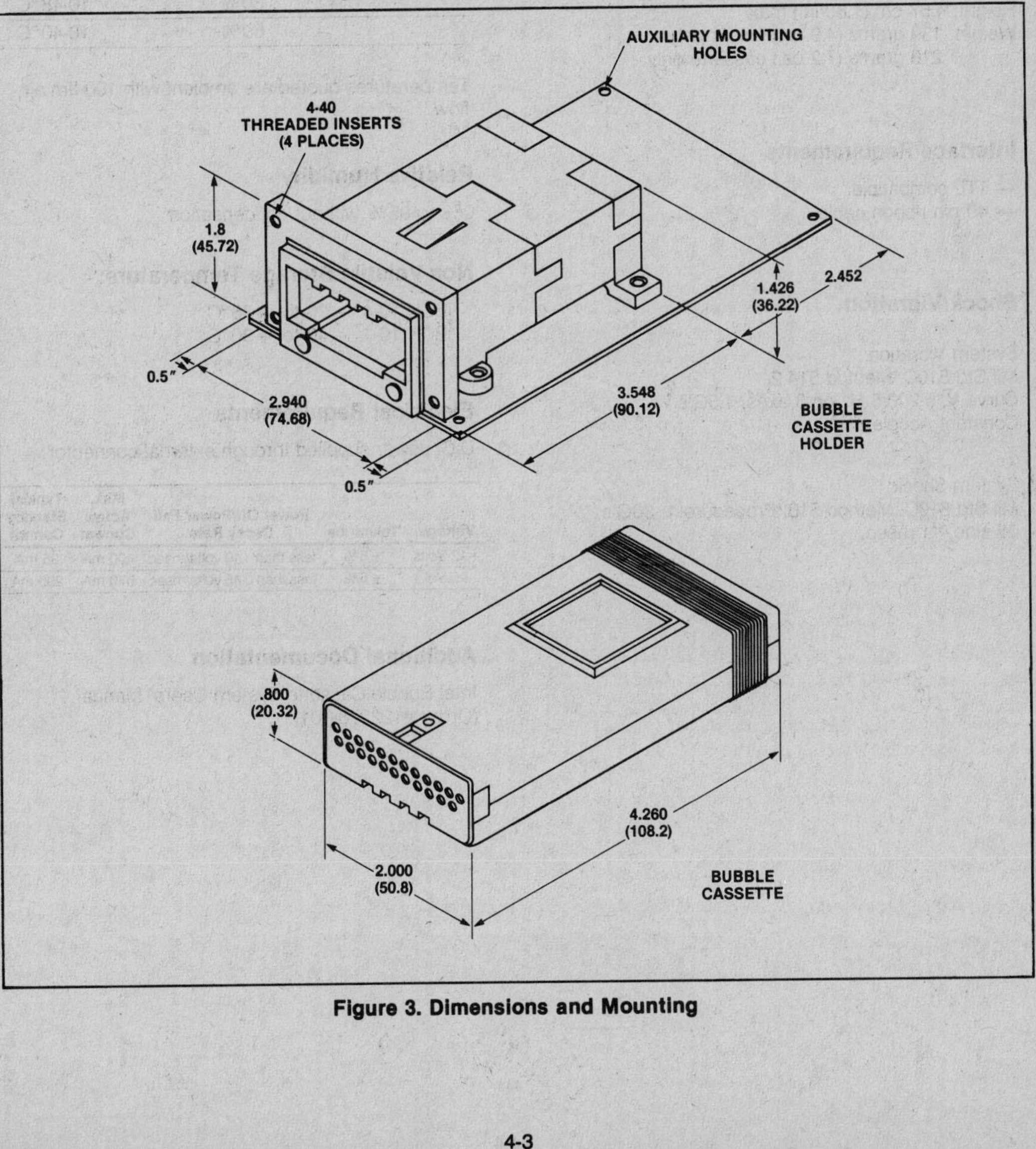

Figure 3. Dimensions and Mounting

4-3

iBCK 10-1 and iBCK 10-4

SPECIFICATIONS

Storage Capacity

— 128K Bytes per cassette
— 2048 Pages
— Page Length:
  64 Bytes with ECC
  68 Bytes without ECC

Physical Characteristics

Width: 10.16 cm (4.00 in.) max.
Length: 15.24 cm (6.00 in.) max.
Height: 4.57 cm (1.80 in.) max.
Weight: 139 grams (4.9 oz.) holder only
        218 grams (7.2 oz.) cassette only

Interface Requirements

— TTL compatible
— 40 pin ribbon cable

Shock/Vibration

System Vibration:
Mil Std 810C, Method 514.2,
Curve V, 5-200-5 Hz on 3 axes, 1.5G's
Constant Acceleration

System Shock:
Mil Std 810C, Method 516, Procedure 1, 30G's,
½ sine, 11 msec.

Operational Modes

Polled, Interrupt Driven, or DMA (with Host DMA Controller)

Environment

	Average Duty Cycle	Operating Temperature
iBCK 10-1	10%	0-65°C
	30%	0-63°C
	60%	0-60°C
iBCK 10-4	10%	10-52°C
	30%	10-48°C
	60%	10-40°C

Temperatures quoted are ambient with 100 lfm air flow.

Relative Humidity

0% to 95% without condensation

Non-Volatile Storage Temperature:

iBCK 10-4: −20 to +75°C
iBCK 10-1: −40 to +90°C

Electrical Requirements

D.C. power supplied through external connector.

Voltage	Tolerance	Power Off/Power Fail Decay Rate	Max. Active Current	Typical Standby Current
+12 Volts	±5%	less than 1.10 volts/msec	400 mA	35 mA
+5 Volts	±5%	less than 0.45 volts/msec	570 mA	200 mA

Additional Documentation

Intel Bubble Cassette System Users' Manual
(Order #122278-001)

iBCK 12
INTEL BUBBLE CASSETTE SYSTEM PROTOTYPING KIT

- Complete iBC System Plus iSBX™ 258 iBC Interface MULTIMODULE™ and Ribbon Cable
- 128 KBytes of Removeable, Reliable, Non-Volatile Bubble Memory storage per Cassette
- Performance:
  — Average Access Time: 48 msec
  — Burst Data Rate: 12.5 KBytes/Sec
- Fastest, easiest way to design with the iBC system; ready to use as a peripheral on the iSBX bus.

The Intel iBCK 12 Intel Bubble Cassette (iBC) System Prototyping Kit contains all the necessary items to begin development with the iBC system. This is a 128 KByte Intel Bubble Cassette (iBC 128), Intel Bubble Cassette Holder (iBCH 110), an iSBX Interface MULTIMODULE for the iBC (iSBX 258), and an 18" ribbon cable to connect them. The kit allows systems designers to prototype the iBC system in their systems with a minimum of time and effort.

The iBC system is described by its data sheet (iBCK 10-1 and iBCK 10-4) in more detail, as is the iSBX 258 by its data sheet.

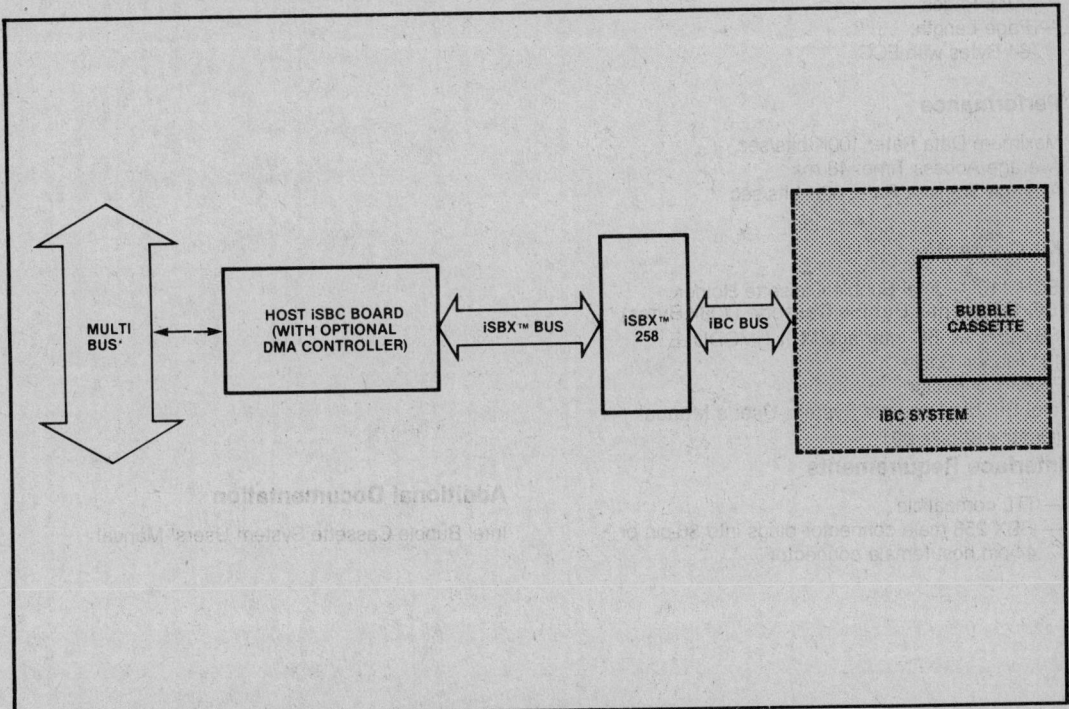

Figure 1. Block Diagram

Intel Corporation Assumes No Responsibility for the Use of Any Circuitry Other Than Circuitry Embodied in an Intel Product. No Other Circuit Patent Licenses are Implied.
© INTEL CORPORATION, 1984

JUNE 1984
ORDER NUMBER: 231086-001

iBCK 12

FUNCTIONAL DESCRIPTION

The iBCK 12 is a complete solution for prototyping with the iBC System. Steps to build up a prototyping system using the iBCK 12 are:

1. Plug iSBX 258 single-wide MULITMODULE onto host board with iSBX connector;
2. Connect the iBC holder board to the iSBX 258 using the the ribbon cable included in the kit;
3. Connect +5V and +12V to the iBC holder board using the power connectors included in the kit;
4. Insert the Intel Bubble Cassette in the iBC holder.

See Figure 1 for a block diagram of the configuration.

SPECIFICATIONS

Storage Capacity

— 128K Bytes per cassette
— 2048 Pages
— Page Length:
  64 Bytes with ECC

Performance

Maximum Data Rate: 100K bits/sec
Average Access Time: 48 ms
Average Transfer Rate: 68K bits/sec

Kit Contents

iBCH 110 — Intel Bubble Cassette Holder
iBC 128 — Intel Bubble Cassette (128KBytes)
iSBX 258 — iBC Interface MULTIMODULE™
18″ Ribbon Cable
Power Connector
Intel Bubble Cassette System User's Manual
(Order #122278-001)

Interface Requirements

— TTL compatible
— iSBX 258 male connector plugs into 36-pin or 44-pin host female connector

Operational Modes

Polled, Interrupt Driven, or DMA (with Host DMA Controller)

Temperature

+20 to +30°C operating @ 30% average duty cycle
−20 to +75°C Non-Volatile Storage

Electrical Requirements

iBC System:
D.C. power supplied through external connector.

Voltage	Tolerance	Power Off/ Power Fail Decay Rate	Max. Active Current	Typical Standby Current
+12 Volts	±5%	less than 1.10 volts/msec	400 mA	35 mA
+5 Volts	±5%	less than 0.45 volts/msec	570 mA	200 mA

iSBX 258:
D.C. power, supplied through SBX connector.
+5V ±5%, 285 mA (max).

Additional Documentation

Intel Bubble Cassette System Users' Manual

PRELIMINARY

iPCB-76 PC-BUBBLE™ CARD
BUBBLE MEMORY EXPANSION BOARD

- Highly Reliable, Non-Volatile Mass Storage for IBM* PC, PC/XT, or Compatibles
- EPROM-Based Driver Provides Transparent Disk Emulation for MS-DOS** or PC-DOS*
- Operating Range 0°C to +60°C
- Available with One or Two 7114 Bubble Memory Devices (512K Bytes or 1-Megabyte)
- Industry's Most Advanced Bubble Memory Controller
- Operates from Standard +5 Vdc ±5% Supply

The iPCB-76 PC-BUBBLE™ Card Expansion Board is a solid-state, non-volatile, mass storage expansion board for the IBM PC, PC/XT, or other compatible systems. PC-BUBBLE Card is available with one or two 7114 devices, yielding storage densities of 512K bytes or 1-Megabyte, respectively.

An integral, EPROM-based I/O driver allows PC-BUBBLE Card to appear to the operating system BIOS as simply another disk drive. The non-volatile nature of bubble memory technology, its capability for wide temperature operation, and its inherent reliability, makes PC-BUBBLE Card suitable for use as mass storage in environments that are much too harsh for disk drives.

*IBM and PC-DOS are trademarks of International Business Machines Corporation.
**MS-DOS is a trademark of Microsoft Corporation.

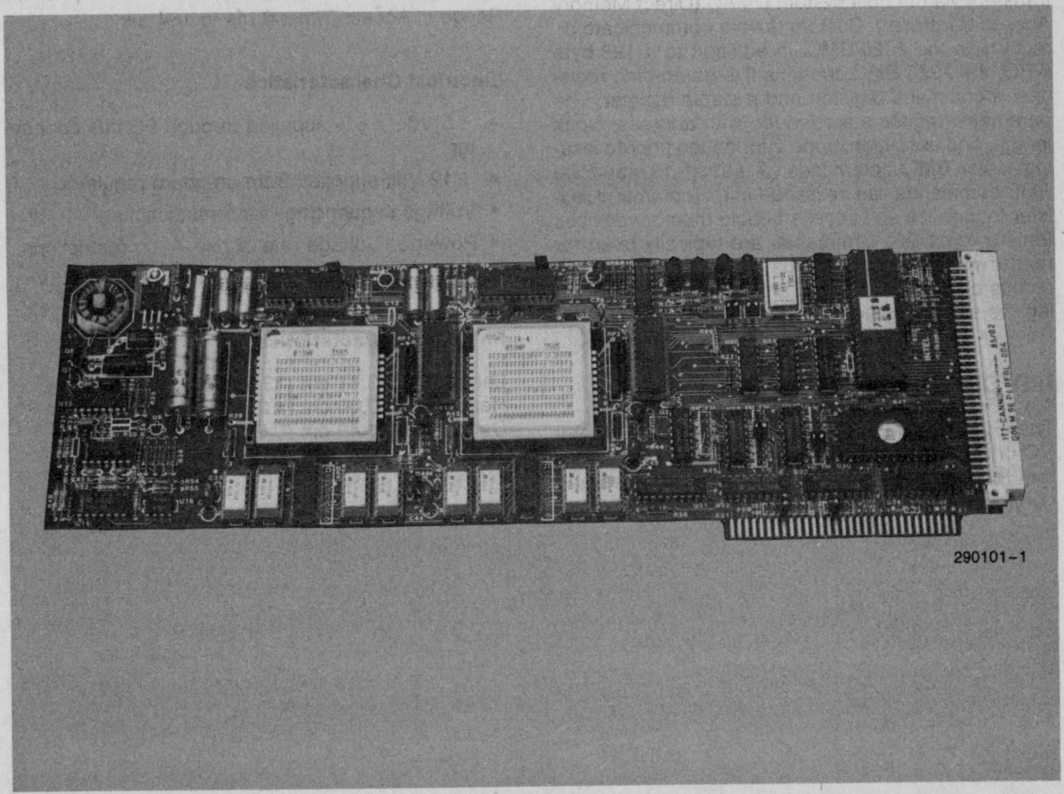

290101-1

Intel Corporation assumes no responsibility for the use of any circuitry other than circuitry embodied in an Intel product. No other circuit patent licenses are implied. Information contained herein supersedes previously published specifications on these devices from Intel. **October 1985**
© Intel Corporation, 1985 **Order Number: 290101-001**

iPCB-76

PRELIMINARY

HARDWARE DESCRIPTION

The iPCB-76 PC-BUBBLE Card contains one or two Intel 7114 4-Megabit Magnetic Bubble Memory devices and their support circuits, a 7225 Bubble Memory Controller, a PC bus interface, and an EPROM-based I/O driver. All data transfers between system memory and the 7114 devices are performed under control of the I/O driver. The iPCB-76 PC-BUBBLE Card includes the following hardware features:

- PC bus interface logic buffers all signals and provides user-selectable I/O address, interrupt request, and DMA handshake signals.
- Automatic power-fail circuit provides data protection.
- Write-protect jumpers allow 7114s to be individually write-protected.
- An on-board +12 Vdc step-up switching regulator allows the board to draw all power from the host system's +5 Vdc ±5% power supply.

For applications that do not require an MS-DOS or PC-DOS driver, PC-BUBBLE Card can be used with a custom software driver that operates in polled or interrupt-driven modes and supports DMA data transfers via the host system DMAC (Direct Memory Access Controller). Custom drivers communicate directly with the 7225 BMC. In addition to a 128-byte FIFO, the 7225 BMC contains five parametric registers, a command register, and a status register. The parametric registers are loaded with address, block length, and execution mode information prior to issuing many BMC commands. A set of 18 separate BMC commands can be issued to the command register to initialize and access bubble memory devices (only a few basic commands are typically used for reads/writes). Current status of the BMC and the results of BMC commands are determined by reading the status register.

I/O DRIVER DESCRIPTION

The iPCB-76 PC-BUBBLE Card includes an integral I/O driver that communicates with the operating system BIOS to allow the bubble memory devices and controller to appear as a mass storage (disk drive-like) device. All hardware-specific operations are transparent to the operating system BIOS and are performed by the on-board EPROM driver. The iPCB-76 PC-BUBBLE Card driver is compatible with Versions 2.0, 2.1, and 3.0 of MS-DOS and PC-DOS.

SPECIFICATIONS

Memory Size

iPCB-76-1	512K Bytes
iPCB-76-2	1-Megabyte

Interface

All address, data, and control signals are TTL-compatible and IBM PC compatible

Performance

Maximum Data Rate: 50K bytes/second (iPCB-76-2)
Average Access Time: 88 ms (single-page access, randomly-accessed pages)
Range of Access Time: 8 ms to 164 ms

Electrical Characteristics

- +5 Vdc ±5% supplied through PC bus connector
- +12 Vdc supplied from on-board regulator
- Voltage sequencing — no restrictions
- Power-on voltage rate of rise — no restrictions
- Power decay rate (max.): 0.45 V/ms for +5V

Physical Characteristics

Length:	33.11 cm (13.038 in.)
Height:	10.66 cm (4.2 in.)
Depth:	1.49 cm (0.59 in.)

iPCB-76

Power Requirements

Specification	iPCB-76-1	iPCB-76-2 (Serial)	iPCB-76-2 (Parallel)
Typ. Active	1.5A	1.69A	2.61A
Typ. Standby	0.58A	0.78A	0.78A
Max. Active	2.07A	2.39A	3.51A
Max. Standby	0.95A	1.27A	1.27A

Environmental Characteristics

Operating Temp. 0°C to +60°C ambient

Non-Volatile
Storage Temp. −20°C to +75°C

Relative Humidity 5 to 95% non-condensing (non-operating)

5 to 90% non-condensing (operating)

External Magnetic
Force 20 Oersteds max.

Available Publications

- *iPCB-76 PC-BUBBLE™ Card User's Guide,* Order Number: 122724

Reference Publications

- *iPCB-75 PC-BUBBLE™ Card Reference Manual,* Order Number: 122710
- *Memory Components Handbook,* Order Number: 210830

iSBC® 012B
RAM MEMORY BOARDS

- iSBC® 86, iSBC® 88 and iSBC® 80 board RAM expansion through direct MULTIBUS® interface
- 512K of read/write memory
- On-board parity generator/checker and error status register
- Requires a single +5 volt power supply
- Assignable anywhere within a 16 megabyte address space
- Jumper selectable base address on any 16K byte boundary
- Auxiliary power bus and memory protect control logic for battery backup RAM requirements

The iSBC 012B RAM memory board is a member of Intel's complete line of iSBC memory and I/O expansion boards. The board interfaces directly to any iSBC 86, iSBC 88 or iSBC 80 Single Board Computer via the MULTIBUS interface to expand system RAM capacity. The iSBC 012B board contains 512K bytes of read/write memory implemented using dynamic RAM components. An on-board dynamic RAM controller refreshes a portion of these components every 16 microseconds. Each refresh cycle utilizes memory for 550 nanoseconds (maximum).

The iSBC 012B board generates byte oriented parity during all write operations and performs parity checking during all read operations. When a parity error is detected, the board can generate an interrupt on the MULTIBUS interface. In addition, the row and bank of the RAM array containing the error are stored in a Parity Flag Register. This register is accessible as a MULTIBUS I/O port. An on-board LED also provides a visual indication that a parity error has occurred.

The following are trademarks of Intel Corporation and may be used to describe Intel products: CREDIT, Index, Insite, Intellec, Library Manager, Megachassis, Micromap, MULTIBUS, PROMPT, UPI, μScope, Promware, MCS, ICE, iRMX, iSBC, iSBX, MULTIMODULE, ICS, iAPX and iMMX. Intel Corporation assumes no responsibility for the use of any circuitry other than circuitry embodied in an Intel product. No other circuit patent licenses are implied.

© INTEL CORPORATION, 1981

July, 1981
143876

iSBC® 012B RAM MEMORY BOARD

SPECIFICATIONS

Word Size
8 bits and 16 bits

Memory Size
524,288 bytes (iSBC 012B)

Access Time
330 nsec (worst case)
300 nsec (typical)

Cycle Times (Worst Case)
Read — 500 ns max.
Write — 500 ns max.
Refresh — 550 ns max.

Interface
All address, data and command signals are TTL compatible.

Address Selection
Memory — Base address is jumper selectable on any 16K byte boundary in a 16 megabyte address space. On-board RAM cannot cross a 4 megabyte address boundary.

Parity Flag Register — The I/O address of the Parity Flag Register is jumper selectable to be between 00H to 0FH or 40H to 4FH.

Connector
Edge connector — 86 pin double-sided PC edge connector with 0.156 in. contact centers.

Mating connector — Viking 3KH43/9AMK12 or equivalent.

Auxiliary Power
An auxiliary power bus is provided to allow separate power to RAM array for systems requiring battery backup of read/write memory. Selection of this auxiliary RAM power bus is made via jumpers on the board.

Memory Protect
An active-low TTL compatible memory protect signal is brought out on the auxiliary connector which, when asserted, disables read/write access to RAM on the board. This input is provided for the protection of RAM contents during system power-down sequences.

Physical Characteristics
Width — 12.00 in. (30.48 cm)
Height — 6.75 in. (17.15 cm)
Depth — 0.50 in. (1.27 cm)
Weight — 14 oz. (397 gm)

Electrical Characteristics
D.C. POWER REQUIREMENTS

All configurations require only +5 volts ±5%.

Normal System Operation (max.)
4.8A (worst case)
3.46A (typical)

Auxiliary Power No RAM Access (max.)
1.35A (worst case)
0.88A (typical)

Environmental Characteristics
Operating Temperature — 0°C to +55°C

Relative Humidity — to 90% (without condensation)

Reference Manual
143865-001 — iSBC 056B/012B Hardware Reference Manual (not supplied)

Manuals may be ordered from any Intel sales representative, distributor office, or from Intel Literature Dept., 3065 Bowers Avenue, Santa Clara, California 95051.

ORDERING INFORMATION

Part Number	Description
SBC 012B	512K-Byte RAM Board with Parity

iSBC® 012C
ECC RAM BOARD

- iSBC® 86, iSBC® 88 RAM expansion through direct, IEEE 796, MULTIBUS® interface
- 512K bytes of read/write memory
- Single bit error correction and double bit error detection via Intel® 8206 ECC device
- Control status register supports multiple ECC operating modes
- Error status register provides error logging by host CPU board
- Base address selectable on 16K byte boundaries
- Supports 8 or 16-bit transfer and 24-bit addressing
- Auxiliary power bus and memory protect logic for battery back-up RAM requirements

The iSBC® 012C RAM board is a member of Intel's complete line of iSBC memory and I/O Expansion boards. The board interfaces directly to any iSBC 88 or iSBC 86 Single Board Computer via the IEEE P796 MULTIBUS® interface to expand system RAM capacity. The iSBC 012C board contains 512K bytes of read/write memory implemented using dynamic RAM components.

Single bit error correction and double bit error detection are provided on the iSBC 012C board via the Intel 8206 Error Checking and Correction (ECC) device. Due to the on-board ECC features of the board it is ideally suited in applications where integrity of the stored data is critical, such as financial transactions, process control and medical equipment applications.

Refresh control of the RAM array is handled on-board by the RAM Array Control Logic. Therefore, no external refresh commands are necessary.

OCTOBER 1984
AFN-00348B

iSBC® 012C

FUNCTIONAL DESCRIPTION

General

The iSBC 012C RAM board is physically and electrically compatible with the MULTIBUS interface standard, IEEE P796, as outlined in the Intel MULTIBUS specification.

System Memory Size

Maximum system memory size with this board is 16 megabytes. On-board jumpers assign the board to one of four 4 megabyte pages. Each page is partitioned into 256 blocks of 16K bytes each. The smallest partition on the board is 16K bytes. Jumpers assign the base address (lowest 16K block) within the selected 4 megabyte page.

Error Checking and Correcting (ECC)

Error Checking and Correction is accomplished with the Intel 8206 Error Checking and Correction device. This ECC component in conjunction with the ECC check bit RAM array provides error detection and correction of single bit errors and detection only of double bit and most multiple bit errors. The ECC circuitry can be programmed to various modes to provide full diagnostic testing of both the storage and check bit RAM arrays.

ECC I/O Address Selection

The processor board communicates with the ECC circuitry via a single I/O port. This port is used for the Control Status Register (CSR) and the Error Status Register (ESR). The Control Status Register is programmed by the user to determine the mode of operation while the Error Status Register provides information about memory errors. The iSBC 012C RAM board is shipped with a Programmed Array Logic (PAL) device which allows selecting one of 9 possible addresses for the I/O port. The actual selection is done by jumper configuration. Additional unprogrammed locations are left in the PAL to allow application specific I/O addresses to be defined.

Battery Back-up/Memory Protect

An auxiliary power bus is provided to allow separate power to the RAM array for systems requiring backup of read/write memory. An active low TTL compatible memory protect signal is brought out on the auxiliary bus connector which, when asserted, disables read/write access to the RAM board. This input is provided for the protection of RAM contents during system power-down sequences.

ERROR CHECKING AND CORRECTION

The iSBC 012C RAM board uses two special registers to pass ECC mode control and status information to and from the system master iSBC board. These registers are called the Control Status Register (CSR) and the Error Status Register (ESR).

CONTROL STATUS REGISTER

There are six ECC modes of operation on the iSBC 012C RAM board. Each mode is obtained by software programming of the CSR from the master iSBC board. The six modes are:

a. Interrupt on any error mode
b. Interrupt on non-correctable error only mode
c. Correcting mode
d. Non-correcting mode
e. Diagnostic mode
f. Examine syndrome word mode

Modes (a) and (b) can be used in conjunction with (c) and (d). The six modes are described below.

Interrupt on Any Error Mode — In this mode the RAM board will interrupt the iSBC processor only when any error (single or multiple bit) is detected by the ECC circuitry.

Interrupt on Non-Correctable Error Mode — In this mode the RAM board will interrupt the iSBC processor only when a non-correctable (multiple bit) error is detected by the ECC circuitry. A multiple bit error is not correctable by the ECC circuitry.

Correcting Mode — In this mode the RAM board corrects any correctable error (single-bit error). Errors which are not correctable are not modified. Interrupts are generated depending on the interrupt mode selected.

Non-Correcting Mode — In this mode the RAM board does not correct any error. The ECC circuitry continues to check for errors, but no corrective action is taken. Interrupts continue as described previously.

Diagnostic Mode — This mode is used for testing the on-board ECC circuitry. In this mode the write enable strobe to the ECC RAM array is continuously disabled. The diagnostic mode can be used to simulate errors and in conjunction with the "Examine Syndrome Word Mode" examine the check bits generated by the ECC circuitry.

iSBC® 012C

Examine Syndrome Word Mode — This mode, in conjunction with the "Diagnostic Mode", is used for testing the ECC memory. In this mode, the syndrome bits/check bits are clocked into the Error Status Register (ESR) on every memory read/write cycle, respectively. The ESR translation PROM switches to a transparent mode in the Examine Syndrome Word Mode. This allows the actual syndrome word generated by the 8206 ECC device to be examined.

ERROR STATUS REGISTER

This 8-bit register contains information about memory errors. The ESR reflects the latest error occurance. Table 1 shows the status register format. Bits 5 & 6 show the failing row while bits 0 through 4 indicate which bit (of the 16-bit data word or the 6-bit ECC syndrome word) is in error. Bit 7 is always high.

Bit 6	Bit 5			Meaning	
0	0			Error in row	0
0	1				1
1	0				2
1	1				3

Bit 4	Bit 3	Bit 2	Bit 1	Bit 0	Meaning	
0	0	0	0	0	Error in data bit	0
0	0	0	0	1		1
0	0	0	1	0		2
0	0	0	1	1		3
0	0	1	0	0		4
0	0	1	0	1		5
0	0	1	1	0		6
0	0	1	1	1		7
0	1	0	0	0		8
0	1	0	0	1		9
0	1	0	1	0		10
0	1	0	1	1		11
0	1	1	0	0		12
0	1	1	0	1		13
0	1	1	1	0		14
0	1	1	1	1		15
1	0	0	0	0	Error in check bit	0
1	0	0	0	1		1
1	0	0	1	0		2
1	0	0	1	1		3
1	0	1	0	0		4
1	0	1	0	1		5
1	1	1	1	0	No Error	
1	1	1	1	1	Non-correctable (multiple-bit error)	

NOTE: Bit 7 is always high

Table 1.

SPECIFICATIONS

Word Size Supported
8 or 16-bits

Memory Size
524,288 Bytes (iSBC 012C)

Access Times (All Densities)
Read/Full Write — 350 ns (max)

Write Byte — 530 ns (max)

Cycle Times (All Densities)
Read/Full Write — 460 ns (max)

Write Byte — 885 ns (max)

NOTE: If an error is detected, read access time and cycle times are extended by 255 ns.

Refresh Times
Refresh Cycle Time — 15.6 μs

Refresh Delay Time — 760 ns

Memory Partitioning
Maximum System RAM size is 16M Bytes

PAGE ADDRESS (4M BYTES)
1 of 4 megabyte pages as follows: 0-4 megabytes; 4-8 megabytes; 8-12 megabytes; 12-16 megabytes

BLOCK ADDRESS (16K BYTES)
iSBC 012C RAM board — 32 contiguous 16K Byte Blocks (512K Bytes)

NOTE: Blocks cannot cross 4K Byte Boundary.

BASE ADDRESS
Any 16K Byte Boundary

Power Requirements
Voltage — 5VDC $\pm$ 5%

Current — iSBC 012C 6.8A max

Standby — iSBC 012C 2.5A max

iSBC® 012C

Environmental Requirements

Operating Temperature — 0°C to 55°C

Operating Humidity — To 90% without condensation

Physical Dimensions

Width — 12 inches (30.48 cm)

Height — 6.75 inches (17.15 cm)

Thickness — 0.50 inches (1.27 cm)

Weight — iSBC 012C 23.5 ounces (6589 gm)

Reference Manuals

145183-001 — iSBC 028C/iSBC 056C/iSBC 012C Hardware Reference Manual

Manuals may be ordered from any Intel Sales Representative, Distributor Office, or from the Intel Literature Department, 3065 Bowers Avenue, Santa Clara, CA 95051.

ORDERING INFORMATION

Part Number	Description
SBC 012C	512K Byte RAM board with ECC

iSBC® 012CX, 010CX, AND 020CX iLBX™ RAM BOARDS

- Dual port capability via MULTIBUS® and iLBX™ Interfaces
- Single bit error correction and double bit error detection utilizing Intel 8206 ECC device
- 512K byte, 1024K byte, and 2048K byte versions available
- Control status register supports multiple ECC operating modes
- Error status register provides error logging by host CPU board
- 16 megabyte addressing capability
- Supports 8- or 16-bit data transfer and 24-bit addressing
- Auxilliary power bus and memory protect logic for battery back-up RAM requirements

The ISBC® 012CX, iSBC 010CX, and iSBC 020CX RAM memory boards are members of Intel's complete line of iSBC memory and I/O expansion boards. Each board interfaces directly to any iSBC 80, iSBC 86, iSBC 186, and iSBC 286 Single Board Computers. The dual port feature of the CX series of RAM-boards allows access to the memory of both the MULTIBUS® and iLBX™ bus interfaces.

In addition to the dual port features the "CX" series of RAM-boards provide Error Checking and Corrections Circuitry (ECC) which can detect and correct single bit errors and detect, but not correct, double and most multiple bit errors.

The iSBC 012CX board contains 512K bytes of read/write memory using 64K dynamic RAM components. The iSBC 010 CX and iSBC 020 CX boards contain 1024K and 2048K bytes of read/write memory using 256K dynamic RAM components.

Due to the iLBX dual port capability and on-board ECC features of the boards they are ideally suited in applications where memory performance and integrity is critical, such as financial transactions, process control and medical equipment applications.

The following are trademarks of Intel Corporation and may be used only to describe Intel products: Intel, ICE, iMMX, iRMX, iSBC, iSBX, iSXM, MULTIBUS, Multichannel and MULTIMODULE. Intel Corporation assumes no responsibility for the use of any circuitry other than circuitry embodied in an Intel product. No other circuit patent licenses are implied. Information contained herein supercedes previously published specifications on these devices from Intel.

© INTEL CORPORATION, 1983

iSBC® 012CX, 010CX, AND 020CX

FUNCTIONAL DESCRIPTION

General

The iSBC 012CX, 010CX, and 020CX RAM boards are physically and electrically compatible with the MULTIBUS interface standard, IEEE-796, as outlined in the Intel MULTIBUS specification. In addition the CX series of RAM-boards are physically and electrically compatible with the iLBX bus (Local Bus Extension) interface as outlined in the Intel iLBX Specification (see Figure 1).

Dual Port Capabilities

The "CX" series of RAM-boards can be accessed by either the MULTIBUS interface or the iLBX interface (see Figure 2). Intel's iLBX interface is an unarbitrated bus architecture which allows direct transfer of data between the CPU and the memory boards without ac-

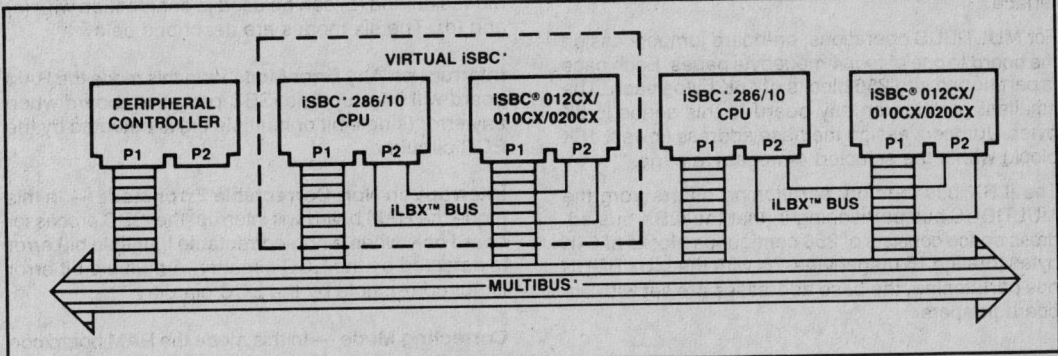

Figure 1. Typical iLBX™ System Configuration

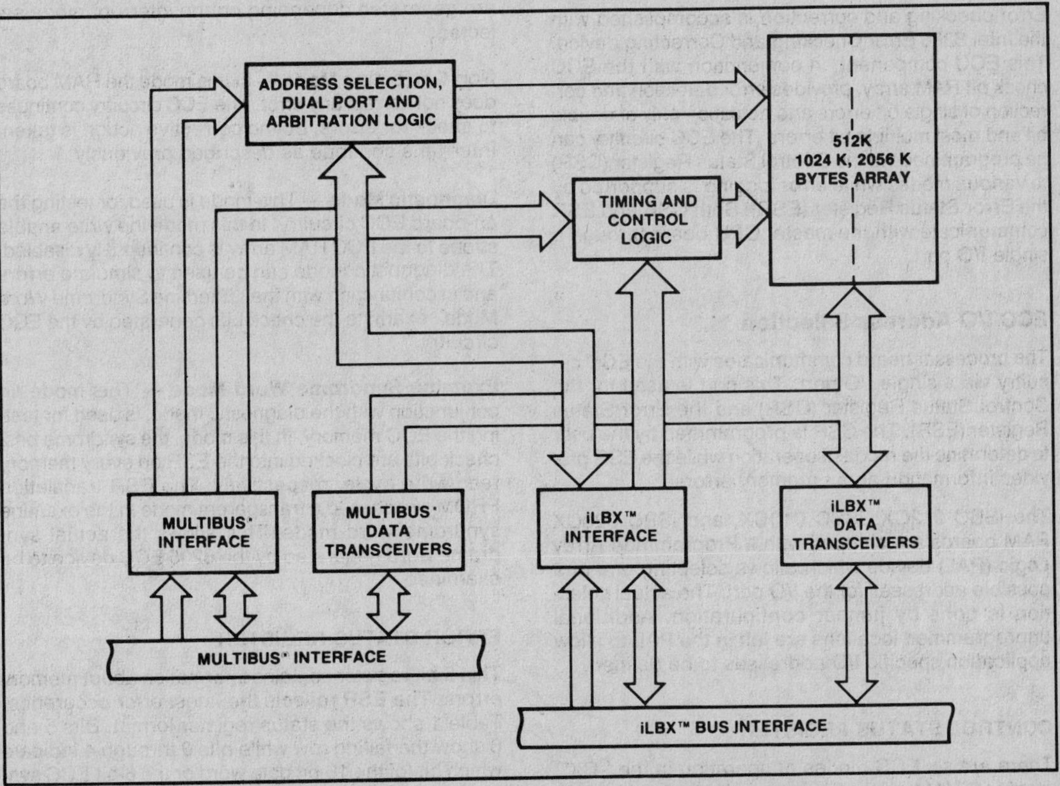

Figure 2. iSBC® 012CX/010CX/020CX Block Diagram

4-17

231023-002

iSBC® 012CX, 010CX, AND 020CX

cessing the MULTIBUS bus. Due to the unarbitrated nature of the iLBX interface significant improvements in memory access times result, typically a 2-6 Wait State improvement over MULTIBUS memory access.

System Memory Size

Maximum system memory size with this series of boards is 16 megabytes. Memory partitioning is independent for the MULTIBUS interface and the iLBX interface.

For MULTIBUS operations, on-board jumpers assign the board to one of four 4-megabyte pages. Each page is partitioned into 256 blocks of 16K bytes each. The smallest partition on any board in this series is 8K bytes. Jumpers assign the base address (lowest 16K block) within the selected 4-megabyte page.

The iLBX bus memory partitioning differs from the MULTIBUS bus partitioning in that the iLBX bus address space consists of 256 contiguous blocks of 64K bytes totaling 16 megabytes. As with the MULTIBUS bus partitioning, the base addresses are set with on-board jumpers.

Error Checking and Correcting (ECC)

Error checking and correction is accomplished with the Intel 8206 Error Checking and Correcting device. This ECC component, in conjunction with the ECC check bit RAM array, provides error detection and correction of single bit errors and detection only of double bit and most multiple bit errors. The ECC circuitry can be programmed via the Control Status Register (CSR) to various modes while error logging is supported by the Error Status Register (ESR). Both CSR and ESR communicate with the master CPU board through a single I/O port.

ECC I/O Address Selection

The processor board communicates with the ECC circuitry via a single I/O port. This port is used for the Control Status Register (CSR) and the Error Status Register (ESR). The CSR is programmed by the user to determine the mode of operation while the ESR provides information about memory errors.

The iSBC 012CX, iSBC 010CX, and iSBC 020CX RAM boards are shipped with a Programmed Array Logic (PAL) device which allows selecting one of 9 possible addresses for the I/O port. The actual selection is done by jumper configuration. Additional unprogrammed locations are left in the PAL to allow application specific I/O addresses to be defined.

CONTROL STATUS REGISTER

There are six ECC modes of operation in the "CX" family of RAM boards. Each mode is obtained by software programming of the CSR from the master iSBC board. The six modes are:

a. Interrupt on any error mode
b. Interrupt on non-correctable error only mode
c. Correcting mode
d. Non-correcting mode
e. Diagnostic mode
f. Examine syndrome word mode

Modes (a) and (b) can be used in conjunction with (c) and (d). The six modes are described below.

Interrupt on Any Error Mode — In this mode the RAM board will interrupt the iSBC processor board when any error (single bit or multiple bit) is detected by the ECC circuitry.

Interrupt on Non-Correctable Error Mode — In this mode the RAM board will interrupt the iSBC processor board only when a non-correctable (multiple bit) error is detected by the ECC circuitry. A multiple bit error is not correctable by the ECC circuitry.

Correcting Mode — In this mode the RAM board corrects any correctable error (single bit error). Errors which are not correctable are not modified. Interrupts are generated depending on the interrupt mode selected.

Non-Correcting Mode — In this mode the RAM board does not correct any error. The ECC circuitry continues to check for errors, but no corrective action is taken. Interrupts continue as described previously.

Diagnostic Mode — This mode is used for testing the on-board ECC circuitry. In this mode the write enable strobe to the ECC RAM array is continuously disabled. The diagnostic mode can be used to simulate errors and in conjunction with the "Examine Syndrome Word Mode" examine the check bits generated by the ECC circuitry.

Examine Syndrome Word Mode — This mode, in conjunction with the diagnostic mode, is used for testing the ECC memory. In this mode, the syndrome bits/check bits are clocked into the ESR on every memory read/write cycle, respectively. The ESR translation PROM switches to a transparent mode in the examine syndrome word mode. This allows the actual syndrome word generated by the 8206 ECC device to be examined.

ERROR STATUS REGISTER

This 8-bit register contains information about memory errors. The ESR reflects the latest error occurence. Table 1 shows the status register format. Bits 5 and 6 show the failing row while bits 0 through 4 indicate which bit (of the 16-bit data word or the 6-bit ECC syndrome) is in error. Bit 7 is always high.

iSBC® 012CX, 010CX, AND 020CX

Table 1. Error Status Register Format

Bit 6	Bit 5	Bit 4	Bit 3	Bit 2	Bit 1	Bit 0	Meaning	
0	0						Error in row	0
0	1							1
1	0							2
1	1							3
		0	0	0	0	0	Error in data bit	0
		0	0	0	0	1		1
		0	0	0	1	0		2
		0	0	0	1	1		3
		0	0	1	0	0		4
		0	0	1	0	1		5
		0	0	1	1	0		6
		0	0	1	1	1		7
		0	1	0	0	0		8
		0	1	0	0	1		9
		0	1	0	1	0	Error in data bit	10
		0	1	0	1	1		11
		0	1	1	0	0		12
		0	1	1	0	1		13
		0	1	1	1	0		14
		0	1	1	1	1		15
		1	0	0	0	0	Error in check bit	0
		1	0	0	0	1		1
		1	0	0	1	0		2
		1	0	0	1	1		3
		1	0	1	0	0		4
		1	0	1	0	1		5
		1	1	1	1	0	No Error	
		1	1	1	1	1	Non-correctable (multiple-bit error)	

Battery Back-up/Memory Protect

An auxillary power bus is provided to allow separate power to the RAM array for systems requiring backup of read/write memory. An active low TTL compatible memory protect signal is brought out on the auxillary bus connector which, when asserted, disables read/write access to the RAM board. This input is provided for the protection of RAM contents during system power-down sequences.

SPECIFICATIONS

Word Size Supported

8- or 16-bits

Memory Size

524,288 bytes (iSBC 012CX board)
1,048,576 bytes (iSBC 010CX board)
2,097,152 bytes (iSBC 020CX board)

Access Times (All densities)

MULTIBUS® System Bus

Read/Full Write — 380 ns (max)
Write Byte — 530 ns (max)

iLBX™ Local Bus

Read/Full Write — 340 ns (max)
Write Byte — 440 ns (max)

Cycle Times (All densities)

MULTIBUS® System Bus

Read/Full Write — 490 ns (max)
Write Byte — 885 ns (max)

iLBX™ Local Bus

Read/Full Write — 375 ns
Write Byte — 740 ns

NOTE: If an error is detected, read access time and cycle times are extended to 255 ns (max)

Memory Partitioning

Maximum System memory size is 16M Bytes for both MULTIBUS and iLBX BUS. MULTIBUS partitioning is by Page, Block and Base, while the iLBX BUS is by Block and Base only.

Page Address

MULTIBUS® — 0-4 megabytes; 4-8 megabytes, 8-12 megabytes; 12-16 megabytes

iLBX™ BUS — N/A

Base Address

MULTIBUS® System Bus — Any 16K byte boundary within the 4M-byte page.

iLBX™ Local Bus — Any 64K byte boundary selectable on board boundaries to 8M-bytes and some 64K-byte boundaries in the first megabyte. Others available if PAL programming is changed.

iSBC® 012CX, 010CX AND 020CX

Power Requirements

Voltage — 5 VDC ± 5%

Product	Current	Standby (Battery Back-up)
iSBC® 012CX Board	4.4A (typ.) 6.8A (max.)	2.2A (typ.) 2.4A (max.)
iSBC® 010CX Board	4.8A (typ.) 7.0A (max.)	2.1A (typ.) 2.3A (max.)
iSBC® 020CX Board	5.3A (typ.) 7.5A (max.)	2.2A (typ.) 2.4A (max.)

Environmental Requirements

Operating Temperature — 0°C to 55°C airflow of 200 linear feet per minute

Operating Humidity — To 90% without condensation

Physical Dimensions

Width — 30.48 cm (12 inches)

Height — 17.15 cm (6.75 inches)

Thickness — 1.27 cm (0.50 inches)

Weight—iSBC 012CX board: 6589 gm (23.5 ounces); iSBC 010CX board: 5329 gm (19.0 ounces); iSBC 020CX board: 6589 gm (23.5 ounces)

Reference Manuals

145158-003 — iSBC® 028CX/iSBC® 056CX/iSBC® 012CX Hardware Reference Manual

144456-001 — Intel iLBX™ 010CX, 020CX Specification

9800683-03 — Intel MULTIBUS® Specification

Manuals may be ordered from any Intel Sales Representative, Distributor Office or from the Intel Literature Department, 3065 Bowers Avenue, Santa Clara, CA. 95051

ORDERING INFORMATION

Part Number	Description
iSBC® 012CX	512K byte RAM board with ECC and iLBX™ Connectors
iSBC® 010CX	1M byte RAM board with ECC and iLBX™ Connectors
iSBC® 020CX	2M byte RAM board with ECC and iLBX™ Connectors

iSBC® 012EX, 010EX, 020EX, and 040EX High Performance RAM Boards

- **0 Wait States at 8 MHz performance with the iSBC® 286/10A, iSBC 286/12 board**
- **Dual port capability via MULTIBUS® and high speed synchronous interface**
- **Configurable to function over iLBX™ bus**
- **On-board parity generator/checker**
- **Independently selectable starting and ending addresses**
- **16 Megabyte addressing capability**
- **512K Byte, 1024K Byte, 2048K Byte, and 4096K Byte densities available**

The iSBC 012EX, iSBC 010EX, iSBC 020EX, and iSBC 040EX RAM memory boards are members of Intel's complete line of iSBC memory and I/O expansion boards. The EX boards are dual ported between the MULTIBUS interface and one of two types of dedicated memory buses. The dedicated buses are the iLBX bus and a high speed interface. The EX series of RAM-boards can be configured to be accessed over the iLBX bus, as well as MULTIBUS bus, to provide memory support for the iSBC 286/10 board, performing at 6 MHz and the iSBC 186/03A board, performing at 8 MHz. The EX boards are default configured to run over the MULTIBUS interface and the high speed interface. This provides 0 wait state 8 MHz memory support for the iSBC 286/10A and iSBC 286/12 boards.

The EX RAM-boards generate byte oriented parity during all write operations and perform parity checking during all read operations. An on-board LED provides a visual indication that a parity error has occured.

The iSBC 012EX, iSBC 010EX, iSBC 020EX, and iSBC 040EX boards contain 512K bytes, 1M byte, 2M bytes, and 4M bytes of read/write memory using 256K dynamic RAM components.

Due to the high speed synchronous interface capability of the boards, they are ideally suited in applications where memory performance is critical.

Intel Corporation assumes no responsibility for the use of any circuitry other than circuitry embodied in an Intel product. No other circuit patent licenses are implied. Information contained herein supersedes previously published specifications on these devices from Intel.

© Intel Corporation, 1985

iSBC® 012EX 010EX 020EX 040EX Board

FUNCTIONAL DESCRIPTION

General

The iSBC 012EX, 010EX, 020EX, and 040EX RAM boards are physically and electrically compatible with the MULTIBUS interface standard, IEEE-796, as outlined in the Intel MULTIBUS architecture specification.

Dual Port Capabilities

The "EX" series of RAM-Boards can be accessed by the MULTIBUS interface, and either the iLBX Bus, or the high speed synchronous interface (see figures 1 and 2). The EX series require jumper and PAL configuration to be accessed over iLBX Bus.

Intel's iLBX interface is an unarbitrated bus architecture which allows direct transfer of data between the CPU and the memory boards without accessing the MULTIBUS bus. Due to the unarbitrated nature of the iLBX interface, significant improvements in memory access times compared to the MULTIBUS bus accesses result. The EX Boards provide 1 wait state performance at 6 MHz and 2 wait states at 8 MHz over the iLBX board. The EX Memory Board Hardware Reference Manual should be consulted for details.

The high speed synchronous interface, like the iLBX Bus, is a bus architecture which allows direct transfer of data between the CPU and the memory boards without accessing the MULTIBUS bus. This high speed interface runs synchronously with the iSBC 286/10A and iSBC 286/12 to provide 0 wait state performance at 8 MHz.

System Memory Size

Maximum system memory size with this series of boards is 16 megabytes. Memory partitioning is independent for the MULTIBUS interface and the iLBX interface.

Address Selection/Memory

SELECTABLE STARTING ADDRESS

A 256K boundary select is implemented on the iSBC 012EX board. A 512K boundary select is implemented on the iSBC 010EX board. A 1M boundary is implemented on the iSBC 020EX and iSBC 040EX boards.

SELECTABLE ENDING ADDRESS

The ending address is selectable as memory size minus select options of 0, 128K, 256K, or 512K on all of the EX boards.

PARITY INTERRUPT CLEAR

The I/O address of the Parity Interrupt Clear circuitry is jumperable to any one of 256 addresses.

SPECIFICATIONS

Word Size Supported

8- or 16-bits

Memory Size

524,288 bytes (iSBC 012EX board)
1,048,576 bytes (iSBC 010EX board)
2,097,152 bytes (iSBC 020EX board)
4,194,304 bytes (iSBC 040EX board)

Access Times (All densities)

MULTIBUS® SYSTEM BUS

Read/Full Write — 375 ns (max)
Write Byte — 375 ns (max)

HIGH SPEED SYNCHRONOUS INTERFACE

Read/Full Write — 167 ns (max)
Write Byte — 132 ns (max)

iLBX™ BUS

Read/Full Write — 295 ns (max)
Write Byte — 116 ns (max)

Cycle Times (All densities)

MULTIBUS® SYSTEM BUS

Read/Full Write — 625 ns (max)
Write Byte — 625 ns (max)

HIGH SPEED SYNCHRONOUS INTERFACE

Read/Full Write — 250 ns (max)
Write Byte — 250 ns (max)

iLBX™ BUS

Read/Full Write — 437.5 ns (max)
Write Byte — 437.5 ns (max)

iSBC® 012EX 010EX 020EX 040EX Board

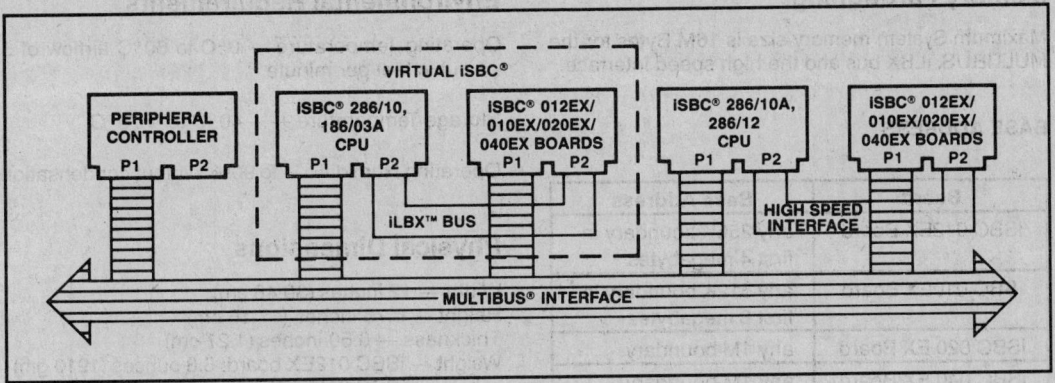

Figure 1. Typical iLBX™ System Configuration

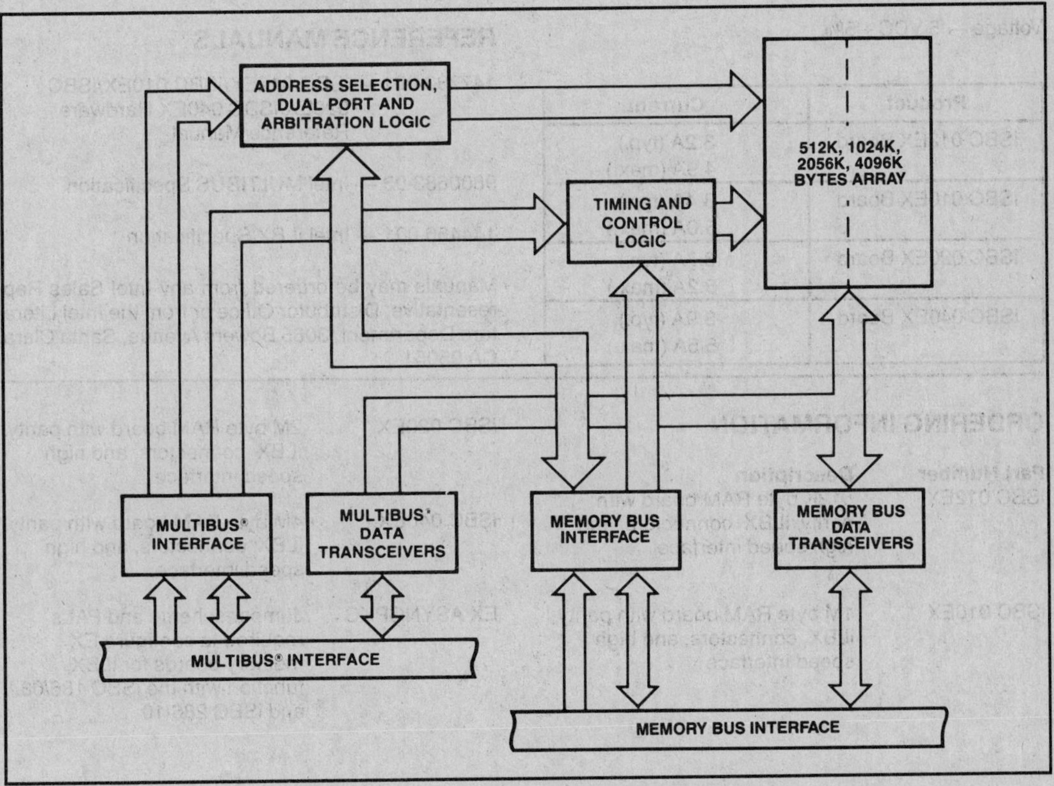

Figure 2. iSBC® EX Memory Board Block Diagram

iSBC® 012EX 010EX 020EX 040EX Board

Memory Partitioning

Maximum System memory size is 16M Bytes for the MULTIBUS, iLBX bus and the high speed interface.

BASE ADDRESS

Board	Base Address
iSBC 012EX Board	any 256K boundary in first 4 megabytes
iSBC 010EX Board	any 512K boundary in first 8 megabytes
iSBC 020 EX Board	any 1M boundary
iSBC 040 EX Board	any 1M boundary

Power Requirements

Voltage — 5 VDC ± 5%

Product	Current
iSBC 012EX Board	3.2A (typ.) 4.9A (max.)
iSBC 010EX Board	3.4A (typ.) 5.0A (max.)
iSBC 020EX Board	3.7A (typ.) 5.2A (max.)
iSBC 040EX Board	3.9A (typ.) 5.5A (max.)

Environmental Requirements

Operating Temperature — 0°C to 60°C airflow of 5 cubic feet per minute

Storage Temperature — −40°C to +75°C

Operating Humidity — To 90% without condensation

Physical Dimensions

Width — 12 inches (30.48 cm)
Height — 6.75 inches (17.15 cm)
Thickness — 0.50 inches (1.27 cm)
Weight — iSBC 012EX board: 6.8 ounces (1910 gm)
   iSBC 010EX board: 9.0 ounces (2550 gm)
   iSBC 020EX board: 13.5 ounces (3830 gm)
   iSBC 040EX board: 18.0 ounces (5100 gm)

REFERENCE MANUALS

147783-001 — iSBC 012EX/iSBC 010EX/iSBC 020EX/iSBC 040EX Hardware Reference Manual

9800683-03 — Intel MULTIBUS Specification

144456-001 — Intel iLBX Specification

Manuals may be ordered from any Intel Sales Representative, Distributor Office or from the Intel Literature Department, 3065 Bowers Avenue, Santa Clara, CA 95051

ORDERING INFORMATION

Part Number	Description
iSBC 012EX	512K byte RAM board with parity, iLBX connectors, and high speed interface
iSBC 010EX	1M byte RAM board with parity, iLBX connectors, and high speed interface
iSBC 020EX	2M byte RAM board with parity, iLBX connectors, and high speed interface
iSBC 040EX	4M byte RAM board with parity, iLBX connectors, and high speed interface
EX ASYNCPKG	Jumper scheme and PAL's required to configure EX memory boards for iLBX function with the iSBC 186/03A and iSBC 286/10

iSBC® 028A/056A
RAM MEMORY BOARDS

- iSBC®86, iSBC®88 and iSBC®80 board RAM expansion through direct MULTIBUS® interface
- 128K or 256K bytes of read/write memory
- On-board parity generator/checker and error status register
- Requires a single +5 volt power supply
- Assignable anywhere within a 16 megabyte address space
- Jumper selectable base address on any 4K byte boundary
- Auxiliary power bus and memory protect control logic for battery backup RAM requirements

The iSBC® 028A and iSBC 056A RAM memory boards are members of Intel's complete line of iSBC memory and I/O expansion boards. Each board interfaces directly to any iSBC 80, iSBC 88 or iSBC 86 Single Board Computer via the MULTIBUS® interface to expand system RAM capacity. The iSBC 028A and iSBC 056A boards contain 128K, or 256K bytes of read/write memory implemented using dynamic RAM components. An on-board LSI dynamic RAM controller refreshes a portion of these components every 14 microseconds. Each refresh cycle utilizes memory for 480 nanoseconds (maximum).

The iSBC 028A and iSBC 056A boards generate byte oriented parity during all write operations and perform parity checking during all read operations. When a parity error is detected, these boards can generate an interrupt on the MULTIBUS interface. In addition, the row and bank of the RAM array containing the error are stored in a Parity Flag Register (see Figure 1). This register is accessible as a MULTIBUS I/O port. An on-board LED also provides a visual indication that a parity error has occurred. To facilitate testing of these boards, parity generation and checking can be changed from even to odd under software control.

The following are trademarks of Intel Corporation and may be used only to describe Intel products: CREDIT, Index, Insite, Intellec, Library Manager, Megachassis, Micromap, MULTIBUS, PROMPT, UPI, μScope, Promware, MCS, ICE, iRMX, iSBC, iSBX, MULTIMODULE, ICS, iAPX and iMMX. Intel Corporation assumes no responsibility for the use of any circuitry other than circuitry embodied in an Intel product. No other circuit patent licenses are implied.

© INTEL CORPORATION, 1981

OCTOBER 1984
ORDER NUMBER: 143877-002

iSBC® 032A/064A/028A/056A

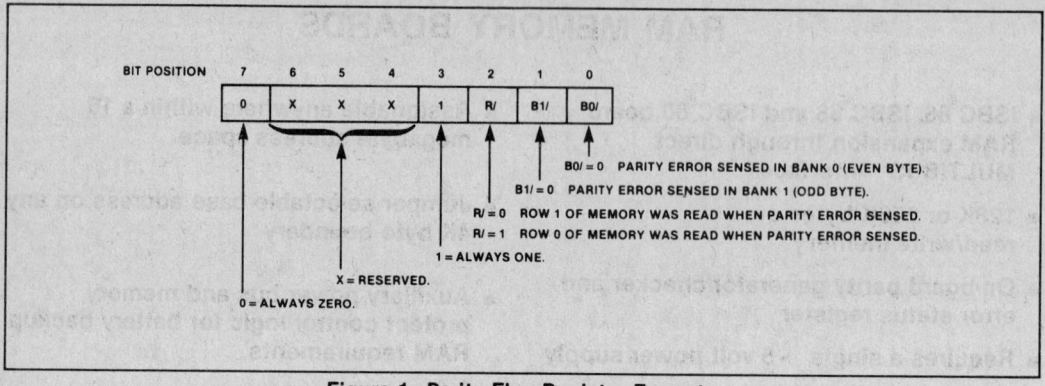

Figure 1. Parity Flag Register Format

SPECIFICATIONS

Word Size
8 bits and 16 bits

Memory Size
131,072 bytes (iSBC 028A); or 262,144 bytes (iSBC 056A)

Access Time

iSBC 028A
  500 ns max. (worst case)
  460 ns max. (typical)

iSBC 056A
  570 ns max. (worst case)
  530 ns max. (typical)

Cycle Times (Worst Case)

Read
  iSBC 028A — 600 ns max.
  iSBC 056A — 650 ns max.

Write
  iSBC 028A — 600 ns max.
  iSBC 056A — 650 ns max.

Refresh
  iSBC 028A — 480 ns max.
  iSBC 056A — 600 ns max.

Interface
All address, data and command signals are TTL compatible.

Address Selection

Memory — Base address is jumper selectable on any 4K byte boundary in a 16 megabyte address space. On-board RAM cannot cross a megabyte address boundary.

Parity Flag Register — The I/O address of the Parity Flag Register is jumper selectable to be between 00H to 0FH or 40H to 4FH.

Connector

Edge connector — 86 pin double-sided PC edge connector with 0.156 in. contact centers.

Mating connector — Viking 3KH43/9AMK12 or equivalent.

Auxiliary Power

An auxiliary power bus is provided to allow separate power to RAM array for systems requiring battery backup of read/write memory. Selection of this auxiliary RAM power bus is made via jumpers on the board.

Memory Protect

An active-low TTL compatible memory protect signal is brought out on the auxiliary connector which, when asserted, disables read/write access to RAM on the board. This input is provided for the protection of RAM contents during system power-down sequences.

4-26   143877-002

iSBC® 032A/064A/028A/056A

Physical Characteristics

Width — 12.00 in. (30.48 cm)
Height — 6.75 in. (17.15 cm)
Depth — 0.50 in. (1.27 cm)
Weight — 14 oz. (397 gm)

Electrical Characteristics

D.C. POWER REQUIREMENTS

All configurations require only +5 volts ±5%.

Normal System Operation (max.)
iSBC 028A/056A — 4.57A (worst case)
3.66A (typical)

Auxiliary Power No RAM Access (max.)
iSBC 028A/056A — 0.55A (worst case)
0.45A (typical)

Environmental Characteristics

Operating Temperature — 0°C to +55°C
Relative Humidity — to 90% (without condensation)

Reference Manual

143572-001 — iSBC 032A/064A/028A/056A Hardware Reference Manual (not supplied)

Manuals may be ordered from any Intel sales representative, distributor office, or from Intel Literature Dept., 3065 Bowers Avenue, Santa Clara, California 95051.

ORDERING INFORMATION

Part Number Description

SBC 028A   128K-Byte RAM Board with Parity
SBC 056A   256K-Byte RAM Board with Parity

iSBC® 254S
BUBBLE MEMORY BOARD

- 0-60°C Operating Temperature
- Capacity up to 512K Bytes of Bubble Memory Storage
- Automatic Error Correction Capability
- Operates from Standard +5V and +12V Power Supplies
- High-Density Storage
- DMA Capability
- Non-Volatile Storage
- High Reliability Even Under Harsh and Rugged Environments
- Average Access Time of 48ms
- Burst Data Rate up to 200K Bytes per Second
- Software Compatible with the iRMX™ Operating System
- Powerfail Data Protection

The iSBC 254S board is a completely assembled and tested non-volatile read/write memory utilizing the Intel 7110 one-megabit bubble memory. This board is offered with one, two, or four 7110 bubble memories, thus yielding capacities of 128K, 256K, or 512K bytes.

Software support is provided under both iRMX/80 and iRMX/86 operating systems, and DMA capability provides the user with considerable flexibility and control. Because of the solid-state nature of this technology, the iSBC 254S board is ideally suited for applications in harsh or rugged environments.

The iSBC 254S board is compatible with 16-bit addressing for 8-bit processors and with 20-bit addressing for 16-bit processors.

The following are trademarks of Intel Corporation and its affiliates and may be used only to identify Intel products: i, Int₉l, INTEL, INTELLEC, MCS, i_m, iCS, ICE, UPI, BXP, iSBC, iSBX, INSITE, iRMX, CREDIT, RMX/80, μScope, Multibus, PROMPT, Promware, Megachassis, Library Manager, MAIN MULTIMODULE, and the combination of MCS, ICE, SBC, RMX, or iCS and a numerical suffix; e.g., iSBC-80.

© INTEL CORPORATION, 1983.

iSBC® 254S BOARD

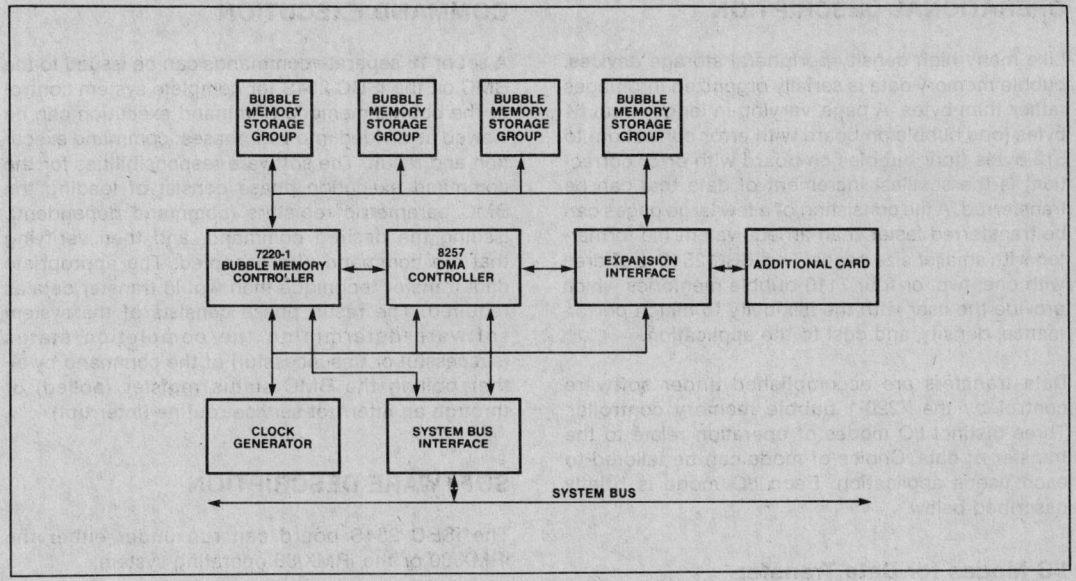

Figure 1. iSBC® 254S Board, Block Diagram

SPECIFICATIONS

Memory Size

128K, 256K, or 512K bytes

Interface

All address, data, and control signals are TTL-compatible and Intel MULTIBUS® system compatible.

Performance

Maximum Data Rate: 200K bytes/second
Average Access Time: 48ms
Power Supply Requirements

Voltage	Tolerance	Power Off/Power Fail Decay Rate	Max. Current
+12 Volts	±5%	less than 1.10 volts/msec	1.4A
+5 Volts	±5%	less than 0.45 volts/msec	3.0A

Electrical Characteristics

D.C. Power, supplied through MULTIBUS® connector

- Voltage sequencing—no restrictions
- Power on voltage rate of rise—no restrictions
- The power supply requirements shown are based on the recommended power fail circuitry.

Connector

86-pin double-sided PC edge connector with 0.40 cm (0.156 in.) contact centers.
Mating Connector: Control Data VFB01E43D0A1 or Viking 2VH43/1ANE5.

Physical Characteristics

Length: 30.48 cm (12 in.)
Height: 17.15 cm (6.75 in.)
Depth: 1.57 cm (0.62 in.)

Note: Because of its depth, the iSBC 254S board requires two card slots in standard MULTIBUS card frame.

Environment

Board Ambient Operating Temperature: 0° to 60°C
Non-Volatile Storage Temperature: −20° to 75°C

Additional Documentation

iSBC 254S Reference Manual (Order No. 113844)
INTEL MULTIBUS Specification (Order No. 9800683)
Memory Components Handbook (Order No. 210830)

iSBC® 254S BOARD

OPERATIONAL DESCRIPTION

Like many high density peripheral storage devices, bubble memory data is serially organized into pages rather than bytes. A page, varying in length from 64 bytes (one bubble on board with error correction) to 512 bytes (four bubbles on board with error correction) is the smallest increment of data that can be transferred. A file consisting of a few large pages can be transferred faster than an equivalent file formatted with smaller size pages. The iSBC 254S is offered with one, two, or four 7110 bubble memories which provide the user with the flexibility to match performance, density, and cost to the application.

Data transfers are accomplished under software control by the 7220-1 bubble memory controller. Three distinct I/O modes of operation relate to the transfer of data. Choice of mode can be tailored to each user's application. Each I/O mode is briefly described below.

I/O Modes for Data Transfer

DMA (Direct Memory Access) I/O Mode is the highest performance mode of data transfer. An on-board INTEL 7220-1 Bubble Memory Controller (BMC) and INTEL 8257 DMA controller work in conjunction to generate the MULTIBUS handshake protocol signals. Once a data block transfer begins in this mode, CPU involvement is not required until the entire transfer is completed. This frees the CPU to perform other tasks during DMA transfers. A single data block transfer can be up to 16K bytes in length.

Interrupt I/O Mode requires moderate CPU involvement for data transfers. The BMC generates an onboard interrupt signal when the BMC FIFO (First In-First Out) buffer is either half full (bubble read operation) or half empty (bubble write operation). The interrupt signal is translated to MULTIBUS interrupt line via a jumper. Using this interrupt-driven scheme, software is responsible for performing the appropriate transfer of data (typically 22 bytes) to or from the FIFO buffer when the interrupt occurs.

Polled I/O Mode is the most simple. However, it is also the most demanding of CPU time. System software must determine when to transfer data to or from the FIFO by continually polling a status bit in the BMC status register. The status bit indicates presence or absence of data in the FIFO on a byte-by-byte basis.

COMMAND EXECUTION

A set of 16 separate commands can be issued to the BMC on the iSBC 254S for complete system control of the bubble memory. Command execution can be viewed as divided into two phases: command execution and result. The software responsibilities for the command execution phase consist of loading the BMC parametric registers (command dependent), issuing the desired command, and then verifying that the command was accepted. The appropriate data transfer technique then would transfer data as required. The result phase consists of the system software determining the completion status (successful or unsuccessful) of the command by either polling the BMC status register (polled) or through an interrupt service routine (interrupt).

SOFTWARE DESCRIPTION

The iSBC 254S board can run under either the iRMX/80 or the iRMX/86 operating system.

Under the iRMX/80 operating system a set of two iRMX/80 software tasks perform data transfers. Bubble I/O (BUBIO) provides the interface routines for data storage and retrieval. A second task, the Bubble Manager (BMGR) keeps track of free or available space on the bubble memory device. BMGR operates very similar to the iRMX/80 free space manager by allocating portions of bubble memory space at the request of a user task. BUBIO can be configured to run independent of BMGR.

Under the iRMX/80 operating system, the iSBC 254S board is supported as an integral part of the I/O System Software. The iRMX 86 I/O System Software is implemented as a set of file drivers to support particular types of files and device drivers to provide support to particular devices (i.e., the iSBC 254S Board). Each type of file has its own file driver and each device has its own device driver. This provides great flexibility and device independence since application tasks communicate with file drivers, not with device drivers.

Bubble memory drivers are included in the standard iRMX/86 and iRMX/88 package. Bubble memory drivers for iRMX 80 are available through Insite™ —INTEL's Software Index and Technology Exchange Library.

PRELIMINARY

iSBC® 264 MAGNETIC BUBBLE MEMORY BOARD

- Up to 2-Megabytes of Non-Volatile Bubble Memory Storage
- Automatic Error Detection and Correction
- Operates from a Standard +5 Vdc Power Supply
- Polled, Interrupt, or DMA Data Transfer Capability
- 128-Byte FIFO Provides Full Page Buffering
- 0–60°C Operating Range
- High Reliability Memory in Harsh and Rugged Environments
- Average Access Time of 88 ms
- Maximum Burst Data Rate of 25K–100K Bytes per Second
- Automatic On-Board Power-Fail Data Protection
- IEEE 796 MULTIBUS® I Interface (with ACLO on P2 Connector)
- Optional iRMX Device Drivers Available

The iSBC 264 is a completely assembled and tested non-volatile memory board utilizing Intel 7114 4-Megabit magnetic bubble memory. The board is available with one, two, or four 7114 devices, yielding storage densities of 512K bytes, 1-Megabyte, and 2-Megabytes, respectively.

Direct Memory Access (DMA) capability provides software flexibility and reduces CPU overhead. The non-volatile nature and reliability of bubble memory technology makes the iSBC 264 ideally suited for applications in harsh or rugged environments.

The iSBC 264 supports 8-bit and 16-bit I/O addressing and 20-bit or 24-bit memory addressing. This makes the iSBC 264 board compatible with standard microprocessors that use the MULTIBUS I system bus interface. Figure 1 shows a block diagram of the board in a system environment.

290096-1

Intel Corporation assumes no responsibility for the use of any circuitry other than circuitry embodied in an Intel product. No other circuit patent licenses are implied. Information contained herein supersedes previously published specifications on these devices from Intel. **August 1985**
© Intel Corporation, 1985   Order Number: 290096-001

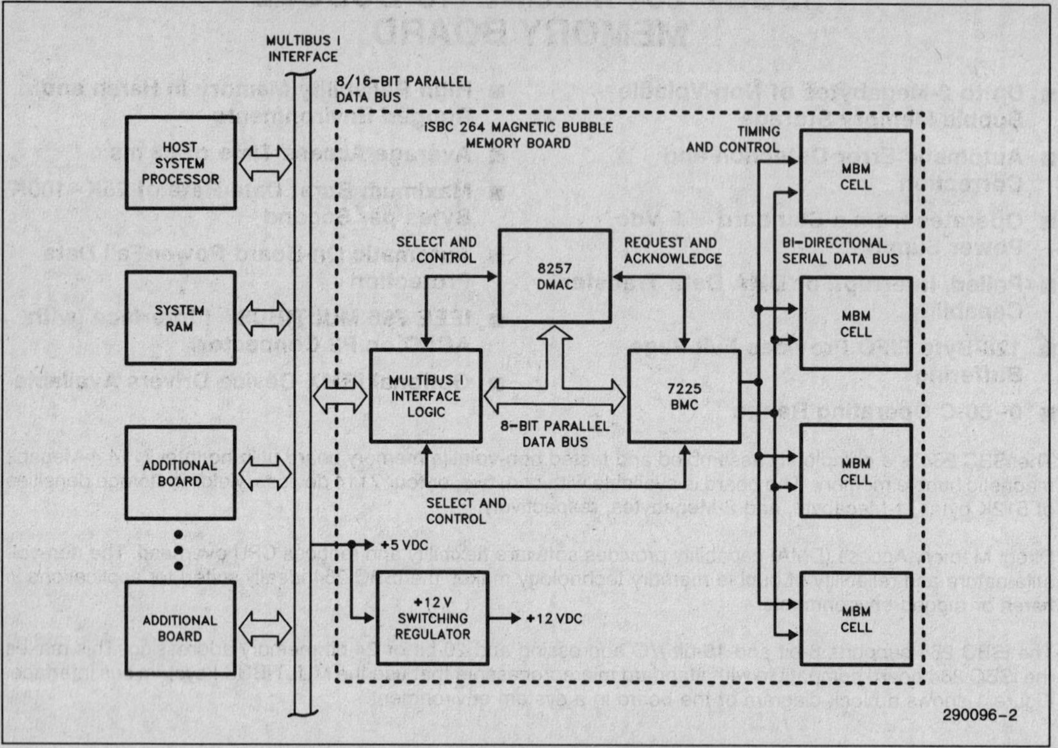

iSBC® 264

PRELIMINARY

Figure 1. iSBC® 264 Board in a System Environment

FUNCTIONAL DESCRIPTION

Like many high-density peripheral devices, bubble memory data is accessed serially as pages of data rather than as individually addressed bytes. A page of data (64, 128, or 256 bytes per page) is the smallest increment of data that can be transferred. Since large pages are transferred in the same time frame as small pages, the overall data rate for large pages is faster than for small pages. Large page sizes assume two or four bubble memory devices operating in parallel (two bubbles in parallel for 128 bytes per page, four bubbles in parallel for 256 bytes per page). The average access time for sequential pages is also much faster than for randomly accessed pages. The iSBC 264 board is available in three densities: 512K bytes (one 7114), 1-Megabyte (two 7114s), and 2-Megabytes (four 7114s).

Data transfers between system memory and the 7114 devices are performed under control of the host CPU and the on-board 7225 BMC (Bubble Memory Controller). An on-board 8257 DMAC (Direct Memory Access Controller) can be programmed to perform the transfers in order to reduce CPU overhead. The iSBC 264 board supports three data transfer modes and two command execution modes.

Data Transfer Modes

DMA mode is the highest performance data transfer mode. In DMA mode, an on-board 8257 DMAC works together with the 7225 BMC to transfer data between the 128-byte BMC FIFO and system memory at high speeds with low CPU overhead. Once a DMA operation is initiated, the CPU may execute other tasks until the transfer completes. An on-board bus controller generates the required MULTIBUS I interface bus handshake signals. The iSBC 264 board supports 20-bit or 24-bit memory addressing in DMA mode.

Interrupt-driven data transfer mode is an extension of interrupt-driven command execution mode. In interrupt-driven data transfer mode, data is transferred by the CPU at the start of the first operation. The BMC generates an interrupt signal for operation complete or operation fail. This interrupt signal is routed to the MULTIBUS I interface via a jumper block. The host CPU responds to this interrupt by reading the BMC Status Register and taking the appropriate action, depending on the desired operation and the current status. For multipage transfers, the host processor typically initiates the next transfer. Up to 128 bytes of data can be transferred between interrupts.

iSBC® 264   PRELIMINARY

Polled mode data transfers are the simplest to implement but require the highest CPU overhead. The CPU determines when to transfer data to and from the BMC FIFO by continuing to poll the BMC Status Register. The FIFO available bit in the Status Register indicates whether an additional byte of data may be read or written. The host CPU transfers the byte, then returns to polling the Status Register.

Command Execution Modes

The BMC contains five parametric registers, a command register, and a status register. The parametric registers are loaded with address, block length, and execution mode information prior to issuing many BMC commands. A set of 18 separate commands can be issued to the command register to initialize and access bubble memory devices (only a few basic commands are typically used for reads/writes). Current status of the BMC and the results of BMC commands are determined by reading the status register. The BMC parametric, command, and status registers can be accessed in either interrupt-driven or polled mode.

Interrupt-driven command execution mode is related to interrupt-driven data transfer mode. An operation complete or operation fail interrupt notifies the host CPU that an operation has completed successfully or has terminated due to an error. The CPU reads the BMC Status Register and tests status bits to determine the current status and to determine what action to take. In the case of a completed operation, a new command can be issued to begin the next data transfer between system memory and the BMC FIFO. In the case of an operation fail interrupt, the CPU can recover from the error by examining the page in error or by retrying the operation.

In polled command execution mode, the CPU continually polls the BMC Status Register to determine the current status of BMC commands. After issuing a command, the CPU verifies that the command has been accepted. After data has been transferred, the CPU polls the Status Register to determine whether an operation has completed successfully or has failed due to errors. The Status Register provides several status bits to indicate the cause for a failed operation.

Additional Hardware Features

The iSBC 264 board includes the following additional hardware features that increase flexibility and enhance operation:

- Data protection provided by automatic power-fail circuit or by ACLO input from P2 edge connector (allows system power supply to provide early warning of power loss)
- Write-protect jumpers to allow 7114s to be individually write-protected
- Bootloop write-protect jumper to prevent accidental bootloop alteration
- LED to indicate the presence of power to the board
- On-board +12 Vdc switching regulator (+12 Vdc ±1% can optionally be sourced from the MULTIBUS I interface)

SOFTWARE DESCRIPTION

The iSBC 264 can run under the iRMX™ 86 operating system. Under iRMX 86, the iSBC 264 board is supported as an integral part of the I/O System Software. The iRMX 86 I/O System Software is implemented as a set of file drivers to support particular types of files and devices, and device drivers to support particular devices (e.g., the iSBC 264 board). Each type of file has its own file driver and each device has its own device driver. This level of granularity provides both flexibility and device independence since application tasks can communicate with file drivers, not device drivers.

SPECIFICATIONS

Memory Size

iSBC 264-1	512K Bytes
iSBC 264-2	1-Megabyte
iSBC 264-4	2-Megabytes

Interface

All address, data, and control signals are TTL-compatible and Intel Multibus I system compatible.

IEEE 796 Compliance: Master/Slave D8 I16 M24 VO

Performance

Maximum Data Rate: 100K bytes/second
Average Access Time: 88 ms (single-page access, randomly-accessed pages)
Range of Access Time: 8 ms to 168 ms

iSBC® 264 PRELIMINARY

Electrical Characteristics
- +5 Vdc supplied through MULTIBUS I P1 connector
- +12 Vdc supplied from on-board regulator or from MULTIBUS I P1 connector
- Voltage sequencing - no restrictions
- Power-on voltage rate of rise - no restrictions
- Power decay rate (max): 0.45 V/ms for +5V (1.1 V/ms for +12V when using external +12V supply)
- ACLO input to allow power supply to provide early warning of power loss (eliminates the voltage decay requirements associated with automatic power-fail circuit)

Mating Connector
P1: Viking 2VN43/9AMK12 or Elfab BS1562D43-PBF
P2: Viking 3VH30/9JNK1 or Elfab BS1020A30-PBF (P2 is used only for ADR14/-ADR17/ and ACLO)

Physical Characteristics
Length: 30.48 cm (12.0 in.)
Height: 17.15 cm (6.75 in.)
Depth: 1.49 cm (0.59 in. - exceeds MULTIBUS I spec.—may require the equivalent of two card slots.)

Power Requirements (Maximum)
264-1 3.4A
264-2 3.7A (serial), 4.7A (parallel)
264-4 4.2A (serial), 5.2A (two 7114s in parallel), 7.0A (four 7114s in parallel)

Environmental Characteristics
Operating Temperature 0° to 60°C ambient @ 80% duty cycle with 100 LFM air flow
Non-Volatile Storage Temperature −20° to +75°C
Relative Humidity 5 to 95% non-condensing (non-operating)
5 to 90% non-condensing (operating)
External Magnetic Force 20 Oersteds max

Available Documentation
- *iSBC 264 Magnetic Bubble Memory Board Reference Manual,* Order Number: 122341-001
- *Intel MULTIBUS® I Specification,* Order Number: 980683-004
- *Memory Components Handbook,* Order Number: 210830-004

4-34

iSBC® 300
32K-BYTE RAM EXPANSION MODULE
iSBC® 340
16K-BYTE EPROM EXPANSION MODULE

- On-board memory expansion for iSBC® 86/12A Single Board Computer
- iSBC® 300 module provides 32K bytes of dual port dynamic RAM and plugs directly into the iSBC® 86/12A board
- iSBC® 340 module provides sockets for up to 16K bytes of additional EPROM and plugs directly into the iSBC 86/12A board
- On-board memory expansion eliminates MULTIBUS® system bus latency and increases system throughput
- Low power requirements
- Simple, reliable mechanical and electrical interconnection

The iSBC 300 32K-byte RAM expansion module and the iSBC 340 16K-byte EPROM expansion module provide simple, low cost expansion of the memory complement available on the iSBC 86/12A single board computer. Each module utilized individually or together can double the iSBC 86/12A board's on-board RAM and EPROM memory capacity. The iSBC 300 32K-byte RAM expansion module and the iSBC 340 16K-byte EPROM expansion module options for the iSBC 86/12A board offer system designers a new level of flexibility in defining and implementing Intel® single board computer systems. These options allow the systems designer to double the memory complement of an iSBC 86/12A board with a minimum of system implications. Because they expand the memory configuration on-board, they can be accessed as quickly as the existing iSBC 86/12A memory by eliminating the need for accessing the additional memory via the MULTIBUS system bus. With the iSBC 86/12A board mounted in the top slot of an iSBC 604 or iSBC 614 cardcage, sufficient clearance exists for mounting both the iSBC 300 and/or the iSBC 340 expansion module option(s). If the iSBC 86/12A board is inserted into some other slot, the combination of boards will physically (but not electrically) occupy two cardcage slots. Incremental power required by the options is minimal; for instance, only 305 mW is needed for the iSBC 300 RAM expansion module.

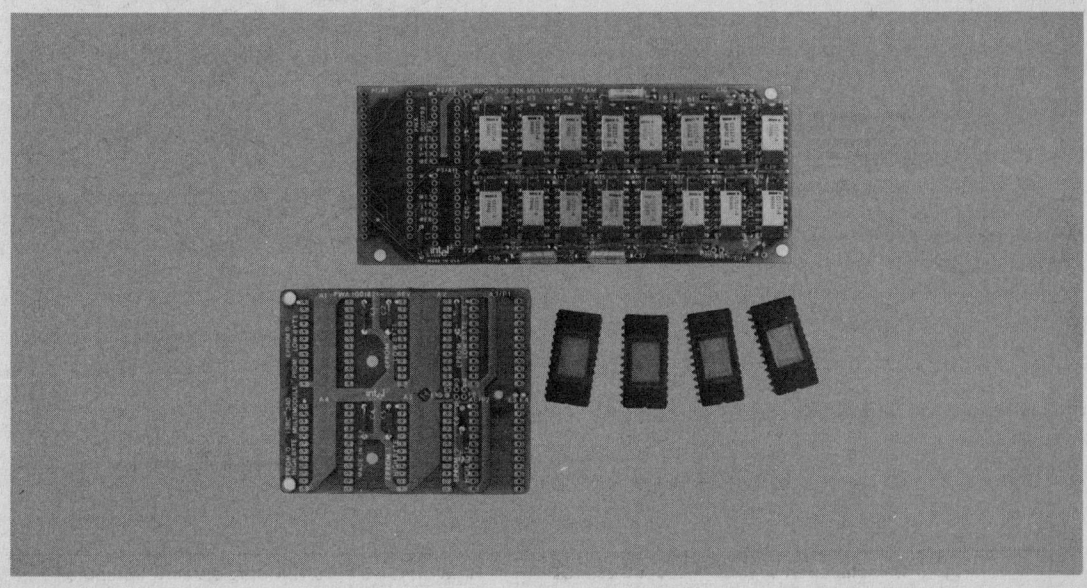

iSBC® 300/340 BOARD

FUNCTIONAL DESCRIPTION

iSBC® 300 32K-Byte MULTIMODULE™ RAM

The iSBC 300 module contains sixteen 16K-byte dynamic RAM devices, sockets for the Intel® 8202A Dynamic computer. It expands the iSBC 86/12A board's on-board dual port RAM capacity from 32K bytes to 64K bytes. The iSBC 300 module contains sixteen 16K-byte dynamic RAM devices, sockets for the Intel® 8202 Dynamic RAM Controller and memory interface latching. To install the iSBC 300 module, the latches and controller from the iSBC 86/12A board are removed and inserted into the sockets on the iSBC 300 module. The add-on board is then mounted onto the iSBC 86/12A board. Pins extending from the controller's and latches' sockets mate with the devices' sockets underneath (see Figure 1). Additional pins mate to supply power and other signals to complete the electrical interface. The module is then secured at three additional points with nylon hardware to insure the mechanical security of the assembly.

To complete the installation, two socketed PROMs are replaced on the iSBC 86/12A board with those supplied with the iSBC 300 kit. These are the on-board memory and MULTIBUS address decode PROMs which allow the iSBC 86/12A board logic to recognize its expanded on-board memory complement.

iSBC® 340 16K-byte MULTIMODULE™ EPROM

The iSBC 340 module expands the iSBC 86/12A Single Board Computer's on-board EPROM capacity from 16K bytes to 32K bytes. It measures 3.3" by 2.8" and consists of a PC board with six 24-pin special sockets. Two of the sockets have extended pins which mate with two of the EPROM sockets on the iSBC 86/12A board. Two of the EPROMs which would have been inserted on the iSBC 86/12A board are then reinserted in the iSBC 340 module. Additional pins also mate for bringing chip selects for the remaining EPROM devices (see Figure 2). The mechanical interface is similar to that used on the iSBC 300 RAM module and consists of two additional mounting holes and the necessary mounting hardware.

The iSBC 340 module supports Intel® 2732A EPROM. One section of the iSBC 86/12A on-board memory and MULTIBUS address decode PROMs (the same decode PROMs mentioned for the iSBC 300 module) is already preprogrammed to support the iSBC 340 module with Intel® 2732A EPROMs. This section is selected through the EPROM configuration switches on the iSBC 86/12A board. The iSBC 340 board can optionally be configured by the user to support Intel® 2758 or 2761 EPROMs by programming new iSBC 86/12A decode PROMs to support these devices. Necessary documentation and PROM map listings are in the iSBC 86/12A Hardware Reference Manual (order number 9803074-01).

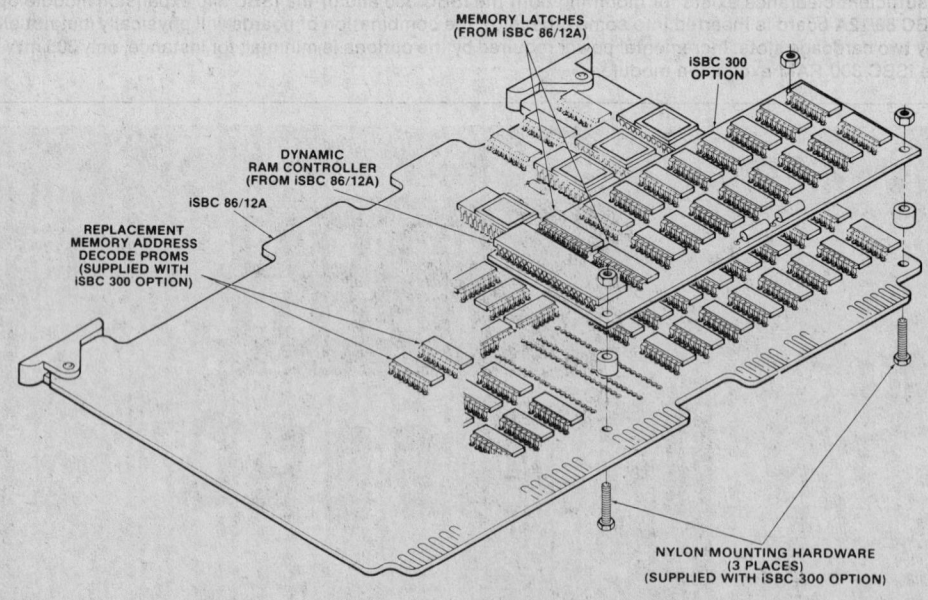

Figure 1. Installation of iSBC® 300 MULTIMODULE™ RAM on iSBC® 86/12A Single Board Computer

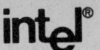

iSBC® 300/340 BOARD

SPECIFICATIONS

Word Size
8 or 16 bits (16-bit data paths)

Memory Size
iSBC 300 Module — 32,768 bytes of RAM
iSBC 340 Module — 16,384 bytes (max) of EPROM

Access Time
iSBC 300 Module — Read: 1 μsec, write: 1.2 μsec
iSBC 340 Module — Standard EPROMs (450 nsec): 1 μsec, fast EPROMs (350 or 390 nsec): 800 nsec

Interface
The interface for the iSBC 300 and iSBC 340 module options is designed only for Intel's iSBC 86/12A Single Board Computer.

Memory Addressing
On-board RAM
  CPU Access
  iSBC 86/12A board only (32K bytes) — 00000-07FFFH.
  iSBC 86/12A board + iSBC 300 module (64K bytes) — 00000-0FFFFH.
  MULTIBUS Access — Jumper selectable for any 8K-byte boundary, but not crossing a 128K-byte boundary.

On-board EPROM
  iSBC 86/12A board only (16K-bytes max.) — FF000-FFFFFH (using 2758 EPROMs); FE000-FFFFFH (using 2316E ROMs or 2716 EPROMs); and FC000-FFFFFH (using 2332A ROMs or 2732A EPROMs).

  iSBC 86/12A board + iSBC 340 module (32K bytes max) — FE000-FFFFFH (using 2758 EPROMs); FC000-FFFFFH (using 2716 EPROMs); F8000-FFFFFH (using 2732A EPROMs).

  On-board EPROM/ROM is not accessible via the MULTIBUS interface.

Auxiliary Power/Memory Protection
The low power memory protection option included on the iSBC 86/12A boards supports the iSBC 300 RAM module.

"Local Only" Memory Protection
The iSBC 86/12A Single Board Computer supports dedication of on-board RAM for on-board CPU access only in 8K, 16K, 24K, or 32K-byte segments. Installation of the iSBC 300 option allows protection of 16K, 32K, 48K, or 64K-byte segments.

Physical Characteristics

	iSBC 300	iSBC 340
Width	5.75″	3.3″
Length	2.35″	2.8″
Height of iSBC 86/12A plus mounted option	.718	.718*
Weight	13 oz.	5 oz.

*Includes EPROMs

All necessary mounting hardware (nylon, screws, spacers, nuts) are supplied with each kit.

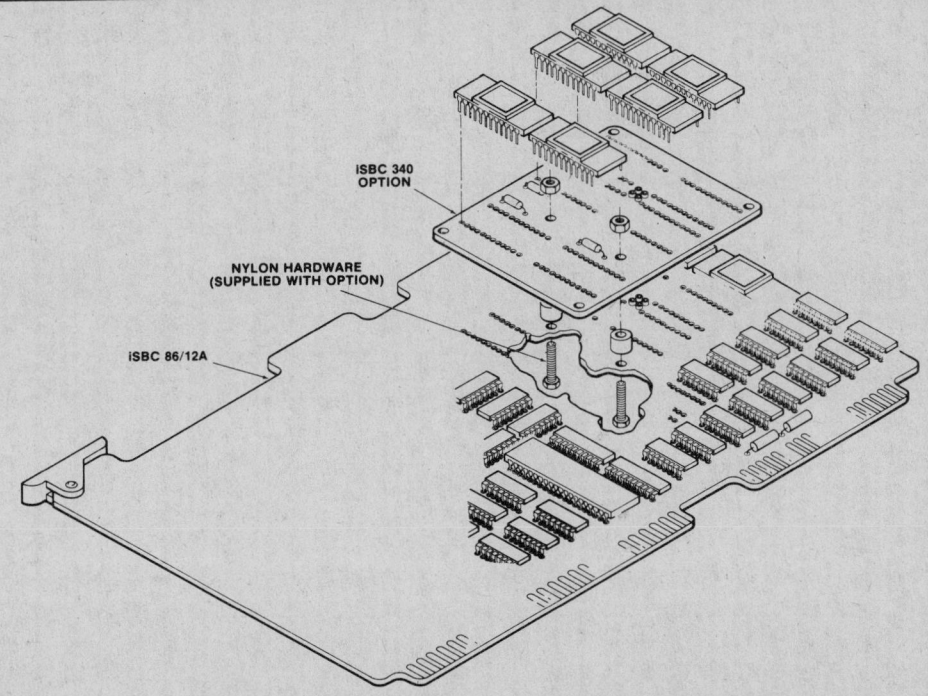

Figure 2. Installation of iSBC® 340 MULTIMODULE ™ EPROM Option on iSBC® 86/12A Single Board Computer

iSBC® 300/340 BOARD

Electrical Characteristics

DC power requirements:

Voltage	iSBC 300	iSBC 340
+5 ±5%	1 mA	120 mA[1]
+12 ±5%	24 mA	—
−12 ±5%	1 mA	—

Note:
1. Loaded with Intel 2732A EPROMs.

Environmental Characteristics

Operating Temperature — 0° to +55°C
Relative Humidity — to 90% (without condensation)

Reference Manuals

All necessary documentation for the iSBC 300 MULTIMODULE RAM and iSBC 340 MULTIMODULE EPROM/ROM is included in the iSBC 86/12A Hardware Reference Manual; order #9803074-01. (NOT SUPPLIED)

Manuals may be ordered from any Intel sales representative distributor office or from Intel Literature Department, 3065 Bowers Avenue, Santa Clara, CA 95051.

ORDERING INFORMATION

Part Number	Description
SBC 300	32K byte MULTIMODULE RAM
SBC 340	16K byte MULTIMODULE EPROM

iSBC® 301
4K-BYTE RAM
MULTIMODULE™ BOARD

- On-board memory expansion to 8K bytes for iSBC® 80/24 and iSBC® 88/40A Single Board Computers

- Provides 4K bytes of static RAM directly on-board

- Uses 5 MHz (8185-2) RAMs

- Single +5V supply

- 0.5 watts incremental power dissipation

- On-board memory expansion eliminates MULTIBUS® system bus latency and increases system throughput

- Reliable mechanical and electrical interconnection

The Intel iSBC 301 4K-byte RAM MULTIMODULE Board provides simple, low cost expansion to double the RAM capacity on the iSBC 80/24 or iSBC 88/40A Single Board Computer to 8K bytes. This offers system designers a new level of flexibility in defining and implementing system memory requirements. Because memory is configured on-board, it can be accessed as quickly as the existing iSBC 80/24 or iSBC 88/40A memory, eliminating the need for accessing the additional memory via the MULTIBUS system bus. As a result, the iSBC 301 board provides a high speed, cost effective solution for systems requiring incremental RAM expansion. Incremental power required by the iSBC 301 module is minimal, dissipating only 0.5 watts.

iSBC® 301

FUNCTIONAL DESCRIPTION

The iSBC 301 Board measures 3.95" by 1.20" and mounts above the RAM area on the iSBC 80/24 or iSBC 88/40A single board computer. It expands the on-board RAM capacity from 4K bytes to 8K bytes. The iSBC 301 MULTIMODULE board contains four 1K byte static RAM devices and a socket for one of the RAM devices on the iSBC 80/24 or iSBC 88/40A board. To install the iSBC 301 MULTIMODULE board, one of the RAMs is removed from the host board and inserted into the socket on the iSBC 301 board. The add-on board is then mounted into the vacated RAM socket on the host board. Pins extending from the RAM socket mate with the device's socket underneath (see Figure 1). Additional pins mate to the power supply and chip select lines to complete the electrical interface. The MULTIMODULE board is then secured at two additional points with nylon hardware to insure mechanical security of the assembly. With the iSBC 80/24 or iSBC 88/40A board mounted in the top slot of an iSBC 604 or iSBC 614 cardcage, sufficient clearance exists for mounting the iSBC 301 option. If the iSBC 80/24 or iSBC 88/40A board is inserted into some other slot, the combination of boards will physically (but not electrically) occupy two cardcage slots.

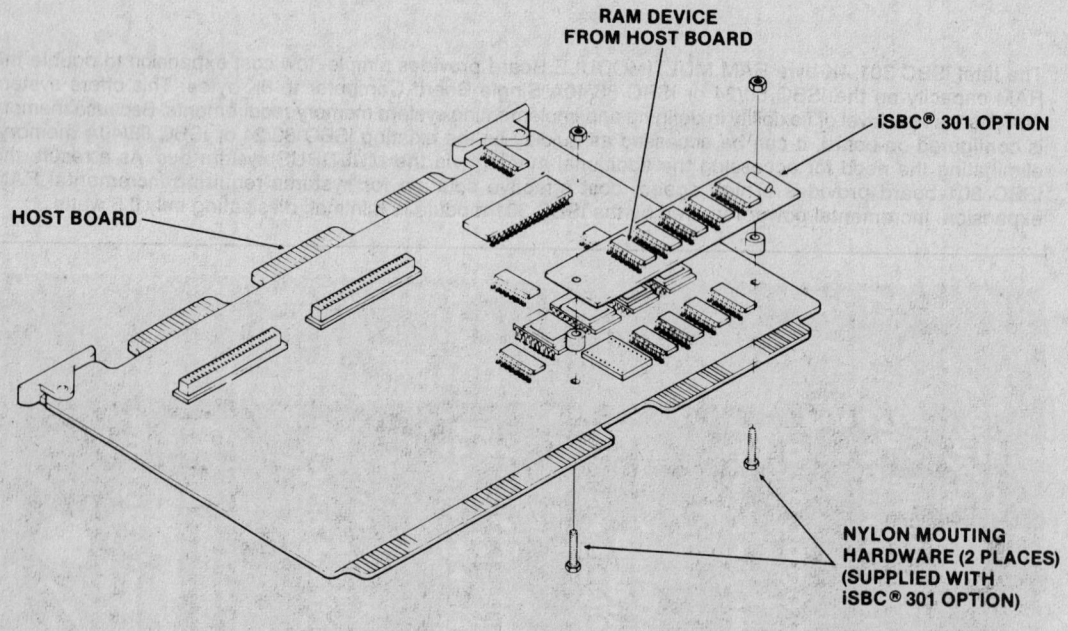

Figure 1. Installation of iSBC® 301 4K-Byte RAM MULTIMODULE™ Board

iSBC® 301

SPECIFICATIONS

Word Size
8 bits

Memory Size
4096 bytes of RAM

Access Time
Read: 140 ns (from READ command)
       200 ns (from ALE)
Write: 150 ns (from READ command)
       190 ns (from ALE)

Memory Addressing
Memory addressing for the iSBC 301 4K-Byte RAM MULTIMODULE Board is controlled by the host board via the address and chip select signal lines and is contiguous with the host board RAM.

   iSBC 80/24 and iSBC 301 board: 02000-02FFF
   iSBC 88/40A and iSBC 301 board: 00000-01FFF

Physical Characteristics
Width — 1.20 in. (3.05 cm)

Length — 3.95 in. (10.03 cm)
Height — .44 in. (1.12 cm) iSBC 301 Board
         .56 in. (1.42 cm)
         iSBC 301 Board + host board
Weight — .69 oz. (19 gm)

Electrical Characteristics
DC Power Requirements:
10 mA at +5 Volts incremental power

Environmental Characteristics
Operating Temperature — 0° to +55° C
Relative Humidity — to 90% (without condensation)

Reference Manuals
All necessary documentation for the iSBC 301 MULTIMODULE board is included in the CPU board Hardware Reference Manual (NOT SUPPLIED).

   iSBC 80/24 — Order No. 142648-001

Manuals may be ordered from any Intel sales representative, distributor office, or from Intel Literature Department, 3065 Bowers Avenue, Santa Clara, California 95051.

SPECIFICATIONS

Part Number	Description
SBC 301	4K Byte RAM MULTIMODULE Board

iSBC® 302
8K-BYTE MULTIMODULE™ RAM

- **Expands on-board memory of the iSBC® 86/05A and iSBC® 88/25 Single Board Computers**
- **Uses four Intel® 2168 static RAMs**
- **Single +5V supply**
- **On-board memory expansion eliminates system bus latency and increases system throughput**
- **Reliable mechanical and electrical interconnection**

The Intel iSBC 302 8K-Byte MULTIMODULE RAM provides simple, low cost expansion to double the RAM capacity on the iSBC 86/05A Single Board Computer to 16K bytes or increase RAM capacity on the iSBC 88/25 Single Board Computer to 12K bytes. This offers system designers a new level of flexibility in implementing system memory. Because the MULTIMODULE memory is configured on-board, it can be accessed as quickly as the standard on-board iSBC 86/05A or iSBC 88/25 memory, eliminating the need for accessing the additional memory via the MULTIBUS system bus. As a result, the iSBC 302 board provides a high-speed, cost-effective solution for systems requiring incremental RAM expansion.

iSBC® 302 BOARD

FUNCTIONAL DESCRIPTION

The iSBC 302 board measures 2.60" by 2.30" and mounts above the RAM area on the iSBC 86/05A or iSBC 88/25 Single Board Computer. The iSBC 302 MULTIMODULE board contains four 4K × 4 static RAM devices and sockets for two of the RAM devices on the iSBC 80/05A board. With the iSBC 302 module mounted on the iSBC 88/25 board, the two sockets on the iSBC module may be filled with 4K × 4 static RAMs. The two sockets on the iSBC 302 module have extended pins which mate with two sockets on the base board. Additional pins mate to the power supply and chip select lines to complete the electrical interface. The mechanical integrity of the assembly is assured with nylon hardware securing the module in two places. With the iSBC 86/05A or iSBC 88/25 board mounted in the top slot of an iSBC 604/614 cardcage, sufficient clearance exists for the mounted iSBC 302 option. If the iSBC 86/05A or iSBC 88/25 board is inserted into some other slot, the combination of boards will physically (but not electrically) occupy two cardcage slots.

SPECIFICATIONS

Word Size
8/16 bits

Memory Size
16,384 bytes of RAM

Cycle Time
Provides "no wait state" memory operations on the iSBC 86/05A board at 5 MHz or 8 MHz or the iSBC 88/25 board at 5 MHz.

5 MHz cycle time — 800 ns
8 MHz cycle time — 500 ns

Memory Addressing
Memory addressing for the iSBC 302 MULTIMODULE board is controlled by the host board via the address and chip select signal lines.

With the iSBC 86/05A board:

The 8K bytes of RAM on the iSBC 302 board occupy the 8K-byte address space immediately after that of the iSBC 86/05A board's 8K RAM (i.e., default configuration —

iSBC 86/05A board's RAM — 00000-01FFF$_H$
iSBC 302 board's RAM — 02000-03FFF$_H$).

With the iSBC 88/25 board:

The 8K bytes of RAM on the iSBC 302 board occupy the 8K byte address space immediately after that of the iSBC 88/25 board's 4K RAM (i.e., default configuration —

iSBC 88/25 board's RAM — 0-0FFF$_H$
iSBC 302 board's RAM — 01000$_H$-02FFF$_H$).

Physical Characteristics
WIDTH — 2.6 in. (6.60 cm)
LENGTH — 2.3 in. (5.84 cm)
HEIGHT — 0.56 in. (1.42 cm) iSBC 302 board + iSBC 86/05A or iSBC 88/25 board
WEIGHT — 1.25 oz (35 gm)

Electrical Characteristics
DC POWER REQUIREMENTS — 720 mA at +5V incremental power

Environmental Characteristics
OPERATING TEMPERATURE — 0°C to +55°C
RELATIVE HUMIDITY — to 90% (without condensation)

Reference Manuals
All necessary documentation for the iSBC 302 MULTIMODULE board is included in the CPU board Hardware Reference Manuals (NOT SUPPLIED).

iSBC 86/05A — Order No.
iSBC 88/25   — Order No. 143825-001

Manuals may be ordered from any Intel sales representative, distributor office, or from Intel Literature Department, 3065 Bowers Avenue, Santa Clara, California 95051.

ORDERING INFORMATION

Part Number	Description
SBC 302	8K-Byte MULTIMODULE RAM

iSBC® 304 128K BYTE RAM MULTIMODULE™ BOARD
iSBC® 300A 32K BYTE RAM MULTIMODULE™ BOARD

- iSBC® 304 module provides 128K bytes of dual port RAM expansion for the iSBC® 86/30 or iSBC® 86/35 board

- iSBC® 300A module provides 32K bytes of dual port RAM expansion for the iSBC® 86/14 board

- Simple, reliable, mechanical and electrical interconnection

- On-board memory expansion for the iSBC® 86/30, iSBC® 86/14 and iSBC® 86/35 Single Board Computers

- On-board memory expansion eliminates MULTIBUS® system bus latency and increases system throughput

- Low power requirements

The iSBC® 304 and iSBC 300A RAM modules provide simple, low cost expansion of the memory compliment available on the iSBC 86/30 and iSBC 86/14 Single Board Computers, respectively. Each module doubles the on-board RAM memory capacity of the host board. Additionally, the iSBC 304 provides 128K bytes ram expansion to the iSBC 86/35 giving a total capacity of 640K bytes ram memory. The RAM MULTIMODULE options for the host boards offer system designers a new level of flexibility in defining and implementing Intel single board computer systems. Because they expand the memory configuration on-board, they can be accessed as quickly as the existing host board memory by eliminating the need for accessing the additional memory via the MULTIBUS system bus.

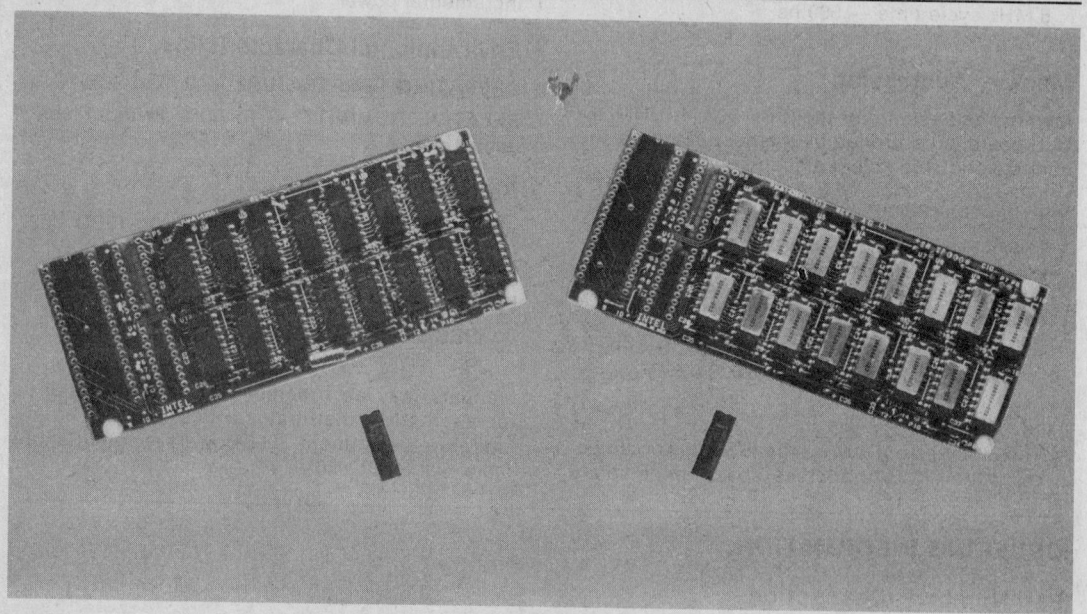

The following are trademarks of Intel Corporation and may be used only to describe Intel products: Intel, CREDIT, Index, Insite, Intellec, Library Manager, Megachassis, Micromap, MULTIBUS, PROMPT, UPI, μScope, Promware, MCS, ICE, iRMX, iSBC, iSBX, MULTIMODULE and iCS. Intel Corporation assumes no responsibility for the use of any circuitry other than circuitry embodied in an Intel product. No other circuit patent licenses are implied.
© INTEL CORPORATION, 1982

iSBC® 304/iSBC® 300A BOARD

FUNCTIONAL DESCRIPTION

Each MULTIMODULE contains dynamic RAM devices and sockets for the Intel 8203 dynamic RAM controller and memory interface latching. To install the module, the latches and controller from the host CPU board are removed and inserted into sockets on the RAM MULTIMODULE. The module is then mounted onto the host board. Pins extending from the controller and latch sockets mate with device sockets underneath (see Figure 1). Additional pins mate to supply other signals to complete the electrical interface.

The module is then secured at three additional points with nylon hardware to ensure the mechanical security of the assembly.

To complete the installation, one socketed PROM is replaced on the host CPU board with the one supplied with the MULTIMODULE kit. This is the MULTIBUS address decode PROM which allows the host board logic to recognize its expanded on-board memory compliment.

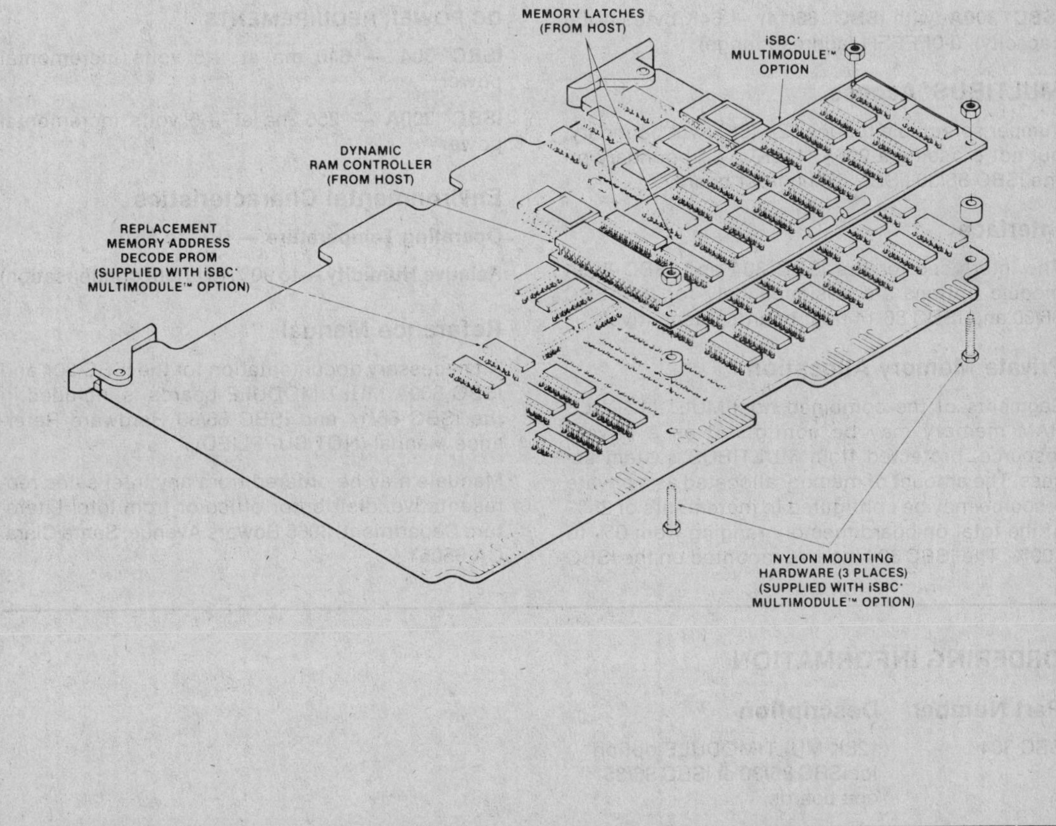

Figure 1. Installation of the MULTIMODULE™ RAM on the Host Single Board Computer

iSBC® 304/iSBC® 300A BOARD

SPECIFICATIONS

Word Size
8 or 16 bits (16-bit data paths)

Memory Size
iSBC® 304 Module — 128K bytes RAM
iSBC® 300A Module — 32K bytes RAM

Cycle Time
iSBC® 304 — 700 nsec (read); 700 nsec (write)
iSBC® 300A — 700 nsec (read); 700 nsec (write)

Memory Addressing
CPU ACCESS
iSBC® 304 (with iSBC® 86/35) — 640K bytes (total capacity); 0-9FFFF$_H$ (address range)
iSBC® 304 (with iSBC® 86/30) — 256K bytes (total capacity); 0-3FFFFH (address range)
iSBC® 300A (with iSBC® 86/14) — 64K bytes (total capacity); 0-0FFFFH (address range)

MULTIBUS® Access
Jumper selectable for any 32K (8K) byte boundary, but not crossing a 256K (128K) byte boundary on the iSBC 86/30 (iSBC 86/14) host board.

Interface
The interfaces for the iSBC 304 and iSBC 300A module options are designed only for the iSBC 86/30 and iSBC 86/14 host boards, respectively.

Private Memory Allocation
Segments of the combined host/MULTIMODULE RAM memory may be configured as a private resource, protected from MULTIBUS system access. The amount of memory allocated as a private resource may be configured in increments of 25% of the total on-board memory ranging from 0% to 100%. The iSBC 304 module mounted on the iSBC 86/30 board, therefore, supports private allocation of 64K, 128K, 192K, or 256K bytes of RAM memory. The iSBC 300A module mounted on the iSBC 86/14 board supports private allocation of 16K, 32K, 48K, or 64K bytes of RAM memory.

Auxiliary Power
The low power memory protection option included on the CPU host boards supports the RAM modules.

Physical Characteristics
Width — 2.4 in. (6.10 cm)
Height — 5.75 in. (14.61 cm)
Depth* — .72 in. (1.83 cm)
Weight — .13 oz. (59 g)

*Note: Combined depth including host board.

Electrical Characteristics
DC POWER REQUIREMENTS
iSBC® 304 — 640 ma at +5 volts incremental power
iSBC® 300A — 256 ma at +5 volts incremental power

Environmental Characteristics
Operating Temperature — 0°C to 55°C
Relative Humidity — to 90% (without condensation)

Reference Manual
All necessary documentation for the iSBC 304 and iSBC 300A MULTIMODULE boards is included in the iSBC 86/14 and iSBC 86/30 Hardware Reference Manual (NOT SUPPLIED).

Manuals may be ordered from any Intel sales representative, distributor office or from Intel Literature Department, 3065 Bowers Avenue, Santa Clara, CA 95051.

ORDERING INFORMATION

Part Number	Description
SBC 304	128K MULTIMODULE option for iSBC 86/30 or iSBC 86/35 cpu boards
SBC 300A	32K MULTIMODULE option for iSBC 86/14 board

iSBC® 307 128K BYTE RAM MULTIMODULE™ BOARD WITH PARITY

- On-board memory expansion for the iSBC® 188/48 Advanced Communicating Computer
- Expands the iSBC® 188/48 on-board RAM to 192K Bytes and provides parity for total 192K Bytes
- iSBC® 307 module provides 128K Bytes of RAM with parity expansion
- Simple, reliable mechanical and electrical interconnection
- Low power requirements

The iSBC® 307 RAM MULTIMODULE board provides simple, low-cost expansion of the iSBC 188/48 board memory. The 128K Bytes of memory provided by the iSBC 307 MULTIMODULE board and the 64K Bytes of memory supplied by the iSBC 188/48 board provides a total of 192K Bytes of on-board RAM. The iSBC 307 MULTIMODULE board generates parity during all write operations and performs parity checking during all read cycles. This MULTIMODULE board offers systems designers flexibility in designing and implementing data communications networks.

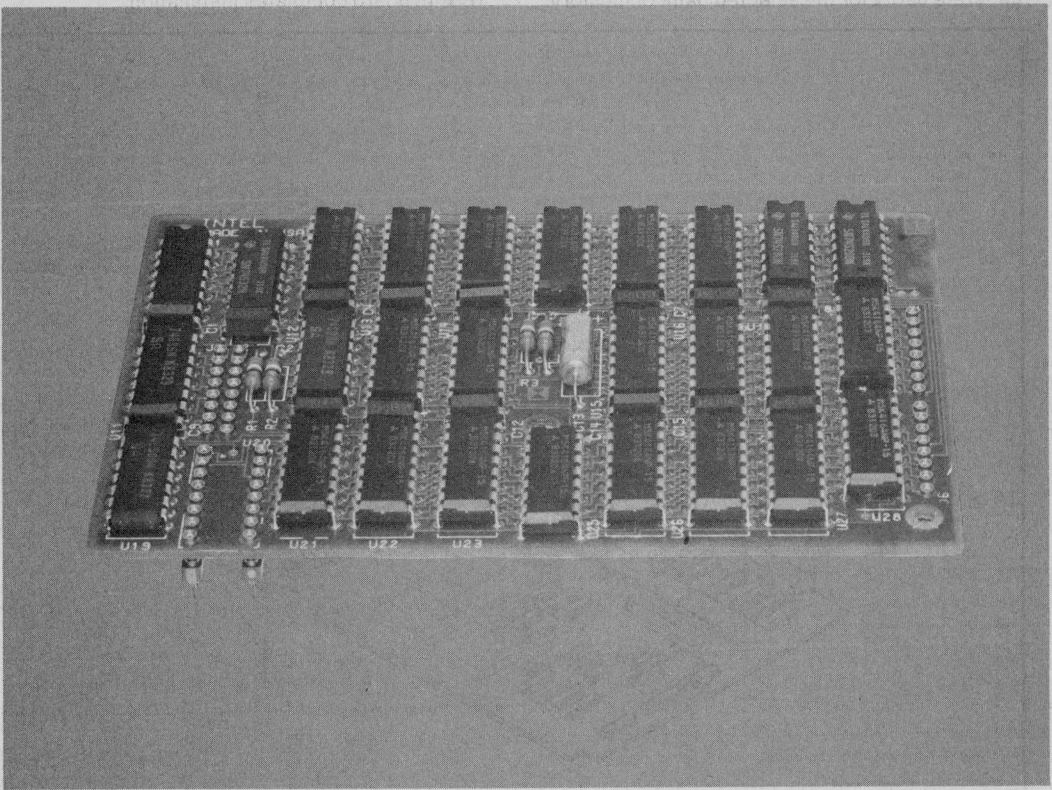

Intel Corporation Assumes No Responsibility for the Use of Any Circuitry Other Than Circuitry Embodied in an Intel Product. No Other Circuit Patent Licenses are Implied. Information Contained Herein Supercedes Previously Published Specifications On These Devices From Intel.

© INTEL CORPORATION, 1984

OCTOBER 1984
ORDER NUMBER: 230970-002

iSBC® 307 MULTIMODULE™ BOARD

FUNCTIONAL DESCRIPTION

The iSBC 307 MULTIMODULE board provides an additional 128K Bytes of on-board RAM to the iSBC 188/48 Advanced Communicating Computer. The iSBC 307 board also provides parity generation and check of all write and read cycles to the total 192K Bytes of on-board memory including the 64K Bytes on the iSBC 188/48 board.

PARITY GENERATION AND CHECKING

The iSBC 307 MULTIMODULE board generates parity during all write operations and performs parity checking during all read operations. When a parity error is detected, the iSBC 307 board generates a parity interrupt. Polarity can be set to even or odd through the Parity Test Pin. For upward capability with future 16-bit Single Board Computer boards, two parity generators are provided. The parity generators (74S20) generate parity for the selected bank of memory.

INSTALLATION:

The iSBC 307 MULTIMODULE board is mounted onto the host board. The board is secured at 1 point with nylon hardware to ensure the mechanical integrity of the assembly. The mounting technique used for the iSBC 188/48 is illustrated below in Figure 1. To install the module, the 2164 Dynamic RAM component from position U101 on the iSBC 188/48 board is removed. This 2164 is then installed into socket U20 on the iSBC 307 board.

The module is then secured by installing one of the supplied screws through the top of the hole above position U24 of the iSBC 307 board. Pins extending from the iSBC 307 MULTIMODULE board mate with connector receptacles located on the iSBC 188/48 board. When all the pins are properly mated, the MULTIMODULE board is seated to the iSBC 188/48 by pressing down firmly and evenly on the iSBC 307 board. Installing the final plastic nut onto the iSBC 307 board securing screw from the trace side of the iSBC 188/48 board completes installation.

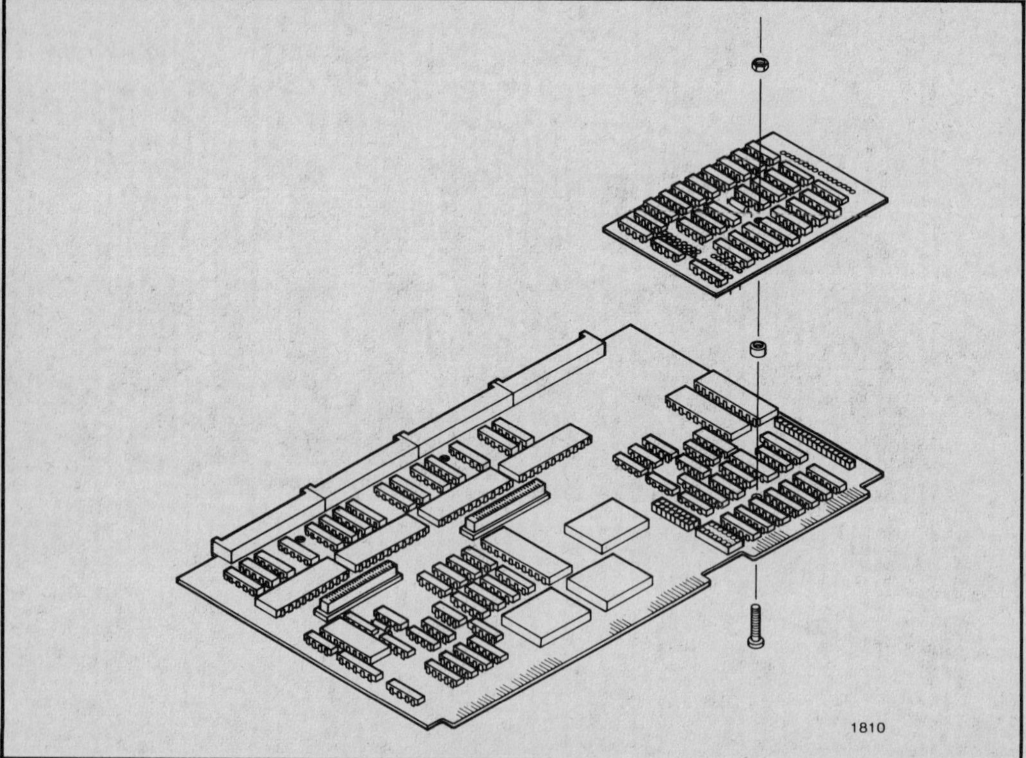

Figure 1. Installation of the iSBC® 307 RAM MULTIMODULE™ board on the iSBC® 188/48 Advanced Communicating Computer

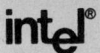 **iSBC® 307 MULTIMODULE™ BOARD**

SPECIFICATIONS

Word Size: 8 bits or 16 bits

Memory Size: 131,072 Bytes

Memory Access Time:

	MIN	MAX
On-Board (Read/Fetch)	0 wait state	1 wait state
On-Board (Write)	0 wait state	2 wait states
MULTIBUS Access (command to xack)	1108 nsec	1275 nsec

Refresh Timing:

Refresh Delay Time: 1002 ns. or 1 μsec. (Increase to normal access time due to a refresh cycle occurring)

Refresh Cycle Time: 1 Refresh cycle ever 15.6 μsec.

Address Selection:

Memory: Fixed by the baseboard.

Interface:

The iSBC 307 MULTIMODULE board option is specifically designed for the iSBC 188/48 Advanced Communication Computer board.

Physical Characteristics:

WEIGHT: 3.00 oz. (85.05 gm.)

WIDTH: 3.00 in. (7.62 cm.)

LENGTH: 4.45 in. (11.30 cm.)

HEIGHT: iSBC 188/48 board plus iSBC 307 MULTIMODULE board combined thickness is .724 inches max. (1.84 cm.) (As measured from the solder side of the iSBC 188/48 to the top of the components on the iSBC 307.)

Electrical Characteristics:

DC Power Requirements: Supplied by iSBC 188/48 board

Main Power (+5v): .44A (iSBC 307 stand-by) .80A (iSBC 307 active)

(Active = memory being accessed either WRITE or READ)

ORDERING INFORMATION:

Part Number: Description
SBC 307   128K Byte RAM MULTIMODULE with Parity

Hardware Reference Manual: Covered in iSBC 188/48 Hardware Reference Manual Order Number: 146218-001

iSBC® 314
512K BYTE RAM MULTIMODULE™ BOARD

- On-board memory expansion for the iSBC® 86/35 Single Board Computer
- iSBC® 314 module provides 512K bytes of dual port RAM expansion for the iSBC® 86/35 board
- Reliable mechanical and electrical interconnection

- Completes iSBC® 86/35 memory array providing a full megabyte page of system memory
- Increases system throughput by reducing accesses to MULTIBUS® global memory
- Low power requirements
- Battery backup capability

The iSBC® 314 512K-Byte RAM MULTIMODULE™ board provides simple, low cost expansion to double the on-board RAM capacity of the iSBC 86/35 Single Board Computer host to one megabyte. This RAM MULTIMODULE option offers system designers a simple, practical solution to expanding and improving the memory capability and performance of the iSBC 86/35 board. The iSBC 314 memory is configured on-board and can be accessed as quickly as the standard iSBC 86/35 memory, eliminating the need for accessing additional memory via the MULTIBUS system bus.

Intel Corporation assumes no responsibility for the use of any circuitry other than circuitry embodied in an Intel product. No other circuit patent licenses are implied. Information contained herein supersedes previously published specifications on these devices from Intel.

© INTEL CORPORATION, 1985

iSBC® 314 MULTIMODULE™ BOARD

FUNCTIONAL DESCRIPTION

The iSBC 314 MULTIMODULE board measures 2.40″ by 5.75″ and mounts above the RAM array on the iSBC 86/35 Single Board Computer. The iSBC 314 board contains sixteen 256Kbit × 1 dynamic RAM devices and three sockets; two for the memory latches and one for the Intel 8203 dynamic RAM controller. The addition of the iSBC 314 memory MULTIMODULE board to the iSBC 86/35 board makes possible a one megabyte single board solution; the full direct addressing capability of the iAPX 86 CPU.

To install the module, the latches and controller from the host iSBC 86/35 board, are removed and inserted into sockets on the iSBC 314 board. The module is then mounted onto the host board. Pins extending from the controller and latch sockets mate with device sockets underneath (see Figure 1). Additional pins mate to supply other signals to complete the electrical interface. The module is then secured at three additional points with nylon hardware to ensure the mechanical security of the assembly.

To complete the installation, one socketed PAL is replaced on the iSBC 86/35 board with the one supplied with the MULTIMODULE kit. This is the PAL which allows the host board logic to recognize its expanded on-board memory compliment.

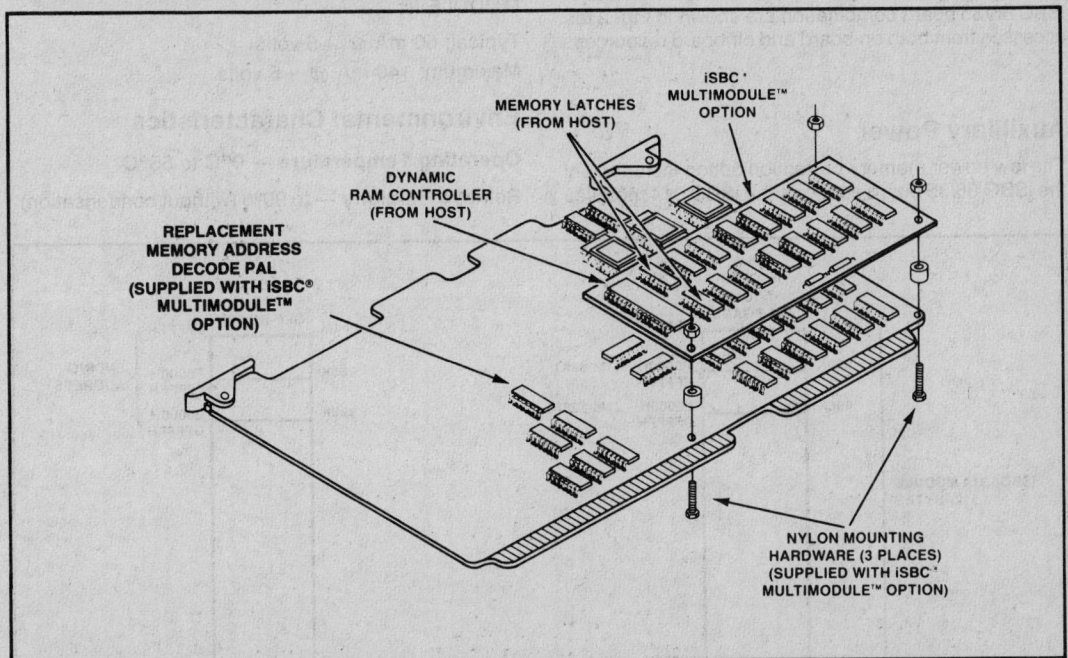

Figure 1. Installation of the MULTIMODULE™ RAM Module on the Host Single Board Computer

SPECIFICATIONS

Word Size
8 or 16 bits (16-bit data paths)

Memory Size
512K bytes RAM

System Cycle Time (8 MHz, 2 Wait States)
750 nsec (read); 750 nsec (write)

NOTE: 1 wait state achieved with jumper change on iSBC 86/35 board.

Memory Addressing
iSBC 314 module with iSBC 86/35 board — 1M bytes (total capacity); 0 — FFFFFH. (See Figure 2., Memory Allocation)

Interface
The interface for the iSBC 314 MULTIMODULE board option is designed only for the iSBC 86/35 host board.

Wait-State Performance
A significant performance advantage of 2 wait-states is achieved when accessing memory on-board the

iSBC® 314 MULTIMODULE™ BOARD

iSBC 86/35 versus the performance of 6 wait-states when accessing memory off-board over the MULTI-BUS. The iSBC 314 puts an additional 512K bytes of system memory on-board the iSBC 86/35 reducing execution time by as much as 70%.

Memory Allocation

Segments of the combined host/MULTIMODULE RAM may be configured to be accessed either from off-board or on-board resources. The amount of memory allocated as either public or private resource may be configured in a variety of sizes. The address range boundaries for the 1 megabyte RAM array of the iSBC 314 and iSBC 86/35 board combination are shown in Fig. 2 for accesses from both on-board and off-board resources.

Auxilliary Power

The low power memory protection option included on the iSBC 86/35 board supports the iSBC 314 module.

Physical Characteristics

Width — 2.4 in. (6.10 cm)

Length — 5.75 in. (14.61 cm)

Depth* — .72 in. (1.83 cm)

Weight — .13 oz. (59g)

***Note:** Combined depth including host board.

Electrical Characteristics

DC Power Requirements*

*Additional power required by the iSBC 314 MULTI-MODULE is:

Typical: 60 mA @ +5 volts
Maximum: 140 mA @ +5 volts

Environmental Characteristics

Operating Temperature — 0°C to 55°C

Relative Humidity — to 90% (without condensation)

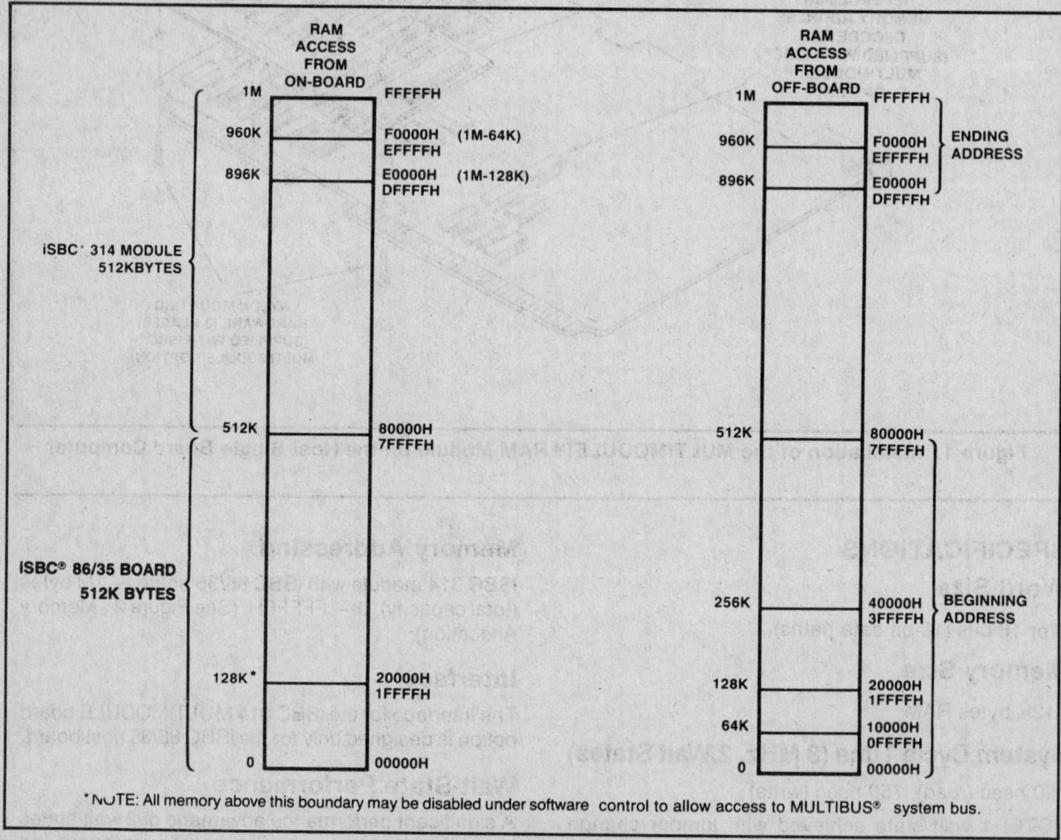

Figure 2. Address Range Selection

*NOTE: All memory above this boundary may be disabled under software control to allow access to MULTIBUS® system bus.

Reference Manual

All necessary documentation for the iSBC 314 MULTI-MODULE board is included in the iSBC 86/35 Hardware Reference Manual (NOT SUPPLIED); Order Number: 146245-001.

Manuals may be ordered form any Intel sales representative, distributor office or from Intel Literature Department, 3065 Bowers Avenue, Santa Clara, CA 95051.

ORDERING INFORMATION

Part Number	Description
iSBC® 314	512K byte Memory MULTIMODULE™ option for iSBC 86/35 board

iSBC® 341
28-PIN MULTIMODULE™ EPROM

- On-board memory expansion for iSBC® 86/05A, iSBC® 88/25, iSBC® 186/03A, iSBC® 286/10A, iSBC® 286/12, and iSBC® 88/40A microcomputers
- Supports JEDEC 24/28-pin standard memory devices, including EPROMs, byte-wide RAMs, and E²PROMs
- Sockets for up to 256K bytes of expansion with Intel® 27512 EPROMs
- On-board expansion provides "no wait state" memory access with selected devices
- Simple, reliable mechanical and electrical interface

The iSBC 341 28-pin MULTIMODULE EPROM board provides simple, low-cost expansion of the on-board EPROM capacity of the iSBC 86/05A Single Board Computer, the iSBC 88/25 Single Board Computer, iSBC 186/03A, iSBC 286/10A, iSBC 286/12 and the iSBC 88/40A Measurement and Control Computer. Four additional 28-pin sockets support JEDEC 24/28-pin standard devices, including EPROMs, byte-wide static and psuedo-static RAMs.

The MULTIMODULE expansion concept provides the optimum mechanism for incremental memory expansion. Mounting directly on the microcomputer, the benefits include low cost, no additional power requirements beyond the memory devices, and higher performance than MULTIBUS-based memory expansion.

iSBC® 341 BOARD

FUNCTIONAL DESCRIPTION

The iSBC 341 28-pin MULTIMODULE EPROM option effectively doubles the number of sockets available for EPROM on the base microcomputer board on which it is mounted. The iSBC 341 board contains six 28-pin sockets. Two of the sockets have extended pins which mate with two of the sockets on the base board. Two of the EPROMs which would have been inserted in the base board are then reinserted in the iSBC 341 sockets. Additional interface pins also connect chip select lines and power. The mechanical integrity of the assembly is assured with nylon hardware securing the unit in two places.

Through its unique interface, the iSBC 341 board can support 8 or 16-bit data paths. The data path width is determined by the base board — being 8 bits for the iSBC 88/40A and iSBC 88/25 microcomputers, and 8/16 bits for the iSBC 86/05A, iSBC 186/03A, iSBC 286/10A, and iSBC 286/12 boards.

SPECIFICATIONS

Word Size

8 or 8/16 bits (determined by data path width of base board).

Memory Size

256K bytes with available technology (JEDEC standard defines device pin-out to 512-bit devices).

Device Size (Bytes)	EPROM Type	Max. iSBC 341 Capacity (Bytes)
2K × 8	2716	8K
4K × 8	2732A	16K
8K × 8	2764	32K
16K × 8	27128	64K
32K × 8	27256	128K
64K × 8	27512	256K

Access Time

Varies according to base board and memory device access time. Consult data sheet of base board for details.

Memory Addressing

Consult data sheet of base board for addressing data.

POWER REQUIREMENTS

Devices[1]	Max. Current @ 5V ±5%
2716	420 mA
2732A	600 mA
2764	600 mA

NOTE:
1. Incremental power drawn from host board for four additional devices.

Auxiliary Power

There are no provisions for auxiliary power (battery backup) on the iSBC 341 option.

Physical Characteristics

WIDTH — 3.4 in. (8.64 cm)
LENGTH — 2.7 in. (6.86 cm)
HEIGHT — 0.78 in. (1.98 cm))*
WEIGHT — 5 oz (141.5 gm)
*Includes height of mounted memory devices and base board.

All necessary mounting hardware (nylon screws, spacers, nuts) is supplied with each kit.

Environmental Characteristics

OPERATING TEMPERATURE — 0°C to +55°C
RELATIVE HUMIDITY — to 90% (without condensation)

Reference Manuals

All necessary documentation for the iSBC 341 module is included in the CPU board Hardware Reference Manuals (NOT SUPPLIED)

    iSBC 186/03A — Order No. 148060-001
    iSBC 86/05A — Order No. 143153-001
    iSBC 88/25 — Order No. 143825-001
    iSBC 88/40A — Order No. 147049-001
    iSBC 286/10A — Order No. 147532-001
    iSBC 286/12 — Order No. 147533-001

Manuals may be ordered from any Intel sales representative, distributor office, or from Intel Literature Department, 3065 Bowers Avenue, Santa Clara, California 95051.

ORDERING INFORMATION

Part Number	Description
SBC 341	28-Pin MULTIMODULE EPROM

PRELIMINARY

iSBC® 428 UNIVERSAL SITE MEMORY EXPANSION BOARD

- **Supports EPROM, ROM, E²PROM, SRAM, IRAM and NVRAM**
- **iLBX™ BUS or MULTIBUS® Selectable**
- **Provides support for Battery Backup/ Memory Protect**
- **Sixteen 28 pin Universal sites**
- **Assignable anywhere within a 16 megabyte address space on 256K byte boundaries**
- **Jumper selectable base address on 4K byte boundaries**

The iSBC® 428 Universal Site Board is a member of Intel's complete line of Memory and I/O Expansion boards. The iSBC 428 Universal Site Memory Expansion Board interfaces directly to the iSBC 80, iSBC 88, or iSBC 86 Single Board Computers via the MULTIBUS® System Bus to expand system memory requirements, while system memory expansion requirements for iSBC 286 Single Board Computer can interface via either the MULTIBUS or the high speed iLBX™ Bus.

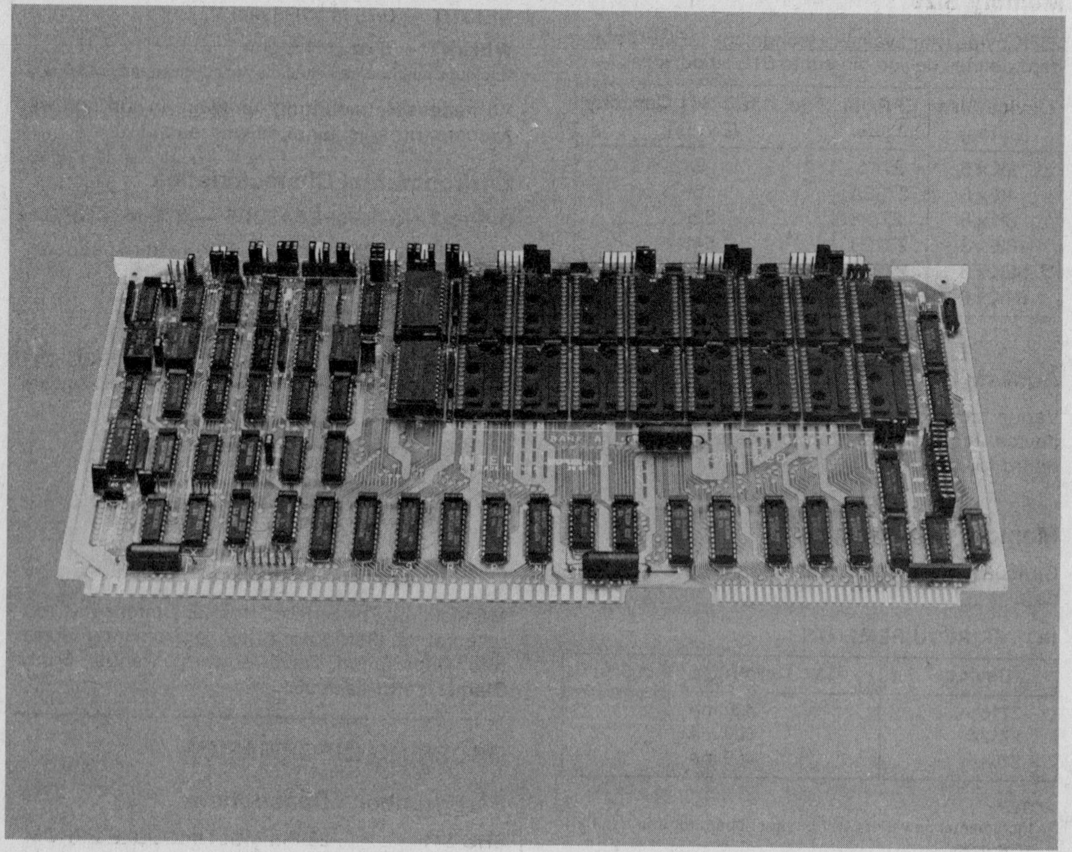

iSBC® 428 BOARD

FUNCTIONAL DESCRIPTION

General

The iSBC 428 board contains sixteen 28 pin sockets. The actual capacity of the board is determined by the type and quantity of components installed by the user. The iSBC 428 board is compatible with five different types and densities of devices: the 2K by 8 thru 64K by 8 EPROM/ROM devices, 2K by 8 thru 8K by 8 "Five Volt Only, Enhanced" E^{2}PROM devices, 512 by 8 thru 16K by 8 NVRAM (Non-Volatile RAM) devices, 2K by 8 thru 32K by 8 SRAM devices, and 8K by 8 IRAM (Integrated RAM) devices. In addition the board can be accessed by either the MULTIBUS System Bus or Intel's new high speed iLBX Bus.

iLBX™ Bus

The iSBC 428 board can be configured via jumpers to communicate with either the MULTIBUS interface or the iLBX Bus interface. Significant memory access time improvements can be realized over the iLBX Bus interface (versus the MULTIBUS interface) due to its dedicated, unarbitrated architecture. Additional information on the iLBX Bus is available in the iLBX Specification #144456-003.

Memory Banks

The sixteen sites on the iSBC 428 board are partitioned into two banks of 8 sites each. Within each bank the 8 sites are further partitioned into 2 groups of 4 sites each. Each group of 4 sites is configurable to each of the six device types described above via a "Configurator". The "Configurator" is an arrangement of push-on jumpers which configures each of the four groups of 4 sites. Within each bank devices of the same density must reside and within each group devices of the same type must reside (i.e. SRAM or EPROM).

Memory Addressing

Addressing of the iSBC 428 board is by pages. There are 64-256K pages which are jumper selectable. Each of the two banks are independently addressable and can reside in any page. Actual beginning and ending addresses within a page are a function of the actual device size and, as with the pages, are determined by jumpers. Because of the paging based memory addressing architecture more than one iSBC 428 board can be placed in a system.

Mode of Operation

The iSBC 428 board can operate in one of two modes: the 8 bit only mode or the 8/16 bit mode. The 8 bit mode provides the most efficient memory configuration for systems handling 8 bit data only. The 8/16 bit mode allows the iSBC 428 board to be compatible with systems employing 8 bit and 16 bit masters. The mode of operation is selected by on board jumpers and is available for both MULTIBUS and iLBX Bus configurations.

Memory Access

The iSBC 428 board has jumper selectable access times which allows the board to be tailored to the performance of the particular devices which are installed in the iSBC 428 board. The board can be configured via jumpers to accept devices with an access time range of 50 ns to 500 ns with a granularity of 50 ns and results in a board access time from 225 ns to 775 ns.

Interrupt

The iSBC 428 board has the capability of generating an interrupt for the write and erase operations of E^{2}PROMS. The interrupt can be configured in two ways: one, to signal completion of the E^{2}PROM write cycle, or two, allow polling by the system to determine the status of the E^{2}PROM during the write programming time.

Inhibits

Inhibits are provided on the iSBC 428 board to allow ROM to overlay RAM for bootstrapping or diagnostic operations. Each bank of the iSBC 428 board can be overlayed with the system RAM by jumpers provided on the board.

Battery Backup

The iSBC 428 board supports battery backup operation via a connector on the board. An auxiliary power bus is provided to allow separate power to the memory array for systems requiring battery backup. Selection of this auxiliary power bus is made via jumpers on the board.

An active-low TTL compatible Memory Protect signal is brought out on the auxiliary connector which, when asserted, disables access to the memory array. This input is provided for the protection of Memory contents during system power-down sequences.

iSBC® 428 BOARD

Devices Supported

Listed below are the current and future devices supported by the iSBC 428 board.

Type	512 × 8	2K × 8	4K × 8	8K × 8	16K × 8	32K × 8	64K × 8	Comments
EPROM	—	2716	2732A	2764	27128	27256	27512	—
ROM	—	X	X	X	X	X	X	—
EEPROM	—	2817A	X	X	X	X	—	5V, Enhanced
SRAM	—	X	X	X	X	X	—	NMOS & CMOS
NVRAM	—	X	X	X	—	—	—	—
IRAM	—	—	—	2186	—	X	—	—

X-Denotes that the iSBC 428 board will support the device indicated but that it is not currently available from Intel.

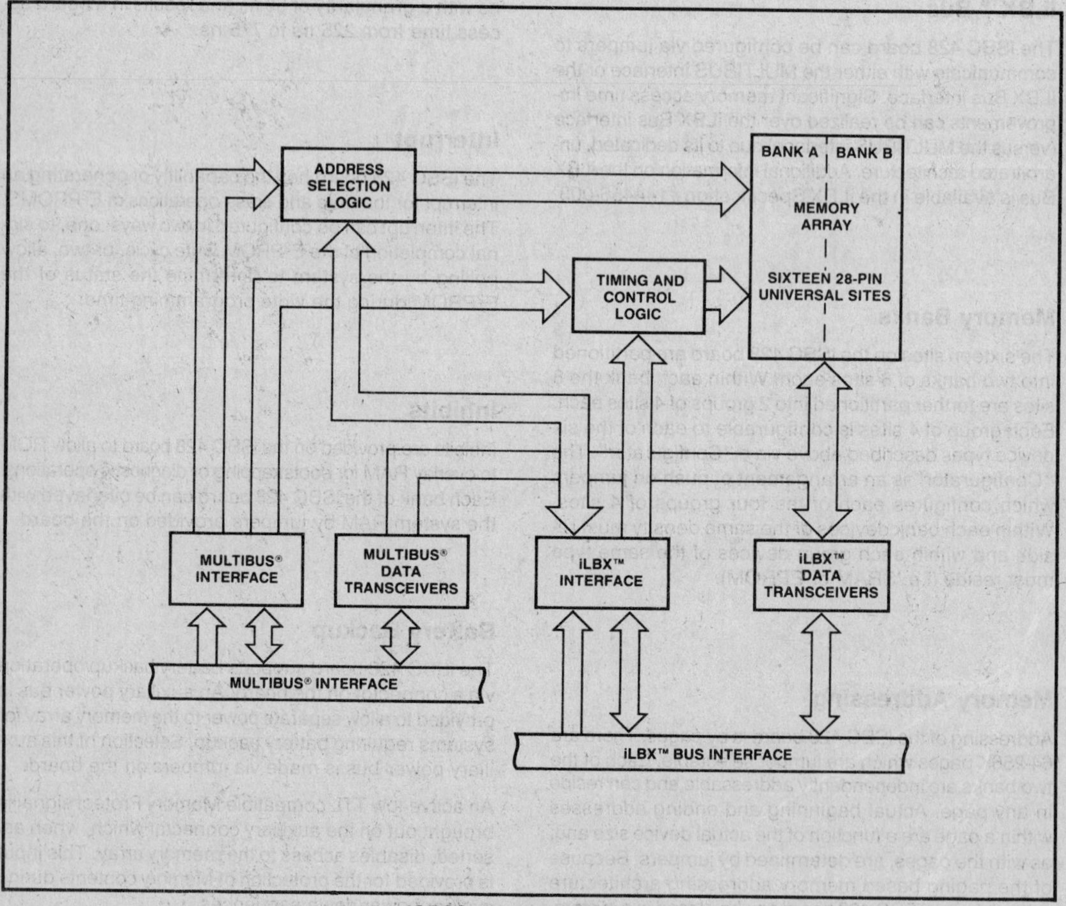

iSBC® 428 Block Diagram

4-58

iSBC® 428 BOARD

SPECIFICATIONS

Word Size
8 or 8/16 bits

Memory Size
Sockets are provided for up-to sixteen 28 pin devices which can provide up to 512K bytes of EPROM/ROM/SRAM.

Access Time
Jumperable from 225 to 775 ns with a granularity of 50 ns and is equivalent for both MULTIBUS and the iLBX Bus.

Power Requirements
V_{CC} = 5 volts ± 5%

I_{CC} = 2.0 amps, maximum, without any memory devices in the board.

Physical Characteristics
Length — 30.48 cm (12 inches)
Width — 17.15 cm (7.05 inches)
Depth — 1.27 cm (0.5 inches)

Environment
Operating Temperature — 0°C to +55°C
Relative Humidity — 90% non-condensing

Reference Manual
145696-001 — iSBC 428 Hardware Reference Manual (NOT SUPPLIED)

Additional Literature
9800683-04 — MULTIBUS Specification
144456-001 — The iLBX Specification

ORDERING INFORMATION

Part Number	Description
SBC 428	Universal Site Memory Expansion Board

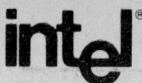

iSBC® 464
64K BYTE EPROM EXPANSION BOARD

- Provides EPROM/ROM expansion of iSBC® 80, iSBC® 86 and iSBC® 88 systems via direct MULTIBUS® interface

- Sockets for up to 64K bytes of EPROM

- Compatible with Intel® 2758, 2716 or 2732/2732A erasable PROMs

- Switch selectable base address on 4K byte boundaries for each memory bank

- Assignable anywhere within a 1 megabyte address space

- EPROM components which are not enabled are placed in standby power mode

- Requires a single +5V power supply

The iSBC 464 is a member of Intel's complete line of iSBC memory and I/O expansion boards. The iSBC 464 board interfaces directly to the iSBC 80, iSBC 86 or iSBC 88 single board computers via the MULTIBUS system bus, to expand system EPROM memory capacity.

iSBC® 464 BOARD

FUNCTIONAL DESCRIPTION

Memory Configuration

The iSBC 464 board contains sixteen sockets which provide a maximum of 64K bytes of memory expansion. The actual capacity of the board is determined by the type and quantity of EPROM components installed by the user. The board is compatible with three different sizes of Intel EPROM devices. These are the 1K byte 2758 EPROM, the 2K byte 2716 EPROM, and the 4K byte 2732 EPROM.

Mode of Operation
The iSBC 464 board can operate in one of two modes: the 8 bit only mode or the 16/8 bit mode. The 8 bit mode provides the most efficient memory configuration for systems handling 8 bit data. The 16/8 bit mode allows 16 bit words to be accessed by 16 bit processors. In the 16/8 bit mode, 16 bit and 8 bit microprocessors may also access either the high order byte or the low order byte of a 16 bit word. The mode of operation is selected by placing two option jumper blocks in the appropriate sockets.

Memory Banks
When used in the 8 bit mode, the iSBC 464 board is organized into four banks (labeled A-D) of four sockets each. Depending on the type of memory components used, each bank may contain a maximum of 4K, 8K or 16K bytes of memory. Unused memory sockets may be deselected by bank or individually in bank D. Deselecting a bank or individual socket frees that address space for use elsewhere in the system. In the 16/8 bit mode, banks A & B and C & D are paired together to form two banks (labeled AB, CD) which are 16 bits wide. Each of these banks has four socket pairs. Bank AB may be deselected as a single unit. Socket pairs in bank CD may be deselected individually. Thus, board configurations using fewer than 16 memory components do not fill memory address space with unused sockets. Selection/deselection is accomplished by setting switches on the board.

Memory Access Time
The iSBC 464 board operates with one of 15 switch selectable memory access times ranging from 35 to 1435 nanoseconds. This feature allows the board to be tailored to the performance of the installed components and the system CPU.

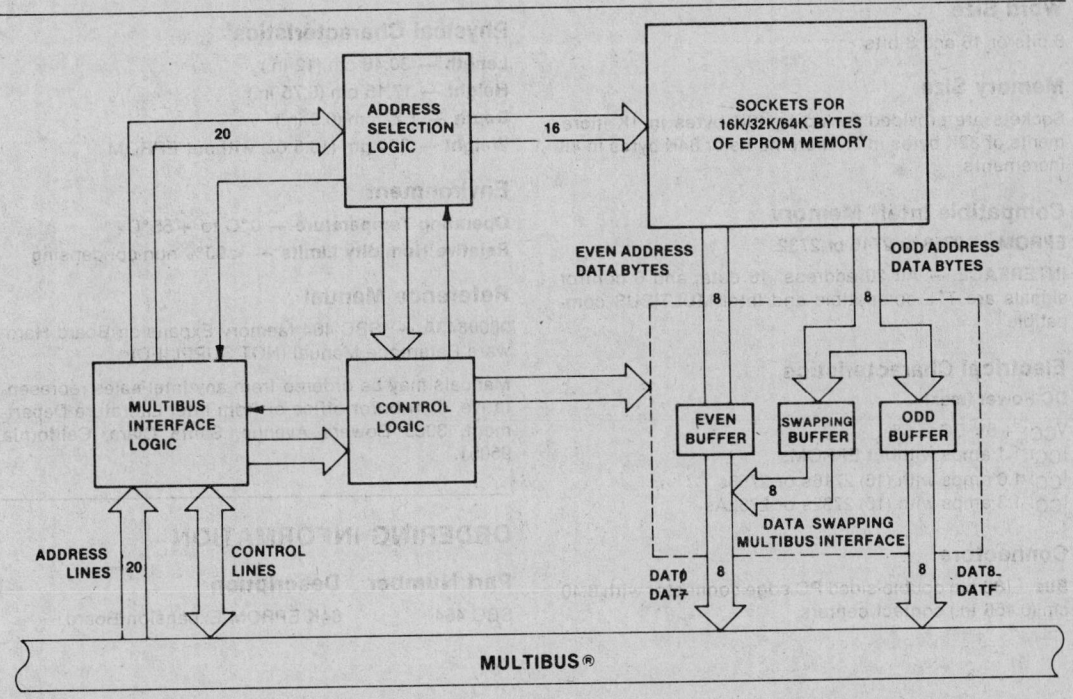

Figure 1. iSBC® 464 Block Diagram

iSBC® 464 BOARD

Memory Addresses

Switch selectable options on the iSBC 464 board allow the board to be assigned anywhere within a 1 megabyte address space. In either operating mode, the base address of each memory bank may be set to any 4K byte boundary within a 64K byte memory page. There is one exception. If the 4K byte devices are used in the 16/8 bit mode, then base addresses are restricted to 8K byte boundaries. If the board is used in a system with an address range greater than 64K bytes, memory on the iSBC 464 board may reside in one or two 64K byte memory pages. Any two pages out of a possible 16 may be chosen by setting switches on the board.

Standby Power Operation

The iSBC 464 board takes advantage of the standby modes of the Intel 2758, 2716 and 2732. When they are not enabled, these components draw as little as 25% of their active level power with no degradation in access time. The iSBC 464 board is designed so that only two memory components are enabled during a read operation.

RAM Overlap

Memory banks of the iSBC 464 board can be overlapped with the addresses of system RAM by setting on-board switches. The process of addressing a memory bank will drive the Inhibit RAM (INH1/) signal true. This signal is issued to the MULTIBUS system bus in order to prevent any MULTIBUS accessable RAM in the system from responding to the current address. If an EPROM is addressed which has its corresponding RAM overlap switch on, an access time of 15 clock cycles is imposed. This allows overlapped dynamic RAM to refresh before the address on the MULTIBUS is changed. The RAM overlap feature does not apply to RAM which is not on the MULTIBUS system bus.

SPECIFICATIONS

Word Size

8 bits or 16 and 8 bits

Memory Size

Sockets are provided for up to 16K bytes in 1K increments or 32K bytes in 2K increments or 64K bytes in 4K increments

Compatible Intel® Memory

EPROM — 2758 or 2716 or 2732

INTERFACE — All 20 address, 16 data, and 6 control signals are TTL compatible and Intel MULTIBUS compatible

Electrical Characteristics

DC Power (max)

V_{CC}: +5V DC ±5%
I_{CC}: 1.1 amps without EPROMs
I_{CC}: 1.6 amps with (16) 2716s or 2758s
I_{CC}: 1.3 amps with (16) 2732s or 2732As

Connectors

Bus — 86-pin double-sided PC edge connector with 0.40 cm (0.156 in.) contact centers

Mating Connector — Viking 3KH43/9AMK12 or compatible connector

Physical Characteristics

Length — 30.48 cm (12 in.)
Height — 17.15 cm (6.75 in.)
Depth — 1.27 cm (0.5 in.)
Weight — 294 gm (10.5 oz) without EPROM

Environment

Operating Temperature — 0°C to +55°C
Relative Humidity Limits — <90% non-condensing

Reference Manual

9800643A — iSBC 464 Memory Expansion Board Hardware Reference Manual (NOT SUPPLIED)

Manuals may be ordered from any Intel sales representative, distributor office or from Intel Literature Department, 3065 Bowers Avenue, Santa Clara, California 95051.

ORDERING INFORMATION

Part Number	Description
SBC 464	64K EPROM Expansion Board

iSBX™ 251 and 251C BUBBLE MEMORY MULTIMODULE™ BOARD

- iSBX™ 251   0-60°C
- iSBX™ 251C   10-40°C
- iSBX™ MULTIMODULE™ Bus Compatible
- Capacity: 128K Bytes Bubble Memory Storage
- Performance:
  —Average Access Time: 48ms
  —Burst Data Rate: Up to 50K Bytes/Sec
- Compatibility with Host DMA Controller
- Non-Volatile Storage
- High Reliability Under Harsh Environments
- Fast Access Storage Option on iPDS™ System
- Automatic Error Correction
- Operates from Standard +5V and +12V Power Supplies
- Power Fail Data Protection
- Low Power Consumption

The Intel iSBX 251 and iSBX 251C bubble memory MULTIMODULE boards are completely assembled and tested Non-Volatile 128K-byte memory boards based on the Intel 7110 one-megabit bubble memory and support chips. The iSBX 251 and iSBX 251C boards are Intel's easiest to use bubble solutions. The iSBX 251 and iSBX 251C MULTIMODULE boards may be designed into Intel SBC products with iSBX connectors as well as into any user manufactured microprocessor board. The bubble memory support circuitry and SBX connector on the iSBX 251 and iSBX 251C boards provide the user with a simple interface to the bubble memory.

The iSBX 251 and iSBX 251C boards are featured as an option on the new Intel Personal Development System as a fast access storage option designed to emulate disk. Typically, the bubble memory option provides a 2X improvement in system performance when compared with a floppy disk. Use of the iSBX 251 or iSBX 251C board with the iPDS system enhances iPDS™ system portability, performance and reliability.

The iSBX 251 and iSBX 251C boards differ in specified operating temperature ranges. The iSBX 251 board operating temperature is 0-60°C. The iSBX 251C boards operating temperature is 10-40°C. These boards plug into any Intel iSBX single board computer or other processor board with an iSBX connector. The iSBX 251 board meets Intel iSBX specifications.

iSBX™ 251/iSBX™ 251C BOARD

FUNCTIONAL DESCRIPTION

The Intel iSBX 251 and iSBX 251C bubble memory MULTIMODULE boards are completely assembled and tested non-volatile memory boards. They consist of the Intel 7110 bubble memory and support circuitry mounted on a double-wide MULTIMODULE board. The bubble memory support circuitry includes the Intel 7220-1 Bubble Memory Controller (BMC) through which the host processor communicates with the bubble storage. See Figure 1 for a system and bubble memory block diagram.

The BMC provides a convenient 8 bit bidirectional bus that requires only two port or I/O addresses. One port is used to transfer data while the other is used to send commands or view operational status. A set of sixteen commands are available to initiate and monitor a bubble memory data transfer. (Refer to the 7220-1 data sheet for more detailed information on the BMC commands).

The iSBX 251 provides the designer with three I/O modes of data transfer for complete flexibility. I/O mode selection is accomplished through the use of on-board jumpers and user software:

1. Polled
2. Interrupt-driven mode
3. Direct Memory Access (DMA) mode

DMA mode requires the use of a DMA controller on the host board.

The iSBX 251 and iSBX 251C boards plug into any Intel iSBC® Single Board Computer or processor board with an iSBX connector. This arrangement frees the MULTIBUS for other traffic while the host iSBC board accesses the bubble memory.

OPERATION

Like many high density peripheral storage devices, bubble memory data is organized serially in pages rather than bytes. Data transfers are accomplished under software control by the 7220-1 BMC. The 7220-1 partitions the one megabit bubble memory into 2048 pages of either 64 or 68 bytes in length. The page length is dependent upon the use of error detection and correction—64 bytes with error correction and 68 bytes without. Data transfers are specified in terms of whole pages. Therefore the minimum amount of data that can be transferred during one read or write command is 64 or 68 bytes. Automatic error correction may be selected by enabling a flag in the 7220-1 BMC.

The iSBX 251 board can be configured to operate in polled mode, interrupt mode, or DMA mode. In the polled mode, the host processor periodically reads the 7220-1 BMC status register to obtain information about completion or termination of commands, error conditions, and the BMC's readiness to transfer data or accept a new command.

In the interrupt-driven mode, an interrupt is issued by the 7220-1 BMC when its internal buffer is ready to accept 22 bytes of data during a write operation. In a read operation, an interrupt is issued whenever 22 bytes of data are available for reading by the host processor in addition to data transfers. The BMC will also issue an interrupt to indicate the completion of a command or the presence of error conditions.

With the assistance of a direct memory access controller on the board hosting the iSBX 251, the BMC can transfer large blocks of data with a single I/O request. DMA mode makes use of the BMC's handshaking ability with a DMA controller.

Regardless of the mode of data transfer, the host processor or DMA controller must be capable of maintaining a data rate of 12.5K bytes/sec.

MOUNTING TECHNIQUE

As shown in Figure 2, the iSBX 251 board plugs into a host board via the iSBX connector and is secured by three spacers with screws. A double-wide iSBX MULTIMODULE board is used and two MULTIBUS card slots are occupied in addition to the card slot for the base board. Dimensions of the board are given in Figures 3 and 4. Although the iSBX 251 board male connector has the standard 36 pins, this board also plugs into the expanded 44-pin female connector.

iSBX™ 251/iSBX™ 251C BOARD

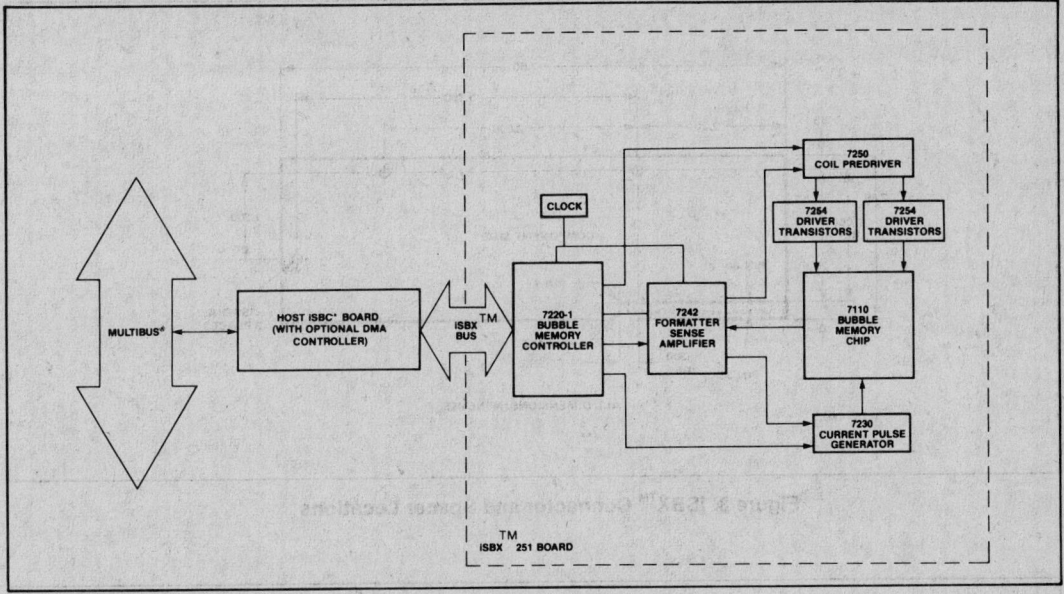

Figure 1. Block Diagram

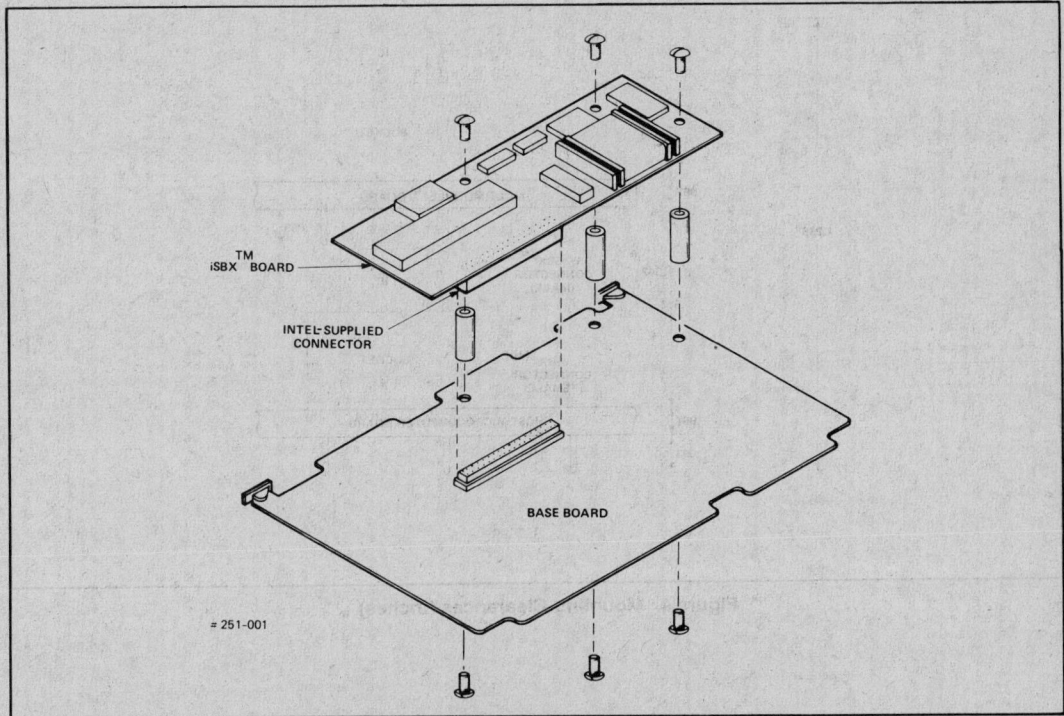

Figure 2. iSBX™ MULTIMODULE™ Board Concept

iSBX™ 251/iSBX™ 251C BOARD

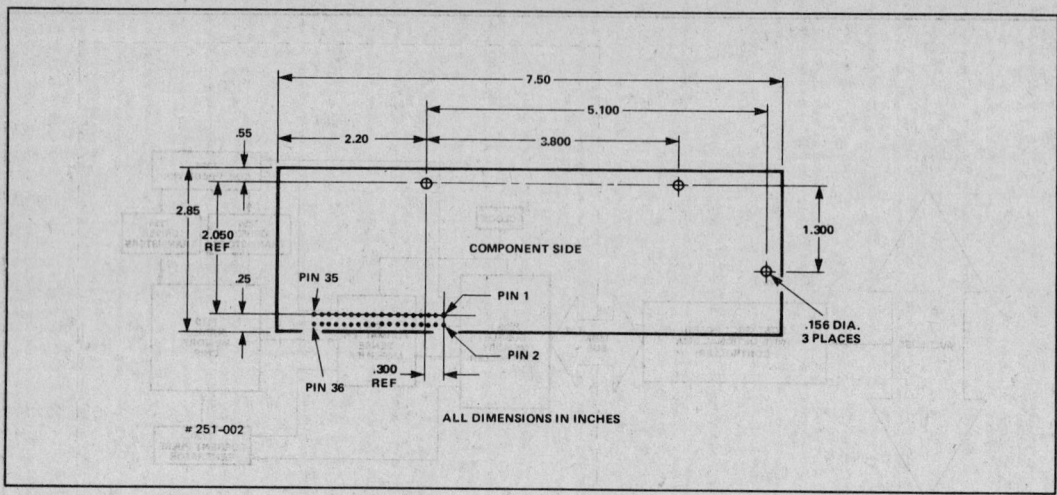

Figure 3. iSBX™ Connector and Spacer Locations

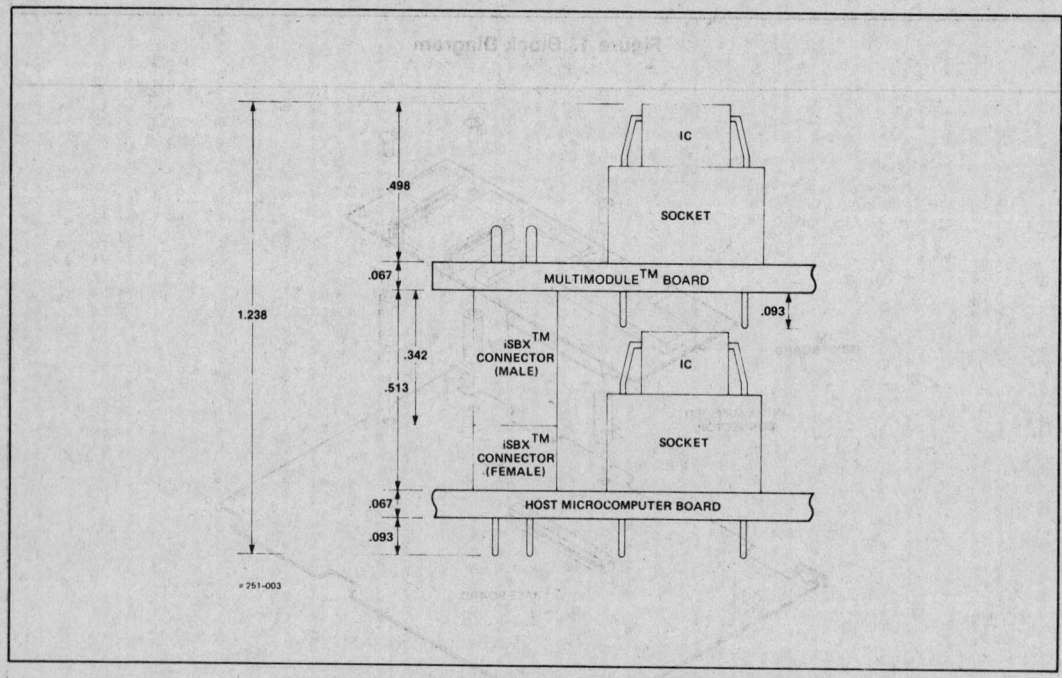

Figure 4. Mounting Clearances (Inches)

iSBX™ 251/iSBX™ 251C BOARD

SPECIFICATIONS

Storage Capacity
—128K Eight-Bit Bytes
—2048 Pages
—Page Length:
  64 bytes with ECC
  68 bytes without ECC

Physical Characteristics
Width....................... 7.24 cm (2.85 in.)
Length..................... 19.05 cm (7.50 in.)
Height...................... 1.27 cm (0.498 in.)
Weight................... 362.9 gm (12.8 oz.)

Environment
iSBX 251 board................ 0-60°C Ambient
iSBX 251C board............ 10°-40°C Ambient
Temperatures quoted are ambient with 100 lfm air flow.

Operational Modes
Polled, Interrupt Driven, or DMA (with Host DMA Controller)

Electrical Requirements
D.C. power, supplied through iSBX connector:

Voltage	D.C. Tolerance	Power Off/Power Fail Decay Rate	Maximum Current
+12 Volts	±5%	less than 1.10 volts/msec	400mA
+5 Volts	±5%	less than 0.45 volts/msec	365mA

Performance
Maximum Data Rate .... 400K bits/sec
Average Access Time................... 48 ms
Average Transfer Rate............. 68K bits/sec

Interface Requirements
—TTL compatible
—iSBX 251 male connector plugs into 36-pin or 44-pin host female connector Intel No. 7906.

Relative Humidity:
0% to 95% without condensation
Non-Volatile Storage temperature:
iSBX 251C board................ −20 to +75°C
iSBX 251 board................. −40 to +90°C

Additional Documentation
iSBX251 Technical Manual (Order Number 112924)
iSBX Bus Specification (Order Number 142686)
Memory Components Handbook
(Order Number 210830)

*MDS is an ordering code and is not used as a product name or trademark. MDS is a registered trademark of Mohawk Data Sciences Corporation.

4-67

iSBX™ 258
iSBX INTERFACE MULTIMODULE™ FOR INTEL BUBBLE CASSETTE SYSTEM

- **Interfaces iBC Bus to iSBX™ Bus**
- **Single-Wide iSBX™ MULTIMODULE™**
- **Drives One or Two iBC Systems**
- **Speeds Design Time with iBC Systems**

The iSBX 258 Interface MULTIMODULE for the Intel Bubble Cassette (iBC) System provides an iSBX interface for the iBC system. Each iSBX 258 can interface up to two daisychained iBC systems in polled or interrupt data transfer modes, or one in the DMA mode.

The iSBX 258 plugs into Intel iSBC® Single Board Computer products which have iSBX connectors or any other processor boards with iSBX connectors. It is included in the iBCK 12 iBC prototyping kit to facilitate design work on the iBC system.

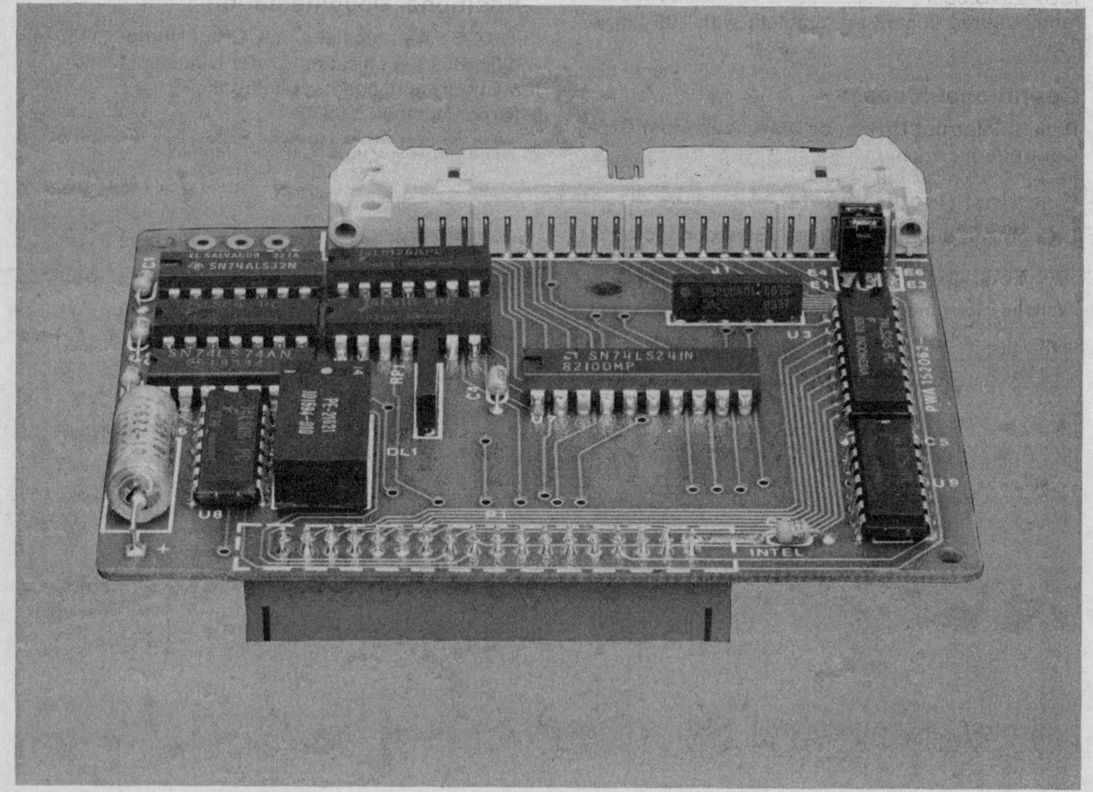

Intel Corporation Assumes No Responsibility for the Use of Any Circuitry Other Than Circuitry Embodied in an Intel Product. No Other Circuit Patent Licenses are Implied.

© INTEL CORPORATION, 1984

JUNE 1984
ORDER NUMBER: 231085-001

iSBX™ 258

FUNCTIONAL DESCRIPTION

The iSBX 258 is a completely assembled and tested iBC bus to iSBX bus interface board. (See Figure 1 for a block diagram of its recommended configuration in an iBC system.) It consists of buffer circuitry mounted on a single-wide iSBX MULTIMODULE card. It is completely iSBX bus compatible and allows easy iSBX interface to an iBC system with up to 18" of ribbon cable.

OPERATION

The operation of the MULTIMODULE is software transparent to the user while maintaining all iSBX bus specifications; +5Vdc ±5% is supplied from the iSBX bus.

MOUNTING TECHNIQUE

As shown in Figure 2, the iSBX 258 plugs into a host board via the iSBX connector and is secured by a spacer with a screw. A single-wide iSBX MULTI-MODULE is used and one Multibus card slot is occupied in addition to the card slot for the host board. Dimensions of the board and host board/MULTI-MODULE height tolerances are given in Figures 3 and 4. Although the iSBX 258 board's male iSBX connector has the standard 36 pins, it will also plug into the expanded 44 pin female iSBX connector.

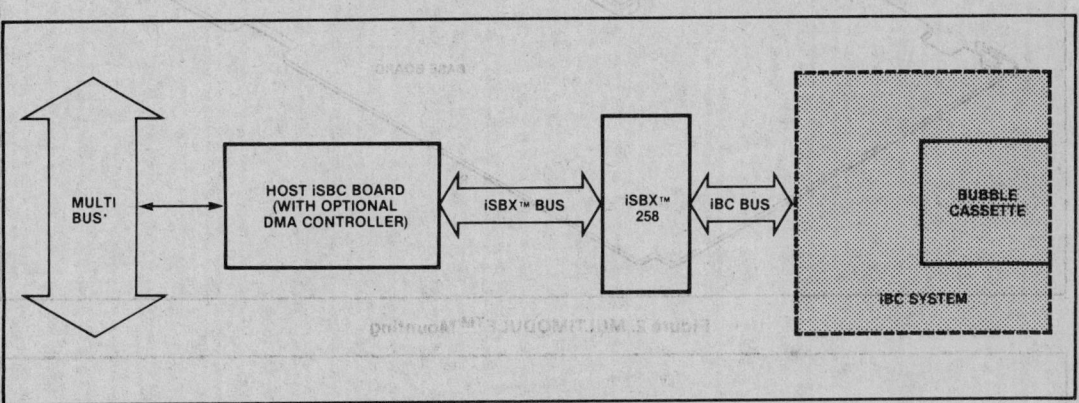

Figure 1. Block Diagram

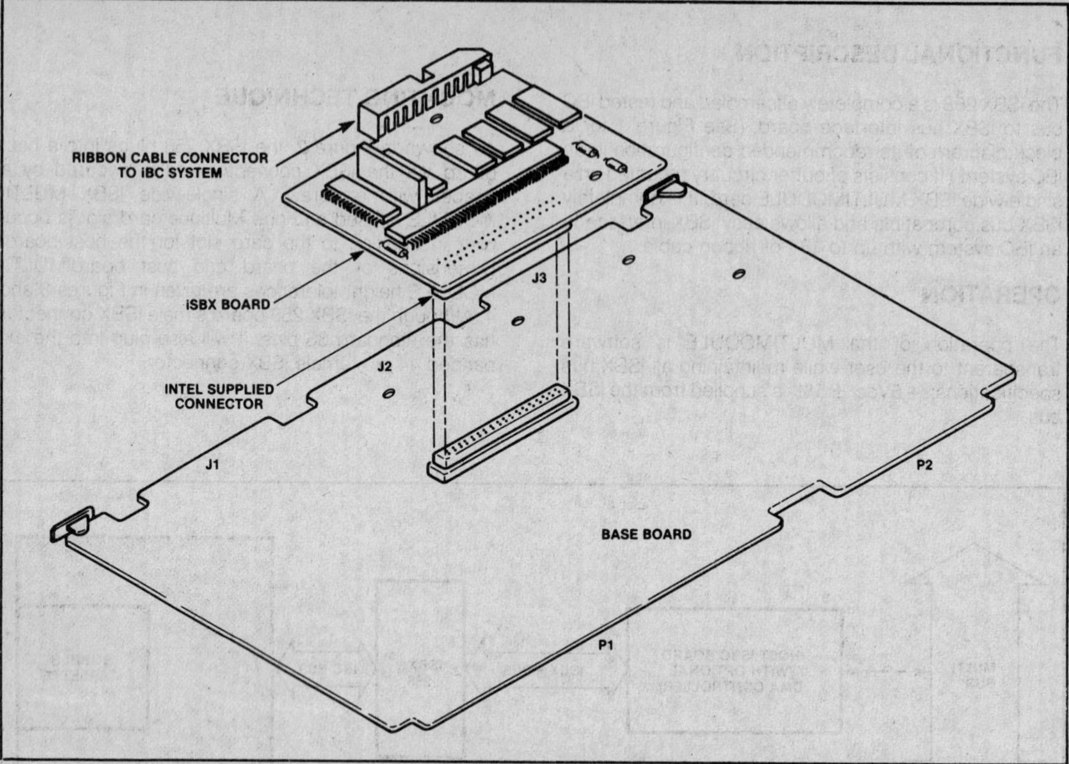

iSBX™ 258

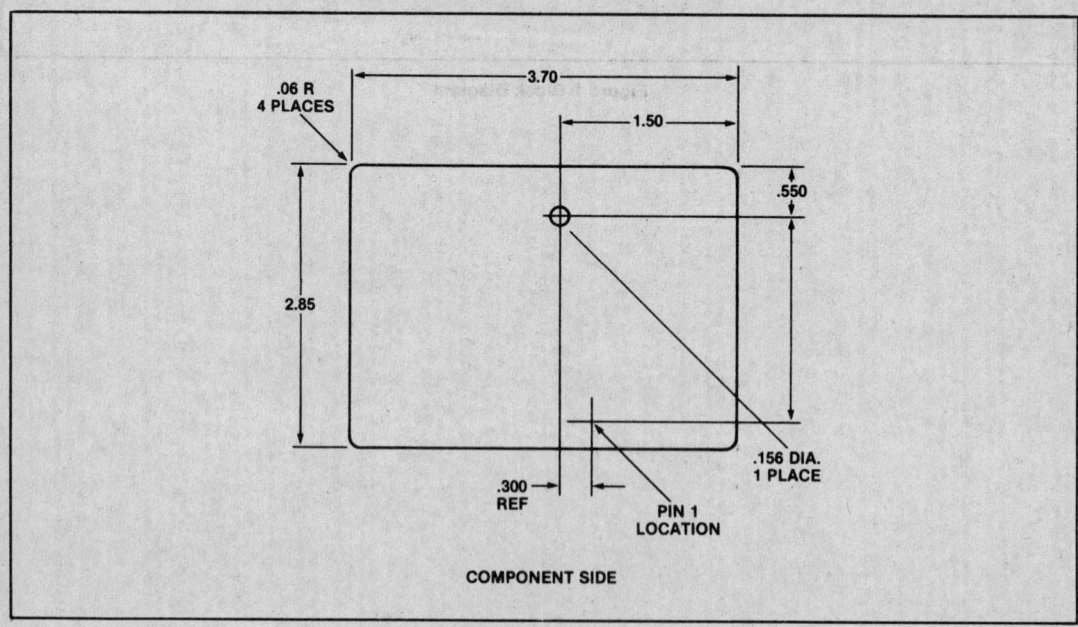

Figure 2. MULTIMODULE™ Mounting

Figure 3. Dimensions

4-70

iSBX™ 258

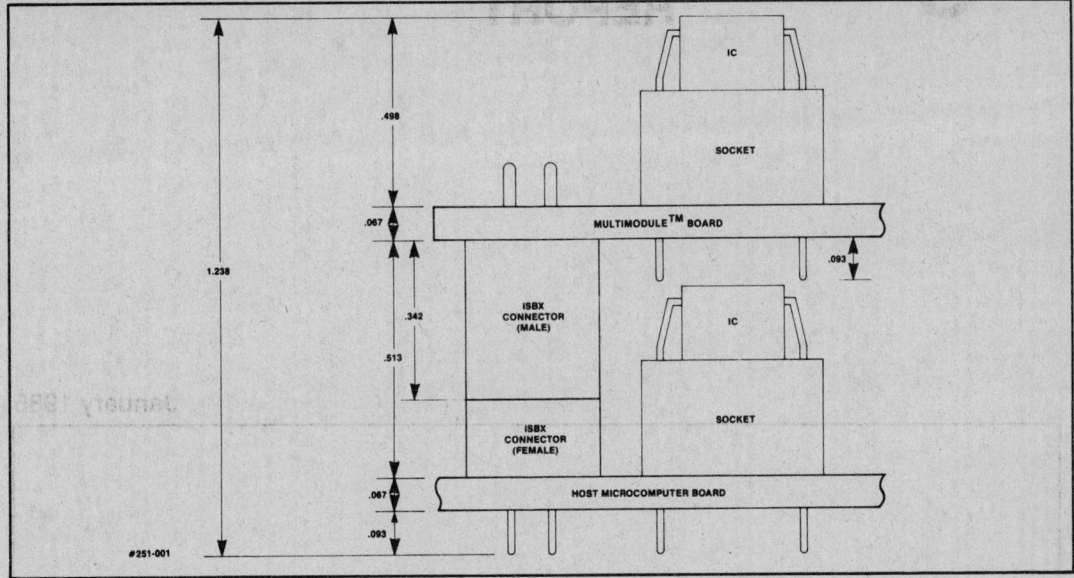

Figure 4. Mounting Clearance

SPECIFICATIONS

Physical Characteristics

Width: 7.24 cm (2.85 in.)
Length: 9.40 cm (3.70 in.)
Height: 2.05 cm (0.81 in.)
Weight: 1.8g

Environment

iSBX 258 Board 0-65°C
Temperatures are ambient in free moving air.

Operational Modes

Supports Polled, Interrupt-Driven, or DMA (with Host DMA controller) transfers with the iBC system.

Electrical Requirements

D.C. power, supplied through iSBX connector: +5Vdc ±5%, 285 mA (max).

Note: Three auxilliary points are provided which supply +5V, +12V and GND. Power available is:

V_{CC} = 5V @ 2.7A (max)
V_{dd} = 12V @ 1.0A (max)

Performance in iBC System

Maximum Data Rate: 100KBits/sec
Average Access Time: 48 msec.
Average Transfer Rate: 68KBits/sec

Interface Requirements

— TTL compatible
— iSBX 258 male iSBX connector plugs into 36-pin or 44-pin host female connector
— iSBX 258 40-pin male ribbon cable connector plugs into 40-pin female ribbon cable connector cabled to iBC system.

Relative Humidity

0% to 95% without condensation

Additional Documentation

Intel Bubble Cassette System Users' Manual (Order #122278-001)
iSBX Bus Specification (Order #142686)

intel

RELIABILITY REPORT

RR-54

January 1985

Series C/CX Memory Board Reliability

CLEONE HAWKINSON
SYSTEMS QUALITY AND RELIABILITY

© 1985, INTEL CORPORATION

Order Number: 280090-001

RR-54

Reliability Report: SERIES C/CX MEMORY BOARD RELIABILITY

RELIABILITY: THE ABILITY OF A PRODUCT TO CONSISTENTLY OPERATE FAILURE-FREE FOR A SPECIFIED AMOUNT OF TIME IN THE ENVIRONMENT FOR WHICH IT WAS DESIGNED

SUMMARY

This report presents the results of the reliability evaluations of the family of iSBC® Series C/CX Memory Boards (iSBC 028C, iSBC 056C, iSBC 012C, iSBC 028CX, iSBC 056CX, iSBC 012CX, iSBC 010CX, and iSBC 020CX boards). This report also reviews Intel's standard component and board Quality Assurance and Reliability qualification program.

The products included in this report have passed reliability and environmental tests (vibration, humidity, temperature, voltage margin, and circuit timing analysis). The evaluations of all the Series C/CX Memory Boards, except the iSBC 010CX and iSBC 020CX boards, were conducted at the same time. The reliability and environmental evaluations of the iSBC 010CX and iSBC 020CX boards, upgrades of the earlier versions, were recently completed. A summary of the Mean Time Between Failures (MTBF) data is shown below and demonstrates the established reliability of these products. Detailed test results with supporting data are presented in the text.

iSBC® Board	MTBF 55°C (hours)	Confidence Level
012CX	9,600	60%
012C	9,600*	60%
056CX	9,600*	60%
056C	9,600*	60%
028CX	9,600*	60%
028C	9,600*	60%
020CX	12,200	60%
010CX	12,200*	60%

* Due to product similarity the MTBF, established on worst-case configurations (iSBC 012CX and iSBC 020CX boards), is inferred as a minimum.

THE SERIES C/CX MEMORY BOARDS

The iSBC Series C/CX Memory Boards (iSBC 028C, iSBC 056C, iSBC 012C, iSBC 028CX, iSBC 056CX, iSBC 012CX, iSBC 010CX, and iSBC 020CX boards) are members of Intel's complete line of iSBC memory and I/O expansion boards. These boards interface directly to various Intel Single Board Computers to expand the RAM capacity. The C RAM-boards interface via the MULTIBUS® system bus interface. The CX RAM-boards have a dual port feature which allows access to the memory via both the MULTIBUS and Intel Local Bus Extension (iLBX™) bus interfaces (Figure 1). Memory size, DRAM device type and interface available for each board are summarized in Table 1.

BOARD PRODUCT QUALITY ASSURANCE

The quality and reliability of products like the Series C/CX Memory Boards are a function of the quality of components used, the care taken in board design and fabrication, and the extent of testing performed on the product before shipment. An examination of each of these functions will provide an understanding of the Intel Quality Assurance program for microcomputer board products.

Component Quality Assurance

Standard Intel Component Quality Assurance processing and 100% screening are applied to all Intel manufactured components before they are assembled on the boards. Once a component has been qualified as reliable and transferred to board-level manufacturing, complete process controls ensure the continuation of high quality.

Intel's Component Quality Assurance flow, shown in Figure 2, combines a series of acceptance gates between process steps and detailed inspection at critical points within the processing areas. For example, during wafer fabrication, processes are routinely monitored for contamination through the use of capacitance versus voltage measurements on test chips. Electrical tests, such as breakdown voltage measurements, are performed on test patterns on each wafer. Routine scanning electron microscope examinations at critical process steps also provide important process control feedback. Full functional testing of all parts precedes final Quality Assurance acceptance. Components are then sent to assembly locations.

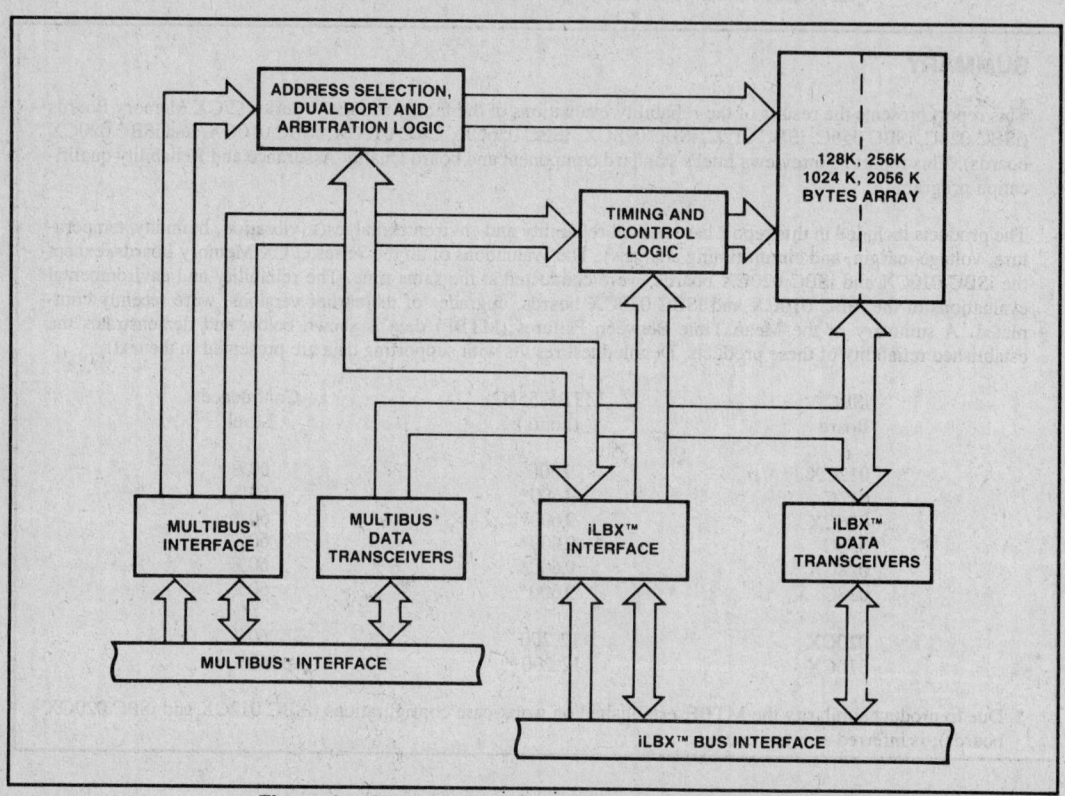

Figure 1. iSBC® 028CX/056CX/012CX Block Diagram

Table 1. Series C/CX Memory Boards

iSBC® Board	Memory Size (K-bytes)	DRAM Devices	Interfaces Via
028C	128	64K-bit	MULTIBUS®
056C	256	2164	bus
012C	512		
028CX	128	64K-bit	MULTIBUS®
056CX	256	2164	& iLBX™
012CX	512		buses
010CX	1024	256K-bit	MULTIBUS®
020CX	2048	21256	& iLBX™ buses

4-74

280090-001

RR-54

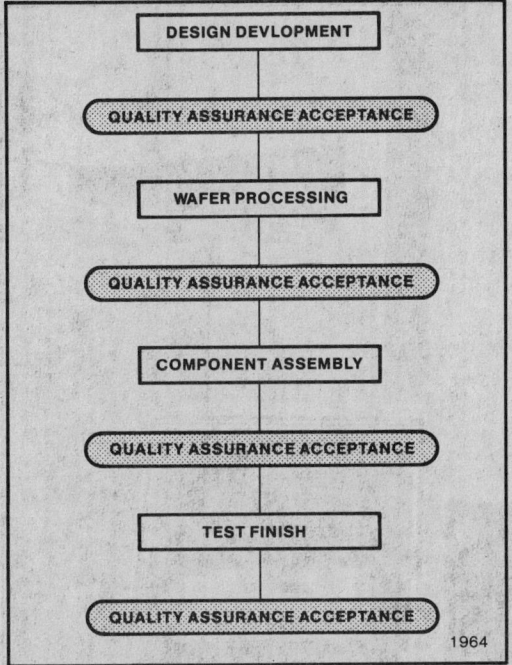

Figure 2. Component Quality Assurance Flow

Board Manufacturing, Testing, and Inspection

The Single Board Computer manufacturing process is closely monitored by Quality Assurance, and inspection occurs at several key stages (Figure 3). Our goal is to achieve 100% acceptance of vendor materials. Source Inspection at selected vendors eliminates some incoming material inspection altogether. However, for commodities such as bare boards and non-Intel components, incoming inspection assures quality specifications are met (see Figure 4 and 5).

After incoming inspection and test, components for an assembly "kit" are pulled together and readied for the assembly operation. Each kit is visually inspected and components are assembled onto the bare board.

Automatic equipment installs most routine components. Machines do repetitive, precision jobs without tiring, which increases productivity and ensures consistent quality. Programmed Dual In-Line Package (DIP) auto-insertion equipment installs integrated circuits onto bare boards (Figure 6). Next, the axial lead inserter is programmed to install capacitors, diodes, and resistors. After automatic stake pin insertion, a three-station robot (Figure 7) puts low profile jumper plugs in place. Finally, a machine masks the areas of the boards which do not need to be soldered.

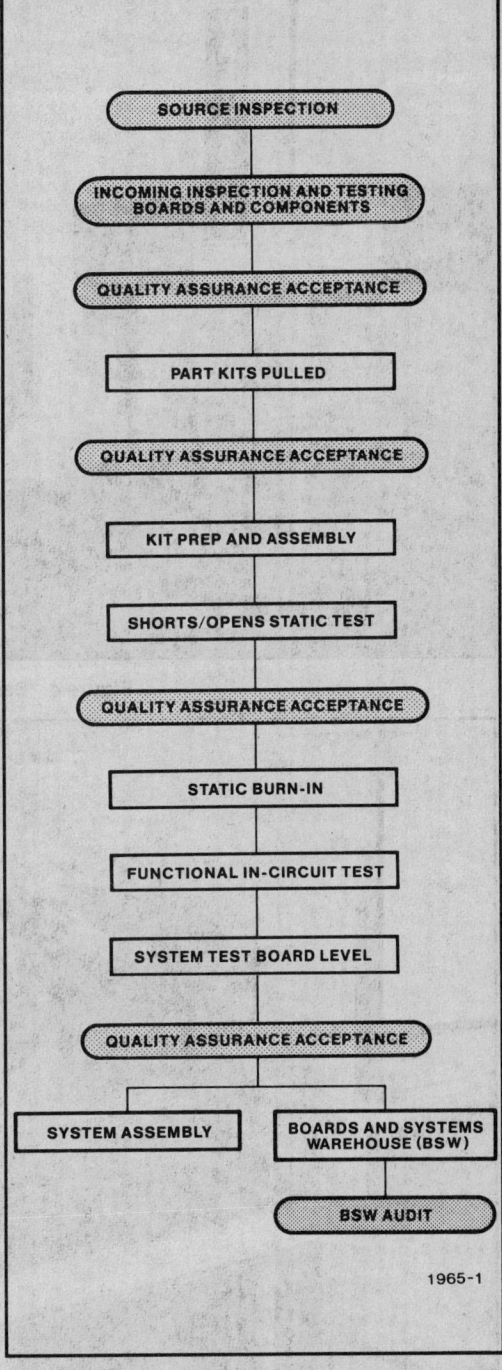

Figure 3. Board Manufacturing, Testing, and Inspection

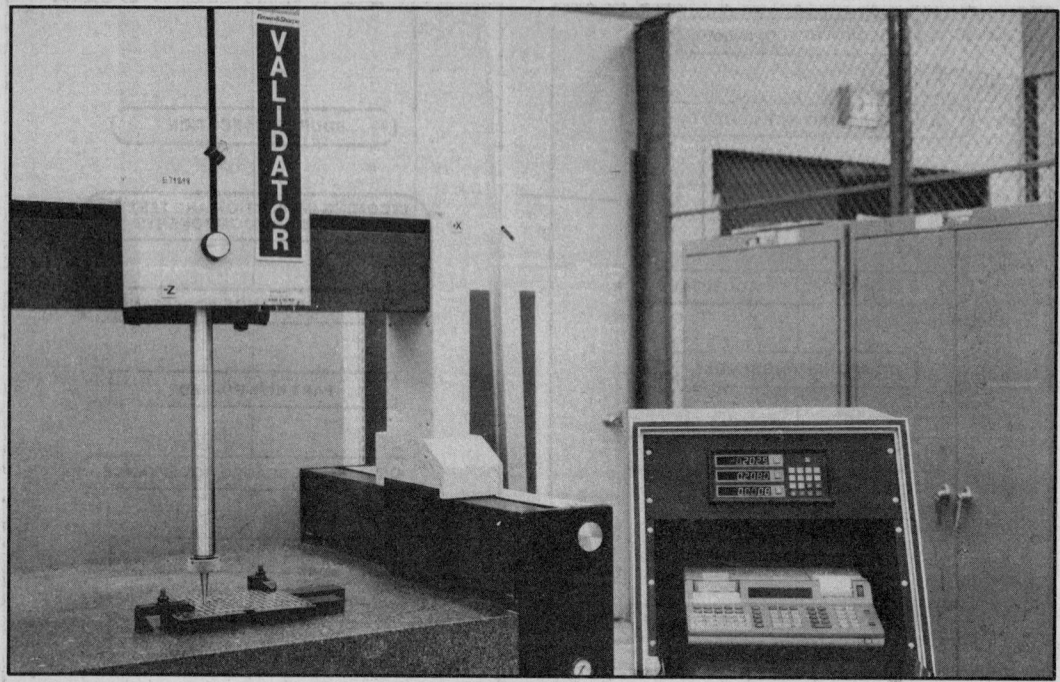

Figure 4. Bare Board Validator

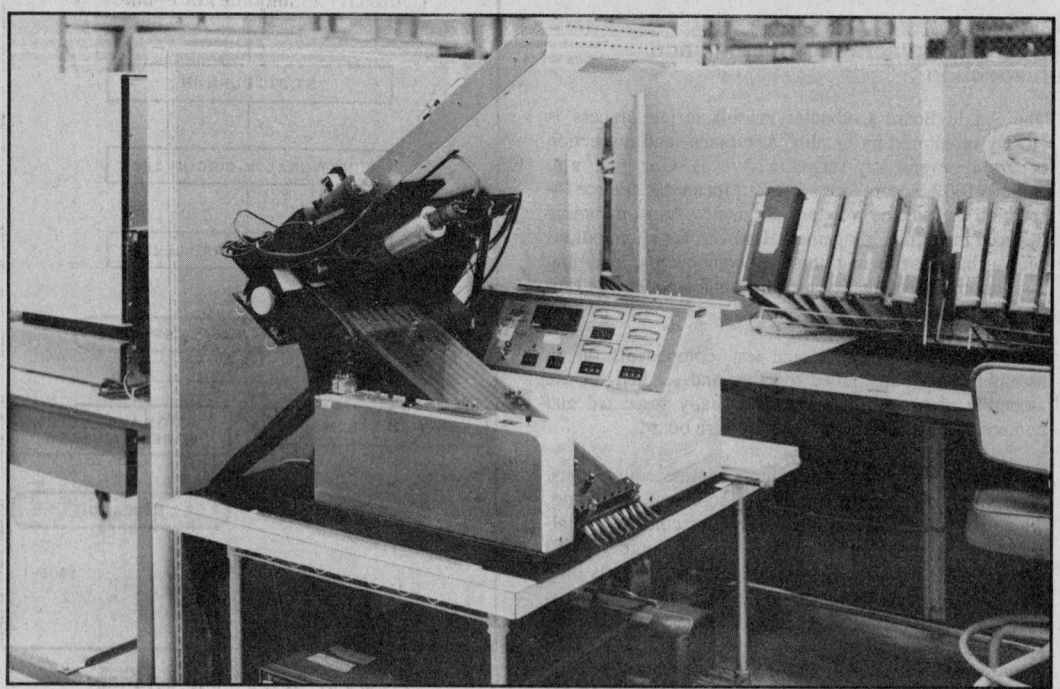

Figure 5. Integrated Circuit Tester

Figure 6 Dual In-Line Package Auto-Insertion Equipment

Parts unsuitable for automatic assembly are manually assembled onto the board. The board is then inspected for accuracy prior to wave solder and for soldering defects after wave solder.

Intel is proud of its wave solder process control. The post solder cleaning process includes detergent and rinse baths monitored and controlled for concentration, temperature, and contamination. Boards are selected at random and then checked under a microscope to ensure compliance to wave solder process and cleanliness standards.

Two other process checks are performed. First, boards are sample tested in an Omegameter (Figure 8), which measures ionic contamination. Second, one board per lot is placed in the Thermotron steady-state environmental chamber at elevated temperature (70°C) and humidity (85% RH) for 96 hours. The board is then checked under a microscope for contamination corrosion. In the rare event that any deviation occurs, the Quality Assurance Auditor stops the process until compliance is restored.

In touch-up and second assembly, such items as connectors and process sensitive components are added to a board. As the final phase of assembly, a board is tested for "shorts" and "opens" on the Teradyne L529 Automatic Test Equipment. Final assembly inspection verifies the boards are acceptable for functional test.

The next stage is static burn-in at elevated temperature and voltage margins (70°C, +6% VDC). Burn-in eliminates temperature- and voltage-related "infant mortality" failures that occur early in the life of a product. All boards are burned-in for 6 1/2 hours in ovens (Figure 9).

Figure 7. Robot

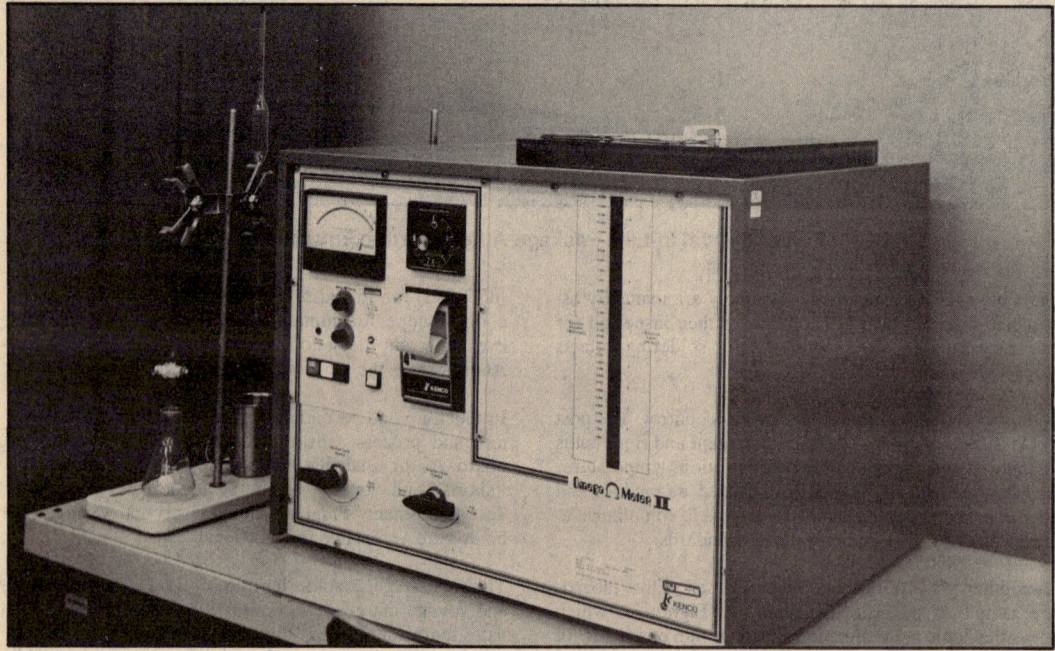

Figure 8. Omegameter: Wave Solder Process Control

Figure 9. Board Burn-in Ovens

Every board is then tested on a Teradyne L125/L135 In-Circuit Tester (Figure 10). This system has a "test the tester" feature that verifies all test points are functioning before actual boards are tested. A special "bed of nails" vacuum fixture ensures that all critical board test points may be accessed by the test system. Any components that fail are replaced, and the boards are retested on the Teradyne system.

Next, each board is functionally tested at System Test Board Level (STBL). For these tests a set of monitor and diagnostic EPROMs are installed. The board is placed in a General Purpose Test Fixture (GPTF) shown in Figure 11. This is a three-phased test. The first test sequence is performed at room temperature and at nominal voltage. The second phase is at elevated temperature (70°C) and +6% VDC voltage. The final phase is at elevated temperature (70°C) and −6% VDC voltage. The STBL program verifies the board's performance throughout these sequences by testing the CPU, the I/O interface, and the MULTIBUS interface in a multiprocessing environment.

After the test sequence, all boards are inspected to ensure that they comply with required quality standards. Boards passing this final screening are then released by Quality Assurance for use in an Intel system product or sent to packaging.

After packaging, a board is sent to the Boards and Systems Warehouse (BSW) to await shipment to the customer. Quality Assurance conducts monthly finished goods audits on randomly selected products in the BSW. This audit reviews documentation, tests for compliance to environmental specifications (temperature, humidity, vibration), and confirms functional performance over time. This finished goods audit is a final in-house monitor of the quality that reaches the customer. Results of the audit are reported back to the factory.

Product performance in the field is also tracked. Results are monitored on a computerized data system, and feedback is used to ensure corrective actions when required.

This rigorous testing, tracking, and corrective action system ensures that Intel's product specifications and the customer's quality and reliability expectations are met.

BOARD PRODUCT RELIABILITY

The Life Curve

Three categories of failures can occur during product life:

- Infant Mortality
- Random
- Wear Out

Each category has a distinct failure distribution when failure frequency is plotted against time. When the three dis-

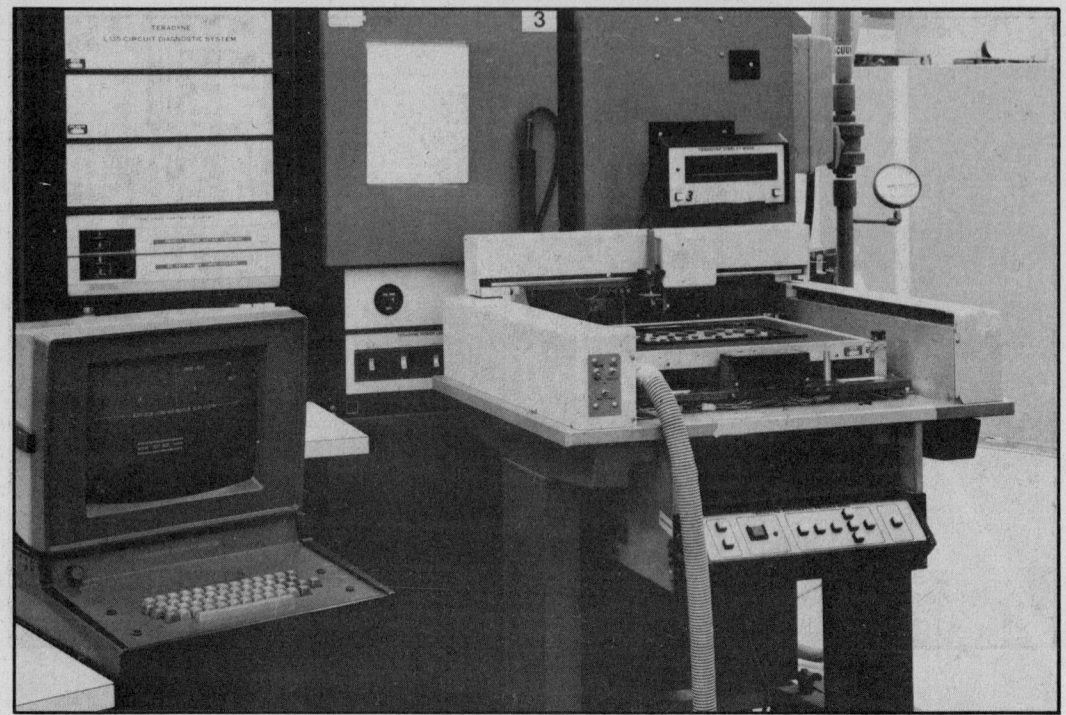

Figure 10. Teradyne Tester

Figure 11. General Purpose Test Fixture

tributions are combined, the resulting failure rate/time distribution produces a characteristic curve known as a "bathtub" curve. The three distributions and the combined bathtub curve are represented in Figure 12.

The boundaries between the categories are less precise than they appear because the failure categories have overlapping distributions. For example, Infant Mortality failures may extend into the Random failure category, but at a low level. Wear Out failures may, in fact, occasionally occur before the expected Wear Out period.

The Infant Mortality area of the curve shows failures caused by manufacturing defects in the components and boards. These are "quality failures," and their frequency decreases with time. Infant Mortality for boards depends on the quality and test history of the components used in manufacturing and is eliminated by burn-in.

Random failures occur during the "useful life" of the product between Infant Mortality and Wear Out. These failures are primarily a function of temperature and circuit complexity. The early phase of the Random failure period is identified during burn-in. As the failure pattern becomes random, it approaches a low constant value (flat distribution).

Wear Out failures are primarily due to mechanical wear or chemical degradation resulting in lack of conformance to specifications. Statistically, Wear Out should not happen until many thousands of hours have elapsed for VLSI-based products.

Mean Time Between Failures and Confidence Levels

In reliability evaluation Mean Time Between Failures (MTBF) is the average time in hours expected to elapse between failures. The point estimate of the MTBF is calculated by dividing the total test operating hours for a sample of system products by the total number of failures during the test period. The demonstrated value at a specific confidence level is calculated using the Chi-Square probability distribution[1]. The confidence level defines the probability of the true MTBF of the product exceeding the demonstrated MTBF value. For board testing the required minimum confidence level defined in the reliability test is 60%. This means that the true product MTBF will be higher than the demonstrated MTBF, 60% of the time.

As the ratio of operating test hours to the true MTBF increases, the confidence that the true MTBF exceeds the specified lower limit also increases. For example, to demonstrate an MTBF of 5000 hours with a confidence level

[1]See Reference 1

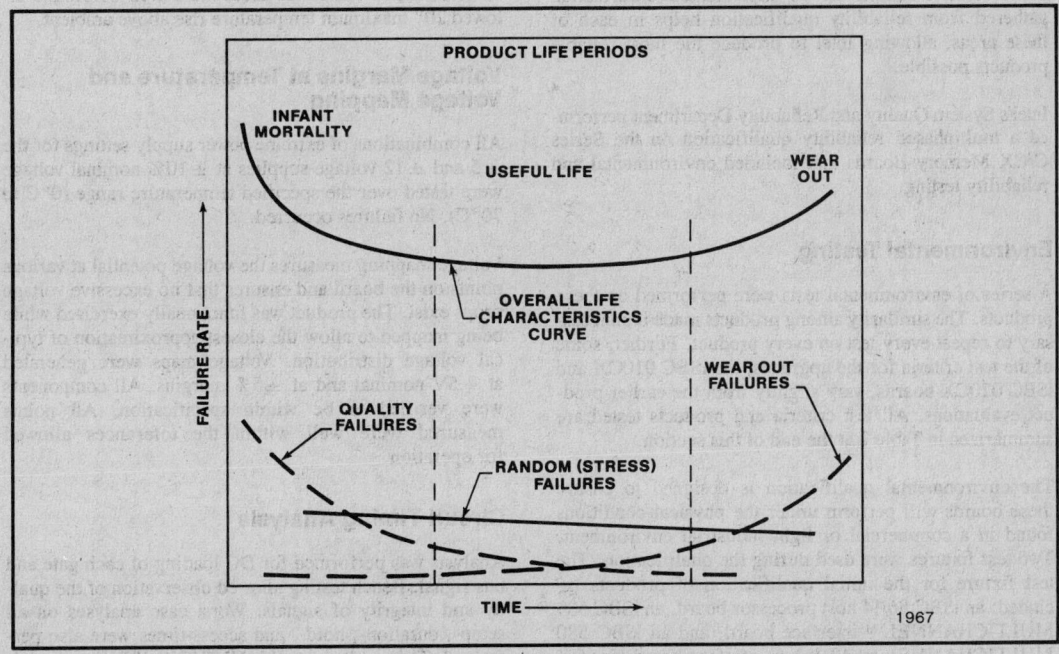

Figure 12. Reliability Life Curve

of 60% takes 10,000 hours of operation with one failure. To demonstrate the same MTBF at a 90% confidence level requires 19,500 hours. The values of MTBF for boards are normally at the 60% confidence level when the product is qualified for full production. Higher confidence level is attained as data are accumulated.

RELIABILITY QUALIFICATION

Reliability qualification serves at least three important functions:

- Provides reliability feedback to product design
- Demonstrates the MTBF and verifies product integrity
- Checks the manufacturing process

First, reliability qualification serves as a feedback mechanism for product design. Lessons learned from building one product can be used to improve the design of new products. Second, the qualification demonstrates the MTBF of a product. Also, a wide range of reliability tests verify that the product performs to specification in the intended environment. This information helps customers to evaluate Intel systems, and helps Intel anticipate customers' product support requirements. Finally, reliability qualification serves as a manufacturing process check. When failures attributed to the manufacturing process occur, they can be quickly identified as exceptions and corrective actions can be implemented. Information gathered from reliability qualification helps in each of these areas, allowing Intel to produce the most reliable products possible.

Intel's System Quality and Reliability Department performed a multiphased reliability qualification on the Series C/CX Memory Boards that included environmental and reliability testing.

Environmental Testing

A series of environmental tests were performed on these products. The similarity among products made it unnecessary to repeat every test on every product. Further, some of the test criteria for the upgrades, the iSBC 010CX and iSBC 020CX boards, vary slightly from the earlier product evaluations. All test criteria and products tested are summarized in Table 2 at the end of this section.

The environmental qualification is designed to ensure these boards will perform under the physical conditions found in a commercial or light industrial environment. Two test fixtures were used during the qualification. The test fixture for the initial qualification of products included: an iSBC 86/14 host processor board, an iSBC 589 MULTICHANNEL™ interface board, and an iSBC 580 MULTICHANNEL to iLBX bus interface board (for CX versions).

The test fixture for the iSBC 010CX/020 upgrades included: an iSBC 286/10 host processor board, an iSBC 614 cardcage, and an iSBC 604 cardcage inter-connected with the iLBX bus. The airflow rate during all tests was 200 linear feet per minute (LFM) ensuring proper cooling during functional tests.

Humidity

The humidity test identifies problems related to high temperature and high humidity environments, such as corrosion and poor mechanical contacts. These conditions not only test the reliability of the product at high humidity and temperature, but also accelerate the effects of moderate humidity over time. The boards were exercised at 90% relative humidity (non-condensing) and 70°C for 48 hours with no failures.

Temperature Tests and Mapping

The boards were tested at two temperature ranges: 0°C to 60°C (functional) and -40°C to 70°C (non-functional). No failures occurred; the boards functioned normally. Temperature test details for each product are given in Table 2.

Temperature maps were made for each board to identify potential "hot spots." Temperatures were measured on selected components representing all areas of the board. The temperature maps were made at 25°C and repeated at 55°C ambient. All tested areas were well below the allowed 20° maximum temperature rise above ambient.

Voltage Margins at Temperature and Voltage Mapping

All combinations of extreme power supply settings for the ±5 and ±12 voltage supplies at ±10% nominal voltage were tested over the specified temperature range (0°C to 70°C). No failures occurred.

Voltage mapping measures the voltage potential at various points on the board and ensures that no excessive voltage drops exist. The product was functionally exercised while being mapped to allow the closest approximation of typical voltage distribution. Voltage maps were generated at +5V nominal and at ±5% margins. All components were verified to be within specification. All points measured were well within the tolerances allowed for operation.

Circuit Timing Analysis

Analysis was performed for DC loading of each gate and bus signal. Bench testing allowed observation of the quality and integrity of signals. Worst case analyses on all setup-, duration-, hold-, and access-times were also performed. The results met all MULTIBUS, iSBX, and product specifications, well within a reasonable guardband.

Table 2. Environmental Qualification Data

THIS INFORMATION, BASED ON SMALL SAMPLES, IS INTERNAL QUALIFICATION TEST DATA GATHERED UNDER CONDITIONS THAT EXCEED SPECIFICATIONS AND SHOULD NOT BE CONFUSED WITH WARRANTED SPECIFICATIONS. ALL CONFIGURATIONS TESTED PASSED ALL TESTS.

iSBC® Board	Sample	Test	Description
		HUMIDITY	
028C	1	Passed	Functional: 90% RH (non-condensing)
056C	1	Passed	70°C for 48 hours
012C	1	Passed	
010CX	1	Passed	90% RH (non-condensing)
020CX	1	Passed	70°C for 72 hours
		TEMPERATURE	
028C	1	Passed	Functional: Two hours each at 0°, 20°, 40°, 60°C
056C	1	Passed	Non-functional: −40°C to +70°C
012C	1	Passed	
010CX	1	Passed	Functional: Two hours at −10°C and eight hours at +70°C
020CX	1	Passed	
		TEMPERATURE MAP	
			Maximum delta:
			25°C 55 °C
012C	2	Passed	32.3°C 61.9°C
056C	2	Passed	34.5°C 63.0°C
028C	2	Passed	39.3°C 69.3°C
010CX	1	Passed	34.5°C 63.0°C
			32 IC test points: 25°C, 55°C
			Maximum temperature rise allowed 20° above ambient
		VOLTAGE MARGINS AT TEMPERATURE	
028C	1	Passed	0°C to 70°C; ±5, ±12 voltage supplies at ±10% nominal voltage for four hours
056C	1	Passed	
012C	1	Passed	
010CX	1	Passed	
		VOLTAGE MAP	
028C	1	Passed	Functional:
056C	1	Passed	Voltage measurement within ±1% of nominal
012C	1	Passed	+5 volts
010CX	1	Passed	No ground shift problems
020CX	1	Passed	
		CIRCUIT TIMING ANALYSIS	
028C	1	Passed	DC loading of each gate and bus signal. Bench testing performed to observe quality and integrity of each signal. Worst-case setup-, duration-, hold-, and access-times. Met all specifications within guardbands
056C	1	Passed	
012C	1	Passed	
010CX	1	Passed	
020CX	1	Passed	
		VIBRATION	
028C	1	Passed	0-55-0 Hz x,y,z axes .01″ PTP displacement with five 1-minute sweeps; two 10-minute dwells at resonance or 55 Hz.
056C	1	Passed	
012C	1	Passed	
010CX	1	Passed	

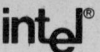

Vibration

Vibration testing identifies mechanically related problems a product could sustain under normal conditions. The areas of concern were the jumpers and components socketed at various locations on the boards. The table displacement was set for .01 inch peak-to-peak excursions on the x, y and z axes. Five one-minute sweeps from 0-55-0 Hz were made on each axis to note all resonance points. Next, each unit was vibrated at resonance on each axis for two ten-minute cycles. If no resonance point was noted, 55 Hz was used. The units functioned normally after vibration testing.

Packaging and Bench Drop Test

Board packaging requirements have been rigorously tested under both laboratory and actual shipping conditions. In the laboratory, packaged products are subjected to worst-case conditions. During the bench drop test, products are monitored for shock, and the package is accepted only after the product meets the shock specification. This portion of the reliability qualification confirms the adequacy of the standard packaging.

Reliability Test Evaluation

Reliability tests verify product reliability by demonstrating the calculated MTBF and qualify a product for full production. The similarity among the Series C/CX Memory Board products made it unnecessary to repeat every test on every product. The 020CX and 010CX, considered to be the worst-case configurations, were chosen for reliability testing.

The test software for the reliability test was designed to evaluate two critical areas. First, the MULTIBUS and iLBX interfaces were tested. Of primary concern was the need to verify that data flow across the bus was reliable. Second, the software was designed to verify that the Error Code Correction (ECC) worked through fault injection.

The reliability evaluations of the Series CX Memory Board products surpassed the minimum calculated MTBFs required for full production. Although the MTBF is demonstrated at 70°C, an MTBF at 55°C can be derived from the test data. The elevated temperature at 70°C during the evaluation provides an accelerated life factor of 2.01 above the 55°C level, based on the Arrhenius equation[1]. Although the Arrhenius equation was developed for semiconductor devices, extending its use to boards is not unreasonable. Historically in board reliability qualifications the most likely failures have been ICs. The two test results are reported separately (Table 3) and are discussed below.

[1]See Reference 2

iSBC® 012CX Memory Board

For the iSBC 012CX board, the reliability qualification required a minimum demonstrated point estimate of 11,300 hours at 55°C. Twenty units were evaluated. The test was terminated after 19,753 hours with one failure, an 8206 ECC device. The test yielded a derived MTBF of 9600 hours at 55°C, 60% confidence level.

The other products in this qualification were the iSBC 028C/CX boards, the iSBC 056C/CX boards, and the iSBC 012C board. Their inferred MTBF is 9600 hours based on the similarity of component parts to those on the iSBC 012CX board, the worst-case configuration. All products were qualified for full production.

Table 3. Reliability Test Results

iSBC® Board (sample)	Operating Hours (55°C)**	Failures	MTBF 55°C (hours)	Confidence Level
012CX (n=20)	19,753	1[1]	9,600	60%
028C	-		9,600*	60%
028CX	-		9,600*	60%
056C	-		9,600*	60%
056CX	-		9,600*	60%
012C	-		9,600*	60%
020CX (n=9)	11,288	0	12,200	60%
010CX	-		12,200*	60%

[1]Failure: 8206 ECC Device

*Due to product similarity the MTBF, established on worst-case configurations (iSBC 012CX and iSBC 020CX boards), is inferred as a minimum.

**Test at 70°C

iSBC® 020CX Memory Board

For the iSBC 020CX board, the reliability qualification required a minimum demonstrated point estimate of 10,500 hours at 55°C. Nine units were evaluated. The test was terminated after 11,288 hours with no failures. The test yielded a derived MTBF of 12,200 hours at 55°C, 60% confidence level.

The other upgrade, the iSBC 010CX board, differs only in that less memory is available. The inferred MTBF is 12,200 hours based on its similarity to the iSBC 020CX board. Both products were qualified for full production.

CONCLUSION

This report has reviewed Intel's Quality Assurance and Reliability program and presented information on the reliability qualification of the Series C/CX Memory Board products. These evaluations demonstrate the high reliability of each of these products. These boards clearly surpass the performance requirements established by Intel.

REFERENCES

1. *Reliability Mathematics: Fundamentals; Practices; and Procedures*, B.L. Amstadler, 1971. McGraw-Hill, Inc.

2. *Semiconductor Device Reliability and the Arrhenius Model*, National Semiconductor Reliability Report G-11, January 1977.

Peripheral Controllers 5

iSBC® 208
FLEXIBLE DISKETTE CONTROLLER

- Compatible with all iSBC®80, iSBC® 86, and iSBC® 88 Single Board Computers
- Controls most single and double density diskette drives
- On-board iSBX™ bus for additional functions
- User-programmable drive parameters allow wide choice of drives
- Phase lock loop data separator assures maximum data integrity
- Read and write on single or multiple sectors
- Single +5V Supply
- Capable of addressing 16M bytes of system memory

The Intel iSBC 208 Flexible Disk Controller is a diskette controller capable of supporting virtually any soft-sectored, double density or single density diskette drive. The standard controller can control up to four drives with up to eight surfaces. In addition to the standard IBM 3740 formats and IBM System 34 formats, the controller supports sector lengths of up to 8192 bytes. The iSBC 208 board's wide range of drive compatibility is achieved without compromising performance. The operating characteristics are specified under user program control. The controller can read, write, verify, and search either single or multiple sectors. Additional capability such as parallel or serial I/O or special math functions can be placed on the iSBC 208 board by utilizing the iSBX bus connection.

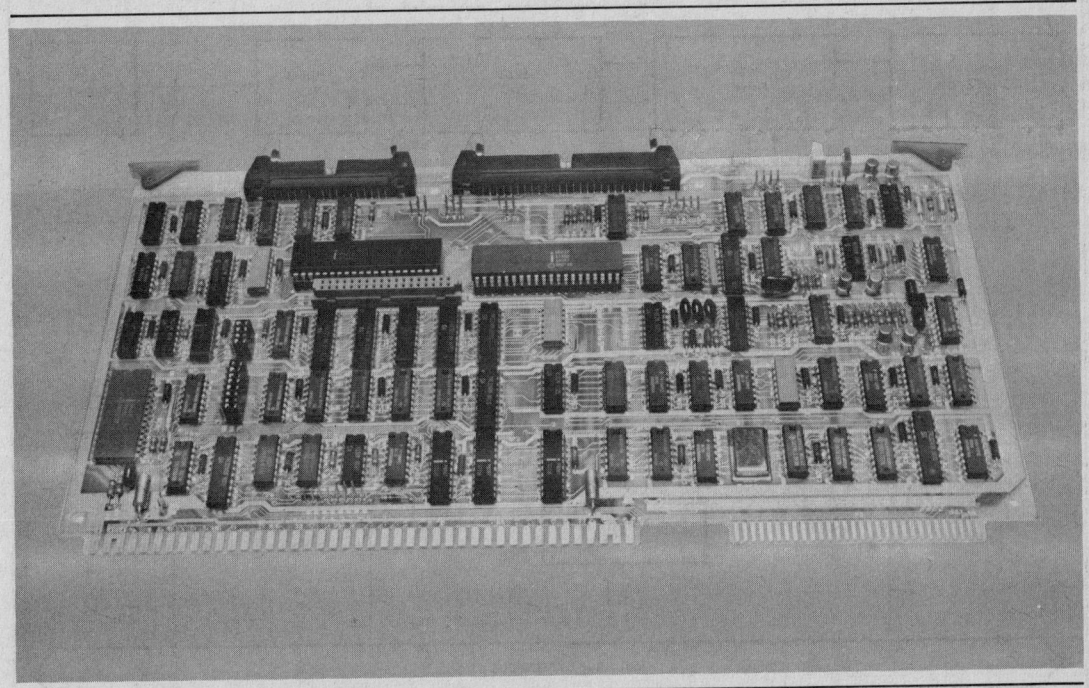

AFN-01629A

iSBC® 208

FUNCTIONAL DESCRIPTION

Intel's 8272 Floppy Disk Controller (FDC) circuit is the heart of the iSBC 208 Controller. On-board data separation logic performs standard MFM (double density) and FM (single density) encoding and decoding, eliminating the need for external separation circuitry at the drive. Data transfers between the controller and memory are managed by a DMA device which completely controls transfers over the MULTIBUS system bus. A block diagram of the iSBC 208 Controller is shown in Figure 1.

Universal Drives and the iSBC® 208 Controller

Because the iSBC 208 Controller has universal drive compatibility, it can be used to control virtually any standard- or mini-sized diskette drive. Moreover, the iSBC 208 Controller fully supports the iSBX bus and can be used with any iSBX module compatible with this bus. Because the iSBC 208 Controller is programmable, its performance is not compromised by its universal drive compatibility. The track-to-track access, head-load, and head-unload characteristics of the selected drive model are program specified. Data may be organized in sectors up to 8192 bytes in length.

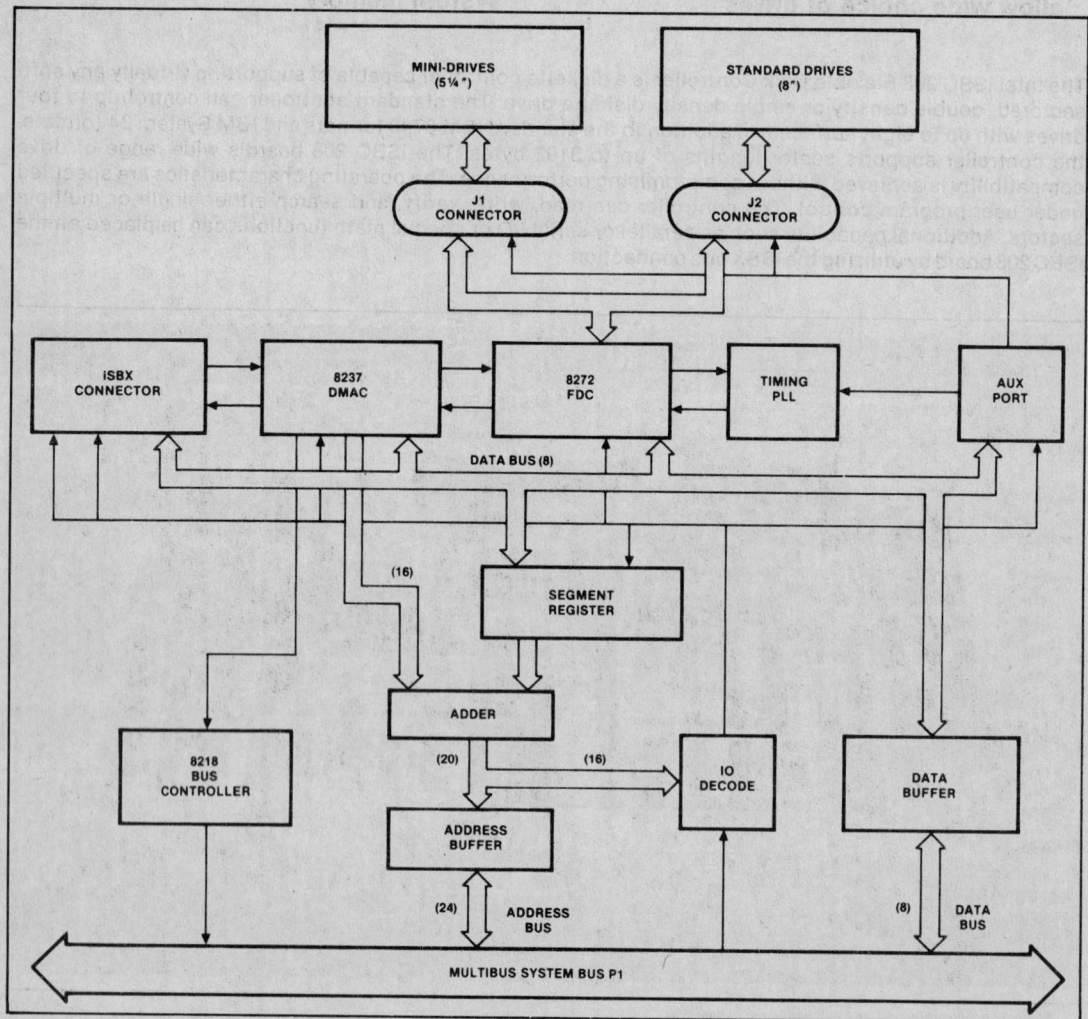

Figure 1. iSBC® 208 Flexible Disk Controller Block Diagram

iSBC® 208

Interface Characteristics

The standard iSBC 208 Controller includes an Intel 8272 Floppy Disk Controller chip which supports up to four drives, single or double sided.

SIMPLIFIED INTERFACE—The cables between the iSBC 208 Controller and the drive(s) may be low cost, flat ribbon cable with mass termination connectors. The mechanical interface to the board is a right-angle header with locking tabs for security of connection.

PROGRAMMING — The powerful 8272 FDC circuit is capable of executing high-level commands that simplify system software development. The device can read and write both single and multiple sectors. CRC characters are generated and checked automatically. Recording density is selected at each Read and Write to support the industry standard technique of recording basic media information on Track 0 of Side 0 in single density, and then switching to double density (if necessary) for operations on other tracks.

Program Initiation—All diskette operations are initiated by standard input/output (I/O) port operations through an iSBC single board computer.

System software first initializes the controller with the operating characteristics of the selected drive. The diskette is then formatted under program control. For subsequent transfers, the starting memory address and transfer mode are specified for the DMA controller. Data transfers occur in response to commands output by the CPU.

Data Transfer—Once a diskette transfer operation has been initiated, the controller acts as a bus master and transfers data over the MULTIBUS at high speed. No CPU intervention is required until the transfer is complete as indicated either by the generation of an interrupt on the bus or by examination of a "done" bit by the CPU.

iSBX BUS SUPPORT — One connector is available on the iSBC 208 board which supports the iSBX system bus. This connector supports single-byte transfer as well as higher-speed transfers supervised by the DMA controller. Transfers may take place in polled or interrupt modes, user-selected. The presence of the iSBX bus allows many different functions to be added to the board. Serial I/O, parallel I/O and various special-purpose math functions are only a few of the capabilities available on iSBX MULTIMODULE boards.

SPECIFICATIONS

Compatibility

CPU—Any iSBC MULTIBUS computer or system main frame

Devices—Double or single density standard (8") and mini (5¼") flexible disk drives. The drives may be single or double sided. Drives known to be compatible are:

Standard (8")		Mini (5¼")	
Caldisk	143M	Shugart	450 SA 400
Remex	RFD 4000	Micropolis	1015-IV
Memorex	550	Pertec	250
MFE	700	Siemens	200-5
Siemens	FDD 200-8	Tandon	TM-100
Shugart	SA 850/800	CDC	9409
Pertec	FD 650	MPI	51/52/91/92
CDC	9406-3		

Diskette—Unformatted IBM Diskette 1 (or equivalent single-sided media); unformatted IBM Diskette 2D (or equivalent double-sided).

Equipment Supplied

iSBC 208 Controller
Reference Schematic
Controller-to-drive cabling and connectors are not supplied with the controller. Cables can be fabricated with flat cable and commercially-available connectors as described in the iSBC 208 Hardware Reference Manual.

Physical Characteristics

Width—6.75 inches (17.15 cm)
Height—0.5 inches (1.27 cm)
Length—12.0 inches (30.48 cm)
Shipping Weight—1.75 pounds (0.80 Kg)
Mounting—Occupies one slot of iSBC system chassis or iSBC 604/614 Cardcage/Backplane. With an iSBX MULTIMODULE board mounted, vertical height increases to 1.13 inches (2.87 cm).

Electrical Characteristics

Power Requirements— +5 VDC @ 3.0A

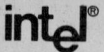

iSBC® 208

Data Organization and Capacity

Standard Size Drives

	Double Density						Single Density					
	IBM System 34			Non-IBM			IBM System 3740			Non-IBM		
Bytes per Sector	256	512	1024	2048	4096	8192	128	256	512	1024	2048	4096
Sectors per Track	26	15	8	4	2	1	26	15	8	4	2	1
Tracks per Diskette	77			256			77			256		
Bytes per Diskette (Formatted, per diskette surface)	512,512 (256 bytes/sector) 591,360 (512 bytes/sector) 630,784 (1024 bytes/sector)			630,784			256,256 (128 byte/sector) 295,680 (256 bytes/sector) 315,392 (512 bytes/sector)			315,392		

Drive Characteristics

	Standard Size	Mini Size
	Double/Single Density	Double/Single Density
Transfer Rate (K bytes/sec)	62.5/31.25	31.25/15.63
Disk Speed (RPM)	360	300
Step Rate Time (Programmable)	1 to 16 msec/track in 1 msec increments	2 to 32 msec/track in 2 msec increments
Head Load Time (Programmable)	2 to 254 msec in 2 msec increments	4 to 508 msec in 4 msec increments
Head Unload Time (Programmable)	16 to 240 msec in 16 msec increments	32 to 480 msec in 32 msec increments

Environmental Characteristics

Temperature—0°C to 55°C (operating); −55°C to +85°C (non-operating)
Humidity—Up to 90% Relative Humidity without condensation (operating); all conditions without condensation or frost (non-operating)

Reference Manual

143078-001—iSBC 208 Flexible Disk Controller Hardware Reference Manual (NOT SUPPLIED). Reference manuals may be ordered from any Intel sales representative, distributor office, or from Intel Literature Department, 3065 Bowers Avenue, Santa Clara, CA 95051.

ORDERING INFORMATION

Part Number	Description
SBC 208	Flexible Disk Controller

iSBC® 214
PERIPHERAL CONTROLLER SUBSYSTEM

- Based on the 80186 Microprocessor
- Controls Up To Two ST506/412 5¼" Winchester Disk Drives
- Controls Up To Four Single/Double Sided and Single/Double Density 5¼" Flexible Disk Drives
- Controls Up To Four QIC-02 Streaming Tape Drives
- Supports 20 or 24-Bit Addressing
- On-Board Diagnostics and Winchester ECC
- Incorporates Track Caching To Reduce Winchester Disk Access Times
- iRMX® and XENIX* Operating System Support

The iSBC® 214 Subsystem is a single-board, multiple device controller that interfaces standard MULTIBUS® systems to three types of magnetic storage media. The iSBC 214 Peripheral Controller Subsystem supports the following interface standards: ST506/412 (Winchester Disk), SA 450/460 (Flexible Disk), and QIC-02 (¼ inch Streaming Tape).

The board combines the functionality of the iSBC 215 Generic Winchester Controller and the iSBC 213 Data Separator, the iSBX™ 218A Flexible Disk Controller, and the iSBX 217C ¼" Inch Tape Drive Interface Module. The iSBC 214 Subsystem emulates the iSBC 215G command set, allowing users to avoid rewriting their software.

The iSBC 214 Peripheral Controller Subsystem offers a single slot solution to the interface of multiple storage devices, thereby reducing overall power requirements, increasing system reliability, and freeing up backplane slots for additional functionality. In addition, the new iSBC 214 Subsystem can be placed in a 16 Megabyte memory space.

Intel Corporation assumes no responsibility for the use of any circuitry other than circuitry embodied in an Intel product. No other circuit patent licenses are implied. Information contained herein supersedes previously published specifications on these devices from Intel.

*XENIX is a registered trademark of MICROSOFT Corp.

© INTEL CORPORATION, 1984

iSBC® 214 CONTROLLER SUBSYSTEM

The iSBC 214 represents a new Peripheral Controller Subsystem architecture which is designed around a dual bus structure and supported by real-time, multitasking firmware. The 80186 controls the local bus and manages the interface between the MULTIBUS and the controller. It is responsible for high speed data transfers of up to 1.6 megabytes per second between the iSBC 214 Subsystem and host memory. The 80186 and the multitasking firmware decode the command request, allocate RAM buffer space, and dispatch the tasks.

A second bus, the I/O Transfer Bus, supports data transfers between the controller and the various peripheral devices. It is this dual bus system that allows the iSBC 214 Subsystem to provide simultaneous data transfers between the controller and storage devices, and between the controller and the MULTIBUS. (See Figure 1).

The iSBC 214 Subsystem implements an intelligent track caching scheme through dynamic allocation of buffer space. This provides reduced access times to the Winchester disk and improved system performance. Operating systems with file management designed to handle sequential data can be supplied directly from the cache without incremental access to the disk.

FUNCTIONAL DESCRIPTION

Winchester Disk Interface

The iSBC 214 Subsystem provides control of one or two ST506/412 compatible Winchester devices and supports up to 16 Read/Write heads per drive. The Intel 82062 acts of the main controller taking care of FM/MFM encoding and decoding, bit stream serialization and deserialization, address mark detection and

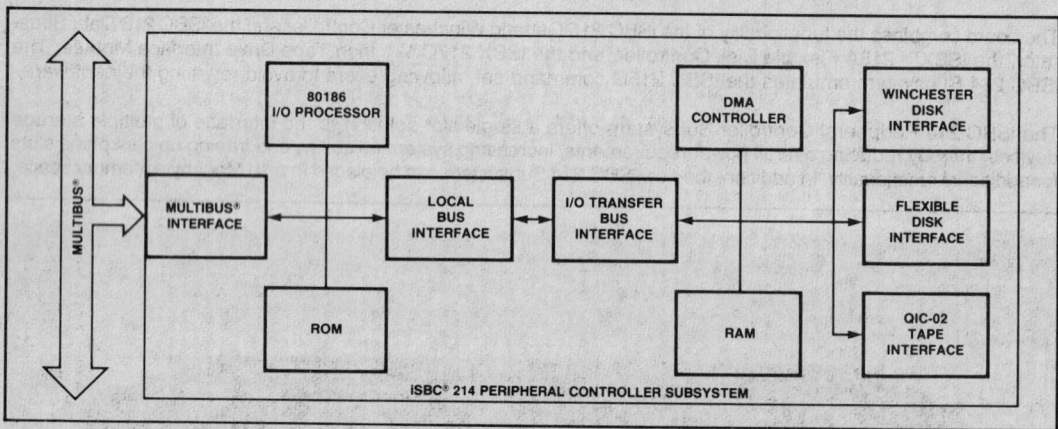

Figure 1. Block Diagram iSBC® 214 Peripheral Controller Subsystem.

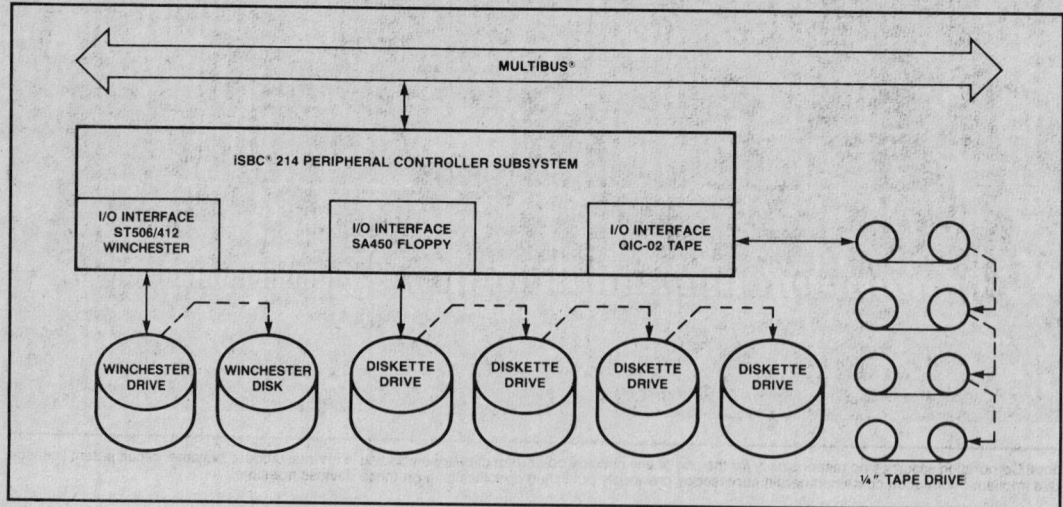

Figure 2. Fully Configured Peripheral Subsystem.

5-6

iSBC® 214 CONTROLLER SUBSYSTEM

generation, sector identification comparisons, CRC error checking and format generation. The board uses a standard daisy-chained control cable and a separate data transfer cable for each device supported.

ECC

High data integrity is provided by on-board Error Checking Code logic. For burst error correction, a 32-bit code is appended to the sector data fields by the controller. During a read operation, the same logic regenerates the ECC polynomial and compares this second code to the appended ECC. The ECC logic can detect an erroneous data burst up to 32 bits in length with correction up to 11 bits.

If an ECC error is detected the controller automatically initiates a retry operation on the data transfer. If the maximum retry count is exceeded, the location of the bad data within the transfer buffer is identified and the 80186 then performs error correction on the data bytes.

Flexible Disk Interface

The Flexible Disk Controller performs all data separation, FM (single density) and MFM (double density) encoding, and CRC support. The 34-pin connector is designed to support the SA450/460 interface directly and up to four flexible disk devices may be connected to the controller.

Tape Controller Interface

The tape controller section of the iSBC 214 Subsystem is based on the 8742 Universal Peripheral Interface (UPI). It is capable of supporting up to four QIC-02 compatible streaming tape drives over a standard 50-pin daisy-chained cable.

All standard QIC-02 commands are supported. All drives must be capable of streaming at 30 or 90 inches per second.

MULTIBUS® Host Interface

The MULTIBUS connection consists of two standard printed circuit board edges that plug into MULTIBUS edge connectors on a backplane in the system bus. An active P1 connector is required and serves as the Host system's communication channel to the controller. An active P2 connector is optional and only required for supporting full 24-bit addressing and power fail signals.

SPECIFICATIONS

Compatibility

CPU — any iSBC MULTIBUS computer or system mainframe.
Winchester disk — Any ST506/412 compatible, 5.25" disk drive.
Flexible disk — Any SA450/460 compatible, 5.25" disk drive.
Tape drive — Any QIC-02 compatible, .25" streaming tape drive.

Controller-to-drive cabling and connectors are not supplied with the controller. Cables can be fabricated with flat cable and commercially-available connectors as described in the iSBC 214 Hardware Reference Manual.

Physical Characteristics

Width — 6.75 in. (17.15cm)
Height — .5 in. (1.27cm)
Length — 12.0 in. (30.48cm)
Shipping Weight — 19 oz. (540g)

Mounting — Occupies one slot of SBC system chassis or cardcage/backplane.

Electrical Characteristics

Power Requirements — +5 VDC @ 4.5A max.

Environmental Characteristics

Temperature — 10°C to 55°C with airflow of 200 linear feet per minute (operating); −55°C to +85°C (non-operating).

Humidity — Up to 90% relative humidity without condensation (operating); all conditions without condensation or frost (non-operating).

Reference Manual

134910-001 — iSBC 214 Peripheral Controller Subsystem Hardware Reference Manual (not supplied). Reference Manual may be ordered from any Intel sales representative, distributor office or from Intel Literature Department, 3065 Bowers Avenue, Santa Clara, CA 95051.

Ordering Information

iSBC 214 Peripheral Controller Subsystem.

iSBC® 215 GENERIC WINCHESTER CONTROLLER

- Controls up to four 5¼", 8" or 14" Winchester disk drives from over ten different vendors
- Compatible with Industry Standard MULTIBUS® (IEEE 796) Interface
- Suports ANSI X3T9/1226 standard interface
- Software drivers available for iRMX™ 86, iRMX™ 88 and Xenix* Operating Systems
- Intel 8089 I/O Processor provides intelligent DMA capability
- On-board diagnostics and ECC
- Full sector buffering on-board
- Capable of directly addressing 16 MB of system memory
- Removable back-up storage available through the iSBX™ 218A Flexible Disk Controller and the iSBX™ 217C ¼" Tape Interface Module†

Using VLSI technology, the iSBC 215 Generic Winchester Controller (GWC) combines three popular Winchester controllers onto one MULTIBUS board: the iSBC 215A open loop controller, the iSBC 215B closed loop controller, and an ANSI X3T9/1226 standard interface controller. The combined functionality of the iSBC 215 Generic Controller supports up to four 5¼", 8" or 14" Winchester drives from over 10 different drive vendors. Integrated back-up is available via two iSBX MULTIMODULE boards; the iSBX 218A module for floppy disk drives and the iSBX 217C module for ¼" tape units.†

From the MULTIBUS side, the iSBC 215 GWC appears as one standard software interface, regardless of the drive type used. In short, the iSBC 215 GWC allows its user to change drive types without rewriting software. The iSBC 215 Generic Controller is totally downward compatible with its predecessors, the iSBC 215A and 215B controller; allowing existing iSBC 215A and 215B users to move quickly to the more powerful iSBC 215 Generic Winchester Controller. In addition, the iSBC 215 GWC directly addresses up to 16 megabytes of system memory.

The following are trademarks of Intel Corporation and may be used only to describe Intel products: Intel, ICE, iMMX, iRMX, iSBC, iSBX, iSXM, MULTIBUS, MULTICHANNEL, MULTIMODULE and iCS. Intel Corporation assumes no responsibility for the use of any circuitry other than circuitry embodied in an Intel product. No other circuit patent licenses are implied. * XENIX is a trademark of Microsoft Corporation. † iSBC® 217 ¼" tape module available late Q4 '82

© INTEL CORPORATION, 1982

OCTOBER 1984
ORDER NUMBER: 210618-002

iSBC® 215

FUNCTIONAL DESCRIPTION

Disk Interface

The iSBC 215 Generic Winchester Controller can interface to over 10 different disk drives. To change drive types the user need only reconfigure a minimal number of board jumpers and, if required, insert the proper formatting information into the command parameter blocks.

The ANSI X3T9/1226 standard interface is a simple one-for-one flat cable connection from drive to controller.

Full On-Board Buffer

The iSBC 215 Generic controller contains enough on-board RAM for buffering one full data sector. The controller is designed to make use of this buffer in all transfers. The on-board sector buffer prevents data overrun errors and allows the iSBC 215 Generic Winchester Controller to occupy any priority slot on the MULTIBUS.

ECC

High data integrity is provided by on-board Error Checking Code (ECC) logic. When writing sector ID or data fields, a 32-bit ECC, for burst error correction, is appended to the field by the controller. During a read operation, the same logic regenerates the ECC polynomial to the appended ECC. The ECC logic can detect an erroneous data burst up to 32 bits in length and using an 8089 algorithm can correct an erroneous burst up to 11 bits in length.

iSBX™ Interface

Two iSBX bus connectors provide I/O expansion capability for the iSBC 215 GWC. With the optional addition of the iSBX 218A Flexible Disk Controller MULTIMODULE™ and or the iSBX 217C ¼" Tape Interface Module, the iSBC 215 GWC can be configured into one of four types of peripheral subsystems, see Table 1.

Table 1. Peripheral Subsystem Configurations

	iSBC® 215	iSBX™ 218A	iSBX™ 217C[1]
Winchester Only	✔		
Winchester + Floppy	✔	✔	
Winchester + ¼"Tape	✔		✔
Winchester + Floppy + ¼"Tape	✔	✔	✔

Expanded I/O Capability

The iSBC 215 GWC controller allows the execution of user-written 8089 programs located in on-board or MULTIBUS system RAM. Thus the full capability of the 8089 I/O processor can be utilized for custom I/O requirements.

MULTIBUS® Interface

The iSBC 215 Generic Controller interfaces to the system CPU(s) through MULTIBUS memory. The iSBC 215 Generic controller directly addresses 16

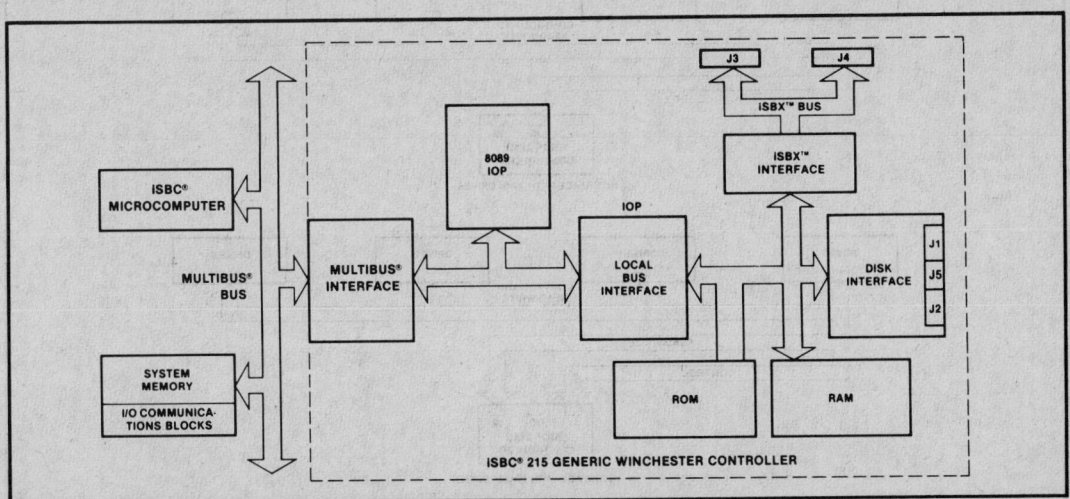

Figure 1. Block Diagram of iSBC® 215 Generic Winchester Disk Controller

iSBC® 215

megabytes of system memory. Commands are passed to and from the iSBC 215 GWC via memory based parameter blocks; these parameter blocks are executed.

directly by the iSBC 215 GWC thus off-loading the system CPU(s). Data transfers to and from the iSBC 215 GWC are done via the high speed DMA capability of the Intel 8089 I/O processor.

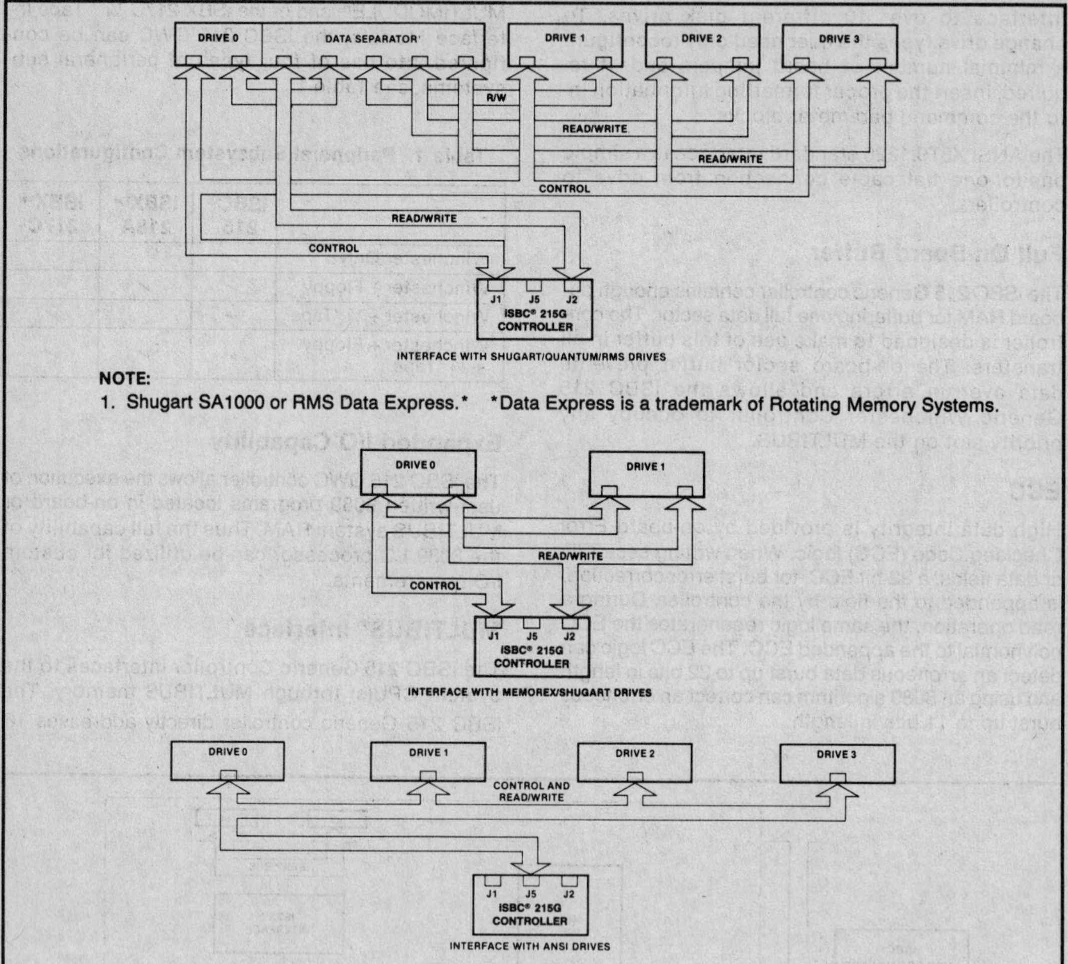

NOTE:
1. Shugart SA1000 or RMS Data Express.* *Data Express is a trademark of Rotating Memory Systems.

Figure 2. Controller to Drive Interfacing

iSBC® 215

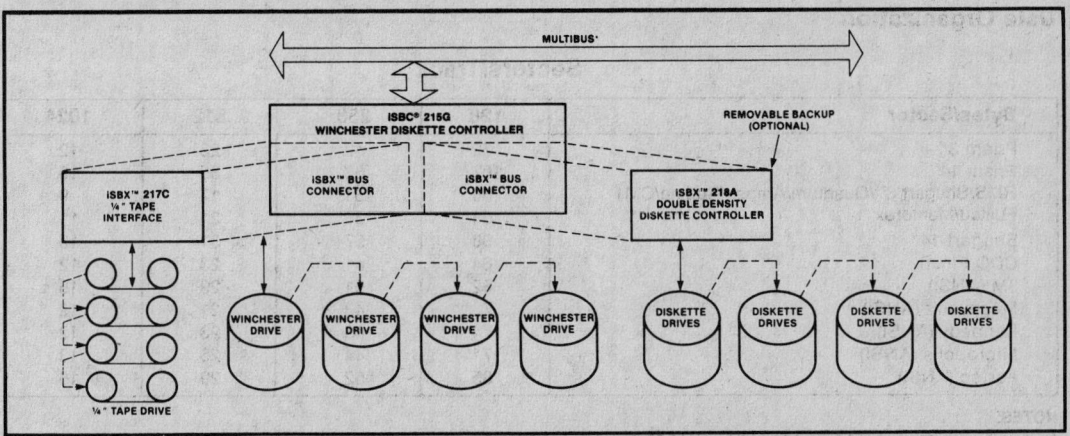

Figure 3. Subsystem Configuration (with Optional Diskette Backup)

SPECIFICATIONS

Compatibility

CPU — Any iSBC MULTIBUS computer or system mainframe.

Disk Drives — Winchester Disk Drives; both open-loop and closed-loop head positioner types. The following drives are known to be compatible:

Open-Loop
Shugart SA 1000 Series
Shugart SA 4000 Series
Memorex 100 Series
Quantum Q2000 Series
Fujitsu 2301, 2302
CDC 9410
RMS 5¼" Series
Rodine 5¼" Series
Ampex 5¼" Series
CMI 5¼" Series
Closed-Loop
Priam 8" and 14" Drive Series
ANSI
3M 8430 Series
Kennedy 6170 Series
Micropolis 8" Series
Pertec Trackstar Series
Priam 8" Series
Megavault (SLI) 8" Series
iSBX™ MULTIMODULE™ Boards
iSBX™ 218A Flexible Disk Controller
iSBX™ 217C ¼" Tape Interface

Equipment Supplied

iSBC 215 Generic Winchester Controller
Reference Schematic

Controller-to-drive cabling and connectors are not supplied with the controller. Cables can be fabricated with flat cable and commercially-available connectors as described in the iSBC 215G Hardware Reference Manual.

Physical Characteristics

Width — 6.75 in. (17.15 cm)
Height — 0.5 in. (1.27 cm)
Length — 12.0 in. (30.48 cm)
Shipping Weight — 19 oz. (.54 kg)
Mounting — Occupies one slot of iSBC system chassis or cardcage/backplane

With an iSBX MULTIMODULE board mounted, vertical height increases to 1.13 in. (2.87 cm).

Electrical Characteristics

Power Requirements

+5 VDC @ 4.52A max
−5 VDC @ 0.015A max[1]
+12 VDC @ 0.15A max[2]
−12 VDC @ 0.055A max[1,2]

Notes:
1. On-board regulator and jumper allows −12 VDC usage from MULTIBUS.
2. Required for some iSBX MULTIMODULE boards.

iSBC® 215

Data Organization

Bytes/Sector	Sectors/Track[1]			
	128	256	512	1024
Priam 8"	72	42	23	12
Priam 14"	107	63	35	18
RMS/Shugart 8"/Quantum/Ampes/Rodine/CM1	54	31	17	9
Fujitsu/Memorex	64	38	21	11
Shugart 14"	96	57	31	16
CDC Finch	64	41	23	12
3M (ANSI)	82	51	29	16
Megavault (ANSI)	73	43	21	12
Kennedy (ANSI)	74	43	23	12
Micropolis (ANSI)	71	44	25	13
Pertec (ANSI)	85	52	29	15

NOTES:
1. Maximum allowable for corresponding selection of bytes per sector.

Drives per Controller

5¼" Winchester Disk Drives — Up to four RMS, CMI, Rodine or Ampex drives.

8" Winchester Disk Drives — Up to four ANSI, Shugart, Quantum or Priam drives; up to two Memorex, CDC, or Fujitsu drives.

14" Winchester Disk Drives — Up to four Priam drivers; up to two Shugart drives.

Flexible Disk Drives — Up to four drives through the optional iSBX 218A Flexible Disk Controller connected to the iSBC 215 GWC board's iSBX connector.

¼" Tape Drives — Up to four drives through the optional iSBX 217C ¼" Tape Interface Module connected to the iSBC 215 GWC board's iSBX connector.

Environmental Characteristics

Temperature — 0° to 55°C (operating); –55°C to +85°C (non-operating)

Humidity — Up to 90% relative humidity without condensation (operating); all conditions without condensation or frost (non-operating)

Reference Manual

144780 — iSBC 215 Generic Winchester Controller Hardware Reference Manual (NOT SUPPLIED)

Reference manuals may be ordered from any Intel sales representative, distributor office, or from Intel Literature Department, 3065 Bowers Avenue, Santa Clara, CA 95051

ORDERING INFORMATION

Part Number	Description
SBC 215G	Generic Winchester Controller

iSBC® 220
SMD DISK CONTROLLER

- Controls up to four soft sectored SMD interface compatible disk drives
- 12 MB to 2.4 GB per controller
- Compatible with all iSBC® 80, iSBC® 88, and iSBC® 86 Single Board Computers
- Intel® 8089 I/O Processor provides two high speed DMA channels as well as controller intelligence
- Software drivers available for iRMX™ 286 and XENIX* operating systems
- On-board diagnostic and ECC
- Full sector buffering on-board
- Capable of addressing 1 MB of system memory
- SMD interface available on Winchester, CMD, SMD and large fixed-media drives

The iSBC 220 SMD Disk Controller brings very large mass storage capabilities to any iSBC 80, iSBC 88, or iSBC 86 MULTIBUS system. The controller will interface to any soft sectored disk drive conforming to the industry standard SMD interface. Using simplified cable connections, up to four drives may be connected to the iSBC 220 Controller Board to give a total maximum capacity of 2.4 gigabytes. The Intel 8089 I/O Processor simplifies programming through the use of memory-based parameter blocks. A linked list technique allows the user to perform multiple disk operations.

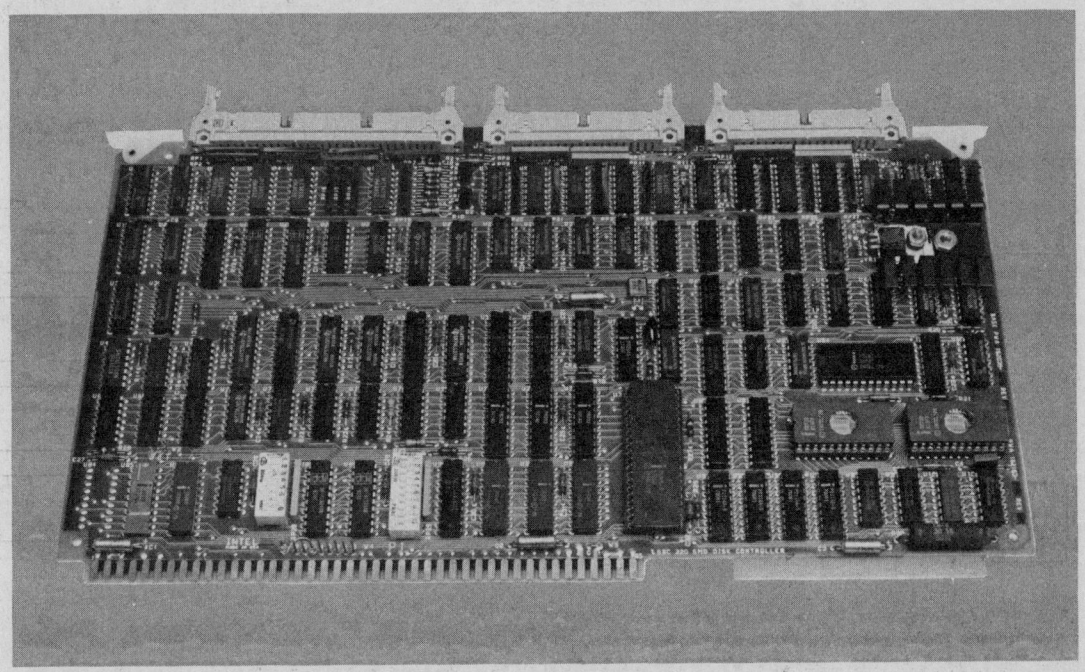

*XENIX is a registered trademark of Microsoft
Intel Corporation assumes no responsibility for the use of any circuitry other than circuitry embodied in an Intel product. No other circuit patent licenses are implied. Information contained herein supersedes previously published specifications on these devices from Intel. Specifications to change without notice
© INTEL CORPORATION, 1980

OCTOBER, 1984
ORDER NUMBER: 143283-002

iSBC® 220

FUNCTIONAL DESCRIPTION

Full On-Board Buffer
The iSBC 220 SMD Controller contains enough on-board RAM for one full sector buffering. The controller is designed to make use of this buffer in all transfers. The on-board sector buffer prevents data overrun errors and allows the iSBC 220 SMD Controller to occupy any priority slot on the MULTIBUS.

ECC
High data integrity is provided by on-board Error Checking Code (ECC) logic. When writing sector ID or data fields, a 32-bit Fire code, for burst error correction, is appended to the field by the controller. During a Read operation, the same logic regenerates the ECC polynomial and compares this second polynomial to the appended ECC. The ECC logic can detect an erroneous data burst up to 32 bits in length and using an 8089 alrogithm can correct an erroneous burst up to 11 bits in length.

SMD Interface
High speed, reliable data transfers are a major benefit of using the SMD interface. A data transfer rate of 1.2 MB is accomplished by using separate (radial) differential data line cabling for each drive. Control signals are daisy-chained from drive to drive.

Defective Track Handling
When a track is deemed defective, the host processor reformats the track, giving it a defective track code and enters the address of the next available alternate track. When the controller accesses a track previously marked defective, the controller automatically seeks to the assigned alternate track. The alternate track seek is totally automatic and invisible to the user.

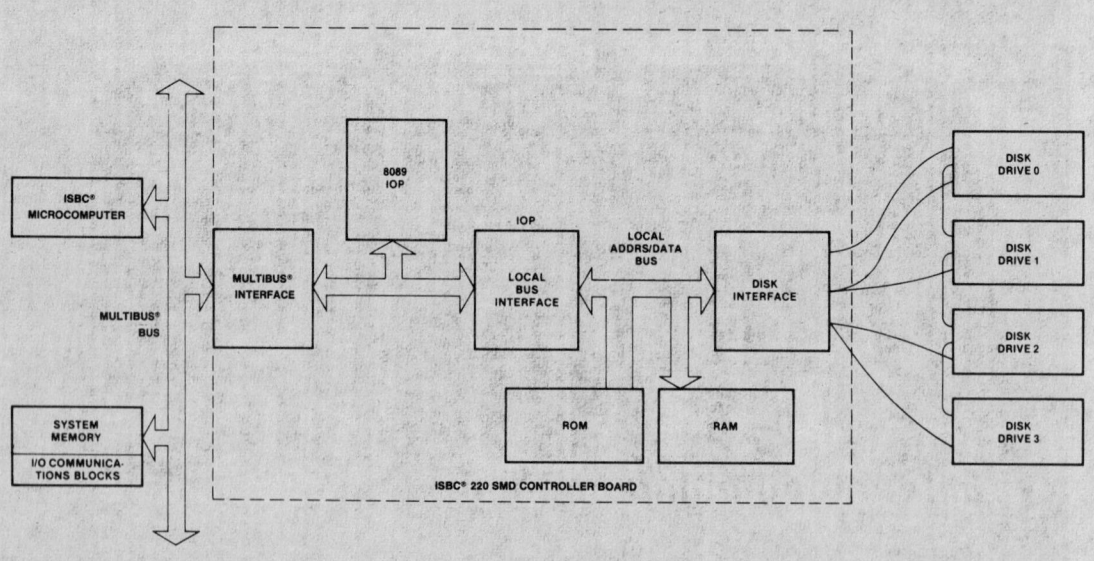

Figure 1. Simplified Block Diagram of iSBC® 220 SMD Disk Controller

iSBC® 220

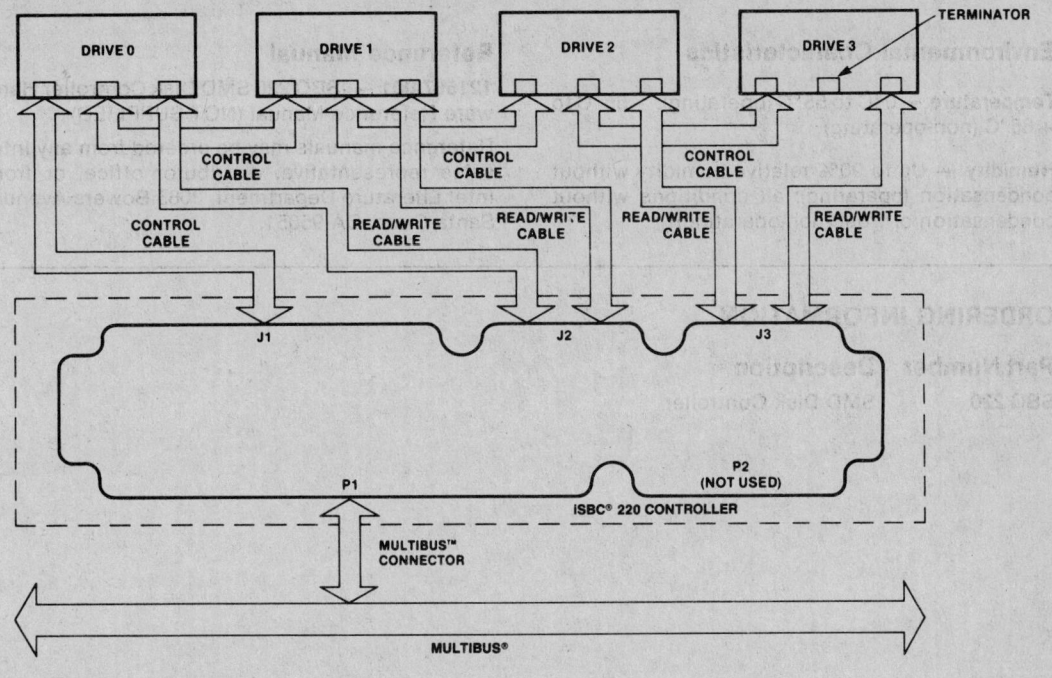

Figure 2. Typical Multiple Drive System

SPECIFICATIONS

Compatibility
CPU — Any iSBC MULTIBUS computer or system mainframe
Disk Drive — Any soft sectored SMD interface-compatible disk drive

Equipment Supplied
iSBC 220 SMD Disk Controller
Reference schematic

Controller-to-drive cabling and connectors are not supplied with the controller. Cables can be fabricated with flat cable and commercially-available connectors as described in the iSBC 220 SMD Disk Controller Hardware Reference Manual.

Physical Characteristics
Width — 6.75 in. (17.15 cm)
Height — 0.5 in. (1.27 cm)
Length — 12.0 in. (30.48 cm)
Shipping Weight — 19 oz (0.54 kg)
Mounting — Occupies one slot of iSBC system chassis or cardcage/backplane

Electrical Characteristics
Power Requirements
+5 VDC @ 3.25A max
−5 VDC @ 0.75A max[1]

Note 1: On-board voltage regulator allows optional −12 VDC usage from MULTIBUS.

Data Organization and Capacity
Bytes per Sector[2] — 128 256 521 1024
Sectors per Track[2] — 108 64 35 18
Note 2: Software selectable.

Table 1. Drive Characteristics (Typical)

Disk (spindle) Speed	3600 rpm
Tracks per Surface	823
Head Positioning	Closed loop servo type, track following
Access Time	Track to Track 6 ms Average 30 ms Maximum 55 ms
Data Transfer Rate	1.2 megabytes/second
Storage Capacity	12 to 2.4 gigabytes

iSBC® 220

Environmental Characteristics

Temperature — 0°C to 55°C (operating); −55°C to +85°C (non-operating)

Humidity — Up to 90% relative humidity without condensation (operating); all conditions without condensation or frost (non-operating)

Reference Manual

121597-001 — iSBC 220 SMD Disk Controller Hardware Reference Manual (NOT SUPPLIED)

Reference manuals may be ordered from any Intel sales representative, distributor office, or from Intel Literature Department, 3065 Bowers Avenue, Santa Clara, CA 95051.

ORDERING INFORMATION

Part Number	Description
SBC 220	SMD Disk Controller

iSBC® 226
High Performance SMD Controller

- Supports one or two SMD or enhanced SMD interface compatible disk drives
- FIFO Buffer on-Board eliminates risk of data overruns
- Supports 24 bit addressing
- Supports implied and implied overlapped seek operations
- On-board diagnostics and 32 bit ECC (with 11 bit correction)
- Supports disk transfer rates up to 2.0 MB per second
- Software drivers available for iRMX™ 86 Operating System
- No −5V requirement; fully IEEE 796 compatible
- Capable of 1:1 interleave

The iSBC® 226 is a single-board, high performance controller that interfaces standard MULTIBUS® systems to the Storage Module Drive (SMD) disk interface. The controller can operate with the latest high-capacity, high speed mass storage devices (up to 2 megabytes per second transfer rate). Using simplified cable connections, one or two drives may be connected to the board. By using multiple I/O Parameter Blocks (IOPB) the iSBC 226 SMD controller implements overlapped seek operations.

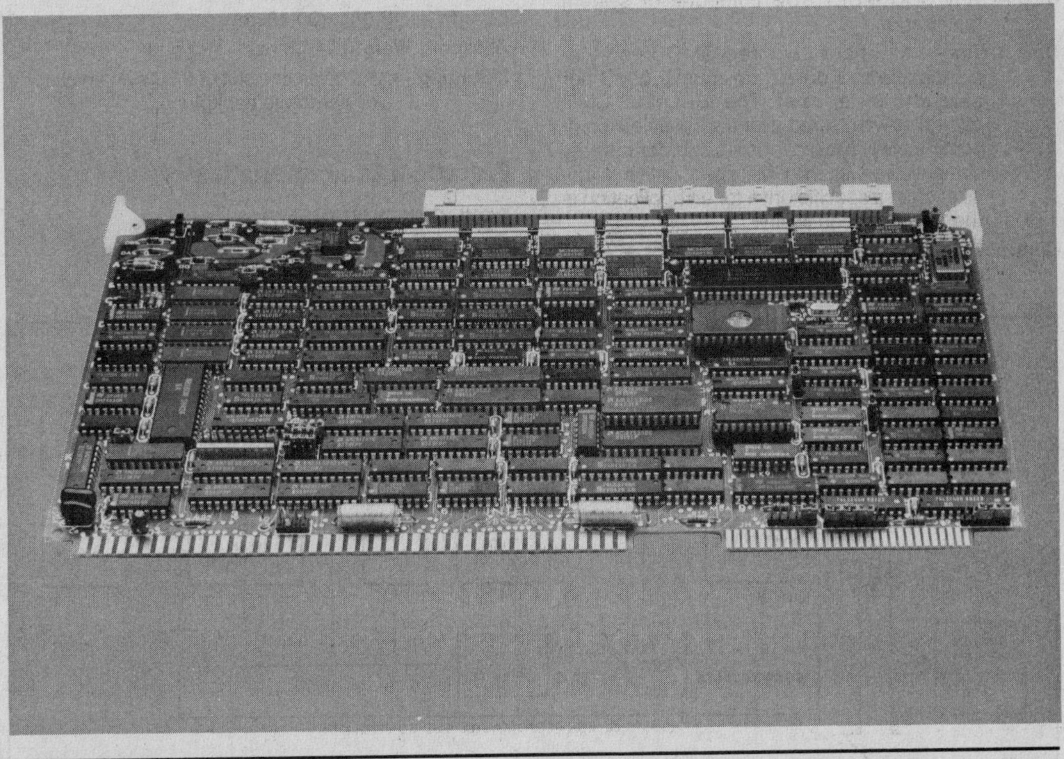

Intel Corporation assumes no responsibility for the use of any circuitry other than circuitry embodied in an Intel product. No other circuit patent licenses are implied. Information contained herein supersedes previously published specifications on these devices from Intel.
©INTEL CORPORATION, 1984.
NOVEMBER, 1984
ORDER NUMBER: 280083-001

iSBC® 226 Controller

FUNCTIONAL DESCRIPTION

On-Board FIFO Buffer

The iSBC 226 High Performance SMD Controller has sufficient on-board RAM for full sector buffering. The controller is designed to make use of this FIFO buffer in all transfers. This buffer prevents data overrun errors and allows the iSBC 226 SMD controller to occupy any priority slot of the MULTIBUS.

ECC

High data integrity is provided by Error Checking Code (ECC) logic. This logic is capable of detecting an erroneous data burst up to 32 bits in length and can correct an erroneous burst up to 11 bits in length. ECC is not limited to the on-board buffer space.

SMD Interface

High speed, reliable data transfers are a major benefit of using the SMD interface. The iSBC 226 SMD controller will support data transfer rates up to 2.0 Megabytes per second and has a DMA capability sufficient to support 1:1 interleave. Actual DMA speed and appropriate interleave factor are dependent on application, memory speed, and bus availability.

Defective Area Handling

The controller is capable of reserving a user-specified number of alternate sectors on each track. When the controller accesses a sector that is identified as defective, it automatically skips the bad sector and reassigns sector numbers for the remainder of the track. By handling defective areas at the sector level, alternate track seek time is eliminated and system performance is enhanced.

SPECIFICATIONS

Compatibility

CPU — Any SBC MULTIBUS computer or system mainframe.

Disk Drive — Any hard sectored SMD interface-compatible disk drive (maximum 2.0 MB per second transfer rate). The iSBC 226 SMD controller was tested with a wide selection of commercially available drives in order to verify compatibility with the SMD specification. Qualification of a specific drive for an application is the user's responsibility.

Controller-to-drive cabling and connectors are not supplied with the controller.

Physical Characteristics

Width — 6.75 in. (17.15cm)
Height — 0.5 in. (1.27cm)
Length — 12.0 in. (30.48cm)
Shipping Weight — 48 oz. (1400 gm)
Mounting — Occupies one slot of SBC system chassis or cardcage/backplane

Electrical Characteristics

POWER REQUIREMENTS

+5 VDC@6.2A max. ±5%
−12 VDC@.6A max. ±5%

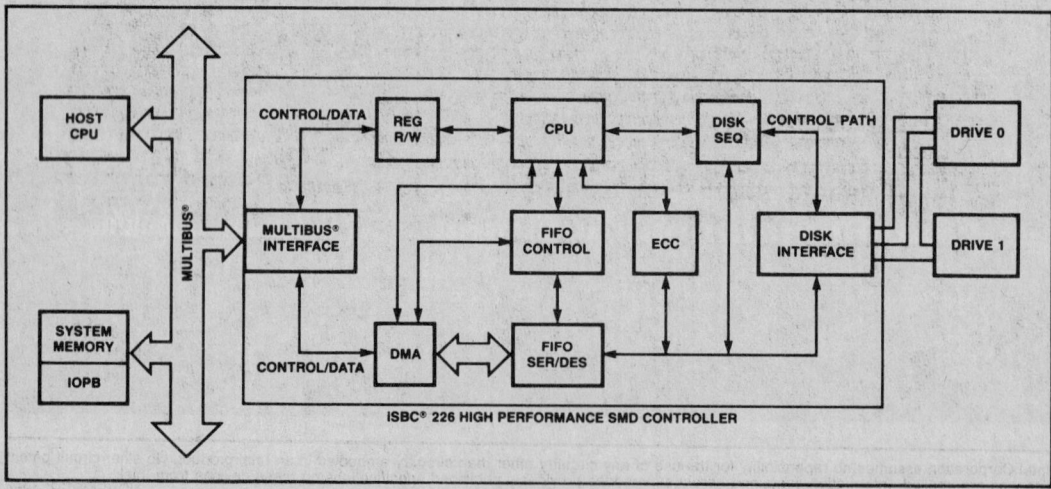

Figure 1. Simplified Block Diagram of iSBC® 226 High Performance SMD Controller.

iSBC® 226 Controller

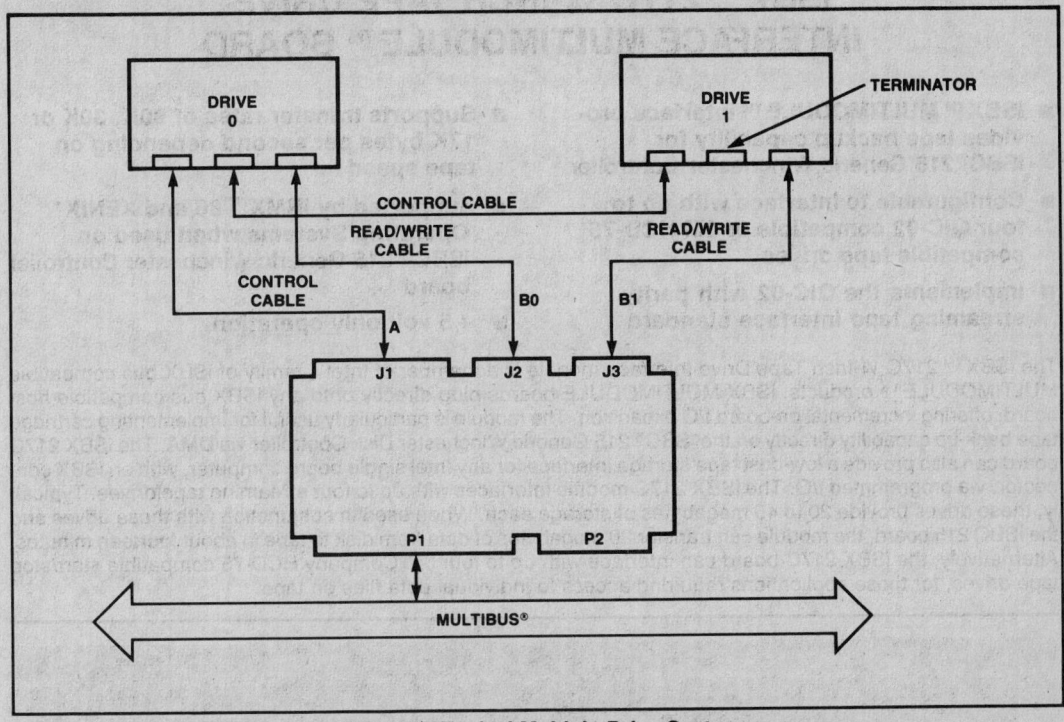

Figure 2. Typical Multiple Drive System

Data Organization and Capacity

Bytes per Sector: 1024 only.

Sectors per Track: Drive type and configuration dependent.

Environmental Characteristics

Temperature — 0°C to 55°C with airflow of 200 linear feet per minute (operating); −55°C to +85°C (non-operating).

Humidity — Up to 90% relative humidity without condensation (operating)' all conditions without condensation or frost (non-operating).

Reference Manuals

147047-001 — iSBC® 226 High Performance SMD Controller Hardware Reference Manual (NOT SUPPLIED)

Reference manuals may be ordered from any Intel sales representative, distributor office, or from Intel Literature Department, 3065 Bowers Avenue, Santa Clara, CA 95051.

ORDERING INFORMATION

Part Number	Description
iSBC® 226	High Performance SMD Controller

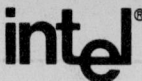

iSBX™ 217C ¼-INCH TAPE DRIVE INTERFACE MULTIMODULE™ BOARD

- **iSBX™ MULTIMODULE™ interface provides tape backup capability for iSBC® 215 Generic Winchester Controller**
- **Configurable to interface with up to four QIC-02 compatible or 3M HCD-75 compatible tape drives**
- **Implements the QIC-02 with parity streaming tape interface standard**
- **Supports transfer rates of 90K, 30K or 17K bytes per second depending on tape speed**
- **Supported by iRMX™ 86 and XENIX* Operating Systems when used on iSBC® 215 Generic Winchester Controller board**
- **+5 volt only operation**

The iSBX™ 217C ¼-Inch Tape Drive Interface module is a member of Intel's family of iSBX bus compatible MULTIMODULE™ products. iSBX MULTIMODULE boards plug directly onto any iSBX bus compatible host board, offering incremental on-board I/O expansion. The module is particularly useful for implementing cartridge tape back-up capability directly on the iSBC® 215 Generic Winchester Disk Controller via DMA. The iSBX 217C board can also provide a low-cost tape storage interface for any Intel single board computer, with an iSBX connector, via programmed I/O. The iSBX 217C module interfaces with up to four streaming tape drives. Typically, these drives provide 20 to 45 megabytes of storage each. When used in conjunction with these drives and the iSBC 215 board, the module can transfer 20 megabytes of data from disk to tape in about fourteen minutes. Alternatively, the iSBX 217C board can interface with up to four 3M Company HCD-75 compatible start/stop tape drives, for those applications requiring access to individual data files on tape.

---

* XENIX is a trademark of Microsoft Corporation.

The following are trademarks of Intel Corporation and may be used only to describe Intel products: Intel, ICE, iMMX, iRMX, iSBC, iSBX, iSXM, MULTIBUS, MULTICHANNEL and MULTIMODULE. Intel Corporation assumes no responsibility for the use of any circuitry other than circuitry embodied in an Intel product. No other circuit patent licenses are implied.
© INTEL CORPORATION, 1984

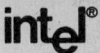

iSBX™ 217C MODULE

FUNCTIONAL DESCRIPTION

The iSBX 217C module implements an interface between a host iSBC board and a cartridge ¼-inch magnetic tape drive, with a minimum of host software overhead. Data transfers may occur in either a direct memory access (DMA) or programmed I/O mode. The DMA mode is available only with host iSBC boards which have DMA capability. In both modes, the host must be able to transfer data at a rate of 90K, 30K or 17K bytes per second, depending on the speed of the tape drive.

Communication with the iSBC® Host

A command plus one-to-five parameter bytes are issued by the host iSBC board to the iSBX 217C module to initiate any tape interface operation. Commands for the QIC-02 and 3M interfaces are summarized in Table 1. If the function is a Read or a Write operation, the host must then be ready to transfer data a byte at a time to or from the module. In programmed I/O mode, with QIC-02 drives, the host polls the iSBX 217C status port to learn when the tape interface is ready for the next 512 byte data block. During the data block transfer, the host is interrupted by MWAIT/ when the interface is ready to transfer a data byte. With 3M tape drives, the host may be interrupted or use MDRQT to detect when the module is ready for the next byte transfer. In DMA mode, the host board uses the DMA Request signal (MDRQT) of the iSBX bus to synchronize the data transfer. At the conclusion of a tape operation, the iSBC host must read one or more of the iSBX 217C module's Sense Bytes to receive status information on the completed operation. When the iSBX 217C module is used on the iSBC 215 Generic Winchester Controller board, these host requirements are fulfilled by the standard on-board firmware and are transparent to the user.

Table 1. Commands required by QIC-02 and 3M tape drives. Number indicates the parameter bytes required by the command. N indicates the command is not supported by the drive.

Hex Code	Command	Parameter Bytes		Type of Command
		QIC-2	3M	
00	RESET iSBX 217C BOARD	1	1	a
01	INITIALIZE DRIVE	1	1	a
02	WRITE A BLOCK	1	3	b
03	WRITE A FILE MARK	1	1	a
04	READ A BLOCK	1	3	b
05	READ FILE MARK COMMAND	1	N	a
06	READ STATUS	1	1	a
07	REWIND	1	N	a
08	RETENSION	1	N	a
09	ERASE TAPE	1	N	a
0C	UNLOAD TAPE	N	1	a
14	CONTINUE	N	1	a
15	WRITE RAM	N	5	b
16	READ RAM	N	5	b
17	VERIFY	N	5	a
18	RUN SELFTEST 1	1	N	a
1A	READ EXTENDED STATUS	1	N	a
1B	SET ALTERNATE SELECT MODE	1	N	a
1C	RETURN RAW DRIVE STATUS	1	N	a
20	RESET BAD PARITY FLAG	0	N	c
40	START OF TRANSFER (SOT)	1	1	c
80	END OF TRANSFER (EOT)	1	1	c
81	PAUSE COMMAND	1	N	c
82	RELEASE PAUSE COMMAND	1	N	c

iSBX™ 217C MODULE

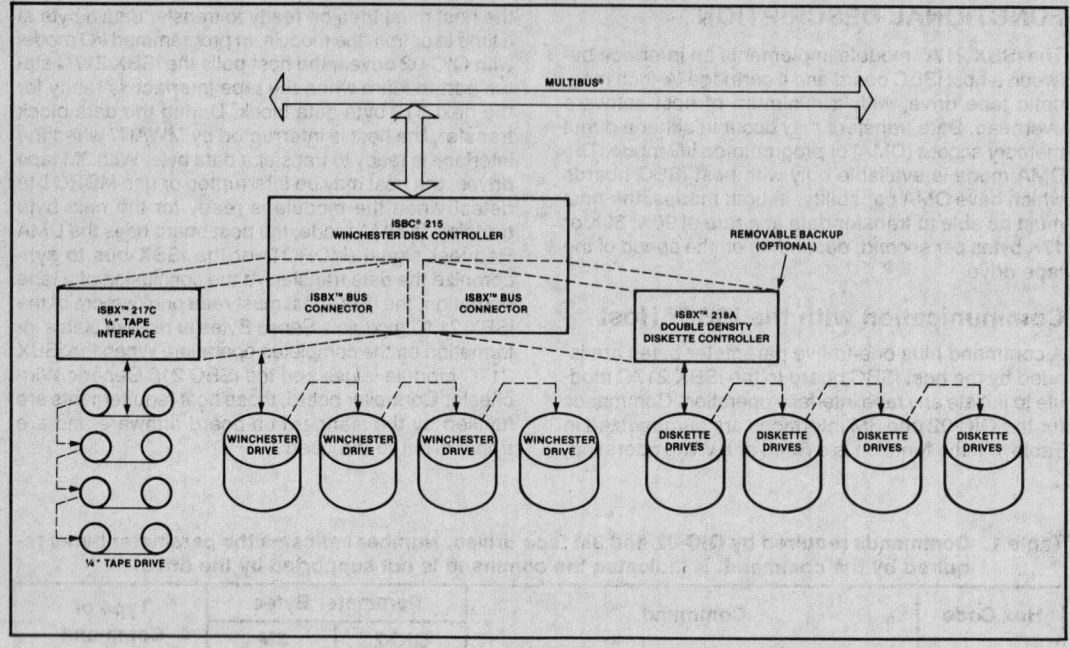

Figure 1. Subsystem Configuration (with optional Diskette and ¼" Tape Backup)

SPECIFICATIONS

Compatibility

Host — Any iSBC single board computer or peripheral controller with an iSBX connector. The iSBC 215 Generic Winchester Controller includes on-board firmware to support the iSBX 217C under either the iRMX 86 or XENIX Operating Systems. The firmware on the iSBC 215A and iSBX 215B Winchester Controllers cannot support the iSBX 217C module.

Drives — Any QIC-02 or 3M HCD-75 interface compatible cartridge ¼-inch magnetic tape drive.

Transfer Rate

90K (one byte every 11 microseconds), 30K (one byte every 33 microseconds) or 17K (one byte every 53 microseconds) depending on tape drive speed.

Equipment Supplied

iSBX 217C Interface Module
Reference Schematic

Controller-to-drive cabling and connectors are not supplied. Cables can be fabricated with flat cable and commercially-available connectors as described in the Hardware Reference Manual.

Nylon mounting bolts

Physical Characteristics

Width — 3.08 inches (7.82 cm)
Height — 0.809 inches (2.05 cm)
Length — 3.70 inches (9.40 cm)
Shipping Weight — 3.5 ounces (99.2 gm)
Mounting — Occupies one single-wide iSBC MULTIMODULE position on boards

Electrical Characteristics

Power Requirements — +5 VDC @ 1.5 A

Environmental Characteristics

Temperature — 0°C to 55°C (operating) @200 LFM; −55°C to +85°C (non operating)

Humidity — Up to 90% relative humidity without condensation (operating); all conditions without condensation or frost (non-operating)

Reference Manual

144260-001 — iSBX 217C Board Hardware Reference Manual (NOT SUPPLIED)

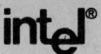

iSBX™ 217C MODULE

ORDERING INFORMATION

Part Number	Description
SBX 217C	Cartridge ¼-Inch Tape Drive Interface

iSBX™ 218A
FLEXIBLE DISK CONTROLLER

- **iSBX™ bus compatible 8" or 5.25" floppy diskette controller module**
- **Hardware and software compatible with iSBX™ 218 module**
- **Controls most single/double density and single/double sided floppy drives**
- **User programmable drive parameters allow wide choice of drives**
- **Motor on/off latch under program control**
- **Drive-ready timeout circuit for 5.25 inch floppy drives**
- **Phase lock loop data separator assures data integrity**
- **Read and write on single or multiple sectors**
- **Single +5 volt supply required**

The Intel iSBX™ 218A Flexible Disk Controller module is a software and hardware compatible replacement for the iSBX 218 module and provides additional features. The iSBX 218A module is a double-wide iSBX module floppy disk controller capable of supporting virtually any soft-sectored, single/double density and single/double sided floppy drives. The controller can control up to four drives. In addition to the standard IBM 3740 and IBM system 34 formats, the controller supports sector lengths up to 8192 bytes. The iSBX 218A module's wide range of drive compatibility is achieved without compromising performance. The operating characteristics are specified under user control. The controller can read and write either single or multiple sectors.

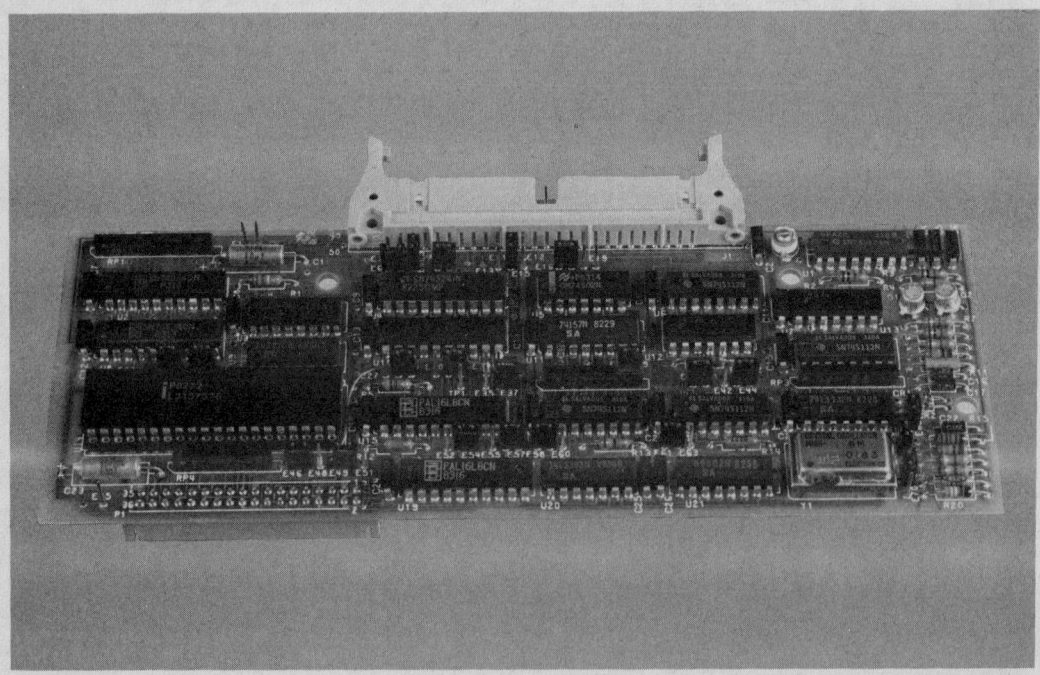

The following are trademarks of Intel Corporation and may be used only to describe Intel products: Intel, ICE, iRMX, iSBC, iSBX, iSXM, MULTIBUS, MULTICHANNEL, MULTIMODULE, and iCS. Intel Corporation assumes no responsibility for the use of any circuitry other than circuitry embodied in an Intel product. No other circuit patent licenses are implied.
©INTEL CORPORATION, 1983

OCTOBER 1984
ORDER NUMBER: 503810-002

iSBX™ 218A CONTROLLER

FUNCTIONAL DESCRIPTION

Intel's 8272 floppy Disk Controller (FDC) chip is the heart of the iSBX 218A Controller. On-board data separation logic performs standard MFM (double density) and FM (single density) encoding and decoding, eliminating the need for external separation circuitry at the drive. Data transfers between the controller and memory are managed by the intelligent device on the host board (usually an Intel 8-bit or 16-bit CPU). A block diagram of the iSBX 218A Controller is shown in Figure 1.

Universal Drive and iSBX™ 218A Controller

Because the iSBX 218A Controller has universal drive compatibility, it can be used to control virtually any standard- or mini-sized diskette drive. Moreover, the iSBX 218A Controller fully supports the iSBX bus and can be used with any single board computer which provides this bus interface. Because the iSBX 218A Controller is programmable, its performance is not compromised by its universal drive compatibility. The track-to-track access, head-load, and head-unload characteristics of the selected drive model are program specified. Data may be organized in sectors up to 8192 bytes in length.

Interface Characteristics

The standard iSBX 218A Controller includes an Intel 8272 Floppy Disk Controller chip which supports up to four drives, single or double sided.

SIMPLIFIED INTERFACE — The cable between the iSBX 218A Controller and the drive(s) may be low cost, flat ribbon cable with mass temination connectors. The mechanical interface to the

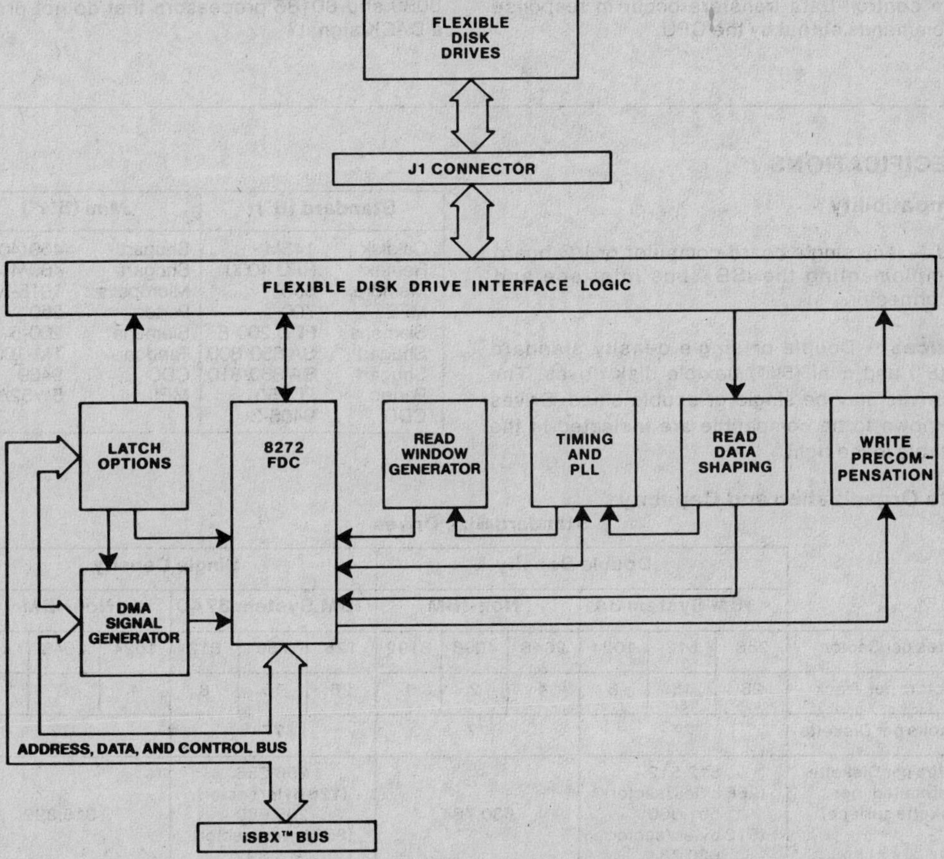

Figure 1. Block Diagram of iSBX™ 218A Board

5-25

503810-002

iSBX™ 218A CONTROLLER

board is a right-angle header with locking tabs for security of connection.

PROGRAMMING — The powerful 8272 FDC circuit is capable of executing high-level commands that simplify system software development. The device can read and write both single and multiple sectors. CRC characters are generated and checked automatically. Recording density is selected at each Read and Write to support the industry standard technique of recording basic media information on Track 0 of Side 0 in single density, and then switching to double density (if necessary) for operations on other tracks.

PROGRAM INITIATION — All diskette operations are initiated by standard iSBX bus input/output (I/O) operations through the host board. System software first initializes the controller with the operating characteristics of the selected drive. The diskette is then formatted under program control. Data transfers occur in response to commands output by the CPU.

DATA TRANSFER — Once a diskette transfer operation has been initated, the controller will require a data transfer every 13 microseconds (double density) or 26 microseconds (single density). Most CPUs will operate in a polled mode, checking controller status and transferring bytes when the controller is ready. Boards utilizing the intel 8080 chip, such as the iSBC 80/10B board, will be restricted to single density operation with the iSBX 218A Controller, due to these speed requirements.

DMA OPERATION — The iSBX 218A module can be used either with or without a DMA controller on the host board. Standard DMA controllers provide a DACK (DMA Acknowledge) signal for proper DMA operation with the 8272. The iSBX 218A's on-board DACK generator provides the interface to allow the iSBX 218A module to be used with DMA controllers such as Intel's 8089 and 80186 processors that do not provide a DACK signal.

SPECIFICATIONS

Compatibility

CPU — Any single board computer or I/O board implementing the iSBX bus interface and connector.

Devices — Double or single density standard (8") and mini (5¼") flexible disk drives. The drives may be single or double sided. Drives known to be compatible are indicated in the table to the right.

Standard (8")		Mini (5¼")	
Caldisk	143M	Shugart	450/400
Remex	RFD 4000	Shugart	460/410
Memorex	550	Micropolis	1015-IV
MFE	700	Pertec	250
Siemens	FDD 200-8	Siemens	200-5
Shugart	SA 850/800	Tandon	TM-100
Shugart	SA 860/810	CDC	9409
Pertec	FD650	MPI	51/52/91/92
CDC	9406-3		

Data Organization and Capacity

Standard Size Drives

	Double Density						Single Density				
	IBM System 34			Non-IBM			IBM System 3740			Non-IBM	
Bytes per Sector	256	512	1024	2048	4096	8192	128	256	512	1024	2048	4096
Sectors per Track	26	15	8	4	2	1	26	15	8	4	2	1
Tracks per Diskette	77			77			77			77		
Bytes per Diskette (Formatted, per diskette surface)	512,512 (256 bytes/sector) 591,360 (512 bytes/sector) 630,784 (1024 bytes/sector)			630,784			256,256 (128 byte/sector) 295,680 (256 bytes/sector) 315,392 (512 bytes/sector)			315,392		

iSBX™ 218A CONTROLLER

Diskette — Unformatted IBM Diskette 1 (or equivalent single-sided media); unformatted IBM Diskette 2D (or equivalent double-sided).

Equipment Supplied

iSBX 218A Controller
Reference Schematic
Controller-to-drive cabling and connectors are not supplied with the controller. Cables can be fabricated with flat cable and commercially-available connectors as described in the iSBX 218A Hardware Reference Manual.
Nylon Mounting Screws and Spacers

Physical Characteristics

Width — 3.15 inches (8.0 cm)
Height — 0.83 inches (2.1 cm)
Length — 7.5 inches (19.1 cm)
Weight — 4.5 ounces (126 gm)
Mounting — Occupies one double-wide iSBX MULTIMODULE™ position on boards; increases board height (host plus iSBX board) to 1.13 inches (2.87 cm).

Electrical Characteristics

Power Requirements — +5VDC @ 1.7A max.

Environmental Characteristics

Temperature — 0°C to +55°C (operating); −55°C to +85°C (non-operating).
Humidity — Up to 90% Relative Humidity without condensation (operating); all conditions without condensation or frost (non-operating).

Reference Manual

145911-001 — iSBX 218A Flexible Disk Controller Hardware Reference Manual (NOT SUPPLIED).

Reference manuals may be ordered from any Intel sales representative, distributor office, or from Intel Literature Department, 3065 Bowers Avenue, Santa Clara, CA 95051.

Drive Characteristics

	Standard Size	Mini Size
	Double/Single Density	Double/Single Density
Transfer Rate (K bytes/sec)	62.5/31.25	31.25/15.63
Disk Speed (RPM)	360	300
Step Rate Time (Programmable)	1 to 16 msec/track in 1 msec increments	2 to 32 msec/track in 2 msec increments
Head Load Time (Programmable)	2 to 254 msec in 2 msec increments	4 to 508 msec in 4 msec increments
Head Unload Time (Programmable)	16 to 240 msec in 16 msec increments	32 to 480 msec in 32 msec increments

ORDERING INFORMATION

Part Number   **Description**
SBX 218A   Flexible Disk Controller

Graphics 6

iSBC® 186/78A
INTELLIGENT VIDEO GRAPHICS CONTROLLER

- 8 MHz 80186 Integrated Microprocessor
- Top Drawing Speeds of 1.25M Pixels/sec Polygon Drawing Rate: 150K Pixels/sec
- Programmable Frame Rate and Size
- Simultaneous Multiwrite into All Planes
- Two iSBX™ Bus Connectors
- DMA to Local Bus from iSBX™ MULTIMODULE™, Local Memory, and MULTIBUS® System Bus
- Optional VDI (Virtual Device Interface) Graphics Software Resides On-Board
- Look-Up Table Generates up to 16 out of a Possible 4096 Colors
- i82720 Graphic Display Controller
- Resolution of 640 x 480 (Non-Interlaced) or 1024 x 800 (Interlaced)
- Eight 28-Pin Memory Sites
- Multiple Co-Resident Frame Buffers
- Serial Input Support for Human Interfaces via iSBX™ MULTIMODULE™ Board
- Full RS-343 or RS-170 Support

The iSBC 186/78A VGC (Video Graphics Controller) is the newest member of Intel's growing family of microcomputer graphics products. It provides an economical, off-the-shelf graphics solution for OEM applications. The local microprocessor (80186) adds on-board intelligence to off-load graphics functions from the host CPU. Powerful bit-mapped graphics are made possible by the Intel 82720 Graphics Display Controller (GDC). This display controller supports high level drawing commands including arcs, circles, rectangles, area filling, zoom, panning and scrolling.

The iSBC 186/78A VGC board functions either as a host CPU with integral graphics, or as a dedicated graphics controller. Graphics applications can communicate directly with the optional on-board VDI (Virtual Device Interface), a standard graphics software interface. Applications that will benefit from the iSBC 186/78A VGC include process control monitoring, automatic test equipment, transaction processing, and instrumentation.

*XENIX is a trademark of MICROSOFT
*UNIX is a trademark of Bell Labs

Intel Corporation assumes no responsibility for the use of any circuitry other than circuitry embodied in an Intel product. No other circuit patent licenses are implied. Information contained herein supersedes previously published specifications on these devices from Intel.

© Intel Corporation, 1985

August 1985
Order Number: 231035-003

iSBC® 186/78A INTELLIGENT VIDEO GRAPHICS CONTROLLER

ARCHITECTURAL OVERVIEW

The iSBC 186/78A integrates both a high performance 80186 microprocessor and a medium resolution graphics display controller on one board, serving both the computational and display requirements of today's interactive applications. The iSBC 186/78A VGC operates with Intel's standard graphics software (iVDI 720), an implementation of the proposed Virtual Device Interface standard.

In the past, MULTIBUS graphics boards combined two functional blocks on a single iSBC board; e.g., graphics control and MULTIBUS interface logic. Now, Intel has integrated a third block; an on-board 80186 microprocessor provides a control center for the local graphics capabilities. In addition, the large display memory area allows multiple buffering of consecutive images for a tremendous improvement in image display performance. Each of these functional areas is highlighted in Figure 1, and detailed in separate sections.

Such high integration results in two significant benefits to the user: (1) increased system performance by off-loading the graphics routines from the host CPU board, and (2) increased savings due to the compact, single board implementation. Distributed graphics processing results in a system cost that is more directly proportional to the number of users serviced, without adversely impacting per-user performance.

In low cost applications, the on-board microprocessor also allows the iSBC 186/78A VGC to function as a host CPU with integral graphics.

GRAPHICS PROCESSOR FUNCTIONS

Graphics Display Controller

The Intel 82720 GDC is an intelligent graphics controller designed to operate as the heart of a raster-scan computer graphics display system. The 82720 GDC performs all the basic timing needed to generate the raster display and manage the display memory. In addition, the 82720 GDC supports several high level graphics figure drawing functions. Table 1 highlights the 82720 command set.

Both the graphics mode and the mixed mode of the 82720 GDC are supported, although the iSBC 186/78A VGC does not use an external character generator. The internal zoom-write feature of the GDC is fully supported. There is no external zoom circuitry. DMA to and from the display memory is supported via the MULTIBUS data bus, the local bus or through the iSBX data bus.

Display Memory

The iSBC 186/78A VGC contains 512K bytes of high-speed display memory, all of which is under the control of the 82720 GDC. The 82720 GDC controls both writing and reading data to and from the display memory and refreshing the screen.

The configuration of on-board display memory may be set under user program control. The display memory may be segmented into multiple frame buffers, for example: three 640 x 480 x 4 frame buffers

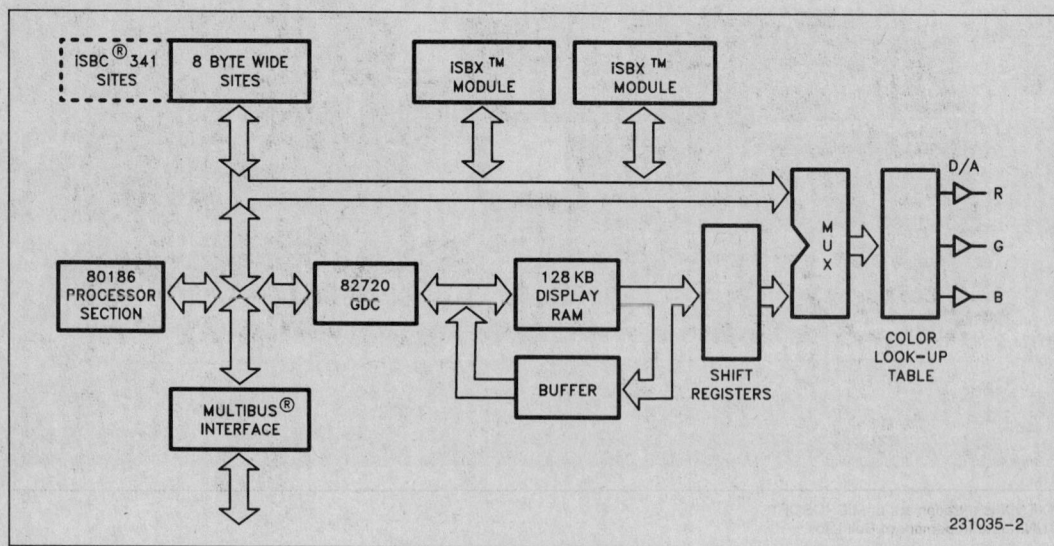

Figure 1. Block Diagram

iSBC® 186/78A INTELLIGENT VIDEO GRAPHICS CONTROLLER

Table 1. 82720 Command Library

Video Control Commands	
RESET:	Resets the GDC to its idle state.
SYNCH:	Specifies the video display format.
Display Control Commands	
START:	Ends idle mode and unblanks the display.
BCTRL:	Controls the blanking and unblanking of the display.
ZOOM:	Specifies the zoom factors for graphics character writing.
CURS:	Sets the position of the cursor in display memory.
PRAM:	Defines the starting address and lengths of display areas, and specifies the eight bytes for the graphics character.
PITCH:	Specifies the width of the X dimension in display memory.
Drawing Control Commands	
WDAT:	Writes data words or bytes into display memory.
MASK:	Sets the mask register contents.
FIGS:	Specifies the parameters for the drawing processor.
FIGD:	Draws the figure as specified.
GCHRD:	Draws the graphics character into display memory.
Data Read Commands	
RDAT:	Reads data words or bytes from display memory.
CURD:	Reads the cursor position.
LPRD:	Reads the light pen address.

or four 512 x 512 x 4 frame buffers. Display memory is read or written 16 bits at a time by the 82720 GDC. Both display cycles and read-modify-write (RMW) cycles may be controlled by the user. During display cycles, data is read from the display memory and sent to the CRT for display, starting at the upper left hand of the screen and moving down toward the bottom right corner. During RMW cycles, data is transferred between the GDC and the display memory.

In monochrome mode, all 256K 16-bit words are treated as a contiguous block of memory, where a logical "1" in memory is displayed as an illuminated pixel. In color mode, four color planes exist in memory and are written into (multi-write) and displayed simultaneously. Each plane consists of 64K 16-bit words.

Video Output

The iSBC 186/78A VGC controls both monochrome and color monitors, providing TTL (0V–5V) or analog (0V–0.7V) signal outputs. The iSBC 186/78A VGC operates with a broad range of CRT horizontal scan-rates. (The scan-rate is related to the pixel clock rate and the desired display resolution.) The pixel clock rate is selected by a jumper on the board, and may be either 20 MHz or 25 MHz. The pixel clock oscillator may be changed by the user to support monitors with lower bandwidths.

MONOCHROME MONITORS

The iSBC 186/78A VGC video outputs and sync signals may be either TTL or analog level signals. The sync signals are available as separate vertical and horizontal sync signals (Vsync and Hsync) or as a composite sync signal (Csync). When the iSBC 186/78A VGC operates in the monochrome mode, the analog video signal can provide a 16-level grey scale.

COLOR MONITORS

When operating in the color mode, the iSBC 186/78A VGC video outputs are Red, Green, and Blue video signals, with a maximum of 16 individual colors displayed at one time. The Red and Blue output signals are always analog. The Green output signal may be analog or TTL. The analog signals are generated in a 12-bit look-up table that provides a possible 4096 colors. When the Green output is analog, it may be combined with the composite sync signal, producing a Sync-on-Green signal. The vertical and horizontal sync signals (Vsync and Hsync) are available on separate outputs or they may be combined to generate a composite sync signal (Csync).

GRAPHICS CONTROL CENTER

Central Processing Unit

The 80186 component is a high-performance, high-integration 16-bit microprocessor. It combines several of the most common components onto a single chip including DMA (Direct Memory Access), interval timers, clock generator, and a PIC (Programmable Interrupt Controller). The 80186 CPU provides up to a 100% performance improvement over the 8086 CPU at an equivalent clock rate.

Three internal 16-bit programmable timers are provided. On the iSBC 186/78A VGC, two of these flexible timers are connected to four external pins (two pins per timer). They can be used to count or time

iSBC® 186/78A INTELLIGENT VIDEO GRAPHICS CONTROLLER

external events, generate nonrepetitive waveforms, etc. The third timer is not connected to any external pins, and is useful for real-time coding and time delay applications. User software can configure each timer independently to select the desired function. Available functions include: Interrupt on terminal count, programmable one-shot, rate generator, square-wave generator, software triggered strobe, hardware triggered strobe, and event counter. In addition, the third timer can be used as a prescaler for the other two timers, or as a DMA request source. The contents of each counter may be read at any time during system operation.

A 6-byte instruction queue provides pre-fetching of sequential instructions and can reduce the 500 ns minimum instruction cycle to 333 ns for queued instructions. The stack oriented architecture readily supports modular programming by facilitating fast, simple intermodule communication along with other programming constructs needed for asynchronous real-time systems.

The 80186 CPU uses a dynamic relocation scheme that allows separation of command procedures from data for efficient memory utilization. Four segment registers (code, stack, data, extra) contain program loaded offset values which are used to map 16-bit addresses to 20-bit addresses. Each register maps 64K bytes at a time. Activation of a specific register is controlled, both explicitly by program control, and implicitly by specific functions and instructions. In addition, the iSBC 186/78A VGC has external logic to provide access to the full 16M byte range of the MULTIBUS address space.

Both DMA channels provided by the 80186 CPU are supported on the iSBC 186/78A VGC. These channels allow a direct path from the MULTIBUS or iSBX bus to local memory. Indirect access to the display memory is also possible under 82720 GDC control.

A flag byte signaling mechanism aids in creating an interprocessor communication scheme. This includes: (1) the ability to set/reset interrupts and (2) board reset.

Instruction Set

The 80186 instruction library is a superset of that for the 8086. Therefore, object code compatibility was maintained while 10 instructions were added. The new instructions include: Block I/O, Enter and Leave subroutines, Push Immediate, Multiply Quick, Array Bounds Checking, Shift and Rotate by Immediate, and Pop and Push All.

Universal Memory Sites for Local Memory

Eight 28-pin JEDEC-compatible sockets are provided for using 2732, 2764, 27128, 27256 and 27512 EPROMs and their respective ROMs. Other JEDEC-standard pinout devices are also supported, including byte-wide static RAMs and iRAMs. Expansion to a total of 12 sockets is available by adding the iSBC 341 memory module. With the iSBC 341 memory module installed, the board supports up to 768K bytes of local storage (using 27512 EPROMs).

The eight sockets are divided into four blocks of two each (for high ahd low byte), or six blocks when using the iSBC 341 memory module. These independent blocks allow the user to mix many different kinds of 28-pin devices for increased application flexibility. Two different kinds of components may be used at any one time and all devices on the optional iSBC 341 memory module must be the same. The memory decode PAL is socketed so that the user may replace it with a custom PAL configured to suit their particular application.

Interrupt Control

The iSBC 186/78A VGC board uses the programmable interrupt controller (PIC) within the 80186 component, and allows 5 on-board vectored interrupt levels. The highest priority interrupt is the Non-Maskable Interrupt (NMI) line which is tied directly to the 80186 CPU. This interrupt is typically used to signal catastrophic events (e.g. power failure). The PIC provides prioritization and vectoring for the other 4 interrupt requests from on-board I/O resources and from the MULTIBUS system bus. The PIC then resolves the requests according to the programmable priority resolution mode, and if appropriate, issues an interrupt to the CPU.

Interrupt service requests to the iSBC 186/78A VGC may originate from 22 sources. Table 2 contains a list of devices and functions capable of generating interrupts. Most of these interrupts may be jumpered (user configurable) to the desired interrupt request level.

iSBX™ MULTIMODULE™ Expansion

The iSBC 186/78A VGC has two iSBX MULTIMODULE connectors, both support the 8-bit and 16-bit iSBX data buses. The addition of iSBX MULTIMODULE boards provides I/O functions to suit most application requirements. These I/O functions can in-

iSBC® 186/78A INTELLIGENT VIDEO GRAPHICS CONTROLLER

Table 2. Interrupt Request Sources

Device	Function	Number Interrupts
MULTIBUS interface INT0–INT7	Requests from resident MULTIBUS CPU or peripheral controller boards	8
Internal 80186 timer and DMA	Timer 0, 1, 2, outputs (function determined by timer mode) and 2 DMA channel interrupts	5
iSBX interfaces	Function determined by iSBX MULTIMODULE boards	6
Bus fail-safe timer	Indicates addressed resident MULTIBUS device has not responded to command within 6 msec	1
GDC vertical retrace	Synchronization of screen blanking	1
Flag Byte	Board identification	1

clude parallel and serial I/O, analog I/O, and mass storage device control. Mounting iSBX MULTIMODULEs directly on the single board computer often results in less interface logic, lower power, simpler packaging, higher performance, and lower costs than an alternative full-size iSBC board solution. See Figure 2 for an example of a minimal system where iSBX MULTIMODULE boards are added to an iSBC 186/78A VGC acting as the host CPU.

Each of the iSBX connectors on the iSBC 186/78A VGC provides all of the signals necessary to interface to the local on-board bus, including 16 data lines for maximum data transfer rates. All iSBX MULTIMODULE boards, designed with 8-bit data paths and using the 8-bit iSBX connector, are also supported on the iSBC 186/78A VGC. A broad range of iSBX MULTIMODULE options are available from Intel.

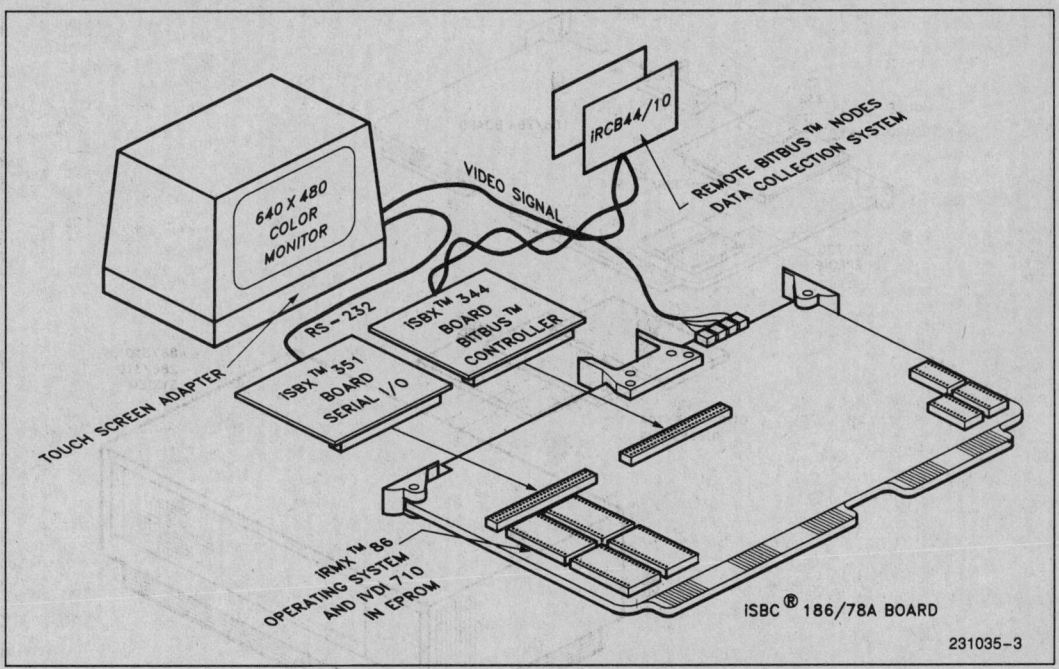

Figure 2. iSBC® 186/78A Board as a Host-CPU

iSBC® 186/78A INTELLIGENT VIDEO GRAPHICS CONTROLLER

MULTIBUS® SYSTEM ARCHITECTURE

System Bus—Overview

The MULTIBUS system bus is Intel's industry standard (IEEE 796) microcomputer bus structure. Both 8-bit and 16-bit single board computers are supported with 24 address and 16 data lines. A MULTIBUS system can be expanded by using a variety of MULTIBUS board products, such as the iSBC 186/78A VGC. The bus structure also allows very powerful distributed processing configurations with multiple processors, including multiple iSBC 186/78A VGC boards, for the most demanding microcomputer applications.

Multimaster Capabilities

For those applications requiring additional processing capacity and the benefits of multiprocessing (i.e. several CPUs and/or controllers logically sharing system tasks), the iSBC 186/78A VGC provides full MULTIBUS bus arbitration control logic. This control logic allows up to three iSBC 186/78A VGCs, or other bus masters, to share the system bus using a serial (daisy chain) priority scheme. Up to 16 bus-masters may share the MULTIBUS system bus with an external parallel priority decoder. In addition to the multiprocessing configurations made possible with multimaster capability, the MULTIBUS system bus also provides an efficient mechanism for all forms of DMA (Direct Memory Access) transfers. Figure 3 shows a multiuser, multimaster configuration.

MULTIBUS® Expansion

Memory and I/O capacity may be increased and additional functions added by using Intel MULTIBUS compatible expansion boards. System memory for the 80186 microprocessor may be expanded by adding RAM boards, EPROM boards, or memory combination boards. Digital I/O and analog I/O expansion boards are available. Floppy disk and hard-disk controllers are available on MULTIBUS expansion boards or iSBX MULTIMODULE boards. Modular, expandable backplanes and cardcages are available to support multi-board systems.

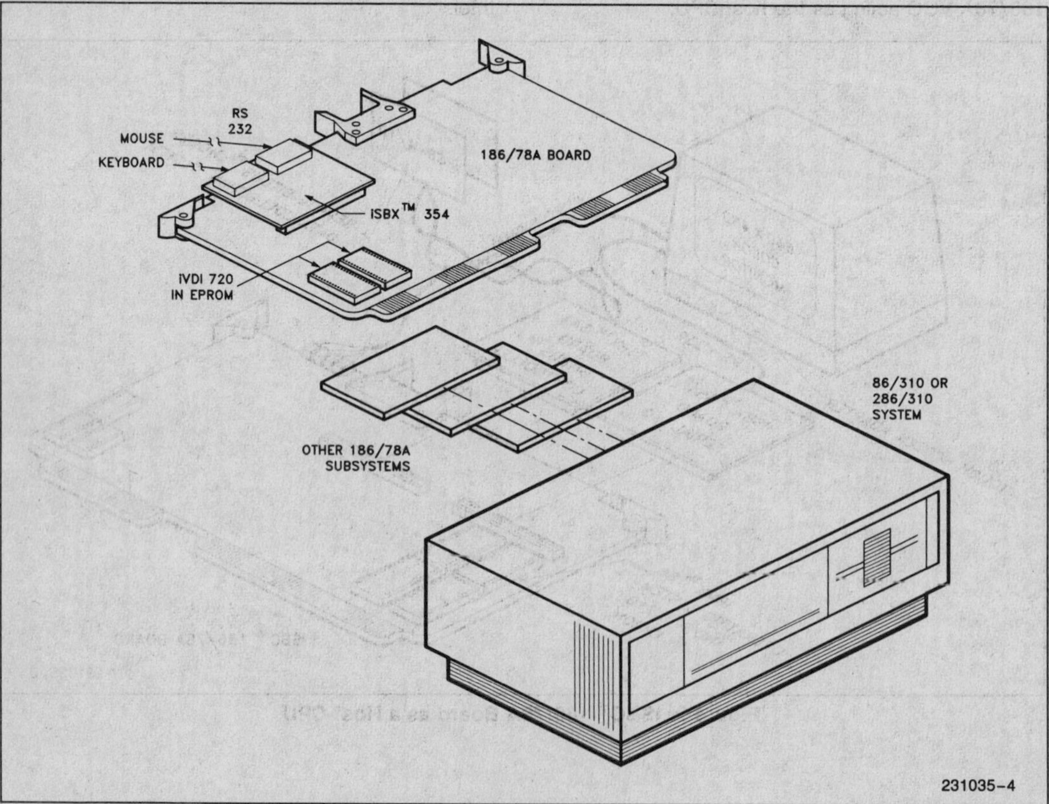

Figure 3.

iSBC® 186/78A INTELLIGENT VIDEO GRAPHICS CONTROLLER

GRAPHICS INTEGRATION KIT

Intel offers a complete graphics integration kit for the iSBC 186/78A VGC.

Hardware

This kit includes static RAMs and a preconfigured version of iVDI 720 graphics software, adding local storage and graphics firmware to the SBC 186/78A VGC. Five video cables connect the board to the back panel of a System 310 or other system enclosure, providing five BNC connectors for external interface to either a color or monochrome monitor. (The user must provide both the monitor and the external video cables.)

Software

In addition to the iVDI 720 graphics software, the kit comes with both iRMS 86 and XENIX* 286 software drivers for the SBC 186/78A VGC. Installation routines and graphics program examples are included for both operating systems. (Customers who wish to pass the iVDI 720 software through to their customer must also purchase an OEM software license and incorporation plan for the iVDI 720 software.)

Documentation

The SBC 186/78A Hardware Reference Manual and the iVDI 720 Software Reference Manual are included in the kit. Complete installation instructions show the user how to configure and install the SBC 186/78A board into a System 310.

In addition to the monitor and external cables, the user must provide a MULTIBUS system (e.g. System 310), equipped with either iRMX 86 or XENIX 286 operating system.

GRAPHICS SOFTWARE (OPTIONAL)

iVDI Command Library

The iVDI 720 Graphics Virtual Device Interpreter provides the iSBC 186/78A VGC with a Virtual Device Interface (VDI) that is consistent with the graphics software standard defined by the ANSI X3 organization. The iVDI 720 software decodes high-level commands to streamline the development of application code. It also supports a variety of input device drivers including digitizing tablets and mice. The standard software interface provides a smooth upgrade path, simplifying the transition to future hardware devices.

The proposed ANSI standard defines the encoding of high-level text and graphics commands. The iVDI 720 software decodes a binary representation of these proposed commands, along with the Virtual Device Metafile (VDM) routines that allow consistent formatting and storage of VDI encoded images.

The compact coding of the iVDI 720 Graphics Virtual Device Interpreter lends itself to EPROM installation on the iSBC 186/78A VGC. Graphics functions can then be off-loaded to the iSBC 186/78A VGC, permitting the host CPU board to concentrate on system level operations such as database management or network communications. A preconfigured PROM version of iVDI 720 software is available in Intel's graphics integration kit.

iRMX™ 86 Software Device Driver

The iRMX 86 software is Intel's real-time, multi-tasking operating system. The iVDI 720 software package furnishes the software device driver required to operate the board in an iRMX 86 software environment (Release 6 or later). It creates a predictable environment for the input and output of high-level commands between the user and system, or among the graphics peripherals attached to the system, such as a mouse, tablet, printer or plotter. The iRMX 86 driver includes a PL/M language binding.

XENIX 286 Software Device Driver

Intel also offers XENIX 286, a UNIX*-like operating system. The XENIX 286 software device driver for the iSBC 186/78A VGC is available in Intel's graphics integration kits. The XENIX 286 driver includes a "C" language binding.

Development Environment

Intel offers a family of tools to aid in the development of iSBC 186/78A VGC based applications. These include full development systems, in-circuit emulators and programming languages. Some of the features of each are described below. Additional information regarding the development environment is available from your Intel representative.

The development cycle of iSBC 186/78A VGC based products can be simplified by using either the System 310, System 380 or the Intellec® Microcomputer Development System. The Assembler, Locating Linker, Library Manager™, Text Editor and System Monitor are all supported by the ISIS-II operating system of the Intellec Microcomputer Development Systems.

iSBC® 186/78A INTELLIGENT VIDEO GRAPHICS CONTROLLER

The Integrated Instrumentation In-Circuit Emulator (I²ICE™) for the 80186 microprocessor provides the necessary link between an Intellec® development system and the target iSBC 186/78A VGC execution system. In addition to providing the mechanism for loading executable code and data into the iSBC 186/78A VGC, the I²ICE 186 emulator provides a sophisticated command set to assist in debugging software and final integration of the user hardware and software. Intel offers two iRMX 86 software systems implementation languages, PL/M-86 and C-86. PL/M-86 provides the capability to program in an algorithmic language and eliminates the need to manage register usage or allocate memory while still allowing direct control of the system's resources when needed. C-86 is especially appropriate in applications requiring portability and code density. FORTRAN 86, PASCAL 86, and BASIC 86 are also available for the iRMX 86 operating system.

Intel also offers several langauges for XENIX 286 systems and software development. These include "C" and FORTRAN.

High-level language bindings provide access to the graphics commands of iVDI 720 software, streamlining the development of graphics application code. A PL/M language binding is available for iRMX 86 systems. A "C" language binding is available for the XENIX 286 operating system.

SPECIFICATIONS

Word Size

Instruction—8, 16, 24, or 32 bits
Data —8 or 16 bits

System Clock

8.00 MHz ±0.1%

Instruction Cycle Time

8 MHz —500 ns
 —333 ns (assumes instruction in queue)

NOTE:
Basic instruction is defined as the fastest instruction time (i.e., two clock cycles).

Memory Response Time

286 ns for zero wait-states (address to data-valid)

Memory Capacity

EPROM   512K bytes (768K with iSBC 341 MULTIMODULE) using 27512s
E²PROM   16K bytes (24K with iSBC 341 MULTIMODULE) using 2817As
iRAM   64K bytes (96K with iSBC 341 MULTIMODULE) using 51C86s

Static RAM same as iRAM

Connectors

Interface	Double-sided	Centers	Supplier
MULTIBUS System	86 pin (P1)	0.156 in.	Viking 3KH43/9AMK12 Wire Wrap
iSBX Bus (8- and 16-bit)	36/44 (J2, J3)	0.100	Viking 000294-0001
Video Interface - or -	26 (J1) 5 pcs. (J7–11)	0.1 SMC-type	3M 3399-6026 flat cable Sealectro 50-007-0000, with Belden 174/U coax

iSBC® 186/78A INTELLIGENT VIDEO GRAPHICS CONTROLLER

PHYSICAL CHARACTERISTICS

Length: 12.00 in. (30.48 cm)
Height: 7.05 in (17.90 cm)
Depth: 0.50 in. (1.78 cm)
　　　　1.13 in. (2.82 cm) with iSBC Memory Expansion and MULTIMODULEs, or iSBX MULTIMODULE boards
Weight: 18.3 ounces (519 gm) excluding any MULTIMODULE boards

ELECTRICAL CHARACTERISTICS

Power Requirements—8.4A @ +5±5% Vdc (Maximum); 4.9A @ +5±5% Vdc (typical)

ENVIRONMENTAL REQUIREMENTS

Operating Temperature—0° to 55°C with 200 lfm air flow

Relative Humidity—to 90% without condensation

ORDERING INFORMATION

Part Number	Description
iSBC 186/78A	Intelligent Video Graphics Subsystem
GXM 278 R1.0	iSBC 186/78A Integration Kit for the System 310

REFERENCE MANUAL

147393-001— iSBC 186/78A Video Graphics Subsystem Hardware Reference Manual

RELATED LITERATURE

210883-001— MULTIBUS Handbook
280002-001— iVDI 720 Data Sheet (Virtual Device Interface)
146717-002— iVDI 720 Graphics Software Reference Manual
142686-001— iSBX Specification
210451-001— iAPX 80186 Data Sheet
210655-001— Intel 82720 Data Sheet

Literature and Hardware Reference Manual may be ordered from an Intel Sales Representative, distributor office or from Intel Literature Department, 3065 Bowers Avenue, Santa Clara, California 95051.

iSBX™ 270
ALPHA-NUMERIC DISPLAY CONTROLLER

- **Complete video display controller on a double-wide iSBX™ MULTIMODULE™ board**
- **Interfaces to either black and white or color display monitors**
- **Displays 7 × 9, 5 × 7 or 6 × 8 character fonts**
- **High level software interface via a pre-programmed 8041A UPI**
- **Interchangeable character fonts available in EPROM**
- **Keyboard and light pen interface provided on-board**
- **50 Hz or 60 Hz frame rate operation**
- **Provides cursor control, reverse video, blinking, underline, highlight and page or scroll mode**
- **Compatible with all 8/16 bit iSBC® boards which support the Intel iSBX™ bus**
- **Graphics capability via pre-defined graphic character fonts**

The iSBX 270 Video Display Controller (VDC) is a complete video controller on a standard double wide Intel iSBX MULTIMODULE board. Providing either black and white (B&W) or eight-color displays, the iSBX 270 VDC brings alphanumeric video control to the iSBX bus. Any computer board or system supporting the Intel iSBX MULTIMODULE bus is compatible with the iSBX 270 VDC, including most board and system products from Intel. Additionally, the iSBX 270 VDC supports keyboard and light pen I/O on-board; this simplifies the design of intelligent terminals.

The iSBX 270 module allows the user to add high level video display capability to his/her computer system with a minimal cost and effort. Typical applications for the iSBX 270 VDC include video displays for industrial operator stations, word processing systems, data base management products and many other uses.

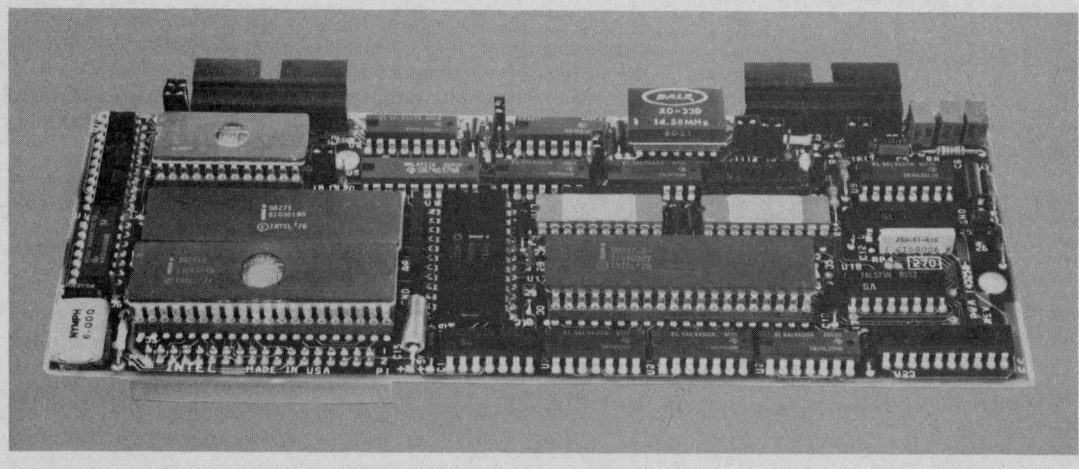

The following are trademarks of Intel Corporation and may be used only to describe Intel products: Intel, CREDIT, Index, Insite, Intellec, Library Manager, Megachassis, Micromap, MULTIBUS, PROMPT, UPI, µScope, Promware, MCS, ICE, iRMX, iSBC, iSBX, MULTIMODULE and iCS. Intel Corporation assumes no responsibility for the use of any circuitry other than circuitry embodied in an Intel product. No other circuit patent licenses are implied.

© INTEL CORPORATION, 1981

iSBX™ 270 ALPHA-NUMERIC GRAPHICS CONTROLLER

FUNCTIONAL DESCRIPTION

iSBX™ Interface

The iSBX 270 VDC interfaces to the Intel iSBX bus via the 8041A Universal Peripheral Interface (UPI) Microcomputer. The 8041A, under firmware control, provides communication between the base board and the iSBX 270 controller circuitry via the iSBX data and control lines. Data may be displayed immediately following power up, using default initialization provided by the 8041A UPI. In addition, eight high-level commands are provided by the iSBX 270 firmware; these eight commands are used to alter the default initialization of the controller and determine status. Following initialization, characters are displayed on the CRT by simply writing to the proper I/O port.

CRT Interface

The iSBX 270 VDC will interface to many B&W and RGB color display monitors. For B&W monitors, the iSBX 270 board provides TTL level signals for video, vertical sync and horizontal sync. Additionally, in B&W, two levels of intensity (normal and highlight) are supported under program control.

When operating in the color mode, the iSBX 270 module provides TTL level 75 ohm line drivers for Red, Green, and Blue Video and sync allowing 8 different colors to be displayed.

Composite video is not provided on the iSBX 270 MULTIMODULE board; however, with minimal external circuitry, composite video can be added (circuit design available; contact the local Intel Sales Office for details).

Table 1 lists several CRT vendors compatible with the iSBX 270 VDC.

Table 1. CRT's (B&W and Color)[1]

TYPE	VENDOR	MODEL #
B&W	Ball Brothers	TTL 120, TV 120, TV 50
	Motorola	M3570
	TSD	MDC-15
	ELSTON	DM30-12B0-51-A04
Color	Ball Brothers	7-015-0131
	IDT	19AC
	CONRAC	5711C13
	NEC	1202DH
	MITSUBISHI	C-3419

[1]**NOTE:** This in no way constitutes an endorsement by Intel Corporation of these companies' products. The companies listed are known to provide products compatible with the iSBX 270 board.

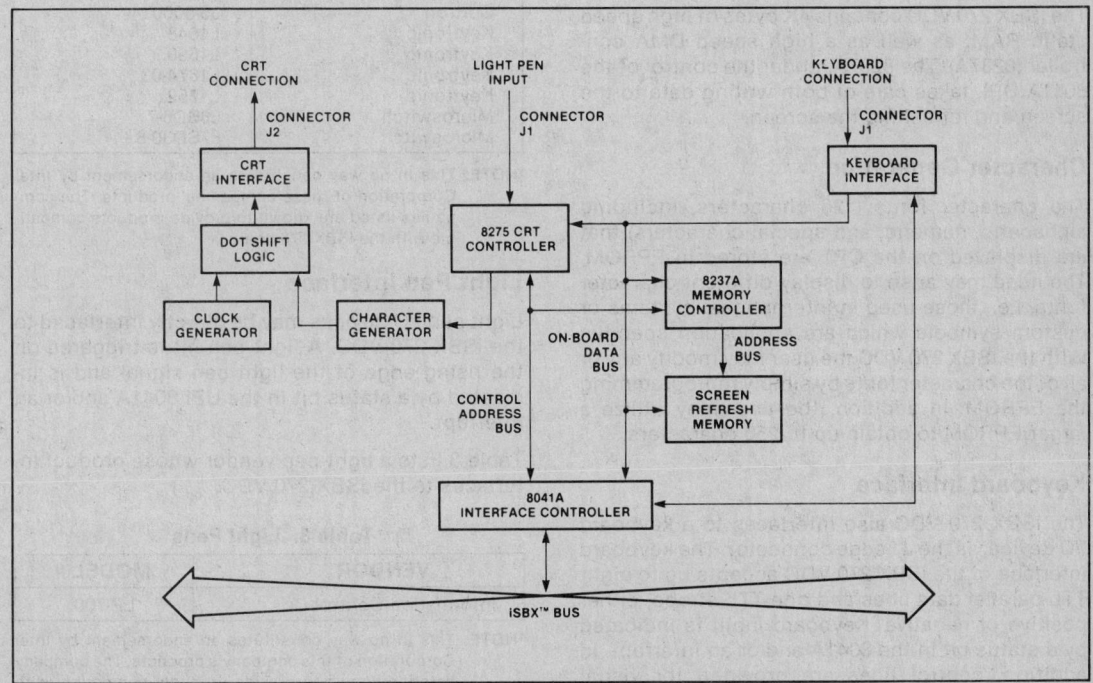

Figure 1. iSBX™ 270 VDC Block Diagram

iSBX™ 270 ALPHA-NUMERIC GRAPHICS CONTROLLER

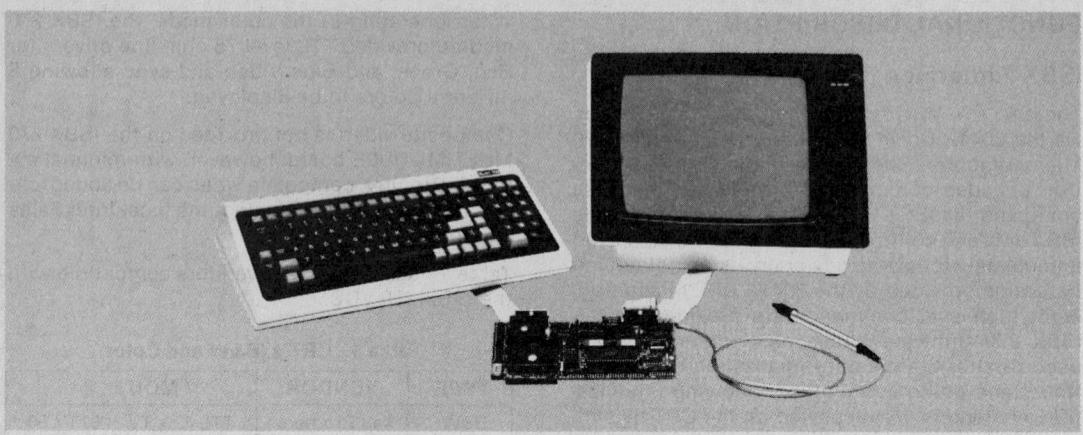

Figure 2. The iSBX™ 270 VDC Interfaces to a User-Supplied Video CRT, Keyboard and Light Pen

CRT Controller

The CRT Controller performs all timing and data buffering functions for the CRT. The iSBX 270 VDC uses the Intel 8275 CRT Controller (for additional details refer to the 8275 data sheet available from Intel).

Screen Refresh

The iSBX 270 VDC contains 4K bytes of high speed static RAM, as well as a high speed DMA controller (8237A). The 8237A, under the control of the 8041A UPI, takes care of both writing data to the screen and refreshing the screen.

Character Generation

The character fonts (128 characters, including alphabetic, numeric, and special characters) that are displayed on the CRT are stored in EPROM. The need may arise to display different character fonts, i.e., those used in international systems or custom symbols which are application specific. With the iSBX 270 VDC the user may modify any or all of the character fonts by simply reprogramming the EPROM. In addition, the user may utilize a larger EPROM to obtain up to 256 characters.

Keyboard Interface

The iSBX 270 VDC also interfaces to a keyboard I/O device via the J1 edge connector. The keyboard interface of the iSBX 270 VDC accepts up to eight TTL parallel data lines and one TTL strobe, either positive or negative. Keyboard input is indicated by a status bit in the 8041A and/or an interrupt. In addition, control lines are provided for visual and/or audible indicators.

Table 2 lists several keyboards that interface to the iSBX 270 VDC.

Table 2. Keyboards[1]

VENDOR	MODEL #
Advanced Input Devices	SK-067
Cherry	B70-05AB
Cherry	CB80-07AA
Chomerics	AN26109/AE26203
Cortron	35-500014
Keytronic	L1648
Keytronic	L1660
Keytronic	L1674-03
Keytronic	L1752
Microswitch	66SD6-7
Microswitch	87SD30-8

[1]NOTE: This in no way constitutes an endorsement by Intel Corporation of these companies' products. The companies listed are known to provide products compatible with the iSBX 270 board.

Light Pen Interface

Light pen I/O devices may be directly interfaced to the iSBX 270 VDC. A light pen hit is triggered on the rising edge of the light pen signal and is indicated by a status bit in the UPI 8041A and/or an interrupt.

Table 3 lists a light pen vendor whose product interfaces to the iSBX 270 VDC.

Table 3. Light Pens[1]

VENDOR	MODEL #
Information Control Co.	LP-700

[1]NOTE: This in no way constitutes an endorsement by Intel Corporation of this company's products. The company listed is known to provide products compatible with the iSBX 270 board.

iSBX™ 270 ALPHA-NUMERIC GRAPHICS CONTROLLER

SPECIFICATIONS

Controller Characteristics

DISPLAY

Programmable to a maximum of 35 rows × 80 columns of characters.

CRT OUTPUTS

B&W — TTL level HSYNC, VSYNC, Video.

Color — TTL level, 75 ohm line drivers for RGB and combined sync provide 8 different display colors.

FRAME RATE

50 Hz or 60 Hz via jumper settings (non-interlaced).

CHARACTER FONTS

5×7, 7×9 or 6×8 jumperable with appropriate crystal. Character generator uses 2716 EPROM. Also compatible with 2732A EPROM's. For generation of special fonts, please refer to iSBX 270 VDC Hardware Reference Manual.

VIDEO CONTROL

Reverse video, blinking, underline, highlight, cursor control and page or scroll mode.

TV MONITOR

Most video display monitors with a 10 MHz bandwidth or better.

LIGHT PEN INPUT

TTL level pulse, maximum 50 ns rise time, minimum 100 ns hold time.

Compatibility

CPU

Any iSBC single board computer or I/O board compatible with the MULTIBUS system bus and implementing the iSBX bus and connector.

Physical Characteristics

Width — 3.08 inches (7.82 cm)
Height — 0.8 inches (2.05 cm)
Length — 7.5 inches (19.05 cm)
Shipping Weight — 0.5 pounds (0.175 Kg)
Mounting — Occupies one double-wide iSBX MULTIMODULE position on boards; increases board height (host plus iSBX board) to 1.14 inches (2.90 cm).

Electrical Characteristics

Power Requirements   +5 Vdc @ 1.3A.

Environmental Characteristics

Temperature — 0°C to 55°C (operating); −55°C to +85°C (non-operating).

Humidity — Up to 90% relative humidity without condensation (operating); all conditions without condensation or frost (non-operating).

Equipment Supplied

iSBX 270 VDC Controller
Reference Schematic

Cabling and connectors from the VDC controller to the CRT, keyboard and light pen are not supplied with the controller. Cables can be fabricated with commercially available cable and connectors as described in the iSBX 270 Hardware Reference Manual.

Reference Manual

143444-001 — iSBX 270 Video Display Controller Hardware Reference Manual (NOT SUPPLIED).

Reference manuals may be ordered from any Intel sales representative, distributor office or from Intel Literature Department, 3065 Bowers Avenue, Santa Clara, CA 95051.

ORDERING INFORMATION

Part Number	Description
SBX 270	Video Display Controller MULTIMODULE Board

iSBX™ 275
VIDEO GRAPHICS CONTROLLER

- Complete video graphics display controller on an iSBX™ MULTIMODULE™ board
- Interfaces to either black and white or color raster scan display monitors
- 50 Hz or 60 Hz frame rate operation
- On-board refresh memory supports 512 × 512 black and white or 256 × 256 eight color display resolution
- High level drawing commands include line, arc, circle, rectangle, character, area fill, pan and scroll
- Includes Intel's 82720 Graphic Display Controller
- Compatible with industry standard iSBX™ bus interface
- Light pen interface

The iSBX 275 Video Graphics Controller (VGC) allows the user to add high level video display capability to his/her computer system with minimal cost and effort. The iSBX 275 module provides a completely self-contained bit-mapped graphics subsystem on a 3″ × 7″ iSBX MULTIMODULE board. This same subsystem supports either black and white or eight color displays.

In addition, iSBX 275 VGC off-loads the system CPU from many of the graphics drawing functions. Under the control of the Intel 82720 Graphics Display Controller (GDC), the iSBX 275 board directly supports high level drawing commands which includes lines, arcs, circles, rectangles, characters, area fill, pan and scroll.

The iSBX 275 MULTIMODULE board is compatible with any computer board or system product supporting the industry standard iSBX bus; this includes most board and system products from Intel. Applications for the iSBX 275 VGC include video displays for industrial operator stations, engineering work stations, videotex, business presentation systems and other information display systems.

iSBX™ 275 VIDEO GRAPHICS CONTROLLER

FUNCTIONAL DESCRIPTION

iSBX™ Interface

The iSBX 275 VGC communicates with the host board through the iSBX bus. The iSBX bus is a standard I/O expansion bus interface (mechanical and electrical) for any microprocessor system. The iSBX standard interface allows system designers to optionally add incremental I/O functionality after the host microprocessor architecture is complete. In the case of the iSBX 275 VGC, the host board passes commands, data and status to and from the 82720 controller via two iSBX bus I/O ports.

The software interface consists of a series of high level commands passed to the 82720 controller. Table 1 contains a summary of 82720 software commands.

CRT Controller

The Intel 82720 is an intelligent graphics controller designed to be the heart of a raster-scan computer graphics display system. The 82720 performs all the basic timing needed to generate the raster display and manage the display memory. In addition, the 82720 supports several high level graphics figure drawing functions.

Table 2 lists several CRT vendors compatible with the iSBX 275 VGC.

Display Screen

The iSBX 275 VGC contains 32K bytes of high speed display memory, all of which is under the control of the 82720. The 82720 takes care of both writing and reading data to and from the screen and refreshing the screen.

The on-board display memory is organized as 16K words of 16-bits each. The 82720 reads or writes 16-bits of display data at a time. When displaying, the 82720 starts at the top left hand corner of the screen and sequences down the screen toward the bottom right hand corner.

In B&W mode all 16K, 16-bit words are treated as a contiguous block of memory, where a logical "1" in memory is displayed as an illuminated pixel.

In the color mode, three color planes, Red, Blue and Green, exist sequentially in memory but are displayed simultaneously. Each plane consists of 4K, 16-bit words where a logical "1" in a plane illuminates the corresponding color in that particular pixel.

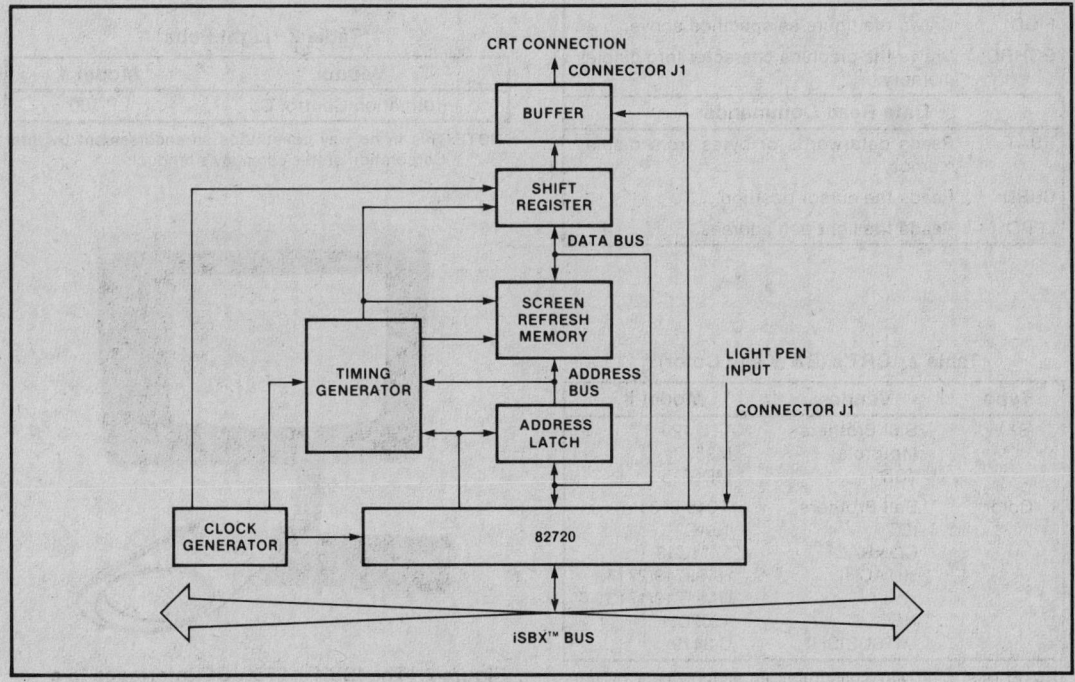

Figure 1. iSBX™ 275 VGC Block Diagram

iSBX™ 275 VIDEO GRAPHICS CONTROLLER

Table 1. 82720 Command Summary

Video Control Commands	
RESET:	Resets the GDC to its idle state.
SYNC:	Specifies the video display format.
CCHAR:	Specifies the cursor and character row heights.
Display Control Commands	
START:	Ends idle mode and unblanks the display.
BCTRL:	Controls the blanking and unblanking of the display.
ZOOM:	Specifies zoom factors for graphics character writing.
CURS:	Sets the position of the cursor in display memory.
PRAM:	Defines starting addresses and lengths of the display areas and specifies the eight bytes for the graphics character.
PITCH:	Specifies the width of the X dimension of display memory.
Drawing Control Commands	
WDAT:	Writes data words or bytes into display memory.
MASK:	Sets the mask register contents.
FIGS:	Specifies the parameters for the drawing processor.
FIGD:	Draws the figure as specified above.
GCHRD:	Draws the graphics character into display memory.
Data Read Commands	
RDAT:	Reads data words or bytes from display memory.
CURD:	Reads the cursor position.
LPRD:	Reads the light pen address.

CRT Interface

The iSBX 275 VGC will interface to many B&W and RGB (Red, Green and Blue) color display monitors. For B&W monitors, the iSBX 275 board provides TTL level signals for video, vertical sync and horizontal sync or combined sync. When operating in the color mode, the iSBX 275 module provides TTL level 75 ohm line drivers for Red, Green, and Blue Video and a combined sync allowing 8 different colors to be displayed.

Composite video is not provided on the iSBX 275 MULTIMODULE board; however, with minimal external circuitry, composite video can be added (sample composite video circuit designs are included in the iSBX 275 Hardware Reference Manual).

Light Pen Interface

Light pen I/O devices may be directly interfaced to the iSBX 275 VGC. A light pen input or "hit" is triggered on the rising edge of the light pen signal and is indicated by a status bit in the 82720. The memory address of the light pen hit is obtained with a LPRD (Light Pen Read) command.

Table 3 lists a light pen vendor whose product interfaces to the iSBX 275 VGC.

Table 3. Light Pens[1]

Vendor	Model #
Information Control Co.	LP-700

[1]**NOTE:** This in no way constitutes an endorsement by Intel Corporation of this company's products.

Table 2. CRT's (B&W and Color)[1]

Type	Vendor	Model #
B&W	Ball Brothers	TTL 120
	Motorola	M3570
	TSD	MDC-15
Color	Ball Brothers	7-015-0131
	IDT	19AC
	CONRAC	5711C13
	HITACHI	HM-2719/2713, HM-1719/1713
	NEC	1202DH
	MITSUBISHI	C-3419

[1]**NOTE:** This in no way constitutes an endorsement by Intel Corporation of these companies' products.

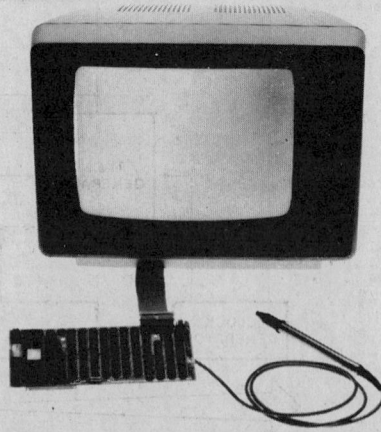

Figure 2. The iSBX™ 275 VGC Interfaces to a User-Supplied Video CRT and Light Pen

iSBX™ 275 VIDEO GRAPHICS CONTROLLER

SPECIFICATIONS

Controller Characteristics

DISPLAY RESOLUTION

Black and White — nominal 512 × 512 × 1, interlaced
Color — nominal 256 × 256 × 3, non-interlaced

CRT OUTPUTS

Black and White — TTL level Video, HSYNC, VSYNC or CSYNC; maximum dot rate 13 MHz
Color — TTL level, 75 ohm line drivers for RGB and combined sync provide 8 different display colors with a 9.75 MHz maximum dot rate

FRAME RATE

50 Hz or 60 Hz via programmable option (non-interlaced)

VIDEO CONTROL

Pan and user selectable display and background color

DRAWING CONTROL

Lines, arcs, circles, rectangles, characters and area fill

CHARACTERS

Any user defined 8 × 8 font

MONITOR

Black and White — Most video display monitors with a TTL interface and a minimum bandwidth of 12 MHz
Color — Most video display monitors with a TTL interface and a minimum bandwidth of 6 MHz

LIGHT PEN INPUT

TTL level pulse, maximum 50 ns rise time, minimum 1.4 µS hold time

Compatibility

CPU

Any iSBC single board computer or I/O board compatible with the MULTIBUS system bus and implementing the iSBX bus and connector

Physical Characteristics

Width — 3.08 inches (7.82 cm)
Height — 0.8 inches (2.05 cm)
Length — 7.5 inches (19.05 cm)
Shipping Weight — 0.5 pounds (0.175 Kg)
Mounting — Occupies one double-wide iSBX MULTIMODULE position on boards; increases board height (host plus iSBX board) to 1.14 inches (2.90 cm)

Electrical Characteristics

Power Requirements — +5 Vdc @ 1.5A

Environmental Characteristics

Temperature — 0° to 55°C (operating); −55°C to +85°C (non-operating)
Humidity — Up to 90% relative humidity without condensation (operating); all conditions without condensation or frost (non-operating)

Equipment Supplied

iSBX 275 VGC Controller

Reference Schematic — Cabling and connectors from the VGC controller to the CRT and light pen are not supplied with the controller. Cables can be fabricated with commercially available cable and connectors as described in the iSBX 275 Hardware Reference Manual.

Reference Manual

144829-001 — iSBX 275 Video Graphics Display Controller Hardware Reference Manual (NOT SUPPLIED)

Reference manuals may be ordered from any Intel sales representative, distributor office or from Intel Literature Department, 3065 Bowers Avenue, Santa Clara, CA 95051.

ORDERING INFORMATION

Part Number	Description
SBX 275	Video Graphics Display Controller MULTIMODULE Board

PRELIMINARY

iVDI 720
VIRTUAL DEVICE
Interpreter

- Provides standardized decoding of high-level graphics commands
- Full iRMX™ 86 compatibility operating system (Rel. 6)
- Standardized input & output drivers
- Compact for EPROM installation
- Support for iSBX™ 275 and iSBC® 186/78A Graphics hardware modules
- Procedural interface from Pascal 86, PL/M 86 and Fortran 86
- Compatible with (proposed) ANSI X3H33 specification
- Virtual Device Metafile interpreter

The Intel iVDI 720 Graphics Virtual Device Interpreter provides both a powerful library of high-level commands, and the drivers necessary to support the iSBX™ 275 or iSBC® 186/78A graphics modules in an iRMX™ 86 (Release 6) environment. It allows the OEM to quickly tailor an Intel system for application into the rapidly growing graphics marketplace, especially low-cost CAD/CAE, CAM, and process control. Individual single-board computer (SBC) modules may also be configured from Intel's broad product family.

For intra-systems graphics control, iVDI 720 is the most powerful and efficient product available that brings (proposed) ANSI X3H33 compatability to an iRMX 86 operating system environment.

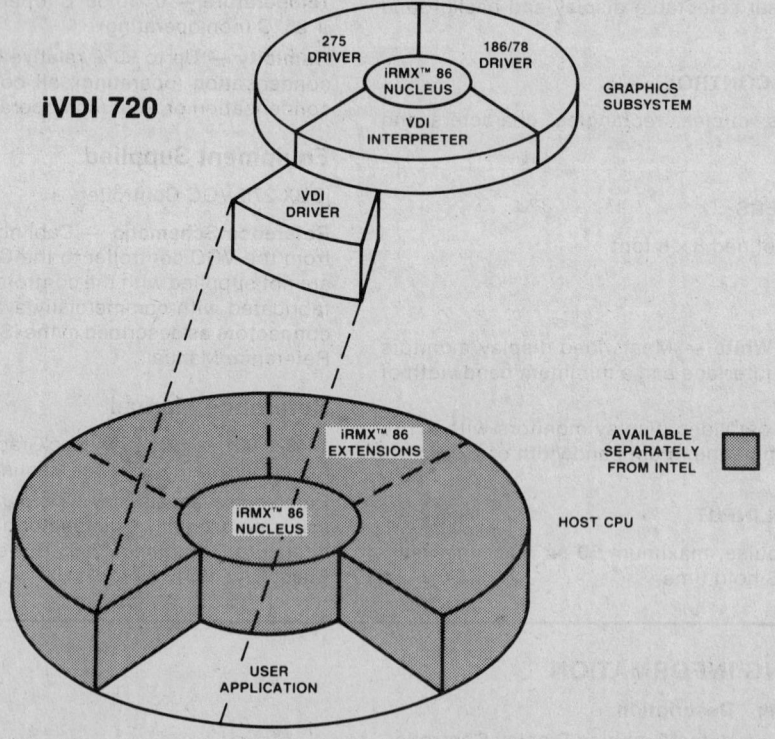

The following are trademarks of Intel Corporation and may only be used to describe Intel Products: Intel, ICE, iRMX, iSBC, iSBX, iSXM, MULTI-BUS, MULTICHANNEL, MULTIMODULE, and iCS. Intel Corporation assumes no responsibility for the use of any circuitry other than the circuitry embodied in an Intel Product. No other circuit patent licenses are implied.

©INTEL CORPORATION, 1984

JUNE, 1984
ORDER NUMBER: 280002-001

iVDI 720 VIRTUAL DEVICE INTERPRETER

PRELIMINARY

FUNCTIONAL DESCRIPTION
Graphics Standard Software

The iVDI 720 Graphics Virtual Device Interpreter implements the proposed ANSI standard on any Intel-based graphics system running under the iRMX 86 operating system, release 6. The proposed standard is a significant advancement in graphics software. It creates a predictable environment for the input and output of high-level commands between the user and system, or among the graphics peripherals attached to the system, such as a mouse, tablet, printer or plotter. The software supports two environments: stand-alone and distributed, depending on the hardware configuration.

All elements of iVDI 720 can run as tasks of the operating system or as part of the graphics application program, hence a stand-alone partitioning of graphics activities such as with the iSBX 275 MULTIMODULE™ attached to a general purpose CPU board like the iSBC 86/30. In a distributed environment, the device driver runs under the iRMX 86 operating system and the remaining application code and VDI interpreter are exercised by a separate processor dedicated to graphics activities. The iSBC 186/78 subsystem was designed especially for the distributed solution.

iSBC® 186/78A Graphics Subsystem Support

By virtue of its on-board, high integration microprocessor (the Intel (80186), the iSBC 186/78A subsystem is an excellent platform on which to perform graphics routines in a distributed environment. This is particularly important in multi-user systems where one iSBC 186/78A subsystem can be dedicated to each user. (see figure 1)

The compact coding of the iVDI 720 Graphics Virtual Device Interpreter lends itself to EPROM installation on the iSBC 186/78A subsystem. The host CPU board is thereby off-loaded from graphics activities so it can direct more global system level operations such as database management or network communications.

iSBX™ 275 Graphics MULTIMODULE™ Support

In single-user applications or where graphics activities are not the major focus of the system, the iSBX 275 MULTIMODULE shares the CPU on the host processor board through the iSBX expansion bus. The subsystem formed in this manner supports either monochrome or eight colors and is a very cost-effective solution. Like the iSBC 186/78A subsystem,

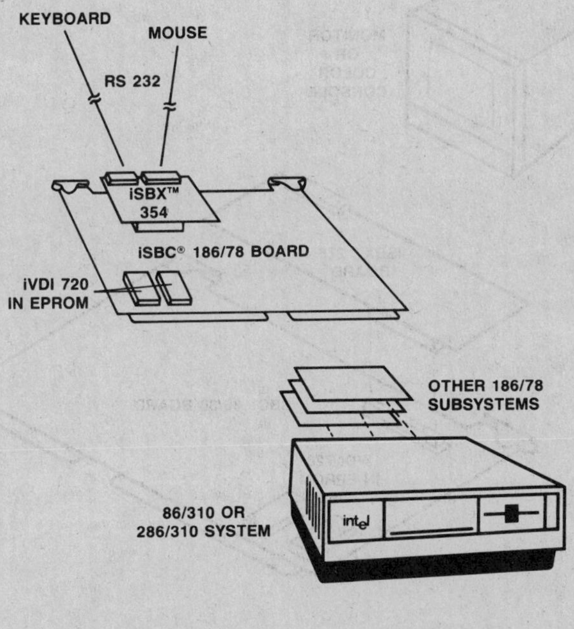

Figure 1. Multi-User Example

6-19

280002-001

iVDI 720 VIRTUAL DEVICE INTERPRETER

PRELIMINARY

this expansion module is based on the Intel 82720 Graphics Display Controller (GDC) component. (see figure 2)

For example using an iSBC 86/30 CPU board, the iVDI 720 library can be installed in EPROM to simplify the application and provide higher performance execution.

82720 Component Designs

The Intel 82720 GDC is an intelligent graphics controller component designed to operate as the heart of a raster-scan computer graphics display system. The 82720 performs all the basic timing needed to generate the raster display and manage the display memory. In addition, it supports several high-level graphics figure drawing functions. The Intel 82720 is an alternative to the NEC 7220 component.

VDI COMMAND LIBRARY

In addition to providing driver support for Intel's growing family of graphics modules, the iVDI 720 Graphics Virtual Device Interpreter decodes a wealth of high-level commands to streamline the development of application code for a variety of graphics devices.

The proposed ANSI standard provides multiple encodings of high-level text and graphics commands and capabilities. The iVDI 720 software decodes a binary representation of these proposed commands, along with the Virtual Device Metafile (VDM) routines that allow consistant formatting and storage of VDI encoded images.

In addition to a full set of inquiry functions, many additional high-level commands are supported in the iVDI 720 software. (See Table 1)

These features are configurable as defined in the iVDI 720 Software Reference Manual. However, they are typically device dependent and therefore reflect the users application. Consequently, the reference manual should be consulted to assure compatability.

DEVELOPMENT ENVIRONMENT

Intel's family of development systems and their extensions are highly recommended for both the development of iVDI 720 and related application code. Languages that are supported include Fortran 86, Pascal 86 and PL/M 86. All iVDI 720 commands can be called from any of these programming languages through the PL/M 86 procedural interface that is integral to the iVDI 720 product.

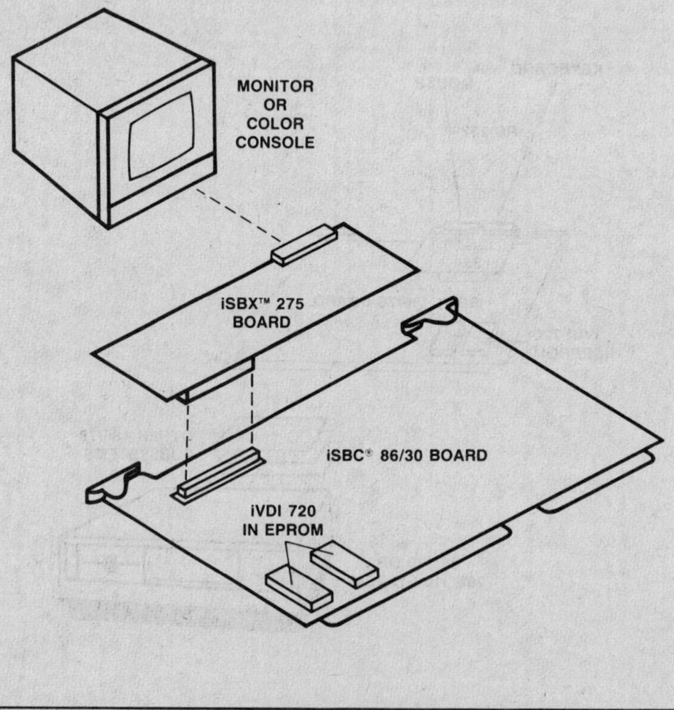

Figure 2. Single-User Example

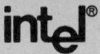

iVDI 720 VIRTUAL DEVICE INTERPRETER

PRELIMINARY

Table 1. iVDI 720 Command Library

Graphical Elements:
- Polyline
- Polygon
- Arc
- Text
- Cell Array
- Polymarker
- Circle
- Arc Close (Pie or Chord)
- Append Text

Attribute Elements:
- Aspect Source Flags
- Character Orientation
- Character Path
- Character Spacing
- Text Alignment
- Perimeter Type & Color
- Hatch Fill
- Pattern Fill
- Pattern Definition
- Text Precision
  - String
  - Character
  - Stroke
- Bundled & Individual Attributes
- Character Height
- Character Expansion Factor
- Interior Style
- Marker Type & Color
- Line Type & Color
- Set Color Table
- Pattern Size
- Pattern Reference Point
- Text Color

Control & Descriptor Elements:
- Begin & End Metafile
- Background Color
- Clip Rectange
- Clear Surface
- Set Device Viewpoint
- Scaling Mode
- Marker Size Mode
- Begin & End Picture
- VDC Extent
- Clip Indicator
- Defaults Replacement
- Color Direct Precision
- Color Specification Mode

Input Elements:
- Initialize Locator
- Sample Locator
- Request Locator
- Set Prompt State
- Release Input Device
- Initialize String
- Sample String
- Request Locator
- Set Echo State
- Set Input Device Mode

SPECIFICATIONS

ANSI X3H33 VDI Specification

The American National Standards Institute (ANSI) administers the standard specification. Requests for information should be directed to:
X3 Secretariat
Computer Business Equipment Manufacturers Association (CBEMA)
311 First Street, NW
Washington, D.C. 20001

Intel is heavily involved in the development of the ANSI X3H33 Virtual Device Interface standard. We will endeavor to bring to our user base the latest revisions through phased introductions and updates. Consequently, it is strongly advised that implementers of iVDI 720 also subscribe to the update service (VDI 720 WX, see below).

iVDI 720 Specifications

Code size — 80 Kbytes in distributed mode (using the iSBC 186/78 subsystem), including the iRMX 86 nucleus

Code size — 64 Kbytes in stand-alone mode (using the iSBX 275 MULTIMODULE)

Source-code language — PL/M 86

Related Literature

Reference material may be ordered from any Intel sales representative, distributor office or from Intel Literature Department, 3065 Bowers Avenue, Santa Clara, Calif., 95051.

- 146717 — iVDI 720 Software Reference Manual
- 210506 — iSBX 275 Video Graphics Controller Data Sheet
- 231035 — iSBC 186/78 Video Graphics Subsystem Data Sheet
- 146666 — iSBC 186/78 Video Graphics Subsystem Hardware Reference Manual
- 210655 — 82720 GDC Component Data Sheet
- 9803126 — iRMX 86 Configuration Guide

Ordering Information

Intel makes available a variety of licensing programs to the iVDI 720 Graphics Virtual Device Interpreter which allow different plans for incorporation of the Intel software into the final product. The Intel Master software Agreement should be consulted to determine which plan is best suited for the particular application and production environment.

The iVDI 720 Graphics Virtual Device Interpreter comes in three formats as shown below, along with source listings and update services. The iRMX 86-Real-time Multitasking Operating System is available separately.

iVDI 720RO OEM license (8 inch single-sided/double density ISIS and iRMX plus 5¼ inch double-sided/double density iRMX formats are supplied)

IVDI 720RF Incorporation fee payment

iVDI 720WX Object code update

Digital and Analog I/O Expansion 7

iSBC® 517
COMBINATION I/O EXPANSION BOARD

- 48 programmable I/O lines with sockets for interchangeable line drivers and terminators
- Synchronous/asynchronous communications interface with RS232C drivers and receivers
- Eight maskable interrupt request lines with a pending interrupt register
- 1 ms interval timer

The iSBC 517 Combination I/O Expansion Board is a member of Intel's complete line of iSBC memory and I/O expansion boards. The board interfaces directly with any iSBC single board computer via the system bus to expand serial and parallel I/O capacity. The combination I/O board contains 48 programmable parallel I/O lines. The system software is used to configure the I/O lines to meet a wide variety of system peripheral requirements. The flexibility of the I/O interface is significantly enhanced by the capability of selecting the appropriate combination of optional line drivers and terminators to provide the required sink current, polarity, and drive/termination characteristics for each application. A programmable RS232C communications interface is provided on the iSBC 517. This interface may be programmed by the system software to provide virtually any asynchronous or synchronous serial data transmission technique (including IBM Bi-Sync). A comprehensive RS232C interface to CRTs, RS232C compatible cassettes, and asynchronous and synchronous modems is thus on the board. An on-board register contains the status of eight interrupt request lines which may be interrogated from the system bus, and each interrupt request line is maskable under program control. The iSBC 517 also contains a jumper selectable 1 ms interval timer and interface logic for eight interrupt request lines.

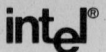

iSBC® 517

FUNCTIONAL DESCRIPTION

Programming Flexibility

The 48 programmable I/O lines on the iSBC 517 are implemented utilizing two Intel 8255 programmable peripheral interfaces. The system software is used to configure these programmable I/O lines in any of the combinations of unidirectional input/output, and bi-directional ports indicated in Table 1. In order to take full advantage of the large number of possible I/O configurations, sockets are provided for interchangeable I/O line drivers and terminators to provide the required sink current, polarity, and drive/termination characteristics for each application. The 48 programmable I/O lines and signal ground lines are brought out to two 50-pin edge connectors that mate with flat, round, or woven cable. Typical I/O read access time is 280 nanoseconds. Typical I/O read cycle time is 600 nanoseconds.

Communications Interface

The programmable communications interface on the iSBC 517 is provided by an Intel 8251 Universal Synchronous/Asynchronous Receiver/Transmitter (USART). The USART can be programmed by the system software to select the desired asynchronous or synchronous serial data transmission technique (including IBM Bi-Sync). The mode of operation (i.e., synchronous or asynchronous), data format, control character format, parity, and asynchronous serial transmission rate are all under program control. The 8251 provides full duplex, double-buffered transmit and receive capability, and parity, overrun, and framing error detection are all incorporated in the USART. The comprehensive RS232C interface on the board provides a direct interface to RS232C compatible equipment. The RS232C serial data lines and signal ground lines are brought out to a 26-pin edge connector that mates with RS232C compatible flat or round cables.

Interrupt Request Lines

Interrupt requests may originate from eight sources. Four jumper selectable interrupt requests can be automatically generated by the programmable peripheral interface when a byte of information is ready to be transferred to the CPU (i.e., input buffer is full) or a character has been transmitted (i.e., output data buffer is empty). Two jumper selectable interrupt requests can be automatically generated by the USART when a character is ready to be transferred to the CPU (i.e., receive buffer is full) or a character has been transmitted (transmit buffer is empty). These six interrupt request lines are all maskable under program control. Two interrupt request lines may be interfaced directly from user designated peripheral devices via the I/O edge connector. An on-board register contains the status of all eight interrupt request lines, and may be interrogated by the CPU. Each interrupt request line is

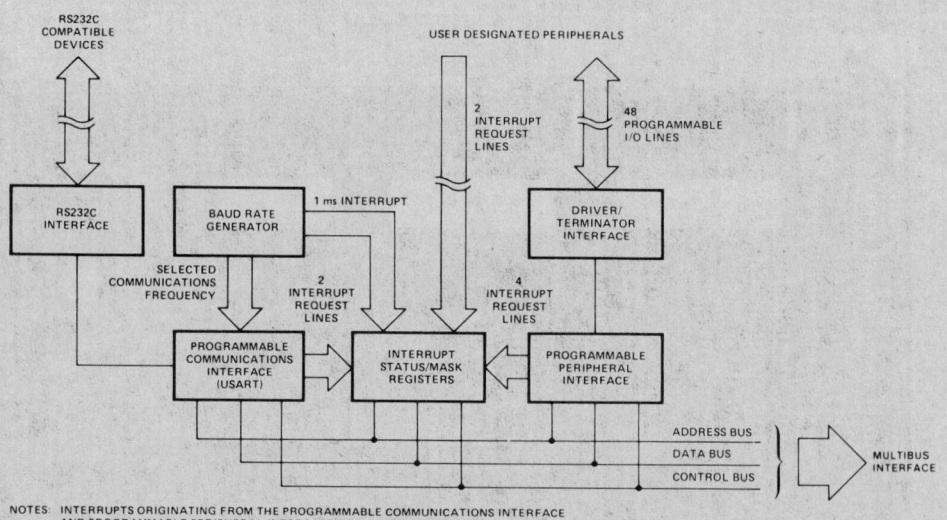

Figure 1. iSBC® 517 Combination I/O Expansion Board Block Diagram

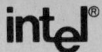 iSBC® 517

Table 1. Input/Output Port Modes of Operation

Ports	Lines (qty)	Unidirectional				Bidirectional	Control
		Input		Output			
		Unlatched	Latched & Strobed	Latched	Latched & Strobed		
1	8	X	X	X	X	X	
2	8	X	X	X	X		
3	4	X		X			X[1]
	4	X		X			X[1]
4	8	X	X	X	X	X	
5	8	X	X	X	X		
6	4	X		X			X[2]
	4	X		X			X[2]

Notes
1. Part of port 3 must be used as control port when either port 1 or port 2 are used as a latched and strobed input or a latched and strobed output port or port 1 is used as a bidirectional port.
2. Part of port 6 must be used as a control port when either port 4 or port 5 are used as a latched and strobed input or a latched and strobed output port or port 4 is used as a bidirectional port.

maskable under program control. Routing for the eight interrupt request lines is jumper selectable. They may be ORed to provide a single interrupt request line for the iSBC 80/10B, or they may be individually provided to the system bus for use by other iSBC single board computers.

Interval Timer
Each board contains a jumper selectable 1 ms interval timer. The timer is enabled by jumpering one of the interrupt request lines from the I/O edge connector to a 1 ms interval interrupt request signal originating from the baud rate generator.

SPECIFICATIONS
I/O Addressing

Port	1	2	3	4	5	6	8255 No. 1 Control	8255 No. 2 Control	USART Data	USART Control
Address	X4	X5	X6	X8	X9	XA	X7	XB	XC	XD

Note
X is any hex digit assigned by jumper selection.

I/O Transfer Rate
Parallel — Read or write cycle time 760 ns max
Serial — (USART)

Frequency (kHz) (Jumper Selectable)	Baud Rate (Hz)		
	Synchronous	Asynchronous (Program Selectable)	
		÷16	÷64
153.6	—	9600	2400
76.8	—	4800	1200
38.4	38400	2400	600
19.2	19200	1200	300
9.6	9600	600	150
4.8	4800	300	75
6.98	6980	—	110

Serial Communications Characteristics
Synchronous — 5-8 bit characters; internal or external character synchronization; automatic sync insertion.
Asynchronous — 5-8 bit characters; peak characters generation; 1, 1½, or 2 stop bits; false start bit detectors.

Interrupts
Eight interrupt request lines may originate from the programmable peripheral interface (4 lines), the USART (2 lines), or user specified devices via the I/O edge connector (2 lines) or interval timer.

Interrupt Register Address
X1 Interrupt mask register
X0 Interrupt status register

Note
X is any hex digit assigned by jumper selection.

Timer Interval
1.003 ms ± 0.1% when 110 baud rate is selected
1.042 ms ± 0.1% for all other baud rates

 **iSBC® 517**

Interfaces

Bus — All signals TTL compatible
Parallel I/O — All signals TTL compatible
Serial I/O — RS232C
Interrupt Requests — All TTL compatible

Connectors

Interface	Pins (qty)	Centers (in.)	Mating Connectors
Bus	86	0.156	CDC VPB01E43A00A1
Parallel I/O	50	0.1	3M 3415-000 or TI H312125
Serial I/O	26	0.1	3M 3462-000 or TI H312113
Auxiliary[1]	60	0.1	AMP PE5-14559 or TI H311130

Note
1. Connector heights and wire-wrap pin lengths are not guaranteed to conform to Intel OEM or system packaging. Auxiliary connector is used for test purposes only.

Line Drivers and Terminators

I/O Drivers — The following line drivers and terminators are compatible with all the I/O driver sockets on the iSBC 517:

Driver	Characteristic	Sink Current (mA)
7438	I,OC	48
7437	I	48
7432	NI	16
7426	I,OC	16
7409	NI,OC	16
7408	NI	16
7403	I,OC	16
7400	I	16

Note
I = inverting; NI = non-inverting; OC = open-collector.

Ports 1 and 4 have 25 mA totem-pole drivers and 1 kΩ terminators.

I/O Terminators — 220Ω/330Ω divider or 1 kΩ pullup

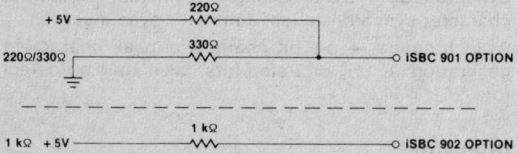

Bus Drivers

Function	Characteristic	Sink Current (mA)
Data	Tri-state	50
Commands	Tri-state	25

Physical Characteristics

Width — 12.00 in. (30.48 cm)
Height — 6.75 in. (17.15 cm)
Depth — 0.50 in. (1.27 cm)
Weight — 14 oz (397.3 gm)

Electrical Characteristics

Average DC Current
$V_{CC} = +5V \pm 5\%$
$V_{DD} = +12V \pm 5\%$
$V_{AA} = -12V \pm 5\%$
$I_{CC} = 2.4$ mA max
$I_{DD} = 40$ mA max
$I_{AA} = 60$ mA max

Note
Does not include power required for optional I/O drivers and I/O terminators. With eight 220Ω/330Ω input terminators installed, all terminator inputs low.

Environmental Characteristics

Operating Temperature — 0°C to +55°C

Reference Manual

9800388B — iSBC 517 Hardware Reference manual (NOT SUPPLIED)

Manuals may be ordered from any Intel sales representative, distributor office or from Intel Literature Department, 3065 Bowers Avenue, Santa Clara, California 95051.

ORDERING INFORMATION

Part Number	Description
SBC 517	Combination I/O Expansion Board

iSBC® 519
PROGRAMMABLE I/O EXPANSION BOARD

- iSBC® I/O expansion via direct MULTIBUS® Interface
- 72 programmable I/O lines with sockets for interchangeable line drivers and terminators
- Jumper selectable I/O port addresses
- Jumper selectable 0.5, 1.0, 2.0, or 4.0 ms interval timer
- Eight maskable interrupt request lines with priority encoded and programmable interrupt algorithms

The iSBC 519 Programmable I/O Expansion Board is a member of Intel's complete line of iSBC memory and I/O expansion boards. The iSBC 519 interfaces directly to any iSBC single board computer via the system bus to expand input and output port capacity. The iSBC 519 provides 72 programmable I/O lines. The system software is used to configure the I/O lines to meet a wide variety of peripheral requirements. The flexibility of the I/O interface is further enhanced by the capability of selecting the appropriate combination of optional line drivers and terminators to provide the required sink current, polarity, and drive/termination characteristics for each application. Address selection is accomplished by using wire-wrap jumpers to select one of 16 unique base addresses for the input and output ports. The board operates with a single +5V power supply.

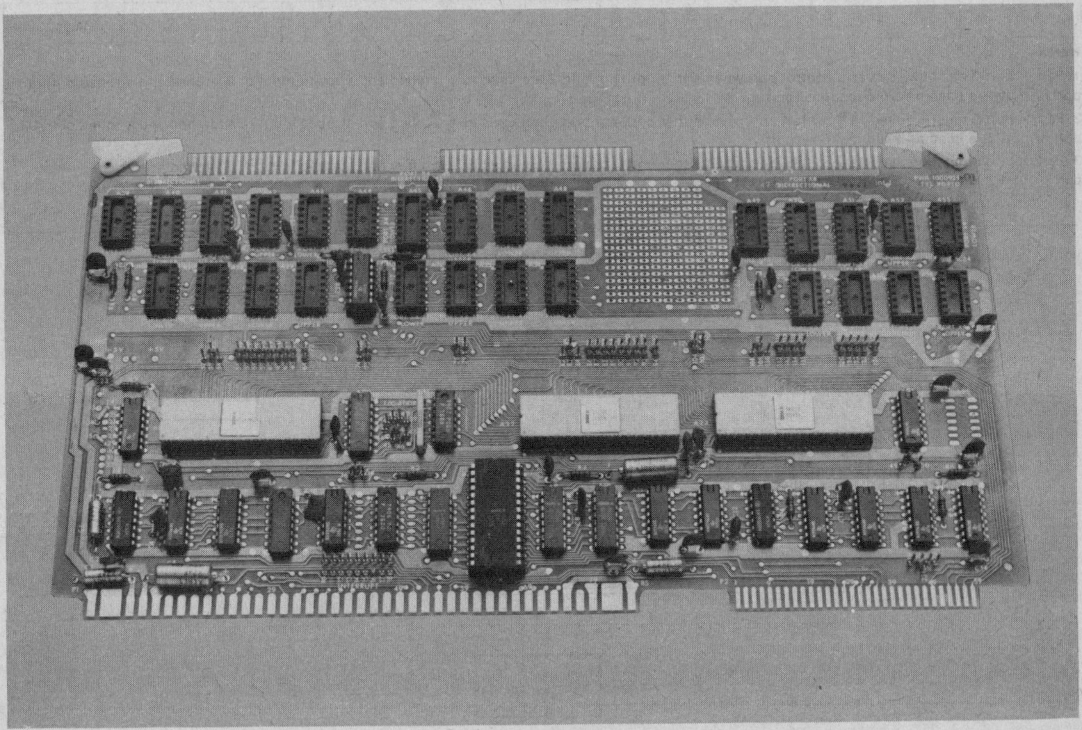

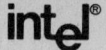

iSBC® 519

FUNCTIONAL DESCRIPTION

The 72 programmable I/O lines on the iSBC 519 are implemented utilizing three Intel 8255A programmable peripheral interfaces. The system software is used to configure the I/O lines in any combination of undirectional input/output and bi-directional ports indicated in Table 1. In order to take full advantage of the large number of possible I/O configurations, sockets are provided for interchangeable I/O line drivers and terminators. The 72 programmable I/O lines and signal ground lines are brought out to three 50-pin edge connectors that mate with flat, round, or woven cable.

Interval Timer

Typical I/O read access time is 350 nanoseconds. Typical I/O read/write cycle time is 450 nanoseconds. The interval timer provided on the iSBC 519 may be used to generate real time clocking in systems requiring the periodic monitoring of I/O functions. The time interval is derived from the constant clock (BUS CCLK) and the timing interval is jumper selectable. Intervals of 0.5, 1.0, 2.0, and 4.0 milliseconds may be selected when an iSBC single board computer is used to generate the clock. Other timing intervals may be generated if the user provides a separate constant clock reference in the system.

Eight-Level Vectored Interrupt

An Intel 8259A programmable interrupt controller (PIC) provides vectoring for eight interrupt levels. As shown in Table 2, a selection of three priority processing algorithms is available to the system designer so that the

Table 1. Input/Output Port Modes of Operation

Ports	Lines (qty)	Unidirectional				Bidirectional	Control
		Input		Output			
		Unlatched	Latched & Strobed	Latched	Latched & Strobed		
1,4,7	8	X	X	X	X	X	
2,5,8	8	X	X	X	X		
3,6,9	4	X		X			X[1,2,3]
	4	X		X			X[1,2,3]

Notes

1. Part of port 3 must be used as a control port when either port 1 or port 2 are used as a latched and strobed input or a latched and strobed output port or port 1 is used as a bidirectional port.
2. Part of port 6 must be used as a control port when either port 4 or port 5 are used as a latched and strobed input or a latched and strobed output port or port 4 is used as a bidirectional port.
3. Part of port 9 must be used as a control port when either port 7 or port 8 are used as a latched and strobed input or a latched and strobed output port or port 7 is used as a bidirectional port.

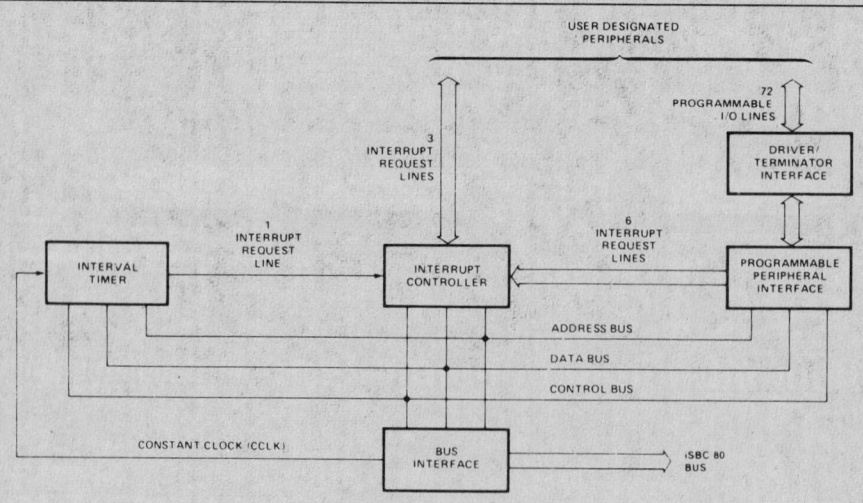

Figure 1. iSBC® 519 Programmable I/O Expansion Board Block Diagram

iSBC® 519

Table 2. Interrupt Priority Options

Algorithm	Operation
Fully nested	Interrupt request line priorities fixed at 0 as highest, 7 as lowest.
Auto-rotating	Equal priority. Each level, after receiving service, becomes the lowest priority level until next interrupt occurs.
Specific priority	System software assigns lowest priority level. Priority of all other levels are based in sequence numerically on this assignment.

manner in which requests are serviced may be configured to match system requirements. Priority assignments may be reconfigured dynamically via software at any time during system operation. The PIC accepts interrupt requests from the programmable parallel I/O interfaces, the interval timer, or direct from peripheral equipment. The PIC then determines which of the incoming requests is of the highest priority, determines whether this request is of higher priority than the level currently being serviced, and if appropriate, issues an interrupt to the system master. Any combination of interrupt levels may be masked through storage, via software, of a single byte to the interrupt mask register of the PIC.

Interrupt Request Generation — Interrupt requests may originate from 10 sources. Six jumper selectable interrupt requests can be automatically generated by the programmable peripheral interfaces when a byte of information is ready to be transferred to the system master (i.e., input buffer is full) or a character has been transmitted (i.e., output data buffer is empty). Three interrupt request lines may be interfaced to the PIC directly from user designated peripheral devices via the I/O edge connectors. One interrupt request may be generated by the interval timer.

Bus Line Drivers — The PIC interrupt request output line may be jumper selected to drive any of the nine interrupt lines on the MULTIBUS. Any of the on-board request lines may also drive any interface interrupt line directly via jumpers and buffers on the board.

SPECIFICATIONS

Addressing

Port	1	2	3	8255 No. 1 Control	4	5	6	8255 No. 2 Control	7	8	9	8255 No. 3 Control
Address	X0	X1	X2	X3	X4	X5	X6	X7	X8	X9	XA	XB

Interrupts

Register Addresses (hex notation, I/O address space)
XD Interrupt request register
XC In-service register
XD Mask register
XC Command register
XD Block address register
XC Status (polling register)

Note
Several registers have the same physical address; sequence of access and one data bit of control word determines which register will respond.

Ten interrupt request lines may originate from the programmable peripheral interface (6 lines), or user specified devices via the I/O edge connector (3 lines), or interval timer (1 line).

Interval Timer

Output Register — Timer interrupt register output is cleared by an output instruction to I/O address XE or XF[1].

Timing Intervals — 500, 1,000, 2,000, and 4,000 ms ± 1%; jumper selectable[2].

Notes
1. X is any hex digit assigned by jumper selection.
2. Assumes constant clock (CCLK) frequency of 9.216 MHz ± 1%.

Interfaces

Bus — All signals TTL compatible
Parallel I/O — All signals TTL compatible
Interrupt Requests — All TTL compatible

Connectors

Interface	Pins (qty)	Centers (in.)	Mating Connectors
Bus	86	0.156	Viking 3KH43/9AMK12
Parallel I/O	50	0.1	3M 3415-000 or TI H312125
Serial I/O	26	0.1	3M 3462-000 or TI H312113
Auxiliary[1]	60	0.1	AMP PE5-14559 or TI H311130

Note
1. Connector heights and wirewrap pin lengths are not guaranteed to conform to Intel OEM or System packaging.

Line Drivers and Terminators

I/O Drivers — The following line drivers and terminators are compatible with all the I/O driver sockets on the iSBC 519:

Driver	Characteristic	Sink Current (mA)
7438	I,OC	48
7437	I	48
7432	NI	16
7426	I,OC	16
7409	NI,OC	16
7408	NI	16
7403	I,OC	16
7400	I	16

Note
I = inverting; NI = non-inverting; OC = open-collector.

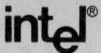

iSBC® 519

I/O Terminators — 220Ω/330Ω divider or 1 kΩ pullup

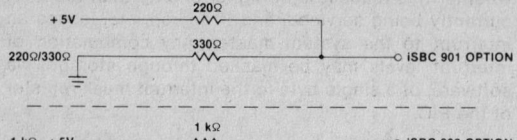

Ports 1, 4, and 7 may use any of the drivers or terminators shown above for unidirectional (input or output) port configurations. Either terminator and the following bidirectional drivers and terminators may be used for ports 1, 4, and 7 when these ports are used as bidirectional ports.

Bidirectional Drivers

Driver	Characteristic	Sink Current (mA)
Intel 8216	NI, TS	25
Intel 8226	I, TS	50

Note
I = inverting; NI = non-inverting; TS = three-state.

Terminators (for ports 1, 4, and 7 when used as bidirectional ports)

Supplier	Product Series
CTS	760-
Dale	LDP14k-02
Beckman	899-1

Bus Drivers

Function	Characteristic	Sink Current (mA)
Data	Tri-state	50
Commands	Tri-state	25

ORDERING INFORMATION

Part Number   Description
SBC 519   Programmable I/O Expansion Board

Physical Characteristics
Width — 12.00 in. (30.48 cm)
Height — 6.75 in. (17.15 cm)
Depth — 0.50 in. (1.27 cm)
Weight — 14 oz (397.3 gm)

Electrical Characteristics
Average DC Current

Voltage	Without Termination[1]	With Termination[2]
$V_{CC} = +5V \pm 5\%$	I_{CC} = 1.5A max	3.5A max

Note
1. Does not include power required for optional I/O drivers and I/O terminators.
2. With 18 220Ω/330Ω input terminators installed, all terminator inputs low.

Environmental Characteristics
Operating Temperature — 0°C to +55°C

Reference Manual

9800385B — iSBC 519 Hardware Reference manual (NOT SUPPLIED)

Manuals may be ordered from any Intel sales representative, distributor office or from Intel Literature Department, 3065 Bowers Avenue, Santa Clara, California 95051.

iSBC®556
OPTICALLY ISOLATED I/O BOARD

- Up to 48 digital optically isolated input/output data lines for MULTIBUS® systems

- Choice of
  — 24 fixed input lines
  — 16 fixed output lines
  — 8 programmable lines

- Provisions for plug-in, optically isolated receivers, drivers, and terminators

- Voltate/current levels
  — Input up to 48V
  — Output up to 30V, 60 mA

- Common interrupt for up to 8 sources

- +5V supply only

The iSBC 556 Optically Isolated I/O Board provides 48 digital input/output lines with isolation between process application or peripheral device and the system CPU board(s). The iSBC 556 contains two 8255A programmable interface devices, and sockets for user supplied optically isolated drivers, receivers, and input resistor terminators, together with common interrupt logic and inteface circuitry for the system bus. Input signals can be single-ended or differential types with user defined input range (resistor terminator and opto-isolated receiver selection), allowing flexibility in design of voltage and threshold levels. The output allows user selection of Opto-Isolated Darlington Pair which can be used as an output driver either as an open collector or current switch.

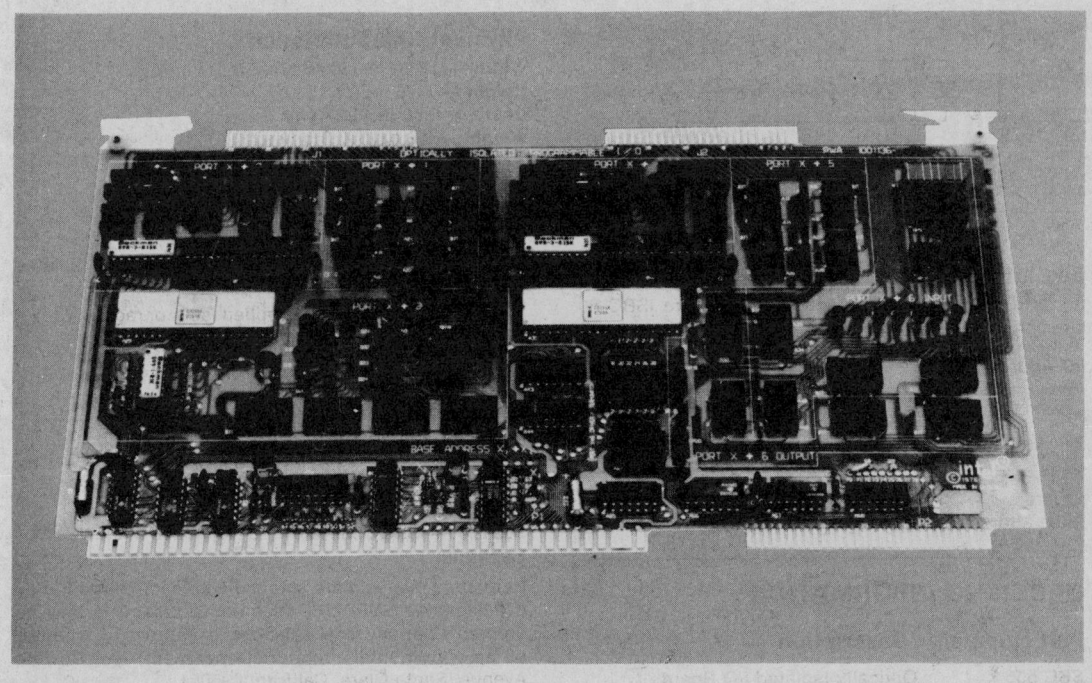

iSBC® 556

Table 1. I/O Ports Opto-Isolator Receivers, Drivers, and Terminators

Port No. X = I/O Base Address	Type of I/O	Lines (qty)	Resistor Terminator Pac-Rp 16-Pin DIP Bourns 4116R-00 or Equivalent	Dual Opto-Isolator 8-Pin DIP Monsanto MC T66 or Equivalent	Driver 7438 or Equivalent	Pull-Up iSBC® 902
X+0	Input	8	1	4	—	
X+1	Output	8			—	
X+2	Input/Control	8	1		—	
X+4	Input	8	1	4	—	
X+5	Output	8			—	
X+6 X+7	Input/Output Control	8	1 if input		2 if output	2 if input

SPECIFICATIONS

Number of Lines
24 input lines
16 output lines
8 programmable lines: 4 input — 4 output

I/O Interface Characteristics
Line-to-Line Isolation — 235V DC or peak AC
Input/Output Isolation — 500V DC or peak AC

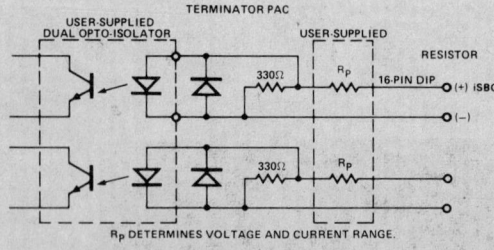

Bus Interface Characteristics
All data address and control commands are iSBC 80 bus compatible.

I/O Addressing

Port	8255 #1			Control	8255 #2			Control
	A	B	C		A	B	C	
Address	X+0	X+1	X+2	X+3	X+4	X+5	X+6	X+7

Where:
base address is from 00H to 1FH (jumper selectable)

ORDERING INFORMATION

Part Number	Description
SBC 556	Optically Isolated I/O Board

Connectors

Interface	Pins (qty)	Centers		Mating Connectors
		in.	cm	
P1 iSBC bus	86	0.156		Viking 3KH43/9AMK12
J1 16 fixed input & 8 fixed output lines	50	0.1		3M 3415-000 or TI M312125
J2 8 fixed output, 8 fixed output, & 8 programmable input/output lines	50	0.1		3M 3415-000 or TI M312125

Physical Characteristics
Width — 12.00 in. (30.48 cm)
Height — 6.75 in. (17.15 cm)
Depth — 0.50 in. (1.27 cm)
Weight — 12 oz (397.3 gm)

Electrical Characteristics
Average DC Current

$V_{CC} = +5V \pm 5\%$, 1.0A without user supplied isolated receiver/driver

$I_{CC} = 1.6A$ max with user supplied isolator receiver/driver

Environmental Characteristics
Temperature — 0°C to 55°C
Relative Humidity — 0 to 90%, non-condensing

Reference Manual
502170 — iSBC 556 Hardware Reference Manual (Order Separately)

Reference manuals are shipped with each product only if designated SUPPLIED (see above). Manuals may be ordered from any Intel sales representative, distributor office or from Intel Literature Department, 3065 Bowers Avenue, Santa Clara, California 95051.

iSBC® 569
INTELLIGENT DIGITAL CONTROLLER

- Single board digital I/O controller with up to four microprocessors to share the digital input/output signal processing

- 3 MHz 8085A central control processor

- Three sockets for 8041/8741A Universal Peripheral Interface (UPI-41A) for distributed digital I/O processing

- Three operational modes
  — Stand-along digital controller
  — MULTIBUS® master
  — Intelligent slave (slave to MULTIBUS® master)

- 2K bytes of dual port static read/write memory

- Sockets for up to 8K bytes of Intel 2758, 2716, 2732 erasable programmable read only memory

- 48 programmable parallel I/O lines with sockets for interchangeable line drivers or terminators

- Three programmable counters

- 12 levels of programmable interrupt control

- Single +5V supply

- MULTIBUS® standard control logic compatible with optional iSBC 80 and iSBC 86 CPU, memory, and I/O expansion boards

The Intel iSBC 569 Intelligent Digital Controller is a single board computer (8085A based) with sockets for three 8041A/8741A Universal Peripherals Interface chips (UPI-41A). These devices, which are programmed by the user, may be used to offload the 8085A processor from time consuming tasks such as pulse counting, event sensing and parallel or serial digital I/O data formatting with error checking and handshaking. The iSBC 569 board is a complete digital controller with up to four processors on a single 6.75 inches x 12.00 inches (17.15cm x 30.48cm) printed circuit board. The 8085A CPU, system clock, read/write memory, non-volatile memory, priority interrupt logic, programmed timers, MULTIBUS control and interface logic, optional UPI processors and optional line driver and terminators all reside on one board.

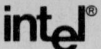 iSBC® 569

FUNCTIONAL DESCRIPTION

Intelligent Digital Controller

Three modes of operation — the iSBC 569 Intelligent Digital Controller is capable of operating in one of three modes; stand alone controller, bus master, or intelligent slave.

Stand alone controller — the iSBC 569 board may function as a stand alone, single board controller with CPU, memory, and I/O elements on a single board. Five volt (+5VDC) only operation allows configuration of low cost controllers with only a single power supply voltage. The on-board 2K bytes RAM and up to 16K bytes ROM/EPROM, as well as the assistance of three UPI-41A processors, allow significant digital I/O control from a single board.

Bus master — in this mode of operation, the iSBC 569 controller may interface with and control iSBC expansion memory and I/O boards, or even other iSBC 569 Intelligent Digital Controllers configured as intelligent slaves (but no additional bus masters).

Intelligent slave — the iSBC 569 controller can perform as an intelligent slave to any 8- or 16-bit MULTIBUS master CPU by offloading the master of digital control related tasks. Preprocessing of data for the master is controlled by the on-board 8085A CPU which coordinates up to three UPI-41A processors. Using the iSBC 569 board as an intelligent slave, multi-channel digital control can be managed entirely on-board, freeing a system master to perform other system functions. The dual port RAM memory allows the iSBC 569 controller to process and store data without MULTIBUS memory contention.

Simplified Programming

By using Intel UPI-41A processors for common tasks such as counting, sensing change of state, printer control and keyboard scanning/debouncing, the user frees up time to work on the more important application programming of machine or process optimization. Controlling the Intel UPI-41A processors becomes a simple task of reading or writing command and data bytes to or from the data bus buffer register on the UPI device.

Central Processing Unit

A powerful Intel 8085A 8-bit CPU, fabricated on a single LSI chip, is the central processor for the iSBC 569 ™ controller. The six general purpose 8-bit registers may be addressed individually or in pairs, providing both single and double precision operations. The program counter can address up to 64K bytes of memory using iSBC expansion boards. The 16-bit stack pointer controls the addressing of an external stack. This stack provides sub-routine nesting bounded only by memory size. The minimum instruction execution time is 1.30 microseconds. The 8085A CPU is software compatible with the Intel 8080A CPU.

Bus Structure

The iSBC 569 Intelligent Digital Controller utilizes a triple bus architecture concept. An internal bus is used for on-board memory and I/O operations. A MULTIBUS interface is available to provide access for all external memory and I/O operations. A dual port bus with controller enables access via the third bus to 2K bytes of static RAM from either the on-board CPU or a system master. Hence, common data may be stored in on-board memory and may be accessed either by the on-board CPU or by system masters. A block diagram of the iSBC 569 functional components is shown in Figure 1.

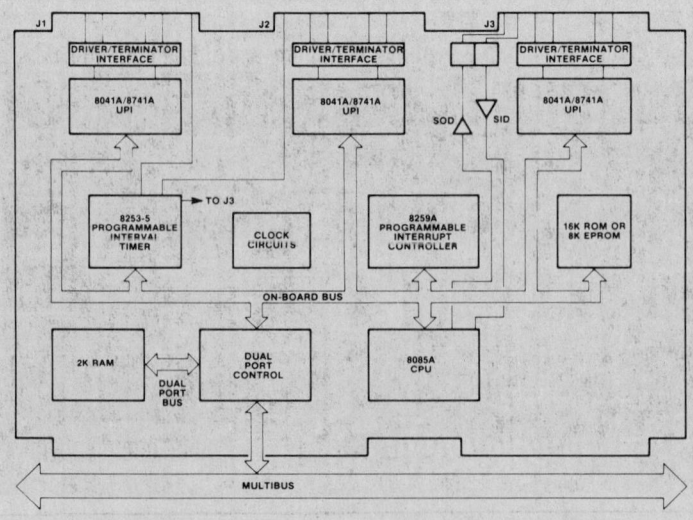

Figure 1. iSBC ®569 Intelligent Digital Controller Block Diagram

iSBC® 569

RAM Capacity

The iSBC 569 board contains 2K bytes of read/write memory using Intel 2114 static RAMs. RAM accesses may occur from either the iSBC 569 controller or from any other bus master interfaced via the MULTIBUS system bus. The iSBC 569 board provides addressing jumpers to allow the on-board RAM to reside within a one megabyte address space when accessed via the system bus. In addition, a switch is provided which allows the user to reserve a 1K byte segment of on-board RAM for use by the 8085A CPU. This reserved RAM space is not accessible via the system bus and does not occupy any system address space.

EPROM/ROM Capacity

Two sockets for up to 16K bytes of nonvolatile read only memory are provided on the iSBC 569 board. Nonvolatile memory may be added in 1K-byte increments up to a maximum of 2K bytes using Intel 2758 erasable and electrically reprogrammable ROMs (EPROMs); in 2K-byte increments up to a maximum of 4K bytes using Intel 2316 ROMs or 2716 EPROMs; in 4K byte increments up to 8K bytes maximum using Intel 2732 EPROMs; or in 8K-byte increments up to 16K bytes maximum using Intel 2364 ROMs (both sockets must contain same type ROM/EPROM). All on-board ROM/EPROM operations are performed at maximum processor speed.

Universal Peripheral Interfaces (UPI-41A)

The iSBC 569 Intelligent Digital Controller board provides three sockets for user supplied Intel 8041A/8741A Universal Peripheral Interface (UPI-41A) chips. Sockets are also provided for the associated line drivers and terminators for the UPI I/O ports. The UPI-41A processor is a single chip microcomputer containing a CPU, 1K bytes of ROM (8041A) or EPROM (8741A), 64 bytes of RAM, 16 programmable I/O lines, and an 8-bit timer/event counter. Special interface registers included in the chip allow the UPI-41A processor to function as a slave processor to the iSBC 569 controller board's 8085A CPU. The UPI processor allows the user to specify algorithms for controlling peripherals directly thereby freeing the 8085A for other system functions. For additional information, including UPI-41A instructions, refer to the UPI-41 User's Manual (Manual No. 9800504).

Programmable Timers

The iSBC 569 Intelligent Digital Controller board provides three independently programmable interval timer/counters utilizing one Intel 8253 Programmable Interval Timer (PIT). The Intel 8253 PIT provides three 16-bit BCD or binary interval timer/counters. Each timer may be used to provide a time reference for each UPI™ processor or for a group of UPI processors. The output of each timer also connects to the 8259A Programmable Interrupt Controller (PIC) providing the capability of timed interrupts. All gate inputs, clock inputs, and timer outputs of the 8253 PIT are available at the I/O ports for external access.

Timer Functions — In utilizing the iSBC 569 controller, the systems designer simply configures, via software, each timer to meet systems requirements. The 8253 PIT modes are listed in Table 1. The contents of each counter may be read at any time during system operation with simple read operations for event counting applications. The contents of each counter can be read "on-the-fly" for time stamping events or time clock referenced program initiations.

Table 1. 8253 Programmable Timer Functions

Function	Operation
Interrupt on terminal count	When terminal count is reached, an interrupt request is generated.
Programmable one-shot	Output goes low upon receipt of an external trigger edge or software command and returns high when terminal count is reached. This function is retriggerable.
Rate generator	Divide by N counter. The output will go low for one input clock cycle, and the period from one low-going pulse to the next is N times the input clock period.
Square-wave rate generator	Output will remain high until one-half the count has been completed, and go low for the other half of the count.
Software triggered strobe	Output remains high until software loads count (N). N counts after count is loaded, output goes low for one input clock period.
Hardware triggered strobe	Output goes low for one clock period N counts after rising edge on counter trigger input. The counter is retriggerable.
Event counter	On a jumper selectable basis, the clock input becomes an input from the external system. CPU may read the number of events occurring after the counting "window" has been enabled or an interrupt may be generated after N counts occur in the system.

iSBC® 569

Interrupt Capability

The iSBC 569 Intelligent Digital Controller provides interrupt service for up to 12 interrupt sources. Any of the 12 sources may interrupt the on-board processor. Four interrupt levels are handled directly by the 8085A CPU and eight levels are serviced from an Intel 8259A Programmable Interrupt Controller (PIC) routing an interrupt request output to the INTR input of the 8085A.

8085A Interrupt — Each of four direct 8085A interrupt inputs has a unique vector memory address. An 8085A jump instruction at each of these addresses then provides software linkage to interrupt service routines located independently anywhere in the memory.

8259A Interrupts — The eight interrupt sources originate from both on-board controller functions and the system bus:

UPI-41A Processors — one interrupt from each of three UPI processor sockets.
8253 PIT — one interrupt from each of three timer outputs.
MULTIBUS System Bus — one of eight MULTIBUS interrupt lines may be jumpered to either of two 8259A PIC interrupt inputs.

Programmable Reset — The iSBC 569 Intelligent Digital Controller board has a programmable output latch used to control on-board functions. Three of the outputs are connected to separate UPI-41A RESET inputs. Thus, the user can reset any or all of the UPI-41A processors under software control. A fourth latch output may be used to generate an interrupt request onto the MULTIBUS interrupt lines. A fifth latch output is connected to a light-emitting diode which may be used for diagnostic purposes.

Expansion Capabilities

When the iSBC 569 controller is used as a single board digital controller, memory and I/O capacity may be expanded using Intel MULTIBUS compatible expansion boards. In this mode, no other bus masters may be in the system. Memory may be expanded to a 64K byte capacity by adding user specified combinations of RAM boards, EPROM boards, or combination boards. Input/output capacity may be increased by adding I/O expansion boards. Multiple iSBC 569 boards may be included in an expanded system using one iSBC 569 Intelligent Digital Controller as the system master and additional controllers as intelligent slaves.

Intelligent Slave Programming

When used as an intelligent slave, the iSBC 569 controller appears as an additional RAM memory module. System bus masters communicate with the iSBC 569 board as if it were just an extension of system memory. To simplify this communication, the user has been given some specific tools:

Flag Interrupt — The Flag Interrupt is generated any time a write command is performed by an off-board CPU to the first location of iSBC 569 RAM. This interrupt provides a means for the master CPU to notify the iSBC 569 controller that it wished to establish a communications sequence. The flag interrupt is cleared when the on-board processor reads the first location of its RAM. In systems with more than one intelligent slave, the flag interrupt provides a unique interrupt to each slave outside the normal MULTIBUS interrupt lines (INT0/-INT7/).

RAM — The on-board 2K byte RAM area that is accessible to both an off-board CPU and the on-board 8085A may be configured for system access on any 2K boundary.

MULTIBUS Interrupts — The third tool to improve system operation as an intelligent slave is access to the MULTIBUS interrupt lines. The iSBC 569 controller can both respond to interrupt signals from an off-board CPU, and generate an interrupt to the off-board CPU via the system bus.

System Development Capability

Software development for the iSBC 569 Intelligent Digital Controller board is supported by the Intellec® Microcomputer Development System including a resident macroassembler, text editor, system monitor, a linker, object code locator, and Library Manager. In addition, both PL/M and FORTRAN language programs can be compiled to run on the iSBC 569 board. A unique in-circuit emulator (ICE-85™) option provides the capability of developing and debugging software directly on the iSBC 569 board. This greatly simplifies the design, development, and debug of iSBC 569 system software.

SPECIFICATIONS

8085A CPU
Word Size — 8, 16 or 24 bits
Cycle Time — 1.30 μsec ± .1% for fastest executable instruction; i.e., four clock cycles.
Clock Rate — 3.07 MHz ± .1%

System Access Time
Dual port memory — 725 nsec

Memory Capacity
On-board ROM/EPROM — 2K, 4K, 8K, or 16K bytes of user installed ROM or EPROM
On-board RAM — 2K bytes of static RAM. Fully accessible from on-board 8085A. Separately addressable from system bus.
Off-board expansion — up to 64K bytes of EPROM/ROM or RAM capacity.

I/O Capacity
Parallel-Timers — Three timers, with independent gate input, clock input, and timer output user-accessible. Clock inputs can be strapped to an external source or to an on-board 1.3824 MHz reference. Each timer is connected to a 8259A Programmable Interrupt Controller and may also be optionally connected to UPI processors.

UPI-I/O — Three UPI-41A interfaces, each with two 8-bit I/O ports plus the two UPI Test Inputs. The 8-bit ports are user-configurable (as inputs or outputs) in groups of four.

iSBC® 569

Serial — 1 TTL compatible serial channel utilizing SID and SOD lines of on-board 8085A CPU

On-Board Addressing
All communications to the UPI-41A processors, to the programmable reset latch, to the timers, and to the interrupt controller are via read and write commands from the on-board 8085A CPU.

Memory Addressing
On-board ROM/EPROM — 0–07FF (using 2758 EPROMs); 0–0FFF (using 2716 EPROMs or 2316 ROMs); 0–1FFF (using 2732 EPROMs); 0–3FFF (using the 2364 ROMs).

On-board RAM — 8000–87FF System access — any 2K increment 00000–FF800 (switch selectable); 1K bytes may be disabled from bus access by switch selection.

I/O Addressing

Source	Addresses
8253	0E0H–0E3H
UPI0	0E4H–0E5H
UPI1	0E6H–0E7H
UPI2	0E8H–0E9H
PROGRAMMABLE RESET	0EAH–0EBH
8259A	0ECH–0EDH

Timer Specifications
Input frequencies — jumper selectable reference
  Internal: 1.3824 MHz ± .1% (.723 μsec, nominal)
  External: User supplied (2 MHz maximum)

Output Frequencies (at 1.3824 MHz)

Function	Min[1]	Max[1]
Real-time interrupt interval	1.45 μsec	47.4 msec
Rate Generator (frequency)	21.09 Hz	691.2 KHz

1. Single 16-bit binary count

Interfaces
MULTIBUS™ Interface — All signals compatible with iSBC and MULTIBUS architecture
Parallel I/O — All signals TTL compatible
Interrupt Requests — All TTL compatible
Timer — All signals TTL compatible
Serial I/O — All signals TTL compatible

Connectors

Interface	Pins (qty)	Centers (in.)	Mating Connectors
Bus	86	0.156	Viking 3KH43/9AMK12
Parallel I/O	50	0.1	3M 3415-000 or TI H312125

Physical Characteristics
Width — 30.48 cm (12.00 inches)
Depth — 17.15 cm (6.75 inches)
Thickness — 1.27 cm (0.50 inch)
Weight — 3.97 gm (14 ounces)

Electrical Characteristics
DC Power Requirements — +5V @ 2.58A with no optional devices installed. For each 8741A add 135 mA. For each 220/330 resistor network, add 60 mA. Add the following for each EPROM/ROM installed.

Type	+5.0V Current Requirement	
	1ROM	2ROMS
2758	100 mA	125 mA
2716	100 mA	125 mA
2316E	120 mA	240 mA
2732	40 mA	55 mA
2364	40 mA	55 mA

Line Drivers and Terminators
I/O Drivers — The following line drivers are all compatible with the I/O driver sockets on the iSBC 569 Intelligent Digital Controller.

Driver	Characteristic	Sink Current (mA)
7438	I,OC	48
7437	I	48
7432	NI	16
7426	I,OC	16
7409	NI,OC	16
7408	NI	16
7403	I,OC	16
7400	I	16

Note I = inverting; NI = non-inverting; OC = open collector.

I/O Terminators — 220Ω/330Ω divider or 1 kΩ pullup (DIP) - user supplied

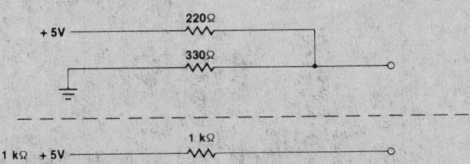

Environmental Characteristics
Operating Temperature — 0°C to 55°C (32°F to 131°F)
Relative Humidity — To 90% without condensation

Reference Manual
502180 — iSBC 569 Intelligent Digital Controller Board Hardware Reference Manual (NOT SUPPLIED)

Reference manuals are shipped with each product only if designated SUPPLIED (see above). Manuals may be ordered from any Intel sales representative, distributor office or from Intel Literature Department, 3065 Bowers Avenue, Santa Clara, California 95051.

ORDERING INFORMATION

Part Number | Description
SBC 569   Intelligent Digital Controller

iSBX™ 311
ANALOG INPUT MULTIMODULE™ BOARD

- Low cost analog input for iSBX™ MULTIMODULE™ compatible iSBC® boards
- 8 differential/16 single-ended, fault protected inputs
- 20 mV to 5V full scale input range, resistor gain selectable
- Unipolar (0 to +5V) or bipolar (−5V to +5V) input, jumper selectable
- 12-bit resolution analog-to-digital converter
- 0.035% full scale accuracy (11 bits) at 25°C
- 18 kHz samples per second throughput to memory
- Connector compatible with iCS 910 Analog Termination Panel

The Intel iSBX 311 Analog Input MULTIMODULE board provides simple interfacing of non-isolated analog signals to any iSBC board which has an iSBX compatible bus and connectors. The single-wide iSBX 311 plugs directly onto the iSBC board, providing data acquisition of analog signals from eight differential or sixteen single-ended voltage inputs, jumper selectable. The iSBX 311 MULTIMODULE is connector and pinout compatible with the Intel iCS 910 Analog Signal Conditioning/Termination panel so that field wiring can easily be terminated and current loop-to-voltage conversion resistors can be mounted for current loop analog signal monitoring. Resistor gain selection is provided for both low level (20mv full scale range) and high level (5 volt FSR) signals. Incorporating the latest high quality IC components, the iSBX 311 MULTIMODULE board provides 12 bit resolution, 11 bit accuracy, and a simple programming interface, all on a low cost iSBX MULTIMODULE board.

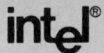

iSBX™ 311

FUNCTIONAL DESCRIPTION

The iSBX 311 Analog Input MULTIMODULE board is a member of Intel's growing family of MULTIMODULE expansion boards, designed to allow quick, easy, and inexpensive expansion for the Intel single board computer product line. The iSBX 311 Analog Input MULTIMODULE Board shown in figure 1, is designed to plug onto any host iSBC microcomputer that contains an iSBX bus connector (P1). The board provides 8 differential or 16 single-ended analog input channels that may be jumper-selected as the application requires. The MULTIMODULE board includes a user-configurable gain, and a user-selectable voltage input range (0 to +5 volts, or −5 to +5 volts). The MULTIMODULE board receives all power and control signals through the iSBX bus connector to initiate channel selection, sample and hold operation, and analog-to-digital conversion.

Input Capacity

Sixteen separate analog signals may be randomly or sequentially sampled in single-ended mode with the sixteen input multiplexers and a common ground. For noisier environments, differential input mode can be configured to achieve 8 separate differential signal inputs, or 16 pseudo-differential inputs.

Resolution

The iSBX 311 MULTIMODULES provide 12-bit resolution with a successive approximation analog-to-digital converter. For bipolar operation (−5 to +5 volts) it provides 11 bits plus sign.

Speed

The A-to-D converter conversion speed is 35 microseconds (28KHZ samples per second). Combined with the sample and hold, settling times and the programming interface, maximum throughput via the iSBX bus and into memory will be 54 microseconds per sample, or 18 KHZ samples per second, for a single channel, a random channel, or a sequential channel scan. A-to-D conversion is initiated via the iSBX connector and programmed command from the iSBC base board. Interrupt on end-of-conversion is a standard feature to ease programming and timing constraints.

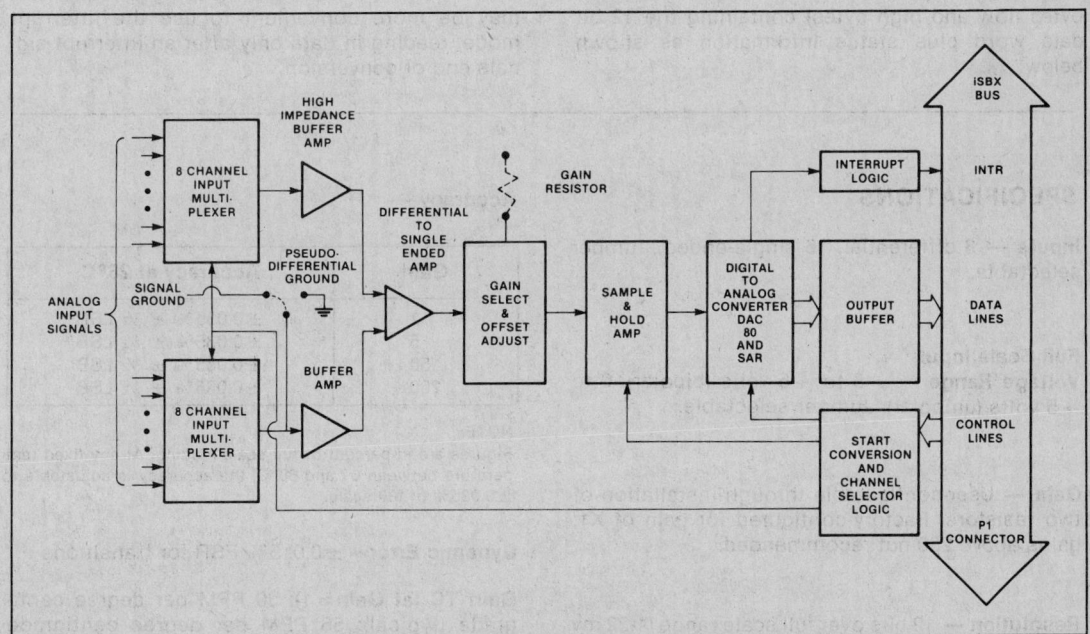

Figure 1. iSBX™ 311 Analog Input MULTIMODULE™ Board

iSBX™ 311

Accuracy

High quality components are used to achieve 12 bits resolution and accuracy of .035% full scale range ± ½ LSB. Offset and gain are adjustable to ± 0.024% FSR ± ½ LSB accuracy at any fixed temperature between 0°C (gain = 1). See specifications for other gain accuracies.

Gain

To allow sampling of millivolt level signals such as strain gauges and thermocouples, gain is made configurable via user inserted gain resistors up to 250× (20 millivolts, full scale input range). User can select any other gain range from 1 to 250 to match his application.

OPERATIONAL DESCRIPTION

The host iSBC microcomputer addresses the iSBX 311 MULTIMODULE board by executing IN or OUT instructions to the iSBX 311 MULTIMODULE as one of the legal port addresses. Analog-to-digital conversions can be programmed in either of two modes: 1. start conversion and poll for end-of-conversion (EOC), or 2. start conversion and wait for interrupt (INTRO/) at end of conversion. When conversion is complete as signaled by one of the above techniques, INput instructions read two bytes (low and high bytes) containing the 12 bit data word plus status information as shown below.

OUTput Command — Select input channel and start conversion.

Bit Position	7	6	5	4	3	2	1	0
Input Channel					C3	C2	C1	C0

INput Data — Read converted data and status (low byte) or Read converted data (high byte). Reads can be with or without reset of interrupt request line (INTRO/).

Bit Position	7	6	5	4	3	2	1	0
Low/status Byte	D3	D2	D1	D0		start/	busy/	EOC/

Bit Position	7	6	5	4	3	2	1	0
High Byte	D11	D10	D9	D8	D7	D6	D5	D4

Fastest data conversion and transfer to memory can be obtained by dedicating the microcomputer to setting the channel address/starting conversion, polling the status byte for EOC/, and when it comes true, read the two bytes of the conversion and send the start conversion/next channel address command. For multitasking situations it may be more convenient to use the interrupt mode, reading in data only after an interrupt signals end of conversion.

SPECIFICATIONS

Inputs — 8 differential. 16 single-ended. Jumper selectable.

Full Scale Input Voltage Range — −5 to +5 volts (bipolar). 0 to +5 volts (unipolar). Jumper selectable.

Gain — User-configurable through installation of two resistors. Factory-configured for gain of X1; gains above 250 not recommended.

Resolution — 12 bits over full scale range (1.22 mv at 0-5 v, 5 μv at 0-20 mv).

Accuracy —

Gain	Accuracy at 25°C
1	± 0.035% ± ½ LSB
5	± 0.035% ± ½ LSB
50	± 0.035% ± ½ LSB
250	± 0.035% ± ½ LSB

NOTE:
Figures are in percent of full scale reading. At any fixed temperature between 0° and 60°C, the accuracy is adjustable to ± 0.035% of full scale.

Dynamic Error — ± 0.015% FSR for transitions

Gain TC (at Gain = 1): 30 PPM per degree centigrade (typical); 56 PPM per degree centigrade (max).

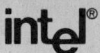

iSBX™ 311

Offset TC (in percent of FSR/°C):

Gain	Offset
1	.0018
5	.0036
50	.024
250	.116

Offset is measured with user-supplied 10 PPM/°C gain resistors installed.

Input Protection — ±30 volts.

Input Impedance — 20 megohms (minimum).

Conversion Speed — 50 microseconds (nominal).

Common Mode Rejection Ratio — 60 db (minimum).

Sample and hold — sample time 15 microseconds.

Aperature — hold aperature time: 120 nanoseconds.

Connectors —

Interface	Pins (Qty)	Centers in	Centers cm	Mating Connectors
P1 iSBX Bus	36	0.1	0.254	iSBC iSBX connector
J1 8/16 channels analog	50	0.1	0.254	3m 3415-000 or T1 H312125 or iCS 910 cable

Physical Characteristics

Width — 9.40 cm (3.7 inches)
Length — 6.35 cm (2.5 inches)
Height — 2.03 cm (0.80 inch) MULTIMODULE board only
2.82 cm (1.13 inches) MULTIMODULE and iSBC board
Weight — 68.05 gm (2.4 ounces)

Electrical Characteristics (from iSBX connector)

V_{cc} = ±5 volts (±0.25V), I_{cc} = 250 mAmax
V_{dd} = +12 volts (±0.6V), I_{dd} = 50 mAmax
V_{ss} = −12 volts (±0.6V), I_{ss} = 55 mAmax

Environmental Characteristics

Operating Temperature — 0° to 60°C (32° to 140°C)

Relative Humidity — to 90% (without condensation)

Reference Manuals

142913-001 — iSBX 311 Analog Input MULTIMODULE Board Hardware Reference Manual (order separately)

Manuals may be ordered from any Intel sales representative, distributor office or from Intel Literature Department, 3065 Bowers Avenue, Santa Clara, California 95051.

ORDERING INFORMATION

Part Number	Description
SBX 311	Analog Input MULTIMODULE Board

iSBX™ 328
ANALOG OUTPUT MULTIMODULE™ BOARD

- Low cost analog output for iSBX™ MULTIMODULE™ compatible iSBC® Boards
- 8 channels output, current loop or voltage in any mix
- 4-20 mA current loop; 5V unipolar or bipolar voltage output
- 12-bit resolution
- 0.035% full scale volage accuracy @ 25°C
- Connector compatible with ICS 910 Analog Termination Panel
- Intel design based on UPI control for high density and low cost
- Programmable offset adjust in current loop mode

The Intel iSBX 328 MULTIMODULE board provides analog signal output for any iSBC board which has an iSBX compatible bus and connectors. The single-wide iSBX 328 plugs directly onto the iSBC board, providing eight independent output channels of analog voltage for meters, CRT control, programmable power supplies, etc. Voltage output can be mixed with current loop output for control of popular 4-20ma industrial control elements. By using an Intel single chip computer LSI (8041) for refreshing separate sample-hold amplifiers through a single 12 bit DAC, eight channels can be contained on a single MULTIMODULE board for high density and low cost per channel. High quality analog components provide 12 bit resolution, 11 bit accuracy, and slew rates per channel of 0.1 volt per microsecond. Programming the iSBX 328 MULTIMODULE board is done via a simple two byte protocol over the iSBX bus. Maximum channel update rates are 5KHZ on a single channel to 1 KHZ on all eight channels. Outputs are compatible for screw termination of field wiring on the ICS 910 Analog Signal Conditioning/Termination Panel.

iSBX™ 328

FUNCTIONAL DESCRIPTION

The iSBX 328 MULTIMODULE board, shown in figure 1 is designed to plug onto any host iSBC microcomputer that contains an iSBX bus connector. The board uses an 8041 UPI device to control eight analog output channels that may be user-configured through jumpers to operate in either bipolar voltage output mode (-5 to $+5$ volts), unipolar voltage output mode (0 to $+5$ volts), or current loop output mode (4 to 20 mA) applications. Channels may be individually wired for simultaneous operation in both current loop output and voltage output applications. The outputs from 50-pin edge connector J1 on the MULTIMODULE board are pin-compatible with the iCS 910 Signal Conditioning/Termination Panel.

Interfacing Through the Intel iSBX Bus

All data to be output through the MULTIMODULE board is transferred from the host iSBC microcomputer to the MULTIMODULE board via the iSBX bus connector. The UPI device on the MULTIMODULE board accepts the binary digital data and generates a 12-bit data word for the Digital-to-Analog Converter (DAC) and a four bit channel decode/enable for selecting the output channel. The DAC transforms the data into analog signal outputs for either voltage output mode or current loop output mode. Offsetting of the DAC voltage in current output mode may be performed by the UPI software offset routine or by the hardware offset adjustments included on the board. The MULTIMODULE board status is available via the iSBX bus connector, to determine if the UPI is ready to receive updates to analog output channels.

OPERATIONAL DESCRIPTION

The host iSBC microcomputer addresses the MULTIMODULE board by executing IN or OUT instructions specifying the iSBX 328 MULTIMODULE as a port address. The UPI on the iSBX 328 is initialized to select whether software or hardware offset is to be used and how many channels will be active. Then a 2 byte transfer to each active channel sets the 12 bit output value, the channel selected and the current or voltage mode.

Commands

OUTput Command — Initialization of UPI/iSBX 328

7							0 Bit
		N	N	D2	D1	D0	

NN: 0,0 = unipolar configuration software current offset
     0,1 = no mixing
     1,0 = bipolar configuration software current offset

D2, D1, D0 = last channel to be output

OUTput Command — Data Bytes

	7							0 Bit
High Byte	D11	D10	D9	D8	D7	D6	D5	D4
Low Byte	D3	D2	D1	D0	A3	A2	A1	V/C

DAC Data | DAC channel to receive data

0 = UPI generates offset
1 = SBC generates offset in current loop mode

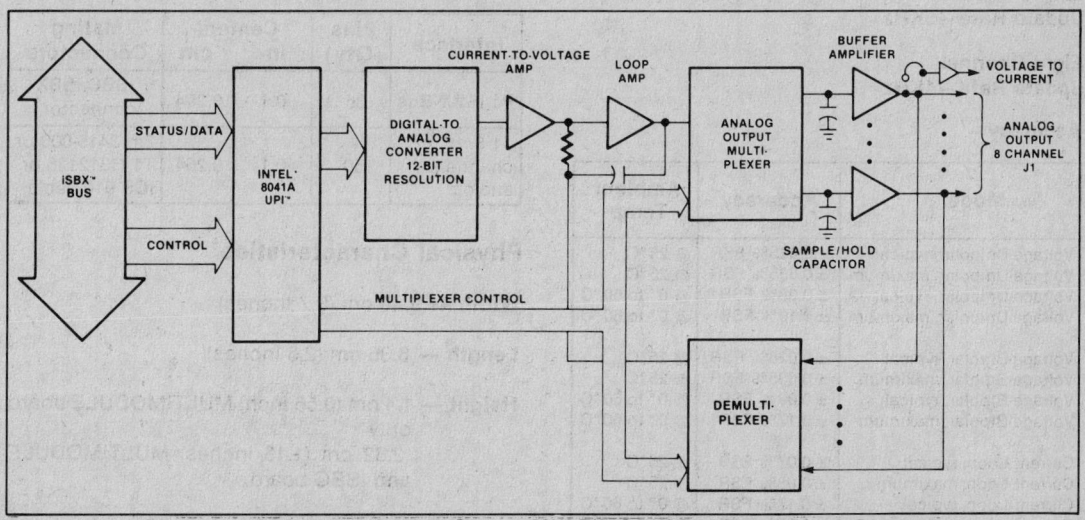

Figure 1. iSBC® 328 Analog Output MULTIMODULE™ Board Block Diagram

iSBX™ 328

INput Command — Status Buffer Read

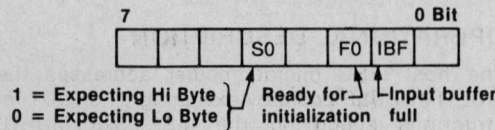

1 = Expecting Hi Byte
0 = Expecting Lo Byte
Ready for initialization
Input buffer full

Interrupts

No interrupts are issued from the iSBX 328 to the host iSBC microcomputer. Data coordination is handled via iSBC software polls of the status buffer.

SPECIFICATIONS

Outputs — 8 non-isolated channels, each independently jumpered for voltage output or current loop output mode.

Voltage Ranges — 0 to +5 volts (unipolar operation)
−5 to +5 volts (bipolar operation)

Current Loop Range — 4 to 20 mA (unipolar operation only)

Output Current — ±5 mA maximum (voltage mode-bipolar operation)

Load Resistance — 0 to 250 ohms with on-board iSBX power. 1000 ohms minimum with 30 VDC max. external supply

Compliance Voltage — 12 V using on-board iSBX power. If supplied by user, up to 30 VDC max

Resolution — 12 bits bipolar or unipolar

Slew Rate — 0.1 volt per microsecond minimum

Single Channel Update Rate — 5KHz

Eight Channel Update Rate — 1KHz

Accuracy —

Mode	Accuracy	Ambient Temp
Voltage-Unipolar, typical	± 0.025% FSR	@ 25°C
Voltage-Unipolar, maximum	± 0.035% FSR	@ 25°C
Voltage-Unipolar, typical	± 0.08% FSR	@ 0° to 60°C
Voltage-Unipolar, maximum	± 0.19% FSR	@ 0° to 60°C
Voltage-Bipolar, typical	± 0.025% FSR	@ 25°C
Voltage-Bipolar, maximum	± 0.035% FSR	@ 25°C
Voltage-Bipolar, typical	± 0.09% FSR	@ 0° to 60°C
Voltage-Bipolar, maximum	± 0.17% FSR	@ 0° to 60°C
Current Loop, typical	± 0.07% FSR	@ 25°C
Current Loop, maximum	± 0.08% FSR	@ 25°C
Current Loop, typical	± 0.17% FSR	@ 0° to 60°C
Current Loop, maximum	± 0.37% FSR	@ 0° to 60°C

Refresh and Throughput Rates**	
Refresh 1 channel (no new data):	80 us
Refresh all 8 channels (no new data):	650 us
Update and refresh 1 channel with new data: firmware program 2	150 us
for each additional channel	130 us
Update and refresh 1 channel with new data: firmware program 1 or 3	200 us
for each additional channel	155 us
Update and refresh all 8 channels (all new data): firmware program 2	1.050 ms
per channel of new data	50 us
Update and refresh all 8 channels (all new data): firmware program 1 or 3	1.280 ms
per channel of new data	80 us

**All times nominal

Output Impedance — 0.1 ohm. Drives capacitive loads up to 0.05 microfarads. (approx. 1000 foot cable)

Temperature Coefficient — 0.005%/°C

Connectors —

Interface	Pins (Qty)	Centers in	cm	Mating Connectors
P1 iSBX Bus	36	0.1	0.254	iSBC iSBX connector
J1 8/16 channels analog	50	0.1	0.254	3m 3415-000 or T1 H312125 or iCS 910 cable

Physical Characteristics

Width — 9.40 cm (3.7 inches)

Length — 6.35 cm (2.5 inches)

Height — 1.4 cm (0.56 inch) MULTIMODULE board only
  2.82 cm (1.13 inches) MULTIMODULE and iSBC board.

Weight — 85.06 gm (3.0 ounces)

iSBX™ 328

Electrical Characteristics

Vcc = ±5 volts (±0.25V), Icc = 140 ma max

Vdd = ±12 volts (±0.6V), Idd = 45 ma max (voltage mode)
= 200 ma max (current loop mode)

Vss = −12 volts (±0.6V), Iss = 55 ma max

Environmental Characteristics

Operating Temperature — 0° to 60°C (32° to 140°C)

Relative Humidity — to 90% (without condensation)

Reference Manuals

142914-002 — Input Power — iSBX 328 Analog Output MULTI-MODULE Board Hardware Reference Manual (Order Separately)

Manuals may be ordered from any Intel sales representative, distributor office or from Intel Literature Department, 3065 Bowers Avenue, Santa Clara, California 95051

ORDERING INFORMATION

Part Number	Description
SBX 328	Analog Output MULTIMODULE Board

iSBX™ 350
PARALLEL I/O MULTIMODULE™ BOARD

- iSBX™ bus compatible I/O expansion

- 24 programmable I/O lines with sockets for interchangeable line drivers and terminators

- Three jumper selectable interrupt request sources

- Accessed as I/O port locations

- Single +5V low power requirement

- iSBX™ bus on-board expansion eliminates MULTIBUS® system bus latency and increases system throughput

The Intel® iSBX 350 Parallel I/O MULTIMODULE Board is a member of Intel's line of iSBX bus compatible MULTIMODULE products. The iSBX MULTIMODULE board plugs directly into any iSBX bus compatible host board offering incremental on-board expansion. The iSBX 350 module provides 24 programmable I/O lines with sockets for interchangeable line drivers and terminators. The iSBX board is closely coupled to the host board through the iSBX bus, and as such, offers maximum on-board performance and frees MULTIBUS system traffic for other system resources. In addition, incremental power dissipation is minimal requiring only 1.6 watts (not including optional driver/terminators).

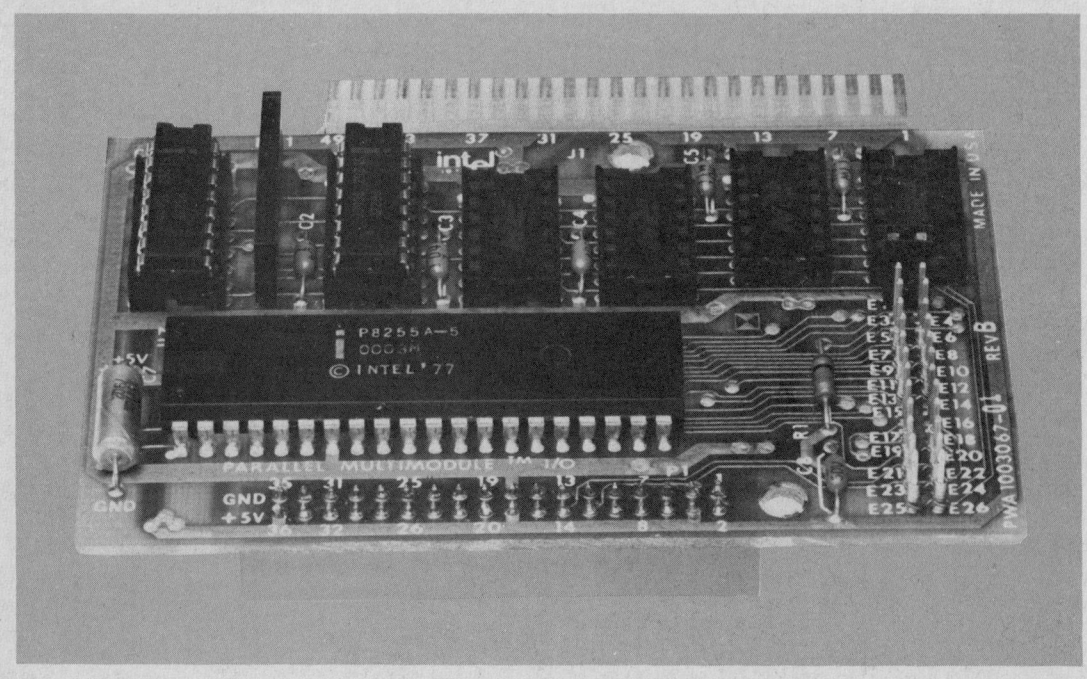

iSBX™ 350

FUNCTIONAL DESCRIPTION

Programmable Interface

The iSBX 350 module uses an Intel® 8255A-5 Programmable Peripheral Interface (PPI) providing 24 parallel I/O lines. The base-board system software is used to configure the I/O lines in any combination of unidirectional input/output and bidirectional ports indicated in Table 1. Therefore, the I/O interface may be customized to meet specific peripheral requirements. In order to take full advantage of the large number of possible I/O configurations, sockets are provided for interchangeable I/O line drivers and terminators. Hence, the flexibility of the I/O interface is further enhanced by the capability of selecting the appropriate combination of optional line drivers and terminators to provide the required sink current, polarity, and driver/termination characteristics for each application. In addition, inverting bidirectional bus drivers (8226) are provided on sockets to allow convenient optional replacement to non-inverting drivers (8216). The 24 programmable I/O lines, signal ground, and +5 volt power (jumper configurable) are brought to a 50-pin edge connector that mates with flat, woven, or round cable.

Interrupt Request Generation

Interrupt requests may originate from three jumper selectable sources. Two interrupt requests can be automatically generated by the PPI when a byte of information is ready to be transferred to the base board CPU (i.e., input buffer is full) or a byte of information has been transferred to a peripheral device (i.e., output buffer is empty). A third interrupt source may originate directly from the user I/O interface (J1 connector).

Installation

The iSBX 350 module plugs directly into the female iSBX connector on the host board. The module is then secured at one additional point with nylon hardware to insure the mechanical security of the assembly (see Figure 1 and Figure 2).

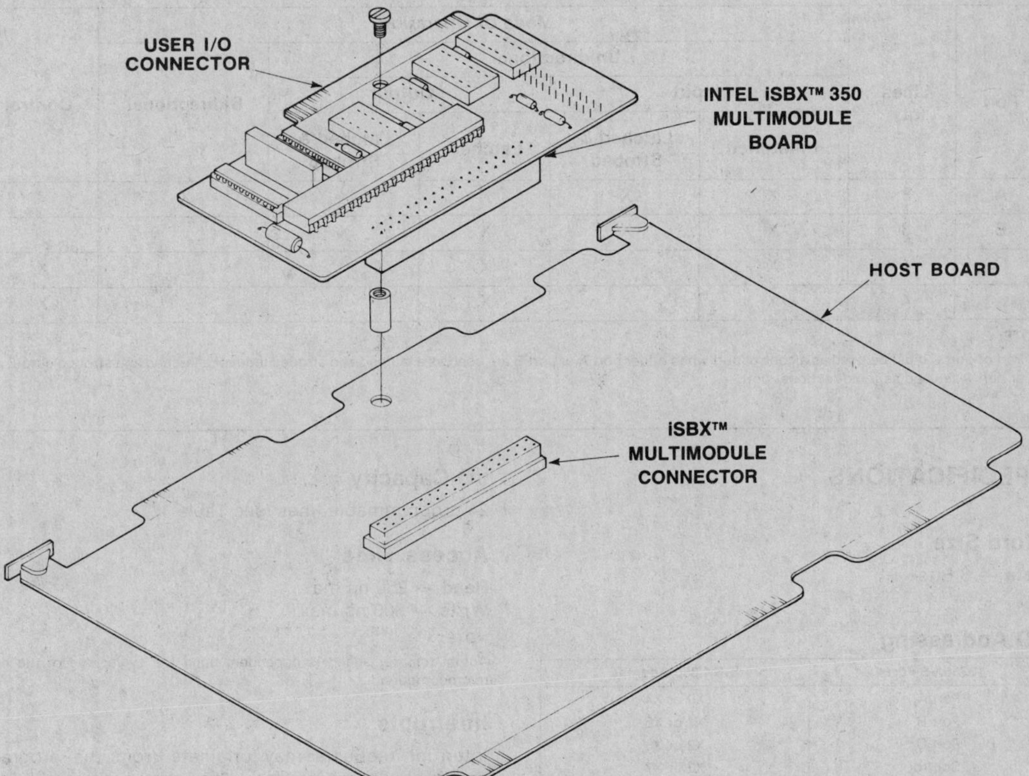

Figure 1. Installation of iSBX™ 350 Module on a Host Board

iSBX™ 350

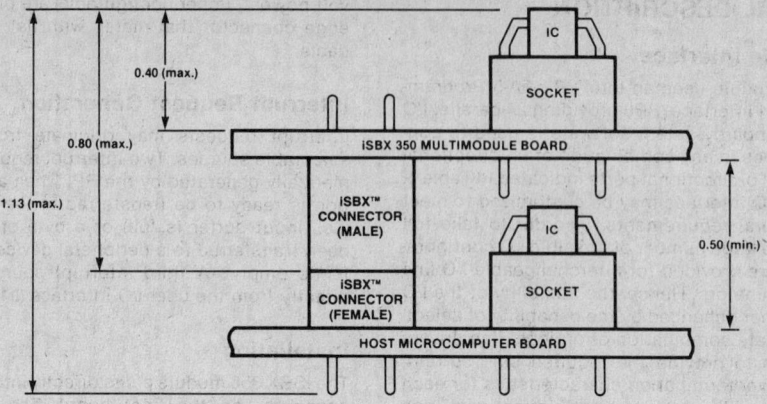

Figure 2. Mounting Clearances (inches)

Table 1. Input/Output Port Modes of Operation

Port	Lines (qty)	Mode of Operation					
		Unidirectional				Bidirectional	Control
		Input		Output			
		Unlatched	Latched & Strobed	Latched	Latched & Strobed		
A	8	X	X	X	X	X	
B	8	X	X	X	X		
C	4	X		X			X[1]
	4	X		X			X[1]

NOTE:
1. Part of port C must be used as a control port when either port A or port B are used as a latched and strobed input or a latched and strobed output port or port A is used as a bidirectional port.

SPECIFICATIONS

Word Size
Data — 8 Bits

I/O Addressing

8255A-5 Ports	iSBX 350 Address
Port A	X0 or X4
Port B	X1 or X5
Port C	X2 or X6
Control	X3 or X7
Reserved	X8 to XF

NOTE:
The first digit of each port I/O address is listed as "X" since it will change dependent on the type of host iSBC microcomputer used. Refer to the Hardware Reference Manual for your host iSBC microcomputer to determine the first digit of the port address.

I/O Capacity
24 programmable lines (see Table 1)

Access Time
Read — 250 ns max.
Write — 300 ns max.
NOTE:
Actual transfer speed is dependent upon the cycle time of the host microcomputer.

Interrupts
Interrupt requests may originate from the programmable peripheral interface (2) or the user specified I/O (1).

Interfaces
iSBX™ Bus — All signals TTL compatible
Parallel I/O — All signals TTL compatible

iSBX™ 350

Parallel Interface Connectors

Interface	No. of Pairs/Pins	Centers (in.)	Connector Type	Vendor	Vendor Part No.
Parallel I/O Connector	25/50	0.1	Female	3M	3415-0001 with Ears
Parallel I/O Connector	25/50	0.1	Female, Soldered	GTE Sylvania	6AD01251A1DD

Note: Connector compatible with those listed may also be used.

Line Drivers and Terminators

I/O Drivers — The following line drivers and terminators are all compatible with the I/O driver sockets on the iSBX 350.

Driver	Characteristic	Sink Current (mA)
7438	I, OC	48
7437	I	48
7432	NI	16
7426	I, OC	16
7409	NI, OC	16
7408	NI	16
7403	I, OC	16
7400	I	16

Note:
I = Inverting, NI = Non-Inverting, OC = Open Collector

Port 1 has 25 mA totem pole drivers and 1 kΩ terminators.

I/O Terminators — 220Ω/330Ω divider or 1 kΩ pull up.

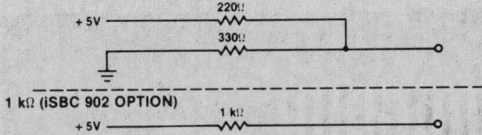

Physical Characteristics

Width — 7.24 cm (2.85 in.)
Length — 9.40 cm (3.70 in.)
Height* — 2.04 cm (0.80 in.) iSBX 350 Board
— 2.86 cm (1.13 in.) iSBX 350 Board + Host Board
Weight — 51 gm (1.79 oz)
*See Figure 2.

Electrical Characteristics
DC Power Requirements

Power Requirement	Configuration
+5V @ 320 mA	Sockets XU3, XU4, XU5, and XU6 empty (as shipped).
+5V @ 500 mA	Sockets XU3, XU4, XU5, and XU6 contain 7438 buffers.
+5V @ 620 mA	Sockets XU3, XU4, XU5, and XU6 contain iSBC 901 termination devices.

Environmental

Operating Temperature — 0°C to 55°C

Reference Manual

9803191-01 — iSBX 350 Parallel I/O MULTIMODULE Manual (NOT SUPPLIED)

Reference Manuals may be ordered from any Intel sales representative, distributor office or from Intel Literature Department, 3065 Bowers Ave., Santa Clara, California 95051.

ORDERING INFORMATION

Part Number	Description
SBX 350	Parallel I/O MULTIMODULE Board

iSBX™ 351
SERIAL I/O MULTIMODULE™ BOARD

- **iSBX™ bus compatible I/O expansion**
- **Programmable synchronous/asynchronous communications channel with RS232C or RS449/422 interface**
- **Software programmable baud rate generator**
- **Two programmable 16-bit BCD or binary timers/event counters**
- **Four jumper selectable interrupt request sources**
- **Accessed as I/O port locations**
- **Low power requirements**
- **Single +5V when configured for RS449/422 interface**
- **iSBX bus on-board expansion eliminates MULTIBUS® system bus latency and increases system throughput**

The Intel® iSBX 351 Serial I/O MULTIMODULE board is a member of Intel's new line of iSBX bus compatible MULTIMODULE products. The iSBX MULTIMODULE board plugs directly into any iSBX bus compatible host board offering incremental on-board I/O expansion. The iSBX 351 module provides one RS232C or RS449/422 programmable synchronous/asynchronous communications channel with software selectable baud rates. Two general purpose programmable 16-bit BCD or binary timers/event counters are available to the host board to generate accurate time intervals under software control. The iSBX board is closely coupled to the host board through the iSBX bus, and as such, offers maximum on-board performance and frees MULTIBUS system traffic for other system resources. In addition, incremental power dissipation is minimal requiring only 3.0 watts (assumes RS232C interface).

iSBX™ 351

FUNCTIONAL DESCRIPTION
Communications Interface

The iSBX 351 module uses the Intel® 8251A Universal Synchronous/Asynchronous Receiver/Transmitter (USART) providing one programmable communications channel. The USART can be programmed by the system software to individually select the desired asynchronous or synchronous serial data transmission technique (including IBM Bi-Sync). The mode of operation (i.e. synchronous or asynchronous), data format, control character format, parity, and baud rate are all under program control. The 8251A provides full duplex, double buffered transmit and receive capability. Parity, overrun, and framing error detection are all incorporated in the USART. The command lines, serial data lines, and signal ground lines are brought out to a double edge connector configurable for either an RS232C or RS449/422 interface (see Figure 3). In addition, the iSBX 351 module is jumper configurable for either point-to-point or multidrop network connection.

16-Bit Interval Timers

The iSBX 351 module uses an Intel 8253 Programmable Interval Timer (PIT) providing 3 fully programmable and independent BCD and binary 16-bit

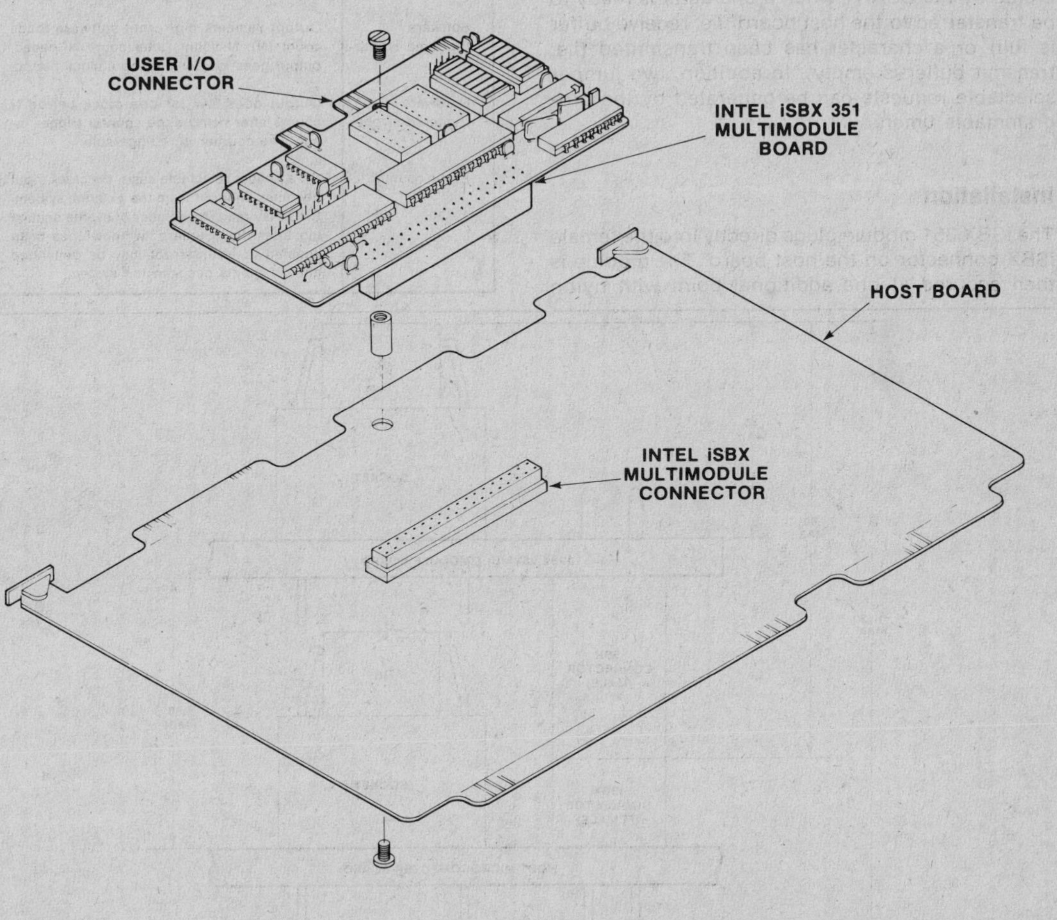

Figure 1. Installation of iSBC® 351 Module on a Host Board

interval timers. One timer is available to the system designer to generate baud rates for the USART under software control. Routing for the outputs from the other two counters is jumper selectable to the host board. In utilizing the iSBX 351 module, the systems designer simply configures, via software, each timer independently to meet system requirements. Whenever a given baud rate or time delay is needed, software commands the programmable timers to select the desired function. The functions of the timers are shown in Table 1. The contents of each counter may be read at any time during system operation.

Interrupt Request Lines

Interrupt requests may originate from four sources. Two interrupt requests can be automatically generated by the USART when a character is ready to be transferred to the host board (i.e. receive buffer is full) or a character has been transmitted (i.e. transmit buffer is empty). In addition, two jumper selectable requests can be generated by the programmable timers.

Installation

The iSBX 351 module plugs directly into the female iSBX connector on the host board. The module is then secured at one additional point with nylon hardware to insure the mechanical security of the assembly (see Figures 1 and 2).

Table 1. Programmable Timer Functions

Function	Operation
Interrupt on terminal count	When terminal count is reached, an interrupt request is generated. This function is useful for generation of real-time clocks.
Programmable one-shot	Output goes low upon receipt of an external trigger edge and returns high when terminal count is reached. This function is retriggerable.
Rate generator	Divide by N counter. The output will go low for one input clock cycle, and the period from one low going pulse to the next is N times the input clock period.
Square-wave rate generator	Output will remain high until one-half the count has been completed, and go low for the other half of the count.
Software triggered strobe	Output remains high until software loads count (N). N counts after count is loaded, output goes low for one input clock period.
Hardware triggered strobe	Output goes low for one clock period N counts after rising edge counter trigger input. The counter is retriggerable.
Event counter	On a jumper selectable basis, the clock input becomes an input from the external system. CPU may read the number of events occurring after the counting "window" has been enabled or an interrupt may be generated after N events occur in the system.

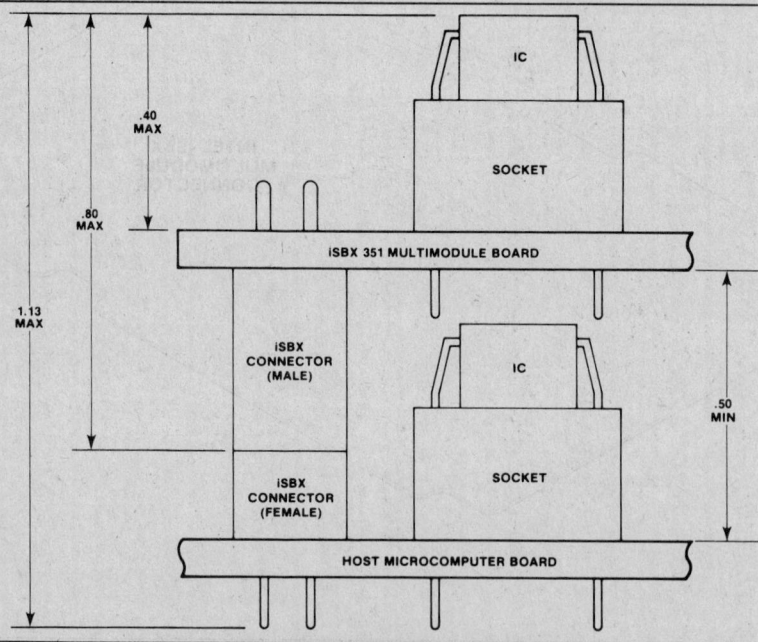

Figure 2. Mounting Clearances (inches)

iSBX™ 351

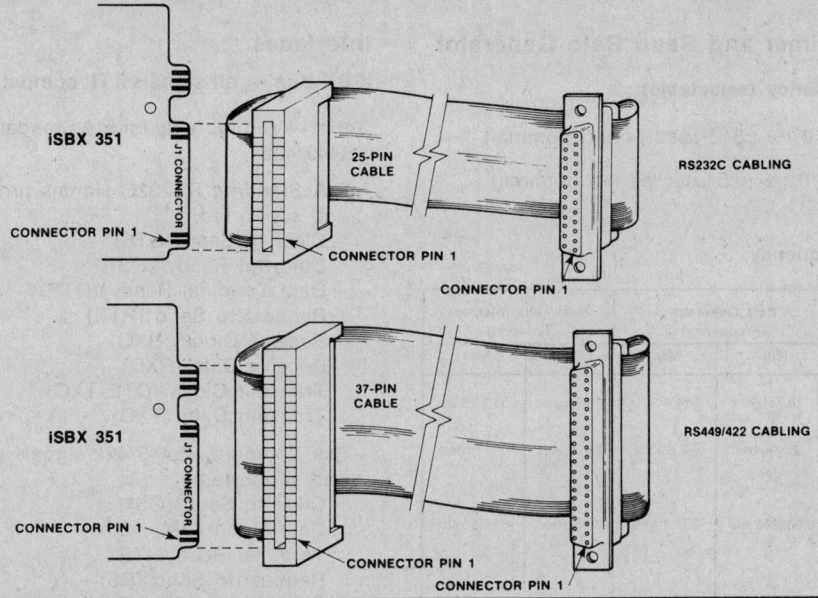

Figure 3. Cable Construction and Installation for RS232C and RS449/422 Interface

SPECIFICATIONS

Word Size
Data — 8 bits

I/O Addressing

I/O Address for an 8-bit host	I/O Address for a 16-bit host	Chip Select	Function
X0, X2, X4 or X6	Y0, Y4, Y8 or YC	8251A USART	Write: Data Read: Data
X1, X3, X5 or X7	Y2, Y6, YA or YE	MCS0/Activated (True)	Write: Mode or command Read: Status
X8 or XC	Z0 or Z8	8253 PIT	Write: Counter 0 Load: Count (N) Read: Counter 0
X9 or XD	Z2 or ZA	MCS1/Activated (True)	Write: Counter 1 Load: Count N Read: Counter 1
XA or XE	Z4 or ZC		Write: Counter 2 Load: Count (N) Read: Counter 2
XB or XF	Z6 or ZE		Write: Control Read: None

Notes: X = The iSBX base address that activates MSC0/ & MSC1 for an 8-bit Host.
Y = The iSBX base address that activates MCS0/ for a 16-bit host.
Z = The iSBX base address that activates MCS1/ for a 16-bit host.

The first digit, X, Y, or Z, is always a variable, since it will depend on the type of host micorcomputer used. Refer to the Hardware Reference Manual for your host microcomputer to determine the first digit of the I/O base address.

NOTE: The first digit of each port I/O address is listed as "X" since it will change depending on the type of host iSBC microcomputer used. Refer to the Hardware Reference Manual for your host iSBC microcomputer to determine the first digit of the I/O address.

Access Time
Read — 250 nsec max
Write — 300 nsec max

Note. Actual transfer speed is dependent upon the cycle time of the host microcomputer.

Serial Communications
Synchronous — 5 - 8-bit characters; internal character synchronization; automatic sync insertion; even, odd or no parity generation/detection.

Asynchronous — 5 - 8-bit characters; break character generation and detection; 1, 1½, or 2 stop bits; false start bit detection; even, odd or no parity generation/detection.

Sample Baud Rate:

8253 PIT Frequency[1] (kHz, Software Selectable)	8251 USART Baud Rate (Hz)[2]	
	Synchronous	Asynchronous
		÷ 16 ÷ 64
307.2	—	19200 4800
153.6	—	9600 2400
76.8	—	4800 1200
38.4	38400	2400 600
19.2	19200	1200 300
9.6	9600	600 150
4.8	4800	300 75
2.4	2400	150 —
1.76	1760	110 —

NOTES:
1. Frequency selected by I/O writes of appropriate 16-bit frequency factor to Baud Rate Register.
2. Baud rates shown here are only a sample subset of possible software-programmable rates available. Any frequency from 18.75 Hz to 614.4 kHz may be generated utilizing on-board crystal oscillator and 16-bit Programmable Interval Timer (used here as frequency divider).

iSBX™ 351

Interval Timer and Baud Rate Generator

Input Frequency (selectable):

1.23 MHz ±0.1% (.813 μsec period nominal)

153.6 kHz ±0.1% (6.5 μsec period nominal)

Output Frequency:

	Rate Generator (Frequency)		Real-Time Interrupt (Interval)	
	Min.	Max.	Min.	Max.
Single Timer[1]	18.75 Hz	614.4 kHz	1.63 μsec	53.3 msec
Single Timer[2]	2.34 Hz	76.8 kHz	13.0 μsec	426.7 msec
Dual Timer[3] (Counters 0 and 1 in series)	0.000286 Hz	307.2 kHz	3.26 μsec	58.25 min
Dual Timer[4] (Counters 0 and 1 in series)	0.0000358 Hz	38.4 kHz	26.0 μsec	7.77 hrs

NOTES: 1. Assuming 1.23 mHz clock input.
2. Assuming 153.6 kHz clock input.
3. Assuming Counter 0 has 1.23 mHz clock input.
4. Assuming Counter 0 has 153.6 kHz clock input.

Interrupts

Interrupt requests may originate from the USART (2) or the programmable timer (2).

Interfaces

ISBX Bus — all signals TTL compatible.

Serial — configurable for EIA Standards RS232C or RS449/422

EIA Standard RS232C signals provided and supported:
   Clear to Send (CTS)
   Data Set Ready (DSR)
   Data Terminal Ready (DTR)
   Request to Send (RTS)
   Receive Clock (RXC)
   Receive Data (RXD)
   Transmit Clock (DTE TXC)
   Transmit Data (TXD)

EIA Standard RS449/422 signals provided and supported:
   Clear to Send (CS)
   Data Mode (DM)
   Terminal Ready (TR)
   Request to Send (RS)
   Receive Timing (RT)
   Receive Data (RD)
   Terminal Timing (TT)
   Send Data (SD)

Physical Characteristics

Width — 7.24 cm (2.85 inches)
Length — 9.40 cm (3.70 inches)
Height* — 2.04 cm (0.80 inches)
   iSBX 351 Board
   — 2.86 cm (1.13 inches)
   iSBX 351 Board and Host Board
Weight — 51 grams (1.79 ounces)
* (See Figure 2)

Serial Interface Connectors

Configuration	Mode[2]	MULTIMODULE Edge Connector	Cable	Connector [8]
RS232C	DTE	26-pin[5], 3M-3462-0001	3M[3]-3349/25	25-pin[7], 3M-3482-1000
RS232C	DCE	26-pin[5], 3M-3462-0001	3M[3]-3349/25	25-pin[7], 3M-3483-1000
RS449	DTE	40-pin[6], 3M-3464-0001	3M[4]-3349/37	37-pin[1], 3M-3502-1000
RS449	DCE	40-pin[6], 3M-3464-0001	3M[4]-3349/37	37-pin[1], 3M-3503-1000

NOTES: 1. Cable housing 3M-3485-4000 may be used with the connector.
2. DTE — Data Terminal mode (male connector), DCE — Data Set mode (female connector).
3. Cable is tapered at one end to fit the 3M-3462 connector.
4. Cable is tapered to fit 3M-3464 connector.
5. Pin 26 of the edge connector is not connected to the flat cable.
6. Pins 37, 39, and 40 of the edge connector are not connected to the flat cable.
7. May be used with cable housing 3M-3485-1000.
8. Connectors compatible with those listed may also be used.

iSBX™ 351

Electrical Characteristics
DC Power Requirements

Mode	Voltage	Amps (Max.)
RS232C	+5V ±0.25V	460 mA
	+12V ±0.6V	30 mA
	−12V ±0.6V	30 mA
RS449/422	+5V ±0.25V	530 mA

Environmental Characteristics
Temperature — 0 - 55°C, free moving air across the base board and MULTIMODULE board.

Reference Manual
9803190-01 — iSBX 351 Serial I/O MULTIMODULE Manual (NOT SUPPLIED)

Reference Manuals may be ordered from any Intel sales representative, distributor office or from Intel Literature Department, 3065 Bowers Ave., Santa Clara, California, 95051.

ORDERING INFORMATION

Part Number   **Description**
SBX 351   Serial I/O MULTIMODULE Board

iSBX™ 352
BIT SERIAL COMMUNICATIONS MULTIMODULE™ BOARD

- **Provides an HDLC/SDLC half/full-duplex communications channel for iSBX™ bus compatible micro-computers**
- **Supports RS232C (including modem support) or RS449/422A interface**
- **Single +5V when configured for RS449/422A interface**
- **Software programmable baud rate generation up to 64K baud synchronous and 9.6K baud self-clocking**
- **Supports synchronous or self-clocking NRZI point-to-point, multidrop and self-clocking NRZI SDLC loop data link interfaces**

The Intel iSBX 352 Bit Serial Communications MULTIMODULE board offers incremental on-board I/O expansion support for ISO/CCITT's HDLC or IBM's SDLC communication. Plugging directly into any iSBX bus compatible host board, the iSBX 352 module provides one RS232C or RS449/422A programmable bit serial communications channel with software selectable baud rates (up to 64K baud for half-duplex synchronous operations). Data link interfaces supported are: synchronous point-to-point, multidrop and SDLC loop. The phase lock loop feature provides NRZI self-clocking 9.6K baud operation.

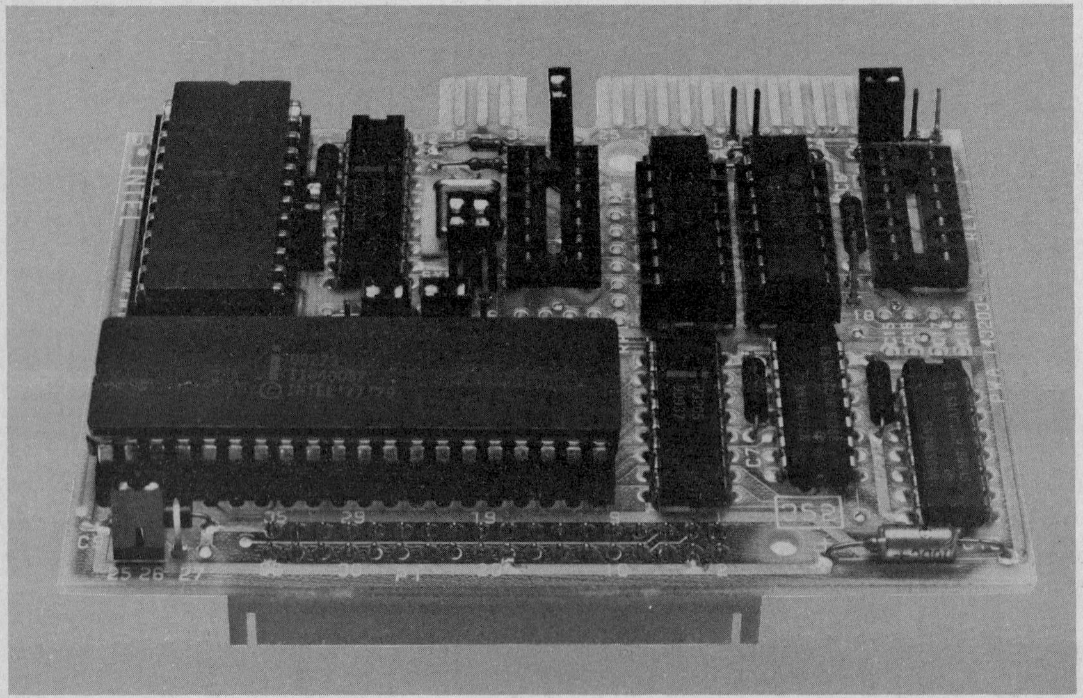

The following are trademarks of Intel Corporation and may be used only to describe Intel products: Intel, CREDIT, Index, Insite, Intellec, Library Manager, Megachassis, Micromap, MULTIBUS, PROMPT, UPI, μScope, Promware, MCS, ICE, iRMX, iSBC, iSBX, MULTIMODULE and iCS. Intel Corporation assumes no responsibility for the use of any circuitry other than circuitry embodied in an Intel product. No other circuit patent licenses are implied.

© INTEL CORPORATION, 1981

iSBX™ 352

FUNCTIONAL DESCRIPTION

Communications Interface

The iSBX 352 module uses the Intel 8273 Programmable HDLC/SDLC Protocol Controller. The iSBX 352 module provides one bit-serial communications channel for iSBX bus compatible host microcomputers. (See Figure 1.) An iSBX microcomputer or MULTIBUS-based application is easily connected to an HDLC/SDLC point-to-point, multidrop, or an SDLC loop configuration.

The High-Level Data Link Control (HDLC) is the International Standards Organization (ISO) standard discipline used to implement X.25 packet switching communications. The Synchronous Data Link Control (SDLC) is an IBM communication protocol used to implement the System Network Architecture (SNA). Both protocols, HDLC and SDLC, are bit oriented, code independent, and support full-duplex operations.

Data Link Interface

The control lines, serial data lines and signal ground lines are brought out to the double edge connector of the iSBX 352 module and are configurable for RS232C or RS449/422A interface (see Figure 2).

Addressing an iSBX 352 board by using a port address, the program performs the 8-bit data transfer required, using buffered or non-buffered transmit/receive and abort sequences.

Serial data transfer control is provided by the 8273 controller of the iSBX 352 module which interfaces the parallel iSBX bus to the serial channel. During a transmit sequence, the iSBX 352 module accepts data and commands from the iSBX bus interface, translates and formats the data into HDLC/SDLC protocol formats, provides the proper RS232C or RS422A interface control signals, and passes data onto the serial channel. The receive operation is the inverse of the previous sequence.

Data Link Configurations

The supported data link configurations are shown in Table 1. The following example configurations provide an overview and a figure for five typical data link configurations:

Table 1. iSBX™ 352 Supported Configurations

Connection	Synchronous		Asynchronous	
	Modem	Direct	Modem*	Direct
point-to-point	X	X	X	X
multidrop	X	X	X	X
loop	NA	NA	X	X

* Modem should not respond to a break.

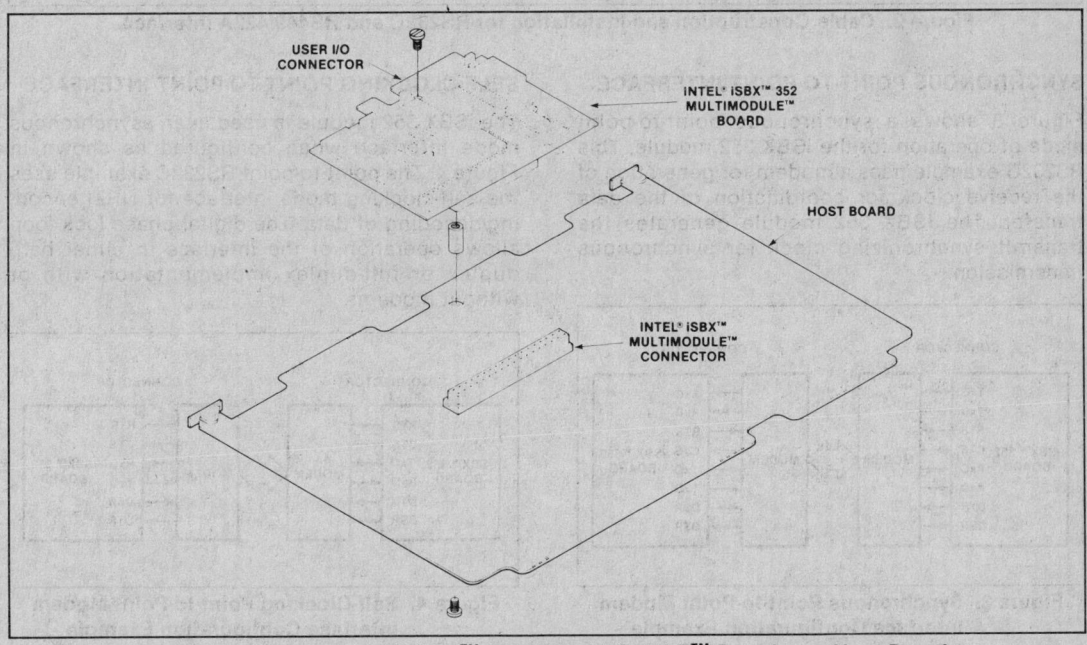

Figure 1. Installation of iSBX™ 352 MULTIMODULE™ Board on a Host Board

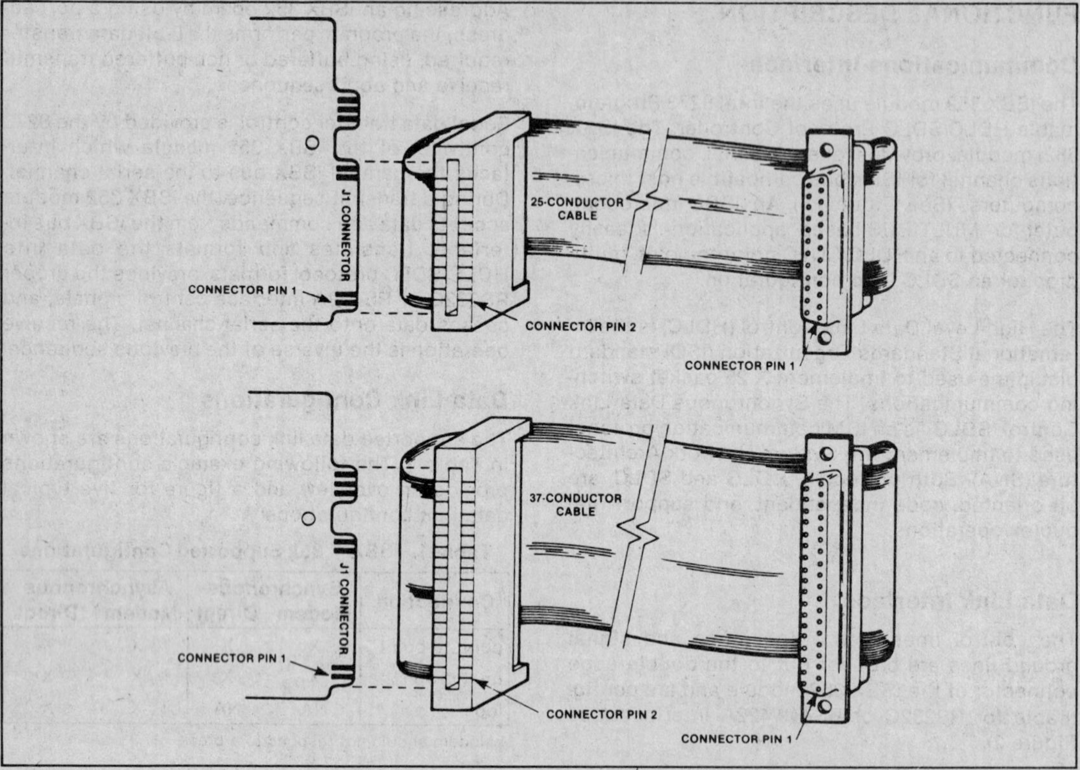

iSBX™ 352

Figure 2. Cable Construction and Installation for RS232C and RS449/422A Interface

SYNCHRONOUS POINT-TO-POINT INTERFACE

Figure 3 shows a synchronous point-to-point mode of operation for the iSBX 352 module. This RS232C example uses a modem for generation of the receive clock for coordination of the data transfer. The iSBX 352 module generates the transmit synchronizing clock for synchronous transmission.

SELF-CLOCKING POINT-TO-POINT INTERFACE

The iSBX 352 module is used in an asynchronous mode interface when configured as shown in Figure 4. The point-to-point RS232C example uses the self-clocking mode interface for NRZI encoding/decoding of data. The digital phase lock loop allows operation of the interface in either half-duplex or full-duplex implementation with or without modems.

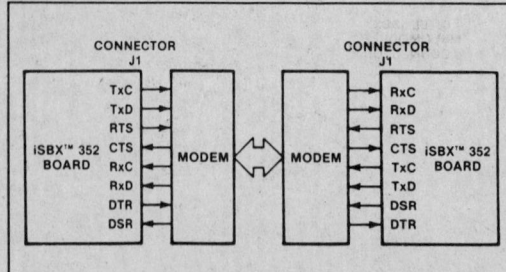

Figure 3. Synchronous Point-to-Point Modem Interface Configuration Example – RS232C

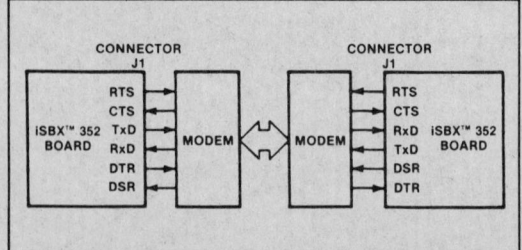

Figure 4. Self-Clocking Point-to-Point Modem Interface Configuration Example – RS232C

iSBX™ 352

SYNCHRONOUS MULTIDROP

The iSBX 352 MULTIMODULE is used in both a master and a slave mode in the RS449/422A example shown in Figure 5. This synchronous multidrop application is effective for high-speed data transfers between slave stations and a central master station.

ASYNCHRONOUS SELF-CLOCKING MULTIDROP

The iSBX 352 MULTIMODULE example in Figure 6 shows a master and multiple slaves in a multidrop configuration. This self-clocking example uses the 8273 digital phase lock loop and NRZI data encoding.

SDLC Loop

The SDLC self-clocking loop configuration shown in Figure 7 permits longer networks since each secondary slave station is a repeater set in one-bit-delay mode. The data sent out by the primary station (the loop controller) are relayed bit-for-bit through each secondary station and finally back to the master station.

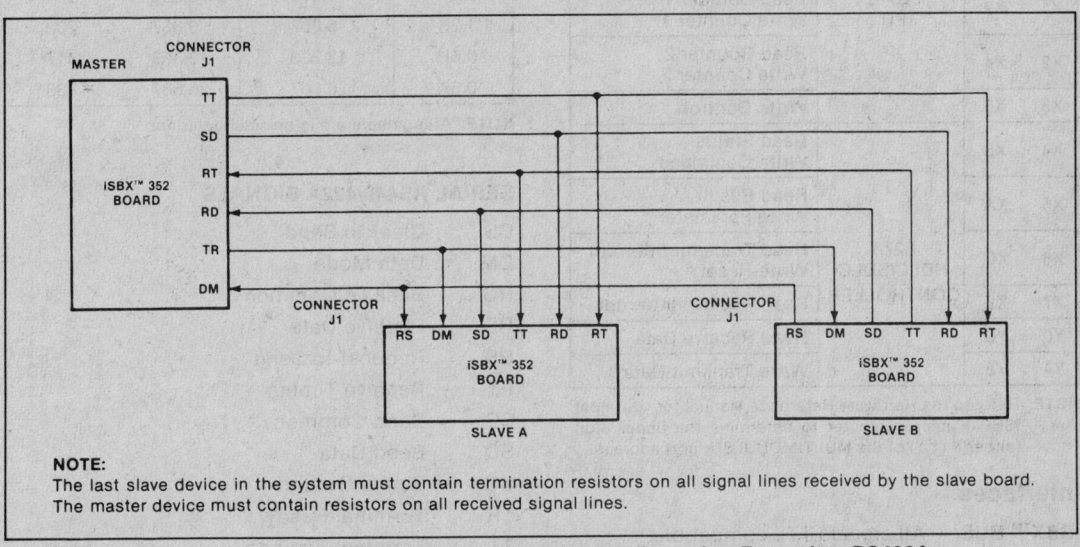

NOTE:
The last slave device in the system must contain termination resistors on all signal lines received by the slave board. The master device must contain resistors on all received signal lines.

Figure 5. Synchronous Multidrop Network Configuration Example – RS422A

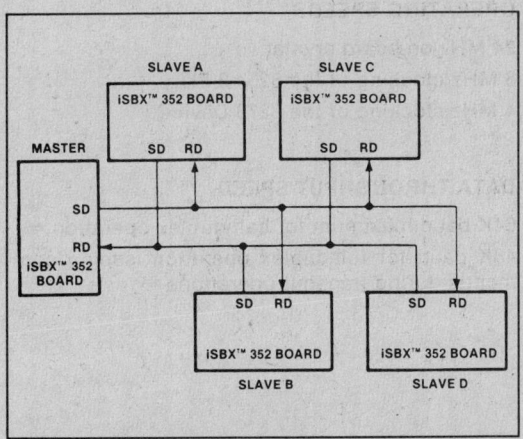

Figure 6. Self-Clocking Multidrop Configuration Example – RS422A

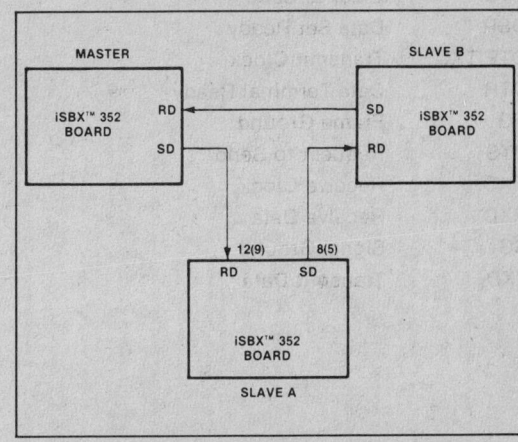

Figure 7. Self-Clocking SDLC Loop Network Configuration Example

iSBX™ 352

SPECIFICATIONS

Data Size
8 Bits

I/O Port Addresses

Port Address 8-bit	Port Address 16-bit	Device Selected	Function Performed
X0	X0		Read Counter 0 / Write Counter 0
X1	X2	8254-2 PIT	Read Counter 1 / Write Counter 1
X2	X4		Read Counter 2 / Write Counter 2
X3	X6		Write Control
X4	X8		Read Status / Write Command
X5	XA		Read Result / Write Parameter
X6	XC	8273 HDLC/SDLC CONTROLLER	Read Transmit Interrupt / Write Reset
X7	XE		Read Receive Interrupt
Y0	Y0		Read Receive Data
Y4	Y8		Write Transmit Data

NOTE: Refer to the Hardware Reference Manual for your host iSBC™ microcomputer to determine the upper digit (either X or Y) of the MULTIMODULE™ port address.

Interfaces
iSBX™ BUS — All signals TTL compatible

SERIAL RS232C SIGNALS

CTS	Clear to Send
DSR	Data Set Ready
DTE TXC	Transmit Clock
DTR	Data Terminal Ready
FG	Frame Ground
RTS	Request to Send
RXC	Receive Clock
RXD	Receive Data
SG	Signal Ground
TXD	Transmit Data

RATE GENERATOR FREQUENCIES

Baud Rate bits/sec	8254-2 Divide Count		
	Synchronous	Self-Clocking	
		TX Clock	32X Clock
64K	125	—	—
56K	143	—	—
48K	167	—	—
19.2K	417	—	—
9.6K	833	833	26
4.8K	1,667	1,667	52
2.4K	3,333	3,333	104
1.2K	6,667	6,667	208
0.6K	13,333	13,333	417
0.3K	26,667	26,667	833

NOTE: All numbers are in decimal notation.

SERIAL RS449/422A SIGNALS

CS	Clear to Send
DM	Data Mode
RC	Receive Common
RD	Receive Data
RS	Request to Send
RT	Receive Timing
SC	Send Common
SD	Send Data
SG	Signal Ground
TR	Terminal Ready
TT	Terminal Timing

OPERATING SPEEDS
24 MHz on-board crystal
8 MHz clocking of the 8254-2 PIT
4 MHz clocking of the 8273 Device

DATA THROUGHPUT SPEED
64K baud maximum for half-duplex operation
48K baud for full-duplex operation issuing commands during transmit operations

iSBX™ 352

SERIAL INTERFACE CONNECTORS

Configuration	Mode[2]	MULTIMODULE™ Edge Connector	Cable	Connector
RS232C	DTE	26-pin[5], 3M-3462-0001	3M[3]-3349/25	25-pin[7], 3M-3482-1000
RS232C	DCE	26-pin[5], 3M-3462-0001	3M[3]-3349/25	25-pin[7], 3M-3483-1000
RS449	DTE	40-pin[6], 3M-3464-0001	3M[4]-3349/37	37-pin[1], 3M-3502-1000
RS449	DCE	40-pin[6], 3M-3464-0001	3M[4]-3349/37	37-pin[1], 3M-3503-1000

NOTES:
1. Cable housing 3M-3485-4000 may be used with the connector.
2. DTE - Data Terminal Equipment mode (male connector); DCE - Data Set Equipment mode (female connector).
3. Cable is tapered at one end to fit the 3M-3462 connector.
4. Cable is tapered to fit 3M-3464 connector.
5. Pin 26 of the edge connector is not connected to the flat cable.
6. Pins 38, 39, and 40 of the edge connector are not connected to the flat cable.
7. May be used with the cable housing 3M-3485-1000.

Electrical Characteristics

DC POWER REQUIREMENTS

Interface	Voltage	Current (max)	Total Power
RS 232C	+5 ± 0.25V	595 mA	3.8 watts
	−12 ± 0.6V	30 mA	
	+12 ± 0.6V	30 mA	
RS 449/422A	+5 ± 0.25V	775 mA	4.1 watts

Environmental Characteristics

Temperature — 0 - 55°C, free moving air across base board and MULTIMODULE board

Humidity — to 90%, without condensation

Physical Characteristics

Width — 7.27 cm (2.85 inches)
Length — 9.40 cm (3.70 inches)
Height — 1.40 cm (0.56 inches)
Weight — 72 gm (2.53 ounces)

Reference Manual (Not Supplied)

143983 — iSBX 352 Bit Serial Communications MULTIMODULE Board Hardware Reference Manual.

Reference manuals may be ordered from any Intel sales representative, distributor office or from Intel Literature Department, 3065 Bowers Ave., Santa Clara, California 95051.

ORDERING INFORMATION

Part Number	Description
SBX 352	HDLC/SDLC Serial I/O MULTIMODULE Board

iSBX™ 354 DUAL CHANNEL SERIAL I/O MULTIMODULE™ BOARD

- Two RS232C or RS422A/449 programmable Synchronous/Asynchronous communications channels
- Programmable baud rate generation for each channel
- Full duplex operation
- iSBX™ Bus compatible I/O expansion
- Supports HDLC/SDLC, NRZ, NRZI or FM Encoding/Decoding
- Three interrupt options for each channel
- Low power requirements

The Intel iSBX™ 354 Serial I/O MULTIMODULE™ board is a member of Intel's line of iSBX compatible MULTIMODULE products. The iSBX MULTIMODULE board plugs directly into any iSBX bus compatible host board offering incremental on-board I/O expansion. Utilizing Intel's 82530 Serial Communications Controller component, the iSBX 354 module provides two RS232C or RS422A/449 programmable synchronous/asynchronous communications channels. The 82530 component provides two independent full duplex serial channels, on chip crystal oscillator, baud-rate generator and digital phase locked loop capability for each channel. The iSBX board connects to the host board through the iSBX bus. This offers maximum on-board performance and frees the MULTIBUS® System bus for use by other system resources.

Intel Corporation Assumes No Responsibility for the Use of Any Circuitry Other Than Circuitry Embodied in an Intel Product. No Other Circuit Patent Licenses are Implied.

©INTEL CORPORATION, 1984

JULY 1984
ORDER NUMBER: 280045-002

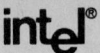

iSBX™ 354 MODULE

FUNCTIONAL DESCRIPTION

Communications Interface

The iSBX 354 module uses the Intel 82530 Serial Communications Controller (SCC) component providing two independent full duplex serial channels. The 82530 is a multi-protocol data communications peripheral designed to interface high speed communications lines using Asynchronous, Byte-Synchronous and Bit-Synchronous protocols to Intel's microprocessor based board and system level products. The mode of operation (i.e. asynchronous or synchronous), data format, control character format, and baud-rate generation are all under program control. The 82530 SCC component can generate and check CRC codes in any Synchronous mode and can be programmed to check data integrity in various modes. The command lines, serial data lines, and signal ground lines are brought out to a double edge connector.

The iSBX 354 module provides a low cost means to add two serial channels to iSBC® boards with 8 or 16 bit MULTIMODULE interfaces. In the factory default configuration, the iSBX 354 module will support two RS232C interfaces. With user supplied drivers and termination resistors, the iSBX 354 module can be reconfigured to support RS422A/449 communication interfaces with support on Channel A only for multidrop control from the base board. Both channels can be configured as DTE or DCE with RS232C interfaces.

Interrupt Request Line

The 82530 SCC component provides one interrupt to the MINTRO signal of the iSBX interface. There are six sources of interrupts in the SCC component (Transmit, Receive and External/Status interrupts in both channels). Each type of interrupt is enabled under program control with Channel A having higher priority than Channel B, and with Receive, Transmit and

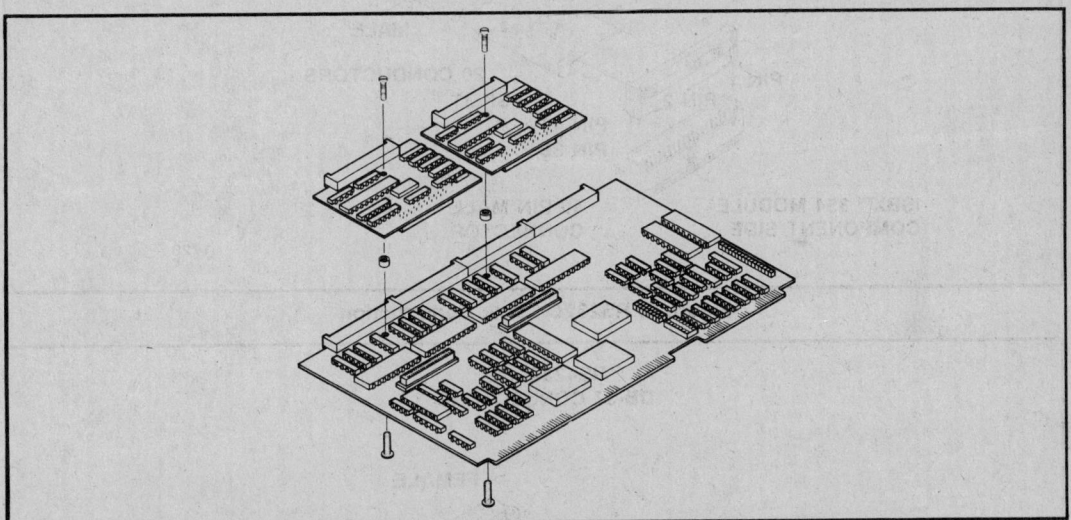

Figure 1. Installation of 2 iSBX™ 354 MULTIMODULE™ Boards on an iSBC® board.

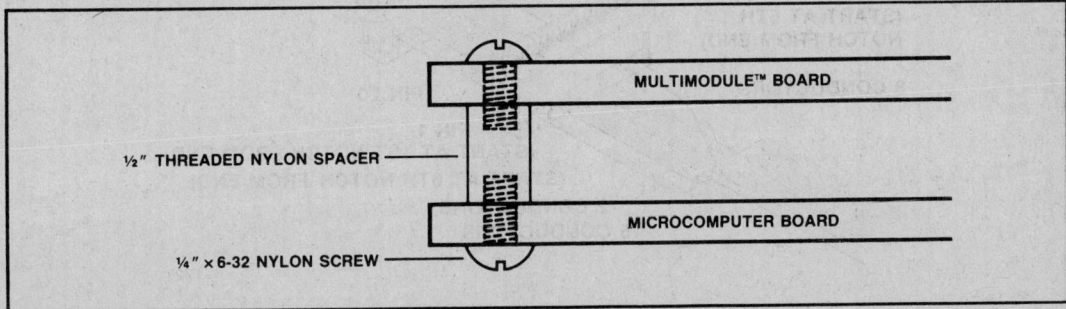

Figure 2. Mounting Technique

iSBX™ 354 MODULE

External/Status interrupts prioritized in that order within each channel.

Installation

The iSBX 354 module plugs directly into the female iSBX connector on the host board. The module is then secured at one additional point with nylon hardware to insure the mechanical security of the assembly. Figures 1 and 2 demonstrate the installation of the iSBX 354 MULTIMODULE board on a Host Board. Figures 3 and 4 provide cabling diagrams.

Programming Considerations

The Intel 82530 SCC component contains several registers that must be programmed to initialize and control the two channels. Intel's iSBX 354 Module Hardware Reference Manual (Order #146531-001) describes these registers in detail.

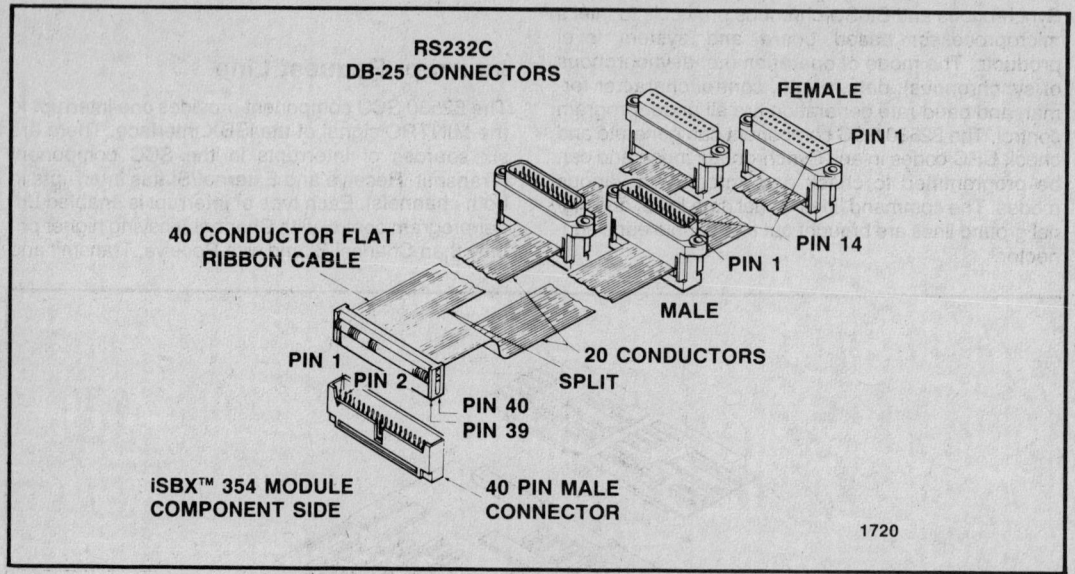

Figure 3. RS232C Cable Construction

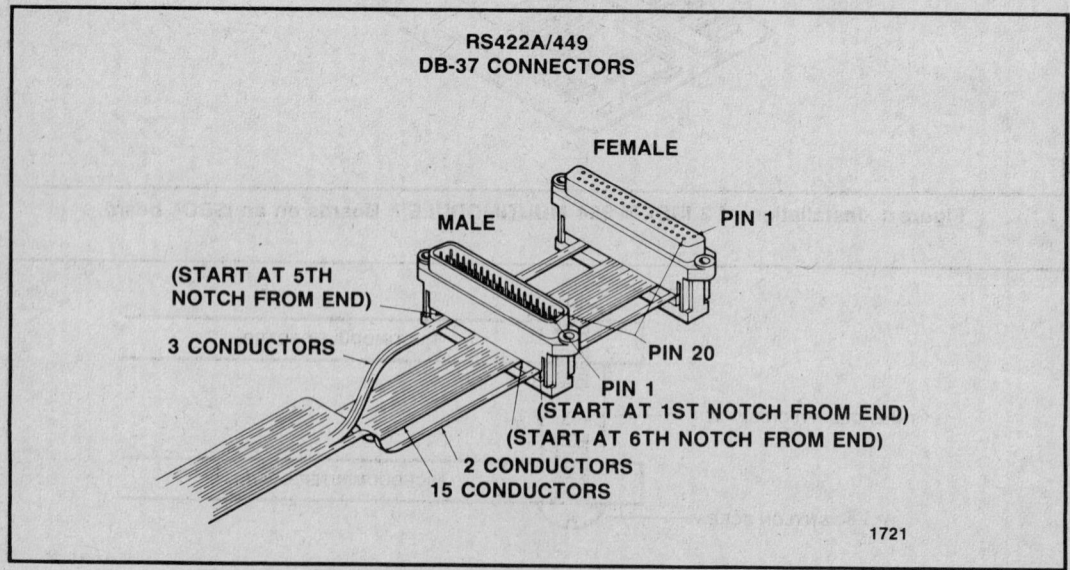

Figure 4. RS422A/449 Cable Construction

iSBX™ 354 MODULE

SPECIFICATIONS

Word Size
Data — 8 Bits

Clock Frequency
4.9152 MHz

Serial Communications

Synchronous — Internal or external character synchronization on one or two synchronous characters

Asynchronous — 5-8 bits and 1, 1½ or 2 stop bits per character; programmable clock factor; break detection and generation; parity, overrun, and framing error detection

Sample Baud Rate:

Synchronous X1 Clock	
Baud Rate	82530 Count Value (Decimal)
64000	36
48000	49
19200	126
9600	254
4800	510
2400	1022
1800	1363
1200	2046
300	8190

Asynchronous X 16 Clock	
Baud Rate	82530 Count Value (Decimal)
19200	6
9600	14
4800	30
2400	62
1800	83
1200	126
300	510
110	1394

INTERFACES

iSBX™ Bus: Meets the iSBX Specification, Compliance Level: D8 I

Serial: Meets the EIA RS232C standard on Channels A and B. Meets the EIA RS422A/449 standard on Channels A and B, Multi-drop capability on Channel A only.

Signals Provided

RS232C DTE
- Transmit Data
- Receive Data
- Request to Send
- Clear to Send
- Data Set Ready
- Signal Ground
- Carrier Detect
- Transmit Clock (2)
- Receive Clock
- Data Terminal Ready
- Ring Indicator

RS232C DCE
- Transmit Data
- Receive Data
- Clear to Send
- Data Set Ready
- Signal Ground
- Carrier Detect
- Transmit Clock (2)
- Receive Clock
- Ring Indicator

RS422A/449
- Send Data
- Receive Timing
- Receive Data
- Terminal Timing
- Receive Common

I/O Port Addresses

Port Address		Function
8-Bit	16-Bit	
X0		Read Status Channel B / Write Command Channel B
X2		Read Data Channel B / Write Data Channel B
X4		Read Status Channel A / Write Command Channel A
X6		Read Data Channel A / Write Data Channel A
Y0		Read Disable RS422A/449 Buffer / Write Enable RS422A/449 Buffer

NOTES:
1. The "X" and "Y" values depend on the address of the iSBX interface as viewed by the base board.
2. "X" corresponds with Activation of the MCS0/interface signal; "Y" corresponds with Activation of the MCS1/ interface signal.

Power Requirements
+5 Volts at .5 Amps
+12 Volts at 50 mA
-12 Volts at 50 mA

Physical Characteristics:
Width: 2.85 inches
Length: 3.70 inches
Height: 0.8 inches
Weight: 85 grams

iSBX™ 354 MODULE

Environmental Characteristics:

Temperature: 0° to 55° C operating at 200 linear feet per minute across baseboard and MULTIMODULE board

Humidity: To 90%, without condensation

Reference Manual

146531-001 — iSBX 354 Channel Serial I/O Board Hardware Reference Manual

Reference manuals may be ordered from any Intel sales representative, distributor office, or from Intel Literature Department, 3065 Bowers Avenue, Santa Clara, CA 95051.

Ordering Information:

Part Number	Description
iSBX 354	Dual Channel I/O MULTIMODULE

iSBX™ 488
GPIB MULTIMODULE BOARD

- **Complete IEEE 488-1978 talker/listener functions including:**
  — Addressing, handshake protocol, service request, serial and parallel polling schemes
- **Complete IEEE 488-1978 controller functions including:**
  — Transfer control, service requests and remote enable
- **Simple read/write programming**

- **Software functions built into VLSI hardware for high performance, low cost and small size**
- **Standard iSBX™ Bus interface for easy connection to Intel iSBC™ boards**
- **IEEE 488-1978 standard electrical interface transceivers**
- **Five volt only operation**

The intel iSBX™ 488 GPIB Talker/Listener/Controller MULTIMODULE™ board provides a standard interface from any Intel iSBC board equipped with an iSBX connector to over 600 instruments and computer peripherals that use the IEEE 488-1978 General Purpose Interface Bus. By taking full advantage of Intel's VLSI technology the single-wide iSBX 488 MULTIMODULE board implements the complete IEEE 488-1978 Standard Digital Interface for Programmable Instrumentation on a single low cost board. The iSBX 488 MULTIMODULE board includes the 8291A GPIB Talker/Listener, 8292 GPIB Controller and two 8293 GPIB Transceiver devices. This board represents a significant step forward in joining microcomputers and instrumentation using industry standards such as the MULTIBUS® system bus, iSBX bus and IEEE 488-1978. The high performance iSBX 488 MULTIMODULE board mounts easily on Intel iSBX bus compatible single board computers.

A simple user programming interface for easy reading, writing and monitoring of all GPIB functions is provided. This intelligent interface minimizes the impact on host processor bandwidth.

The following are trademarks of Intel Corporation and may be used only to describe Intel products: Intel, MULTIBUS, iRMX, iSBC, iSBX, MULTIMODULE, iCS and iEBC, and the combination of MCS, ICE, iRMX, iSBC, iSBX, iCS or iEBC, and a numerical suffix. Intel Corporation assumes no responsibility for the use of any circuitry other than circuitry embodied in an Intel product. No other circuit patent licenses are implied.
© INTEL CORPORATION, 1981

iSBX™ 488

FUNCTIONAL DESCRIPTION

The iSBX 488 Multimodule board is a single-wide iSBX bus compatible I/O expansion board that provides a complete implementation of the IEEE 488-1978 Standard Digital Interface for Programmable Instrumentation. The iSBX 488 Multimodule board may be configured to be a GPIB controller, talker, listener or talker/listener. The hardware implementation of the iSBX 488 board takes full advantage of Intel's VLSI çapability by using the Intel 8292 GPIB controller, 8291A talker/listener and two (2) 8293 bus transceivers. All communication between the host iSBC board and the iSBX 488 Multimodule board is executed via the Intel standard iSBX connector. Many of the functions that previously were performed by user software have been incorporated into VLSI hardware for high performance and simple programming. Both the Intel 8291A GPIB Talker/Listener device and the 8292 device can each communicate independently with the host processor on the iSBC board depending on configuration. Communication from the host iSBC board to either device on the iSBX 488 board is flexible and may be either interrupt or poll driven depending on user requirements. Data transfers to or from the GPIB may be executed by the host processor's I/O Read and I/O Write commands or with DMA handshaking techniques for very high speed transfers.

GPIB Talker/Listener Capabilities

The Intel 8291A device on the iSBX 488 Multimodule board handles all talker/listener communications between the host iSBC processor board and the GPIB. Its capabilities include data transfer, bus handshake protocol, talker/listener addressing procedures, device clearing and triggering, service requests, and both serial and parallel polling schemes. In executing most procedures the iSBX 488 board does not interrupt the microprocessor on the iSBC processor board unless a byte of data is waiting on input or a byte is sent to an empty output buffer, thus offloading the host CPU of GPIB overhead chores.

SIMPLE PROGRAMMING INTERFACE — The GPIB talker/listener functions can be easily programmed using the high level commands made available by the Intel 8291A on the iSBX 488 Multimodule board. The 8291A device architecture includes eight registers for input and eight registers for output. One each of these read and write registers is used for direct data transfers. The remaining write registers are used by the pro-

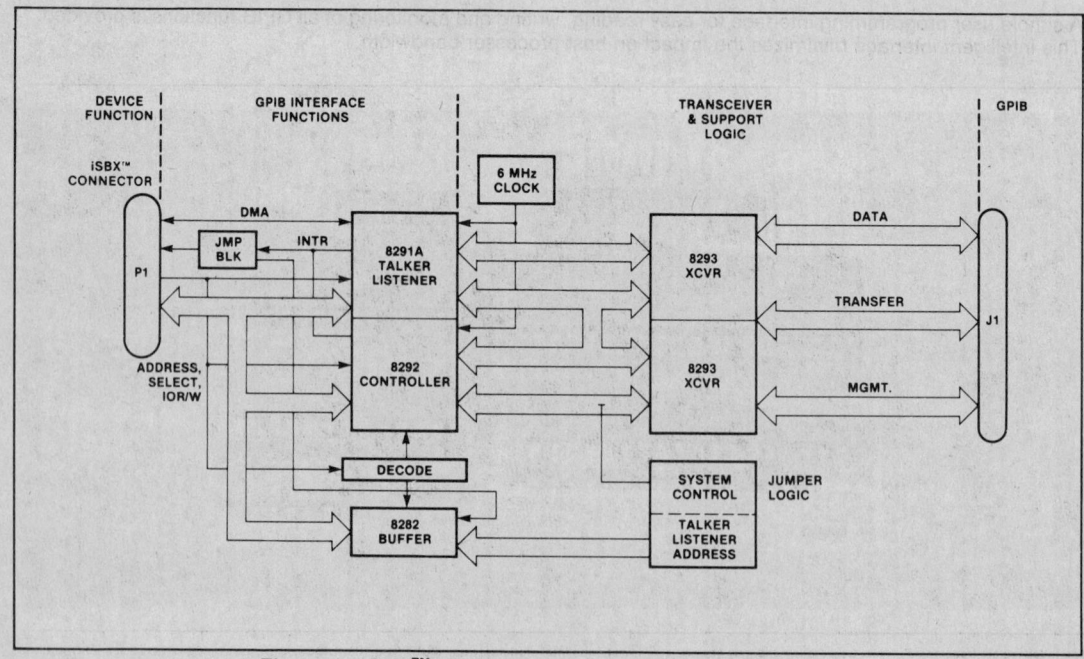

Figure 1. iSBX™ 488 Multimodule™ Board Block Diagram

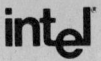

iSBX™ 488

grammer to control the various interface features of the Intel 8291A device. The remaining read registers provide the user with a monitor of GPIB states, bus conditions and device status.

SOFTWARE FUNCTIONS BUILT INTO VLSI HARDWARE — Additional features that have migrated from discrete logic and software into Intel VLSI include programmable data transfer rate and three addressing modes that allow the iSBX board to be addressed as either a major or a minor talker/listener with primary or secondary addressing. The iSBX 488 Multimodule board can be programmatically configured into almost any bus talker, listener, or talker/listener configuration. Writing software to control these and other iSBX 488 board functions is simply a matter of reading or writing the control registers.

IEEE 488-1978 Functions[1]

Function	iSBX™ 488 Supported IEEE Subsets
Source Handshake (SH)	SH0, SH1
Acceptor Handshake (AH)	AH0, AH1
Talker (T)	T0 through T8
Extended Talker (TE)	TE0 through TE8
Listener (L)	L0 through L4
Extended Listener (LE)	LE0 through LE4
Service Request (SR)	SR0, SR1
Remote Local (RL)	RL0, RL1
Parallel Poll (PP)	PP0, PP1, PP2
Device Clear (DC)	DC0 through DC2
Device Trigger (DT)	DT0, DT1
Controller (C)	C0 through C28

[1] For detailed information refer to IEEE Standard Digital Interface for Programmable Instrumentation published by The Institute of Electrical and Electronics Engineers, Inc., 1978.

Controller Capabilities

The GPIB controller functions supplied by the iSBX 488 board are provided by the Intel 8292 GPIB controller device. The 8292 is actually an Intel 8041A eight bit microcomputer that has been preprogrammed to implement all IEEE 488-1978 controller functions. The internal RAM in the 8041A is used as a special purpose register bank for the 8292 GPIB Controller. Just as with the 8291A GPIB Talker/Listener device, these registers are used by the programmer to implement controller monitor, read and write commands on the GPIB.

When configured as a bus controller the iSBX 488 board will respond to Service Requests (SRQ) and will issue Serial Polls. Parallel Polls are also issued to multiple GPIB instrument devices for receiving simultaneous responses. In applications requiring multiple bus controllers, several iSBX 488 boards may each be configured as a controller and pass the active control amongst each other. An iSBX 488 board configured for a System Controller has the capability to send Remote Enable (REN) and Interface Clear (IFC) for initializing the bus to a known state.

GPIB Physical Interface

The iSBX 488 Multimodule board interfaces to the GPIB using two Intel 8293 bidirectional transceivers. The iSBX 488 board meets or exceeds all of the electrical specifications defined in IEEE 488-1978 including the required bus termination specifications. In addition, for direct connection to the GPIB, the iSBC 988 cable, a 26 conductor 0.5 meter GPIB interface cable is also available from Intel. The cable is terminated with a 26-pin edge connector at the iSBX end and a 24-pin GPIB connector at the other. The cable is also supplied with shield lines for simple grounding in electrically noisy environments.

Installation

The iSBX 488 Multimodule board plugs directly onto the female iSBX connector available on many Intel iSBC boards. The Multimodule board is then secured at one additional point with nylon hardware (supplied) to insure the mechanical security of the assembly.

SPECIFICATIONS

Interface Information

iSBX™ Bus — All signals TTL compatible
26-pin edge connector — Electrical levels compatible with IEEE 488-1978.

Physical Characteristics

Width — 3.70 in (.94 cm)
Length — 2.85 in (7.24 cm)
Height — 0.8 in (2.04 cm)
Weight — 3.1 oz (87.8 gm)

iSBX™ 488

GPIB Data Rate*

300K bytes/sec transfer rate with DMA host iSBC board

50K bytes/sec transfer rate using programmed I/O

730 nsec Data Accept Time

*Data rates are iSBX board maximum. Data rates will vary and can be slower depending on host iSBC board and user software driver.

Electrical Characteristics

DC power requirements —

$V_{CC} = +5$ Vdc $\pm 5\%$

$I_{CC} = 600$ milliamps maximum

GPIB Electrical and Mechanical Specifications

Conforms to IEEE 488-1978 standard electrical levels and mechanical connector standard when purchased with the iSBC 988 GPIB cable.

Environmental Characteristics

Operating Temperature — 0° to 60°C (32° to 140°F)

Relative Humidity — Up to 90% R.H. without condensation.

Reference Manual

143154-001 — iSBX 488 GPIB Multimodule Board Hardware Reference Manual (not supplied).

ORDERING INFORMATION

Part Number	Description
SBX 488	GPIB Multimodule
SBC 988	0.5 meter GPIB cable for iSBX 488 Multimodule Board

APPLICATION NOTE

AP-96

July 1980

Designing iSBX™ MULTIMODULE™ Boards

Stephen Grubb
OEM Microcomputer
Systems Applications

AFN-01931A

AP-96

INTRODUCTION

Intel's single board computers and the MULTIBUS system bus have become de facto industry standards in the microcomputer board market. The speed and capability of the bus coupled with the functionality and performance of the boards have been used to solve a large number of problems. iSBC products are in applications ranging from simple single board relay replacement to sophisticated multi-board business systems supporting large hard disk files. However, even with the range of functionality provided by standard iSBCs and expansion boards, designers have felt the need to design custom MULTIBUS-compatible boards to fit their application. Until the introduction of the iSBX concept, these custom boards had to be implemented using a separate MULTIBUS form factor board.

Intel has recently introduced a new line of board products and a new bus which are destined to become another industry standard because of the niche they fill. The new iSBX MULTIMODULE boards are designed to extend the functional capabilities of single board computers at a much lower cost than previously possible. iSBX MULTIMODULE boards are supported by a new bus — the iSBX bus, which allows the MULTIMODULE boards to be added directly to the on-board microprocessor bus. iSBX MULTIMODULE boards are from 10 to 20 square inches in size, therefore permitting small modular increments to a single board computer's capabilities.

System designers now have the capabilities of using either standard iSBCs or iSBX MULTIMODULE boards, or designing custom MULTIBUS compatible or iSBX MULTIMODULE boards. Cost-effective solutions are easily realized because of this added flexibility.

This application note discusses the iSBX MULTIMODULE concept, currently available MULTIMODULE boards and the iSBCs which support these boards. The iSBX bus interface specifications are discussed next, followed by consideration for designing custom iSBX MULTIMODULE boards. A specific design example using an Intel® 8279 Programmable Keyboard/Display Controller is presented.

The objective of the note is to introduce the reader to the iSBX MULTIMODULE concept for expanding iSBC functionality and to illustrate how a designer can effectively use this concept with either standard or custom iSBX boards.

References to further documentation on the iSBX bus, specific iSBX MULTIMODULE boards and iSBC host boards currently available may be found in the Related Intel Publications section in the front overleaf of this application note.

iSBX™ MULTIMODULE™ BOARD CONCEPT

The iSBX MULTIMODULE board concept was developed to provide the users of Intel single board computers (iSBCs) with a convenient method to incrementally expand the I/O or the computing capabilities of a single board computer. This expansion is done through the use of a new interface called the iSBX bus interface. This interface gives the user the capability of adding I/O mapped functions directly onto the microprocessor bus via plug-in modules that connect to the iSBC board by means of a special iSBX connector. With the use of this new bus interface, it is now possible to expand or add new features to your iSBC system without incurring large costs and long engineering development times.

There are a number of unique advantages to using the iSBX bus interface for system expansion rather than adding a separate expansion board to your system. First, when expansion is required, the user needs only to buy what is required for the application. Second, it is now possible to return to one board solutions for small systems. One board solutions eliminate the need for expensive backplanes and cardcages. Next, the iSBX interface connects directly to the microprocessor or local bus, as opposed to interfacing to the MULTIBUS system bus, therefore I/O expansion does not require system bus cycles. To the CPU, the iSBX board looks like any other on-board I/O device (Figure 1). Address decode logic exists on the iSBC host board for each iSBX connector on the host board.

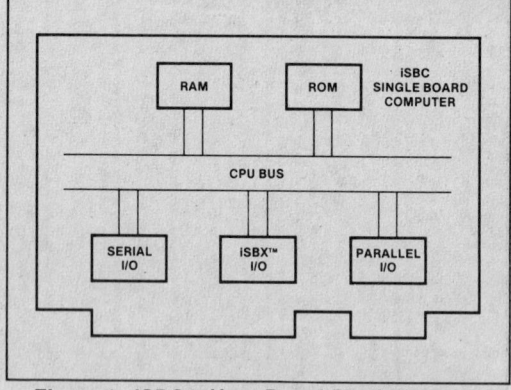

Figure 1. iSBC® Host Board Block Diagram

Third, if there is no iSBC or MULTIBUS compatible expansion board available to fit the needs of your application or if the expansion boards available offer more capability than required, then it is possible to design a custom iSBX MULTIMODULE board. Custom iSBX boards offer several advantages over custom MULTIBUS boards: they require less board real estate (10 or 20 square inches versus 81 square inches) and less engineering design time; consequently, they cost considerably less to implement. Additional capability is therefore achieved with maximum productivity.

Currently available Intel iSBX MULTIMODULE Boards include:

1) iSBX 350 Parallel I/O MULTIMODULE board which contains 24 programmable I/O lines with sockets for line drivers and terminators.
2) iSBX 351 Serial I/O MULTIMODULE board containing one RS232 or RS449/422 programmable synchronous/asynchronous communications channel and two timers.
3) iSBX 331 Fixed/Floating Point Math MULTIMODULE board which permits fixed or floating point mathematics via the Intel 8231 device.
4) iSBX 332 Floating Point Math MULTIMODULE board which permits floating point mathematics using the Intel and proposed IEEE floating point standards via an Intel 8232 device.

With these iSBX MULTIMODULE boards and other soon-to-be-announced boards, the capability now exists to economically tailor a single board computer to the application using off-the-shelf products.

iSBX™ MULTIMODULE™ SYSTEM INTERFACE

This section begins by describing the basic system elements used in an iSBX MULTIMODULE interface configuration and then defines the interface signals used for the communication between these elements. The specifications contained in this application note are included for descriptive and tutorial purposes only. The ultimate source for this information is the iSBX Bus Specification which is referenced in the front overleaf of this note.

Host Boards

The host board provides an electrical and mechanical interface for the iSBX expansion module. The host board is the master of the communications between the host and iSBX board, it controls the address and command signals.

A new generation of iSBX bus compatible host boards are evolving. The first board available from Intel is the iSBC 80/10B Single Board Computer. The 80/10B contains an 8080A CPU operating at 2 MHz, 1K bytes of RAM with sockets available for expansion to 4K bytes of RAM, sockets for up to 16K bytes of EPROM, 24 parallel I/O lines, a programmable synchronous/asynchronous communications interface and a fixed 1.04 msec timer. The 80/10B has one iSBX connector, permitting the use of an iSBX MULTIMODULE board.

The second iSBC board available supporting iSBX boards is the iSBC 80/24 Single Board Computer. The 80/24 board, which supports two iSBX MULTIMODULE boards, contains an 8085A-2 CPU operating at 4.8 or 2.4 MHz, 4K bytes of RAM, sockets for up to 32K bytes of EPROM, 48 parallel I/O lines, a programmable synchronous/asynchronous communications interface, three programmable interval timers and a programmable interrupt controller. Further RAM expansion on the 80/24 board is accomplished by the addition of an iSBC 301 4K byte RAM MULTIMODULE board which expands the RAM by an additional 4K bytes for a total of 8K bytes. The iSBC 301 MULTIMODULE board is not iSBX bus compatible; it is attached via pins and sockets in the RAM section of the host board.

iSBX™ MULTIMODULE™ Boards

The iSBX MULTIMODULE boards communicate with the host boards via the iSBX bus interface. These iSBX boards are I/O mapped through pre-defined select lines to specific port addresses. The iSBX bus currently defines an 8-bit data path compatible with both 8 and 16-bit future iSBC host boards. Examples of possible iSBX expansion boards include a floppy disk controller, a cassette interface, analog-to-digital converter or digital-to-analog converter boards, an interface to the IEEE 488 Bus and a video graphics display interface board.

There are two standard sizes of iSBX boards: a single-wide board measuring 7.24 by 9.40 cm (2.85 by 3.70 inches) and a double-wide board measuring 7.24 by 19.05 cm (2.85 by 7.50 inches). The iSBX MULTIMODULE boards mount onto any microcomputer board containing an iSBX connector and mounting hole. The iSBX boards physically plug into the iSBX connector on the host board and are secured with a nylon stand-off and screws. The mounting hardware supplied as part of the iSBX board includes:

1) One nylon spacer, 1/2" threaded
2) Two nylon screws, 1/4" 6-32
3) One 36-pin connector, factory-installed onto the iSBX module. (These may also be purchased from Intel.)

The interconnection between the host board and iSBX board, as well as the mounting clearances, may be seen in Figures 2 and 3.

NOTE

The iSBX board, when installed onto a host board, occupies an additional card slot adjacent to the base board in an iSBC 604/614 Cardcage. However, the base board may be inserted in the top card slot of the cardcage. If this is done, no additional slots are required.

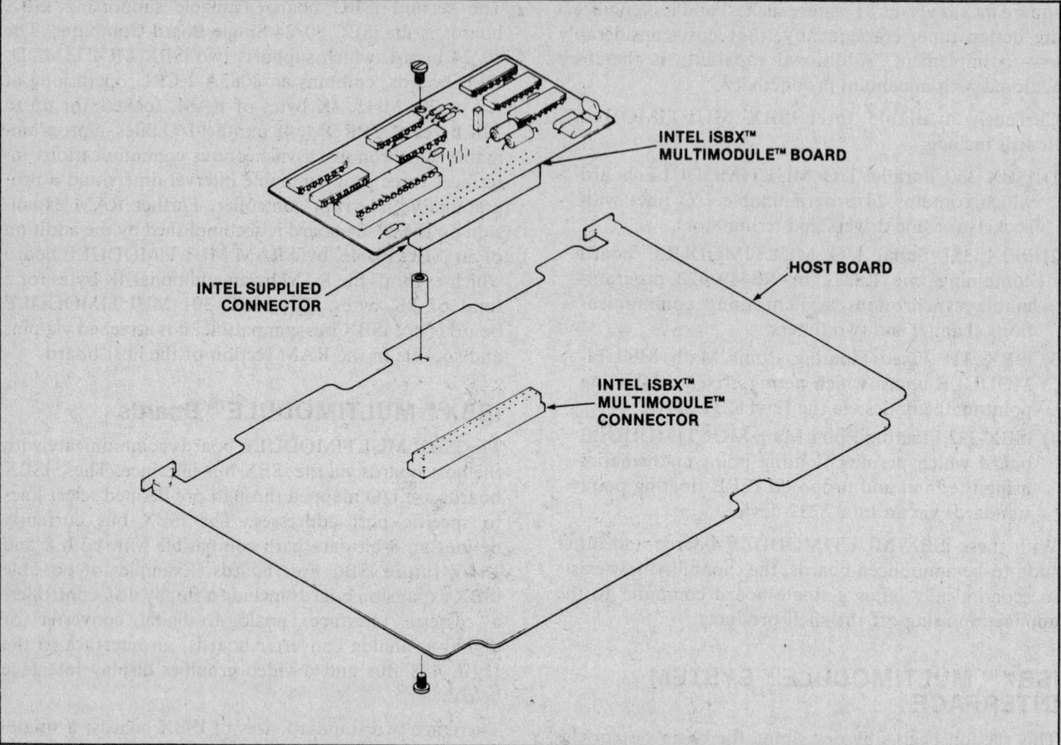

AP-96

Figure 2. Connection of iSBX™ MULTIMODULE™ to Host Board

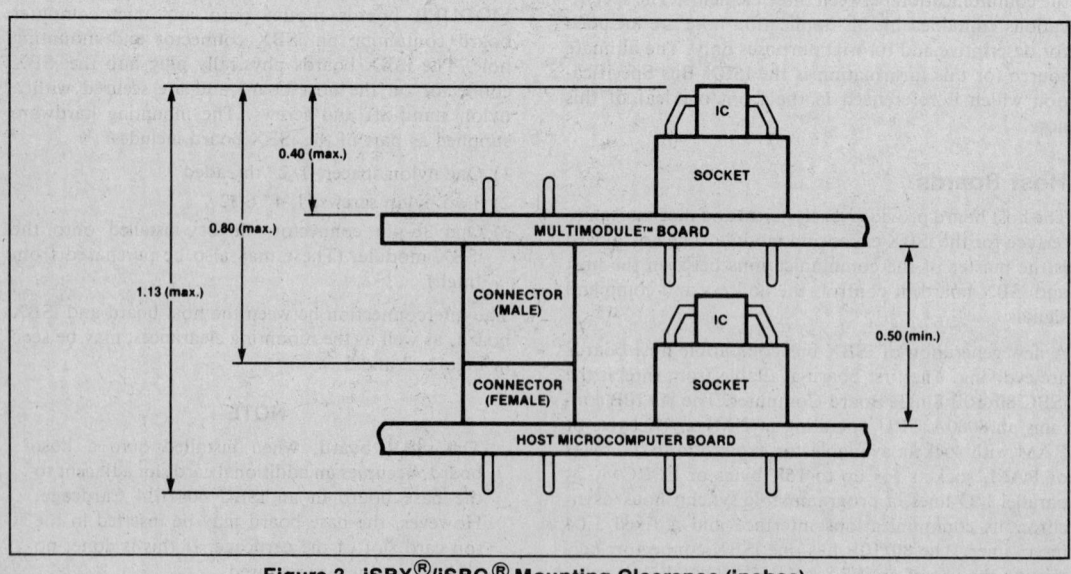

Figure 3. iSBX®/iSBC® Mounting Clearance (inches)

AP-96

iSBX™ Connector

The iSBX interface connector is a 36-pin custom made connector that was designed by Intel especially for this interface. The connector is plastic with gold plated contact pins for maximum reliability. The connector for the iSBX interface was designed for high reliability and durability. The connection between the host board and the iSBX MULTIMODULE board was extensively tested for vibration, shock, humidity, and temperature to insure that the connection is rugged enough to be used in severe environments. This connection was tested for the following environment:

Vibration: Sweeping from 10 Hz to 55 Hz and back to 10 Hz at a distance of 0.010 inches peak-to-peak, lasting 15 minutes in each of the three planes.

Shock: 30g's of force for an 11-msec duration, three times in three planes, both sides (total of 18 drops).

Humidity: 90% maximum relative (no condensation).

Temperature: 0 to 55°C (32-131°F) free moving air across the base board and the iSBX MULTIMODULE board.

Further information on the reliability testing that was done on this inter-connection, or reliability information on the iSBX MULTIMODULE boards in general, is contained in the Reliability Report, RR-29, "Intel iSBX MULTIMODULE Boards and iSBC 80/10B Single Board Computer," listed in the overleaf of this note.

The male half of this connector is available from Intel in the form of the iSBX 960-5 package which contains five of the connectors.

iSBX™ Bus Interface Signals

The iSBX bus interface signals are grouped into six basic groups, or classes, according to the functions performed relative to the interface:

These signals are:
 CONTROL LINES
 ADDRESS LINES
 DATA LINES
 INTERRUPT LINES
 OPTIONAL LINES
 POWER LINES

Many of the signals on the iSBX bus are active-low, meaning a low level on a control signal of the bus indicates a logic "1" value, while a low level on an address or data signal of the bus represents a logic "0" value.

NOTE
In this application note, an active-low signal will be designated by placing a slash (/) after the mnemonic for the signal.

Appendix A contains a pin assignment list of the following signals:

CONTROL LINES

The following signals are classified as control lines:
1) COMMANDS — IORD/, IOWRT/
2) DMA — DMRQT, MDACK/, TDMA
3) INITIALIZE — RESET
4) CLOCK — MCLK
5) SYSTEM CONTROL — MWAIT/, MPST/

Command Lines (I/O READ, I/O WRITE)

The command lines are active-low signals which control the communication link between the host board and the iSBX board. An active command line conditioned by chip select indicates to the iSBX board that the address lines are valid and the iSBX board should perform the specified operation.

DMA Lines (MDRQT, MDACK/, TDMA)

The DMA lines control the communication link between the DMA device on the host board and the iSBX module. DMRQT is an active-high output signal from the iSBX board to the host board's DMA device requesting a DMA cycle. MDACK/ is an active-low input signal to the iSBX board from the host board DMA device acknowledging that the requested DMA cycle has been granted. TDMA is used by the iSBC board to terminate DMA activity. The use of the DMA lines is optional as not all host boards will provide DMA channels nor will all iSBX boards be capable of supporting them.

Initialize Line (RESET)

This active-high input line to the iSBX board is generated by the host board to put the iSBX board into a known internal state.

Clock Line (MCLK)

This input line to the iSBX board is a timing signal. The clock frequency is 10 MHz (+0%, −10%), and the clock is asynchronous with respect to all other iSBX bus signals.

System Control Lines (MWAIT/, MPST/)

These output signals from the iSBX board control the state of the system. Active MWAIT/ (active-low) will put the CPU on the host board into a wait state, providing additional time for the iSBX board to perform the requested operation. MPST/ is an active-low signal (usually tied to signal ground) that informs the host board I/O decode logic that an iSBX module has been installed.

ADDRESS AND CHIP SELECT LINES

The address and chip select lines are made up of the following signals:

1) ADDRESS LINES — MA0, MA1, MA2
2) CHIP SELECT LINES — MCS0/, MCS1/

Address Lines (MA0, MA1, MA2)

These active-high input lines to the iSBX boards are generally the least three significant bits of the I/O addresses. In conjunction with the command and chip select lines, they establish the I/O port address being accessed.

Chip Select Lines (MCS0/, MCS1/)

These active-low input lines to the iSBX board are the result of the host board I/O decode logic. When active, the MCS/ lines condition the I/O command signals and thus enable communication between the iSBX board and the host board.

DATA LINES (MD0–MD7)

There are eight bidirectional data lines. These active-high lines are used to transmit or receive information to or from the iSBX ports. MD0 is the least significant bit.

INTERRUPT LINES (MINTR0, MINTR1)

These active-high output lines from the iSBX board are used to make interrupt requests to the host board. These lines are jumper enabled and disabled on the host board via wire wrap posts.

OPTION LINES (OPT0, OPT1)

These two signals are reserved lines that are connected to wire wrap posts on both the host board and the iSBX MULTIMODULE board. They are for unique requirements where a user needs a host board or MULTIBUS bus signal on the iSBX module.

POWER LINES

All host boards provide +5 volts as well as ±12 volts to the iSBX MULTIMODULE board along with signal ground. All power supply voltages are ±5%. Table 1 gives the power supply specifications for the iSBX interface.

Table 1. Power Supply Specifications

Minimum (volts)	Nominal (volts)	Maximum (volts)	Maximum (current)*
+4.75	+5.0	+5.25	3.0A
+11.4	+12	+12.6	1.0A
−12.6	−12	−11.4	1.0A
—	GND	—	6.0A

*Per iSBX MULTIMODULE board mounted on base board.

iSBX™ BUS INTERFACING

This section of the application note focuses on the iSBX interface and design considerations related to interfacing with the iSBX bus. It discusses the way the major operations like READ, WRITE, and DMA work, and the timing diagrams associated with each. There is also a discussion on other considerations for designing with the iSBX bus.

Bus Timing

The AC timing specifications for the iSBX bus interface can be found in Appendix B of this application note. It should be emphasized that the interface timing between the host board and the iSBX MULTIMODULE board is very critical. This is largely due to the fact that the iSBX board is attached directly to the microprocessor bus. If the timing specifications are not met, unpredictable and possibly intermittent operation of the host board may result.

Command Operations

The command lines (IORD/, IOWRT) are driven from the host board by three-state drivers with pull-up resistors or standard TTL totem-pole drivers. These lines indicate to the iSBX board that action is being requested. There are two types of operations for each command line and it is the iSBX board that determines which operation is to be performed.

READ OPERATIONS (IORD/)

Two different types of read operations are possible. The first type of read is called a full speed I/O READ. The host board generates a valid I/O address (MA0–MA2) and a valid chip select signal (MCS1/) which is then sent to the iSBX board; after the set-up times are met, the host board activates the IORD/ line. At this time, the iSBX board must generate valid data from the addressed I/O port in less than 250 ns. The host board then reads the data and removes the READ command, address and chip selects. These are shown in the timing diagram for this operation (Figure 4). The second type of read operation is called an I/O READ with Wait. This READ is used by iSBX boards that cannot perform a full speed read operation. Under this operation the host board generates the valid address and chip select signals, as in the full speed read. But this time the iSBX board will activate the MWAIT/ signal, which in turn removes the READY input to the CPU, putting it into a Wait state. The CPU, however, first activates the IORD/ signal before going into the Wait state. After valid data is placed on the iSBX data bus by the iSBX board, the iSBX board will remove the MWAIT/ signal. The host board will then read the data and remove the command, address, and chip select lines. This I/O READ with Wait operation is shown in Figure 5.

WRITE OPERATIONS (IOWRT/)

There are also two types of write operations possible: the type performed is again determined by the iSBX board. In the full speed I/O WRITE operation, the host board generates a valid I/O address and chip select and then activates the IOWRT/ line after the necessary set-up times are met. The IOWRT/ line, after being activated, will remain active for 300 ns and the data will be valid for 250 ns before the IOWRT/ command is removed. The host board will then remove the data, address, and chip select lines after the hold times are met, as shown in the timing diagram of this operation (Figure 6).

This second write operation is the I/O WRITE with Wait operation. This WRITE is used by the iSBX boards that cannot write into an I/O port with the full speed write specifications. The host board again generates valid address and chip select signals as in the full speed write operation. However, this time the iSBX board generates the MWAIT/ signal based on address information (chip select and MA0–MA1). The activation of MWAIT/ causes the removal of READY to the CPU, thus causing the CPU to go into a Wait state. The iSBX board removes the MWAIT/ signal (allowing the CPU to leave its Wait state) when it has satisfied the WRITE pulse width requirements. At this time the board removes the WRITE command, followed by the data, address, and chip select lines. This I/O WRITE with Wait operation can be seen in Figure 7.

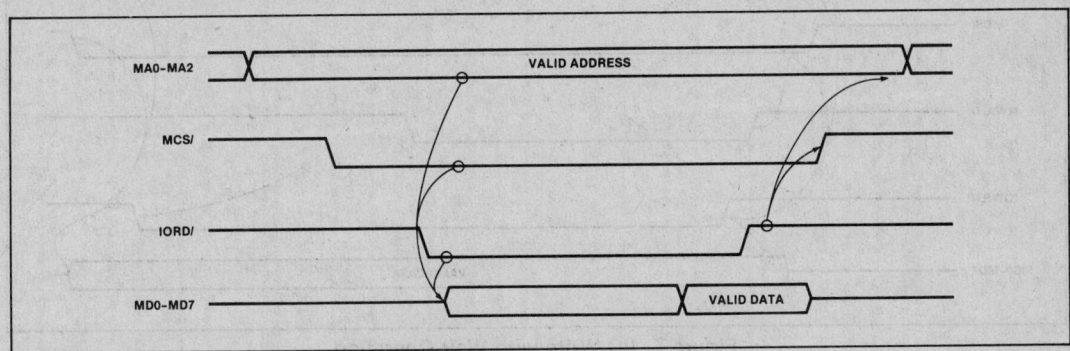

Figure 4. Full Speed I/O Read Operation

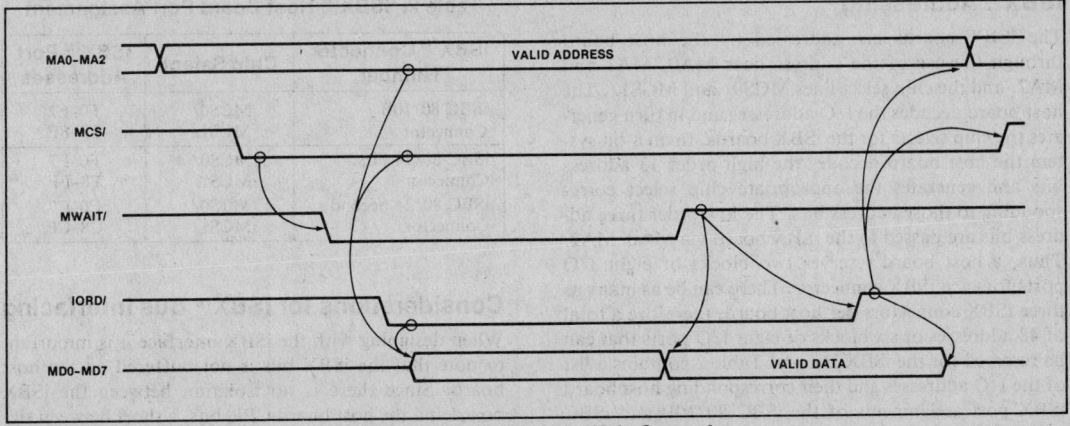

Figure 5. I/O Read with Wait Operation

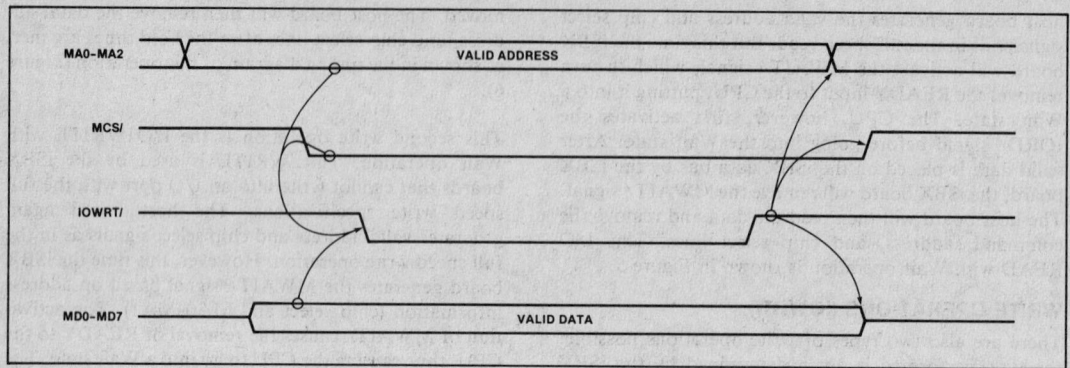

Figure 6. Full Speed I/O Write Operation

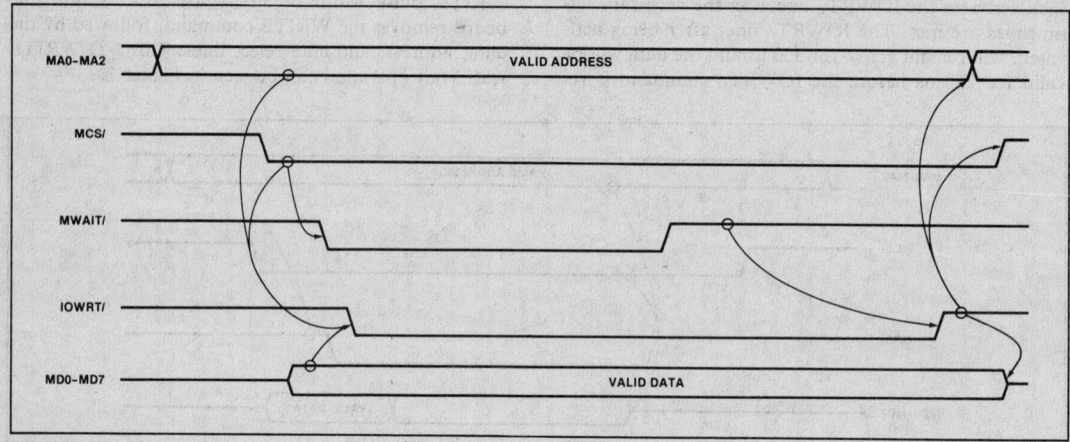

Figure 7. I/O Write with Wait Operation

iSBX™ Addressing

The iSBX boards are addressed by the host board through the use of the address lines MA0, MA1 and MA2, and the chip select lines MCS0/ and MCS1/. The host board decodes the I/O addresses and in turn generates the chip selects for the iSBX boards. In an 8-bit system the host board decodes the high order 13 address bits and generates the appropriate chip select corresponding to those address bits. The low order three address bits are passed to the iSBX board via MA0–MA2. Thus, a host board reserves two blocks of eight I/O ports for each iSBX connector. There can be as many as three iSBX connectors per host board, therefore a total of 48 addresses or six blocks of eight I/O ports that can be reserved for the iSBX boards. Table 2 contains a list of the I/O addresses and their corresponding host board iSBX port assignments of the iSBC 80/10B and iSBC 80/24 host boards.

Table 2. iSBX™ Host Board Port Assignment

iSBX™ Connector Number	Chip Select	iSBX™ Port Addresses
iSBC 80/10B Connector	MCS0/ MCS1/	F0–F7 F8–FF
iSBC 80/24 First Connector	MCS0/ MCS1/	F0–F7 F8–FF
iSBC 80/24 Second Connector	MCS0/ MCS1/	C0–C7 C8–CF

Considerations for iSBX™ Bus Interfacing

When designing with the iSBX interface it is important to note that the iSBX bus is not buffered on the host board. Since there is no isolation between the iSBX board and the host board CPU bus, a short between signal lines and power or ground could have a direct effect on the CPU or the drivers and receivers associated with the CPU on the host board. This must be taken into consideration, especially when designing and debugging any custom designed iSBX MULTIMODULE board. It is usually during the development states of a product that these types of problems occur. One advantage to not buffering the iSBX bus is increased speed of data and command transfers. Applications requiring buffering may add the buffers on the iSBX board. A second advantage to not buffering is the saving of parts costs, board real estate and development time for the host board. Another consideration when designing with the iSBX interface is, if the application to be designed requires high throughput, like a floppy disk controller or a CRT controller, the designer may consider putting some type intelligent control of buffer RAM onto the iSBX board. By doing this, the transfer information can be stored in this buffer and the throughput of the system increased.

iSBX™ BUS LOADING REQUIREMENTS

Loading requirements for the iSBX bus have been broken up into two basic categories, output specifications and input specifications, which can be viewed in Tables 3 and 4. The output specifications are the requirements on the output drivers of the iSBX board and are the minimum drive requirements necessary. A good example of this would be that the data bus output drivers must be able to sink a minimum of 1.6 mA and maintain V_{OL} at a maximum of 0.5 volts and a minimum source of 200 μA, while providing a minimum output of 2.4 volts. The input specifications are the requirements on the receivers of the iSBX board. An example of this would be that the loading of the address lines (MA0–MA2) can be no greater than 0.5 mA with a minimum low threshold of 0.8 volts.

Optional Interface Lines

The iSBX interface has two optional lines which were included for the user to configure the iSBX board for special application needs. These two lines can be used in a number of ways helpful in unique situations. For example, they could be used as a way to get two extra interrupt lines down to the host board, thus yielding a total of four interrupt lines running between the iSBX MULTIMODULE board and the host board. They could also be used to get extra address lines, or even another clock signal to the iSBX board. They could also

Table 3. Output Specifications

Bus Signal Name	Type[2] Drive	I_{OL} Max – Min (mA)	@ Volts (V_{OL} Max)	I_{OH} Max – Min (μA)	@ Volts (V_{OH} Min)	C_O Min (pF)
MD0–MD7	TRI	1.6	0.5	–200	2.4	130
MINTR0-1	TTL	2.0	0.5	–100	2.4	40
MDRQT	TTL	1.6	0.5	–50	2.4	40
MWAIT/	TTL	1.6	0.5	–50	2.4	40
OPT1-2	TTL	1.6	0.5	–50	2.4	40
MPST/	TTL	Note 3				

Table 4. Input Specifications

Bus Signal Name	Type[2] Receiver	I_{IL} Max (mA)	@ Volts (V_{IN} Max)	I_{IH} Max (μA)	@ Volts (V_{IN} Min)	C_I Max (pF)
MD0–MD7	TRI	–0.5	0.4	70	2.4	40
MA0–MA2	TTL	–0.5	0.4	70	2.4	40
MCS0/–MCS1/	TTL	–4.0	0.4	100	2.4	40
MRESET	TTL	–2.1	0.4	100	2.4	40
MDACK/	TTL	–1.0	0.4	100	2.4	40
IORD/ IOWRT/	TTL	–1.0	0.4	100	2.4	40
MCLK	TTL	2.4	0.4	100	2.4	40
OPT1–OPT2	TTL	2.0	0.4	100	2.4	40

NOTES:
1. Per iSBX MULTIMODULE board.
2. TTL = standard totem-pole output. TRI = three-state.
3. iSBX MULTIMODULE board must connect this signal to ground.

be used to send a special status line to or from the iSBX MULTIMODULE board.

iSBX™ MULTIMODULE™ DESIGN EXAMPLE

This section covers the description of a custom iSBX MULTIMODULE board which uses the Intel 8279 Programmable Keyboard/Display Controller. This iSBX board, when added to an iSBC host board, provides an interface to a keyboard and display. A description of the hardware design considerations for breadboarding the hardware is presented. Following this, a software exerciser, useful for debugging the board, is described. A listing for the exerciser is contained in Appendix C.

Since the iSBX MULTIMODULE board was designed using the Intel 8279 Programmable Keyboard/Display Controller, a brief description of the 8279 is presented. The 8279 is a general purpose programmable keyboard and display I/O controller which was designed for use with the Intel microprocessors. The keyboard portion of this device is capable of providing a scanned interface to a 64-contact key matrix. It is also possible to interface to an array of sensors or a strobed keyboard, such as those of the Hall Effect or the ferrite variety. The 8279 provides a variety of keyboard inputs (i.e., 2-key lockout and N-key rollover), and all key entries are debounced and strobed into an 8-character FIFO. The display portion provides the user with a scanned display interface for LED, incandescent, and other popular display technologies. Both numeric and alphanumeric segment displays may be used, as well as simple indicators. The 8279 is used in this iSBX design example to provide an interface of 2-key lockout with key debounce to a 64-character keyboard, and an interface for a 16-character, 18-segment alphanumeric display.

iSBX™ MULTIMODULE™ Board Design

The iSBX board that was designed for this application note contains a total of three IC's, the keyboard/display controller, a flip-flop, and a 3-to-8-line decoder. Figure 8 contains a block diagram of the hardware used in this design example. Figure 9 contains a schematic for the portion of the design example resident on the custom iSBX board.

The design offers the user some flexibility as to the type of display or keyboard to be attached. For example, if the application design was defined to be for a 7-segment, 16-character display (as the 8279 is designed to drive), a 4-to-16-line decoder along with the display drivers could be added to the iSBX board. Another idea would be to include everything except the display drivers and the display on the iSBX board, and to put the dis-

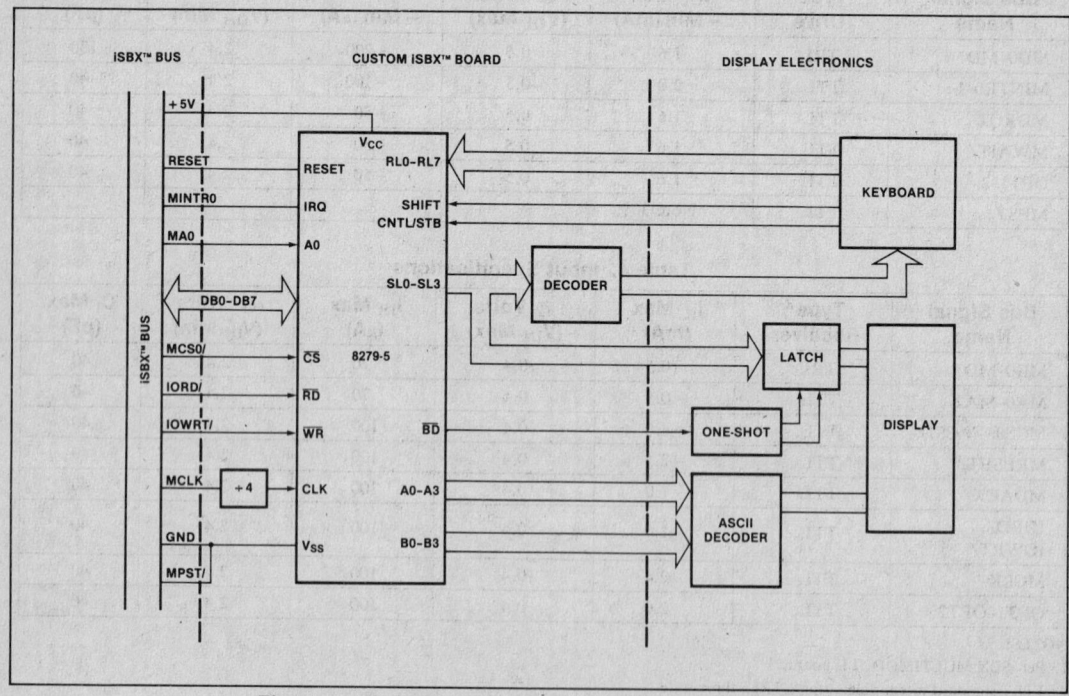

Figure 8. Block Diagram of the iSBX™ Design Example

play and drivers in with the keyboard. It is possible, and probably desirable in some applications, to incorporate some of the display electronics onto the iSBX MULTI-MODULE board. Some of the IC's found in the display portion of this design could also have been placed on the iSBX board, as there is enough room on the finished product for doing so.

The design was very easy to implement because, with the exception of one signal, all of the iSBX bus signals necessary to drive the 8279 are connected directly without any extra logic needed. The one signal that would not connect directly to the interface is the clock signal MCLK from the bus to CLK on the controller. It is not possible to connect these two together as MCLK is a 10 MHz signal and the 8279 requires a maximum clock signal of 3.1 MHz to generate its internal timings. It is necessary to add a 74LS74 dual D-type flip-flop to divide the MCLK signal by 4 for the controller. With this exception, all other signals, DB0–DB7 to MD0–MD7, A_0 to MA0, CS/ to MCS0/, etc., are connected directly to the iSBX interface. To meet the timing requirements of the iSBX bus, a high speed version of the 8279, the 8279-5, is used.

The keyboard interface side of the iSBX board consists of a 3-to-8-line decoder, which is used for scanning the keyboard matrix. The 8279 scan lines SL0–SL2 are decoded by a 74LS156 open-collector output decoder and sent to the keyboard via a connector.

The display interface of the iSBX board consists of sending the scan lines and the display outputs to the display module via a connector. The scan lines SL0–SL3 are sent to the display drivers, and the display outputs A0–A3 and B0–B3 are sent to an ASCII to 18-segment decoder driver. The display is discussed in further detail in the next section of this application note.

Display Module Design

The display module design (Figure 10) consists of two 8-digit HDSP 6805 Alphanumeric Displays by Hewlett

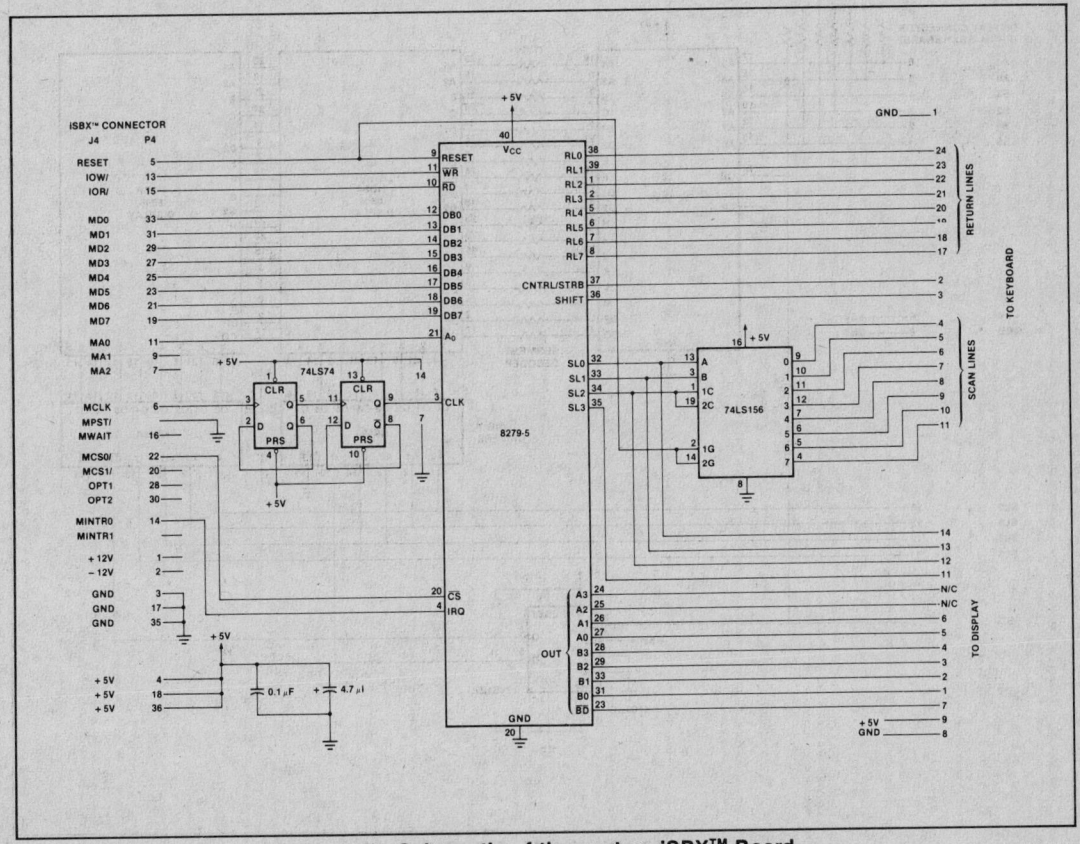

Figure 9. Schematic of the custom iSBX™ Board

AP-96

Packard, the AC5947 ASCII to 18-segment decoder driver by Texas Instruments, two Signetics NE590 Peripheral Drivers, and a 74LS122 monostable multivibrator. The display is scanned by the outputs A0–A1 and B0–B3, which are connected to the inputs of the AC5947, and the SL0–SL3 outputs which are connected to the NE590 digit scanning circuitry. The interdigit blanking is provided by the 74LS122, which prevents a display ghosting type effect. With the 8279 display controller it is possible for the display to have either left entry, where the data enters from left to right across the display, overflowing in the left most display position, or right entry, where the data enters from the right side of the display and all previous data shifts left. Left entry was chosen for this example. The controller also provides commands for blanking or clearing the display.

Keyboard Interface Design

The eight output lines from the decoder on the iSBX board select 1-of-8 keyboard matrix rows for testing by the controller to see if a key depression has been made in the selected row. The keyboard matrix column output lines are connected directly to the return lines of the 8279, RL0–RL7. Open-collector outputs presented by individual keys within the matrix eliminate the need for isolation diodes when two keys in a given column are depressed. The keyboard/display controller has the option of using either scan keyboard, scan sensor matrix, or strobed input as modes of operation. With the scan keyboard mode there is a choice of using either 2-key lockout or N-key rollover for keyboard entry. The scan keyboard with 2-key lockout mode is used for this ex-

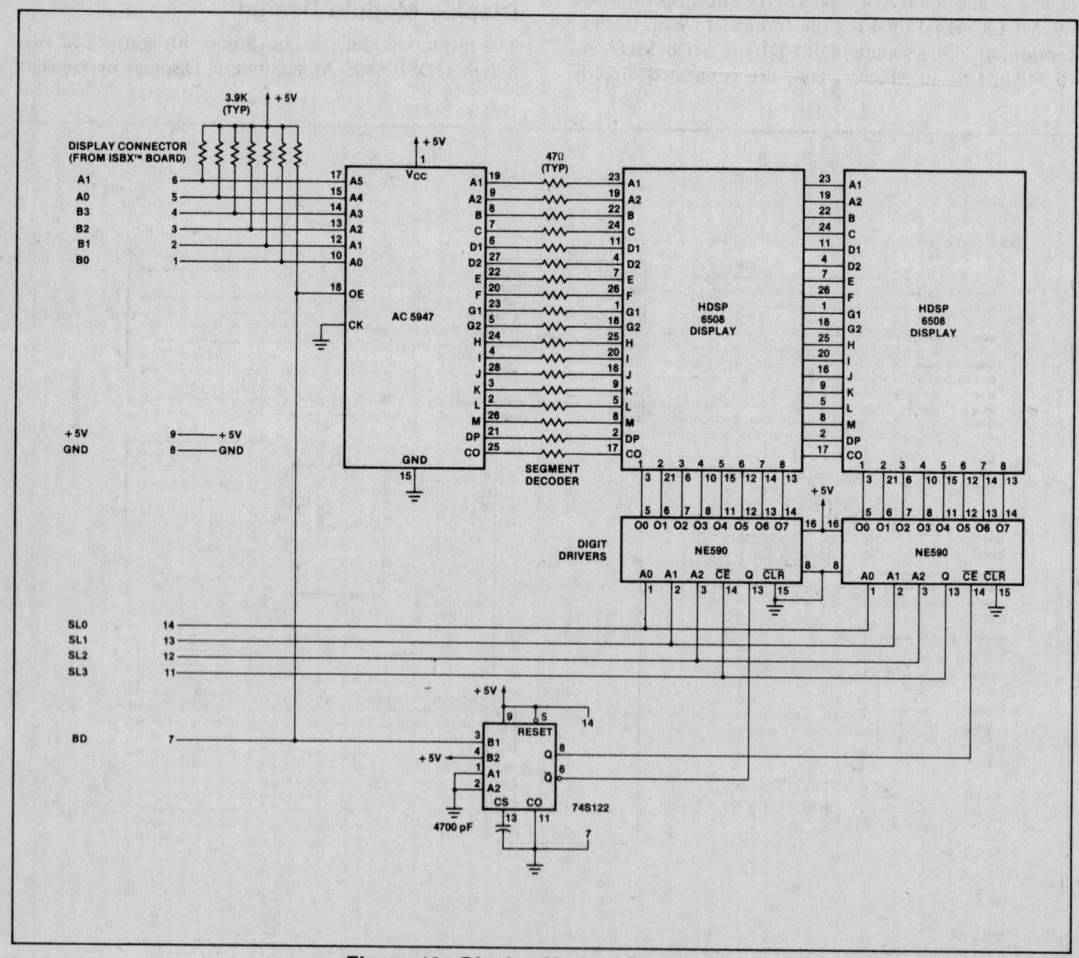

Figure 10. Display Module Schematic

ample. A diagram of the keyboard interfaces and matrix can be seen in Figure 11.

Operation with the iSBC® 80/10B Single Board Computer

The 8279 on the iSBX expansion board is initialized to its mode of operation following a system reset. The keyboard mode of operation is to scan the keyboard with 2-key lockout, and the display mode is set for the 16-character left entry mode of operation. Upon receiving a character from the keyboard, the 8279 generates an interrupt along the MINTR0 line of the iSBX bus to the CPU. At this time the iSBC 80/10B board commences I/O read operations to the iSBX board by generating valid I/O address and chip select commands on the MA0 and MCS0/ signal lines. After the setup times are met, the 80/10B issues an I/O read command by asserting the IORD/ line on the bus, and the base board reads the data from the iSBX board and removes the IORD/, MA0, and MCS0/ signals from the bus. After the data has been read in from the keyboard, it must be output to the display. The iSBC 80/10B board starts an I/O write operation by generating a valid I/O address and the chip select signal with the MA0 and MCS0/ lines. After the valid setup times are met, the IOWRT/ line is activated by the base board. When the data has been valid for a minimum of 250 ns, the host board removes the IOWRT/ line. When the hold times have been met, the data, address and chip select lines are also removed. Figure 12 shows the timing diagrams just discussed.

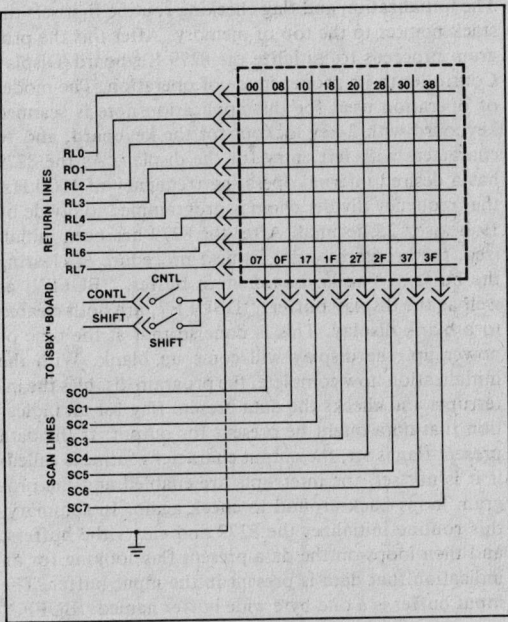

Figure 11. Keyboard Matrix Schematic

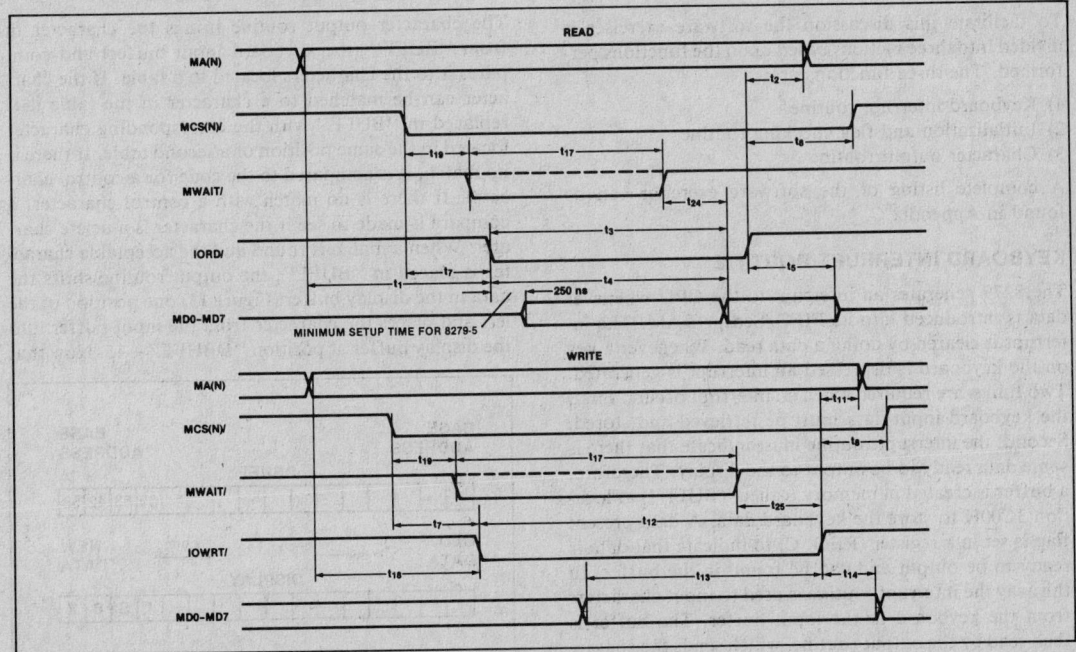

Figure 12. System Timing Diagrams

Breadboarding the Design

When doing the layout of the breadboard, it is also necessary to take into consideration the space required by the mounting holes and to plan the positioning of the components accordingly. (This information is available in the iSBX Bus Specification Manual.)

When attaching the breadboarded design, which typically contains raised wirewrap posts, it is necessary to raise the breadboard well above the host board. This can be accomplished by building a small cable and putting the breadboard on longer nylon standoffs. It is not recommended that the cable be longer than 15 cm (6 in.), otherwise bus timing problems could result.

With the breadboarding finished it is a good idea to re-check all wiring connections for possible errors. Also check all signal lines with an ohmmeter between power, and then ground, for potential shorts. An error at this point can cause serious damage to the host board!

Software Considerations

The software written for this application is an exerciser that is used for hardware checkout. It is a small program designed to echo characters from the keyboard to the display. The software was edited, assembled, linked and located with an Intel development system; it was then debugged with an in-circuit emulator. Both the software and the hardware debug is covered in the next section of this application note.

To facilitate this discussion the software exerciser is divided into three sections based upon the functions performed. The three functions are:

1) Keyboard interrupt routine
2) Initialization and flag checking routine
3) Character output routine

A complete listing of the software exerciser can be found in Appendix C.

KEYBOARD INTERRUPT ROUTINE

The 8279 generates an interrupt to the CPU whenever data is introduced into its FIFO/Sensor RAM. The interrupt is cleared by doing a data read. Whenever a key on the keyboard is depressed an interrupt is generated. Two things are required when an interrupt occurs. First, the keyboard input data must be retrieved and stored. Second, the interrupt routine must indicate that there is some data ready to be output to the display. Therefore, a buffer is created in memory (called "BUFF") at location 3C00H to store the keyboard data. A data present flag is set in a register (REG. C) to indicate that data is ready to be output and can be found in the buffer. In this way the interrupt routine is used to input characters from the keyboard to the input buffer. The buffer is then read by the output routine, which sends the characters to the display.

INITIALIZATION AND FLAG CHECKING ROUTINE

The initialization and flag checking routine first sets the stack pointer to the top of memory. After this the program proceeds to initialize the 8279 Keyboard/Display Controller to its proper mode of operation. The modes of operation used for this application note is scanned keyboard with 2-key lockout for the keyboard, and 16 characters with left entry for the display. As the 8279 has a desired internal operating frequency of 100 kHz, the frequency divider chain is programmed to divide by 19 hex, or 25 decimal. After the 8279 has been initialized, the program begins its next procedure of clearing the buffers. The keyboard input buffer, "BUFF", as well as the display buffer, "DBUFF", are both cleared to a blank display. This is done so that at the time of power up, the display will come up blank. With the initialization now complete, the program disables the interrupts and checks the data present flag for an indication that data might be present for output. If the data present flag is set, the output character routine is called; if it is not set, the interrupts are enabled and the program loops back around to check again. In summary, this routine initializes the 8279 and clears the buffers, and then loops on the data present flag looking for an indication that data is present in the input buffer. The input buffer is a one-byte wide buffer named "BUFF."

CHARACTER OUTPUT ROUTINE

The character output routine brings the character in from "BUFF" (the keyboard input buffer) and compares it to the characters located in a table. If the character can be matched to a character in the table it is replaced in "BUFF" with the corresponding character located in the same position of a second table. If there is no match, it is compared to the code for a control character. If there is no match with a control character, a compare is made to see if the character is a delete character. When a match is found and the acceptable character is placed in "BUFF", the output routine shifts the data in the display buffer (Figure 13) one position to the left and places the character from the input buffer into the display buffer at position "DBUFF" + 15. Now that

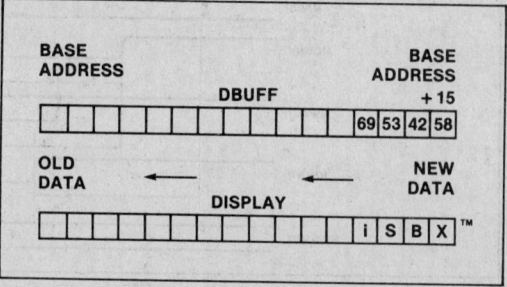

Figure 13. Display Buffer

the new information is in the display, the routine copies the complete contents of the display buffer, "DBUFF", to "DBUFF" + 15 to the display. In the case of the input character being matched up with a delete character, all information in the display buffer is shifted to the right one position and the ASCII code for a blank character is placed into the left-most position or the base address of "DBUFF", thus making the next character sent to the display a blank character. In the case of a control character, nothing is done and the program returns to the flag checking routine.

Debug Considerations

Hardware and software debug was accomplished using an iSBC 80/10B Single Board Computer, an iSBC 655 Chassis, an Intellec® Series II Model 230 Microcomputer Development System, and an ICE-80™ In-Circuit Emulator.

The software was down-loaded from the disk to the iSBC 80/10B board using the in-circuit emulator. The ICE™ module gives the engineer the capability of interrogating the iSBC system by allowing the user to access and display the CPU register contents, status, system memory contents, and all I/O devices and their data.

The iSBC 80/10B board was configured to enable interrupts from the iSBC board via the interrupt 0 line (MINTR0), which is connected to the interrupt pin of the 8080 CPU. The iSBX board was attached to the iSBC 80/10B board via the iSBX connector. The iSBC 80/10B board was powered-up and the iSBX board was checked for proper power and ground connections. The ICE-80 emulator was connected to the iSBC 80/10B board. Using the interrogation mode of the emulator, it is possible to check proper functioning of the iSBX board by sending and receiving data to/from the 8279. The keyboard can be tested by depressing a key on the keyboard and then examining the FIFO/Sensor RAM to see if the data was entered. The display RAM can also be read and written to for testing the interface to the display.

After this initial checking of the iSBX board, the software exerciser can then be down-loaded with the ICE module to further check the board.

SUMMARY

The objective of this application note is to introduce the reader to the iSBX MULTIMODULE concept for expanding a single board computer's functionality, and to illustrate how a designer can use this concept with either standard or custom iSBX boards. In contrast to system expansion using MULTIBUS-compatible boards, iSBX MULTIMODULE boards provide smaller, lower cost, incremental expansion. This application note explains how a custom iSBX board can be designed and debugged. Using this capability, it is now possible to more quickly add new VLSI technology to systems as the technology becomes available. Intel will continue to provide new iSBX MULTIMODULE boards and, because of the the publication of the iSBX Bus Specification and this application note, it will be easier for Intel's customers to also design and build their own custom iSBX boards.

APPENDIX A
iSBX™ SIGNAL PIN ASSIGNMENTS

Pin	Mnemonic	Description	Pin	Mnemonic	Description
35	GND	Signal Ground	36	+5V	+5 Volts
33	MD0	MDATA Bit 0	34	MDRQT	M DMA Request
31	MD1	MDATA Bit 1	32	MDACK/	M DMA Acknowledge
29	MD2	MDATA Bit 2	30	OPT0	Option 0
27	MD3	MDATA Bit 3	28	OPT1	Option 1
25	MD4	MDATA Bit 4	26	TDMA	Terminate DMA
23	MD5	MDATA Bit 5	24		Reserved
21	MD6	MDATA Bit 6	22	MCS0/	M Chip Select 0
19	MD7	MDATA Bit 7	20	MCS1/	M Chip Select 1
17	GND	Signal Ground	18	+5V	+5 Volts
15	IORD/	I/O Read Command	16	MWAIT/	M Wait
13	IOWRT/	I/O Write Command	14	MINTR0	M Interrupt 0
11	MA0	M Address 0	12	MINTR1	M Interrupt 1
9	MA1	M Address 1	10		Reserved
7	MA2	M Address 2	8	MPST/	iSBX MULTIMODULE Board Present
5	RESET	Reset	6	MCLK	M Clock
3	GND	Signal Ground	4	+5V	+5 Volts
1	+12V	+12 Volts	2	−12V	−12 Volts

All undefined pins are reserved for future use.

APPENDIX B
iSBX™ MULTIMODULE™ BOARD I/O AC SPECIFICATIONS

Symbol*	Parameter	Min (ns)	Max (ns)
t_1	Address stable before read	50	—
t_2	Address stable after read	30	—
t_3	Read pulse width	300	—
$t_4^{(2)}$	Data valid from read	0	250
$t_5^{(2)}$	Data float after read	0	150
t_6	Time between RD and/or WRT	—	Note 3
t_7	CS stable before CMD	25	—
t_8	CS stable after CMD	30	—
t_9	Power up reset pulse width	50 ms	—
t_{10}	Address stable before WRT	50	—
t_{11}	Address stable after WRT	30	—
$t_{12}^{(2)}$	Write pulse width	300	—
$t_{13}^{(2)}$	Data valid to write	250	—
t_{14}	Data valid after write	30	—
t_{15}	MCLK cycle	100	110
t_{16}	MCLK width	35	65
$t_{17}^{(1)}$	MWAIT/ pulse width	0	4 ms
t_{18}	Reset pulse width	50 ms	—
t_{19}	MCS/ to MWAIT/ valid	0	75
t_{20}	DACK set up to I/O CMD	100	—
t_{21}	DACK hold	30	—
t_{22}	CMD to DMA RQT removed to end of DMA cycle	—	200
t_{23}	TDMA pulse width	500	—
$t_{24}^{(1)}$	MWAIT/ to valid read data	—	0
$t_{25}^{(1)}$	MWAIT/ to WRT CMD	0	—

NOTES:
1. Required only if WAIT is activated.
2. If MWAIT/ not activated.
3. To be specified by each iSBX MULTIMODULE board.
* For a more complete definition of symbols refer to iSBX Bus Specification, 142686-001.

APPENDIX C
LISTING FOR THE iSBX™ DESIGN EXAMPLE SOFTWARE EXERCISER

```
LOC     OBJ         LINE    SOURCE STATEMENT

                    1    ;************************************************************************
                    2    ;*
                    3    ;*         THIS PROGRAM WAS USED AS AN EXAMPLE FOR EXERCISING THE        *
                    4    ;*         8279 iSBX MULTIMODULE BUILT FOR THIS APPLICATION NOTE.        *
                    5    ;*
                    6    ;************************************************************************
                    7
                    8
                    9    ;************************************************************************
                    10   ;                       PROGRAM EQUATES
                    11   ;************************************************************************
                    12
00F0                13   DATAAD      EQU         0F0H        ; PORT ADDRESS TO READ OR WRITE
                    14                                       ;/DATA TO/OR FROM KEYBOARD/DISPLAY
00F1                15   CMDAD       EQU         0F1H        ; PORT ADDRESS TO SEND COMMANDS
                    16                                       ;/TO KEYBOARD/DISPLAY
0008                17   MODE0       EQU         08H         ; CONTROL CHAR. TO SET
                    18                                       ;/KEYBOARD/DISPLAY MODE FOR
                    19                                       ;/(2 KEY LOCKOUT,16 CHAR LEFT ENTRY
0039                20   PROGCK      EQU         39H         ; CONTROL CHAR. TO SET 8279 CLK
                    21                                       ;/TO 100 KHz INTERNAL TIMING
0040                22   RDFIFO      EQU         40H         ; CONTROL CHAR. TO READ KEYBOARD
0060                23   RDRAM       EQU         60H         ; CONTROL CHAR. TO READ DISPLAY RAM
0070                24   RDRAMA      EQU         70H         ; CONTROL CHAR. TO READ DISPLAY RAM
                    25                                       ;/AUTO INCREMENT
0080                26   WRRAM       EQU         80H         ; CONTL CHAR. TO WRITE TO DISPLAY RAM
0090                27   WRRAMA      EQU         90H         ; CONTL CHAR. TO WRITE TO DISPLAY
                    28                                       ;/RAM AUTO INCREMENT
00D8                29   CLR         EQU         0D8H        ; CONTROL CHAR. TO CLEAR OR BLANK
                    30                                       ;/DISPLAY
3C00                31   BUFF        EQU         3C00H       ; ADDRESS OF KEYBOARD INPUT BUFFER
3D00                32   DBUFF       EQU         3D00H       ; ADDRESS OF DISPLAY BUFFER
                    33
                    34   ;************************************************************************
                    35
0000 F3             36   START:      DI
0001 C33B00         37               JMP         BEGIN
                    38
                    39   ;********************  RST 7 ENTRY POINT  ******************************
                    40
0038                41               ORG         38H
0038 C3D100         42               JMP         INT
                    43
                    44   ;************************************************************************
                    45   ;                       INITIALIZE PROGRAM
                    46   ;               AND KEY BOARD DISPLAY CONTROLLER
                    47   ;
003B 31FF3F         48   BEGIN:      LXI         SP,3FFFH    ; INITIALIZE STACK PT
003E 3E08           49               MVI         A,MODE0     ; GET CONTROL CHAR.
0040 D3F1           50               OUT         CMDAD       ; SET KEYBOARD/DISPLAY MODE
0042 3E39           51               MVI         A,PROGCK    ; GET CONTROL CHAR.
0044 D3F1           52               OUT         CMDAD       ; SET 8279 CLK FOR 100 KHz
0046 3ED8           53               MVI         A,CLR       ; GET CONTROL CHAR.
0048 D3F1           54               OUT         CMDAD       ; CLEAR OR BLANK DISPLAY
004A 0EE0           55               MVI         C,0E0H
004C 21003C         56               LXI         H,BUFF      ; SET POINTER TO INPUT BUFFER
004F 71             57               MOV         M,C         ; CLEAR INPUT BUFFER TO BLANK CODE
0050 060F           58               MVI         B,0FH       ; SET COUNTER = 15
0052 210F3D         59               LXI         H,DBUFF+0FH ; SET POINTER TO DBUFF +15
0055 71             60   ZDBUFF:     MOV         M,C         ; CLEAR DISPLAY BUFFER TO
0056 2B             61               DCX         H           ;/DISPLAY BUFFER +15 TO CODE
0057 05             62               DCR         B           ;/FOR CLEARING OR BLANKING OUT
0058 C25500         63               JNZ         ZDBUFF      ;/THE DISPLAY
                    64
                    65   ;************************************************************************
                    66   ;               THIS IS THE BACKGROUND PROGRAM
                    67   ;       WHICH LOOPS CHECKING FOR THE DATA PRESENT FLAG
                    68   ;
005B F3             69   CKFLAG:     DI                      ; DISABLE INTERRUPTS
005C AF             70               XRA         A           ;/CLEAR A REG AND COMPARE WITH
005D B9             71               CMP         C           ;/C REG CHECKING FOR DATA PRESENT
005E CA6400         72               JZ          LABEL       ;/IF PRESENT CALL OUTPT
0061 CD6800         73               CALL        OUTPT       ;/TO DISPLAY CHAR.
0064 FB             74   LABEL:      EI                      ;/IF NO DATA PRESENT ENABLE
0065 C35B00         75               JMP         CKFLAG      ;/INTERRUPTS AND JMP BACK
                    76
```

```
                77 ;******************************************************************
                78 ;                     OUTPUT CHARACTER TO DISPLAY
                79 ;
0068 3A003C     80 OUTPT:     LDA    BUFF           ; LOAD A WITH KEYBOARD DATA
006B 062B       81            MVI    B,2BH          ; SET COUNTER MAX POSSIBLE CHAR.
006D 21DE00     82            LXI    H,TABLE1       ; SET POINTER TO INPUT TABLE
0070 110901     83            LXI    D,TABLE2       ; SET POINTER TO OUTPUT TABLE
0073 BE         84 COMPARE:   CMP    M              ; COMPARE KEYBD DATA TO INPUT
0074 CA8000     85            JZ     MATCH          ;/TABLE IF = JMP TO MATCH
0077 05         86            DCR    B              ;/ELSE DECREMENT COUNTER IF 0
0078 CAC600     87            JZ     CONTROL        ;/JMP TO CONTROL
007B 23         88            INX    H              ;/ELSE INCREMENT BOTH TABLE
007C 13         89            INX    D              ;/POINTERS AND JMP TO COMPARE
007D C37300     90            JMP    COMPARE
0080 EB         91 MATCH:     XCHG                  ; IF MATCH CHANGE INPUT WITH
0081 7E         92            MOV    A,M            ;/OUTPT DATA AND PLACE IN BUFF
0082 21003C     93            LXI    H,BUFF
0085 77         94            MOV    M,A
0086 060F       95            MVI    B,0FH          ; SET COUNTER = TO 15
0088 11003D     96            LXI    D,DBUFF        ; POINTER TO FIRST LOC IN DBUFF
008B 21013D     97            LXI    H,DBUFF+1      ; POINTER TO 2ND LOC IN DBUFF
008E 7E         98 LOOP1:     MOV    A,M            ; READ HIGH POINTER FROM DBUFF
008F 23         99            INX    H              ;/UPDATE HIGH POINTER
0090 EB        100            XCHG
0091 77        101            MOV    M,A            ; SHIFT DATA LEFT IN D BUFF
0092 23        102            INX    H              ; UPDATE LOW POINTER
0093 EB        103            XCHG
0094 05        104            DCR    B              ; TEST IF DONE
0095 C28E00    105            JNZ    LOOP1          ;/AND GO BACK IF NOT
0098 3A003C    106            LDA    BUFF           ;/ELSE READ KEYBOARD DATA
009B 320F3D    107            STA    DBUFF+0FH      ;/AND PLACE IT IN THE DBUFF
009E 0610      108 LOOPA:     MVI    B,10H          ; SET COUNTER = 16
00A0 21003D    109            LXI    H,DBUFF        ; SET POINTER = DBUFF 1ST POS.
00A3 7E        110 LOOP2:     MOV    A,M            ;/READ 1 BYTE FROM DBUFF
00A4 D3F0      111            OUT    DATAAD         ;/AND SENT IT TO DISPLAY
00A6 23        112            INX    H              ; UPDATE POINTER
00A7 05        113            DCR    B              ;/AND TEST IF DONE
00A8 C2A300    114            JNZ    LOOP2          ;/GO BACK IF NOT DONE
00AB 0E00      115            MVI    C,0H           ;/ELSE CLR DATA PRESENT FLAG
00AD C9        116            RET                   ;/AND RETURN
                117 ;******************************************************************
                118 ;                         CHARACTER DELETE
                119 ;                           OR RUB OUT
                120 ;
00AE 060F      121 DELETE:    MVI    B,0FH          ; SET COUNTER =15
00B0 110F3D    122            LXI    D,DBUFF+0FH    ; SET POINTER = DBUFF+15
00B3 210E3D    123            LXI    H,DBUFF+0EH    ; SET POINTER = DBUFF+14
00B6 7E        124 LOOPB:     MOV    A,M            ; READ LOW POINTER FROM DBUFF
00B7 2B        125            DCX    H              ;/UPDATE LOW POINTER
00B8 EB        126            XCHG
00B9 77        127            MOV    M,A            ; SHIFT DATA RIGHT IN DBUFF
00BA 2B        128            DCX    H              ;/UPDATE HIGH POINTER
00BB EB        129            XCHG
00BC 05        130            DCR    B              ; TEST IF DONE
00BD C2B600    131            JNZ    LOOPB          ;/AND GO BACK IF NOT
00C0 EB        132            XCHG                  ;/ELSE SET DBUFF FOR
00C1 36E0      133            MVI    M,0E0H         ;/CODE TO BLANK DISPLAY
00C3 C39E00    134            JMP    LOOPA          ;/AND JMP TO LOOPA
                135
                136 ;******************************************************************
                137 ;                      CHECK IF CHARACTER IS
                138 ;                    A CONTROL OR DELETE CHARACTER
                139 ;
00C6 FEFA      140 CONTROL:   CPI    0FAH           ; COMPARE FOR CONTROL CHAR.
00C8 CA3B00    141            JZ     BEGIN          ;/IF CONTROL JMP TO BEGIN
00CB FEF9      142            CPI    0F9H           ;/ELSE COMP. FOR DELETE CHAR.
00CD CAAE00    143            JZ     DELETE         ;/IF DELETE JMP TO DELETE
00D0 C9        144            RET                   ;/ELSE RETURN
                145
                146 ;******************************************************************
                147 ;                         KEYBOARD INPUT
                148 ;                         INTERRUPT ROUTINE
                149 ;
00D1 3E40      150 INT:       MVI    A,RDFIFO       ; GET CONTL CHAR. TO READ FIFO
00D3 D3F1      151            OUT    CMDAD          ; SET 8279 FOR READ MODE
00D5 DBF0      152            IN     DATAAD         ; READ KEYBOARD DATA IN
00D7 21003C    153            LXI    H,BUFF         ; SET POINTER TO BUFF
00DA 77        154            MOV    M,A            ;/AND STORE KEYBOARD DATA
00DB 0EFF      155            MVI    C,0FFH         ;/THEN SET DATA PRESENT FLAG
00DD C9        156            RET                   ;/AND RETURN
                157
```

AP-96

```
                       158 ;**********************************************************************
                       159 ;
                       160 ;                        TABLE 1
                       161 ;             ACCEPTABLE INPUT CHARACTERS FROM KEYBOARD
  00DE DE              162 TABLE1:   DB      0DEH,0FFH,0EFH,0EEH,0E5H,0F6H,0FEH,0C6H
  00DF FF
  00E0 EF
  00E1 EE
  00E2 E5
  00E3 F6
  00E4 FE
  00E5 C6
  00E6 C9              163           DB      0C9H,0CAH,0D2H,0DAH,0D3H,0C7H,0D1H,0D9H
  00E7 CA
  00E8 D2
  00E9 DA
  00EA D3
  00EB C7
  00EC D1
  00ED D9
  00EE D5              164           DB      0D5H,0EDH,0E6H,0F5H,0C1H,0F7H,0DDH,0E7H
  00EF ED
  00F0 E6
  00F1 F5
  00F2 C1
  00F3 F7
  00F4 DD
  00F5 E7
  00F6 FD              165           DB      0FDH,0DFH,0CCH,0D4H,0DCH,0E4H,0ECH,0F4H
  00F7 DF
  00F8 CC
  00F9 D4
  00FA DC
  00FB E4
  00FC EC
  00FD F4
  00FE FC              166           DB      0FCH,0C0H,0C8H,0D0H,098H,0A2H,0CFH,0AAH
  00FF C0
  0100 C8
  0101 D0
  0102 98
  0103 A2
  0104 CF
  0105 AA
  0106 EB              167           DB      0EBH,0E3H,0D8H
  0107 E3
  0108 D8
                       168
```

```
                        169 ;************************************************************
                        170 ;                         TABLE 2
                        171 ;              ACCEPTABLE OUTPUT CHARACTERS TO DISPLAY
                        172 ;
0109 C1                 173 TABLE2:     DB      0C1H,0C2H,0C3H,0C4H,0C5H,0C6H,0C7H,0C8H
010A C2
010B C3
010C C4
010D C5
010E C6
010F C7
0110 C8
0111 C9                 174             DB      0C9H,0CAH,0CBH,0CCH,0CDH,0CEH,0CFH,0D0H
0112 CA
0113 CB
0114 CC
0115 CD
0116 CE
0117 CF
0118 D0
0119 D1                 175             DB      0D1H,0D2H,0D3H,0D4H,0D5H,0D6H,0D7H,0D8H
011A D2
011B D3
011C D4
011D D5
011E D6
011F D7
0120 D8
0121 D9                 176             DB      0D9H,0DAH,0F1H,0F2H,0F3H,0F4H,0F5H,0F6H
0122 DA
0123 F1
0124 F2
0125 F3
0126 F4
0127 F5
0128 F6
0129 F7                 177             DB      0F7H,0F8H,0F9H,0F0H,0FDH,0EBH,0E0H,0EAH
012A F8
012B F9
012C F0
012D FD
012E EB
012F E0
0130 EA
0131 EF                 178             DB      0EFH,0EEH,02DH
0132 EE
0133 2D
0000                    179             END     START
```

PUBLIC SYMBOLS

EXTERNAL SYMBOLS

```
USER SYMBOLS
BEGIN  A 003B    BUFF   A 3C00    CKFLAG A 005B    CLR    A 00D8    CMDAD  A 00F1    COMPAR A 0073    CONTRO A 00C6
DATAAD A 00F0    DBUFF  A 3D00    DELETE A 00AE    INT    A 00D1    LABEL  A 0064    LOOP1  A 008E    LOOP2  A 00A3
LOOPA  A 009E    LOOPB  A 0086    MATCH  A 0080    MODE0  A 0008    OUTPT  A 0068    PROGCK A 0039    RDFIFO A 0040
RDRAM  A 0060    RDRAMA A 0070    START  A 0000    TABLE1 A 00DE    TABLE2 A 0109    WRRAM  A 0080    WRRAMA A 0090
ZDBUFF A 0055
```

ASSEMBLY COMPLETE,   NO ERRORS

Communication Controllers 8

iDCM 911-1 INTELLINK™
ETHERNET* CLUSTER MODULE

- Eliminates need for transceivers and Ethernet coaxial cable for a local cluster of workstations
- Enables local cluster of nine workstations to connect to main Ethernet cable with only one transceiver
- Permits clustering of up to nine workstations in a smaller area
- Enables workstations to be up to 100M from main Ethernet cable
- Complies with the Ethernet Specification, Version 1.0, September 1980

The Intellink™ Ethernet Cluster Module is a device used as a means of interconnecting up to nine Ethernet devices without the need for Ethernet coaxial cable and transceivers. The Intellink module forms a standalone Ethernet local area network with "interconnection" communication capability. The Intellink module (and attached devices) can optionally be connected to the Ethernet coaxial cable through a single transceiver

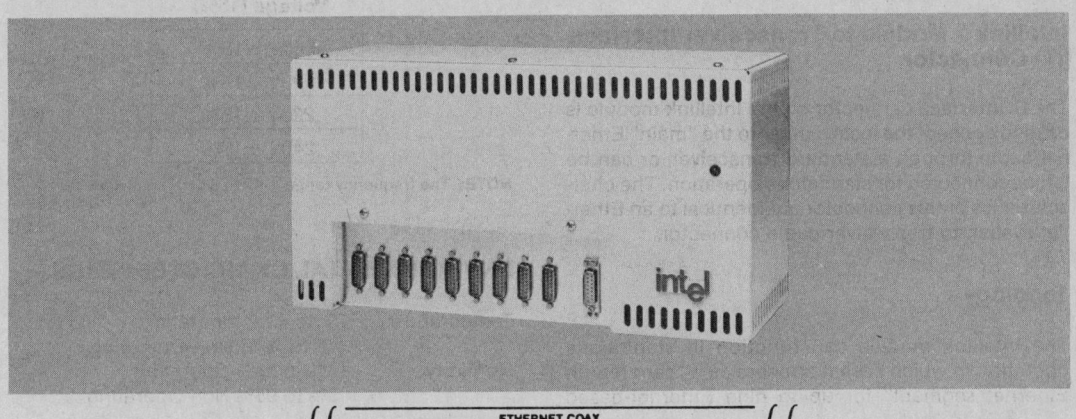

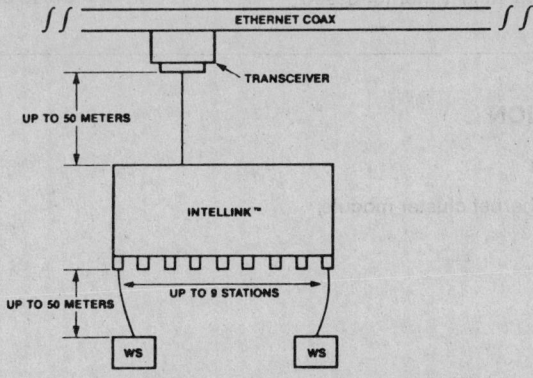

Figure 1. Intellink™ Configuration

*Ethernet is a trademark of Xerox Corporation.

Intel Corporation Assumes No Responsibility for the Use of Any Circuitry Other Than Circuitry Embodied in an Intel Product. No Other Circuit Patent Licenses are implied. Information Contained Herein Supercedes Previously Published Specifications On These Devices From Intel.
© INTEL CORPORATION, 1983.

iDCM 911-1 INTELLINK™ ETHERNET* CLUSTER MODULE

PRELIMINARY

FUNCTIONAL DESCRIPTION

Intellink module performs the same functions as a standard Ethernet transceiver. It buffers receive and transmit data, detects attempts by two or more stations to gain access to the line simultaneously, signals the presence of a collision to the transmitting stations, and transmits the jam signal prior to initiation of the random back-off algorithm. It complies with all of the interface parameters set forth in "The Ethernet Specification," 1.0 Version, September 1980.

Ethernet Work Station to Intellink™ Interface (WI) Connectors

There are nine WI interface connectors into which Ethernet-based systems can be connected. Each connector has the same signal pairs as does the equivalent connector on a standard Ethernet transceiver.

Intellink™ Module to Transceiver Interface (IT) Connector

The IT interface connector on the Intellink module is used to connect the local cluster to the "main" Ethernet cable through a standard transceiver, or can be left unconnected for standalone operation. The characteristics of this connector are identical to an Ethernet system to transceiver cable connector.

Topology

The Intellink module can function in standalone operation in which case it appears as a "zero length Ethernet segment" for up to nine Ethernet-based systems, or optionally can be connected to the "main" Ethernet coaxial cable through a single transceiver. When connected to the "main" Ethernet coaxial cable, it extends the Ethernet system interface to the transceiver from 50 meters to 100 meters. (Figure 1).

Physical Characteristics

Width .... 14 in. (35.56 cm)
Height .... 7.8 in. (19.81 cm)
Depth .... 5.5 in. (13.97 cm)
Weight .... 10 lb. (4.52 kg)

ELECTRICAL CHARACTERISTICS

Input Voltage Range:
(Voltages AC RMS)

Voltage (15%)
100V ±15%
120V ±15%
220V ±15%
240V ±15%

NOTE: The frequency range is 47 to 64 Hz, single phase.

ENVIRONMENTAL CHARACTERISTICS

Temperature: 10° to 40°C Operating
              −40° to 70°C Non-Operating
Humidity: 10% to 85% Operating
              5% to 95% Non-Operating

ORDERING INFORMATION

Part Number	Description
iDCM 911-1	Intellink, Ethernet cluster module, Version 1.0

iSBC® 88/45
ADVANCED DATA COMMUNICATIONS PROCESSOR BOARD

- Three HDLC/SDLC half/full-duplex communication channels — optional ASYNC/SYNC on two channels

- Supports RS232C (including modem support), CCITT V.24, or RS422A/449 interfaces

- On-board DMA supports 800K baud operation

- Self-clocking NRZI SDLC loop data link interface
  — point-to-point
  — multidrop

- Software programmable baud rate generation

- iAPX 88/10 (8088-2) Microprocessor operates at 8 MHz

- iSBC® 337 Numeric Data Processor option supported

- 16K bytes static RAM (12K bytes dual-ported)

- Four 28-pin JEDEC sites for EPROM/RAM expansion; four additional 28-pin JEDEC sites added with iSBC® 341 board

- Two iSBX™ bus connectors

- MULTIBUS® interface supports Multimaster configuration

The iSBC 88/45 Advanced Data Communications Processor (ADCP) Board adds 8 MHz, iAPX 88/10 (8088-2) 8-bit microprocessor-based communications flexibility to the Intel line of OEM microcomputer systems. The iSBC 88/45 ADCP board offers asynchronous, synchronous, SDLC, and HDLC serial interfaces for gateway networking or general purpose solutions. The iSBC 88/45 ADCP board provides the CPU, system clock, EPROM/RAM, serial I/O ports, priority interrupt logic, and programmable timers to facilitate higher-level application solutions.

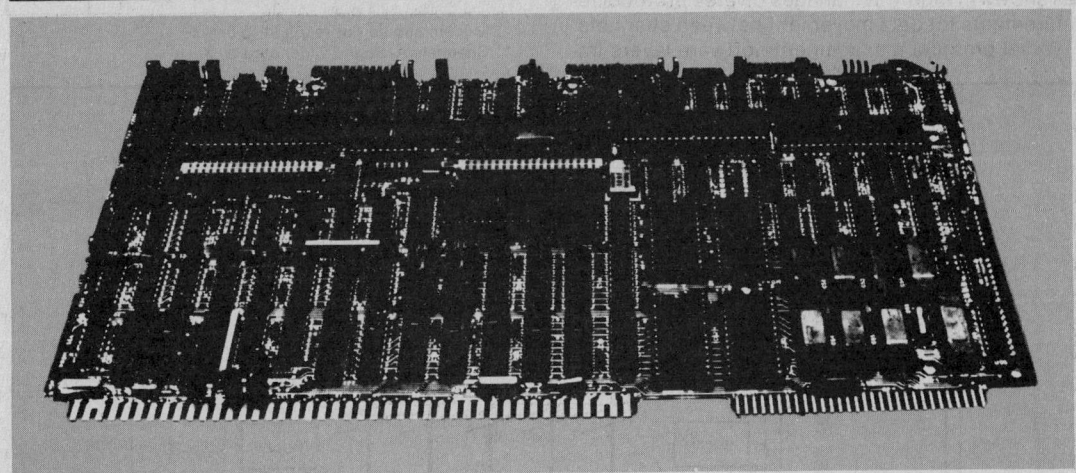

The following are trademarks of Intel Corporation and may be used only to describe Intel products: Intel, CREDIT, Index, Insite, Intellec, Library Manager, Megachassis, Micromap, MULTIBUS, PROMPT, UPI, µScope, Promware, MCS, ICE, iRMX, iSBC, iSBX, MULTIMODULE and iCS. Intel Corporation assumes no responsibility for the use of any circuitry other than circuitry embodied in an Intel product. No other circuit patent licenses are implied.

iSBC® 88/45

FUNCTIONAL DESCRIPTION

Three Communication Channels

Three programmable HDLC/SDLC serial interfaces are provided on the iSBC 88/45 ADCP board. The SDLC interface is familiar to IBM system and terminal equipment users. The HDLC interface is known by users of CCITT's X.25 packet switching interface.

One channel utilizes an Intel 8273 controller to manage the serial data transfers. Accepting the 8-bit data bytes from the local bus, the 8273 controller translates the data into the HDLC/SDLC format. The channel operates in half/full-duplex mode.

In addition to the synchronous mode, the 8273 controller operates asynchronously with NRZI encoded data which is found in systems such as the IBM 3650 Retail Store System. An SDLC loop configuration using iSBX 352 and iSBC 88/45 products is shown in Figure 1.

The two additional channels utilize the Intel 8274 Multi-Protocol Serial Controller (MPSC). The MPSC provides two independent half/full-duplex serial channels which provide asynchronous, synchronous, HDLC or SDLC protocol operations. The sync and async protocol operations are commonly used to communicate with inexpensive terminals and systems.

The three serial channels of the iSBC 88/45 ADCP board offer communications capability to manage a gateway application. The gateway application, as shown in Figure 1, manages diverse protocol requirements for data movement between channels. Typical protocol management software layers implemented by the user include SNA terminal interfaces to IBM systems.

On-Board DMA

For high-speed communications, one MPSC channel has a DMA capacity to support an 800K baud rate. The second channel attached to the MPSC is capable of simultaneous 800K baud operation when configured with DMA capability, but is connected to an RS232C interface which is defined as 20K baud maximum. Figure 2 shows an RS422A/449 multidrop application which supports high-speed operation.

Interfaces Supported

The iSBC 88/45 ADCP board provides an excellent foundation to support these electrical and diverse software drivers protocol interfaces. The control lines, serial data lines, and signal ground lines are brought out to the three double-edge connectors. Figure 3 shows the cable to connector construction. Two connectors are pre-configured for RS422A/449. All three channels are configurable for RS232C/CCITT V.24 interfaces as shown in Table 1.

Table 1. iSBC® 88/45 Supported Configurations

Connection	Synchronous		Asynchronous	
	Modem	Direct	Modem*	Direct
point-to-point	X**	X	X	X
multidrop	X	X	X	X
loop	N.A.	N.A.	C (only)	C (only)

* Modem should not respond to break.
** Channels A, B, and C denoted by X.

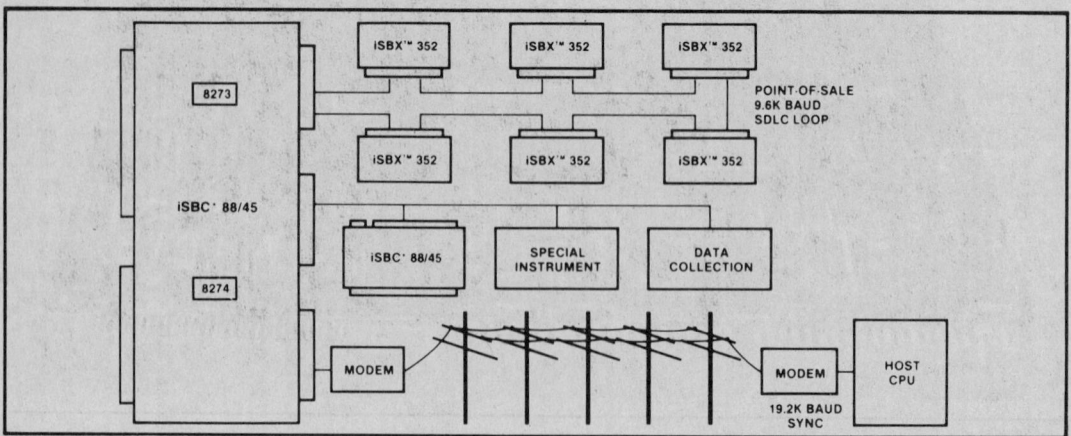

Figure 1. iSBC® 88/45 Gateway Processor Example

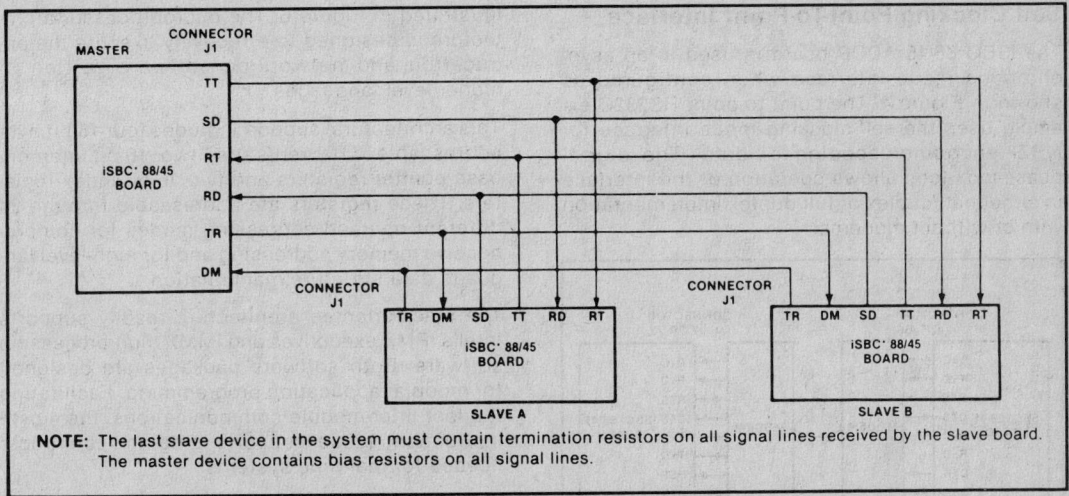

Figure 2. Synchronous Multidrop Network Configuration Example – RS422A

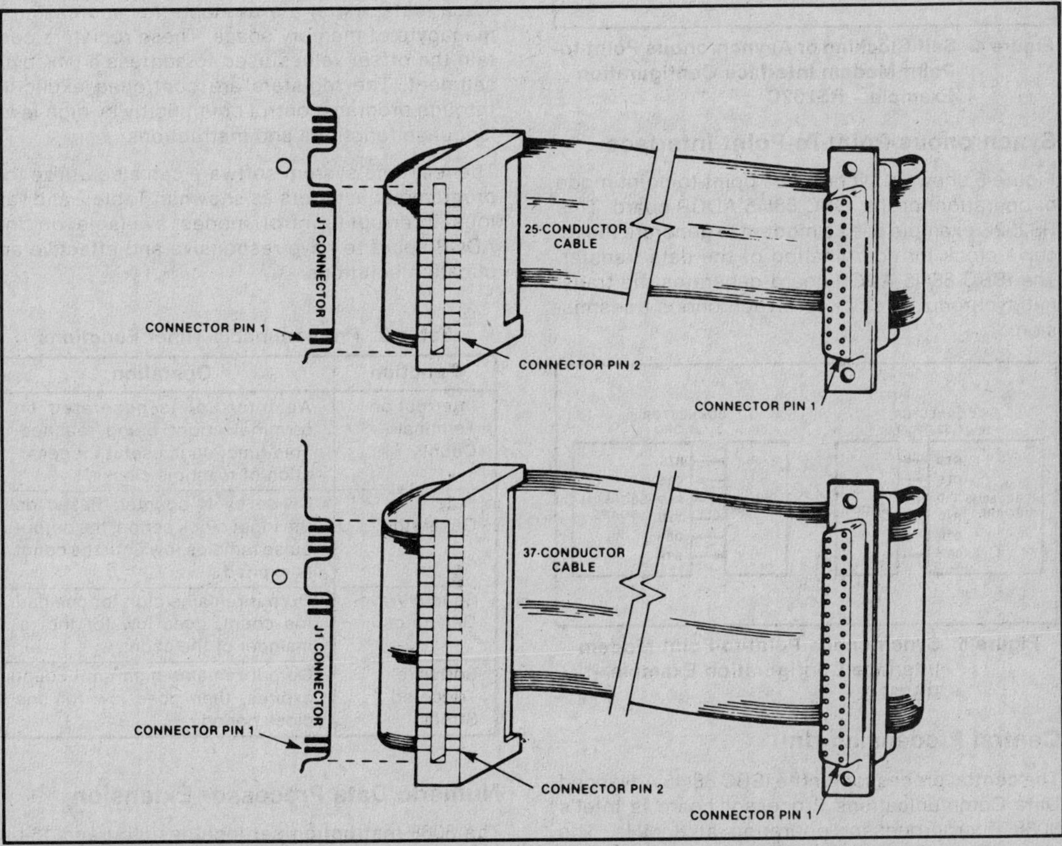

Figure 3. Cable Construction and Installation for RS232C and RS422A/449 Interface

Self Clocking Point-To-Point Interface

The iSBC 88/45 ADCP board is used in an asynchronous mode interface when configured as shown in Figure 4. The point-to-point RS232C example uses the self-clocking mode interface for NRZI encoding/decoding of data. The digital phase-lock loop allows operation of the interface in either half/duplex or full/duplex implementation with or without modems.

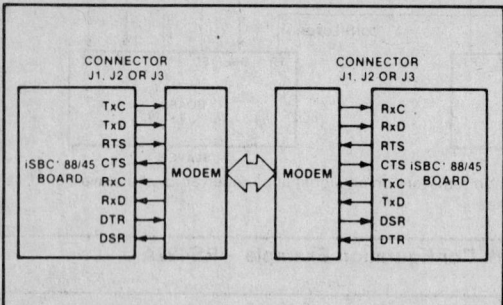

Figure 4. Self-Clocking or Asynchronous Point-to-Point Modem Interface Configuration Example - RS232C

Synchronous Point-To-Point Interface

Figure 5 shows a sychronous point-to-point mode of operation for the iSBC 88/45 ADCP board. This RS232C example uses a modem to generate the receive clock for coordination of the data transfer. The iSBC 88/45 ADCP board generates the transmit sychronizing clock for synchronous transmission.

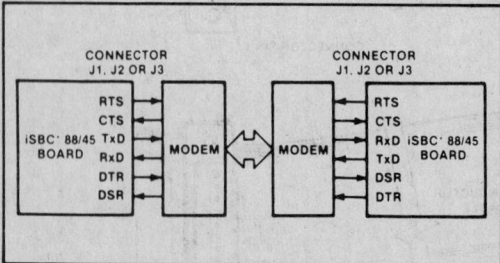

Figure 5. Synchronous Point-to-Point Modem Interface Configuration Example - RS232C

Central Processing Unit

The central processor for the iSBC 88/45 Advanced Data Communications Processor board is Intel's 8088 microprocessor operating at 8 MHz. The microprocessor interface to other functions is illustrated in Figure 6. The microprocessor architecture is designed to effectively execute the application and networking software written in higher-level languages.

This architectural support includes four 16-bit byte addressable data registers, two 16-bit memory base pointer registers and two 16-bit index registers. These registers are addressable through 24 different operand addressing modes for comprehensive memory addressing and for high-level language data structure manipulation.

The stack-oriented architecture readily supports Intel's iRMX executives and iMMX multiprocessing software. Both software packages are designed for modular application programming. Facilitating the fast inter-module communications, the 4-byte instruction queue supports program constructs needed for real-time systems.

Since programs are segmented between pure procedure and data, four segment registers (code, stack, data, extra) are available for addressing 1 megabyte of memory space. These registers contain the offset values used to address a 64K byte segment. The registers are controlled explicitly through program control or implicitly by high-level language functions and instructions.

The real-time system software can also utilize the programmable timers as shown in Table 2 and various interrupt control modes available on the ADCP board to have responsive and effective application solutions.

Table 2. Programmable Timer Functions

Function	Operation
Interrupt on Terminal Count	An interrupt is generated on terminal count being reached. This function is useful for generation of real-time clocks.
Rate Generator	Divide by N counter. Based on the input clock period, the output pulse remains low until the count is expired.
Square Wave Generator	Output remains high for one-half the count, goes low for the remainder of the count.
Software Triggered Strobe	Output remains high until count expires, then goes low for one clock period.

Numeric Data Processor Extension

The 8088 instruction set includes 8-bit and 16-bit signed and unsigned arithmetic operators for bi-

iSBC® 88/45

nary, BCD, and unpacked ASCII data. For enhanced numerics processing capability, the iSBC 337 MULTIMODULE Numeric Data Processor extends the 8088 architecture and data set[1].

The extended numerics capability includes over 60 numeric instructions offering arithmetic, trigonometric, transcendental, logarithmic, and exponential instructions. Many math-oriented applications utilize the 16-, 32-, and 64-bit integer, 32- and 64-bit floating point, 18-digit packed BCD, and 80-bit temporary data types.

16K Bytes Static Ram

The iSBC 88/45 ADCP board contains 16K bytes of high-speed static RAM, with 12K bytes dual-ported which is addressable from other MULTIBUS devices. When coupled with the high-speed DMA capability of the iSBC 88/45 ADCP board, the dual-ported memory provides effective data communication buffers. The dual-ported memory is useful for interprocessor message transfers.

The iSBC 337 board requires the iSBC 88/45 ACDP board be jumpered to provide 4 MHz operation.

Interrupt Capability

The iSBC 88/45 ADCP board provides nine vectored interrupt levels. The highest level is the NMI (Non-Maskable Interrupt) line. The additional eight interrupt levels are vectored via the Intel 8259A Programmable Interrupt Controller (PIC). As shown in Table 3, four priority processing modes are available to match interrupt servicing requirements. These modes and priority assignments are dynamically configurable by the system software.

Table 3. Programmable Interrupt Modes

Mode	Operation
Nested	Interrupt request line priorities fixed; interrupt 0 is the highest and 7 is the lowest.
Auto-Rotating	The interrupt priority rotates; once an interrupt is serviced it becomes the lowest priority.
Specific Priority	System software assigns lowest level priority. The other levels are sequenced based on the level assigned.
Polled	System software examines priority interrupt via interrupt status register.

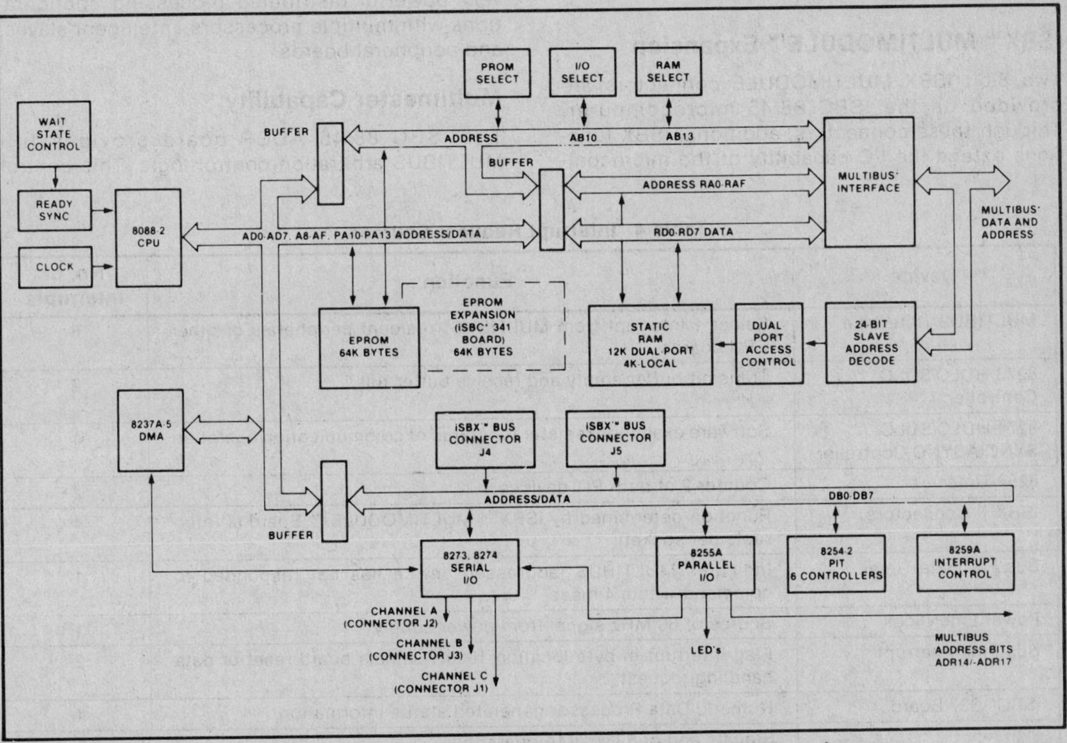

Figure 6. Block Diagram of the iSBC® 88/45 ADCP Board

8-7

210372-002

iSBC® 88/45

Interrupt Request Generation

Listed in Table 4 are the devices and functions supported by interrupts on the iSBC 88/45 ADCP board. All interrupt signals are brought to the interrupt jumper matrix. Any of the 23 interrupt sources are strapped to the appropriate 8259A PIC request level. The PIC resolves requests according to the software selected mode and, if the interrupt is unmasked, issues an interrupt to the CPU.

EPROM/RAM Expansion

In addition to the on-board RAM, the iSBC 88/45 ADCP board provides four 28-pin JEDEC sockets for EPROM expansion. By using 2764 EPROMs, the board has 32K bytes of program storage. Three of the JEDEC standard sockets also support byte-wide static RAMs or iRAMs; using 8K x 8 static RAMs provides an additional 24K bytes of RAM.

Inserting the optional iSBC 341 MULTIMODULE EPROM expansion board onto the iSBC 88/45 ADCP board provides four additional 28-pin JEDEC sites. This expansion doubles the available program storage or extends the RAM capability by 32K bytes.

iSBX™ MULTIMODULE™ Expansion

Two 8-bit iSBX MULTIMODULE connectors are provided on the iSBC 88/45 microcomputer. Through these connectors, additional iSBX functions extend the I/O capability of the microcomputer. The iSBX connectors provide the necessary signals to interface to the local bus.

In addition to specialized or custom designed iSBX boards, the customer has a broad range of Intel iSBC MULTIMODULEs available, including parallel I/O, analog I/O, IEEE 488 GPIB, floppy disk, magnetic bubbles, video, and serial I/O boards.

The serial I/O MULTIMODULE boards include the iSBX 351 (one ASYNC/SYNC serial channel) the iSBX 352 (one HDLC/SDLC serial channel) and the iSBX 354 (two SYNC/ASYNC, HDLC/SDLC serial channels) boards. Adding two iSBX 352 MULTIMODULE boards to the iSBC 88/45 ADCP provides a total of five HDLC/SDLC channels.

MULTIBUS® Multimaster Capabilities

OVERVIEW

The MULTIBUS system is Intel's industry standard microcomputer bus structure. Both 8- and 16-bit single board computers are supported on the MULTIBUS structure with 24 address and 16 data lines. In addition to expanding functions contained on a single board computer (e.g., memory and digital I/O), the MULTIBUS structure allows very powerful distributed processing configurations with multiple processors, intelligent slaves, and peripheral boards.

Multimaster Capability

The iSBC 88/45 ADCP board provides full MULTIBUS arbitration control logic. This control

Table 4. Interrupt Request Sources

Device	Function	No. of Interrupts
MULTIBUS* Interface	Select 1 interrupt from MULTIBUS* resident peripherals or other CPU boards	8
8273 HDLC/SDLC Controller	Transmit buffer empty and receive buffer full	2
8274 HDLC/SDLC SYNC/ASYNC Controller	Software examines register for status of communication operation	1
8254-Timer	Counter 2 of both PIT devices	2
iSBX™ Connectors	Function determined by iSBX™ MULTIMODULE™ Board (2 interrupts per socket)	4
Bus Fail Safe Timer	Indicates MULTIBUS* addressed device has not responded to command within 4 msec	1
Power Line Clock	Source of 60 MHz signal from power supply	1
Bus Flag Interrupt	Flag interrupt in byte location 1000H signals board reset or data handling request	2
iSBC* 337 Board	Numeric Data Processor generated status information	1
8237A-5	Signals end of 8237 DMA operation	1

iSBC® 88/45

logic allows up to three iSBC 88/45 ADCP boards or other bus masters, including iSBC 286, iSBC 86 and iSBC 86 family boards to share the system bus using a serial (daisy chain) priority scheme. By using an external parallel priority decoder, the MULTIBUS system bus could be shared among sixteen masters.

The Intel standard MULTIBUS Interprocessor Protocol (MIP) software, implemented as the Intel iMMX 800 package for iRMX 86 and iRMX 88 Real-Time Executives, fully supports multiple 8-and 16-bit distributed processor functions. The software manages the message passing protocol between microprocessors.

System Development Capabilities

The application development cycle for an iSBC 88/45 ADCP board is reduced and simplified through the usage of several Intel tools. The tools include the Intellec Series Microcomputer Development System, the ICE-88 In-Circuit Emulator, the iSDM 86 debug monitor software, and the iRMX 86 and iRMX 88 run-time support packages.

The Intellec Series Microcomputer Development System offers a complete development environment for the iSBC 88/45 software. In addition to the operating system, assembler, utilities and application debugger features provided with the system, the user optionally can utilize higher-level languages like PL/M, PASCAL, and FORTRAN.

The ICE-88 In-Circuit Emulator provides a link between the Intellec system and the target iSBC 88/45-based system for code loading and execution. The ICE-88 package assists the developer with the debugging and system integrating processes.

Run-Time Building Blocks

Intel offers run-time foundation software to support applications which range from general purpose to high-performance solutions. The iRMX 88 Real-time Multitasking Executive provides a multi-tasking structure which includes task scheduling, task management, intertask communications, and interrupt servicing for high-performance applications. The highly configurable modules make the system tailoring job easier whether one uses the compact executive or the complete executive with its variety of peripheral devices supported.

The iRMX 86 Operating System provides a very rich set of features and options to support sophisticated applications solutions. In addition to supporting real-time requirements, the iRMX 86 Operating System has a powerful, but easy-to-use human interface. When added to the sophisticated I/O system, the iRMX 86 Operating System is readily extended to support assembler, PL/M, PASCAL, and FORTRAN software development environments. The modular building block software lends itself well to customized application solutions.

SPECIFICATIONS

Word Size

Instruction — 8, 16, 24, or 32 bits
Data — 8 or 16 bits

System Clock

8 MHz — ±0.1%
NOTE: Jumper selectable for 4 MHz operation with iSBC 337 Numeric Data Processor module or ICE-88 product.

Cycle Time

Basic Instruction Cycle at 8.00 MHz — 1.25 μsec, 250 nsec (assumes instruction in the queue)
NOTE: Basic instruction cycle is defined as the fastest instruction time (i.e., two clock cycles).

Memory Cycle Time

RAM — 500 nsec (no wait states)
EPROM — jumper selectable from 500 nsec to 625 nsec.

On-Board RAM* —

K Bytes	Hex Address Range
16 (total)	0000-3FFF
12 (dual-ported)	1000-3FFF

* Four iSBC 88/45 EPROM sockets support JEDEC 24/28-pin standard EPROMs and RAMs (3 sockets); iSBC 341 (4 sockets)

Environmental Characteristics

Temperature — 0-55°C, free moving air across the base board and MULTIMODULE board
Humidity — 90%, non-condensing

Physical Characteristics

Width	— 30.48 cm (12.00 in)
Length	— 17.15 cm (6.75 in)
Height	— 1.50 cm (0.59 in)
Weight	— 6.20 gm (22 oz)

iSBC® 88/45

Memory Capacity/Addressing

On-Board EPROM* —

Device	Total K Bytes	Hex Address Range
2716	8	FE000-FFFFF
2732A	16	FC000-FFFFF
2764	32	F8000-FFFFF
27128	64	F0000-FFFFF

With optional iSBC® 341 MULTIMODULE™ EPROM —

Device	Total K Bytes	Hex Address Range
2716	16	FC000-FFFFF
2732A	32	F8000-FFFFF
2764	64	F0000-FFFFF
27128	128	E0000-FFFFF

* Four iSBC 88/45 EPROM sockets support JEDEC 24/28-pin standard EPROMs and RAMs (static and iRAM, 3 sockets); iSBC 341 sockets also support EPROMs and RAMs.

Timer Input Frequency — 8.00 MHz ± 0.1%

Interfaces

iSBX™ Bus — All signals TTL compatible

Serial RS232C Signals —

CTS	CLEAR TO SEND
DSR	DATA SET READY
DTE TXC	TRANSMIT CLOCK
DTR	DATA TERMINAL READY
FG	FRAME GROUND
RTS	REQUEST TO SEND
RXC	RECEIVE CLOCK
RXD	RECEIVE DATA
SG	SIGNAL GROUND
TXD	TRANSMIT DATA

Serial RS422A/449 Signals —

CS	CLEAR TO SEND
DM	DATA MODE
RC	RECEIVE COMMON
RD	RECEIVE DATA
RS	REQUEST TO SEND
RT	RECEIVE TIMING
SC	SEND COMMON
SD	SEND DATA
SG	SIGNAL GROUND
TR	TERMINAL READY
TT	TERMINAL TIMING

Electrical Characteristics

DC Power Dissipation — 28.3 Watts

DC Power Requirements —

Configuration	Current Requirements (all voltages ±5%)		
	+5V	+12V	-12V
without EPROM[1]	5.1A	20 mA	20 mA
with 8K EPROM (using 2716)	+0.14A	—	—
with 16K EPROM (using 2732A)	+0.20A	—	—
with 32K EPROM (using 2764)	+0.24A	—	—
with 64K EPROM (using 27128)	+0.24A	—	—

NOTE 1: AS SHIPPED - no EPROMs in sockets, no iSBC 341 module. Configuration includes terminators for two RS422A/449 and one RS232C channels.

Serial Communication Characteristics

Channel	Device	Supported Interface	Max. Baud Rate
A	8274[1]	RS442A/449 RS232C CCITT V.24	800K SDLC/HDLC 125K Synchronous 50K Asynchronous
B	8274	RS232C CCITT V.24	125K Synchronous[2] 50K Asynchronous
C	8273[3]	RS442A/449 RS232C CCITT V.24	64K SDLC/HDLC[3] 9.6K SELF CLOCKING

NOTES:
1. 8274 supports HDLC/SDLC/SYNC/ASYNC multiprotocol
2. Exceed RS232C/CCITT V.24 rating of 20K baud
3. 8273 supports HDLC/SDLC

BAUD RATE EXAMPLES (Hz)

8254 Timer Divide Count N	Synchronous K Baud	Asynchronous ÷16 ÷32 ÷64 K Baud		
10	800	50.0	25.0	12.5
26	300	19.2	9.6	4.8
31	256	16.1	8.06	4.03
52	154	9.6	4.8	2.4
104	76.8	4.8	2.4	1.2
125	64	4.0	2.0	1.0
143	56	3.5	1.7	.87
167	48	3.0	1.5	.75
417	19.2	—	—	—
833	9.6	—	—	—
EQUATION	$\dfrac{8{,}000{,}000}{N}$	$\dfrac{500K}{N}$	$\dfrac{250K}{N}$	$\dfrac{125K}{N}$

iSBC® 88/45

SERIAL INTERFACE CONNECTORS

Interface	Mode[1]	MULTIMODULE™ Edge Connector	Cable	Connector
RS232C	DTE	26-pin[4], 3M-3462-0001	3M[2]-3349/25	25-pin[6], 3M-3482-1000
RS232C	DCE	26-pin[4], 3M-3462-0001	3M[2]-3349/25	25-pin[6], 3M-3483-1000
RS449	DTE	40-pin[5], 3M-3464-0001	3M[3]-3349/37	37-pin[7], 3M-3502-1000
RS449	DCE	40-pin[5], 3M-3464-0001	3M[3]-3349/37	37-pin[7], 3M-3503-1000

NOTES:
1. DTE — Data Terminal Equipment mode (male connector); DCE — Data Circuit Equipment mode (female connector) requires line swaps.
2. Cable is tapered at one end to fit the 3M-3462 connector.
3. Cable is tapered to fit 3M-3464 connector.
4. Pin 26 of the edge connector is not connected to the flat cable.
5. Pins 38, 39, and 40 of the edge connector are not connected to the flat cable.
6. May be used with the cable housing 3M-3485-1000.
7. Cable housing 3M-3485-4000 may be used with the connector.

Line Drivers (supplied)

Device	Characteristic	Qty	Installed
1488	RS232C	3	1
1489	RS232C	3	1
3486	RS422A	2	2
3487	RS422A	2	2

Reference Manual

143824 — iSBC 88/45 Advanced Data Communications Processor Board Hardware Reference Manual (not supplied).

Reference manuals may be ordered from any Intel sales representative, distributor office or from Intel Literature Department, 3065 Bowers Avenue, Santa Clara, CA 95051

ORDERING INFORMATION

Part Number   Description

SBC 88/45   8-bit 8088-based Single Board Computer with 3 HDLC/SDLC serial channels

iSBC® 186/51
COMMUNICATING COMPUTER
MEMBER OF THE OpenNET™ PRODUCT FAMILY

- 6 MHz iAPX 186 Microprocessor
- 128K Bytes of dual-ported RAM expandable on-board to 256K Bytes
- 82586 Local Area Network Coprocessor for CSMA/CD applications and 82501 Ethernet serial interface for Ethernet/IEEE 802.3 specifications
- Two serial interfaces, RS-232C and RS-422A/RS-449 compatible
- Sockets for up to 192K Bytes of JEDEC 28 pin standard memory devices
- Supports transport layer software (iNA 960) and higher layer communications software (such as RMX-NET)
- Two iSBX™ bus connectors
- 16M Bytes address range of MULTIBUS®
- MULTIBUS® interface for multimaster configurations and system expansion
- Supported by a complete family of single board computers, peripheral controllers, digital & analog I/O, memory, packaging and software

The iSBC® 186/51 COMMUNICATING COMPUTER, THE COMMputer™, is a member of Intel's OpenNET family of products, and supports Intel's network software. The COMMputer utilizes Intel's VLSI technology to provide an economical self-contained computer for applications in processing and local area network control. The combination of the iAPX 186 Central Processing Unit and the 82586 Local Area Network Coprocessor/82501 Ethernet Serial Interface makes it ideal for applications which require both communication and processing capabilities such as networked workstations, factory automation, office automation, communications servers, and many others. The CPU, Ethernet interface, serial communications interface, 128K Bytes of RAM, up to 192K Bytes of ROM, I/O ports and drivers and the MULTIBUS interface all reside on a single 6.75"x12.00" printed circuit board.

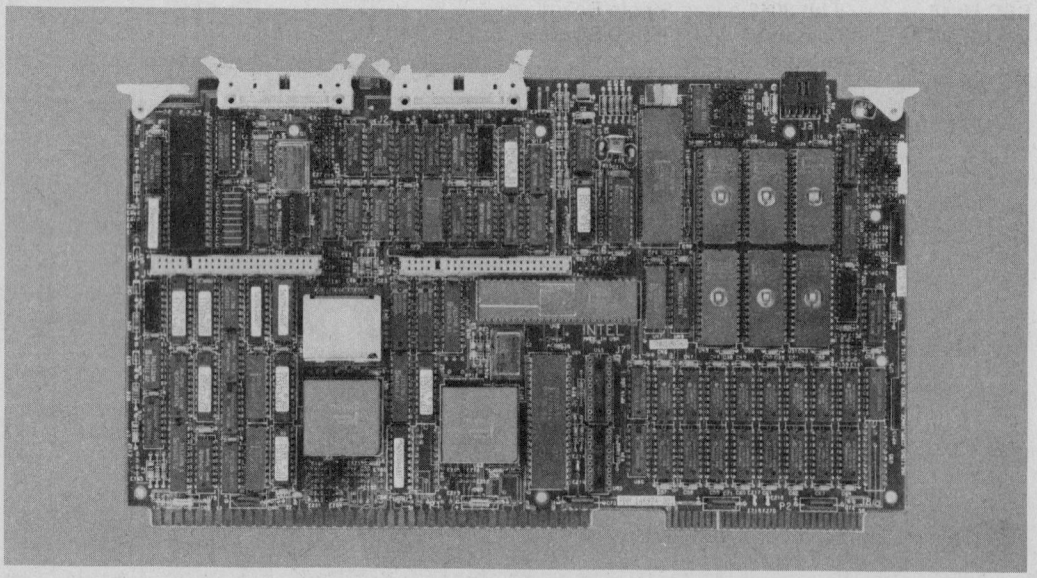

Intel Corporation Assumes No Responsibility for the Use of Any Circuitry Other Than Circuitry Embodied in an Intel Product. No Other Circuit Patent Licenses are Implied. Information Contained Herein Supercedes Previously Published Specifications On These Devices From Intel.

© INTEL CORPORATION 1985

iSBC® 186/51 COMMUNICATING COMPUTER

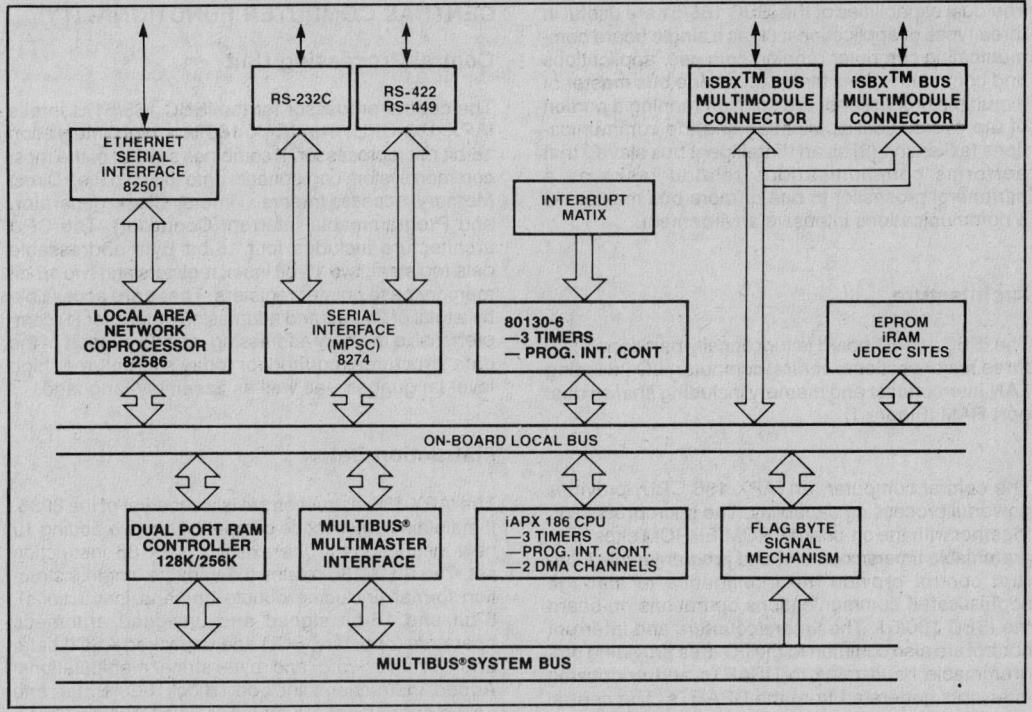

Figure 1. iSBC® 186/51 Block Diagram

FUNCTIONAL DESCRIPTION

Communicating Computer

Intel's OpenNET strategy provides the user with building blocks to implement all seven layers of the International Standards Organization's (ISO) Open Systems Interconnect (OSI) model (see figure 2.) The iSBC 186/51 is a part of the OpenNET product family. The iSBC 186/51 can host iNA 960 transport layer software to provide ISO 8073 class 4 standard protocol on IEEE 802.3 LAN. In conjunction with the transport file access software, RMX-NET, the iSBC 186/51 and iNA 960 provide a complete seven layer communications solution.

The iSBC 186/51 board integrates a programmable processor and communications capability onto one board, serving both computational and networking capacities as dictated by the application. The communications coprocessor (82586) aids in this task by accomplishing as much of the communications task as possible before the processor intervenes (thus reducing the overhead load of the 80186 processor).

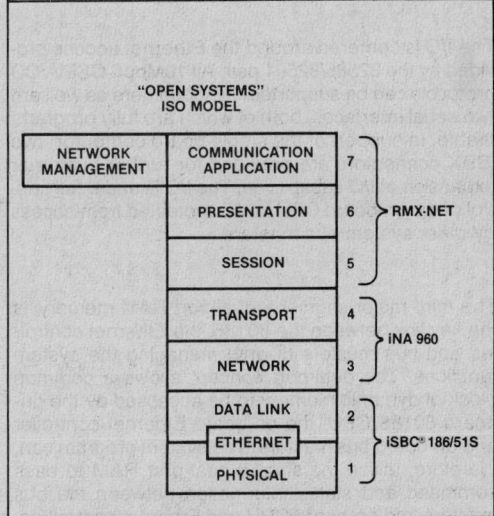

Figure 2. iSBC® 186/51 Implementation of ISO Standard Model

8-13

iSBC® 186/51 COMMUNICATING COMPUTER

The dual capabilities of the iSBC 186/51 are useful in three types of applications: (1) as a single board communicating computer running both user applications and communications tasks; (2) as one bus master of a multiple processor board solution running a portion of the overall user application and the communications tasks; and (3) as an "intelligent bus slave" that performs communications related tasks as a peripheral processor to one or more bus masters in a communications intensive environment.

Architecture

The iSBC 186/51 board is functionally partitioned into three major sections: central computer, I/O including LAN interconnect and memory including shared dual port RAM (Figure 1).

The central computer, an iAPX 186 CPU, provides powerful processing capability. The microprocessor, together with the on-board PROM/EPROM sites, programmable timers/counters, and programmable interrupt control provide the intelligence to manage sophisticated communications operations on-board the iSBC 186/51. The timers/counters and interrupt control are also common to the I/O area providing programmable baud rates to USARTs and prioritizing interrupts generated from the USARTs. The central computer functions are protected for access by the on-board 80186 only.

The I/O is centered around the Ethernet access provided by the 82586/82501 pair. All 10MbpS CSMA/CD protocols can be supported. Included here as well are two serial interfaces, both of which are fully programmable. In support of the single board computer, two iSBX connectors are provided for further customer expansion of I/O capabilities. The I/O is under full control of the on-board CPU and is protected from access by other system bus masters.

The third major segment, dual-port RAM memory, is the key link between the 80186, the Ethernet controller, and bus masters (if any) managing the system functions. The dual-port concept allows a common block of dynamic memory to be accessed by the on-board 80186 CPU, the on-board Ethernet controller and off-board bus masters. The system program can, therefore, utilize the shared dual-port RAM to pass command and status information between the bus masters and on-board CPU and Ethernet controllers. In addition, the dual-port concept permits blocks of data transmitted or received to accumulate in the on-board shared RAM, minimizing the need for a dedicated memory board.

CENTRAL COMPUTER FUNCTIONALITY

Central Processing Unit

The central processor for the iSBC 186/51 is Intel's iAPX 186 CPU. The iAPX 186 is a high integration 16-bit microprocessor. It combines several of the most common system components onto the chip (i.e., Direct Memory Access, Interval Timers, Clock generator, and Programmable Interrupt Controller). The CPU architecture includes four 16-bit Byte addressable data registers, two 16-bit index registers and two 16-bit memory base pointer registers. These are accessible by a total of 24 operand addressing modes for (1) comprehensive memory addressing, and (2) support of the data structures required for today's structured, high level languages—as well as assembly language.

Instruction Set

The iAPX 186 instruction set is a superset of the 8086. It maintains object code compatibility while adding 10 new instructions to the existing iAPX 86 instruction set. The iAPX 186 retains the variable length instruction format (including double operand instructions), 8-bit and 16-bit signed and unsigned arithmetic operators for binary, BCD and unpacked ASCII data, and iterative word and byte string manipulations. Added instructions include: Block I/O, Enter and Leave subroutines, Push Immediate, Multiply Quick, Array Bounds Checking, Shift and Rotate by Immediate, and Pop and Push All.

Architectural Features

A six-byte instruction queue provides prefetching of sequential instructions and can reduce the 1000 nsec minimum instruction cycle to 333 nsec for queued instructions. The stack oriented architecture readily supports modular programming by facilitating fast, simple intermodule communication, and other programming constructs needed for asynchronous real-time systems. Using a windowing technique and external logic, the full 16M Bytes addressing range of the IEEE-796 MULTIBUS Standard is available to the user. The dynamic relocation scheme allows ease in segmentation of pure procedure and data for efficient memory utilization. Four segment registers (code, stack, data, extra) contain program loaded offset values which are used to map 16-bit addresses to 20-bit addresses. Each register maps 64K Bytes at a time and activation of a specific register is controlled both explicitly by program control, and implicitly by specific functions and instructions. A flag byte signaling mechanism aids in creating an interprocessor communication scheme. This includes (1) the ability to set/reset interrupts with MULTIBUS commands and (2) board reset.

Programmable Timers

The 80186 provides three internal 16-bit programmable timers. Two of these are highly flexible and are connected to four external pins (two per timer). They can be used to count external events, time external events, generate nonrepetitive waveforms, etc. The third timer is not connected to any external pins, and is useful for real-time coding and time delay applications. In addition, this third timer can be used as a prescaler to the other two, or as a DMA request source. The factory default configuration for timer 0 is baud rate generator.

The 80130-6 provides three more programmable timers. One is a factory default baud rate generator and outputs an 8254 compatible square wave to the RS232 Channel B. The other two timers are assigned to the use of the Operating System and should not be altered by the user.

The system software configures each timer independently to select the desired function. Examples of available functions are shown in Table 3. The contents of each counter may be read at any time during system operation.

Table 3. 80186 Programmable Timer Functions

Function	Operation
Interrupt on terminal count	When terminal count is reached, an interrupt request is generated. This function is extremely useful for generation of real-time clocks.
Programmable one-shot	Output goes low upon receipt of an external trigger edge or software command and returns high when terminal count is reached. This function is retriggerable.
Rate generator	Divide by N counter. The output will go low for one input clock cycle, and the period from one low going pulse to the next is N times the input clock period.
Square-wave rate generator	Output will remain high until 1/2 the count has been completed, and go low for the other half of the count.
Software triggered strobe	Output remains high until software loads count (N). N periods after count is loaded, output goes low for one input clock period.
Hardware triggered strobe	Output goes low for one clock period N counts after rising edge counter trigger input. The counter is retriggerable.
Event counter	On a jumper selectable basis, the clock input becomes an input from the external system. CPU may read the number of events occurring after the counter "window" has been enabled or an interrupt may be generated after N events occur in the system.

iSBC® 186/51 COMMUNICATING COMPUTER

Interrupt Capability

The iSBC 186/51 has two programmable interrupt controllers (PICs): one in the 80186 component and one in the 80130-6 component. In the iRMX mode, the 80186 interrupt controller acts as a slave to the 80130-6. The 80186 interrupt controller in this mode uses all of its external interrupt pins. It therefore services only internally generated interrupts (i.e., three timers, two DMA channels). The 80130-6 interrupt controller operates in the master mode and has eight prioritized inputs that can be programmed either edge or level sensitive.

The iSBC 186/51 board provides 9 vectored interrupt levels. The highest level is the NMI (Non-Maskable Interrupt) line which is directly tied to the 80186 CPU. This interrupt is typically used for signaling catastrophic events (e.g., power failure). The Programmable Interrupt Controllers (PIC) provide control and vectoring for the next eight interrupt levels. As shown in Table 4, a selection of four priority processing modes is available for use in designing request processing configurations to match system requirements for efficient interrupt servicing with minimal latencies. Operating modes and priority assignments may be reconfigured dynamically via software at any time during system operation. The PIC accepts interrupt requests from all on-board I/O resources and from the MULTIBUS system bus. The PIC then resolves requests according to the selected mode and, if appropriate, issues an interrupt to the CPU.

Table 4. iSBC® 186/51 Programmable Interrupt Modes

Mode	Operation
Fully nested	Interrupt request line priorities fixed at 0 as highest, 7 as lowest.
Special fully nested	Allows multiple interrupts from slave PICs to the master PIC. Used in the case of cascading where the priority has to be conserved within each slave.
Specific priority	System software assigns lowest priority level. Priority of all other levels based in sequence numerically on this assignment.
Polled	System software examines priority-encoded system interrupt status via interrupt status register.

iSBC® 186/51 COMMUNICATING COMPUTER

Interrupt Request Generation

iSBC 186/51 Interrupt Service requests may originate from 25 sources. Table 5 contains a list of devices and functions supported by interrupts. All interrupts are jumper configurable with either suitcase or wire wrap to the desired interrupt request level.

I/O FUNCTIONALITY

Local Area Network Coprocessor

The 82586 is a local communications controller designed to relieve the iAPX 186 of many of the tasks associated with controlling a local network. The 82586 provides most of the functions normally associated with the data link and physical link layers of a local network architecture. In particular, it performs framing (frame boundary delineation, addressing, and bit error detection), link management, and data modulation. It also supports a network management interface.

The iAPX 186 and the 82586 communicate entirely through a shared memory space. To the user, the 82586 appears as two independent but communicating units: the Command Unit (CU) and the Receive Unit (RU). The CU executes the commands given by

Table 5. Interrupt Request Sources

Device	Function	Number of Interrupts
MULTIBUS® interface	Requests from MULTIBUS® resident peripherals or other CPU	2
8274	Transmit buffer empty, receive buffer full and channel errors	8
Internal 80186 PIC	Timer 0, 1, 2 outputs (function determined by timer mode) and 2 DMA channel interrupts	5
82586	Communications processor needs attention	1
Flag byte interrupt	Flag byte interrupt set by MULTIBUS master	1
Systick	80130-6, RMX system timer	1
Edge to level trigger	Converts EDGE interrupts to level interrupts	1
iSBX™ connectors MULTIMODULE™	Function determined by iSBX™	4 (2 per iSBX™ connector)
Bus fail safe timer	Indicates addressed MULTIBUS® resident device has not responded to command within 6 msec	1
OR-gate matrix	Outputs of OR-gates on-board for multiple interrupts	1

iSBC® 186/51 COMMUNICATING COMPUTER

the 80186 to the 82586. The RU handles all activities related to packet reception, address recognition, CRC checking, etc. The two are controlled and monitored by the CPU via a shared memory structure called the System Control Block (SCB). Commands for the CU and RU are placed into the SCB by the host processor. Status information is placed into the SCB by the CU and RU (via the CU). The Channel Attention and Interrupt lines are used by the CPU and the 82586 to get the other to look into the SCB. See Figure 3.

The 82586 features a high level diagnostic or maintenance capability. It automatically gathers statistics on CRC errors, frame alignment errors, overrun errors, and frames lost due to lack of reception resources. In addition, the user can output the status of all internal registers to facilitate system design.

Upon initialization, the 82586 obtains the address of its System Control Block through the Initialization Root which begins at location 0FFFFF6H. See Figure

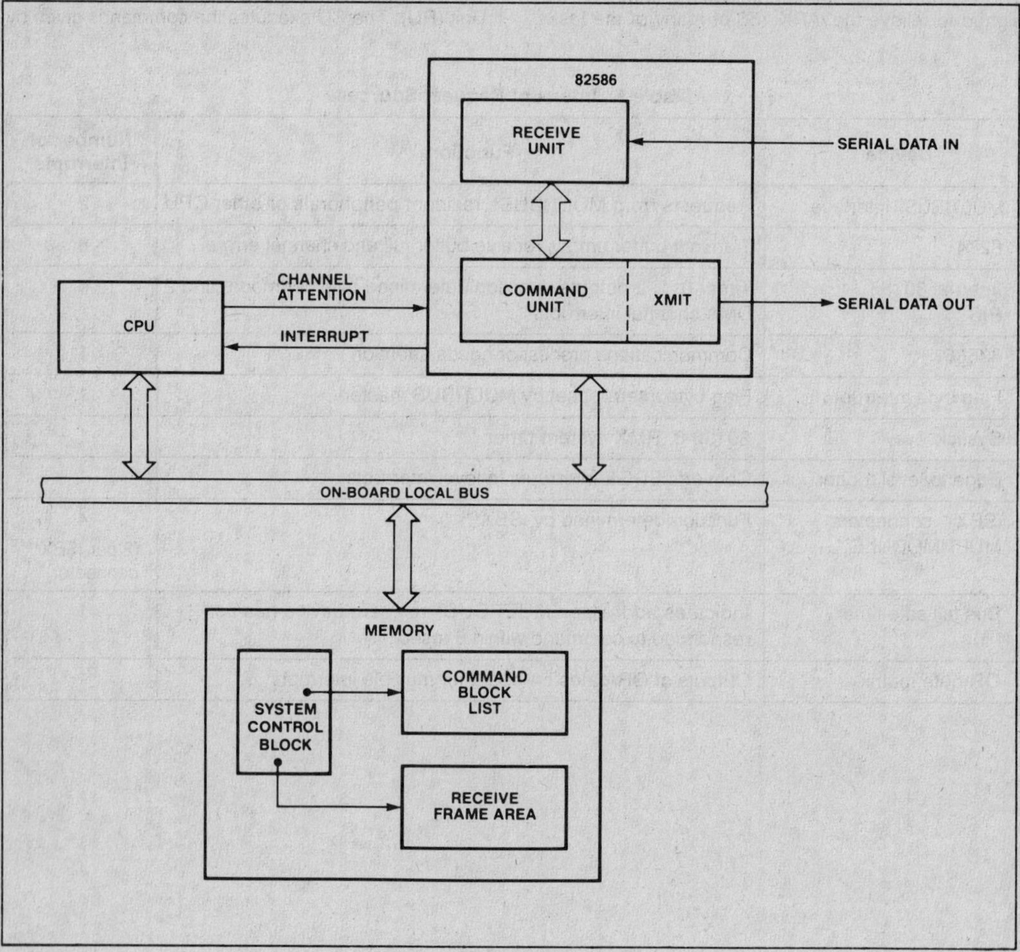

Figure 3. System Overview

8-18

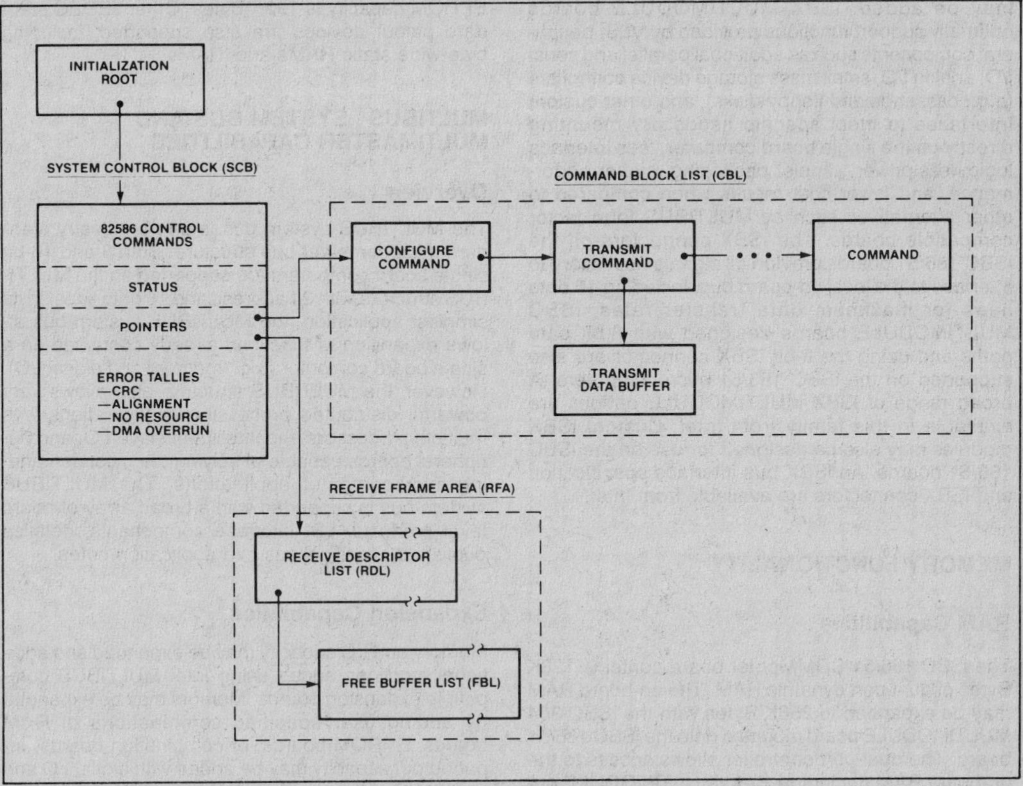

iSBC® 186/51 COMMUNICATING COMPUTER

Figure 4. 82586 Memory Structures

4. The SCB contains control commands, status register, pointers to the Command Block List (CBL) and Receive Frame Area (RFA), and tallies for CRC, Alignment, DMA Overrun and No Resource errors. Through the SCB, the 82586 is able to provide status and error counts for the iAPX 86, execute "programs" contained in the CBL and receive incoming frames in the Receive Frame Area (RFA).

Serial I/O

Two programmable communications interfaces using the Intel 8274 Multi-Protocol Serial Controller (MPSC) are contained on the iSBC 186/51. Two independent software selectable BAUD rate generators provide the channels with all the common communications frequencies. The mode of operation (for example, Asynchronous, Byte Synchronous or Bisynchronous protocols), data format, control character format, parity, and baud rate are all under program control. The 8274 provides full duplex, double buffered transmit and receive capability. Parity, overrun, and framing error detection are all incorporated in the MSPC. The iSBC 186/51 supports operation in the polled, interrupt and DMA driven interfaces through jumper options. The board is delivered previously configured with channel A in RS-422/RS-449. Channel B in RS-232C. Channel A may be configured to support RS-232C.

iSBX™ MULTIMODULE™ On-Board Expansion

Two 8/16-bit iSBX MULTIMODULE connectors are provided in the iSBC 186/51 microcomputer. Through these connectors, additional on-board I/O functions

iSBC® 186/51 COMMUNICATING COMPUTER

may be added. iSBX MULTIMODULE boards optimally support functions provided by VLSI peripheral components such as additional parallel and serial I/O, analog I/O, small mass storage device controllers (e.g., cassettes and floppy disks), and other custom interfaces to meet specific needs. By mounting directly on the single board computer, less interface logic, less power, simpler packaging, higher performance, and lower cost results when compared to other alternatives such as MULTIBUS form factor compatible boards. The iSBX connectors on the iSBC 186/51 boards provide all signals necessary to interface to the local on-board bus, including 16 data lines for maximum data transfer rates. iSBC MULTIMODULE boards designed with 8-bit data paths and using the 8-bit iSBX connector are also supported on the iSBC 186/51 microcomputers. A broad range of iSBX MULTIMODULE options are available in this family from Intel. Custom iSBX modules may also be designed for use on the iSBC 186/51 boards. An iSBX bus interface specification and iSBX connectors are available from Intel.

MEMORY FUNCTIONALITY

RAM Capabilities

The iSBC 186/51 COMMputer board contains 128K Bytes of dual-port dynamic RAM. The on-board RAM may be expanded to 256K Bytes with the iSBC 304 MULTIMODULE board mounted onto the iSBC 186/51 board. The dual-port controller allows access to the on-board RAM (including RAM MULTIMODULE options) from the iSBC 186/51 board and from any other MULTIBUS master via the system bus. Segments of on-board RAM may be configured as a private resource, protected from MULTIBUS system access. The amount of memory allocated as a private resource may be configured in increments of 25% of the total on-board memory ranging from 0% to 100% (optional RAM MULTIMODULE board doubles the increment size). These features allow the multiprocessor systems to establish local memory for each processor and shared system memory configurations where the total system memory size (including local on-board memory) can exceed one megabyte without addressing conflicts.

Universal Memory Sites for Local Memory

Six 28-pin sockets are provided for the use of Intel's 2732, 2764, 27128, 27256 EPROMs and their respective ROMs. When using the 27256s, the on-board EPROM capacity is 192K Bytes. Other JEDEC standard pinout devices are also supported, including byte-wide static RAMs and iRAMs.

MULTIBUS® SYSTEM BUS AND MULTIMASTER CAPABILITIES

Overview

The MULTIBUS system bus is Intel's industry standard microcomputer bus structure. Both 8 and 16-bit single board computers are supported on the MULTIBUS structure with 24 address and 16 data lines. In its simplest application, the MULTIBUS system bus allows expansion of functions already contained on a single board computer (e.g., memory and digital I/O). However, the MULTIBUS structure also allows very powerful distributed processing configurations with multiple processors and intelligent slave I/O, and peripheral boards capable of solving the most demanding microcomputer applications. The MULTIBUS system bus is supported with a broad array of board level products, LSI interface components, detailed published specifications and application notes.

Expansion Capabilities

Memory and I/O capacity may be expanded and additional functions added using Intel MULTIBUS compatible expansion boards. Memory may be expanded by adding user specified combinations of RAM boards, EPROM boards, or combination boards. Input/output capacity may be added with digital I/O and analog I/O expansion boards. Mass storage capability may be achieved by adding single or double density diskette controllers, or hard disk controllers. Modular expandable backplanes and cardcages are available to support multiboard systems.

Multimaster Capabilities

For those applications requiring additional processing capacity and the benefits of multiprocessing (i.e., several CPU's and/or controllers logically sharing system tasks through communication of the system bus), the iSBC 186/51 boards provide full MULTIBUS arbitration control logic. This control logic allows up to three iSBC 186/51 boards or other bus master, including iSBC 80 family MULTIBUS compatible 8-bit single board computers to share the system bus using a serial (daisy chain) priority scheme. This allows up to 16 masters to share the MULTIBUS system bus with an external parallel priority decoder. In addition to the multiprocessing configurations made possible with

iSBC® 186/51 COMMUNICATING COMPUTER

multimaster capability, it also provides a very efficient mechanism for all forms of DMA (Direct Memory Access) transfers.

MISCELLANEOUS FUNCTIONALITY

Power-Fail Control and Auxiliary Power

An active-low TTL compatible memory protect signal is brought out on the auxiliary connector which, when asserted, disables read/write access to RAM memory on the board. This input is provided for the protection of RAM contents during system power-down sequences. An auxiliary power bus is also provided to allow separate power to RAM for systems requiring battery back-up of read/write memory. Selection of this auxiliary RAM power bus is made via jumpers on the board.

System Development Capabilities

The development cycle of iSBC 186/51 products can be significantly reduced and simplified by using either the System 86/3XX or the Intellec Series Microcomputer Development Systems. The Assembler, Locating Linker, Library Manager, Text Editor and System Monitor are all supported by the ISIS-II disk-based operating system. To facilitate conversion of the 8080A/8085A assembly language programs to run on the iSBC 186/51 boards, CONV-86 is available under the ISIS-II operating system.

In-Circuit Emulator

The Integrated Instrumentation In-Circuit Emulator (I^2ICE) provides the necessary link between the software development environment provided by the Intellec system and the "target" iSBC 186/51 execution system. In addition to providing the mechanism for loading executable code and data into the iSBC 186/51 boards, the I^2ICE-186 provides a sophisticated command set to assist in debugging software and final integration of the user hardware and software.

PL/M-86 and C-86

Intel has two systems implementation languages, PL/M-86 and C-86. Both are standard in the System 86/3XX and are also available as Intellec Microcomputer Development System options. PL/M-86 provides the capability to program in algorithmic language and eliminates the need to manage register usage or allocate memory while still allowing explicit control of the system's resources when needed. C-86 is especially appropriate in applications requiring portability and code density. FORTRAN 86 and PASCAL 86 are also available on Intellec or 86/3XX systems.

Run-Time Support

Intel also offers two run-time support packages: iRMX 88 Realtime Multitasking Executive and the iRMX 86 Operating System. The iRMX 88 executive is a simple, highly configurable and efficient foundation for small, high performance applications. Its multitasking structure establishes a solid foundation for modular system design and provides task scheduling and management, intertask communication and synchronization, and interrupt servicing for a variety of peripheral devices. Other configurable options include terminal handlers, disk file system, debuggers and other utilities. The iRMX 86 Operating System is a highly functional operating system with a very rich set of features and options based on an object-oriented architecture. In addition to being modular and configurable, functions beyond the nucleus include a sophisticated file management and I/O system, and a powerful human interface. Both packages are easily customized and extended by the user to match unique requirements.

iSBC® 186/51 COMMUNICATING COMPUTER

SPECIFICATIONS

Word Size
Instruction—8, 16, 24, or 32 bits
Data—8, 16 bits

System Clock
6.00 MHz ± 0.1%

Cycle Time
Basic Instruction Cycle
6 MHz—1000ns
333ns (assumes instruction in the queue)

Note: Basic instruction cycle is defined as the fastest instruction time (i.e., two clock cycles).

Memory Capacity/Addressing
Six Universal Memory Sites support JEDEC 24/28 pin EPROM, PROM, iRAM and static RAM.

Example for EPROM:

Device	Total Capacity	Address Range
2732	24K Bytes	F8000-FFFFF$_H$
2764	48K Bytes	F0000-FFFFF$_H$
27128	96K Bytes	E0000-FFFFF$_H$
27256	192K Bytes	C0000-FFFFF$_H$

On-Board RAM

Board	Total Capacity	Address Range
iSBC 186/51	128K Bytes	0-1FFFF$_H$

With MULTIMODULE™ RAM

Board	Total Capacity	Address Range
iSBC 304	256K Bytes	0-3FFFF$_H$

I/O Capacity
Serial—two programmable channels using one 8274
iSBX™ Multimodule™—two 8/16-bit iSBX™ connectors allow use of up to 2 single-wide modules or 1 single-wide module and 1 double-wide iSBX module.

Serial Communications Characteristics
Synchronous —5-8 bit characters; internal or external character synchronization; automatic sync insertion
Asynchronous —5-8 bit characters; break character generation; 1, 1/2, or 2 stop bits; false start bit detection

Baud Rates

Frequency (KHz) (S/W Selectable)	Baud Rate (Hz)		
	Synchronous	Asynchronous	
	÷1	÷16	÷64
153.6	—	9600	2400
76.8	—	4800	1200
38.4	38,400	2400	600
19.2	19,200	1200	300
9.6	9,600	600	150
4.8	4,800	300	75
2.4	2,400	150	—
1.76	1,760	110	2400

NOTE:
Frequency selected by I/O write of appropriate 16-bit frequency factor to baud rate register (80186 timer 0 & 80130 baud timer).

Timers

Input Frequencies
Reference 1.5 MHz ± 0.1% (.5μSec period nominal)
Event Rate: 1.5 MHz max.

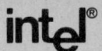

iSBC® 186/51 COMMUNICATING COMPUTER

80186 Output Frequencies/Timing Intervals

Function	Single Timer/Counter		Dual (Cascaded) Timer/Counter	
	Min	Max	Min	Max
Real-time Interrupt	667ns	43.69ms	667ns	47.72 minutes
Programmable one-shot	1000ns	43.69ms	1000ns	47.72 minutes
Rate generator	22.889 Hz	1.5 MHz	.0003492 Hz	1.5 MHz
Square-wave rate generator	22.889 Hz	1.5 MHz	.0003492 Hz	1.5 MHz
Software triggered strobe	1000ns	43.69ms	1000ns	47.72 minutes
Event counter	—	1.5 MHz	—	—

Interfaces
Ethernet—IEEE 802.3 compatible
MULTIBUS® —IEEE 796 compatible
MULTIBUS® —Master D16 M24 I16 V0 EL

Compliance
iSBX™ Bus—IEEE P959 compatible
Serial I/O—RS-232C compatible, configurable as a data set or data terminal, RS-422A/RS-449

Connectors

Interface	Double-Sided Pins	Centers (in.)	Mating Connectors
Ethernet	10	0.1	AMP87531-5
MULTIBUS® SYSTEM	86 (P1)	0.156	Viking 3KH43/9AMK12 Wire Wrap
	60 (P2)	0.1	Viking 3KH30/9JNK
iSBX™ Bus 8-Bit Data	36	0.1	iSBX™ 960-5
16-Bit Data	44	0.1	iSBX™ 960-5
Serial I/O	26	0.1	3M 3452-0001 Flat or AMP88106-1 Flat

iSBC® 186/51 COMMUNICATING COMPUTER

Physical Characteristics

Width—12.00 in. (30.48 cm)
Height—6.75 in. (17.15 cm)
Depth—0.70 in. (1.78 cm)
Weight—18.7 ounces (531 g.)

Environmental Characteristics

Operating Temperature—0°C to 55°C
Relative Humidity—10% to 90% (without condensation)

Electrical Characteristics

DC Power Supply Requirements

Configuration	Maximum Current (All Voltages ± 5%)		
	+5	+12	−12
SBC 186/51 as shipped:			
Board Total	7.45A	40mA	40mA
With separate battery back-up	6.30A	40mA	40mA
Battery back-up	1.15A	—	—
With SBC-304 Memory Module Installed:			
Board Total	7.55A	40mA	40mA
With separate battery back-up	6.30A	40mA	40mA
Battery back-up	1.25A	—	—

NOTES:
1. Add 150 mA to 5V current for each device installed in the 6 available Universal Memory Sites.
2. Add 500 mA to 12V current if Ethernet transceiver is connected.
3. Add additional currents for any SBX modules installed.

Reference Manual

122330-001—iSBC 186/51 Hardware Reference Manual (NOT SUPPLIED)

Manuals may be ordered from any Intel sales representative, distributor office or from Intel Literature Department, 3065 Bowers Avenue, Santa Clara, California 95051.

ORDERING INFORMATION

Part Number	Description
SBC 186/51	Communicating Computer

iSBC® 188/48 ADVANCED COMMUNICATING COMPUTER

- iSBC® Single Board Computer or Intelligent Slave Communication board
- 8 Serial Communications channels, expandable to 12 channels on a single MULTIBUS® board
- 6 MHz 80188 Microprocessor
- Supports RS232C interface on 6 channels, RS422A/449 or RS232C interface configurable on 2 channels
- Supports Async, Bisync HDLC/SDLC, on-chip baud rate generation, half/full-duplex, NRZ, NRZI or FM encoding/decoding
- 7 on-board DMA channels for serial I/O, 2 80188 DMA channels for iSBX™ MULTIMODULE™ board
- MULTIBUS® Interface for system expansion and Multimaster configuration
- 2 iSBX™ connectors for low cost I/O expansion
- 64K Bytes Dual-ported RAM expandable to 192K Bytes with Parity using the iSBC® 307 RAM MULTIMODULE™ board
- 2 28-pin JEDEC PROM sites expandable to 6 sites with the iSBC® 341 MULTIMODULE™ board for a maximum of 192K Bytes EPROM
- Resident firmware to handle up to 12 RS232C Async lines

The iSBC® 188/48 Advanced Communicating Computer (COMMputer™) is an intelligent 8-channel single board computer. This iSBC board adds 6MHz 80188 microprocessor-based communications flexibility to the Intel line of OEM microcomputer systems. Acting as a stand-alone CPU or intelligent slave for communication expansion, this board provides a high performance, low-cost solution for multi-user systems. The features of the iSBC 188/48 board are uniquely suited to manage higher-layer protocol requirements needed in today's data communications applications. This single board computer takes full advantage of Intel's VLSI technology to provide state-of-the-art, economic, computer-based solutions for OEM communications-oriented applications.

Intel Corporation assumes no responsibility for the use of any circuitry other than circuitry embodied in an Intel product. No other circuit patent licenses are implied. Information contained herein supersedes previously published specifications on these devices from Intel.

© INTEL CORPORATION, 1983

SEPTEMBER, 1984
ORDER NUMBER: 230890-004

iSBC® 188/48

OPERATING ENVIRONMENT

The iSBC 188/48 COMMputer™ features have been designed to meet the needs of numerous communications applications. Typical applications include:

1. Terminal/cluster controller
2. Front-end processor
3. Stand-alone communicating computer

Terminal/cluster controller

A terminal/cluster controller concentrates communications in a central area of a system. Efficient handling of messages coming in or going out of the system requires sufficient buffer space to store messages and high speed I/O channels to transmit messages. More sophisticated applications, such as cluster controllers, also require character and format conversion capabilities to allow different types of terminals to be attached.

The iSBC 188/48 Advanced Communicating Computer is well suited for multi-terminal systems (See Figure 1). Up to 12 serial channels can be serviced in multi-user or cluster applications by adding two iSBX 354 MULTIMODULE boards. The dual-port RAM provides a large onboard buffer to handle incoming and outgoing messages at data rates up to 19.2K Baud. Two channels are supported for continuous data rates greater than 19.2K Baud. Each serial channel can be individually programmed for different Baud rates to allow system configurations with differing terminal types. The firmware supplied on the iSBC 188/48 board supports up to 12 asynchronous RS232C serial channels, provides modem control and performs power-up diagnostics. The high performance of the onboard CPU provides intelligence to handle protocols and character handling typically assigned to the system CPU. This distribution of intelligence results in optimizing system performance by releasing the system CPU of routine tasks.

Front-end Processor

A front-end processor off-loads a system's central processor of tasks such as data manipulation and text editing of characters collected from the attached terminals. A variety of terminals require flexible terminal interfaces. Program code

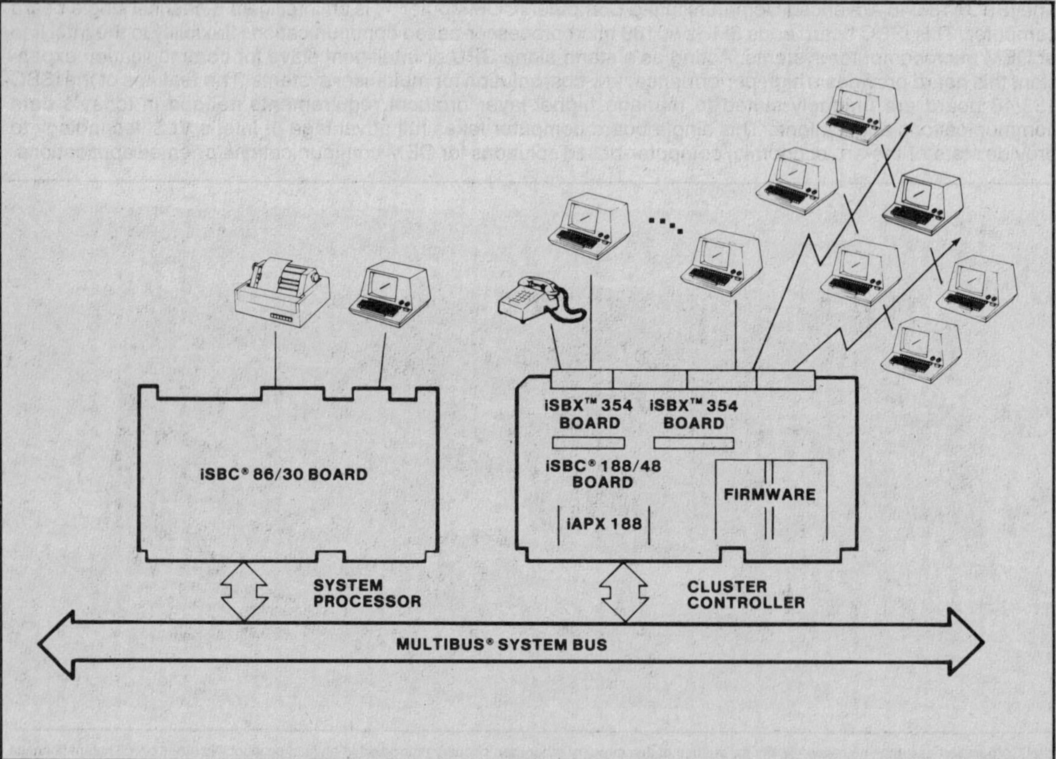

Figure 1. Terminal/Cluster Controller Application

iSBC® 188/48

is often dynamically down-loaded to the front-end processor from the system CPU. Downloading code requires sufficient memory space for protocol handling and program code. Flow control and efficient handling of interrupts require an efficient operating system to manage the hardware and software resources.

The iSBC 188/48 board features are designed to provide a high performance solution for front-end processor applications (see Figure 2). A large amount of random access memory is provided for dynamic storage of program code. In addition, local memory sites are available for storing routine programs such as X.25, SNA or bisync protocol software. The serial channels can be configured for links to mainframe systems, point-to-point terminals, modems or multi-drop configurations.

STAND-ALONE COMMputer™ APPLICATION

A stand-alone communicating computer is a complete computer system. The CPU is capable of managing the resources required to meet the needs of multi-terminal, multi-protocol applications. These applications typically require multi-terminal support, floppy disk control, local memory allocation, and program execution and storage.

To support stand-alone applications, the iSBC 188/48 COMMputer board uses the computational capabilities of an on-board CPU to provide a high-speed solution controlling 8 to 12 channels of serial I/O (see Figure 3). The local memory available is large enough to handle special purpose code, execution code and routine protocol software. The MULTIBUS interface can be used to access additional system functions. Floppy disk control and graphics capability can be added to the iSBC stand-alone computer through the iSBX connectors.

ARCHITECTURE

The four major functional areas are Serial I/O, CPU, Memory and DMA. These areas are illustrated in Figure 4.

Serial I/O

Eight HDLC/SDLC serial interfaces are provided on the iSBC 188/48 board. The serial interface can be expanded to 12 channels by adding 2

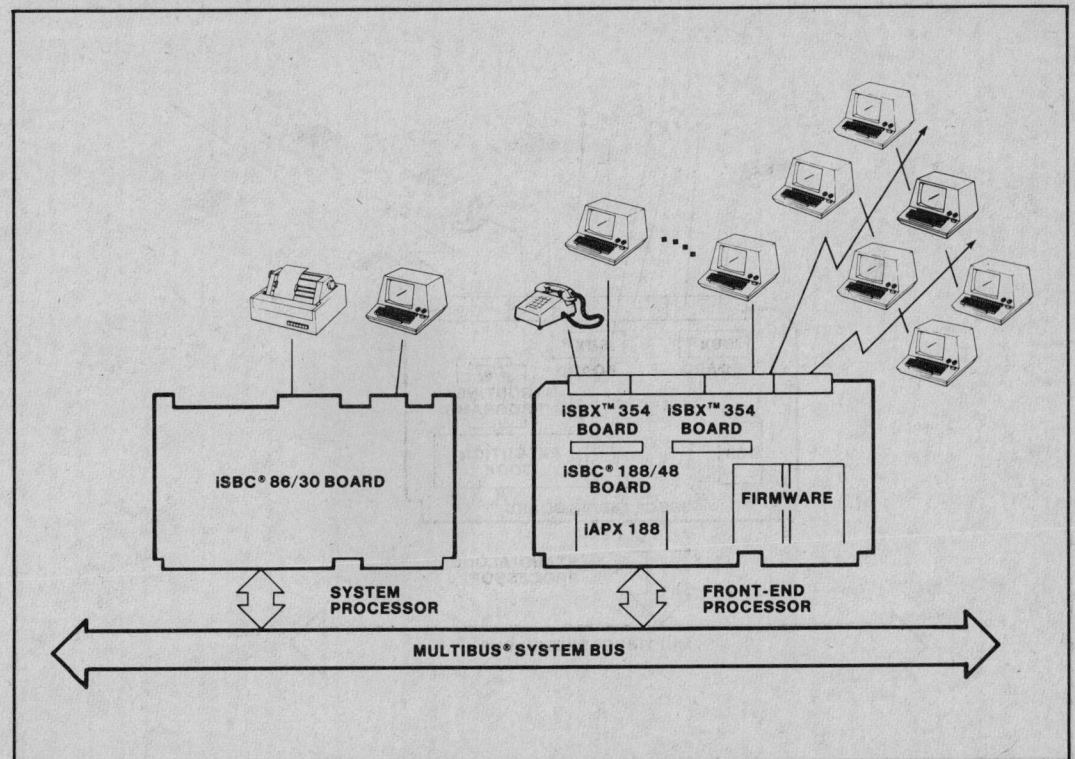

Figure 2. Front-end Processor Application

iSBC® 188/48

iSBX 354 MULTIMODULE boards. The HDLC/SDLC interface is compatible with IBM system and terminal equipment and with CCITT's X.25 packet switching interface.

Four 82530 Serial Communications Controllers (SCC) provide eight channels of half/full duplex serial I/O. Six channels support RS232C interfaces. Two channels are RS232C/422/449 configurable and can be tri-stated to allow multidrop networks. The 82530 component is designed to satisfy several serial communications requirements: asynchronous, byte-oriented synchronous, and bit-oriented synchronous (HDLC/SDLC) modes. The increased capability at the serial controller point results in off-loading the CPU of tasks formerly assigned to the CPU or its associated hardware. Configurability of the 82530 allows the user to configure it to handle all asynchronous data formats regardless of data size, number of start and stop bits, or parity requirements. An on-chip Baud rate generator allows independent Baud rates on each channel.

The clock can be generated either internally with the SCC chip, with an external clock or via the NRZ1 clock encoding mechanism.

All eight channels can be configured as Data Terminal Equipment (DTE) or Data Communication Equipment (DCE). Table 1 lists the interfaces supported.

Central CPU

The 80188 central processor component provides high performance, flexibility and powerful processing power. The 80188 component is a highly integrated microprocessor with an 8-bit data bus interface and a 16-bit internal architecture to give high performance. The 80188 is upward compatible with 8086 and 80186 software.

The 80188/82530 combination with on-board PROM/EPROM sites, and dual-port RAM provide the intelligence and speed to manage multi-user, multi-protocol communications operations.

Memory

There are two areas of memory on-board: dual-port RAM and universal site memory. The iSBC 188/48 board contains 64K bytes of dual-port

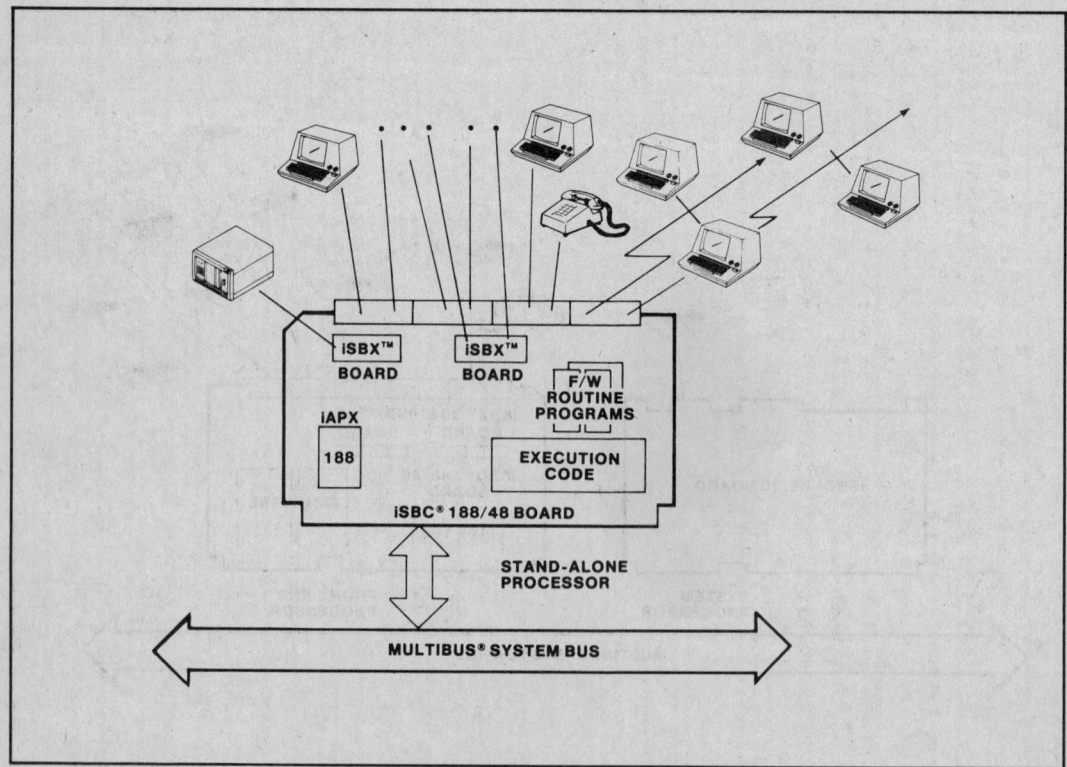

Figure 3. Stand-alone COMMputer™ Application

iSBC® 188/48

RAM that is addressable by the 80188 on-board. The dual-port memory is configurable anywhere in a 16M Byte address space on 64K Byte boundaries as addressed from the MULTIBUS port. Not all of the 64K bytes are visible from the MULTIBUS side. The amount of dual-port memory visible to the MULTIBUS side can be set (with jumpers) to none, 16K bytes, or 48K bytes. The on-board RAM is expandable to a total of 192K bytes with parity by adding the iSBC 307 MULTIMODULE board. In a multiprocessor system these features provide local memory for each processor and shared system memory configurations where the total system memory size can exceed one megabyte without addressing conflicts.

The second area of memory is universal site memory providing flexible memory expansion. Two 28-pin JEDEC sockets are provided. One of these sockets is used for the resident firmware as described in the FIRMWARE section on Page 7.

The default configuration of the board supports 16K Byte EPROM devices such as the Intel 27128 component. However, these sockets can contain ROM, EPROM, Static RAM, or EEPROM. Both sockets must contain the same type of component (i.e. as the first socket contains an EPROM for the resident firmware, the second must also contain an EPROM with the same pinout). Up to 32K bytes can be addressed per socket giving a maximum universal site memory size of 64K bytes. By using the iSBC 341 MULTIMODULE board, a maximum of 192K bytes of universal site memory is available. This provides sufficient memory space for on-board network or resource management software.

Table 1. iSBC® 188/48 Interface Support

Connection	Synchronous Modem or Direct	Asynchronous Modem or Direct
Point-to-point	X**	X
Multidrop	Channels 0 and 1	Channels 0 and 1
Loop	X	N/A

** All 8 channels are denoted by X.

On-Board DMA

Seven channels of Direct Memory Access (DMA) are provided between serial I/O and on-board

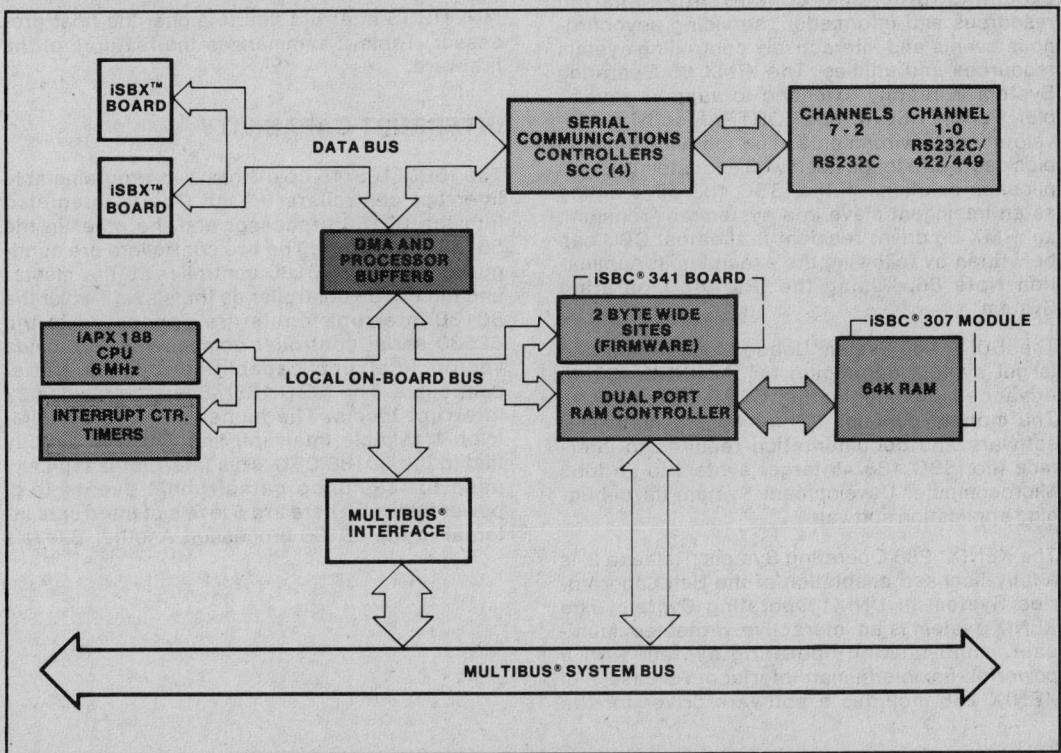

Figure 4. Block Diagram of iSBC 188/48 Board

iSBC® 188/48

dual-port RAM by two 8237-5 components. Each of channels 0, 1, 2, 3, 5, 6, and 7 is supported by their own DMA line. Serial channels 0 and 1 are configurable for full duplex DMA. Configuring the full duplex DMA option for Channels 0 and 1 would require Channels 2 and 3 to be interrupt driven or polled. Channel 4 is interrupt driven or polled only.

Two DMA channels are integrated into the iAPX 188 processor. These additional channels can be connected to the iSBX interfaces to provide DMA capability to iSBX MULTIMODULE boards such as the iSBX 218A Floppy Disk Controller MULTIMODULE board.

OPERATING SYSTEM SUPPORT

Release 6 of the iRMX 86 Operating System provides a rich set of features and options to support sophisticated stand-alone communications applications on the iSBC 188/48 Advanced Communicating Computer. In addition to supporting real-time requirements, the iRMX 86 Operating System Release 6 has a powerful, yet easy to use human interface. Services provided by the iRMX 86 Operating System include facilities for executing programs concurrently, sharing resources and information, servicing asynchronous events and interactively controlling system resources and utilities. The iRMX 86 Operating System is readily extended to support assembler, PL/M, PASCAL, and FORTRAN software development environments. The modular building block software lends itself well to customized application solutions. If the iSBC 188/48 is acting as an intelligent slave in a system environment, an iRMX 86 driver resident in the host CPU can be written by following the examples in Application Note 86, "Using the iRMX86 Operating System".

The iSDM™ 86 System Debug Monitor supports target system debugging for the iSBC 188/48 Advanced Communicating COMMputer board. The monitor contains the necessary hardware, software and documentation required to interface the iSBC 188/48 target system to an Intel Microcomputer Development System for debugging application software.

The XENIX* 286 Operating System, Release 2, is a fully-licensed adaptation of the Bell Laboratories System III UNIX* Operating System. The XENIX system is an interactive, protected, multiuser, multi-tasking operating system with a powerful, flexible human interface. Release 2 of XENIX 286 includes a software driver for the iSBC 188/48 board (and up to two iSBX354 Multimodule Boards) acting as an intelligent slave for multi-user applications requiring multiple persons running independent, terminal-oriented jobs. Example applications include distributed data processing, business data processing, software development and engineering or scientific data analysis. XENIX 286 Release 2 Operating System services include device independent I/O, tree-structured file directory and task hierarchies, re-entrant/shared code and system accounting and security access protection.

FIRMWARE

The iSBC 188/48 Communicating COMMputer board is supplied with resident firmware that supports up to 12 RS232C asynchronous serial channels. In addition, the firmware provides a facility for a host CPU to download and execute code on the iSBC 188/48 board. Simple power-up confidence tests are also included to provide a quick diagnostic service. The firmware converts the iSBC 188/48 COMMputer to a slave communications controller. As a slave communications controller, it requires a separate MULTIBUS host CPU board and requires the use of a MULTIBUS interrupt line to signal the host processor. Table 2 summarizes the features of the firmware.

INTERRUPT CAPABILITY

The iSBC 188/48 board has two programmable interrupt controllers (PICs). One is integrated into the 80188 processor and the other in the 80130 component. The two controllers are configured with the 80130 controller as the master and the 80188 controller as the slave. Two of the 80130 interrupt inputs are connected to the 82530 serial controller components to provide vector interrupt capablities by the serial controllers. The iSBC 188/48 board provides 22 interrupt levels. The highest level is the NMI (Non-Maskable Interrupt) line which is directly tied to the 80188 CPU. This interrupt is typically used for signaling catastrophic events (e.g. power failure). There are 5 levels of interrupts internal to the 80188 processor. Another 8 levels

---

*UNIX is a trademark of Bell Laboratories.

iSBC® 188/48

Table 2. Features of the iSBC® 188/48 Firmware

Feature	Description
Asynchronous Serial Channel Support	Supports the serial channels in asynchronous ASCII mode. Parameters such as baud rate, parity generation, parity checking and character length can be programmed independently for each channel.
Block Data Transfer (On Output)	Relieves the host CPU of character-at-a-time interrupt processing. The iSBC 188/48 board accepts blocks of data for transmission and interrupts the processor only when the entire block is transmitted.
Limited Modem Control	Provides software control of the Data Terminal Ready (DTR) line on all channels. Transitions on the Carrier Detect (CD) line are sensed and reported to the host CPU.
Tandem Mode Support	Transmits an XOFF character when the number of characters in its receive buffer exceeds a threshold value and transmits an XON character when the buffer drains below some other threshold.
Download and execute capability	Provides a capability for the host CPU to load code anywhere in the address space of the iSBC 188/48 board and to start executing at any address in its address space.
Power Up Confidence Tests	On board reset, the firmware executes a series of simple tests to establish that crucial components on the board are functional.

of interrupts are available from the 80130 component. Of these 8, one is tied to the programmable interrupt controller (PIC) of the 80188 CPU. An additional 8 levels of interrupts are available at the MULTIBUS interface. The iSBC 188/48 board does not support bus vectored interrupts. Table 3 lists the possible interrupt sources.

SUPPORT FOR THE 80130 COMPONENT

Intel does not support the direct processor execution of the iRMX nucleus primitives from the 80130 component. The 80130 component provides timers and interrupt controllers only.

EXPANSION

EPROM/RAM Expansion

Memory may be expanded by adding Intel compatible memory expansion boards. The universal site memory can be expanded to six sockets by adding the iSBC 341 MULTIMODULE board for a maximum total of 192K bytes of universal site memory. The 64K bytes of on-board dual-port RAM can be expanded to a maximum total of 192K bytes by adding the iSBC 307 MULTIMODULE board. The iSBC 307 MULTIMODULE board also provides parity for all 192K bytes of on-board RAM.

iSBX™ MULTIMODULE™ Expansion

Two 8-bit iSBX MULTIMODULE connectors are provided on the iSBC 188/48 board. Using iSBX modules additional functions can be added to extend the I/O capability of the board. In addition to specialized or custom designed iSBX boards, there is a broad range of iSBX MULTIMODULE boards from Intel including parallel I/O, analog I/O, IEEE 488 GPIB, floppy disk, magnetic bubbles, video and serial I/O boards.

The serial I/O MULTIMODULE boards available include the iSBX 354 Dual Channel Expansion

iSBC® 188/48

MULTIMODULE board. Each iSBX 354 MULTIMODULE board adds two channels of serial I/O to the iSBC 188/48 board for a maxmimum of twelve serial channels. The 82530 serial communications controller on the MULTIMODULE handles a large variety of serial communications protocols. This is the same serial controller as is used on the iSBC 188/48 board to offer directly compatible expansion capability for the iSBC 188/48 COMMputer board.

MULTIBUS® INTERFACE

The iSBC 188/48 Advanced COMMputer board can be a MULTIBUS master or intelligent slave in a multimaster system. The iSBC 188/48 board incorporates a flag byte signalling mechanism for use in multiprocessor environments where the iSBC 188/48 board is acting as an intelligent slave. This mechanism provides an interrupt handshake from the MULTIBUS System Bus to the on-board processor and vice-versa.

The Multimaster capabilities of the iSBC 188/48 board offers easy expansion of processing capacity and the benefits of multiprocessing. Memory and I/O capacity may be expanded and additional functions added using Intel MULTIBUS compatible expansion boards.

Table 3. Interrupt Request Sources

Device	Function	Number of Interrupts
MULTIBUS® Interface INT0 - INT7	Requests from MULTIBUS resident peripherals or other CPU boards.	8
82530 Serial Controllers	Transmit buffer empty, receive buffer full and channel errors 1 and external status	8 per 82530 Total = 32
Internal 80188 Timer and DMA	Timer 0,1,2 outputs and 2 DMA channel interrupts	5
80130 Timer Outputs	Timer 0,1,2, outputs of 80130	3
Interrupt from Flag Byte Logic	Flag byte interrupt set by MULTIBUS master (through MULTIBUS® I/O Write)	1
Bus Flag Interrupt	Interrupt to MULTIBUS® (Selectable for INT0 to INT7) generated from on-board 80188 I/O Write	1
iSBX™ connectors	Function determined by iSBX™ MULTIMODULE™ board	4 (Two per connector)
iSBX™ DMA	DMA interrupt from iSBX™(TDMA)	2
Bus fail-safe timeout Interrupt	Indicates iSBC® 188/48 board timed out either waiting for MULTIBUS® access or timed out from no acknowledge while on MULTIBUS System Bus	1
Latched Interrupt	Converts pulsed event to a level interrupt. Example: 8237A-5 EOP	1
OR-gate Matrix	Concentrates up to 4 interrupts to 1 interrupt (selectable by stake pins)	1
Ring Indicator Interrupt	Latches a ring indicator event from serial channels 4,5,6, or 7	1
NOR-Gate Matrix	Inverts up to 2 interrupts into 1 (selectable by stake pins)	1

iSBC® 188/48

SPECIFICATIONS

Word Size

Instruction — 8, 16, 24 or 32 bits
Data Path — 8 bits

Processor Clock	82530 Clock	DMA Clock
6 MHZ	4.9152 MHz	3 MHz

MEMORY CAPACITY/ADDRESSING

Dual-Port RAM

iSBC® 188/48 Board — 64K bytes

As viewed from the iAPX 188 — 64K

As viewed from the MULTIBUS® System Bus —
Choice: 0, 16K or 48K

EPROM

Using:

iSBC® 188/48 Board	Size	On Board Capacity	Address Range
2732	4K	8K	FE000-FFFFF$_H$
2764	8K	16K	FC000-FFFFF$_H$
27128	16K	32K	F8000-FFFFF$_H$
27256	32K	64K	F0000-FFFFF$_H$

Memory Expansion

1. **Ram Memory** — with iSBC 307 Board

   Total Capacity — 192K

   As viewed from the MULTIBUS® System Bus —
   Choice: 0, 16K or 48K Public
   16K to 192K Private
   64K or 192K Total

2. | EPROM with iSBC® board using: | Total Capacity | Address Range |
   |---|---|---|
   | 2732 | 24K | F8000-FFFFF$_H$ |
   | 2764 | 48K | F0000-FFFFF$_H$ |
   | 27128 | 96K | E0000-FFFFF$_H$ |
   | 27256 | 192K | C0000-FFFFF$_H$ |

I/O Capacity

Serial — 8 programmable lines using 4 82530 components

iSBX™ MULTIMODULE™ Board — 2 iSBX™ single-wide boards

Serial Communications Characteristics

Synchronous — Internal or external character synchronization on one or two synchronous characters

Asynchronous — 5-8 bits and 1, 1½ or 2 stop bits per character; programmable clock factor; break detection and generation; parity, overrun, and framing error detection

Baud Rates

Synchronous X1 Clock	
Baud Rate	82530 Count Value (Decimal)
64000	36
48000	49
19200	126
9600	254
4800	510
2400	1022
1800	1363
1200	2046
300	8190

Asynchronous X 16 Clock	
Baud Rate	82530 Count Value (Decimal)
19200	6
9600	14
4800	30
2400	62
1800	83
1200	126
300	510
110	1394

iSBC® 188/48

INTERFACES

iSBX™ Bus

The iSBC 188/48 board meets iSBX compliance level D8/8 DMA

MULTIBUS® System Bus

The iSBC 188/48 board meets MULTIBUS compliance level Master/Slave D8 M24 I16 V0 EL

Serial RS232C Signals

CD	Carrier Detect
CTS	Clear to Send
DSR	Data Set Ready
DTE TXC	Transmit Clock
DTR	Data Terminal Ready
RTS	Request to Send
RXC	Receive Clock
RXD	Receive Data
SG	Signal Ground
TXD	Transmit Data
RI	Ring Indicator

RS422A/449 Signals

RC	Receive Common
RD	Receive Data
RT	Receive Timing
SD	Send Data
TT	Terminal Timing

ENVIRONMENTAL CHARACTERISTICS

Temperature — 0 to 55°C, at 200 Linear Feet/Min. (LFM) Air Velocity

Humidity — to 90%, non-condensing (25°C to 70°C)

PHYSICAL CHARACTERISTICS

Width:	30.48 cm (12.00 in)
Length:	17.15 cm (6.75 in)
Height:	1.04 cm (.41 in)
Weight:	595 gm (21 ounces)

ELECTRICAL CHARACTERISTICS

The power required per voltage for the iSBC 188/48 board is shown below. These numbers do not include the current required by universal memory sites or expansion modules.

Voltage (Volts)	Current (Amps) typ.	Power (Watts) typ.
+5	4.56A	22.8W
+12	.12A	1.5W
−12	.11A	1.3W

ORDERING INFORMATION

Part Number	Description
iSBC 188/48	8-Serial Channel Advanced Communicating Computer

REFERENCE MANUAL

iSBC 188/48 Advanced Communications Computer Reference Manual
Order Number 146218-002

PRELIMINARY

iSBC® 188/56 ADVANCED COMMUNICATING COMPUTER

- iSBC® Single Board Computer or Intelligent Slave Communication Board
- 8 Serial Communications Channels, Expandable to 12 Channels on a Single MULTIBUS® Board
- 8 MHz 80188 Microprocessor
- Supports RS232C Interface on 6 Channels, RS422A/449 or RS232C Interface Configurable on 2 Channels
- Supports Async, Bisync HDLC/SDLC, On-chip Baud Rate Generation, Half/full-duplex, NRZ, NRZI or FM Encoding/decoding

- 7 On-board DMA Channels for Serial I/O, 2 80188 DMA Channels for the iSBX™ MULTIMODULE™ Board
- MULTIBUS® Interface for System Expansion and Multimaster Configuration
- Two iSBX Connectors for Low Cost I/O Expansion
- 256K Bytes Dual-ported RAM On-board
- Two 28-pin JEDEC PROM Sites Expandable to 6 Sites with the iSBC 341 MULTIMODULE Board for a Maximum of 192K Bytes EPROM
- Resident Firmware to Handle up to 12 RS232C Async Lines

The iSBC 188/56 Advanced Communicating Computer (COMMputer™) is an intelligent 8-channel single board computer. This iSBC board adds the 8 MHz 80188 microprocessor-based communications flexibility to the Intel line of OEM microcomputer systems. Acting as a stand-alone CPU or intelligent slave for communication expansion, this board provides a high performance, low-cost solution for multi-user systems. The features of the iSBC 188/56 board are uniquely suited to manage higher-layer protocol requirements needed in today's data communications applications. This single board computer takes full advantage of Intel's VLSI technology to provide state-of-the-art, economic, computer-based solutions for OEM communications-oriented applications.

Intel Corporation assumes no responsibility for the use of any circuitry other than circuitry embodied in an Intel product. No other circuit patent licenses are implied. Information contained herein supersedes previously published specifications on these devices from Intel. Specifications to change without notice.
© INTEL CORPORATION, 1985

iSBC® 188/56

PRELIMINARY

OPERATING ENVIRONMENT

The iSBC 188/56 COMMputer™ features have been designed to meet the needs of numerous communications applications. Typical applications include:

1. Terminal/cluster controller
2. Front-end processor
3. Stand-alone communicating computer

Terminal/Cluster Controller

A terminal/cluster controller concentrates communications in a central area of a system. Efficient handling of messages coming in or going out of the system requires sufficient buffer space to store messages and high speed I/O channels to transmit messages. More sophisticated applications, such as cluster controllers, also require character and format conversion capabilities to allow different types of terminals to be attached.

The iSBC 188/56 Advanced Communicating Computer is well suited for multi-terminal systems (See Figure 1). Up to 12 serial channels can be serviced in multi-user or cluster applications by adding two iSBX 354 MULTIMODULE boards. The dual-port RAM provides a large on-board buffer to handle incoming and outgoing messages at data rates up to 19.2K baud. Two channels are supported for continuous data rates greater than 19.2K baud. Each serial channel can be individually programmed for different baud rates to allow system configurations with differing terminal types. The firmware supplied on the iSBC 188/56 board supports up to 12 asynchronous RS232C serial channels, provides modem control and performs power-up diagnostics. The high performance of the on-board CPU provides intelligence to handle protocols and character handling typically assigned to the system CPU. The distribution of intelligence results in optimizing system performance by releasing the system CPU of routine tasks.

Front-end Processor

A front-end processor off-loads a system's central processor of tasks such as data manipulation and text editing of characters collected from the attached terminals. A variety of terminals require flexible terminal interfaces. Program code is often dynamically downloaded to the front-end processor from the system CPU. Downloading code requires sufficient memory space for protocol handling and program code. Flow control and efficient handling of interrupts require an efficient operating system to manage the hardware and software resources.

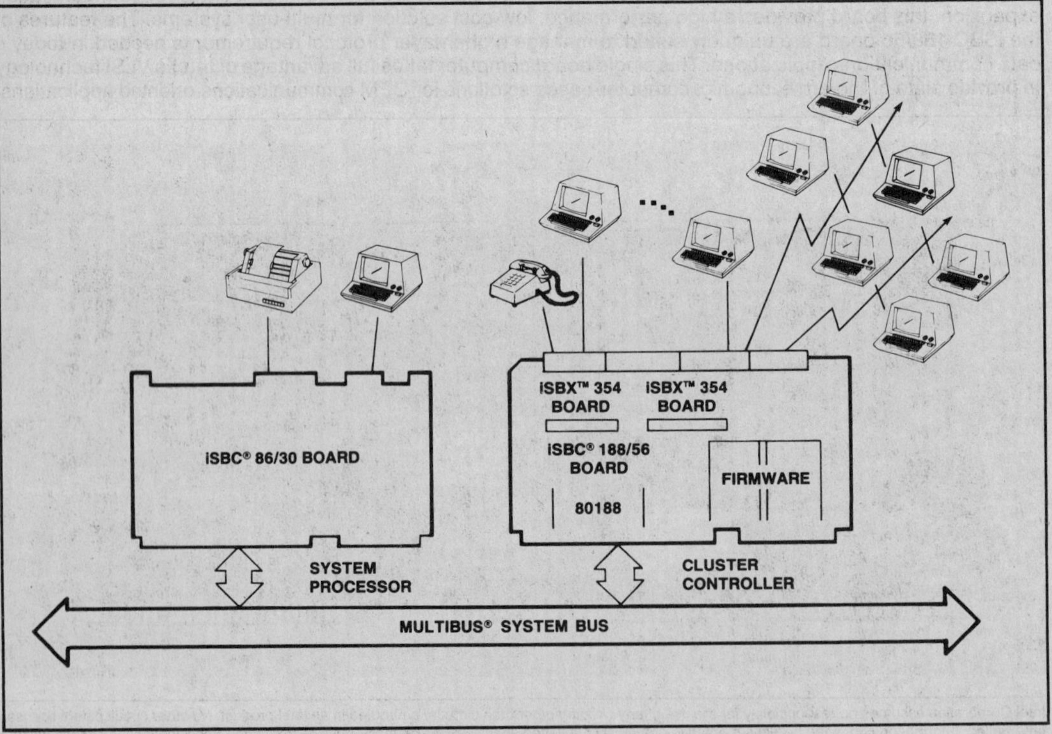

Figure 1. Terminal/Cluster Controller Application

iSBC® 188/56

The iSBC 188/56 board features are designed to provide a high performance solution for front-end processor applications (see Figure 2). A large amount of random access memory is provided for dynamic storage of program code. In addition, local memory sites are available for storing routine programs such as X.25, SNA or bisync protocol software. The serial channels can be configured for links to mainframe systems, point-to-point terminals, modems or multi-drop configurations.

Stand-Alone COMMputer™ Application

A stand-alone communicating computer is a complete computer system. The CPU is capable of managing the resources required to meet the needs of multi-terminal, multi-protocol applications. These applications typically require multi-terminal support, floppy disk control, local memory allocation, and program execution and storage.

To support stand-alone applications, the iSBC 188/56 COMMputer board uses the computational capabilities of an on-board CPU to provide a high-speed system solution controlling 8 to 12 channels of serial I/O (see Figure 3). The local memory available is large enough to handle special purpose code, execution code and routine protocol software. The MULTIBUS interface can be used to access additional

*IBM is a registered trademark of International Business Machines

system functions. Floppy disk control and graphics capability can be added to the iSBC stand-alone computer through the iSBX connectors.

ARCHITECTURE

The four major functional areas are Serial I/O, CPU, Memory and DMA. These areas are illustrated in Figure 4.

Serial I/O

Eight HDLC/SDLC serial interfaces are provided on the iSBC 188/56 board. The serial interface can be expanded to 12 channels by adding 2 iSBX 354 MULTIMODULE boards. The HDLC/SDLC interface is compatible with IBM* system and terminal equipment and with CCITT's X.25 packet switching interface.

Four 82530 Serial Communications Controllers (SCC) provide eight channels of half/full duplex serial I/O. Six channels support RS232C interfaces. Two channels are RS232C/422/449 configurable and can be tri-slated to allow multidrop networks. The 82530 component is designed to satisfy several serial communications requirements; asynchronous, byte-oriented synchronous (HDLC/SDLC) modes. The increased capability at the serial controller point results in off-loading the CPU of tasks formerly

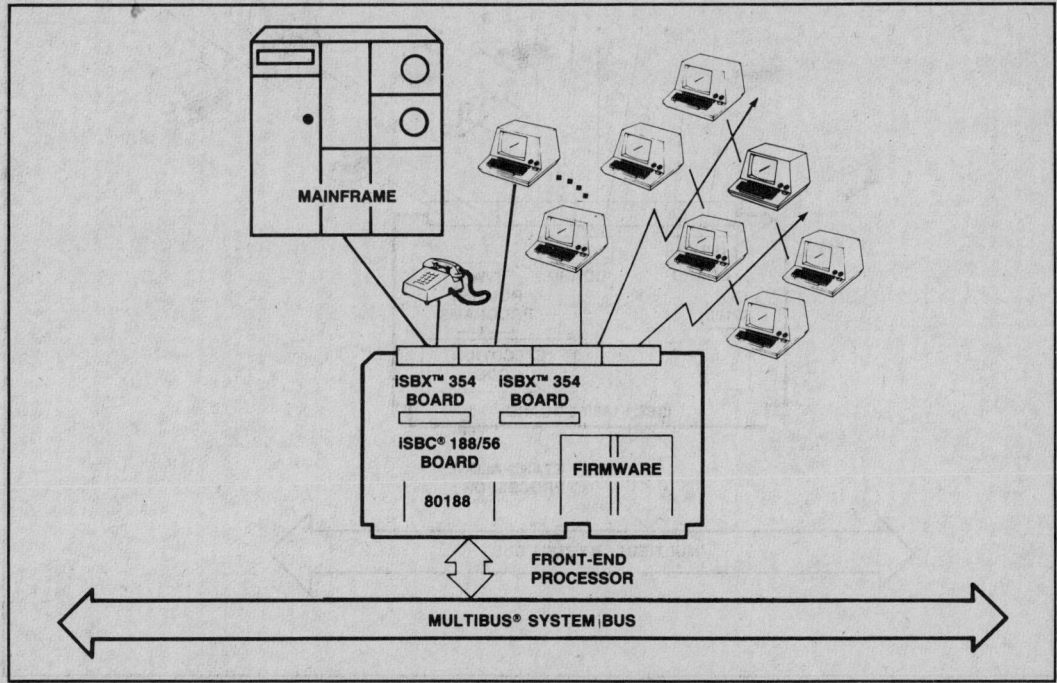

Figure 2. Front-end Processor Application

iSBC® 188/56

PRELIMINARY

assigned to the CPU or its associated hardware. Configurability of the 82530 allows the user to configure it to handle all asynchronous data formats regardless of data size, number of start or stop bits, or parity requirements. An on-chip baud rate generator allows independent baud rates on each channel.

The clock can be generated either internally with the SCC chip, with an external clock or via the NRZ1 clock encoding mechanism.

All eight channels can be configured as Data Terminal Equipment (DTE) or Data Communications Equipment (DCE). Table 1 lists the interfaces supported.

Table 1. iSBC® 188/56 Interface Support

Connection	Synchronous Modem or Direct	Asynchronous Modem or Direct
Point-to-point	X**	X
Multidrop	Channels 0 and 1	Channels 0 and 1
Loop	X	N/A

** All 8 channels are denoted by X.

Central CPU

The 80188 central processor component provides high performance, flexibility and powerful processing. The 80188 component is a highly integrated microprocessor with an 8-bit data bus interface and a 16-bit internal architecture to give high performance. The 80188 is upward compatible with 86 and 186 software.

The 80188/82530 combination with on-board PROM/EPROM sites, and dual-port RAM provide the intelligence and speed to manage multi-user, multi-protocol communications operations.

Memory

There are two areas of memory on-board: dual-port RAM and universal site memory. The iSBC 188/56 board contains 256K bytes of dual-port RAM that is addressable by the 80188 on-board. The dual-port memory is configurable anywhere in a 16M byte address space on 64K byte boundaries as addressed from the MULTIBUS port. Not all of the 256K bytes are visible from the MULTIBUS bus side. The amount of

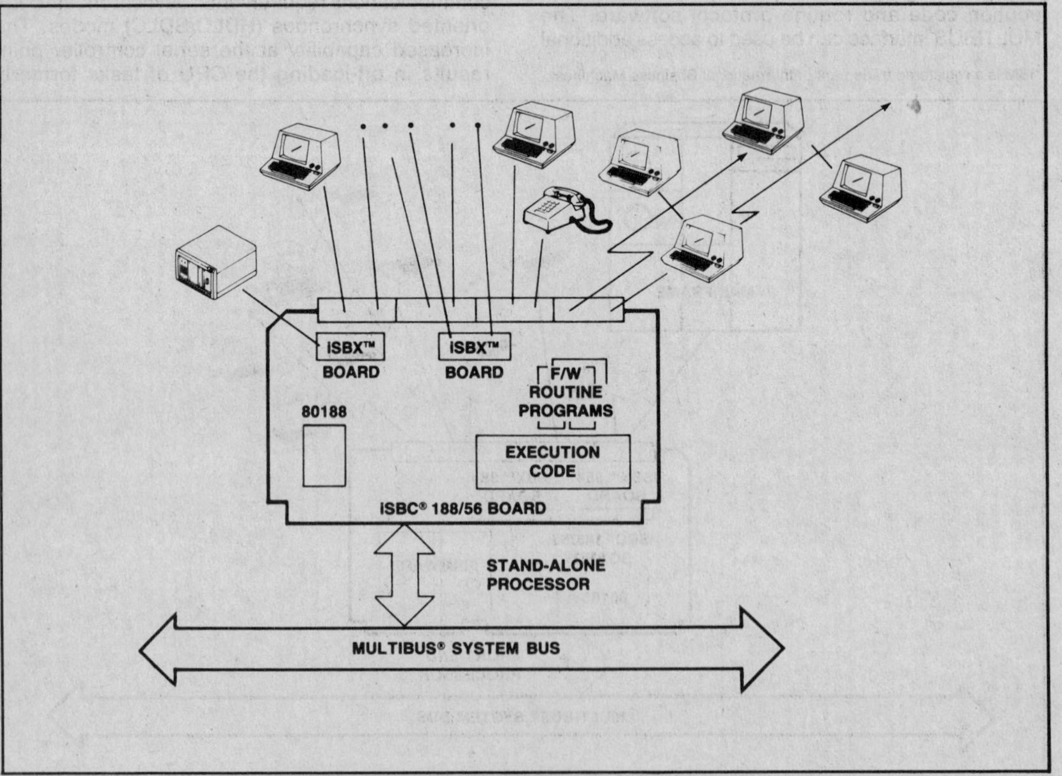

Figure 3. Stand-alone COMMputer™ Application

8-38

280715-001

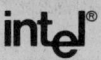

iSBC® 188/56

PRELIMINARY

dual-port memory visible to the MULTIBUS side can be set (with jumpers) to none, 16K bytes, or 48K bytes. In a multiprocessor system these features provide local memory for each processor and shared system memory configurations where the total system memory size can exceed one megabyte without addressing conflicts.

The second area of memory is universal site memory providing flexible memory expansion. Two 28-pin JEDEC sockets are provided. One of these sockets is used for the resident firmware as described in the FIRMWARE section.

The default configuration of the boards supports 16K byte EPROM devices such as the Intel 27128 component. However, these sockets can contain ROM, EPROM, Static RAM, or EEPROM. Both sockets must contain the same type of component (i.e. as the first socket contains an EPROM for the resident firmware, the second must also contain an EPROM with the same pinout). Up to 32K bytes can be addressed per socket giving a maximum universal site memory size of 64K bytes. By using the iSBC 341 MULTIMODULE board, a maximum of 192K bytes of universal site memory is available. This provides sufficient memory space for on-board network or resource management software.

On-Board DMA

Seven channels of Direct Memory Access (DMA) are provided between serial I/O and on-board dual port RAM by two 8237-5 components. Each of channels 0, 1, 2, 3, 5, 6, and 7 is supported by their own DMA line. Serial channels 0 and 1 are configurable for full duplex DMA. Configuring the full duplex DMA option for Channels 0 and 1 would require Channels 2 and 3 to be interrupt driven or polled. Channel 4 is interrupt driven or polled only.

Two DMA channels are integrated in the 80188 processor. These additional channels can be connected to the iSBX interfaces to provide DMA capability to iSBX MULTIMODULE boards such as the iSBX 218A Floppy Disk Controller MULTIMODULE board.

OPERATING SYSTEM SUPPORT

Intel offers run-time foundation software to support applications that range from general purpose to high-performance solutions.

Release 6 of the iRMX 86 Operating System provides a rich set of features and options to support sophisticated stand-alone communications applications on the iSBC 188/56 Advanced Communicating Computer. In addition to supporting real-time require-

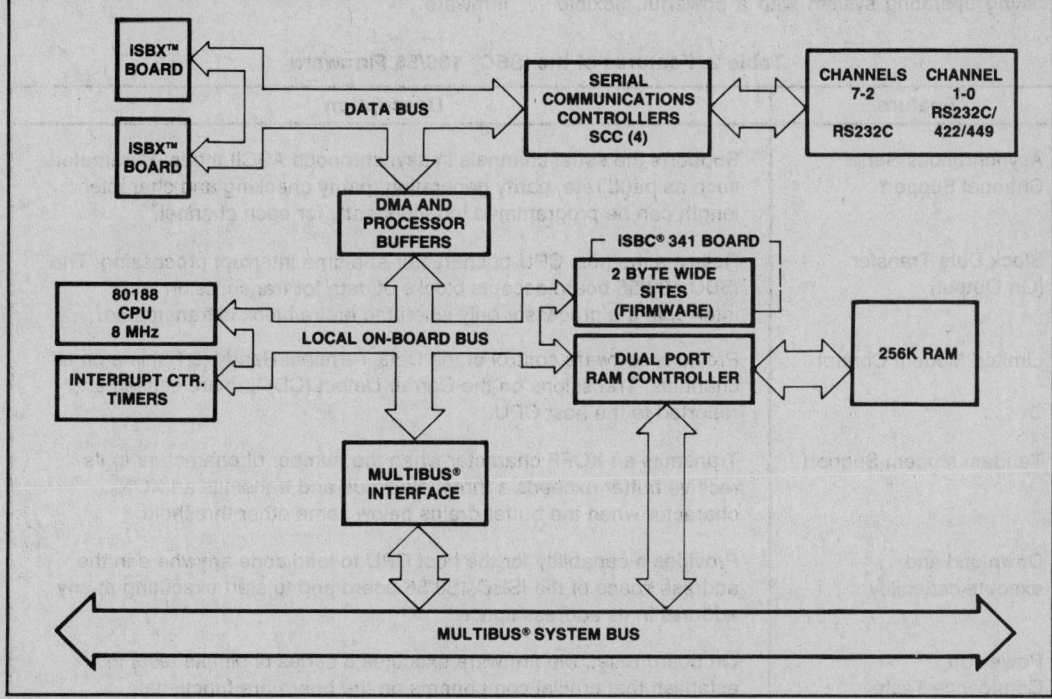

Figure 4. Block Diagram of iSBC® 188/56 Board

iSBC® 188/56

ments, the iRMX 86 Operating System Release 6 has a powerful, yet easy to use human interface. Services provided by the iRMX 86 Operating System include facilities for executing programs concurrently, sharing resources and information, servicing asynchronous events and interactively controlling system resources and utilities. The iRMX 86 Operating System is readily extended to support assembler, PL/M, PASCAL, and FORTRAN software development environments. The modular building block software lends itself well to customized application solutions. If the iSBC 188/56 board is acting as an intelligent slave in a system environment, an iRMX 86 driver resident in the host CPU can be written by following the examples in the manual "Guide to Writing Device Driven for iRMX 86 and iRMX 88 I/O Systems".

The iSDM™ 86 System Debug Monitor supports target system debugging for the iSBC 188/56 Advanced Communicating COMMputer board. The monitor contains the necessary hardware, software and documentation required to interface the iSBC 188/56 target system to an Intel microcomputer development system for debugging application software.

The XENIX* 286 Operating System, Release 3, is a fully licensed adaptation of the Bell Laboratories System III UNIX* Operating System. The XENIX system is an interactive, protected, multi-user, multi-tasking operating system with a powerful, flexible human interface. Release 3 of XENIX 286 includes a software driver for the iSBC 188/56 board (and up to two iSBX 354 MULTIMODULE Boards) acting as an intelligent slave for multi-user applications requiring multiple persons running independent, terminal-oriented jobs. Example applications include distributed data processing, business data processing, software development and engineering or scientific data analysis. XENIX 286 Release 3 Operating System services include device independent I/O, tree-structured file directory and task hierarchies, re-entrant/shared code and system accounting and security access protection.

FIRMWARE

The iSBC 188/56 Communicating COMMputer board is supplied with resident firmware that supports up to 12 RS232C asynchronous serial channels. In addition, the firmware provides a facility for a host CPU to download and execute code on the iSBC 188/56 board. Simple power-up confidence tests are also included to provide a quick diagnostic service. The firmware converts the iSBC 188/56 COMMputer board to a slave communications controller. As a slave communications controller, it requires a separate MULTIBUS host CPU board and requires the use of a MULTIBUS interrupt line to signal the host processor. Table 2 summarizes the features of the firmware.

Table 2: Features of the iSBC® 188/56 Firmware

Feature	Description
Asynchronous Serial Channel Support	Supports the serial channels in asynchronous ASCII mode. Parameters such as baud rate, parity generation, parity checking and character length can be programmed independently for each channel.
Block Data Transfer (On Output)	Relieves the host CPU of character-at-a-time interrupt processing. The iSBC 188/56 board accepts blocks of data for transmission and interrupts the processor only when the entire block is transmitted.
Limited Modem Control	Provides software control of the Data Terminal Ready (DTR) line on all channels. Transitions on the Carrier Detect (CD) line are sensed and reported to the host CPU.
Tandem Modem Support	Transmits an XOFF character when the number of characters in its receive buffer exceeds a threshold value and transmits an XON character when the buffer drains below some other threshold.
Download and execute capability	Provides a capability for the host CPU to load code anywhere in the address space of the iSBC 188/56 board and to start executing at any address in its address space.
Power Up Confidence Tests	On board reset, the firmware executes a series of simple tests to establish that crucial components on the board are functional.

*UNIX is a trademark of Bell Laboratories
*XENIX is a trademark of Microsoft Corporation

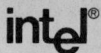

iSBC® 188/56

INTERRUPT CAPABILITY

The iSBC 188/56 board has two programmable interrupt controllers (PICs). One is integrated into the 80188 processor and the other in the 80130 component. The two controllers are configured with the 80130 controller as the master and the 80188 controller as the slave. Two of the 80130 interrupt inputs are connected to the 82530 serial controller components to provide vector interrupt capabilities by the serial controllers. The iSBC 188/56 board provides 22 interrupt levels. The highest level is the NMI (Non-Maskable Interrupt) line which is directly tied to the 80188 CPU. This interrupt is typically used for signaling catastrophic events (e.g. power failure). There are 5 levels of interrupts internal to the 80188 processor. Another 8 levels of interrupts are available from the 80130 component. Of these 8, one is tied to the programmable interrupt controller (PIC) of the 80188 CPU. An additional 8 levels of interrupts are available at the MULTIBUS interface. The iSBC 188/56 board does not support bus vectored interrupts. Table 3 lists the possible interrupt sources.

Table 3. Interrupt Request Sources

Device	Function	Number of Interrupts
MULTIBUS® Interface INT0 - INT7	Requests from MULTIBUS resident peripherals or other CPU boards.	8
82530 Serial Controllers	Transmit buffer empty, receive buffer full and channel errors 1 and external status	8 per 82530 Total = 32
Internal 80188 Timer and DMA	Timer 0,1,2 outputs and 2 DMA channel interrupts	5
80130 Timer Outputs	Timer 0,1,2, outputs of 80130	3
Interrupt from Flag Byte Logic	Flag byte interrupt set by MULTIBUS master (through MULTIBUS® I/O Write)	1
Bus Flag Interrupt	Interrupt to MULTIBUS® (Selectable for INT0 to INT7) generated from on-board 80188 I/O Write	1
iSBX™ connectors iSBX™ DMA	Function determined by iSBX™ MULTIMODULE™ board DMA interrupt from iSBX™(TDMA)	4 (Two per connector) 2
Bus fail-safe timeout Interrupt	Indicates iSBC® 188/48 board timed out either waiting for MULTIBUS® access or timed out from no acknowledge while on MULTIBUS System Bus	1
Latched Interrupt	Converts pulsed event to a level interrupt. Example: 8237A-5 EOP	1
OR-gate Matrix	Concentrates up to 4 interrupts to 1 interrupt (selectable by stake pins)	1
Ring Indicator Interrupt	Latches a ring indicator event from serial channels 4,5,6, or 7	1
NOR-Gate Matrix	Inverts up to 2 interrupts into 1 (selectable by stake pins)	1

iSBC® 188/56

PRELIMINARY

SUPPORT FOR THE 80130 COMPONENT

Intel does not support the direct processor execution of the iRMX nucleus primitives from the 80130 component. The 80130 component provides timers and interrupt controllers only.

EXPANSION

EPROM Expansion

Memory may be expanded by adding Intel compatible memory expansion boards. The universal site memory can be expanded to six sockets by adding the iSBC 341 MULTIMODULE board for a maximum total of 192K bytes of universal site memory.

iSBX™ MULTIMODULE™ Expansion Module

Two 8-bit iSBX MULTIMODULE connectors are provided on the iSBC 188/56 board. Using iSBX modules additional functions can be added to extend the I/O capability of the board. In addition to specialized or custom designed iSBX boards, there is a broad range of iSBX MULTIMODULE boards from the Intel including parallel I/O, analog I/O, IEEE 488 GPIB, floppy disk, magnetic bubbles, video and serial I/O boards.

The serial I/O MULTIMODULE boards available include the iSBX 354 Dual Channel Expansion MULTIMODULE board. Each iSBX 354 MULTIMODULE board adds two channels of serial I/O to the iSBC 188/56 board for a maximum of twelve serial channels. The 82530 serial communications controller on the MULTIMODULE board handles a large variety of serial communications protocols. This is the same serial controller as is used on the iSBC 188/56 board to offer directly compatible expansion capability for the iSBC 188/56 COMMputer board.

MULTIBUS® INTERFACE

The iSBC 188/56 Advanced COMMputer board can be a MULTIBUS master or intelligent slave in a multimaster system. The iSBC 188/56 board incorporates a flag byte signalling mechanism for use in multiprocessor environments where the iSBC 188/56 board is acting as an intelligent slave. The mechanism provides an interrupt handshake from the MULTIBUS System Bus to the on-board-processor and vice-versa.

The Multimaster capabilities of the iSBC 188/56 board offers easy expansion of processing capacity and the benefits of multiprocessing. Memory and I/O capacity may be expanded and additional functions added using Intel MULTIBUS compatible expansion boards.

SPECIFICATIONS

Word Size

Instruction—8, 16, 24 or 32 bits
Data Path—8 bits

Processor Clock	82530 Clock	DMA Clock
8 MHz	4.9152 MHz	4 MHz

Dual Port RAM

iSBC 188/56 Board—256 bytes

As viewed from the 80188—64K bytes

As viewed from the MULTIBUS System Bus—
 Choice: 0, 16K or 48K

EPROM

iSBC® 188/56 Board using:	Size	On Board Capacity	Address Range
2732	4K	8K bytes	FE000-FFFFF$_H$
2764	8K	16K bytes	FC000-FFFFF$_H$
27128	16K	32K bytes	F8000-FFFFF$_H$
27256	32K	64K bytes	F0000-FFFFF$_H$

Memory Expansion

EPROM with iSBC® Board using:	Capacity	Address Range
2732	24K bytes	F8000-FFFFF$_H$
2764	48K bytes	F0000-FFFFF$_H$
27128	96K bytes	E0000-FFFFF$_H$
27256	192K bytes	C0000-FFFFF$_H$

I/O Capacity

Serial—8 programmable lines using four 82530 components

iSBX MULTIMODULE—2 iSBX single-wide boards

Serial Communications Characteristics

Synchronous—Internal or external character synchronization on one or two synchronous characters.

Asynchronous—5-8 bits and 1, 1½, or 2 stop bits per character; programmable clock factor; break detection and generation; parity, overrun, and framing error detection.

iSBC® 188/56

Baud Rates

Synchronous X1 Clock	
Baud Rate	82530 Count Value (Decimal)
64000	36
48000	49
19200	126
9600	254
4800	510
2400	1022
1800	1363
1200	2046
300	8190

Asynchronous X 16 Clock	
Baud Rate	82530 Count Value (Decimal)
19200	6
9600	14
4800	30
2400	62
1800	83
1200	126
300	510
110	1394

Interfaces

iSBX™ BUS

The iSBC 188/56 board meets iSBX compliance level D8/8 DMA

MULTIBUS® SYSTEM BUS

The iSBC 188/56 board meets MULTIBUS compliance level Master/Slave D8 M24 I16 VO EL

SERIAL RS232C SIGNALS

CD	Carrier Detect
CTS	Clear to Send
DSR	Data Set Ready
DTE TXC	Transmit Clock
DTR	Data Terminal Ready
RTS	Request to Send
RXC	Receive Clock
RXD	Receive Data
SG	Signal Ground
TXD	Transmit Data
RI	Ring Indicator

RS422A/449 SIGNALS

RC	Receive Common
RD	Receive Data
RT	Receive Timing
SD	Send Data
TT	Terminal Timing

Environmental Characteristics

Temperature—0 to 55°C at 200 Linear Feet/Min. (LFM) Air Velocity

Humidity—to 90%, non-condensing (25°C to 70°C)

Physical Characteristics

Width—30.48 cm (12.00 in)
Length—17.15 cm (6.75 in)
Height—1.04 cm (.41 in)
Weight—595 gm (21 oz)

Electrical Characteristics

The power required per voltage for the iSBC 188/56 board is shown below. These numbers do not include the current required by universal memory sites or expansion modules.

Voltage (Volts)	Current (Amps) typ.	Power (Watts) typ.
+5	4.56A	22.8W
+12	.12A	1.5W
-12	.11A	1.3W

ORDERING INFORMATION

Part Number	Description
iSBC 188/56	8-Serial Channel Advanced Communicating Computer

Reference Manuals

iSBC 188/56 Advanced Communications Computer Reference Manual Order Number 148209-001

iSBC® 534
FOUR CHANNEL COMMUNICATION EXPANSION BOARD

- Serial I/O expansion through four programmable synchronous and asynchronous communications channels

- Individual software programmable baud rate generation for each serial I/O channel

- Two independent programmable 16-bit interval timers

- Sixteen maskable interrupt request lines with priority encoded and programmable interrupt algorithms

- Jumper selectable interface register addresses

- 16-bit parallel I/O interface compatible with Bell 801 automatic calling unit

- RS232C/CCITT V.24 interfaces plus 20 mA optically isolated current loop interfaces (sockets)

- Programmable digital loopback for diagnostics

- Interface control for auto answer and auto originate modems

The iSBC 534 Four Channel Communication Expansion Board is a member of Intel's complete line of memory and I/O expansion boards. The iSBC 534 interfaces directly to any single board computer via the MULTIBUS to provide expansion of system serial communications capability. Four fully programmable synchronous and asynchronous serial channels with RS232C buffering and provision for 20 mA optically isolated current loop buffering are provided. Baud rates, data formats, and interrupt priorities for each channel are individually software selectable. In addition to the extensive complement of EIA Standard RS232C signals provided, the iSBC 534 provides 16 lines of RS232C buffered programmable parallel I/O. This interface is configured to be directly compatible with the Bell Model 801 automatic calling unit. These capabilities provide a flexible and easy means for interfacing Intel iSBC based systems to RS232C and optically isolated current loop compatible terminals, cassettes, asynchronous and synchronous modems, and distributed processing networks.

Intel Corporation Assumes No Responsibility for the Use of Any Circuitry Other Than Circuitry Embodied in an Intel Product. No Other Circuit Patent Licenses are Implied. Information Contained Herein Supercedes Previously Published Specifications On These Devices From Intel.

© INTEL CORPORATION 1985

iSBC® 534

FUNCTIONAL DESCRIPTION
Communications Interface
Four programmable communications interfaces using Intel's 8251A Universal Synchronous/Asynchronous Receiver/Transmitter (USART) are contained on the board.* Each USART can be programmed by the system software to individually select the desired asynchronous or synchronous serial data transmission technique (including IBM Bisync). The mode of operation (i.e., synchronous or asynchronous), data format, control character format, parity, and baud rate are all under program control. Each 8251A provides full duplex, double buffered transmit and receive capability. Parity, overrun, and framing error detection are all incorporated in each USART. Each set of RS232C command lines, serial data lines, and signal ground lines are brought out to 26-pin edge connectors that mate with RS232C flat or round cables.

16-Bit Interval Timers
The iSBC 534 provides six fully programmable and independent BCD and binary 16-bit interval timers utilizing two Intel 8253 programmable interval timers.* Four timers are available to the systems designer to generate baud rates for the USARTs under software control. Routing for the outputs from the other two counters is jumper selectable. Each may be independently routed to the programmable interrupt controller to provide real time clocking or to the USARTs (for applications requiring different transmit and receive baud rates). In utilizing the iSBC 534, the systems designer simply configures, via software, each timer independently to meet system requirements. Whenever a given baud rate or time delay is needed, software commands to the programmable timers select the desired function. Three functions of these timers are supported on the iSBC 534, as shown in Table 1. The contents of each counter may be read at any time during system operation.

Table 1. Programmable Timer Functions

Function	Operation
Interrupt on terminal count	When terminal count is reached an interrupt request is generated. This function is used for the generation of real-time clocks.
Rate generator	Divide by N counter. The output will go low for one input clock cycle and high for N – 1 input clock periods.
Square wave rate generator	Output will remain high for one-half the count and low for the other half of the count.

Interrupt Request Lines
Two independent Intel 8259A programmable interrupt controllers (PIC's) provide vectoring for 16 interrupt levels.* As shown in Table 2, a selection of three priority processing algorithms is available to the system designer. The manner in which requests are serviced may thus be configured to match system requirements. Priority assignments may be reconfigured dynamically via software at any time during system operation. Any combination of interrupt levels may be masked through storage, via software, of a single byte to the interrupt mask register of each PIC. Each PIC's interrupt request

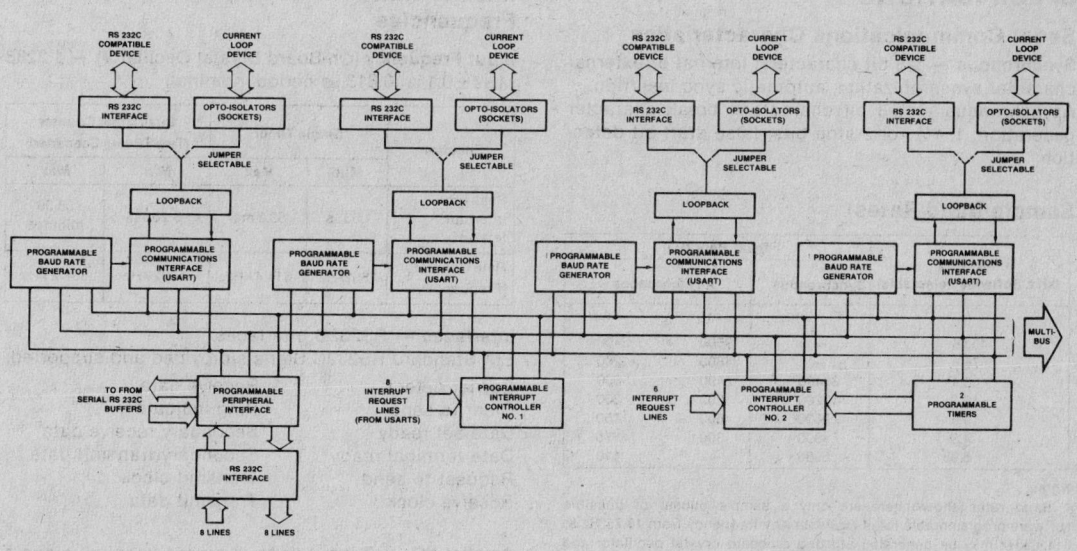

Figure 1. iSBC® 534 Four Channel Communications Expansion Board Block Diagram

iSBC® 534

output line may be jumper selected to drive any of the nine interrupt lines on the MULTIBUS.

Table 2. Interrupt Priority Options

Algorithm	Operation
Fully nested	Interrupt request line priorities fixed at 0 as highest, 7 as lowest.
Auto-rotating	Equal priority. Each level, after receiving service, becomes the lowest priority level until next interrupt occurs.
Specific priority	System software assigns lowest priority level. Priority of all other levels based in sequence numerically on this assignment.

Table 3. Interrupt Assignments

Interrupt Request Line	PIC 0	PIC 1
0	PORT 0 R_X RDY	PIT 1 counter 1
1	PORT 0 T_X RDY	PIT 2 counter 2
2	PORT 1 R_X RDY	Ring indicator (all ports)
3	PORT 1 T_X RDY	Present next digit
4	PORT 2 R_X RDY	Carrier detect port 0
5	PORT 2 T_X RDY	Carrier detect port 1
6	PORT 3 R_X RDY	Carrier detect port 2
7	PORT 3 T_X RDY	Carrier detect port 3

Interrupt Request Generation — As shown in Table 3, interrupt requests may originate from 16 sources. Two jumper selectable interrupt requests (8 total) can be automatically generated by each USART when a character is ready to be transferred to the MULTIBUS system bus (i.e., receive buffer is full) or a character has been transmitted (transmit buffer is empty). Jumper selectable requests can be generated by two of the programmable timers (PITs), and six lines are routed directly from peripherals to accept carrier detect (4 lines), ring indicator, and the Bell 801 present next digit request lines.

Systems Compatibility

The iSBC 534 provides 16 RS232C buffered parallel I/O lines implemented utilizing an Intel 8255A programmable peripheral interface (PPI) configured to operate in mode 0.* These lines are configured to be directly compatible with the Bell 801 automatic calling unit (ACU). This capability allows the iSBC 534 to interface to Bell 801 type ACUs and up to four modems or other serial communications devices. For systems not requiring interface to an ACU, the parallel I/O lines may also be used as general purpose RS232C compatible control lines in system implementation.

---

* Complete operational details on the Intel 8251A USART, the Intel 8253 Programmable Interval Timer, the Intel 8255A Programmable Peripheral Interface, and the Intel 8259A Programmable Interrupt Controller are contained in the Intel Component Data Catalog.

SPECIFICATIONS

Serial Communications Characteristics

Synchronous — 5-8 bit characters; internal or external character synchronization; automatic sync insertion.
Asynchronous — 5-8 bit characters; break character generation; 1, 1½, or 2 stop bits; false start bit detection.

Sample Baud Rates[1]

Frequency[2] (kHz, Software Selectable)	Baud Rate (Hz)		
	Synchronous	Asynchronous	
		÷ 16	÷ 64
153.6	—	9600	2400
76.8	—	4800	1200
38.4	38400	2400	600
19.2	19200	1200	300
9.6	9600	600	150
4.8	4800	300	75
6.98	6980	—	110

Notes:
1. Baud rates shown here are only a sample subset of possible software-programmable rates available. Any frequency from 18.75 Hz to 614.4 kHz may be generated utilizing on-board crystal oscillator and 16-bit programmable interval timer (used here as frequency divider).
2. Frequency selected by I/O writes of appropriate 16-bit frequency factor to Baud Rate Register.

Interval Timer and Baud Rate Generator Frequencies

Input Frequency (On-Board Crystal Oscillator) — 1.2288 MHz ± 0.1% (0.813 μs period, nominal).

Function	Single Timer		Dual/Timer Counter (Two Timers Cascaded)	
	Min	Max	Min	Max
Real-Time Interrupt Interval	1.63 μs	53.3 ms	3.26 μs	58.25 minutes
Rate Generator (Frequency)	18.75 Hz	614.4 kHz	0.0029 Hz	307.2 kHz

Interfaces — RS232C Interfaces
EIA Standard RS232C Signals provided and supported:

Carrier detect	Receive data
Clear to send	Ring indicator
Data set ready	Secondary receive data
Data terminal ready	Secondary transmit data
Request to send	Transmit clock
Receive clock	Transmit data

Parallel I/O — 8 input lines, 8 output lines, all signals RS232C compatible
Bus — All signals MULTIBUS system bus compatible

iSBC® 534

I/O Addressing
The USART, interval timer, interrupt controller, and parallel interface registers of the iSBC 534 are configured as a block of 16 I/O address locations. The location of this block is jumper selectable to begin at any 16-byte I/O address boundary (i.e., 00H, 10H, 20H, etc.).

I/O Access Time
400 ns USART registers
400 ns Parallel I/O registers
400 ns Interval timer registers
400 ns Interrupt controller registers

Compatible Connectors

Interface	Pins (qty.)	Centers (in.)	Mating Connectors
Bus	86	0.156	Viking 2KH43/9 AMK12
Serial and parallel I/O	26	0.1	3M 3462-0001 or TI H312113

Compatible Opto-Isolators

Function	Supplier	Part Number
Driver	Fairchild General Electric Monsanto	4N33
Receiver	Fairchild General Electric Monsanto	4N37

Physical Characteristics
Width — 12.00 in. (30.48 cm)
Height — 6.75 in. (17.15 cm)
Depth — 0.50 in. (1.27 cm)
Weight — 14 oz (398 gm)

Electrical Characteristics
Average DC Current

Voltage	Without Opto-Isolators	With Opto-Isolators[1]
$V_{CC} = +5V$	1.9 A, max	1.9 A, max
$V_{DD} = +12V$	275 mA, max	420 mA, max
$V_{AA} = -12V$	250 mA, max	400 mA, max

Note
1. With four 4N33 and four 4N37 opto-isolator packages installed in sockets provided to implement four 20 mA current loop interfaces.

Environmental Characteristics
Operating Temperature — 0°C to +55°C

Reference Manual
502140-002 — iSBC 534 Hardware Reference Manual (NOT SUPPLIED)

Reference manuals are shipped with each product only if designated SUPPLIED (see above). Manuals may be ordered from any Intel sales representative, distributor office or from Intel Literature Department, 3065 Bowers Avenue, Santa Clara, California 95051.

ORDERING INFORMATION

Part Number	Description
SBC 534	Four Channel Communication Expansion Board

ISBC® 544
INTELLIGENT COMMUNICATIONS CONTROLLER

- iSBC® Communications Controller acting as a single board communications computer or an intelligent slave for communications expansion

- On-board dedicated 8085A Microprocessor providing communications control and buffer management for four programmable synchronous/asynchronous channels

- Sockets for up to 8K bytes of EPROM

- 16K bytes of dual port dynamic read/write memory with on-board refresh

- Extended MULTIBUS® addressing permits iSBC 544 board partitioning into 16K-byte segments in a 1-megabyte address space

- Ten programmable parallel I/O lines compatible with Bell 801 Automatic Calling Unit

- Twelve levels of programmable interrupt control

- Individual software programmable baud rate generation for each serial I/O channel

- Three independent programmable interval timer/counters

- Interface control for auto answer and auto originate modem

The iSBC 544 Intelligent Communications Controller is a member of Intel's family of single-board computers, memory, I/O, and peripheral controller boards. The iSBC 544 board is a complete communications controller on a single 6.75 × 12.00 inch printed circuit card. The on-board 8085A CPU may perform local communications processing by directly interfacing with on-board read/write memory, nonvolatile read only memory, four synchronous/asynchronous serial I/O ports, RS232/RS366 compatible parallel I/O, programmable timers, and programmable interrupts.

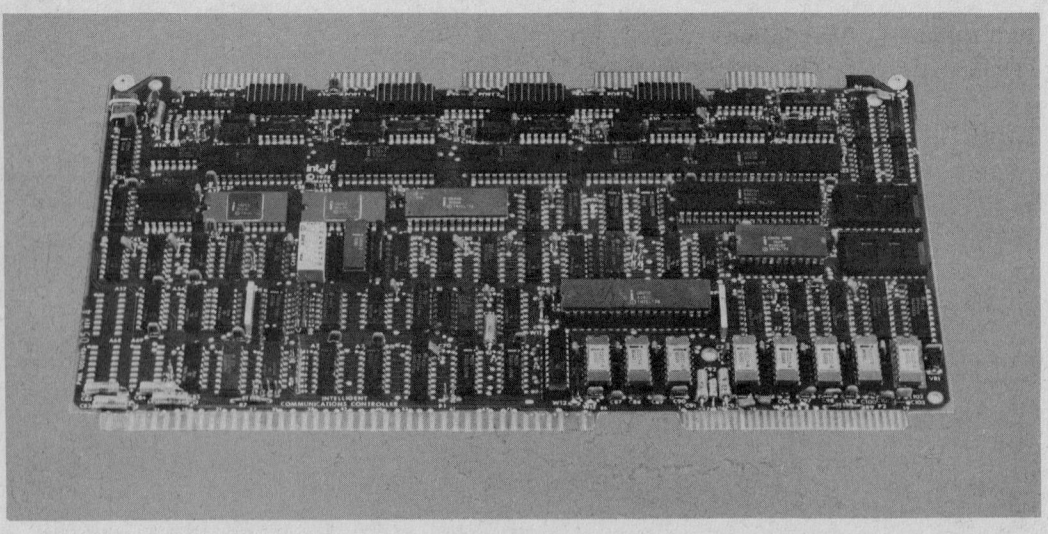

Intel Corporation Assumes No Responsibility for the Use of Any Circuitry Other Than Circuitry Embodied in an Intel Product. No Other Circuit Patent Licenses are Implied. Information Contained Herein Supercedes Previously Published Specifications On These Devices From Intel.

© INTEL CORPORATION 1985

iSBC® 544

FUNCTIONAL DESCRIPTION

Intelligent Communications Controller

Two Mode Operation — The iSBC 544 board is capable of operating in one of two modes: 1) as a single board communications computer with all computer and communications interface hardware on a single board; 2) as an "intelligent bus slave" that can perform communications related tasks as a peripheral processor to one or more bus masters. The iSBC 544 may be configured to operate as a stand-alone single board communications computer with all MPU, memory and I/O elements on a single board. In this mode of operation, the iSBC 544 may also interface with expansion memory and I/O boards (but no additional bus masters). The iSBC 544 performs as an intelligent slave to the bus master by performing all communications related tasks. Complete synchronous and asynchronous I/O and data management are controlled by the on-board 8085A CPU to coordinate up to four serial channels. Using the iSBC 544 as an intelligent slave, multichannel serial transfers can be managed entirely on-board, freeing the bus master to perform other system functions.

Architecture — The iSBC 544 board is functionally partitioned into three major sections: I/O, central computer, and shared dual port RAM memory (Figure 1). The I/O hardware is centered around the four Intel 8251A USART devices providing fully programmable serial interfacing. Included here as well is a 10-bit parallel interface compatible with the Bell 801 automatic calling unit, or equivalent. The I/O is under full control of the on-board CPU and is protected from access by system bus masters. The second major segment of the intelligent communications controller is a central computer, with an 8085A CPU providing powerful processing capability. The 8085A together with on-board EPROM / ROM, static RAM, programmable timers/counters, and program-

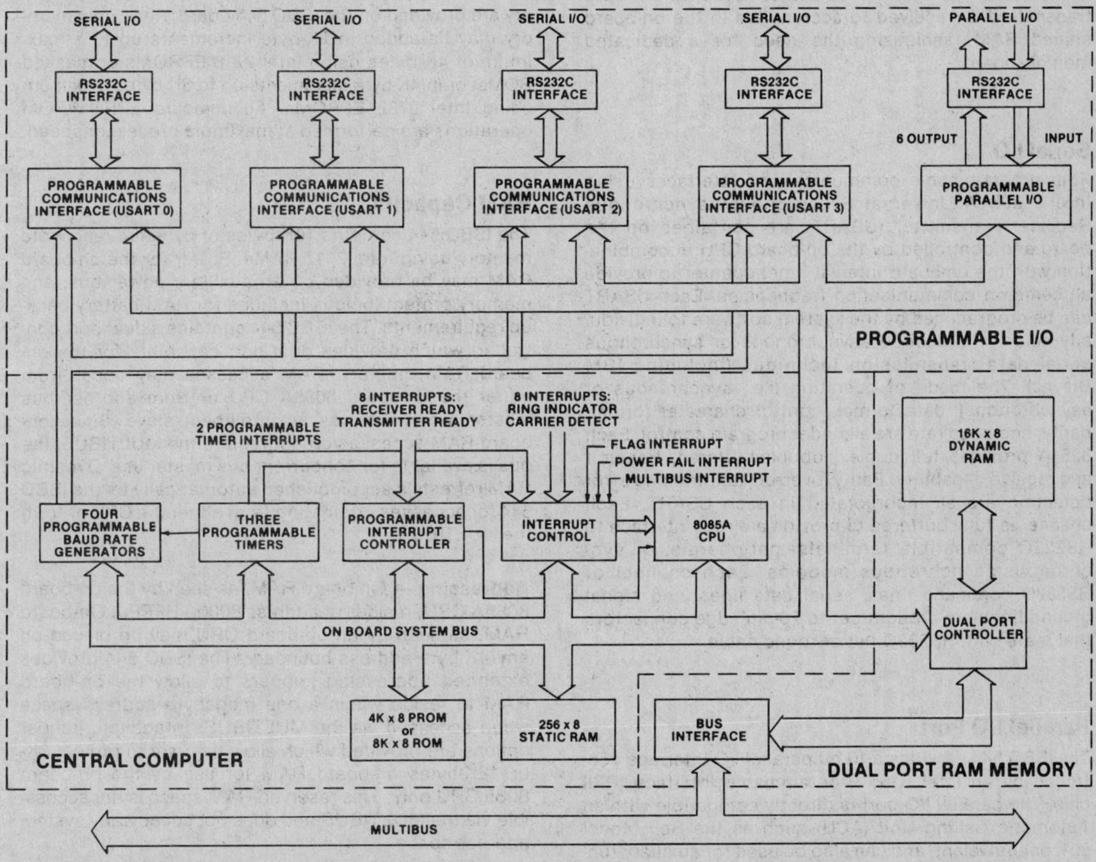

Figure 1. iSBC® 544 Intelligent Communications Controller Block Diagram

iSBC® 544

mable interrupt control provide the intelligence to manage sophisticated communications operations on-board the iSBC 544 board. The timer/counters and interrupt control are also common to the I/O area providing programmable baud rates to the USARTs and prioritizing interrupts generated from the USARTs. The central computer functions are protected for access only by the on-board 8085A. Likewise, the on-board 8085A may not gain access to the system bus when being used as an intelligent slave. When the iSBC 544 is used as a bus master, the on-board 8085A CPU controls complete system operation accessing on-board functions as well as memory and I/O expansion. The third major segment, dual port RAM memory, is the key link between the iSBC 544 intelligent slave and bus masters managing the system functions. The dual port concept allows a common block of dynamic memory to be accessed by the on-board 8085A CPU and off-board bus masters. The system program can, therefore, utilize the shared dual port RAM to pass command and status information between the bus masters and on-board CPU. In addition, the dual port concept permits blocks of data transmitted or received to accumulate in the on-board shared RAM, minimizing the need for a dedicated memory board.

Serial I/O

Four programmable communications interfaces using Intel's 8251A Universal Synchronous/Asynchronous Receiver/Transmitter (USART) are contained on the board and controlled by the on-board CPU in combination with the on-board interval timer/counter to provide all common communication frequencies. Each USART can be programmed by the system software to individually select the desired asynchronous or synchronous serial data transmission technique (including IBM Bisync). The mode of operation (i.e., synchronous or asynchronous), data format, control character format, parity, and baud rate are all under program control. Each 8251A provides full duplex, double-buffered, transmit and receive capability. Parity, overrun, and framing error detection are all incorporated in each USART. Each channel is fully buffered to provide a direct interface to RS232C compatible terminals, peripherals, or synchronous/asynchronous modems. Each channel of RS232C command lines, serial data lines, and signal ground lines are brought out to 26-pin edge connectors that mate with RS232C flat or round cable.

Parallel I/O Port

The iSBC 544 provides a 10-bit parallel I/O interface controlled by an Intel 8155 Programmable Interface (PPI) chip. The parallel I/O port is directly compatible with an Automatic Calling Unit (ACU) such as the Bell Model 801, or equivalent, and can also be used for auxiliary functions. All signals are RS232C compatible, and the interface cable signal assignments meet RS366 specifications. For systems not requiring an ACU interface, the parallel I/O port can be used for any general purpose interface requiring RS232C compatibility.

Central Processing Unit

Intel's powerful 8-bit n-channel 8085A CPU, fabricated on a single LSI chip, is the central processor for the iSBC 544. The 8085A CPU is directly software compatible with the Intel 8080A CPU. The 8085A contains six 8-bit general purpose registers and an accumulator. The six general purpose registers may be addressed individually or in pairs, providing both single and double precision operators. The minimum instruction execution time is 1.45 microseconds. The 8085A CPU has a 16-bit program counter. An external stack, located within any portion of iSBC 544 read/write memory, may be used as a last-in/first-out storage area for the contents of the program counter, flags, accumulator, and all of the six general purpose registers. A 16-bit stack pointer controls the addressing of this external stack. This stack provides subroutine nesting bounded only by memory size.

EPROM/ROM Capacity

Sockets for up to 8K bytes of nonvolatile read only memory are provided on the iSBC 544 board. Read only memory may be added in 2K-byte increments up to a maximum of 4K bytes using Intel 2716 EPROMs or masked ROMs; or in 4K-byte increments up to 8K bytes maximum using Intel 2732 EPROMs. All on-board EPROM/ROM operations are performed at maximum processor speed.

RAM Capacity

The iSBC 544 contains 16K bytes of dynamic read/write memory using Intel 2117 RAMs. Power for the on-board RAM may be provided on an auxiliary power bus, and memory protect logic is included for RAM battery back-up requirements. The iSBC 544 contains a dual port controller, which provides dual port capability for the on-board RAM memory. RAM accesses may occur from either the on-board 8085A CPU or from another bus master, when used as an intelligent slave. Since on-board RAM accesses do not require the MULTIBUS, the bus is available for concurrent bus master use. Dynamic RAM refresh is accomplished automatically by the iSBC 544 for accesses originating from either the CPU or from the MULTIBUS.

Addressing — On board RAM, as seen by the on-board 8085A CPU, resides at address 8000_H-$BFFF_H$. On-board RAM, as seen by an off-board CPU, may be placed on any 4K-byte address boundary. The iSBC 544 provides extended addressing jumpers to allow the on-board RAM to reside within a one megabyte address space when accessed via the MULTIBUS. In additon, jumper options are provided which allow the user to protect 8K- or 12K-bytes on-board RAM for use by the on-board 8085 CPU only. This reserved RAM space is not accessible via the MULTIBUS and does not occupy any system address space.

Static RAM — The iSBC 544 board also has 256 bytes of static RAM located on the Intel 8155 PPI. This memory is only accessible to the on-board 8085A CPU and is located at address $7F00_H$-$7FFF_H$.

iSBC® 544

Programmable Timers

The iSBC 544 board provides seven fully programmable and independent interval timer/counters utilizing two Intel 8253 Programmable Interval Timers (PIT), and the Intel 8155. The two Intel 8253 PITs provide six independent BCD or binary 16-bit interval timer/counters and the 8155 provides one 14-bit binary timer/counter. Four of the PIT timers (BDG0-3) are dedicated to the USARTs providing fully independent programmable baud rates.

Three General Use Timers — The fifth timer (BDG4) may be used as an auxiliary baud rate to any of the four USARTs or may alternatively be cascaded with timer six to provide extended interrupt intervals. The sixth PIT timer/counter (TINT1) can be used to generate interrupt intervals to the on-board 8085A. In addition to the timer/counters on the 8253 PITs, the iSBC 544 has a 14-bit timer available on the 8155 PPI providing a third general use timer/counter (TINT0). This timer output is jumper selectable to the interrupt structure of the on-board 8085A CPU to provide additional timer/counter capability.

Timer Functions — In utilizing the iSBC 544 board, the systems designer simply configures, via software, each timer independently to meet systems requirements. Whenever a given baud rate or interrupt interval is needed, software commands to the programmable timers select the desired function. The on-board PITs together with the 8155 provide a total of seven timer/counters and six operating modes. Mode 3 of the 8253 is the primary operating mode of the four dedicated USART baud rate generators. The timer/counters and useful modes of operation for the general use timer/counters are shown in Table 1.

Interrupt Capability

The iSBC 544 board provides interrupt service for up to 21 interrupt sources. Any of the 21 sources may interrupt the intelligent controller, and all are brought through the interrupt logic to 12 interrupt levels. Four interrupt levels are handled directly by the interrupt processing capability of the 8085A CPU and eight levels are serviced from an Intel 8259A Programmable Interrupt Controller (PIC) routing an interrupt request output to the INTR input of the 8085A (see Table 2).

Interrupt Sources — The 22 interrupt sources originate from both on-board communications functions and the Multibus. Two interrupts are routed from each of the four USARTs (8 interrupts total) to indicate that the transmitter and receiver are ready to move a data byte to or from the on-board CPU. The PIC is dedicated to accepting these 8 interrupts to optimize USART service request. One of eight interrupt request lines are jumper selectable for direct interface from a bus master via the system bus. Two auxiliary timers (TINT0 from 8155 and TINT1 from 8253) are jumper selectable to provide general purpose counter/timer interrupts. A jumper selectable Flag Interrupt is generated to allow any bus master to interrupt the iSBC 544 by writing into the base address of the shared dual port memory accessable to the system. The Flag Interrupt is then cleared by the iSBC 544 when the on-board processor reads the base address. This interrupt provides an interrupt link between

Table 1. Programmable Timer Functions

Function	Operation	Counter
Interrupt on Terminal Count (Mode 0)	When terminal count is reached, an interrupt request is generated. This function is useful for generation of real-time clocks.	8253 TINT1
Rate Generator (Mode 2)	Divide by N counter. The output will go low for one input clock cycle and high for N-1 input clock periods.	8253 BDG4 *
Square-Wave Rate Generator (Mode 3)	Output will remain high until one-half the TC has been completed, and go low for the other half of the count. This is the primary operating mode used for generating a Baud rate clocked to the USARTs.	8253 BDG0-4 TINT1
Software Triggered Strobe (Mode 4)	When the TC is loaded, the counter will begin. On TC the output will go low for one input clock period.	8253 BDG4 * TINT1
Single Pulse	Single pulse when TC reached.	8155 TINT0
Repetitive Single Pulse	Repetitive single pulse each time TC is reached until a new command is loaded.	8155 TINT0

* BDG4 is jumper selectable as an auxiliary baud rate generator to the USARTs or as a cascaded output to TINT1. BDG4 may be used in modes 2 and 4 only when configured as a cascaded output.

Table 2. Interrupt Vector Memory Locations

Interrupt Source		Vector Location	Interrupt Level
Power Fail	TRAP	24$_H$	1
8253 TINT1 8155 TINT0	RST 7.5	3C$_H$	2
Ring Indicator (1) Carrier Detect	RST 6.5	34$_H$	3
Flag Interrupt INT0/-INT7/ (1 of 8)	RST 5.5	2C$_H$	4
RXRDY0 TXRDY0 RXRDY1 TXRDY1 RXRDY 2 TXRDY2 RXRDY3 TXRDY3	INTR	Programmable	5-12

(1) Four ring indicator interrupts and four carrier detect interrupts are summed to the RST 6.5 input. The 8155 may be interrogated to inspect any one of the eight signals.

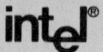

iSBC® 544

a bus master and intelligent slave (See System Programming). Eight inputs from the serial ports are monitored to detect a ring indicator and carrier detect from each of the four channels. These eight interrupt sources are summed to a single interrupt level of the 8085A CPU. If one of these eight interrupts occur, the 8155 PPI can then be interrogated to determine which port caused the interrupt. Finally, a jumper selectable Power Fail Interrupt is available from the Multibus to detect a power down condition.

8085 Interrupt — Thirteen of the twenty-two interrupt sources are available directly to four interrupt inputs of the on-board 8085A CPU. Requests routed to the 8085A interrupt inputs, TRAP, RST 7.5, RST 6.5 and RST 5.5 have a unique vector memory address. An 8085A jump instruction at each of these addresses then provides software linkage to interrupt service routines located independently anywhere in the Memory. All interrupt inputs with the exception of the TRAP may be masked via software.

8259A Interrupts — Eight interrupt sources signaling transmitter and receiver ready from the four USARTs are channeled directly to the Intel 8259A PIC. The PIC then provides vectoring for the next eight interrupt levels. Operating mode and priority assignments may be reconfigured dynamically via software at any time during system operation. The PIC accepts transmitter and receiver interrupts from the four USARTs. It then determines which of the incoming requests is of highest priority, determines whether this request is of higher priority than the level currently being serviced, and, if appropriate, issues an interrupt to the CPU. The output of the PIC is applied directly to the INTR input of the 8085A. Any combination of interrupt levels may be masked, via software, by storing a single byte in the interrupt mask register of the PIC. When the 8085A responds to a PIC interrupt, the PIC will generate a CALL instruction for each interrupt level. These addresses are equally spaced at intervals of 4 or 8 (software selectable) bytes. Interrupt response to the PIC is software programmable to a 32- or 64-byte block of memory. Interrupt sequences may be expanded from this block with a single 8085A jump instruction at each of these addresses.

Interrupt Output — In addition, the iSBC 544 board may be jumper selected to generate an interrupt from the on-board serial output data (SOD) of the 8085A. The SOD signal may be jumpered to any one of the 8 MULTIBUS interrupt lines (INT0/-INT7/) to provide an interrupt signal directly to a bus master.

Power-Fail Control

Control logic is also included to accept a power-fail interrupt in conjunction with the AC-low signal from the iSBC 635 Power Supply or equivalent.

Expansion Capabilities

When the iSBC 544 board is used as a single board communications controller, memory and I/O capacity may be expanded and additional functions added using Intel MULTIBUS™ compatible expansion boards. In this mode, no other bus masters may be configured in the system. Memory may be expanded to a 65K byte capacity by adding user specified combinations of RAM boards, EPROM boards, or combination boards. Input/output capacity may be increased by adding digital I/O and analog I/O expansion boards. Furthermore, multiple iSBC 544 boards may be included in an expanded system using one iSBC 544 board as a single board communications computer and additional controllers as intelligent slaves.

System Programming

In the system programming environment, the iSBC 544 board appears as an additional RAM memory module when used as an intelligent slave. The master CPU communicates with the iSBC 544 board as if it were just an extension of system memory. Because the iSBC 544 board is treated as memory by the system, the user is able to program into it a command structure which will allow the iSBC 544 board to control its own I/O and memory operation. To enhance the programming of the iSBC 544 board, the user has been given some specific tools. The tools are: 1) the flag interrupt, 2) an on-board RAM memory area that is accessible to both an off-board CPU and the on-board 8085A through which a communications path can exist, and 3) access to the bus interrupt line.

Flag Interrupt — The Flag Interrupt is generated anytime a write command is performed by an off-board CPU to the base address of the iSBC 544 board's RAM. This interrupt provides a means for the master CPU to notify the iSBC 544 board that it wishes to establish a communications sequence. In systems with more than one intelligent slave, the flag interrupt provides a unique interrupt to each slave outside the normal eight MULTIBUS interrupt lines (INT0/-INT7/).

On-Board RAM — The on-board 16K byte RAM area that is accessible to both an off-board CPU and the on-board 8085A can be located on any 4K boundary in the system. The selected base address of the iSBC 544 RAM will cause a flag interrupt when written into by an off-board CPU.

Bus Access — The third tool to improve system operation as an intelligent slave is access to the Multibus interrupt lines. The iSBC 544 board can both respond to interrupt signals from an off-board CPU, and generate an interrupt to the off-board CPU via the MULTIBUS.

System Development Capability

The development cycle of iSBC 544 board based products may be significantly reduced using the Intellec series microcomputer development systems. The Intellec resident macroassembler, text editor, and system monitor greatly simplify the design, development and debug of iSBC 544 system software. An optional ISIS-II diskette operating system provides a linker, object code locater, and library manager. A unique in-circuit emulator (ICE-85) option provides the capability of developing and debugging software directly on the iSBC 544 board.

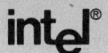

iSBC® 544

SPECIFICATIONS

Serial Communications Characteristics

Synchronous — 5-8 bit characters; automatic sync insertion; parity.

Asynchronous — 5-8 bit characters; break character generation; 1, 1½, or 2 stop bits; false start bit detection; break character detection.

Baud Rates

Frequency (KHz)[1] (Software Selectable)	Baud Rate (Hz)[2] Synchronous	Asynchronous ÷16	÷64
153.6	— —	9600	2400
76.8	— —	4800	1200
38.4	38400	2400	600
19.2	19200	1200	300
9.6	9600	600	150
4.8	4800	300	75
6.98	6980	— —	110

Notes:
1) Frequency selected by I/O writes of appropriate 16-bit frequency factor to Baud Rate Register.
2) Baud rates shown here are only a sample subset of possible software programmable rates available. Any frequency from 18.75 Hz to 614.4 KHz may be generated utilizing on-board crystal oscillator and 16-bit Programmable Interval Timer (used here as a frequency divider).

8085A CPU

Word Size — 8, 16 or 24 bits/instruction; 8 bits of data

Cycle Time — 1.45/usec ± .1% for fastest executable instruction; i.e. four clock cycles.

Clock Rate — 2.76 MHz ± .1%

System Access Time

Dual port memory — 740 nsec
Note: Assumes no refresh contention

Memory Capacity

On-Board ROM/PROM — 4K, or 8K bytes of user installed ROM or EPROM.

On-Board Static RAM — 256 bytes on 8155.

On-Board Dynamic RAM (on-board access) — 16K bytes. Integrity maintained during power failure with user-furnished batteries (optional).

On-Board Dyanmic RAM (MULTIBUS access) — 4K, 8K, or 16K-bytes available to bus by switch selection.

Memory Addressing

On-Board ROM/PROM — 0-0FFF (using 2716 EPROMs or masked ROMs); 0-1FFF (using 2732A EPROMs)

On-Board Static Ram — 256 bytes: 7F00-7FFF

On-Board Dynamic RAM (on-board access) — 16K bytes: 8000-BFFF.

On-Board Dynamic RAM (MULTIBUS access) — any 4K increment 00000-FF000 which is switch and jumper selectable. 4K- 8K- or 16K-bytes can be made available to the bus by switch selection.

I/O Capacity

Serial — 4 programmable channels using four 8251A USARTs.

Parallel — 10 programmable lines available for Bell 801 ACU, or equivalent use. Two auxiliary jumper selectable signals.

I/O Addressing

On-Board Programmable I/O

Port	Data	Control
USART 0	D0	D1
USART 1	D2	D3
USART 2	D4	D5
USART 3	D6	D7
8155 PPI	E9 (Port A)	E8
	EA (Port B)	
	EB (Port C)	

Interrupts

Addresses for 8259A Registers (Hex notation, I/O address space)

- E6 Interrupt request register
- E6 In-service register
- E7 Mask register
- E6 Command register
- E7 Block address register
- E6 Status (polling register)

Note: Several registers have the same physical address: Sequence of access and one data bit of the control word determines which register will respond.

Interrupt levels routed to the 8085 CPU automatically vector the processor to unique memory locations:

- 24 TRAP
- 3C RST 7.5
- 34 RST 6.5
- 2C RST 5.5

Timers

Addresses for 8253 Registers (Hex notation, I/O address space)

Programmable Interrupt Timer One

D8	Timer 0	BDG0
D9	Timer 1	BDG1
DA	Timer 2	BDG2
DB	Control register	

Programmable Interrupt Timer Two

DC	Timer 0	BDG3
DD	Timer 1	BDG4
DE	Timer 2	TINT1
DF	Control register	

Address for 8155 Programmable Timer

- E8 Control
- ED Timer (LSB)   TINT0
- EC Timer (MSB)   TINT0

iSBC® 544

Input frequencies — Jumper selectable reference 1.2288 MHz ± .1% (.814 usec period nominal) or 1.843 MHz ± .1% crystal (0.542 usec period, nominal)

Output Frequencies (at 1.2288 MHz)

Function	Single timer/counter		Dual timer/counter (two timers cascaded)	
	Min	Max	Min	Max
Real-time interrupt interval	1.63 usec	53.3 usec	3.26 usec	58.25 min
Rate Generator (frequency)	18.75 Hz	614.4 KHz	0.00029 Hz	307.2 KHz

Interfaces

Serial I/O — EIA Standard RS232C signals provided and supported:

Carrier Detect	Receive Data
Clear to Send	Ring Indicator
Data Set Ready	Secondary Receive Data *
Data Terminal Ready	Secondary Transmit Data *
Request to Send	Transmit Clock
Receive Clock	Transmit Data
	DTE Transmit Clock

* Optional if parallel I/O port is not used as Automatic Calling Unit.

Parallel I/O — Four inputs and eight outputs (includes two jumper selectable auxiliary outputs). All signals compatible with EIA Standard RS232C. Directly compatible with Bell Model 801 Automatic Calling Unit, or equivalent.

MULTIBUS — Compatible with iSBC MULTIBUS.

On-Board Addressing

All communications to the parallel and serial I/O ports, to the timers, and to the interrupt controller, are via read and write commands from the on-board 8085A CPU.

Auxiliary Power

An auxiliary power bus is provided to allow separate power to RAM for systems requiring battery backup of read/write memory. Selection of this auxiliary RAM power bus is made via jumpers on the board.

Connectors

Interface	Pins (qty)	Centers (in.)	Mating Connectors
Bus	86	0.156	Viking 2KH43/9AMK12
Parallel I/O	50	0.1	3M 3415-000 or AMP 88083-1
Serial I/O	26	0.1	3M 3462-000 or AMP 88373-5

Memory Protect

An active-low TTL compatible memory protect signal is brought out on the auxiliary connector which, when asserted, disables read/write access to RAM memory on the board. This input is provided for the protection of RAM contents during the system power-down sequences.

Bus Drivers

Function	Characteristic	Sink Current (mA)
Data	Tri-state	50
Address	Tri-state	15
Commands	Tri-state	32

Note: Used as a master in the single board communications computer mode.

Physical Characteristics

Width: 30.48 cm (12.00 inches)
Depth: 17.15 cm (6.75 inches)
Thickness: 1.27 cm (0.50 inch)
Weight: 3.97 gm (14 ounces)

Electrical Characteristics

DC Power Requirements

	Current Requirements			
Configuration	$V_{CC} = +5V$ ± 5% (max)	$V_{DD} = ±12V$ ± 5% (max)	$V_{BB} = -5V$(3) ± 5% (max)	$V_{AA} = -12V$ ± 5% (max)
With 4K EPROM (using 2716)	I_{CC} = 3.4 max max	I_{DD} = 350mA max	I_{BB} = 5mA max	I_{AA} = 200mA max
Without EPROM	3.3A max	350 mA max	5 mA max	200 mA max
RAM only (1)	390 mA max	176 mA max	5 mA max	—
RAM (2) refresh only	390 mA max	20 mA max	5 mA max	

Notes: 1. For operational RAM only, for AUX power supply rating.
2. For RAM refresh only. Used for battery backup requirements. No RAM accessed.
3. V_{BB} is normally derived on-board from V_{AA}, eliminating the need for a V_{BB} supply. If it is desired to supply V_{BB} from the bus, the current requirement is as shown.

Environmental Characteristics

Operating Temperature: 0°C to 55°C (32°F to 131°F)
Relative Humidity: To 90% without condensation

Reference Manual

502160 — iSBC 544 Intelligent Communications Controller Board Hardware Reference Manual (NOT SUPPLIED)

Reference manuals are shipped with each product only if designated SUPPLIED (see above). Manuals may be ordered from any Intel sales representative, distributor office or from Intel Literature Department, 3065 Bowers Avenue, Santa Clara, California 95051.

ORDERING INFORMATION

Part Number	Description
iSBC 544	Intelligent Communications Controller

ISBC® 550
ETHERNET COMMUNICATIONS CONTROLLER

- **Meets the version 1.0 tri-corporate Ethernet specification**
- **Ethernet data link layer support**
  - Data encapsulation
  - Framing and packet control
  - Buffer management
- **Ethernet physical link layer support**
  - Serial/deserialization
  - 10 Mbits per second data rate
  - CRC generation/check
  - Carrier-sense multiple-access with collision detection (CSMA/CD)
  - Transceiver interface compatibility
- **Easy-to-use MULTIBUS® interprocessor protocol supported in firmware**
- **Power-up confidence test assures integrity of on-board memory and programmable LSI**
- **Traffic, errors and collision information maintained for network management**
- **Excellent foundation for Ethernet local area end-to-end network**

The iSBC 550 Ethernet Communications Controller meets the tri-corporate (DEC, Xerox, Intel) specification for Ethernet local area networks. All the functions of the Ethernet data link layer and physical link layer are provided on two 6.75 × 12" circuits boards and associated firmware. The MULTIBUS compatible controller can be utilized as the foundation for a single board computer (iSBC)-based Ethernet local area network or as a prototype for Intel® 8085, iAPX™ 88, or iAPX 86 component-based Ethernet applications. The iSBC 550 controller's firmware (supplying the Ethernet and system interface) has an easy-to-use MULTIBUS Interprocessor Protocol (MIP) facility, which is readily accessed from another iSBC Board using a custom run-time software system or Intel's iRMX™ 80/88/86 Real-Time Executive software and the iMMX™ 800 (MULTIBUS Message Exchange) software package. The Ethernet data link functions are divided between the processor board which provides the data link layer's software to control the data encapsulation and the link management, and the serial/deserialization (SerDes) board which provides the 10-MBit per second serial interface to the Ethernet transceiver.

The following are trademarks of Intel Corporation and may be used to describe Intel products. CREDIT, Index, Insite, Intellec, Library Manager, Megachassis, Micromap, MULTIBUS, PROMPT, UPI, µScope, Promware, MCS, ICE, iRMX, iSBC, iSBX, MULTIMODULE, ICS, iAPX and iMMX. Intel Corporation assumes no responsibility for the use of any circuitry other than circuitry embodied in an Intel product. No other circuit patent licenses are implied.

© INTEL CORPORATION, 1981
*Ethernet™ is a trademark of Xerox Corporation

iSBC® 550

FUNCTIONAL DESCRIPTION

The iSBC 550 Ethernet Communications Controller is a two-board MULTIBUS-compatible set that offers high-speed Ethernet-compatible data transfer between digital devices operating at a 10-Mbit per sec data rate. The iSBC 550 controller can effectively support the needs of local area network applications, such as office automation, distributed data processing, factory data collection, research data collection, intelligent terminal and other EDP-related products.

Ethernet Specification

The Ethernet network is a local area network concept that is jointly being supported by Intel Corporation, Digital Equipment Corporation, and Xerox Corporation. The network is designed to link systems over a distance of up to 2500 meters using an available 50-ohm coaxial cable. Several hundred stations may be connected to the cable which supports a data rate of 10 Megabits per second. The data is encapsulated in a packet message format. The data signal is a base-band, Manchester-encoded type that is self-synchronizing.

The jointly developed Ethernet specification, "The Ethernet, A Local Area Network Data Link Layer and Physical Link Layer Specification, Version 1.0, September 30, 1980", precisely defines the two lower layers of a local area network architecture where the system is a series of independent layers. The lowest layer, the physical link layer, is concerned with coaxial cable interface. The data link layer supports the peer protocol's statistical contention resolution (CSMA/CD) and link management functions. All additional network layers are defined by the user during the implementation of the application-specific layers.

Ethernet Data Link Layer Support

The iSBC 550 processor board provides the data link layer's software to control the data encapsulation and the link management, including frame delimitation, address handling, error detection, and collision handling. After the iSBC 550 processor board is initialized upon system start-up or reset, the data link firmware is ready to service the local area network commands. An example of a command structure sent the iSBC controller to receive a packet of data from the Ethernet link is shown in Figure 1. The message passed via the MIP (MULTIBUS Interprocessor Protocol) interface is composed of two parts, the iSBC 550 controller information (including the command and associated data), and the required Ethernet information.

```
iSBC 550        ⎧ RESERVED DATA    (14 bytes)
CONTROLLER      ⎨ COMMAND          (1 byte)
INFORMATION     ⎩ RESERVED DATA    (7 bytes)

                ⎧ DESTINATION      (6 bytes)
ETHERNET        ⎨ SOURCE           (6 bytes)
INFORMATION     ⎪ TYPE             (2 bytes)
                ⎩ DATA             (46-1500 bytes)
```

Figure 1. Data Link for SUPPLYBUF Command Format

Shown in Table 1 are eight external Ethernet controller commands available to a user's application via the MIP interface. The commands manage the Ethernet multicast address recognition, message type connection, message flow, and overall network statistics.

Table 1. External Controller Commands

Command	Function
CONNECT	Indicates the data link message TYPE to be *connected* to user program.
DISCONNECT	*Disconnects* the data link TYPE from the user's application.
ADDMCID	*Adds* a multicast ID for recognition.
DELETEMCID	*Delete* the specified multicast ID.
TRANSMIT	*Transmit* a data packet to the Ethernet link.
SUPPLYBUF	*Supplies* a buffer for packet reception from the Ethernet link ("receive" function).
READ	*Read* the statistical variables maintained by data link layer.
READC	*Read* and *clear* the statistical variables.

Ethernet Physical Link Layer Support

The Serialization/Deserialization (SerDes) board provides the required electrical characteristics of the physical link layer of the Ethernet architecture for a transceiver interface. The transceiver is a device physically attached to the coax cable which does signal conditioning for transmitting and receiving.

Many major functions are controlled by the SerDes board. These functions include serialization/deserialization, packet framing, Manchester encoding/decoding, transmit data flow control, receive data flow control, destination address decoding for received message, CRC generation and

iSBC® 550

checking, and diagnostics for CRC error, loopback, transmit timeout, and CSMA/CD (Carrier-Sense Multiple-Access with Collision-Detection).

Easy-To-Use Interface

One of the iSBC 550 controller boards is an iAPX 88-based processor board which has firmware support for the user's application interface. The programmatic interface utilizes the MULTIBUS Interprocessor Protocol (MIP) interface to the processor board. This interface is concerned with the message-passing protocol between multiple-processors. The iMMX 800 (MULTIBUS Message Exchange) software supports the MIP interface and offers a convenient quick-start method for users of Intel's iRMX 80, iRMX 88 executives and iRMX 86 operating system products for an Ethernet-based application.

Confidence Test

An effective diagnostic function is implemented in firmware on the processor board. This function is invoked at system initialization during both power-up and system reset time. These functions include: packet CRC checking, memory test, controller loopback, and other error tests. The tests provide a fundamental level of controller integrity.

Network Statistics

Statistics maintained by the data link firmware include packet traffic counts, collision information and error totals. This information can be effectively utilized by the user's application to understand the network's operation.

End-To-End Networking Foundation

The iSBC 550 controller provides the foundation data link layer and the physical link layer for a local area network architecture. Typically, the higher levels are user-defined and include the transport and the session control layers. The transport control layer is concerned with the end-to-end communications and the virtual channel connection via a port-to-port address. The session control layer provides the process-to-process control function which includes symbolic name binding and the establishment of the virtual connection via the transport control layer. In addition, the session control provides the specific error and recovery control responsible for message delivery.

The higher levels of the local area network architecture (see Figure 2) which use the data link layer are outside of the Ethernet standard, but can be implemented quickly on companion iSBC boards (e.g., iSBC 80/24, iSBC 88/25, iSBC 86/12A) running under the iRMX 80/88/86 Real-Time Multitasking Executives, respectively, and associated iMMX MULTIBUS Message Exchange (iMMX 800) software. Special iSBC 550 device driver software compatible with the iRMX 86 and iRMX 88 file systems is provided in the iMMX 800 package.

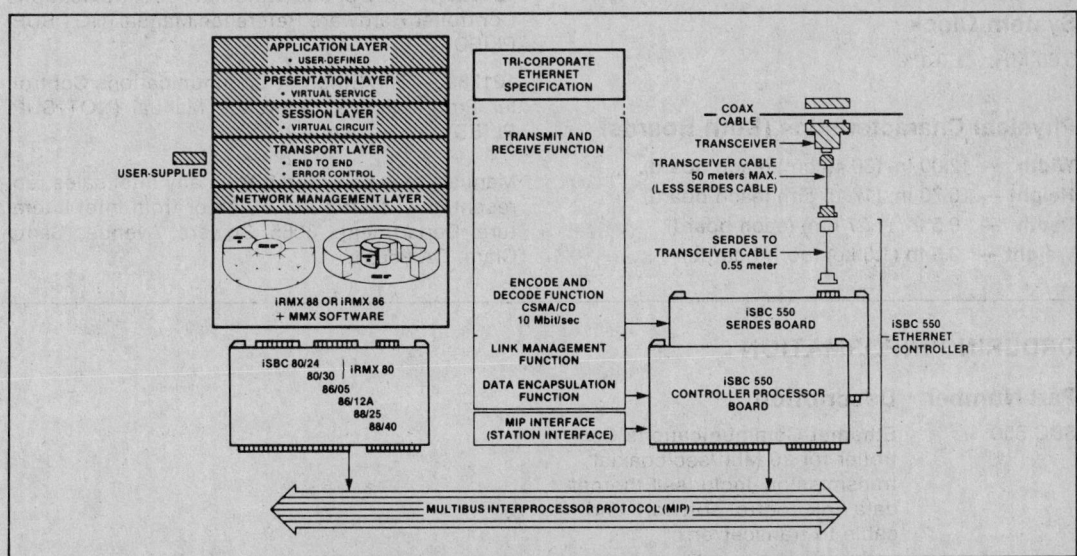

Figure 2. Ethernet Architecture and Implementation

8-57

iSBC® 550

SPECIFICATIONS

Memory Addressing Capability
MULTIBUS System Bus — (00000–EFFFF)

Ethernet I/O Channels
One Ethernet electrically-compatible transceiver line on the SerDes board.

Interface Specifications
MULTIBUS System Bus — All signals TTL compatible.

Transceiver — All signals Ethernet specifications transceiver compatible.

Serial Communications Characteristics
Bit Serial Frame — Provides 64-bit *preamble*, 48-bit *destination* address, 48-bit *source* address, 16-bit *type*, 46–1500 bytes for *data*, and a *frame* check sequence of 32 bits.

Ethernet Network Specifications Supported
Coax Cable Length — 500-meter max.
Transceiver Cable Length — 50-meter max.
Number of Stations — 100 max.
Baud Rate — 10-Mbit/sec

System Clock
5.00 MHz, ± 0.1%

Physical Characteristics (Both Boards)
Width — 12.00 in. (30.48 cm) (each board)
Height — 6.75 in. (17.15 cm) (each board)
Depth — 0.5 in. (1.27 cm) (each board)
Weight — 3.5 lb (1.6 kg) (both boards)

SerDes to Transceiver Cable
Length — 0.55 meter (22 in.). Four pair twisted-wire cable with SerDes connector and transceiver interface connector.

Electrical Characteristics
Power requirements for both boards
 + 5 VDC @ 9.0A max.
 + 12 VDC @ 0.5A max.

Environmental Characteristics
Operating Temperature — 0°C to 55°C
Relative Humidity — To 90% (without condensation)

Connectors

Interface	Pins (qty)	Centers (in.)	Mating Connectors
MULTIBUS System	86	0.156	Viking 2KH43/9AMK12
SerDes Edge Connector	10	0.1	AMP 87631-5 Housing AMP 87195-9 Pins
Transceiver	15	0.1	Cinch Type DA 51220-1

Reference Manuals
121746 — iSBC 550 Ethernet Communications Controller Hardware Reference Manual (NOT SUPPLIED)

121769 — The Ethernet Communications Controller Programmer's Reference Manual (NOT SUPPLIED)

Manuals may be ordered from any Intel sales representative, distributor office or from Intel Literature Department, 3065 Bowers Avenue, Santa Clara, CA 95051.

ORDERING INFORMATION

Part Number   Description
SBC 550   Ethernet Communications Controller for 10 Mbit/sec coaxial transmission. Includes Ethernet data link control software and cable to transceiver.

iSBC® 552 AND iSXM™ 552 ETHERNET COMMUNICATIONS ENGINE PRODUCTS
MEMBERS OF THE OpenNET™ PRODUCT FAMILY

- Provides networking capability for all MULTIBUS® systems regardless of the operating system of the host
- Supports XENIX*- and RMX-Network File Service (XNX-NET and RMX-NET) products
- Available in two versions
  — Turn-key controller implementing ISO 8073 Class 4 Standard Transport functionality (iSXM™ 552 board) on IEEE 802.3 LANs
  — Flexible, intelligent communications controller for iSBC® 552 board for custom configurations on IEEE 802.3 LANs
- iSXM™ 552 board is fully qualified as system extension module for the 86/310, 286/310, 86/380 and 286/380 Intel systems
- Resident network software can be down loaded (SXM) or stored in on-board PROMs (SBC)
- Runs iNA 960 and iNA 961 (SXM) transport software
- On-board diagnostic and boot firmware (SXM)

The iSBC 552 and iSXM 552 COMMengine products are designed for communications front end processor applications connecting MULTIBUS systems onto IEEE 802.3/Ethernet LANs. COMMengines are dedicated to the communications tasks within a system allowing the host to spend more time processing user applications. A major advantage of COMMengines is that they can be used to network existing systems and established designs without forcing the redesign of the entire system architecture.

The iSBC and iSXM 552 boards can be used with any operating system because they require only a high level interface to communicate with the host (eg. transport commands in case of the iSXM 522 board). The result is a powerful system building block which enables the OEM to connect MULTIBUS-based systems with different operating systems to the same network. Applications for the 552 products include networked multiuser XENIX 286 based systems for the office and iRMX-based systems for real time applications. The iSXM version is a transport engine complete with on board RAM and ROM memory preconfigured to run iNA 961 transport software. iNA 961 software is a version of Intel's iNA 960 LAN software implementing the ISO 8073 Class 4 protocol specifically configured to support the iSXM 552 board. The iSBC 552 board is a "de-bundled" version of the iSXM 552 board; it comes without memory and software allowing greater flexibility for the user to adapt the board for his special requirements.

Intel Corporation assumes no responsibility for the use of any circuitry other than circuitry embodied in an Intel product. No other circuit patent licenses are implied. Information contained herein supersedes previously published specifications on these devices from Intel. **February 1985**
© Intel Corporation, 1985   *XENIX is a trademark of MICROSOFT CORP.

iSBC 552 /iSXM 552

The iSBC® Board vs. the iSXM™ 552 Board

The fundamental difference between the two versions is the iSBC 552 board offers the hardware necessary for the user to construct an Ethernet front-end processor for his unique requirements and the iSXM 552 board provides full ISO standard transport services ready to plug in and to be used without any additional configuration effort. The SXM version is arrived at by populating the iSBC 552 board with 16K bytes of ROM and 80K bytes of iRAM, and by providing iNA 961, a directly downloadable transport software module. The iSXM 552 board is configured for Intel's 86/286-310 systems and fully qualified to run in these systems. iSXM 552 customers receive the iNA software with the purchase of the iNA 961 license which is an integral part of the SXM offering.

ARCHITECTURE DESCRIPTION

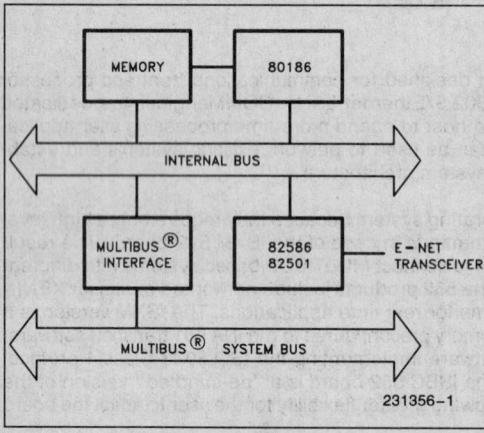

Figure 1.

The iSBC and iSXM 552 boards consist of the following major architectural blocks (see Figure 1): an 80186 processor running at 6 MHz, the Ethernet I/O channel based on the 82586 LAN coprocessor and the 82501 Ethernet serial interface, the on-board memory consisting of ROM and iRAM, and the MULTIBUS interface.

Processor

The iSBC 552 board contains an 80186 processor operating in the maximum mode at 6 MHz. It is responsible for implementing the intelligent interface between the iSBC 552 board and a host processor. The 80186 processor runs the iNA 961 (iSXM 552) and iNA 960 (iSBC 552) transport software and delivers data between user buffers in MULTIBUS memory and iNA960/961 buffers on the iSBC and iSXM 552 boards. iNA 960 and 961 software is responsible for the reliable transfer of information across Ethernet.

The 80186 and 82586 both use asynchronous ready logic. The 80186 chip select lines are used to select memory mapped I/O locations.

The 80186 supplies the timers and the interrupt controller on iSBC 552. The interrupt controller is used in the fully nested mode. The inputs and the outputs of the 80186 timers are not connected to external sources and destinations. Timer clocking and timer interrupts are generated internally in the 80186.

Memory

The one megabyte address space of the 80186 is divided into four quadrants (see Figure 2). The first (0-256K Byte) and the last (768-1000K Byte) quadrants are reserved for local memory. The second quadrant (256-512K Byte) is used for memory mapped I/O. The iSBC 552 board is totally memory mapped. The third quadrant (512-768K Byte) maps into a 256K Byte MULTIBUS window. This window allows the iSBC 552 board to access a total of 16M Byte of MULTIBUS memory in 256K Byte segments. The iSBC 552 board does not contain any memory which is accessible from MULTIBUS.

The 256K Byte MULTIBUS window starts on 64K Byte boundaries anywhere in the 16M byte MULTIBUS memory. The starting location of this window is determined by a memory mapped I/O latch described in "iSBC 552 User Interface" section.

Local memory on the iSBC 552 board (quadrants one and four) is made up of twelve 28-pin memory sockets. Either EPROM (2764, 27128), Intel iRAM (2186) or equivalent static RAM memory can occupy these sockets. The only limitations are that the lowest pair of sockets corresponding to the bottom memory location must be RAM and the highest pair of sockets corresponding to the top memory location must be EPROM or ROM. The intermediate pairs of sockets can be jumper-configured to be either RAM or EPROM.

Memory mapped I/O locations are selected by the PCS and the MCS control lines of the 80186 processor. Functions controlled by memory mapped I/O are discussed in "iSBC 552 User Interface" section.

Ethernet Interface

The Ethernet Interface on the iSBC 552 is implemented by the 82586 LAN Coprocessor and the 82501 Ethernet Serial Interface. Data is transferred be-

iSBC 552 /iSXM 552

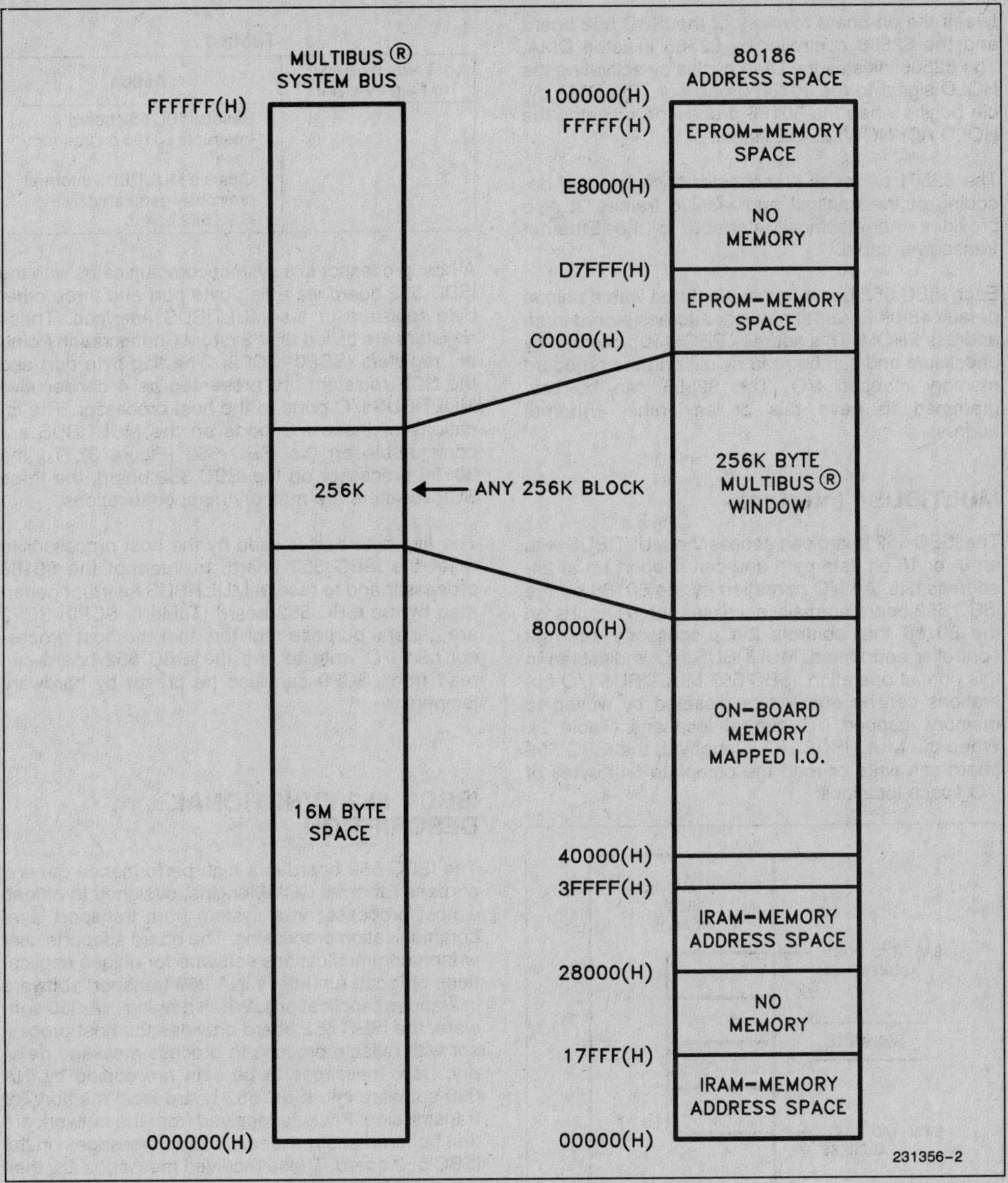

Figure 2. iSBC 552 Memory Configuration

tween the on-board memory of the iSBC 552 board and the 82586 controller by 82586 initiated DMA. The 82586 initiates the DMA cycles by activating the HOLD signal to the 80186 processor. The DMA cycle begins when the 80186 processor activates the HOLD ACKNOWLEDGE signal.

The 82501 performs Manchester encoding and decoding of the transmit and receive frames. It also provides the electrical interface to the Ethernet transceiver cable.

Each iSBC 552 board is manufactured with a unique default 48-bit Ethernet network address stored in an address PROM. This address PROM is protected by checksum and can be read by utilizing the on board memory mapped I/O. The 82586 can be programmed to have this or any other Ethernet address.

MULTIBUS® Interface

The iSBC 552 board can access the MULTIBUS with an 8- or 16-bit data path and can support up to 24-address bits. An I/O operation by the 80186 on the iSBC 552 board normally accesses the I/O ports on the 80186 that controls the processor's interrupt controller and timers. MULTIBUS I/O is disabled in this normal operation. iSBC 552 MULTIBUS I/O operations can be enabled or disabled by writing to memory mapped I/O control locations (Table 2). When the MULTIBUS I/O is enabled, the iSBC 552 board can write or read the complete 64k bytes of I/O space locations.

Table 1.

Value written to Flag byte port	Action
1	Resets iSBC 552 board
2	Interrupts 80186 on Interrupt Level 1
4	Clears a MULTIBUS interrupt previously generated by the iSBC 552 board

A host processor in a system communicates with the iSBC 552 board via a flag byte port and three other byte registers in the MULTIBUS interface. These registers are called the "System Configuration Pointer" registers (SCP0–SCP2). The flag byte port and the SCP registers are presented as 4 consecutive MULTIBUS I/O ports to the host processor. The locations of these I/O ports on the MULTIBUS are configurable on the iSBC 552 (Figure 3). To the 80186 processor on the iSBC 552 board, the three SCP registers are memory mapped locations.

The flag byte port is used by the host processor to reset the iSBC 552 board, to interrupt the 80186 processor and to reset a MULTIBUS interrupt generated by the iSBC 552 board (Table I). SCP0–SCP2 are general purpose registers that the host processor can I/O write to and the iSBC 552 board can read from. SCP0 can also be preset by hardware jumpers.

iSBC® 552 FUNCTIONAL DESCRIPTION

The iSBC 552 board is a high performance general purpose Ethernet COMMengine, designed to offload a host processor in a system from transport layer communication processing. The board supports user written communications software for unique applications or it can run Intel's iNA 960 transport software in standard applications. When running iNA 960 software, the iSBC 552 board provides the host processor with reliable process to process message delivery. User messages to be sent are copied by iNA 960 software into iSBC 552 board local memory for transmission. Packets received from the network are first buffered and reassembled into messages on the iSBC 552 board. These received messages are then delivered to the user.

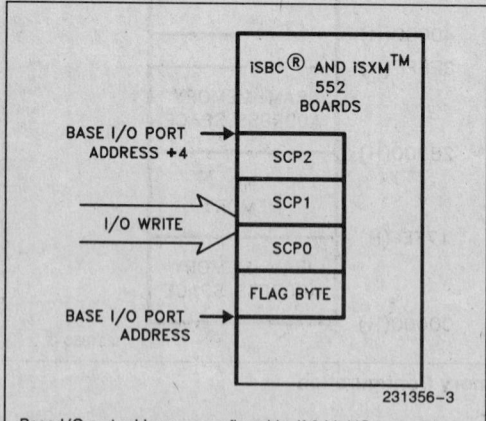

Base I/O port address = configurable. If 8 bit I/O is used, base port address is configurable from 0-0FCH. If 16 bit I/O is used, base port address is configurable from 0-0FFFCH.
Flag byte: see Table I.
SCP0–SCP2: I/O written by host processor and read by 80186 on iSBC and iSXM 552 SCP0 can be jumper preset.

Figure 3. iSBC® 552 MULTIBUS® Communication Interface

The iSBC 552 board makes use of the functions on the 82586 and 82501 to implement a number of network functions. These functions include reprogramming the iSBC 552 station address, Multicast packet reception filtering, Time Domain Reflectometer tests and Loopback diagnostics. The 82586 also records a number of network statistics information. Information stored include the number of CRC and alignment errors, the number of

iSBC 552 /iSXM 552

occurrences of no receive buffer resources and the number of DMA overruns/underruns.

The iSBC 552 can be configured to have a range of local memory configurations, from 16K Byte RAM (160K Byte EPROM/ROM) to 80K Byte RAM (16K Byte EPROM/ROM).

The iSBC 552 board and iNA 960 software combination offers a flexible and configurable transport COMMengine, and allows a user to optimally configure his system for highest performance. The iSXM 552 and iNA 961 combination offers a preconfigured turn-key solution. In both cases, iNA 960 software and the 552 significantly reduces the design cycle involved in designing and implementing a transport COMMengine.

iSBC® 552 User Interface

The iSBC 552 board communicates with a host processor through a handshake of interrupts. The host processor can generate flag byte interrupts to the 80186 on the iSBC 552 and the iSBC 552 can generate MULTIBUS interrupts to the host processor. The host processor and the iSBC 552 can also communicate through shared MULTIBUS system memory. None of the on-board buffer on the iSBC 552 is accessible to the host processor but the iSBC 552 can read and write all of 16M byte of MULTIBUS system memory.

The host processor and the iSBC 552 board further communicate through the SCP registers. These byte registers can be I/O written by the host and can be read through memory mapped I/O by the iSBC 552 processor.

The 80186 processor controls the iSBC 552 through memory mapped I/O. Functions that are controlled are listed in Table 2.

OPERATING ENVIRONMENTS

The iSBC 552 is designed to function in any MULTIBUS systems as a communications processor. It can function as both a MULTIBUS bus master or a slave. As a MULTIBUS master, it can access up to 16M byte of host memory and 64K byte of I/O address. As a MULTIBUS slave, it occupies four consecutive I/O locations on the MULTIBUS. These locations are reserved for the flag byte and the three SCP registers.

iSXM™ 552 FUNCTIONAL DESCRIPTION

The iSXM 552 board is a preconfigured iSBC 552 with 16K Bytes of boot firmware and 80K Bytes of iRAM. The iSXM 552 board is offered with iNA 961 preconfigured ISO 8073 transport software. The iSXM 552 firmware provides the capabilities to load iNA 961 onto the 552 from either a buffer in the local host or remotely from another Ethernet station. It also performs a variety of Ethernet and on-board diagnostics (see sections on iNA 961 User Interfaces and Operating Systems Environment).

iNA 961 software and the iSXM 552 board together provide the functionality of a preconfigured operating system independent transport engine. In addition to transport services, iNA 961 software also includes extensive Data Link and Network Management Facility services. Figure 4 shows the configuration of iNA 961. Table 3 shows some examples of functions provided by iNA 961. iNA 961 is a preconfigured version of iNA 960. Refer to the iNA 960 data sheet for more iNA 961 information.

User programs that use iNA 960 and the iSBC 186/51 board can be run on a host processor with iNA 961 and iSXM 552 as a transport engine. The user programs will require minimal changes in most cases.

Table 2. iSBC® 552 Memory Mapped Functions

80186 Chip Select Lines	Read/Write by 80186	Functions
MCS	R	MULTIBUS® Interface registers (System Configuration Pointer registers, see "MULTIBUS® Interface")
PCS	W	Channel Attention to 82586
	R	Reading iSBC® 552 Ethernet Address PROMS
	W	Controlling loopback of 82501
	W	Disabling and Enabling MULTIBUS® I/O
	W	Generating and Clearing iSBC® 552 interrupts to the MULTIBUS® System Bus
	W	Controlling the on-board LED
	W	Latches the MULTIBUS® window segment (8 most significant bits of 24 bit address)

iSBC® 552/iSXM™ 552

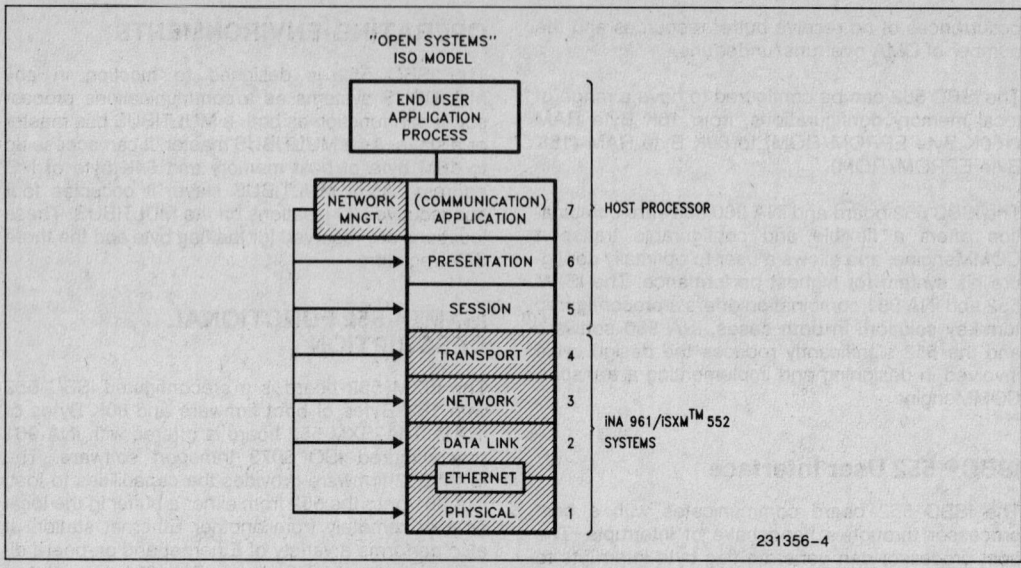

Figure 4. iNA 961 CONFIGURATION ON iSXM 552 Board

Table 3. iNA 961 Services

Transport	Virtual circuit
	   open: establish a virtual circuit database
	   send connect: actively try to establish a virtual connection
	   await connect: passively awaits the arrival of a connection request
	   send: send a message
	   receive: post a buffer to receive a message
	   close: close a virtual circuit
	Datagram
	   send: send a datagram message
	   receive: post a buffer to receive a datagram message

Data Link	Transmit: transmit a data link packet Receive: post a buffer to receive a data link packet Connect: make a data link logical connection (link service access point, IEEE802.3/802.2) Disconnect: disconnect a data link logical connection Change Ethernet address: change the Ethernet address Add multicast address: add a multicast address Delete multicast address: remove a multicast address Configure 82586: configure the 82586 controller

Network Management	Read/Clear/Set network objects (local/remote):
	   read/clear/set local or remote iNA 960 network parameters
	Read/Set network memory (local/remote):
	   read/set memory of the local or a remote station.
	   Useful in network debug process.
	Boot consumer: requests a network boot server to
	   load a boot file into this station
	Echo: Echo a packet between this station and
	   another remote station on the network

iSBC 552 /iSXM 552

iSXM™ Boot Firmware User Interface

The iSXM 552 boot firmware is used to load iNA 961 or other software onto the 552 from either local MULTIBUS memory or a remote network station. The firmware performs a number of local and network diagnostics. Table 4 describes the functions of the boot firmware.

The iSXM 552 boot firmware interfaces with the host processor through a configurable command buffer location in MULTIBUS memory. This location can be either jumper or program configured. The host processor updates the command byte in the command buffer and expects the firmware to update the response byte when the command is done. The host processor signals to the firmware to examine this command buffer by writing a 2 to the flag byte port. The firmware will update the response byte when the command is completed.

The iSXM 552 boot firmware commands fully support the initialization of the MIP Interface. The MIP interface is used by the host processor to communicate with the iNA 961 once it is loaded and started. (See section "iNA 961 User Interfaces" for details.)

iNA 961 User Interfaces

User programs give iNA 960 commands to the iNA 961 software on the iSXM 552 board via the MULTIBUS Interface Protocol (MIP). MIP is an Intel reliable process to process message delivery protocol between MULTIBUS processors. Figure 5 illustrates how this message delivery functions. Commands are passed between the iSXM 552 and the host processor in the form of request blocks. A request block is a buffer that contains a command specification and the command parameters. Each request block (or equivalently, each command) is reliably delivered from the host processor to iNA 961 via the MIP facility. iNA 961 will extract the command information and carry out the command. After a command is done, iNA 961 will use the MIP facility to return the command result to the user program.

iNA 961 request blocks are in the same formats as iNA 960 commands. Refer to the iNA 960 data sheet and reference manuals for more details on iNA 961 software.

Table 4. iSXM™ 552 Boot Firmware Commands

Command	Function
Presence	This command will indicate that the boot firmware is functional by returning the version number of the firmware, the power on diagnostic result, and the default Ethernet address of the iSXM 552.
Load	Load a program from MULTIBUS memory into a designated location in the iSBC 552 memory.
Start	Load a program from MULTIBUS bus memory into a designated location in the iSXM 552 memory. Proceed to start this program once it is loaded. This command also initializes the MIP interface on the iSXM 552 board.
Echo	Echo a packet between this iSXM 552 board and another station on the network.
Remote Boot	This command requests a remote boot server station to download software onto the iSXM 552.
and start MIP initialize	Used after a remote boot. This command initializes the MIP interface on the iSXM552 and then start the software loaded by the remote boot command.

iSBC 552 /iSXM 552

Operating Systems Environment

The iSXM 552 board and iNA 961 software can function in any MULTIBUS environment. The communication between the iSXM 552 and the host processor is entirely independent of any host operating systems. iNA 961 uses the MIP protocol to interface with the host processor. The MIP is a reliable, host operating system independent, process to process communication scheme between any processors on the MULTIBUS System Bus. iNA 961 can service multiple processes utilizing its services at the same time.

A host processor passes iNA 961 commands and buffers in the MULTIBUS system memory to the iNA 961 software. iNA 961 is responsible for updating the response fields of these commands. It is responsible for copying the user send buffer in MULTIBUS system memory into its on board buffers for transmission and for copying received messages to user buffers in MULTIBUS system memory.

Diagnostics

The iSXM 552 board offers a range of power up diagnostics designed to ensure that the 80186 processor, the memory (EPROM and iRAM), and the Ethernet serial interface are functioning properly. Table 5 describes these diagnostics.

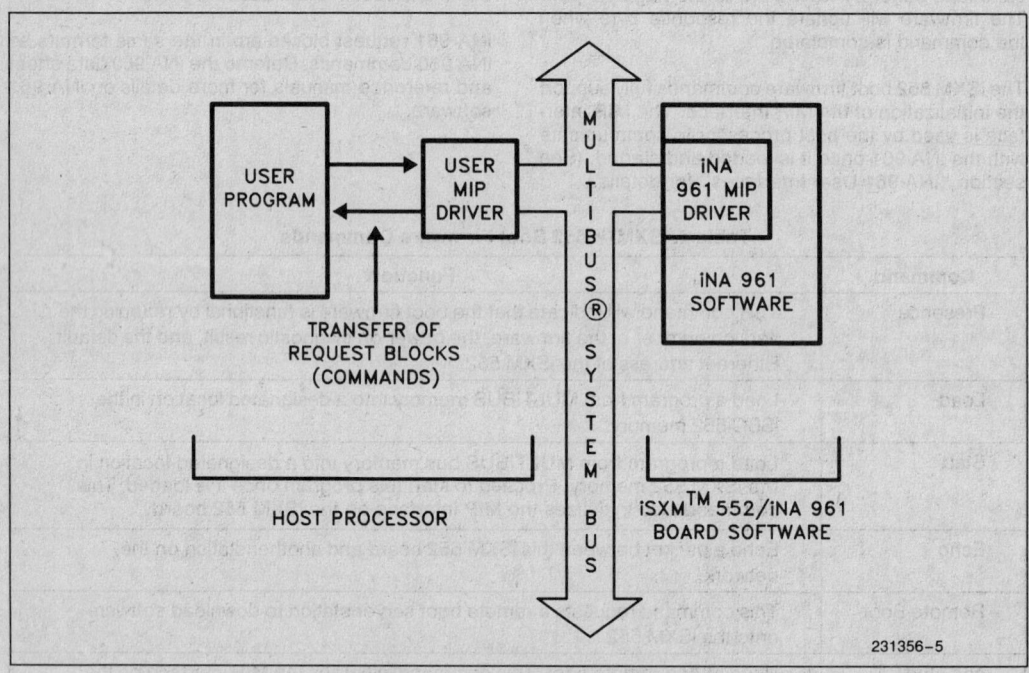

Figure 5. iNA 961 MIP Interface

8-66

iSBC 552 / iSXM 552

Table 5. Functions Checked by iSXM™ 552 Diagnostics

1. Insufficient RAM
2. Ram match pattern test
3. Ram ripple data test
4. Boot firmware PROM checksum
5. Address PROM checksum
6. 80186 interrupt controller
7. 80186 timer controller
8. 82586 initialization
9. 82586 CRC check
10. 82586 broadcast packet recognition
11. 82586 external loopback
12. 82586 individual address recognition
13. 82586 multicast address recognition
14. 82586 reset
15. 82586 diagnose check

DEVELOPMENT ENVIRONMENT

The iSXM 552 board is a turn-key product that allows a user to emphasize the development of high level software, such as a network file server. The iSXM 552 board and iNA 961 software together form a transport COMMengine that integrates into any MULTIBUS system. iNA 961 is supplied in a boot loadable file format. This file can be loaded into the iSXM 552 by a host processor or through a remote boot server. The boot firmware on the iSXM 552 supports both functions.

The iSBC 552 allows a user to fine tune iNA 960 and put the software on the board. Both iNA 960 and the iSBC 552 can be flexibly configured to best meet the users' requirements. An Intel development system, together with an Intel I2ICE or equivalent product is usually needed if the user desires to do extensive development work on the iSBC 552. Intel also supplies a wide range of host processor boards and systems (such as the iSBC 286/10 and system 310) that will function well both with the iSBC 552 or the iSXM 552.

iNA 960 can be put into PROMs and run on the iSBC 552.

ORDERING INFORMATION

Part Number	Description
SXM 552	Ethernet Transport Engine
SBC 552	Ethernet COMMengine

SPECIFICATIONS

MULTIBUS Interface
The iSBC 552 and iSXM 552 boards conform to all AC and DC requirements outlined in the Intel MULTIBUS Specification, Order Number 142686-002 with the following exceptions:

Signal	Specification
DAT0 – DAT7:	IIH = 180µA, IIH = 125µA

Transceiver Interface
IEEE 802.3 compatible

DC Power Requirements
All voltages supplied by the MULTIBUS Interface
+5.0V ± 5%, 5.9A maximum
+12.0 ± 5%, 0.5A maximum

Environmental

Temperature	0°C to 55°C Operating
	–40°C to 65°C Non-Operating
Humidity	5% to 90% Operating
	5% to 95% Non-Operating

ADVANCE INFORMATION

iSXM™ 554 MAP COMMUNICATIONS ENGINE

- Provides Networking Capability for MULTIBUS® Based Systems Running Under any Operating System
- Serves as a Complete Front End Communication Engine With the Capacity to Provide MAP Layers 1 Through 7 Capability for MULTIBUS® Based Hosts
- Runs Intel's Proven iNA 961 Rel 2.0 Providing the ISO 8073 Transport Software and ISO 8473 Internet Software for IEEE 802.4 LANs
- On Board Diagnostic and Boot Firmware
- Supported by Intels' Implementation of MAP Software for Layers 5–7 Which Can Be Run on Board

- 8 MHz 80186 Processor
- 256 KBytes of RAM of Which 128 KBytes are Dual Portable
- 10 Mbps IEEE 802.4/Token Bus Interface
- Sockets for up to 4 JEDEC 28 Pin Memory Devices, up to Maximum of 160 KBytes EPROM Storage
- One iSBX™ Bus Connector for I/O Expansion Capability
- Can Be Configured as Either a Master or a Slave in MULTIBUS®

The iSXM 554 COMMengine product is designed to fit into front end LAN Communication processor applications. It allows the connection of MULTIBUS-based systems onto a MAP/IEEE 802.4 (Token Bus) LAN. COMMengines are dedicated communication processor boards. They allow the host processor board to offload LAN communication related tasks onto the front end COMMengine. Therefore the host has more processing capability for user applications or other tasks. COMMengines also allow the networking of existing systems without forcing a redesign of the entire system architecture.

The iSXM 554 board can be used as a front end COMMengine for a MULTIBUS-based host running any operating system. This is because the on board software provides a high level interface to the host (e.g., transport level commands). This results in a powerful system building block which enables an OEM to connect MULTIBUS-based systems onto IEEE 802.4 10 Mbps LANs. Applications for the iSXM 554 include networked iRMX™-based systems for real time applications and networked XENIX* systems for laboratory and data base application. The iSXM 554 is preconfigured to run iNA 961 R2.0 transport and network software. iNA 961 R2.0 is a preconfigured version for the iSXM 554 of Intel's iNA 960 LAN software which implements the ISO 8073 Class 4 transport protocol and the ISO 8473 internet network layer protocol.

The iSXM 554 has the processing and memory capacity to accommodate an on board implementation of the MAP software for layers 3 through 7 of the ISO OSI model. Intel will provide an implementation of the MAP layers 5 through 7 as a product. This will be available in a version preconfigured to run on the iSXM 554. The iSXM 554 coupled with iNA 961 R2.0 (layers 3 and 4) and the MAP layer 5–7 software will be an ideal turn key solution for OEMs requiring a 7 layer MAP specification communication engine.

iSXM™ 554 FUNCTIONAL DESCRIPTION

The iSXM 554 board is a preconfigured MAP Communication Engine with boot firmware and 256K bytes of RAM. The iSXM 554 board is offered for use with iNA 961 R2.0 preconfigured ISO 8073 transport plus ISO 8473 network layer software. The iSXM 554 firmware provides the capabilities to load iNA 961 R2.0 onto the iSXM 554 from either a buffer in the local host or remotely from another Token Bus station. It also performs a variety of on-board diagnostics.

---

*XENIX is a trademark of Microsoft Corporation.

Intel Corporation assumes no responsibility for the use of any circuitry other than circuitry embodied in an Intel product. No other circuit patent licenses are implied. Information contained herein supersedes previously published specifications on these devices from Intel.   **August 1985**
© Intel Corporation, 1985   Order Number: 231594-001

iSXM™ 554   ADVANCE INFORMATION

The iNA 961 R2.0 software and the iSXM 554 board together provide the functionality of a preconfigured OS independent transport engine. In addition to transport services, iNA 961 R2.0 software also includes ISO 8473 Internet network layer, extensive data link and network management facilility services. Figure 1 shows the configuration of iNA 961 R2.0. Table 1 shows some examples of functions provided by iNA 961 R2.0. iNA 961 R2.0 is a preconfigured version of iNA 960. Refer to the iNA 960 data sheet for more iNA 961 R2.0 information.

Intel will also provide an implementation of the MAP software for layers 5 through 7 as a product. Refer to the MAP version 2.1 specification for more information. This implementation of layers 5 through 7 will run on the iSXM 554 along with iNA 961 R2.0. The iSXM 554 coupled with the software packages will be a high performance, 7-layer communication engine (see Figure 1).

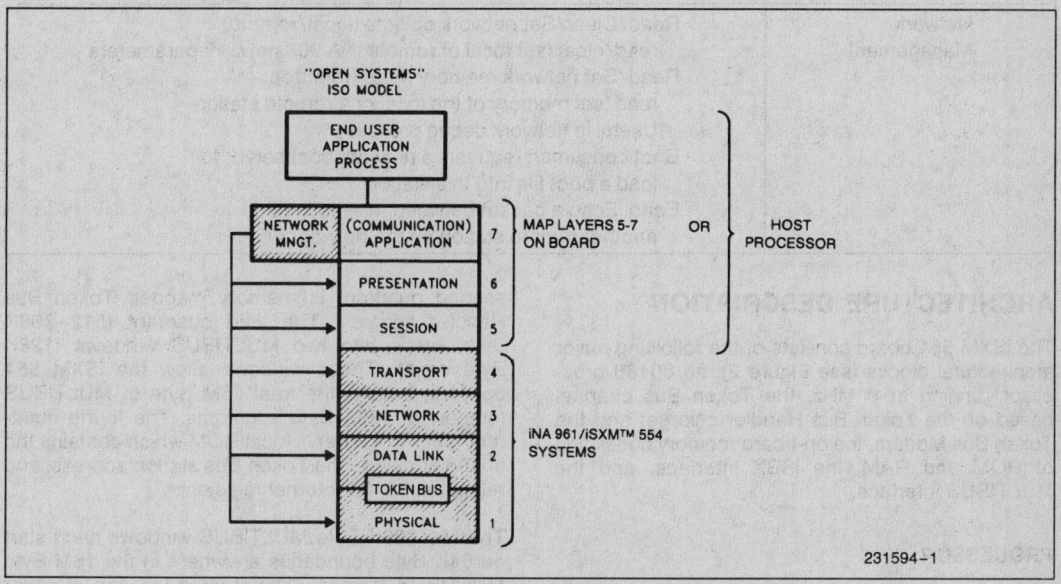

Figure 1. iNA 961 Configuration on iSXM™ 554 Board

Table 1. iNA 961 R2.0 Services

Transport	Virtual circuit
	   open: establish a virtual circuit database
	   send connect: actively try to establish a virtual connection
	   await connect: passively awaits the arrival of a connection request
	   send: send a message
	   receive: post a buffer to receive a message
	   close: close a virtual circuit
	Datagram
	   send: send a datagram message
	   receive: post a buffer to receive a datagram message

Network	Internetworking
	   routing between multiple lans
	   segmentation/reassembly
	   user defined routing tables
	Multiple subnets supported
	   user supplied
	   802.3, 802.4

iSXM™ 554 — ADVANCE INFORMATION

Table 1. iNA 961 R2.0 Services (Continued)

Data Link	Transmit: transmit a data link packet Receive: post a buffer to receive a data link packet Connect: make a data link logical connection (link service access point. IEEE802.4) Disconnect: disconnect a data link logical connection Change token bus address Add multicast address Delete multicast address Configure TBH

Network Management	Read/Clear/Set network objects (local/remote):
	   read/clear/set local or remote iNA 960 network parameters
	Read/Set network memory (local/remote):
	   read/set memory of the local or a remote station
	   Useful in network debug process
	Boot consumer: requests a network boot server to load a boot file into this station
	Echo: Echo a packet between this station and another remote station on the network

ARCHITECTURE DESCRIPTION

The iSXM 554 board consists of the following major architectural blocks (see Figure 2): an 80186 processor running at 8 MHz, the Token Bus channel based on the Token Bus Handler chip set and the Token Bus Modem, the on-board memory consisting of ROM and RAM, the iSBX interface, and the MULTIBUS interface.

PROCESSOR

The iSXM 554 board contains an 80186 processor operating at 8 MHz. It is responsible for implementing the intelligent interface between the iSXM 554 board and a host processor. The 80186 processor runs the iNA 961 R2.0 transport software and the data link software needed by the Token Bus Handler chip set. It is responsible for the delivery of data between user buffers in MULTIBUS memory and iNA buffers on the iSXM 554 board. The iNA software is responsible for the reliable transfer of information across the Token Bus LAN.

MEMORY

The one megabyte address space of the 80186 is divided into four quadrants (see Figure 3). The first quadrant (0–256K Byte) is local RAM memory. The second quadrant is memory mapped Token Bus Handler address. The third quadrant (512–768K Byte) maps into two MULTIBUS windows (128K Byte each). These windows allow the iSXM 554 board to access the total 16M Byte of MULTIBUS memory in 128K Byte segments. The fourth quadrant (768–1M Byte) is local ROM which contains the 80186 firmware, the Token Bus station address, and relocated 80186 internal registers.

The two 128K Byte MULTIBUS windows each start on 64K Byte boundaries anywhere in the 16M Byte MULTIBUS memory. The starting location of either window is determined by writing to a local I/O mapped latch.

Options on the iSXM 554 allow up to 128K Byte of RAM to be accessible by the host. This dual port RAM is jumper selectable to appear anywhere in the MULTIBUS 16M Byte memory space on 128K Byte boundaries. The dual port RAM memory is a data link between the on board 80186, the token bus controller, and the bus master (if any) managing the systems functions. This shared dual port RAM can be used to transfer command, status and data between the on board 80186 processor and the host. This feature minimizes the necessity for the 80186 to access MULTIBUS while acquiring shared information. This has a direct positive effect on performance, serving to eliminate bus contention.

iSXM™ 554 ADVANCE INFORMATION

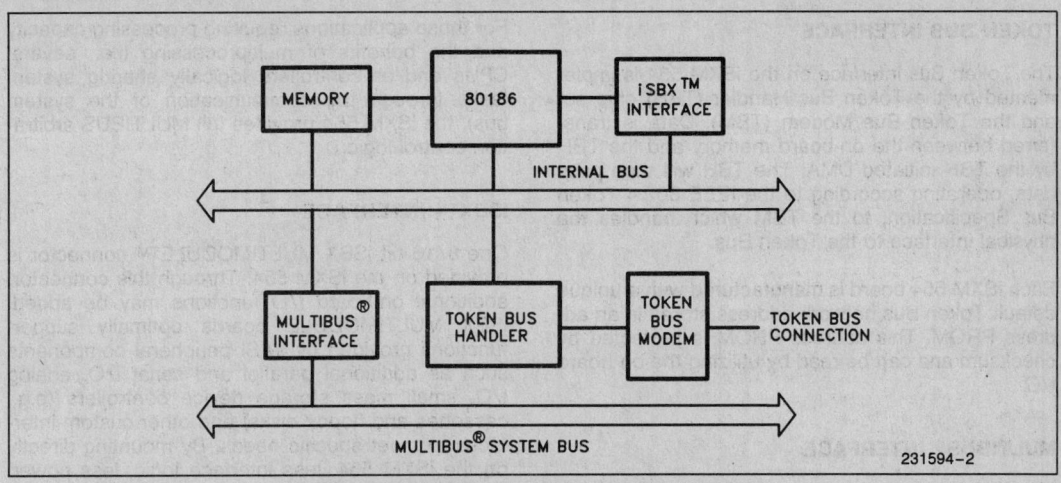

Figure 2. iSXM™ 554 Architectural Blocks

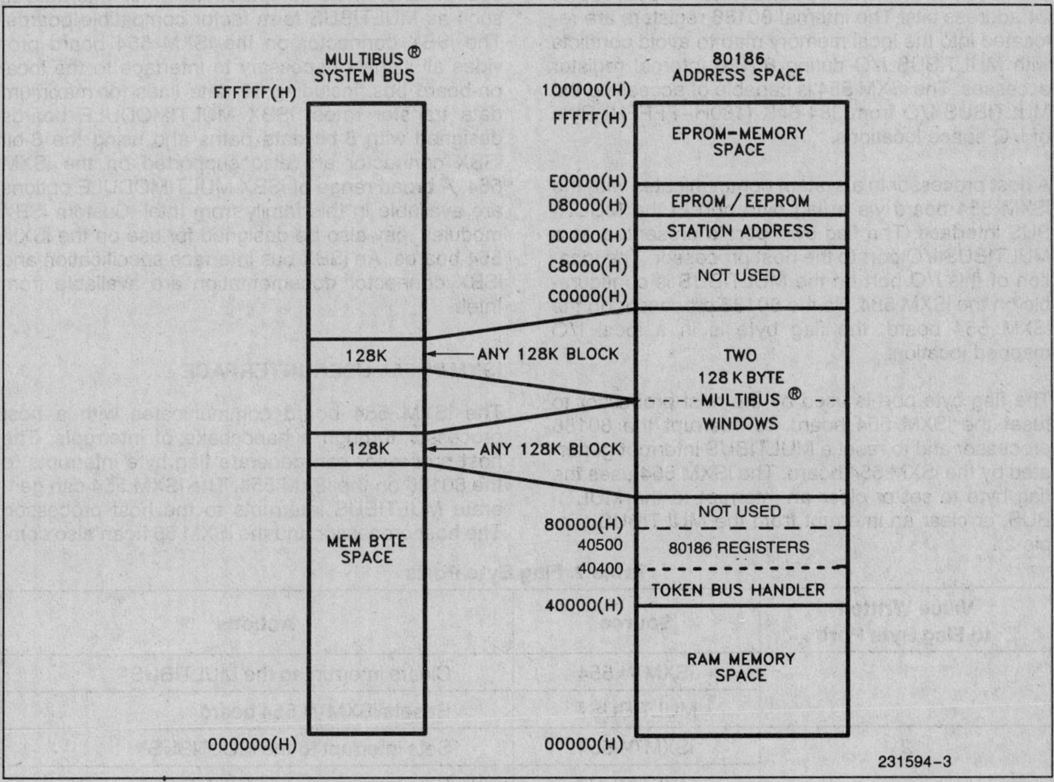

Figure 3. iSXM™ 554 Memory Configuration

iSXM™ 554 — ADVANCE INFORMATION

TOKEN BUS INTERFACE

The Token Bus interface on the iSXM 554 is implemented by the Token Bus Handler (TBH) chip set and the Token Bus Modem (TBM). Data is transferred between the on-board memory and the TBH by the TBH initiated DMA. The TBH will then pass data, operating according to the IEEE 802.4 Token Bus Specification, to the TBM which handles the physical interface to the Token Bus.

Each iSXM 554 board is manufactured with a unique default Token Bus network address stored in an address PROM. This address PROM is protected by checksum and can be read by utilizing the on board I/O.

MULTIBUS® INTERFACE

The iSXM 554 board can access the MULTIBUS with an 8- or 16-bit data path and can support up to 24 address bits. The internal 80186 registers are relocated into the local memory map to avoid conflicts with MULTIBUS I/O during 80186 internal register accesses. The iSXM 554 is capable of accessing the MULTIBUS I/O from 384-64K (180H–FFFFH) Byte of I/O space locations.

A host processor in a system communicates with the iSXM 554 board via a flag byte port in the MULTIBUS interface. The flag byte port is presented as a MULTIBUS I/O port to the host processor. The location of this I/O port on the MULTIBUS is configurable on the iSXM 554. To the 80186 processor on the iSXM 554 board, the flag byte is in a local I/O mapped location.

The flag byte port is used by the host processor to reset the iSXM 554 board, to interrupt the 80186 processor and to reset a MULTIBUS interrupt generated by the iSXM 554 board. The iSXM 554 uses the flag byte to set or clear an interrupt to the MULTIBUS, or clear an interrupt from the MULTIBUS (Table 2).

For those applications requiring processing capacity and the benefits of multiprocessing (i.e., several CPUs and/or controllers logically sharing system tasks through the communication of the system bus), the iSXM 554 provides full MULTIBUS arbitration control logic.

iSBX™ INTERFACE

One 8/16 bit iSBX MULTIMODULE™ connector is provided on the iSXM 554. Through this connector, additional on-board I/O functions may be added. iSBX MULTIMODULE boards optimally support functions provided by VLSI peripheral components such as additional parallel and serial I/O, analog I/O, small mass storage device controllers (e.g., cassettes and floppy disks) and other custom interfaces to meet specific needs. By mounting directly on the iSXM 554, less interface logic, less power, simpler packaging, higher performance, and lower cost results when compared to other alternatives such as MULTIBUS form factor compatible boards. The iSBX connector on the iSXM 554 board provides all signals necessary to interface to the local on-board bus, including 16 data lines for maximum data transfer rates. iSBX MULTIMODULE boards designed with 8-bit data paths and using the 8-bit iSBX connector are also supported on the iSXM 554. A broad range of iSBX MULTIMODULE options are available in this family from Intel. Custom iSBX modules may also be designed for use on the iSXM 554 boards. An iSBX bus interface specification and iSBX connector documentation are available from Intel.

iSXM™ 554 USER INTERFACE

The iSXM 554 board communicates with a host processor through a handshake of interrupts. The host processor can generate flag byte interrupts to the 80186 on the iSXM 554. The iSXM 554 can generate MULTIBUS interrupts to the host processor. The host processor and the iSXM 554 can also com-

Table 2. Flag Byte Ports

Value Written to Flag Byte Port	Source	Actions
1	iSXM™ 554	Clears interrupt to the MULTIBUS®
	MULTIBUS®	Resets iSXM™ 554 board
2	iSXM™ 554	Sets interrupt to the MULTIBUS®
	MULTIBUS®	Sets interrupt to the iSXM™ 554 board
3	iSXM™ 554	Clears interrupt to the iSXM™ 554 board
	MULTIBUS®	Clears interrupt to the MULTIBUS®

iSXM™ 554

municate through shared MULTIBUS system memory. As much as 128K byte of the on-board RAM on the iSXM 554 is accessible to the host processor and the iSXM 554 can read and write all of the 16M byte of MULTIBUS system memory.

OPERATING ENVIRONMENTS

The iSXM 554 is designed to function in any MULTIBUS system as a communication processor. It can function as both a MULTIBUS bus master or a slave. As a MULTIBUS master, it can access up to 16M Byte of host memory and 64K byte of I/O address. As a MULTIBUS slave, it occupies one location reserved for the flag byte.

iNA 961 R2.0 USER INTERFACES

User programs give iNA 960 commands to the iNA 961 R2.0 software on the iSXM 554 board via the MULTIBUS Interface Protocol (MIP). MIP is an Intel reliable process to process message delivery protocol between MULTIBUS processors. An implementation of the MIP protocol is provided on the iSXM 554 for communication with the host. The corresponding MIP protocol implementation will have to be provided by the user on the host side for communicating with the iSXM 554. Figure 4 illustrates how this message delivery functions. Commands are passed between the iSXM 554 and the host processor in the form of request blocks. A request block is a buffer that contains a command specification and the command parameters. Each request block (or equivalently, each command) is reliably delivered from the host processor to iNA 961 R2.0 via the MIP facility. iNA 961 R2.0 will extract the command information and carry out the command. After a command is done, iNA 961 R2.0 will use the MIP facility to return the command result to the user program.

iNA 961 R2.0 request blocks are in the same formats as iNA 960 commands. Refer to the iNA 960 data sheet and reference manuals for more details on the iNA 961 R2.0 software.

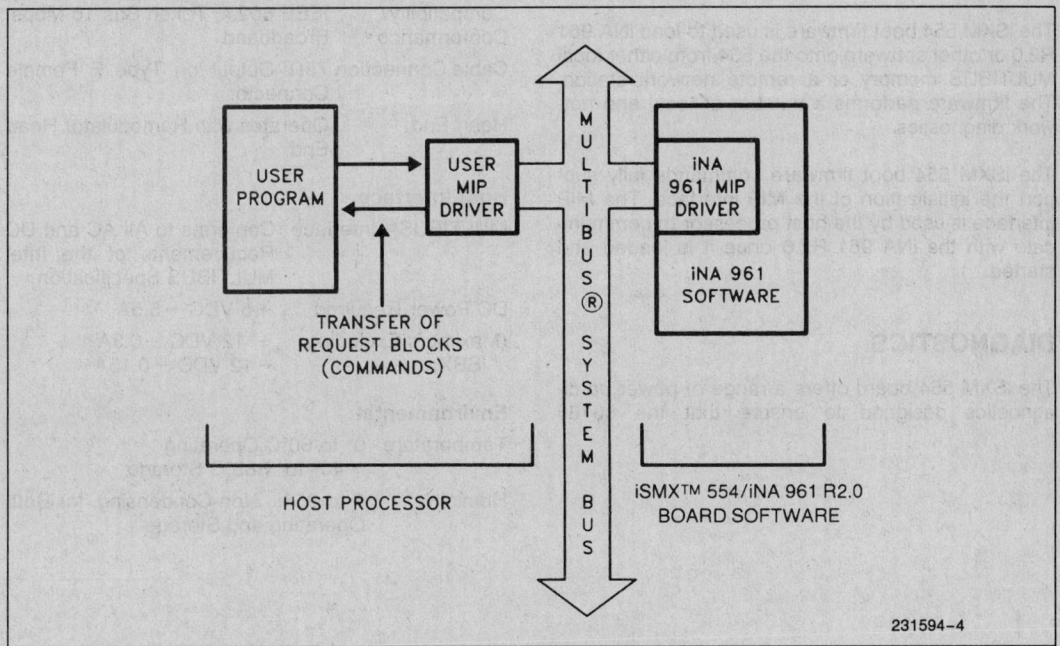

Figure 4. iNA 961 MIP Interface

iSXM™ 554   ADVANCE INFORMATION

OPERATING SYSTEMS ENVIRONMENT

The iSXM 554 board and iNA 961 R2.0 software can function in any MULTIBUS environment. The communication between the iSXM 554 and the host processor is entirely independent of any host operation systems. iNA 961 R2.0 uses the MIP protocol to interface with the host processor. iNA 961 R2.0 can service multiple processes utilizing its services at the same time.

A host processor passes iNA 961 R2.0 commands and buffers in the MULTIBUS system memory to the iNA 961 R2.0 software. iNA 961 R2.0 is responsible for updating the response fields of these commands. It is responsible for copying the user send buffer in MULTIBUS system memory into its on board buffers for transmission and for copying received messages to user buffers in MULTIBUS system memory.

iSXM™ BOOT FIRMWARE USER INTERFACE

The iSXM 554 boot firmware is used to load iNA 961 R2.0 or other software onto the 554 from either local MULTIBUS memory or a remote network station. The firmware performs a number of local and network diagnostics.

The iSXM 554 boot firmware commands fully support the initialization of the MIP interface. The MIP interface is used by the host processor to communicate with the iNA 961 R2.0 once it is loaded and started.

DIAGNOSTICS

The iSXM 554 board offers a range of power up diagnostics designed to ensure that the 80186 processor, the memory (EPROM and RAM), and the Token Bus Interface are functioning properly.

ORDERING INFORMATION

Part Number Modem Frequencies/Channel Pairs

SXM 554-1 Transmit: 59.75 to 71.75 MHz/Ch. 3 and 4

Receive: 252 to 264 MHz/Ch. P and Q

SXM 554-2 Transmit: 71.75 to 83.75 MHz/Ch. 4A and 5

Receive: 264 to 276 MHz/Ch. R and S

SXM 554-3 Transmit: 83.75 to 95.75 MHz/Ch. 6 and FM1

Receive: 276 to 288 MHz/Ch. T and U

SPECIFICATIONS

Network Interface

Compatiblity/Conformance IEEE 802.4, Token Bus 10 Mbps Broadband

Cable Connection 75Ω Output on Type F Female Connector

Head End Operates with Remodulator Head End

Host Interface

MULTIBUS® Interface Conforms to All AC and DC Requirements of the Intel MULTIBUS Specification

DC Power Required (Maximum Excluding iSBX)
+5 VDC −5.5A
+12 VDC −0.3A
−12 VDC −0.15A

Environmental

Temperature 0° to 60°C Operating
−40° to +85°C Storage

Humidity 5 to 95%, Non-Condensing, for Both Operating and Storage

iSBC® 561
SOEMI (Serial OEM Interface)
CONTROLLER BOARD

- Dedicated I/O controller provides a direct connection of MULTIBUS®-based systems to an IBM 4361 Mainframe host via IBM's SOEMI (Serial OEM Interface) protocol
- Physical interface is via IBM 3270 coax with a maximum distance of 1.5 km
- Maximum transmission rate of 2.36 Megabits/second
- Dual I/O processors manage both SOEMI and MULTIBUS® interfaces
- Includes a SMC-to-BNC cable assembly to attach into the IBM 3270 Information Display System
- On-board diagnostic capability provides operational status of board function and link with the Host
- Supported by a complete family of single board computers, memory, digital and analog I/O, peripheral and graphics controllers' packaging and software

The Intel iSBC® 561 SOEMI (Serial OEM Interface) Controller Board is a member of Intel's family of single board computers, memory, I/O, peripheral and graphics controller boards. It is a dedicated intelligent I/O controller on a MULTIBUS form-factor printed circuit card. The board allows OEMs of MULTIBUS-based systems a direct, standard link to an IBM System 4361 environment via the SOEMI (Serial OEM Interface). The iSBC 561 Controller also provides 4361 users access to the broad range of applications supported by hundreds of MULTIBUS vendors.

The SOEMI interface is comprised of an IBM System/370 programming interface and a 3270 coax interface. It is a flexible, high speed, point-to-point serial interface offered as a standard feature on the 4361 processor family. The iSBC 561 SOEMI Controller Board contains two processors and provides the necessary intelligence for conversion, control functions, and buffer management between the IBM mainframe and the MULTIBUS system. This board allows an IBM user to distribute control and information to MULTIBUS compatible systems for a variety of applications including factory automation, data acquisition, measurement, control, robotics, process control, communications, local area networking, medical instrumentation, and laboratory automation.

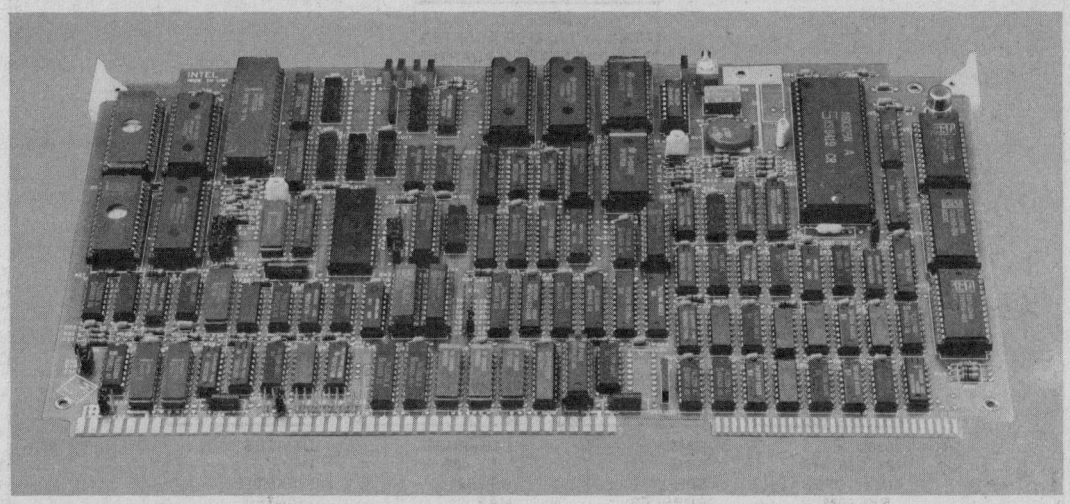

*IBM is a trademark of International Business Machine Corp.

Intel Corporation assumes no responsibility for the use of any circuitry other than circuitry embodied in an Intel product. No other circuit patent licenses are implied. Information contained herein supersedes previously published specifications on these devices from Intel.

© INTEL CORPORATION, 1985

APRIL, 1985
ORDER NUMBER: 280114-001

iSBC® 561 SOEMI Controller Board

SOEMI INTERFACE OVERVIEW

The Serial OEM Interface (SOEMI) is a new means of connecting Original Equipment Manufacturer (OEM) MULTIBUS-based systems and subsystems to an IBM 4361 mainframe. Previously, the only low-cost way to attach non-IBM equipment into the IBM mainframe environment was to use 3270 emulation software and hardware adaptors. This type of interface is low-speed (approx. 19.6K bits/sec.) and not very flexible as to the type and format of data that can be transferred. The 3270 emulators must mimic the device formats of the displays and printers that are typically attached on this interface; stripping out command characters, carriage return and line feed characters, etc. The SOEMI Protocol is much faster and more flexible, in that any type of raw data or formatted data may be sent across the connecting coax cable.

The SOEMI attachment into the MULTIBUS system architecture, via the iSBC 561 SOEMI Controller Board, extends the attachment capabilities of the IBM 4361 to a variety of systems, boards, and I/O devices provided by other manufacturers. Figure 1 is an example of the variety achievable on Intel's MULTIBUS (IEEE 796) system architecture.

The SOEMI interface utilizes the System/370 Programming Interface on the IBM 4361 to create the protocols and formats required by a given application for connection to and communication with virtually any type of OEM device.

The System/370 Programming Interface provides the standard System/370 I/O instructions for exchanging data between the host and the MULTIBUS-based system. System/370 applications see MULTIBUS system memory as one or more entities called "spaces." The 4361 host system program writes to and reads from these spaces. The user can define the number of spaces or the layout of fields in the SOEMI interface at his discretion and as required by the application and the MULTIBUS system configuration.

The 3270 coax interface provides the physical connection between the OEM MULTIBUS system and the IBM 4361 host. The coax cable (type RG62AU) can operate over a distance of 1.5 kilometers at a maximum transfer rate of 2.3587 Mbits/second. The distance of 1.5 kilometers can be increased to a maximum of 3 kilometers by installing an IBM 3299 Terminal Multiplexer (repeater) between the IBM 4361 and the MULTIBUS system. The protocol at the coax interface includes a polling mechanism, a set of Write and Read commands, and requires a buffer with an address register at the OEM controller end.

The actual connection to the IBM 4361 is made via the IBM 3270 Information Display System's Display/Printer Adapter (DPA) and/or Work Station Adapter (WSA) coax ports. The DPA can drive up to sixteen 3270/SOEMI coax ports, and is the standard configuration. The WSA is an optional add-on to the IBM 4361 that increases the total number coax ports supported to 40. A typical 4361 configuration can support an aggregate data rate of approximately 45K Bytes/second (approx. 360K bits/second).

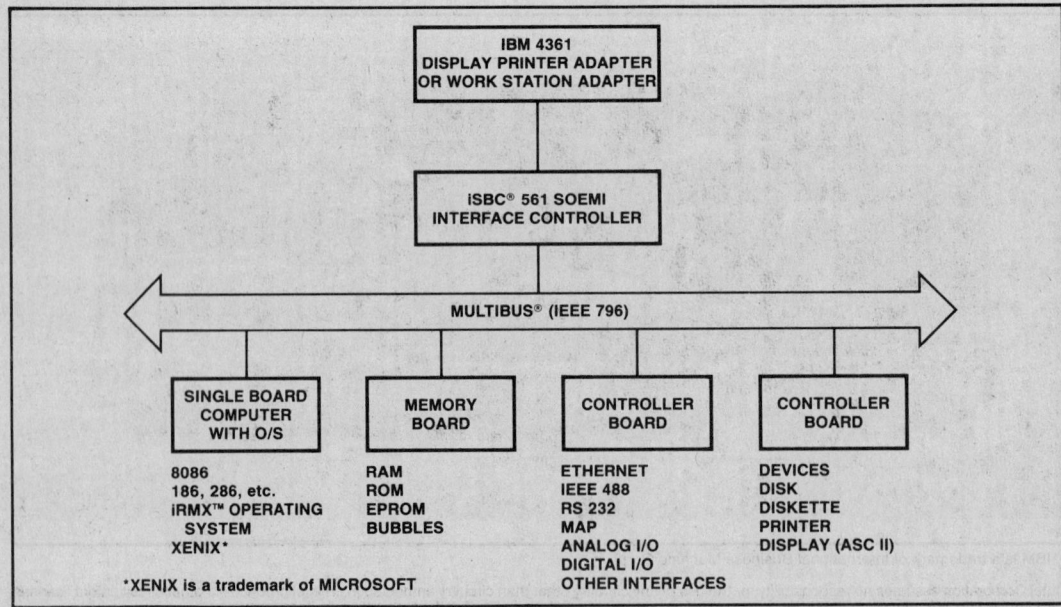

Figure 1. IBM 4361-to-MULTIBUS® Attachment Capability Block Diagram

iSBC® 561 SOEMI Controller Board

OPERATING ENVIRONMENT

The iSBC 561 board functions as a slave to the host mainframe, reacting and executing under System/370 program control as a mainframe resource. In addition, it has a full multimaster MULTIBUS interface that allows the board to arbitrate for bus ownership, generate bus clocks, respond to and generate interrupts, etc. With the iSBC 561 controller connected to the 4361 mainframe, all MULTIBUS system resources are available to the IBM host program/controller. From the IBM 4361 side, the mainframe is capable of accessing the entire 16 MBytes of MULTIBUS system memory, 64K Bytes of I/O space, and all on-board resources of the iSBC 561 board. Other intelligent MULTIBUS boards access iSBC 561 controller services through normal interrupt mechanisms.

Using the SOEMI interface in a relatively low-level application may simply require the user to write System/370 application control programs that reside in the IBM 4361 mainframe. A more elaborate implementation would also involve application programs that reside in the MULTIBUS system under its "native" operating environment (i.e., iRMX or XENIX operating systems) and an end-to-end protocol that ties both sets of application programs together.

ARCHITECTURE

The iSBC 561 board is functionally partitioned into three major sections: the front-end section, the common section, and the back-end section (see Figure 2).

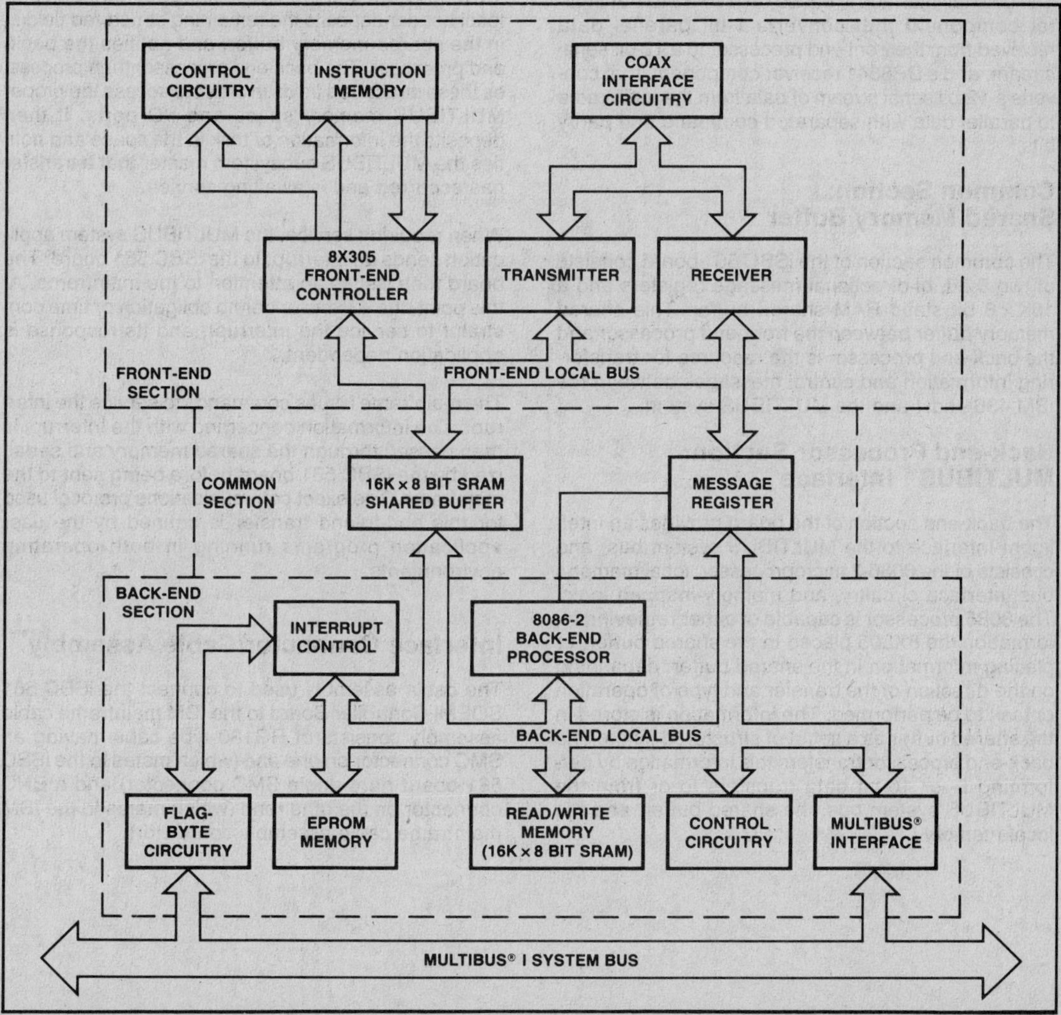

Figure 2. iSBC® 561 SOEMI (Serial OEM Interface) Controller Board Functional Block Diagram

8-77

Order Number: 280114-001

iSBC® 561 SOEMI Controller Board

Front-end Processor Section:
IBM 4361 Interface

The front-end section of the iSBC 561 Controller board interfaces with the IBM mainframe via the IBM 3270 Information Display System, and consists of an 8X305 Signetics microcontroller, the 8X305 instruction memory, and the coaxial interface. The 8X305 executes the coax commands and places the structured field's instructions in shared memory buffers for subsequent execution by the back-end processor. The front-end instruction memory consists of three $2K \times 8$ bit PROMs which provide the instruction code for the 8X305 processor and the information needed to generate the various control signals required by the 8X305 to elicit system functions. The information contained in each PROM is not modifiable by the user. The coaxial interface is based on a DP8340 transmitter component that converts 8-bit parallel data received from the front-end processor to a 12-bit serial stream, and a DP8341 receiver component, that converts a 12-bit serial stream of data from the mainframe to parallel data with separated command and parity bits.

Common Section:
Shared Memory Buffer

The common section of the iSBC 561 board consists of two 8 bit, bi-directional message registers and a $16K \times 8$ bit static RAM shared buffer. This shared memory buffer between the front-end processor and the back-end processor is the resource for transferring information and control messages between the IBM 4361 host and the MULTIBUS system.

Back-end Processor Section:
MULTIBUS® Interface

The back-end section of the board provides an intelligent interface to the MULTIBUS system bus, and consists of the 8086-2 microprocessor, local memory, bus interface circuitry, and memory-mapped logic. The 8086 processor is capable of either retrieving information the 8X305 placed in the shared buffer, or placing information in the shared buffer, depending on the direction of the transfer and type of operation or task to be performed. The information is stored in the shared buffer as a set(s) of structured fields. The back-end processor transfers this information by performing 8- or 16-bit data transfers to or from the MULTIBUS system bus, the shared buffer, and the local memory.

The control program for this high-speed, back-end processor is resident in two local ROM sites. The processor also has access to 16K bytes of static RAM for local data storage.

The back-end section interfaces to other MULTIBUS boards through two bus controllers, a bus arbiter, and the address, data, and command buffers for access over the 24 address lines and 16 data lines of the MULTIBUS system bus.

OPERATION FLOW

The commands and information passed along the coax by the IBM 4361 host to the iSBC 561 controller represent what is known as a "structured field." The iSBC 561 front-end processor strips out the 12-bit protocol header deposits the remaining structured field(s) in the shared memory buffer, and notifies the back-end processor. The back-end processor then processes these structured fields in order to access the proper MULTIBUS memory space and I/O ports. It then deposits the information or task in the space and notifies the MULTIBUS subsystem master that a transfer has occurred and is awaiting service.

When requiring service, the MULTIBUS system application sends an interrupt to the iSBC 561 board. The board then issues an attention to the mainframe. At this point, the 4361 is under no obligation or time constraint to service the interrupt, and its response is application dependent.

The mainframe issues commands to service the interrupt. The information concerned with the interrupt is then passed through the shared memory and serialized by the iSBC 561 board before being sent to the mainframe. The exact communications protocol used for this end-to-end transfer is defined by the user application programs running in both operating environments.

Interface Connector/Cable Assembly

The cable assembly used to connect the iSBC 561 SOEMI Controller Board to the IBM mainframe cable assembly consists of RG180 type cable having an SMC connector on one end (which mates to the iSBC 561 board right angle SMC connector) and a BNC connector on the other end (which mates to the IBM mainframe cable assembly connector).

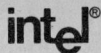

iSBC® 561 SOEMI Controller Board

SPECIFICATIONS

Operational Characteristics

Back-end processor — Intel 8086-2/5 MHz
    — 20-bit address path; 8/16-bit data path

Front-end processor — Signetics 8X305/8 MHz
    — 16-bit instruction path; 8-bit data path

Serial Transfer Rate — 2.3587 Mbits/second (max. bit rate)
    — 360K bits/second (approx. aggregate throughput)

Serial Transfer Rate — Binary dipulse (with 12-bit serial stream)

Memory Capacity — All iSBC 561 controller board memory is available to on-board firmware only.

Common memory — 16K Bytes of Shared Buffer memory (SRAM @ 0 wait state access)

8086-2 memory — 16K Bytes of EPROM; 16K Bytes of SRAM

8X305 memory — 4K Bytes of Instruction memory (EPROM)
    — 2K Bytes of Control memory (EPROM)

Physical Characteristics

Width: 30.48 cm (12.00 in)
Height: 17.15 cm (6.75 in)
Depth: 1.78 cm (0.70 in)
Weight: 510 gm (18 oz)

Electrical Characteristics

DC Power Requirements:
    Voltage — +5V
    Current (Max) — 6.28A
    Current (Typ) — 5.46A
    Power Dissipation (Max) — 35.5VA

Cable Characteristics

Impedance: coax connector – 50 ohms (nominal)
    external cable (user furnished) – 95 ohms (nominal)

Capacitance: 35 pF/ft

Propagation: 1.6 ns/ft

Environmental Characteristics

Operating Temperature: 0° to 55°C at 200 LFM air velocity

Operating Humidity: 10 to 85% non-condensing (0° to 55°C)

Non-Operating Temperature: −40° to 75°C

Shock: 30G for a duration of 11 ms with ½ sinewave shape.

Vibration: 0 to 55 Hz with 0.0 to 0.010 inches peak to peak excursion.

Reference Manuals

147048-001 — iSBC 561 SOEMI (Serial OEM Interface) Controller Board Hardware Reference Manual (NOT SUPPLIED)

Reference manual may be ordered from any Intel sales representative, distributor office, or from Intel Literature Department, 3065 Bowers Avenue, Santa Clara, California 95051.

GA33-1585-0 (File No. S370-03) — IBM Serial OEM Interface (SOEMI) Reference Manual (NOT SUPPLIED)

Reference manual may be ordered from IBM Advanced Technical Systems; Dept. 3291, 7030-16; Schoenaicherstr. 220; 7030 Boeblingen. Federal Republic of Germany.

ORDERING INFORMATION

Part Number	Description
iSBC 561	SOEMI (Serial OEM Interface) Controller Board

iSBC® 570, 576, 577
INTEL SPEECH TRANSACTION FAMILY

- **Friendly man-machine interface**—speech is the most natural and most easily learned form of interaction for man.
- **Lower data entry cost**—source data capture
- **Higher accuracy**—operator mental encoding is eliminated.
- **Freedom of Movement**—More efficient work flow
- **Hands and eyes free**—ability to perform another primary task
- **Easier training**—interactive, generic terminology
- **Complements keyboard/CRT**—new dimension to data entry

Users world wide are recognizing the many advantages of having Automatic Speech Recognition (ASR) and Electronic Speech Synthesis (ESS) in their products and applications. Speech I/O is a new dimension in data entry/control that complements other I/O mechanisms.

Speech I/O as a direct man-machine interface can be used for a broad range of applications, such as office and factory automation, computer-aided design, QC inspection stations, inventory control—and many more. Whatever your application is, the benefits of speech I/O are measured in dollars saved, improved productivity and improved product quality.

The following are trademarks of Intel Corporation and its affiliates and may be used only to identify Intel products: BXP, CREDIT, i, ICE, iCS, im, Insite, Intel, INTEL, Intelevision, Intellec, iMMX, iOSP, iPDS, iRMX, iSBC, iSBX, Library Manager, MCS, MULTIMODULE, Megachassis, Micromainframe, Micromap, MULTIBUS, Multichannel, Plug-A-Bubble, PROMPT, Promware, RMX/80, System 2000, UPI, and the combination of iCS, iRMX, iSBC, iSBX, ICE, MCS, or UPI and a numerical suffix. Intel Corporation Assumes No Responsibility for the use of Any Circuitry Other Than Circuitry Embodied in an Intel Product. No Other Patent Licenses are implied. ©INTEL CORPORATION, 1982. FEBRUARY 1983

ORDER NUMBER: 210598

iSBC® 570, 576, 577

In computer-aided design and manufacturing (CAD/CAM), design commands by speech allow the design engineer to keep his attention focused on the actual graphic elements.

In manufacturing, speech transactions provide important advantages in productivity. Defect tracing, production line monitoring and synchronization, and factory data collection, all benefit from direct human speech to computer communication.

In the automated office, ever-increasing machine intelligence can be controlled without mastering of typing skills.

The basic concept of a speech I/O system is shown in Figure 1. The speech I/O system provides a human-oriented interface with a machine-oriented computer-based information system or process. The speech I/O system recognizes speech inputs, provides visual/audio prompts and verification, and handles message editing and buffering. Depending on what was recognized, digitally coded data is then used to interact with the machine-oriented computer-based system.

The functional blocks of a speech I/O system are shown in Figure 2.

A complete system includes not just the capabilities for signal conditioning, Automatic Speech Recognition (ASR), and Electronic Speech Synthesis (ESS), but must include speech transaction processing as well. The Speech Transaction Processing task includes:

—The conversion between spoken language and coded representation
—Operator prompting and feedback
—Message editing
—Message buffering

In addition, development tools should be available for the generation of speech transaction files that will define the operations of the speech I/O system. Figure 3 shows the function of each member of the Intel Speech Transaction Family.

The Intel Speech Transaction Family, iSBC® 570, iSBC® 576 and iSBC® 577, is a family of products that provides a minimal risk path to add speech Input/Output (I/O) to your product line. The Speech Transaction Family will allow you to move from evaluation to integral speech driven products without major redesigns. Depending on your stage of product development, whether it is an evaluation, or a product simulation, or an add-on speech option, or a

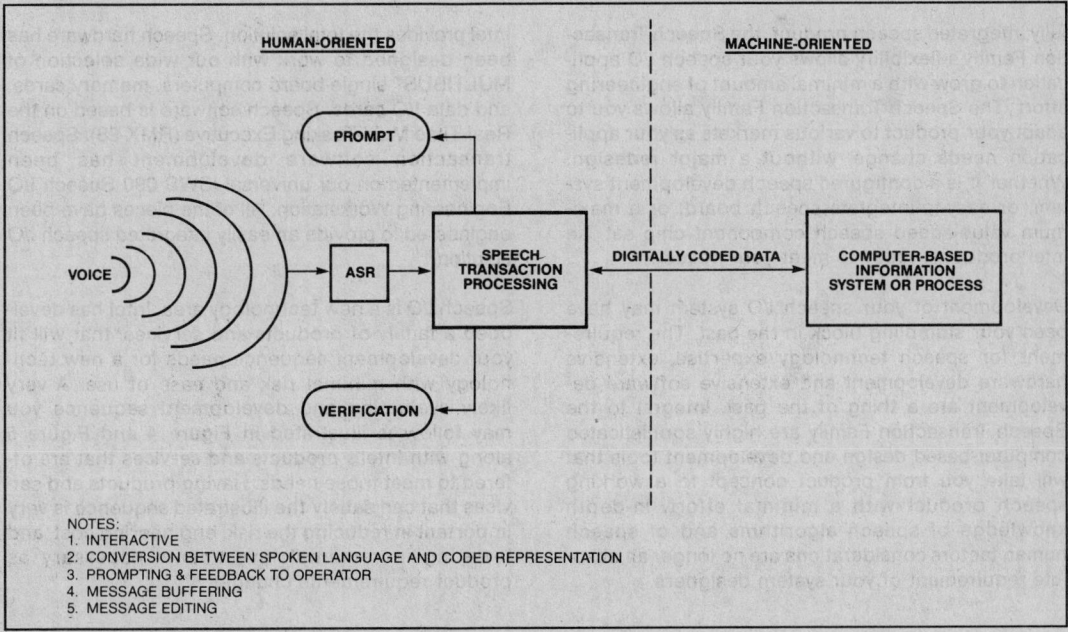

NOTES:
1. INTERACTIVE
2. CONVERSION BETWEEN SPOKEN LANGUAGE AND CODED REPRESENTATION
3. PROMPTING & FEEDBACK TO OPERATOR
4. MESSAGE BUFFERING
5. MESSAGE EDITING

Figure 1. Basic Concept

iSBC® 570, 576, 577

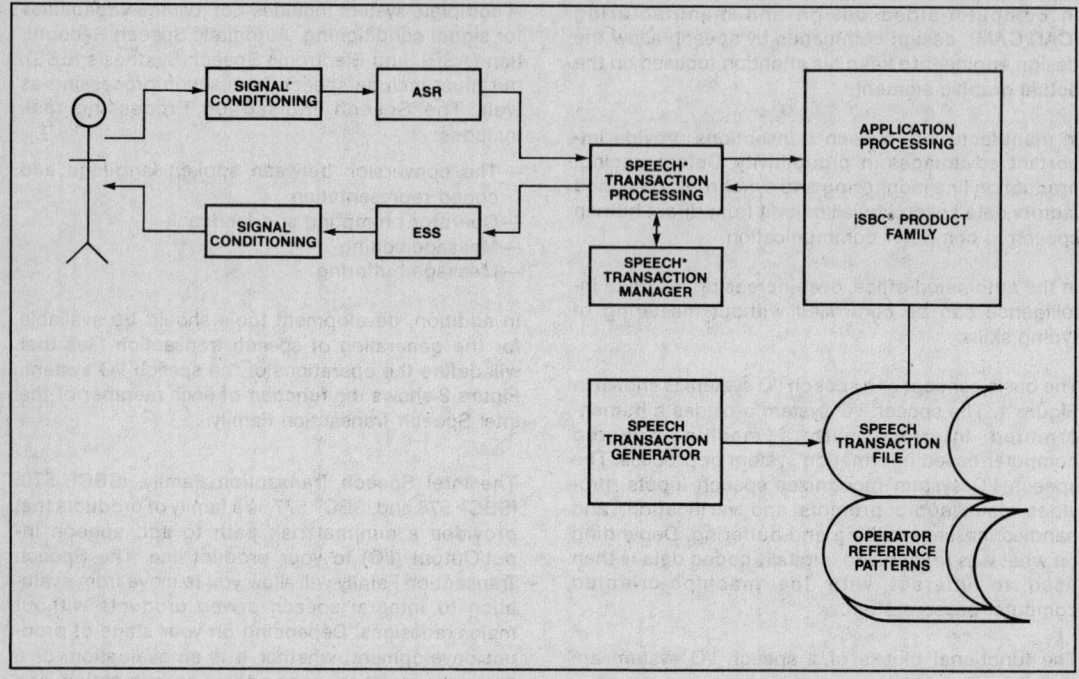

Figure 2. Functional Blocks of Speech I/O System.

fully integrated speech product, the Speech Transaction Family's flexibility allows your speech I/O application to grow with a minimal amount of engineering effort. The Speech Transaction Family allows you to adapt your product to various markets as your application needs change, without a major redesign. Whether it is a configured speech development system, or easy-to-integrate speech board, or a maximum value-added speech component chip set, an Intel product is ready to meet your needs.

Development of your speech I/O system may have been your stumbling block in the past. The requirement for speech technology expertise, extensive hardware development and extensive software development are a thing of the past. Integral to the Speech Transaction Family are highly sophisticated computer-based design and development tools that will take you from product concept to a working speech product with a minimal effort. In-depth knowledge of speech algorithms and of speech human factors considerations are no longer an absolute requirement of your system designers.

Intel provides the total solution. Speech hardware has been designed to work with our wide selection of MULTIBUS® single-board computers, memory cards, and data I/O cards. Speech software is based on the Real-Time Multi-Tasking Executive (RMX-88). Speech transaction software development has been implemented on our universal iSWS 090 Speech I/O Engineering Workstation. All of the pieces have been engineered to provide an easily integrated speech I/O solution.

Speech I/O is a new technology area. Intel has developed a family of products and services, that will fit your development sequence needs for a new technology with minimal risk and ease of use. A very likely evaluation and development sequence you may follow is illustrated in Figure 4 and Figure 5 along with Intel's products and services that are offered to meet those needs. Having products and services that can satisfy the illustrated sequence is very important in reducing the risk, engineering cost, and lowering incremental investments necessary as product requirements change.

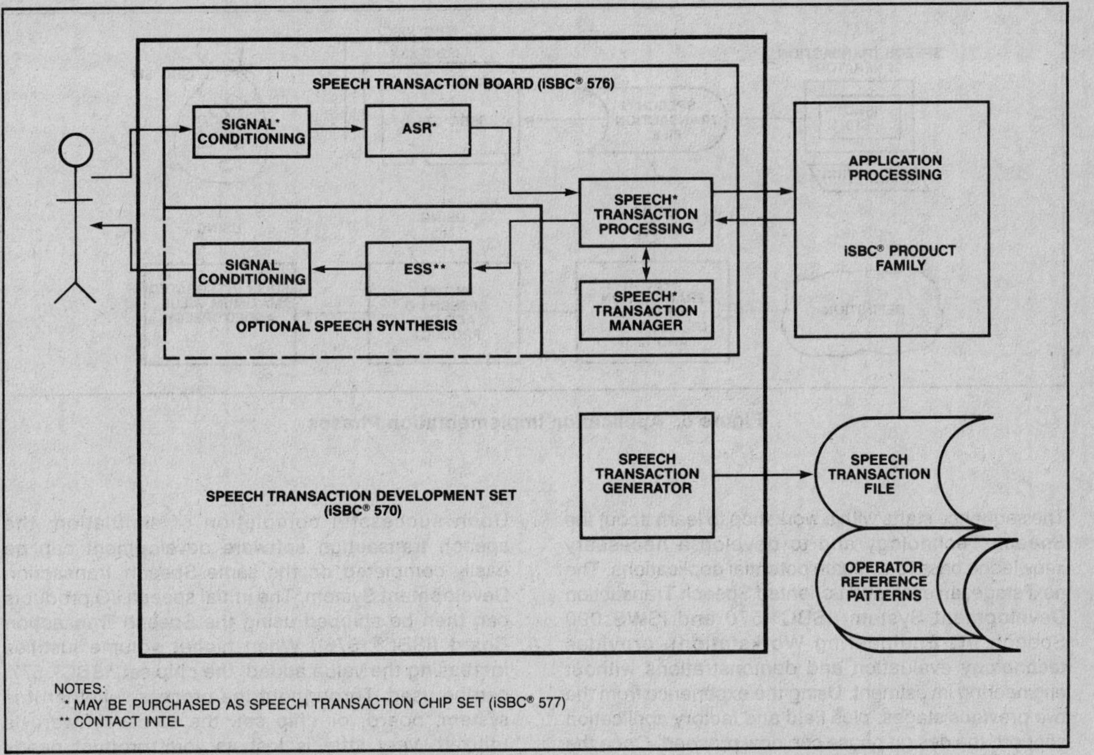

iSBC® 570, 576, 577

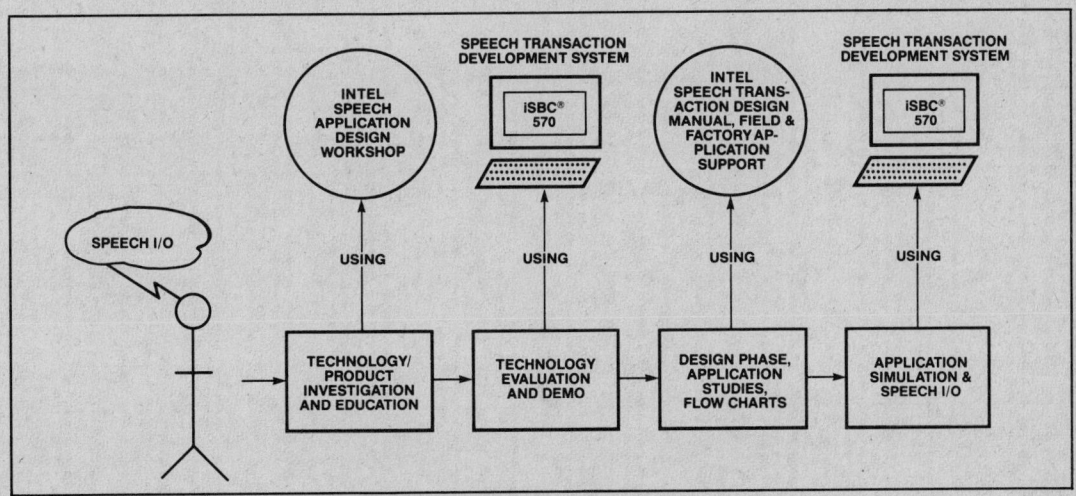

Figure 3. Functional Blocks of the Intel Speech Transaction Family.

Figure 4. Application Definition Phases

iSBC® 570, 576, 577

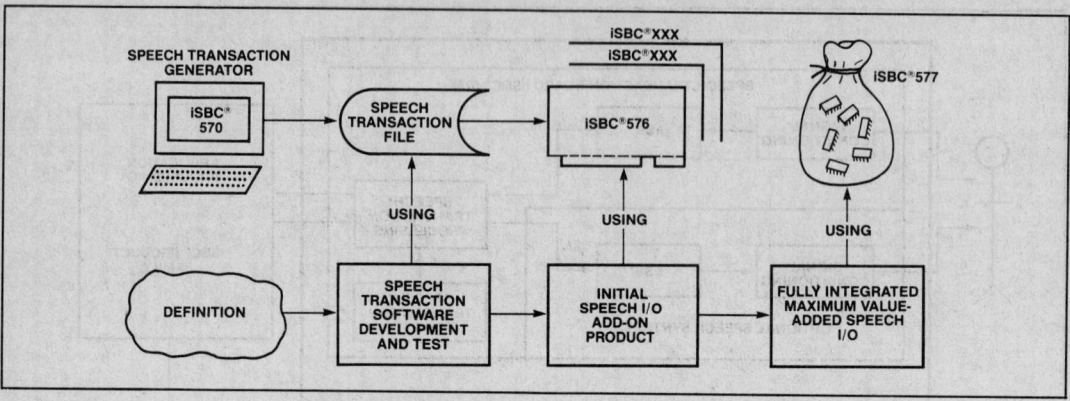

Figure 5. Application Implementation Phases

The sequence starts with a workshop to learn about the Speech Technology and to develop a necessary knowledge base to evaluate potential applications. The next stage, an evaluation-oriented Speech Transaction Development System (iSBC® 570 and iSWS 090 Speech I/O Engineering Workstation), provides technology evaluation and demonstrations without engineering investment. Using the experience from the two previous stages, plus field and factory application support, the design phase can now proceed. Once the application framework has been established, application simulation can be performed using the Speech Transaction Development System.

Upon successful completion of simulation, the speech transaction software development can be easily completed on the same Speech Transaction Development System. The initial speech I/O products can then be shipped using the Speech Transaction Board (iSBC® 576). When higher volume justifies increasing the value added, the chip set, iSBC® 577, can be used. Throughout the process, whether it is system, board, or chip set, the same software is utilized. Very little is lost as your product needs change. The level of investment required tracks the stage of product development. Your risk and exposure is kept to a minimum.

iSBC® 570
SPEECH TRANSACTION DEVELOPMENT SET

- **Complete Development Support Set for the Intel Speech Product Family. Includes:**
  - Speech Transaction Generator
  - iSBC® 576 Speech Transaction Board
  - iSBC® 575 Operator Control Unit
  - Microphone
  - Demo program
  - Speech Transaction Design Manual

- **iSWS 090 Speech I/O Engineering Workstation based**

- **Speech Transaction Generator provides:**
  - Interactive design environment
  - A speech transaction structure embodying good human factors engineering
  - Automatic error checking of transaction design
  - Symbolic labeling for easy system designer reference
  - Speech Transaction File data base manager facilitates Speech Transaction File changes

The Speech Transaction Development Set, iSBC® 570, provides an easy-to-use package for speech transaction evaluation, design simulation and application development. Along with Intel's Speech Design Workshop, the Speech Transaction Development Set becomes the starter kit that will move you into the forefront of speech I/O systems. Using the demo program supplied, you are quickly introduced to the important attributes of speech. Using the iSWS 090 Speech I/O Engineering Workstation and writing/modifying software based on examples provided, you can quickly simulate your application without hardware development. And finally, with the Speech Transaction Generator, your speech transaction structure, definition, transaction file coding and management become a well-defined automated task.

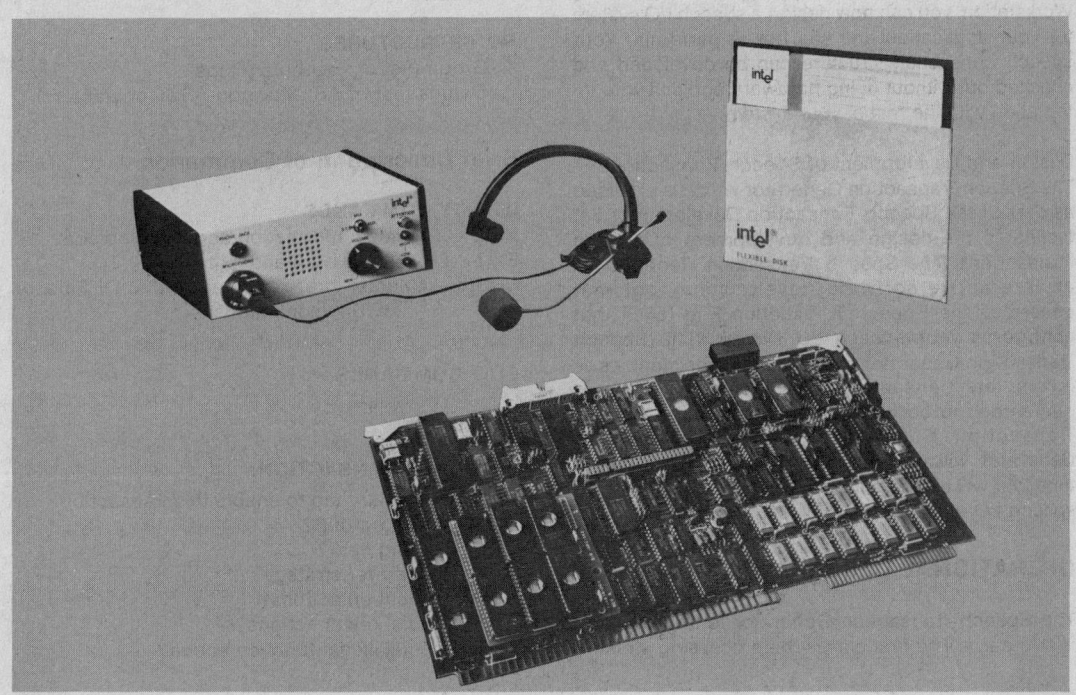

iSBC® 570

FUNCTIONAL DESCRIPTION

The iSBC® 570 Speech Transaction Development Set has been designed to meet your speech I/O needs as your level of involvement with speech I/O system grows. The Speech Transaction Development Set serves three very important functions. The three functions are: 1) Technology Evaluation and Demonstration, 2) Application Simulation of Speech I/O, and 3) Design and Development of Speech Transaction Software. These three functions are discussed below.

Technology Evaluation and Demonstration — A complete demo package is provided for you to demonstrate the capabilities of speech I/O. This package allows you to evaluate the speech technology without investing engineering design and development time. It is easy to use. Major attributes of a speech I/O system are highlighted and fully documented. The host system for the demonstration is the iSWS 090 Speech I/O Engineering Workstation.

Application Simulation of Speech I/O — The Speech Transaction Development Set provides the necessary tools and program examples for you to easily simulate your speech I/O system using the iSWS 090 Speech I/O Engineering Workstation as the host. With the iSBC® 570 and the iSWS 090 Speech I/O Engineering Workstation, you can now design a speech I/O system for your application and see how it performs. Your speech transaction structure can be developed and checked out without doing hardware and software integration with the rest of your system.

Design and Development of Speech Transactions — The Speech Transaction Generator which is provided as part of the Speech Transaction Development Set facilitates the design and development of speech transactions. The Speech Transaction Generator is an interactive software development tool that generates the Speech Transaction File (STF) that configures your speech I/O system. The Speech Transaction Generator checks for inconsistencies or incomplete transactions. The generated code is guaranteed to be fully compatible with the Speech Transaction Board. The Speech Transaction Generator will not only shorten your development time, but will also facilitate a well human-engineered speech I/O interface.

OPERATIONAL DESCRIPTION

The Speech Transaction Generator is implemented in two parts. The first part is the processing element of the STG and resides on EPROM in an STB environment. The second part is the data base manager for the STG and resides as an executable file under ISIS. The STG allows a system designer (with appropriate knowledge of transaction, fields, vocabulary and synthesis) to specify a STF easily. The STG maintains a set of files on the iSWS 090 Speech I/O Engineering Workstation as the data base. In this manner, the STG is the customization tool used by the speech system designers to prepare application-unique speech transactions that will execute on the STB under the supervision of the Speech Transaction Manager (STM). The STG also allows the system designer to dump portions of this data base in an ASCII-text format to a file. This ASCII-text file is useful for transporting data base entries between the STG implemented on other than an ISIS environment.

The things that a system designer can manipulate with the STG are termed "objects." Objects can be catagorized into structures and non-structures. Structures are generally a string of characters or a list of tags. Objects are classified as follows:

STRUCTURES
1. Transaction
2. Fields
3. Vocabulary
4. Synthesis

NON-STRUCTURES
1. Group (list of vocabulary tags)
2. Strings (list of ASCII or non-ASCII characters)

Brief Description of Commands

UTILITY COMMANDS
HELP—Provides information about the objects
EXIT—Close data base and exit STG
PREfix—Specify prefix character for DEFine or MODify commands

EDIT COMMANDS

DEFine

   DEFINE TRANSACTION:
    1. Vocabulary tag to enable this transaction?
    2. Training group?
    3. Starting field?
    4. Host buffer strategy?
    5. Verification actions?
    6. Special reject actions?
    7. Special illegal function action?

iSBC® 570

DEFINE FIELD:
1. Prompt?
2. Help message?
3. Prefix for host message?
4. Suffix for host message?
5. Special functions enable?
6. Valid sources?
7. Multiple utterance path?
   If yes,
   a) Vocabulary words?
   b) Next field?
   c) Maximum number of utterances?
   d) Fixed or variable?
8. Vocabulary words?
9. Next field?

DEFINE VOCABULARY:
1. Name?
2. Visual verify?
3. Audio verify?
4. Host message?
5. Visual train?
6. Audio train?
7. Special functions?

DEFINE SYNTHESIS:
1. Function?
2. Duration?
3. Delay?

DELete
Removes objects from the data base.

MODify
Modifies objects already entered into the data base with the DEFine command.

VALIDATION AND GENERATION COMMANDS

VALidate
Sequences through each of the transactions specified and validates them for completeness and proper definition.

GENerate
Takes the result of a successful validate command and produces a memory image of the STF. The STF can now be executed.

INTERROGATION COMMANDS

DISplays
Displays the contents of the objects

LISts
Lists the directory of the objects

FILE INTERFACE COMMANDS

DUMp
Passes results of current validation and outputs it to the host in a .DMP file.

USE
Takes command input from the specified file.

SPECIFICATIONS

Operating Environment

iSWS 090 Speech I/O Engineering Workstation (Model 800, Series II, and Series III with 64K byte of RAM).

SUPPLIED EQUIPMENT
iSBC® 576—Speech Transaction Board with Speech Transaction Manager Firmware.
—Speech Transaction Generator software and firmware.
—Speech I/O Demo Software.
—iSBC® 575 Operator Control Unit.
—Shure SM-10A Microphone.
—Speech Transaction Design Manual.

OPTIONAL EQUIPMENT
iSBX®-351—RS232 Multimodule
iSBC®-342—EPROM expansion module
—SBX synthesizers

ORDERING INFORMATION

Part Number Description

iSBC® 570   Speech Transaction Development Set

iSBC® 576
SPEECH TRANSACTION BOARD

- Up to 200 recognition words or phrases
- Automatic ASR and ESS handling
- On-board Speech Transaction Manager
- 8086, 16-bit CPU
- On-board diagnostic
- Multibus or serial host interface
- iSBX® interface
- Built-in buffer editing functions

The iSBC® 576 Speech Transaction Board is the heart of a speech I/O system. Beside providing Automatic Speech Recognition (ASR) capabilities, a ROM-resident Speech Transaction Manager (STM) is included on the board. This provides a flexibile operating structure for the system designer with a fully buffered speech-generated input-transaction handling capability. Flexibility has been designed into the STM to allow integration into existing applications without a major rewrite/redesign of host application software and hardware. The Speech Transaction Manager accommodates a Speech Transaction File which configures the iSBC® 576 Speech Transaction Board for each application. Also included on the board are three selectable audio feedback tones, visual feedback/control via a CRT terminal or printer, and an optional Electronic Speech Synthesis (ESS) capability.

iSBC® 576   PRELIMINARY

FUNCTIONAL DESCRIPTION

Figure 6 shows the functional structure of the Speech Transaction Board.

Input Signal Conditioning—Microphone input signal is amplified and low-pass filtered. The conditioned signal is then digitized and passed through 16 bandpass digital filters implemented by 2920/21 analog signal processors. The 2920/21s are synchronized and are operating in parallel. The bandpass filter information is then assembled by an 8048 microcomputer for algorithm processing by an 8086 processor. System-to-system portability is guaranteed by the usage of digital signal processing techniques.

ASR—Automatic Speech Recognition is accomplished by the 8086 processor in conjunction with two 2920/21 digital signal processors and an 8048 microcomputer. ASR handling is done completely under the control of the Speech Transaction Manager. This task is transparent to the system designers. Automatic statistics are also provided to track system performance.

Tone Generator—3 audio tones are available for use as a prompt. The tones are generated within a 2920 analog signal processor. The tone generator also generates test patterns for use by the diagnostic section.

Diagnostic—Under the control of the Speech Transaction Manager, a diagnostic check of the speech recognition hardware and software can be performed. System integrity is automatically determined to insure repeatable performance.

Output Signal Conditioning—Output amplifiers are provided to drive a speaker for the audio tones. Volume can be varied by a potentiometer.

Terminal Driver—Under the control of the Speech Transaction Manager, a CRT terminal/keyboard can be connected directly to the Speech Transaction Board. The terminal can be used for visual feedback as well as data entry/control. The interface is RS232 compatible.

Operator Control—Two LED lights to indicate recognition status and an operator attention button are provided. These functions are programmable under the control of the Speech Transaction Manager.

Operator Reference Patterns—Speech patterns for recognition are normally contained in RAM. The patterns are downloaded from the host processor under the control of the Speech Transaction Manager. The operator reference patterns are also generated under the control of the Speech Transaction Manager.

Speech Transaction Manager—The Speech Transaction Manager is the heart of the Speech Transaction Board. The Speech Transaction Manager controls all of the functions within the board. This firmware is

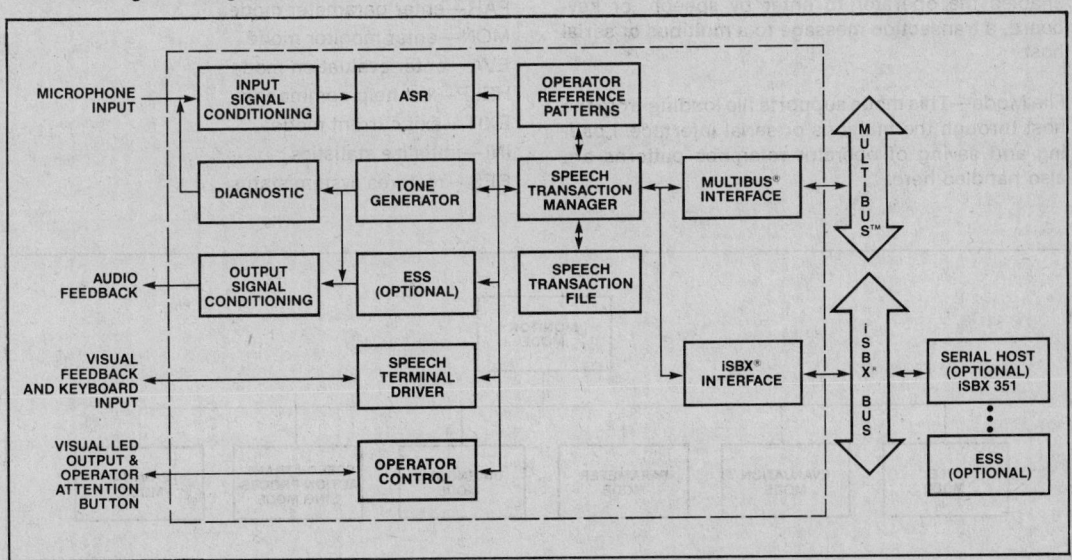

Figure 6. Functional Structure of the Speech Transaction Board

contained in 27128 EPROMs and is RMX®-88 (Real-Time Multi-Tasking Executive) based. Processing is provided by the 8086 processor.

Speech Transaction File—The Speech Transaction File determines the configuration of the board for each application. The Speech Transaction Manager executes this file which is normally downloaded from the host and stored in RAM. The file can also be stored in ROM/EPROM on the Speech Transaction Board itself. These files are generated by the Speech Transaction Generator.

Multibus® Interface—A slave multibus® interface is implemented. On the multibus the Speech Transaction Board looks like a data port.

iSBX® Interface—One SBX® interface has been implemented. This interface is controlled by the Speech Transaction Manager. Interface with a non-Multibus® host can be implemented via this channel.

Diagnostic Mode—This mode tests the hardware. The diagnostics will test the 2920/8048 interface and the 8048/8086 interface.

Terminal Mode—This mode provides for direct communication between the host and the Speech Transaction Board terminal. All response from the operator (through the terminal) is passed directly to the host. ALL host messages are passed directly to the terminal.

Parameter Mode—This mode lets the user define a limited set of configuration information and to set various other system parameters.

Evaluation Mode—This mode lets the user evaluate the recognition performance of an STF vocabulary or a vocabulary entered from the STB terminal. Use of this mode will facilitate evaluation of training strategies, vocabulary choices and parameter settings. In this mode statistics and automatic scoring of results are all standard features.

OPERATIONAL DESCRIPTION

The operation of the Speech Transaction Board is determined by the Speech Transaction Manager. The Speech Transaction Manager has several specific modes of operation as described below.

Speech Transaction Processing Mode—This mode enables the operator to enter by speech, or keyboard, a transaction message to a multibus or serial host.

File Mode—This mode supports file loading from the host through the multibus or serial interface. Loading and saving of operator reference patterns are also handled here.

LIST OF COMMANDS

Monitor Mode Commands

STP—enter speech transaction processing mode
FIL—enter file mode
DIA—enter diagnostic mode
TER—enter terminal mode
PAR—enter parameter mode
MON—enter monitor mode
EVA—enter evaluation mode
HELP—list help commands
EXIT—exit current mode
INI—initialize statistics
RES—restores system status

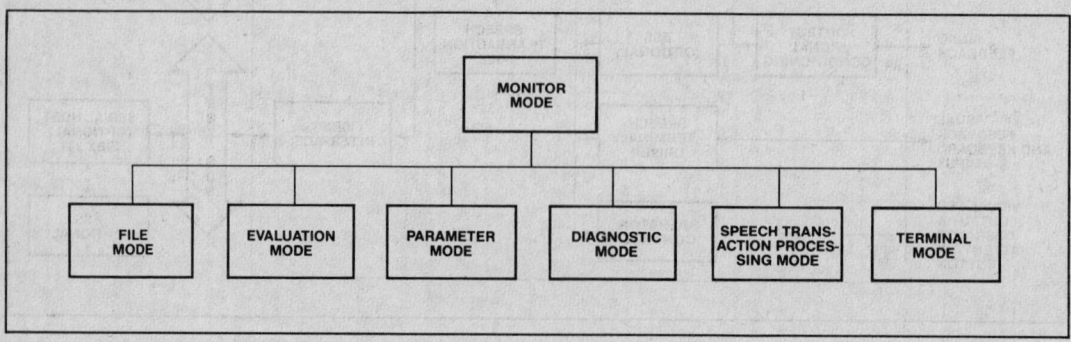

iSBC® 576   PRELIMINARY

Speech Transaction Processing Mode Function

Buffer Editing Functions

Forward   Erase Field
Backup   Continue
Correction   Beginning
Replace   Cancel
Forward Field   Finish
Backup Field

Utility Functions

Help—operator assistance at each field
Display—current transaction buffer
Next—go to next field
Detach—put terminal in "Terminal Mode"
Attach—get terminal out of "Terminal Mode"
Exit—exit STP mode
Up—raise rejection threshold
Down—lower rejection threshold
Relax—put system in not-ready state
Ready—first of two utterances to exit not-ready state
Attention—second of two utterances to exit not-ready state
Enable Transaction "N"—initiate transaction
Macro—performs a series of commands automatically in any mode

Operator Speech Pattern Maintenance Functions

Test Group   Train
Test All   Train Group
Retrain   Train All
Retrain Group   Update
Retrain All   Update Group
Delete   Update All
Delete All   Test

File Mode Commands

LST—load Speech Transaction File
SST—save speech transaction file
LRP—load operator speech patterns
SRP—save operator speech patterns
CRP—clear operator speech pattern RAM area
HELp—list help commands
CST—clear speech transaction

EXIt—exit current mode
LDI—load dictionary
SDI—save dictionary

Diagnostic Commands

FET—front end test
EXIt—exit mode
HELp—list help commands

Parameter Mode Commands

BLO—block size of transfer
CHS—communication header
CON—display all configuration parameters
DIS—discrimination level
DRE—small delta rejection
EST—display extended statistics
HOS—specifies host and characteristics
HTE—host terminator string
HTO—host time-out
INS—initialize statistics
MTP—minimum training passes
RPT—operator reference pattern names
SHC—serial host baud rate
STA—displays statistics
STF—STF name
STR—ROM STF name
TST—STB terminal status
WRD—word gap and word length
FEG—front-end gain
HELp—list help commands
EXIt—exit current mode

Evaluation Mode Commands

DEF—define
MVO—modify vocabulary
RVO—remove vocabulary
RRP—remove reference pattern
RET—retrain
LIS—list vocabulary
TRAin—train
UPDate—update
TESt—test
RECognition—recognition
STA—statistics
COR—cross correlation
INS—initialize statistics
HELp—list help commands
EXIt—exit current mode

SPECIFICATIONS

Operating Environment

Host Processor—any iSBC® Multibus® computer
 —any RS232 serial host interface
Audio Input—475Ω input impedence
 —50 m.v. p–p max.
 —differential or single-ended

Equipment Supplied

iSBC® 576 Speech Transaction Board with Speech Transaction Manager Firmware

Optional Equipment

iSBX®-351	RS232 Multimodule
iSBX®-342	EPROM expansion
	SBX synthesizer
iSBC®-575	Operator Control Unit

Performance Specifications

Recognition vocabulary—200 words or phrases
Utterance duration—user selectable > 100 msec., minimum
 —user selectable < 2 sec. maximum
Rejection Threshold—user selectable
Word gap—user selectable > 50 msec., minimum
 —user selectable < 250 msec., maximum
Recognition Accuracy (50 state names)—99+%
Response Time (for vocabulary up to 200 words with maximum node length 50 words) — < 500 msec.

Physical Characteristics

Width—6.75 in. (17.15 cm)
Height—0.5 in. (1.27 cm)
Length—12.0 in. (30.48 cm)
Shipping weight—TBD
Mounting—occupies one slot of iSBC® system chasis in cardcage/backplane. With iSBX® Multimodule™ board mounted, vertical height increases to 1.13 in. (2.87 cm)

Electrical Characteristics

Power Requirements
+5V DC @ 3 A
+10V DC @ TBD   *Multimodule™
−12V DC @ 0.02 A   *Multimodule™
+12V DC @ 0.5 A

Environmental Characteristics

Temperature—0 to 55°C (operating): −55°C to 85°C (non-operating)
Humidity—up to 90% relative humidity without condensation (operating); all conditions without condensation or frost (non-operating)

Reference Manual

Speech Transaction Design Manual (supplied)

ORDERING INFORMATION

Part Number	Description
iSBC® 576	Speech Transaction Board

iSBC® 577
SPEECH TRANSACTION RECOGNITION CHIP SET

- High-volume solution for speech I/O
- Fully compatible with iSBC 570, 576-generated software

The iSBC® 577 Speech Recognition Chip Set is a solution for your high-volume/maximum value-added speech I/O solution. The Chip Set contains the Intel-developed proprietary components from the iSBC® 576 Speech Transaction Board. With these components you can build the equivalent of the Speech Transaction Board into your own system. The Chip Set contains the digital front-end processors, a preprogrammed 8048 interface processor, the Speech Transaction Manager Firmware on 27128 EPROMs, and the 8086 microprocessor.

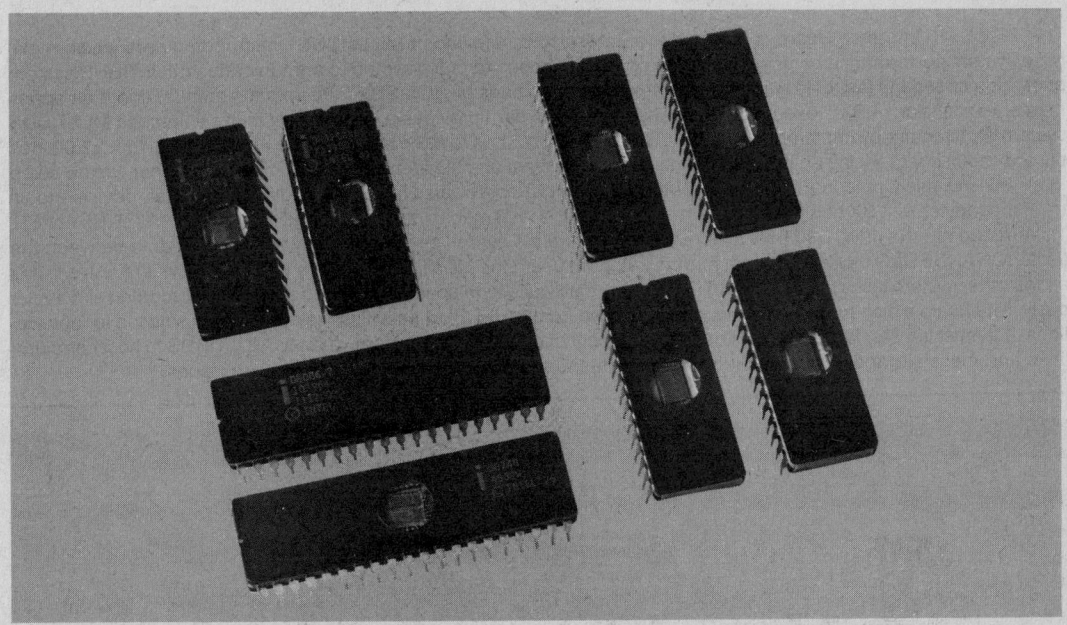

SPECIFICATIONS

Performance

—Refer to iSBC® 570 and iSBC® 576 performances.

Equipment Supplied

2—Preprogrammed 2920/21s (Digital Front-end Processor)
4—Preprogrammed 27128 (Speech Transaction Manager)
1—Preprogrammed 8048 (Interface Processor)
1—8086

ORDERING INFORMATION

Part Number   Description

iSBC® 577   Speech Transaction Recognition Chip Set

iSBC® 580 MULTICHANNEL™ BUS TO iLBX™ BUS INTERFACE

- MULTICHANNEL™ I/O bus 16-bit Talker/Listener interface
- iLBX™ bus master interface (primary or secondary)
- Supports MULTIBUS® interrupts
- Data rates up to 5.3 megabytes per second
- Addresses up to 16 megabytes of iLBX™ bus memory
- MULTIBUS® form factor

The iSBC® 580 Interface Board is a member of Intel's complete line of MULTIBUS® microcomputers which maximize system performance by using separate optimized buses for intra-system communication (MULTIBUS system bus), high speed I/O (MULTICHANNEL™ DMA I/O bus), expansion I/O (iSBX™ I/O expansion bus) and high-speed memory expansion (iLBX™ execution bus). The iSBC 580 board provides a key element in the enhanced MULTIBUS system architecture by implementing a MULTICHANNEL I/O bus to iLBX bus interface on a single 6.75 × 12.00 inch printed circuit board. Using an LSI state machine with standard on-chip firmware to maximize throughput, the on-board Intel® 8048 Single Component Microcomputer transfers data between a MULTICHANNEL Controller, device and up to 16 megabytes of iLBX bus resident memory at rates up to 5.3 megabytes per second. Acting as a MULTICHANNEL Talker/Listener, the iSBC 580 board increases the system's overall performance by transferring data between the MULTICHANNEL I/O bus and system memory without using the MULTIBUS system bus. As shown in Figure 1, this allows other system tasks to utilize MULTIBUS resources while high-speed I/O block transfers are occurring simultaneously. The board's high throughput and independence from MULTIBUS activities make it an ideal solution for applications that must transfer large amounts of data in and out of a MULTIBUS system, such as MULTIBUS to host computer links and mass storage, graphics display and high-speed data acquisition subsystem interfaces.

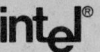

iSBC® 580

FUNCTIONAL DESCRIPTION

MULTICHANNEL™ Interface Capabilities

The MULTICHANNEL I/O bus is designed to provide a general purpose, high-speed data path between a microcomputer system and up to 15 block transfer devices. Using a 16-bit wide data bus and a simple asynchronous handshaking scheme, the MULTICHANNEL bus can operate over distances up to 15 meters (50 feet) with a maximum burst throughput of 8 megabytes/second. The bus consists of 16 address/data lines, 6 control lines, 2 interrupt lines, parity lines and reset. Via these signals, a MULTICHANNEL Supervisor or Controller may configure and then initiate a block data transfer with any other device on the bus.

The iSBC 580 board acts as a 16-bit only Talker/Listener device on the MULTICHANNEL I/O bus. As a Talker/Listener, the board will respond to Register Read or Write and DMA requests issued by the MULTICHANNEL Supervisor (typically an iSBC 589 board) or by a MULTICHANNEL Controller device.

The iSBC 580 board implements 32 MULTICHANNEL Device Registers. The first three registers are the standard STO Status, SRQ Status and SRQ Mask Registers, as defined by the MULTICHANNEL Bus Specification. The remaining registers are used to communicate with the on-board firmware and for user data storage. The firmware operations which may be initiated by writing to the Command Register are listed in Table 1. The iSBC 580 board always sends and receives a 16-bit word on the MULTICHANNEL interface but, the iSBC®

580 device registers (see Table 2) are 8-bit only. Register Write operations use only the low order 8-bits (AD0-AD7). Register Read operations place the data on the low order data lines of the MULTICHANNEL I/O bus and set the high order data lines to FFH.

Command Code (Hex)	Operation
0	No Operation
1	Go off line forever
2	STO poll (diagnostic)
3	SRQ poll (diagnostic)
4	Set on-board timer
5	Read on-board timer
6	Start on-board timer
7	Stop on-board timer
8	Generate Task Complete interrupt
9	Perform checksum on firmware (diagnostic)
A	Turn on-board LED on
B	Turn on-board LED off
C	Reset
D, E	Reserved
F	Set interrupt mask
10	Read interrupt mask
11-1F	Reserved

Table 1. iSBC® 580 Firmware Commands

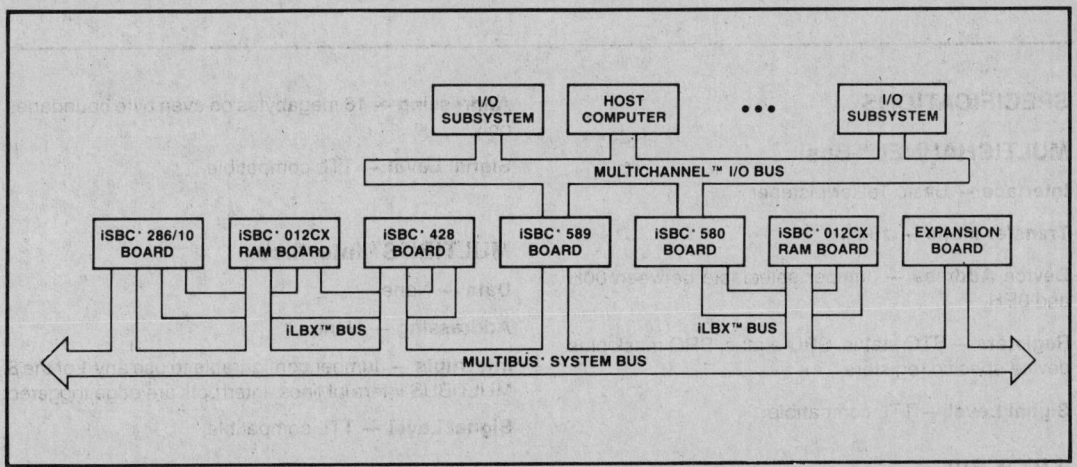

Figure 1. iSBC® 580 board, configured as an iLBX™ Bus Primary Master, transfers data between iLBX™ memory and MULTICHANNEL™ devices without using the system bus. The iSBC® 589 board acts as the MULTICHANNEL™ Supervisor and performs data transfers between MULTIBUS® memory and MULTICHANNEL™ devices.

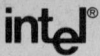

iSBC® 580

The iSBC 580 board can generate maskable MULTI-CHANNEL STO interrupts when the board detects a parity error in incoming MULTICHANNEL data, when the board attempts to address non-existent iLBX memory or when the board detects a MULTIBUS interrupt from the system in which it resides. The last type of interrupt allows a single board computer to send an interrupt via the iSBC 580 board to the MULTICHANNEL Supervisor located in another MULTIBUS system. The board can also generate a number of SRQ interrupts on the MULTI-CHANNEL bus as shown in Figure 2.

```
 7                                    0
┌───┬───┬───┬────┬─────┬─────┬─────┐
│ X │ X │ X │ LM │ TOM │ PEM │ MIM │ FPE
└───┴───┴───┴────┴─────┴─────┴─────┘
```

X   : Don't care
LM : iLBX™ lock/mask
TOM : Time out mask (STO)
PEM : Parity error mask (STO)
MIM : MULTIBUS® interrupt mask (STO)
FPE : Forced Parity Error mask

Figure 2. iSBC® 580 Interrupt Mask Register (14H)

iLBX™ Bus Interface Capabilities

Used in conjunction with the MULTIBUS interface, the iLBX bus is designed to provide off-board memory and I/O expansion for single board computers while maintaining on-board performance. The iLBX bus provides high-speed access to compatible expansion boards by granting privileged use of the bus to a single Primary Master. The bus also provides limited access to iLBX bus expansion boards for, at most, one Secondary Master that requires only occasional or non-concurrent access to iLBX resources. The iLBX bus, with 16 data lines, 24 address lines plus control, parity and interrupt signals, utilizes all the pins on the P2 connector except the four pins dedicated to the high-order address lines of the MULTIBUS interface. The non-multiplexed address and data lines provide access to up to 16 megabytes of iLBX bus resident memory, on up to 4 separate expansion boards, at speeds comparable to that of a single board computer's on-board resources.

The iSBC 580 board is configurable as either a Primary or a Secondary Master on the iLBX bus. Figure 1 shows a typical system configuration, with an iSBC 580 board acting as a Primary Master. The board can access up to 16 megabytes of iLBX memory. Supporting 16-bit transfers on the MULTICHANNEL bus, the board accesses memory as 16-bit words on even byte iLBX address boundaries. To increase the performance of iLBX memory read operations, the iSBC 580 board prefetches data from memory while the current data word is being transferred over the MULTICHANNEL I/O bus.

Register	Address
STO Status	00H
SRQ Status	01H
SRQ Mask	02H
RESERVED	03H-0FH
General Purpose Registers	10H*-1FH

* **NOTE:** 10H used as Command Register.

Table 2. iSBC® 580 MULTICHANNEL™ Device Register Set

SPECIFICATIONS

MULTICHANNEL™ Bus

Interface — Basic Talker/Listener

Transfer Mode — 16-bit

Device Address — Jumper selectable between 00H and 0EH

Registers — STO status, SRQ status, SRQ mask plus device specific registers

Signal Level — TTL compatible

iLBX™ Bus

Interface — Primary or Secondary (default) Master

Transfer Mode — 16-bit

Addressing — 16 megabytes on even byte boundaries only

Signal Level — TTL compatible

MULTIBUS® Interface

Data — None

Addressing — None

Interrupts — Jumper configurable to use any 1 of the 8 MULTIBUS interrupt lines. Interrupts are edge triggered.

Signal Level — TTL compatible

Throughput

5.3 megabytes/sec (2.65 megatransfers) max.

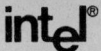

iSBC® 580

Connectors

iLBX™ BUS INTERFACE

Double-Sided Pins — 60

Centers — 0.100 in.

Mating Connectors* — Kelam RF30-2803-5
T&B Ansley A3020
(609-6025 modified)

MULTICHANNEL™ BUS INTERFACE

Pins — 60

Centers — 0.100 in.

Mating Connectors* — 3M 3334-6000
Berg 65949-960

* Connectors compatible with those listed may also be used.

Physical Characteristics

Width — 12.00 inches (30.5 cm)

Height — 6.75 inches (17.1 cm)

Depth — 0.60 inches (1.5 cm)

Weight — 12 ounces (340 gm)

Environmental Characteristics

Operating Temperature — 0° to 55°C

Relative Humidity — to 90% (without condensation)

DC Power Requirements

Voltage — +5 volt only ± 5%

Current — 2.5 amps (typical)

Reference Manuals

144457-001 — iSBC 580 MULTICHANNEL to iLBX Bus Interface Board Hardware Reference Manual (NOT SUPPLIED)

143269-001 — Intel MULTICHANNEL Bus Specification (NOT SUPPLIED)

144456-001 — Intel iLBX Bus Specification (NOT SUPPLIED)

142996-001 — iSBC 589 Intelligent DMA Controller Board Hardware Reference Manual (NOT SUPPLIED)

Manuals may be ordered from any Intel sales representative, distributor office or from Intel Literature Department, 3065 Bowers Avenue, Santa Clara, CA 95051

ORDERING INFORMATION

Part Number	Description
SBC 580	MULTICHANNEL to iLBX Bus Interface Board

iSBC® 589
INTELLIGENT DMA CONTROLLER

- Configurable as either an intelligent slave or MULTIBUS® master
- 5 MHz 8089 I/O Processor
- MULTICHANNEL™ DMA I/O bus interface with Supervisor, Controller or Basic Talker/Listener capabilities
- Two 8/16-bit iSBX™ bus connectors
- DMA transfer rates up to 1.25 megabytes per second
- User Command Interface Firmware Package provides high level I/O commands
- 8K bytes of high-speed dual-ported static read/write memory
- Sockets for up to 32K bytes of read only memory or additional byte-wide static RAMs
- Three programmable timers

The iSBC 589 Intelligent DMA Controller is a member of Intel's complete line of MULTIBUS microcompter systems which take full advantage of VLSI technology to provide economical computer based solutions for OEM applications. The iSBC 589 board is a general purpose, programmable, high-speed DMA controller on a single 6.75 × 12.00 inch printed circuit board. Using the board's dual-port RAM and standard EPROM resident firmware, the on-board Intel 8089 I/O Processor can perform memory to memory block transfers and complex I/O operations via two iSBX connectors and the MULTICHANNEL I/O bus at DMA transfer rates up to 1.25 megabytes per second. Acting as an intelligent slave to one or more iSBC 286, iSBC 186, iSBC 86, iSBC 88 or iSBC 80, single board computers, the iSBC 589 board enhances the sytem's overall performance by relieving the host CPU of time consuming I/O operations. The board's unique combination of performance, on-board intelligence and flexible hardware I/O interfaces make the iSBC 589 board the ideal solution for applications with specialized I/O requirements, such as high-speed data acquisition, graphics, instrument automation and specialized peripheral control, that previously would have necessitated an expensive custom designed I/O controller.

The following are trademarks of Intel Corporation and may be used only to describe Intel products: Intel, CREDIT, Index, Insite, Intellec, Library Manager, Megachassis, Micromap, MULTIBUS, PROMPT, UPI, µScope, Promware, MCS, ICE, iRMX, iSBC, iSBX, MULTIMODULE and iCS. Intel Corporation assumes no responsibility for the use of any circuitry other than circuitry embodied in an Intel product. No other circuit patent licenses are implied.

© INTEL CORPORATION, 1982

iSBC® 589

FUNCTIONAL DESCRIPTION

Two Modes of Operation

The iSBC 589 Intelligent DMA Controller is capable of operating either as a stand-alone, high-speed data acquisition controller or as an intelligent slave. In stand-alone mode, external requests cause the Intel 8089 I/O Processor to execute I/O programs contained in its on-board memory. As an intelligent slave to one or more Intel single board computers, the IOP can perform sophisticated DMA operations in response to high level commands issued by the host processor. While operating in either mode, the iSBC 589 board may act as a MULTIBUS master to access any system memory or I/O resources.

Input/Output Processor

The iSBC 589 board contains a 5 MHz Intel 8089 HMOS I/O Processor, whose architecture and instruction set have been optimized for performing DMA operations. The DMA function of the 8089 IOP uses a two cycle approach where the information actually flows through the 8089 IOP. This approach to DMA vastly simplifies the bus timings and enhances compatibility with memory and peripherals, in addition to allowing operations to be performed on the data as it is transferred. Operations can include such constructs as translate, where the 8089 automatically vectors through a lookup table and mask compare, both on the "fly". This DMA capability includes flexible termination conditions (such as external terminate, mask compare, single transfer and byte count expired).

The 8089 IOP supports two logically and physically separate I/O channels. The IOP maintains separate register sets for each I/O channel which allows the processor to alternate operation between the two channels without incurring context switching overhead delays.

DMA Capabilities

The iSBC 589 board supports both individual byte or word data transfers and DMA block transfer operations among its MULTICHANNEL interface, two iSBX connectors, on-board RAM and the MULTIBUS interface. Each of these devices may be combined

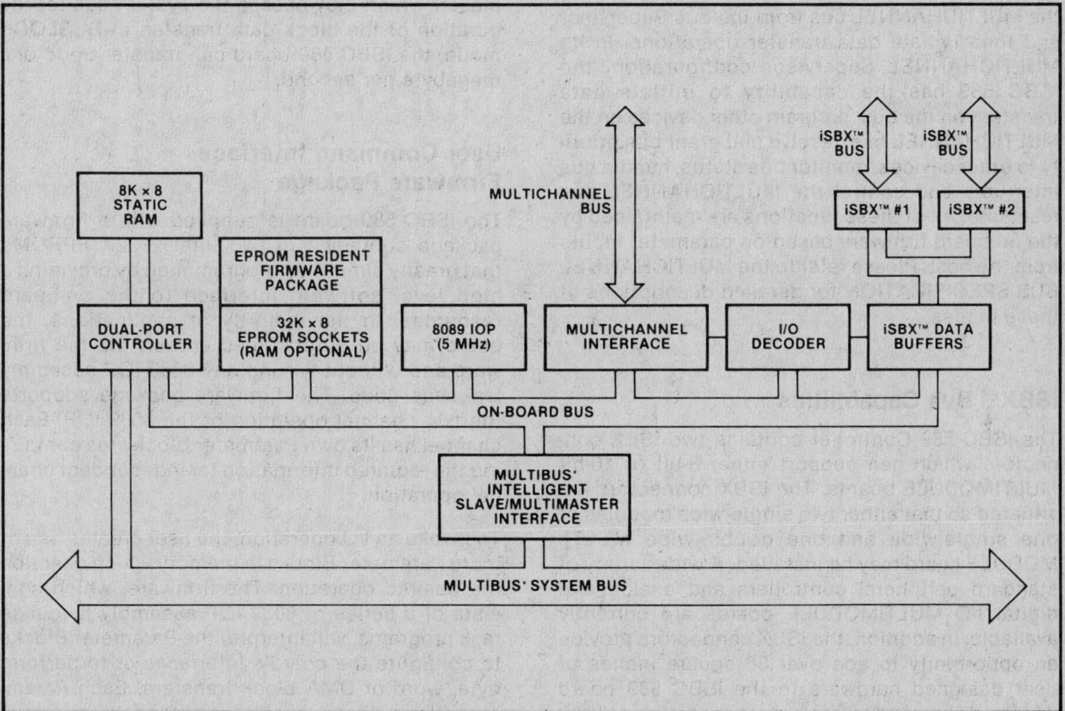

8-99

210354-001

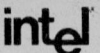

iSBC® 589

with any other as the source and destination for a DMA operation. The same firmware commands are used for all of the DMA source and destination combinations.

MULTICHANNEL Capabilities

The MULTICHANNEL bus provides a high-speed 8-bit or 16-bit wide data path for block data transfers between external devices, such as instruments, peripherals and other computers, and the iSBC 589 board. The iSBC 589 board can access up to 15 other devices on the MULTICHANNEL bus at distances of up to 15 meters and has the ability to address up to 16 megabytes of memory and 16 megabytes of I/O on each device.

The iSBC 589 Intelligent DMA Controller can interface to the MULTICHANNEL bus in one of three modes: as a Basic Talker/Listener, a Controller, and a Supervisor. In Basic Talker/Listener Mode, the iSBC 589 board monitors the MULTICHANNEL for requests from a Controller or the bus Supervisor to perform a read or a write operation, but it has no bus control capabilities. In Controller Mode, the board can request temporary control of the MULTICHANNEL bus from the bus Supervisor and thus initiate data transfer operations. In its MULTICHANNEL Supervisor configuration, the iSBC 589 has the capability to initiate data transfers on the bus, program other devices on the MULTICHANNEL bus, resolve and grant bus priority to other devices, monitor bus status, handle bus interrupts and control the MULTICHANNEL bus reset line. All of these functions are maintained by the on-board firmware based on parameter inputs from the host. Please refer to the MULTICHANNEL BUS SPECIFICATION for detailed descriptions of these modes.

iSBX™ Bus Capabilities

The iSBC 589 Controller contains two iSBX connectors which can support either 8-bit or 16-bit MULTIMODULE boards. The iSBX connectors are situated so that either two single-wide modules or one single-wide and one double-wide MULTIMODULE board may be installed. A wide variety of standard peripheral controllers and analog and digital I/O MULTIMODULE boards are currently available. In addition, the iSBX connectors provide an opportunity to add over 30 square inches of user designed hardware to the iSBC 589 board which can be used to implement specialized I/O interfaces. For more information on specific iSBX MULTIMODULE boards, consult the Intel OEM Microcomputer System Configuration Guide.

MULTIBUS® Capabilities

MULTIBUS system memory and I/O resources may be used as the source or the destination for an iSBC 589 board transfer operation. The iSBC 589 DMA Controller may also be used as a high-speed data mover to transfer blocks of data from one MULTIBUS system RAM area to another. MULTIBUS system memory may also be used to store Parameter Blocks to be executed by the on-board firmware package. The iSBC 589 board, acting as a MULTIBUS Master, can access up to 16 megabytes of MULTIBUS memory and up to 64K MULTIBUS I/O locations.

Two MULTIBUS transfer modes are available. Selection of the desired mode is done via the Parameter Block. Transfer rates of up to 900K bytes per second may be achieved in shared bus mode, where the iSBC 589 board requests access to the system bus for 1.4 microseconds to transfer one byte or word to or from memory. In BUSLOCK mode, the iSBC 589 is established as the sole master which may access the system bus for the duration of the block data transfer. In BUSLOCK mode, the iSBC 589 board can transfer up to one megabyte per second.

User Command Interface Firmware Package

The iSBC 589 board is supplied with a firmware package contained in two Intel 2732A EPROMs that greatly simplifies programming by providing a high level software interface to the on-board resources. In the majority of applications, the board may be programmed entirely via the firmware and without writing any 8089 IOP assembly language code. The firmware package supports the two channel operation of the 8089 IOP. Each channel has its own Parameter Block area containing the required information for independent channel operation.

To invoke an I/O operation, the user creates one or more Parameter Blocks in memory which describe the desired operation. The firmware, which consists of a series of 8089 IOP assembly language task programs, will interpret the Parameter Blocks to configure the board's interfaces or to perform byte, word or DMA block transfers. Each Parameter Block consists of a command byte, status byte, data source and destination pointers and other information as shown in Table 1. Commands recognized by the firmware package are listed in Table 2. The Execute User Task command is of special interest because it allows the user to extend the capabilities of the iSBC 589 board by adding his own 8089 IOP assembly language routines to the firmware package, while retaining the structure and standard functions supplied by the firmware.

Table 1. User Command Interface Firmware Parameter Block Byte Format

Command Byte
Status Byte
Command Chaining Pointer
Command Chaining Pointer
Command Chaining Pointer
Command Chaining Pointer
Device Number
MULTICHANNEL Data Type
Memory Pointer or Register Number
Memory Pointer or Register Number
Memory Pointer or Data Storage Location
Memory Pointer or Data Storage Location
Device Number
MULTICHANNEL Data Type
Memory Pointer or Register Number
Memory Pointer or Register Number
Memory Pointer
Memory Pointer
Byte Counter
Byte Counter
Byte Counter

In addition to executing transfer operations, the firmware package executes an initialization sequence which prepares the 8089 IOP and the on-board RAM, EPROM and I/O resources for further firmware execution.

RAM Capabilities

In its standard configuration, the iSBC 589 board contains 8K bytes of high-speed, dual-ported static RAM. The first 256 bytes are dedicated for use by the on-board firmware. The remaining on-board RAM may be used for storing additional Parameter Blocks for the firmware or as a data buffer for I/O operations. This memory is always addressed by the 8089 IOP as locations 0000H to 1FFFH. However, for MULTIBUS accesses through the dual-port, the RAM base address may be configured on any 8K-byte boundary in the first megabyte page of the MULTIBUS memory space. Users may install additional on-board RAM by placing two byte-wide RAMs in the 28-pin JEDEC standard sockets. The additional RAM is accessible only by the on-board 8089 IOP.

EPROM Capabilities

The iSBC 589 board can be configured with up to 32K bytes of non-volatile read only memory. Four 28-pin sockets are provided for the use of Intel 2716, 2732 and 2764 EPROMs or byte-wide RAMs.

Table 2. User Command Interface Firmware Package Commands

Command	Description
NO-OP	Test the intelligent slave interface on the iSBC 589 board. The board reads the Parameter Block, generates status and interrupts the host on completion.
REGISTER WRITE	Write either a word or byte of data from the Data Storage Location within the Parameter Block to the location specified by the Parameter Block Device Number and Register Number.
REGISTER READ	Read either a word or byte of data from the location specified by the Parameter Block Device Number and Register Number to the Data Storage Location within the Parameter Block.
PERFORM DMA	Transfer data beginning at the location specified by the source Memory Pointer, Device Number and Register Number parameters to the location specified by the destination Memory Pointer, Device Number and Register Number parameters. The number of transfers is specified by the Byte Count parameter. A Byte Count of 0 enables DMA until an external terminate condition is sensed.
EXECUTE USER TASK	Transfer 8089 IOP program execution from the Firmware Package to a user defined 8089 assembly language routine beginning at the location specified by the Memory Pointer parameter. Upon completion, the user task returns control to the firmware.

iSBC® 589

In the default configuration, the board is jumpered for 32K devices, and, two 2732A EPROMs containing the firmware package are installed. Users who wish to extend the capabilities of the firmware may do so by programming unused locations in the firmware PROMs, installing two additional 2732A PROMs or copying the firmware into 2764s along with their own code. As an alternative, two byte-wide RAMs of equal or smaller capacity may be installed in the open sockets and used in conjunction with the firmware PROMs.

Programmable Interval Timers

Three independent, fully programmable 16-bit interval/event counters are provided by an 8254-12 Programmable Interrupt Timer. Each counter may operate in either BCD or binary mode. One counter is used by the firmware package, leaving two counters available to the firmware user. These timers may be used for a variety of on-board and off-board functions including timed-interval DMA requests and terminations or fail safe time out control for I/O operations.

System Development Capabilities

For applications where it is necessary to extend the User Command Firmware Package by writing additional 8089 IOP assembly language code, the development cycle can be significantly reduced and simplified by using the Intellec Series Microcomputer Development Systems. The 8089 IOP Software Support Package which includes a Macro assembler, linker, locater and PROM mapper is supported by the ISIS-II disk-based operating system.

In-Circuit Emulator

The ICE-86A or ICE-86 and ICE-86U upgrade kit provide the necessary link between the software development environment provided by the Intellec system and the "target" iSBC 589 execution system. In addition to providing a mechanism for loading executable code and data into the iSBC 589 board, the In-Circuit Emulator provides a sophisticated command set to assist in debugging software and in final integration of the user hardware and software.

SPECIFICATIONS

8089 IOP

WORD SIZE

Instruction — 16 to 40-bits

Data — 8, 16-bits

SYSTEM CLOCK

5.0 MHz ± 0.1%

CYCLE TIME

2.2 microseconds for the fastest instructions

System Access Time

Dual-port Memory — 550 nanoseconds (worst case, without contention from on-board access)

I/O Capacity

MULTICHANNEL I/O Bus — 1 MULTICHANNEL port which supports 8 and 16-bit transfers and can be configured as a Basic Talker/Listener, Controller or Supervisor

iSBX™ MULTIMODULE™ — Two (2) iSBX MULTIMODULE boards

I/O Addressing

Interface	I/O Addresses
iSBX Connector #1	FF80 thru FF9F
iSBX Connector #2	FFA0 thru FFBF
MULTICHANNEL	FFD0 thru FFEE
Interval Timer	FFC8 thru FFCE
Other On-board Devices	FFC0 thru FFC6 FFF0 thru FFFE

Memory Capacity

ON-BOARD EPROM

Device	Total Capacity	Address Range
2716	8K bytes	FE000-FFFFF$_H$
2732A	16K bytes	FC000-FFFFF$_H$
2764	32K bytes	F8000-FFFFF$_H$

ON-BOARD RAM

Total Capacity — 8K bytes

On-Board Address — 00000-01FFF$_H$

MULTIBUS® Address — Jumper selectable on 8K byte boundaries. Default is 0$_H$.

iSBC® 589

I/O Transfer Rates (microseconds/tranfer)

	MULTICHANNEL	iSBX™	MULTIBUS® Shared	MULTIBUS® Buslock	On-Board RAM
MULTICHANNEL	—	2.0	2.4	2.2	1.8
iSBX	2.0	2.0	2.4	2.2	2.0
MULTIBUS (Shared)	2.4	2.4	2.8	—	2.2
MULTIBUS (Buslock)	2.2	2.2	—	2.4	2.0
On-Board RAM	1.8	1.8	2.2	2.0	1.6

Timers

Input Frequencies — Jumper selectable at 1.25 MHz, 625 KHz or 312.5 KHz

Output Frequencies/Timing Intervals —

Function	Single Timer/Counter Minimum	Single Timer/Counter Maximum	Dual Timer/Counter (Two Timers Cascaded) Minimum	Dual Timer/Counter (Two Timers Cascaded) Maximum
Real-time delay	1.6 usec	210 msec	3.2 usec	1.37×10^4 sec
Programmable one-shot	1.6 usec	210 msec	3.2 usec	1.37×10^4 sec
Rate generator	4.76 Hz	625 KHz	7.3×10^{-5} Hz	312.5 KHz
Square-wave rate generator	4.76 Hz	625 KHz	7.3×10^{-5} Hz	312.5 KHz
Software triggered strobe	1.6 usec	210 msec	3.2 usec	1.37×10^4 sec
Hardware triggered strobe	1.6 usec	210 msec	3.2 usec	1.37×10^4 sec

Connectors

Interface	Double-Sided Pins (qty.)	Centers (in.)	Mating Connectors*
MULTIBUS System Bus	86	0.156	ELFAB BS1562043PBB Viking 2KH43/9AMK12 Soldered PCB Mount EDAC 337086540201 ELFAB BW1562D43PBB EDAC 337086540202 ELFAB BW1562A43PBB Wire Wrap
Auxiliary Bus	60	0.100	EDAC 345060524802 ELFAB BS1020A30PBB EDAC 345060540201 ELFAB BW1020D30PBB Wire Wrap
iSBX Bus (2)	36	0.100	iSBX 960-5
MULTICHANNEL Bus	60	0.100	3M 3334-6000 BERG 65949-960

*NOTE: Connectors compatible with those listed may also be used.

iSBC® 589

Interfaces

MULTIBUS® — All signals TTL compatible
MULTICHANNEL — All signals TTL compatible
iSBX™ Bus — All signals TTL compatible
Timers — All signals TTL compatible

Auxiliary Power/Memory Protect

There is no provision made on the iSBC 589 board for battery backup of RAM or for power fail detection.

MULTIBUS® Bus Drivers

Function	Characteristic	Sink Current (mA)
Data	Tri-state	32
Address	Tri-state	32
Commands	Tri-state	32

Physical Characteristics

Width — 12.00 in (30.48 cm)
Height — 7.05 in (17.9 cm)
Depth — .50 in (1.27 cm)
Weight — 16 oz (453.6 gm)

Environmental Characteristics

Operating Temperature — 0°C to 55°C

Relative Humidity — to 90% (without condensation)

Electrical Characteristics

DC POWER REQUIREMENTS

Configuration	Current Requirements (+5V +5% maximum)
Without EPROM	4.7 amps
With 8K EPROM (using four 2716s)	5.4 amps
With 8K EPROM* (using two 2732As)	5.0 amps
With 16K EPROM (using four 2732As)	5.3 amps
With 32K EPROM (using four 2164s)	5.3 amps

*Factory default configuration

Reference Manuals

142996-001 — iSBC 589 Intelligent DMA Controller Board Hardware Reference Manual (Not Supplied)

142686-001 — Intel iSBX Bus Specification (Not Supplied)

143269-001 — Intel MULTICHANNEL Bus Specification (Not Supplied)

Manuals may be ordered from any Intel sales representative, distributor office or from Intel Literature Department, 3065 Bowers Avenue, Santa Clara, California 95051

ORDERING INFORMATION

Part Number	Description
SBC 589	Intelligent DMA Controller Board

Communication Software 9

iNA 960 TRANSPORT SOFTWARE
MEMBER OF THE OpenNET™ PRODUCT FAMILY

- ISO Transport (8073) Class 4 services
  — Guaranteed message integrity
  — Data rate matching (flow control)
  — Multiple connection capability
  — Variable length messages
  — Expedited delivery
  — Negotiation of virtual circuit characteristics during opens
- Additional functionality
  — Connectionless transport (Datagram)
  — External Data Link
- IEEE 802.3 Data Link protocol (CSMA/CD) supported
- Comprehensive Network Management services
- — Collection of network usage statistics
  — Setting and inspecting of transport and data link parameters
  — Fault isolation and detection
  — Boot Server
- Compatible with multiple system environments
  — Runs as an iRMX™ 86 job
  — Supports host operating system independent designs based on 8086, 8088 or 80168 and 82586 components
- Runs on iSBC® 186/51 COMMputer™ Board
- Preconfigured version runs on SXM 552 Transport Engine

iNA 960 is a general purpose local area network software package implementing the class 4 services of the ISO transport specification and network management functions in system designs based on the 8086, 8088 and 80186 microprocessors and the 82586 communications co-processor. iNA 960 also supports Intel's board level LAN products, the iSBC® 552, iSXM™ 552, and the iSBC® 186/51. Combined with these board products iNA 960 provides a cost effective, high performance industry standard transport capability supporting the OpenNET higher layer software or other user application.

iNA 960 is a ready-to-use software building block for OEM suppliers of networked systems for both technical and commercial applications. Examples for such applications include networked design stations, manufacturing process control, communicating word processors, and financial services workstations. Using the iNA 960 software the OEM can minimize development cost and time while achieving compatibility with a growing number of equipment suppliers adapting the IEEE and ISO standards.

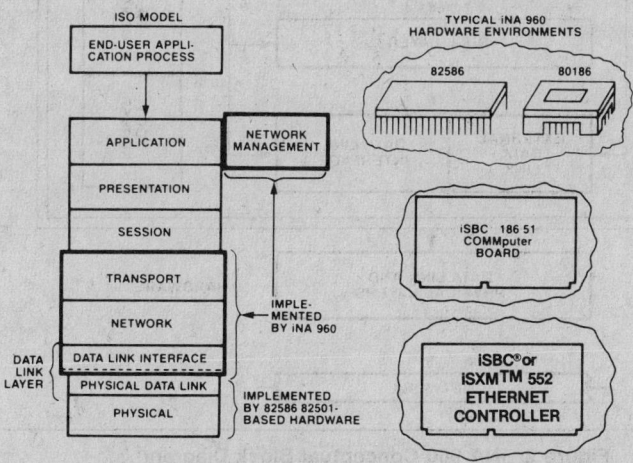

Figure 1.

iNA 960

FUNCTIONAL OVERVIEW

The iNA 960 design is a standard implementation of the Class 4 transport protocol defined by the ISO OSI model. The Transport Layer provides a reliable full-duplex message delivery service on top of the "best effort" IEEE 802.3 standard packet delivery service implemented by the 82586 (or equivalent) physical and data link functions.

Consisting of linkable modules, the software can be configured to implement a range of capabilities and interface protocols. In addition to reliable process-to-process message delivery, the capabilities include a datagram service, a boot server, a direct user access to the Data Link Layer, and a comprehensive network management facility.

iNA 960 can be configured to run under iRMX 86 along with the user software, or to run on top of a dedicated 8086, 8088 or 80186 processor coupled with an 82586 to provide a communications front end processor.

The software also includes a Network Management service. This facility enables the user to monitor and adjust the network's operation in order to optimize its performance.

The current release of iNA 960 includes a "null" Network Layer supporting the Data Link and Transport Layers without providing internetwork routing service. This capability will be implemented in later releases of iNA 960.

For a conceptual block diagram of iNA 960, refer to Figure 2.

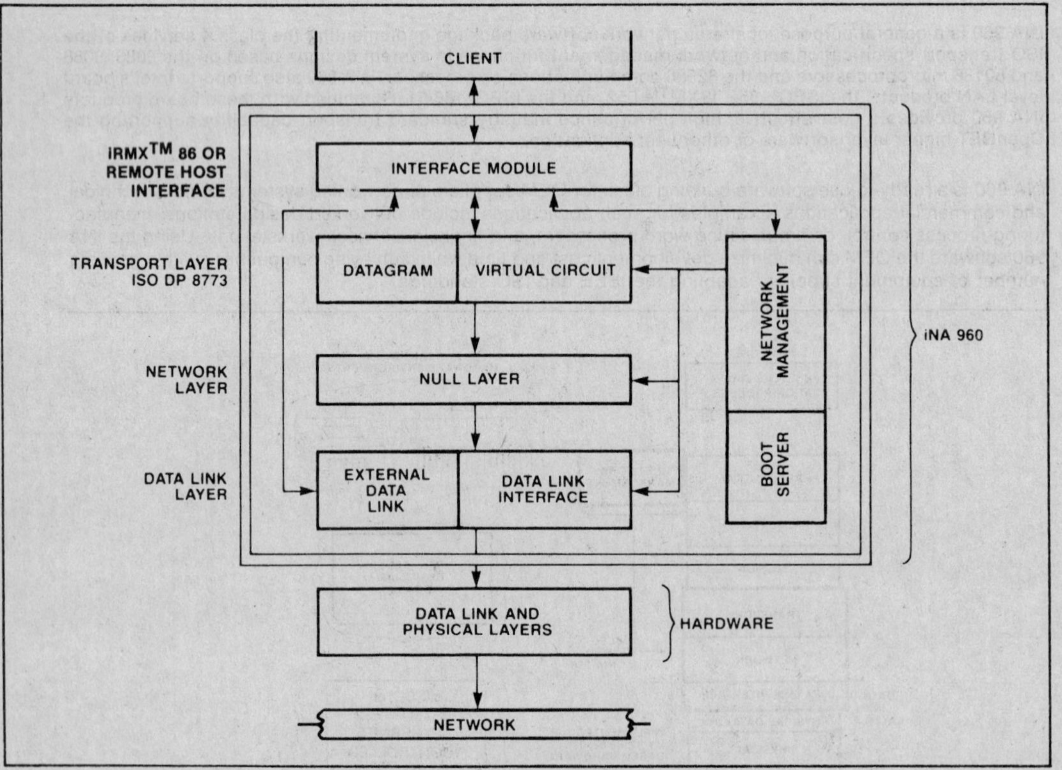

Figure 2. iNA 960 Conceptual Block Diagram

TRANSPORT LAYER

The Transport Layer provides message delivery services between client processes running on computers (network "hosts" or "nodes") anywhere in the network.

Client processes are identified by a combination of a network address defining the node and a transport service access point defining the interface point through which the client accesses the transport services. The combined parameters, called the transport address, are supplied by the user for both the local and the remote client processes to be connected.

The iNA 960 transport layer implements two kinds of message delivery services: virtual circuit and datagram. The virtual circuit provides a reliable point-to-point message delivery service ensuring maximum data integrity, and it is fully compatible with the ISO 8073 Class 4 protocol. The datagram service provides a best effort message delivery between client processes requiring less overhead and therefore allowing higher throughput than virtual circuits.

Both the datagram and the virtual circuit services are optional and can be included when configuring iNA 960.

Virtual Circuit Services

—Reliable Delivery: Data is delivered to the destination in the exact order it was sent by the source, with no errors, duplications or losses, regardless of the quality of service available from the underlying network service.

—Data Rate Matching (flow control): The Transport Layer attempts to maximize throughput while conserving communication subsystem resources by controlling the rate at which messages are sent. That rate is based on the availablity of receive buffers at the destination and its own resources.

—Multiple Connection Capability (Process Multiplexing): Several processes can be simultaneously using the Transport Layer with no risk that progress or lack of progress by one process will interfere with others.

—Variable Length Messages: The client software can submit arbitrarily short or long messages for transmittal without regard for the minimum or maximum network service data unit (NSDU) lengths supported by the underlying network services.

—Expedited Delivery (optional). With this service the client can transmit up to 16 bytes of urgent data bypassing the normal flow control. The expedited data is guaranteed to arrive before any normal data submitted afterward.

Connectionless Transport (Datagram) Service

The datagram service transfers data between client processes without establishing a virtual circuit. The service is a "best effort" capability and data may be lost or misordered. Data can be transferred at one time to a single destination or to several destinations (multicast).

NETWORK MANAGEMENT FACILITY (NMF)

The network management facility provides the users of the network with planning, operation, maintenance and initialization services described below.

—Planning: This service captures network usage statistics on the various layers to help plan network expansion. Statistics are maintained by the layers themselves and are made available to users via an interface with the NMF.

—Operation: This service allows the user to monitor network functions and to inspect and adjust network parameters. The goal is to provide the tools for performance optimization on the network.

—Maintenance: This service deals with detecting isolating and correcting network faults. It also provides the capability to determine the presence of hosts and the viability of their connection to the network.

—Initialization: NMF provides initialization and remote loading facilities.

Network management provides distributed management of the network; the user can request any of the services to be performed on a remote as well as a local node. The NMF interfaces to every other network layer both to utilize their services and to access their internal data bases.

In support of the above services, the NMF capabilities include layer management, echo testing, limited debugging facilities, and the ability to down line load and dump a remote system.

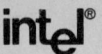

iNA 960

Layer management deals with manipulating the internal database of a layer. The elements of these data bases are termed objects. Some examples for objects are the number of collisions, retransmission time-out limit, the number of packets sent, and the list of nodes to boot. NMF can examine and modify objects in a layer's data base.

An echo facility is provided. Using this facility the host can determine if a node is present on the network or not, test the communication path to that node and determine whether the remote node is functional.

NMF enables the user to read or write memory in any host present on the network. This feature is provided as an aid to debugging.

NMF can down line load any system present on the network. A simple Data Link protocol is used to ensure reliability. This facility can be used to load databases, to boot systems without local mass storage or to boot a set of nodes remotely, thus ensuring that they have the same version of software, etc.

Dumping is an operation equivalent to memory read from the user's standpoint; however, dumping uses the Data Link facilities while memory read uses the transport facilities.

EXTERNAL DATA LINK (EDL)

The External Data Link option allows the user to access the functionalities of the Data Link Layer directly instead of having to go through the network and transport layers. This flexibility is useful when the user needs custom higher layer software, or does not need the Network Layer and Transport Layer services (e.g., when sending "best effort" messages, or running customer diagnostics).

Through the EDL the capabilities supporting the lower layers in iNA 960 are made directly available to the user. EDL enables the user to establish and delete data link connections, transmit packets to individual and multiple receivers, and configure the data link software to meet the requirements of the given network environment.

USER ENVIRONMENT

iNA 960 is designed to run on hardware based on the 8086, 8088 or 80186 microprocessors and the 82586 LAN Coprocessor. The software can be configured to run under iRMX 86 or on a dedicated 8086, 8088 or 80186 processor separately from the host. The following section describes these two operating environments.

iRMX™ Environment

In this configuration, both the user program and iNA 960 are running under iRMX 86. The communications software is implemented as an iRMX 86 job requiring the nucleus only for most operations. The only exception is the boot server option which also needs the Basic I/O System. iNA 960 will run in any iRMX environment including configurations based on the 80130. See Figure 3 and 4 for an illustration of iNA 960 running under iRMX 86.

Operating System/Processor Independent Implementation

In those systems where iRMX 86 is not the primary operating system, where off-loading the host of the communications tasks is necessary for performance reasons, or where an existing communications front-end processor configuration is being upgraded, the user may wish to dedicate a processor for communications purposes. iNA 960 can be configured to support such implementations by providing network services on an 8086, 8088 or 80186 processor. Figure 5 depicts the conceptual block diagram of this configuration. The SBC & SXM 552 are MULTIBUS® implementations of this architecture.

This approach provides the component and system designer with an ISO standard communications software building block that can be adapted to his system's needs with a minimum interfacing effort. For added flexibility, iNA 960 provides the user with the alternative of using the included interface module or writing his own module, if necessary.

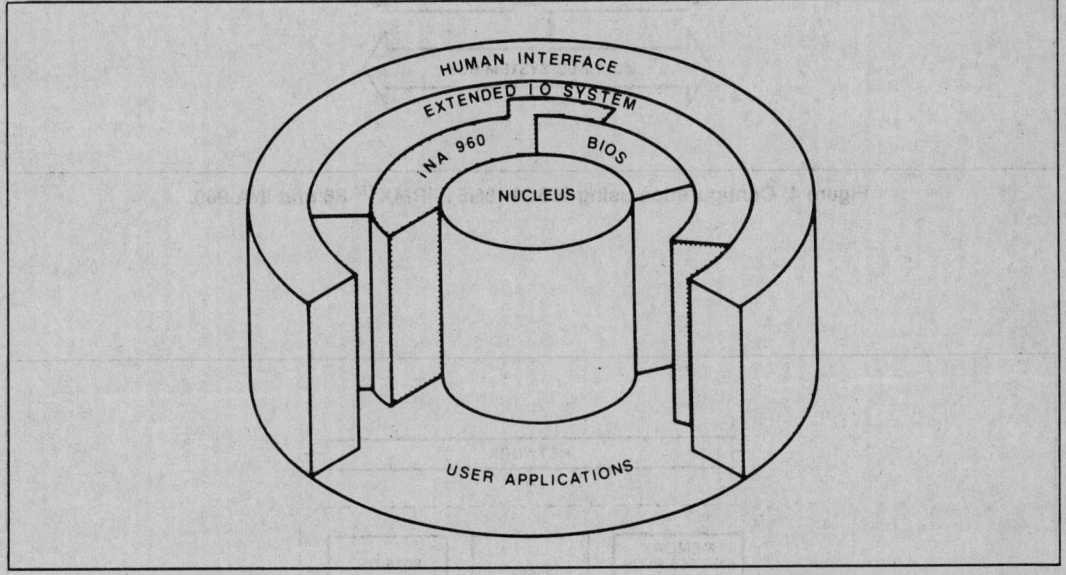

Figure 3. As an iRMX™ job, iNA 960 uses nucleus calls and, when the Boot Server is present, BIOS calls.

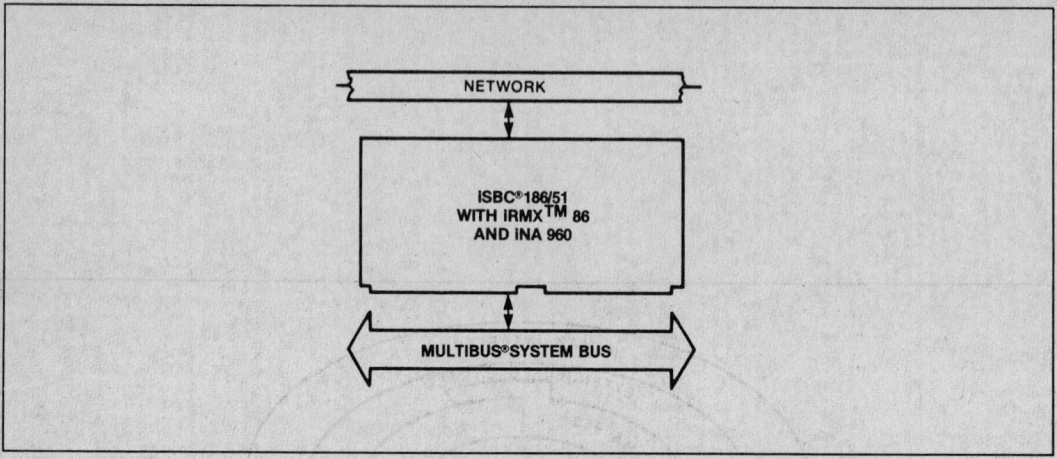

Figure 4. Configuration using iSBC® 186/51, iRMX™ 86 and iNA 960.

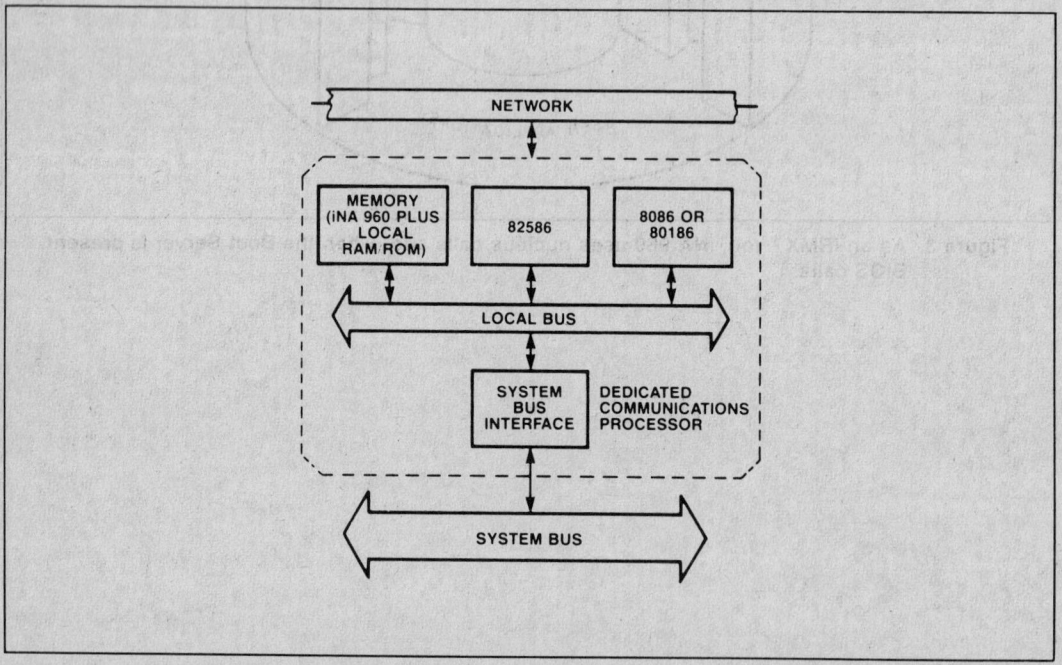

Figure 5. In the operating system/processor independent implementation iNA 960 is running on a dedicated 8086, 8088 or 80186 processor.

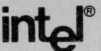

iNA 960

USER INTERFACE

iNA 960 is designed to run both under iRMX 86 and on a dedicated communications front end processor separately from the host. In both environments, the interface is based on exchanging memory segments called request blocks between iNA 960 and the client. The format and contents of the request blocks remain the same in both configurations; only the request block delivery mechanism changes. See Figure 6 for a simplified interface diagram.

Request blocks are memory segments containing the data to be passed from the user to iNA 960 (commands), or from iNA 960 to the user (responses). The iNA 960 request blocks consist of fixed format fields identical across all user commands and argument fields unique to the individual commands. Refer to Figure 7 for the standard request block format.

Issuing an iNA 960 command consists of filling in the request block fields and transferring the block to iNA 960 for execution. After processing the command, iNA 960 returns the request block with one of the pre-defined response codes placed in the response code field of the request block. The response code indicates whether the command was executed successfully or whether an error occurred. By examining the response code, the user can take appropriate action for that command.

For iRMX users, iNA 960 also provides a procedural interface option to simplify writing the application software interface. In this case, the allocation and formatting of request blocks are replaced by a procedure call with parameters that specify the user's command options. The procedure execution will create a request block and fill in the appropriate fields from the user's parameter list.

For component users the request block delivery mechanism is the means by which the host processor and the communications processor running iNA 960 software exchange the request blocks. iNA 960 provides three such mechanisms: the MIP (Multibus Inter-process Protocol), the BCB (Base Control Block) and a user-defined mechanism. The MIP interface is included for use in systems already supporting this protocol; the BCB is a simple interface for single host environments, and the user-defined interface accommodates unique application requirements.

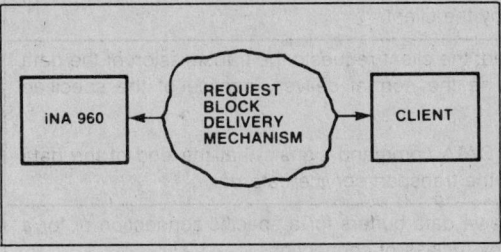

Figure 6.

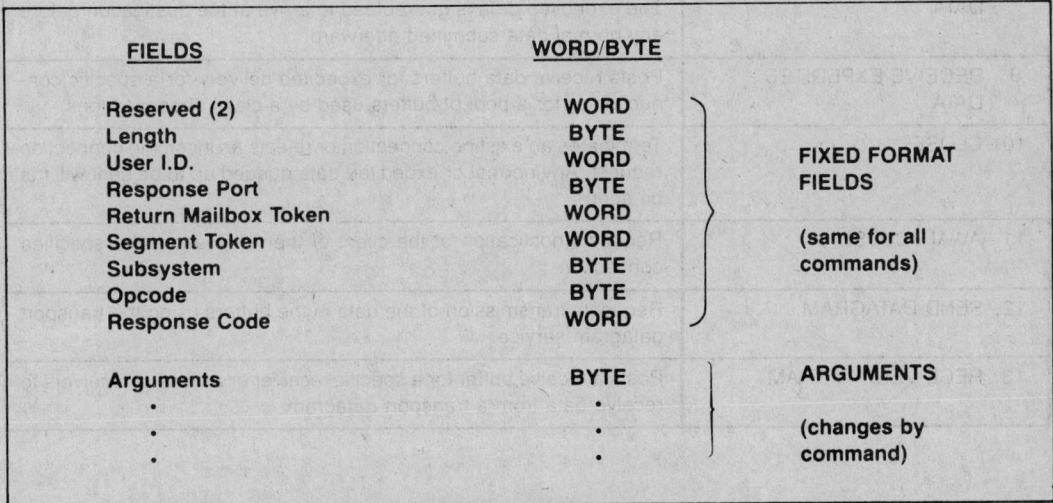

FIELDS	WORD/BYTE	
Reserved (2)	WORD	
Length	BYTE	
User I.D.	WORD	FIXED FORMAT
Response Port	BYTE	FIELDS
Return Mailbox Token	WORD	
Segment Token	WORD	(same for all
Subsystem	BYTE	commands)
Opcode	BYTE	
Response Code	WORD	
Arguments • • •	BYTE • • •	ARGUMENTS (changes by command)

Figure 7. iNA 960 Request Block Format

iNA 960

Transport Layer User Interface

The following table summarizes the user commands and the corresponding transport layer responses.

Command	Function
1. OPEN	Allocates memory for the connection data base of a virtual circuit (or connection) to be established. The connection database contains data concerning the connection.
2. SEND CONNECT REQUEST	Requests connection to a fully specified remote transport address using specified ISO connection negotiation options.
3. AWAIT CONNECT REQUEST TRAN	Indicates that the transport client is willing to consider incoming connection requests based on pre-established acceptance criteria.
4. AWAIT CONNECT REQUEST USER	Indicates that the transport client is willing to consider incoming connection requests. If the request meets the address and negotiation option criteria, it is passed to the client for further consideration.
5. ACCEPT CONNECT REQUEST	Indicates that the connection requested by a remote transport service is accepted by the client.
6. SEND DATA or SEND EOM DATA	With this command, the client requests the transmission of the data in the buffers using the normal delivery service of the specified connection. The SEND EOM DATA command signals that the end of the data marks the end of the transport service data unit.
7. RECEIVE DATA	Posts normal receive data buffers for a specific connection or for a buffer pool used by a class of connections.
8. SEND EXPEDITED DATA	Transmits up to 16 bytes of data using the expedited delivery service. The expedited data is guaranteed to arrive at the destination before any normal data submitted afterward.
9. RECEIVE EXPEDITED DATA	Posts receive data buffers for expedited delivery for a specific connection or for a pool of buffers used by a class of connections.
10. CLOSE	Terminates an existing connection or rejects an incoming connection request. Any normal or expedited data queued up to be sent will not be sent.
11. AWAIT CLOSE	Requests notification of the client of the termination of a specified connection.
12. SEND DATAGRAM	Requests transmission of the data in the buffers using the transport datagram service.
13. RECEIVE DATAGRAM	Posts a receive buffer for a specific receiver or a class of receivers to receive data from a transport datagram.

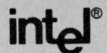

iNA 960

Network Management Layer User Interface

Command	Function
1. READ OBJECT	Returns the value of the specified object to the client.
2. SET OBJECT	Sets the value of an object as specified by the client.
3. READ AND CLEAR OBJECT	Returns the value of the specified object to the client then clears the object.
4. ECHO	This function is used to determine the presence of a node, to test the communication path to the node and to ascertain the viability and functionality of the remote host addressed.
5. UP LINE DUMP	Requests a remote node to dump a specified memory area.
6. READ MEMORY	Reads memory of the specified network node.
7. SET MEMORY	Sets memory of the specified network node.
8. FORCE LOAD	Causes a node to attempt a remote load from another node.

External Data Link Interface

Command	Function
1. CONNECT	With this command the client establishes a data link connection.
2. DISCONNECT	Eliminates a previously established connection.
3. TRANSMIT	Transmits data contained in buffers specified by the client.
4. POST RECEIVE PACKET DESCRIPTOR	Allocates memory for maintaining records on receive data buffers. Also may be used to allocate memory for buffering receive data.
5. POST RECEIVE BUFFER	Allocates memory for buffering receive data.
6. ADD MULTICAST ADDRESS	Adds an address to the list of data link multicast addresses.
7. REMOVE MULTICAST ADDRESS	Removes an address from the list of data link multicast addresses.
8. SET DATA LINK I.D.	Sets up a unique data link I.D. for the station.

iNA 960

CONFIGURING iNA 960

In order to adapt iNA 960 to his specific application, the user must configure the software to define the desired functions, to select the appropriate interface, to set the layer parameters and to set up for the required hardware configuration.

There are a number of capability combinations the user may elect to implement in his application. At the transport layer level the options are: virtual circuit service with or without expedited delivery, or datagram service, or both. At the data link level, the user may include or exclude the External Data Link interface.

The Network Management Facility is also optional. When it is configured in, the user may also include the boot server module. These capabilities can be made available simply by linking in the corresponding software modules. The interface options are also implemented in a modular fashion; the user links in the desired module to set up for the iRMX 86 or the operating system independent configurations.

Layer parameters and confiuration options are first edited into layer configuration files, then assembled and linked into iNA 960. Layer parameters adjust the network's operation to match the usage pattern and the available resources. For example, within the Transport Layer, the flow control parameters, the retransmission timer parameters, the transport data base parameters, etc. can be set via this process.

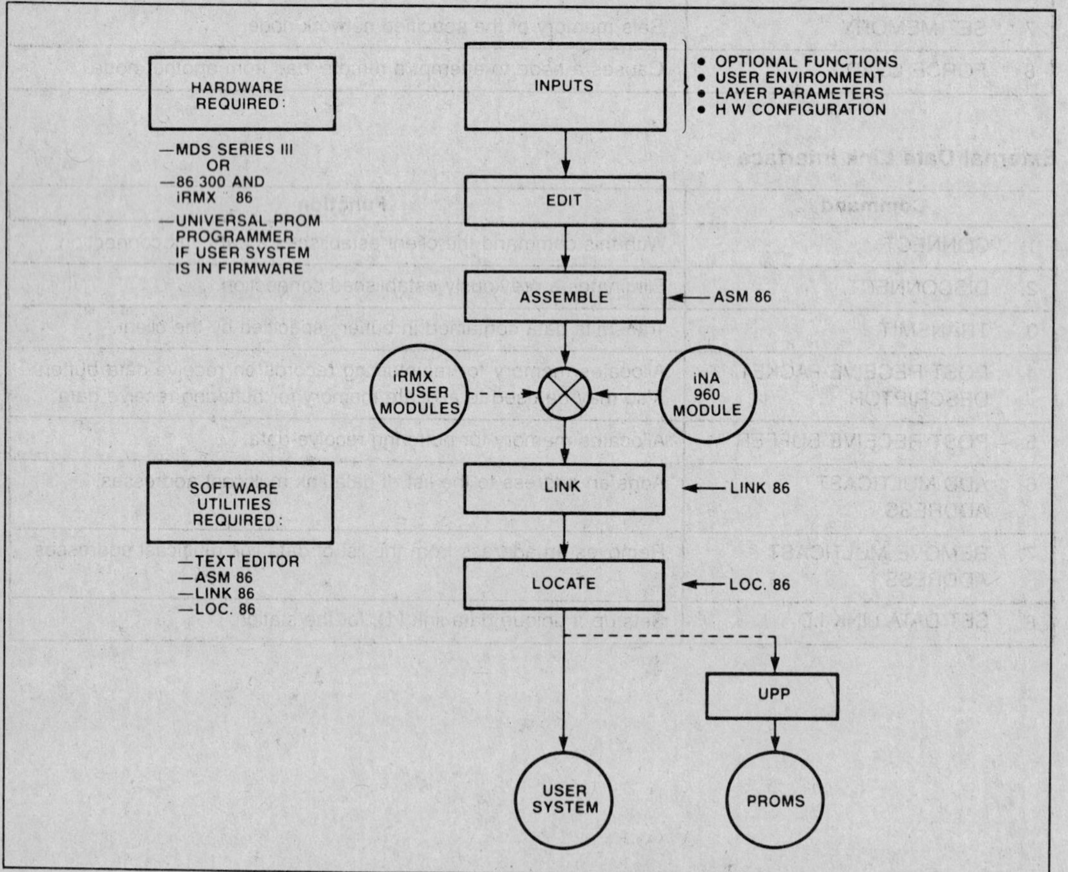

```
HARDWARE REQUIRED:
—MDS SERIES III
   OR
—86 300 AND
   iRMX 86
—UNIVERSAL PROM
   PROGRAMMER
   IF USER SYSTEM
   IS IN FIRMWARE

SOFTWARE
UTILITIES
REQUIRED:
—TEXT EDITOR
—ASM 86
—LINK 86
—LOC. 86
```

INPUTS:
- OPTIONAL FUNCTIONS
- USER ENVIRONMENT
- LAYER PARAMETERS
- H W CONFIGURATION

EDIT → ASSEMBLE ← ASM 86

iRMX USER MODULES + iNA 960 MODULE → LINK ← LINK 86 → LOCATE ← LOC. 86 → USER SYSTEM

UPP → PROMS

Figure 8. The Configuration Process for iNA 960

9-10

iNA 960

The user also sets up for the required hardware configuration, such as port addresses and interrupt levels, during this process. For the flow diagram of configuring iNA 960, refer to Figure 8.

SPECIFICATIONS

Hardware Supported:
— iSBC 186/51 Communicating Computer
— SBC 552 COMMengine
— SXM 552 Transport Engine (runs with preconfigured transport software)
— Custom designs based on 8086, 8088 and 80186 microprocessors and the 82586 Local Communications Controller.

Typical Throughput at transport:

Environments:
186 51 and iRMX 86	50K to 200K bytes sec
Dedicated 80186 82586 COMMengine	100K to 300K bytes sec

Memory Requirements: (in bytes)

Base System	12K plus configurable Buffer Memory
Normal Virtual Circuit Option	18K plus configurable Buffer Memory
Expedited Delivery Option	2K
Datagram Option	3K plus Data Base Memory
Net Management Option	1K to 5K
External Data Link Option	5K
Boot Server Option	5K

Available Literature/Reference Materials:
— iNA 960 Programmer's Reference Manual (11/83)
— iSBC 186/51 Data Sheet (Now)
— iSBC 186/51 Hardware Reference Manual (11/83)

ORDERING INFORMATION

The following is a list of ordering options for the iNA 960 Transport Software. All options include a full year of update service that provides a periodic NEWSLETTER, Software Problem Report Service, and copies of system updates that occur during this period. All of the object code options listed are available on either ISIS or RMX compatible double density diskettes.

As with all Intel software, purchase of any of these options requires the execution of a standard Intel Master Software License. The specific rights granted to users depend on the specific option and the License signed.

iNA 960

Order Code	Description
iNA 960 YRO	OEM object code license requiring the payment of incorporation fees for each derivative work based on iNA 960; ISIS and RMX formatted diskettes
iNA 960 YST	Object code license to use the product at a second site or facility; ISIS and RMX formatted diskettes
iNA 960 YBY	Object code buy-out license requiring no further payment of incorporation fees; ISIS and RMS formatted diskettes
iNA 960 YSU	Object code single use license only; ISIS and RMS formatted diskettes
iNA 960 ESR	License for machine readable source code if iNA 960. RMX and 51V formatted diskettes
iNA 960 LST	Source listing of iNA 960 provided on microfiche under a special source code license agreement
iNA 960 RF	Order code for the payment of incorporation fees

9-12

PRELIMINARY

iRMX™ NETWORKING SOFTWARE-iRMX™-NET
MEMBER OF THE OpenNET™ PRODUCT FAMILY

- **Transparent Network File Access**
  — Remote files can be worked with as if they were local
- **Connects iRMX™, XENIX* and DOS systems on the LAN***
  — Compatible with XENIX Networking Software (XENIX* NET) and MS-NET/IBM PC Networking program
- **Runs under iRMX™ 86 Operating System**
- **Existing applications can be distributed without change**
- **Supports OpenNET™—Ethernet hardware and software**
  — iSXM™ 552 Transport Engine
  — iSBC® 552 COMMengine
  — iSBC® 186/51 COMMputer™
  — iNA 960 Transport software
- **Supports file server applications**
  — Based on iRMX™ 86 Basic I/O system
- **Distributed name server**

The Intel OpenNET™ iRMX™ Network File access software provides transparent file access between iRMX and XENIX* and iRMX and MS/DOS systems across a LAN. Users can use local file systems commands to read, write, open, close, etc. files residing at remote iRMX, MS/ or PC/DOS and XENIX systems. IRMX NET implements the upper layer ISO OSI protocols used by the IBM PC Network Program and XENIX NET. Interoperation among these systems is supported by Intel's LAN product line including the iSXM 552 Transport engine, the iSBC® 552 COMMengine, the iSBC® 186/51 COMMputer™ and the iNA 960 Transport software. Networked iRMX systems serve in a wide range of applications including real time transactions, automated testing, data collection, communications switching, etc.

*XENIX is a trademark of Microsoft Corp.
**RMX to XENIX interoperation will be fully qualified only in R1.1 and up.

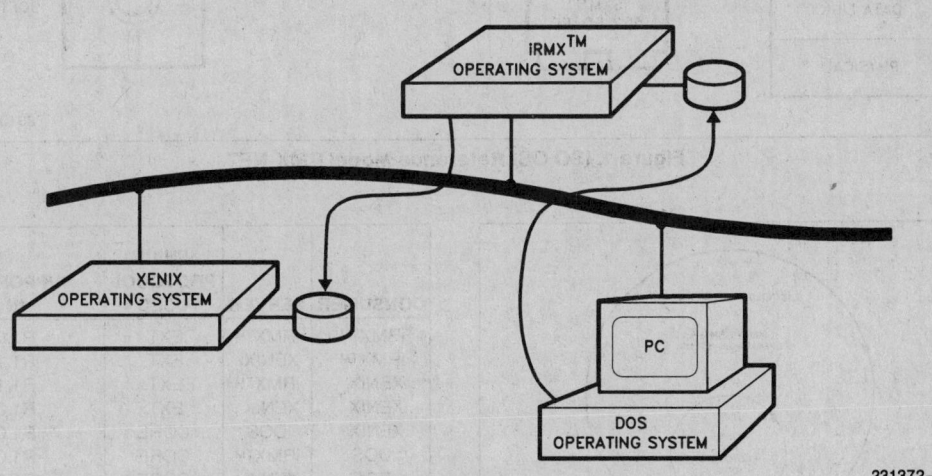

231372-1

Intel Corporation assumes no responsibility for the use of any circuitry other than circuitry embodied in an Intel product. No other circuit patent licenses are implied. Information contained herein supersedes previously published specifications on these devices from Intel. **February 1985**
© Intel Corporation, 1985

iRMX™-NET

PRELIMINARY

iRMX™-NET FUNCTIONAL DESCRIPTION

iRMX™-NET provides transparent remote file access capability through a file consumer and a file server module. The consumer intercepts file commands from the local user and transmits them across the LAN to the server at the node where the target file resides. The server receives, interprets and executes the command acting as a user to its local file system. The user has the option of configuring either or both in his target system.

RMX-NET also includes a name server which provides name-to-address mapping. The iRMX-NET file consumer uses the name server to find the physical address of the referenced system.

The capabilities allow iRMX systems to interoperate over the LAN with XENIX systems configured with XENIX-NET or DOS systems using MS-NET or IBM PC Network Program. This interoperation entails accessing data and loading programs through the network, sharing common servers and communication between users.

The network file service requires the support of an underlying ISO 8073 compatible transport service provided by the iNA 960 network software running on the iSBC 186/51 COMMputer or the iSXM 552/iSBC 552 boards. In terms of the ISO OSI reference model iRMX-NET, in conjunction with the transport service and Ethernet/IEEE 802.3 hardware, provide complete seven layer functionality and serves as the fundamental building block for the development of a host of other services such as mail or virtual terminal (see Figure 1).

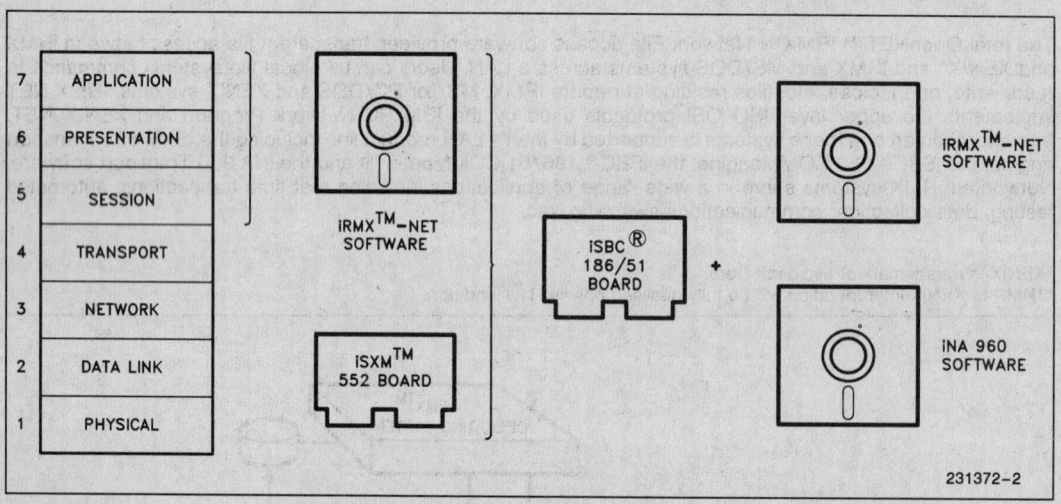

Figure 1. ISO OSI Reference Model RMX-NET

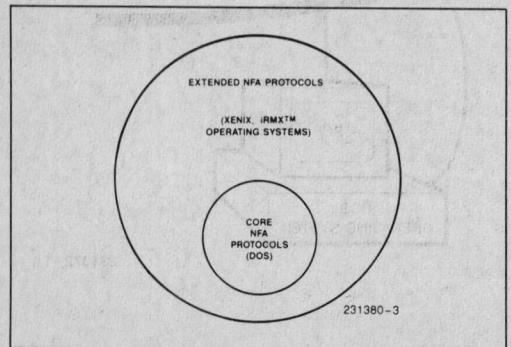

Figure 2. Protocols and Interoperation

CONSUMER	SERVER	WHICH PROTOCOL USED	SUPPORTED IN
iRMX™	iRMX™	EXT.	R1.0
iRMX™	XENIX	EXT.	R1.1
XENIX	iRMX™	EXT.	R1.1
XENIX	XENIX	EXT.	R1.0
XENIX	DOS	CORE	R1.0
DOS	iRMX™	CORE	R1.0
DOS	XENIX	CORE	R1.0
DOS	DOS	CORE	M/S NETWORK, IBM PC NETWORK SOFTWARE

Table 1. Protocols

iRMX™-NET

PRELIMINARY

TRANSPARENT REMOTE FILE ACCESS

iRMX-NET provides transparent remote file access at the BIOS, EIOS and Human Interface level. This means that all iRMX 86 applications written using BIOS, EIOS or HI commands can be used in a networked environment where the referenced files may reside at other nodes of the network.

With Release 1 of RMX-NET the user (file consumer) can transparently access files resident at remote systems configured with iRMX-NET or XENIX-NET (file servers). On the other hand, an RMX file server supports remote nodes configured with iRMX-NET, XENIX-NET, Microsoft Networks and IBM PC Network Software file consumers. For a table showing the combinations supported with the initial Open-NET product line please refer to Figure 2.

Transparent remote file access enables the user to manipulate and use remote files as if they were local. This capability can be used to develop key network services, such as mail, print server or virtual terminal with minimum additional effort.

PROTOCOLS

File sharing among different operating systems across the network is made possible through implementing a common set of file access (or file sharing) protocols under these operating systems. Network file sharing protocols are a set of rules governing the interaction between a file consumer and a file server on the same local area network. The file access protocols used by the OpenNet product line were jointly developed Intel, Microsoft and IBM.

Since the file systems of DOS, XENIX 286 and iRMX 86 are not identical, two protocol sets have been devised to support transparency in the various server-consumer combinations. The so-called "core protocols" support transparent file access between two DOS nodes on the network. The "extended protocols" support transparent file access between iRMX and XENIX nodes. The extended protocols contain the core protocols as a subset. See Figure 2 for an illustration. The core and extended protocols are in public domain and can be implemented under other operating systems, thus enabling a host of otherwise incompatible systems to share data and resources and to communicate across the network.

NETWORK HIERARCHICAL FILE SYSTEM

The file sharing protocols implemented in a network extend the file systems of the individual nodes into a so-called network hierarchical file system. Within a network any user can access each of the "public" files through a unique path of the network directory. For an illustration of the latter, please refer to Figure 3. Note that a directory can be designated as public (accessible from other nodes of the network) or private (accessible only locally) when SYSGEN-ing the server. Within a network hierarchical file system the same access right options are available as under RMX 86, that is a remote file can be read only, written into or searched depending on how it is set up.

IMPLEMENTATION

iRMX-NET implements file access across the network through introducing a new file type, the "remote file." The iRMX operating system originally supports physical, stream and named files through the respective file drivers contained within the Basic I/O system (BIOS). iRMX-NET adds a new file driver called remote file driver (RFD). All local commands referencing remote files are intercepted at the BIOS level and are redirected through the RFD to the network.

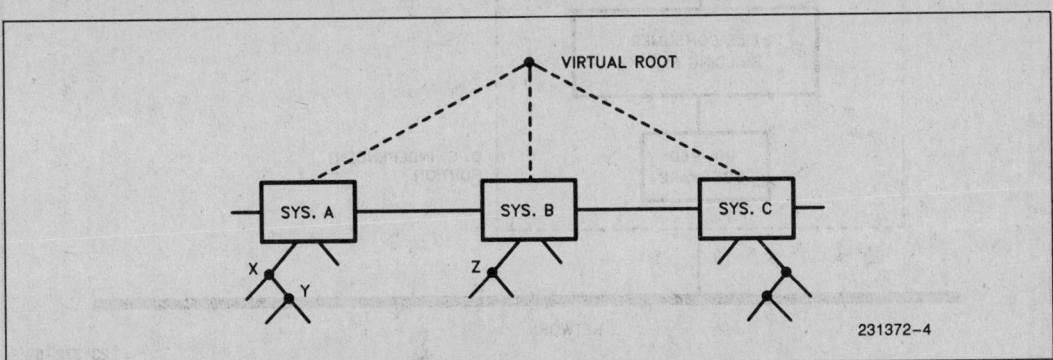

Figure 3. Network Hierarchical File System

iRMX™-NET

PRELIMINARY

The server receives the command from the network and forwards it to the local operating system acting as a user for the local file system. For an implementation block diagram please refer to Figures 4 and 5.

The consumer consists of two basic building blocks. The RFD is operating system dependent and must be configured to run under the host. The file consumer building block is supported by the special executive of iNA 960 and can run on a separate processor along with iNA 960.

The server includes a file server building block and a name server module which are configured to run with iNA 960 and are operating system independent. The server interfaces to the host operating system through the File Access interface which runs under the host operating system.

NAME SERVER

The Name Server provides name to network address mapping for the users. iRMX-NET implements a distributed or "protocol based" name server scheme in which every node "knows" its own name and address and thus there is no "master directory" file within the system.

When a user is referencing a remote node on the network by its name the file consumer broadcasts a request for that name across the network. The only node having the name called will respond by sending its address to the requestor.

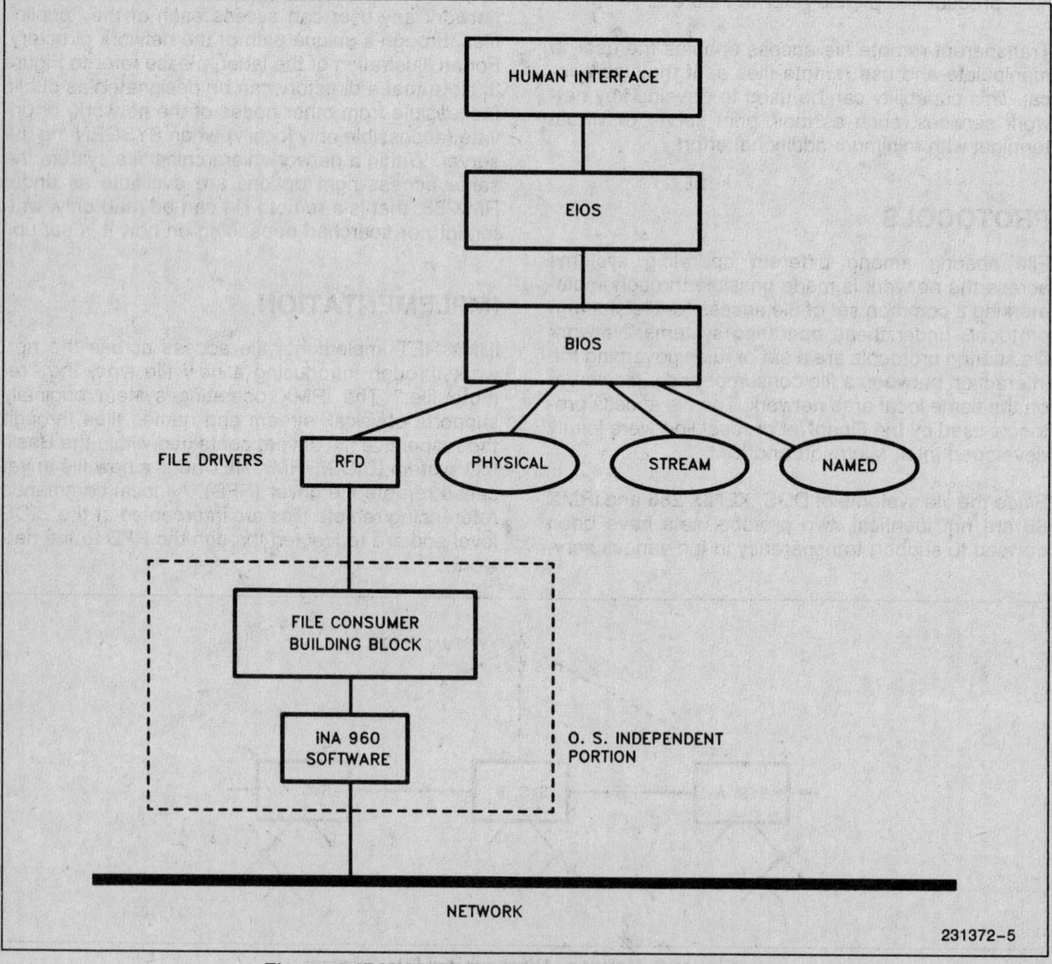

Figure 4. iRMX-NET File Consumer Implementation

iRMX™-NET

PRELIMINARY

SYSTEM ENVIRONMENT

iRMX-NET is supported by any system in which iRMX 86 is at release level 6.0 or later and in which the iNA 960 transport software is already configured in.

iRMX-NET is included at sysgen time as a first level job if the extended I/O system is not present or as an I/O job if it is present. iRMX-NET contains a number of user-defined parameters which must be set up when configuring the system, These parameters include the size of buffers, the number of consumers served concurrently or the maximum permissible number of outstanding processes.

USING iRMX-NET

When first referencing a remote directory the user has to issue an "attachdevice" command just like in the case of attaching a new local device under RMX 86. For example if the remote system is SYSB the user will need to issue the following command:

Attachdevice SYSB as :f5: Remote.

In this case :f5: is chosen to designate the newly opened "network volume." The "attachfile" command in fact opens a virtual circuit between the consumer and the server to support the subsequent communication between these two nodes. Once the remote device is "attached" the user can access his remote and local files alike. As a file server to a DOS consumer, iRMX-NET functions just like a PC AT file server. As a server to XENIX consumer there are a few limitations to transparency, for example, the "LOCK" and "LINK" XENIX commands are not supported under iRMX. As a file consumer to a XENIX server iRMX-NET provides full transparency.

SPECIFICATIONS
— Code size: about 40 KB
— System requirements: - RMX 86 R6.0 or later
                                                - iNA 960
— Throughput: T. B. D.

ORDERING INFORMATION
iRMX-NET WRO

Object code on double density RMX diskettes with OEM license.

iRMX-NET WSU

Object code on double density RMX diskettes with single user development license.

iRMX-NET LST

Source listing on microfiche. (Available for R1.1 and up.)

iRMX-NET SRC

Machine readable source
(Available for R1.1 and up.)

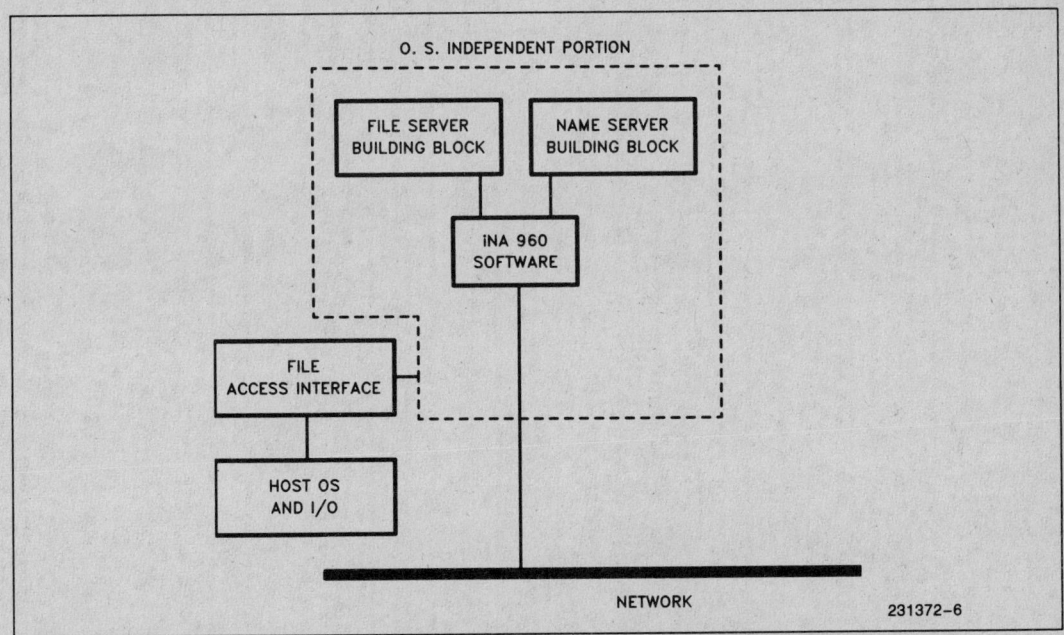

Figure 5. File Server Implementation

iRMX™-NET

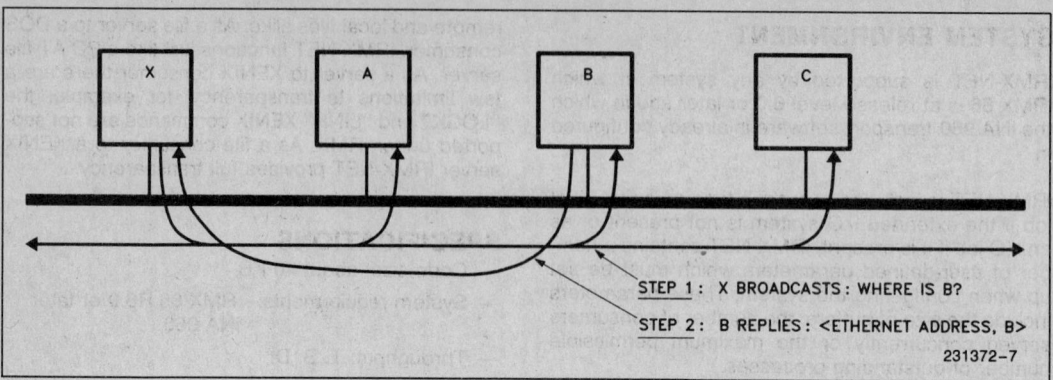

Figure 6. Distributed Name Server Scheme

XENIX* NETWORKING SOFTWARE
MEMBER OF THE OpenNET PRODUCT FAMILY

- **Transparent Network File Access Allows Existing Applications to be Distributed without Change**
- **Interoperation between iRMX™, XENIX and MS/DOS* Based Systems over a Local Area Network (LAN).**
  — Interoperation between XENIX and DOS by Rel 1.0
  — Interoperation between XENIX and iRMX by Rel 1.1
- **Runs under XENIX 3.0 on 286/310 and 286/380 Systems**
- **Supports OpenNET™ Hardware and Software**
  — iSXM™ 552 Ethernet COMMengine
  — iNA 961 Transport Software
- **Supports File Server Applications**

XENIX Networking software is a part of Intel's OpenNET Product Family which provides transparent file access between iRMX, XENIX and MS/DOS systems across a LAN. Users can use local file systems commands to read, write, open, close, etc. files residing at remote iRMX, MS/DOS and XENIX systems. The XENIX Networking Software implements the upper layer protocols used by Microsoft Networks, Interoperation among these systems is supported by Intel's OpenNET LAN product line including the iSXM 552 Transport Engine, iNA 961 (a preconfigured version of iNA 960 transport software), the iSBC® 186/51 COMMputer™ and the iNA 960 Transport software. Networked XENIX systems serve in a wide range of applications, such as distributed data processing, development, scientific and engineering applications, and graphics. Below is a diagram of the OpenNET Local Area Network.

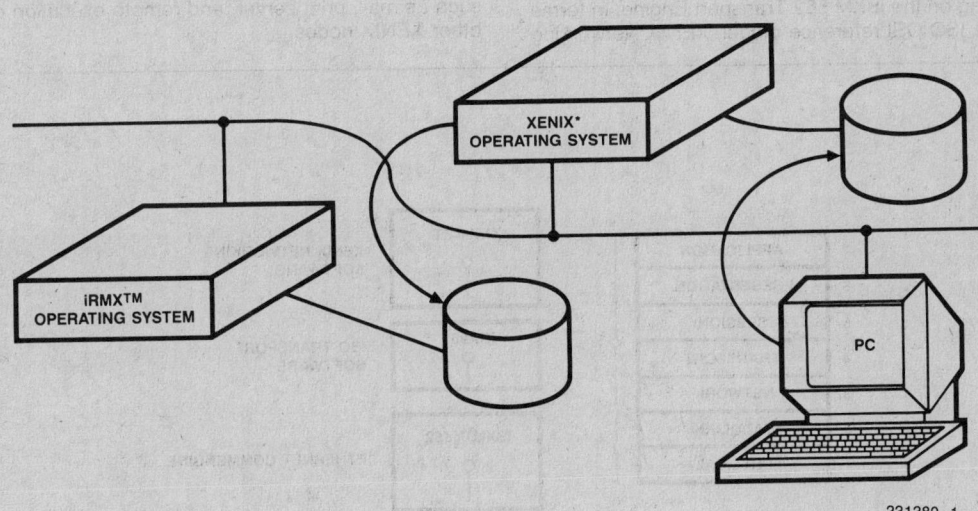

231380-1

* XENIX and MS/DOS are trademarks of Microsoft Corporation.

Intel Corporation assumes no responsibility for the use of any circuitry other than circuitry embodied in an Intel product. No other circuit patent licenses are implied. Information contained herein supersedes previously published specifications on these devices from Intel. **February 1985**
© Intel Corporation, 1985

XENIX

XENIX—NETWORKING FUNCTIONAL DESCRIPTION

The XENIX Networking software provides transparent remote file access capability through a file consumer and a file server module. The consumer intercepts file commands from the local user application and transmits them across the LAN to the server at a network system or node where the target file resides. The server receives, interprets, and executes the command acting as a user to its local file system. The user has the option of configuring either or both the consumer and server in his target system.

The XENIX Networking Software also includes a name server which allows a logical name to be used to refer to remote nodes instead of the physical LAN address.

The capabilities allow XENIX systems to interoperate over the LAN with RMX systems (with release 1.1) configured with RMX Networking software or MS/DOS systems (with release 1.0) using Microsoft Networks. This interoperation entails accessing data and loading programs through the network, sharing common servers, and communication between users.

The XENIX Networking Software requires the support of an underlying ISO 8073 compatible transport service provided in the iNA 960 network software running on the iSXM 552 Transport Engine. In terms of the ISO OSI reference model, XENIX Networking in conjunction with the transport service and Ethernet hardware provides complete seven layer functionality and serves as the fundamental building block for the development of other services such as mail and remote execution (see Figure 1).

TRANSPARENT REMOTE FILE ACCESS

XENIX Networking provides transparent remote file access at the application interface level. This means that all XENIX 3.0 applications written using operating system file access commands can be used without change in a networked environment where the referenced files may reside at other nodes of the network.

With release 1.0 of the XENIX Networking software, the user (file consumer) can transparently access files resident at remote systems configured with XENIX or MS/DOS file servers. While a XENIX file server supports remote nodes configured with both XENIX and Microsoft Networks and file consumers. For a table showing the combinations supported with the initial OpenNET product line, please refer to Figure 2.

Transparent remote file access enables the user to manipulate and use remote files as if they were local. This capability is used for key network services, such as mail, print server, and remote execution on other XENIX nodes.

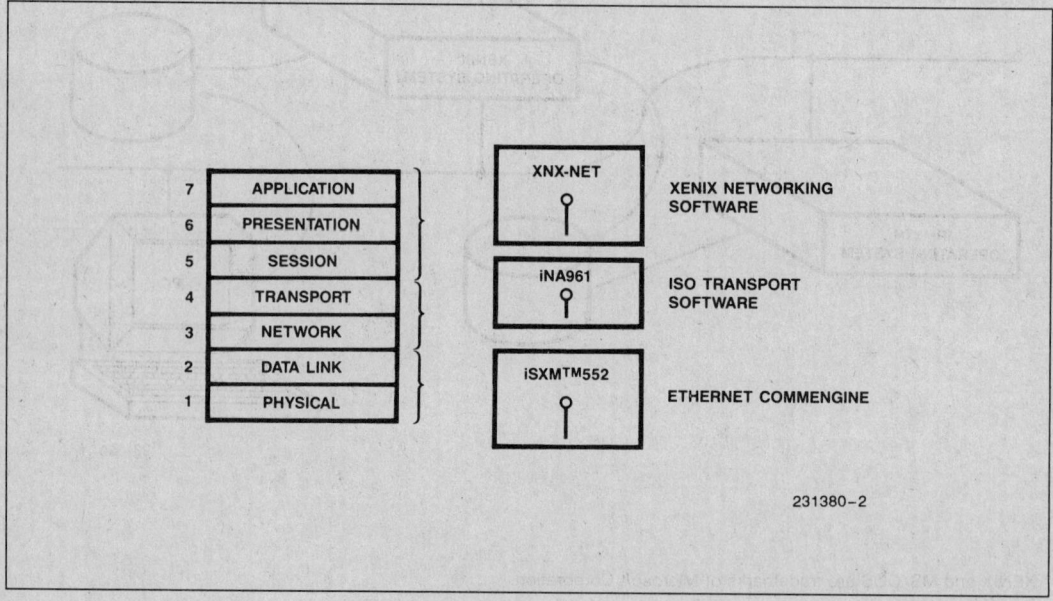

Figure 1. OpenNET™ Product Offerings

XENIX

Consumer	Server	Protocol Used	Supported In
iRMX™	iRMX™	EXT.	R1.0
iRMX™	XENIX	EXT.	R1.1
XENIX	iRMX™	EXT.	R1.1
XENIX	XENIX	EXT.	R1.0
XENIX	MS/DOS	CORE	R1.0
MS/DOS	iRMX™	CORE	R1.0
MS/DOS	XENIX	CORE	R1.0
MS/DOS	•MS/DOS	CORE	MICROSOFT NETWORKS

Figure 2. Interoperation

NETWORK FILE ACCESS PROTOCOLS

File sharing among different operating systems across the network is made possible through implementing a common set of file access (or file sharing) protocols under these operating systems. Network file sharing protocols are a set of rules governing the interaction between a file consumer and a file server on the same local area network. The file access protocols used by the OpenNET product line were jointly developed by Intel, Microsoft, and IBM.

Since the file systems of DOS, XENIX, and iRMX are not identical, two protocol sets have devised to support transparency in the various server-consumer combinations. The core protocols support transparent file access between a MS/DOS consumer and remote server. The "extended protocols" support transparent file access between RMX and XENIX nodes. The extended protocols contain the core protocols as a subset. See Figure 3 for an illustration.

The core and extended protocols are in public domain and can be implemented under other operating systems, thus enabling a host of otherwise incompatible systems to share data resources and to communicate across the network.

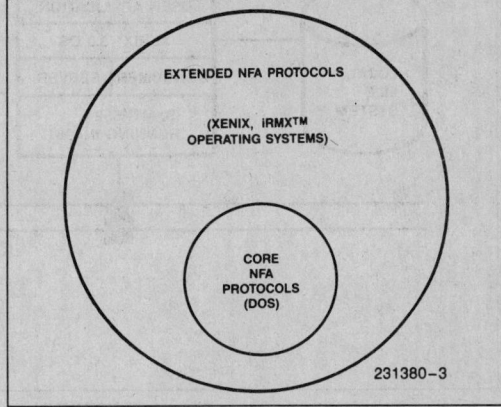

Figure 3. Network File Access Protocols

NETWORK HIERARCHICAL FILE SYSTEM

The file sharing protocols implemented in a network extend the file systems of the individual nodes into a hierarchical file system. Within a network any user can access each of the "public" files through a unique path of the network directory. For an illustration of the latter, refer to Figure 4. Within a network hierarchical file system the same access right options are available as under XENIX 3.0, that is a remote file can be read only, written into or searched if the requesting user has the appropriate permissions.

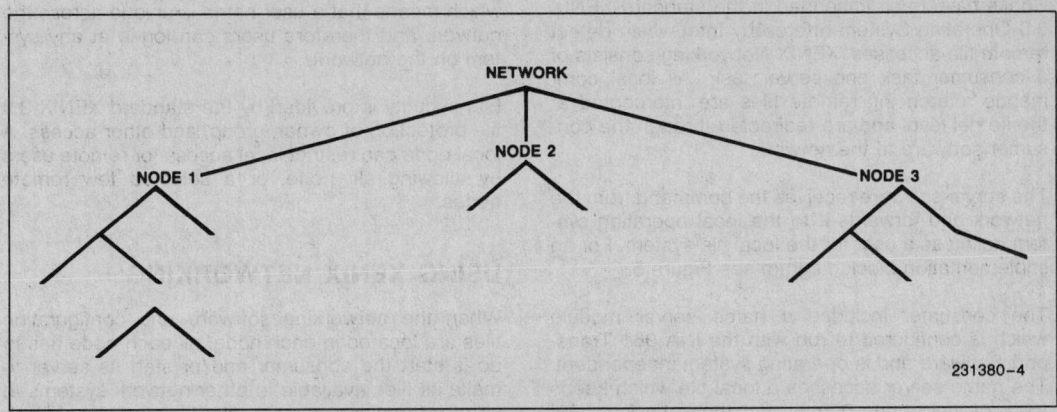

Figure 4. Network Hierarchical File System

XENIX

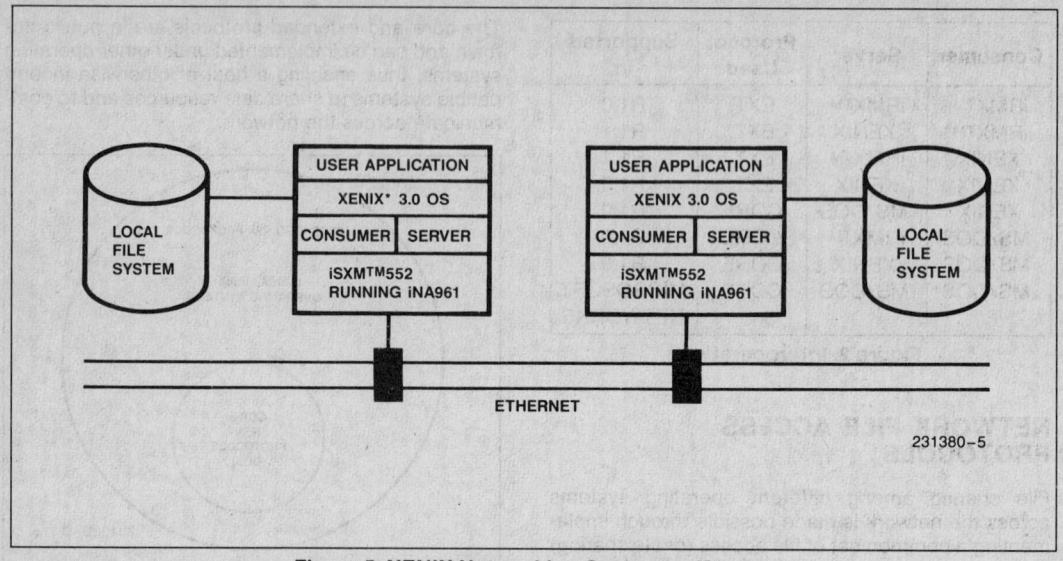

Figure 5. XENIX Networking Consumer/Server

IMPLEMENTATION

The XENIX Networking software implements file access across the network through enhancing the file naming syntax. The logical name associated with a remote system (or node) is appended by the user to the path name of the required file. This nomenclature is distinguished from normal path names by a double slash (//). A similar technique is used for MS/DOS and RMX.

    //<node name>/<path name>

Hooks have been imbedded in the standard XENIX 3.0 Operating System offered by Intel which detect remote file accesses. XENIX Networking consists of a consumer task and server task. All local commands referencing remote files are intercepted at the kernel level and are redirected through the consumer software to the network.

The server software receives the command from the network and forwards it to the local operating system acting as a user for the local file system. For an implementation block diagram see Figure 5.

The consumer includes a name server module which is configured to run with the iNA 961 Transport Software and is operating system independent. The name server accesses a local file which keeps track of valid node names and their physical LAN address.

SYSTEM ENVIRONMENT

The XENIX Networking software can be used on any system running Intel's XENIX 3.0. This includes the 286/310 and 286/380 systems. Since networking "hooks" are already included in the operating system nothing other than loading the XENIX Networking software onto the local system is necessary. Special network utilities are included for building and maintaining the network configuration files so that the network can be tailored to meet each customers needs.

The network supports a single community of users which means that a user name is unique across the network and therefore users can log-in at any system on the network.

File security is provided by the standard XENIX 3.0 file protection of owner, group, and other access. A local node can restrict local access for remote users by allowing all, none, or a selected few remote nodes.

USING XENIX NETWORKING

When the networking software and configuration files are located in each node, all each node has to do is start the consumer and/or start its server to make its files available to other network systems to start referencing remote files immediately. Each node can talk to as many as 20 other nodes at

XENIX

the same time. This is dynamic and a node can switch to any other nodes at any time as long as it doesn't exceed 20. This limit is only for consumer tasks talking to server tasks and vice versa and in no way limits the number of users at a node which can have remote file access, i.e., all user requests from a single node are multiplexed through a single consumer.

The standard XENIX 3.0 mail works via XENIX Networking across the LAN as well as remote execution on XENIX 3.0 systems via the AT command.

As a consumer to RMX servers there are a few limitations to transparency, for example, the "LOCK" and "LINK" XENIX commands are not supported under RMX. As a file server to a RMX consumer, XENIX Networking does provide full transparency.

SPECIFICATIONS

—Code size: —about 60 KB plus 40 K for buffers

—System requirements—XENIX 3.0
—iNA 961

— XENIX Networking along with the iNA 961 software and the iSXM 552 have been qualified for the 286/310-17, 286/310-41, and 286/380 systems.

ORDERING INFORMATION

XNX-NET-NSO	XENIX Networking Software (both 8″ and 5¼″ double sided, double density) plus rights for eight copies
XNX-NET-961-NSU	XENIX Networking and iNA 961 Object Software (both 8″ and 5¼″ double sided, double density) plus rights for 8 copies
XNX-NET-KIT-NRI	XENIX Networking and iNA 961 Object Software (both 8″ and 5¼″ double sided, double density) plus iSXM 552 Transport Engine for pass through use
XNX-NET-RO	XENIX Networking and iNA 961 Object Software (both 8″ and 5¼″ double sided, double density) plus license rights
XNX-NET-RF	Software Incorporation Fee
XNX-NET-NSR	Machine Readable source code for the XENIX Networking Software. (both 8″ and 5¼″ double sided, double density)
iNA-961-RO	iNA 961 Transport Software plus license rights
iSXM 552	Ethernet Transport Engine plus one iNA 961 Software Incorporation Fee
SYS 310-41XN	XENIX System 286/310-41 with Xenix Networking Software, iNA961 Transport Software and iSXM 552 Transport Engine
SYS 310-17XN	XENIX System 286/310-17 with Xenix Networking Software, iNA 961 Transport Software and iSXM 552 Transport Engine
iMDX 457	Ethernet Transceiver Cable
iMDX 3015	Ethernet Transceiver
iMDX 3016-1	Ethernet Cable
iDCM 911-1	Intellink™

Ethernet hardware and software for the IBM Personal Computer is available from Ungermann Bass, Inc.

System Packaging and Power Supplies 10

10

System Packaging and Power Supplies

iCS™80 INDUSTRIAL CHASSIS
KIT 635, KIT 640

- Available with iSBC® 640 power supply

- Accommodates from 1 to 3 iSBC® 604/614 cardcage assemblies for 4-12 MULTIBUS® board capacity

- Vertical board orientation and four fans for high efficiency cooling

- Front access to iSBC® boards, power supply, and signal conditioning panels

- 19-inch wide RETMA rack mounting or NEMA type backwall mounting brackets

- UL and CSA approved

- Multi-voltage operation

- Lockable service panel

- Recessed mounting space for signal conditioning/wire termination panels

The iCS 80 Industrial Chassis provides industrially oriented mounting space for Intel single board computer (iSBC) products, associated iSBC power supplies, and related analog and digital conditioning/termination panels. The base unit provides a 4-slot MULTIBUS backplane (iSBC 604) with expansion space and cabling to expand to 12 MULTIBUS backplane slots by adding additional 4-slot iSBC 614s as needed (up to two). Full MULTIBUS compatability in the iCS 80 chassis allows configuration of multiple single board computers to share system tasks through communication over the bus (through multimaster bus arbitration built on the multiple iSBC processors).

iCS™ 80

FUNCTIONAL DESCRIPTION

iCS™ 80 Kit 640

This chassis uses the higher power iSBC 640 power supply, and is designed to power higher board count systems. By installing one or two additional iSBC 614 cardcages, this chassis will accommodate up to 8 or 12 MULTIBUS boards. Signal conditioning panels may attach directly in the iCS 80.

Engineered for Industrial Applications

The MULTIBUS slots are mounted vertically to improve convection cooling and the top, bottom and sides are engineering to allow maximum air flow over the boards. Four fans are provided to increase air flow, allowing users to eliminate or minimize the need for supplementary fans or air conditioning.

Power Supply Flexibility

The power supplies are mounted on slide in/out mounting rails, and quick disconnect cabling and connectors are provided for rapid service replacement. An AC wiring barrier strip allows simple wiring connections for integration into larger systems (see Figure 4).

Industrial Rack Mounting

The chassis mounts directly into 19-inch standard width RETMA (Radio-Electronics-Television Manufacturers Association) customer provided rack. Alternately, mounting brackets and power cabling access are provided for mounting directly on a backwall, such as the backwall panel of a NEMA-type (National Electrical Manufacturers Association), front-access-only cabinet.

Front Access Serviceability

To simplify serviceability, front access is provided for all iSBC boards, the power supply, operation indicator lights, interrupt and reset buttons, and the AC power fuse.

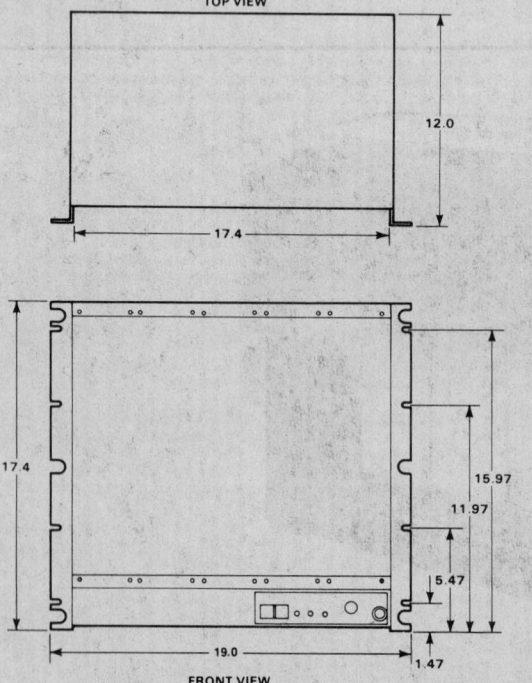
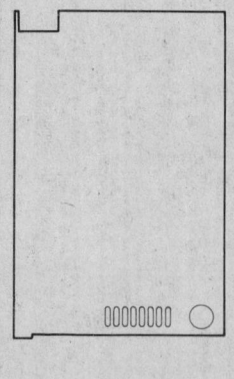

Figure 1. iCS™ 80 Chassis Dimensions

iCS™ 80

Typical Small Configuration

- iSBC 88/40A Test and Measurement Computer
- iCS 910 Analog I/O Signal Conditioning Panel
- iCS 930 AC/DC Control Interface Panel

Figure 2. Small Configuration iCS™ 80 Kit.

Typical Maximum Configuration

- 16-bit 8086 processor (iSBC 86/30 w/RAM MULTIMODULE)
- 768K bytes RAM (2 - iSBC 056A)
- 128K bytes EPROM (or 16K E^2PROM)
- 240 analog inputs (3 - iSBC 88/40A w/2 ea. iSBX 311)
- 24 analog voltage outputs

OR

- 24 analog current outputs (4-20 mA)
- 72 isolated digital inputs/outputs
- 144 TTL digital inputs/outputs (2 - iSBC 519s)

(All iCS 9XX Signal Conditioning/Termination Panels shown mounted to cabinet)

Figure 3. iCS™ 80 Kit 640 with 12 MULTIBUS® Card Slots Mounted in NEMA Cabinet

Figure 4. Rear View iCS™ 80 Chassis Showing Power Distribution Panel (detached to show terminal block), and Cabling from iCS 80 Chassis to iCS 9XX RETMA Mounted Signal Conditioning Panels (Top of iCS 80 Chassis)

10-3

AFN-01280C

iCS™ 80

Lockable Service Panel

To assist in development, checkout and service, two pushbuttons are provided. The RESET button pulls low the initialize line (INIT) on the MULTIBUS backplane. The INTERRUPT button pulls low one interrupt line on the MULTIBUS backplane (INT1). Logic within the iCS 80 ensures that these buttons function with all versions of Intel single board computers. From the front of the iCS 80 chassis, without a CRT or other panel, an operator or service person can reset or interrupt on-going iCS 80 system operations to get attention, signal an alarm, or start a self-test operation.

A front panel key provides three positions: OFF (AC power off and key removable), ON (AC power on, pushbuttons enabled, key unremovable), and LOCK (AC power on, pushbuttons disabled, key removable).

Three indicator light emitting diodes record basic chassis status. POWER ON (GREEN); RUN (GREEN); and HALT (RED); the RESET or INTERRUPT buttons will remove the HALT state.

U.L. Approved

The iCS 80 chassis has received full Underwriters Laboratory approval (F.6 #E70842) as a U.L. listed component under the Underwriters Laboratories Safety Standard for Process Control Equipment, UL1092. When installed as described in the iCS 80 Hardware Reference Manual, the iCS 80 chassis provides adequate protection against shock, fire and casualty hazards, and should comply with most local and regional requirements for installation in ordinary locations. In addition, the iCS 80 chassis was designed to comply with the UL requirements for Data Processing Equipment, UL478. The iCS 80 has also been approved by the Canadian Standards Association under CSA category C22.2 No. 142, the Canadian Standard for Safety for Process Control Equipment and C22.2 No. 154 for Data Processing Equipment.

Mounting Space for Signal Conditioning/Wire Terminations

The cardcages and power supplies in the iCS 80 chassis are recessed behind the front edge of the rack mounting ears to provide mounting space for the iCS 9XX series signal conditioning/termination panels and field wiring. For smaller systems with only one or two iSBC 604/614 cardcages (4 to 8 slots), up to two iCS 910, iCS 920, or iCS 930 signal conditioning/termination panels can be mounted vertically over the area where the second or third cardcage would mount (see Figure 2). The benefit of this design is a completely self-contained industrial chassis with iSBC cards, power supply, signal conditioning and field wiring terminations, all in one enclosure.

SPECIFICATIONS

Capacity

Four slots for MULTIBUS compatible single board computers, memory, I/O or other expansion boards
Expandable to 12 slots using two iSBC 614 cardcages
(Order Separately)

Front Panel Controls

Pushbuttons
RESET: Connected to Initialize/ on MULTIBUS backplane
INTERRUPT: Connected to Interrupt 1/ line on MULTIBUS backplane.

Panel Indicator Lights (LEDs)
POWER ON (green): +5V power exists on the MULTIBUS backplane
RUN (green): CPU is executing an instruction. Light goes out if CPU is in WAIT or HALT state
HALT (red): CPU has executed a HALT instruction

Keylock
OFF: AC power off, key removable
ON: AC power on, pushbuttons enabled, key unremovable
LOCK: AC power on, pushbuttons disabled, key removable

Fuse — AC power (6A)

Equipment Supplied

iCS 80 industrial chassis, three fans for cardcages, one fan for power supply, 4-slot cardcage with MULTIBUS backplane, control panel with switches, indicators, keylock, power distribution barrier strip, AC power fuse, line filter, 115V power cable, and logic for interrupt and reset buttons. An installation package is also provided, including a NEMA cabinet mounting kit, power supply extension cables, and RETMA cabinet mounting screws, 100/120/220/240 VAC operation.

Software

See the RMX/80 Real-time Multitasking Executive specifications for industrial related applications. In addition, system monitors for most of the Intel single board computers are available in the INSITE (Intel's Software Index and Technology Exchange) User's Program Library.

Physical Characteristics

Height — 39.3 cm (15.7 in.)
Width — 48.5 cm (19.0 in.) at front panel
43.5 cm (17.4 in.) behind front panel
Depth — 30.0 cm (12.0 in.) with all protrusions
Weight — 16.8 kg (37.0 lb) without power supplies

Environmental Characteristics

(Ambient at iCS-80 air intake, bottom of chassis)

Temperature (Ambient)
Operating: 0°C to 50°C (32°F to 122°F)
Non-operating: −40°C to +85°C

Humidity — Up to 90% relative, noncondensing at 40°C

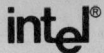

iCS™ 80

Electrical Characteristics

The iCS 80 chassis provides mounting space for the iSBC 640 power supply. Unless otherwise stated, electrical specifications apply to both power supplies when installed by user in iCS 80 chassis.

Input Power

Frequency: 47 to 63 Hz. Voltage (Nominal) Voltage (Single Phase, Jumper Selectable) iCS 80 Kit 640: 100, 120, 220, 240 VAC (±10%)

Current (Including fans)	With iSBC 640	Input Voltage
	5.6A max	103 VAX
	2.8A max	206 VAX
Power, max:	580 watts	

Output Power

Voltage	Output Current (max)	Overvoltage Protection
	iSBC 640	iSBC 640
+12V	4.5A	+14V to +16V
+5V	30.0A	+5.8V to +6.6V
-5V	1.75A	-5.8V to -6.6V
-12V	1.75A	-14V to -16V

Combined Line/Load Regulation — ±1% at ±10% static line change and ±50% static load change, measured at the output connector (±0.2% measured at the power supply under the same conditions).

Remote Sensing — Provided for +5 VDC output line regulation.

Output Ripple and Noise — 10mV (iSBC 640 supply) peak-to-peak, max (DC to 500 kHz)

Output Transient Response — Less than 50 μsec for ±50% load change.

Maximum Watts Dissipation (load plus losses) — 500W (iSBC 640 supply)

Installation

Complete instructions for installation are contained in the iCS 80 Site Planning and Installation Guide, including RETMA and NEMA cabinet mounting, and field signal, ground wiring and cooling suggestions.

Warranty

The iCS 80 Industrial Chassis is warranted to be free from defects in materials and workmanship under normal use and service for a period of 90 days from date of shipment.

Reference Manuals

9800799A — iCS 80 Industrial Chassis Hardware Reference Manual (SUPPLIED)

9800708A — iSBC 604/614 Cardcage Hardware Reference Manual (SUPPLIED)

ORDERING INFORMATION

Part Number	Description
iCS 80 Kit 640	iCS 80 system consisting of: iCS 80 Industrial Chassis iSBC 640 Power Supply

iSBC® 604/614
MODULAR CARDCAGE ASSEMBLIES

- Interconnects and houses up to four MULTIBUS® boards per cardcage
- Connectors allow interconnection of up to four cardcage assemblies for 16 board systems
- Strong cardcage structure helps protect installed boards from warping and physical damage
- Cardcage mounting holes facilitate interconnection of units
- Compatible with 3.5-inch RETMA rack mount increments
- Interleaved grounds on backplane minimize noise and crosstalk
- Up to 3 CPU boards per system for multiprocessing applications

The iSBC 604 and iSBC 614 Modular Cardcage Assemblies units provide low-cost, off-the-shelf housing for OEM products using two or more MULTIBUS® boards. Each unit interconnects and houses up to four boards. The base unit, the ISBC 604 Cardcage Assembly, contains a male backplane PC edge connector and bus signal termination circuits, plus power supply connectors. It is suitable for applications requiring a single unit, or may be interconnected with up to three iSBC 614 cardcage assemblies for a four cardcage (16 board) system. The iSBC 614 contains both male and female backplane connectors, and may be interconnected with iSBC 604/614 units. Both units are identical, with the exception of the bus signal terminator feature. A single unit may be packaged in a 3.5 inch RETMA rack enclosure, and two interconnected units may be packaged in a 7 inch enclosure. The units are mountable in any of three planes.

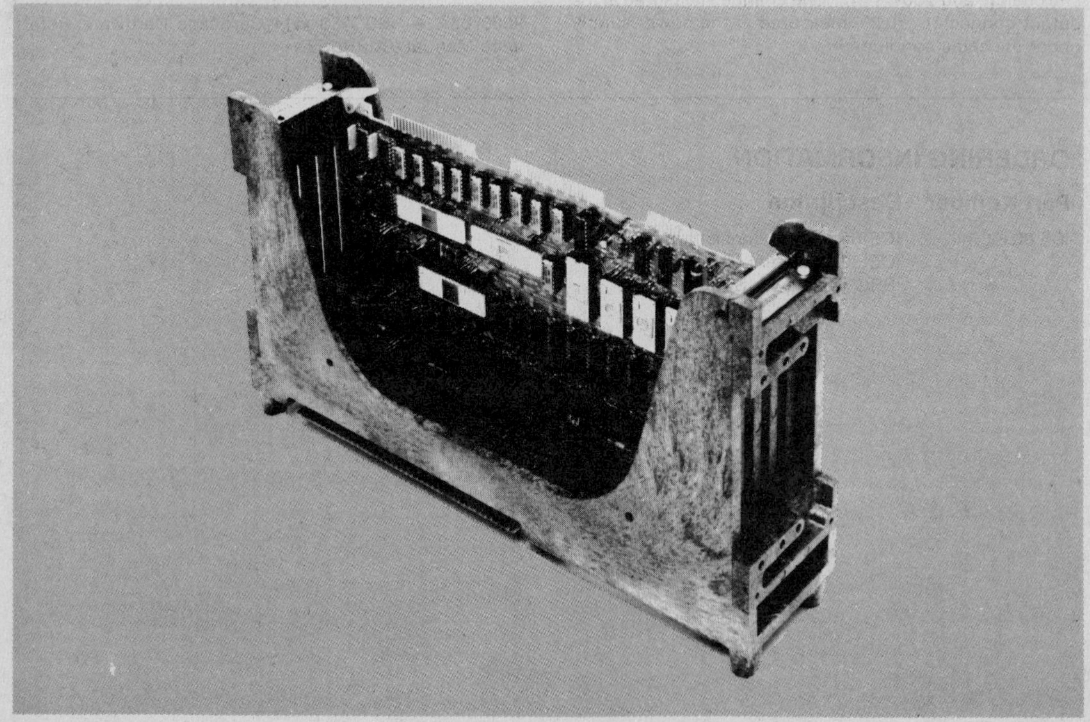

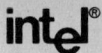

iSBC® 604/614

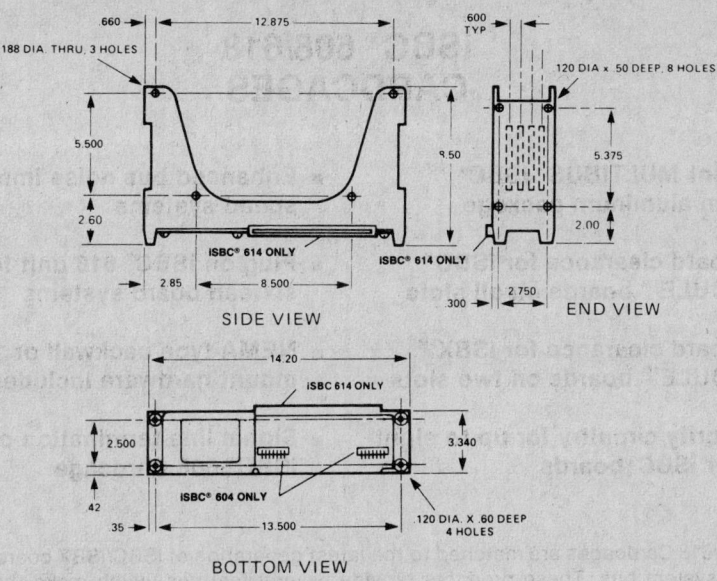

Figure 1. iSBC® 604/814 Cardcage Assembly Dimensions

SPECIFICATIONS
Backplane

Bus Lines — All MULTIBUS system bus address, data, and command bus lines are bussed to all four connectors on the printed circuit backplane

Power Connectors — G for ground, +5V, −5V, +12V, −12V, and −10V power supply lines

iSBC 604 — Bus signal terminators, backplane male PC edge connector only, and power supply headers

iSBC 614 — Backplane male and female connectors and power supply headers

Mating Power Connectors

	Connector	87159-7
AMP	Pin	87023-1
	Polarizing key	87116-2
	Connector	09-50-7071
Molex	Pin	08-50-0106
	Polarizing key	15-04-0219

Note
1. Pins from a given vendor may only be used with connectors from the same vendor.

ORDERING INFORMATION

Part number	Description
SBC 604	Modular Cardcage Assembly (Base Unit)

Bus Arbitration — Serial; up to 3 CPU masters

Equipment Supplied
iSBC 604 or iSBC 614 Cardcage
Schematic

Physical Dimensions

Height — 8.5 in. (21.59 cm)
Width — 14.2 in. (36.07 cm)
Depth — 3.34 in. (8.48 cm)
Weight — 35 oz. (992.23 gm)
Card Slot Spacing — 0.6 in.

Environmental Characteristics

Operating Temperature — 0°C to 55°C

Reference Manual

9800708 — iSBC 604/614 Cardcage Hardware Reference Manual (ORDER SEPARATELY)

Part Number	Description
SBC 614	Modular Cardcage Assembly (Expansion Unit)

iSBC® 608/618 CARDCAGES

- Houses eight MULTIBUS® iSBC® boards in an aluminum package
- Board-to-board clearance for iSBC® MULTIMODULE™ boards on all slots
- Board-to-board clearance for iSBX™ MULTIMODULE™ boards on two slots
- Parallel priority circuitry for up to eight Multimaster iSBC® boards
- Enhanced bus noise immunity for high speed systems
- Plug on iSBC® 618 unit for up to sixteen board systems
- NEMA-type backwall or 19-inch rack mount hardware included
- Signal line termination circuitry on iSBC® 608 Cardcage

Intel's iSBC 608/618 Cardcages are matched to the latest generation of iSBC/iSBX boards which mount in the MULTIBUS system bus. These products provide several features which make them the industry's leading price/performance cardcage product. MULTIMODULE board clearance, parallel priority circuitry, enhanced backplane noise immunity, and precision fit card guides are a few of the distinctions which make this the industry's better product.

The iSBC 608 Cardcage is the base unit, housing up to eight iSBC boards and their MULTIMODULE boards. Additionally, this base unit includes mounting hardware and fan mounting bracketry. The iSBC 618 is the expansion unit, providing eight additional iSBC board slots to the iSBC 608 Cardcage for a total of sixteen board slots which can be NEMA-type backwall or 19-inch rack mounted. This is accomplished with the mounting hardware of the iSBC 608 Cardcage. The iSBC 618 expansion unit also includes fan mounting bracketry.

The following are trademarks of Intel Corporation and may be used only to describe Intel products: Intel, CREDIT, Index, Insite, Intellec, Library Manager, Megachassis, Micromap, MULTIBUS, PROMPT, UPI, μScope, Promware, MCS, ICE, iRMX, iSBC, iSBX, MULTIMODULE, and iCS. Intel Corporation assumes no responsibility for the use of any circuitry other than circuitry embodied in an Intel product. No other circuit patent licenses are implied.

©INTEL CORPORATION, 1982

iSBC® 608/618

FUNCTIONAL DESCRIPTION

Mechanical Aspects

The iSBC 608/618 Cardcages provide housing and a MULTIBUS system bus for up to sixteen single board computers and their MULTIMODULE boards. The iSBC 608 unit and iSBC 618 unit offer board-to-board clearance (0.8 inches or greater) on all eight slots for iSBC MULTIMODULE boards. Two slots provide clearance (1.2 inches or greater) for iSBX MULTIMODULE boards as shown in Figure 1. Each cardcage includes precision fitted nylon cardguides for secure board fit and accurate MULTIBUS board pin alignment. Fan mounting bracketry is also included with each cardcage. This bracketry allows the mounting of several industry standard fans. The iSBC 608 Cardcage base unit includes aluminum mounting hardware for NEMA-type backwall mounting, or anchoring a sixteen slot iSBC 608/618 combination in a standard 19-inch rack.

Electrical Aspects

The iSBC 608/618 Cardcages implement a parallel priority resolution scheme by using plug-in jumper connections. There are six different priority schemes allowed, each requiring a different jumper configuration. In systems where an iSBC 618 Cardcage is attached to the base unit, the base unit will have lower priority overall. That is, master boards in the iSBC 608 base unit may gain control of the MULTIBUS lines only when no boards in the iSBC 618 expansion unit are asserting the bus request (BREQ/) signal.

Noise-minimizing ground traces are strategically interleaved between signal and address lines on these backplanes. This provides the enhanced noise immunity and minimized signal-to-signal coupling which is important in high speed, high board count microcomputer systems.

The iSBC 608/618 Cardcages provide power connector lug bolts for +5 VDC and ground. The lug bolts, compared to other power connection methods, help transfer higher amounts of current. Other voltages (±12 VDC, −5 VDC) are connected via a mating power connector plug as shown in Figure 2.

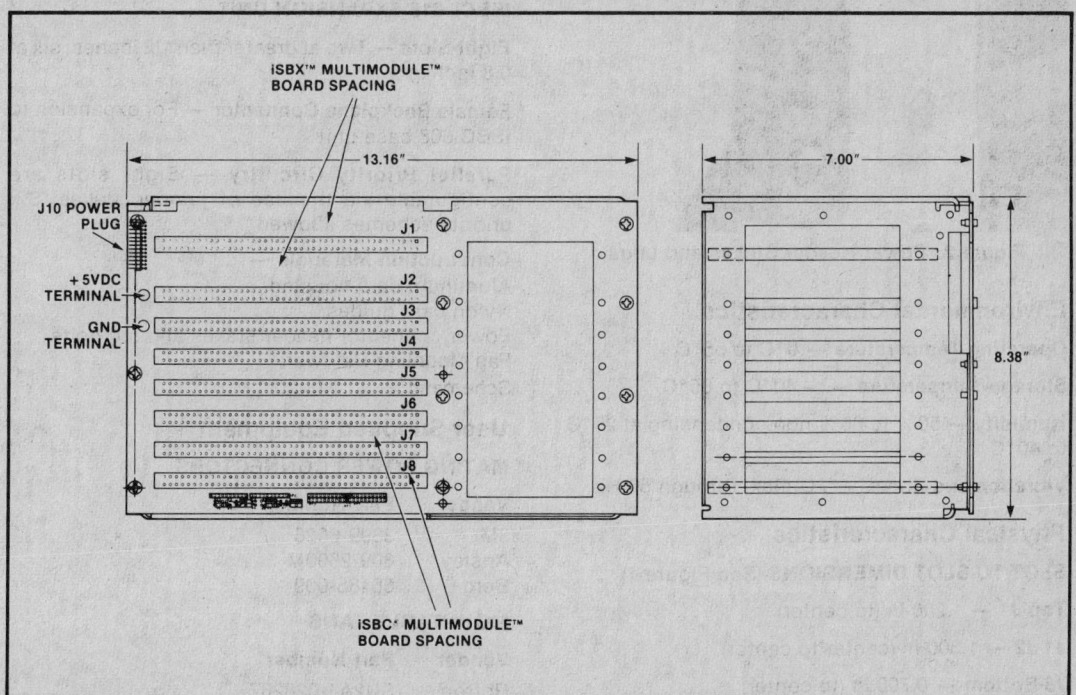

Figure 1. iSBC® 608/618 Cardcages Dimensions

iSBC® 608/618

SPECIFICATIONS

Bus Lines

All MULTIBUS (IEEE 796) system bus address and command lines are bussed to each of the eight MULTIBUS connectors on the backplane. Ground traces are interleaved among these signal lines and bussed to the backplane edge connector for interconnection of the iSBC 608 and iSBC 618 backplane.

Power Connectors

Ground (0V), +5V, −5V, +12V, −12V power supply header stakes and power lug bolts are provided on the iSBC 608/618 Cardcages as shown in Figure 2.

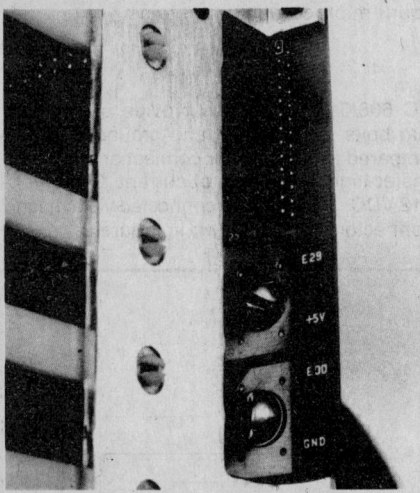

Figure 2. Power Header Stakes and Lugs

Environmental Characteristics

Operating Temperature — 0°C to 55°C

Storage Temperature — −40°C to 85°C

Humidity — 50% to 95% non-condensing at 25°C to 40°C

Vibration and Shock — 2G max. through 50 Hz

Physical Characteristics

SLOT-TO-SLOT DIMENSIONS (See Figure 1)

Top-J1 — 1.200 in (to center)

J1-J2 — 1.300 in (center to center)

J8-Bottom — 0.700 in (to center)

All Others — 0.800 (center to center)

PHYSICAL DIMENSIONS

Height — 8.38 in (21.29 cm)

Length — 13.16 in (33.43 cm)

Width — 7.50 in (19.05 cm)

Weight — 3.50 lbs (1.59 kg)

Shipping Weight — 5.75 lbs (2.61 kg)

Equipment Supplied
iSBC® 608 BASE UNIT

Eight-Slots — Two at greater than 1.2 inches; six at 0.8 inches

Male Backplane Connector — For expansion with iSBC 618 cardcage

Parallel Priority Circuitry — Eight slots are configurable via the use of jumper stakes. Six priority schemes allowed

Construction Materials —
Aluminum card housing
Nylon card guides
Power connector header stakes and lug bolts

Accessories
iSBC® 618 EXPANSION UNIT

Eight-Slots — Two at greater than 1.2 inches; six at 0.8 inches

Female Backplane Connector — For expansion to iSBC 608 base unit

Parallel Priority Circuitry — Eight slots are configurable via the use of jumper stakes. Six priority schemes allowed

Construction Materials —
Aluminum card housing
Nylon card guides
Power connector header stakes and lug bolts
Fan Mounting Hardware
Schematic

User-Supplied Equipment
MATING POWER CONNECTORS

Vendor	Part Number
3M	3399-6026
Ansley	609-2600M
Berg	65485-009

MOUNTABLE FANS

Vendor	Part Number
Rotron	SU2A1-028267
Torin	TA300-A30473-10
Pamotor	8506D

iSBC® 608/618

Reference Manual

144261-001 — iSBC 608/618 Cardcages Hardware Reference Manual (order separately)

Manuals may be ordered from any Intel sales representative, distributor office or from Intel Literature Department, 3065 Bowers Avenue, Santa Clara, California 95051

ORDERING INFORMATION

Part Number	Description
SBC 608	Cardcage (base unit)
SBC 618	Cardcage (expansion unit for iSBC 608)

iSBC® 640
POWER SUPPLY

- ±5V and ±12V output voltage
- Sufficient power for 8-12 MULTIBUS® computer, memory, and peripheral boards
- Current limiting and overvoltage protection on all outputs
- UL Listed and CSA Certified
- "AC low" power failure TTL logic level output provided for system power-down control
- DC power cables and connectors mate directly to iSBC 604/614 and iSBC 608/618 Modular Cardcage/Backplane assemblies
- 100, 120, 220, and 240V AC operation, 50 Hz or 60 Hz input

The iSBC 640 Power Supply provides low cost, off-the-shelf, single chassis power generation for OEM and industrial system products using Intel single board computers. The iSBC 640 supply provides regulated DC output power at +12V, +5V, and −5V and −12V levels. The current capabilities of each of these output levels has been chosen to provide power over a 0°C to +55°C temperature range for one fully loaded Intel single board computer, plus residual capability for most combinations of up to eleven iSBC memory, I/O, or combination expansion boards. Current limiting and overvoltage protection is provided on all outputs. Access for AC input is provided via a standard 4-pin keyed connector. DC output power levels are provided on cables with keyed connectors directly compatible with the iSBC 604/614 and iSBC 608/618 Modular Backplane/Cardcage assemblies. The iSBC 640 supply includes logic whose purpose is to sense system AC power failure and generate a TTL signal for clean system power-down control.

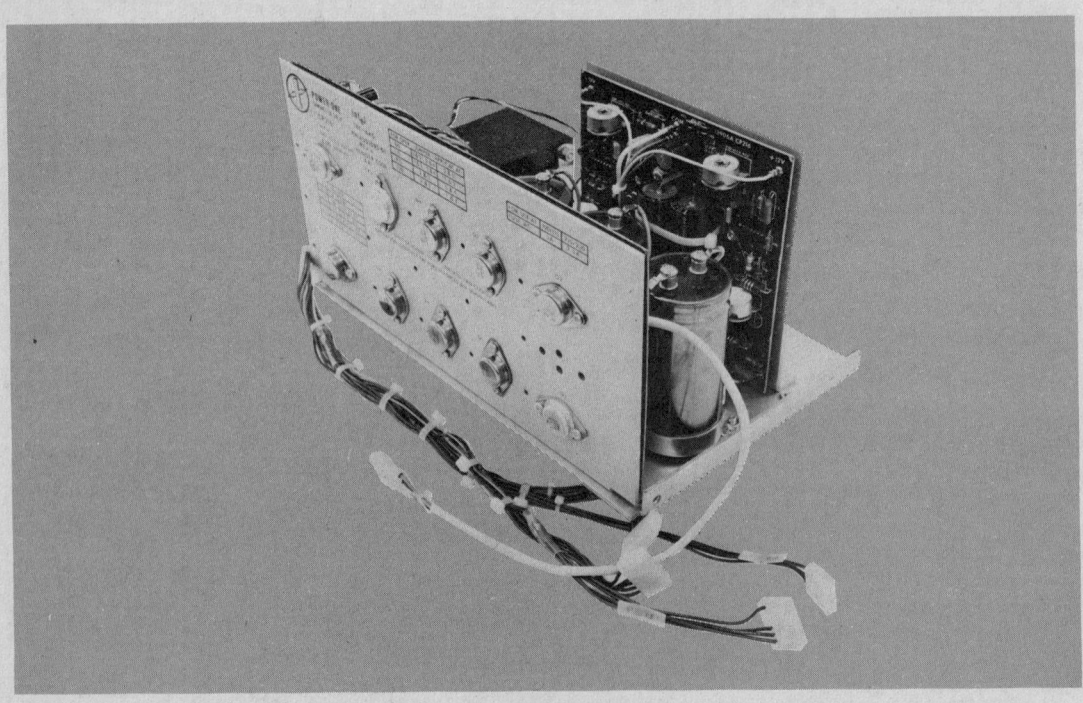

iSBC® 640

SPECIFICATIONS

Electrical Characteristics

Input Power
Frequency: 50 Hz ± 5%, 60 Hz ± 5%
Voltage: 100/120/220/240 VAC ± 10%
Via user configured wiring options

Output Power

Nominal Voltage	Current (Amps)(Max)	Current Limit Range (Amps)	Short Circuit (Amps)(Max)	Overvoltage Protection
+12V	4.5A	4.7- 6.8	2.3	15V ± 1V
+ 5V	30A	31.5-45.0	15.0	6.2V ± 0.4V
- 5V	1.75A	1.8- 3.2	0.9	-6.2V ± 0.4V
-12V	1.75A	1.8- 3.2	0.9	-15V ± 1V

Combined Line/Load Regulation — ±1% at ±10% static line change and ±50% static load change, measured at the output connector (±0.2% measured at the power supply under the same conditions).

Remote Sensing — Provided for +5 VDC output line regulation.

Output Ripple and Noise — 10 mV peak-to-peak maximum (DC to 500 KHz)

Output Transient Response — Less than 50 μsec for ±50% load change.

Output Transient Deviation — Less than ± 10% of initial voltage for ± 50% load change.

Power Failure Indication (AC Low) — A TTL open collector high signal is provided when the input voltage drops below 90% of its nominal value. DC voltages will remain within 5% of their nominal values for 3.0 milliseconds (minimum, 7.5 ms typical) after AC Low goes true.

The "AC Low" signal will reset to a TTL low level when the AC input voltage is restored and after all output voltages are within specified regulation.

The "AC Low" threshold is adjustable for optimum powerdown performance at other input combinations (i.e. 100 VAC, 220 VAC, 50 Hz).

Mating Connectors[1]

AC Input

Housing	Molex	03-09-2042 or equivalent
Pin	Molex	02-09-2118 or equivalent (18 to 22 gauge wire)

DC Output[2]

Housing	Molex	26-03-3071
	Amp	3-87025-3
Pins	Molex	08-50-0187 or 08-50-0189
	Amp	87023-1
Key	Molex	15-04-9209
	Amp	87116-2

Compatible with Molex 09-66-1071 Header

Notes
1. Pins from given vendor may only be used with connectors from the same vendor.
2. iSBC 640 DC output connectors are directly compatible with input power connectors on iSBC 604/614 and iSBC 608/618 Modular Cardcage/Backplane assemblies. Four connectors are provided.

Physical Characteristics
Height — 6.66 in. max. (16.92 cm)
Width — 8.19 in. max. (20.80 cm)
Depth — 12.65 in. max. (32.12 cm)
Weight — 30 lbs. max (13.63 kg)

Environmental Characteristics
Temperature — 0°C to 55°C with 55 CFM moving air
Non-Operating — -40°C to +85°C

Equipment Supplied
iSBC 640 Power Supply with AC and DC cables with keyed connectors.

Reference Manuals
9800803 — iSBC 640 Power Supply Hardware Reference Manual (order separately)

9800798 — iCS 80 Systems Site Planning and Installation Manual (for installation of iSBC 640 supply into iCS 80 Industrial Chassis) (Order Separately)

Manuals may be ordered from any Intel sales representative, distributor office or from Intel Literature Department, 3065 Bowers Avenue, Santa Clara, California 95051.

ORDERING INFORMATION

Part Number	Description
SBC 640	Power Supply

iSBC® 660 SYSTEM CHASSIS

- **Eight-slot cardcage and backplane for iSBC® computers and expansion boards**
- **Heavy duty power supply with all standard iSBC® voltages**
- **Compatible with all Intel single board computers**
- **Forced-air cooling**
- **Attractive, versatile pop-off front panel**
- **19-inch wide rack mountable chassis**
- **Horizontal board mounting for compactness**
- **100/120/220/240 VAC, 50/60 Hz operation**

The iSBC 660 System Chassis is an attractive, 7-inch high system chassis designed for use with Intel OEM computers. It has eight slots for single board computers, memory, I/O, or other expansion modules. The iSBC 660 is ideal for applications requiring multiple board solutions. DC power output is provided at +12V, +5V, −12V, and −5V levels. The current capabilities of each of these output levels have been chosen to provide power over a 0°C to 50°C temperature range for the majority of applications requiring combinations of computers, memories, peripherals, and other I/O capabilities. Current limiting and over-voltage protection is provided at all outputs. Standard logic recognizes a system AC power failure and generates a TTL signal for use in power-down control. For user convenience, a reset switch is provided on the front panel. The reset signal generated and sent to the system bus can be used for external system control.

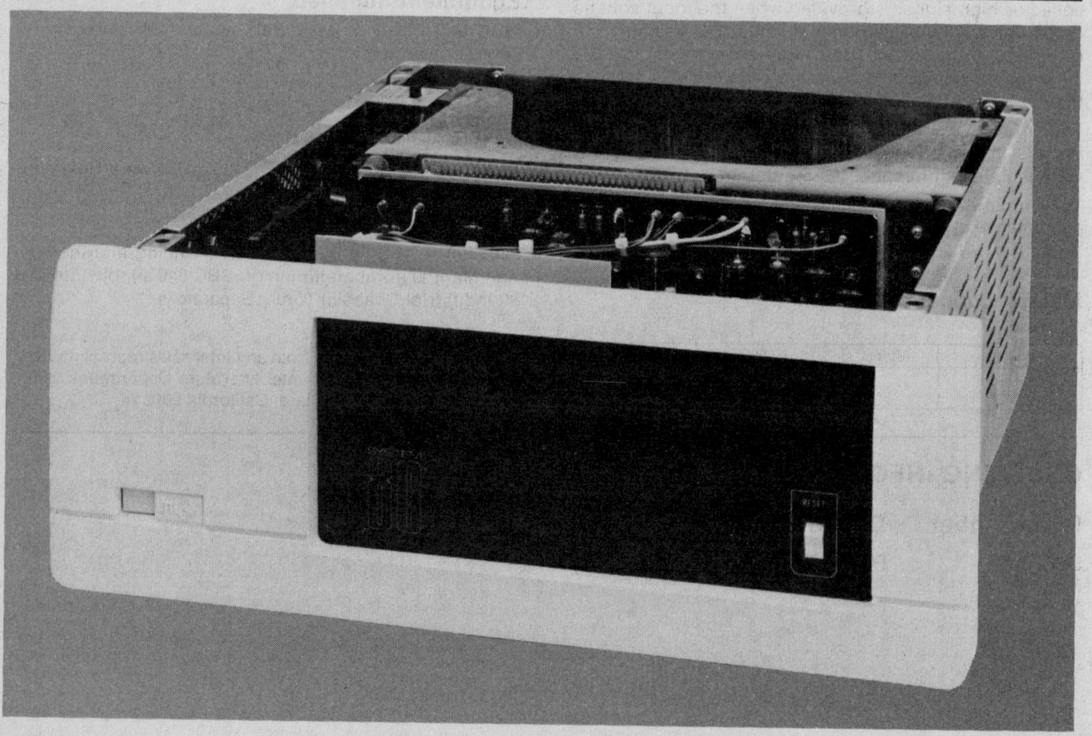

intel

iSBC® 660

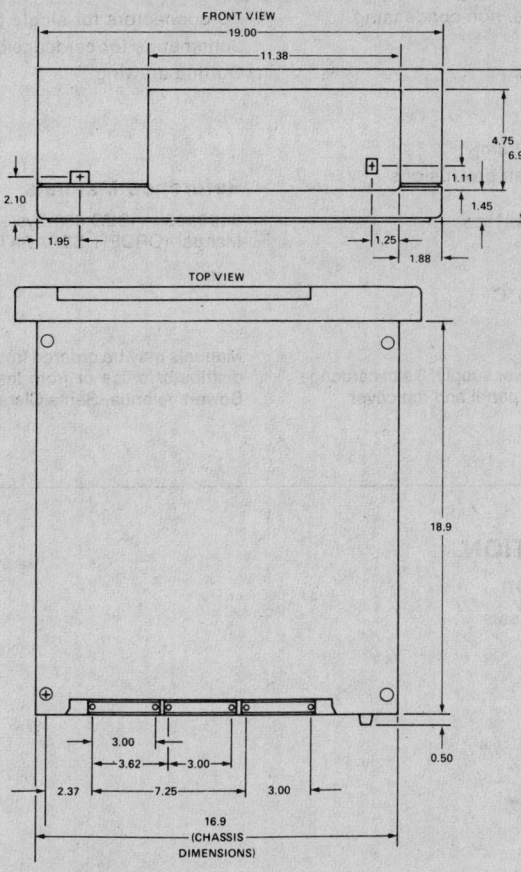

Figure 1. iSBC® System Chassis Dimensions

SPECIFICATIONS

Electrical Characteristics

Input Power

Frequency: 50 Hz ±5%, 60 Hz ±5%

Voltage: 100/120/220/240 VAC ±10% via user configured wiring options

Output Power

Power	Output Current (Max)	Current Limit (Amps)	Over-Voltage Protection
+12V	4.5A	5.4	15V ± 1V
+5V	30A	3.6	6.2V ± 0.4V
−5V	1.75A	2.1	−6.2V ± 0.4V
−12V	1.75A	2.1	−15V ± 1V

Combined Line/Load Regulation — ±1% at ±10% static line change and ±50% static load change, measured at the output connector (±0.2% measured at the power supply under the same conditions).

Remote Sensing — Provided for +5 VDC output line regulation.

Output Ripple and Noise — 10 mV peak-to-peak maximum (DC to 500 kHz).

Output Transient Response — Less than 50 μs for ±50% load change.

Output Transient Deviation — Less than ±5% of linitial voltage for ±50% load change.

Power Failure Indication (AC Low) — A TTL open collector high signal is provided when the input voltage drops below 90% of its nominal value. DC voltages will remain within 5% of their nominal values for 3.0 milliseconds (minimum) after AC low goes true.

The "AC Low" signal will reset to a TTL low level when the AC input voltage is restored and after all output voltages are within specified regulation.

The "AC Low" threshold is adjustable for optimum power-down performance at other input combinations (i.e. 100 VAC, 220 VAC, 50 Hz).

 iSBC® 660

Humidity — Up to 90% relative, non-condensing
Physical Characteristics
Height — 7 in. (17.8 cm)
Width
At Front Panel: 19 in. (48.3 cm)
Behind Front Panel: 17 in. (43.2 cm)
Depth — 20 in. (50.8 cm) with all protrusions

Environmental Characteristics
Temperature
Operating: 0°C to 50°C
Non-Operating: −40°C to +85°C

Equipment Supplied
iSBC 660 System Chassis with power supply, 8 slot cardcage assembly, dual fans, pop-off front panel and top cover

I/O connectors for single board computers
Schematics for cardcage/backplane, chassis
Outline drawing

Reference Manuals
9800505 — iSBC 660 System Chassis Hardware Reference Manual (ORDER SEPARATELY)

Manuals may be ordered from any Intel sales representative, distributor office or from Intel Literature Department, 3065 Bowers Avenue, Santa Clara, California 95051.

ORDERING INFORMATION
Part Number	Description
SBC 660	System Chassis

iSBC® 661 SYSTEM CHASSIS

- Eight-slot MULTIBUS® chassis with parallel priority circuitry
- UL, FCC and CSA approved for data processing equipment
- 230 watt power supply with power fail warning
- Designed for slide rack mounting or table-top use
- Extra-wide cardcage slot spacing for iSBX™ MULTIMODULE™ board clearance
- Configurable for front or rear access to MULTIBUS® circuit boards
- Five connector ports for I/O cabling
- Operational from 47 Hz to 63 Hz, 100/120/220/240 VAC ± 10%

The iSBC® 661 System Chassis is an advanced MULTIBUS® (IEEE) 796 chassis which incorporates unique usability and service features not found on competitive products. This chassis is designed for rack-mount or table-top applications and reliably operates up to an ambient temperature of 50°C. Additionally, this system chassis is certified by UL, CSA, and FCC for data processing equipment.

An application requiring multiprocessing will find this eight-slot MULTIBUS chassis particularly well suited to its needs. Parallel priority bus arbitration circuitry has been integrated into the backplane. This permits a bus master to reside in each slot. Extra-wide inter-slot spacing on the cardcage allows the use of plug-on MULTIMODULE™ boards without blocking adjacent slots. For this reason, the iSBC 661 System Chassis provides the slot-functionality of most 16-slot chassis. Standard logic recognizes a system AC power failure and generates a TTL signal for use in power-down control. Additionally, current limiting and over-voltage protection are provided at all outputs.

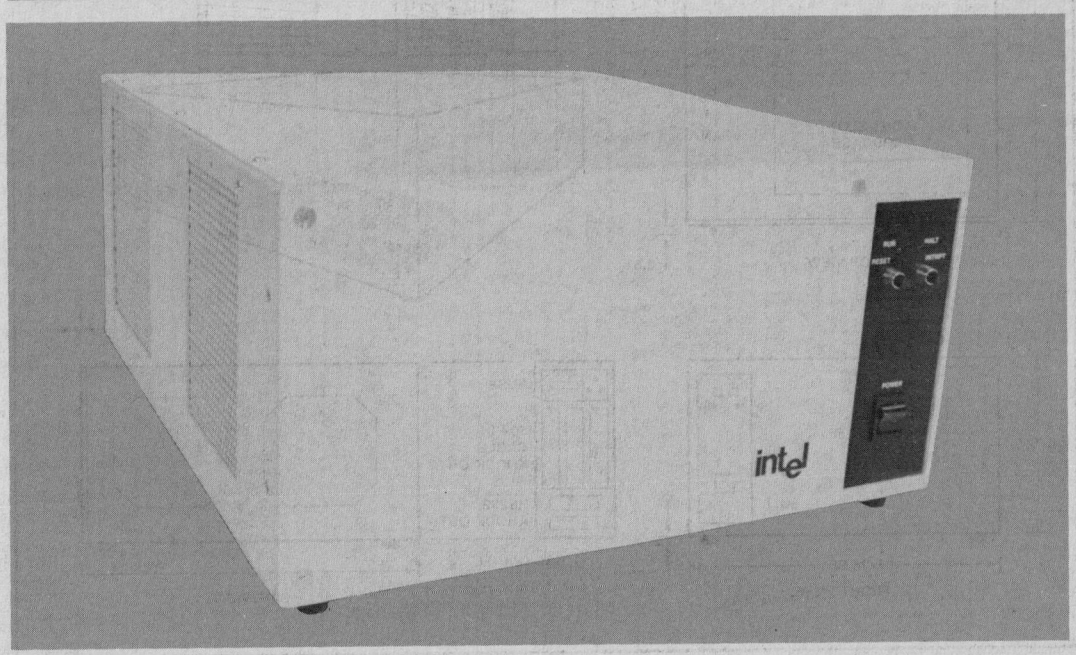

The following are trademarks of Intel Corporation and may be used only to describe Intel products: Intel, ICE, iMMX, iRMX, iSBC, iSBX, iSXM, MULTIBUS, MULTICHANNEL and MULTIMODULE. Intel Corporation assumes no responsibility for the use of any circuitry other than circuitry embodied in an Intel product. No other circuit patent licenses are implied.

© INTEL CORPORATION, 1983

OCTOBER 1984
ORDER NUMBER: 210866-002

iSBC® 661

FUNCTIONAL DESCRIPTION

Mechanical Features

The iSBC 661 System Chassis houses, cools, powers, and interconnects up to eight iSBC single board computers and their MULTIMODULE boards for the MULTIBUS System Bus. Based on Intel's iSBC 608 Cardcage, the chassis provides 0.8 inches of board center-to-center clearance on six slots, and 1.2 inches or more of center-to-center clearance on two slots. This permits the users of standard MULTIMODULE boards and custom wire-wrap boards to plug into the MULTIBUS System Bus without blocking adjacent slots. All slots provide enough clearance for iSBC MULTIMODULE boards, and two slots can accommodate iSBX MULTIMODULE boards.

High-technology MULTIBUS applications requiring rack-mount, or laboratory table-top use will find the iSBC 661 System Chassis ideal. Standard 19″ slide-rack mounting is possible with user-provided slides attached to the side panels. Slide mounting holes are provided in the chassis for the slide-rails listed under User Supplied Options. Rubber feet are included on the chassis for convenient table-top use.

The chassis is constructed of burnished aluminum which has been coated with corrosion-resistant chromate. It contains a system control module which presents the front panel control switches to the user, and holds the I/O cabling bulkhead to the rear. The chassis has the unique feature of being configurable for either front or rear access to MULTIBUS circuit boards.

This is accomplished by a simple procedure involving removal of the system control module, reversing it end-for-end, and re-securing it to the chassis. The system chassis is shipped in a configuration such that the MULTIBUS boards are installed from the front.

Electrical Features

The iSBC 661 System Chassis is powered by the iSBC 640 power supply. This is a standard Intel power supply which has been adopted by several MULTIBUS vendors throughout the industry. It supplies 230 watts of

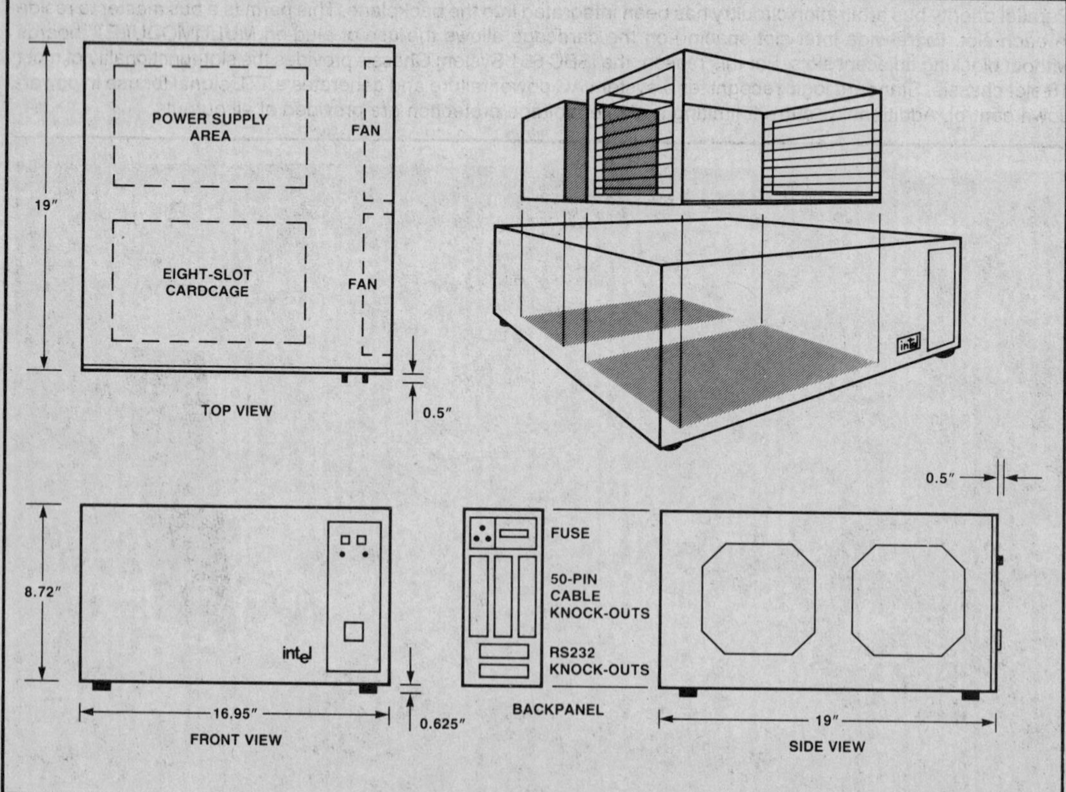

Figure 1. iSBC® 661 System Chassis Dimensions

10-18

210866-002

iSBC® 661

power, power fail warning, and remote sensing of +5 volts. Its electrical and operational parameters are listed under Specifications.

The cardcage of the iSBC 661 System Chassis implements a user-changeable parallel priority bus arbitration scheme by using plug-in jumper connections. Six different priority schemes are allowed, each scheme fixing the priority of the eight MULTIBUS board slots. Bus contention among eight bus-masters in a multiprocessing environment can be be managed using this approach.

Noise minimizing ground traces are strategically interleaved between signal and address lines on the system bus. This provides the enhanced noise immunity and minimized signal-to-signal coupling which is particularly important in high speed, high board count microcomputer systems.

SPECIFICATIONS

Electrical Parameters

OUTPUT POWER

Table 1. Output Power Levels iSBC® 661-1

Voltage	Output Current (max.)	Current Limits (amps)	Over-Voltage Protection
+12V	4.5A	4.7-6.8	15V ± 1V
+5V	30.0A	31.5-45.0	6.2V ± 0.4V
−5V	1.75A	1.8-3.2	−6.2V ± 0.4V
−12V	1.75A	1.8-3.2	−15V ± 1V

OPERATIONAL PARAMETERS

Input AC Voltage — 100/120/220/240 VAC ± 10% (User selects via external switch), 47-63 Hz

Power-Fail Indication and Hold-Up Time (triggered at 90% of VAC in) — TTL O.C. High 3 msec. (min.)

Output Ripple and Noise — 1% Peak-to-Peak output nominal (DC to 0.5 MHz)

Operational Temperature — 0°C to 50°C

Storage Temperature — −40°C to 70°C

Operational Humidity — 10% to 85% relative, non-condensing

Remote Sensing — Provided for +5 VDC

Output Transient Response — 50 μsec or less for ±50% load change

PHYSICAL CHARACTERISTICS

Width — 16.95 inches (43.05 cm)

Height — 8.72 inches (22.2 cm)

Depth — 19.00 inches (48.3 cm)

Weight — 41 pounds (21 kg)

Shipping Weight (approx.) — 50 pounds (25 kg)

Equipment Supplied

iSBC® 661-1 — Eight-slot MULTIBUS system chassis chassis with parallel priority arbitration circuitry and 230 watt linear power supply

REFERENCE MANUAL (Not included: order separately)

145340-001 — iSBC 661 System Chassis Hardware Reference Manual

Reference manual may be ordered from any Intel sales representative, distributor office or from Intel Literature Department.

In North America: Intel Corp. Literature Department
3065 Bowers Ave.
Santa Clara, California 95051
Phone: (408) 987-8080

In Europe: Intel Corp. S.A. Literature
 Department
Rue du Moulin A Papier 51
Boite 1
B-1160 Brussels, Belgium
Phone: 322-661-07-11

In the Orient: Intel Corp. Literature Department
5-6 Tokodai, Toyosato-cho
Tsukuba-gun, Ibaragi-ken 300-26
Japan
Phone: 81-29747-8591

iSBC® 661

User Supplied Options

Compatible Rack-Mount Slides — Chassis Trak, Inc., P.O. Box 39100, Indianapolis, IN 46239; Part No. C 300 S 122

ORDERING INFORMATION

Part Number	Description
SBC 6611	Eight-slot MULTIBUS system chassis with parallel priority arbitration circuitry and 230 watt Linear Power Supply

iSBC® 655 SYSTEM CHASSIS

- A rack-mountable package for Intel microcomputer system
- Provides the Intel MULTIBUS® structure used on the single board computers
- Compact single chassis power supply with all standard iSBC® board voltages
- Attractive front panel with control switches and indicator lights
- 100, 120, 220, and 240V A.C.
- 19-inch rach mountable
- Forced-air cooling

The iSBC® 665 System Chassis is an attractive 3.5" high unit designed for use in Intel Microcomputer Systems. The Chassis' four slots accommodate both single board computers and expansion boards which provide additional I/O, memory, or peripheral controller functions. The iSBC 655 System Chassis will accept all Intel boards using the MULTIBUS® architecture. DC power is provided at ±5VDC and ±12VDC levels, at current levels commensurate with typical combinations of four boards. The chassis is designed to provide adequate cooling to both power supply and circuit boards over external temperatures ranging from 0°C to 50°C. Current limiting and over-voltage protection are provided on all outputs. The power supply recognizes an AC power failure condition and provides a TTL signal sufficiently in advance of DC power failure to allow orderly system shut-down. For user convenience, system RESET and INTERRUPT switches are provided on the front panel to facilitate system restarts and provide for operator intervention. RUN and HALT LED indicators are driven to indicate the operational status of the single board computer.

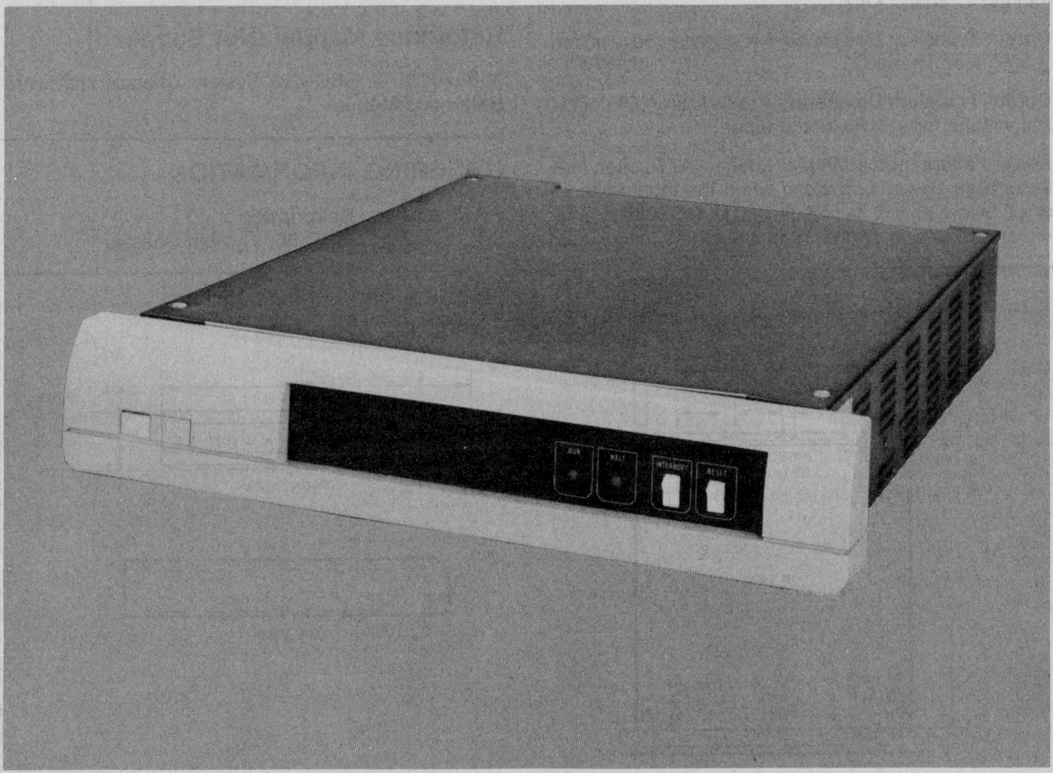

The following are trademarks of Intel Corporation and may be used only to describe Intel products: Intel, ICE, iMMX, iRMX, iSBC, iSBX, MULTIBUS, MULTICHANNEL, and MULTIMODULE. Intel Corporation assumes no responsibility for the use of any circuitry other than circuitry embodied on an Intel product. No other circuit patent licenses are implied. Information contained herein supercedes previously published specifications on these devices from Intel.

©INTEL CORPORATION, 1984

SEPTEMBER, 1984
ORDER NUMBER 280068-001

iSBC® 655

SPECIFICATIONS

Electrical

Input Power — Frequency: 47-63 Hz. Voltage (Nominal) (Single Phase): 100, 115, 215, or 230 VAC ± 10%

Output Power:

Nominal Voltage	Current (AMPS) (MAX)	Current Limit Range (AMPS)	Max Short Circuit (AMPS)	Over-Voltage Protection
+12	2.0	2.1-3.0	1.0 (Foldback)	+14 to +16 V
+5	14.0	14.7-21.0	7.0 (Foldback)	+5.8 to +6.6 V
+5	0.9	0.9-1.4	1.4	−5.8 to −6.6 V
+12	0.8	0.8-1.2	1.2	−14 to −16 V

Combined Line/Load Regulation — ±1% at ±10% static line change and ±50% static load change, measured at the output connector (±0.2% measured at the power supply under the same conditions).

Remote Sensing — Provided for +5VDC output line regulation.

Output Ripple and Noise — 10 mV peak-to-peak maximum (DC to 500 KHz)

Output Transient Response — Less than 50 μsec for ±50% load change

Output Transient Deviation — Less than ±5% of initial voltage for ±50% load change

Power Failure Indication (AC Low) — A TTL open collector high signal is provided when the input voltage drops below 90% of its nominal value. DC voltages will remain within 5% of their nominal values for 3.0 milliseconds (minimum, 7.5 ms typical) after AC LOW goes true.

Mechanical

Height — 3.5 inches (8.9 cm)

Width — 19 inches (48.3 cm) at Front Panel, 17 inches (43.2 cm) behind Front Panel

Depth — 20 inches (50.8 cm) with all protrusions

Weight — 37 pounds (17 Kg)

Cardcage — 4 board capacity at 0.6 in spacing

Environmental

Temperature — Operating: 0°C to 50°C.
Non-Operating: 40°C to 85°C

Relative Humidity — Up to 90%, non-condensing

Equipment Supplied

iSBC 655 System Chassis with power supply, cardcage/backplane, dual fans, pop-off front panel and top cover

Reference Manual (Not Supplied)

9800709A — iSBC 655 System Chassis Hardware Reference Manual

ORDERING INFORMATION

Part Number	Description
SBC 655	iSBC 655 System Chassis

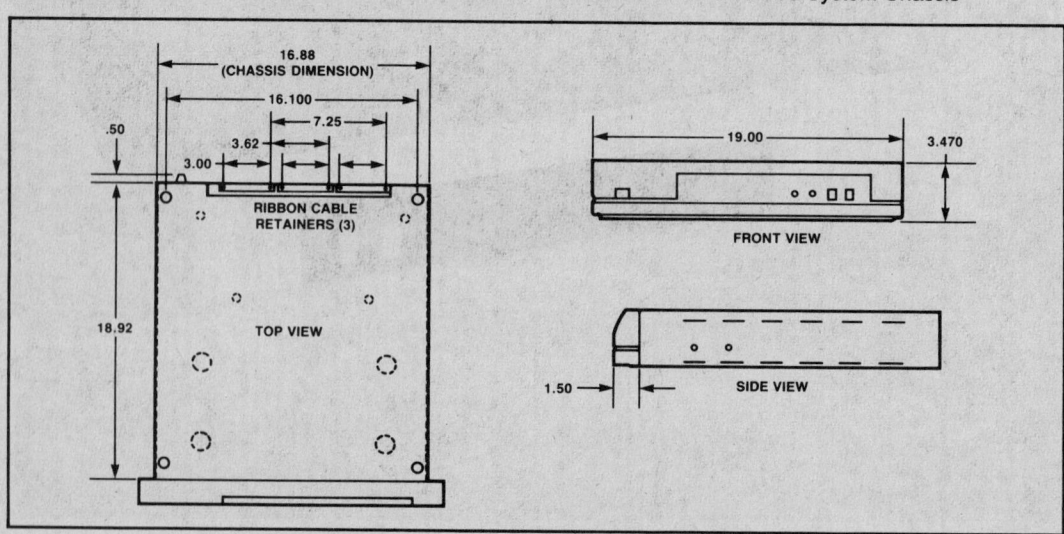

Figure 1. iSBC® 655 Dimensions (inches)

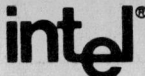

iSYP 384
SYSTEM CHASSIS

- **Fourteen-slot MULTIBUS® chassis with parallel priority circuitry and low noise/high speed backplane**
- **500 watt power supply provides 70 amps output at 5 volts**
- **Operates on 92-126 VAC, 47-63 Hz lines**
- **UL, CSA, FCC approved for data processing equipment — meets IEC-435**
- **Extra-wide cardcage slot spacing for iSBC® and iSBX™ MULTIMODULES™**
- **Fourteen connector ports for I/O cabling**

The iSYP 384 chassis is designed for the user who needs a reliable, easily configured chassis for high board count microcomputer applications. The iSYP 384 features a 14 slot cardcage, a 500 watt power supply, power cabling, system status controls and indicators, all fully integrated together in an attractively styled chassis.

The iSYP 384 chassis has many unique features which make it the best large system chassis on the market. First, the cardcage uses a parallel priority, low noise, high speed backplane. This allows the designer to install up to 7 CPU boards in the system and operate them at speeds up to 10 MB/sec. with full data integrity. Also for maximum reliability in the toughest environments, the chassis is cooled by three fans and powered by a conservatively rated, high efficiency switching power supply. Finally, the user can easily access the cardcage, power supply, I/O connectors and all chassis wiring by removing the pop-off top cover. This greatly simplifies initial system configuration, future upgrades, and field service.

Intel Corporation Assumes No Responsibility for the Use of Any Circuitry Other Than Circuitry Embodied in an Intel Product. No other Circuit Patent Licenses are implied.

©INTEL CORPORATION, 1984

iSYP 384 SYSTEM CHASSIS

FUNCTIONAL DESCRIPTION

Mechanical Features

CHASSIS

The welded aluminum chassis is lightweight, strong, and rigid. To aid servicing and board/connector installation, the front, rear, top, bottom, and side covers are all removable. The chassis may be mounted on a bench top or installed in a rack, using an optionally available rack mount kit. The rack mount kit includes a wider front trim bezel to cover the mounting rails.

CARDCAGE

The 14 slot cardcage has 11 slots at 0.8" spacing, which will accommodate MULTIBUS® boards with iSBC® MULTIMODULES™; and 3 slots at 1.2" spacing, which will accommodate either the higher profile MULTIBUS boards with iSBX MULTIMODULES or prototype (wire wrapped) boards. All boards are held firmly in place with board retainers. The assembly uses an extruded, aluminum channel construction for strength, rigidity, and to ensure a solid electrical contact between the backplane and the MULTIBUS boards. Access to the cardcage is through the top cover of the chassis (see Figure 2).

COOLING

The chassis is cooled using three 100 CFM fans. A fully loaded chassis can be operated over a temperature range of 0° to −50°C (ambient).

I/O CONNECTORS

The removable back panel has 14 connector cutouts: 3 cutouts for 50 pin "D-ribbon" style connectors; 1 cutout for a 36 pin printer connector; and 10 cutouts for 25 pin, RS-232 type connectors. Each cutout has its own cover plate. Additional space is provided on the panel for the user to punch cutouts for any other size connector (see Figure 3).

Electrical Features

CHASSIS

The chassis is designed for domestic and international applications and will operate over a wide range of input voltages. The unit has been certified to meet

Figure 2. Cardcage in the iSYP 384 Chassis

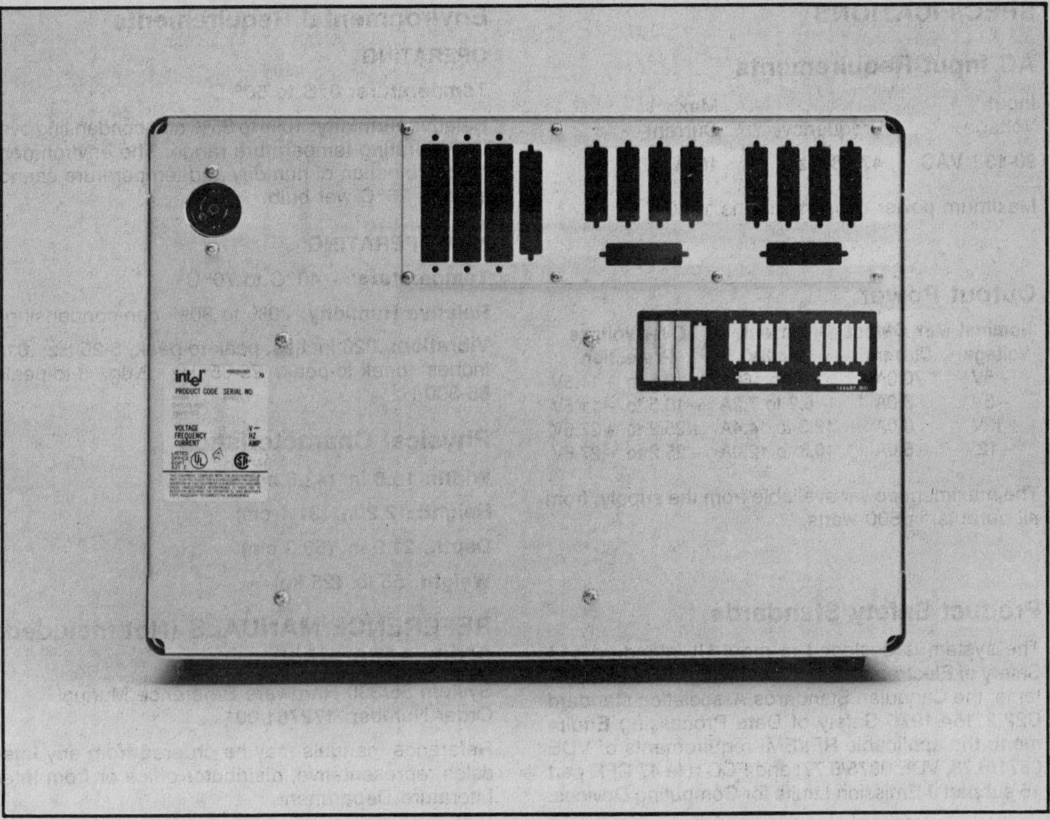

iSYP 384 SYSTEM CHASSIS

Figure 3. Back panel of the iSYP 384 Chassis

UL, CSA, and FCC requirements for data processing equipment, and has been designed to meet IEC-435 requirements. Three RFI filters, including one built into the power supply, keep conducted and radiated RFI/EMI emissions well below accepted limits. Furthermore, the filtering enables the chassis to operate reliably on the "noisy" power lines common in industrial environments.

POWER SUPPLY

The power supply is rated for 500 watts of power output, offering high current output over four DC voltages. All outputs are current limited and over-voltage protected.

A power fail circuit, incorporated in the power supply, measures the AC input voltage and generates an AC LOW signal during deep "brownout" or power fail situations. This signal, which is generated at least 10 msec before the DC voltages go out of regulation, can be used by the system software for memory protection and to execute an orderly shutdown.

CARDCAGE

The 14 slot cardcage/backplane is designed to ensure quiet operation of the bus. This is done by interleaving ground traces between all signal traces on the backplane and by providing a ground plane on the connector side of the board. The backplane uses a parallel bus arbitration scheme which allows up to 7 CPU boards to be installed in the system for multiprocessing applications. The priority of the board locations is set by jumpers on the backplane.

FRONT PANEL

On the front panel of the chassis are three LED indicators and two push button switches. The "POWER" LED monitors the +5V output and will remain on as long as both the AC input and the +5V output from the power supply are within limits. The RESET and INTERRUPT push button switches generate RESET/ and INT1/ signals on the MULTIBUS when depressed. The "RUN" LED (green) is on when the CPU is executing an instruction, and the "HALT" LED (red) is on whenever the processor executes a HALT instruction.

iSYP 384 SYSTEM CHASSIS

SPECIFICATIONS

AC Input Requirements

Input Voltage	Frequency	Max Current
90-132 VAC	47-63 Hz	10 A

Maximum power consumption is 1250W.

Output Power

Nominal Voltage	Max Output Current	Current Limits	Over-Voltage Protection
+5V	70.0A	143 to 168A	+10.5 to +11.5V
−5V	3.0A	6.2 to 7.2A	−10.5 to −11.5V
+12V	6.0A	12.3 to 14.4A	+25.2 to +27.6V
−12	5.0A	10.3 to 12.0A	−25.2 to −27.6V

The maximum power available from the supply, from all outputs, is 500 watts.

Product Safety Standards

The system is designed to meet UL standard 114 Safety of Electronics Data Processing Units and Systems; the Canadian Standards Association standard C22.2 154-1975 Safety of Data Processing Equipment; the applicable RFI/EMI requirements of VDE 0871/6.78, VDE 0875/6.77; and FCC rule 47 CFR part 15 subpart J Emission Limits for Computing Devices.

Environmental Requirements

OPERATING

Temperature: 0°C to 50° C

Relative Humidity: 10% to 85% non-condensing over the operating temperature range. The environmental combination of humdity and temperature cannot exceed 26°C wet bulb.

NON-OPERATING

Temperature: −40°C to 70°C

Relative Humidity: 20% to 80% non-condensing

Vibration: .020 inches, peak-to-peak, 5-25 Hz; .010 inches, peak-to-peak, 25-65 Hz; 2.0g, 0-to-peak, 65-300 Hz

Physical Characteristics

Width: 16.8 in. (42.6 cm)
Height: 12.2 in. (31.1 cm)
Depth: 21.0 in. (53.3 cm)
Weight: 55 lb. (25 kg)

REFERENCE MANUALS (Not included: order separately)

System 86/380 Hardware Reference Manual
Order Number: 172761-001

Reference manuals may be ordered from any Intel sales representative, distributor office or from Intel Literature Department.

ORDERING INFORMATION

ORDER CODE

iSYP 384-7

DESCRIPTION

Fourteen-slot MULTIBUS system chassis with parallel priority bus arbitration circuitry and 500 watt switching power supply, 90-132 VAC, 47-63 Hz

BITBUS™ Architecture   11

INTRODUCTION TO THE DISTRIBUTED CONTROL MODULES

Overview

Intel's Distributed Control Module (iDCM) products provide building blocks for construction of real-time distributed control systems based on the BITBUS™ interconnect. This new serial bus architecture addresses many of the limitations inherent in traditional connection methods. For instance, future system cost reductions are limited in systems based on parallel bus structures due to their electrical and mechanical characteristics. Other traditional connection methods such as current loops and RS 232 C do not provide sufficient performance or flexibility for complex industrial control applications. In addition, although there are numerous industry standards for connecting microprocessors, the MULTIBUS® and the STD-bus for example, there is no standard connection for microcontrollers. The BITBUS interconnect (Table 1) combines existing standards with new standard interfaces to provide the optimal solution for difficult distributed control problems.

The iDCM products combine hardware and software for use in applications that would benefit most from employing distributed architectures. Applications such as robotics, process control, data acquisition and control, and environmental control are a few examples.

Table 1. Standard BITBUS™ Interfaces

Interface	Specification
Electrical	RS485
Cable	10-conductor flat ribbon or 1 to 2 wire twisted pair
Back-plane connector	64-pin Standard DIN
End-cable connector	3M #3446-1302 female
Control-board form-factor	Single-height, Double-depth Eurocard
Data Link control	Synchronous Data-link Control
Data transfer rate	62.5K baud, 375K baud and 2.4M baud
Message formats	Compatible with iDCX format command/response/status
Common command sequences	Integral Remote Access and Control (RAC) function
Operating systems	S/W drivers for iRMX 86, 88, 286R and ISIS (for iPDS only)

Benefits of Distributed Architectures

Distributed architectures are intrinsically more reliable than centralized architectures. In a centralized control system a central controller failure results in a system-wide failure. Distributed systems can be configured to prevent this. Also, distributed systems are more cost effective and more easily modified. For instance, performance improvements in centralized systems are expensive and do not concentrate improvements in the areas where they are needed most. In distributed systems, only the specific parts of the system that require enhancement need be modified. Most importantly, control systems based on distributed architectures have less difficulty responding to the external environment because they have less to manage.

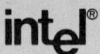

iDCM Introduction

The BITBUS™ Interconnect

The BITBUS interconnect is a serial bus optimized for high speed transfer of short control messages in a hierarchical system. In order to provide an easy to use high performance serial interconnect, transparent to the applications programmer, high-level interfaces are specified. These interfaces include: the message structure and protocol for a multitasking environment, and a set of high-level commands for remote I/O access and application task control. As with traditional bus specifications, the electrical and data protocol levels have been defined.

The BITBUS interconnect supports up to 250 nodes and three bit rates dependent on application performance requirements. Different BITBUS segments may support different bit rates.

A Simple and Reliable Solution

The BITBUS architecture supplies the system designer with a simple and reliable foundation. Some key features of this architecture are: defined high-level interfaces that provide all communication and user program management, the reliable SDLC protocol, power-up diagnostics, standard industrial packaging, compact software and hardware provided in the high performance 12MHz 8044 microcontroller, and a board-level integrated solution. In addition, complex, expensive, and awkward connection problems are no longer a factor because the BITBUS interconnect is a serial bus requiring a simple twisted wire pair.

Open Systems — An Answer to Obsolescence

Intel's Open Systems philosophy requires systems be open to: future VLSI, all levels of integration, third party suppliers, and special requirements. In order to facilitate this design strategy, the BITBUS interconnect was developed as a standard microcontroller interface. The same benefits realized by users of Intel's MULTIBUS architecture will be realized by users of the BITBUS architecture — the ability to exploit VLSI technology without having to pay premiums for new system design, multiple supply sources, wide product selections, and competitive prices.

The Open Systems philosophy characterizes the iDCM product line. Distributed Control Modules are compatible (open) at three levels of integration: components, boards, and systems. This multilevel approach enables OEM's to adapt to new business environments and opportunities as VLSI technology evolves.

Distributed Control Modules

The iDCM product line consists of both software and hardware products: the iDCX 51 Executive, iRMX 510 Support Package, BITBUS Toolbox Software, iSBX™ 344 BITBUS MULTIMODULE™ Board, the iRCB 44/10 Digital I/O Controller Board, and the iRCB 44/20 Analog I/O Controller Board, and all iDCM hardware products include integral firmware to implement the high-level BITBUS interfaces: message formats, command sequences, and operating system environments.

iDCX™ 51 Executive

The iDCX 51 Executive is a compact, easy to use, software tool for development and implementation of applications built on the high performance 8-bit family of 8051 microcontrollers. A pre-configured version of the Executive is included in firmware of the iDCM hardware products. During run-time, some of the services provided by this event driven Executive are: task scheduling, interrupt handling, and message passing. Streamlined code, the simpler user interface and modular design of the iDCX 51 Executive enhance system reliability.

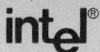 iDCM Introduction

iRMX™ 510 iDCM Support Package and BITBUS Toolbox Software

The iRMX 510 iDCM Support Package provides the software development and run-time support for BITBUS systems. Also included are the software interfaces for other operating systems: iRMX 86, iRMX 286R, iRMX 88, and the iPDS ISIS. These software interfaces ease integration of a BITBUS system into MULTIBUS or iPDS environments. The BITBUS Toolbox Software includes an interactive BITBUS monitor and high performance interfaces to: iRMX 86, 286, DOS 3.0, and ISIS operating systems.

iSBX™ 344 BITBUS™ Intelligent MULTIMODULE™ Board

The iSBX 344 board facilitates expansion of MULTIBUS and iPDS systems via the BITBUS interconnect. This board is the iDCM hardware interface. MULTIBUS system capabilities can be expanded to include low-cost remote control using the iSBX 344 MULTIMODULE board and the iRMX 510 iDCM Support Package. Also, BITBUS system capabilities can be expanded using this board with user supplied software. The iSBX 344 board's integral firmware reduces application development time, ensures real time response, eases system integration, and lowers system cost.

iRCB 44/10 BITBUS™ Digital I/O Remote Controller Board

The iRCB 44/10 BITBUS Remote Controller module is a low-end, single-board computer with 24 lines of parallel I/O. The board has a single-high Eurocard form factor with a DIN connector for increased reliablity and integration with standard industrial packaging. One iSBX I/O Expansion connector will accommodate one of many iSBX MULTIMODULE Boards for I/O expansion. Also, sockets for repeaters are provided for extending the BITBUS interconnect beyond the length limits of one BITBUS segment. This board lowers distributed system cost via the BITBUS interconnect support and the same integral firmware provided on the iSBX 344 BITBUS Controller MULTIMODULE board.

iRCB 44/20 BITBUS™ Analog I/O Remote Controller Board

For controlling real-time Analog I/O, the iRCB 44/20 Controller is an ideal solution. Capable of receiving 16 single-ended, or 8 differential inputs, the iRCB 44/20 can also manage two analog output channels. An 8-bit iSBX I/O expansion connector can support many different modules. In particular, the iSBX 311 would double the analog input capability, while the iSBX 328 provides 8 more analog outputs. Programmable gain allows modification on the fly, 12-bit resolution assures accuracy.

Expanding a MULTIBUS® System with Distributed Control Modules

An example of how a MULTIBUS system can be expanded with iDCM Modules is shown in Figures 1 and 2. Figure 1 shows a basic MULTIBUS system: processor board, memory module, and I/O controller. Figure 2 illustrates the expanded system. Some advantages of the expanded system follow: The burden on the central processor has been reduced, thereby increasing overall system performance. System cost reduction is realized because the BITBUS architecture removes the necessity of adding expensive centralized systems to handle increased performance demands. Also, the BITBUS architecture enables implementation of a more efficient and flexible system that is insensitive to the addition of more nodes, or changes in node job functions.

iDCM Introduction

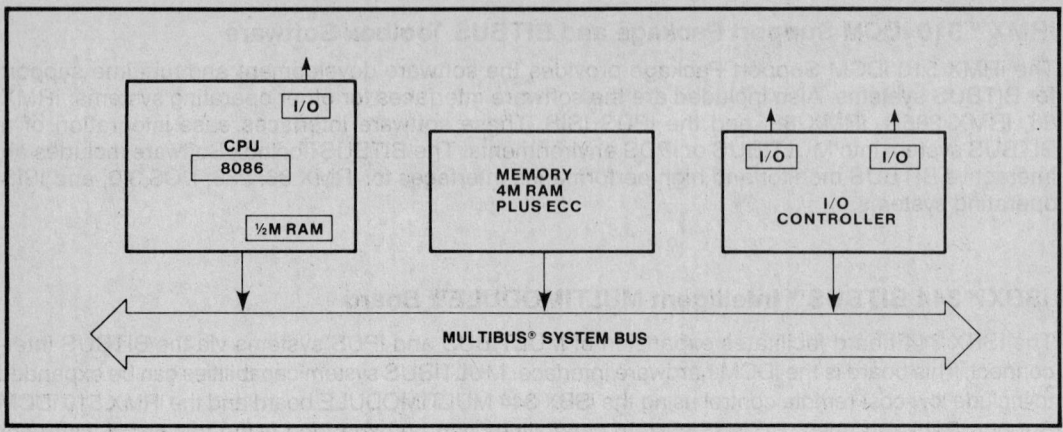

Figure 1. Basic MULTIBUS® System

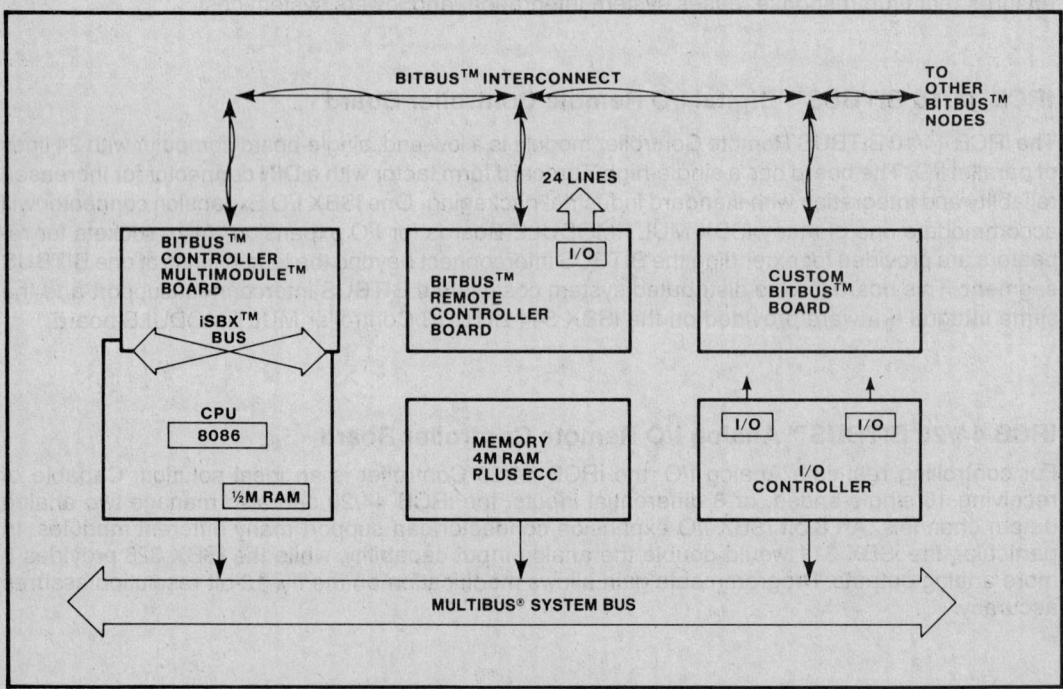

Figure 2. MULTIBUS® System Expanded with BITBUS™ Interconnect and Distributed Control Modules

Summary

This overview has introduced the attributes and advantages of the BITBUS Interconnect and Distributed Control Modules. These core iDCM products (the iDCM 51 Executive, the iRMX 510 iDCM Support Package, iSBX 344 BITBUS Controller MULTIMODULE and iRCB 44/10 BITBUS Remote Controller boards) are intended to allow rapid assimilation of this new technology. Data sheets describing the individual iDCM products are included in the next section of this document. The final section presents the BITBUS Specification (supported by the iDCM products).

8044 BITBUS™ Enhanced Microcontroller

- **8044 Dual Processor Microcontroller with High Performance 8-Bit CPU for Real-Time Control**

- **Extends Distributed Control Capabilities via Embedded Parallel Communications Firmware**

- **BITBUS™ Firmware Simplifies Design of of Real-Time Distributed Control Systems**

- **Increased Reliability with Single Chip Distributed Controller Solution and Power-Up Diagnostics**

- **Powerful Multitasking Capability with the iRMX™ 51 Executive and 8051 CPU Core**

The 8044 BITBUS Enhanced Microcontroller (BEM) is an 8044 microcontroller with on-chip firmware. The dual processor architecture of the 8044 combined with the on-chip firmware supply the processing power of an 8051 CPU as well as a superset of the features required for complete BITBUS compatibility. The firmware includes facilities for: diagnostics, task management, message passing, and user-transparent parallel and serial communication services. Figure 1 is a block diagram of the BEM component.

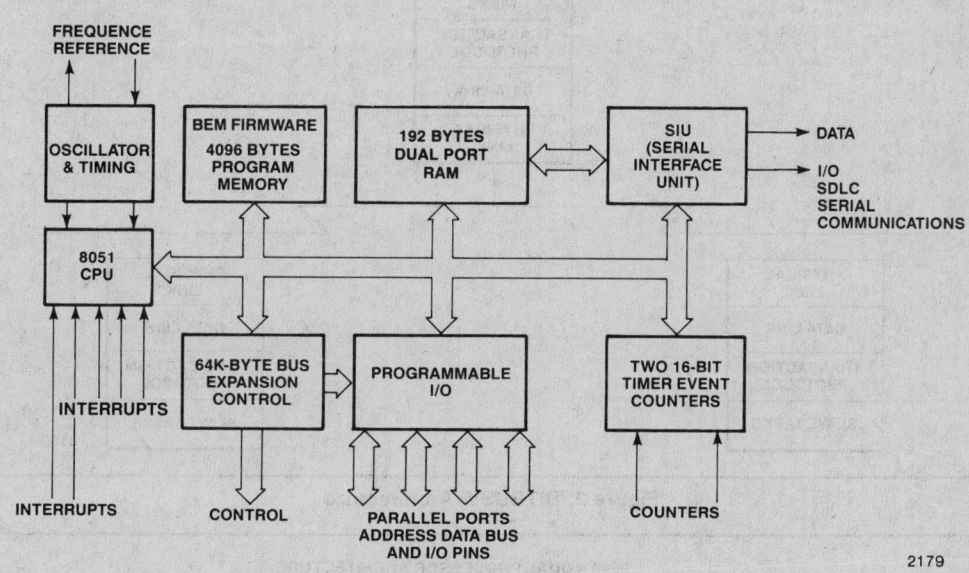

Figure 1. BEM Block Diagram

Intel Corporation assumes no responsibility for the use of any circuitry other than circuitry embodied in an Intel product. No other circuit patent licenses are implied. Information contained herein supersedes previously published specifications on these devices from Intel.

© INTEL CORPORATION, 1985

APRIL, 1985
ORDER NUMBER: 280129-001

8044 BITBUS™ Enhanced Microcontroller

OPERATING ENVIRONMENT

Introduction

The BITBUS™ Interconnect Serial Control Bus Specification defines an integrated architecture optimized for implementing real-time distributed control systems. The architecture includes a message structure and protocol for multitasking environments, and a pre-defined interface for I/O access and control. As with traditional bus specifications the mechanical, electrical, and data protocols have been defined. Over a twisted pair of wires the bus can support up to 250 nodes at three different bit rates dependent on application performance requirements. Figure 2 illustrates the BITBUS Interconnect architecture.

The 8044 BITBUS Enhanced Microcontroller (BEM) or DCM Controller provides the user with the smallest BITBUS building block – a BITBUS component solution. With its dual processor architecture, this unique single chip provides both communication and computational engines (Figure 3). Real-time control and computational power are provided by the on-chip 8-bit 8051 CPU. The Serial Interface Unit (SIU) executes a majority of the communications functions in hardware resulting in a high performance solution for distributed control applications where communication and processing power are equally important. The BEM's firmware implements the BITBUS message structure and protocol, and the pre-defined I/O command set.

Firmware

The 8044 microcontroller requires specific hardware to interface to BITBUS. The BEM's firmware also requires a particular hardware environment in order to execute correctly, just as the iRMX 86 Operating System or other operating systems require a specific hardware environment, ie. interrupt controller, timers, etc. Based upon the hardware provided, Basic or Extended firmware environments result.

The Basic firmware environment supports the minimum configuration for the BEM to execute as a BITBUS device. The Extended firmware environment requires hardware incremental to the Basic environ-

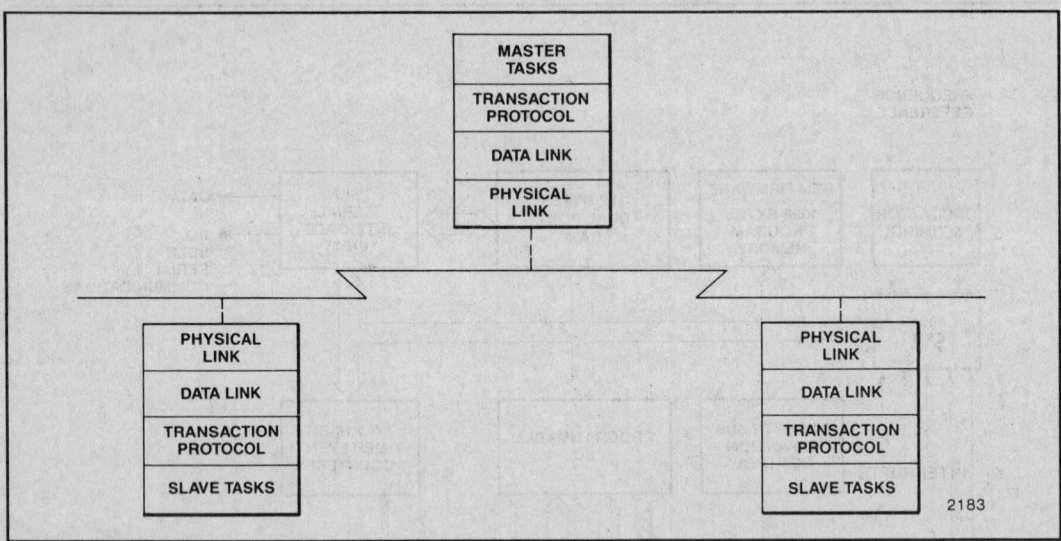

Figure 2. BITBUS™ Architecture

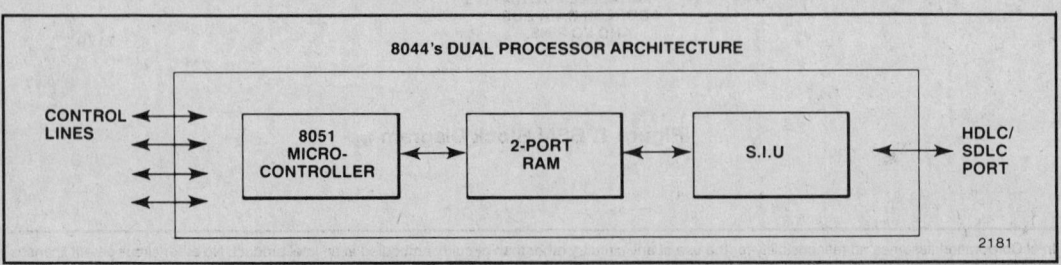

Figure 3. 8044's Dual Processor Architecture

8044 BITBUS™ Enhanced Microcontroller

ment and allows the user to take full advantage of all the features included in the BEM's firmware. The designer may implement the Basic or Extended firmware environment as desired as long as the programmatic requirements of the firmware are met (see below).

Figure 4 shows one example of an Extended firmware environment. This particular example represents the BITBUS Core as used on Intel's iSBX™ 344 BITBUS Controller MULTIMODULE™ Board and iRCB 44/10 BITBUS Remote Controller Board.

BASIC FIRMWARE ENVIRONMENT	
Memory bus	Parallel ports of 8044
BITBUS Node Address	0FFFFH external data space
Configuration	0FFFEH external data space
System RAM	0-02FFH external data space
Diagnostic LED #1	Port 1.0 (Pin 1)
Diagnostic LED #2	Port 1.1 (Pin 2)
EXTENDED FIRMWARE ENVIRONMENT	
Memory bus	Parallel ports of 8044
BITBUS Node Address	0FFFFH external data space
Configuration	0FFFEH external data space
System RAM	0-02FFH external data space
Diagnostic LED #1	Port 1.0 (Pin 1)
Diagnostic LED #2	Port 1.1 (Pin 2)
User Task Interface	First Task Descriptor – 0FFF0H to 0FFFFH in External data space Other Task Descriptors and User Code – 01000H to 0FFEFH in external code space
User RAM Availability	On-Chip – 02AH to 02FH bit space Off-Chip – BITBUS Master: 0400H to 0FFEFH external data space BITBUS Slave: 0100H to 0FFEFH external data space
Remote Access and Control Interface	Memory-Mapped I/O – 0FF00H to 0FFFFH external data space
Parallel Interface to Extension Device	Fifo Command Byte – 0FF01H external data space Fifo Data Byte – 0FF00H external data space Receive Data Intr – INT0 (pin 12) Transmit Data Intr – INT1 (pin 13) Command/Data Bit – P1.2

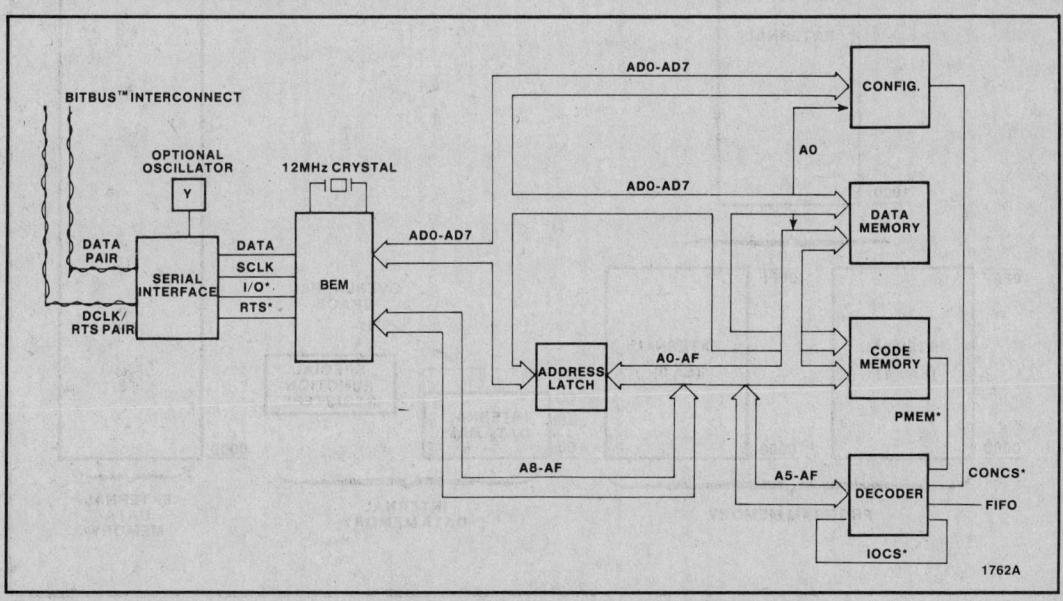

Figure 4. Extended Firmware Environment Example

8044 BITBUS™ Enhanced Microcontroller

FUNCTIONAL DESCRIPTION

High Performance 8044 Microcontroller

The 8044 combines the powerful 8051 microcontroller with an intelligent serial communications controller to provide a single-chip solution that efficiently implements distributed processing or distributed control systems. The microcontroller is a self-sufficient unit containing ROM, RAM, ALU, and peripherals. The 8044's architecture and instruction set are identical to the 8051's. The serial interface of the 8051 is replaced with an intelligent communications processor, the Serial Interface Unit (SIU), on the 8044. This unique dual processor architecture results in high performance and reliability for distributed control and processing environments. The intelligent SIU offloads the CPU from communication tasks, thus dedicating more of its compute power to external processes.

Major features of the 8051 microcontroller are:

- 8-bit CPU
- On-chip oscillator
- 4K bytes of RAM
- 192 bytes of ROM
- 32 I/O lines
- 64K address space external data memory
- 64K address space external program memory
- Two Programmable 16-bit counters
- Five source interrupt structure with two priority levels
- Bit addressability for Boolean functions
- 1 usec instruction cycle time for 60% instructions
  2 usec instruction cycle time for 40% instructions
- 4 usec cycle time for 8 by 8 unsigned multiple and divide

As noted in the Operating Environment discussion, the BITBUS firmware requires various CPU resources, ie. memory, timers, and I/O dependent upon the firmware environment selected.

Memory Architecture

The 8044 microcontroller maintains separate data and code memory spaces. Internal data memory and program memory reside on the controller. External memory resides outside the controller. The BEM firmware uses the available internal code memory space and most of the remaining internal data memory with the exception of bit space 02AH to 02FH. Figure 5 shows the BEM's memory map.

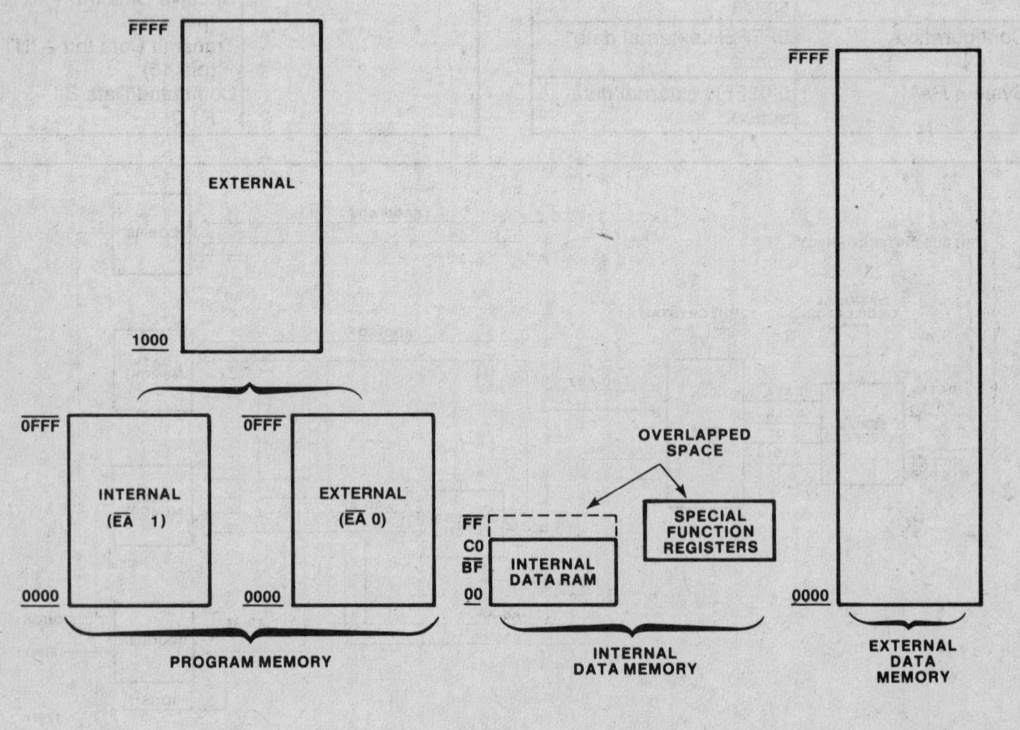

Figure 5. BEM Memory Map

8044 BITBUS™ Enhanced Microcontroller

I/O ADDRESSING REQUIREMENTS

The table below provides the BEM's I/O port addresses.

Table 1. BEM I/O Addressing

Function	Address	Bit	Byte
Red LED P1.0	90H	X	
Green LED P1.1	91H	X	
TCMD	92H	X	
RFNF#	B3H	X	
TFNF #	B2H	X	
RDY/NE*	B4H	X	
Node Address	FFFFH		X
Configuration	FFFEH		X
Reserved	FFE0H-FFFDH		X
Digital I/O	FFC0H-FFDFH		X
SBX #4	FFB0H-FFBFH		X
SBX #3	FFB0H-FFAFH		X
SBX #2	FF90H-FF9FH		X
SBX #1	FF80H-FF8FH		X
User Defined	FF40H-FF7FH		X
Reserved	FF02H-FF3FH		X
FIFO Command	FF01H		X
FIFO Data	FF00H		X

SIGNAL FUNCTIONS

The 8044 BEM's pin configuration and pin description follow.

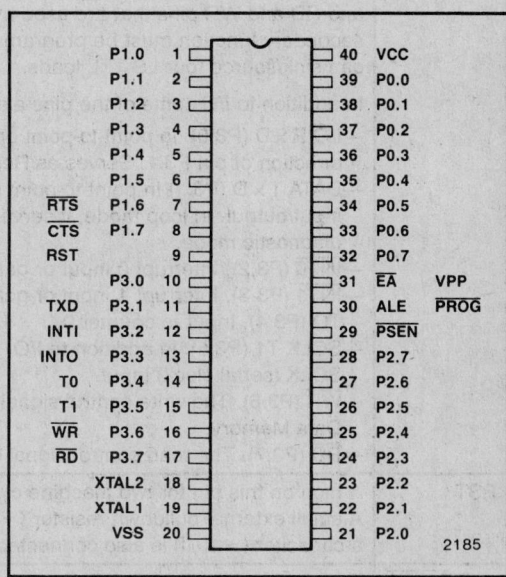

Figure 6. BEM Pin Configuration

Table 2. BEM Pin Description

Name	Description
VSS	Circuit ground potential.
VCC	+5V power supply during operation and program verification.
PORT 0	Port 0 is an 8-bit open drain bidirectional I/O port. It is also the multiplexed low-order address and data bus when using external memory. It is used for data output during program verification. Port 0 can sink/source eight LS TTL loads.
PORT 1	Port 1 is an 8-bit quasi-bidirectional I/O port. It is used for the low-order address byte during program verification. Port 1 can sink/source four LS TTL loads. In non-loop mode two of the I/O lines serve alternate functions: —$\overline{RTS}$ (P1.6) Request-to-Send output. A low indicates that the 8044 is ready to transmit. —$\overline{CTS}$ (P1.7) Clear-to-Send input. A low indicates that a receiving station is ready to receive.
PORT 2	Port 2 is an 8-bit quasi-bidirection I/O port. It also emits the high-order address byte when accessing external memory. It is used for the high-order address and the control signals during program verification. Port 2 can sink/source four LS TTL loads.

8044 BITBUS™ Enhanced Microcontroller

Table 2. BEM Pin Description (Con't.)

Name	Description
PORT 3	Port 3 is an 8-bit quasi-bidirectional I/O port. It also contains the interrupt, timer, serial port and RD and WR pins that are used by various options. The output latch corresponding to a secondary function must be programmed to a one (1) for that function to operate. Port 3 can sink/source four LS TTL loads. In addition to I/O some of the pins also serve alternate functions as follows: —I/$\overline{O}$ R x D (P3.0). In point-to-point or multipoint configurations, this pin controls the direction of pin P3.1. Serves as Receive Data input in loop and diagnostic modes. —DATA T x D (P3.1) In point-to-point or multipoint configurations, this pin functions as data input/output. In loop mode, it serves as transmit pin. A '0' written to this pin enables diagnostic mode. —$\overline{INT0}$ (P3.2). Interrupt 0 input or gate control input for counter 0. —$\overline{INT1}$ (P3.3). Interrupt 1 input or gate control input for counter 1. —T0 (P3.4). Input to counter 0. —SCLK T1 (P3.5). In addition to I/O, this pin provides input to counter 1 or serves as SCLK (serial clock) input. —$\overline{WR}$ (P3.6). The write control signal latches the data byte from Port 0 into the External Data Memory. —$\overline{RD}$ (P3.7). The read control signal enables External Data Memory to Port 0.
RST	A high on this pin for two machine cycles while the oscillator is running resets the device. A small external pulldown resistor ($\approx 8.2 K\Omega$) from RST to V_{SS} permits power-on reset when a capacitor ($\approx 10 \mu f$) is also connected from this pin to V_{CC}.
ALE/$\overline{PROG}$	Provides Address Latch Enable output used for latching the address into external memory during normal operation. It is activated every six oscillator periods except during an external data memory access. It also receives the program pulse input for programming the EPROM version.
$\overline{PSEN}$	The Program Store Enable output is a control signal that enables the external Program Memory to the bus during external fetch operations. It is activated every six oscillator periods, except during external data memory accesses. Remains high during internal program execution.
$\overline{EA}$/VPP	When held at a TTL high level, the 8044 executes instructions from the internal ROM when the PC is less than 4096. When held at a TTL low level, the 8044 fetches all instructions from external Program Memory. The pin also receives the 21V EPROM programming supply voltage on the 8744.
XTAL 1	Input to the oscillator's high gain amplifier. Required when a crystal is used. Connect to VSS when external source is used on XTAL 2.
XTAL 2	Output from the oscillator's amplifier. Input to the internal timing circuitry. A crystal or external source can be used.

Firmware

The BEM's Basic firmware environment provides two services: BITBUS Communications and Power-Up Diagnostics. The Extended firmware environment provides the Basic firmware services plus Parallel Communications and User Software Services (iRMX 51 Executive, Remote Access and Control functions). A discussion of each service follows.

Basic Firmware Services

POWER-UP DIAGNOSTICS INCREASE RELIABILITY

For added reliability and simplified system start up, the BEM firmware includes power-up diagnostics. At chip reset the BEM diagnostic firmware checks the integrity of the 8044's instruction set, ROM, internal RAM, and

external RAM. LED indicator lights may be used to show the progress of the diagnostics. Intel's BITBUS boards use one red LED, and one green LED as indicators for test progress. Since the test halts if a fault is found, the last LED state indicates the trouble area.

No programmatic interface exists for the power-up diagnostics. Only LEDs (or other indicators) connected to the outputs of Port 1 of the 8044 are required. For the test sequence shown in Table 3, the red LED is connected to pin P1.0, and the green LED is connected to pin P1.1.

Table 3. Power-Up Test Sequence

Test Sequence	State of Port* After Test Completion	
	Red LED (Pin 1.0)	Green LED (Pin 1.1)
Power-on	On	On
Prior to Start of Tests	Off	Off
Test 1 – Instruction Set	On	On
Test 2 – ROM Checksum Test	On	Off
Test 3 – Internal RAM	Off	Off
Test 4 – External RAM	Off	On

*Ports are Active Low.

BITBUS™ INTERFACE SIMPLIFIES DESIGN OF DISTRIBUTED CONTROL SYSTEMS

The BITBUS Serial Control Bus is a serial bus optimized for high speed transfer of short messages in a hierarchical system. From the perspective of systems using the BITBUS bus there are three external protocols that must be adhered to: physical, data link, and transaction control as shown in Figure 2. The physical interface includes all bus hardware requirements, e.g. cable and connector definition, transceiver specification. The data link interface refers to the device to device transfer of frames on the bus. The transaction control interface identifies the rules for transmitting messages on the bus as well as the format of the messages passed.

For maximum reliability and to facilitate standardization the following existing standards were chosen as portions of the BITBUS Specification: International Electrotechnical Commission (IEC) mechanical board and connector specifications, the Electronic Industry Association (EIA) RS-485 Electrical Specification and IBM*'s Serial Data Link Control protocol for the physical and data link levels of the BITBUS interface.

*IBM is a trademark of International Business Machines Corporation.

BITBUS™ Physical Interface

Implementation of the electrical interface to BITBUS requires external hardware. Specifically, an EIA Standard RS-485 driver and transceiver and an optional clock source for the synchronous mode of operation. A self clocked mode of operation is also available. Different modes of operation facilitate a variety of performance/distance options as noted in Table 4. Figure 7 illustrates the BEM's BITBUS interface hardware requirements.

Table 4. BITBUS™ Interconnect Modes of Operation

	Speed Kb/s	Max. Dist Between Repeaters M/ft	Max # Nodes Between Repeaters	Max # Repeaters
Synchronous	2400	30/100	28	0
Self-Clocked	375	300/1000	28	2
	62.5	1200/4000	28	10

BITBUS™ Data Link Service

The 8044's serial interface unit (SIU) implements a majority of the data link interface, a subset of IBM's Serial Data Link Protocol (SDLC), in hardware resulting in a significant performance advantage compared with multichip solutions. Multichip solutions require both hardware and software glue that degrade performance, decrease reliability, and increase cost. This portion of the BITBUS interface requires no user involvement for execution.

For a detailed discussion of the protocol executed by the BITBUS data link service refer to "The BITBUS Interconnect Serial Control Bus Specification". A basic subset of SDLC with the REJECT option is implemented. The standard frame format transferred across the BITBUS is shown in Figure 8. The information field carries the BITBUS message.

BITBUS™ Transaction Control Service

For added reliability, the BITBUS interface incorporates error checking at the message level in addition to the imbedded error checking provided by SDLC at the data link level. The message control interface defines the format and function of messages transmitted in frames across the BITBUS bus. (Figure 9)

The transaction protocol requires that for every order message transmitted across the bus a reply message must be transmitted in return. Error types and error detection mechanisms are also designated by this interface.

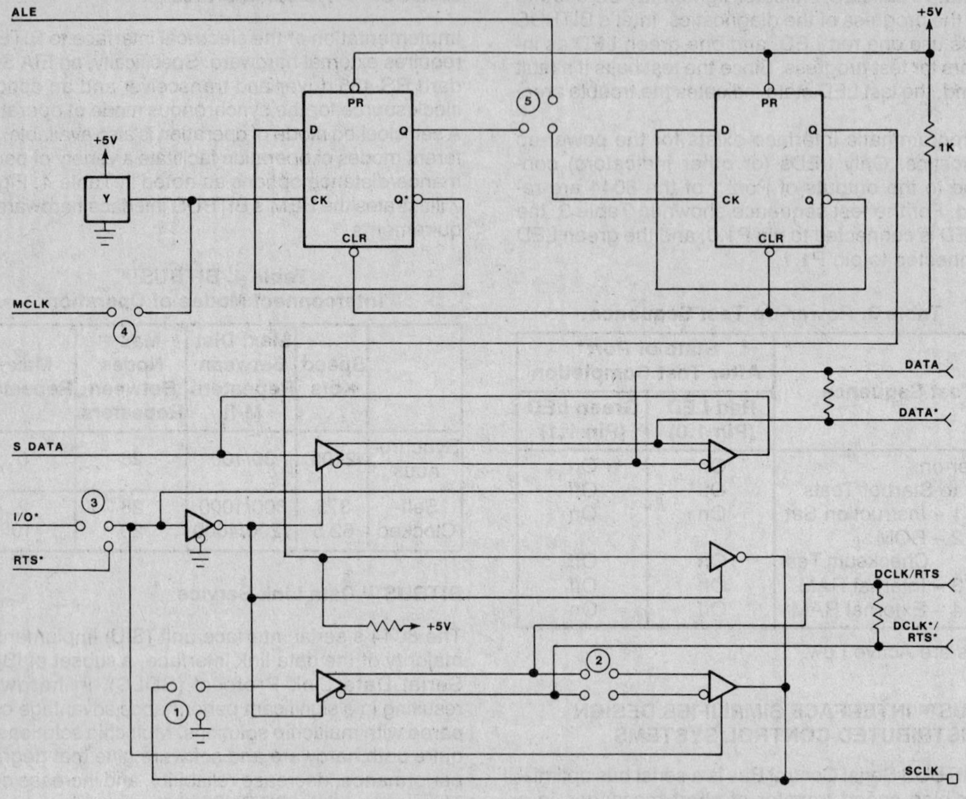

8044 BITBUS™ Enhanced Microcontroller

NOTES:
1. Connect to ground for self-clocked mode and SCLK for synchronous mode.
2. Remove for self-clocked operation with repeater(s).
3. Connect to RTS* for synchronous mode or I/O* for self-clocked mode.
4. Selects MCLK as serial clock source.
5. Selects ALE or oscillator as serial clock source.

Figure 7. BITBUS™ Interface Hardware Requirements

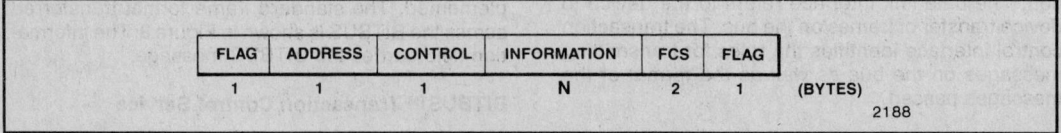

Figure 8. BITBUS™ Frame Format

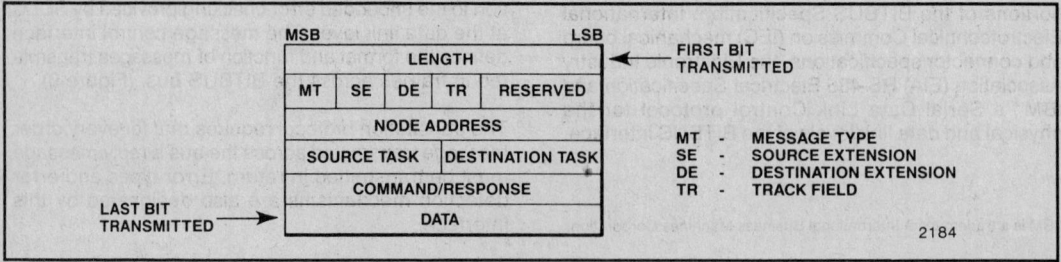

MT - MESSAGE TYPE
SE - SOURCE EXTENSION
DE - DESTINATION EXTENSION
TR - TRACK FIELD

Figure 9. BITBUS™ Message Format

8044 BITBUS™ Enhanced Microcontroller

BITBUS™ Interface Configuration

The BEM's firmware also simplifies designation of the bus mode of operation (speed/distance option) as well as the node address, memory configuration and parallel interface parameters by reading two external locations for this information as shown in Figure 10. The designer no longer needs to directly manipulate the 8044's serial mode register (SMD), status/command register (STS), and send/receive count register (NSNR). These two 8-bit locations are derived by multiplexing the 8044's port 0 address lines AD0-AD7.

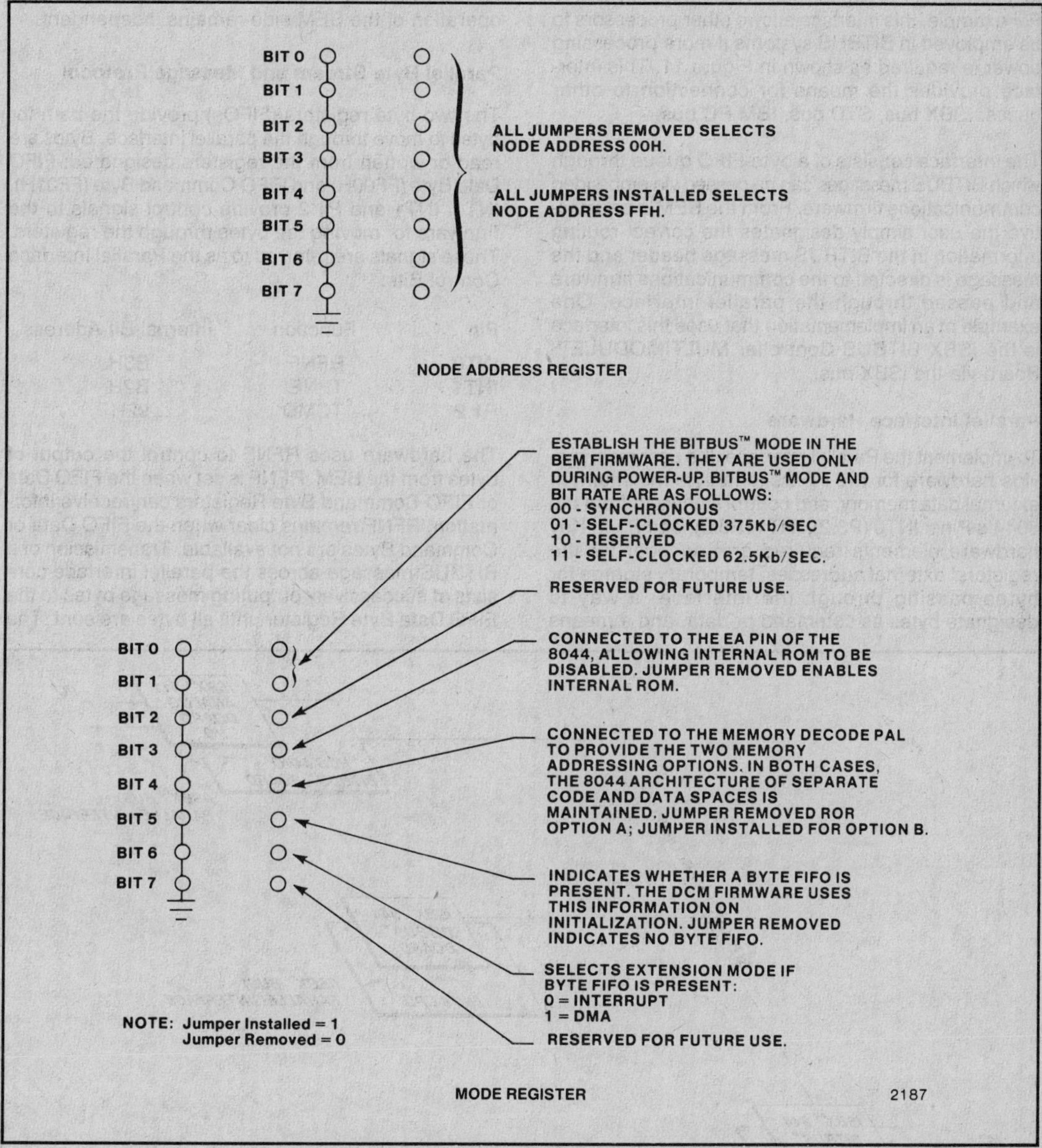

```
BIT 0  ─┐
BIT 1  ─┤
BIT 2  ─┤   ALL JUMPERS REMOVED SELECTS
BIT 3  ─┤   NODE ADDRESS 00H.
BIT 4  ─┤
BIT 5  ─┤   ALL JUMPERS INSTALLED SELECTS
BIT 6  ─┤   NODE ADDRESS FFH.
BIT 7  ─┘
```

NODE ADDRESS REGISTER

BIT 0, BIT 1: ESTABLISH THE BITBUS™ MODE IN THE BEM FIRMWARE. THEY ARE USED ONLY DURING POWER-UP. BITBUS™ MODE AND BIT RATE ARE AS FOLLOWS:
- 00 - SYNCHRONOUS
- 01 - SELF-CLOCKED 375Kb/SEC
- 10 - RESERVED
- 11 - SELF-CLOCKED 62.5Kb/SEC.

BIT 2: RESERVED FOR FUTURE USE.

BIT 3: CONNECTED TO THE EA PIN OF THE 8044, ALLOWING INTERNAL ROM TO BE DISABLED. JUMPER REMOVED ENABLES INTERNAL ROM.

BIT 4: CONNECTED TO THE MEMORY DECODE PAL TO PROVIDE THE TWO MEMORY ADDRESSING OPTIONS. IN BOTH CASES, THE 8044 ARCHITECTURE OF SEPARATE CODE AND DATA SPACES IS MAINTAINED. JUMPER REMOVED FOR OPTION A; JUMPER INSTALLED FOR OPTION B.

BIT 5: INDICATES WHETHER A BYTE FIFO IS PRESENT. THE DCM FIRMWARE USES THIS INFORMATION ON INITIALIZATION. JUMPER REMOVED INDICATES NO BYTE FIFO.

BIT 6: SELECTS EXTENSION MODE IF BYTE FIFO IS PRESENT:
- 0 = INTERRUPT
- 1 = DMA

BIT 7: RESERVED FOR FUTURE USE.

NOTE: Jumper Installed = 1
      Jumper Removed = 0

MODE REGISTER

Figure 10. BITBUS™ Firmware Configuration

8044 BITBUS™ Enhanced Microcontroller

Extended Firmware Services

PARALLEL COMMUNICATION INTERFACE EXTENDS DISTRIBUTED CONTROL CAPABILITY

The BEM's firmware also includes a parallel interface for expanding the capabilities of distributed systems. For example, this interface allows other processors to be employed in BITBUS systems if more processing power is required as shown in Figure 11. This interface provides the means for connection to other buses: iSBX bus, STD bus, IBM PC bus.

The interface consists of a byte-FIFO queue through which BITBUS messages can be passed via embedded communications firmware. From the BEM's perspective the user simply designates the correct routing information in the BITBUS message header and the message is directed to the communications firmware and passed through the parallel interface. One example of an implementation that uses this interface is the iSBX BITBUS Controller MULTIMODULE™ Board via the iSBX bus.

Parallel Interface Hardware

To implement the Parallel Interface, the user must provide hardware for two FIFOs (one byte minimum) in external data memory, and control signals to/from the 8044's Pins: INT0 (P3.2), INT1 (P3.3), and P1.2. Key hardware elements required are: decoder for the registers' external addresses, temporary storage for bytes passing through the interface, a way to designate bytes as command or data, and a means to generate the control signals. FIFO's must be used to move the data through the interface although the depth of the FIFO need not exceed one byte.

Interface hardware must also be provided for the 'extension' side of the interface. Implementation of this hardware is left to the user with the restriction that the operation of the BEM side remains independent.

Parallel Byte Stream and Message Protocol

The two byte registers (FIFOs) provide the path for bytes to move through the parallel interface. Bytes are read or written from the registers designated: FIFO Data Byte (FF00H) and FIFO Command Byte (FF01H). INT0, INT1 and P1.2 provide control signals to the firmware for moving the bytes through the registers. These signals are referred to as the Parallel Interface Control Bits:

Pin	Function	Internal Bit Address
INT0	RFNF	B3H
INT1	TFNE	B2H
P1.2	TCMD	92H

The hardware uses RFNF to control the output of bytes from the BEM. RFNF is set when the FIFO Data or FIFO Command Byte Registers can receive information. RFNF remains clear when the FIFO Data or Command Bytes are not available. Transmission of a BITBUS message across the parallel interface consists of successively outputing message bytes to the FIFO Data Byte Register until all bytes are sent. The

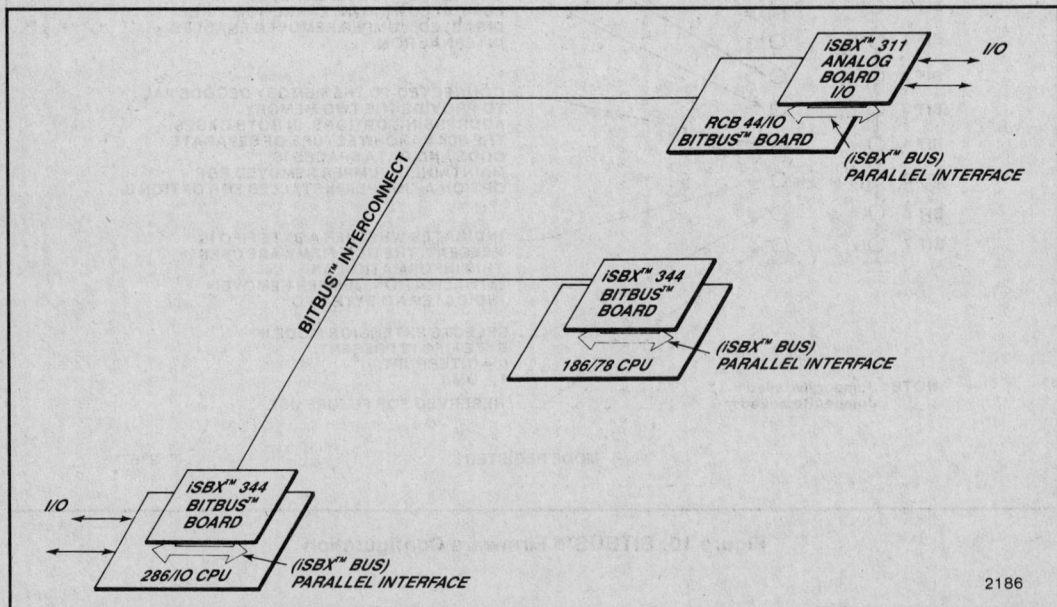

Figure 11. Extending the Capability of BITBUS™ System with the Parallel Communications Interface

8044 BITBUS™ Enhanced Microcontroller

firmware then writes a value of 0 to the Command Byte register indicating all the message bytes have been sent. The first data byte in the message indicates the number of bytes in the message.

TFNE controls the input of data bytes to the BEM. This bit is set when bytes are available for reading. When no bytes are available this bit is clear. TCMD indicates whether the next byte read is a Data Byte or Command Byte. BITBUS messages are received by inputing data bytes until a command byte is received. Data bytes are read from the FIFO Data Byte Register. Command Bytes are read from the FIFO Command Byte Register.

Figure 12 provides one example of a Byte FIFO Interface. This specific example illustrates the interface provided on the iSBX 344 BITBUS Controller MULTIMODULE Board. Figure 13 shows transmission of bytes from the BEM across the parallel interface. Figure 14 shows transmission of bytes to the BEM.

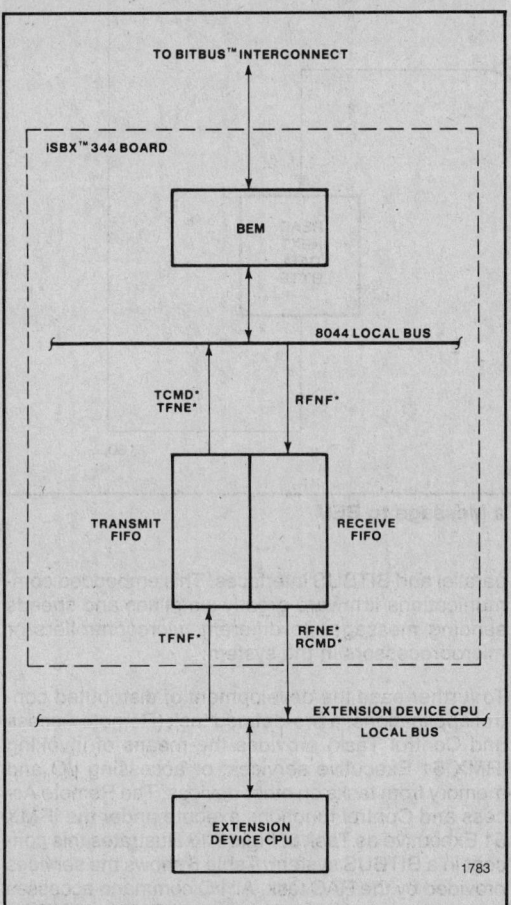

Figure 12. Byte FIFO Interface Example

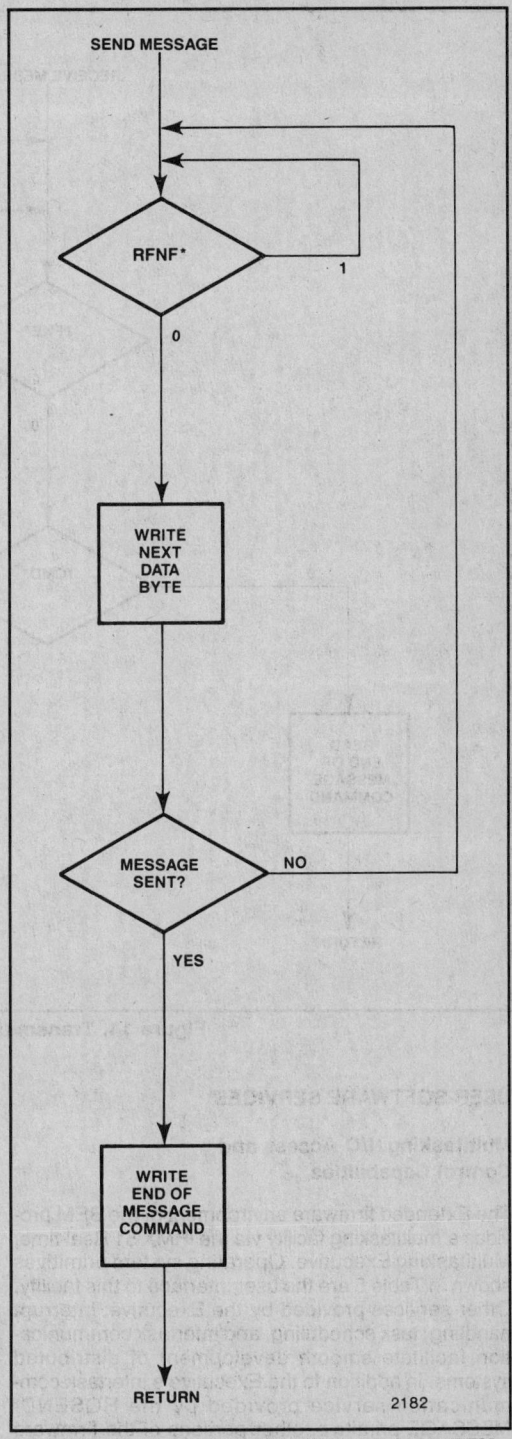

Figure 13. Transmitting a Message from BEM

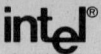

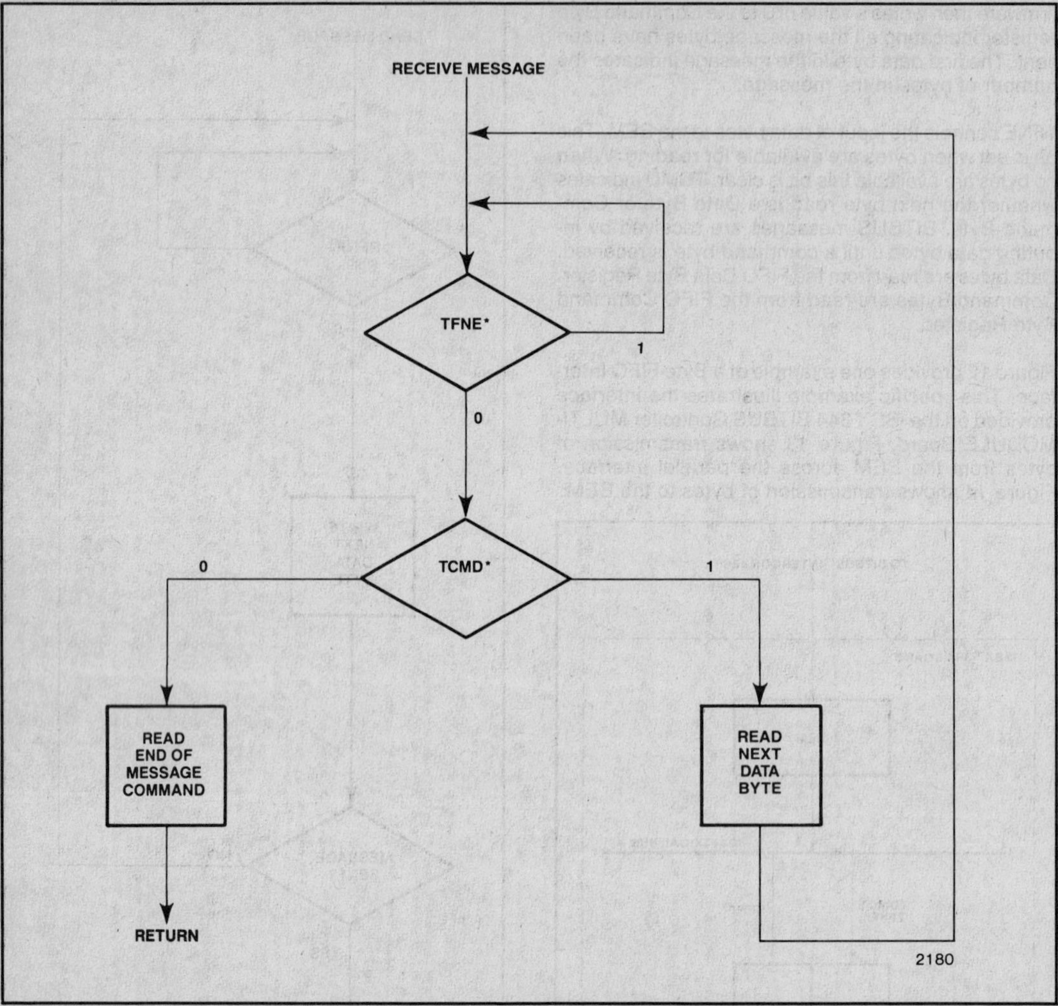

8044 BITBUS™ Enhanced Microcontroller

Figure 14. Transmitting a Message to BEM

USER SOFTWARE SERVICES

Multitasking, I/O Access and Control Capabilities

The Extended firmware environment of the BEM provides a multitasking facility via the iRMX 51 Real-time, Multitasking Executive. Operating system primitives shown in Table 5 are the user interface to this facility. Other services provided by the Executive: interrupt handling, task scheduling, and intertask communication facilitate smooth development of distributed systems. In addition to the Executive's intertask communication service provided by the RQSEND-MESSAGE primitive, other portions of the firmware extend the communication capability across the parallel and BITBUS interfaces. This embedded communications firmware greatly simplifies and speeds sending messages to different microcontrollers or microprocessors in the system.

To further ease the development of distributed control applications, a pre-defined task (Remote Access and Control Task) provides the means of invoking iRMX 51 Executive services, or accessing I/O and memory from tasks on other devices. The Remote Access and Control functions execute under the iRMX 51 Executive as Task 0. Figure 13 illustrates this concept in a BITBUS system. Table 6 shows the services provided by the RAC task. All I/O command accesses are memory mapped to locations 0FF00H to 0FFFFH in the BEM's external memory.

8044 BITBUS™ Enhanced Microcontroller

Table 5. iRMX™ 51 Interfaces

COMMAND	DESCRIPTION
RQ SEND MESSAGE	Sends a message (a command from the BITBUS master, a response from a slave, or a simple message between tasks on the same BITBUS component) to another task.
RQ WAIT	Waits for an interrupt, and event time-out, a message, or any combination of the three.
RQ CREATE TASK	Causes a new sequence of code to be run as an iRMX 51 task with a specific function identification code and priority.
RQ DELETE TASK	Stops the specified task and removes it from all execution lists.
RQ ALLOCATE	Allocates a fixed-length buffer from the on-chip, scratch-pad RAM for general use, or, in BITBUS applications, for a BITBUS message buffer.
RQ DEALLOCATE	Returns an on-chip buffer to the system.
RQ SET INTERVAL	Set the time interval to be used as a separate event-timer for the task.
RQ ENABLE INTERRUPT	Allow external interrupts to signal the microcontroller.
RQ DISSABLE INTERRUPT	Stops all external interrupts from signalling the microcontroller.
RQ GET FUNCTION ID	Provides a list of the 8 function identification codes representing the tasks currently operating on the microcontroller.

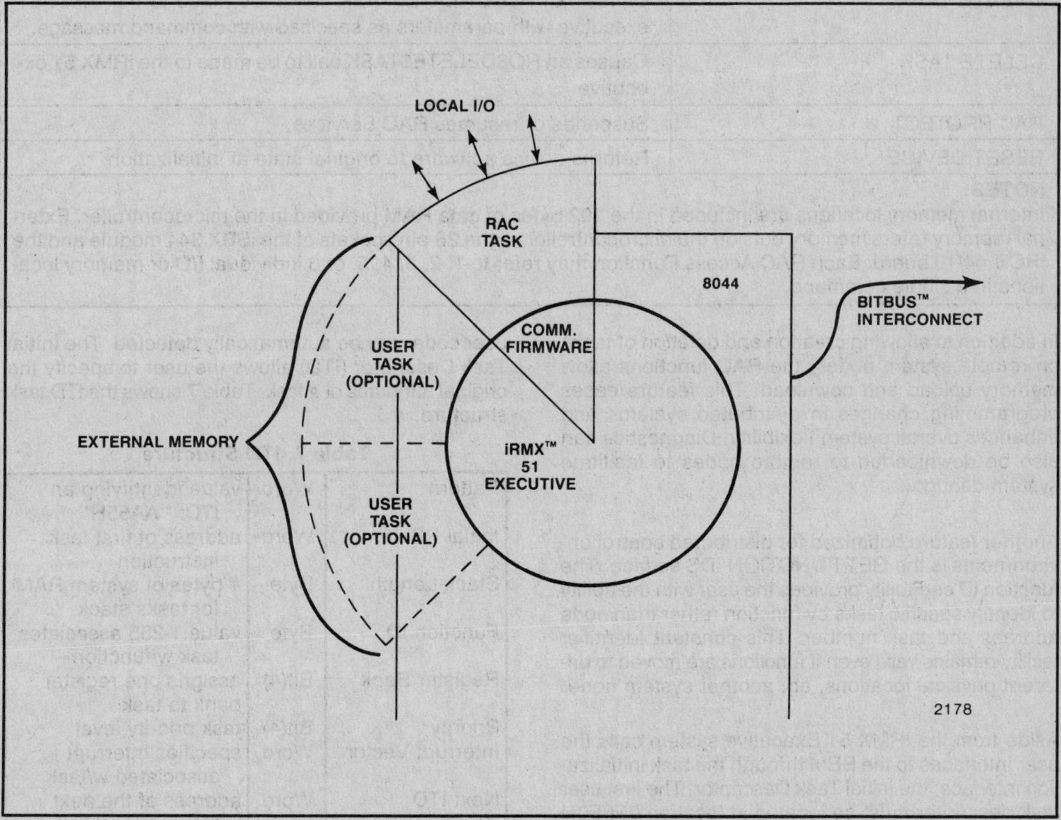

Figure 15. BEM Communication Firmware

8044 BITBUS™ Enhanced Microcontroller

Table 6. RAC Services

COMMAND	DESCRIPTION
READ I/O	Read external I/O location. Return result in reply message.
WRITE I/O	Write byte to external I/O location.
UPDATE I/O	Write byte to, then read byte from external I/O location. Return result in reply message.
OR I/O	OR data with contents of external I/O location. Return OR'd value.
AND I/O	AND data with contents of external I/O location. Return AND'd value.
XOR I/O	XOR data with contents of external I/O location. Return XOR'd value.
READ INTERNAL MEMORY	Read contents of internal memory location. Return result in reply message.
WRITE INTERNAL MEMORY	Write data to internal memory location.
DOWNLOAD EXTERNAL MEMORY	Write data starting at external memory location.
UPLOAD EXTERNAL MEMORY	Read data starting at external memory location. Return result in reply message.
GET FUNCTIONS	Provides a list of the 8 function identification codes representing the tasks currently operating on the microcontroller.
CREATE TASK	Causes an RQ$CREATE$TASK call to be made to the iRMX 51 executive with parameters as specified with command message.
DELETE TASK	Causes an RQ$DELETE$TASK call to be made to the iRMX 51 executive.
RAC PROTECT	Suspends or resumes RAC Services.
RESET DEVICE	Returns device software to original state at initialization.

NOTES:
Internal memory locations are included in the 192 bytes of data RAM provided in the microcontroller. External memory refers memory outside the microcontroller — the 28-pin sockets of the iSBX 344 module and the iRCB 44/10 board. Each RAC Access Function may refer to 1, 2, 3, 4, 5, or 6 individual I/O or memory locations in a single command.

In addition to allowing creation and deletion of tasks on remote system nodes, the RAC functions allow memory upload and download. This feature eases programming changes in distributed systems and enhances overall system flexibility. Diagnostics can also be downloaded to remote nodes to facilitate system debug.

Another feature optimized for distributed control environments is the GET FUNCTION IDS service. The function ID capability provides the user with the ability to identify specific tasks by function rather than node address and task number. This constant identifier facility remains valid even if functions are moved to different physical locations, eg. another system node.

Aside from the iRMX 51 Executive system calls the user interfaces to the BEM through the task initialization interface; the Initial Task Descriptor. The first user task descriptor must be located at location 0FFF0H in external memory code space so that on power up user code may be automatically detected. The Initial Task Descriptor (ITD) allows the user to specify the original attributes of a task. Table 7 shows the ITD task structure.

Table 7. ITD Structure

Pattern	Word	value identifying an ITD: "AA55H"
Initial PC	Word	address of first task instruction
Stack-Length	Byte	# bytes of system RAM for tasks stack
Function ID	Byte	value 1-255 associates task w/function
Register Bank	Bit(4)	assigns one register bank to task
Priority	Bit(4)	task priority level
Interrupt Vector	Word	specifies interrupt associated w/task
Next ITD	Word	address of the next ITD in linked-list

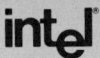

8044 BITBUS™ Enhanced Microcontroller

ABSOLUTE MAXIMUM RATINGS*

Ambient Temperature Under Bias............0 to 70°C
Storage Temperature............. −65°C to +150°C
Voltage on Any Pin With
 Respect to Ground (V$_{SS}$)............. −0.5V to +7V
Power Dissipation.........................2 Watts

*Notice: Stresses above those listed under "Absolute Maximum Ratings" may cause permanent damage to the device. This is a stress rating only and functional operation of the device at these or any other conditions above those indicated in the operational sections of this specification is not implied. Exposure to absolute maximum rating conditions for extended periods may affect device reliability.

DC CHARACTERISTICS (T$_A$ = 0°C to 70°C, V$_{CC}$ = 5V ± 10%, V$_{SS}$ = 0V)

Symbol	Parameter	Min	Typ	Max	Units	Test Conditions
VIL	Input Low Voltage	−0.5		0.8	V	
VIH	Input High Voltage (Except RST and XTAL2)	2.0		VCC + 0.5	V	
VIH1	Input High Voltage To RST For Reset, XTAL2	2.5		VCC to .5	V	XTAL1 to VSS
VOL	Output Low Voltage Ports 1, 2, 3 (Note 1)			0.45	V	IOL = 1.6mA
VOL1	Output Low Voltage Port 0 ALE, \PSEN (Note 1)			0.45	V	IOL = 3.2mA
VOH	Outpt High Voltage Ports 1, 2, 3	2.4			V	IOH = −80µA
VOH1	Output High Voltage Port 0, ALE, \PSEN	2.4			V	IOH = −400µA
IIL	Logical 0 Input Current Ports 1, 2, 3			−500	µA	XTAL1 at VSS Vin = 0.45V
IIH1	Input High Current.T0 RST/VPD For Reset			500	µA	Vin = VCC − 1.5V
ILI	Input Leakage Current To Port 0, \EA			10	µA	0.45V < Vin < VCC
ICC	Power Supply Current		125	170	mA	All Outputs Disconnected, EA = VCC
CIO	Capacitance of I/O Buffer			10	pF	fc = 1MHz
IIL2	Logical 0 Input Current XTAL 2			3.6	mA	XTAL1 at VSS Vin = 0.45V

NOTE 1: Capacitive loading on Ports 0 and 2 may cause spurious noise pulses to be superimposed on the VOLs of ALE and Ports 1 and 3. The noise is due to external bus capacitance discharging into the Port 0 and Port 2 pins when these pins make 1-to-0 transitions during bus operations. In the worst cases (capacitive loading > 100 pF), the noise pulse on the ALE line may exceed 0.8V. In such cases it may be desirable to qualify ALE with a Schmitt Trigger, or use an address latch with a Schmitt Trigger STROBE input.

8044 BITBUS™ Enhanced Microcontroller

A.C. CHARACTERISTICS (T_A 0 °C to 70 °C, VCC = 5V ± 10% VSS = OV, C_L for Port 0, ALE and $\overline{PSEN}$ Outputs = 100pF; C_L for All Other Outputs = 80 pF)

Program Memory

Symbol	Parameter	12 MHz Clock			Variable Clock 1/TCLCL = 1.2 MHz to 12 MHz		
		Min	Max	Units	Min	Max	Units
TLHLL	ALE Pulse Width	127		ns	2TCLCL-40		ns
TAVLL	Address Setup to ALE	43		ns	TCLCL-40		ns
TLLAX[1]	Address Hold After ALE	48		ns	TCLCL-35		ns
TLLIV	ALE To Valid Instr In		233	ns		4TCLCL-100	ns
TLLPL	ALE To $\overline{PSEN}$	58		ns	TCLCL-25		ns
TPLPH	$\overline{PSEN}$ Pulse Width	215		ns	3TCLCL-35		ns
TPLIV	$\overline{PSEN}$ To Valid Instr In		125	ns		3TCLCL-125	ns
TPXIX	Input Instr Hold After $\overline{PSEN}$	0		ns	0		ns
TPXIZ[2]	Input Instr Float After $\overline{PSEN}$		63	ns		TCLCL-20	ns
TPXAV[2]	Address Valid After $\overline{PSEN}$	75		ns	TCLCL-8		ns
TAVIV	Address To Valid Instr In		302	ns		5TCLCL-115	ns
TAZPL	Address Float To $\overline{PSEN}$	-25		ns	-25		ns

NOTES:
1. TLLAX for access to program memory is different from TLLAX for data memory.
2. Interfacing RUPI-44 devices with float times up to 75 ns is permissible. This limited bus contention will not cause any damage to Port 0 drivers.

External Data Memory

Symbol	Parameter	12 MHz Clock			Variable Clock 1/TCLCL = 1.2 MHz to 12 MHz		
		Min	Max	Units	Min	Max	Units
TRLRH	$\overline{RD}$ Pulse Width	400		ns	6TCLCL-100		ns
TWLWH	$\overline{WR}$ Pulse Width	400		ns	6TCLCL-100		ns
TLLAX[1]	Address Hold After ALE	48		ns	TCLCL-35		ns
TRLDV	$\overline{RD}$ To Valid Data In		252	ns		5TCLCL-165	ns
TRHDX	Data Hold After $\overline{RD}$	0		ns	0		ns
TRHDZ	Data Float After $\overline{RD}$		97	ns		2TCLCL-70	ns
TLLDV	ALE To Valid Data In		517	ns		8TCLCL-150	ns
TAVDV	Address To Valid Data In		585	ns		9TCLCL-165	ns
TLLWL	ALE To $\overline{WR}$ or $\overline{RD}$	200	300	ns	3TCLCL-50	3TCLCL+50	ns
TAVWL	Address To $\overline{WR}$ or $\overline{RD}$	203		ns	4TCLCL-130		ns
TWHLH	$\overline{WR}$ or $\overline{RD}$ High To ALE High	43	123	ns	TCLCL-40	TCLCL+40	ns
TQVWX	Data Valid To $\overline{WR}$ Transition	23		ns	TCLCL-60		ns
TQVWH	Data Setup Before $\overline{WR}$	433		ns	7TCLCL-150		ns
TWHQX	Data Hold After $\overline{WR}$	33		ns	TCLCL-50		ns
TRLAZ	$\overline{RD}$ Low to Address Float		25	ns		25	ns

NOTE 1: TLLAX for access to program memory is different from TLLAX for access data memory.

Serial Interface

Symbol	Parameter	Min	Max	Units
TDCY	Data Clock	420		ns
TDCL	Data Clock Low	180		ns
TDCH	Data Clock High	100		ns

8044 BITBUS™ Enhanced Microcontroller

Serial Interface (Continued)

tTD	Transmit Data Delay		140	ns
tDSS	Data Setup Time	40		ns
tDHS	Data Hold Time	40		ns

WAVEFORMS

Memory Access

Program Memory Read Cycle

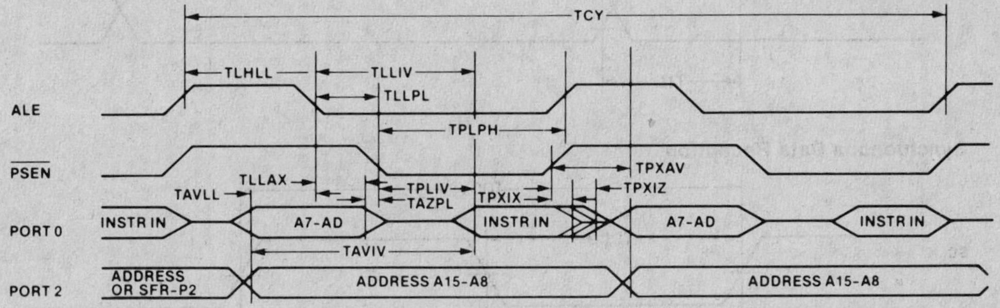

Data Memory Read Cycle

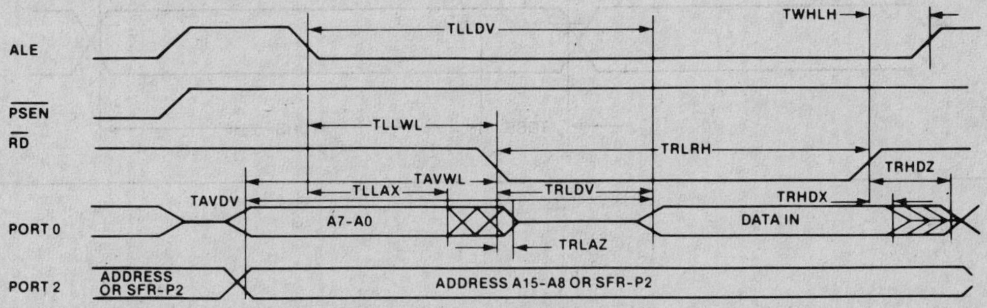

Data Memory Write Cycle

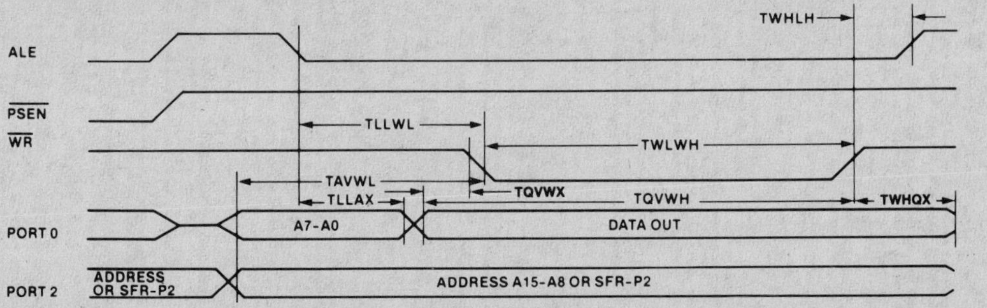

8044 BITBUS™ Enhanced Microcontroller

SERIAL I/O WAVEFORMS

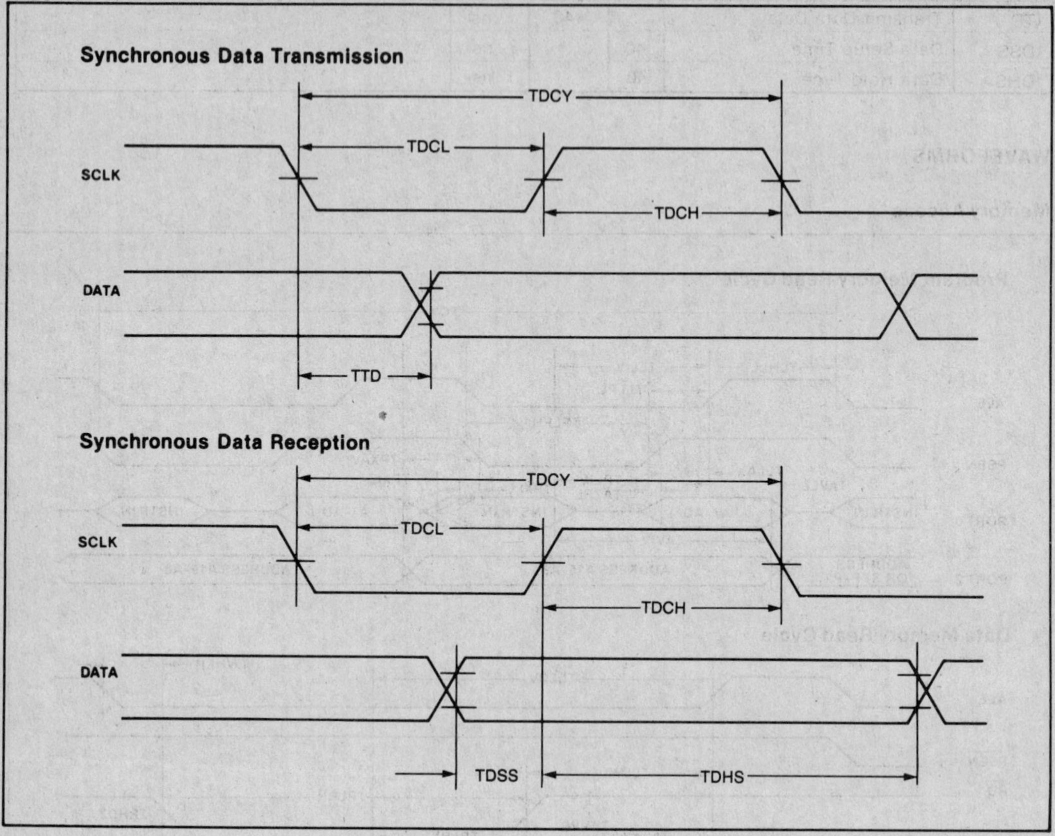

Synchronous Data Transmission

Synchronous Data Reception

8044 BITBUS™ Enhanced Microcontroller

CLOCK WAVEFORMS

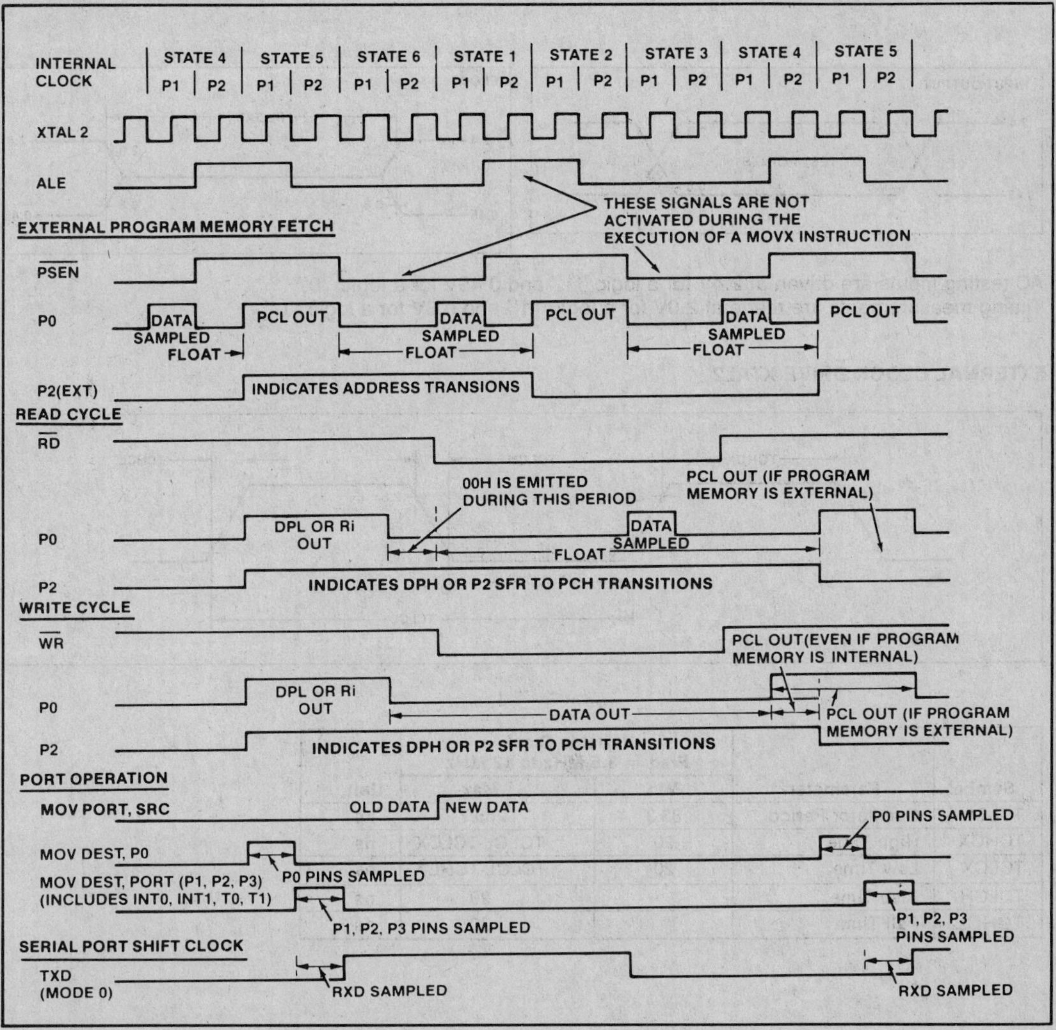

[Clock waveform timing diagram showing INTERNAL CLOCK states 4-5 with P1/P2 phases, XTAL 2, ALE, EXTERNAL PROGRAM MEMORY FETCH (PSEN, P0, P2(EXT)), READ CYCLE (RD, P0, P2), WRITE CYCLE (WR, P0, P2), PORT OPERATION (MOV PORT,SRC; MOV DEST,P0; MOV DEST,PORT (P1,P2,P3) (INCLUDES INT0, INT1, T0, T1)), and SERIAL PORT SHIFT CLOCK (TXD (MODE 0), RXD SAMPLED).]

This diagram indicates when signals are clocked internally. The time it takes the signals to propagate to the pins, however, ranges from 25 to 125 ns. this propagation delay is dependent on variables such as temperature and pin loading. Propagation also varies from output to output and component to component. Typically though, ($T_A = 25°C$, fully loaded) RD and WR propagation delays are approximately 50 ns. The other signals are typically 85 ns. Propagation delays are incorporated in the AC specifications.

8044 BITBUS™ Enhanced Microcontroller

AC TESTING INPUT, OUTPUT, FLOAT WAVEFORMS

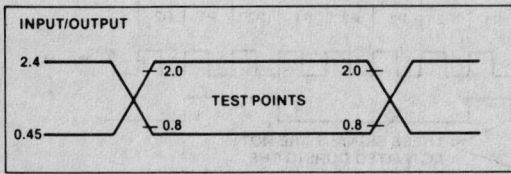
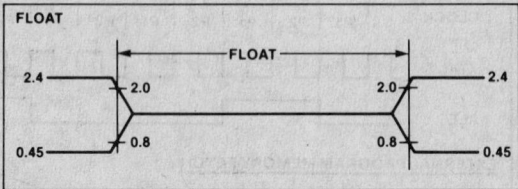

AC testing inputs are driven at 2.4V for a logic "1" and 0.45V for a logic "0"
Timing measurements are made at 2.0V for a logic "1" and 0.8V for a logic "0"

EXTERNAL CLOCK DRIVE XTAL2

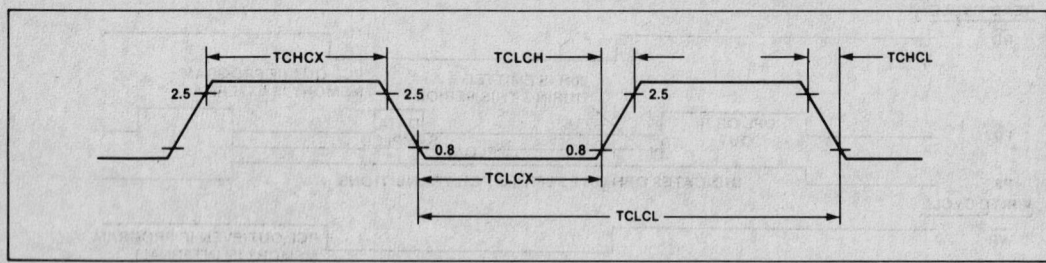

Symbol	Parameter	Variable Clock Freq = 3.5 MHz to 12 MHz		Unit
		Min	Max	
TCLCL	Oscillator Period	83.3	285.7	ns
TCHCX	High Time	20	TCLCL-TCLCX	ns
TCLCX	Low Time	20	TCLCL-TCHCX	ns
TCLCH	Rise Time		20	ns
TCHCL	Fall Time		20	ns

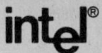

8044 BITBUS™ Enhanced Microcontroller

BEM PARALLEL INTERFACE LOGIC TIMING

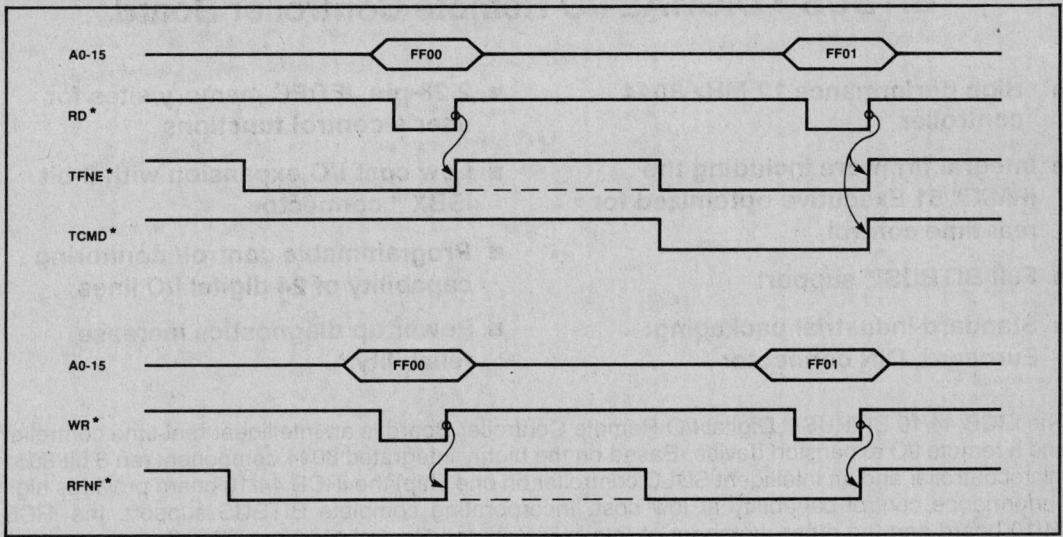

SPECIFICATIONS

Package: 40 pin DIP
Process: +5 volt, silicon gate HMOSII

RELATED DOCUMENTS
(NOT SUPPLIED)

Order Number

230973-001 — Distributed Control Modules Data Book (includes BITBUS Interconnect Specification)

146312-001 — Guide to Using the Distributed Control Modules

210941-003 — OEM System Handbook

210918-003 — Microcontroller Handbook

231166-001 — VLSI Solutions for Distributed Control Applications

ORDERING INFORMATION

Part Number	Description
P,8044AH,R 0100	BITBUS Enhanced Microcontroller

iRCB 44/10
BITBUS™ DIGITAL I/O Remote Controller Board

- High performance 12 MHz 8044 controller
- Integral firmware including the iRMX™ 51 Executive optomized for real-time control
- Full BITBUS™ support
- Standard industrial packaging: Eurocard, DIN connector
- 2 28-pin JEDEC memory sites for user's control functions
- Low cost I/O expansion with 8-bit iSBX™ connector
- Programmable control/monitoring capability of 24 digital I/O lines
- Power up diagnostics increase reliability

The iRCB 44/10 BITBUS™ Digital I/O Remote Controller Board is an intelligent real-time controller and a remote I/O expansion device. Based on the highly integrated 8044 component (an 8 bit 8051 microcontroller and an intelligent SDLC controller on one chip) the iRCB 44/10 board provides high performance control capability at low cost. Incorporating complete BITBUS support, the iRCB 44/10 board and the other members of Intel's Distributed Control Modules (iDCM) family expand Intel's OEM microcomputer system capabilities to include distributed real-time control. Like all members of the iDCM family, the iRCB 44/10 board includes many features that make it well suited for industrial control applications such as: data acquisition and monitoring, process control, robotics, and machine control.

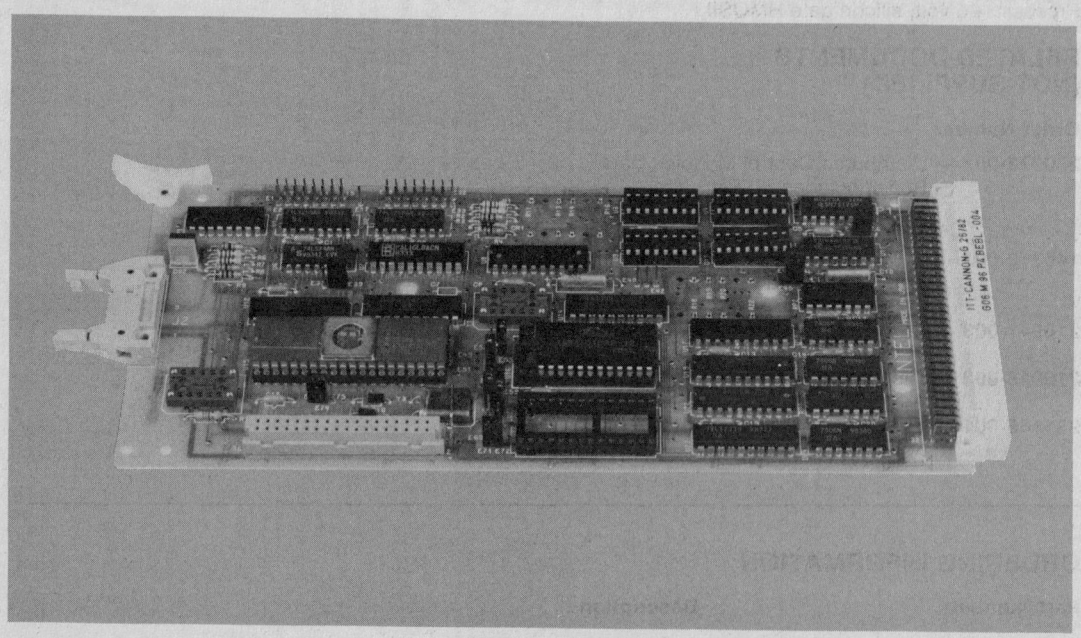

Intel Corporation Assumes No Responsibility for the Use of Any Circuitry Other Than Circuitry Embodied in an Intel Product. No other Circuit Patent Licenses are implied.

iRCB 44/10

OPERATING ENVIRONMENT

Intel's Distributed Control Modules (iDCM) product family contains the building blocks to implement real-time distributed control applications. The iDCM family incorporates the BITBUS interconnect to provide standard high speed serial communication between microcontrollers. The iDCM hardware products, the iSBX 344 BITBUS controller MULTIMODULE™ board and the iRCB 44/10 BITBUS Remote Controller Board (and other iRCB boards), communicate in an iDCM system via the BITBUS interconnect as shown in Figure 1.

The iRCB 44/10 board can be used as an intelligent remote controller or an I/O expansion device. When performing as an intelligent controller the iRCB 44/10 board not only monitors the status of multiple process points, but it can execute varied user supplied control algorithms. When functioning as an I/O expansion device, the iRCB 44/10 board simply collects data from multiple I/O ports and transmits this information via the BITBUS or iSBX bus interface to the system controller for analysis or updating purposes.

As a member of the iDCM product line the iRCB 44/10 board fully supports the BITBUS microcontroller interconnect. Typically, the iRCB 44/10 board would be a node in a BITBUS system. The iRCB 44/10 board could be part of a master or slave node. (The BITBUS system supports a multidrop configuration: one master, many slaves.)

ARCHITECTURE

Figure 2 illustrates the major functional blocks of the iRCB 44/10 board: 8044 BITBUS Enhanced Microcontroller, memory, BITBUS microcontroller interconnect, parallel I/O, iSBX expansion, initialization and diagnostic logic.

8044 BITBUS™ Enhanced Microcontroller

The heart of the iRCB 44/10 board's controlling and communication capability is the highly integrated 12 MHz 8044 microcontroller. The 8044 consists of the advanced 8-bit 8051 microcontroller and a SDLC controller called the Serial Interface Unit (SIU). This dual processor architecture allows complex control and high speed communication functions to be realized cost effectively.

Another essential part of the BEM is the integral firmware that resides on-chip to implement the BITBUS interface. In the operating environment of the iRCB 44/10 board, the 8044's SIU acts as a SDLC controller which offloads the on-chip 8051 microcontroller of communication tasks; freeing the 8051 to concentrate on real-time control.

The BEM (8044 microcontroller and on-chip firmware) provides, in one package, a simple user interface, and high performance communications and control capabilities to efficiently and economically build a complex control system.

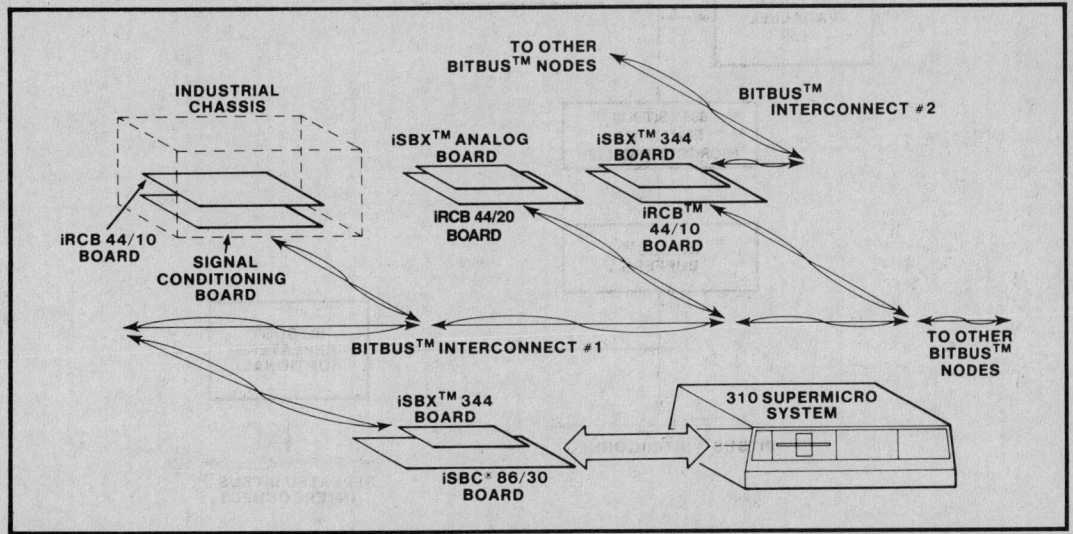

Figure 1. iDCM Operating Environment

iRCB 44/10

Memory

The iRCB 44/10 board memory consists of two sections: internal and external. Internal memory is located in the on-chip memory of the BEM. The iDCX 51 Executive and the remaining BEM firmware ration this resource. However, eight bytes of bit addressable internal memory are reserved for the user. Ample space is reserved for user programs and data in the iRCB 44/10 board external memory.

Two 28 pin JEDEC sites comprise the iRCB 44/10 board external memory. One site has been dedicated for data, the other for code. Table 1 lists the supported memory devices for each site. Intel's 2764, 27128, and 2817A are a few examples. The user may choose one of two memory configurations and specify different memory sizes by placing the proper jumpers at system initialization. The most flexible configuration option provides the user with access to the code site for program download or upload. This feature ensures expansion of an existing system is easily accomodated.

Table 1. Supported Memory Devices

DEVICE	DATA SITE	CODE SITE
4K × 8-64K × 8 EPROM/ROM	NO	YES
2K × 8-32K × 8 SRAM	YES	YES
2K × 8-16K × 8 NVRAM and E2PROM	NO	YES

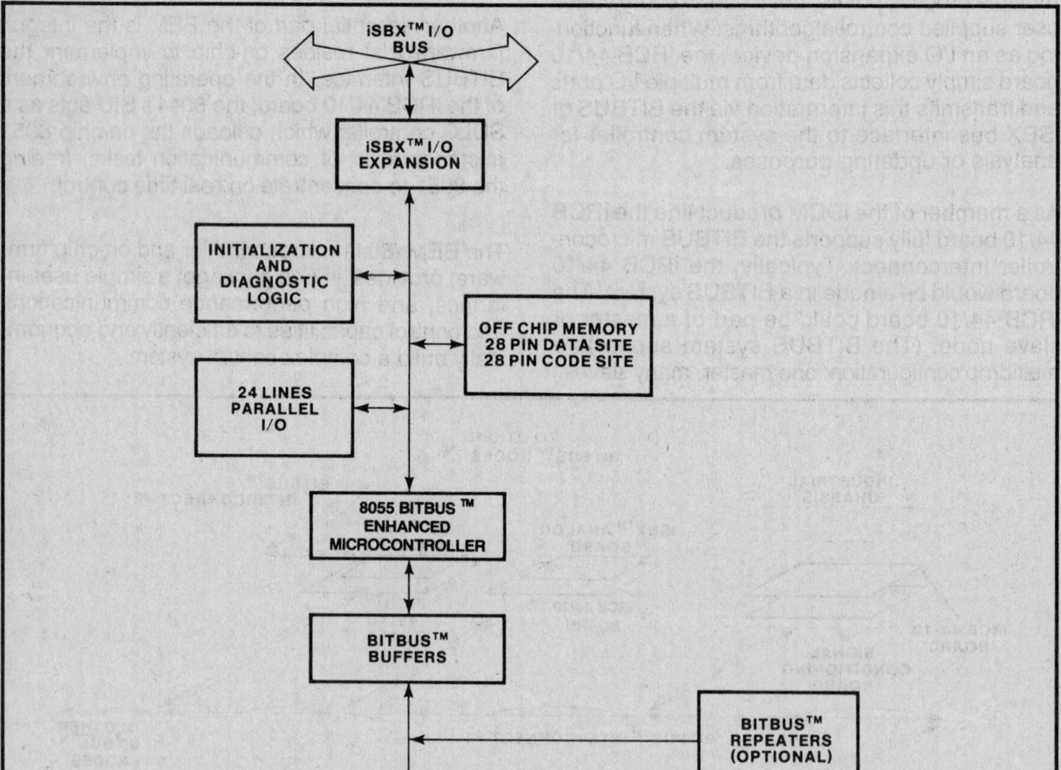

Figure 2. iRCB™ 44/10 Block Diagram

11-28

iRCB 44/10

BITBUS™ Microcontroller Interconnect

The iRCB 44/10 board serial interface fully supports the BITBUS microcontroller interconnect. The BITBUS interconnect is a serial bus optimized for control applications. The bus supports both synchronous and self-clocked modes of operation. These modes of operation are selectable dependent on application requirements as are the transmission speeds. Table 2 shows the different combinations of modes of operation, transmission speeds, and distances. The SDLC protocol, BITBUS message format, and compatibility with Intel's other software and hardware products comprise the remainder of the BITBUS architecture. These features contribute to BITBUS system reliability and usefulness as a microcontroller interconnect.

The BITBUS connection consists of one or two differential pair(s) of wires. The serial (BITBUS) interface of the iRCB 44/10 board consists of: a half-duplex RS 485 tranceiver, an optional BITBUS repeater and an optional clock source for the synchronous mode of operation.

Digital Parallel I/O

In order to provide an optimal parallel I/O interface for control applications, the iRCB 44/10 board supports 24 software programmable parallel I/O lines. This feature supplies the flexibility and simplicity required for control and data acquisition systems. Sixteen of these lines are fully programmable as inputs or outputs, with loopback, on a bit by bit basis so that bit set, reset, and toggle operations are streamlined. The remaining eight lines are dedicated as inputs. Figure 3 depicts the general I/O port structure.

The parallel I/O lines can be manipulated by using the Remote Access and Control (RAC) function (in BEM firmware) from a supervisory node or locally by a user program. The user program can also access the RAC function or directly operate the I/O lines. Input, output, mixed — input and output, and bit operations are possible simply by reading or writing a particular port.

iSBX™ Expansion

One iSBX I/O expansion connector is provided on the iRCB 44/10 board. This connector can be used to extend the I/O capability of the board. In addition to specialized and custom designed iSBX boards, a full line of compatible high speed, 8-bit expansion MULTIMODULE boards, both single and double wide, are available from Intel. The only incompatible modules are those that require the MWAIT* signal or DMA operation. A few of Intel's iRCB 44/10 board compatible iSBX MULTIMODULE boards include: parallel I/O, serial I/O, BITBUS expansion, IEEE 488 GPIB, analog input, analog output, and magnetic bubble.

With the iSBX 344 BITBUS Controller MULTIMODULE board and user supplied software, the iRCB 44/10 board can act as an intelligent BITBUS repeater facilitating the transition between two BITBUS segments operating at different speeds.

Initalization and Diagnostic Logic

Like the other members of Intel's Distributed Control Modules (iDCM) product line, the iRCB 44/10 board includes many features which make it well suited for industrial control applications. Power up diagnostics is just one of these features. Diagnostics simplify system startup considerably, by immediately indicating an iDCM controller or external bus failure. The LEDs used for power up diagnostics are available for user diagnostics after power up as well to further contribute to reliable operation of the system.

Initial iRCB 44/10 board parameters are set by positioning jumpers. The jumpers determine the

Table 2. Modes of Operation

	Speed Kb/s	Maximum Distance Between Repeaters M/ft	Maximum # Nodes Between Repeaters	Maximum # Repeaters
Synchronous	2400	30/100	28	0
Self Clocked	375	300/1000	28	2
	62.5	1200/4000	28	10

iRCB 44/10

BITBUS mode of operation: synchronous, self clocked, transmission speed, and address of the iRCB 44/10 board in the BITBUS system. This minimizes the number of spare boards to be stocked for multiple nodes, decreasing stocking inventory and cost.

INTEGRAL FIRMWARE

The iRCB 44/10 board contains resident firmware located in the 8044 BEM. The on-chip firmware consists of: a pre-configured iDCX 51 Executive for user program development; a Remote Access and Controller (RAC) function that enables user communication and control of different microcontrollers and I/O points; a communications gateway to connect the BITBUS interconnect, iSBX bus, and iDCX 51 tasks; and power up diagnostics.

The iDCX 51 Executive is an event-driven software manager that can respond to the needs of multiple tasks. This real-time multitasking executive provides: task management, timing, interrupt handling, and message passing services. Table 3 shows the iDCX 51 user interfaces. Both the Executive and the communications gateway allow for the addition of up to seven user tasks at each node while making BITBUS operations transparent.

The Remote Access and Control Function is a special purpose task that allows the user to trans-

Table 3. iDCX™ 51 Interfaces

COMMAND	DESCRIPTION
RQ SEND MESSAGE	Sends a message (a command from the BITBUS master, a response from a slave, or a simple message between tasks on the same BITBUS component) to another task.
RQ WAIT	Waits for an interrupt, and event time-out, a message, or any combination of the three.
RQ CREATE TASK	Causes a new sequence of code to be run as an iDCX 51 task with a specific function identification code and priority.
RQ DELETE TASK	Stops the specified task and removes it from all execution lists.
RQ ALLOCATE	Allocates a fixed-length buffer from the on-chip, scratch-pad RAM for general use, or, in BITBUS applications, for a BITBUS message buffer.
RQ DEALLOCATE	Returns an on-chip buffer to the system.
RQ SET INTERVAL	Set the time interval to be used as a separate event-timer for the task.
RQ ENABLE INTERRUPT	Allow external interrupts to signal the microcontroller.
RQ DISSABLE INTERRUPT	Stops all external interrupts from signalling the microcontroller.
RQ GET FUNCTION ID	Provides a list of the 8 function identification codes representing the tasks currently operating on the microcontroller.

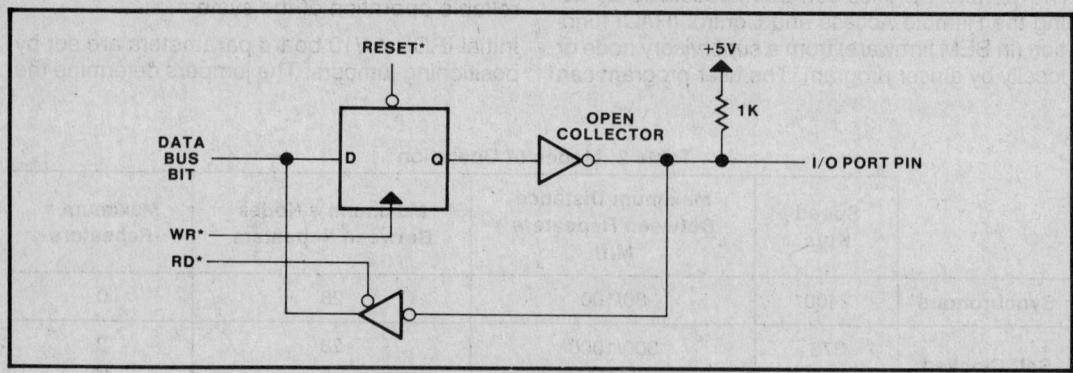

Figure 3. I/O Port Structure

iRCB 44/10

fer commands and program variables to remote BITBUS controllers, obtain the status of a remote I/O line(s), or reverse the state of a remote I/O line. Table 4 provides a complete listing of the RAC services. No user code need be written to use this function. Power up tests provide a quick diagnostic service.

The services provided by the iRCB 44/10 board integral firmware simplify the development and implementation of complex real-time control application systems. All iDCM hardware products contain integral firmware thus supplying the user with a total system solution.

INDUSTRIAL PACKAGING

The iRCB 44/10 form factor is a single high, 220mm deep Eurocard as shown in Figure 4. The Eurocard form factor supports most standard industrial packaging schemes as well as Intel's MULTIBUS® II packaging scheme. The Eurocard form factor specifies reliable DIN connectors. A standard 64 pin connector is included on the iRCB 44/10 board.

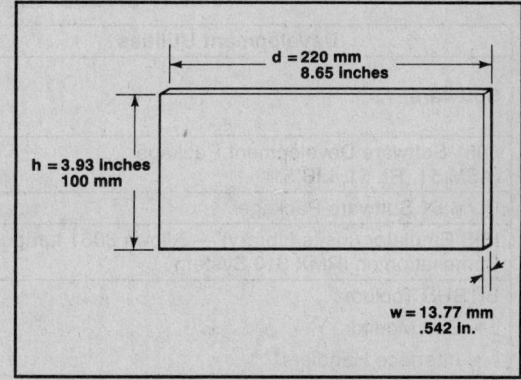

Figure 4. Eurocard Single High Form Factor

Table 4. RAC Services

COMMAND	DESCRIPTION
READ I/O	Read external I/O location. Return result in reply message.
WRITE I/O	Write byte to external I/O location.
UPDATE I/O	Write byte to, then read byte from external I/O location. Return result in reply message.
OR I/O	OR data with contents of external I/O location. Return OR'd value.
AND I/O	AND data with contents of external I/O location. Return AND'd value.
XOR I/O	XOR data with contents of external I/O location. Return XOR'd value.
READ INTERNAL MEMORY	Read contents of internal memory location. Return result in reply message.
WRITE INTERNAL MEMORY	Write data to internal memory location.
DOWNLOAD EXTERNAL MEMORY	Write data starting at external memory location.
UPLOAD EXTERNAL MEMORY	Read data starting at external memory location. Return result in reply message.
GET FUNCTIONS	Provides a list of the 8 function identification codes representing the tasks currently operating on the microcontroller.
CREATE TASK	Causes an RQ$CREATE$TASK call to be made to the iDCX 51 executive with parameters as specified with command message.
DELETE TASK	Causes an RQ$DELETE$TASK call to be made to the iDCX 51 executive.
RAC PROTECT	Suspends or resumes RAC Services.
RESET DEVICE	Returns device software to original state at initialization.

NOTES:
Internal memory locations are included in the 192 bytes of data RAM provided in the microcontroller. External memory refers memory outside the microcontroller — the 28-pin sockets of the iSBX 344 module and the iRCB 44/10 board. Each RAC Access Function may refer to 1, 2, 3, 4, 5, or 6 individual I/O or memory locations in a single command.

iRCB 44/10

DEVELOPMENT ENVIRONMENT

Intel provides a complete development environment for the iRCB 44/10 board.

Table 7. BITBUS™ Development Environments

Development Utilities	Development System			
Software	INTELLEC® Series III/IV Systems	iPDS™ System	iRMX™ System 310	IBM PC
8051 Software Development Package (ASM 51, RL 51, LIB 51)	X	X		X**
PL/M 51 Software Package	X	X		X**
ISIS Emulator (Insite Library) — Allows 8051 Language Compilation on iRMX 310 System			X	
BITBUS Toolbox:				
• Bus Monitor		X	X	X
• Interface Handlers*	X	X	X	X
DCM Debug (Insite Library)			X	
Hardware				
EMV-44, Emulation Vehicle	X			
ICE-44, 8044 In-Circuit Emulator	X			
iUP-2000A/201A Universal Prom Prog.	X		Contact Factory	X
Prom Programmer Personality Modules		X		X

* XENIX BITBUS Driver Provided Separately   ** Requires third party ISIS Emulation Software.

SPECIFICATIONS

Word Size
Instruction — 8 bit
Data — 8 bit

Processor Clock 12 MHz
Instruction Execution Times
1 μsec 60% instructions
2 μsec 40% instructions
4 μsec Multiply & Divide

Memory Capacity/Addressing
iDCM Controller — 64 K

Address Range

	Option 1	Option 2
External Memory Data	0000H-7FFFH	0000H-7FFFH
Code	1000H-0FFFFH	8000H-0FFEFH
Internal Memory Code	0000H-0FFFH	0000H-0FFFH

I/O Capacity
iSBX MULTIMODULE™ board — one single or doublewide not requiring MWAIT* or DMA
24 Digital Lines Programmable Parallel I/O

Interrupt Sources
Two external — iSBX I/O Expansion bus sources or other sources.
BITBUS Microcontroller Interconnect.

Terminations
Sockets provided on board for ¼ Watt 5% Carbon type resistors. Resistor value to match characteristic impedance of cable as closely as possible — 120 ohms or greater.

Repeaters
Sockets provided on board — Devices 75174 and 75175

iRCB 44/10

8044 BITBUS™ Enhanced Microcontroller I/O Addressing

FUNCTION	ADDRESS	READ	WRITE	BIT
PORT A	FFC0H	✓	✓	
PORT B	FFC1H	✓		
PORT C	FFC2H	✓	✓	
MCS0	FF80H-FF87H FF00, FF01	✓	✓	
MSC1	FF88H-FF8F	✓	✓	
LED #1	90H	✓	✓	✓
LED #2	91H	✓	✓	✓
RDY/NE*	B4H	✓	✓	✓
NODE ADDRESS	FFFFH	✓		
CONFIGURATION	FFFEH	✓		
OPT0	92H	✓	✓	✓
OPT1	93H	✓	✓	✓
INT0	B2H	✓		✓
INT1	B3H	✓		✓

Connector Options

10 Pin Plug

Flat Cable — 3M 3473-6010, TB Ansley 609-1001M, or equal

Discrete Wire — BERG 65846-007, ITT Cannon 121-7326-105, or equal

DIN Connector Plug

Flat Cable — GW Elco 00-8259-096-84-124, Robinson Nugent RNE-IDC64C-TG30, or equal

Discrete Wire — ITT Cannon G06 M96 P3 BDBL-004 GW Elco 60 8257 3017, or equal

10 Pin Repeater Connector Pin Out

PIN	SIGNAL
1	+12V
2	+12V
3	GND
4	GND
5	DATA*
6	DATA
7	DCLK*/RTS*
8	DCLK/RTS
9	RGND
10	RGND

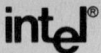

iRCB 44/10 Pin Out

DIN Connector

DIN PIN #	PIN & SOCKET PIN #	FUNCTION	DIN PIN #	PIN & SOCKET PIN #	FUNCTION
1a		GND	1c		GND
2a		+5V	2c		+5V
3a		DATA	3c		DATA*
4a		DLCK/RT	4c		DLCK*/RTS*
5a	1	EXTINT	5c		RGND
6a	3	PB7	6c	2	GND
7a	5	PB6	7c	4	GND
8a	7	PB5	8c	6	GND
9a	9	PB4	9c	8	GND
10a	11	PB3	10c	10	GND
11a	13	PB2	11c	12	GND
12a	15	PB1	12c	14	GND
13a	17	PB0	13c	16	GND
14a	19	PC3	14c	18	GND
15a	21	PC2	15c	20	GND
16a	23	PC1	16c	22	GND
17a	25	PC0	17c	24	GND
18a	27	PC4	18c	26	GND
19a	29	PC5	19c	28	GND
20a	31	PC6	20c	30	GND
21a	33	PC7	21c	32	GND
22a	35	PA7	22c	34	GND
23a	37	PA6	23c	36	GND
24a	39	PA5	24c	38	GND
25a	41	PA4	25c	40	GND
26a	43	PA3	26c	42	GND
27a	45	PA2	27c	44	GND
28a	47	PA1	28c	46	GND
29a	49	PA0	29c	48	GND
30a		+12V	30c		−12V
31a		+5V	31c		+5V
32a		GND	32c		GND

iRCB 44/10

Electrical Characteristics

Interfaces

iSBX I/O expansion bus — supports the standard I/O Expansion Bus Specification with compliance level D8/8F

Memory Sites — Both code and data sites support the electrical Universal Memory Site specification

BITBUS™ Interconnect — The iRCB 44/10 Remote Controller Board supports the BITBUS Specification as follows:
Fully supported synchronous mode at 2.4 Mbits/second and self clocked mode for 375 kbits/second and 62.5 kbits/second.

The iRCB 44/10 Remote Controller Board presents one standard load to the BITBUS bus without repeaters, with repeaters two standard loads
Message length of 18 bytes supported
RAC Function support as shown in Table 4

Parallel I/O — See the Table 5 for Electrical Specifications of the interface.

Power Requirements

.9A at +5V ±5% iRCB 44/10 board only — memory, repeater, or iSBX board NOT included

Physical Characteristics

Single high, 220mm deep Eurocard Form Factor
Dimensions
Width — 13.77 mm (.542 in) maximum component height
Height — 100 mm (3.93 in)
Depth — 220 mm (8.65 in)
Weight — 169 gm (6 ounces)

Environmental Characteristics

Operating Temperature — 0°C to 55°C at 200 Linear Feet/Minute Air Velocity
Humidity — 90% non-condensing

Reference Manual (NOT Supplied)

146312 — Guide to Using the Distributed Control Modules

Table 5. Parallel I/O Electrical Specification

PARAMETER	CONDITION	MIN	MAX	UNITS
V_{OL}	I_{OL} = 16 mA		0.5	V
V_{OH}	I_{OH} = −2 mA	2.4		V
V_{IH}		2.0	7.0	V
V_{IL}		−1.0	0.8	V
I_{IL}	V_{IL} = 0.5V		6.0	mA
I_{IH}	V_{IH} = logic high		.0	mA
I_I	V_{IH} = 7V		−2.2	mA

Ordering Information

Part Number **Description**
iRCB 44/10   BITBUS Digital I/O Remote Controller board

ADVANCED INFORMATION

iRCB 44/20
ANALOG I/O CONTROLLER

- Distributed Intelligence Via BITBUS™ Serial Bus
- Integral 8044 8-bit Microcontroller
- 12-bit Analog Resolution
- 20 kHz Acquisition Rate (50 msec.)
- Industrial (Eurocard) Packaging With DIN Connector
- Two 28-pin JEDEC Memory Sites
- 16 Single-ended Input Channels, Configurable as 8 Differential Channels
- Two Output Channels
- Software Programmable Gain: 1, 10, 100, 500
- ±10V Range or 4-20 mA
- Expandable Via iSBX™ Connector
- Low Power Consumption

The iRCB 44/20 is a fully programmable analog I/O subsystem on a single board. The resident 8044 microcontroller operating at 12 MHz provides a means of executing data acquisition routines remote from the host computer. Real-time capability is made possible by the iDCX 51 Distributed Control Executive, resident in the 8044 microcontroller. Distribution of real-time control is implemented by the BITBUS serial bus protocol, which is also managed integrally by the 8044.

Offering high performance, low-cost, and improved system bandwidth via distributed intelligence, the iRCB 44/20 analog I/O controller is ideal for data acquisition and control in both laboratory and industrial environments.

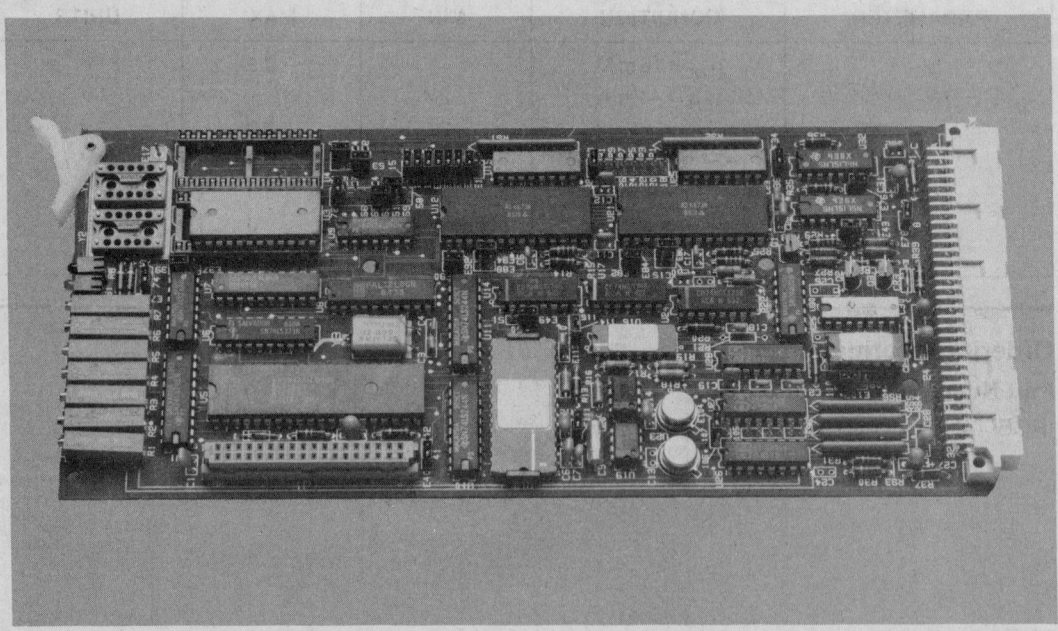

Intel Corporation assumes no responsibility for the use of any circuitry other than circuitry embodied in an Intel product. No other circuit patent licenses are implied. Information contained herein supersedes previously published specifications on these devices from Intel.

© Intel Corporation, 1985

October 1985
Order Number: 280721-001

iSBX™ 344
BITBUS™ INTELLIGENT MULTIMODULE™ BOARD

- **High performance 12MHz 8044 controller**
- **Integral firmware including the iDCX™ 51 Executive optimized for real-time control applications**
- **Full BITBUS™ support**
- **2 28-pin JEDEC memory sites for user's control functions**
- **Low cost, double-wide iSBX™ BITBUS™ expansion MULTIMODULE™ board**
- **Power up diagnostics increase reliablity**

The iSBX™ 344 BITBUS™ Intelligent MULTIMODULE™ board is the BITBUS gateway to all Intel products that support the iSBX I/O Expansion Interface. Based on the highly integrated 8044 component (an 8 bit 8051 microcontroller and an SDLC controller on one chip) the iSBX 344 MULTIMODULE board extend the capability of other microprocessors via the BITBUS interconnect. With the other members of Intel's Distributed Control Modules (iDCM) family, the iSBX 344 MULTIMODULE board expands Intel's OEM microcomputer system capabilities to include distributed real-time control. Like all members of the iDCM family, the iSBX 344 MULTIMODULE board includes many features that make it well suited for industrial control applications such as: data acquisition and monitoring, process control, robotics, and machine control.

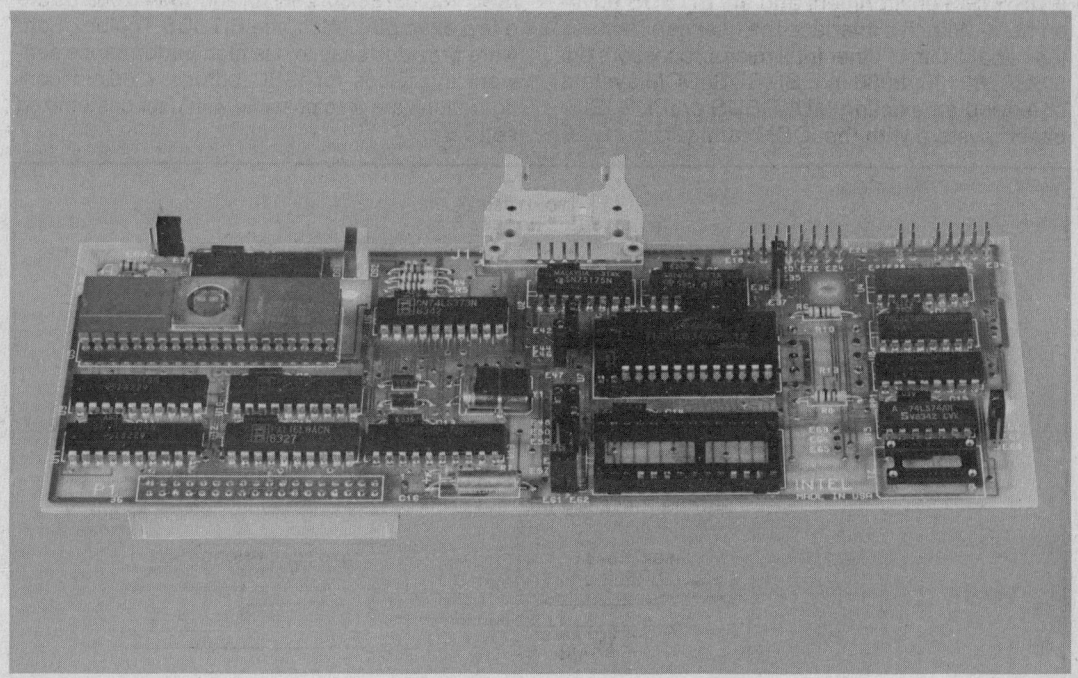

Intel Corporation Assumes No Responsibility for the Use of Any Circuitry Other Than Circuitry Embodied in an Intel Product. No other Circuit Patent Licenses are implied.

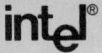

iSBX™ 344

OPERATING ENVIRONMENT

Intel's Distributed Control Modules (iDCM) product family contains the building blocks to implement real-time distributed control applications. The iDCM family incorporates the BITBUS interconnect to provide standard high speed serial communication between microcontrollers. The iDCM hardware products, the iSBX 344 MULTIMODULE board and the iRCB 44/10 BITBUS Remote Controller Board (or other iRCB boards), communicate in an iDCM system via the BITBUS interconnect as shown in Figure 1.

As a member of the iDCM product line the iSBX 344 MULTIMODULE board fully supports the BITBUS microcontroller interconnect. Typically, the iSBX 344 MULTIMODULE board would be part of a node (master or slave) on the BITBUS interconnect in an iDCM system. As shown in Figure 2 the iSBX 344 MULTIMODULE board plugs into any iSBC® board with an iSBX connector.

The iSBX 344 MULTIMODULE board is the hardware interface between Intel's MULTIBUS® and iPDS™ ISIS environment and the BITBUS environment. With this interface the user can harness the capabilities of other Intel microprocessors eg: 80286, 80186, 8086 in a BITBUS/iDCM system or extend an existing MULTIBUS or iPDS ISIS-based system with the iDCM family.

MULTIBUS® and iPDS™ I/O Expansion

Typically, MULTIBUS iSBC boards have a maximum of two iSBX I/O expansion connectors. These connectors facilitate addition of one or two iSBX I/O MULTIMODULE boards with varying numbers of I/O lines. The iSBX 344 MULTIMODULE board increases the number of I/O lines that can be accommodated by a MULTIBUS system by at least an order of magnitude. The iSBX 344 MULTIMODULE board extends the I/O of Intel's Personal Development System (iPDS) or other systems products in a similar manner.

Extending BITBUS™/iDCM System Processing Capability

The iSBX 344 MULTIMODULE board allows utilization of other processors in a BITBUS/iDCM system to accommodate particular application requirements. The MULTIMODULE board is compatible with any iSBX connector so that any board having a compatible connector can potentially enhance system performance. Intel's iRMX 510 iDCM Support Package provides the software interface required for a variety of iSBC boards. The iSBC 186/03, 86/30, 286/10, and 188/48 boards are a few examples. Also, the BITBUS Toolbox Software provides easy to use high performance software interfaces for iSBC boards. Custom configurations are also possible with user customized software.

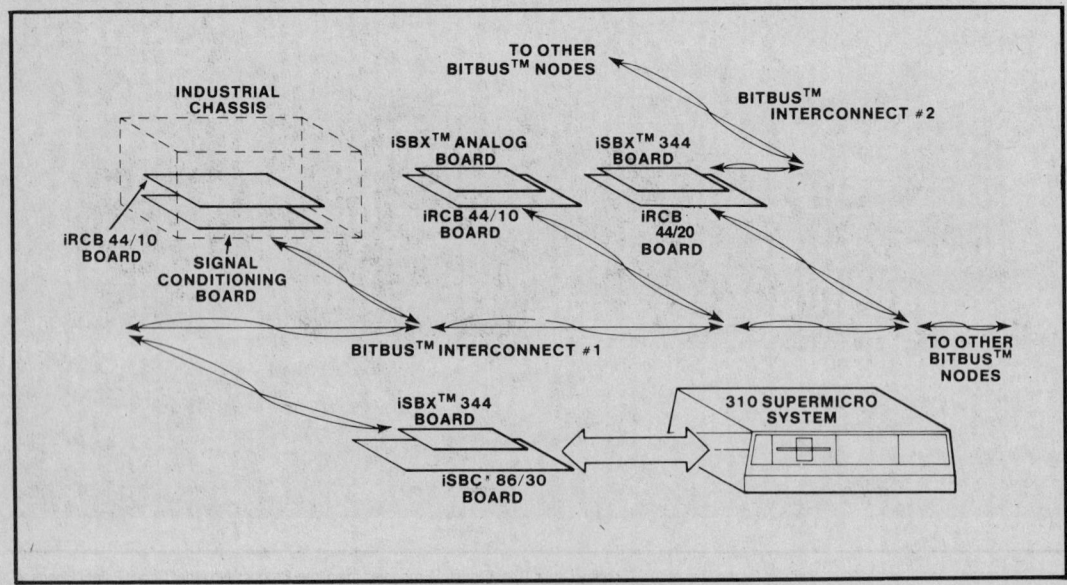

Figure 1. iDCM Operating Environment

intel® iSBX™ 344

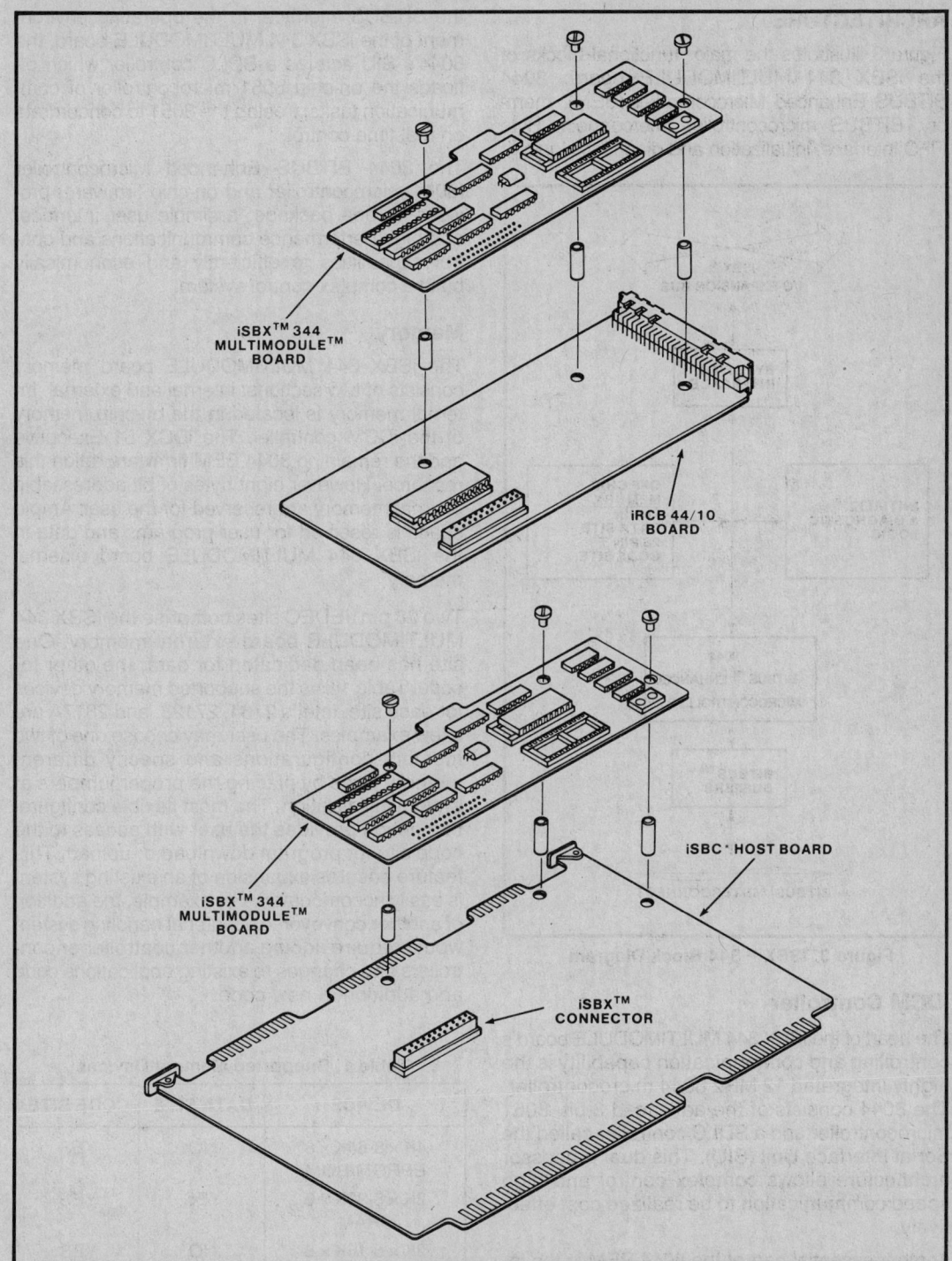

Figure 2. iSBX™ 344 Installation

11-39

iSBX™ 344

ARCHITECTURE

Figure 3 illustrates the major functional blocks of the iSBX 344 MULTIMODULE board: 8044 BITBUS Enhanced Microcontroller (BEM), memory, BITBUS microcontroller interconnect, Byte FIFO interface, initialization and diagnostic logic.

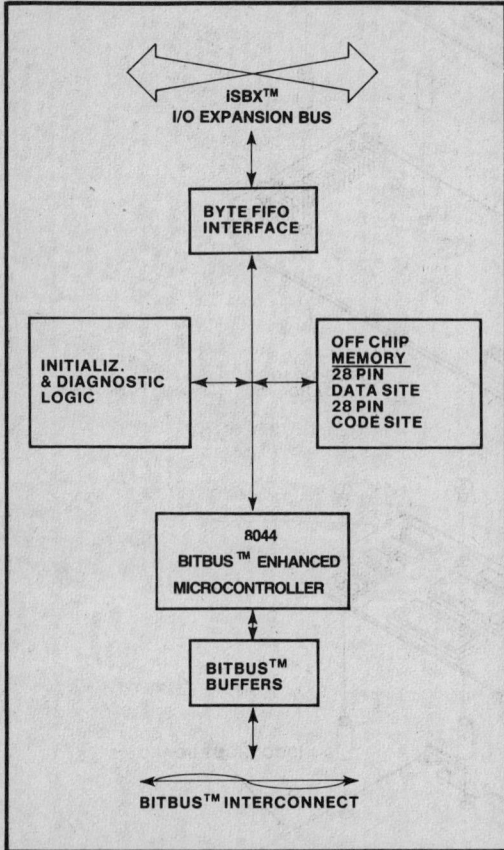

Figure 3. iSBX™ 344 Block Diagram

iDCM Controller

The heart of the iSBX 344 MULTIMODULE board's controlling and communication capability is the highly integrated 12 MHz 8044 microcontroller. The 8044 consists of the advanced 8-bit, 8051 microcontroller and a SDLC controller called the Serial Interface Unit (SIU). This dual processor architecture allows complex control and high speed communication to be realized cost effectively.

Another essential part of the 8044 BEM is the integral firmware that resides on-chip to implement the BITBUS interface. In the operating environment of the iSBX 344 MULTIMODULE board, the 8044's SIU acts as a SDLC controller which offloads the on-chip 8051 microcontroller of communication tasks; freeing the 8051 to concentrate on real-time control.

The 8044 BITBUS Enhanced Microcontroller (8044 microcontroller and on-chip firmware) provides, in one package, a simple user interface, and high performance communications and control capabilities to efficiently and economically build a complex control system.

Memory

The iSBX 344 MULTIMODULE board memory consists of two sections: internal and external. Internal memory is located in the on-chip memory of the iDCM controller. The iDCX 51 Executive and the remaining 8044 BEM firmware ration this resource. However eight bytes of bit addressable internal memory are reserved for the user. Ample space is reserved for user programs and data in the iSBX 344 MULTIMODULE board external memory.

Two 28 pin JEDEC sites comprise the iSBX 344 MULTIMODULE board external memory. One site has been dedicated for data; the other for code. Table 1 lists the supported memory devices for each site. Intel's 2764, 27128, and 2817A are a few examples. The user may choose one of two memory configurations and specify different memory sizes by placing the proper jumpers at system initialization. The most flexible configuration option provides the user with access to the code site for program download or upload. This feature ensures expansion of an existing system is easily accomodated. For example, the addition of another conveyor to a material handling system would require adding another controller or controllers and changes to existing applications code and addition of new code.

Table 1. Supported Memory Devices

DEVICE	DATA SITE	CODE SITE
4K × 8-64K × 8 EPROM/ROM	NO	YES
2K × 8-32K × 8 SRAM	YES	YES
2K × 8-16K × 8 NVRAM and E2PROM	NO	YES

iSBX™ 344

BITBUS™ Microcontroller Interconnect

The iSBX 344 MULTIMODULE board fully supports the BITBUS microcontroller interconnect. The BITBUS interconnect is a serial bus optimized for control applications. The interconnect supports both synchronous and self-clocked modes of operation. These modes of operation are selectable dependent on application requirements as are the transmission rates. Table 2 shows different combinations of modes of operations, transmission rates, and distances. The SDLC protocol, BITBUS message format, and compatibility with Intel's other software and hardware products comprise the remainder of this established architecture. These features contribute to BITBUS reliability and usefulness as a microcontroller interconnect.

The BITBUS connection consists of one or two differential pair(s) of wires. The BITBUS interface of the iSBX 344 MULTIMODULE board consists of a half-duplex RS 485 tranceiver and an optional clock source for the synchronous mode of operation.

Byte FIFO Interface

The Byte FIFO Interface on the iSBX 344 MULTIMODULE board implements the required hardware buffering between the 8044 BEM and an extension. An extension is defined as a device attached to the iSBX I/O expansion interface on the iSBX 344 MULTIMODULE board. In an iDCM system, an example of an extension is an iSBC 86/30 board which may be considered the host board in a MULTIBUS system. When used with the software handlers in the iRMX 510 iDCM Support Package or the BITBUS Toolbox, implementation of this interface is complete.

For particular applications, the user may wish to develop a custom software interface to the extension or host board. On the iSBX 344 MULTIMODULE board side of the interface the iDCM firmware automatically accepts messages for the FIFO. No user code is required increasing the time available for application system development.

The Byte FIFO supports both byte and message transfer protocol in hardware via three register ports: data, command, and status. The extension side supports polled, interrupt, and limited DMA modes of operation (e.g. 80186 type DMA controllers).

Initalization and Diagnostic Logic

Like the other members of Intel's Distributed Control Modules (iDCM) product line, the iSBX 344 MULTIMODULE board includes many features which make it well suited for industrial control applications. Power up diagnostics is just one of these features. Diagnostics simplify system startup considerably, by immediately indicating an 8044 BEM or external bus failure. The LEDs used for power up diagnostics are available for user diagnostics after power up as well as to further contribute to reliable operation of the system.

Initial iSBX 344 MULTIMODULE board parameters are set by positioning jumpers. The jumpers determine the BITBUS mode of operation: synchronous, self-clocked, transmission rate, and address of the iSBX module in the BITBUS system. This minimizes the number of spare boards to be stocked for multiple nodes, decreasing stocking inventory and cost.

INTEGRAL FIRMWARE

The iSBX BITBUS Controller MULTIMODULE board contains resident firmware located in the 8044 BEM. The on-chip firmware consists of: a pre-configured iDCX 51 Executive for user program development; a Remote Access and Control (RAC) function that enables user communication and control of different microcontrollers and I/O points; a communications gateway to

Table 2. BITBUS™ Microcontroller Interconnect Modes of Operation

	Speed Kb/s	Maximum Distance Between Repeaters M/ft	Maximum # Nodes Between Repeaters	Maximum # Repeaters
Synchronous	2400	30/100	28	0
Self Clocked	375	300/1000	28	2
	62.5	1200/4000	28	10

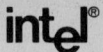

iSBX™ 344

connect the BITBUS interconnect, iSBX bus, and iDCX 51 Executive tasks; and power up diagnostics.

The iDCX 51 Executive is an event-driven software manager that can respond to the needs of multiple tasks. This real-time multitasking executive provides: task management, timing, interrupt handling, and message passing services. Table 3 shows the iDCX 51 user interfaces. Both the executive and the communications gateway allow for the addition of up to seven user tasks at each node while making BITBUS operations transparent.

The Remote Access and Control Function is a special purpose task that allows the user to transfer commands and program variables to remote BITBUS controllers, obtain the status of a remote I/O line(s), or reverse the state of a remote I/O line. Table 4 provides a complete listing of the RAC services. No user code need be written to use this function. Power up tests provide a quick diagnostic service.

The services provided by the iSBX 344 MULTIMODULE board integral firmware simplify the development and implementation of complex real-time control application systems. All iDCM hardware products contain integral firmware thus supplying the user with a total system solution.

DEVELOPMENT ENVIRONMENT

Intel provides a complete development environment for the iSBX 344 MULTIMODULE board. Software development support consists of: the 8051 Software Development Package, the iRMX 510 iDCM Support Package, and the BITBUS Toolbox. The 8051 Software Development Package provides the RL 51 Linker and Relocator Program, and ASM 51. PL/M 51 is also available. The iRMX 510 Support Package includes the iDCX 51 libraries. Hardware tools consist of the In-Circuit Emulator (ICE-44), Intel's Portable Development System (iPDS), and Intellec Series II or III Development Systems.

Table 3. iDCX 51 Interfaces

COMMAND	DESCRIPTION
RQ SEND MESSAGE	Sends a message (a command from the BITBUS master, a response from a slave, or a simple message between tasks on the same BITBUS component) to another task.
RQ WAIT	Waits for an interrupt, and event time-out, a message, or any combination of the three.
RQ CREATE TASK	Causes a new sequence of code to be run as an iDCX 51 task with a specific function identification code and priority.
RQ DELETE TASK	Stops the specified task and removes it from all execution lists.
RQ ALLOCATE	Allocates a fixed-length buffer from the on-chip, scratch-pad RAM for general use, or, in BITBUS applications, for a BITBUS message buffer.
RQ DEALLOCATE	Returns an on-chip buffer to the system.
RQ SET INTERVAL	Set the time interval to be used as a separate event-timer for the task.
RQ ENABLE INTERRUPT	Allow external interrupts to signal the microcontroller.
RQ DISSABLE INTERRUPT	Stops all external interrupts from signaling the microcontroller.
RQ GET FUNCTION ID	Provides a list of the 8 function identification codes representing the tasks currently operating on the microcontroller.

iSBX™ 344

Table 4. RAC Services

COMMAND	DESCRIPTION
READ I/O	Read external I/O location. Return result in reply message.
WRITE I/O	Write byte to external I/O location.
UPDATE I/O	Write byte to, then read byte from external I/O location. Return result in reply message.
OR I/O	OR data with contents of external I/O location. Return OR'd value.
AND I/O	AND data with contents of external I/O location. Return AND'd value.
XOR I/O	XOR data with contents of external I/O location. Return XOR'd value.
READ INTERNAL MEMORY	Read contents of internal memory location. Return result in reply message.
WRITE INTERNAL MEMORY	Write data to internal memory location.
DOWNLOAD EXTERNAL MEMORY	Write data starting at external memory location.
UPLOAD EXTERNAL MEMORY	Read data starting at external memory location. Return result in reply message.
GET FUNCTIONS	Provides a list of the 8 function identification codes representing the tasks currently operating on the microcontroller.
CREATE TASK	Causes a new sequence of code to be run as in the iDCX™ 51 interface.
DELETE TASK	Stops the specified task and removes it from all execution lists as in the iDCX™ 51 interface.
RAC PROTECT	Suspends or resumes RAC Services.
RESET DEVICE	Returns device software to original state at initialization.

NOTES:
Internal memory locations are included in the 192 bytes of data RAM provided in the microcontroller. External memory refers memory outside the microcontroller — the 28-pin sockets of the iSBX 344 module and the iRCB 44/10 board. Each RAC Access Function may refer to 1, 2, 3, 4, 5, or 6 individual I/O or memory locations in a single command.

SPECIFICATIONS

Word Size

Instruction — 8 bit
Data — 8 bit

Processor Clock 12 MHz

Instruction Execution Times
1 μsec 60% instructions
2 μsec 40% instructions
4 μsec Multiply & Divide

Memory Capacity/Addressing

iDCM Controller — 64 K

Address Range

	Option 1	Option 2
External Memory		
Data	0000H-7FFFH	0000H-7FFFH
Code	1000H-0FFFFH	8000H-0FFEFH
Internal Memory		
Code	0000H-0FFFH	0000H-0FFFH

Terminations

Sockets provided on board for ¼ Watt 5% Carbon type resistors. Resistor value to match characteristic impedance of cable as closely as possible — 120 ohms or greater.

iSBX™ 344

8044 BITBUS™ Enhanced Microcontroller (8044 + firmware) I/O Addressing as viewed from the 8044

FUNCTION	ADDRESS	READ	WRITE	BIT	COMMENTS
Data	FF00H	✓	✓		
Command	FF01H	✓	✓		Write sets command to extension — Read clears command from extension
Status					
-RFNF*	B3H	✓		✓	Also INT1 Input
-TFNE*	B2H	✓		✓	Also INT0 Input
-TCMD*	92H	✓		✓	
LED #1	90H	✓	✓	✓	
LED #2	91H	✓	✓	✓	
RDY/NE*	B4H	✓	✓	✓	
Node Address	FFFFH	✓			
Configuration	FFFEH	✓			

iSBX™ 344 MULTIMODULE™ board I/O Addressing as viewed from the iSBX™ 344 MULTIMODULE™ board

REGISTER FUNCTION	ADDRESS	COMMENTS
Data	Base	Read/Write
Command	Base + 1	Write sets command from extension
		Read clears command to extension
Status	Base + 2	Read Only

NOTES:
1. Base is determined by MCS0* on extension device

Interrupt/DMA Lines

SIGNAL	LOCATION	INTERFACE OPTION
RINT	MDRQ/MINT0	INT
TINT	MINT1	INT
RCMI	OPT0	INT OR DMA
RDRQ	MDRQ/MINT0	DMA
TDRQ	MINT1	DMA

Status Register Interface

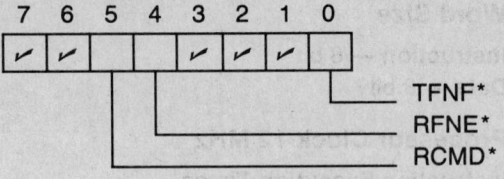

11-44

iSBX™ 344

Connector Options

10 Pin Plug
Flat Cable — 3M 3473-6010, TB Ansley 609-1001M, or equal
Discrete Wire — BERG 65846-007, ITT Cannon 121-7326-105, or equal

Pin Out

PIN	SIGNAL
1	+12V
2	+12V
3	GND
4	GND
5	DATA*
6	DATA
7	DCLK*/RTS*
8	DCLK/RTS
9	RGND
10	RGND

Electrical Characteristics

Interfaces

iSBX™ I/O expansion bus — supports the standard I/O Expansion Bus Specification with compliance level D8

Memory Sites — Both code and data sites support the electrical Universal Memory Site specification

BITBUS™ Interconnect — The iSBX 344 MULTIMODULE board supports the BITBUS Specification as follows:

Fully supported synchronous mode at 2.4 Mbits/sec and self clocked mode for 375 kbits/sec and 62.5 kbits/sec

The iSBX 344 MULTIMODULE board presents one standard load to the BITBUS bus

Message length of 18 bytes supported

RAC Function support as shown in Table 4

Power Requirements

.9A at +5V ± 5% iSBX™ 344 MULTIMODULE™ board only — memory NOT included

Physical Characteristics

Double-wide iSBX™ MULTIMODULE™ Form Factor

Dimensions
Height — 10.16 mm (0.4 in) maximum component height
Width — 63.5 mm (2.50 in)
Depth — 190.5 mm (7.50 in)
Weight — 113 gm (4 ounces)

Environmental Characteristics

Operating Temperature — 0°C to 55°C at 200 Linear Feet/Minute Air Velocity
Humidity — 90% non-condensing

Reference Manual (NOT Supplied)

146312 — Guide to Using the Distributed Control Modules

Ordering Information

Part Number	Description
iSBX 344	BITBUS Intelligent MULTIMODULE board

APPLICATION NOTE

AP-224

September 1984

The BITBUS™ Interconnect: From Flight Simulation To Process Control, It Simplifies Distributed Intelligence

SHANKER MUNSHANI
RICHARD MCALISTER
PETER MACWILLIAMS

Reprinted from Solutions July/August 1984

Order Number 280072-001

AP-224

APPLICATION NOTE

The BITBUS™ Interconnect: From Flight Simulation To Process Control, It Simplifies Distributed Intelligence

By Shanker Munshani, Richard McAlister and Peter MacWilliams

A large portion of microcontroller applications demand distributed modes of operation. Physically, this distribution can stretch from a few meters to several kilometers. The environment of operation varies from a very peaceful electrical environment to a very variable industrialized environment.

To accommodate changing application needs and technological advances, designers need a *flexible* interconnect for such systems that causes minimal impact to performance. Compatibility and the implementation of standards are key. Adhering to a standard has several advantages: designers of equipment need not waste time defining and testing their own standard, and end-users are more comfortable if the manufacturer has followed an industry standard. At the same time, another important feature is the capability of handling reliable communication activity without impacting CPU performance.

Intel's Distributed Control Modules (DCM) family accomplishes such goals for distributed applications. DCM defines an interconnect architecture and consists of:

The BITBUS interconnect – Interconnect serial control bus
iSBX™ 344 – BITBUS controller multimodule board
iRCB 44/10 – BITBUS remote controller board
iRMX™ 51 – Real-time multitasking executive
iRMX™ 510 – DCM support package
8044AH – 8-bit microcontroller with on-chip serial communication support

This application note will explain the structure and function of the BITBUS interconnect and explore its use in aircraft simulation and chemical process control.

The BITBUS Interconnect: Rationale and Structure

To connect microcontrollers in a distributed application, two common approaches involve either building a custom interface and a custom cabling mechanism, or using other interfaces such as RS 232.

Yet, custom interfaces are faced with several disadvantages. They are generally very expensive, and a designer must design an interface in addition to designing the system. They also lack flexibility. For example, it is often impossible to add more input/output connections to a custom interface once it is implemented. Finally, custom interfaces pose problems for the end-user: they require considerable support; the cabling is generally cumbersome and slow; and the distance over which they can be used is usually quite limited and their reliability may not be sufficient. Interfaces such as RS 232 are not an ideal alternative, either, because of the large amount of software support and cabling required.

The BITBUS interconnect avoids many of these problems. The BITBUS specification defines the data link protocol, message structure, protocol for a multitasking environment and a set of high-level commands for remote I/O access and application task control. This makes it very convenient to write high-level software interfaces. The BITBUS interconnect's high-level of definition means that the interface requirements can be implemented in silicon with minimal real estate at a low cost. This in turn reduces the complexity level.

The BITBUS in its simplest form is a pair of twisted wires. The BITBUS operates in a half duplex mode and can be used either in point-to-point operation or in a multi-drop environment. Figure 1 illustrates these two forms of connection. The BITBUS architecture supports a subset of the Synchronous Data Link Control (SDLC) protocol.

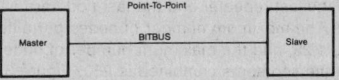

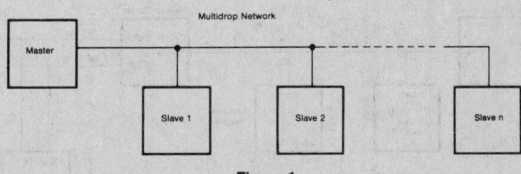

Figure 1.

There are three main objectives to be considered when using the BITBUS interconnect: speed of operation, distance over which communications has to take place, and number of nodes in the network. The BITBUS has two modes to meet these objectives: synchronous and self-clocked.

Synchronous mode
The synchronous mode is used for high speed operation. The distance over which this mode can be used is limited to 30 meters, and the number of modes in this set-up is restricted to 28 nodes. The speed of transmission in this mode is between 500 Kbits/sec to 2.4 Mbits/sec. To use this mode of operation, two pairs of twisted wires are required. One pair is used for the differential data clock signal (DCLK), while the other is used for the differential data signal (DATA). Figure 2 shows a typical synchronous mode interconnect.

Self-Clocked mode
In the self-clocked mode, as the name suggests, the clock is embedded in the data stream. In its simplest form, the

280072-001

intel AP-224

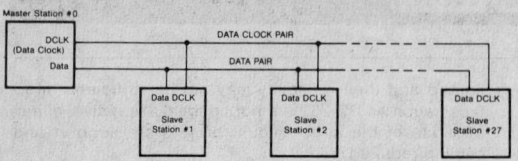

Figure 2. Synchronous Mode Network.

self-clocked mode requires just one pair of twisted wires. The speeds of operation in the self-clocked mode are 62.5 Kbits/sec and 375 Kbits/sec. The maximum distance of operation at 62.5 Kbits/sec is 1200 meters, and at 375 Kbits/sec is 300 meters. The maximum number of nodes in either case is 28. The self-clocked mode can be used to transmit over longer distances and to support more nodes by the use of repeaters. This, however, requires the use of an additional twisted pair of cables. This pair is used for Request To Send (RTS), which is the differential signal for transceiver control. The maximum number of repeaters allowed at 62.5 Kbits/sec are 10 and at 375 Kbits/sec are 2. Hence, at 62.5 Kbits/sec the distance over which the BITBUS link can be used is 13.2 kilometers, or 8.25 miles. The distance between the first node and the first repeater, the distance between two adjacent repeaters, and the distance between the last repeater and the last node are all called a segment. The maximum number of nodes permitted in any segment is 28, and the maximum number of nodes permitted in all the segments combined is 250. Figure 3 shows a self-clocked mode interconnect.

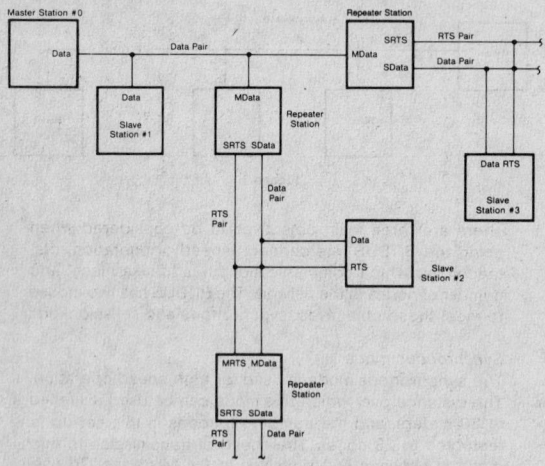

Figure 3. Self-Clocked Mode Interconnect.

The functions of the other parts of the BITBUS interconnect are described below:

iSBX 344 The iSBX 344 is a BITBUS controller multimodule board. This board can be used as either a master or a slave node in a BITBUS environment. This board has an iSBX connector and can be mounted on any iSBC board which has an iSBX connector and operates under any one of the following operating systems: iRMX 86, iRMX 286, iRMX 88, and ISIS-iPDS™ (Personal Development System). When the iSBX 344 multimodule board is used as a master node it is called a master extension, and when it is used as a slave node it is called a slave extension.

iRCB 44/10 The iRCB 44/10 board is a stand-alone BITBUS node. Unlike the iSBX 344 board, this board does not need a base board upon which to operate. The iRCB 44/10 board has a Eurocard single high-form factor and can be used as a stand-alone board. This board has 8 dedicated input lines and 16 programmable input/output lines.

iRMX 51 The iRMX 51 is a real-time, multitasking executive designed to monitor and control real-time events. A pre-configured version of the iRMX 51 Executive implements the BITBUS message format and provides all iRMX 51 facilities: task management, interrupt handling, and message passing.

iRMX 510 The iRMX 510 is a package of software aids to interface MULTIBUS™ and iPDS ISIS systems to BITBUS systems in both run-time and development environments. It provides a simple software interface for iRMX 86, 88, 286 and iPDS ISIS operating systems compatibility. It provides a means for inexpensive remote control and communication in MULTIBUS-based systems.

8044AH The 8044AH with the DCM firmware provides the basic BITBUS interface. The 8044AH integrates a high performance 8-bit microcontroller, the Intel 8051 core, with an intelligent/high performance serial communication controller, called the Serial Interface Unit. The on-chip ROM can be used for the DCM firmware.

By virtue of these products, support for the BITBUS interconnect comes at various levels. The 8044AH chip with the DCM firmware provides the designer with the facility to integrate the BITBUS into the system at the very lowest level. Alternatively, the iSBX 344 multimodule board with an iSBX connector can be plugged into a system design at the highest level. Since the BITBUS interconnect is intelligent, it is capable of handling reliable communication activity with minimal interaction with the host processor.

Setting up a BITBUS Network

Figure 4 shows a typical BITBUS network. iPDS, Intel's Personal Development System, can be used as a master station to control the BITBUS network. The iPDS is a stand-alone development system with a CRT, a keyboard and a 5-1/4" floppy disk drive. The iSBX 344 board can act as a master extension on the iPDS base-processor board. This master station is capable of controlling up to 249 slave stations in a multi-drop fashion. The iSBX 344 is numbered as station #0 and is connected via the BITBUS to station 1, which is an iRCB 44/10 board. The BITBUS is then used to connect to slave station number 2, which is another iRCB 44/10 board. From here the BITBUS is routed to an iSBX 344 board mounted on an iSBC 86/30 board, a MULTIBUS-based board. This is termed as station #4. (Note there is no station #3; the station numbering does not have to follow a sequential order). The BITBUS then routes over to station #9, an iSBX 344 board on an iRCB 44/10 board. After this the BITBUS travels to another iRCB 44/10 board, station #10. From here the BITBUS goes to station #15, which is an iRCB 44/10 board with an analog multimodule

280072-001

board. Thus, there is one master station number 0, and six slave stations with the following numbers: 1, 2, 4, 9, 10, 15.

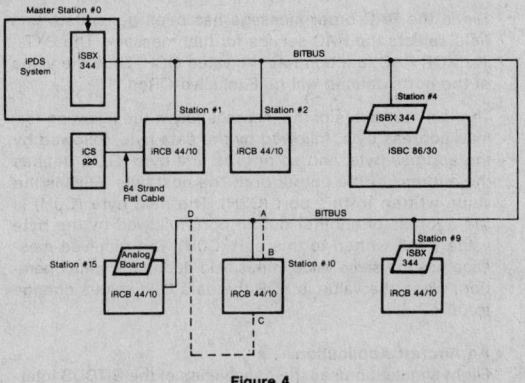

Figure 4.

If the distance from station 0 to 15 is less than 30 meters, this network can operate in either the synchronous mode or self-clocked mode. Assume the distance between stations 0 and 10 to be 200 meters, between stations 10 and 15 to be 250 meters and the speed required for the operation of the network to be 375 Kbit/sec. Since the maximum distance of a segment at 375 Kbits/sec is 300 meters, a repeater must be placed in the network. Since the iRCB 44/10 has on-board repeaters, station 10 could serve the function of a repeater. If this is the case, the BITBUS route then follows the direction of ABCD, as opposed to AD, as was the case in the previous example. Station 10 exists as a slave station and also as a repeater. Thus, the network has two segments, each less than 300 meters long. As a result, the network will work in asynchronous mode at 375 Kbits/s. It should be noted that stub lengths play an important role in a multi-drop network. Stub length is the distance from the drop point on the network to the node. Care should be taken to keep this as small as possible.

Creating a Task
Each individual station is now set up as an individual node. Since each BITBUS interconnect is an intelligent node, each node has its own tasks. Each station can have up to eight tasks. The Remote Access and Control (RAC) task is designated as task 0, so there can be seven more user-defined tasks. Using the same set-up as in figure 4, assume station 1 has only task 0 and no other user-defined tasks. This station could be used to perform any of the RAC Access or Control functions. A simple example could be to write a set of 1's to an output port and then flip this value to 0's. This could be achieved by using the EXT_I0_Write RAC function to write a set of 1's to an output port and then using the EXT_0I_XOR function to flip these bits. If an iCS 920 Digital Signal Conditioning board is connected to the output port of the iRCB 44/10 board, the LEDs (Light-Emitting Diodes) on that port of the iCS 920 board will turn on and off. If this task is run at a station, this will cause the LEDs to flash continuously. This demonstrates the simplicity of the I/O capabilities.

Message Structure The iRMX 51 Executive allows tasks to interface with one another via a simple message-passing facility.

Link: is a 2-byte field used by the executive.

Message_Length: is a byte value specifying the number of bytes in the message. This is 7 bytes of header information plus the number of bytes of user data. The maximum message size is configurable.

Message_Type: is a bit that determines whether this is an order message (=0) or a reply to a message (=1). If it is an order, the nucleus will use the consumer address as the destination. If it is a reply it will use the producer address as the destination.

Src_ext: is a bit value which indicates whether the sending task of an order message is located on an extension (=1) or on a device (=0).

Dest_ext: is a bit value which indicates whether the receiving task of an order message is located on an extension (=1) or on a device (=0).

Trk: is a bit field used during BITBUS transfer for tracking the message. Trk is set to 0 before sending an order message.

Station_address: For messages delivered locally (on the same chip), this field is 0. For messages delivered over a parallel interface only, this field is OFFH. For order types of messages, to be delivered from a master device or its extension to a slave device or its extension, this field is the SDLC station address of the slave device.

Source_task_id: is a byte value containing the task i.d. for the message originator. Upon reply, this value is interpreted as the reply destination.

Destination_task_id: is a byte value containing the task i.d. for the message destination. Upon reply, this value is interpreted as the reply source.

Command/response: is a byte field which is available for use by the sending and receiving tasks. It can be used for sending command or reply information. This field has pre-defined functions when communicating with the RAC function.

Message_information: is a user-defined field following the 7 bytes of message header information. For messages destined for the RAC task, this area has a fixed structure.

280072-001

Considering the example mentioned above to flash LEDs, the message sent and received would be (in Hex):

Message Sent   00 00 0B 40 01 00 0C C2 FF C0 FF
Message Received XX XX 0B C0 01 00 00 C2 FF C0 FF
                                                00 00

The first two bytes are the Link field. This field is reserved. The next byte specifies the message length, which is 7 bytes of header information plus 4 bytes of user-defined message. Therefore, the total message length is 11 bytes (i.e., 0BH).

In the next byte, the first bit is set to 0 to indicate an order type and the second bit is set to 1, since the order message resides on an extension (the iSBX 344 is on an extension). The third bit is set to 0, since the task which receives the order message resides on a device (iRCB 44/10). The fourth bit is always set to zero before sending a message. The last four bits are reserved and set to 0's. This byte in binary is then equal to 01000000, i.e., 40H. In the received message the only field changed is the first bit, because now this bit is a reply and hence changes to 1. The received byte in binary is therefore equal to 11000000, i.e., C0H.

The next byte defines the slave station address. Since the slave station address was 1, this field and its reply field are both 01.

The next byte is broken into two nibbles. Since the sending task and the receiving tasks were both RAC tasks (Task 0), this field is 00. (Note: this is not strictly the case for extensions).

Since the RAC order message has been generated, this field selects the RAC service for that message. The EXT_10_XOR RAC function has the value 0CH. Thus the value at the ports defined will be Exclusive-ORed.

The last four bytes of the message follow the following format: address byte, followed by the data byte, followed by the address byte, and so on. The first byte (C2H) defines the address of the output port. The next byte (FFH) is the value written to this port (C2H). The next byte (C0H) is the address of another output port, followed by the byte value (FFH) written to this port (C0H). The received message has the same value in this field during the write operation. When the value is XOR the data field values change to 00H.

An Aircraft Application
Flight simulation uses the capabilities of the BITBUS interconnect. Figure 5 shows an implementation for flight simulation. As the figure demonstrates, flight simulation can be broken down into a block diagram level consisting of six sections, namely:

1) Pitch: This section is responsible for the vertical movements of the aircraft. The inputs required for this section

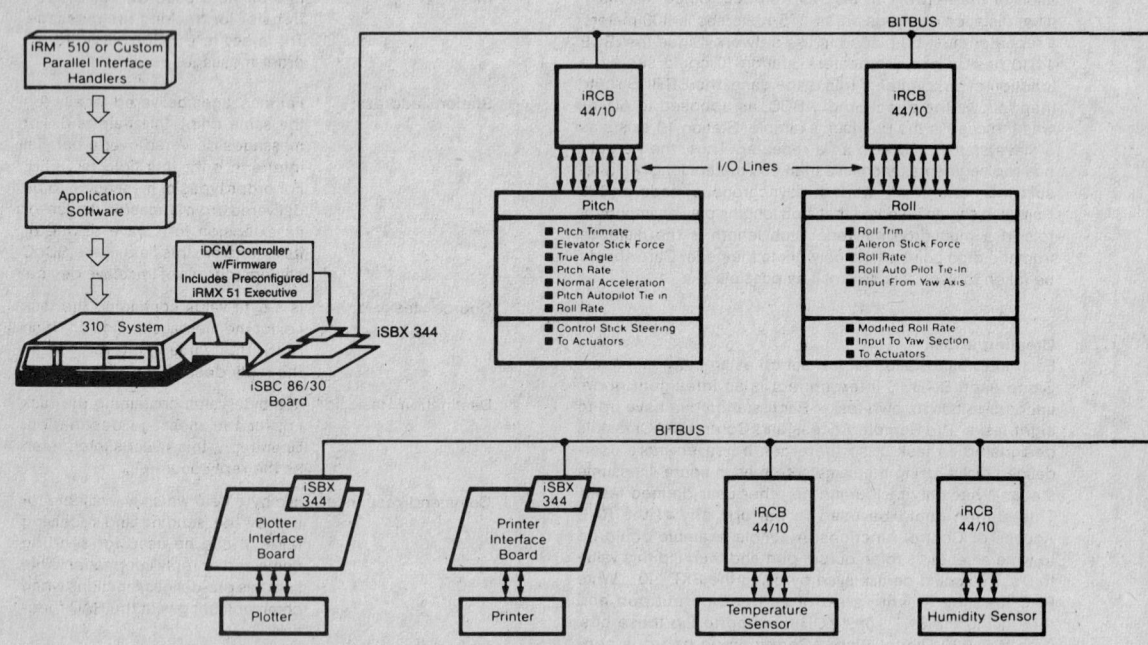

Figure 5.

are pitch trim rate, elevator stick force, true angle, pitch rate, normal acceleration, pitch autopilot tie-in, and roll rate. The outputs of this section are: control stick steering and input to the actuators.

2) Roll: The Roll section is responsible for the rolling movement of the aircraft about its belly. The inputs required for this section are: roll trim, aileron stick force, roll rate, roll autopilot tie-in, and input from yaw axis. The outputs of this section are the modified roll rate, input to the yaw section, and input for the actuators.

3) Yaw: This section is responsible for the horizontal movements of the aircraft. The inputs for the yaw section are: yaw trim, rudder pedal force, yaw rate, lateral acceleration and yaw axis. The outputs of this section are input to the aileron rudder interconnect and input to the actuators.

4) Trailing Edge Flap: The trailing edge flap section is responsible for the drag on the aircraft, mainly during take-off and landing. The inputs to this section are: trailing edge flap command, and transonic flap. The output of this section is input to the actuators.

5) Aileron Rudder Interconnect: When an aircraft rolls, its center of gravity shifts. Therefore, a force is required to counteract the gravitational force in order to keep the aircraft stable. This is achieved by the Aileron Rudder Interconnect. The inputs for this section are input from the pitch and turn coordination. The output of this section is input to the yaw section.

6) Actuators: Actuators are basically transducers which constantly monitor the aircraft. Their inputs are the various forces and factors currently acting on the aircraft and their outputs are the command signals for the next position of the aircraft.

In this example, Intel's 310 system is used as the master station. This is achieved by plugging an iSBX 344 board onto the iSBC 86/30 board inside the 310 system. The iSBX 344 board provides the BITBUS interconnect. Each section of the aircraft block diagram is controlled via an iRCB 44/10 board. (Depending on the device used to take the measurements and the accuracy desired, several iRCB 44/10s could be used in one section.) With this simple insertion, the BITBUS can be used to monitor each section. The actuators are also connected via the BITBUS, providing the control mechanism.

The BITBUS model monitors sections in the following manner: Each node (iRCB 44/10) has several tasks (a maximum of 8) residing on it. These tasks monitor the various parameters in each section. I/O ports on the iRCB 44/10 can be used to read the value of the different parameters in each section. They then perform the necessary computation and return the output parameters of that section to the master node. For example, in the "Pitch section", there would be a task to read the input port which is connected to a sensor monitoring the pitch trim rate. Similarly, there would be a task to compute the output of the pitch sec-

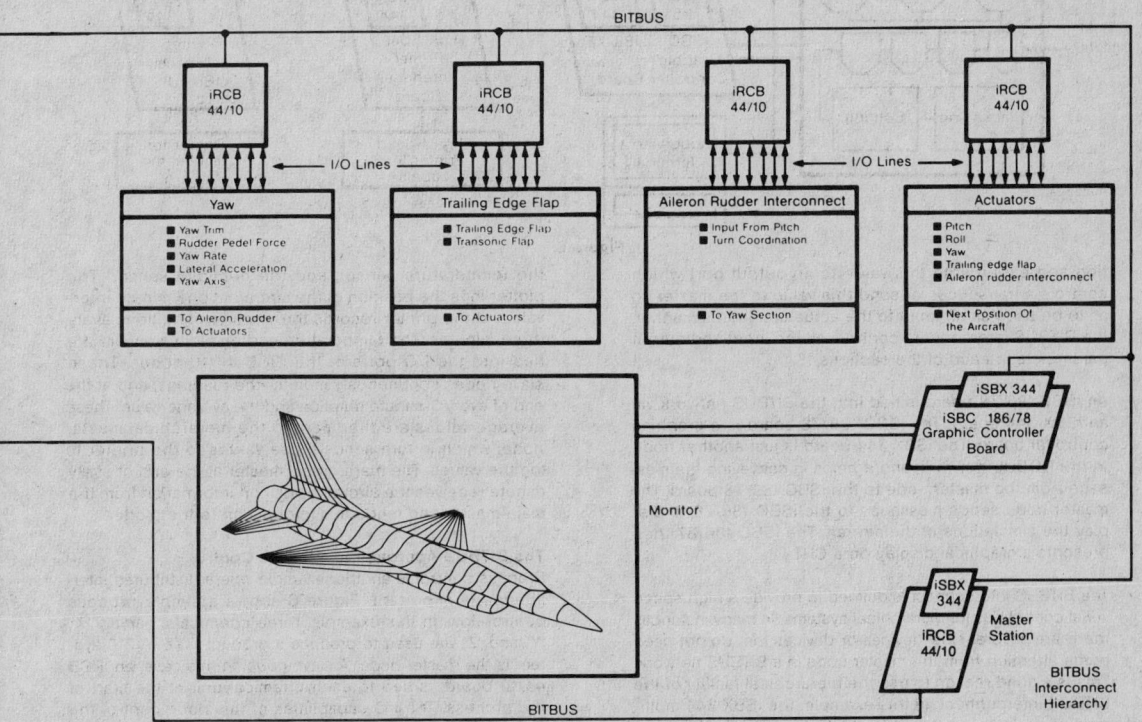

AP-224

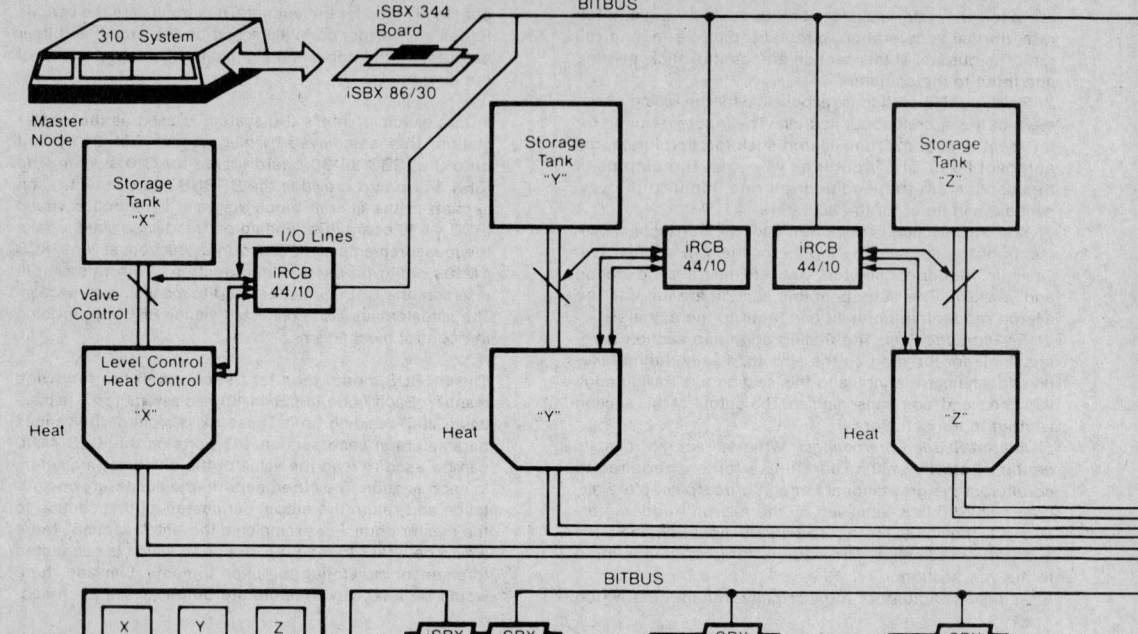

Figure 6.

tion and either write this value to an output port which controls a transducer, or send this value to the master so as to be used as an input to the actuators. In this manner, the BITBUS interconnect controls all the input and output parameters in each of the sections.

An iSBC 186/78 board is tied into the BITBUS network via an iSBX 344 board. The iSBC 186/78 board is a graphics controller board. The iSBX 344 board is just another node in the BITBUS network, and it helps in conveying the message from the master node to the iSBC 186/78 board. The master node sends messages to the iSBC 186/78 to display the simulations of the aircraft. The iSBC 186/87 then presents a graphical display on a CRT.

The BITBUS interconnect is defined to provide a high speed serial control bus for hierarchical systems. In many instances there are several slow devices or devices that do not need prime attention from the master node in a BITBUS network. This is a good reason to use the hierarchical facility of the BITBUS interconnect. In this example, the iSBX 344 multi-module residing on the iRCB 44/10 board uses this hierarchical interconnect. This iRCB 44/10 is now the master node for the four nodes that control the printer, the plotter, the temperature sensor, and the humidity sensor. The plotter logs the position of the aircraft at one minute intervals and the printer records the weather conditions every three minutes. The temperature and humidity sensors are tied into the I/O ports of the iRCB 44/10 nodes. These slave nodes continuously monitor the readings, and at the end of every 3-minute duration find the average value. These average values are then sent to the hierarchical master node, which in turn sends these values to the printer to log the values. The hierarchical master at the end of every minute receives the aircraft's position information from the main master and feeds this information to the plotter.

The BITBUS Approach to Process Control
Process control is another example where distributed intelligence is important. Figure 6 shows a simple process control flow. In this example, three chemicals, namely 'X', 'Y', and 'Z', are used to produce a product 'XYZ'. A 310 system is the master node. A slave node, in this case, an iRCB 44/10 board, is tied to each chemical unit at the start of the process. The I/O capabilities of this node control the flow of the chemical from the storage tank and the level of the chemical in the heating tank. Once the chemical reaches the required level in the heating tank, this node

280072-001

intel AP-224

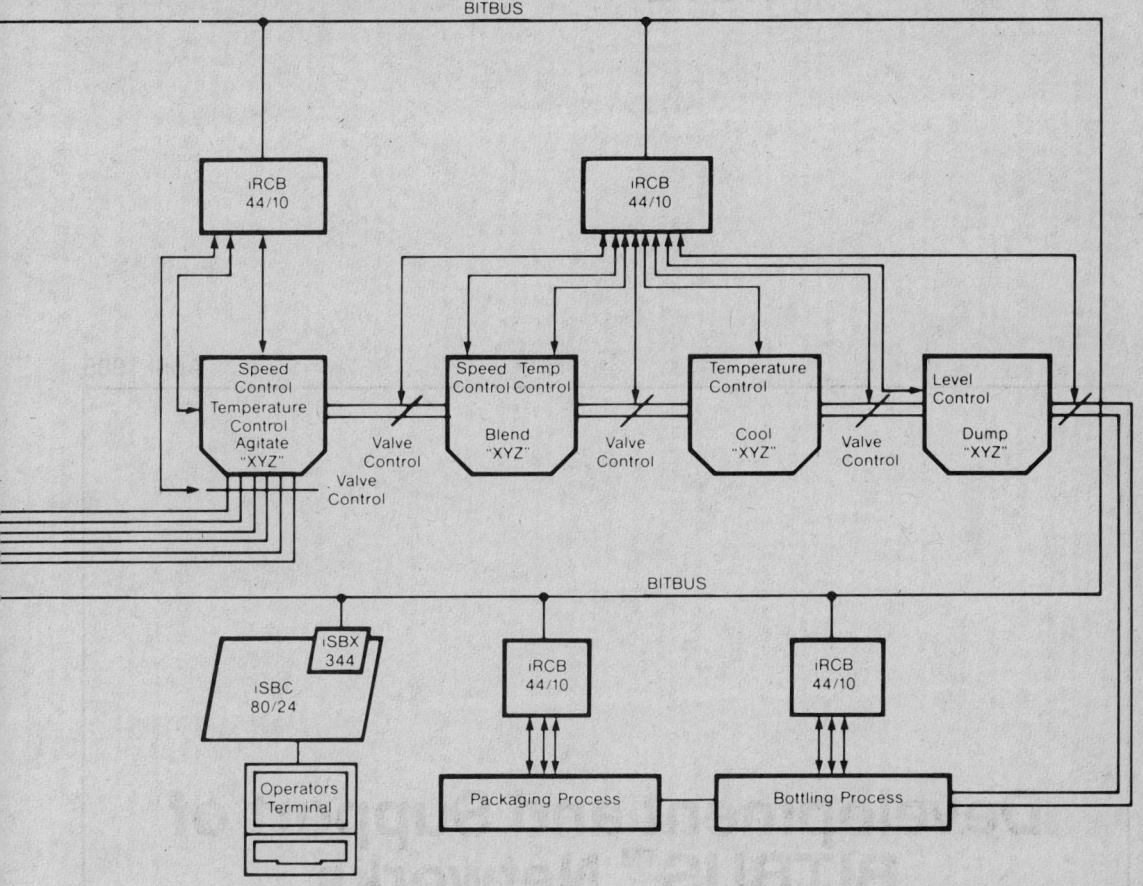

also closes the storage tank valve. After closing this valve, this node then turns the heater on in the tank and controls its temperature. At the end of the heating period, it opens the valve to the next tank.

Another node at the Agitate tank monitors the activities of this tank. This node controls the flow of the chemicals into the tank, the temperature of the chemicals, and the speed of the agitation motor.

Another node controls all the Blend, Cool and Dump stages. In the blend tank, the node controls the speed, temperature and the flow into and out of the tank. In the cooling tank, temperature and flow are controlled. The dump tank control monitors the level of the final product in this tank. If it reaches a near-full stage, it sends a message to the master station which then either stops the process momentarily or else diverts the action onto another dump tank. The BITBUS network then goes on to control the assembly line by controlling the bottling process and the packaging process. The same network is also used to log the packaged product information onto a line printer. Another node could be used to control a high-speed printer which would print labels with the batch number, the date of manufacture

and the expiration date. If desired, an iSBX 344 node could be connected to an iSBC 186/78 board, which would run a color monitor in a supervisor's office, giving the supervisor a pictorial view of the entire manufacturing line. The BITBUS set up could also accommodate operators having a node at their benches to do any form of human interaction that is desired.

Conclusion

The BITBUS interconnect is capable of handling reliable communication activity without impacting CPU performance. It is a low-cost, high-performance approach that is easy to use. It does not require expensive cabling or special cables. It provides intelligent I/O capabilities. It has several speeds of operation in two modes and can be used over long distances at comparable speeds. The flexibility of the BITBUS interconnect makes it very attractive, since more slave nodes can be added with minimal effort. It is intended to be an important tool in an industrial environment, and, by virtue of its open architecture and standardized implementation, to continue to be of use as application needs evolve over time.

intel

APPLICATION NOTE

AP-251

April 1985

Development and Support of BITBUS™ Networks Using the Intel Personal Development System (iPDS™)

BARRY POTTER
DSO TECHNICAL PUBLICATIONS

INTEL CORPORATION, 1985

Order Number 280115-001

AP-251

INTRODUCTION

Development of a network of microcontrollers that communicate using the BITBUS™ interconnect involves key tasks: software development, hardware development, and hardware and software integration. Once development is complete, there will be a need for troubleshooting and field service support of the individual systems that comprise the network.

The purpose of this application note is to illustrate the advantages of using the low cost Intel Personal Development System (iPDS™) to develop, test, and service 8044-based systems connected to the BITBUS interconnect.

This application note is divided into two parts. In the first part, background information on Intel's distributed control modules (iDCM) and the iPDS system is presented.

In the second part, the development tasks associated with developing a BITBUS network are discussed. A BITBUS design example (with a PL/M-80 control task) is also presented showing how the iPDS system can be used in a BITBUS environment. The application note also provides a list of related publications that the reader can reference for further information on the iPDS system, the 8044 microcontroller, and the BITBUS interconnect.

BACKGROUND INFORMATION

The following sections explain how the iDCM products and the iPDS system can be combined to create a low cost distributed control network that communicates over the BITBUS interconnect.

Intel Distributed Control Modules

Intel's family of distributed control modules (iDCM) contain the components, boards, and software needed to create a high-speed distributed control system. The iDCM modules include the following items:

- BITBUS interconnect
- 8044 BITBUS enhanced microcontroller (DCM controller)
- iSBX™ 344 BITBUS MULTIMODULE™ board
- iRCB 44/10 BITBUS remote controller board
- iRMX™ 51 multitasking executive
- iRMX 510 DCM software support package

These modules are briefly described in the following sections.

BITBUS™ INTERCONNECT

The BITBUS interconnect is a serial bus that was developed to provide a standard for connecting microcontrollers using serial communication. Serial communication is better suited for microcontroller networking because it is less expensive (i.e., it requires fewer wires) and it performs reliably over much longer distances than parallel communication.

The BITBUS interconnect supplies the system designer with a simple and reliable foundation for developing a network of distributed control modules. Some of the features of the BITBUS interconnect are as follows:

- Optimized serial bus for high-speed transfer of short control messages and responses
- Based on Intel's 8044 microcontroller with a high-speed synchronous data link controller
- Supports the ISIS-PDS and iRMX operating systems
- Defined high-level commands for remote I/O access and task control
- Ease of expansion and low cost implementation

The individual systems that are connected to the BITBUS interconnect are called nodes. A node can consist of a device, a device and an extension, or a repeater. An extension is a secondary processor board with an iSBX connection that is used to host the iSBX 344 BITBUS MULTIMODULE board. There are two types of devices: the master device and the slave device. In a BITBUS segment there can be a maximum of 28 devices attached to the interconnect. A segment is defined as being the maximum operating distance allowed between a node (master or slave) and a repeater. The BITBUS interconnect provides two modes of operation that can be configured for different speeds and distance of operation as shown in Table 1.

8044 MICROCONTROLLER

Intel introduced the 8044 microcontroller as a stand-alone high performance single-chip computer intended for use in real-time applications such as instrumentation, industrial control, and intelligent peripherals. The 8044 microcontroller combines onto a single chip the 8051 microcontroller with a high-level data link/synchronous data link control (HDLC/SDLC) serial communication controller, called the serial interface unit (SIU). Figure 1 shows a simplified diagram of the 8044 microcontroller.

With the dual controller architecture, the 8044 microcontroller can perform complex control tasks and high-speed communication in a distributed control environment. The 8044's architecture and instruction set is identical to the 8051 microcontroller's.

AP-251

Table 1 BITBUS™ Interconnect Modes of Operation

Feature	Synchronous Mode	Self-Clocked Mode
Maximum nodes allowed in a segment	28	28
Repeater nodes allowed in a BITBUS™ network	0	2 at 375K bps 10 at 62.5K bps
Maximum nodes allowed in a BITBUS™ network	28	250
Range of transfer rates	500K/2.4M bps	62.5K/375K bps
Wire pairs needed	2	1 (no repeaters) 2 (with repeaters)
Maximum operating distance allowed in a BITBUS segment	30 meters	300 meters at 375K bps 1200 meters at 62.5K bps
Maximum operating distance allowed in a BITBUS network	30 meters	900 meters at 375K bps 13.2 Km at 62.5K bps

iSBX™ 344 BITBUS™ MULTIMODULE™ BOARD

The iSBX 344 BITBUS board is the hardware interface that enables the iPDS system to be used as a master or slave extension in a BITBUS network. The iSBX 344 BITBUS board is an iSBX MULTIMODULE board that is used with any Intel single-board computer (iSBC®-computer) that supports iSBX expansion I/O. The iSBX 344 board contains a firmware enhanced 8044 microcontroller, called the 8044 BITBUS enhanced microcontroller (BEM). The firmware contains a preconfigured version of the iRMX 51 multitasking executive, power-up diagnostics, a communications buffer, and a remote access and control function (RAC) that enables users to communicate with and control different microcontrollers and I/O devices. The iSBX 344 BITBUS board can be used as a master or slave node in a BITBUS network.

iRCB 44/10 BITBUS REMOTE CONTROLLER BOARD

The iRCB 44/10 is a stand-alone BITBUS node based on the DCM controller. Unlike the iSBX 344 BITBUS board, the iRCB 44/10 board does not require a host iSBC board upon which to operate. This board can be used as a master or slave device in a BITBUS network. The iRCB 44/10 can also be used with the iSBX 344 BITBUS board to create a master or slave extension device.

iRMX™ 51 MULTITASKING EXECUTIVE

The iRMX 51 executive is a real-time multitasking software tool designed to monitor and control real-time events. The iRMX 51 executive provides the protocol for task management, passing control messages, and interrupt handling in a BITBUS environment.

iRMX™ 510 SOFTWARE SUPPORT PACKAGE

The iRMX 510 support package contains the software for interfacing the iPDS system to the iSBX 344 BITBUS board during run time and during software development. Support of iRMX 51 executive applications is provided via the iRMX 51 libraries incorporated in the iRMX 510 package. With the iRMX 51 libraries, users can create iRMX 51 compatible control tasks and store them in EPROM memory devices located on the iDCM boards.

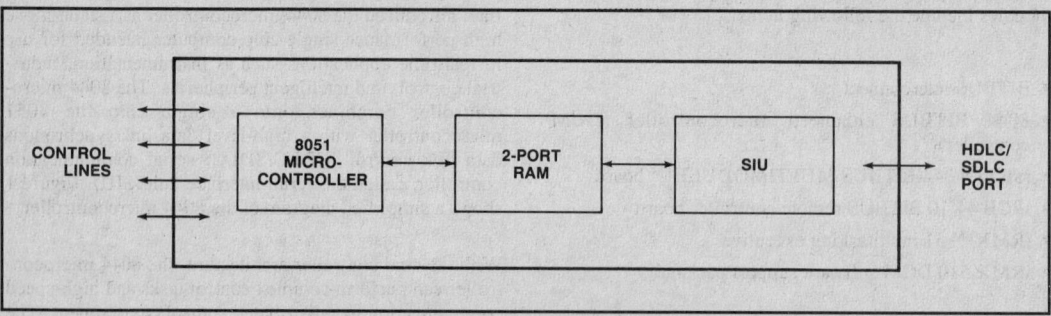

Figure 1 8044 Microcontroller Architecture

The iRMX 510 package contains the DCM controller firmware in a loadable object file. This file is used with the EMV-44 emulator to debug the systems connected to the interconnect.

Intel Personal Development System

Intel's iPDS system is an integrated portable development system that can be used for solving the tasks associated with developing a BITBUS network. The following sections briefly describe the iPDS system.

BASIC iPDS™ SYSTEM

The iPDS system is comprised of the 8085A microprocessor, 64K bytes of RAM, a 640K-byte integral floppy disk drive (expandable to 2.4M bytes), a nine-inch CRT screen, and a full ASCII keyboard.

The ISIS-PDS operating system included with the iPDS system is based on the ISIS II operating system. The following software is included with the iPDS system:

- CREDIT™ text editor
- 8080/8085 macro assembler
- Software utility programs
- Power-up diagnostics

iPDS™ SYSTEM EXPANSION TOOLS

A wide range of expansion tools are available for the iPDS system. These tools include the following:

- Optional processor board — A second 8085A-based processor board can be added to the iPDS system to create a single-user dual processor computer.
- Add-on mass storage — Up to three 640K-byte disk drives can be daisy chained to the iPDS system. This brings total disk storage up to 2.4 M bytes.
- iSBX MULTIMODULE adapter board — With this adapter board, up to four iSBX MULTIMODULE boards can be plugged into the iPDS system at one time. The iSBX 344 BITBUS board is connected to the iPDS system via this board.
- Bubble memory — Up to two iSBX 251 bubble memory MULTIMODULE boards can be connected to the iPDS system's MULTIMODULE adapter board for a combined memory storage capacity of 256K bytes.
- EMV/PROM programming adapter board — This board provides the interface between the iPDS base processor board and the EMV-44 emulator and PROM programming modules.

Figure 2 shows the iPDS system with some of the available development tools.

iPDS™ System Development Tools for 8044-Based Systems

In addition to the options previously described, Intel offers a variety of tools that enable you to perform the development tasks associated with 8044-based systems.

EMV-44 CON CONVERSION PACKAGE

The EMV-44 CON conversion package converts an EMV-51A emulator to an EMV-44 emulator. The resulting EMV-44 interfaces to any 8044 system (via the 8044 microcontroller socket) and assists in the software and hardware development and debugging of 8044 systems. The EMV-44 has a special bondout chip that duplicates the behavior of the 8044 microcontroller.

EPROM PROGRAMMING PERSONALITY MODULES

A family of state-of-the-art personality modules are available for programming a wide range of EPROM and ROM devices. These personality modules provide the necessary support for programming the control software into a BITBUS node's EPROMs and E^2PROMs. Table 2 lists the personality modules available for use with the iPDS system.

SOFTWARE SUPPORT PACKAGES

The remote access and control (RAC) functions included with the DCM controller's firmware can be used for controlling devices attached to the BITBUS interconnect. The iPDS system can access these functions from an ISIS program. The iSBX 344 board uses the iSBX connector to interface the ISIS operating system and the BITBUS interconnect. The iPDS system can control a BITBUS network using these built-in RAC functions.

If the built-in RAC tasks do not meet the requirements of the control application, additional control tasks can be written and stored in EPROM memory devices on the BITBUS node. The DCM controller will support user-written instructions in either ASM-51 or PL/M-51. ASM-51 and PL/M-51 software development packages are available to use with the iPDS system for writing and compiling 8051-based control tasks.

BITBUS™ DEVELOPMENT CYCLE

To illustrate the advantages of using the iPDS system to develop and service a BITBUS network, the following sections discuss the development tasks, describing how the iPDS system and its family of development tools can be used to streamline these tasks. Figure 3 shows the development cycle for the BITBUS network, with tasks supported by the iPDS system shaded in gray.

Figure 2 iPDS™ System with Optional Development Tools

BITBUS™ Network Operating Parameters

There are several factors that need to be considered in developing the individual nodes that will attach to the BITBUS interconnect. The following list describes the areas that need to be considered.

- Range of operation — Consider the distance over which the network is expected to communicate. Does the BITBUS interconnect support this distance (see Table 1)? Will repeater nodes be needed to extend the capabilities of the BITBUS interconnect beyond the length limits of one segment?

Table 2 EPROM Programming Personality Modules

Personality Module	EPROM Type	Devices Supported
iUP-Fast 27/K with U2 Upgrade Kit	EPROM/E^{2}PROM/KEPROM	2764, 2764A, 27128, 27256, 27C64, 87C64, 27128A, 27C256, 27512, 27513, 2817A, and 27916
iUP-F27/128	E^{2}PROM	2716, 2732, 2732A, 2764, 27128, 2815, and 2816
iUP-F87/51A	Microcontroller	8748, 8748H, 8048, 8749H, 8049, 8048H, 8049H, 8050H, 8751, 8751H, and 8051
iUP-F87/44A	Peripheral	8741A, 8041A, 8742, 8042, 8744H, 8044AH, and 8755A

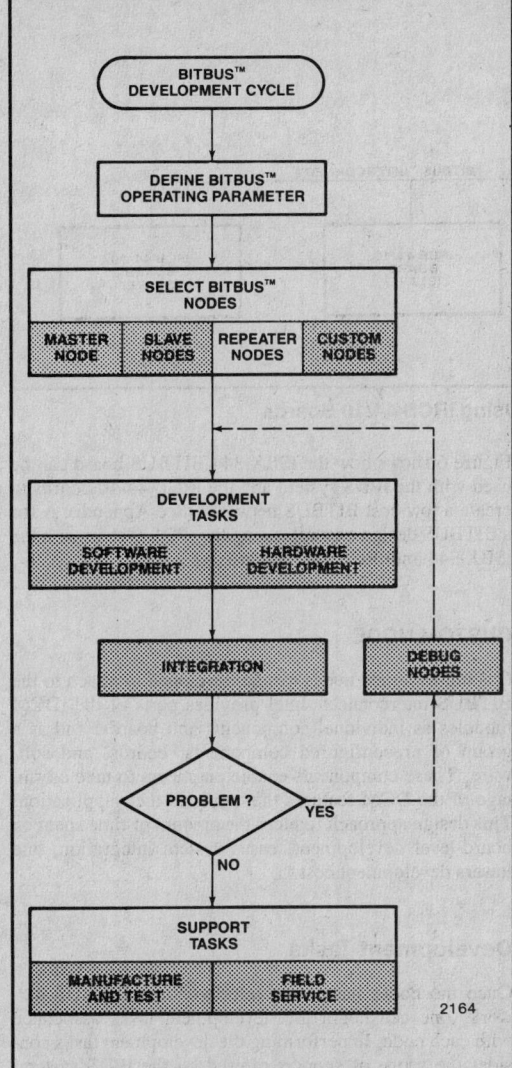

Figure 3 BITBUS™ Development Cycle

- Node functions — Consider the tasks that each node in the network is to perform. Can one of the preconfigured iDCM boards be used to perform the tasks? Perhaps a custom-designed node will be needed to perform the tasks. Will user-written control tasks be needed?
- Future expansion — Additional devices can be added to the BITBUS network without affecting the performance of the existing network devices. Consider the operating parameters of these additional nodes. Will the new devices operate in a different mode and at a different speed than the other devices? The BITBUS interconnect is designed to operate in a hierarchical network. This means that there can be different segments of the network operating in different modes and speeds of operation. A secondary master station can be configured to control the new segment of devices connected to the network.
- Cost of development — Consider the cost of development and of the final product. The iDCM modules offer a low cost approach to developing a BITBUS network. But what about the development tools needed to support the devices attached to the network? Tools are needed that support hardware and software development, debugging, and integration. System integration will need tools that can test the operation of individual devices as well as test the overall operation of the network devices. Field service and manufacturing tasks need tools for testing and troubleshooting the systems connected to the network.

Selecting the BITBUS™ Nodes

The next step in the development cycle is to select (or build in the case of custom nodes) the devices that will comprise the nodes in the network.

MASTER AND SLAVE NODES

Intel's iDCM hardware modules (iRCB 44/10 BITBUS remote controller board and iSBX 344 BITBUS MULTIMODULE board) can be used to create low cost master and slave devices. The iRCB 44/10 is a single-board computer with 24 parallel digital I/O lines that can be used to monitor and control outside events. In addition, the iSBX expansion connector will host one MULTIMODULE board for I/O expansion.

The iRCB 44/10 board has sockets for a BITBUS repeater. It also has on-board ROM and RAM sockets for the DCM controller's external memory needs and for storing user created control tasks. A simple control network that is capable of controlling many processes can be created by connecting iRCB 44/10 boards as shown in Figure 4.

- Speed of operation — At what speed is the network to operate? Will segments of the network operate under different speeds? (See Appendix C for a list of related publications on the BITBUS interconnect.)
- Number of nodes — How many nodes are needed? Keep in mind that the number of nodes allowed in any one segment of a BITBUS network is 28. In the self-clocked mode of operation, up to 250 nodes can be connected together. This is done using repeater stations to extend the number of nodes in the network beyond the length limits of a BITBUS segment (see Table 1).

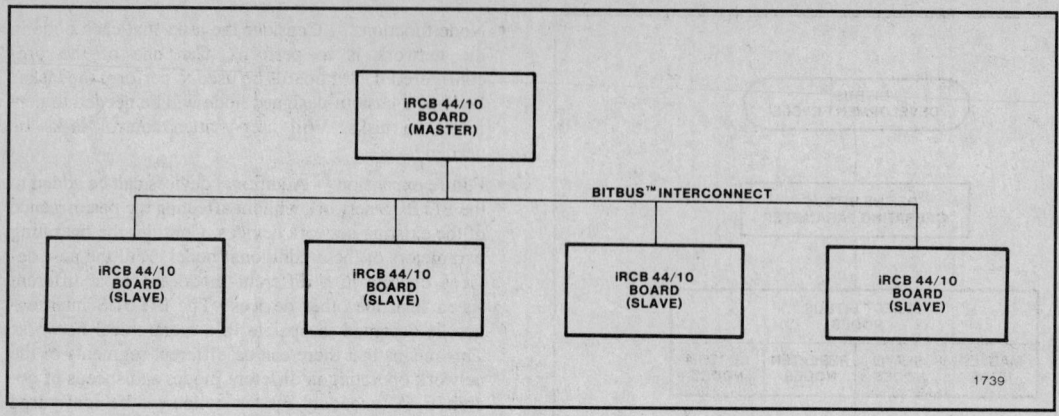

Figure 4 BITBUS™ Network Using iRCB 44/10 Boards

The iSBX 344 BITBUS board contains a BITBUS connection and an iSBX parallel connector. The BITBUS connection allows the iSBX 344 board to be part of the BITBUS network. The iSBX parallel connector allows the iSBX 344 board to communicate with any iSBC board that supports the iSBX I/O expansion bus. The iSBX 344 board is mounted to an iSBC MULTIMODULE adapter board via the parallel connector. The iSBX parallel connector enables master or slave extensions with different capabilities than the 8044 to use the BITBUS network. The iSBX 344 board also features ROM and RAM sockets for the DCM controller's external memory needs and for storing additional user tasks.

The iSBX 344 BITBUS board is capable of communicating with Intel operating systems that run on the iSBC board to which the iSBX 344 board is mounted. The iRMX 510 software package included with the iDCM boards contains the operating system handlers that enable the iSBX 344 board to operate under the ISIS-PDS, iRMX 86, iRMX 88, or iRMX 286 operating systems.

Figure 5 shows how the iSBX 344 BITBUS board can be used with the iPDS system to create a master extension device for controlling a BITBUS network.

REPEATER NODE

Typically, repeaters are used to extend the number of nodes and the operating distance of the network beyond the length limits of one segment. The iRCB 44/10 board has sockets for adding user-supplied components for setting up the repeater function. The iRCB 44/10 board can be used as a stand-alone repeater station in addition to performing local control tasks. It can be interfaced with an iSBX 344 BITBUS board and used as an extension device for repeating the transmission of BITBUS messages at a different mode and speed of operation.

Figure 6 shows how the iSBX 344 BITBUS board can be used with the iPDS system and the iRCB 44/10 boards to create a low cost BITBUS network. (See Appendix A for a BITBUS design example using the iPDS system with the iSBX 344 and iRCB 44/10 boards.)

CUSTOM NODE

Custom-designed nodes can be developed to attach to the BITBUS interconnect. Intel provides parts of the iDCM modules as individual components and boards, and as a group of preconfigured components, boards, and software. These components enable engineers to take advantage of the DCM features that apply to their application. This design approach reduces the amount of time spent on board-level development, eases system integration, and lowers development cost.

Development Tasks

Once the nodes have been selected for a BITBUS network, one can begin the development tasks associated with each node. In performing the development tasks consider the scope of support offered by the iPDS system. The iPDS system and its family of 8044-based development tools offer the support needed to develop individual BITBUS nodes as well as service the network once it is operational.

SOFTWARE DEVELOPMENT

Software development involves writing and debugging the software for each node that will attach to the network. Software development support required includes text editors for writing the source code, assemblers and compilers for converting source code into machine language, utility programs that aid in compiling and locating the software, and software emulators to debug the code.

AP-251

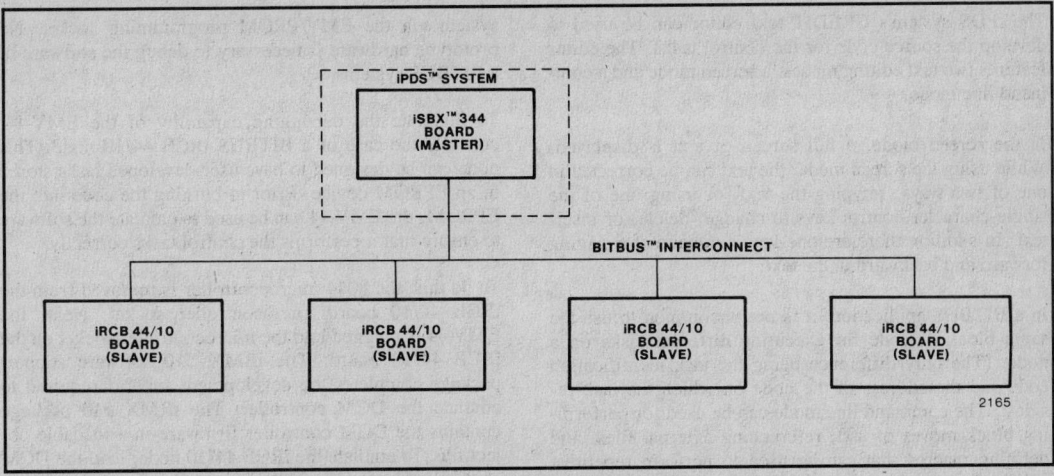

Figure 5 iPDS™ System Used as a Master Extension Device

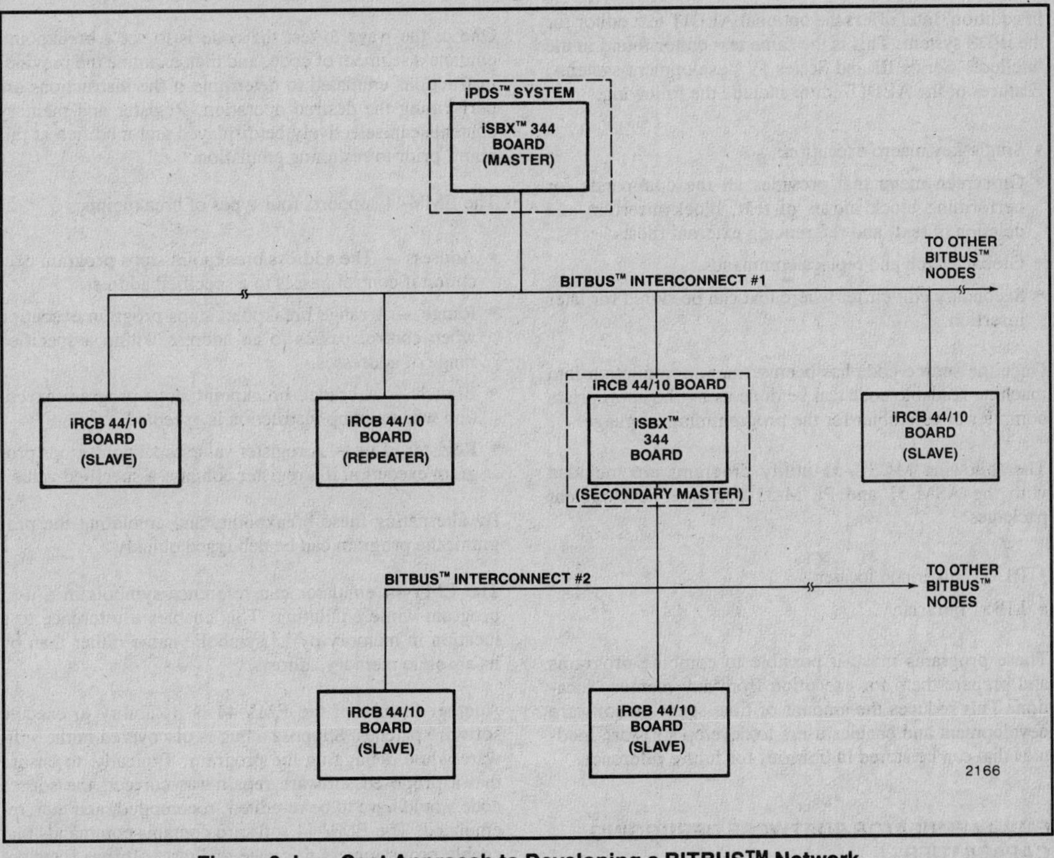

Figure 6 Low Cost Approach to Developing a BITBUS™ Network

The iPDS system's CREDIT text editor can be used to develop the source code for the control tasks. The editor features two text editing modes, a screen mode and a command line mode.

In the screen mode, a full screen of text is displayed. While using the screen mode, the text can be corrected in one of two ways: retyping the text, or using one of the single-character control keys to change, delete, or insert text. In addition there are one-key commands for paging forward and backward in the text.

In a BITBUS application, it is not uncommon to use the same block of code for executing different tasks on a node. (The only difference being the task identification code and the address of the node on which the task resides.) The command line mode can be used for performing block moves of text, referencing external files, and defining macros that can be used to perform repetitive editing functions.

In addition, Intel offers the optional AEDIT text editor for the iPDS system. This is the same text editor found in the Intellec® Series III and Series IV development systems. Features of the AEDIT editor include the following:

- Single-key macro execution.
- On-screen menu that provides all the commands for performing block moves of text, block insertion and deletion of text, and referencing external files.
- Global search and replace commands.
- Secondary edit buffer where text can be stored for later insertion.

Once the source code has been written, compilation into machine readable code can be done using the appropriate compiler or assembler for the programming language.

The following MCS® -51 utility programs are included with the ASM-51 and PL/M-51 software development packages:

- RL 51 linker and locater
- LIB51 librarian

These programs make it possible to combine programs and prepare them for execution from any memory location. This reduces the amount of time spent on software development and enables users to develop software modules that can be stored in libraries for future reference.

EMV-44 EMULATOR SOFTWARE DEBUGGING CAPABILITIES

The EMV-44 emulator can be used to debug 8051-based object code. The EMV-44 plugs into the side of the iPDS system via the EMV/PROM programming socket. No prototype hardware is necessary to debug the software of a BITBUS system.

To illustrate the debugging capability of the EMV-44, consider the case of a BITBUS iRCB 44/10 node. This node can be designed to have user-developed tasks stored in an EPROM device. Prior to burning the code into the EPROM, the EMV-44 can be used to emulate the software to ensure that it performs the control tasks correctly.

To do this, the 8044 microcontroller is removed from the iRCB 44/10 board microcontroller socket. Next, the EMV-44 is plugged into the microcontroller socket on the iRCB 44/10 board. The iRMX 510 software support package completes the development support required to emulate the DCM controller. The iRMX 510 package contains the DCM controller firmware in a loadable object file. To emulate the iRCB 44/10 node, load the DCM controller object file and the user-written control software into the EMV-44's system memory.

One of the ways to test the code is to set a breakpoint, emulate a segment of code, and then examine the previous instructions emulated to determine if the instructions are performing the desired operation. Register and memory contents can selectively be displayed and modified at this point, prior to resuming emulation.

The EMV-44 supports four types of breakpoints:

- Address — The address breakpoint stops program execution if control passes to a specified address.
- Range — A range breakpoint stops program execution when control passes to an address within a specified range of addresses.
- Branch — A branch breakpoint stops program execution when a jump instruction is executed.
- Register value — A register value breakpoint stops program execution if a register contains a specified value.

By alternating these breakpoints and emulating the program, the program can be debugged quickly.

The EMV-44 emulator can reference symbols in a user program while emulating. This enables a reference to a location in memory by its symbolic name rather than by its absolute memory address.

Another feature of the EMV-44 is its ability to execute software patches. Suppose a bug is discovered in the software while debugging the program. Typically, to ensure that a proposed software repair was correct, the source code would have to be re-edited, recompiled, and then re-emulated. The EMV-44 software contains commands that enable programmers to create and test software fixes before making changes in the source file. To create a software patch, have the EMV-44 break emulation at the location of the error in the program. Using the EMV command ASM, insert a jump to an address in free memory where the patch is to be stored. Next, using the ASM command, insert the instructions for the software patch in the free memory space. As the last command in the patch, insert a jump back to the first error-free address of the main program. Now the program can be re-emulated to ensure that the patch fixed the error. The remaining program can be debugged and fixed in this manner.

After successfully debugging the program, the emulation session can be saved to a file on disk for future reference.

HARDWARE DEVELOPMENT SUPPORT

The hardware development tasks associated with the pre-configured iDCM boards include configuring the boards for speed and mode of operation, addressing of external memory, and selecting the address of the node with respect to the master device. If the iSBX 344 board is used with an iSBC board, the two boards will have to be configured so they are compatible with one another. Repeater nodes have to be configured with user supplied components to enable the repeater function on the iRCB 44/10 boards. All of these tasks can be performed by setting jumper pins on the iDCM boards.

For custom nodes, hardware development involves designing and developing the circuits that will make up the systems connected to the network (8044 microcontroller, iSBX 344 and iRCB 44/10 boards, memory, input/output circuits).

The EMV-44 has six terminal posts that supply test signals to the user prototype system. These signals indicate the internal state of various operations in the 8044 microcontroller. External test equipment can be connected to these test terminals to help debug the hardware of a BITBUS node.

Suppose, for example, there was a custom-designed BITBUS node with user-written control tasks attached to the BITBUS interconnect. The EMV-44 can be used to debug this node. The EMV-44 can be used to read and write I/O ports, read and write internal memory locations, access and change the contents of registers, and perform data analysis — all in a controlled environment. Emulation can take place in the single-step or real-time emulation mode. If an error is detected, the EMV-44 can be used with a logic analyzer to determine whether the problem is in the hardware of the node or in the software code. The EMUL test signal on the EMV-44 can be used to trigger an input to the logic analyzer. The logic analyzer then feeds a signal to the EXTBRK (external break) input terminal, causing emulation to halt.

As each part of the hardware prototype becomes available, it can be added to the system. In this way, modules can be tested as they are developed. The EMV-44's ability to execute in single-step mode, to read and write data at I/O ports, to examine or modify memory or 8044 registers, to trace program flow, and to break in real-time mode provides the power needed to debug the hardware.

INTEGRATION

Integration is a two-step process. Step one involves testing the software and hardware of each node to ensure compatibility. Step two involves testing the operation of the nodes on the BITBUS interconnect to ensure that the nodes are working properly. The overall operation of the BITBUS network needs to be tested to see if all nodes are communicating with one another. Some questions that need to be answered are

Do the nodes rely on input from other nodes?

Are they receiving this data?

Is the master sending the control mesages to the correct node?

Are the slave devices responding correctly?

Support needed during this phase of the development cycle involves the use of hardware and software emulators, PROM programmers, text editors, and software utility programs.

Integration of a BITBUS node can be carried out using the EMV-44 emulator. This enables the programmer to test and verify the compatibility of the software with the hardware in a real-time controlled environment. As each node is developed and tested, it can be added to the network.

For nodes that will have external user-written control tasks stored in memory devices, the EMV-44 can be used to emulate these control tasks to ensure that the nodes are performing the tasks correctly. If problems are found, the EMV-44 can be used to diagnose and locate the source of the problem.

After testing, the appropriate PROM programming personality module can be used to program the control software into the 8044 system's PROMs and EPROMs devices.

The iPDS system can be used to test the overall operation of a BITBUS network. Diagnostic and integration routines can be developed using the ASM-80 or PL/M-80 languages. These programs can access the built-in RAC functions on the iSBX 344 board to send control tasks to the nodes attached to the network. (Appendix A describes how the iPDS system can be configured to operate in a BITBUS network. Appendix B presents a PL/M-80 program that is used to control the operation of I/O devices attached to a BITBUS node.)

For example, the iPDS CREDIT text editor can be used to create a menu-driven test program that allows users to enter and change control tasks at will. In these sessions, control order messages can be sent to a BITBUS node causing it to perform one of the RAC functions. The user can (using an input menu) have the program execute just once or have it loop forever, sending control messages to the nodes attached to the network. The iPDS system can monitor and keep track of nodes that did not respond to a task. The on-board diagnostic LED's on the iDCM boards can also be programmed to provide visual verification of a node's response to a control task. In addition, these programs can read and write I/O ports and, based on the input, send control tasks that enable another node on the network to begin or stop operating.

SUPPORT TASKS

The last stage of the development cycle is providing the necessary services needed to support the BITBUS network. Typically, these support tasks fall under two areas: (1) manufacturing and testing, and (2) field service.

Manufacturing and Testing

During this stage, final checks can be made on each system that is to be attached to the BITBUS interconnect. Diagnostic test routines developed in the debugging of the software and hardware can be used for testing a board prior to network operation.

The optional iPDS PROTO design kit can be used to develop customized plug-in test equipment that is compatible with the EMV/PROM programming adapter socket. The DCM controller can be used to develop an 8044-based plug-in test module for testing custom BITBUS boards as they are developed. The RAC functions in the DCM controller can be used to test these boards prior to attaching it to the network. The tests performed in this stage can reduce system integration of the hardware once it is connected to the network.

FIELD SERVICE

The last area of concern for developing a BITBUS network is ensuring the availability of diagnostic and repair tools for servicing (both in the repair depot and in the field) the BITBUS network and its control systems. These tools should be flexible enough to offer portability, software and hardware emulation, software upgrade support, and tests that can be used to isolate a problem to a replaceable portion of the node (e.g., board, module, or component).

The EMV-44 emulator can be used to troubleshoot a defective node in the network without removing it from the network. One simply removes the node's microcontroller and replaces it with the EMV-44 emulator. The ability to connect into the network and emulate the defective node in its operating environment enables field engineers to quickly locate the source of the problem. Figure 7 shows the iPDS system and EMV-44 being used to troubleshoot a defective node in a typical BITBUS interconnect environment.

The EMV MACRO command can be used to write in-depth diagnostic routines to test the defective node. Figure 8 shows a sample screen display of a test macro written to test an I/O device address line.

The EMV-44 provides a method of running diagnostic control routines and, when conditions for breaking are met, going in and tracing the flow of execution prior to the break.

The EMV-44's ability to execute software patches enables the testing of repair code before committing the changes to the source file 0 for recompilation or assembling. If software changes are necessary, the CREDIT text editor can be used to make the changes. Then, after recompiling, the iPDS system can be used with the appropriate PROM programming personality module to program upgrades or patches to user developed code that is stored in the system's EPROM memory devices.

Using the iPDS system and its optional development tools allows repairs and troubleshooting to take place on-line rather than pulling a control node from the network. This results in savings to the company in terms of man-hours necessary to troubleshoot and repair, and cost savings in stocking of spare boards for the network. It also reduces down time of the overall BITBUS network because the defective node does not have to be removed from the network for diagnostics and repair at a repair depot.

In the repair depot, the iPDS system can be used to troubleshoot defective boards using diagnostic test routines developed during hardware debugging and field service support.

An iPDS system with an optional bubble memory board offers a stable, nonvolatile form of mass storage that is often more acceptable than disk storage in hostile environments. Diagnostic test routines for debugging a BITBUS node can be written and stored in the bubble memory.

iPDS™ SYSTEM GENERAL PURPOSE FEATURES

In addition to the development support offered by the iPDS system, it can also be used as a general purpose computer.

The iPDS system can be used to maintain inventory records, perform failure analysis and other manufacturing tasks, and other general purpose tasks — all while the iPDS system is controlling the BITBUS network. (The iPDS system can be equipped with an optional second processor board. This enables one to control the BITBUS

Figure 7 Troubleshooting a BITBUS™ Node

```
   *DEFINE : IO_TEST
  .*BR0=F004H             (SET BREAKPOINT)
  .*GO FROM .READ_STATUS      (START EMULATION AT LABEL READ_STATUS)
  .*IF RBYTE .ACC < > 01 AND RBYTE .P1 < > 00 THEN        (TEST A REG)
  .*WRITE 'IO TEST FAILED'
  .*ELSE
  .*WRITE 'IO TEST PASSED'
  .*ENDIF
  .*EM
  *:IO_TEST
                         : 0F00H=RET              GO=BREAK
IO TEST PASSED
```

Figure 8 Sample EMV-44 Test Macro

nodes with the A processor, while using the B processor for other functions.) The popularity of the system has prompted a number of third-party vendors to provide both software and hardware support modules for the iPDS system. The iPDS system is CP/M* compatible, making it possible for one to choose from a large list of software packages that include word processing, project management packages, financial accounting tools, executive/time planning tools, and several high-level programming languages.

Also available is the Intel Insite™ user's program library. This is a collection of user designed and supplied non-licensed software available for use with Intel products.

*CP/M is a registered trademark of Digital Research, Inc.

For example, there is an Insite program that enables the iPDS system to be used as a dumb terminal for entering user input to devices attached to a BITBUS network.

SUMMARY

The iPDS system and its family of 8044 development tools can be used to develop and support BITBUS network applications. The versatility of the iPDS system, combined with its portability, allows it to function as a complete development tool — for software and hardware development of BITBUS nodes, integration of these nodes, and manufacturing and field service support of nodes that communicate using the BITBUS interconnect. Table 3 summarizes the support offered by the iPDS system in developing and servicing a BITBUS network.

Table 3 iPDS™ System Features and BITBUS™ Development Tasks

Task	iPDS™ System Feature
Software development	The iPDS system's CREDIT or optional AEDIT text editor is designed for software development. ASM-51, PL/M-51, and CP/M*-based compilers (for FORTH, LISP, PASCAL, C, and FORTRAN) are available.
Software debugging	The iPDS system used with the EMV-44 emulator effectively debugs programs programmed in ASM-51 or PL/M-51.
Develop/debug hardware	The EMV-44 provides a window to registers, memory I/O ports, and logic signals of the 8044 microcontroller that are normally inaccessible to the user.
Hardware/software integration	The iPDS system can be used as a master extension to send control tasks to the slave node while using the EMV-44 to monitor the interaction of the hardware and software.
Program PROM/EPROM memory chips	A family of PROM programming personality modules provides an easy-to-use, cost-effective approach in programming the latest nonvolatile memory devices.
Monitor BITBUS node operation	The iPDS system and the EMV-44 can be used with the iSBX 344 BITBUS board, and the iRMX 510 software support package to monitor the operation of the BITBUS node.
Production tests of BITBUS nodes	The EMV-44 can be used with the iPDS system, the iSBX 344 BITBUS board, and the iRMX 510 software support package to test individual nodes as they are developed.
Field service support of BITBUS nodes	The iPDS system is used with the EMV-44, iSBX 344 BITBUS board, the iRMX 510 software support package, and other support tools to troubleshoot and repair BITBUS nodes.
Master node	The iPDS system can be interfaced with the iSBX 344 BITBUS board and the iRMX 510 software support package and used as a master extension device to control the operation of a BITBUS network.
Slave node	The iPDS system can be interfaced with the iSBX 344 MULTIMODULE board and the iRMX 510 software support package for use as a slave extension device.

*CP/M is a registered trademark of Digital Research, Inc.

APPENDIX A:
BITBUS™ NETWORK DESIGN EXAMPLE

AP-251

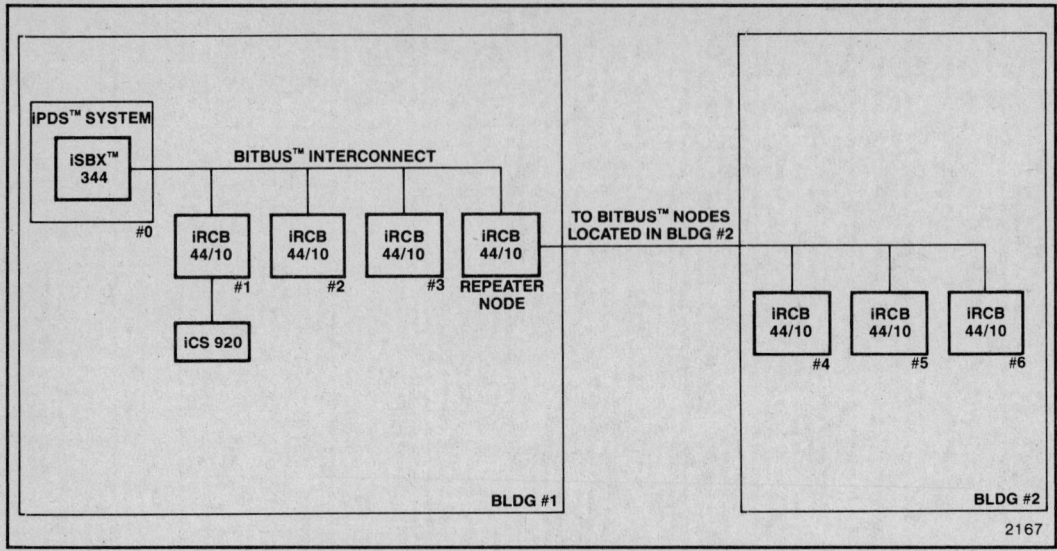

Figure A-1 An Example BITBUS™ Network

BITBUS™ NETWORK DESIGN EXAMPLE

This section contains a design example of a BITBUS network that uses the iPDS system to control the nodes attached to the network. Also included in this section are instructions for configuring the various BITBUS nodes for operation.

Figure A-1 illustrates a simple BITBUS network. Assume that the network is designed to operate in a factory environment that extends over two buildings. Also assume that the distance between the master and the slave devices located in building #2 is greater than 300 meters. This network is designed to operate in the self-clocked mode of operation at a speed of 375K bps. For this network to operate at the speed desired, a repeater station is needed (see Table 1) to extend the BITBUS electrical signals from the master station to the slave devices in building #2. The iRCB 44/10 remote controller board has on-board repeater capability, so it will be used as a repeater node in the network.

The network's master station is the iPDS system interfaced with an iSBX 344 BITBUS MULTIMODULE board. The slave devices attached to the network are iRCB 44/10 stand-alone remote controller boards. The iPDS system is used as the master node for controlling the BITBUS nodes.

The iSBX 344 BITBUS board attached to the iPDS system is labeled device #0 and is connected via the BITBUS interconnect to slave devices #1, #2, and #3. The BITBUS interconnect is then routed from device #3 to the iRCB 44/10 repeater node. From the repeater node, the BITBUS interconnect is connected to the first node in building #2 (device #4). From this board, the BITBUS interconnect is attached to the remaining two devices in the network (#5 and #6). Thus, the network has one master node (device #0), a repeater node, and six slave nodes (#1 through #6).

HARDWARE INSTALLATION/CONFIGURATION

This section explains how to configure the BITBUS network shown in Figure A-1 for operation.

NOTE

In the network example, the I/O hardware interfaces required to support the tasks at each node were not presented. Typical I/O hardware interfaces for these nodes include analog signal boards, digital signaling boards, optical sensors, and custom-designed I/O devices.

iPDS™ System Configuration

To configure the iPDS system for use with the iSBX 344 BITBUS board, perform the following:

- Install an iPDS-120 MULTIMODULE adapter board to the base processor board inside the iPDS system. This enables the iPDS system to host the iSBX 344 BITBUS board. Refer to Appendix A in the *iPDS™ User's*

intel AP-251

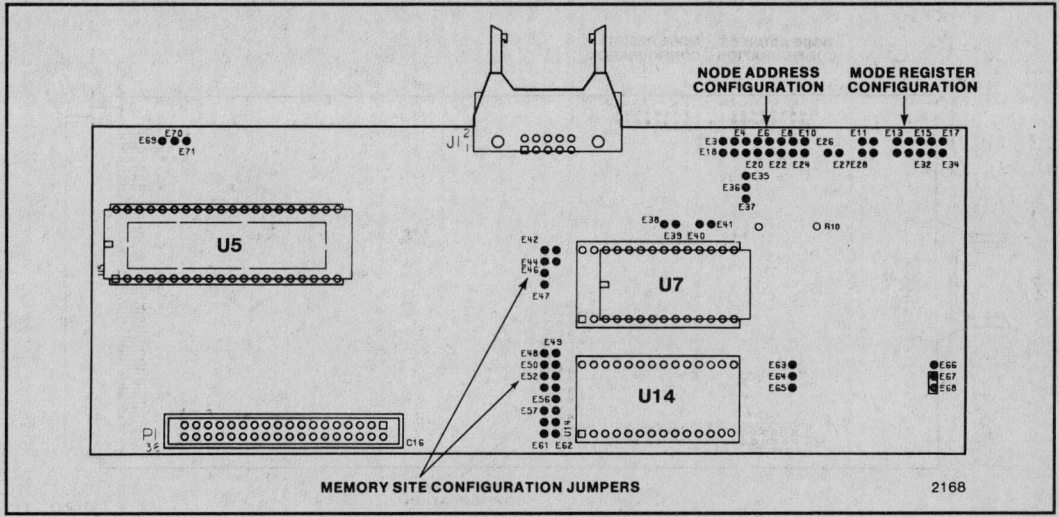

Figure A-2 iSBX™ 344 Jumper Locations

Guide for instructions on mounting the MULTI-MODULE adapter board and iSBX boards in the iPDS system.

If the iPDS system is going to be used with an EMV-44 or PROM programming module, perform the following:

- Install a plug-in module adapter board (ιPDS-140) in the main chassis of the iPDS system. This enables the iPDS system to host the EMV-44 and the PROM programming personality modules. Refer to Appendix A of the *iPDS™ User's Guide* for installation instructions.

The iPDS is now ready to accept the iSBX 344 BITBUS board.

iSBX™ 344 BITBUS™ MULTIMODULE™ Board Configuration

To configure the iSBX 344 BITBUS MULTIMODULE board for use with the iPDS system, refer to Figure A-2 and perform the following steps.

1. Install a resistor (minimum value of 120 ohm) in socket R10 of the iSBX 344 BITBUS board. This resistor is used to terminate the data signals on the master extension end of the BITBUS network.

2. Remove all jumpers from the jumper pair pins (E3/E18 through E10/E24) of the node address register on the iSBX 344 BITBUS board. This sets the node address of the iSBX 344 BITBUS board to address 00H.

3. Place a jumper across jumper pair pins E17/E34 of the mode register on the iSBX 344 BITBUS board.

This sets the mode of operation to self-clocked and the speed of operation to 375K bps. Remove all other jumpers from the mode register on the iSBX 344 BITBUS board.

NOTE

In the BITBUS example shown in Figure A-1, it is assumed that none of the devices will store user tasks on an external memory device. Therefore, you do not have to configure the memory pins on the mode register on the iDCM boards.

4. Mount the iSBX 344 BITBUS board in the J3 connector of the MULTIMODULE adapter board inside the iPDS chassis. (Instructions are given in Appendix A of the *iPDS™ User's Guide* for mounting the iSBX boards to the adapter board.)

5. Attach one end of the BITBUS cable to socket J1 of the iSBX 344 BITBUS board (see Figure A-2). Feed the cable out of one of the I/O expansion slots on the back of the iPDS chassis box. The remaining nodes will be connected to the BITBUS cable. For information on the characteristics and property requirements to consider in selecting a BITBUS cable, refer to the section on cable characteristics in the **Distributed Control Modules Databook**.

The iSBX 344 BITBUS board is now ready for operation with the iPDS system.

AP-251

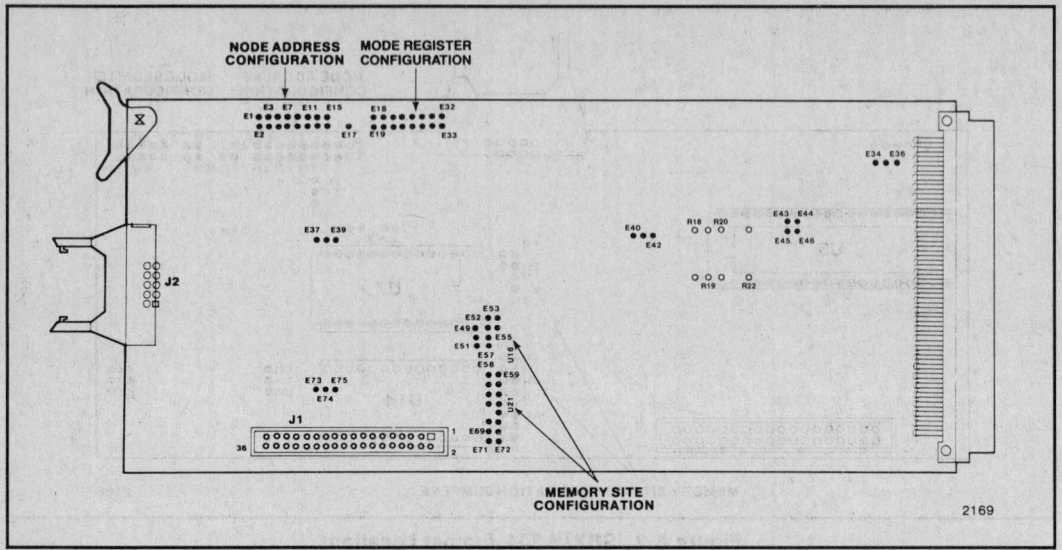

Figure A-3 iRCB 44/10 Board Jumper Locations

iRCB 44/10 Slave Node Configuration

To configure the iRCB 44/10 boards for use with the BIT-BUS network shown in Figure A-1, refer to Figure A-3 and perform the following steps.

Device #1

1. Install a jumper across jumper pins E15/E16 of the node address register on the iRCB 44/10 board. Remove all other jumpers from the node address register. This sets the address of the node to 01H.

2. Install a jumper across jumper pins E32/E33 of the mode register on the iRCB 44/10 board. This sets the mode of operation to self-clocked and the speed of operation to 375K bps. Remove all other jumper pins from the mode register.

3. Install a 75174 IC (RS485 transmitter) in socket U9 on the iRCB 44/10 board. This IC repeats the data signals from the master connector (J2) on the iRCB 44/10 board to the I/O port (P1) on the iRCB 44/10 board.

4. Install a 75175 IC (RS485 receiver) in socket U10 on the iRCB 44/10 board. This IC repeats the data signals from the master connector (J2) on the iRCB 44/10 board to the I/O port (P1) on the iRCB 44/10 board.

5. Install a 470 ohm resistor in sockets R18 and R22 on the iRCB 44/10 board. These resistors act as biasing resistors for the RTS signals on the iRCB 44/10 board.

Device #2

1. Repeat the instructions given for device #1, except place the jumpers across jumper pins E13/E14 of the node address register on the iRCB 44/10 board. This sets the address of this node to 02H.

Device #3

1. Repeat the instructions given for device #1, except place the jumpers across jumper pins E13/E14 and E15/E16 of the node address register. This sets the address of this node to 03H.

Device #4

1. Repeat the instructions given for device #1, except place the jumpers across jumper pins E11/E12 of the node address register on the iRCB 44/10 board. This sets the address of this node to 04H.

Device #5

1. Repeat the instructions given for device #1, except place the jumpers across jumper pins E11/E12 and E15/E16 of the node address register on the iRCB 44/10 board. This sets the address of this node to 05H.

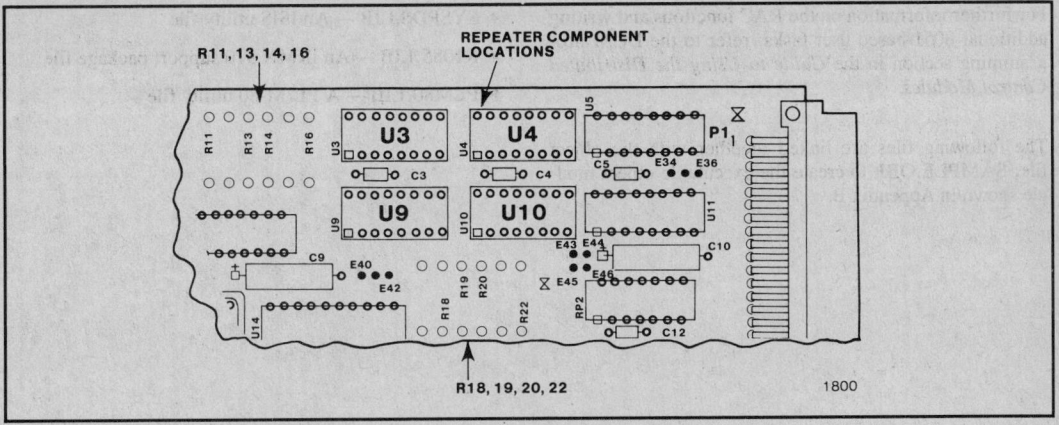

Figure A-4 iRCB 44/10 Repeater Socket Locations

Device #6

1. Repeat the instructions given for device #1, except place the jumpers across jumper pins E11/E12, E13/E14 of the node address register on the iRCB 44/10 board. This sets the address of this node to 06H.
2. Install a 120 ohm resistor in sockets R19 and R20 on the iRCB 44/10 board. These resistors are used to terminate the DATA and DCLK/RTS signals from the master device.

iRCB 44/10 Repeater Node Configuration

To configure the iRCB 44/10 board for use as a repeater node, refer to Figure A-4 and perform the following steps.

1. Install a 75174 IC (RS485 transmitter) in sockets U3 and U9 on the iRCB 44/10 board. These ICs are used to repeat the BITBUS electrical signals from the master device to the nodes in building #2.
2. Install a 75175 IC (RS485 receiver) in sockets U4 and U10 on the iRCB 44/10 board. These ICs are used to repeat the BITBUS electrical signals from the master device to the nodes in building #2.
3. Install a 120 ohm resistor in sockets R13 and R14 on the iRCB 44/10 board. These resistors are used to terminate the RTS and DATA signals on the iRCB 44/10 repeater board.
4. Install a 470 ohm resistor in sockets R11, R16, R18, and R22 on the iRCB 44/10 board. These resistors act as biasing resistors for the RTS signal on the iRCB 44/10 board.

The BITBUS boards are now configured for operation with the iPDS system.

Connecting the Nodes to the BITBUS™ Interconnect

The next step is to connect all of the BITBUS nodes to the BITBUS interconnect cable attached to the iPDS system. After this, apply power to the boards, and observe the green and red LED's on each of the boards. These LED's indicate if a malfunction has been detected by the power-up diagnostics. If the system checks out, the green LED will be on and the red LED will be off. For more information on the power-up diagnostics, refer to the DCM hardware section in the *Guide to Using the Distriubuted Control Modules*.

CREATING A BITBUS™ TASK

This section explains how the iPDS system makes use of the DCM controller's RAC functions to perform a control task.

NOTE

Assume that device #1 has an ICS 920 digital signaling board attached to it.

The built-in RAC functions on the DCM controller of the iSBX 344 BITBUS board enable the iPDS system to control the nodes attached to the network. These RAC functions are sent to the individual nodes as control messages. An example of a program used to send a RAC control task to device #1 is shown in Appendix B. The instructions for this task are written in PL/M-80. The program writes a set of 1's to Port A and Port C of device #1. It then goes into a delay loop, at the end of which it sends a command to change the 1's to 0's. This is done using the EXT_IO XOR function. The program is designed to have the LED's on the iCS 920 board flash continuously.

For further information on the RAC functions and writing additional 8051-based user tasks, refer to the DCM programming section in the *Guide to Using the Distributed Control Modules*.

The following files are linked together with the object file, SAMPLE.OBJ, to create the executable object module shown in Appendix B.

- SYSPDS.LIB — An ISIS utility file
- R1085.LIB — An iRMX 510 support package file
- PLM80.LIB — A PL/M-80 utility file

APPENDIX B:
PROGRAM LISTING FOR
BITBUS™ CONTROL TASK

AP 251

PROGRAM LISTING FOR THE BITBUS™ CONTROL TASK

PL/M-80 COMPILER

PAGE 1

ISIS-II PL/M-80 V3.1 COMPILATION OF MODULE TASK1
OBJECT MODULE PLACED IN SAMPLE.OBJ
COMPILER INVOKED BY: :F1:PLM*) SAMPLE

```
            $ TITLE ('iPDS/BITBUS RAC TASKS')

            /* THIS PROGRAM SHOWS HOW THE iPDS SYSTEM CAN USE THE
               RAC FUNCTIONS TO CONTROL A BITBUS NODE */

1           TASK1:DO;

2     1     DECLARE LIT        LITERALLY       'LITERALLY',
                    DCL        LIT             'DECLARE',
                    FOREVER    LIT             'WHILE 1',
                    I                          BYTE,
                    MSG$PTR                    ADDRESS,
                    TR$STATUS                  BYTE,
                    MESSAGE BASED MSG$PTR STRUCTURE (
                                               LINK       ADDRESS,
                                               LENGTH     BYTE,
                                               ROUTE      BYTE,
                                               NODE       BYTE,
                                               TASKS      BYTE,
                                               CMD$RSP    BYTE,
                                               TEXT(13)   BYTE);

3     1     CQ$DCM$RECEIVE: PROCEDURE (BUFFER$ADDR) EXTERNAL;
4     2         DCL BUFFER$ADDR ADDRESS;
5     2     END CQ$DCM$RECEIVE;

6     1     CQ$DCM$TRANSMIT: PROCEDURE (DCM$MESSAGE$ADDR) EXTERNAL;
7     2         DCL DCM$MESSAGE$ADDR ADDRESS;
8     2     END CQ$DCM$TRANSMIT;

9     1     CQ$DCM$STATUS$CHECK: PROCEDURE BYTE EXTERNAL;
10    2     END CQ$DCM$STATUS$CHECK;

11    1         TR$STATUS = 01;

                /* SEND RAC COMMAND TO NODE 1 */
12    1         MESSAGE.LINK          = 0000H;  /*BUILD A MESSAGE*/
13    1         MESSAGE.LENGTH        = 0DH;
14    1         MESSAGE.ROUTE         = 40H;
15    1         MESSAGE.NODE          = 1;
16    1         MESSAGE.TASKS         = 00H;
17    1         MESSAGE.CMD$RSP       = 06H;    /*WRITE TO EXTERNAL I/O*/
18    1         MESSAGE.TEXT(0)       = 0C0H;   /*WRITE TO PORT A*/
19    1         MESSAGE.TEXT(1)       = 0FFH;
20    1         MESSAGE.TEXT(2)       = 0C2H;   /*WRITE TO PORT C*/
21    1         MESSAGE.TEXT(3)       = 0FFH;
22    1         CALL CQ$DCM$TRANSMIT (.MESSAGE.LINK);
23    1         DO WHILE TR$STATUS < > 0;
24    2             TR$STATUS = CQ$DCM$STATUS$CHECK;
25    2         END;
26    1         CALL CQ$DCM$RECEIVE (MESSAGE.CMD$RSP);
```

AP 251

PL/M-80 COMPILER   IPDS BITBUS RAC TESTS
                          PAGE 2

```
27  1   DO FOREVER;

                /* WAIT FOR A FEW MOMENTS */
28  2       DO I = 1 to 200;
29  3           CALL TIME (250);
30  3       END;

31  2       TR$STATUS = 01;

32  2       MESSAGE.LINK          = 0000H;   /*BUILD A MESSAGE*/
33  2       MESSAGE.LENGTH        = 0DH;
34  2       MESSAGE.ROUTE         = 40H;
35  2       MESSAGE.NODE          = 1;
36  2       MESSAGE.TASKS         = 00H;
37  2       MESSAGE.CMD$RSP       = 0CH;     /*X'OR EXTERNAL I/O*/
38  2       MESSAGE.TEXT(0)       = 0C0H;    /*X'OR PORT A*/
39  2       MESSAGE.TEXT(1)       = 0FFH;
40  2       MESSAGE.TEXT(2)       = 0C2H;    /*X'OR PORT C*/
41  2       MESSAGE.TEXT(3)       = 0FFH;

42  2       CALL CQ$DCM$TRANSMIT (.MESSAGE.LINK);
43  2       DO WHILE TR$STATUS < > 0;
44  3           TR$STATUS = CQ$DCM$STATUS$CHECK;
45  3       END;
46  2       CALL CQ$DCM$RECEIVE (MESSAGE.CMD$RSP);

47  2       END;    /* DO FOREVER */
48  1   END TASK1;
```

MODULE INFORMATION:

```
    CODE AREA SIZE      = 0129H   297D
    VARIABLE AREA SIZE  = 0004H   4D
    MAXIMUM STACK SIZE  = 0002H   2D
    93 LINES READ
    0 PROGRAM ERROR(S)
```

END OF PL/M-80 COMPILATION

APPENDIX C:
ADDITIONAL PUBLICATIONS

AP-251

ADDITIONAL PUBLICATIONS

The following publications contain additional information on the iPDS system, the EMV-44 emulator, the BITBUS interconnect, and the iDCM family of control modules.

- *iPDS^{TM} Personal Development System User's Guide*, order number 162606
- *Microcontroller Handbook*, order number 210918
- *PROM Programming With the Intel Personal Development System (iPDS^{TM})*, order number 280015
- *Distributed Control Modules Databook*, order number 230973-001
- *Guide to Using the Distributed Control Modules*, order number 146312
- *Insite User's Program Library*, order number 121707
- *EMV-44 CON Conversion Guide Installation Manual*, order number 165726
- *EMV-51A Emulation Vehicle User's Guide*, order number 165624

ARTICLE REPRINT

AR-347

September 1984

BITBUS™ Promises to Standardize Control

MARK C. BUDZINSKI,
SR. TECHNICAL MARKETING ENGINEER

Reprinted with permission from July, 1984 issue of Systems & Software, Copyright, Hayden Publishing Company, 1984.

Order Number: 280053-001

intel® AR-347

Illustration John Trotta

Bitbus promises to standardize control

With a quartet of software and hardware modules, distributed control becomes much easier in the manufacturing environment.

The world of control systems is a rather confused one currently. Though the system designer has several excellent tools trying to meet the rigorous real-time requirements demanded by today's control applications and tomorrow's factory-automation desires, he is still put off by the lack of communications standards. Networks like Ethernet and IEEE-supported ones for token ring and bus find a niche in the manufacturing environment but do not specifically address problems residing in the control process. What is needed is a network that meets the needs of the control process and data com.

However, the Bitbus serial-network architecture represents a flexible solution to this problem (see "Specifications shoot for a flexible standard"). With just a simple twisted-pair, Bitbus may be configured in a multidrop set up with hardware- and software-interconnect modules and defined protocol support. The bus ranges from 30 meters to 10 kilometers in maximum length with speeds of 2.4 Mbaud to 62.5 kbaud, respectively; up to 250 nodes are possible with Bitbus (Fig. 1).

The key behind this standard is in the silicon of the 8044 microcontroller, which integrates an 8051 microcontroller and a serial interface unit that

Mark C. Budzinski, Sr. Technical Marketing Engineer
Intel Corp.
5200 NE Elam Young Pkwy
Hillsboro, Ore. 97123

Systems & Software•July 1984   280053-001

Bitbus architecture

arbitrates control and interface functions, respectively. The 8051 can run closely to its 12-MHz clock rate because many babysitting functions, which in other systems are controlled by the main processor, are coordinated by the serial interface unit. Because the 8051 microcontroller will be placed locally at each control point, real-time control and task execution is now possible—a goal unattainable with more commonly used distributed architectures.

Control problems. Typically in control systems, it is desirable for a host computer to communicate with microcontrollers at remote locations. Bus-arbitration schemes like carrier-sense, multiple-access with collision detection are useful for local networks in many applications but are not suited for or even needed in the industrial environment. The overhead embedded in bus contention may thus be eliminated through a master-slave relationship between the host and remote microcontrollers—the master simply polls all of the microcontrollers.

There are a few applications that address the master-slave model: data acquisition, factory automation, and process control. Data acquisition usually deals with large amounts of input, and the input sites tend to have a limited amount of intelligence. Host-to-remote microcontoller transactions occur quickly so that all nodes may be polled often. The host computer can compile the required information and respond to the slave nodes with the appropriate acknowledgments or signals.

Factory automation requires more substantial remote intelligence, but a host computer still maintains overall system control. Readouts from I/O devices are generally dependent upon the conditions of their peers. For instance, a conveyer belt's speed is directly dependent on inputs from sensor devices located on the belt. As a result, communication must be both fast and reliable.

A process-control application usually involves the same peer interdependence as factory automation, but more wiring and local communications are required. Input devices can affect linked output devices without host intervention because a control system essentially resides at each remote node. The host acts as the system's global watchdog. Thus, communication must be fast, reliable, and cover significant distances.

Generally, control messages are short, concise statements that can be encoded in a few bytes. Remote controllers just idle until stimulated by the host that is controlling the system. The control message lets a microcontroller influence a process.

Data-acquisition messages originate differently. The host polls each microcontroller to send back temperature, pressure, or whatever type of information that it wants to examine. Again, the reply data can usually be encoded into a few bytes.

Because there may be many I/O points in a system, it is desirable to poll all of the microcontrollers as quickly as possible. For instance, process control would require more frequent polling than an environmental control system.

Transmission considerations. Transmitting and collating this data is not a trivial matter. Parallel buses provide the needed bandwidth but at a high price. In addition, the number of slots in a backplane is always limited. Serial buses are cheaper but suffer from the fact that RS-232-C is just a connection standard, not a protocol, and can offer only point-to-point communications.

The control environment presents fairly specific requirements to the more global field of data communications. Master-slave relationships, short messages, and many I/O points are typical of control systems. Unfortunately, there is no standard method available to bring all these elements together.

Bitbus arrives. Bitbus's architecture addresses many of these problems. At the physical level, RS-485 is utilized. This is a superset of the more popular RS-422 and provides multidrop support over a twisted pair. Logical states 0 and 1 are derived from the voltage across the pair. Any noise will raise the absolute potential, but the differential voltage potential will remain constant throughout the bus thus making the line fairly noise resistant. RS-485 is used instead of RS-422 because it allows more nodes over a given distance. Bitbus networks support 32 nodes in each 1200-m segment.

The data-link level is supported by a subset of IBM's synchronous-data-link-control (SDLC) protocol, which is well-suited for the control environment. First, it provides a header field for addressing the remote nodes in a system. Second, it provides excellent reliability through its cyclic-

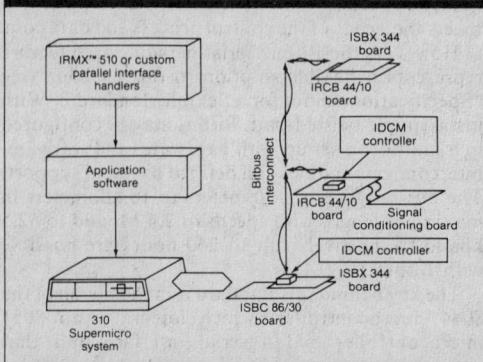

1. The typical system configuration of Bitbus comprises iRMX 510 or custom parallel interface handlers, several iRCB 44/10 boards, a iSBX 344 board, and firmware containing the iRMX 51 executive. Bitbus links all these elements into a communicating multidrop network.

redundancy-check algorithm—the probability of passing an erroneous bit is less than 10^{-10}. Third, it provides frame-for-frame reliability by keeping track of outstanding frames, as well as maintaining an acknowledge mechanism. The protocol is well-accepted throughout the data-communications field, thus contributing to a potential standardization for control applications.

Most common data-communications packages, particularly those in the microcontroller area, end their support at this level. The Bitbus architecture goes an additional step and establishes end-to-end communications through a defined message header and efficient routing. The message header contains information that routes the message to the correct

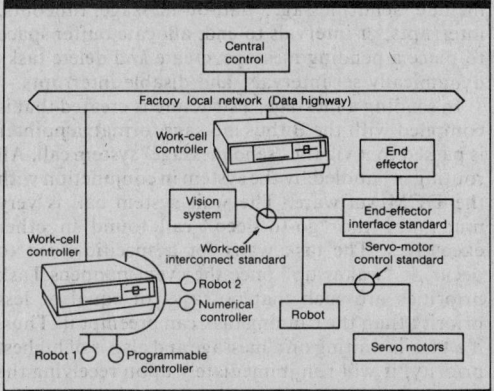

2. Bitbus's architecture is quite useful in the factory where it can be used to link dissimilar devices like robots, programmable controllers, and vision systems. Because all the interface levels—from the physical to the protocol—are defined, interconnection is easy and straightforward.

node and in turn to the correct process running at that node. Message length is specified so that dynamic structures can be used to create messages. Maximum message size is currently 18 bytes and includes the header information.

Only 4 bytes out of the initial 18 are used for the message header. Because control applications require only short message lengths, typically, the header-field requirement does not weaken the network.

Bitbus is set up so that the master node keeps track of outstanding order messages that have to be polled. Thus, when an order is sent to a slave node, a reply is guaranteed in a subsequent poll. There are no wasted polls, which adds to system efficiency.

Distributed control modules. A quartet of software and hardware components support Bitbus communication and are called distributed control modules (DCMs). The two board-level products are the iSBX 344 and iRCB 44/10. The software components comprise the iRMX 51 real-time

multitasking executive and the iRMX 510 Bitbus utility package.

The 344 is a single-height, double-wide multi-module board designed to interface with a Multibus-compatible central-processing-unit board. The 44/10 remote controller board serves by itself as a good solution for a stand-alone controller node in a system. Twenty-four lines of I/O are provided from the board in addition to Bitbus communications capabilities. Both boards are based on the 8044 microcontroller, which is composed of an 8051 CPU and a serial-interface unit; they provide 64-kbytes of both data and instruction memory. The software is provided on both boards in the form of preconfigured firmware.

Designing a control system with these modules is very straightforward. Initially a host computer must be selected. For instance, the Intel system 310 running the iRMX 86 operating system is a good choice. It is easily implemented into a Bitbus system by adding just one iSBX 344 board.

The heart of the entire DCM scheme is the real-time control provided by the microcontroller. The iRMX 51 operating system offers an environment where eight tasks can run on the same microcontroller. It is an interrupt-driven executive that utilizes a convenient interface through system calls. It supports the Bitbus message format, allowing easy implementation into a distributed control system. Also, it is included as part of the firmware available with the DCM board-level products.

The iRMX 51 executive is an excellent development tool. The functions that have to be explicitly coded can be greatly reduced by making system calls. Once the system is up and running, the executive handles all interrupts, context switching, message passing, buffer management, and timer management transparently.

Real-time support is another characteristic of the iRMX 86 operating system, which is run at the host. A Bitbus driver runs under the operating system,

3. The heart of the Bitbus specification is the 8044 microcontroller. It combines the 8051 microprocessor and a serial interface unit on one chip so that interface demands and control needs are separated. This arrangement leads to quicker response times.

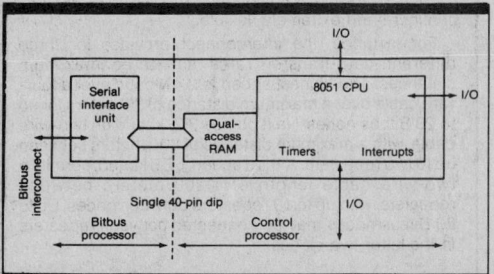

Bitbus architecture

which allows message passing across the iSBX interface and on down the Bitbus network. This allows 8051 messages to be transmitted to and from the iRMX 86 host conveniently.

Routing operations. The 4-byte message header has the routing and control information that travels with every message. The first byte represents the length of the transmitted message. This overhead byte quickly pays for itself when smaller messages are transmitted—statically defined space is not wasted.

The next field provides a level of routing information. Four flags are set: message type, source extended, destination extended, and track bit. Message type specifies whether the message is going from master to slave or vice versa. Source- and destination-extended bits allow a level of routing across another bus interface (the iSBX bus, in the DCM case). If a non-Bitbus interface is required in the system, the extended bit is set so it is clear that the message has to be routed across another interface. The track bit is used to keep messages going forward across multiple-extended interfaces.

The third byte in the header specifies the station address, which is the SDLC address, of the destination node. The fourth byte identifies the 8051 sending and receiving task. Under the iRMX 51 executive there are up to eight tasks running on the microcontroller.

The routing strategy is directly related to the defined message format. First, a node is specified to receive a message. A task is then sent a message from the node and, if necessary, an extended interface is configured. If the message is an order, it will go to the destination task; if it is a reply, it will come back to the appropriate task at the master.

iRMX 51 interfacing. Interfacing with the 51 executive is quite easy. The executive is small, having only 12 system calls. Available functions include, send message; wait-on-message, timeouts, interrupts, or intervals to end; allocate buffer space to place a pending message; create and delete tasks dynamically set intervals; and disable interrupts.

In sending a message, a structure is created that is compiled with the Bitbus message format; a pointer is passed to it via the "send message" system call. All routing is handled by the system in conjunction with the DCM software. The wait system call is very much like the "go-to-sleep" call found in other executives. The task waits for a specific event to occur; it "wakes up" once the event happens. Task priorities are such that no tasks of equal or less priority than the running task can preempt it. Thus, if a task is waiting on a message and also is of highest priority, it will run immediately upon receiving the message.

Allocate system calls permit a user to easily send messages across the Bitbus network. Upon allocating a buffer for the message, it is simply sent—the system expects to see it in the buffer and then sends the message. Create-and-delete-task system calls provide the system with the capability to ring up code during runtime. In addition, a task may be deleted during runtime in response to a condition like an error.

The iRMX 51 executive is designed to run on 8044 processors as well as 8051s. As a result, firmware is provided in the board-level products to handle communication over the Bitbus network transparently. When a communication interrupt occurs, the DCM code flags it and sends a message across either the Bitbus or the iSBX bus. Since Bitbus accommodates the iRMX 51 executive, the task is straightforward. The DCM software is implemented as Task 0 under the iRMX operating system.

In addition, the DCM code provides a user interface (destination Task 0) that can send redefined messages. These messages allow reading and writing to certain memory locations. The I/O locations on the iRCB 44/10 board are memory-mapped in these same locations. Thus the I/O ports of a remote controller can be accessed without writing any code at that node.

In addition, a task may be created at a remote

Specifications shoot for a flexible standard

Though bus and network products for industrial applications abound, few if any can claim to be inexpensive and sufficiently defined so that any two implementations of such a product can be linked easily. But with Bitbus, everything from the electrical interface to the operating system is specified. As a result, compatibility between dissimilar products adopting the standard is ensured. Manufacturers such as Mitsubishi, Westinghouse, and Unimation have already expressed support for this specification.

The Bitbus interconnect method was developed to use a range of industry-standard approaches for simplicity of design and use. The Bitbus physical connection uses inexpensive twisted-pair wiring (2 pairs and 10-conductor flat ribbon are also specified) and the RS-485-compatible electrical characteristics. Besides the SDLC protocol, Intel's open-system software interfaces for the iSBX, Bitbus drivers, and intertask message passing are included. This setup is easy to configure and extremely flexible.

For instance, the interconnect provides for three different data-transfer rates and three maximum distances. The highest speed is 2.4 Mbaud over a four-wire cable over a maximum distance of 30 meters for up to 28 Bitbus nodes. Next comes 375 kbaud on two-wire cable, with a maximum distance of 300 meters between up to two repeaters. A third speed, 62.5 kbaud, permits a two-wire cable length of 1,200 meters between repeaters, with up to 10 repeaters between nodes. Up to 28 Bitbus nodes may be connected between repeaters in the latter two modes.

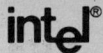

Bitbus architecture

location through the same interface. This feature lets task code be downloaded to a remote node and be created in real time from the master node. The task can later be deleted from the master by sending a similar message to Task 0.

Though the software flexibility contributes much to the desirability of Bitbus, the 8044 microcontroller (Fig. 3) is the heart of the system. It consists of an 8051 microcontroller with an SDLC controller, which share a dual-port RAM area. The 8051 section controls processes without the overhead of communications responsibilities. The SDLC controller or the serial interface unit (SIU), can generate frame acknowledgments, maintain frame-sequence counters, and other such things in hardware without the assistance of the main processor.

Because of this splitting of chores, Bitbus speed is relatively high. The slave end never has to interrupt the processor unless it has a valid message for input. All negative acknowledgments are transparent to the 8051 portion of the chip.

Message buffers, task stack space, iRMX 51 variables, and register banks sit in the dual-port RAM area, which is 192 bytes—sufficient for most applications. The system is optimized to a certain extent so that when an interrupt occurs, no context switch to off-chip RAM takes place unless the running task is preempted. If a running task continues to run after an interrupt occurs, there is no context switch to external memory.

iRCB 44/10 interfacing. The iRCB 44/10 boards have a single-width Eurocard form-factor with a 64-pin DIN connector. Power, ground signals, the Bitbus interface, and 24 I/O lines are physically connected to the DIN plug. The I/O lines are not optically isolated or conditioned in any fashion but provide simple binary 0s and 1s. To interface the I/O lines with real-world devices requires an intermediate interface like an optical isolator. Analog signaling is possible when an iSBX multimodule board is included.

The beauty of the I/O-line setup is not the direct-indirect interface to real devices, but their co-location with the controller board and their memory-mapped addressing that can be accessed from both the remote node as well as the host. Because the board is designed to stand alone, no backplane is necessary.

Development of application code may proceed with either assembly language or PL/M 51, which is a more sophisticated high-level language.□

ARTICLE REPRINT

AR-351

September 1984

Intel's BITBUS™ Microcontroller Interconnect

PETER WOLOCHOW
PRODUCT MARKETING MANAGER

Reprinted by permission from June 1984 Robotics Age Magazine, Robotics Age, Inc.

Order Number: 280069-001

INTEL'S BITBUS MICROCONTROLLER INTERCONNECT

A Modern Method of Robot Communication

Peter I. Wolochow
Intel Corporation
5200 NE Elam Young Parkway
Hillsboro, OR 97124

In February 1984, Intel introduced a new bus communication architecture aimed at enhancing microcontroller-based applications. This article describes Intel's Bitbus—an interconnect scheme specifically designed to match the needs of high-performance, cost-conscious microcontroller applications. The Bitbus, along with the accompanying Distributed Control Module (iDCM™) family, provides the latest steps toward making the best use of VLSI technology in control applications.

BITBUS USES

Microcontrollers are a driving force in modernizing mechanical and electrical systems. They have replaced relays, wheels, and gears in applications ranging from automated manufacturing to process control. By incorporating at least one microcontroller, the total system cost of most control-oriented applications can be lowered while improving performance and leaving room for useful options. However, without an industry-wide standard on which to rely, most microcontroller applications lack a simple connection to other microcontrollers and control equipment.

Through advances in silicon technology, control systems have already made many evolutionary changes. Early systems relied on relay sequencers and simple alarm indicators. The PDP-8™ from Digital Equipment Corp. provided the first commonly used tool for coordinating many real-time controls. Microprocessors provided a simple way to reduce computer costs, but did not change system architectures until standard buses became popular. Industry standard bus architectures such as the Multibus® and STD-Bus™ have allowed designers to divide control tasks between many processors while taking advantage of standard modules from many vendors.

Microcontrollers have paved the road for the next step—distributed control. Most control-oriented systems distribute control functions to minimize system cost while improving system performance, responsiveness, and reliability. There are several ways to distribute control: a parallel bus structure, a simple set of control signals on individual control lines, a serial communications link, or custom technology. Each of these solutions requires considerable design effort, and often results in a performance-limiting interconnect matched to current applications but ill-suited for expansion or connection to a different control system.

Applications best suited for the Bitbus interconnect include robotics, numerically-controlled machines, process control, security systems, environmental control, and other distributed control and data collection systems. These applications typically use multiple controllers to physically distribute control, to improve system performance and reliability, and to reduce total system and maintenance cost. Existing data networks such as Ethernet, Token Bus, and various custom technologies are useful for transferring large data blocks at high speed, but also at a relatively high cost. What is still missing is a low-cost bus for local control environments. Combining the strengths of existing hardware and protocol standards with complete firmware and software support, the Bitbus interconnect provides a simple, standard technology for connecting distributed controllers.

BITBUS CONFIGURATIONS

The Bitbus microcontroller interconnect can connect a single master controller to a number of local or remote slave controllers. A multidrop configuration connects controllers (8044s) to a common bus. The single-chip *8044 microcontroller* contains two functional elements: an 8051 processor and an SDLC Serial Interface Unit (SIU). The onboard processor contains 4 Kbytes of read-only memory, 192 bytes of read/write memory, clock, timers, interrupt controller, and memory expansion bus. In Bitbus applications, the read-only memory is filled with special firmware routines that support the message-passing protocol, interact with user application tasks, and perform a series of power-up self-diagnostics.

Integral firmware allows each Bitbus controller to act as either a master or slave.

RAC Function Commands

Every member of the 8044 family is programmed for Bitbus operation by including the iRMX 51 Executive and one system task, called the Remote Access and Control (RAC) function. The system task, responsible for managing the interface, provides a number of utilities to ensure that all Bitbus controllers can communicate with each other. The utilities also allow a master node to interact with slave controllers without having to write any 8051 code. The RAC function provides ten commands that let a remote master access local resource and status information and five commands specifically designed for intelligent remote control. Tables 3 and 4 describe the available access and control RAC functions.

The control functions can be used for higher-level utilities. For example, the Bitbus master can determine the existence of a special service task at a remote slave, and download programs depending on high-level system requirements or environmental influences such as service options or power failures. This test-and-program function could be accomplished by sending a GET__FUNCTION__IDS command and sending a group of WRITE__EXTERNAL__MEMORY messages to download an appropriate program, and then starting the program by sending a CREATE__TASK command.

Table 3. Remote Access and Control (RAC) Access Functions

COMMAND	OPERATION
READ I/O	Read external I/O location. Return result in reply message.
WRITE I/O	Write byte to external I/O location.
UPDATE I/O	Write byte to, then read byte from external I/O location. Return result in reply message.
OR I/O	OR data with contents of external I/O location. Return OR'd value.
AND I/O	AND data with contents of external I/O locaton. Return AND'd value.
XOR I/O	XOR data with contents of external I/O location. Return XOR'd value.
READ INTERNAL MEMORY	Read contents of internal memory location. Return result in reply message.
WRITE INTERNAL MEMORY	Write data to internal memory location.
DOWNLOAD EXTERNAL MEMORY	Write data starting at external memory location.
UPLOAD EXTERNAL MEMORY	Read data starting at external memory location. Return result in reply message.

NOTES:
Internal memory locations are included in the 192 bytes of data read/write memory provided in the microcontroller. External memory refers memory outside the microcontroller—the 28-pin sockets of the iSBX 344 module and the iRCB 44/10 board. Each RAC Access Function may refer to 1, 2, 3, 4, 5 or 6 individual I/O or memory locations in a single command.

Table 4. RAC Control Functions

COMMAND	OPERATION
GET FUNCTION IDS	Execute iRMX 51 GET_FUNCTION_IDS command. Return resulting list in reply message.
CREATE TASK	Execute iRMX 51 CREATE_TASK command using the specified Task Descriptor. Return resulting status in reply message.
DELETE TASK	Execute iRMS 51 DELETE_TASK primitive using specified Task Identification. Return resulting status in reply message.
RAC PROTECT	Suspend or Resume Remote Access types of service. Return resulting status in reply message.
RESET STATION	Jump to initial code reset address. **NO REPLY IS RETURNED.**

master and slave starts with an exchange of U-frames to synchronize the frame sequence counters and other controls. The data exchange is accomplished with the I-frame and S-frame. The I-frame contains data for a slave or a response from a slave. S-frames are used to acknowledge data receipt or to poll a slave for data.

Bitbus Messages. The *user data* contained in the I-frames conform to a standard Bitbus message format. All messages contain a five-byte header describing the source and destination, along with other status and control information. Messages sent to, or from, the standard Bitbus firmware (see the RAC Function Commands text box) may also contain special information to perform common I/O operations. Up to 13 user data bytes may be transmitted at one time.

Bitbus controllers *require* each message to be answered—not just acknowledged. The SIU provides an SDLC acknowledgement for each message. Only the application task to which the message is sent can send a meaningful reply. The Bitbus master enforces this rule by continuing to poll a slave for its reply to each transmitted message. Separating the replies and acknowledgements helps give Bitbus systems additional performance by freeing the control link while a reply is generated.

Figure 1 shows how several overlapping conversations can occur between the Bitbus master and slaves. The Bitbus master maximizes throughput by taking advantage of each slave's SIU ability to immediately acknowledge a message, without interrupting the 8051 processor. This removes the need to tie up the bus while waiting for the slave to calculate a response. The master can send commands to a controller and come back for the response later.

Bitbus traffic patterns and rules reflect the primary Bitbus purpose—control. The master controls all message traffic and initiates all messages. Slaves answer each message with either an immediate acknowledgement to confirm correct recognition, or with a response message associated with a previously received command. Whereas many SDLC-based systems suffer from large and unpredictable delays between a poll and a slave's acknowledgement, Bitbus slave controllers use the SIU to send an immediate answer. Because the response time is always short and predictable, no Bitbus bandwidth is wasted.

AR-351

The master/slave relationship can be changed in real time. This provides a simple method for allowing backup master controllers. For example, you could program a backup master to wait for a poll from the primary master every second. If the master missed several polls, the backup could take control and switch itself from a slave to a master.

TRANSFER PROTOCOL AND MESSAGE FORMAT

The Bitbus interconnect is based on the SDLC (IBM's Synchronous Data Link Control) standard supported by the 8044. SDLC is commonly used by many vendors concerned about data integrity and interface standards. Since the SDLC protocol has limited overhead and a built-in data security and acknowledgement protocol, it is ideally suited for reliable transmission of short, control-oriented messages. To ensure a workable standard interface between Bitbus systems, additional protocol standards are included in the published Bitbus specifications.

The 8044 Bitbus microcontroller supports a large subset of the standard SDLC protocol. The 8044 manages SDLC traffic in Auto and Non-Auto modes with a minimum of interruption to the 8051 half of the microcontroller. In Auto mode (used by all Bitbus slaves), all SDLC functions are managed automatically with minimal effect on controller performance. In the Non-Auto mode (used by the Bitbus master), the controller can initiate transmissions and polls to slaves as well as process parts of the protocol not managed by the SIU (such as responding directly to each message and checking other status conditions). The 8044 component automatically manages all SDLC frame control, sequencing, and transmission procedures. In Bitbus applications, the 8044 also provides the message formats and sequence checks needed to guarantee proper delivery of critical control signals.

SDLC Protocol. SDLC is a bit-oriented data-link control protocol that defines a specific structure for each type of data and control exchange. As shown in table 1, each transmission type (I-frame, S-frame, and U-frame) is divided into identifiable fields. Each field contains one or more bytes of data and/or control information to accomplish the corresponding function.

Normal transmission between an SDLC

Transmission Modes

The Bitbus operates in either of two transmission modes: synchronous or self-clocking. In the synchronous mode, an external clock provides a data clock to transmit data at rates between 375 K and 2.4 M bits per second. In the self-clocking mode, the clock is derived from transition in the data using the NRZI (Non-Return to Zero, Inverted) encoding technique. Characteristics of each mode are shown below:

Synchronous Mode:
2.4 bits per second with external clock
  Maximum of 30 m distance
  Maximum of 28 Bitbus nodes

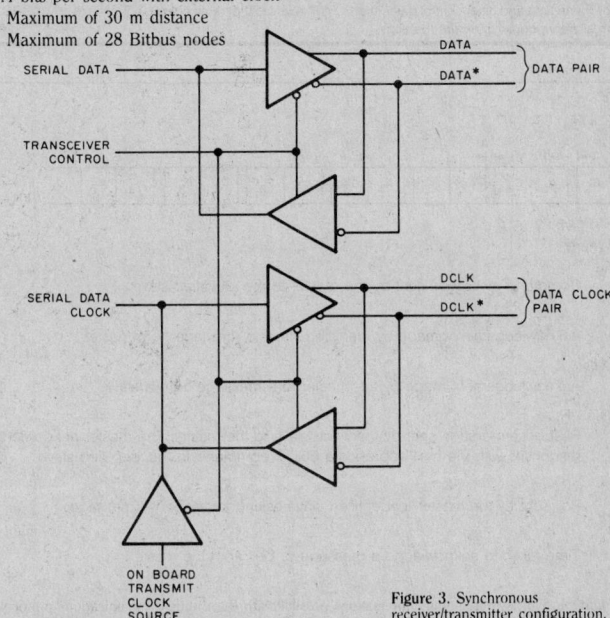

Figure 3. Synchronous receiver/transmitter configuration.

Self-Clocking Mode:
375K bits per second NRZI encoding:
  Maximum of 300 m between repeaters (total limit 900 m)
  Maximum of 28 Bitbus nodes between repeaters (limit 250)
  Maximum of 2 repeaters between the master and any slave

62.5K bits per second NRZI encoding:
  Maximum of 1200 m between repeaters (total limit 4800 km)
  Maximum of 28 Bitbus nodes between repeaters (limit 250)
  Maximum of 10 repeaters between the master and any slave

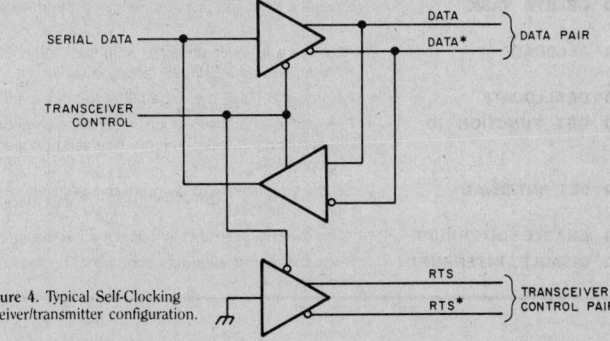

Figure 4. Typical Self-Clocking receiver/transmitter configuration.

AR-351

Table 1. Synchronous Data Link Control (SDLC) Frame Formats.

FRAME-TYPE	FORMAT	FUNCTION
I-frame	F A C—user data—FCS F	Information Transfer
S-frame	F A C FCS F	Supervisory Control
U-frame	F A C FCS F	Receiver/Transmitter Synchronization

NOTES:
'F' refers to the SDLC Flag byte; 'A' refers to the slave station's address; 'C' refers to the control field identifying the frame-type and other control parameters; 'FCS' refers to the frame check sequence (a 16-bit CRC calculated on all frame contents except the flags).

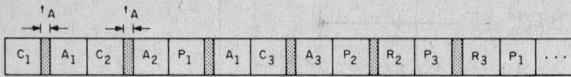

Where:
$C_1 \ldots C_n =$
Command messages sent by the master to the identified slave.

$A_1 \ldots A_n =$
Acknowledgements made by identified slave to message from master.

$A_m =$
Acknowledgement made by the master to a message from a slave.

$R_1 \ldots R_n =$
Response message sent by identified slave to the master. The master acknowledges these responses with the next appropriate poll or command to the identified slave.

$P_1 \ldots P_n =$
Poll sent by the master to identified slave asking for response message.

$t_A =$
Time taken to acknowledge a message or poll from the master.

Figure 1. Typical overlapping conversations possible with the Bitbus communications protocol.

Table 2. iRMX 51 Commands

COMMAND	FUNCTION
RQ SEND MESSAGE	Sends a message (a command from the BITBUS master, a response from a slave, or a simple message between tasks on the same BITBUS component) to another task.
RQ WAIT	Waits for an interrupt, an event time-out, a message, or any combination of the three.
RQ CREATE TASK	Causes a new sequence of code to be run as an iRMX 51 task with a specific Function Identification Code.
RQ DELETE TASK	Stops the specified task and removes it from all execution lists.
RQ ALLOCATE	Allocates a fixed-length buffer from the internal 8044 RAM for use as a BITBUS message buffer.
RQ DEALLOCATE	Returns a BITBUS message buffer to the system.
RQ GET FUNCTION ID	Provides a list of the 8 function identification codes representing the tasks currently operating on the microcontroller.
RQ SET INTERVAL	Set the time interval to be used as a separate event-timer for the task.
RQ ENABLE INTERRUPT	Allow external interrupts to signal the microcontroller.
RQ DISABLE INTERRUPT	Stops all external interrupts from signalling the microcontroller.

Bitbus Message Passing. Messages are an integral part of any control-oriented application. Intel's entire Digital Control Module family supports the passing of short control commands, responses to these commands, and status information. A small executive program provides multiple tasking capability so that messages can be managed on a task-by-task basis. All Bitbus components and boards offer the same, simple, message-based interface to user applications that produce and act on control information in small messages. By using standard messages, 8044 tasks can perform I/O operations such as inverting a single I/O bit at a distant Bitbus node, without specially coded communications or bus management software.

BITBUS SPECIFICATIONS

The Bitbus hardware and software interfaces were selected to match distributed control requirements while conforming to established standards supportable with currently available electrical interfaces, cables, and operating systems. However, since some applications require different electrical and mechanical interfaces, the Bitbus connectors and bus interfaces provide additional signals such as power, RTS, DLCK, etc. By using these additional signals, other extensions such as simple fiber-optic communication links and optical isolators can easily be adapted to standard Bitbus connectors.

The Bitbus software interfaces also provide extra customization "hooks." For example, the Function ID Codes and the ability to create new tasks dynamically allow application tasks to take advantage of standard Bitbus services in custom—even proprietary—fashions. To assist in typical and custom designs, a complete Bitbus specification has been published which identifies all facets of Bitbus design.

The Bitbus uses the RS-485 interface as the physical link between controllers. The RS-485 electrical interface is an accepted variation of the common RS-422 interface that allows longer cable segments with more multidrop connections. Repeater stations make it possible to link concentrated control stations with additional remote data collection points. Repeaters are not supported in the Synchronous Mode.

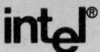

AR-351

Bitbus Backplane Configurations

Although the Bitbus interconnect is designed as a simple two-wire microcontroller interconnect, it can also be distributed over a backplane. The iRCB 44/10 Remote Controller Board uses a single-wide, 220 mm-deep, Eurocard format and DIN connectors as interface to power, other controllers, and I/O. Table 5 defines the pin-out of the 64-pin DIN connector which facilitates board insertion and maintenance; all I/O and bus connections are on the same connector. The connections are compatible with the standard Intel parallel port adopted by many other vendors. The power pins are compatible with standard Eurocard designations except for the ±12 V provided for the possible use of iSBX modules mounted on Bitbus controller boards.

Since the power and Bitbus connections occupy only a small number (14) of the backplane pins, many custom functions can be implemented on iRCB-type modules. Each module can include a controller and dedicated I/O circuitry designed for a particular application. The iDCM Controller manages all the Bitbus interface and provides the on-chip 8051 controller for local control.

Table 5. Eurocard Connector Pin-Out

DIN PIN #	PIN & SOCKET PIN #	FUNCTION	DIN PIN #	PIN & SOCKET PIN #	FUNCTION
1c		GND	1a		GND
2c		+5V	2a		+5V
3c		DATA*	3a		DATA
4c		DLCK*/RTS*	4a		DLCK/RTS
5c		RGND	5a	1	EXTINT
6c	2	GND	6a	3	PB7
7c	4	GND	7a	5	PB6
8c	6	GND	8a	7	PB5
9c	8	GND	9a	9	PB4
10c	10	GND	10a	11	PB3
11c	12	GND	11a	13	PB2
12c	14	GND	12a	15	PB1
13c	16	GND	13a	17	PB0
14c	18	GND	14a	19	PC3
15c	20	GND	15a	21	PC2
16c	22	GND	16a	23	PC1
17c	24	GND	17a	25	PC0
18c	26	GND	18a	27	PC4
19c	28	GND	19a	29	PC5
20c	30	GND	20a	31	PC6
21c	32	GND	21a	33	PC7
22c	34	GND	22a	35	PA7
23c	36	GND	23a	37	PA6
24c	38	GND	24a	39	PA5
25c	40	GND	25a	41	PA4
26c	42	GND	26a	43	PA3
27c	44	GND	27a	45	PA2
28c	46	GND	28a	47	PA1
29c	48	GND	29a	49	PA0
30c		−12V	30a		+12V
31c		+5V	31a		+5V
32c		GND	32a		GND

INITIAL BITBUS PRODUCTS

The Bitbus microcontroller interconnect is supported by a number of new products. Using a preprogrammed 8044 called the iDCM Controller, the following products provide firmware, additional software, and flexible board-level support for distributed control applications. System-level controllers can take advantage of these modules to extend their I/O into the Bitbus realm. Component-level solutions can make use of the iDCM Controller, or use the software to configure unique solutions that are still compatible with different Bitbus systems.

iRMX 51 Real-Time Executive. The Bitbus firmware is based on a new member of Intel's iRMX Real-Time Operating System family, the iRMX 51 Executive, a very small multitasking executive that supports up to eight user tasks on any of the 8051 family of processors (8051, 8031, 8044, 8744, 8751, etc.). The Executive provides the basic utilities for users to create and maintain tasks, manage interrupts and time intervals, and pass messages between local and remote tasks. Table 2 shows all ten available commands.

The primary operation of the Executive centers around its ability to send messages between tasks residing on the same microcontroller or on another one. As the supporting system for Bitbus firmware, the Executive has been optimized to transfer messages with a minimum of delay. As a general-purpose, real-time executive, it directly supports user tasks located in memory. The first task (task 0) is reserved for a system task, called the RAC function that performs all Bitbus-related functons and provides some user, application-level services.

iRMX 510 DCM Support Package. The package contains software utilities to assist 8044 users in implementing Bitbus-based applications. They include software drivers for interfacing Intel's iRMX 86, 88, 286R, and iPDS ISIS operating systems to Bitbus boards and components. Remote I/O points, from a high-level task, may be controlled using the supplied drivers just as though they were attached directly to the master processor. The 510 package also includes developmental aids, such as a collection of literal definitions and a copy of the Bitbus firmware for use with in-circuit emulators, like the ICE-44, for Intel development systems.

iSBX 344 Bitbus Expansion Module. The module is an 8044-based, double-wide iSBX module, having two 28-pin memory expansion sockets, for driving distributed control systems as either masters or slaves. One socket is equipped with 2 Kbytes of user-accessible memory that is expandable to 8 Kbytes. The other socket may house an additional 64 Kbytes. Users may take advantage of the 8044's features to off-load control and polling functions from the base-board unit.

iRCB 44/10 Bitbus Controller Multimodule. The remote controller board is an 8044-based single-wide Eurocard form-factor board providing the standard Bitbus interface, memory expansion sockets, and clock-support circuitry found on the iSBX 344 Module. It also provides an expansion

AR-351

Bitbus Robot Example

The Bitbus microcontroller interconnect is well suited for a number of different robot applications. Figure 2 shows a typical robot workstation that includes a machine tool, two robots, a conveyer belt, and a central work-cell controller. The hierarchy of devices shown reflects the recent factory automation trend of connecting more machines to central accounting and control systems. One standard interface (labelled A) at the face-plate of each robot lets users select end-effectors from a variety of sources while maintaining a common control interface to the robot controller. The other standard interface (labelled B) ensures a coordinated work-cell by providing a way to connect robots, conveyers, etc. to the same work-cell controller with a simple and standard control interface.

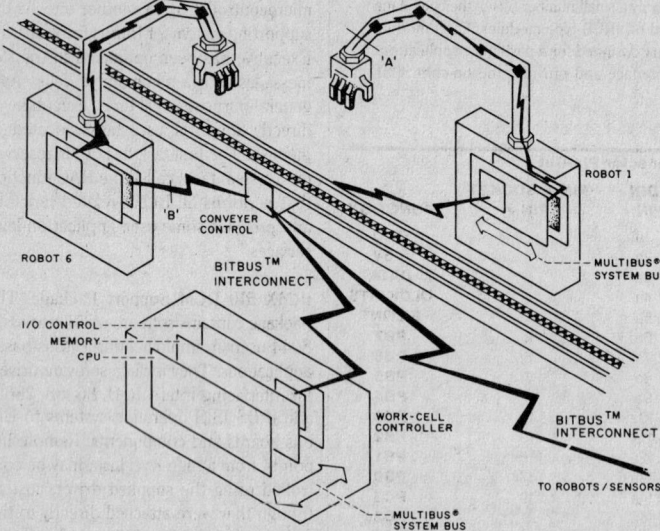

Figure 2. The Bitbus microcontroller interconnect is well suited for a number of different robot applications. Typical robot workstations include a machine tool, two robots, a conveyer belt, and a central work-cell controller. One standard interface (labelled A) at the face-plate of each robot lets users select end-effectors from a variety of sources while maintaining a common control interface to the robot controller. The other standard interface (labelled B) ensures a coordinated work-cell by providing a way to connect robots, conveyers, etc. to the same work-cell controller with a simple and standard control interface.

connector, and 24 lines of bit-programmable I/O. Connection is made by either a standard 10-pin connector or Eurocard 64-pin DIN connector. The iRCB 44/10 form-factor was selected to allow multiple concentrations of controllers.

DESIGNING A FLEXIBLE BITBUS ROBOT

Board and chip level modules can simplify many of the control problems inherent in robot architectures. High-speed central processors are necessary to manipulate positional coordinates and direct individual motor controllers to proper attitudes. Figure 2 shows the Bitbus approach to distributing the control while providing for future expansion and performance enhancements. In this example, the Multibus-based robot controller contains the iSBC 286/10 single board computer,

an iSBC 012CX memory expansion board, an iSBC 186/03 single board computer, and two iSBX 344 Bitbus expansion modules. Each board performs a particular system function. The robot drive electronics are housed in a separate Eurocard housing mounted within the robot base. Bitbus connections link the robot controller to the robot, teaching pendant, and work-cell controller. An RS-232 interface is provided to support communication with existing display and control equipment.

Robot Controller. The iAPX 286/287-based computer board provides high-speed computational power to control overall robot motion. Simple high-level commands can be sent over the iSBX connector without regard to their eventual destination because no special software is needed to drive the robot link. The Bitbus controller

will automatically send the command to the appropriate control node, ensure proper transmission, and continue polling the slave (interleaved with other commands) until an adequate response is relayed back to the base-board processor. If the computer board uses a multitasking operating system, message traffic can be maintained while the processor is calculating new position information and interacting with the RS-232 link and other processors.

Robot Drive Electronics. A collection of iRCB-style boards in the base of the robot provides servomotor control and sensory feedback to the robot controller. The custom servomotor drive card provides maximum flexibility for each axial motor. Each axial motor control card contains an iDCM Controller that maintains the Bitbus link to the master while performing all the required loop-control calculations. The card also contains inputs for individual limit sensors to maintain desired safety margins. The board is also capable of driving up to 24 auxilliary connections in end-effectors and other peripherals.

The number of degrees of freedom may be increased by adding another axial control card. The Bitbus interface to the robot controller makes it possible to enhance, change, and substitute different robots without having to change hardware or software in the master controller.

CONCLUSION

The Bitbus microcontroller interconnect provides a method of connecting controllers in distributed control applications. By means of standard interfaces and specification of new and useful hardware and software interfaces, the Bitbus interconnect can link together many intelligent parts of industrial work-cells, distributed motor and device control, data acquisition, and distributed process control systems. Looking for a standard interconnect, Westinghouse, Unimation, Yasakawa Electric, Mitsubishi Electric, and other well-known industrial control vendors have already turned to the Bitbus as a possible means to remove the final obstacle preventing proper synchronization of high-performance distributed control systems. Using a standard interconnect allows previously isolated controllers to interact with other parts of a distributed control system—even when those parts are from many different vendors.

ROBOTICS AGE June 1984

intel

ARTICLE REPRINT

AR-358

September 1984

Serial Bus Simplifies Distributed Control

PETER D. MACWILLIAMS

Reprinted with permission from June, 1984 issue of Control Engineering, Copyright ©, Technical Publishing, A Company of the Dun & Bradstreet Corporation.

Order Number: 280080-001

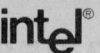

AR-358

Serial Bus Simplifies Distributed Control

As VLSI technology advances, making distribution of control to the single chip level a reality, there is a need for a low cost, reliable, and easy-to-use interconnect between these devices. Intel has addressed this need with its 8044 microcontroller and supporting product line. The resulting "Bitbus" is a silicon SDLC protocol subset for communication between microcontrollers.

PETER D. MacWILLIAMS, Intel Corp., Hillsboro, OR

Key technologies that have made distributed control possible are VLSI and standard distributable communications interconnects. VLSI has reduced the cost of a processing element such that it is now cost effective to use multiple elements per system. Standard interconnects, such as data highways and local area networks (LANs), have complemented VLSI by allowing process elements to be efficiently distributed.

Taken to its extreme, the trend to producing higher levels of VLSI integration at lower costs will eventually provide distribution down to the level of a single VLSI device. But single-chip controllers will need a lower level of distribution than existing architectures provide. In other words, if data highways and LANs interconnect distributed systems, a low end interconnect is needed to connect subsystems within a system. The goal of the "Bitbus" architecture described here is to provide a standard interconnect for distribution of single VLSI controllers.

Low end interconnect considerations

The interconnect below a data highway or LAN is in existence, but most implementations are in the form of parallel buses such as Multibus or STD bus. These are useful and will continue to be, but, for low end applications, can have undesirable mechanical, electrical, and cost constraints. An interconnect which can be implemented as a small piece of a VLSI controller is needed.

A significant factor in the cost of an interconnect is the number of signal lines it requires. For a given transfer rate and protocol, the cost of an interconnect is roughly proportional to the number of signal lines. This is demonstrated in the implementation of parallel buses today.

As a bus approaches a single line (serial) implementation the physical constraints of a backplane are relaxed, allowing physical distribution of nodes which can reduce wiring and packaging costs. However, interface logic to encode and decode address, data, and control signals on a common line becomes more complex. This tends to offset the savings of reducing the number of signal lines. If the logic is implemented as a small portion of a VLSI device rather than discretely, the cost of the interconnect becomes roughly proportional to the cable, connector, and transceiver costs.

Cost is also affected by architecture. The two basic choices are a peer structure, in which a group of nodes communicate with each other as required, or a hierarchical architecture, in which a master node communicates with slave nodes. The trade-off between the two architectures is capability versus complexity and cost. The peer architecture provides a higher level of capability for nodes that need to interact with one another. However the need to provide a complex access protocol (CSMA/CD or Tokens) and software to manage the many possible communication paths adds complexity and cost. In the hierarchical architecture, slave nodes are simplified since they only need to keep track of a single communication path. The master node remains at a complexity comparable to the peer architecture, but its costs can be distributed across the slave nodes in the system.

Low end interconnects are needed for distributed I/O points or intelligent controllers. These applications tend to be hierarchical in nature. Slave nodes are dedicated to a specific task while the master node coordinates all interactions. This reduces the complexity of the slave node by minimizing its requirement to know details about the system.

VLSI plays an important role in selecting interconnect architecture as well. The desire to have low cost nodes tends to favor simplifying the interface. By adopting the hierarchical structure, it is possible to provide high level protocol support cost effectively, in silicon for the slave nodes. This high level integration not only reduces cost, but can increase performance since a protocol supported in hardware is faster than one supported in software. This increased performance can make the hierarchical architecture perform as well as or better than peer systems in many applications.

The Bitbus interconnect

The Bitbus interconnect is designed to be a low-cost serial control bus optimized for the high speed transfer of short control messages between tasks in a hierarchical system. It provides a high level, easy-to-use interface while maintaining low cost characteristics.

Today's standard serial interconnects are either supported at a very low level or supported by a highly structured layered protocol. An RS-232

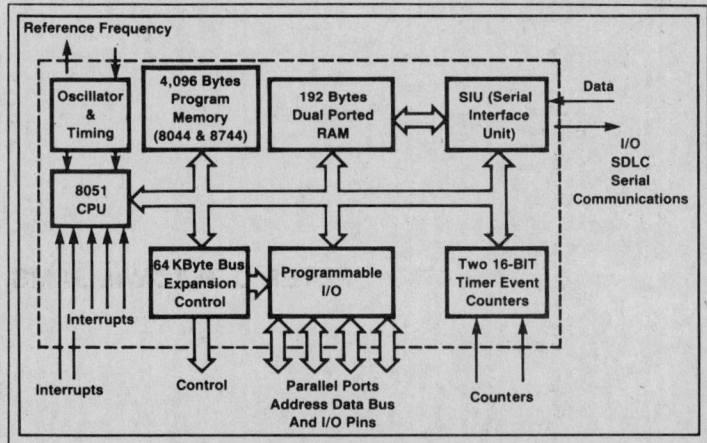

The Intel 8044 incorporates two processing units. An 8051 CPU performs the control tasks, and the SIU handles SDLC serial communications.

CONTROL ENGINEERING/JUNE 1984

AR-358

asynchronous link is a specific example of a low level standard. It provides for byte transfers. Any higher level protocol must be implemented in software.

An example of the highly structured layered protocol is an LAN. LANs are typically based on the seven-layer International Standards Organization (ISO) communication model. This model provides six standard interfaces to allow protocols to be redefined at multiple levels while maintaining compatibility. This flexibility requires overhead, however, to maintain the structure and support all the features of the various layers.

Requirements of the Bitbus demand a high level easy-to-use interface. Interfaces of an RS-232 asynchronous line are not acceptable from an ease-of-use perspective as well as for performance. The highly structured layered protocol is unacceptable due to the performance penalty paid for the multiple standard interfaces. The ISO definition provides many capabilities within the layers that are not required for low-end interconnections.

The solution for the Bitbus interconnect is to provide the high-level interface, but eliminate the many intermediate standard interfaces. This provides the high level support without performance impact. Additionally, the ability to integrate the simple high level interface into silicon will provide for future performance enhancements.

The Bitbus interconnect is defined at four levels: electrical interface, data link protocol, message protocol, and application. A special application task is also defined for slave nodes. It is called Remote Access and Control (RAC). This allows remote I/O access and task control operations to be performed without adding specific application tasks at slave nodes.

The Bitbus electrical interface is based on the RS-485 standard. It supports up to 28 nodes on a cable segment using standard off-the-shelf transmitters and receivers. These devices operate with differential signal drivers, providing a high degree of noise immunity. Both receivers and disabled transmitters can withstand dc common mode voltages of up to ±7 V. For applications requiring more isolation, optical isolators may be incorporated. The electrical interface is optimized for low-cost implementations. It is designed to use low-cost twisted pair cable and standard off-the-shelf connectors. Additional flexibility is obtained by providing two modes of operation. The synchronous mode provides the highest performance over a relatively short distance. The self-clocked mode of provides for longer distance

Data packets can contain three operation types—unnumbered, supervisory, and information.

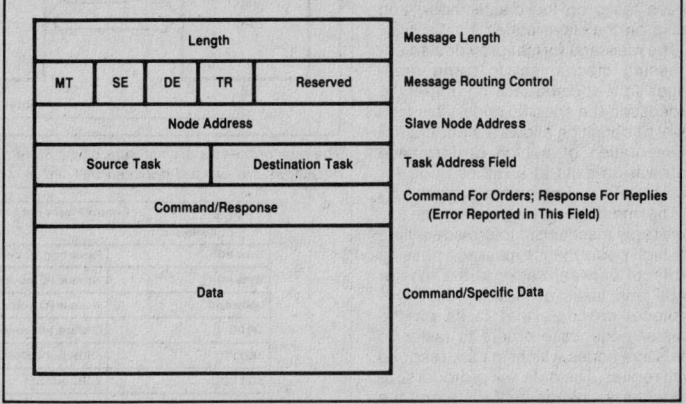

The message format provides an addressing mechanism to route messages.

operation and increased node count.

The Bitbus data link protocol is based on a subset of the IBM Synchronous Data Link Control (SDLC) standard. SDLC is a proven reliable protocol for interconnecting a master node to multiple slave nodes in a multidrop structure, and it can be easily integrated into a VLSI device.

The standard data link frame format supports node addressing, data link control functions, message transfer and error detection. Frames are delimited by flags which contain the bit pattern 01111110. This unique bit pattern is guaranteed by using zero bit insertion/deletion throughout the rest of the fields in the frame. Bitbus messages are transferred in the information field of the frame. This field format is defined by the Bitbus message protocol. The data link protocol supports reliable message transfer with this frame format in two ways: bit error detection in the frame check sequence (FCS) field and sequencing of transfers in the control field.

The FCS field contains a 16-bit cyclic redundancy check (CRC) used to detect bit errors on the link. Any node receiving a frame with an invalid CRC ignores it since the cause of error is unknown. If the error was in the address field the wrong node, or even multiple nodes, may have received the message. The master node recovers from this condition automatically by timing out on the slave response. If this time out occurs, the transfer is automatically tried a second time.

Error detection at a higher level is provided by sequencing transfers. After a reset the master node must synchronize with any slave to which it wishes to send messages. This synchronization is performed using standard SDLC unnumbered control fields. Messages cannot be transferred until this process is complete. Additionally, if at any time synchronization is lost, the data link protocol requires the slave to be resynchronized before transferring further messages.

Once synchronized, the master node may exchange messages with a slave node using standard SDLC supervisory and information control fields. Each transfer contains SDLC sequence counts in the control field to verify synchronization. Information control fields are used to transfer messages while supervisory control fields are used to perform data link control functions when messages are not available. These include a slave node acknowledging receipt of a frame from the master node or the master node polling a slave node for a message. These capa-

CONTROL ENGINEERING/JUNE 1984

bilities allow messages sent to slave nodes to be immediately acknowledged by the hardware interface. Automatic acknowledgment frees up the link for the master node to perform other operations such as sending another message or polling another slave node. This maximizes the serial bus utilization and thus system performance.

The Bitbus message protocol is defined on top of the data link protocol. It defines the message structure for the information field and an order/reply mechanism for communication between tasks on the master node and tasks on the slave nodes.

The message format provides an addressing mechanism to route messages to a specific task on a specific processor at a specific node. This high level of definition allows a standard implementation of a high performance gateway to exist at a Bitbus node for completely routing all messages.

The message protocol uses an order/reply mechanism to provide a simple high performance message passing protocol between tasks at the master node and tasks at slave nodes. This protocol specifies that tasks on the master node issue orders to tasks on the slave nodes which, in turn, respond with replies. The data link protocol supports the exchange by transferring the order message in an information frame that is immediately acknowledged by the receiving slave node with either a supervisory frame or an information frame if the reply from a previous order is available. The master node then polls the slave node until the corresponding reply message is returned. This polling may be performed with supervisory frames or, if additional order messages are available, with information frames. This algorithm minimizes unnecessary polling since a slave is only polled when one or more (maximum of seven) orders are outstanding to it and maximizes performance by allowing polls and acknowledges to be piggybacked on order and reply messages respectively. Also note that this allows the master node to interleave orders and polls to multiple slave nodes.

Application tasks interface directly to the message protocol. In general, these tasks are defined by the user. One exception is the Remote Access and Control (RAC) task that is defined at slave nodes. The RAC task provides a standard set of high level commands to perform remote I/O access and task control. This interface allows operation of a Bitbus system without specific application tasks at the slave nodes.

The 8044 microcontroller

The 8044 microcontroller is a member of the 8051 microcontroller family. The 8044 provides a basic 8051 CPU core, and a highly capable serial interface unit (SIU). The SIU is an independent processor that implements a subset of the SDLC data link protocol directly in hardware. This unique two-processor architecture off-loads the 8051 CPU of all routine communication overhead, allowing it to be dedicated to control.

In addition to the SIU and CPU, this device integrates two timers/counters, an interrupt controller, up to 32 bits of parallel I/O, 4 kbytes of EPROM/ROM

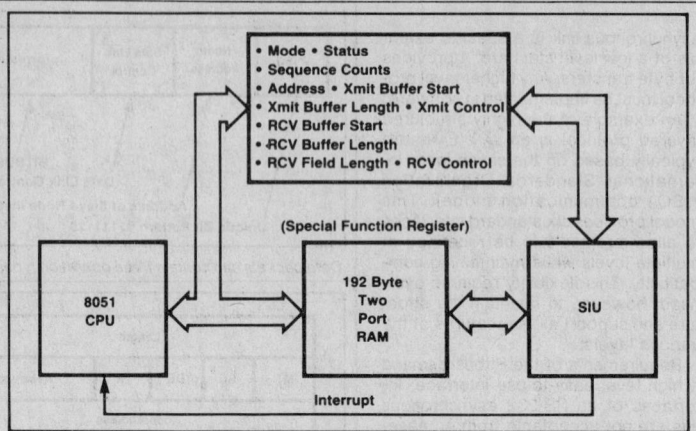

The dual processor architecture of the 8044 reduced communication overhead. Only actual messages are passed between the CPU and the serial interface unit (SIU).

Remote Access and control (RAC) Commands	
Command	Description
Read I/O	Reads from I/O locations and returns results.
Write I/O	Writes to I/O locations and returns original values.
Update I/O	Writes to I/O locations then rereads and returns results.
OR I/O	ORs data with contents of I/O. Rereads and returns results.
AND I/O	ANDs data with contents of I/O. Rereads and returns results.
XOR I/O	XORs data with contents of I/O. Rereads and returns results.
Download memory	Writes block of data to memory.
Upload memory	Reads block of data from memory.
Status read	Reads from locations in memory or I/O and returns results.
Status write	Writes to locations in memory or I/O and returns values.
Reset slave	Causes slave node to reinitialize.
Create task	Causes new task to be recongnized and queued for execution.
Delete task	Permanently terminates execution of a task.
Get function IDs	Returns a list of function IDs for tasks currently recognized.
RAC protect	Enables or disables the remote access functions.

Remote access commands perform remote I/O access and remote task control. This allows the Bitbus to operate without specific tasks at the slave nodes.

ICM Products Available	
Product	Description
Firmware	Firmware for the 8044, including iRMX 51, power up diagnostics, Bitbus interconnect driver, and Remote Access and Control tasks.
iSBX 344	Bitbus controller multimodule allowing any product with iSBX interface to attach to the Bitbus interconnect.
iRCB 44/10	Low cost remote controller board supporting iRMX 51 tasks, 24 lines of parallel I/O and iSBX I/O expansion.
iRMX 510	Support package for Bitbus products with operating system drivers and iRMX 51 development support modules.
iRMX 51	Small, fast real-time operating system kernel for the 8051 mocrocontroller family.

The iDCM product line consists of hardware and software products to support the Bitbus interconnect at multiple levels of integration.

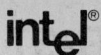

AR-358

and 192 bytes of RAM. This level of integration makes it possible to implement the "single chip node" previously discussed. The 8044 can literally be used with a power source, a crystal and a transceiver to build a Bitbus slave node. For this implementation, a user simply generates an application program and minimal Bitbus interface code for the internal EPROM/ROM.

The most significant feature in the 8044 is the intelligent SIU. This device is actually a second processor that complements the 8051 CPU by off-loading a significant portion of the SDLC communication protocol. The two processors communicate through a time multiplexed two-port RAM and a group of special function registers. This interface allows both the CPU and SIU to execute at full speed simultaneously. The only interaction required is to exchange transmit and receive buffers and to handle infrequent protocol conditions that are not supported in hardware.

Under normal conditions, passing information between the CPU and SIU is extremely easy. To send a message, an application running on the CPU simply creates a data structure in the internal RAM and passes a pointer to the SIU through the special function register interface. The SIU transmits the message and awaits an acknowledgment. If the acknowledgment is negative, the SIU can automatically retransmit the message. Only after the message has been successfully transmitted and acknowledged is the CPU interrupted. To receive a message, an application running on the CPU simply assigns a receive buffer by passing a pointer to the SIU through a special function register. Only after an error-free message has been received and acknowledged will the CPU be interrupted.

Functions handled by the SIU without CPU intervention include framing, address recognition, CRC generation and checking, sequence count generation and checking, and automatic acknowledgment. Automatic acknowledgment provides a significant performance improvement for the link when the 8044 is used as a slave node. This feature generates a response to a valid incoming frame immediately, with absolutely no software overhead. The incoming frame may be an information frame with a message or a supervisory frame used as a poll. If a message is available the response is an information frame. If a message is not available the response is a supervisory frame. In either case this feature quickly returns control of the link to the master node so that it can perform another operation such as sending another message or polling another slave node.

The 8051 CPU in the 8044 is only required to perform minimal protocol processing to complement the SIU functions. In addition to irrecoverable protocol errors that may be detected during normal operation, the CPU is responsible for initialization. This is not a significant overhead since it is performed only after reset or after an irrecoverable protocol error. The result for this architecture is that almost 100 percent of the CPU bandwidth is available to process the application task(s) at slave nodes. Additionally, the time spent servicing an SIU interrupt is minimal, allowing the CPU to efficiently process high-speed real-time events.

The 8044 may be used as either a slave or master node. In this case, the SIU cannot perform the automatic acknowledgment function and the 8051 CPU must be used to process the additional protocol. As a result, the 8051 CPU is dedicated to the protocol implementation and a second processor is used for tasks. Note that even in non-AUTO mode, the 8044 still does framing, address recognition, CRC generation and checking and sequence count generation and checking.

The 8044 reaps many benefits as a member of the standard 8051 family. It shares a common CPU, instruction set and peripheral architecture. This leads to a wealth of support tools and software. All standard development software for the 8051, such as ASM 51, PL/M 51, and RL51 may be used without modification for 8044 development. Most hardware tools, such as in-circuit emulators, are easily modified to provide development support.

The iDCM product line

Support of the Bitbus interconnect is based on the open system concept. Solutions are available at the component, board, and software levels. Users choose the implementation that best meets the needs of the application. The Bitbus interconnect specification is published by Intel to allow any manufacturer to build compatible products.

For support of the Bitbus interconnect, Intel provides the 8044 microcontroller component and the Distributed Control Modules (iDCM) products. The 8044 provides the lowest level component solution. This provides the lowest possible cost implementation (i.e., "single chip"); however, the user must write application software as well as Bitbus interconnect interface software. Other iDCM products support the Bitbus interconnect at higher levels.

The iDCM product line consists of hardware and software products that support the Bitbus interconnect at multiple levels of integration. These products are based on the 8044 microcontroller whose on-chip program memory contains a small, fast, real-time operating system Kernel (iRMX 51), and communication protocol drivers that fully support Bitbus interconnect, power up diagnostics, and the Remote Access and Control task.

Bitbus in the factory

The Bitbus interconnect in the factory complements existing data highways. Presently, the data highways are used to distribute islands of automation throughout the factory. Due to the cost of a connection to a data highway, each island of automation typically consists of many individual controllers. The Bitbus interconnect can be used to further distribute these controllers.

As an example, consider a system that controls a continuous process. It requires many individual control loops. Using the Bitbus interconnect, each loop can be controlled by an individual processor. The master controller is used to interface to the data highway and to supervise the individual loop controllers. The supervision role includes monitoring and recording operations, optimizing the process by altering appropriate setpoints and, if required, switching to back up devices. If the master controller were to fail the slave nodes could contain sufficient intelligence to continue operation at reduced efficiency or at least bring the process to an orderly shutdown. The master controller could also download control programs or tables. This would allow the process to be altered easily to produce different end products.

Implementing a control system using the Bitbus is extremely flexible. The existing method of a single cabinet or cabinet group may be used, allowing a central power source for all controllers. In this case, the Bitbus interconnect provides a cost reduction due to the simplicity of the interconnect. At the other extreme, each controller may be distributed to the point of control. This may also save cost by eliminating the large enclosure and the wiring between it and remote I/O points.

Realistically most applications will be in the middle. Controllers will tend to be clustered with a few scattered from the main groups. The extent of the distribution is a cost trade off. However, the flexibility of the Bitbus interconnect simplifies the solution. Possibly the most important example of this is the software transparency of nodes local to the master controller and nodes in remote locations. This allows easy migration of a controller anywhere on the interconnect as well as easy expansion for additional nodes in the future. ☐

intel

RELIABILITY REPORT

RR-57

April 1985

iSBX™ 344 BITBUS™ Controller MULTIMODULE™ Board and iRCB 44/10 BITBUS™ Remote Controller Board Reliability

CLEONE HAWKINSON
SYSTEMS QUALITY AND RELIABILITY

INTEL CORPORATION, 1985

Order Number 280113-001

RR-57

RELIABILITY IS THE PROBABILITY OF A PRODUCT PERFORMING A SPECIFIED FUNCTION WITHOUT FAILURE UNDER GIVEN CONDITIONS FOR A GIVEN PERIOD PERIOD OF TIME.

SUMMARY

This report presents the results of the reliability evaluations of the iSBX™ 344 BITBUS™ Controller MULTIMODULE™ Board and iRCB 44/10 BITBUS™ Remote Controller Board. This report also reviews Intel's board Quality Assurance and Reliability qualification program.

The iSBX 344 board and the iRCB 44/10 board have successfully met requirements for reliability, environment (vibration, humidity, temperature), voltage margins, and circuit timing.

The summary of the Mean Time Between Failures (MTBF) data below demonstrates the established reliability of these products. If the iSBX 344 board (36,000 hours MTBF) were used eight hours a day, five days a week, the expected MTBF is 18 years. If the same product were used twenty-four hours a day, seven days a week the expected MTBF is 4.1 years. For the iRCB 44/10 board, (29,000 hours MTBF) the expected MTBF at eight hours a day, five days a week is 14.1 years. At twenty-four hours a day, seven days a week, the expected MTBF is 3.3 years. Detailed test results with supporting data are presented in the text.

	MTBF 55°C* (hours)	Confidence Level	MTBF 55°C 40 Hrs/Wk (years)	MTBF 55°C 168 Hrs/Wk (years)
iSBX 344 board	36,000	60%	18	4.1
iRCB 44/10 board	29,000	60%	14.5	3.3

*test performed at 70°C (158°F) to accelerate test time

THE iSBX™ 344 BOARD AND THE iRCB 44/10 BOARD

The iSBX 344 BITBUS Controller MULTIMODULE Board and the iRCB 44/10 BITBUS Remote Controller Board communicate in an Intel Distributed Control Module (iDCM) system via the BITBUS interconnect. Both hardware products are based on the highly integrated 8044 BITBUS controller. The iSBX 344 board provides a BITBUS connection to all Intel Single Board Computers that support the iSBX I/O Expansion Interface. The iSBX 344 board is part of a node (master or slave) on the BITBUS interconnect. Figure 1 illustrates the major functional blocks of the iSBX 344 MULTIMODULE board.

The iRCB 44/10 board can be used as an intelligent remote controller or an I/O expansion device. As a stand-alone BITBUS node, the iRCB 44/10 board provides communications and CPU power via the 8044 BITBUS Controller, as well as digital I/O capability. The iRCB 44/10 can be part of a master or of a slave node in a BITBUS system. Figure 2 illustrates the major functional blocks of the iRCB 44/10 board.

Both products have features well suited for industrial control applications (data acquisition and monitoring, process control, robotics, and machine control) where distributed control architectures are most beneficial. Figure 3 illustrates the Distributed Control Module operating environment.

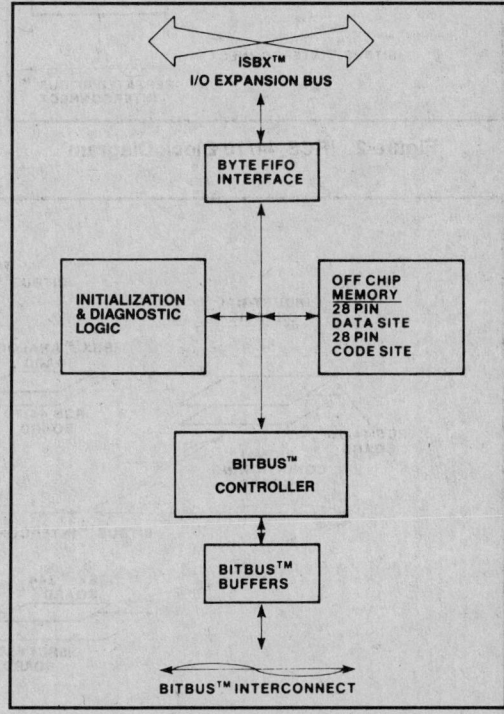

Figure 1. iSBX™ 344 Block Diagram

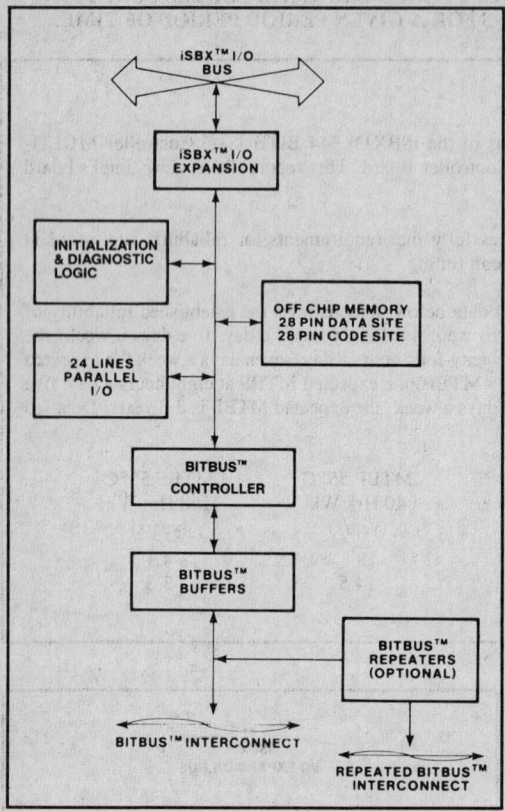

Figure 2. iRCB 44/10 Block Diagram

BOARD PRODUCT QUALITY ASSURANCE

The quality and reliability of products like the iSBX 344 and iRCB 44/10 boards are a function of the quality of components used, the care taken in product design and manufacturing, and the extent of testing performed on the product before shipment. Examining these functions illustrates the Intel Quality Assurance program for microcomputer board products.

The Single Board Computer manufacturing process is audited by Quality Assurance, and manufacturing inspection occurs at every step. First, a high quality product requires high quality material. Our goal is to achieve 100% acceptance of vendor materials. Source Inspection at selected vendors eliminates some incoming material inspection altogether. However, for commodities such as bare boards and non-Intel components, incoming inspection assures quality specifications are met. After incoming inspection, components for an assembly kit are pulled together for assembly onto the bare board.

Next, automatic equipment installs most routine components. Machines do repetitive, precision jobs without tiring, which increases productivity and ensures consistent quality. Programmed Dual In-Line Package (DIP) auto-insertion equipment installs integrated circuits onto bare boards (Figure 4). Next, the axial lead inserter is programmed to install capacitors, diodes, and resistors. After automatic stake pin insertion, a three-station robot (Figure 5) puts low profile jumper plugs in place. Finally, a machine masks the areas of the boards which do not need to be soldered.

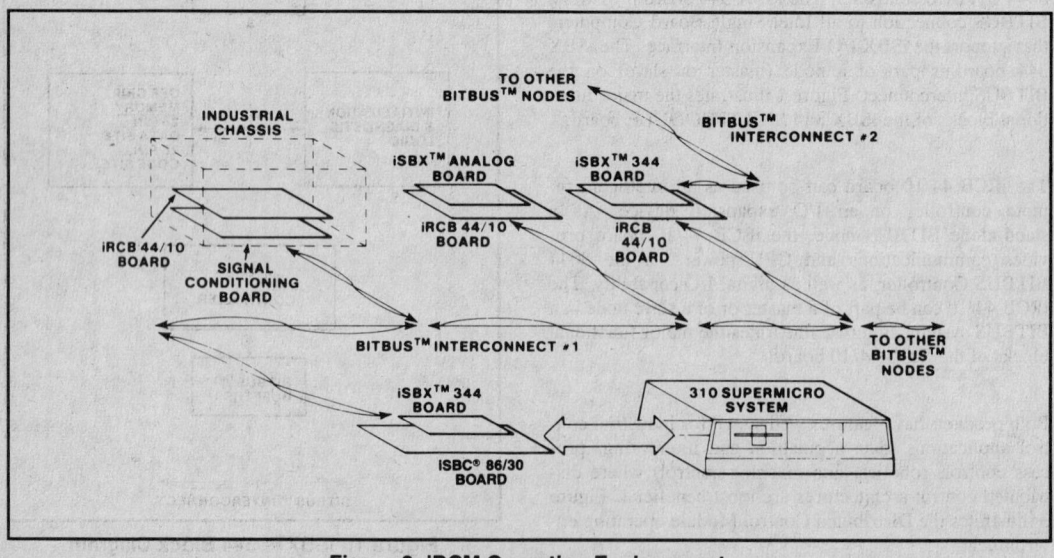

Figure 3. iDCM Operating Environment

Figure 4. Dual In-Line Package Auto-Insertion Equipment

After this, parts unsuitable for automatic assembly are manually assembled onto the board. The board is then inspected for conformance to standards prior to wave solder and for soldering defects after wave solder.

Intel is proud of its wave solder process control. The post-wave cleaning process begins with a detergent wash. Next, boards pass through two rinse cycles; the second uses deionized water. The final step is hot air drying. Statistical process control techniques are used throughout this operation.

Two additional process checks are performed. First, boards are sample tested in an Omegameter, which measures ionic contamination of the rinse water. Second, one board per lot is placed in the Thermotron steady-state environmental chamber at elevated temperature (70°C, 158°F) and humidity (85% RH) for 96 hours. The board is then checked under a microscope for corrosion or other deposits. In the rare event that any deviation occurs, the process is stopped until compliance to specification is restored.

In touch-up and second assembly, such items as connectors and process sensitive components are added to a board. As the final phase of assembly, a board is tested for "shorts" and "opens" on the Teradyne L529 or the Teradyne L260 Automatic Test Equipment. Final assembly inspection verifies the boards are acceptable for functional test. Quality Assurance audits the process.

Figure 5. Robot placing jumper plugs on a MULTIBUS® iSBC® 428 Universal Memory Site Board

Figure 6. Board Burn-in Ovens

Figure 7. Teradyne Tester

The next stage is static burn-in at elevated temperature and voltage margins (70°C, +6% VCC). Burn-in eliminates "infant mortality" failures that occur early in the life of a product. All boards are burned-in for 6 1/2 hours in ovens (Figure 6).

Boards are then functionally tested on a Teradyne L125/L135 (Figure 7) or a Teradyne L260 In-Circuit Tester. These systems have a "test the tester" feature that verifies all test points are functioning before actual boards are tested. A special "bed of nails" vacuum fixture ensures that all board test points may be accessed by the test system. Any components that fail are replaced, and the boards are retested on the Teradyne system.

Next, each board undergoes a three phase operational test at System Test Board Level (STBL). For these tests, a set of monitor and diagnostic EPROMS are installed. The board is placed in a General Purpose Test Fixture (GPTF) shown in Figure 8. The first test sequence is performed at room temperature and at nominal voltage. The second phase is at elevated temperature (70°C) and +6% VCC voltage. The final phase is at elevated temperature (70°C) and -6% VCC voltage. The STBL program verifies the board's performance throughout these sequences by testing the CPU, the I/O interface, and other major functional blocks of the board.

After the test sequence, all boards are visually inspected to ensure that they comply with required quality standards. Boards passing this final screening are then released for use in an Intel system product or sent to packaging.

After packaging, a board is sent to the Boards and Systems Warehouse (BSW) to await shipment to the customer. Quality Assurance conducts monthly finished goods audits on randomly selected products in the BSW. This audit reviews documentation, tests for compliance to temperature specifications, and confirms functional performance.

The boards are functionally tested on 64-board audit racks equipped with appropriate Audit Test Fixtures (Figure 9). The auto-logging center tracks the number of tests run and records any failures which may occur. In 1985, Intel replaced these audit test racks with a temperature controlled board audit chamber, similar to the environmental chamber used for Intel system products.

This finished goods audit is a final in-house monitor of the quality that reaches the customer. Results of the audit are reported back to the factory on a regular basis. This feedback system ensures problems are identified for corrective action.

Figure 8. Intel MULTIBUS™ iSBC® Board in the General Purpose Test Fixture

Figure 9. Board Audit System

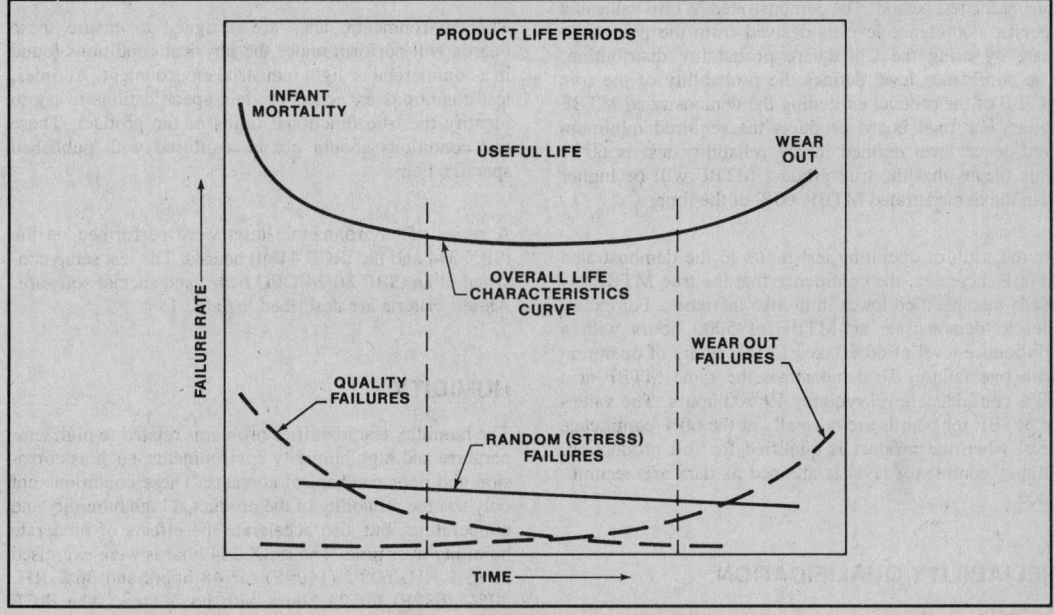

Figure 10. Reliability Life Curve

Performance in the field is also tracked. A Systems Quality and Reliability (SQR) field auditor contacts customers according to monthly product shipments. The auditor communicates all problems to a "DOA" (Defective on Arrival) Team within SQR for resolution.

This rigorous testing, tracking, and corrective action system ensures that Intel's product specifications and the customer's quality and reliability expectations are met.

BOARD PRODUCT RELIABILITY

The Life Curve

Three categories of failures can occur during product life:
- Infant Mortality
- Random
- Wear Out

Each category has a distinct failure distribution when failure frequency is plotted against time. When the three distributions are combined, the resulting failure rate/time distribution produces a characteristic curve known as a "bathtub" curve. The three distributions and the combined reliability life curve are represented in Figure 10.

The boundaries between the categories are less precise than they appear because the failure categories have overlapping distributions. For example, Infant Mortality failures may extend into the Random failure category, but at a very low level. Wear Out failures may, in fact, occasionally occur before the expected Wear Out period.

The Infant Mortality area of the curve shows failures caused by manufacturing defects in the components and boards. These are "quality failures," and their frequency decreases with time. Infant Mortality for boards depends on the quality and test history of the components used in manufacturing. Burn-in minimizes the chance that a customer will receive a product that will fail because of manufacturing defects.

Random failures occur during the "useful life" of the product between Infant Mortality and Wear Out. Most often, these failures are a function of temperature and circuit complexity. The failure pattern becomes random at a low constant value (flat distribution).

Wear Out failures are primarily due to mechanical wear or chemical degradation. Statistically, Wear Out should not happen until many thousands of hours have elapsed for VLSI-based products.

MEAN TIME BETWEEN FAILURES AND CONFIDENCE LEVELS

In reliability evaluation Mean Time Between Failures (MTBF) is the average time in hours expected to elapse between failures. The point estimate of the MTBF is derived by dividing the total test operating hours for a sample of system products by the total number of failures during the test period. The demonstrated MTBF value at a specific confidence level is derived from the point estimate by using the Chi-square probability distribution. The confidence level defines the probability of the true MTBF of the product exceeding the demonstrated MTBF value. For Intel board products the required minimum confidence level defined in the reliability test is 60%. This means that the true product MTBF will be higher than the demonstrated MTBF, 60% of the time.

As the ratio of operating test hours to the demonstrated MTBF increases, the confidence that the true MTBF exceeds the specified lower limit also increases. For example, to demonstrate an MTBF of 5000 hours with a confidence level of 60% takes 10,000 hours of operation with one failure. To demonstrate the same MTBF at a 90% confidence level requires 19,500 hours. The values of MTBF for boards are normally at the 60% confidence level when the product is qualified for full production. Higher confidence level is attained as data are accumulated.

RELIABILITY QUALIFICATION

Reliability qualification serves at least three important functions:

- Provides reliability feedback to product design
- Demonstrates the MTBF and verifies product integrity
- Checks the manufacturing process

First, reliability qualification serves as a feedback mechanism for product design. Lessons learned from building one product can be used to improve the design of new products.

Second, the qualification demonstrates the MTBF of a product. Also, a wide range of reliability tests verify that the product performs to specification in the intended environment. The test information helps customers to evaluate Intel systems, and helps Intel anticipate customers' product support requirements.

Finally, reliability qualification serves as a manufacturing process check. When failures attributed to the manufacturing process occur, they can be quickly identified as exceptions and corrective actions can be implemented.

Information gathered from reliability qualification helps in each of these areas, allowing Intel to produce the most reliable products possible. Intel's Systems Quality and Reliability Department performed a multiphased reliability qualification on the iSBX 344 and the iRCB 44/10 boards, which included environmental and reliability testing.

ENVIRONMENTAL TESTING

The environmental tests are designed to ensure these boards will perform under the physical conditions found in a commercial or light industrial environment. At times, test conditions exceeded product specifications to try to identify the true functional limits of the product. These test conditions should not be confused with published specifications.

A series of environmental tests were performed on the iSBX 344 and the iRCB 44/10 boards. The test setup consisted of an iSBC 80/24 CPU board and special software. All test criteria are described in Table 1.

HUMIDITY

The humidity test identifies problems related to high temperature and high humidity environments, such as corrosion and poor mechanical contacts. These conditions not only test the reliability of the product at high humidity and temperature, but also accelerate the effects of moderate humidity over time. The iSBX 344 boards were exercised at 86% RH, 60°C (140°F) for 48 hours and 36% RH, 20°C (68°F) for 24 hours with no failures. The iRCB 44/10 board was exercised at 85% RH, 65°C (149°F) for 72 hours with no failures.

TEMPERATURE TEST

Two units of each product were functionally tested at two temperatures: 0°C (32°F) for four hours, and 55°C (131°F) for four hours. All four units passed these tests.

A non-functional test (storage) was conducted in an environmentally controlled chamber on one unit of each product. The boards were taken to −40°C (−104°F) and stored for twelve hours. The temperature was returned to room temperature, and the boards were functionally tested for two hours. The temperature was then increased to 70°C (158°F) and was maintained for twenty-four hours. The temperature was again returned to room temperature, and the boards were functionally tested for two hours. The boards functioned normally during and after the storage test.

TEMPERATURE MAPPING

Temperature maps were made for each board to identify potential "hot spots." Case temperatures were measured on selected components representing all areas of the board. The temperature maps were made under several different conditions. Readings were taken at three ambient temperatures, (23°, 50°, 70°C) with and without the use of a cooling fan. The fan produced airflow of 200 linear feet per minute (LFM). Further, the map of the iRCB 44/10 board was made with an iSBX 344 board mounted on it. Details of test conditions are presented in Table 1.

The UTI 9000 Thermal Imaging System (Figure 11) plays an important role in reliability evaluation at Intel. This scanner is more accurate than traditional thermocouple techniques, providing complete coverage of the product instead of selected points. Airflow, ambient temperature, and the ability to locate "hotspots" are under precise control. Accurate measurements (to 0.1°) can be made in a few minutes. The entire board surface can be scanned at once, identifying precisely those areas which deserve a closer look. The board temperatures can be easily, quickly, and thoroughly assessed.

VOLTAGE MARGINS AT TEMPERATURE AND VOLTAGE MAPPING

Voltage margins were tested. Both products were subjected to two hours at 25°C and 70°C each at ±10% margins on all voltages. The products passed all tests.

Voltage mapping measures the voltage potential at various points on the board and ensures that no excessive voltage drops exist. The products were functionally exercised while being mapped to allow the closest approximation of

Table 1. Environmental Qualification Data

THIS INFORMATION, BASED ON SMALL SAMPLES, IS INTERNAL QUALIFICATION TEST DATA GATHERED UNDER CONDITIONS THAT EXCEED SPECIFICATIONS AND SHOULD NOT BE CONFUSED WITH WARRANTED SPECIFICATIONS. ALL CONFIGURATIONS TESTED PASSED ALL TESTS.

PRODUCT (n = sample size)	TEST	DESCRIPTION
	HUMIDITY	
iSBX 344 Board (n = 2)	Passed	Functional: 85% RH 60°C 48 Hours 36% RH 20°C 24 Hours
iRCB 44/10 Board (n = 1)	Passed	Functional: 85% RH 55°C 72 Hours
	TEMPERATURE	
iSBX 344 Board (n = 2)	Passed	Functional: 55°C 4 Hours 0°C 4 Hours
iRCB 44/10 Board (n = 1)	Passed	Non-functional: (1 board each) −40°C, 12 hours, return to room temperature, functionally tested for 2 hours; 70°C for 24 hours, return to room temperature, functionally tested for 2 hours.
	TEMPERATURE MAP	
iSBX 344 Board (n = 1)	Passed	Maps at 23°C, 50°C, 70°C ambient; 15 test points with maximum temperature rise allowed 20° above ambient. 　　　　　Maximum Temperature 　　　　23°C　　50°C　　70°C 　　　　39.8　　62.1　　81.5
iRCB 44/10 Board (n = 1)	Passed	Maps at 23°C, 55°C, 70°C ambient; 9 test points, with and without fan. With fan: 200 LFM airflow across board 　　　　Maximum Temperature (with fan) 　　　　23°C　　55°C　　70°C 　　　　31.8　　62.2　　77.1 Test run at 23°C (without fan). Maximum Temperature: 48.2°C. Test run at 55°C (with fan) with an iSBX 344 board mounted on an iRCB 44/10 board. Maximum Temperature: 62°C. Same test run at 55°C (without fan). Maximum Temperature: 70.3°C.

Table 1. Environmental Qualification Data (continued)

PRODUCT (n = sample size)	TEST	DESCRIPTION
	VOLTAGE MARGINS AT TEMPERATURE	
iSBX 344 Board (n = 2)	Passed	±10% margins on all voltages; 25°C and 70°C for 2 hours each
iRCB 44/10 Board (n = 2)	Passed	
	VOLTAGE MAP	
iSBX 344 Board (n = 1)	Passed	Voltage measurement within ±5% of nominal +5 volts. No ground shift problems, within operational specifications
iRCB 44/10 Board (n = 1)	Passed	
	CIRCUIT TIMING ANALYSIS	
iSBX 344 Board (n = 1)	Passed	DC loading of each gate and bus signal. Bench testing performed to observe quality and integrity of each signal. AC timing analyses of setup-, duration-, hold-, and access-times. Met all specifications within guardbands. Measurements performed at 25°C.
iRCB 44/10 Board (n = 1)	Passed	
	VIBRATION	
iSBX 344 Board (n = 2)	Passed	15 one minute cycles 0-50-0 Hz. Vibration at resonance for five minutes at .01″ PTP excursion. Axis Resonance X 27.8 Hz Y 21.2 Hz Z 19.3 Hz

typical voltage distribution. Voltage maps were generated at +5% nominal and at ±5% margins. All components were verified to be within specification. All points measured were well within the tolerances allowed for operation.

CIRCUIT TIMING ANALYSIS

Analysis was performed for DC loading of each gate and bus signal. Bench testing allowed observation of the quality and integrity of 13 signals. AC timing analyses on all setup-, duration-, hold-, and access-times were also performed. The results met all specifications, well within a reasonable guardband. Measurements were performed at 25°C.

VIBRATION

Vibration testing identifies mechanically related problems a product could sustain under normal conditions. The areas of concern were the jumpers and components socketed at various locations on the boards. The table displacement was set for .01 inch peak-to-peak excursions on the X, Y, and Z axes. Fifteen one-minute sweeps from 0-55-0 Hz were made on each axis to note all resonance points. Next, each unit was vibrated at resonance on each axis for five minutes. The units functioned normally after vibration testing.

PACKAGING AND BENCH DROP TEST

Board packaging requirements have been rigorously tested under both laboratory and actual shipping conditions. In the laboratory, packaged products are subjected to worst-case conditions. During the bench drop test,

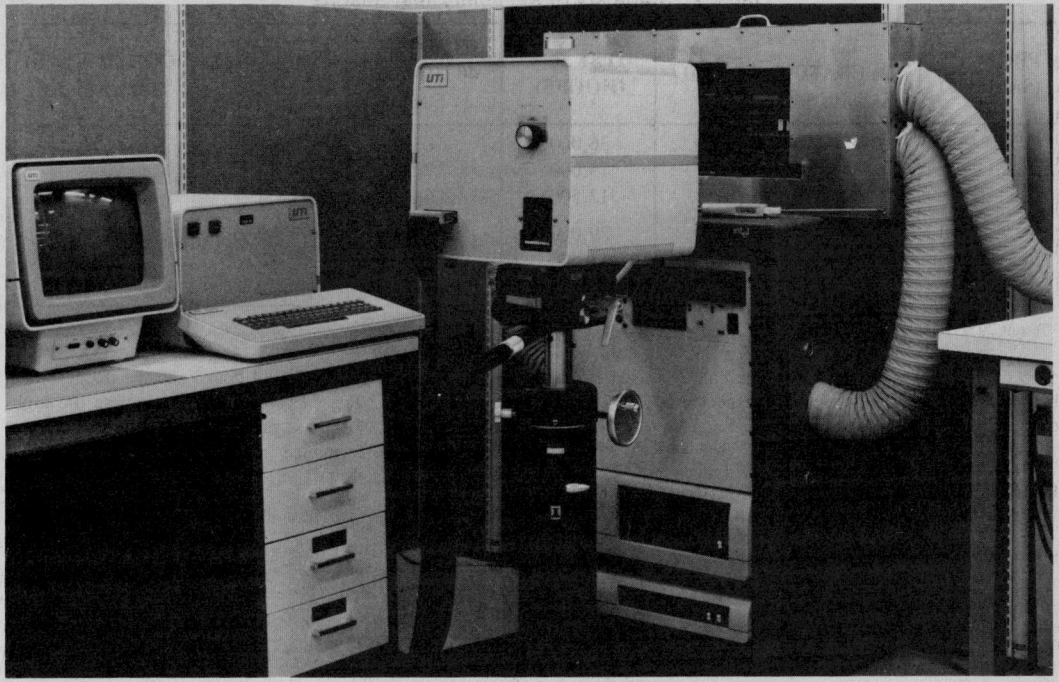

Figure 11. The UTI 9000 Thermal Imaging System

products are monitored for shock, and the package is accepted only after the product meets the shock specification. This portion of the reliability qualification confirms the adequacy of the packaging.

RELIABILITY TEST

Reliability tests verify product reliability by demonstrating the MTBF, an required step to qualify the product for full production. A board product must achieve a demonstrated MTBF of at least 25,000 hours. Both the iSBX 344 and iRCB boards achieved the required minimum MTBF without failing, so the tests were terminated. Therefore, the demonstrated MTBF for these two products is a conservative estimate of the true product reliability. The iSBX 344 board has a higher MTBF because the test ran longer.

Although the MTBF is demonstrated at 70°C, an MTBF at 55°C can be derived from the test data. The elevated temperature during the evaluation provides an accelerated life factor above the 55°C level, based on the Arrhenius equation. Although this equation was developed for semiconductor devices, extending its use to boards is reasonable. Historically in board reliability qualifications the most common failures have been ICs. The test results are are discussed below and are summarized in Table 2.

iSBX™ 344 BOARD

The reliability qualification required the iSBX 344 board product to demonstrate a minimum MTBF of 25,000 hours at 55°C, 60% confidence level. The test was run on 20 units at 70°C. The test ran for 16,620 unit hours with no failures. Converting to 55°C hours, the test yields a derived MTBF of 36,000 hours at 60% confidence level.

The iSBX 344 board is a highly reliable product. If this board is used twenty-four hours a day, seven days a week, the expected mean time between failures (with 60% confidence) is 4.1 years. If this board is used eight hours a day, five days a week, the expected MTBF (60% confidence) is 18 years.

iRCB 44/10 BOARD

The reliability qualification required the iRCB 44/10 board product to demonstrate a minimum MTBF of 25,000 hours at 55°C, 60% confidence level. The test was run on 30 units at 70°C. The test ran for 13,456 unit hours with no failures. Converting to 55°C hours, the test yields a derived MTBF of 29,000 hours at 60% confidence level.

If iRCB 44/10 board is used twenty-four hours a day, seven days a week, the expected mean time between failures (with

Table 2. Summary of Reliability Test Results

PRODUCT (SAMPLE)	UNIT OPERATING HOURS 55°C	FAIL	MTBF 55°C (HOURS)	MTBF 55°C 40 HR/WK (YEARS)	MTBF 55°C 168 HR/WK (YEARS)	CONFIDENCE LEVEL
iSBX 344 Board (n = 20)	33,407	0	36,000	18.0	4.1	60%
			15,000	7.5	1.7	90%
			12,500	6.3	1.4	95%
iRCB 44/10 Board (n = 30)	27,047	0	29,000	14.5	3.3	60%
			11,500	5.8	1.3	90%
			9,000	4.5	1.0	95%

*Test at 70°C to accelerate test time

60% confidence) is 3.3 years. If this board is used eight hours a day, five days a week, the expected MTBF (60% confidence) is 14.5 years.

CONCLUSION

This report describes Intel's Quality Assurance and Reliability program and presents information on the reliability qualification of the iSBX 344 board and the iRCB 44/10 board products. These evaluations demonstrate the high reliability of each of these products. These boards clearly surpass the performance requirements established by Intel.

Distributed Control Software   12

iDCX™ 51
DISTRIBUTED CONTROL EXECUTIVE

- **Software for family of 8051 microcontroller based applications**
- **Real-time, multitasking executive**
- **Supports remote task communication**
- **Small — 2.2K Bytes**

- **Reliable**
- **Simple user interface**
- **Compatible with BITBUS™/Distributed Control Modules (iDCM) product line: iSBX™ 344 & iRCB boards**

The iDCX™ 51 Executive is compact, easy to use, software for development and implementation of applications built on the high performance 8-bit family of 8051 microcontrollers. A few members of this expansive family are the 8051, 8044, and 8052 microcontrollers. Like the 8051 family, the iDCX 51 Executive incorporates many features that make it exceptionally well suited for real-time control applications requiring manipulation and scheduling of more than one job, and fast response to external stimuli.

The 8051 microcontroller family is the family of choice for applications such as: data acquisition and monitoring, process control, robotics, and machine control. Using the iDCX 51 Executive for a foundation can significantly reduce applications development time. Also, the iDCX 51 Executive fully supports Intel's BITBUS™ microcontroller interconnect expressly designed for reliable high performance real-time control.

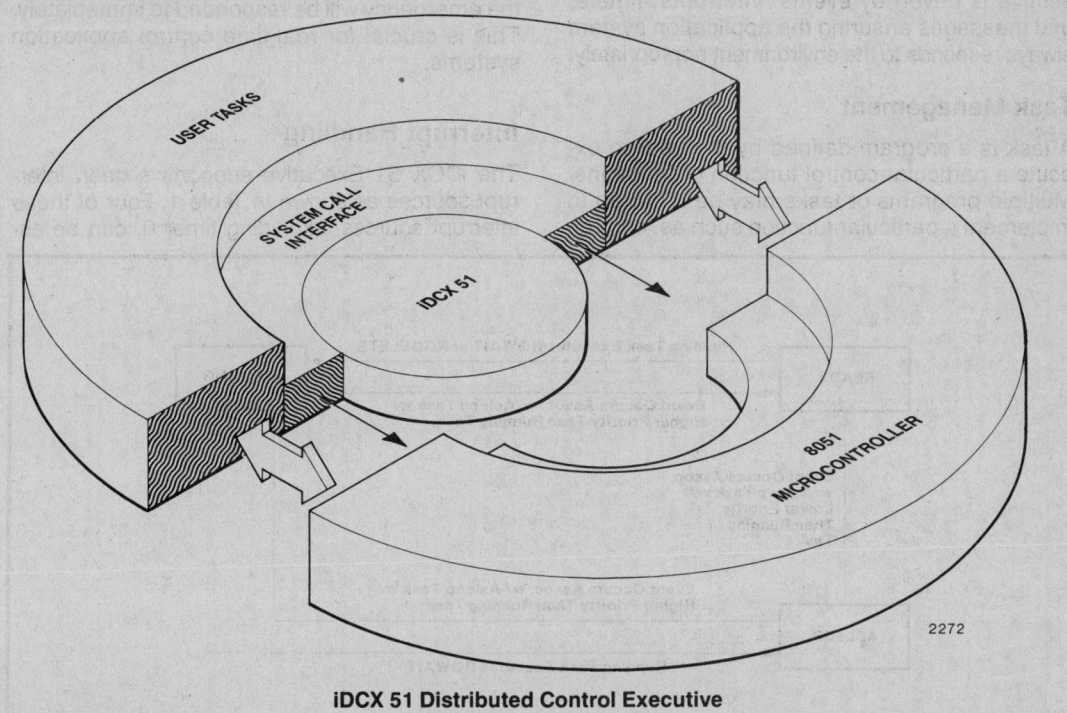

iDCX 51 Distributed Control Executive

Intel Corporation assumes no responsibility for the use of any circuitry other than circuitry embodied in an Intel product. No other circuit patent licenses are implied. Information contained herein supersedes previously published specifications on these devices from Intel. Specifications to change without notice.
© INTEL CORPORATION, 1985

ORDER NUMBER: 280176-001

iDCX™ 51

ARCHITECTURE

Real-time and Multitasking

Real-time control applications must be responsive to the external environment and typically involve the execution of more than one activity (task or set of tasks) in response to different external stimuli. Control of an industrial drying process is an example. This process could require monitoring of multiple temperatures and humidity; control of fans, heaters, and motors that must respond accordingly to a variety of inputs, The iDCX 51 Executive fully supports applications requiring response to stimuli as they occur ie. in real-time. This real-time response is supported for multiple tasks often needed to implement a control application.

Some of the facilities precisely tailored for development and implementation of real-time control application systems provided by the iDCX 51 Executive are: task management, interrupt handling, message passing, and when integrated with communications support, message passing with different microcontrollers. Also, the iDCX 51 Executive is driven by events: interrupts, timers, and messages ensuring the application system always responds to the environment appropriately.

Task Management

A task is a program defined by the user to execute a particular control function or functions. Multiple programs or tasks may be required to implement a particular function such as 'controlling Heater 1.' The iDCX 51 Executive recognizes three different task states as one of the mechanisms to accomplish scheduling of up to eight tasks. Figure 2 illustrates the different task states and their relationship to one another.

The scheduling of tasks is priority based. The user can prioritize tasks to reflect their relative importance within the overall control scheme. For instance, if Heater 1 must go off line prior to Heater 2 then the task associated with Heater 1 shutdown could be assigned a higher priority ensuring the correct shutdown sequence. The RQ WAIT system call is also a scheduling tool. In this example the task implementing Heater 2 shutdown could include an instruction to wait for completion of the task that implements Heater 1 shutdown.

The iDCX 51 Executive allows for PREEMPTION of a task that is currently being executed. This means that if some external event occurs such as a catastrophic failure of Heater 1, a higher priority task associated with the interrupt, message, or timeout resulting from the failure will preempt the running task. Preemption ensures the emergency will be responded to immediately. This is crucial for real-time control application systems.

Interrupt Handling

The iDCX 51 Executive supports sixteen interrupt sources as shown in Table 1. Four of these interrupt sources, excluding timer 0, can be as-

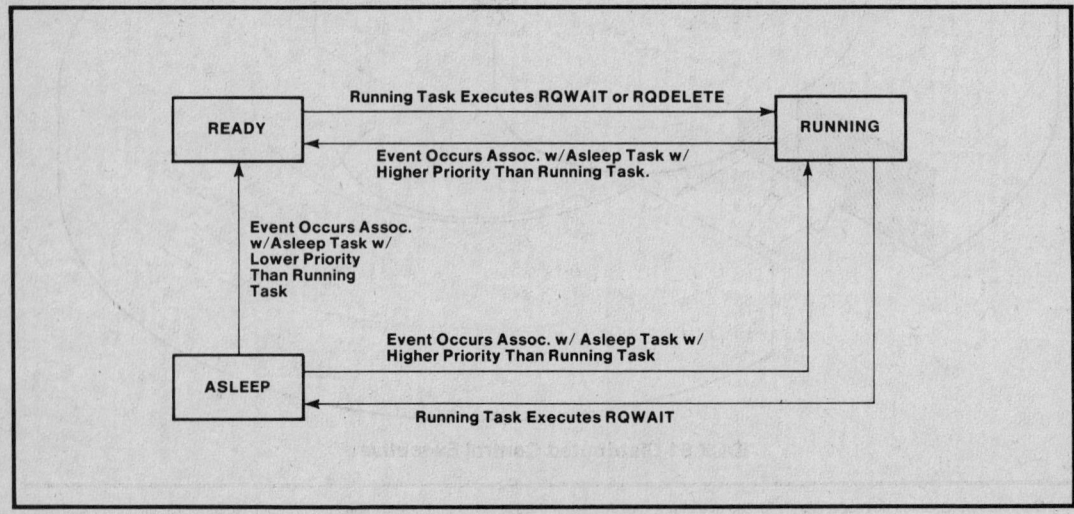

Figure 2. Task State Transition Diagram

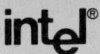

signed to a task. When one of the interrupts occurs the task associated with it becomes a running task (if it were the highest priority task in a ready state). In this way, the iDCX 51 Executive responds to a number of internal and external stimuli including time intervals designated by the user.

Table 1. iDCX™ 51 Interrupt Sources

INTERRUPT SOURCE	INTERRUPT NUMBER
External Request 0	00H
Timer 0	01H
External Request 1	02H
Timer 1	03H
Internal Serial Port 1	04H
Reserved	05H
Reserved	06H
Reserved	07H
Reserved	08H
Reserved	09H
Reserved	0AH
Reserved	0BH
Reserved	0CH
Reserved	0DH
Reserved	0EH
Reserved	0FH

Message Passing

The iDCX 51 Executive allows tasks to interface with one another via a simple message passing facility. This message passing facility can be extended to different processors when communications support is integrated within a BITBUS/iDCM system, for example. This facility provides the user with the ability to link different functions or tasks. Linkage between tasks/functions is typically required to support development of complex control applications with multiple sensors (inputs variables) and drivers (output variables). For instance, the industrial drying process might require a dozen temperature inputs, six moisture readings, and control of: three fans, two conveyor motors, a dryer motor, and a pneumatic conveyor. The data gathered from both the temperature and humidity sensors could be processed. Two tasks might be required to gather the data and process it. One task could perform a part of the analysis, then include a pointer to the next task to complete the next part of the analysis. The tasks could continue to move between one another.

REMOTE TASK COMMUNICATION

The iDCX 51 Executive system calls can support communication to tasks on remote controllers. This feature makes the iDCX 51 Executive ideal for applications using distributed architectures. Providing communication support saves significant application development time and allows for more effective use of this time. Intel's iDCM product line combines hardware and software to provide this function.

In an iDCM system, communication between nodes occurs via the BITBUS microcontroller interconnect. The BITBUS microcontroller interconnect is a high performance serial control bus specifically intended for use in applications built on distributed architectures. The iDCX 51 Executive provides BITBUS support.

BITBUS™/iDCM COMPATIBLE

A pre-configured version of the iDCX 51 Executive implements the BITBUS message format and provides all iDCX 51 facilities mentioned previously: task management, interrupt handling, and message passing. This version of the Executive is supplied in firmware on the 8044 BEM with the iDCM hardware products: the iSBX 344 BITBUS Controller MULTIMODULE and the iRCB boards. It is also supplied on diskette as part of the iRMX 510 DCM Support Package to ease development of BITBUS systems.

SIMPLE USER INTERFACE

The iDCX 51 Executive's capabilities are utilized through system calls. These interfaces have been defined for ease of use and simplicity. Table 2 includes a listing of these interfaces and their functions. Note tasks may be created at system initialization or run-time using the CREATE TASK call.

Functions such as GET FUNCTION IDS, ALLOCATE/DEALLOCATE BUFFER, and SEND MESSAGE (Messages in the iDCX 51 Executive have a maximum size of 255 bytes.), support communication for distributed architectures. Architectures that define multiple remote stations requiring intelligent and dumb I/O manipulation. The remaining

iDCX™ 51

Table 2. iDCX™ 51 System Interfaces

COMMAND	DESCRIPTION
RQ SEND MESSAGE	Sends a message (a command from the BITBUS master, a response from a slave, or a simple message between tasks on the same BITBUS component) to another task.
RQ WAIT	Waits for an interrupt, an event time-out, a message, or any combination of the three.
RQ CREATE TASK	Causes a new sequence of code to be run as an iDCX 51 task with a specific function identification code and priority.
RQ DELETE TASK	Stops the specified task and removes it from all execution lists.
RQ ALLOCATE	Allocates a fixed-length buffer from the on-chip, scratch-pad RAM for general use, or, in BITBUS applications, for a BITBUS message buffer.
RQ DEALLOCATE	Returns an on-chip buffer to the system.
RQ SET INTERVAL	Set the time interval to be used as a separate event-timer for the task.
RQ ENABLE INTERRUPT	Allow external interrupts to signal the microcontroller.
RQ DISSABLE INTERRUPT	Stops all external interrupts from signaling the microcontroller.
RQ GET FUNCTION ID	Provides a list of the 8 function identification codes representing the tasks currently operating on the microcontroller.

interfaces allow the user to specify the system's response to the external environment — a must for real-time control.

Another feature that eases application development is automatic register bank allocation. The Executive will assign tasks to register banks automatically unless a specific request is made. The iDCX 51 Executive keeps track of the register assignments allowing the user to concentrate on other activities.

The user configures an iDCX 51 system simply by: specifying the initial set of task descriptors and configuration values, and linking the system via the RL 51 Linker and Locator Program with user programs. The nature of the task descriptors allows the user to develop programs, locate them in off-chip ROM, and access them without writing additional code. Programs may be written in ASM 51 or PL/M 51. (Intel's 8051 Software Development Package contains both ASM 51 and RL 51. The iDCX 51 Executive supplies the configuration file and macro defining initial task descriptors.) Figure 3 shows the relationships that exist in the system generation process.

RELIABLE

Real-time control applications require reliability. The nucleus requires about 2K bytes of code space, 40 bytes on-chip RAM, & 218 bytes external RAM. Streamlined code increases performance and reliability, and flexibility is not sacrificed as code may be added to either on-chip or external memory.

The iDCX 51 architecture and simple user interface further enhance reliability and lower cost. For example, the straightforward structure of the user interfaces, and the transparent nature of the scheduling process contribute to reliability of the overall system by minimizing programming effort. Also, modularity increases reliability of the system and lowers cost by allowing user tasks to be refined independent of the system. In this way, errors are identified earlier and can be easily corrected in each isolated module.

In addition, users can assign tasks a Function ID that allows tracking of the tasks associated with a particular control/monitoring function. This feature reduces maintenance and trouble shooting time thus increasing system run time and decreasing cost.

OPERATING ENVIRONMENT

The iDCX 51 Executive supports applications development based on any member of the high performance 8051 family of microcontrollers. The Executive is available on diskette with user linkable libraries or in the 8044 BITBUS Enhanced Microcontroller preconfigured in on-

iDCX™ 51

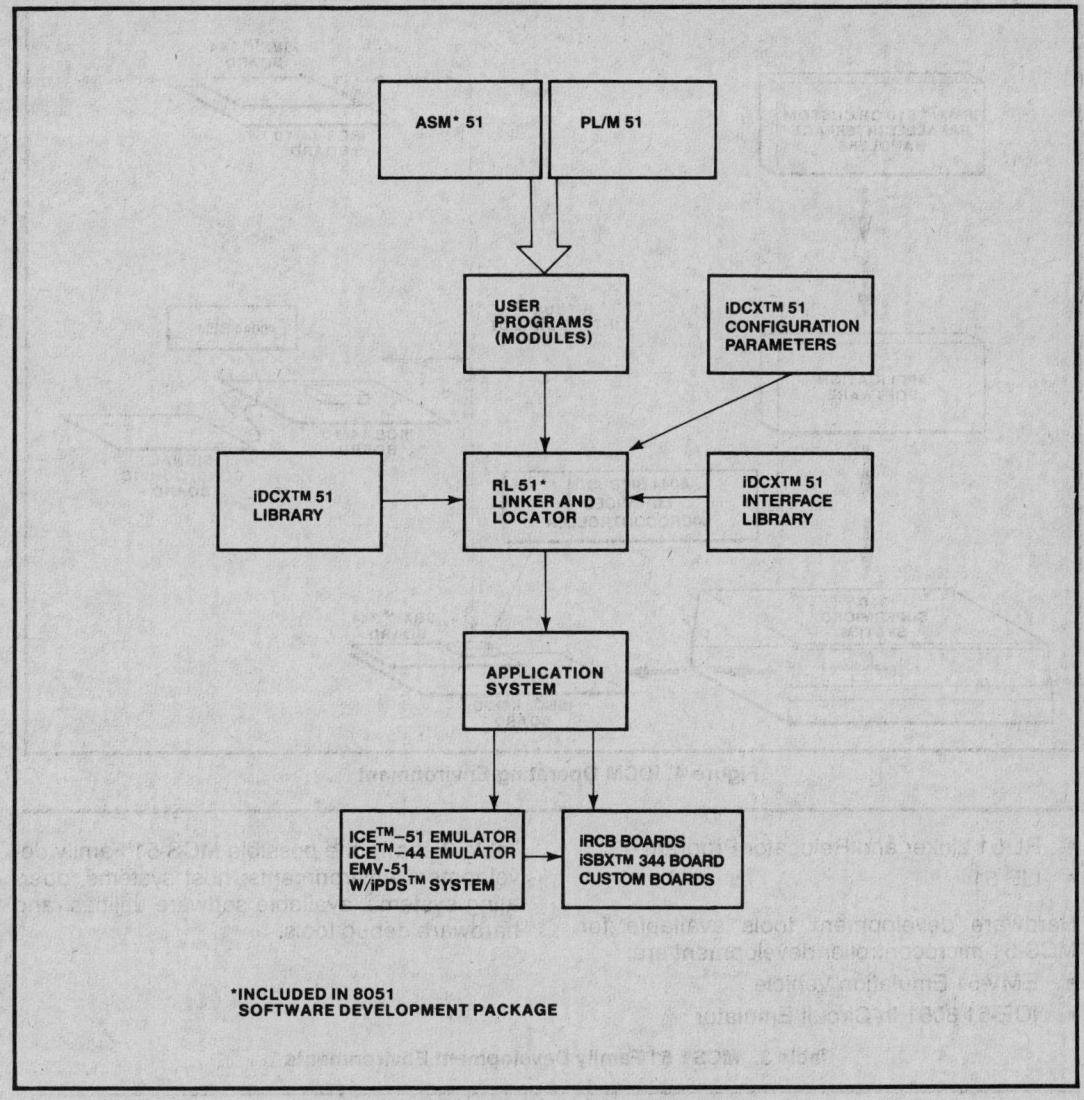

Figure 3. System Generation Process

chip ROM. (The 8044 BEM is an 8044 component that consists of an 8051 microcontroller and SDLC controller on one chip with integral firmware.)

When in the iDCM environment (Figure 4), the iDCX 51 Executive can communicate with iRMX based systems like the System 286/310 or ISIS based systems like the Intel Portable Development System (iPDS) by using the BITBUS™ Software Toolbox.

DEVELOPMENT ENVIRONMENT

Intel provides a complete development environment for the MCS-51 Family of microcontrollers. The iDCX 51 Executive is only one of many of the software development products available. The executive is compatible with the following software development utilities available from Intel:

- 8051 Macro Assembler (ASM 51)
- PL/M 51 Compiler

intel® iDCX™ 51

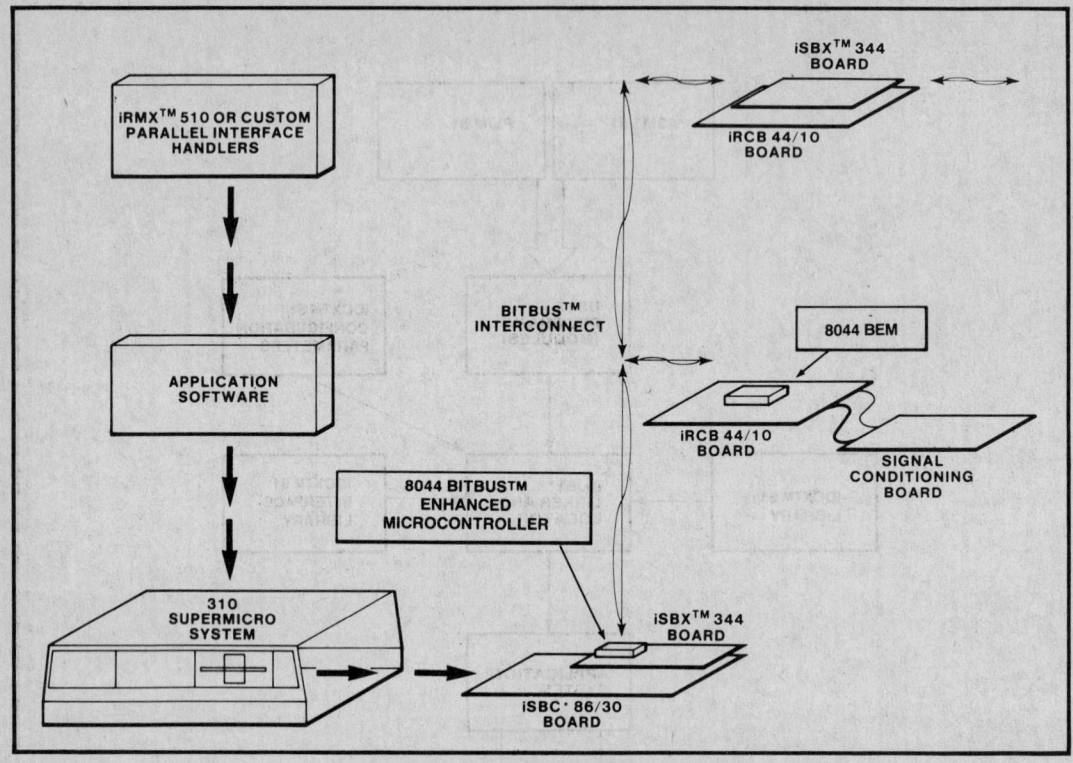

Figure 4. iDCM Operating Environment

- RL 51 Linker and Relocator Program
- LIB 51

Hardware development tools available for MCS-51 microcontroller development are:
- EMV-51 Emulation Vehicle
- ICE-51 8051 In-Circuit Emulator

Table 3 shows the possible MCS-51 Family development environments: host systems, operating systems, available software utilities, and hardware debug tools.

Table 3. MCS® 51 Family Development Environments

Development Utilities	Host Systems		
Software	Intellec® Series III/IV Systems	iPDS™ System	IBM**-PC System
8051 Software Development (ASM 51)	X	X	X
PL/M 51 Software Package	X	X	X
iDCX 51 Executive	X	X	X
Hardware			
EMV 51 Emulation Vehicle		X	
ICE 51, 8051 In-Circuit Emulator	X		X

*Products of U.S. Software, Portland, OR
**IBM is a registered trademark of International Business Machines.

iDCX™ 51

SPECIFICATIONS

Supported Hardware

Microcontrollers

8051	80C51
8052	8044
8751	8744
8031	80C31
8032	8344

iDCM Product Line

iSBX 344 MULTIMODULE Board
iRCB 44/10 Digital I/O Remote Controller Board
iRCB 44/20 Analog I/O Remote Controller Board

Compatible Software
iRMX™ 510 iDCM Support Package

Development Tools
ICE™ 51 or ICE 44 Emulators
Intellec Series Development Systems
iPDS System w/EMV-51
iRMX 510 iDCM Support Package
8051 Software Development Package

Reference Manual (Supplied)
146312-001 — Guide to Using the Distributed Control Modules

Ordering Information

Part Number	Description
iDCX 51 SU	Executive for 8051 Family of Microcontrollers. Single User License, Development Only. Media Supplied: B, F
iDCX 51 BY	Executive for 8051 Family of Microcontrollers. OEM License, Derivative Products. Media Supplied: B, F

iDCX 96
DISTRIBUTED CONTROL EXECUTIVE

- **High Performance, Real-time, Multitasking Executive**
- **Speeds Development of MCS®-96 Microcontroller Applications**
- **Configurable for User Customization**
- **Provides Task Management, Timing, Interrupt and Message Passing Services**
- **Reliable, Compact 2.9K bytes**
- **Simple User Interface**

The iDCX 96 Distributed Control Executive is compact, configurable, easy-to-use software for developing and implementing applications built on the high performance 16-bit family of 8096 microcontrollers (MCS-96). As a real-time, multitasking nucleus, the iDCX 96 Executive enhances the users ability to efficiently design MCS-96 microcontroller applications requiring handling of multiple asynchronous events, and real-time response.

In addition to the features integrated into most microcontrollers (CPU, RAM, ROM, and I/O) the MCS-96 family provides analog to digital conversion, pulse width modulation, and high-speed I/O facilities. Some examples of applications well-suited to the feature set and performance of the 8096 microcontrollers are: motor control, medical instrumentation, automotive transmission control, and machine control. Using the iDCX 96 Distributed Control Executive in these environments will significantly reduce application development time and expense. The iDCX 96 Executive performs equally well in stand-alone applications as well as distributed applications.

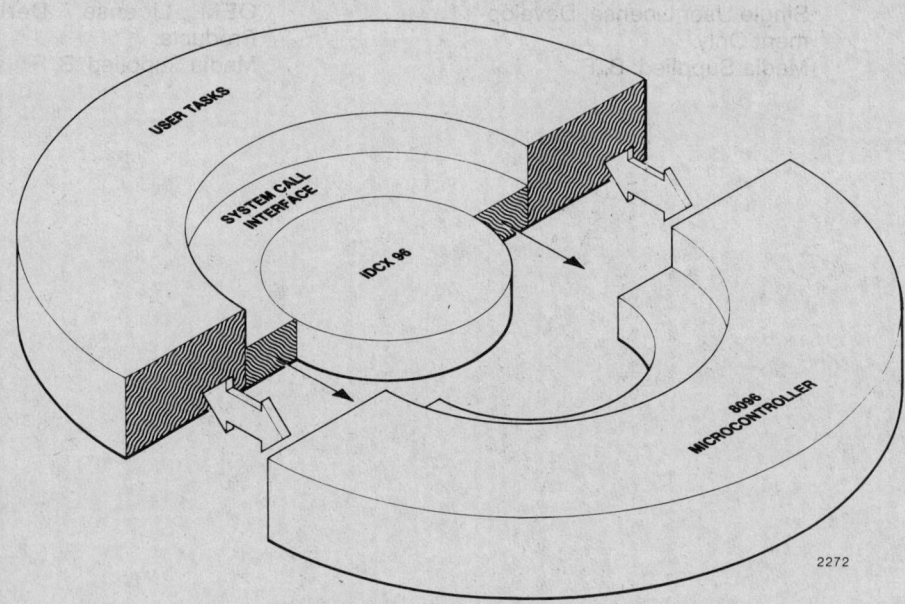

Figure 1. iDCX 96 Distributed Control Executive System

iDCX 96 DISTRIBUTED CONTROL EXECUTIVE

ARCHITECTURE

Real-time and Multitasking

Real-time control systems must be responsive to the external environment and typically involve the execution of more than one function (task or set of tasks) in response to different external stimuli. Control of manufacturing process is an example. These processes can require the monitoring of multiple temperatures and pressures; control of heaters, fans, and motors all responding to many seemingly random inputs. The iDCX 96 Distributed Control Executive fully supports applications requiring response to inputs as they occur ie. in real-time. Multiple tasks in control applications require real-time response. The iDCX 96 Executive helps the user implement these multitasking time-critical applications.

Some of the executive's facilities specifically tailored for developing and implementing standalone and distributed control systems are: task management, timing and interrupt handling, and message passing. When integrated with communications software, the iDCX 96 Executive provides message passing to tasks on different microcontrollers. Response to the environment is guaranteed due to the event-driven nature of the executive. Interrupts, timers, or messages can initiate tasks for proper system response.

Task Management

A task can be thought of as a block of code that performs a specific activity. This activity is one that can occur in parallel with other activities in the system. A task starts at a single point and executes indefinitely, usually in a loop. The iDCX 96 Executive's multitasking facility allows the user to partition system applications code into manageable activities or tasks. Each task competes for processor resources. The executive provides all synchronization, control, and scheduling to ensure each task gets the processor time it requires. A priority mechanism used by the executive determines when a task accesses the processor. Up to 16 tasks can be managed by the executive.

All tasks in an iDCX 96 Executive application are in one of three states as shown in Figure 2. For example, when an RQ WAIT system call is made, the calling task becomes ASLEEP until one of the events upon which it is waiting occurs. These events can be messages, timeouts, time intervals, or interrupts. When an event occurs the task becomes READY or RUNNING.

Also, the executive allows for PREEMPTION of a task currently using processor resources so that emergencies will be responded to immediately. For example, suppose a conveyor in a manufacturing system

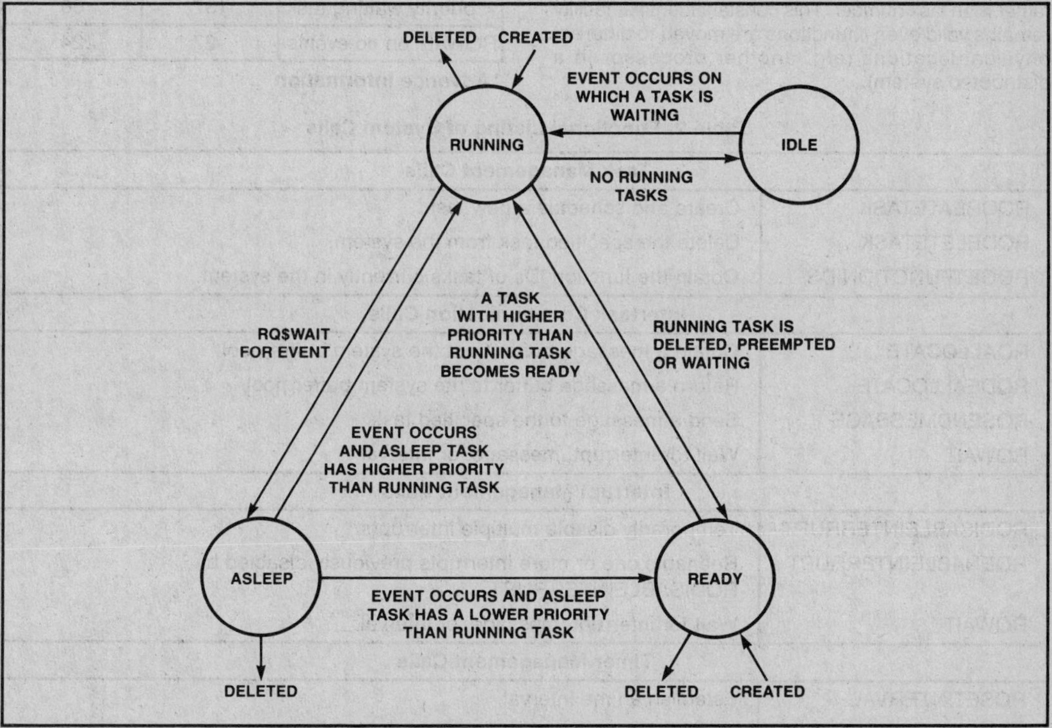

Figure 2. iDCX 96 Executive Task States

iDCX 96 DISTRIBUTED CONTROL EXECUTIVE

incorporate iDCX 96 Executive systems into a BITBUS Interconnect environment. Thus the executive supports communications in standalone and distributed control systems. Although users need to provide some communications software to implement communication between different microcontrollers, the support already provided in the executive gives users a head start in applications development.

HIGH PERFORMANCE AND EASE OF USE

To meet the dual requirements of high performance and ease of use, two interfaces are provided for each system call: a PL/M 96 interface and a register interface. The PL/M 96 interface provides a higher degree of ease of use thus speeding development time. For extremely demanding applications the register interface provides greater run-time speed and can be used with either PL/M 96 or ASM 96.

The iDCX 96 Executive's capabilitites are invoked through a set of system calls. Table 2 includes a listing of these interfaces and their functions. All the system calls with the exception of RQ GET FUNCTION IDS have already been referenced in this document as part of the interrupt handling, message passing, and timing support facilities. The RQ GET FUNCTION IDS call allows the user to reference tasks by function rather than task number. This constant identifier facility remains valid even if functions are moved to different physical locations (e.g. another processor in a distributed system).

The iDCX 96 Distributed Control Executive executes a variety of services in about half the time the iDCX 51 Executive (formally iRMX™ 51 Executive) can. (The iDCX 96 Executive is a functional port of the iDCX 51 Executive to the MCS-96 family of microcontrollers.) Table 3 shows ADVANCE performance information for the iDCX 96 Executive.

Table 3. iDCX 96 Executive Performance

Function	iDCX 51 Time (microsecs.)	iDCX 96 Time* (microsecs.)
Interrupt Latency w/context switch	130	70
Interrupt Latency from idle stage	46	42
Interrupt Latency w/custom handler	N/A	16
RQALLOCATE	18	16
RQSEND = > non-waiting task	98	46
RQSEND = > >priority waiting task	172	90
RQSEND = > <priority waiting task	137	66
RQWAIT on no events	27	24

*Advance Information

Table 2. Functional Listing of System Calls

Task Management Calls	
RQCREATETASK	Create and schedule a new task.
RQDELETETASK	Delete the specified task from the system.
RQGETFUNCTIONIDS	Obtain the function IDs of tasks currently in the system.
Intertask Communication Calls	
RQALLOCATE	Obtain a message buffer from the system buffer pool.
RQDEALLOCATE	Return a message buffer to the system buffer pool
RQSENDMESSAGE	Send a message to the specified task.
RQWAIT	Wait for interrupt, message, or interval.
Interrupt Management Calls	
RQDISABLEINTERRUPT	Temporarily disable multiple interrupts.
RQENABLEINTERRUPT	Reenable one or more interrupts previously disabled by RQDISABLEINTERRUPT.
RQWAIT	Wait for interrupt, message, or interval.
Timer Management Calls	
RQSETINTERVAL	Establish a time interval.
RQWAIT	Wait for interrupt, message, or interval.

iDCX 96 DISTRIBUTED CONTROL EXECUTIVE

suddenly developed a fault and began running out of the normal range. The other parts of the system cannot compensate, and an alarm is triggered. Immediate response is a must to minimize losses. The executive's task prioritization scheme, task state definitions, and preemption facility reflect the asynchronous nature of events in real-time systems as well as the need to respond to the most critical events first.

Interrupt Handling

Interrupts signal the occurrence of an external event and are typically asynchronous with respect to the processor. In real-time control systems interrupt handling plays a major factor in the responsiveness and performance of the system. The iDCX 96 Distributed Control Executive provides the following interrupt handling services and features:

- Interrupt source assignment to a task at system configuration.
- Ability to disable all or some interrupts using the RQ DISABLEINTERRUPT system call.
- Ability to enable disabled interrupts using the RQ ENABLEINTERRUPT system call.
- Synchronization of events using the RQ WAIT system call.
- Configuring a custom interrupt handler into the system.

In keeping with the executive's preemptive priority-based scheduling scheme for an interrupt to occur its associated task must have a higher priority than the present running task. The executive will mask all interrupts of lower priority.

The eight interrupt sources provided by the 8096 architecture are shown in Table 1. The iDCX 96 Executive architecture provides interrupt handlers for each source but allows users to substitute custom interrupt handlers if desired.

Table 1. 8096 Hardware Interrupt Sources

Source
EXTINT
Serial Port
HSI.0
High Speed Outputs
HSI Data Available
A/D Conversion Complete
Timer Overflow
Software Interrupt

Timer Management

The iDCX 96 Executive supplies timing management facilities for synchronizing timed control loops and determining how long tasks wait on an event. In multitasking environments tasks compete for timing resources. The executive eliminates contention for this resource by reserving one of the 8096 on-chip timers for software timing services. A software clock is maintained from this on-chip timer, and is used for system timing functions. Tasks request interval timing or timeout timing services via the iDCX 96 Executive appropriate system calls.

Message Passing

The iDCX 96 Distributed Control Executive facilitates intertask communication that allows tasks to:

- communicate with other tasks via messages
- wait indefinitely on a message event
- synchronize task operations throughout a system
- manage system resources

These services greatly simplify design of multitasking, real-time control applications by providing an extremely flexible method of communication. Because tasks in an iDCX 96 Executive system exchange messages via message queues the communicating tasks are independent of one another. Tasks can store messages not yet received and put messages in a buffer that have not yet been sent. The user simply invokes the relevant system calls when required (RQ ALLOCATE, RQ DEALLOCATE, RQ SENDMESSAGE, RQ WAIT).

The format of iDCX 96 messages follows the standard BITBUS™ Interconnect message format. Figure 3 shows the iDCX 96 Executive message format. By implementing communications software, users can

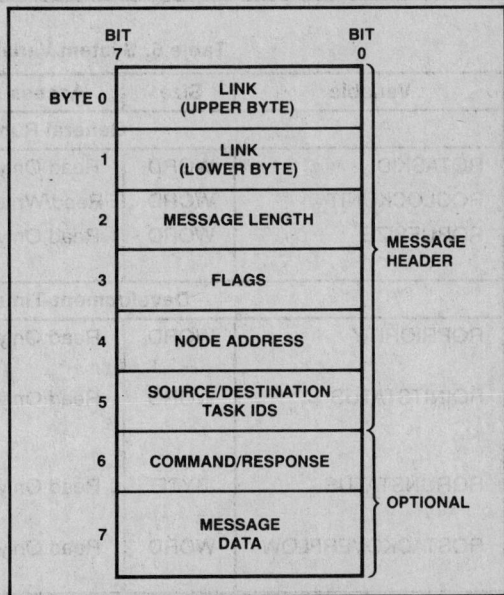

Figure 3. iDCX 96 Message Format

iDCX 96 DISTRIBUTED CONTROL EXECUTIVE

CONFIGURABLE

Aside from the interrupt handler variables noted previously, other system variables are made available to the user for system customization. Most of these variables must be defined during initial system configuration. Task-specific attributes like task priority, interrupt vectors, and function ID are assigned via the Initial Task Descriptor structure at configuration time. Table 4 shows the configuration constants accessible to the user. These configuration constants give the iDCX 96 Executive added flexibility to satisfy the users needs. Table 5 shows other USER AVAILABLE variables. Run-time variables reflect the condition of the running system. Development-time diagnostic variables also reflect conditions of the running environment, but are usually helpful during application development.

Also, the executive allows for adding additional tasks to an already configured system or changing initial configuration constants via an Initial Data Descriptor (IDD). The IDD structure lets the user redefine existing configuration constants without reconfiguring the entire system. Constants that may be redefined are the system: clock unit, clock priority, buffer pool address, buffer pool size, and buffer size.

Table 4. Configuration Constants

Constant Name	Description
RQMAXTASKS	The maximum number of tasks that can exist in the system at any given time.
RQMAXPRIORITY	The highest priority level that can be assigned to a task or to the system clock.
RQCLOCKPRIORITY	The priority level of the system clock.
RQCLOCKTICK	The number of time cycles in the system clock basic time unit (a "tick").
RQSTACKPOOLADR	The starting address of the system stack pool.
RQSTACKPOOLLEN	The length, in bytes, of the system stack pool.
RQSYSPOOLADR	The starting address of the system buffer pool.
RQSYSPOOLLEN	The length, in bytes, of the system buffer pool.
RQSYSBUFSIZE	The size, in bytes, of each buffer in the system buffer pool.
RQFIRSTITD	The absolute address of the first ITD in the ITD/IDD chain.
RQDIAGNOSTICS	An entry point in which user-written power-up diagnostic code is added.

Table 5. System Variables Available to the User

Variable	Size	Access	Description
General Run-Time Variables			
RQTASKID	WORD	Read Only	Contains the ID of the running task
RQCLOCKUNIT	WORD	Read/Write	Specifies the unit of time for the system clock
RQBUFSIZE	WORD	Read Only	Specifies the size of the buffers in the system buffer pool
Development-Time Diagnostic Variables			
RQPRIORITY	WORD	Read Only	Contains the priority of the running task, or zero if the system is idle
RQINITSTATUS	WORD	Read Only	Specifies the system status at the end of the system initialization (low byte), and the ID of the last task initialized (high byte)
RQRUNSTATUS	BYTE	Read Only	Specifies certain occurences and conditions which exist during runtime
RQSTACKOVERFLOW	WORD	Read Only	Specifies which tasks, if any, may have stack overflow conditions

iDCX 96 DISTRIBUTED CONTROL EXECUTIVE

RELIABLE AND COMPACT

Real-time control applications require reliability. The iDCX 96 Distributed Control Executive requires 2.9K bytes of code space, 75 bytes of on-chip register RAM, and a minimum of 56 bytes of data RAM. This streamlined executive increases performance and reliability by providing a range of services in a minimal amount of code. The compact nature of the executive, in addition to its architecture, allows for incorporating it into PROM or the memory of the 8096 microcontroller further reducing component count of the total system.

The iDCX 96 Executive is completely tested and verified by Intel's stringent software evaluation process. Thus the user realizes higher system reliability with reduced effort by incorporating fully functional and tested software. Using the iDCX 96 Executive allows the software development team to focus on the application-specific parts of a project.

The modular nature of the executive also enhances reliablity by allowing user tasks to be refined independently. In this way, errors can be isolated more easily and corrected in each specific module. Using the iDCX 96 Executive for MCS-96 microcontroller application development reduces risk and development time.

OPERATING ENVIRONMENT

The iDCX 96 Executive will operate on any of the MCS-96 Family of microcontrollers. Tables 6 and 7 show the product family and a summary of the MCS-96 Family features and benefits.

Table 6. MCS®-96 Family of Products

Options		68 Pin	48 Pin
Digital I/O	ROMless	8096	8094
	ROM	8396	8394
Analog and Digital I/O	ROMless	8097	8095
	ROM	8397	8395

The 48 pin version is available in DIP (dual inline) package.
The 68 pin version comes in two packages, the plastic Flatpack and the Pin Grid Array.

Table 7. MCS®-96 Features and Benefits Summary

Features	Benefits
16-Bit CPU	Efficient machine with higher throughput.
8K Bytes ROM	Large program space for more complex, larger programs.
232 Bytes RAM	Large on-board register file.
Hardware MUL/DIV	Provides good math capability 16 by 16 multiply or 32 by 16 divide in 6.5 μs @ 12 MHz.
6 Addressing Modes	Provides greater flexibility of programming and data manipulation

High Speed I/O Unit
  4 dedicated I/O lines
  4 programmable I/O lines
	Can measure and generate pulses with high resolution (2 μs @ 12 MHz).

10-Bit A/D Converter	Reads the external analog inputs.
Full Duplex Serial Port	Provides asynchronous serial link to other processors or systems.
Up to 40 I/O Ports	Provides TTL compatible digital data I/O including system expansion with standard 8 or 16-bit peripherals.
Programmable 8 Source Priority Interrupt System	Respond to asynchronous events.
Pulse Width Modulated Output	Provides a programmable pulse train with variable duty cycle. Also used to generate analog output.
Watchdog Timer	Provides ability to recover from software malfunction or hardware upset.
48 Pin (DIP) & 68 Pin (Flatpack, Pin Grid Array) Versions	Offers a variety of package types to choose from to better fit a specific application need for number of I/O's and package size.

iDCX 96 DISTRIBUTED CONTROL EXECUTIVE

DEVELOPMENT ENVIRONMENT

Intel provides a complete development environment for the MCS-96 Family of microcontrollers. The iDCX 96 Executive is only one of many of the software development products available. Figure 4 shows the iDCX 96 Executive development environment. The executive is compatible with the following software development utilities available from Intel:

- 8096 Macro Assembler (ASM 96)
- PL/M 96 Compiler
- RL 96 Linker and Relocator Program
- LIB 96
- FPAL 96 Floating Point Arithmetic Library

Hardware development tools available for MCS-96 microcontroller development are:

- iSBE-96, Single Board Emulator for the MCS-96 Family of Microcontrollers
- VLSiCE-96 In-Circuit Emulator

Table 8 shows the possible MCS-96 Family development enviroments: host systems, operating systems, available software utilities, and hardware debug tools.

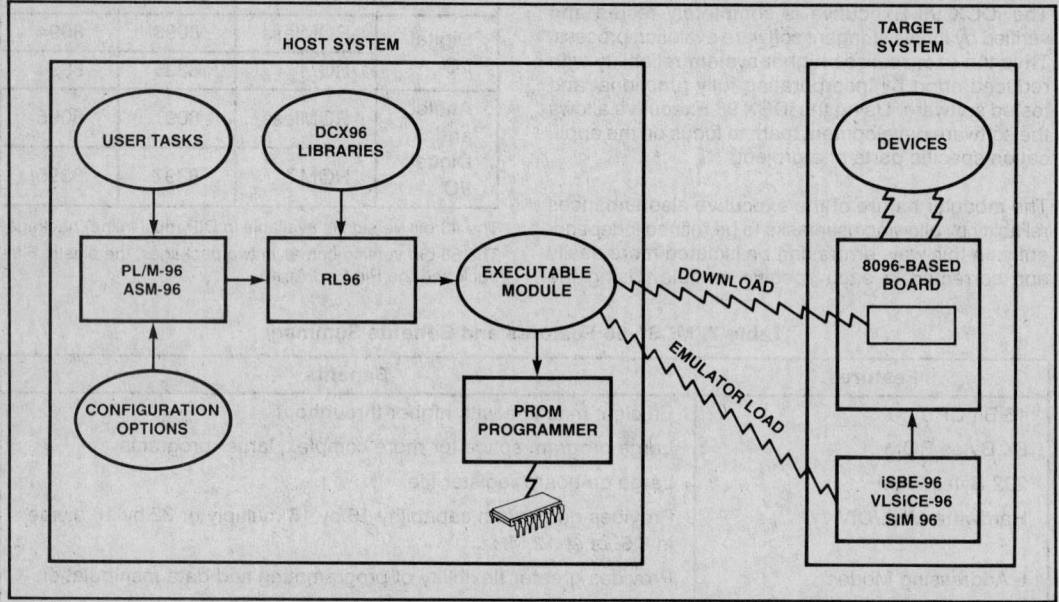

Figure 4. iDCX 96 Development Environment

Table 8. MCS®-96 Family Development Environments

Development Utilities	Host Systems		
Software	Intellec® Series III/IV Systems	iPDS™ System	IBM**-PC System
MCS® 96 Software Support Package (ASM96)	X		X
PL/M 96 Software Package	X		X
iDCX 96 Executive	X	X	X
XASM96, COMM96, ATOP 96*		X	
Hardware			
iSBE-96, Single Board Emulator	X	X	X
VLSiCE-96, In-Circuit Emulator	X		X

*Products of U.S. Software, Portland, OR
**IBM is a registered trademark of International Business Machines

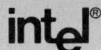

iDCX 96 DISTRIBUTED CONTROL EXECUTIVE

SPECIFICATIONS

Hardware

MCS-96 Family of Microcontrollers
8094	8394
8095	8395
8096	8396
8097	8397

DEVELOPMENT ENVIRONMENT

Software

MCS-96 Software Support Package
PL/M-96 Software Package

iPDS System Host:

*XASM96   Assembles MCS-96 programs on the iPDS™
*COM96   iPDS host communication software. Use with XASM96
*ATOP96   Performs host communications and assembly/disassembly of iSBE-96 instructions. Use with XASM96.

*Products of U.S. Software
5470 N.W. Innisbrook, Portland, OR 97229
Phone: 503-645-5043
Telex: 4993875

Hardware

SYSTEMS

Intellec Microcomputer Development System, Series III/IV
iPDS Intel Personal Development System
IBM Personal Computer

DEBUG TOOLS

SBE-96 Single Board Emulator for MCS-96 Family of Microcontrollers
VLSiCE 96 In-Circuit Emulator

Reference Manual (Supplied)

148107-001   iDCX 96 Distributed Control Executive User's Guide

ORDERING INFORMATION

Part Number	Description
iDCX96SU	Executive for the MCS-96 Family of Microcontrollers Single User License, Development Only Media Supplied: B, E, F, J and I
iDCX96BY	Executive for the MCS-96 Family of Microcontrollers OEM License, Derivative Products Media Supplied: B, E, F, J and I

iRMX™ 510
iDCM SUPPORT PACKAGE

- Low cost remote communication/control expansion for MULTIBUS® based systems

- Extends functionality of BITBUS™/iDCM systems

- Software development support for BITBUS™/iDCM products: iSBX™ 344 and iRCB 44/10 boards

- Simple software interface for iRMX™ 86, 286, 88, and iPDS™ ISIS operating system compatibility

The iRMX™ 510 iDCM Support Package contains the necessary software tools to interface MULTIBUS®, and iPDS™ ISIS systems to BITBUS™ systems in both a development environment and during runtime. With other members of the Distributed Control Modules family, the iRMX 510 iDCM Support Package expands Intel's OEM Microcomputer Systems capabilities to include distributed real-time control.

The iRMX 510 Package software interface handlers and the iSBX™ 344 BITBUS Controller MULTI-MODULE™ board extend the capabilities of other microprocessors such as the 8086, 80186, or 80286 in iDCM, MULTIBUS, or iPDS systems. Support of iRMX 51 applications is provided via the iRMX 51 libraries incorporated in the iRMX 510 Support Package. Also, the Support Package completes the development environment for BITBUS/iDCM products : iSBX 344 and iRCB 44/10 boards. When used with an ICE-44 Emulator the iDCM controller is accurately simulated resulting in a highly effective product development effort.

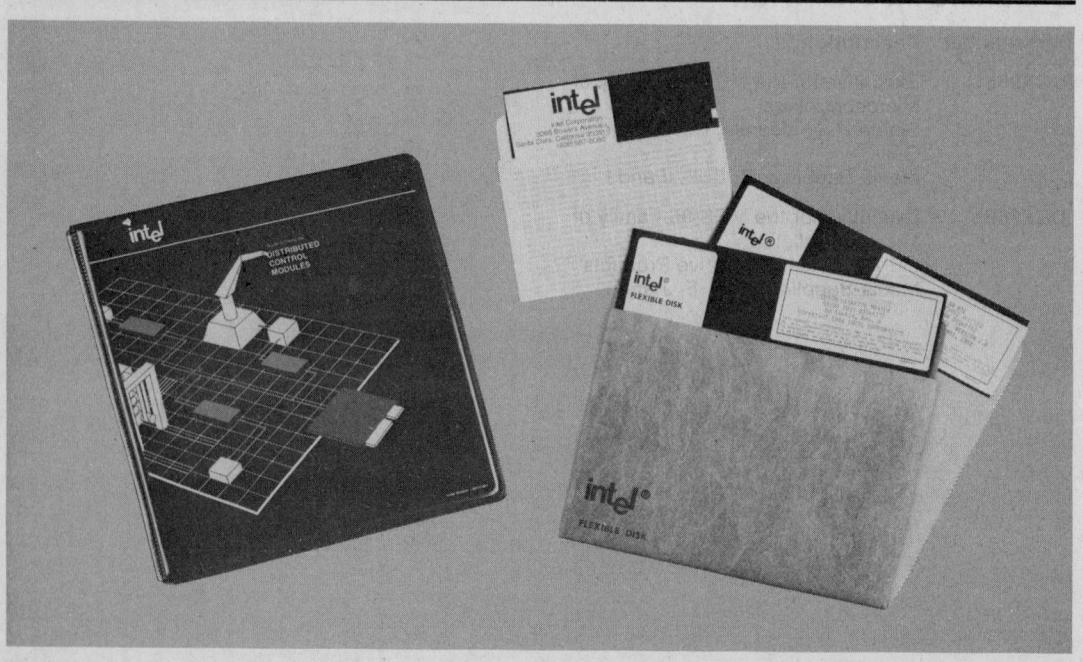

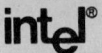

iRMX™ 510

MULTIBUS®, iPDS,™ and iDCM SYSTEM EXPANSION

The iRMX 510 Support Package provides the software interface between Intel's MULTIBUS and iPDS environment, and the BITBUS environment. With Intel's Distributed Control Modules hardware interface, the iSBX 344 MULTIMODULE board, this capability enables the user to expand the existing functionality of an iRMX-based SYSTEM 310, for example, to include control and monitoring of a material handling operation. Intel's Personal Development System (iPDS) can be used as a central supervisory station for data acquistion in a laboratory or for program development. The iRMX 510 iDCM Support Package provides a general purpose interface. For custom applications, users may wish to develop a custom interface.

OPERATING ENVIRONMENT

The iRMX 510 Support Package is supplied on diskettes formated for iRMX, Intellec® Series II or III and iPDS ISIS development systems. Application programs or tasks residing on an extension in the iDCM environment may use the iRMX 510 interface. (Application programs or tasks are written in iRMX 88, 86 or ISIS compatible code.) Some examples of extensions in an iDCM system are the iSBC 86/05, 88/25, 186/03 boards and the iPDS system. Figure 2 shows how the iRMX 510 interface is integrated into an iDCM system.

For iRMX 86, 88, or 286R-based systems, configuration of the iRMX 510 interface requires two steps: configuring the interface to the hardware and then the supporting executive. Hardware configuration requires creating a file of configuration parameters, compiling it, and linking the result with the application program. When using the iRMX 510 Package with the iPDS ISIS system, hardware configuration is not required.

ARCHITECTURE

The major functional blocks of the iRMX 510 Support Package are: iRMX 86, 286R, 88 and iPDS ISIS parallel interface handlers, iDCM Controller firmware files, and iRMX 51 include files.

Simple Parallel Interface Handlers

The iRMX 510 Support Package includes parallel interface handlers for systems using the iRMX 86 or 286R Operating System, the iRMX 88 Executive, or Intel's Personal Development System ISIS Operating System. These software handlers pass iRMX 51 messages to and from the iSBX 344 parallel interface (Byte FIFO). In iRMX 86, 286R or 88 — based systems, the interface executes as two tasks: one to transmit, the other to receive the message. In iPDS systems the interface is a procedural call: DCM TRANSMIT, DCM RECIEVE, or DCM STATUS CHECK. In both cases the handlers are straightforward and easy to use. Figure 1 illustrates transmission of a message in an iRMX-based system.

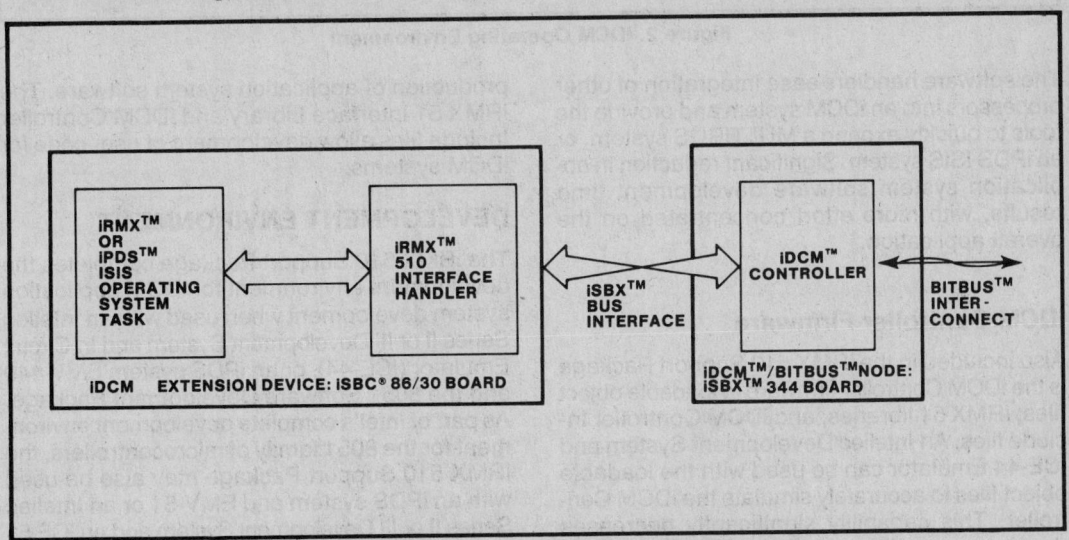

Figure 1. Message Transfer to an iDCM System

intel

iRMX™ 510

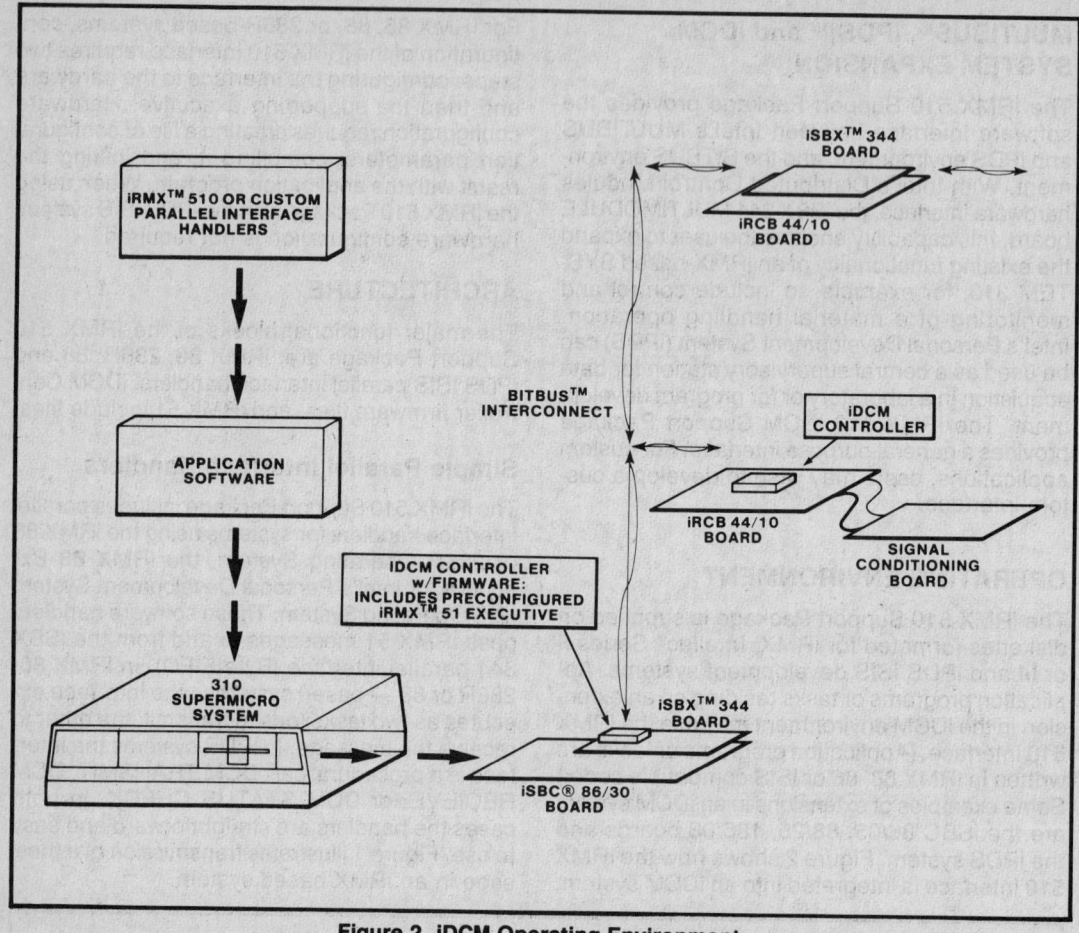

Figure 2. iDCM Operating Environment

The software handlers ease integration of other processors into an iDCM system and provide the tools to quickly expand a MULTIBUS system, or an iPDS ISIS system. Significant reduction in application system software development time results, with more effort concentrated on the overall application.

iDCM Controller Firmware

Also included in the iRMX 510 Support Package is the iDCM Controller firmware in loadable object files, iRMX 51 libraries, and iDCM Controller Include files. An Intellec Development System and ICE-44 Emulator can be used with the loadable object files to accurately simulate the iDCM Controller. This capability significantly decreases development effort by reducing trial and error production of application system software. The iRMX 51 Interface Library and iDCM Controller Include files allow development of user code for iDCM systems.

DEVELOPMENT ENVIRONMENT

The iRMX 510 Support Package completes the development environment for iDCM application system development when used with an Intellec Series II or III Development System and In-Circuit Emulator (ICE-44), or an iPDS system EMV-440 and the 8051 Software Development Package. As part of Intel's complete development environment for the 8051 family of microcontrollers, the iRMX 510 Support Package may also be used with an iPDS system and EMV-51 or an Intellec Series II or III Development System and an ICE-51 Emulator.

iRMX™ 510

SPECIFICATIONS

Supported Hardware/Software for iDCM Systems

Operating System	Supported Extension*
iRMX 86 Release 5.0	iSBC 86/05, 86/14, 86/30, 186/03, 186/51, 188/48, 88/25, 88/45 boards
iRMX 88 Release 3.0	iSBC 86/05, 86/14, 86/30, 186/03, 186/51, 188/48, 88/25, 88/45 boards
iRMX 286R	iSBC 286/10 board
ISIS Release 1.0 (PDS)	iPDS System

*Each extension device uses an iSBX 344 BIT-BUS Controller MULTIMODULE Board

Supported Hardware — 8051 Microcontroller Family

8051	80C51
8052	8044
8751	8744
8031	80C31
8032	8344

Compatible Software
iRMX 86 Release 5.0
iRMX 286R
iRMX 88 Release 3.0
iPDS ISIS Release 1.0
iRMX 51 Release 1.0

Development Tools
ICE-51 or ICE-44 Emulators
iPDS System with EMV-51
Intellec Series II or III Development System
8051 Software Development Package

Reference Manual
146312-001 — Guide to Using the Distributed Control Modules (Supplied)

Ordering Information

Part Number	Description
iRMX 510BY	iDCM Support Package w/ Reference Manual A,B,E, and F Media Formats Supplied.

intel

ARTICLE REPRINT

AR-410

February 1985

Real-time Executive Juggles Multicontrol Systems Like a Pro

RONALD M. SMITH
SENIOR SOFTWARE ENGINEER
INTEL CORPORATION

Copyright 1985. Reprinted by permission from Electronic Products, February 1, 1985.

Order Number: 280723-001

Software

Real-time executive juggles multicontrol systems like a pro

Ronald M. Smith
Senior Software Engineer
Intel Corp., Hillsboro, OR

Designing control applications around a real-time multitasking executive—such as Intel's iRMX 51—can considerably simplify the effort to map several control functions into a microprocessor's architecture. With such a system, the designer can maintain each control function as a separate task.

Executives also provide system services that allow these tasks to interact with both external hardware and each other. In these ways, the complexity and size of the designer's own application code are significantly reduced, the reliability of the system is increased, and development time is minimized.

However, when the designer begins to incorporate multiple control functions into a single microprocessor with conventional standalone software, mapping them into the processor's architecture can be a problem. Individual control functions must be integrated into a more complex control environment and lose their individuality as a result. The added complexity decreases the overall reliability of the system while significantly increasing development time.

There are several steps to developing control software even when dealing with a single function (or loop) such as the one shown in *Fig. 1*. Moving a simple control function from an analog device to a microprocessor is a relatively straightforward procedure. Microprocessor architectures are generally amenable to implementing the initialization, monitoring, and controlling functions required in a typical control loop.

Initializing the loop

The first step is to initialize the control environment. This consists of internally initializing the state of the control software and externally initializing the instruments or machinery to be controlled. This initialization takes place before the control loop itself is executed.

The next step is to monitor the activity of the controlled device. Monitoring begins the actual loop. This monitoring can be either the active process of obtaining data from the monitoring device at regular intervals, the passive process of being interrupted by the device whenever a significant event has occurred, or a combination of the two. The net result of monitoring is that the control process becomes aware of some aspect of the state of the device that is to be controlled.

The third step is to control device activity in response to the results of monitoring. The control activity may or may not affect the value of subsequent monitoring.

Figure 2a depicts a hypothetical machine with both digital and analog I/O. The design goal is to control this machine by periodically reading the analog output (from the machine) and adjusting the analog input value (to the machine) accordingly. Additionally, there is a single digital input line for resetting the machine.

A control loop directs the machine according to the requirements (see *Fig. 2b*). After both the machine and the controller are initialized, the controller enters the loop and waits for work to do. Work is required when the designated control time period has elapsed. When this occurs,

---

Specialized multitask machine-control-managing software simplifies the required application codes, thereby easing the programmer's job, and increasing the system's reliability

---

the controller reads the analog output value from the machine and sends analog input to the machine in response. The loop is then repeated in this manner continuously.

Implementing the control loop

Figure 3a is an example of code that a programmer might provide to handle this application without the help of executive software—a standalone operating environment. In this approach, the main-line code is the code executed in response to a hardware reset on the microprocessor, and it continues to run for the life of the system. Upon reset, the system, therefore, initializes the controlled machine and its internal data structures and continuously monitors for a true-condition time interval. When encountered, the monitor and control routines are commanded to be executed.

The timer-interrupt-handler code is executed in response to an external interrupt from a hardware timer to indicate that so many microseconds have elapsed. Upon entry, the handler must first perform housekeeping tasks such as saving the present context—the main-line code must resume execution when the handler is finished—and resetting the timer. It then updates the software clock and checks to see if a time interval has elapsed. If it has, then the software clock is reset and a flag is set to indicate to the main routine that an interval has lapsed. After this is done, additional housekeeping must be performed before the return to where execution was interrupted in the main routine.

Executive code simpler

However, the code that a programmer would create for use with a multitasking executive, such as iRMX 51, is no longer partitioned into main-line and interrupt routines, but is organized into task segments (see *Fig. 3b*). The code is simplified considerably because the executive handles both timer interrupts and clock functions. The task only has to wait for a time-interval event.

When two machines, as described in Fig. 2, are controlled by stand-alone software, the timer-interrupt routine now must maintain two software clocks and signal the mainline routine through two sets of flags. In the main-line routine, the two control loops are integrated into one software loop (see *Fig. 4a*).

However, in *Fig. 4b*, another machine has been added to the executive-based software by duplicating the software for the single task in Fig. 3b. It is evident that the com-

280723-001

plexity of the standalone algorithm increases as more control functions are added, whereas the complexity of executive-supported routines remains about the same.

Another important difference in these implementations is in the capability to execute functions concurrently. With the standalone software, the control functions within the main-line code loop are executed sequentially. In the example, the monitoring and controlling of machine 1 must be completed before the monitoring and controlling of machine 2 can begin. While monitoring or controlling, any time spent waiting—whether done with a hardware timer or in a program loop—is time that cannot be used to accomplish anything else.

This is not true with executive-supported software. For example, if during the control procedure for one task a 10-ms pause were required, then the executive would allow another task to execute during that time. For this reason, tasks are said to be concurrent.

Advantages of executives

From the general notion of a real-time executive presented thus far, the benefits of executives can be summarized as follows.

The first advantage is that control functions are segregated into separate code segments. The executive implements additional control functions into code without concern for the other software functions. No overall reorganization of the present code is required when a new function is incorporated, unlike the case with the standalone approach.

The second advantage is that significantly less application code is required. Since the executive provides various high-level services to the application, the need for user code is minimized.

Another advantage is that several control functions can be executed concurrently because of the multitasking nature of the executive. The executive does not require that control functions be placed sequentially within a main control loop and allows them to be organized as tasks that contend for the available processing resources.

Because less code has to be developed, software development time is minimized. Of course, since less code need be developed, less code has to be tested. The tight correspondence between control functions and tasks also allows the resulting implementation to be less complex than equivalent standalone software.

Because of segregated control functions and the need for less code, product reliability is maximized. There is less chance of introducing errors to the software.

Another benefit is that the developer need not generate or test the most complex and crucial part of the application—it is a rare development effort that can afford to invest as much time in testing standalone software as has already been spent testing an executive like iRMX 51.

Synchroneity is needed to implement and support the advantageous task feature on executives. Because tasks are in effect decoupled from each other and the system in time, the real-time executive must provide concurrency by keeping track of which tasks need the processor's attention and which don't. Of those which do, it must select a task for execution when an opportunity arises.

Successful multitasking depends

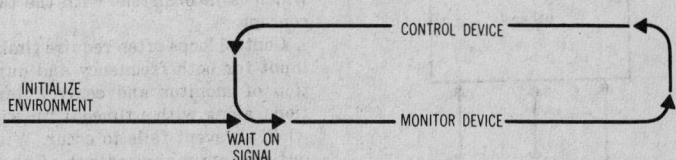

Fig. 1. Even a simplified control loop must include the basic requirements of initialization, monitoring, and control. A program switch causes the process to stop and wait for a signal from the device.

System call codes

CODE	FUNCTION
RQSENDMESSAGE	Sends a message to another task.
RQWAIT	Waits on any combination of interrupt, time-interval, or message events.
RQCREATETASK	Causes the specified code block to be executed as a new task.
RQDELETETASK	Halts all present and future execution of the specified task.
RQALLOCATE	Allocates a fixed-length buffer from the free-space pool.
RQDEALLOCATE	Deallocates the specified fixed-length buffer back to the free-space pool.
RQSETINTERVAL	Sets the time period associated with the task for time-interval events.
RQDISABLEINTERRUPT	Temporarily disables the specified interrupt.
RQENABLEINTERRUPT	Reenables the interrupt disabled by RQDISABLEINTERRUPT.
RQGETFUNCTIONID	iRMX 51 allows the user to associate a unique function ID with each task. This allows a task to be associated with the function it performs. This call returns the function IDs of all existing tasks.

Software

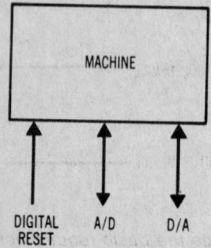

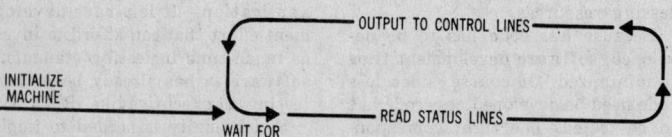

Fig. 2. In a hypothetical machine that handles both analog and digital I/O (a), analog output is read and analog input is adjusted. A single digital signal controls machine reset. A control loop guides the machine (b).

among two or more blocks of code, which is inconsistent with the task concept.

Control loops often require timing input for both frequency and duration of monitor and control iterations, along with a timeout function when an event fails to occur. Without system management of these timing functions, each task would need its own software clock, which would require an iterative loop waiting on a specific number of timer interrupts. Doing so would increase the size of the application code and the focus from the application itself. For this reason the executive should implement its own software clock

and provide high-level timing services to the tasks.

Since tasks run asynchronously with respect to both external events and other tasks, the system can encounter problems if the task is not provided with a way to synchronize with an event or communicate with another task. Polling is untenable in this environment, because the processor is a shared resource.

Supporting the control elements

The goal of the executive software for use with Intel's family of 8-bit microcontrollers is to provide and support the user with all of these multitasking features when implemented in iRMX 51.

Associated with each task is a descriptor—a block of information that tells the executive such things as the initial program counter value for the task, the relative priority to assign to the task, and the interrupts associated with the task. Tasks can be created either automatically at system initialization time or during run time by another task. The tasks created at initialization are those whose descriptors have been chained together at configuration time.

These tasks then start competing for processor time on a priority basis after the system is initialized. Tasks

on the assumption that enough processing resources will be available to go around. This assumption is usually accurate, because most control loops spend a significant amount of time waiting for something to occur externally and therefore require access to the processor only part of the time. Additionally, the system must manage task priorities, interrupts, timing and timeout resources, as well as synchronizing all the functions and tasks.

Establishing priorities

When two or more tasks are ready to use the processor at the same time, the executive must decide which task gets processing time first. Because some tasks may be more time-critical to the controlled machinery than others, they should gain first use of the processor. For this reason, tasks are assigned priorities to allow the executive to decide which task to execute next.

When an external event causes a processor interrupt, the executive provides the interrupt code, as well as a means of notifying the current task that a particular event has occurred. If this job were left to the application programmer, the resulting control loops would be dispersed

Main-line code	Timer-interrupt handler

(initialize machine)
(initialize data structures)
loop
  if time-interval flag = true
    time-interval flag = false
    call monitor routine
    call control routine
  end if
end loop.
	(save interrupted context)
	(mask off lower priority
	  interrupts)
	enable interrupts
	(reset timer)
	increment clock count
	if clock count = time interval
	  clock count = 0;
	  time interval flag = true.
	end if.
	(restore context)
	(unmask lower-priority interrupts)
	return from interrupt.

(a)

Executive implementation

(initialize machine)
(initialize data structures)
loop
  wait for time interval
  call monitor routine
  call control routine
end loop.

(b)

Fig. 3. Implementing a single control loop without an executive requires that both main-line code and interrupt handler be user-developed (a). However, implementing the same single control loop with an executive is much simpler (b).

```
(initialize data structures)           ( save interrupted context )
(initialize machine 1)                 ( mask-off lower priority
(initialize machine 2)                   interrupts)
loop                                   enable interrupts.
  if time interval flag 1 = true       ( reset timer )
    time interval flag 1 = false.      increment clock count 1.
    call machine-1-monitor routine     increment clock count 2.
    call machine-1-control routine     if clock count 1 = time interval 1
  end if.                                time interval flag 1 = true.
  if time interval flag 2 = true         clock count 1 = 0.
    time interval flag 2 = false       if clock count 2 = time interval 2
    call machine-2-monitor routine       time interval flag 2 = true
    call machine-2-control routine       clock count 2 = 0
  end if                               ( restore context )
end loop.                              ( unmask lower-priority interrupts )
                                       return from interrupt.
```
(a)

```
       Task 1                                 Task 2

(initialize machine)                  (initialize machine)
(initialize data structures)          (initialize data structures)
loop                                  loop
  wait for time interval                wait for time interval
  call machine-1-monitor routine        call machine-2-monitor
  call machine-1-control routine        call machine-2-control
end loop.                             end loop.
```
(b)

Fig. 4. When multiple control loops are involved without an executive, control software becomes complex and must be revised extensively as more devices to control are added (a). However, implementing multiple control loops with an executive limits user code to relatively small and simple task modules (b).

are created during run time by use of the RQCREATETASK system call (see *table*). This call adds the new task to the list of tasks waiting to use the processor. System-interface calls provide essentially real-time services that otherwise would have to be implemented in elaborate user codes.

Deleting a task from the system consists simply of issuing a RQDELETETASK system call, specifying which task to eliminate. Up to eight tasks can coexist in the system at any one time. An existing task is either in the ready, running, or asleep state (see *Fig. 5*).

A ready task is any one that is not waiting for an event and is therefore ready for execution. The running task is the ready task with the highest priority, or, if all tasks have equal priority, the first task in the ready list. Its code is executed until either it must wait for an event or a task with a higher priority becomes ready and preempts the task that is running.

If no task is running, and there are no ready tasks, the system is said to be in the idle state. An asleep task is a task that is waiting for an event to occur. When that event occurs, the task becomes ready or running.

Task priorities

Under iRMX 51, a task can exist at one of four priority levels. This means that a priority-4 ready task will not be the running task only when another priority-4 task is running, and a priority-1 ready task will become the running task only when no tasks of priority-2 and above are ready or running.

The iRMX 51 removes the overhead of handling interrupts from the user code by providing two services. First, it supplies the code that is executed in response to an interrupt. Then, it controls the enabling and disabling of particular interrupt sources according to the priority of the running task.

In the first case, when an interrupt occurs, the executive's interrupt code associates the interrupt source with its assigned task and updates its data base to record the event. The event remains posted until the assigned task calls an RQWAIT for that event.

In the second case, the iRMX 51 executive enables, at any given time, only those interrupt sources that are associated with tasks having higher priority than the running task. This reduces execution overhead by allowing only those interrupts to occur that may result in a preemption by a higher-priority task.

Software clocks provided

The iRMX 51 maintains a software system clock that is implemented around one of two 8051-resident timers. Clock services are offered to the user tasks in the form of time intervals and timeouts. The time unit is selectable and is usually 1 to 10 ms.

A time interval is the frequency with which a task requires that a time-interval event be posted and is set by the RQSETINTERVAL system call. When set, the time-interval event is posted at regular intervals until it is reset. A timeout is the period specified in an RQWAIT call that states the maximum amount of time that the task can wait for an event.

Tasks are able to synchronize with each other and trade information by means of messages. When one task sends a message to a second using the RQSENDMESSAGE system call, the message is added to a FIFO queue associated with the second task, and a message event is posted for that task. iRMX 51 messages may be of any length.

Software

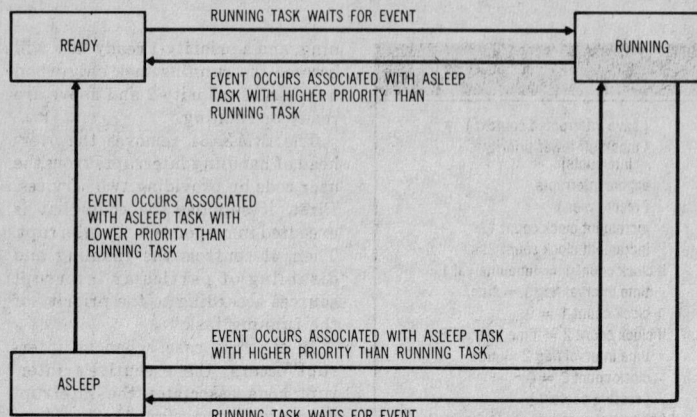

Fig. 5. Under iRMX 51, tasks are executed according to their assigned priorities and state of readiness as managed by the executive.

Tasks synchronize with the environment by means of the RQWAIT system call. This call allows a task to wait for the occurrence of any combination of the three events mentioned previously: interrupts, time intervals, and messages. If the particular event has already occurred when the RQWAIT call is made, then synchronization is reached and the task proceeds. Otherwise, the task is put into the asleep state until one of the specified events occurs.

A distributed system

Developing control applications around the iRMX 51 executive provides, in addition to the benefits previously noted, the ability to upgrade to a distributed control environment that allows both interprocessor and intertask message passing, as well as the ability for a task to read and modify the resources of another processor environment.

This ability is made possible by the Intel iDCM series, which includes the iSBX 344 and iRCB 44/10 boards. These boards support distributed processing through control firmware configured around iRMX 51. iDCM components communicate over the Bitbus serial interconnect, a bus optimized for high-speed transfer of short control messages in a hierarchical system. □

Integrated Microcomputer Systems 13

SYSTEM 310 MICROCOMPUTER SYSTEM

- High-performance, expandable OEM microcomputer system based on Intel's 80286/80287 supermicro and 8086/8087 world-standard processor
- Open MULTIBUS® architecture for flexibility, future growth
- 5¼" Winchester disks and diskette drives for data storage, backup, and interchange
- Industry-standard operating systems and programming languages
- Total system support from Intel's worldwide field service and support organization.

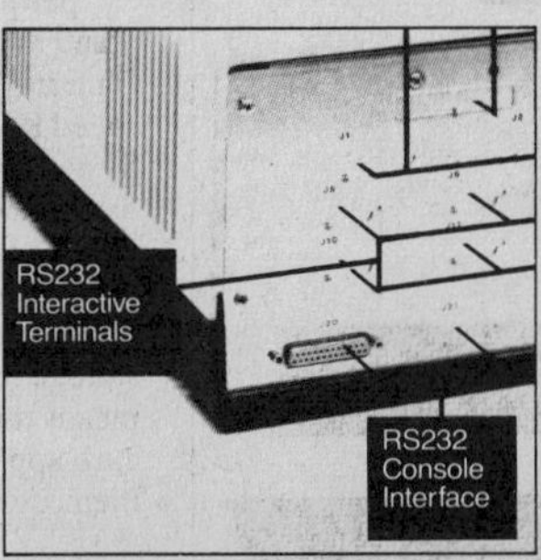

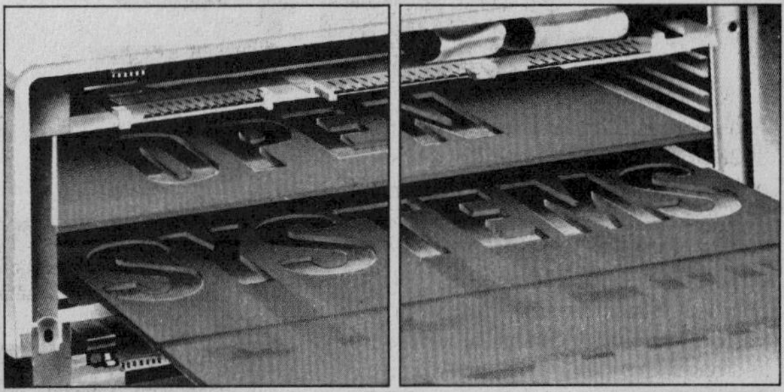

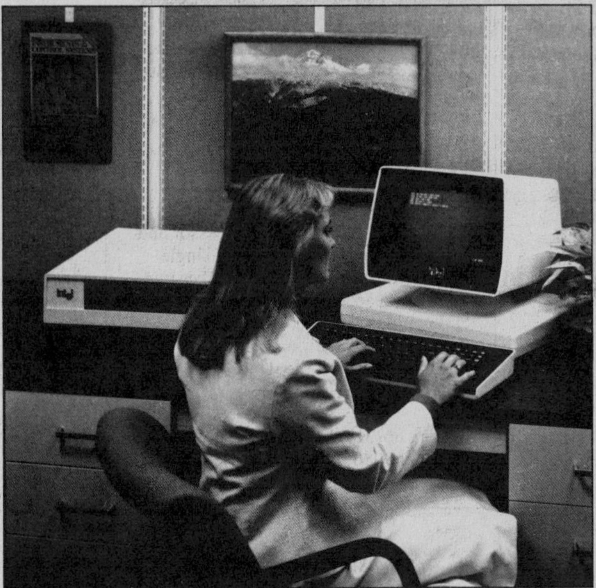

©INTEL CORPORATION 1985

ORDER NUMBER 230753-005

High-performance, Expandable Microcomputer System for the OEM

Intel's System 310 microcomputer offers OEMs an open, MULTIBUS-based microcomputer system for high-speed real-time applications and interactive multi-user commercial and technical environments. Everything about System 310 is standard—buses, interfaces, peripherals, and software—and open to new VLSI expansion, to special application-specific configurations, to aftermarket hardware and software suppliers' products, and to all levels of integration.

Available with either the super-fast 80286 or the industry-standard 8086 microprocessors, System 310 offers an unprecedented range of price/performance. The iRMX™, and XENIX* operating systems and open MULTIBUS board slots reinforce Intel's system performance with unbeatable software and hardware flexibility and expansion for the industrial or commercial OEM. Also, System 310 may be placed on a desktop, rackmounted, or installed in an optional floorstand.

Finally, everything in the System 310 is supported by Intel: boards, chassis, software and peripherals are purchased and serviced through one-stop shopping. When you buy a system from Intel, we don't send you to one outside vendor for software support and to another for hardware repairs. One phone call is all you need.

Two "Micro-Engines" to Choose From

At the heart of the 310 systems, Systems 286/310 and 86/310, are the industry's leading microprocessors: the Intel 80286 and 8086, respectively. The OEM can select the optimal price/performance hardware mix for each application.

System 286/310 is based on the Intel 80286, the outstanding supermicro on the OEM market today. Residing on an Intel single board computer, the 80286 delivers more than twice the performance of the 8086 while its teammate, the 80287 numeric coprocessor, assists in providing System 286/310 with unmatched throughput in its price class for numeric-based applications.

Intel's iLBX™ (Local Bus Extension) on System 286/310 turns the processor and memory boards into a "virtual single board" for the fastest possible data and instruction access in high-performance applications, and the OEM can expand with up to two additional memory boards that exploit the iLBX bus's fast-access characteristics.

System 86/310, based on the industry-standard 8086, offers new low cost levels for 16-bit integrated systems while leaving the path open to move 86-based applications up to higher performance on System 286/310. System compatibility maintained at the operating system level protects your software investment as your needs change.

Ample, Flexible Storage for Unlimited Application Growth

Industry-standard 5¼ inch peripheral drives furnish data and program storage: a 320KB diskette drive in all systems, and depending on the configuration, no Winchester hard disk drive, a 19MB or 40MB Winchester hard disk drive. Increases in available disk storage will keep pace with advances in Winchester and other peripheral technologies; System 310-compatible peripheral chassis also offers tape and multiple Winchester drive configurations. All systems ship with high-speed RAM memory: 1MB in the largest System 286/310, 640KB in the largest System 86/310 with the ability to increase memory to a total of 8.0MB (286-based) and 896KB (86-based), respectively. The variety and quantity of storage media available for System 310 means that the OEM will never have to curb application growth due to lack of memory.

Expandable to Meet Diverse OEM Application Needs

Intel's System 310 offers the OEM system expansion and flexibility because it is MULTIBUS-based. Intel's industry leadership in standardizing the bus (IEEE 796) is supported by 170 vendors with over 1,000 currently-available products.

System 310 configurations offer between three and six MULTIBUS board slots for expansion and customization. The expansion possibilities are almost limitless: disk controllers, communications boards, graphics interfaces, memory expansion boards, and many other specialized single board computer products are available to the OEM con-

*XENIX is a trademark of Microsoft Corporation.

figuring unique functionality into this product.

If the time comes that a System 310 configuration needs even more performance, the OEM can take advantage of MULTIBUS' multiprocessing architecture. Multiple processors can share computing and I/O loads, with standard system software in support of real-time communication between boards. Multiprocessing is a standard feature of MULTIBUS when one processor isn't enough.

Building end-user systems on an industry-standard foundation such as MULTIBUS means much more than having a smorgasbord of available third-party options. It is a guarantee of continued system compatibility and expandability for years to come. OEMs can absorb state-of-the-art technology as quickly as it becomes available.

System Extension Modules for Easy I/O Expansion

For further expansion Intel provides System Extension Modules (iSXM™). iSXMs are factory-configured board, peripheral, and accessory products designed for installation in Intel System products to add I/O capability. For example, the iSXM 544 Intelligent Communications board supports four RS232 channels for multiterminal operations with iRMX or XENIX, plus it furnishes a parallel I/O interface compatible with the Bell 801 Automatic Calling Unit for auto-dial functions. Firmware coupling the iSXM 544 board with both operating systems is resident on the board as delivered. Other iSXM products provide low-cost or very-high-performance communications interfaces, I/O cable sets, and other expansion products.

Worldwide Compatibility

The System 310 is designed to be a "good citizen" throughout the world, operating on commercially-available power sources and adhering to a broad set of standards laid down by many nations for safety and signal radiation. The system meets UL and CSA safety requirements, as well as FCC standards for radio-frequency emissions (RFI) and electromagnetic interference (EMI). Additionally, it is designed to allow the OEM to be confident that he can meet the requirements of IEC 435 and VDE 0806 for safety and VDE 0871 for RFI/EMI.

Industry-standard Operating Systems and Languages Increase the OEM's Options

Intel's Open Systems standards philosophy extends to the System 310's software. Two industry-standard operating systems, iRMX and XENIX, allow the OEM to optimize systems for real-time or interactive commercial applications. A wide range of popular high-level languages enable application developers to program in multiple languages and still link modules together.

Intel's XENIX operating system is Bell Laboratories' System III UNIX† with a blend of enhancements from Microsoft and Intel to specifically suit OEM interactive, multi-user applications. Benchmark figures show Intel's XENIX 286 to be at the leading edge of UNIX performance on a microsystem. For application areas such as distributed data processing, business data processing, and software development, XENIX offers superior human-machine interaction and performance.

The iRMX operating system optimizes System 310 products for real-time, multitasking, time-critical applications such as factory automation, industrial control, and communications networks where rapid response to the "real world" is required.

Both operating systems are supported by a range of high-level languages for rapid and easy applications development. FORTRAN, COBOL, C, Pascal, PL/M, Intel Assemblers and popular utilities round out System 310's software offerings, providing the OEM with a comprehensive development tool kit for getting applications to market before the competition. In addition, a wide range of independent software vendors (ISV) are available on the System 310, both under iRMX and XENIX.

Full System Support

Quality. Since Intel's systems are built from Intel boards and components, quality is checked and double-checked all along the way. All systems are run in to eliminate potential problems with "infant mortality"; our philosophy is that if a system component is going to break down, we want it to break down on us.

†UNIX is a trademark of Bell Laboratories.

13-3

Every System 310 contains a comprehensive, two-part diagnostic package to assist in problem isolation and to further ensure system reliability. A System Confidence Test (SCT) automatically checks out the boards on power-up; a System Diagnostic Test (SDT) provides detailed diagnostics on bugs identified by the SCT.

OEMs also receive the System Analysis Test (SAT) with their XENIX and iRMX software. This test tool stresses both hardware and software to isolate hardware/software interaction problems.

Service. All hardware is warranted for 90 days. Maintenance contracts are available, or customers can opt for service on a per-call basis. If on-site repair is not required, 48-hour factory repair is available on a limited basis, as well as our economical direct-return service. Additionally, "Family Plan" service, covering non-Intel portions of the system as well as Intel-supplied parts, is available on a negotiated basis.

Software service is offered by a factory-resident group with consulting support, response to problem reports, and a Hot Line for critical problems that just won't wait.

Application support. Intel's application engineering organization is one of the largest in the world. We have Field Application Engineers specializing in everything from system software to complex peripherals. These professionals are dedicated to supporting OEMs in the pre-sales development environment. A separate group, Systems Engineers, is dedicated to post-sales consulting support. Intel's built-in quality, our 75-plus worldwide field service locations, and staff of trained hardware and software applications engineers are major advantages for the OEM trying to get an application running and, once running, having the systems maintained.

VLSI Systems Leadership —Today and Tomorrow

Intel is the undisputed leader in microprocessor VLSI; we invented both the microprocessor and the industry-standard MULTIBUS, and we are the world's largest producer of MULTIBUS board-level products.

With the System 310 and other products, we're expanding our leadership into the OEM microcomputer systems market. It's not unfamiliar turf. Intel has been in the systems business for a number of years; we're the largest supplier of micro-processor development systems in the world!

We've also introduced an end-user-oriented data base information system (iDIS) that accesses mainframe-resident data bases.

Intel is uniquely able to offer VLSI technology leadership to OEMs at the low-risk, quick-to-market systems level. The System 310's openness and industry-standard MULTIBUS are guarantees of continued system compatibility and expandability for years to come. With Intel systems, there are no dead ends lurking in the OEM's product future; rather, he can now absorb new VLSI advances and functionality almost as quickly as they become available.

Intel is committed to the Open Systems concept, in which industry standards pave the way into future applications and future markets. For the OEM seeking product wins in today's fiercely competitive markets, Open Systems from Intel are the only way to build.

Specifications

Central Processor: System 286/310 models provide an 80286 General Purpose Processor; System 86/310s provide an 8086 General Purpose Processor. Instructions are 8, 16, or 32 bits in length, data are 8- or 16-bits long; numeric processing (with Numeric Co-Processors) is carried out in 80-bit-words.

Mass Storage: See Configuration Summary for standard configurations; all drives are 5¼-inch format; the Winchester controller provides complete ECC write/read checks for data integrity.

System Expansion: Three to six Multibus (IEEE 796) slots for customizing and expansion based on over 80 boards available from Intel and more than 900 offered by independent hardware vendors.

Environmental Specifications:
Operating: 10°C to 40°C (Winchester Only); to 35°C (With Diskette) (26°C maximum wet bulb temperature) (20% to 80% Relative Humidity, non-condensing)
Altitude: Sea Level to 8,000 feet

Regulatory Agency Specifications:
Meets: UL 114—Safety; CSA 22.2—Safety; FCC Docket 20780 Class A—RFI/EMI.
Designed To Meet: IEC 435—Safety; VDE 0871 Class A—RFI/EMI
AC Power Input: 88-132VAC or 180-264VAC, 47-63Hz (user-selectable on chassis)

310 Dimensions: Height: 6½", Width: 17", Depth: 22"

Optional Floorstand Dimensions: Height: 24.4", Width: 8.5", Depth: 23"

Weight: Less than 60 lbs. (Varies with configuration)

Configuration Summary

	System 286/310-41	System 286/310-40	System 286/310-17	System 286/310-4	System 86/310-35,	System 86/310-1
Microprocessor	80286 (6 MHz)	80286 (6 MHz)	80286 (6 MHz)	80286 (6 MHz)	8086 (8 MHz)	8086 (5 MHz)
Numeric Coprocessor	80287 (4 MHz)	80287 (4 MHz)	80287 (4 MHz)	80287 (4 MHz)	8087 (8 MHz)	N/A
RAM Memory, Expandable To	1MB 8.0MB	896KB 8.0MB	512KB 6.0MB	512KB 6.0MB	640KB 896KB	128KB 896KB
Mass Storage	320KB Diskette (Formatted) 40MB Wini (Unformatted)	320KB Diskette (Formatted) 40MB Wini (Unformatted)	320KB Diskette (Formatted) 19MB Wini (Unformatted)	320KB Diskette (Formatted)	320KB Diskette (Formatted) 19MB Wini (Unformatted)	320KB Diskette (Formatted)
I/O Ports	(10) RS232 (1) Centronics	(2) RS232 (1) Centronics	(2) RS232 (1) Centronics	(2) RS232 (1) Centronics	(1) RS232 (1) Centronics	(1) RS232 (1) Centronics
MULTIBUS® Expansion Slots	2 @ 0.65 in.	3 @ 0.65 in.	4 @ 0.65 in. 4 @ 0.65 in.	1 @ 1.20 in.	5 @ 0.65 in.	1 @ 1.20 in. 5 @ 0.65 in.
DC Power Output	270 Watts Maximum +5V @45A +12V @4.7A −12V @4.7A	270 Watts Maximum +5V @45A +12V @4.7A −12V @4.7A	220 Watts Maximum +5V @30A +12V @4.7A −12V @4.7A	220 Watts Maximum +5V @30A +12V @4.7A −12V @4.7A	220 Watts Maximum +5V @30A +12V @4.7A −12V @4.7A	220 Watts Maximum +5V @30A +12V @4.7A −12V @4.7A

Ordering Information—System Hardware

System Description	Order Code
System 286/310-41	SYS310-41A
System 286/310-40	SYS310-40A
System 286/310-17	SYS310-17A
System 286/310-4	SYS310-4A
System 86/310-3A	SYS310-3A
System 86/310-1	SYS310-1A
Optional Floorstand	SYP312

SYSTEM 380 MICROCOMPUTER SYSTEMS

- High-performance, highly expandable OEM microcomputer systems, iAPX 86- or iAPX 286-based
- High-performance floating point math capabilities with 8087/80287 numeric coprocessors
- Unmatched system flexibility with eleven MULTIBUS® expansion slots, 8-inch peripheral slot, and 13 back-panel knock-out ports
- 35MB Winchester disk and 1 MB flexible diskette for data storage and backup
- Total system support from Intel's worldwide field service and support organization

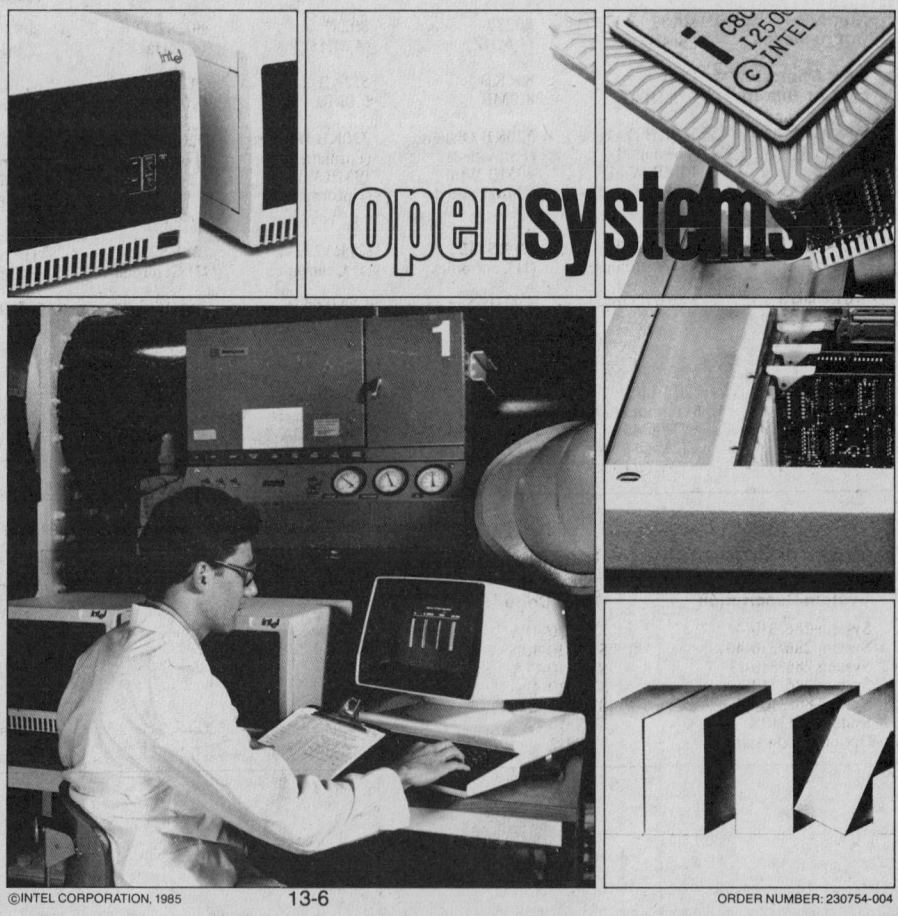

©INTEL CORPORATION, 1985

ORDER NUMBER: 230754-004

Highest Performance, Most Expandable Microcomputer System on the Market

Intel's System 380 microcomputer system is a MULTIBUS-based, integrated package targeted at OEM's needing a powerful, flexible, expandable base product upon which to add value.

Available in either iAPX 86 or a superfast iAPX 286-based version, the System 380 offers high performance and expandability to the industrial or commercial OEM. With an industry-standard 35 MB Winchester, 1 MB diskette, eleven board slots and one peripheral slot for system expansion, the System 380 provides unmatched flexibility in a MULTIBUS system.

And, with optional iRMX or XENIX* operating systems and a broad array of popular languages and utilities, the System 380 meets the software needs of technical or commercial applications.

The System 380 is an open system; a system built around industry standards. This means that the OEM's product can easily incorporate the next generations of Very Large Scale Integration (VLSI) or take advantage of industry-standard hardware and application software for maximum configuration flexibility and quick time-to-market advantages. With today's fast-paced, rapidly changing technology, an open system just makes good business sense.

And to help reduce the risk of ownership, everything in the System 380 is supported by Intel: boards, software and peripherals are all under our one-stop support program. When you buy a system from Intel, you don't go to one outside vendor for software support and to another for hardware repairs. One phone call is all you need to keep your systems at peak-performance.

Two High-Performance "Micro-Engines" to Choose From

At the heart of System 86/380 and System 286/380 are the industry's leading microprocessors: the Intel iAPX 86 and iAPX 286, respectively. The OEM can select the optimum price/performance hardware mix that best fits the application.

System 86/380 is based on the Intel 8086, the industry's most popular 16-bit microprocessor.

The single board computer that houses the central processor also contains Intel's 8087 Numeric Data Processor. Working together, the 8086 and 8087 perform floating point processing at 50 times the throughput of an 8086 system alone.

System 286/380 is based on the Intel 80286. Residing on a single board computer, the 80286 is capable of delivering more than twice the performance of the 8086. When teamed with the 80287 math coprocessor, an 80286-based system is virtually unmatched in numeric-intensive applications. In addition, Intel's iLBX (Local Bus Extension) makes extremely fast memory access possible for high-performance applications.

Both systems contain a standard 35MB, 8-inch Winchester hard disk as well as a 1MB diskette disk drive for program and data storage. Both come with high-speed RAM memory (384 KB in the 86/380 and 512 KB ECC memory in the 286/380), expandable to more than ten megabytes. Systems are designed to meet UL/CSA/VDE safety regulations and FCC/VDE EMI/RFI requirements.

System 380 is available as a desktop or rack-mount dual-chassis package. The processor chassis contains processor, RAM, and disk controller boards, while the peripheral chassis contains the disk drive peripherals. One parallel printer connection and RS-232C serial ports are included for I/O.

The 380 systems are available as hardware only for the OEM's volume production needs or as hardware kitted with iRMX or XENIX system software with everything needed to get an application designed and into production.

The System 380's processing performance together with generous allocations of Winchester, flexible disk and RAM storage offer OEMs the resources to develop sophisticated industrial or commercial applications.

Highly Expandable to Meet Diverse OEM Applications

Intel's System 380 has more system expansion alternatives than any other microcomputer system on the market; Intel's MULTIBUS architecture is one of the reasons why. Intel's industry-standard MULTIBUS (IEEE 796) is supported by 150 vendors with over 1000 currently available products.

System 380 contains eleven MULTIBUS board slots for system expansion and customization. The expansion possibilities for an Intel MULTIBUS-based

---

*XENIX is a trademark of Microsoft Corporation.

system are nearly limitless: disk controllers, communications controllers, graphics controllers, bubble memory, memory expansion boards, and many other specialized MULTIBUS boards are available to the OEM configuring unique functionality into his product. And the MULTIBUS specification is widely published to encourage OEMs to build custom boards for their system.

In addition to adding MULTIBUS boards, the System 380's mass storage can be expanded by adding an eight-inch hard disk drive in the open peripheral slot. The additional peripheral, controlled by the system's internal controller board, can be added without an extra power supply; the existing one has plenty of power!

For flexibility and low-risk expandability, the System 380 can't be beat.

System Extension Modules for Easy I/O Expansion

For data communications expansion, Intel provides System Extension Modules (iSXMs). Intel's iSXMs are factory-configured MULTIBUS boards that plug directly into the System 380 expansion slots to allow the addition of more terminals and I/O devices.

For example, when installed in the System 380, the iSXM 534 module provides four additional fully programmable RS-232C serial communications channels, plus a parallel I/O interface that is compatible with the Bell 801 automatic calling unit (ACU).

The iSXM 544 module is an intelligent version of the iSXM 534 module acting as a communications controller or an intelligent slave for multi-terminal applications. The iSXM 953 module provides necessary cabling for four RS-232C serial ports. The iSXM 534 or iSXM 544 module plus an iSXM 953 module is the easiest way to add multiple terminals to a 380 system.

Industry-Standard Operating Systems and Languages Shorten Development Time

Intel's open systems, standards-only philosophy extends to the System 380's software. Two industry-standard operating systems, iRMX and XENIX, allow the OEM to adapt systems to real-time or interactive applications and a wide range of popular high-level languages enable easy development.

The iRMX operating system (available for both System 86/380 and the 286/380) is geared towards real-time, multitasking, time-critical applications such as factory automation, industrial control and communications networks where rapid response to machine-generated interrupts is required.

Software developed on 86-based systems is totally upward portable to the 286-based systems.

Intel's XENIX operating system, also available for both systems, is Bell Laboratory's System III UNIX* with a blend of enhancements from Microsoft

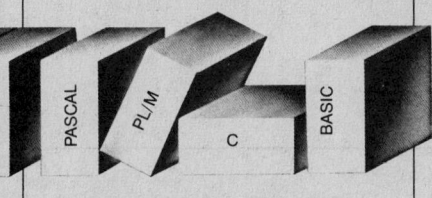

and Intel to suit interactive, multiuser applications. For application areas such as distributed data processing, business data processing and software development, XENIX offers superior user-machine interaction and performance.

Both operating systems are supported by a range of high-level languages for rapid and easy application development. FORTRAN, COBOL, Pascal, PL/M, "C", BASIC, Intel Assemblers and popular utilities round out the System 380's software offerings, providing the OEM with comprehensive development tools for getting applications to market fast. Additionally, Program Libraries and Users Groups link the entire community of system users together, leveraging each other's software investments.

Quality Systems with Support to Match

Intel's reputation for quality holds true at the systems level. Intel builds their systems from field-proven Intel MULTIBUS boards and operating systems.

Integrated peripherals and components must pass Intel's rigorous qualification standards before becoming part of an Intel system. Extensive life-cycle and environmental tests are performed during the development process to verify reliability. During production, functional operation is tested at the module and system levels for every unit. Extensive environmental testing is done periodically on product samples to maintain quality. Regular audits of customer and field service reports are used to continually monitor the reliability of field units. Intel understands how vital reliability is at the systems level, and we're committed to building it into our products.

Every System 380 also contains a comprehensive, tri-level diagnostic package to assist in problem isolation and assure system reliability. The System Confidence Test (SCT) automatically checks out all boards and peripherals on power-up; the System Diagnostic Tests can isolate problems identified by the SCT to the board level; and the System Analysis Test stresses both hardware and software to isolate related problems.

All hardware is warranted for 90 days. Should repair service be required, the customer can choose on-site service under a maintenance agreement or on a per-call basis. If on-site repair is not required, 48-hour factory repair is available, in addition to our economical direct-return service.

Provided the necessary training and diagnostics, Intel will actually service non-Intel products such as terminals or printers in addition to our own 300 family systems. This is a real problem solved for OEMs who must provide a service solution in order to sell their value-added products!

Intel's application engineering organization is one of the largest in the world. We have application engineers specializing in everything from system software to complex peripherals. These professionals are dedicated to supporting OEMs in the pre-sales development environment. Another such group is dedicated to post-sales consulting support.

Intel's built-in quality, army of trained hardware and software application engineers, and over 75 worldwide field service locations are substantial advantages to the OEM trying to get an application off the ground and maintained in the marketplace.

VLSI Technology Leadership at the Systems Level... Today and Tomorrow

Intel is the undisputed leader in microprocessor VLSI; we invented both the microprocessor and the industry-standard MULTIBUS and are the world's largest producer of MULTIBUS board-level products.

Intel is now making a major thrust into the OEM microcomputer systems market. The fact is, we've been in the systems business for a number of years; we're the largest supplier of microprocessor development systems in the world!

Intel is uniquely positioned to offer VLSI technology leadership to OEMs at the low-risk, quick-to-market systems level. The System 380's industry-standard MULTIBUS is a guarantee of continued system compatability and expandability for years to come. With Intel systems, there are no dead ends lurking in the future for the OEM's product. An Intel system can absorb new VLSI advances and functionality almost as quickly as they become available.

Intel is committed to industry standards which lay the foundation for easy access to future technologies, future applications and future markets. For the OEM seeking to stay ahead in today's fiercely competitive markets, Intel Open Systems are the only systems to build upon.

*UNIX is a trademark of Bell Laboratories.

Specifications

Central Processor: System 380-2A, 2B, 2C models provide an 80286 General Purpose Processor and 80287 Numeric Data CoProcessor; System 380 AA, AB, AC models provide an 8086 General Purpose Processor and 8087 Numeric Data CoProcessor. Instructions are 8-, 16-, or 32-bits in length, data are 8- or 16-bits long; numeric processing (with Numeric CoProcessors) is carried out in 80-bit words.

Peripheral Interfaces: See Configuration Summary for serial port configurations; one Centronics-compatible printer interface is provided on all System 380 models.

Mass Storage: See Configuration Summary for standard configurations; all drives are 8-inch format; the Winchester controller provides complete ECC write/read checks for data integrity.

System Expansion: Eleven MULTIBUS (IEEE 796) slots for customizing and expansion using boards available from Intel and independent hardware vendors.

Environmental Specifications:
Operating: 15°C to 35°C, 20% to 80% Relative Humidity, non-condensing (26°C maximum wet bulb temperature),
Altitude: Sea Level to 8,000 feet

Regulatory Agency Specifications: **Meets:** UL 114—Safety; CSA 22.2—Safety; FCC Docket 20787—RFI/EMI; VDE 0871—RFI/EMI

AC Power Input: 92-126 VAC, or 184-252 VAC, 47-63 HZ (user selectable upon ordering).*†

† 80286 Systems sold in three versions: A (120 VAC/60HZ), B (220 VAC/50Hz) and C (100 VAC/50Hz).
*8086 Systems sold in three versions: AA (120 VAC/60HZ), AB (220 VAC/50Hz), and AC (100 VAC/50HZ).

Configuration Summary

	System 286/380†	System 86/380*
Microprocessor	80286 (6 MHz)	8086 (5 MHz)
Numeric Coprocessor	80287 (4 MHz)	8087 (5 MHz)
RAM Memory	512KB W/ECC	384KB
Expandable To:	10 MB using IMB RAM boards	896 KB
Mass Storage	1 MB Diskette Drive	1 MB Diskette Drive
	35 MB Winchester Drive	35 MB Winchester Drive
Multibus Expansion Slots	Nine @ 0.8 inch spacing	Nine @ 0.8 inch spacing
	Two @ 1.2 inch spacing	Two @ 1.2 inch spacing
Serial Ports	Two RS-232C	One RS-232C
Expansion Power Available:		
Processor Box		
Amps @ +5VDC	53.8A	55.1A
−5VDC	2.2A	2.8A
+12VDC	5.2A	5.6A
−12VDC	2.9A	3.0A
Total Expansion Power	377 Watts	394 Watts
Peripherals Box		
Amps @ +5VDC	26.5A	26.5A
−5VDC	1.3A	1.3A
+12VDC	2.0A	2.0A
−12VDC	2.6A	2.6A
+24VDC	3.7A	3.7A
−24VDC	1.6A	1.6A
Total Expansion Power	321 Watts	321 Watts
AC Input Power Max. Req. (Approx.)		
Processor Box	1250 Watts	1250 Watts
Peripherals Box	820 Watts	820 Watts

†Sold in three versions: A(120 VAC/60HZ), B(220 VAC/50Hz), C(100 VAC/50Hz).
*Sold in three versions: AA (120 VAC/60HZ), AB (220 VAC/50Hz), and AC (100 VAC/50HZ).

Documentation

Title	Literature Number
System 86/380 Overview Manual	144720-001
System 86/380 Hardware Reference Manual	172761-001
System 86/380 Installation and Maintenance Manual	144721-001
System 286/380 Installation and Operation Guide	134589
System 286/380 Hardware Maintenance Manual	134595
System 286/380 Processor Configuration Guide	135033
System 286/380 Memory Configuration Guide	135034
System 286/380 Disk Configuration Guide	134594
System 286/380 Hardware Integration Guide	134590

Manuals may be ordered directly from the Intel Literature Department.

Ordering Information

System Description	Order Code
OEM Hardware System 86/380	SYS380-1A*
iRMX™ System 86/380	SYS380A-AR-Kit*
OEM Hardware System 286/380	SYS380-2A†
iRMX™ System 286/380	SYS380-2AR†
XENIX Multiuser System 286/380@	SYS380-2AMX†

* Sold in three versions = AA (120VAC/60Hz), AB (220 VAC/50Hz), AC (100 VAC/50Hz)
† Sold in three versions = A (120VAC/60Hz), B (220 VAC/50Hz), C (100 VAC/50 Hz)
@ Includes 4-Channel Intelligent Terminal Controller Board

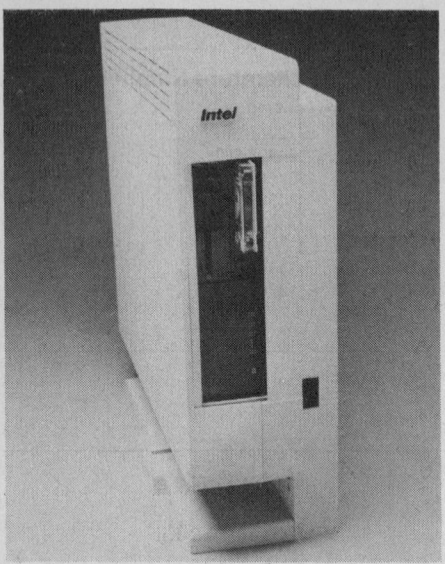

310 AP
XENIX* SYSTEMS

- Advanced Processor — based on the 8MHz 80286 CPU and 80287 numeric coprocessor with zero wait state access memory
- Advanced Peripherals — 3 peripherals in one system: tape backup, Winchester storage, floppy
- Advanced Performance — 80% performance increase over 6MHz 310
- Open System MULTIBUS® architecture for upgradeability and growth
- Winchester storage expandable to 420MB using the 311 Peripheral Subsystem
- XENIX Operating System with all of the latest independent software vendor packages
- Total hardware and software support from Intel's worldwide customer support organization

THE 310 AP DELIVERS PERFORMANCE

The System 310 AP is faster than many minicomputers. Powerful dedicated processors for communications and mass storage input/output control allow the 8MHz 80286 CPU to concentrate on your application software. The System 310 AP can even accommodate additional CPUs to deliver up to 4.8 MIPS using Intel's APEX Series products.

310 AP MULTIUSER AND SERVER SYSTEMS

The 310 AP is delivered in various multiuser system and OpenNET™ server configurations. XENIX on the 310 AP meets the microsystems marketplace head on with industry standards delivered at high performance.

310 AP EXPANDABILITY

The 310 AP is an Intel open system designed with expansion in mind. It accommodates up to 9MB of parity checked RAM, all accessible with no wait states across Multibus's Local Bus Extension (LBX™).

The 310 AP supports 40MB-140MB of Winchester storage on a single disk drive. Mass storage can be expanded to 420MB using the 311 Peripheral Subsystem. The 310 AP also supports a 320KB 5¼" floppy drive and a 65MB streaming tape cartridge drive.

For terminal communications, up to a total of 18 (+2) RS232 serial ports are supported in 310AP. Intel's OpenNET local area network is also supported on 310 AP XENIX systems. Many 310 AP systems can interoperate over OpenNET for large installations.

THE 310 AP IS THE NEXT STEP IN OPEN SYSTEMS

System 310 AP is open, which means you can upgrade performance and/or functionality in the future without purchasing a new system. The open system's design protects your investment from becoming obsolete. Open systems design also means modularity for easy system customization and third-party Multibus board integration.

310 AP SUPPORTS A FULL RANGE OF SOFTWARE

The System 310 AP runs the most popular microsystem version of UNIX** — XENIX. That means lots of languages, utilities and application packages are available. Intel's Xenix also features an optimized file I/O system, Intel's Universal Development Interface for support of all Intel UDI compatible languages and utilities and a configuration and tuning utility.

INTEL SERVICE AND SUPPORT

The System 310 AP is backed by Intel's worldwide service and support organization. Total hardware and software support is there, including a hotline number for when you need it *fast*.

© INTEL CORPORATION, 1985
*TRADEMARK OF MICROSOFT CORPORATION
**TRADEMARK OF BELL LABORATORIES

THE RIGHT CONFIGURATION TO MEET YOUR NEEDS

	SYSTEM 310 AP-41 (8 user)	SYSTEM 310 AP-44 (4 user)	SYSTEM 310 AP-42 (8 user with integrated tape)	SYSTEM 310 AP-142 (8 user with large mass storage and integrated tape)
Microprocessor	80286 8MHz	80286 8MHz	80286 8MHz	80286 8MHz
Numeric Processor	80287	80287	80287	80287
RAM Memory	1MB	1MB	1MB	2MB
• Expandable To:	9MB	9MB	9MB	9MB
Mass Storage (unformatted)	40MB Winchester	40MB Winchester	40MB Winchester	140MB Winchester
Serial I/O Ports	10	6	10	10
• Expandable To:	18	14	18	18
Tape Backup	NA	NA	45MB*	45MB*
Parallel Ports	1	1	1	1

*60MB capacity is possible with the use of a 600-foot tape length cartridge.

OPTIONAL FEATURES

OpenNET™ Express Kit: Fully integrated, high performance, network of interconnect PCs and other 310 AP systems. Includes Intel installation and training.

XENIX Express Kit: XENIX already loaded and pre-configured on your Winchester mass storage device.

iDIS Software: Menu-driven office productivity software package which provides word processing, spreadsheet, and database management capabilities.

Floorstand: Space-saving device that allows you to vertically stand your 310 AP on the floor.

Host Communications: Several Host Communications packages, including 3270 BSC, 2780/3780 RJE, and 3270 HASP/RJE, 3270SNA.*

311 Peripheral Subsystem: Separate peripheral system to accommodate a tape backup unit and up to two additional Winchester mass storage devices.

APEX: Advanced Processor EXtensions for advanced performance: Transparently increase processing power. APEX multi-CPU products deliver CPU power for 310 AP up to 4.8 MIPS through dual, tri, and quad 286 CPU systems.

Over 400 Intel Multibus Boards: Add unique capabilities to the 310 AP through the use of Multibus boards inserted in the system.

*Available Dec. 1985

SPECIFICATIONS

System Expansion
2 to 4 Multibus (IEEE796) slots for adding Memory, Additional Communication Controllers and/or other MB boards.

Environmental Specifications
10°C to 35°C (Winchester only); to 35°C (with diskette) (26°C maximum wet bulb temp) (20% to 70% relative humidity, non-condensing. Altitude: sea level to 8,000 feet.

DC Power Output
360 watts maximum

REGULATORY AGENCY SPECS
Meets: UL 114 — Safety; CSA 22.2 — Safety; FCC Docket 20780 Class A — RFI/EMI

Designed to Meet: IEC435 — Safety; VDE0871 Class A — RFI/EMI

AC Power Input: 88-132VAC or 180-264VAC, 47-63Hz (user-selectable on chassis)

310 Dimensions: Height, 6½"; Width, 17"; Depth, 22"

Weight: Approximately 55 lbs.

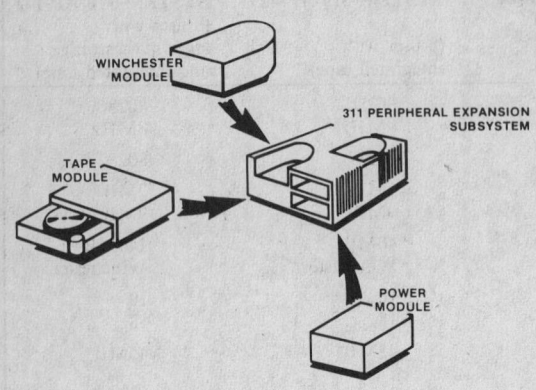

311 PERIPHERAL EXPANSION SUBSYSTEM

- 3 full-height peripheral bays, offering
  — tape back-up and archiving
  — high capacity Winchester drive expansion
- Ergonomically compatible with System 310 Product Family design
- High degree of configurability and upgradeability
- Vehicle for custom peripheral configurations
- Support of high-capacity devices
- Worldwide service and support from Intel

Intel's 311 is a flexible peripheral expansion subsystem for the Intel 310 Product Family. With three full-height 5.25" bays, the 311 provides a wide range of peripheral expansion options.

45MB STREAMING TAPE BACK-UP

The 5.25" half-height streaming tape option provides the user with 45MB of back-up capacity (or up to 60MB with a 600' tape cartridge). Thus, a 40MB Winchester disk drive can be quickly, conveniently, and reliably backed up with a single tape cartridge. The tape option also presents the user with convenient removable archiving capability. One tape cartridge functionally replaces more than one hundred floppy diskettes.

INCREASED DISK STORAGE CAPACITY

Users requiring higher Winchester disk storage capacities than those provided by a host system now have the option of adding two full height 5.25" Winchester disk drives. The 311 can be configured with a choice of 40 or 140MB drives, thus providing as much as 280MB of additional disk storage.

HIGH DEGREE OF CONFIGURABILITY AND UPGRADEABILITY

The 311 can be configured to most combinations of 5.25" peripherals desired by users. The 311 can be ordered in its maximum configuration, with two full height Winchester drives and tape, or in many subsets of that configuration (for example, a "tape only" configuration or a "Winchester disk/tape" configuration).

OPEN TO 5.25" PERIPHERALS

The 311 serves as an excellent base for OEMs who wish to integrate and remarket non-Intel qualified peripherals. Upgrade kits are available that provide the OEM with all the necessary brackets, cabling, power supply upgrades and documentation to integrate most non-Intel supplied 5.25" Winchester disks.

A COMPLETE SOLUTION

The 311 provides the user with a complete solution. It comes with all the external cables, power and documentation that are necessary to connect the 311 to its host system.

"Host controller kits," for preparing the host 310 with appropriate cabling, are sold separately. Both 215/218/217- and 214-based hosts are supported.

THE POWER SUPPLY

The 311 power system consists of five independent power supplies. The fully configured "Wini/Wini/tape" 311 uses all five power supplies, whereas the "tape only" and the "Wini only" configurations require only two. Each power supply provides 2.5A of +12V, 2.5A of +5V and 0.1A of −12V. To reconfigure the power supply between 115V and 220V requires one jumper change.

WORLDWIDE COMPATIBILITY

The 311 adheres to a broad set of worldwide safety and signal radiation regulations. It meets class A FCC standards for radio frequency interference (RFI) and electromagnetic interference (EMI), and is designed to comply with the UL, CSA, and the European TUV and IEC-435 safety regulations.

ENVIRONMENTAL SPECIFICATION
Operating: 10°C to 40°C (Winchester Only); to 35°C (With Diskette) (26°C maximum wet bulb temperature) (20% to 80% Relative Humidity, non-condensing)
Altitude: Sea Level to 8,000 feet

WORLDWIDE SERVICE
All hardware is warranteed for 90 days. Maintenance contracts are available, or customers can opt for service available on a per-call basis. If on-site repair is not required, 48-hour factory repair is available as well as economical direct-return service. Additionally, "Open Systems" service covers non-Intel portions of the system as well as Intel supplied parts.

Intel's service organization has over 80 offices worldwide.

DOCUMENTATION
The 311 Peripheral Expansion Subsystem Service Manual #134923

ORDERING INFORMATION

Peripheral Expansion Subsystem for System 310 Product Family (A = 110V, B = 220V)
All include external cables for connection to host 310 backpanel

PSYS311A02 or B02	One streaming cartridge tape drive, two empty 5.25" peripheral bays. *Requires separate purchase of one Tape Host Controller SXM.*
PSYS311A14 or B14	One streaming cartridge tape drive, one 40MB Winchester disk drive. *Requires separate purchase of one Tape Host Controller SXM and one Winchester Host Controller SXM.*
PSYS311A17 or B17	One streaming cartridge tape drive, two 40MB Winchester disk drives. *Requires separate purchase of one Tape Host Controller SXM and one Winchester Host Controller SXM.*
PSYS311A33 or B33	One 140MB Winchester disk drive. *Requires separate purchase of one Winchester Host Controller SXM.*
PSYS311A34 or B34	One streaming cartridge tape drive, one 140 MB Winchester disk drive. *Requires separate purchase of one Tape Host Controller SXM and one Winchester Host Controller SXM.*
PSYS311A36 or B36	Two 140MB Winchester disk drives. *Requires separate purchase of one Winchester Host Controller SXM.*
PSYS311A37 or B37	One streaming cartridge tape drive, two 140MB Winchester disk drives. *Requires separate purchase of one Tape Host Controller SXM and one Winchester Host Controller SXM.*

Tape Host Controller SXMs

PSXM217C	311 streaming tape controller kit *Rom 215/218-based host* 310 systems. Consists of iSBX217C tape controller, iSBC215G firmware PROMs, and cables and connectors for the 310 backpanel.
PSXM311TCBL	311 streaming tape controller kit for *214-based host* 310 systems. Consists of cables and connectors for the 310 backpanel.

Winchester Host Controller SXMs

PSXM311HCS	311 Winchester Controller cable kit *for 215/218-based host* 310 systems. Consists of Winchester daisy-chain cables and connectors to the 310 backpanel, and a replacement 310 scrambler card.
PSXM311WDCBL	311 Winchester controller cable kit *for 214-based host* 310 systems. Consists of Winchester daisy-chain cables and connectors to the 310 backpanel.

311 Upgrade Kits

PSYS311W1K	Kit for adding the first 40MB Winchester drive to the 311. Consists of forward mounting bracket, all internal and external cables, and one power supply module. Does *not* include Winchester drive. *Requires separate purchase of one Winchester Host Controller SXM.*
PSYS311W2K	Kit for adding the second 40MB Winchester drive to the 311. Consists of rear mounting bracket, all internal cables, 311 data mux board and one power supply module. Does *not* include Winchester drive.
PSYS311W14K	Kit for adding the first 140MB Winchester drive to the 311. Consists of forward mounting bracket, all internal and external cables, and two power supply modules. Does *not* include Winchester drive. *Requires separate purchase of one Winchester Host Controller SXM.*
PSYS311W24K	Kit for adding the second 140MB Winchester drive to the 311. Consists of rear mounting bracket, all internal cables, 311 data mux board and two power supply modules. Does not include Winchester drive.
PSYS311TK	Kit for adding a streaming tape drive to the 311. Consists of forward mounting bracket, all internal and external cables, two power supply modules, one 90 ips streaming tape drive, and one 450-foot tape cartridge. *Requires separate purchase of one Tape Host Controller SXM.*

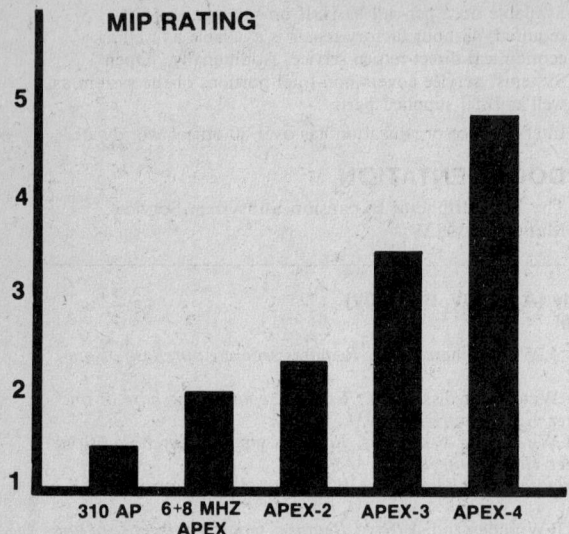

APEX* ADVANCED PROCESSOR EXTENSION SERIES

- Configure up to four 8MHz CPUs
- Automatic CPU workload balancing
- Graphic display of CPU, memory and I/O load
- Intel's 8MHz 286 and 287 per CPU
- From 2.4 to 4.8 MIPS processing power
- Configure up to 16MB of zero wait state memory
- Assured future XENIX† compatibility
- Transparent to users and applications
- Upgrade kits for System 310 and 310 AP

VERY HIGH PERFORMANCE XENIX SYSTEMS

The Advanced Processor EXtension series (APEX) adds processing power to Intel's XENIX-based microcomputer systems. The APEX architecture is designed for as many as four CPUs in a system. The addition of a second, third or fourth processor results in a broad range of processing power from 2.4 MIPS extending up to 4.8 MIPS. The processing power of multi-CPUs can be sized to accommodate applications with a wide range of requirements, whether to support a large number of users, CPU-intensive programs or the distributed processing needs of a large-scale OpenNET™ local area network.

PROTECT YOUR SOFTWARE INVESTMENT

Intel's multiple processor technology is completely transparent to your XENIX software investment, and will remain compatible with future Intel XENIX enhancements.

With APEX, you no longer have to wait for the next generation of VLSI technology to get greater processing power and application capabilities.

PROTECT YOUR HARDWARE INVESTMENT

The 8MHz APEX processors come with zero wait state memory and can be installed in existing systems with 6MHz or 8MHz 286/287 CPUs by a trained Intel Customer Engineer. This system upgrade capability provides your customers with a smooth and totally transparent migration path to the latest Intel System technology.

THE APEX ARCHITECTURE

The APEX architecture is engineered to handle multi-computing processes executed in parallel. To accomplish this, APEX divides the system processes between application tasks, and operating system and I/O tasks. APEX automatically balances the workload over the number of processors in the system. Any process that is created is sent to the least utilized CPU. No special programming is required to take advantage of this processing architecture.

AN OPEN SYSTEM ENGINEERED TO BE CONFIGURABLE

Each processor has its own memory with a dedicated LBX memory bus to maximize the performance of each CPU. Additionally, portions of memory may be configured into RAM disk for the ultimate in performance. The amount of memory associated with each CPU can vary.

Intel's Open System design also allows integration of Multibus I boards for SMD disk drives, 9 track tape, host communication and OpenNET networking.

THE APEX ARCHITECTURE IS ADDRESSABLE BY CPU

Programs can be directed to execute on a specific CPU within a multiprocessor system. A programmer can use this feature to optimize special processing requirements or to interleave execution of two or more programs. The APEX architecture permits tandem execution of programs scheduled automatically and programs are directed to specific CPUs. Analysis of the CPU utilization can easily be made using the graphic performance monitor.

© INTEL CORPORATION, 1985
*AVAILABLE ONLY WITH THE INTEL XENIX OPERATING SYSTEM
† TRADEMARK OF MICROSOFT CORPORATION

APEX PERFORMANCE MONITOR

```
CPU            # PROCESSES   0     10    20    30    40    50    60    70    80    90   100
   main            15        |]]]]]]]]]]]]]]]]]]]]]]]|     |     |     |     |     |
   Apex 1          35        |]]]]]]]]]]]]]]]]]]]]]]]]]]]]]]]]]]|    |     |     |     |
   Apex 2        offline     |     |     |     |     |     |     |     |     |     |     |
   Apex 3          67        |]]]]]]]]]]]]]]]]]]]]]]]]]]]]]]]]]]]]]]]]]]]]]]]]|     |     |
MEMORY         TOTAL MEM (K) |     |     |     |     |     |     |     |     |     |     |
   main           1024       |]]]]]]]]]]]]|    |     |     |     |     |     |     |     |
   Apex 1         2048       |]]]]]]]]]]]]]]]]]]]]|  |     |     |     |     |     |     |
   Apex 2        offline     |     |     |     |     |     |     |     |     |     |     |
   Apex 3         4096       |]]]]]]]]]]]]]]]]]]]]]]]]]]]]]]]]]]]]]]]]]]]]]]]]]]]]]]]]]]]|
DISK                         |***************************|  |     |     |     |     |
```

DISTRIBUTED PROCESSING USING APEX ON AN OPENNET NETWORK

The APEX architecture is compatible with the OpenNET network. Thus, an Intel system with multiple APEX processors can be used as a distributed "super processing node" on a XENIX OpenNET network. This feature also permits large programs or data files to be downloaded from a mainframe computer and processed locally in the network.

SPECIFICATIONS

Central Processors: Up to 4 processors, each containing both an 80286 microprocessor, and an 80287 math co-processor on each Multibus I (IEEE 796) single board computer.

Mass Storage: System 310 Product Family: from 20MB through 140MB Winchesters. System 311 Peripheral chasis: from 40MB through 420MB storage.

System Expansion: System 310 Product Family: up to 4 Multibus I card slots. System 313 Expansion chasis: up to 6 additional Multibus I card slots available for APEX processors, memory or other boards. Integration capabilities include boards for SMD disk drives, 9 track tape, host communication, networking, graphics and custom boards.

Environmental Specifications: From 10°C to 35°C (with diskette), 26°C maximum wet bulb temperature, 20% to 80% relative humidity, non-condensing. Altitude: sea level to 8,000 feet.

Regulatory Specifications: Meets UL 114 Safety, CSA 22.2 Safety; IEC 435 Safety, FCC docket 20780 RFI/EMI; VDE 0871 Class A RFI/EMI.

AC Power Input: 88-132 VAC or 180-264 VAC, 47-63HZ (user selectable).

Required Hardware: SBC 286/10 based systems with 270 W power supplies.

Required Software: Intel's XENIX 286 R 3.0 with update 3 applied.

ORDERING INFORMATION

APEX Systems
- 310APEX-2 Dual 8MHz APEX Processor System, 2MB RAM, 40MB Winchester, 45/60MB Tape, 320KB Floppy and preconfigured for 8 users.
- 310APEX-4 Quad 8MHz APEX Processor System, 8MB RAM, 140MB Winchester, 45/60MB Tape, 320KB Floppy and preconfigured for 16 users.

APEX 8MHz Upgrade Kits*
- APEX21-6 First 1MB kit for 6MHz 310s
- APEX22-6 First 2MB kit for 6MHz 310s
- APEX24-6 First 4MB kit for 6MHz 310s
- APEX21-8 First 1MB kit for 8MHz 310 APs
- APEX22-8 First 2MB kit for 8MHz 310 APs
- APEX24-8 First 4MB kit for 8MHz 310 APs
- APEX32   Second 2MB kit for 310s and 310 APs
- APEX34   Second 4MB kit for 310s and 310 APs
- APEX42   Third 2MB kit for 310s and 310 APs
- APEX44   Third 4 MB kit for 310s and 310 APs
- SYS313   APEX Expansion Chassis for 6 additional board slots†

*All upgrade kits require a minimum power supply of 270 Watts.
†APEX Expansion Chassis required for expansion of System 310 and 310 AP to Tri and Quad APEX system.

PRELIMINARY

iSXM™ SERIES
SYSTEM EXTENSION MODULES

- iSXM™ 534 Four-channel Serial Communication Extension Module for multi-user systems

- iSXM™ 544A Intelligent Four-channel Serial Communication Extension Modules for high-performance multi-user systems

- iSXM™ 951 RS232 Serial I/O Cable Extension Module for use with iSXM 534 or 544 in Intel SYSTEM 310 Family microcomputer systems

- iSXM™ 953 RS232 Serial I/O Cable Extension Module for use with iSXM™ 534 or 544 in Intel SYSTEM 380 Family microcomputer systems, or as a second cable set for the SYSTEM 86/330A

- iSXM™ 955 Communication Cabling for use with the iSBC® 188/48 Eight Channel Communication board in the SYSTEM 310 Family

The iSXM™ family of System Extension Modules is designed to extend the hardware capability of the SYSTEM 86/300 and SYSTEM 286/300 Series microcomputers. All hardware is fully configured and can easily be installed in the system. An easy-to-follow installation manual as well as all hardware documentation is included in each package.

---

† XENIX is a trademark of Microsoft Corporation.

The following are trademarks of Intel Corporation and may be used only to describe Intel products: Intel, ICE, iMMX, iRMX, iSBC, iSBX, iSXM, MULTIBUS, Multichannel and MULTIMODULE. Intel Corporation assumes no responsibility for the use of any circuitry other than circuitry embodied in an Intel product. No other circuit patent licenses are implied. Information contained herein supercedes previously published specifications on these devices from Intel.
© INTEL CORPORATION, 1983

OCTOBER 1984
ORDER NUMBER: 230877-002

iSXM™ SERIES

PRELIMINARY

iSXM™ 534 Four-Channel I/O Extension Module, and iSXM™ 544A Intelligent Four-Channel I/O Extension Module

The iSXM 534 contains the iSBC 534 Four-channel Serial Communications Board, fully configured for use in Intel SYSTEM 300 Series microcomputer systems, installation instructions and a Hardware Reference Manual.

The iSXM 544A Intelligent Four-Channel Serial I/O Module contains the iSBC 544A board, fully configured for use in Intel SYSTEM 300 Series microcomputer systems, two 2732A EPROMS containing firmware to control the iSBC 544A, installation instructions and Hardware Reference Manual.

Installation of these modules adds four serial I/O channels to the one already resident on the 86/35 processor board, or to the two resident on the 286/12 processor board. They interface directly to the system through the MULTIBUS® system bus. The four serial ports fully support RS232C (configured) asynchronous communications.

The iSXM 544A provides much higher I/O performance, making it particularly suited for multiuser requirements.

These System Extension Modules are fully supported by iRMX™ 86 Release 6 and XENIX 286.

Cables and mounting hardware are required for use in Intel microcomputer systems. Order the iSXM 951, 952, or 953 depending on your system type.

For a full explanation of the iSBC 534 or iSBC 544, please refer to the respective data sheets.

iSXM™ 951 RS232 Serial I/O Cables

This module contains four 1-foot cables for use from the edge connectors of the iSXM 534 or 544 to the back of the SYSTEM 86/310 Series or SYSTEM 286/310 Series chassis. An installation guide is also included.

iSXM™ 953 RS232 Serial I/O Cables

This module contains four 2-foot cables for use from the edge connectors of the iSXM 534 or 544 to the back of the SYSTEM 86/380 Series or SYSTEM 286/380 Series chassis, and an installation guide.

Reference Manuals

173177-001	System Terminal Communication Installation Guide
980450	iSBC 534 Hardware Reference Manual
980616	iSBC 544 Hardware Reference Manual
173074-001	iSXM 951 Installation Guide
173076-001	iSXM 953 Installation Guide

Ordering Information

iSXM 534 or	PSXM 534	4-channel I/O Extension Module
iSXM 544 or	PSXM 544	Intelligent 4-channel I/O Extension Module
iSXM 544A or	PSXM 544A	16 MB Intelligent 4 Channel I/O Extension Module
iSXM 951 or	PSXM 951	Cables for SYSTEM 86/310, SYSTEM 286/310
iSXM 953 or	PSXM 953	Cables for SYSTEM 86/380, SYSTEM 286/380
iSXM 955 or	PSXM 955	Cables for the iSBC 188/48 in any SYSTEM 310

intel®

RELIABILITY REPORT

RR-52

July 1984

SYSTEM 310 RELIABILITY

CLEONE HAWKINSON
OREGON SYSTEMS QUALITY AND RELIABILITY

© INTEL CORPORATION, 1984

Order Number 280044-001

SYSTEM 310 RELIABILITY REPORT

RELIABILITY: THE ABILITY OF A PRODUCT TO CONSISTENTLY OPERATE FAILURE FREE IN THE ENVIRONMENT FOR WHICH IT WAS DESIGNED

SUMMARY

This report describes the Intel System 310 microcomputer and presents the results of the system's reliability evaluation. This report also reviews the component, board, and system Quality Assurance and Reliability qualification programs.

Five configurations of the System 310 were evaluated: the SYP310-1, -2, and -3 (8086-based product) and the SYP310-4 and -17 (80286-based product). These System 310 products have passed a series of reliability tests that include accelerated life, environmental, (temperature, humidity, shock, vibration, altitude) and shipping tests. A summary of the Mean Time Between Failures (MTBF) data is below. Supporting data are presented in the text.

Configuration	Goal MTBF 35°C (in hours)	MTBF 35°C (in hours)	MTBF 25°C (in hours)	Confidence Level
−1	3500	4200	7385	60%
−2, −3	2000	4680	8190	60%
−4	3156	5100	8925	60%
−17	1960	2875	5031	60%

DESCRIPTION OF THE SYSTEM 310

Intel's System 310 microcomputer (Figure 1) is a user-configurable, MULTIBUS®-based, 16-bit microcomputer intended for real-time applications and interactive multiuser commercial and technical environments. Various configurations are available to meet the customer's optimal price and performance requirements. These configurations are presented in Table 1.

Four key elements of the open system give it power and flexibility:

- iSBC® 86/30 or 286/10 processor boards
- MULTIBUS interface
- XENIX* and iRMX™ operating systems
- Diagnostics

Processor Boards: The heart of the System 310 is the processor board. For the SYP310-1, -2, and -3 the iSBC 86/30 offers the system 128K-byte, dual-port dynamic RAMs, which may be doubled to 256K bytes by adding the iSBC 304C MULTI-MODULE™ board, as in the -2 configuration. The -3 version contains an iSBC 012B memory board, extending RAM to 640K bytes. The iSBC 337 MULTIMODULE Math Coprocessor provides arithmetic and logical instruction extensions to the 8086 CPU. The iSBC 337 is optional in the -1 configuration and is standard in the -2 and -3 configurations.

For the SYP310-4 and -17, the iSBC 286/10 provides sites for EPROM, which contains bootstrap and diagnostic code. The 012CX is a 512K-byte RAM board with error correction, connected to the 286/10 on the local bus extension (iLBX™). The iLBX bus provides improved performance by avoiding MULTIBUS arbitration delays. All memory addressable by the processor can be accessed over the iLBX bus (16 M-bytes) and appears to the processor as though it were resident on the processor board.

The MULTIBUS Interface: As industry bus standard IEEE 796, it provides the physical framework and conceptual foundation of Intel's total open system architecture. With a guarantee of future system expansion compatibility, the customer can choose from a wide range of MULTIBUS products. This general-purpose system bus, in conjunction with the iSBC 86/30 or 286/10 processor board, provides a flexible mechanism for intermodule processing, control, and communication. The MULTIBUS interface supports modular memory and I/O expansion. When new peripherals are added, more processing power can be applied to handle them without degrading

*XENIX is a trademark of MicroSoft Corp.

RR-52

Figure 1. The System 310

Table 1. System 310 Configurations

	-1	-2	-3	-4	-17
iSBC® 86/30 CPU	x	x	x		
iSBC 286/10 CPU				x	x
iSBC 337 math coprocessor		x	x		
Numeric data processor (80287)				x	x
iSBC 304C memory board		x			
iSBC 012B RAM board			x		
iSBC 012CX RAM board				x	x
Flexible diskette drive	x	x	x	x	x
iSBX 218A flexible diskette controller	x	x	x	x	x
Winchester drive (12M-byte)			x	x	
(19M-byte)					x
iSBC 215G Winchester controller			x	x	x
iSBC 213 Data Separator			x	x	x
System 310 Chassis (including 220W power supply)	x	x	x	x	x

existing processor performance. Figure 2 is a block diagram of the System 310, illustrating the MULTIBUS interface.

Operating Systems: The System 310 operates with the industry-standard iRMX and XENIX operating systems. The iRMX operating system optimizes the System 310 for real-time multitasking, time-critical applications where rapid response is required. XENIX offers conversational access to the System 310 for multiple users in a time-shared environment. A wide range of popular high-level languages enables applications developers to program in multiple languages and still link modules together. The system also supports the Universal Development Interface (UDI), which provides the Independent Software Vendor (ISV) access to the iRMX operating system for developing languages and applications.

Diagnostics: The System 310 includes a comprehensive diagnostic package. A System Confidence Test (SCT) automatically checks the hardware on power-up or RESET. Two separate software packages are also available: the System Diagnostics Tests (SDTs) and the System Analysis Tests (SATs). The SDTs provide detailed diagnostics on problems identified by the SCT and allow the user to isolate a problem on a specific board or drive - often to the component level. The SATs for the iRMX and XENIX operating systems allow the user to interactively exercise the system hardware with the operating system for extended periods of time. Thus, subtle problems can be isolated to a given area within the system.

SYSTEM PRODUCT QUALITY ASSURANCE

The quality and reliability of system products like the System 310 are a function of the quality of components used, the care taken in board and system design and fabrication, and the extent of testing performed on the product before shipment. Examining these functions illustrates the Intel Quality Assurance program for microcomputer system products.

Component Quality Assurance

Standard Intel Component Quality Assurance processing and 100% screening are applied to all Intel components before they are assembled on the boards. Once a component has been qualified as reliable and transferred to systems-level

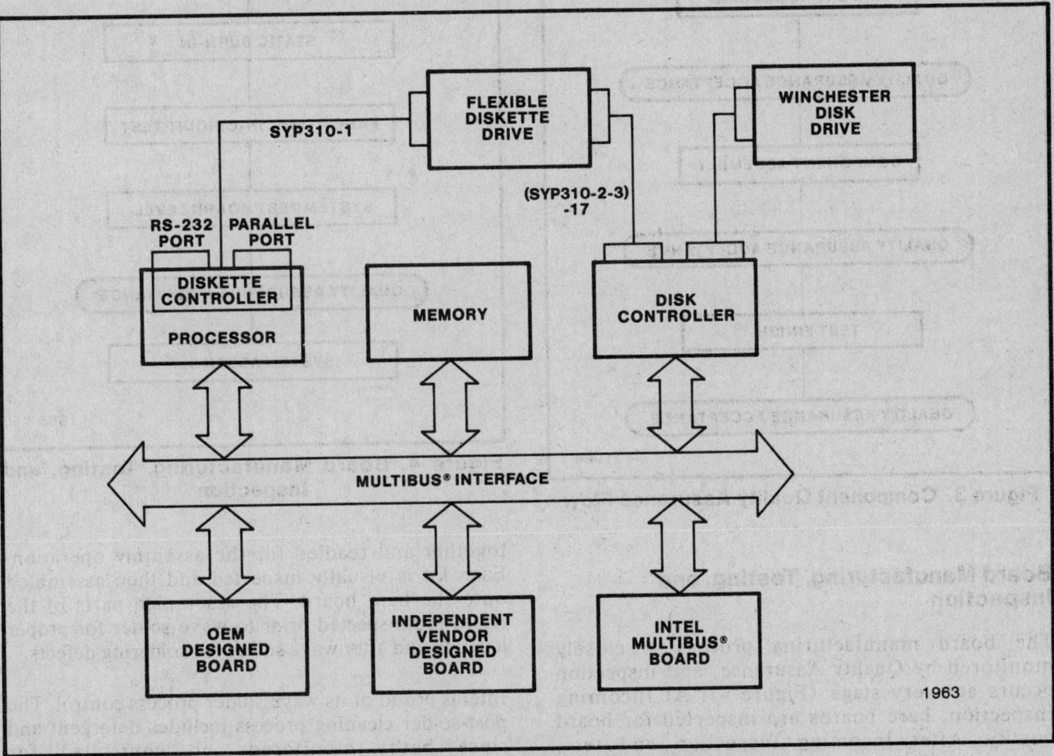

Figure 2. System 310 MULTIBUS® Interface

manufacturing, complete process controls assure the continuation of high quality.

Intel's Component Quality Assurance flow, shown in Figure 3, combines a series of acceptance gates between process steps and detailed inspection at critical points within the processing areas. For example, during wafer fabrication, processes are routinely monitored for contamination through the use of capacitance versus voltage measurements on test chips. Electrical tests, such as breakdown voltage measurements, are performed on test patterns on each wafer. Routine electron microscope examinations at critical process steps also provide important process control feedback. Full functional testing of all parts precedes final Quality Assurance acceptance. Qualified components are then sent to assembly locations.

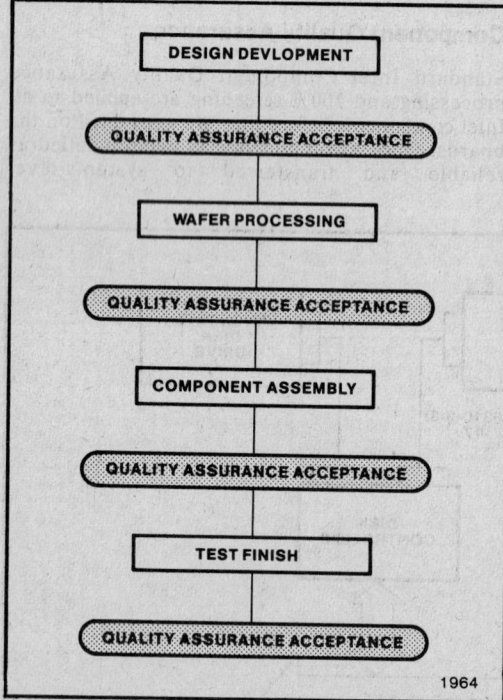

Figure 3. Component Quality Assurance Flow

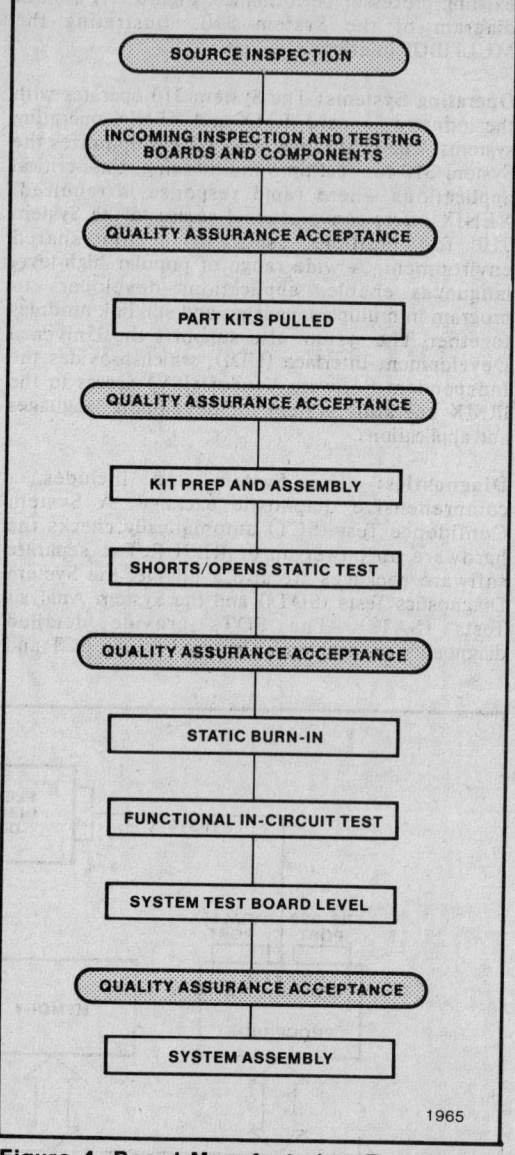

Figure 4. Board Manufacturing, Testing, and Inspection

Board Manufacturing, Testing, and Inspection

The board manufacturing process is closely monitored by Quality Assurance, and inspection occurs at every stage (Figure 4). At Incoming Inspection, bare boards are inspected for board quality. After Incoming Inspection and test, components for an assembly "kit" are then pulled together and readied for the assembly operation. Each kit is visually inspected and then assembled onto the bare board. The assembled parts of the board are inspected prior to wave solder for proper location and after wave solder for soldering defects.

Intel is proud of its wave solder process control. The post-solder cleaning process includes detergent and rinse baths monitored and controlled for concentration, temperature, and contamination.

Boards are selected at random and then checked under a microscope to assure compliance with Intel's wave solder process and cleanliness standards. Boards are also sample tested in an Omegameter (Figure 5), which measures ionic contamination. In the rare event any deviation occurs, the Quality Assurance Inspector stops the process until compliance is restored.

In touch-up and second assembly such items as connectors and process sensitive components are added to a board. As the final phase of kit assembly, a board is tested for circuit "shorts" and "opens" on the Teradyne L529 Automatic Test Equipment (Figure 6). Final assembly inspection certifies the boards are acceptable for test.

The next stage is static burn-in at elevated temperature and voltage margins (70°C, +6% VDC). Burn-in eliminates temperature- and voltage-related "infant mortality" failures that occur early in the life of a product.

The boards are then tested on a Teradyne L125/L135 In-Circuit Tester. This system has a "test the tester" feature that verifies all test points are functioning before actual boards are tested. Use of a special "bed of nails" vacuum fixture ensures that all critical board test points may be accessed by the test system. Any components that fail are replaced, and the boards are retested on the Teradyne system.

Next, boards are functionally tested at System Test Board Level (STBL), a three-stage test. The first stage is at room temperature and nominal voltage. The next two stages are at elevated temperature (70°C) and voltage: first at +6% VDC and then repeated at -6% VDC. For these tests a set of monitor and diagnostic EPROMs are installed, the board is installed into a General Purpose Test Fixture (GPTF) and the board's performance is monitored with a CRT terminal (Figure 7). The monitor/diagnostic exerciser program tests the CPU, I/O interface, and MULTIBUS interface in a multiprocessing environment, which guarantees MULTIBUS interface integrity.

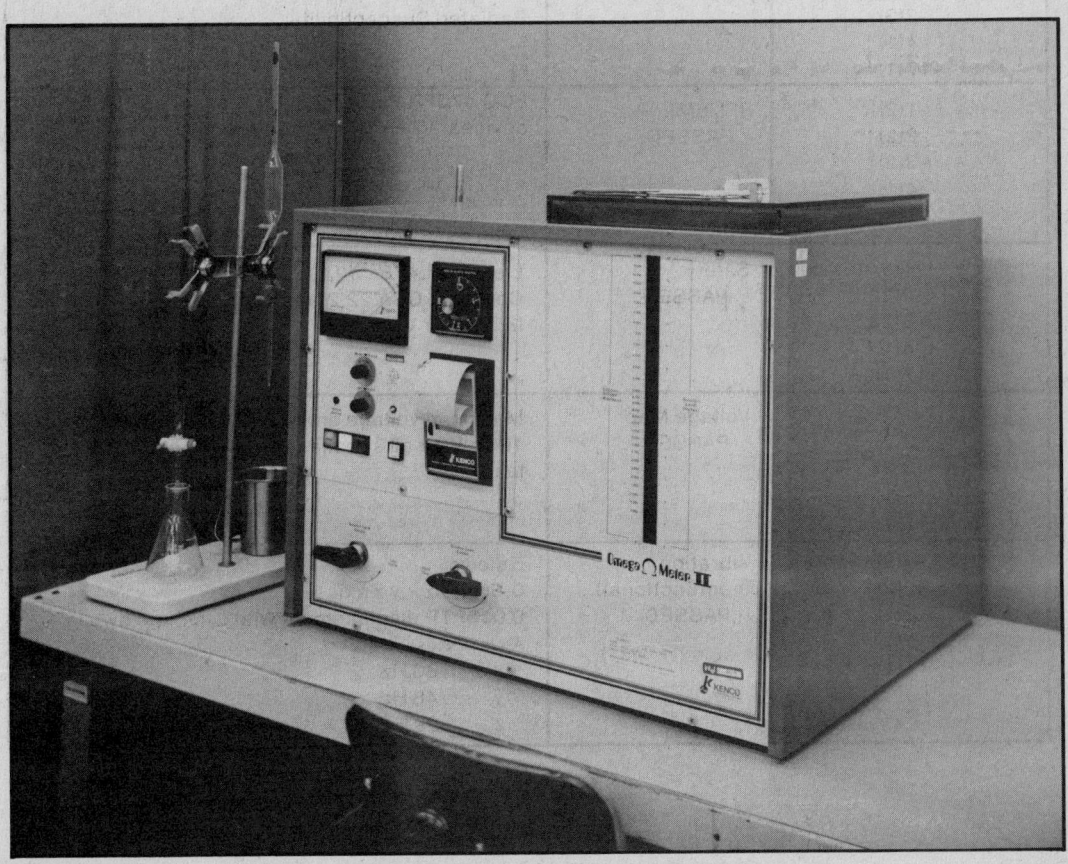

Figure 5. Omegameter: Wave Solder Process Control

Table 2. Environmental Qualification Data

THIS INFORMATION, BASED ON SMALL SAMPLES, IS INTERNAL QUALIFICATION TEST DATA GATHERED UNDER CONDITIONS THAT EXCEED SPECIFICATIONS AND SHOULD NOT BE CONFUSED WITH WARRANTED SPECIFICATIONS. ALL CONFIGURATIONS TESTED PASSED ALL TESTS.

Configuration(Sample)	Test	Description
-1(1) -2(1) -3(4) -4(1) -17(1)	Temperature Map (fully loaded) PASSED	Maximum temperature delta above external system ambient: Semiconductor case temperature +24.4°C (8089 on iSBC 215G) Power supply +19.6°C Internal Winchester +4.5°C
-3(2) -17(1)	Humidity (functional) PASSED (nonfunctional) PASSED	63 hours/unit 29°C (84.2°F) 76% RH noncondensing 90 hours/unit, 26°C wet bulb 95% RH noncondensing
-1(2) -2(2) -3(3) -4(1) -17(1)	ESD PASSED	Direct Discharge Conducted Susceptibility Radiated Susceptibility
-1(2) -2(2) -3(2) -4(1) -17(1)	RFI/EMI PASSED	FCC 47CFR Part 15, "J" for Class A computing devices; VDE 0871, Class A limits
-1(2) -2(2) -3(2) -4(1) -17(1)	Safety PASSED	Listed: UL478 Certified: CSA 22.2 No. 154 IEC435 or VDE0806
-1(2) -2(2) -3(2) -4(1) -17(1)	Voltage Map PASSED	Maximum voltage drop: 100 mv for all supplies at full load at component lead

-1(2)
-2(2)
-3(4)
-4(1)
-17(1)
	Vibration
	(nonfunctional)
	PASSED
		5 slews
		0-55-0 Hz x,y,z axis
		0.01" PTP displacement with 3-minute dwells
		Axis Resonance
		  x 30 Hz
		  y 48 Hz
		  z 29 Hz

Figure 6. Teradyne Tester

Figure 7. General Purpose Test Fixture

After test, the boards are inspected to ensure that they comply with required specifications and quality standards. Boards passing this final screening are then released by Intel Quality Assurance for use in a system product like the System 310.

System Manufacturing, Testing, and Inspection

Quality Assurance closely monitors the system manufacturing process (Figure 8). After electromechanical assembly, Quality Assurance inspects the systems to ensure compliance with engineering documentation and Intel Workmanship Standards.

The HYPOT (Hypotronics) test verifies primary circuit integrity and ensures compliance with various safety agency requirements. Next, a power-up test, with load boards, checks power supply output voltages and system power distribution integrity. After the system passes the power-up test, the required boards are installed in the system.

Pre run-in System Test System Level (STSL), a "handshake" test using the System Confidence Test (SCT), is the first test of system integration. This test determines if any major components of the system are malfunctioning. If a problem occurs, it is isolated and corrected, and the system is retested.

STSL, the run-in phase for systems, is functionally equivalent to burn-in for boards. During run-in the system is tested to verify that infant mortality failures have been eliminated. Although the boards have already been rigorously tested, run-in verifies the reliability of the integrated system, which includes power supplies and disk drives. The systems are tested at specification temperature and voltage and are continuously monitored to record any malfunctions. Run-in time is determined by system reliability characterization during the product's development stage. Data collected during the run-in of all subsequent systems are continuously reviewed to assure appropriate run-in time.

At post run-in STSL, Quality Assurance performs a final inspection to certify that all quality standards have been met. After the system passes this inspection, the diskette drive heads are cleaned. As a final step before packaging, drive heads are repositioned to avoid shipping damage.

After packaging, a system is sent to the Boards and Systems Warehouse (BSW) to await shipment to the customer. Quality Assurance conducts monthly finished goods audits on products before shipping. This audit reviews documentation, tests for compliance to environmental specifications (temperature, humidity, shock, vibration), and confirms functional performance over time. Audit systems are run for 48 hours at 35°C. This finished goods audit is a final in-house monitor of the quality that reaches the customer.

Product performance in the field is also tracked. All processes are monitored on a computerized data system, and feedback is used to assure corrective actions when required. This rigorous testing, tracking, and corrective action system assures Intel's product specifications are met, and therefore, the customer's quality and reliability expectations are met.

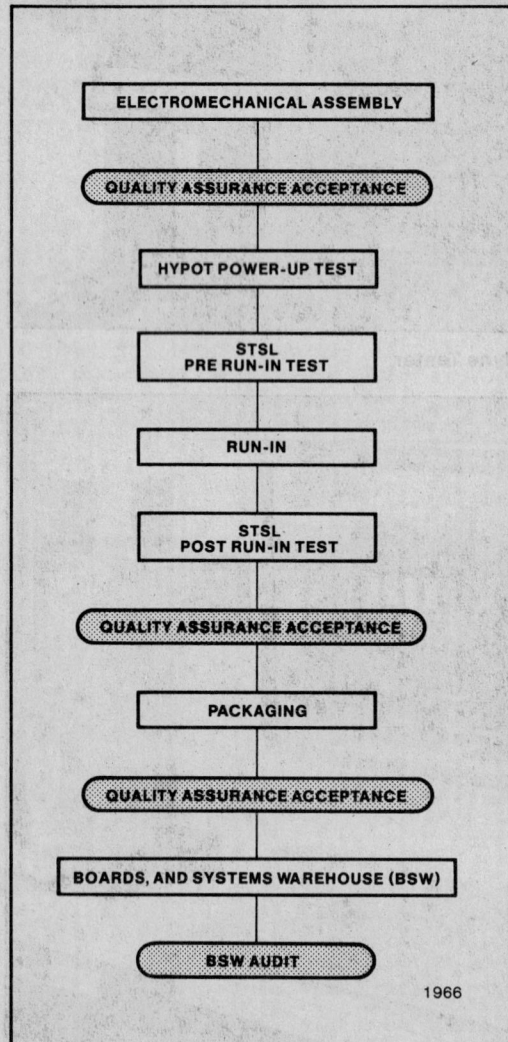

Figure 8. System Manufacturing, Testing, and Inspection

SYSTEM PRODUCT RELIABILITY

The Life Curve

Three categories of failures can occur during system product life:

- Infant Mortality
- Random
- Wear Out

Each category has a distinct distribution when failure frequency is plotted against time. When the three distributions are combined, the resulting failure rate/time distribution produces a characteristic curve known as a "bathtub" curve. The three distributions, as well as the combined bathtub curve, are represented in Figure 9.

However, the boundaries between the categories are less precise than they appear because the failure categories have overlapping distributions. For example, Infant Mortality failures may extend into the expected Random failure period, but at a very low level. Wear Out failures may, in fact, occasionally occur before the expected Wear Out period. As additional long-term product information becomes available, these boundaries may change.

The Infant Mortality area of the curve shows failures caused by manufacturing defects in the components, boards, and systems. These are "quality failures," and their frequency decreases with time. Infant Mortality for systems depends on the quality and test history of the components and assemblies used in systems manufacturing.

System run-in characterization explores failure modes to identify the change from Infant Mortality to Random failure patterns. The systems are run and failure data collected. Run-in is then defined to include the point at which the instantaneous failure rate falls below a defined limit. Thus, the length of time required for system run-in is closely tied to the Infant Mortality failure rate. In this way, the length of run-in time is defined for future System 310 builds. This point becomes the boundary between the Infant Mortality and Random failure modes.

Random failures occur during the "useful life" of the product, between Infant Mortality and Wear Out. These stress-related failures are primarily a function of temperature, circuit complexity, and device loading. The early phase of the Random failure period is explored during run-in characterization. As the failure pattern becomes random, it approaches a low constant value (flat distribution). For Intel systems this period lasts for many thousands of operating hours. The limiting factors are usually the power supplies, fans, and disk drives, which tend to have higher electrical stress levels and mechanical failures.

To gain insight into system performance, data collected during run-in characterization is extensive. During the original System 310 characterization, the data indicated that run-in should be 40 hours to eliminate Infant Mortality failures. On the

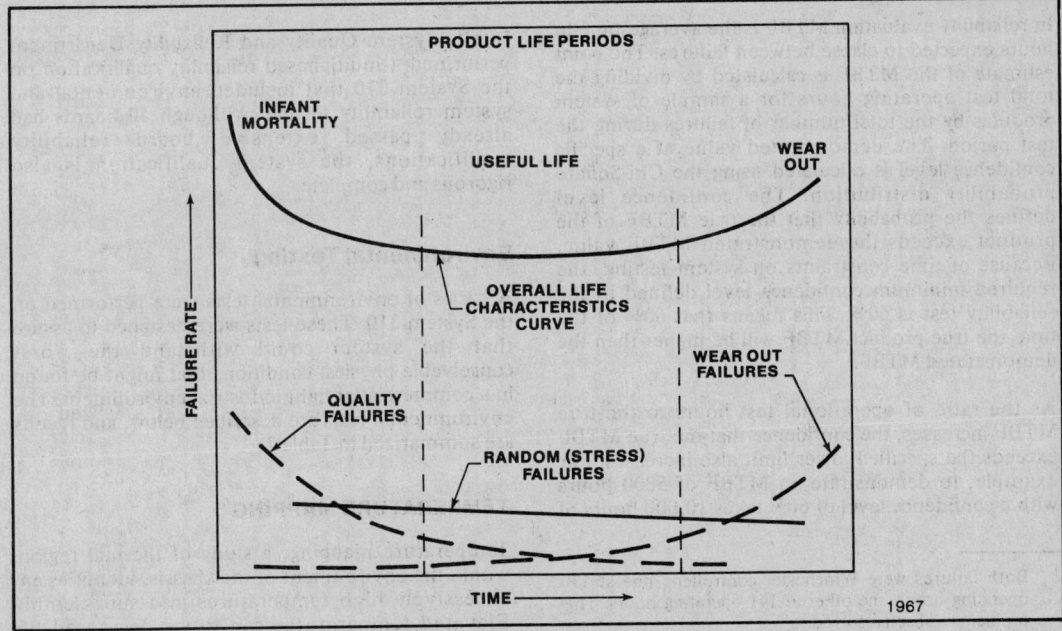

Figure 9. Reliability Life Curve

production floor, after completing the 40 hours of run-in time, we used 145 System 310's to accumulate an additional 19,140 system operating hours with two failures[1], at approximately 25°C. This resulted in a demonstrated 6100 hour MTBF (Mean Time Between Failures; see explanation next section) at 60% confidence level using a Chi-Square distribution[2], and a 3610 hour MTBF at 90% confidence level. This characterization data validated the run-in time for the System 310 and provided some early insights into the Random failure mode.

While run-in defines the starting boundary of useful product life, the end boundary is less easily defined. Until accelerated life testing is completed, the Wear Out period must be estimated, based on known device limitations. As can be seen in Figure 9, Wear Out failure frequency increases with time.

Wear Out failures are primarily due to mechanical wear or chemical degradation. Each can cause the system to lose conformance to specifications. Obviously, not all parts of a system have identical life expectancies. Statistically, Wear Out will not happen until hundreds of years have elapsed for VLSI-based products; however, the life expectancy for peripherals and mechanical devices, such as fans, is in the tens of thousands of hours. Intel identifies these system elements and puts preventive maintenance programs in place.

Mean Time Between Failures and Confidence Levels

In reliability evaluation MTBF is the average time in hours expected to elapse between failures. The point estimate of the MTBF is calculated by dividing the total test operating hours for a sample of system products by the total number of failures during the test period. The demonstrated value at a specific confidence level is calculated using the Chi-Square probability distribution. The confidence level defines the probability that the true MTBF of the product exceeds the demonstrated MTBF value. Because of time constraints on system testing, the required minimum confidence level defined in the reliability test is 60%. This means that 60% of the time the true product MTBF will be higher than the demonstrated MTBF.

As the ratio of operational test hours to the true MTBF increases, the confidence that the true MTBF exceeds the specified lower limit also increases. For example, to demonstrate an MTBF of 5000 hours with a confidence level of 60% takes 10,000 hours of operation with one failure. To demonstrate the same MTBF at a 90% confidence level requires 19,500 hours. The values of MTBF for specific system configurations are normally at the 60% confidence level when the product is qualified for full production. The higher confidence level is attained later in product life, with data from the accelerated life test. As this information becomes available, it will be reported.

RELIABILITY QUALIFICATION

Reliability evaluation serves at least three important functions:

- Demonstrates the MTBF
- Checks the manufacturing process
- Provides system design feedback

First, the evaluation demonstrates the MTBF of a product. This information helps customers to evaluate Intel systems, and helps Intel anticipate customers' product support requirements. Second, it serves as a manufacturing process check. When failures attributed to the manufacturing process occur, they can be quickly identified as exceptions and corrective actions can be implemented. Finally, reliability evaluation serves as a feedback mechanism for system design. Lessons learned from building one system can be used to improve the design of new products. Information gathered from reliability evaluation helps in each of these areas, ensuring Intel will continue to produce the most reliable products possible.

Intel's System Quality and Reliability Department performed a multiphased reliability qualification on the System 310 that included environmental and system reliability testing. Although all boards had already passed extensive board reliability qualifications, the system qualification is also rigorous and complete.

Environmental Testing

A series of environmental tests were performed on the System 310. These tests were designed to assure that the system could withstand the worst conceivable physical conditions that might be found in a commercial or light industrial environment. The environmental tests are described below, and results are summarized in Table 2.

TEMPERATURE MAPPING

Temperature mapping, a study of thermal regions within the environment of the chassis, identifies any excessively high temperatures in a subassembly. Elevated temperatures can cause decreased life expectancy and lower system reliability. All

---

[1] Both failures were Winchester controllers: one at 130 operating hours, the other at 141 operating hours. This problem has been resolved.
[2] See Reference 1.

Table 2. Environmental Qualification Data (continued)

Configuration (Sample)	Test	Description
-1(2)	Vibration (functional) PASSED	7-55 Hz, in 1 Hz steps 1 minute dwell per step 30 minute dwell at the resonant frequency or 55 Hz Axis Resonance PTP x 49 Hz .0045" y,z 55 Hz .0045"
-3(2) -4(1) -17(1)		x 44 Hz .003" y 48 Hz .003" z 54 Hz .001"
-3(3)	Shock (nonfunctional) PASSED	15G, 1 drop per face (6)
-3(2)	Thermal Shock (non-functional) PASSED	8 cycles 60°C to −40°C
-3(1)	Altitude (functional) PASSED	Altitude chamber: 8000 feet 35°C, 220W maximum load
-3(5)	Packaging PASSED	Tested to National Safe Transit Requirements
-3(1)	Package Drop PASSED	Republic Packaging: 30", 15G maximum, 6 faces
-3(12)	Shipping PASSED	Inspection and functional test before and after round trip shipment: Portland, OR - San Jose, CA (plane change at San Jose)

measurements were taken in a walk-in environmental chamber at 35°C (Figure 10). The iRMX 86 System Analysis Test (RSAT) exercised the system during temperature mapping. Measurements on all subassemblies within the chassis (boards, drives, and power supply) were well within their individual maximum operating temperature specifications.

HUMIDITY

The humidity test identifies problems related to high temperature and high humidity environments, such as corrosion and poor mechanical contacts. These conditions not only test the reliability of the systems at high humidity and temperature, but also accelerate the effects of moderate humidity over time. The humidity test confirmed that the system operates properly at its maximum 26°C wet bulb specification. No evidence of system deterioration was found at the end of the test.

Note, however, that the system may not function correctly if operated at its maximum temperature specification (35°C) and its maximum humidity specification (80% relative humidity) simultaneously. These conditions fall outside the maximum 26°C wet bulb specification (a disk drive limitation) and the defined operating environment of expected system use. The temperature and humidity boundaries for 26°C wet bulb are illustrated in Figure 11.

EMI, RFI, ESD

Electro Magnetic Interference (EMI) and Radio Frequency Interference (RFI) evaluation measures the emitted and conducted radiation from the product to the outside world. Electro Static Discharge (ESD) evaluation measures a system's ability to withstand static discharges of electricity without failure or component damage. An independent laboratory confirmed that the System 310 passes FCC (Federal Communications Commission) and VDE (Verband Deutscher Elektrotechniker) conducted and radiated emission requirements. ESD specifications were verified internally.

Figure 10. Environmental Chamber

VOLTAGE MAPPING

Voltage mapping measures the voltage potential at various points within the system and ensures no excessive voltage drops exist in the system. All points measured were well within the tolerances allowed for operation.

VIBRATION AND SHOCK

Vibration and shock testing identifies mechanically related problems a system could sustain under normal conditions. The diskette and Winchester drives' vibration and shock specifications are lower than those of the remainder of the system (boards, fans, power supply, chassis structure); the system limits are essentially those of the peripherals. Functional and non-functional vibration tests were performed both at Intel and in an independent laboratory. Non-functional shock tests were performed at two independent facilities.

The test system passed the functional and non-functional vibration tests from 5Hz to 55Hz. As expected, the critical point in the system was the Winchester drive head assembly. No damage resulted, nor did the tests have any permanent effect on the performance of the system.

ALTITUDE

The altitude test evaluates the system's performance at altitude and temperature extremes. The system was operated at maximum altitude (8000 ft.) and maximum temperature (35°C) with maximum power supply loading (220W) without exceeding the temperature specifications of the various components.

PACKAGING AND SHIPPING

System packaging requirements are rigorously tested under both laboratory and actual shipping conditions. In the laboratory, packaged systems were subjected to worst-case conditions. Systems were monitored for shock, and the package was accepted only after shock to the system met the specification.

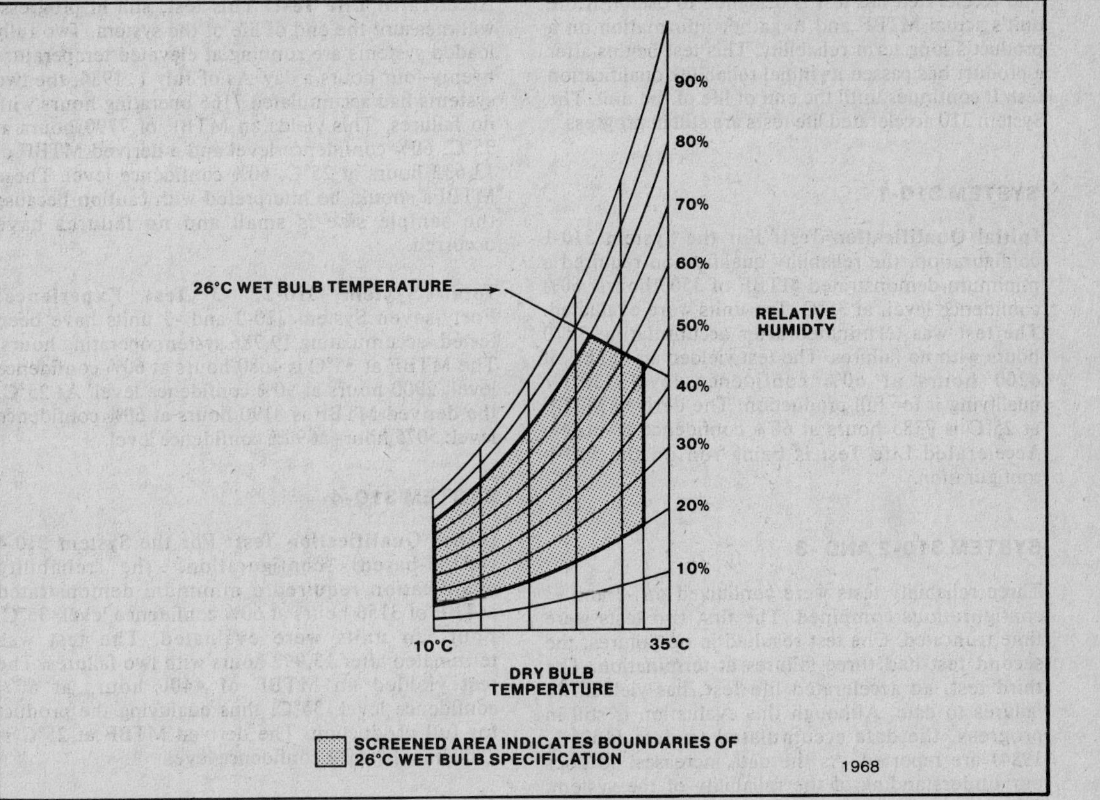

Figure 11. Operational Temperature and Humidity Specification, 26°C Wet Bulb

The reliability evaluation confirms the adequacy of packaging for commercial transportation conditions. Twelve systems were shipped round trip by truck and air from Hillsboro, Oregon, to Santa Clara, California, (approximately 1600 miles). During this test they were subjected to the typical handling conditions of commercial carriers. Before and after the test the systems were visually inspected and mechanically tested; no damage resulted.

The results of these environmental tests are summarized in Table 2.

Reliability Test Evaluation

Reliability test data were collected on System 310 configurations:

- 310-1
- 310-2, -3
- 310-4
- 310-17

Because of differences in system complexity and the Winchester drive in the 310-2, -3, and -17, each configuration had a different minimum MTBF qualification goal.

All System 310 reliability evaluations surpassed their designated minimum MTBF qualifications. The qualification requirements were at 35°C with a confidence level of 60%. The minimum MTBF requirements and the actual MTBFs attained are summarized in Table 3.

The elevated temperature (35°C) during the evaluation accelerates the wear on a system. Although the MTBF is demonstrated at 35°C, an MTBF at 25°C can be derived from the test data using a factor of 1.75 based on the Arrhenius equation[1]. This information is also presented.

Two types of tests are performed: the initial reliability qualification test and the accelerated life test. The initial reliability test qualifies a product for full production. This test is time truncated; the test is terminated when the product has met its minimum required MTBF. At that time, the product is qualified for full production.

---

[1] See Reference 2.

The accelerated life test is designed to establish the unit's actual MTBF and to gather information on a product's long term reliability. This test begins after a product has passed its initial reliability qualification test. It continues until the end of life of the unit. The System 310 accelerated life tests are still in progress.

SYSTEM 310-1

Initial Qualification Test: For the System 310-1 configuration, the reliability qualification required a minimum demonstrated MTBF of 3500 hours, 60% confidence level, at 35°C. Ten units were evaluated. The test was terminated after accumulating 3870 hours with no failures. The test yielded an MTBF of 4200 hours at 60% confidence level (35°C) qualifying it for full production. The derived MTBF at 25°C is 7385 hours at 60% confidence level. No Accelerated Life Test is being run on the 310-1 configuration.

SYSTEM 310-2 AND -3

Three reliability tests were conducted on -2 and -3 configurations combined. The first two tests were time truncated. One test resulted in no failures; the second test had three failures at termination. The third test, an accelerated life test, has yielded no failures to date. Although this evaluation is still in progress, the data accumulated to date (July 1, 1984) are reported. As the data increases, so does our understanding of the reliability of the system. The accelerated life test data will continue to accumulate, and they will be reported.

Initial Qualification Test: For the System 310-2 and -3 configurations, the reliability qualification required a minimum demonstrated MTBF of 2000 hours, 60% confidence level, at 35°C. Twenty-five units were evaluated. The test was terminated after accumulating 1870 system hours with no failures. The test met an MTBF of 2020 hours at 60% confidence level, and this product was qualified for full production. The derived MTBF at 25°C is 3552 hours at 60% confidence level.

The complexity of the -2 and -3 system configurations required more complete evaluation. Failure patterns of complex systems are largely unknown, so two further tests were designed: one to be terminated at about 10,000 hours; the other an accelerated life test, still in progress. The 10K-hour test logged 10,750 system hours at 35°C with three failures. Twenty units were evaluated. This was a rigorous test with the systems fully loaded to simulate maximum power load conditions. At 35°C this test yielded a 2570-hour MTBF at 60% confidence level. The 25°C derived MTBF is 4519 hours at 60% confidence level.

Accelerated Life Test: This test, still in progress, will measure the end of life of the system. Two fully loaded systems are running at elevated temperature twenty-four hours a day. As of July 1, 1984, the two systems had accumulated 7166 operating hours with no failures. This yields an MTBF of 7790 hours at 35°C, 60% confidence level and a derived MTBF of 13,632 hours at 25°C, 60% confidence level. These MTBFs should be interpreted with caution because the sample size is small and no failures have occurred.

Total System 310-2, -3 Test Experience: Forty-seven System 310-2 and -3 units have been tested, accumulating 19,786 system operating hours. The MTBF at 35°C is 4680 hours at 60% confidence level; 2900 hours at 90% confidence level. At 25°C, the derived MTBF is 8190 hours at 60% confidence level; 5075 hours at 90% confidence level.

SYSTEM 310-4

Initial Qualification Test: For the System 310-4 (80286-based) configuration, the reliability qualification required a minimum demonstrated MTBF of 3156 hours at 60% confidence level, 35°C. Fourteen units were evaluated. The test was terminated after 13,992 hours with two failures. The test yielded an MTBF of 4400 hours at 60% confidence level, 35°C, thus qualifying the product for full production. The derived MTBF at 25°C is 7700 hours at 60% confidence level.

Accelerated Life Test: This test was started on two 310-4 units. These units are running twenty-four hours a day at 35°C. As of July 1, 1984, the two systems had accumulated 2021 operating hours with no failures. The MTBF is 2200 hours at 35°C, 60% confidence level; the derived MTBF at 25°C is 3850 hours, 60% confidence level.

Total System 310-4 Test Experience: A total of 16,013 operating hours with two failures have been accumulated on the 16 System 310-4 units. This yields an MTBF of 5100 hours at 35°C, 60% confidence level; 3000 hours at 90% confidence level. The derived MTBF at 25°C is 8925 hours at 60% confidence level; 5250 hours at 90% confidence level.

SYSTEM 310-17

Initial Qualification Test: The System 310-17 qualification required a minimum demonstrated MTBF of 1960 hours at 60% confidence level, 35°C. Thirteen units were evaluated. The test was terminated after 13,434 hours with four failures. The test yielded an MTBF of 2500 hours at 60% confidence level, 35°C. The derived MTBF at 25°C was 4375 at 60% confidence level.

Accelerated Life Test: This test is still in progress with two 310-17 units; conditions are identical to those for the 310-4 units. As of July 1, 1984, 2021 operating hours have been accumulated on the two units with no failures. The MTBF at 35°C is 2200 hours at 60% confidence level; the derived MTBF at 25°C is 3850 hours at 60% confidence level.

Total System 310-17 Test Experience: A total of 15,455 operating hours with four failures have been accumulated on the 15 System 310-17 units. This yields an MTBF of 2875 hours at 35°C, 60% confidence level; 1800 hours at 90% confidence level. The derived MTBF at 25°C is 5031 hours at 60% confidence level; 3150 hours at 90% confidence level.

REFERENCES

1. *Reliability Mathematics: Fundamentals; Practices; and Procedures*, B. L. Amstadler, 1971. McGraw-Hill, Inc.

2. *Semiconductor Device Reliability and the Arrhenius Model*, National Semiconductor Reliability Report G-11, January 1977.

Table 3. Summary of Reliability Tests

-1 CONFIGURATION					
Operating Hours	Failures	MTBF Goal 35°C (in hours)	MTBF 35°C (in hours)	MTBF 25°C (in hours)	Confidence Level
3,870 (time truncated) n=10	0	3500	4200	7385	60%

-2, -3 CONFIGURATIONS					
Operating Hours	Failures	MTBF Goal 35°C (in hours)	MTBF 35°C (in hours)	MTBF 25°C (in hours)	Confidence Level
1,870 (time truncated) n=25	0	2000	2020	3,552	60%
10,750 (time truncated) n=20	3*		2570	4,519	60%
7,166 (on-going) n=2	0		7790	13,632	60%
TOTAL FOR -2, -3					
19,786 n=47	3		4680 2900	8190 5075	60% 90%

* Failures include
1) Resettable Winchester control error
2) Winchester control error (marginal crystal oscillator)
3) Power supply failure

Table 3. Summary of Reliability Tests (continued)

-4 CONFIGURATION					
Operating Hours	Failures	MTBF Goal 35°C (in hours)	MTBF 35°C (in hours)	MTBF 25°C (in hours)	Confidence Level
13,992 (time truncated) n=14	2*	3156	4400	7700	60%
2,021 (on-going) n=2	0		2200	3850	60%
TOTAL FOR -4					
16,013 n=16	2		5100 3000	8925 5250	60% 90%

* Failures
  1) Flexible diskette drive intermittent
  2) Response failure; occurred once, no reoccurrence

-17 CONFIGURATION					
Operating Hours	Failures	MTBF Goal 35°C (in hours)	MTBF 35°C (in hours)	MTBF 25°C (in hours)	Confidence Level
13,434 (time truncated) n=13	4*	1960	2500	4375	60%
2,021 (on-going) n=2	0		2200	3850	60%
TOTAL FOR -17					
15,455 n=15	4		2875 1800	5031 3150	60% 90%

* Failures
  1) Winchester drive
  2) 215G intermittent
  3) System halt, user resettable
  4) RAM malfunction, user resettable

System Software   14

iRMX™ 86 OPERATING SYSTEM

- Real-time processor management for time-critical iAPX 86, iAPX 88, iAPX 186, iAPX 188, and iAPX 286 (Real Address Mode) applications
- On-target system development with Universal Development Interface (UDI)
- Configurable system size and function for diverse application requirements
- All iRMX™ 86 code can be (P)ROM'ed to support totally solid state designs
- Compatible operating system services for iAPX 86/30, 88/30, 186/30 and 188/30 Operating System Processors (iOSP™ 86)
- Configured systems for the iAPX 86 and iAPX 286 processors in Intel integrated system products (iSYS 86/300 and iSYS 286/300)
- Multi-terminal support with multi-user human interface
- Broad range of device drivers included for industry standard MULTIBUS® peripheral controllers
- Complete support of 8087 and 80287 processor extension
- Powerful utilities for interactive configuration and real-time debugging

The iRMX™ 86 Operating System is an easy-to-use, real-time, multi-tasking and multi-programming software system designed to manage and extend the resources of iSBC® 86, iSBC 88, iSBC 186, iSBC 188, and iSBC 286 Single Board Computers, as well as other iAPX 86, iAPX 88, iAPX 186, iAPX 188, and iAPX 286 (Real Address Mode) based microcomputers. iRMX 86 functions are available in silicon with the iAPX 86/30, 88/30, 186/30 and 188/30 Operating System Processors, in a user configurable software package. iRMX 86 functions are also fully integrated into the SYSTEM 86/300 and SYSTEM 286/300 Family of Microcomputer Systems. The Operating System provides a number of standard interfaces that allow iRMX 86 applications to take advantage of industry standard device controllers, hardware components, and a number of software packages developed by Independent Software Vendors (ISVs). Many high-performance features extend the utility of iRMX 86 Systems into applications such as data collection, transaction processing, and process control where immediate access to advances in VLSI technology is paramount. These systems may deliver real-time performance and explicit control over resources; yet also support applications with multiple users needing to simultaneously access terminals. The configurable layers of the System provide services ranging from interrupt management and standard device drivers for many sophisticated controllers, to data file maintenance commands provided by a comprehensive multi-user human interface. By providing access to the standard Universal Development Interface (UDI) for each user terminal, Original Equipment Manufacturers (OEMs) can pass program development and target application customization capabilities to their users.

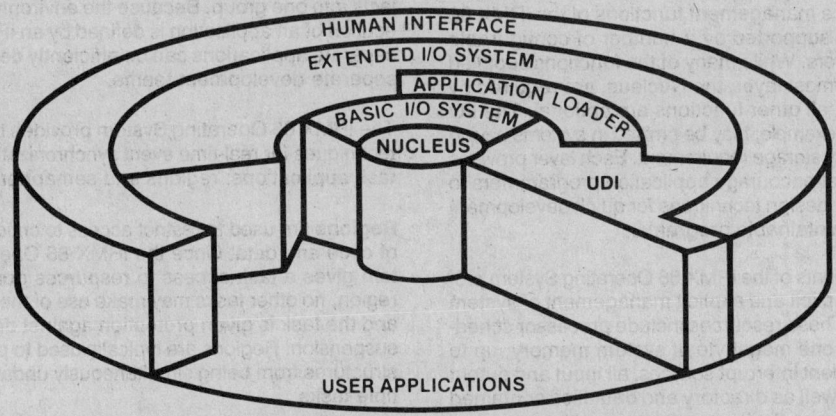

iRMX™ VLSI Operating System

The following are trademarks of Intel Corporation and may be used only to describe Intel products: Intel, ICE, iMMX, iRMX, iSBC, iSBX, iSXM, MULTIBUS, MULTICHANNEL, and MULTIMODULE. Intel Corporation assumes no responsibility for the use of any circuitry other than circuitry embodied in an Intel product. No other circuit patent licenses are implied. Information contained herein supercedes previously published specifications on these devices from Intel.

© INTEL CORPORATION, 1984   April, 1984   Order Number: 210885-002

iRMX™ 86 OPERATING SYSTEM

The iRMX 86 Operating System is a complete set of system software modules that provide the resource management functions needed by computer systems. These management functions allow Original Equipment Manufacturers (OEMs) to best use resources available in microcomputer systems while getting their products to market quickly, saving time and money. Engineers are relieved of writing complex system software and can concentrate instead on their application software.

This data sheet describes the major features of the iRMX 86 Operating System. The benefits provided to engineers who write application software and to users who want to take advantage of improving microcomputer price and performance are explained. The first section outlines the system resource management functions of the Operating System and describes several system calls. The second section gives a detailed overview of iRMX 86 features aimed at serving both the iRMX 86 system designer and programmer, as well as the end users of the product into which the Operating System is incorporated.

FUNCTIONAL DESCRIPTION

To take best advantage of iAPX 86, 88, 186, 188, and 286 (Real Address Mode) microprocessors in applications where the computer is required to perform many functions simultaneously, the iRMX 86 Operating System provides a multiprogramming environment in which many independent, multi-tasking application programs may run. The flexibility of independent environments allows application programmers to separately manage each application's resources during both the development and test phases.

The resource management functions of the iRMX 86 System are supported by a number of configurable software layers. While many of the functions supplied by the innermost layer, the Nucleus, are required by all systems, all other functions are optional. The I/O systems, for example, may be omitted in systems having no secondary storage requirement. Each layer provides functions that encourage application programmers to use modular design techniques for quick development of easily maintainable programs.

The components of the iRMX 86 Operating System provide both implicit and explicit management of system resources. These resources include processor scheduling, up to one megabyte of system memory, up to 57 independent interrupt sources, all input and output devices, as well as directory and data files contained on mass storage devices and accessed by a number of independent users. Management of these system resources and methods for sharing resources between multiple processors and users is discussed in the following sections.

Process Management

To implement multi-tasking application systems, programmers require a method of managing the different processes of their application, and for allowing the processes to communicate with each other. The Nucleus layer of the iRMX 86 System provides a number of facilities to efficiently manage these processes, and to effectively communicate between them. These facilities are provided by system calls that manipulate data structures called tasks, jobs, regions, semaphores and mailboxes. The iRMX 86 System refers to these structures as "objects".

Tasks are the basic element of all applications built on the iRMX 86 Operating System. Each task is an entity capable of executing CPU instructions and issuing system calls in order to perform a function. Tasks are characterized by their register values (including those of an optional 8087 or 80287 Numeric Processor Extension), a priority between 0 and 255, and the resources associated with them.

Each iRMX 86 task in the system is scheduled for operation by the iRMX 86 Nucleus. Figure 1 shows the five states in which each task may be placed, and some examples of how a task may move from one state to another. The iRMX 86 Nucleus ensures that each task is placed in the correct state, defined by the events in its external environment and by the task issuing system calls. Each task has a priority to indicate its relative importance and need to respond to its environment. The Nucleus guarantees that the highest priority ready-to-run task is the task that runs.

Jobs are used to define the operating environment of a group of tasks. Jobs effectively limit the scope of an application by collecting all of its tasks and other objects into one group. Because the environment for execution of an application is defined by an iRMX 86 job, separate applications can be efficiently developed by separate development teams.

The iRMX 86 Operating System provides two primary techniques for real-time event synchronization in multi-task applications: regions and semaphores.

Regions are used to restrict access to critical sections of code and data. Once the iRMX 86 Operating System gives a task access to resources guarded by a region, no other tasks may make use of the resources, and the task is given protection against deletion and suspension. Regions are typically used to protect data structures from being simultaneously updated by multiple tasks.

Semaphores are used to provide mutual exclusion between tasks. They contain abstract "units" that are sent between the tasks, and can be used to implement the cooperative sharing of resources.

iRMX™ 86 OPERATING SYSTEM

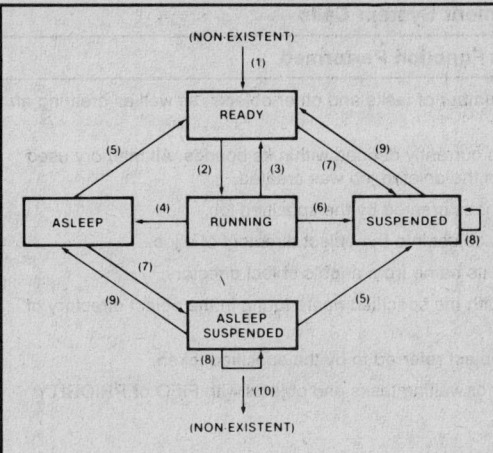

NOTES:
(1) Task is created
(2) Task becomes highest priority ready task
(3) Task gets pre-empted by one with higher priority
(4) Task calls SLEEP or task waits at an exchange
(5) Task sleep period has ended, message was sent to waiting task or wait has ended
(6) Task calls SUSPEND on self
(7) Task suspended by other than self
(8) Task suspended by other than self or a resume that did not bring suspension depth to zero
(9) Task was resumed by other task
(10) Task is deleted

Figure 1. Task State Diagram

Multi-tasking applications must communicate information and share system resources among cooperating tasks. The iRMX 86 Operating System assigns a unique 16-bit number, called a token, to each object created in the System. Any task in possession of this token is able to access the object. The iRMX 86 Nucleus allows tasks to gain access to objects, and hence system resources, at run-time with two additional mechanisms: mailboxes and object directories.

Mailboxes are used by tasks wishing to share objects with other tasks. A task may share an object by sending the object token via a mailbox. The receiving task can check to see if a token is there, or can wait at the mailbox until a token is present.

Object Directories are also used to make an object available to other tasks. An object is made public by cataloging its token and name in a directory. In this manner, any task can gain access to the object by knowing its name, and job environment that contains the directory.

Two example jobs are shown in Figure 2 to demonstrate how two tasks can share an object that was not

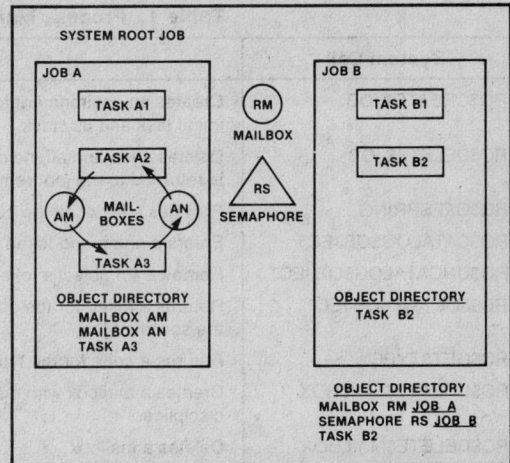

Figure 2. Multiple Jobs Example

known to the programmer at the time the tasks were developed. Both Job 'A' and Job 'B' exist within the environment of the 'Root Job' that forms the foundation of all iRMX 86 systems. Each job possesses a directory in which tasks may catalog the name of an object. Semaphore 'RS', for example, is accessable by all tasks in the system, because its name is cataloged in the directory of the Root Job. Mailbox 'AN' can be used to transfer objects between Tasks 'A2' and 'A3' because its token is accessable in the object directory for Job 'A'.

Table 1 lists the major functions of the iRMX 86 Nucleus that manage system processes.

Memory Management

Each job in an iRMX 86 System defines the amount of the one megabyte of addressable memory to be used by its tasks. The iRMX 86 Operating System manages system memory and allows jobs to share this critical resource by providing another object type: segments.

Segments are contiguous pieces of memory between 16 Bytes and 64K Bytes in length, that exist within the environment of the job in which they were created. Segments form the fundamental piece of system memory used for task stacks, data storage, system buffers, loading programs from secondary storage, passing information between tasks, etc.

The example in Figure 2 also demonstrates when information is shared between Tasks 'A2' and 'A3'; 'A2' only needs to create a segment, put the information in the memory allocated, and send it via the Mailbox 'AM' using the RQ$SEND$MESSAGE system call (see Table 1). Task 'A3' would get the message by using the RQ$RECEIVE$MESSAGE system call. The Figure also shows how the receiving task could signal the sending task by sending an acknowledgement via the second Mailbox 'AN'.

iRMX™ 86 OPERATING SYSTEM

Table 1. Process Management System Calls

System Call	Function Performed
RQ$CREATE$JOB	Creates an environment for a number of tasks and other objects, as well as creating an initial task and its stack.
RQ$DELETE$JOB	Deletes a job and all the objects currently defined within its bounds. All memory used is returned to the job from which the deleted job was created.
RQ$OFFSPRING	Provides a list of all the current jobs created by the specified job.
RQ$CATALOG$OBJECT	Enters a name and token for an object into the object directory of a job.
RQ$UNCATALOG$OBJECT	Removes an object's token and its name from a job's object directory.
RQ$LOOKUP$OBJECT	Returns a token for the object with the specified name found in the object directory of the specified job.
RQGETTYPE	Returns a code for the type of object referred to by the specified token.
RQ$CREATE$MAILBOX	Creates a mailbox with queues for waiting tasks and objects with FIFO or PRIORITY discipline.
RQ$DELETE$MAILBOX	Deletes a mailbox.
RQ$SEND$MESSAGE	Sends an object to a specified mailbox. If a task is waiting, the object is passed to the appropriate task according to the queuing discipline. If no task is waiting, the object is queued at the mailbox.
RQ$RECEIVE$MESSAGE	Attempts to receive an object token from a specified mailbox. The calling task may choose to wait for a specified number of system time units if no token is available.
RQ$DISABLE$DELETION	Prevents the deletion of a specified object by increasing its disable count by one.
RQ$ENABLE$DELETION	Reduces the disable count of an object by one, and if zero, enables deletion of that object.
RQ$FORCE$DELETE	Forces the deletion of a specified object if the disable count is either 0 or 1.
RQ$CREATE$TASK	Creates a task with the specified priority and stack area.
RQ$DELETE$TASK	Deletes a task from the system, and removes it from any queues in which it may be waiting.
RQ$SUSPEND$TASK	Suspends the operation of a task. If the task is already suspended, its suspension depth is increased by one.
RQ$RESUME$TASK	Resumes a task. If the task had been suspended multiple times, the suspension depth is reduced by one, and it remains suspended.
RQ$SLEEP	Causes a task to enter the ASLEEP state for a specified number of system time units.
RQGETTASK$TOKENS	Gets the token for the calling task or associated objects within its environment.
RQSETPRIORITY	Dynamically alters the priority of the specified task.
RQGETPRIORITY	Obtains the current priority of a specified task.
RQ$CREATE$REGION	Creates a region, with an associated queue of FIFO or PRIORITY ordering discipline.
RQ$DELETE$REGION	Deletes the specified region if it is not currently in use.
RQ$ACCEPT$CONTROL	Gains control of a region only if the region is immediately available.
RQ$RECEIVE$CONTROL	Gains control of a region. The calling task may specify the number of system time units it wishes to wait if the region is not immediately available.
RQ$SEND$CONTROL	Relinquishes control of a region.
RQ$CREATE$SEMAPHORE	Creates a semaphore.
RQ$DELETE$SEMAPHORE	Deletes a semaphore.
RQ$SEND$UNITS	Increases a semaphore counter by the specified number of units.
RQ$RECEIVE$UNITS	Attempts to gain a specified number of units from a semaphore. If the units are not immediately available, the calling task may choose to wait.

iRMX™ 86 OPERATING SYSTEM

Each job is created with both maximum and minimum limits set for its memory pool. Memory required by all objects and resources created in the job is taken from this pool. If more memory is required, a job may be allowed to borrow memory from the pool of its containing job (the job from which it was created). In this manner, initial jobs may efficiently allocate memory to jobs they subsequently create, without knowing their exact requirements.

The iRMX 86 Operating System supplies other memory managment functions to search specific address ranges for available memory. The System performs this search at system initialization, and can be configured to ignore non-existent memory and addresses reserved for I/O devices and other application requirements.

Table 2 lists the major system calls used to manage the system memory.

Interrupt Management

Real-time systems, by their nature, must respond to asynchronous and unpredictable events quickly. The iRMX 86 Operating System uses interrupts and the event-driven Nucleus described earlier to give real-time response to events. Use of a pre-emptive scheduling technique ensures that the servicing of high priority events always takes precedence over other system activities.

The iRMX 86 Operating System gives applications the flexibility to optimize either interrupt response time or interrupt response capability by providing two tiers of Interrupt Management. These two distinct tiers are managed by Interrupt Handlers and Interrupt Tasks.

Interrupt Handlers are the first tier of interrupt service. For small simple functions, interrupt handlers are often the most efficient means of responding to an event. They provide faster response than interrupt tasks, but must be kept simple since interrupts (except the iAPX 86, 88, 186, 188, and 286 non-maskable interrupt) are masked during their execution. When extended service is required, interrupt handlers "signal" a waiting interrupt task that, in turn, performs more complicated functions.

Interrupt Tasks are distinct tasks whose priority is associated with a hardware interrupt level. They are permitted to make any iRMX 86 system call. While an interrupt task is servicing an interrupt, interrupts of lower priority are not allowed to pre-empt the system.

Table 3 shows the iRMX 86 System Calls provided to manage interrupts.

Table 2. Memory Management System Calls

System Call	Function Performed
RQ$CREATE$SEGMENT	Dynamically allocates a memory segment of the specified size.
RQ$DELETE$SEGMENT	Deletes the specified segment by deallocating the memory.
RQGETPOOL$ATTRIBUTES	Returns attributes such as the minimum and maximum, as well as current size of the memory in the environment of the calling task's job.
RQGETSIZE	Returns the size (in bytes) of a segment.
RQSETPOOL$MIN	Dynamically changes the minimum memory requirements of the job environment containing the calling task.

Table 3. Interrupt Management System Calls

System Call	Function Performed
RQSETINTERRUPT	Assigns an interrupt handler and, if desired, an interrupt task to the specified interrupt level. Usually the calling task becomes the interrupt task.
RQ$RESET$INTERRUPT	Disables an interrupt level, and cancels the assignment of the interrupt handler for that level. If an interrupt task was assigned, it is deleted.
RQGETLEVEL	Returns the number of the highest priority interrupt level currently being processed.
RQ$SIGNAL$INTERRUPT	Used by an interrupt handler to signal the associated interrupt task that an interrupt has occurred.
RQ$WAIT$INTERRUPT	Used by an interrupt task to SLEEP until the associated interrupt handler signals the occurrence of an interrupt.
RQ$EXIT$INTERRUPT	Used by an interrupt handler to relinquish control of the System.
RQ$ENABLE	Enables the hardware to accept interrupts from a specified level.
RQ$DISABLE	Disables the hardware from accepting interrupts at or below a specified level.

iRMX™ 86 OPERATING SYSTEM

INTERRUPT MANAGEMENT EXAMPLE

Figure 3 illustrates how the iRMX 86 Interrupt System may be used to output strings of characters to a printer. In the example, a mailbox named 'PRINT' is used by all tasks in the system to queue messages to be printed. Application tasks put the characters in segments that are transmitted to the printer interrupt task via the PRINT Mailbox. Once printing is complete, the same interrupt task passes the messages on to another application via the FINISHED Mailbox so that an operator message can be displayed.

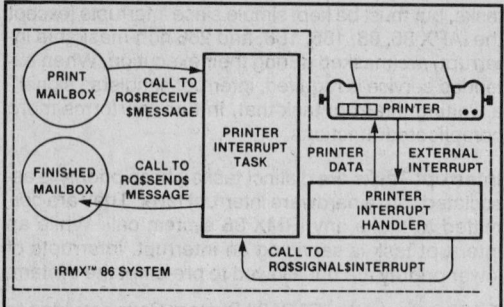

Figure 3. Interrupt Management Example

Basic I/O System

The Basic I/O System (BIOS) provides the direct access to I/O devices needed by real-time applications. The BIOS allows I/O functions to overlap other system functions. In this manner, application tasks make asynchronous calls to the iRMX 86 BIOS, and proceed to perform other activities. When the I/O request must be completed before an application can continue, the task waits at a mailbox for the result of the operation.

Some system calls provided by the BIOS are listed in Table 4.

The Basic I/O System communicates with peripheral devices through device drivers. These device drivers provide the System with four basic functions needed to control and communicate with devices: Initialize I/O, Finish I/O, Queue I/O, and Cancel I/O. Using the device driver interface, users of non-standard devices may write custom drivers compatible with the I/O System.

The iRMX 86 Operating System includes a number of device drivers to allow applications to use standard USART serial communications devices, multiple CRTs and keyboards, bubble memories, diskettes, disks, a Centronics-type parallel printer, and many of Intel's iSBC and iSBX™ device controllers (see Table 8). If an application requires use of a non-standard device, users need only write a device driver to be included with the BIOS, and access it as if it were part of the standard system. For most common random-access devices, this job is further simplified by using standard routines provided with the System. Use of this technique ensures that applications can remain device independent.

Multi-Terminal Support

The iRMX 86 Terminal Support provides line editing and terminal control capabilities. The Terminal Support communicates with devices through simple drivers that do only character I/O functions. Dynamic terminal reconfiguration is provided so that attributes such as terminal type and line speed may be changed without modifying the application or the Operating System. Dynamic configuration may be typed in, generated programmatically or stored in a file and copied to a terminal I/O connection.

Table 4. Key BIOS I/O Management System Calls

System Call	Function Performed
RQAATTACH$FILE	Creates a Connection to an existing file.
RQACHANGE$ACCESS	Changes the types of accesses permitted to the specified user(s) for a specific file.
RQACLOSE	Closes the Connection to the specified file so that it may be used again, or so that the type of access may be changed.
RQACREATE$DIRECTORY	Creates a Named File used to store the names and locations of other Named Files.
RQACREATE$FILE	Creates a data file with the specified access rights.
RQADELETE$CONNECTION	Deletes the Connection to the specified file.
RQAGET$FILE$STATUS	Returns the current status of a specified file.
RQAOPEN	Opens a file for either read, write, or update access.
RQAREAD	Reads a number of bytes from the current position in a specified file.
RQASEEK	Moves the current data pointer of a Named or Physical file.
RQAWRITE	Writes a number of bytes at the current position in a file.
RQ$WAIT$IO	Synchronizes a task with the I/O System by causing it to wait for I/O operation results.

iRMX™ 86 OPERATING SYSTEM

The iRMX 86 Terminal Support provides automatic translation of control characters to specific control sequences for each terminal. This translation enables applications using standard control characters to function with non-standard terminals. The translation requirements for each terminal can be stored in terminal description files and copied to a connection, as described above.

Disk I/O Performance

Figure 4 shows iRMX 86 performance obtained using the iSBC 215 Winchester Disk and iSBX 218A Diskette Controllers under the specified conditions. The vertical axis is a linear scale of throughput in units of 10,000 bytes per second. The horizontal axis is a logrithmic scale showing the transfer size for the reads and writes. Each data point on the graph indicates the time required for a read/write request of 64K bytes. Therefore each transfer size on the horizontal scale less than 64K was repeated until a total request of 64K was read or written.

Each device driver can be used to interface to a number of separate and, in some cases, different devices (see Figure 5). The iSBC 215 Device Driver, supplied with the system, is capable of supporting the iSBC 215 Winchester Disk Controller, the iSBC 220 SMD Disk Controller, and the iSBX 218A Flexible Disk Controller (when mounted on an iSBC 215 board). Each device controller may, in turn, control a number of separate device units. In addition, each driver may control a number of like device controllers. This capability allows the use of large storage systems with a minimum of I/O system code to write or maintain.

Extended I/O System

The iRMX 86 Extended I/O System (EIOS) adds a number of I/O management capabilities to simplify access to files. Whereas the BIOS provides users with the basic system calls needed for direct management of I/O resources, many users prefer to have the system perform all the buffering and synchronization of I/O requests automatically. The EIOS allows users to access I/O devices without having to write procedures for buffering data, or to specify particular devices with constant device names.

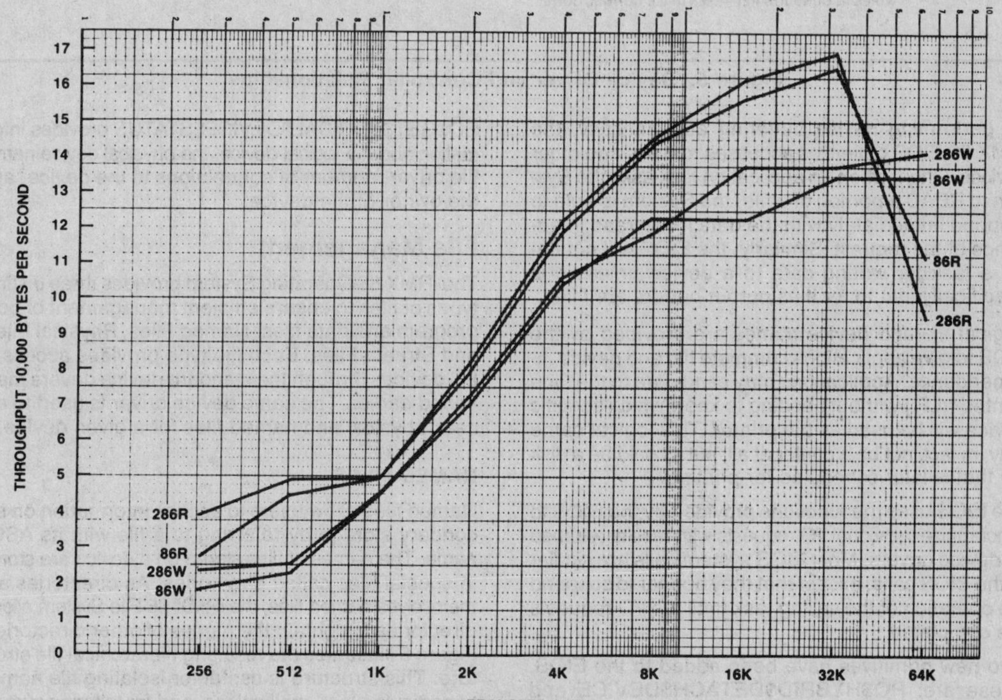

Figure 4. iRMX™ 86 Disk I/O Performance

iRMX™ 86 OPERATING SYSTEM

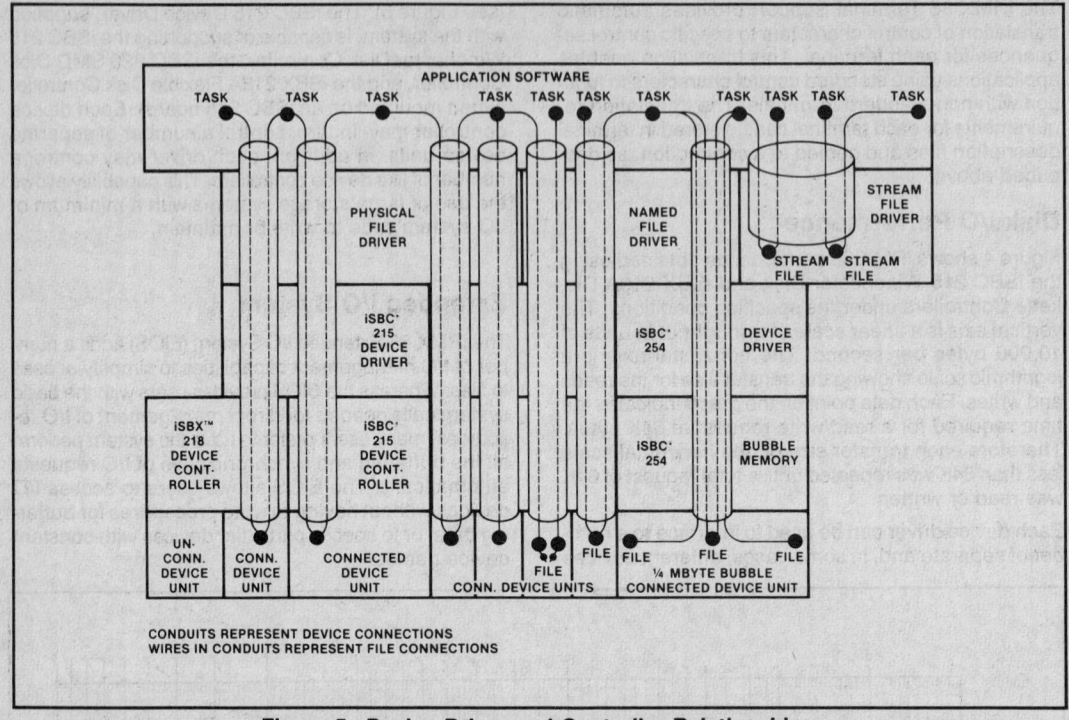

Figure 5. Device Driver and Controller Relationships

By performing device buffering automatically, the iRMX 86 EIOS optimizes accesses to disks and other devices. Often, when an application task asks the System to READ a portion of a file, the System is able to respond immediately with the data it has read in advance of the request. Similarly, the EIOS will not delay a task for writing data to a device unless it is specifically told to, or if its output buffers are filled.

Logical file and device names are provided by the EIOS to give applications complete file and device independence. Applications may send data to the 'line printer' (:LP:) without needing to know which specific device will be used as the printer. This logical name may, in fact, not be a printer at all, but it could be a disk file that is later scheduled for printing.

The EIOS uses the functions provided by the BIOS to synchronize individual I/O requests with results returned by device drivers. Most EIOS system calls are similar to the BIOS calls, except that they appear to suspend the operation of the calling task until the I/O requests are completed.

Two new primitives have been added to the EIOS. These are: RQ$HYBRID$DETACH$DEVICE and RQ$GET$LOGICAL$DEVICE$STATUS.

RQ$HYBRID$DETACH$DEVICE allows a programmer to temporarily detach a device physically so it can be temporarily attached another way.

RQGETLOGICAL$DEVICE$STATUS provides information about a logical device: the physical device name, file driver, number of connections to the device, and the owner of the device.

File Management

The iRMX 86 Operating System provides three distinct types of files to ensure efficient management of both program and data files: Named Files, Physical Files, and Stream Files. Each file type provides access to I/O devices through the standard device drivers mentioned earlier. The same device driver is used to access physical and named files for a given device.

NAMED FILES

Named files allow users to access information on secondary storage by referring to a file with its ASCII name. The names of files stored on a device are stored in special files called directories. As directories are themselves named files, the iRMX 86 File System allows directories to contain the names of other directories. Figure 6 illustrates the resulting hierarchical file structure. This structure is useful for isolating file names to particular user applications, and for tailoring system data to the requirements of users and applications sharing storage devices. Using different branches on the directory tree, different users do not have to coordinate in naming their files to ensure unique names.

iRMX™ 86 OPERATING SYSTEM

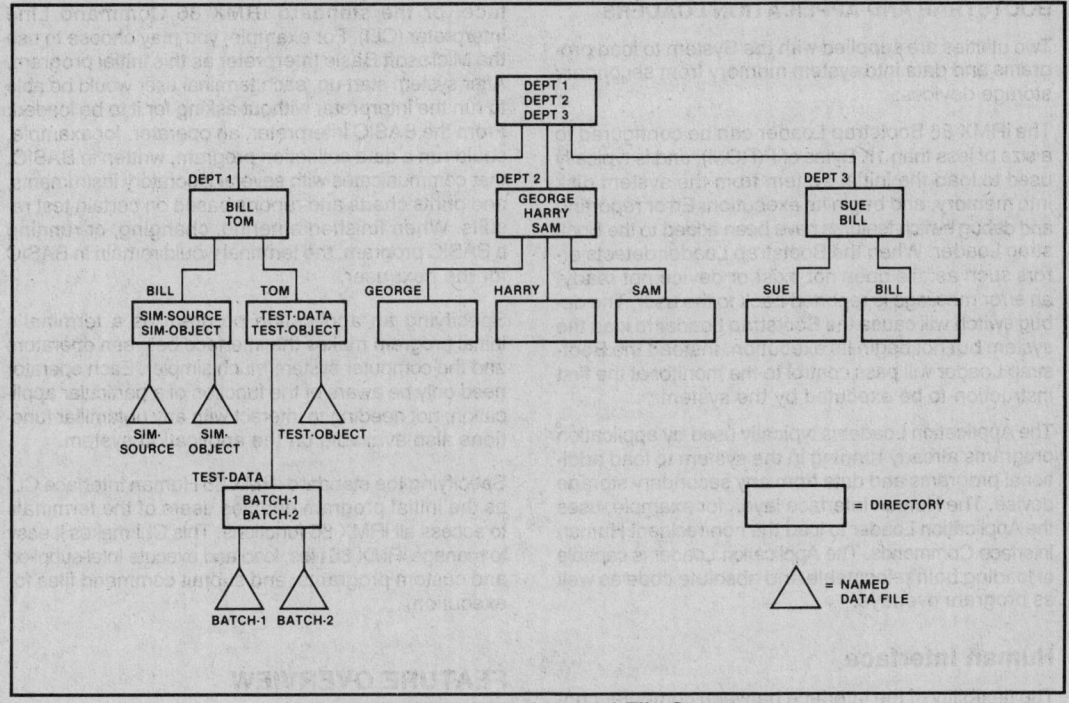

Figure 6. Hierarchical Named File Structure

Whenever a request is made involving a file name, the System will search the appropriate directory in order to find the necessary information about the file's size, access rights, and specific location on the storage device.

The iRMX 86 BIOS uses an efficient format for writing the directory and data information into secondary storage. This standard iRMX 86 format is fully compatible with the ISO Media standard, and other Intel systems such as the iRMX 88 Operating System. This structure enables the system to directly access any byte in a file, often without having to do additional I/O to access space allocation information. The maximum size of an individual file is 4.3 billion bytes.

EASE OF ACCESS

The hierarchical file structure is provided to isolate and organize collections of named files. To give operators fast and simple access to any level within the file tree, an ATTACHFILE command is provided. This command allows operators to create a logical name to a point in the tree so that a long sequence of characters need not be typed each time a file is referred to.

ACCESS PROTECTION

Access to each Named File is protected by the rights assigned to each user by the owner of the file. Rights to read, append, update, and delete may be selectively granted to other users of the system. In general, users of Named Files are classified into one of two categories: User and World. Users are used when different programmers and programs need to share information stored in a file. The World classification is used when rights are to be granted to all who can use the system.

PHYSICAL FILES

Physical Files allow more direct device access than Named Files. Each Physical File occupies an entire device, treated as a single stream of individually accessable bytes. No access control is provided for Physical Files as they are typically used for such applications as driving a printing device, translating from one device format to another, driving a paper tape device, realtime data acquisition, and controlling analog mechanisms.

STREAM FILES

Stream Files provide applications with a method of using iRMX 86 file management methods for data that does not need to go into secondary storage. Stream Files act as direct channels, through system memory, from one task to another. These channels are very useful to programs, for example, wishing to preserve file and device independence allowing data sent to a printer one time, to a disk file another time, and to another program on a different occasion.

iRMX™ 86 OPERATING SYSTEM

BOOTSTRAP AND APPLICATION LOADERS

Two utilities are supplied with the System to load programs and data into system memory from secondary storage devices:

The iRMX 86 Bootstrap Loader can be configured to a size of less than 1K Bytes of P(ROM), and is typically used to load the initial system from the system disk into memory, and begin its execution. Error reporting and debug switch features have been added to the Bootstrap Loader. When the Bootstrap Loader detects errors such as: file does not exist or device not ready, an error message is reported back to the user. The debug switch will cause the Bootstrap Loader to load the system but not begin its execution. Instead the Bootstrap Loader will pass control to the monitor at the first instruction to be executed by the system.

The Application Loader is typically used by application programs already running in the system to load additional programs and data from any secondary storage device. The Human Interface layer, for example, uses the Application Loader to load the non-resident Human Interface Commands. The Application Loader is capable of loading both relocatable and absolute code as well as program overlays.

Human Interface

The flexibility of the interface between computer controlled machines and their users often determines the usability and ultimate success of the machines. Table 11 lists iRMX 86 Human Interface functions giving users and applications simple access to the file and system management capabilities described earlier. The process, interrupt, and memory managment functions described earlier, are performed automatically for Human Interface users.

MULTI-USER ACCESS

Using the multi-terminal support provided by the BIOS, the iRMX 86 Human Interface can support several simultaneous users. The real-time nature of the system is maintained by providing a priority for each user, and using the event-driven iRMX 86 Nucleus to schedule tasks. High-performance interrupt response is guaranteed even while users interact with various application packages. For example, multi-terminal support allows one person to be using the iRMX 86 Editor, while another compiles a FORTRAN 86 or PASCAL 86 program, while several others load and access applications.

Each terminal attached to the iRMX 86 multi-user Human Interface is automatically associated with a user, a memory pool, and an initial program to run when the terminal is connected. This association is made using a file that may be changed at any time. Changes are effective the next time the system is initialized.

The initial program specified for each terminal can be a special application program, a custom Human Interface, or the standard iRMX 86 Command Line Interpreter (CLI). For example, you may choose to use the Microsoft Basic Interpreter as this initial program. After system start-up, each terminal user would be able to run the interpreter without asking for it to be loaded. From the BASIC interpreter, an operator, for example, could run a data collection program, written in BASIC, that communicates with several laboratory instruments, and prints charts and reports based on certain test results. When finished entering, changing, or running a BASIC program, the terminal would remain in BASIC for the next user.

Specifying an application program as a terminal's initial program makes the interface between operators and the computer system much simpler. Each operator need only be aware of the function of a particular application; not needing to interact with any unfamiliar functions also available on the application system.

Specifying the standard iRMX 86 Human Interface CLI as the initial program enables users of the terminals to access all iRMX 86 functions. This CLI makes it easy to manage iRMX 86 files, load and execute Intel-supplied and custom programs, and submit command files for execution.

FEATURE OVERVIEW

The iRMX 86 Operating System is well suited to serve the demanding needs of real-time applications executing on complex microprocessor systems. The iRMX 86 System also provides many tools and features needed by real-time system developers and programmers. The following sections describe features useful in both the development and execution environments. The description of each feature outlines the advantages given to hardware and software engineers concerned with overall system cost, expandability with custom and industry standard options, and long-term maintenance of iRMX 86-based systems. The development environment features also describe the ease with which the iRMX 86 Operating System can be incorporated into overall system designs.

Execution Environment Features

REAL-TIME PERFORMANCE

The iRMX 86 Operating System is designed to offer the high performance, multi-tasking functions required by real-time systems. Designers can make use of the latest VLSI devices such as the 8087 or 80287 Numeric Processor Extension, and the 80130 Operating System Firmware Component to improve their system cost/performance ratio or the iMMX™ 800 MULTIBUS® Message Exchange software package to divide and coordinate various system activities among multiple processors. Typical iRMX 86 system performance characteristics are shown in Table 5.

iRMX™ 86 OPERATING SYSTEM

Many real-time systems require high performance operation. To meet this requirement, all of iRMX 86 can be put into zero wait-state P(ROM). This approach eliminates the possibility of disk access times slowing down performance, while allowing system designers to take advantage of high performance memory devices.

CONFIGURABILITY

The iRMX 86 Operating System is configurable by system layer, and by system call within each layer. In addition all the I/O port addresses used by the System are configurable by the user. This flexibility gives designers the freedom to choose configurations of hardware and software that best suit their size and functional requirements. Two example configurations are shown in Figure 7.

Table 5. iRMX™ Real-Time Performance Using iSBC® 86/30 and iSBC® 286/10 Single Board Computers

Real-Time Function	iSBC® 86/30 Execution Time (msec)	iSBC® 286/10 Execution Time (msec)
Suspend Task	1.02	0.83
Interrupt Latency (to handler)	0.29 (Max)	0.20 (Max)
Interrupt Latency (to handler)	0.02 (Typical)	0.03 (Typical)
Context Switch Caused By Interrupt	0.84 (Max)	0.78 (Max)
Send Message (no context switch)	0.32	0.25
Send Message (with context switch)	0.58	0.49
Send Control (no context switch)	0.21	0.16
Send Control (with context switch)	0.64	0.54
Receive Control (no waiting)	0.26	0.19

Context switch time is the time between executing in the context of a task, and the first instruction to execute in the context of another task.

The execution times shown in Column 2 were measured using an 8MHz iSBC Single Board Computer, 256K on-board RAM, and all program and data stored in on-board RAM.

The execution times shown in Column 3 were measured using a 5MHz iSBC 286/10 Single Board Computer, no on-board RAM, and all program and data stored in LBX RAM.

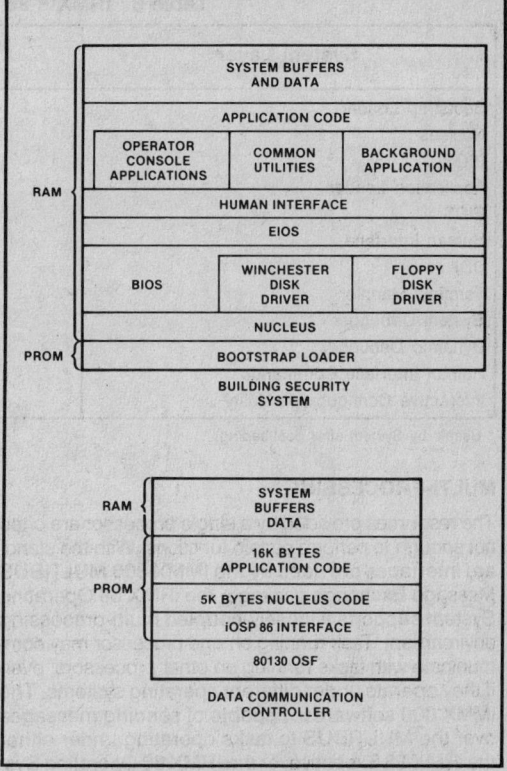

Figure 7. Typical iRMX™ 86 Configurations

Most configuration options are selected during system design stages. Others may be selected during system operation. For example, the amount of memory devoted to queues within a Mailbox can be specified at the time the Mailbox is created. Devoting more memory to the Mailbox allows more messages to be transmitted to other tasks without having to degrade system performance to allocate additional memory dynamically.

The chart shown in Table 6 indicates the actual memory size required to support these different configurations of the iRMX 86 System. Systems requiring only Nucleus level functions may require no more than 13K bytes for the Operating System. (Use of the iAPX 86/30 requires only 4K bytes of RAM, 7K bytes of initialization code in EPROM and the 16K bytes of code in the 80130.) Other applications, needing I/O management functions, may select portions of additional layers that fit their needs and size constraints.

This configurability also applies to the Terminal Handler, Dynamic Debugger, and System Debugger. The Terminal Handler provides a serial terminal interface in a system that otherwise doesn't need an I/O system. Either one of the debuggers need to be included only as debugging tools (usually only during system development).

iRMX™ 86 OPERATING SYSTEM

Table 6. iRMX™ 86 Configuration Size Chart

System Layer	Min. ROMable Size	Max. Size	Data Size
Bootstrap Loader	1K	1.5K	6K*
Nucleus	10.5K	24K	2K
BIOS	26K	78K	1K
Application Loader	4K	10K	2K
EIOS	10.5K	12.5K	1K
Human Interface	22K	22K	15K
UDI	8K	8K	0
Terminal Handler	3K	3K	0.3K
System Debugger	20K	20K	1K
Dynamic Debugger	28.5K	28.5K	1K
Human Interface Commands			116K
Interactive Configuration Utility			308K

* Usable by System after bootloading.

MULTI-PROCESSING

The resources provided by a single processor are often not enough to perform certain functions. With the standard interfaces provided by the iMMX 800 MULTIBUS Message Exchange package, the iRMX 86 Operating System supports a loosely-coupled multi-processing environment. Task running on one processor may communicate with tasks running on other processors, even if they operate under different operating systems. The iMMX 800 software is capable of sending messages over the MULTIBUS to tasks operating under either the iRMX 88 Executive, or the iRMX 86 Operating System. Using this message exchange mechanism, applications may increase their system performance quite easily, improve overall interrupt response, gain access to the iSBC® 550 Ethernet Controller, and leave room for future product enhancements.

MULTI-USER ACCESS

Many real-time systems must provide a variety of users access to system control functions and collected data. The iRMX 86 System provides easy-to-use support for applications to access multiple terminals. It also enables multiple and different users to access different applications concurrently.

Figure 8 illustrates a typical iRMX 86 application simultaneously supporting multi-terminal data collection and real-time environments. Shown is a group of terminals used by machinists on a shop floor to communicate with a job management program, a building security system that constantly monitors energy usage requirements, a system operator console capable of accessing all system functions, and a group of terminals in the Production Engineering department used to monitor job costs while developing new device control specifications instructions. The iSBC 544 Intelligent Terminal Interface supports multiple user terminals without degrading system performance to handle character I/O.

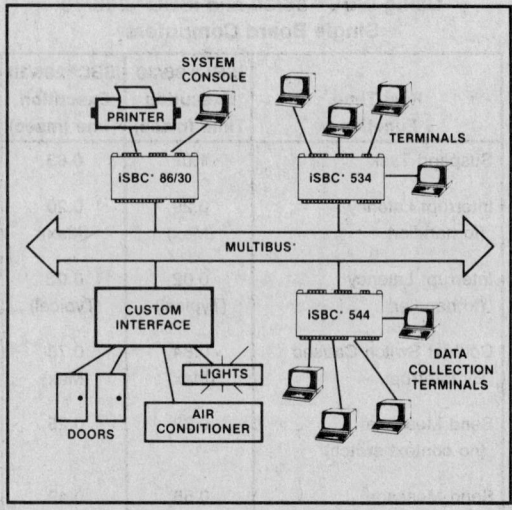

Figure 8. Multi-Terminal and Multi-User Real-Time System

EXTENDABILITY

The iRMX 86 Operating System provides three means of extensions. This extendability is essential for support of OEM and volume end user value added features. This ability is provided by: user-defined operating system calls, user-defined objects (similar to Jobs, Tasks, etc.), and the ability to add functions later in the product life cycle. The modular, layered structure of the System easily facilitates later additions to iRMX 86 applications. User-defined objects are supported by the functions listed in Table 7.

Using standard iRMX 86 system calls, users may define custom objects, enabling applications to easily manipulate commonly used structures as if they were part of the original operating system.

iRMX™ 86 OPERATING SYSTEM

Table 7. User Extension System Calls

System Call	Function Performed
RQ$CREATE$COMPOSITE	Creates a custom object built of previously defined objects.
RQ$DELETE$COMPOSITE	Deletes the custom object, but not the various objects from which it was built.
RQ$INSPECT$COMPOSITE	Returns a list of Token Identifiers for the component objects from which the specified composite object is built.
RQ$ALTER$COMPOSITE	Replaces a component object of a composite object.
RQ$CREATE$EXTENSION	Creates a new type of object and assigns a mailbox used for collecting these objects when they are deleted.
RQ$DELETE$EXTENSION	Deletes an extension definition.

EXCEPTION HANDLING

The System includes predefined exception handlers for typical I/O and parameter error conditions. The error handling mechanism is both configurable and extendable.

SUPPORT OF STANDARDS

The iRMX 86 Operating System supports the many hardware and software standards needed by most application systems to ensure that commonly available hardware and software packages may be interfaced with a minimum of cost and effort. The iRMX 86 System supports the iSBC family of products built on the Intel MULTIBUS (IEEE Standard 796), and a number of standard software interfaces such as the UDI and the common device driver interface (See Figure 9). The procedural interfaces of the UDI are listed in Table 9.

The Operating System includes support for the proposed IEEE 80-bit extended real-variable format of the 8087 Numeric Data Processor, and the IEEE 796 (MULTIBUS) hardware interface. Other standards such as the iMMX 800 MULTIBUS Message Exchange, and an Ethernet communication interface are supported by optional software packages available to run on the iRMX 86 System.

SPECTRUM OF CPU PERFORMANCE

The iRMX 86 Operating System supports a broad range of Intel processors. In addition to support for iAPX 86 and 88 based systems, the iRMX 86 system has been enhanced to support iAPX 186, 188, and 286 (Real Address Mode)-based Systems. This new support enables the user to take advantage of the faster speed and higher performance of Intel's 286 based microprocessors such as the iSBC 286/10 single board computer. By choosing the appropriate CPU, designers can choose from a wide range of performance options, without having to change application software.

COMPONENT LEVEL SUPPORT

The iRMX 86 System may be tailored to support specific hardware configurations. In addition to system memory,

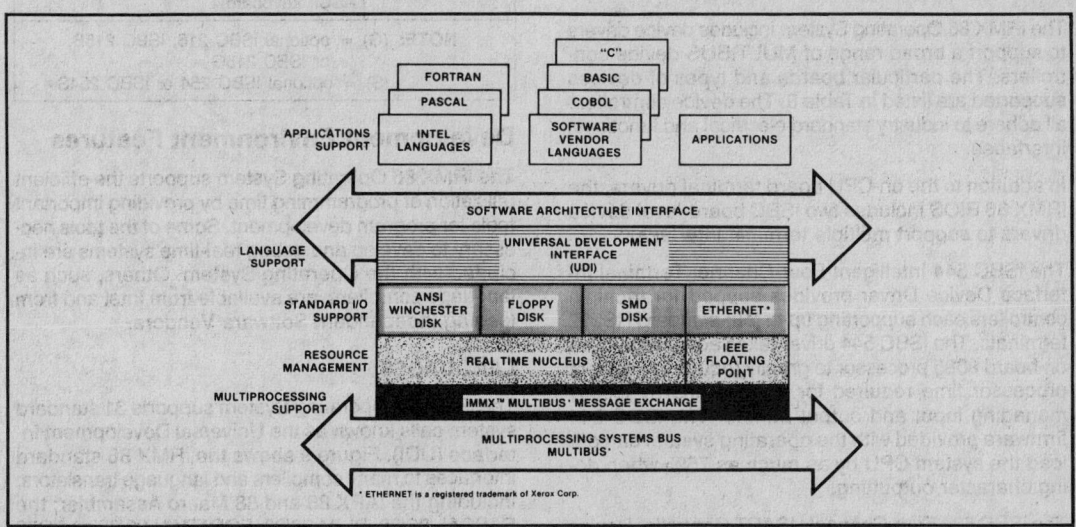

Figure 9. iRMX™ 86 Standard Interfaces

iRMX™ 86 OPERATING SYSTEM

only an iAPX 86, iAPX 88, iAPX 186, iAPX 188, or iAPX 286 microprocessor, an 8259A Programmable Interrupt Controller (PIC), and either an 8253, 8274, or 82530 Programmable Interval Timer (PIT) are required as follows:

- iAPX 86 and iAPX 88 systems need either:
  - 8253 PIT and 8259A PIC (master) or
  - 80130 firmware (PIC is master)

- iAPX 186 and iAPX 188 systems where 186 PIC is slave, needs either:
  - 8253 PIT and 8259A PIC (master) or
  - 80130 firmware (PIC is master)

  where 186 PIC is master:
  - Uses 186 PIT for the system clock; no external PIT is needed
  - Can use either
    186 PIC (master) only or
    8259A/80130 PIC (slave)

- iAPX 286 systems need
  - 8253 PIT and 8259A PIC.

Alternatively, the iRMX 86 Operating System may be used in conjunction with the 80130 Operating System Firmware Component that not only provides these hardware functions, but eliminates the need for approximately 16K bytes of the iRMX 86 Nucleus code (see Figure 7). For systems requiring extended mathematics capability, an 8087 or 80287 Numeric Data Processor may be added to perform these functions up to 100 times faster than equivalent software. For applications servicing more than 8 interrupt sources, additional 8259A's may be configured as slave controllers.

BOARD LEVEL SUPPORT

The iRMX 86 Operating System includes device drivers to support a broad range of MULTIBUS device controllers. The particular boards and types of devices supported are listed in Table 8. The device controllers all adhere to industry standard electrical and functional interfaces.

In addition to the on-CPU board terminal drivers, the iRMX 86 BIOS includes two iSBC board-level device drivers to support multiple terminal interfaces:

The iSBC 544 Intelligent Four-Channel Terminal Interface Device Driver provides support for multiple controllers each supporting up to four standard RS232 terminals. The iSBC 544 driver takes advantage of an on-board 8085 processor to greatly reduce the system processor time required for terminal I/O by locally managing input and output buffers. The iSBC 544 firmware provided with the operating system can off-load the system CPU by as much as 75% when doing character outputting.

The iSBC 534 Four-Channel USART Controller Device Driver also provides support for multiple controller boards each supporting up to four standard RS232 terminals.

The new RAM disk feature in iRMX 86 makes a portion of the memory address space look like a disk drive to the I/O system.

Table 8. Supported Devices

iSBC® Device Controller	Description
iSBC® 86,88	Serial Port to CRT, Parallel Port to Centronics-type Printer, Interval Timer and Interrupt Controller.
iSBC® 186/03	Small Computer System Interface (SCSI) Supporting All Random Access "Extended Standard" SCSI/SASI hard disk controllers.
iSBC® 204	Single Density Diskette.
iSBC® 206	Cartridge-Type Hard Disk.
iSBC® 208	Single & Double Density, Single & Double Sided, 8" & 5.25" Diskettes.
iSBC® 215(G)	Standard Winchester Disks.
iSBX® 218	Single or Double density, Single or double sided, 8-inch diskettes (when used on an iSBC 215(G)).
iSBX® 218A	Single or Double Density, Single or Double Sided, 8" & 5.25" Diskette (when used on an iSBC 215G Winchester Controller).
iSBC® 220	Standard Storage Module Board.
iSBX® 251	Bubble Memory Multimodule Board.
iSBC® 254(S)	Bubble Memory Board.
iSBX® 351	1-Channel Serial Port to CRTs, Modems.
iSBC® 534,544	4-Channel Serial Ports to CRTs, Modems.
iSBX™ 270	Black and White CRTs and full ASCII keyboards.

NOTE: (G) = optional iSBC 215, iSBC 215B, or iSBC 215G
(S) = optional iSBC 254 or iSBC 254S

Development Environment Features

The iRMX 86 Operating System supports the efficient utilization of programming time by providing important tools for program development. Some of the tools necessary to develop and debug real-time systems are included with the Operating System. Others, such as language compilers, are available from Intel and from leading Independent Software Vendors.

LANGUAGES

The iRMX 86 Operating System supports 31 standard system calls known as the Universal Development Interface (UDI). Figure 9 shows the iRMX 86 standard interfaces to many compilers and language translators, including the iAPX 86 and 88 Macro Assembler; the PASCAL 86/88, PL/M 86/88, FORTRAN 86/88 and C86 compilers available from Intel. Also included are other

iRMX™ 86 OPERATING SYSTEM

Intel development tools, language translators and utilities available from other vendors. Any application that ran on the iRMX 86 Release 5 Universal Runtime Interface (URI) will run on the iRMX 86 Release 6 UDI. The full set of UDI calls (which includes the URI system calls) is required to run a compiler.

These standard software interfaces (the UDI) ensure that users of the iRMX 86 Operating System may transport their applications to future releases of the iRMX 86 Operating System and other Intel and independent vendor software products. The calls available in the UDI are shown in Table 9.

Table 9. UDI System Calls

System Call	Function Performed
Memory Management:	
DQ$ALLOCATE	Creates a Segment of a specified size.
DQ$FREE	Returns the specified segment to the System.
DQGETSIZE*	Returns the size of the specified Segment.
DQ$RESERVE$IO$MEMORY*	Reserves memory to OPEN and ATTACH files.
File Management:	
DQ$ATTACH	Creates a Connection to a specified file.
DQ$CHANGE$ACCESS*	Changes the user access rights associated with a file or directory.
DQ$CHANGE$EXTENSION	Changes the extension of a file name in memory.
DQ$CLOSE	Closes the specified file Connection.
DQ$CREATE	Creates a Named File.
DQ$DELETE	Deletes a Named File.
DQ$DETACH	Closes a Named File and deletes its Connection.
DQ$OPEN	Opens a file for a particular type of access.
DQGETCONNECTION$STATUS*	Returns the current status of the specified file Connection
DQ$FILE$INFO*	Returns data about a file Connection.
DQ$READ	Reads the next sequence of bytes from a file.
DQ$RENAME*	Renames the specified Named File.
DQ$SEEK	Moves the position pointer of a file.
DQ$TRUNCATE	Truncates a file.
DQ$WRITE	Writes a sequence of bytes to a file.
Process Management:	
DQ$EXIT	Exits from the current application job.
DQ$OVERLAY*	Causes the specified overlay to be loaded.
DQ$SPECIAL	Performs special I/O related functions on terminals with special control features.
DQ$TRAP$CC	Captures control when CNTRL/C is typed.
Exception Handling:	
DQGETEXCEPTION$HANDLER	Returns a pointer to the program currently being used to process errors.
DQ$DECODE$EXCEPTION	Returns a short description of the specified error code.
DQ$TRAP$EXCEPTION	Identifies a custom exception processing program for a particular type of error.
Application Assistance:	
DQ$DECODE$TIME	Returns system time and date in binary and ASCII character format.
DQGETARGUMENT*	Returns the next argument from the character string used to invoke the application program.
DQGETSYSTEM$ID*	Returns the name of the underlying operating system supporting the UDI.
DQGETTIME*	Returns the current time of day as kept by the underlying operating system.
DQ$SWITCH$BUFFER	Selects a new buffer from which to process commands.

* Calls available only through the UDI.

iRMX™ 86 OPERATING SYSTEM

The high performance of the iRMX 86 Operating System enhances the throughput of compilers and other development utilities. Table 10 indicates the average performance of typical development environment functions operating in the same configuration described in Figure 4.

Table 10. Development Environment Performance

Function	Average Execution Time
Directory Command (S Format with 25 files)	5.3 sec
Load the COPY Command	1.2 sec
Copy a 1K Byte File (Winchester to Winchester)	1.0 sec
Copy a 16K Byte File	1.7 sec
Copy a 64K Byte File	3.9 sec
Copy a 1K Byte File (Winchester to Diskette)	1.4 sec
Compile PL/M 86	393 lpm
Compile PASCAL 86 Program	453 lpm

TOOLS

Certain tools are necessary for the development of microcomputer applications. The iRMX 86 Human Interface includes many of these tools as non-resident commands. They can be included on the system disk of a application system, and brought into memory when needed to perform functions as listed in Table 11.

Table 11. Major Human Interface Utilities

Command	Function
BACKUP	Copy directories and files from one device to another.
COPY	Copy one or more files to one or more destination files.
CREATEDIR	Create a directory file to store the names of other files.
DIR	List the names, sizes, owners, etc. of the files contained in a directory.
ATTACHFILE	Give a logical name to a specified location in a file directory tree.
PERMIT	Grant or rescind user access to a file.
RENAME	Change the name of a file.
SUBMIT	Start the processing of a series of commands stored in a file.
SUPER	Change operator's ID to that of the System Manager with global access rights and privileges.

Table 11. Major Human Interface Utilities (Con.t.)

Command	Function
TIME	Set the system time-of-day clock.
VERIFY	Verify the structure of an iRMX™ 86 Named File volume, and check for possible disk data errors.

INTERACTIVE CONFIGURATION UTILITY

The iRMX 86 Operating System is designed to provide OEMs the ability to configure for specific system hardware and software requirements. The Interactive Configuration Utility (ICU) builds iRMX 86 configurations by asking appropriate questions and making reasonable assumptions. It runs on either an Intellec® Series III development system or iRMX 86 development system that includes a hard disk and the UDI. Table 12 lists the hardware and support software requirements of different iRMX 86 development system environments.

Table 12. iRMX™ Development Environment

Intellec® Series III: MDS 313 PL/M 86/88 Compiler   One hard disk and one diskette drive

iRMX™ 86 Development System
   iRMX™ 860 ASM 86 Assembler and Utilities
   iRMX™ 863 PL/M 86/88 Compiler
   iSDM 86 or 286 System Debug Monitor
   512K Bytes of RAM
   5M Byte On-Line Storage and one double-density diskette drive

SYSTEM 86/300 or 286/300 Series Microcomputer System Basic configuration

Figure 10 shows one of the many screens displayed during the process of defining a configuration. It shows the abbreviations for each choice on the left, a more complete description with the range of possible answers in the center, and the current (sometimes default) choice on the right. The bottom of the screen shows three changes made by the operator (lower case lettering), and a request for help on the Exception Mode question. In response to a request for help, the ICU displays an additional screen outlining possible choices and some overall system effects.

The ICU requests only information required as a result of previous choices. For example, if no Extended I/O System functions are required, the ICU will not ask any further questions about the EIOS. Once a configuration session is complete, the operator may save all the information in a file. Later when small changes are necessary, this file can be modified. A completely new session is not required.

iRMX™ 86 OPERATING SYSTEM

```
Nucleus
(ASC)     All Sys Calls [Yes/No]                              Yes
(PV)      Parameter Validation [Yes/No]                       Yes
(ROD)     Root Object Directory Size [0 – 0FF0h]              0014H
(MTS)     Minimum Transfer Size [0 – 0FFFFH]                  0040H
(DEH)     Default Exception Handler [Yes/No/Deb/Use]          Yes
(NEH)     Name of Ex Handler Object Module {1 – 32chs}
(EM)      Exception Mode [Never/Program/Environ/All]          Never
(NR)      Nucleus in ROM [Yes/No]                             No

Enter Changes [Abbreviations ?/ = new-value] : ASC = N
:pv = no
:rod = 48
:em ?
```

Figure 10. ICU Screen for iRMX™ 86 Nucleus

REAL-TIME DEBUGGING TOOLS

The iRMX 86 Operating System supports three distinct debugging environments: Static, Dynamic, and Post-Mortem. While the iRMX 86 Operating System does support a multi-user Human Interface, these real-time debugging aids are usually most useful in a single-user environment where modifications made to the system cannot affect other users.

System Debugger

The static debugging aid is the iRMX 86 System Debugger. This debugger is an extension of the iSDM 86 and the iSDM 286 System Debug Monitors. The System Debugger provides static debugging facilities when the system hangs or crashes, when the Nucleus is inadvertently overwritten or destroyed, or when synchronization requirements prevent the debugging of certain tasks. The System Debugger stops the system and allow you to examine the state of the system at that instant, and allows you to:

— Identify and interpret iRMX 86 system calls.
— Display information about iRMX 86 objects.
— Examine a task's stack to determine system call history.

iRMX™ 86 Dynamic Debugger

The iRMX 86 Dynamic Debugger runs as part of an iRMX 86 application. It may be used at any time during program development, or may be integrated into an OEM system to aid in the discovery of latent errors. The Dynamic Debugger can be used to search for errors in any task, even while the other tasks in the system are running. The iRMX 86 Dynamic Debugger communicates with the developer via a terminal handler that supports full line editing.

System Crash/Dump Analyzer

The often difficult job of debugging real-time applications is made much simpler with the System Crash/Dump Analyzer. The analyzer allows program developers to record system memory for later analysis even if the system has halted. This analysis lists such vital information as which jobs have active tasks, which system queues contain which tasks, and what segments contain which data.

PARAMETER VALIDATION

Some iRMX 86 System Calls require parameters that may change during the course of developing iRMX 86 applications. The iRMX 86 Operating System includes an optional set of routines to validate these parameters to ensure that correct numeric values are used and that correct object types are used where the System expects to manipulate an object. For systems based only on the iRMX 86 Nucleus, these routines may be removed to improve the performance and code size of the System once the development phase is completed.

START-UP SYSTEMS

Two ready-to-run, multi-user start-up systems are included in the iRMX 86 Operating System package. These iRMX 86 start-up systems are fully configured, multi-user iRMX 86 Operating Systems ready to be loaded into memory by the Bootstrap Loader. Both start-up systems are configured to include all of the system calls for each layer and most of the features provided by iRMX 86. iRMX start-up systems include UDI support so that users may run languages such as PL/M-86, Pascal, FORTRAN, and software packages from independent vendors.

The start-up system for the iAPX 86 processor is configured for Intel SYSTEM 86/300 Series microcomputers with a minimum of 384K bytes of RAM. The following devices are supported.

- iSBC 215/iSBX 218 or iSBC 215G/iSBX 218A
- iSBC 254(S)
- Line Printer
- 8251A Terminal Driver
- iSBC 544 Terminal Driver

The start-up system for the iAPX 286 processor is configured for Intel SYSTEM 286/300 Series microcomputers with a minimum of 512K bytes and a maximum of 896K bytes of RAM. The following devices are supported.

- iSBC 208
- iSBC 215/iSBX 218 or iSBC 215G/iSBX 218A
- iSBC 254(S)
- Line Printer for iSBC 286/10
- 8274 Terminal Driver
- iSBC 544 Terminal Driver

Either system will run without hardware or software configuration changes and can be reconfigured on a standard system with at least 512K bytes of RAM. Definition files are also included for iSBC 186/03, 186/51 and 188/48 configurations.

This start-up system may be used to run the ICU (if a Winchester disk is attached to the system) to develop custom configurations such as those pictured in Figure 8. As shipped, the Human Interface supports a single user terminal. However, the Start-up System terminal configuration file may be altered easily to support from two to five users.

iRMX™ 86 OPERATING SYSTEM

SPECIFICATIONS

Supported Software Products

iRMX 860	iRMX 86 Development Utilities Package, including the iAPX 86 and 88 Linker, Locater, Macro Assembler, Librarian, and the iRMX 86 Editor.
iRMX 861	PASCAL 86/88 Compiler
iRMX 862	FORTRAN 86/88 Compiler
iRMX 863	PL/M 86/88 Compiler
iRMX 864	TX Screen-oriented Editor
iMMX 800	MULTIBUS Message Exchange software package for iRMX 86, and 88 application systems
iOSP 86	Support Package for iAPX 86/30, 88/30, 186/30, and 188/30 Operating System Processors
iRMX PSCOPE 86	High Level Language Debugger

Supported Hardware Products

COMPONENTS

iAPX 86 and 88 Microprocessors
iAPX 186 and 188 Microprocessors
iAPX 286 Microprocessors (Real Address Mode only)
8087 Numeric Data Processor Extension
80287 Numeric Data Processor Extension
iAPX 86/30 (80130) Operating System Firmware Component
8253 and 8254 Programmable Interval Timers
8259A Programmable Interrupt Controller
8251A USART Terminal Controller
8255 Programmable Parallel Interface
8274 Terminal Controller
82530 Serial Communications Controller

iSBC® MULTIBUS BOARD AND SYSTEM PRODUCTS

iSBC 86/12A, 86/05, 86/14, 86/30, 86/35, 88/25, and 88/40 Single Board Computers
iSBC 186/03 Single Board Computer
iSBC 186/51 Ethernet Controller
iSBC 188/48 Communications Controller
iSBC 286/10 Single Board Computer (Real Address Mode only)
iSBC 204 Diskette Controller
iSBC 206 Hard Disk Controller
iSBC 208 Diskette Controller
iSBC 215(G) Winchester Disk Controller
iSBX 218(A) Flexible Diskette Multi-Module Controller
iSBC 220 SMD Disk Hard Controller
iSBC 254(S) Bubble Memory System
iSBC 534 4-Channel Terminal Interface
iSBC 544 Intelligent 4-Channel Terminal Interface and Controller
iSBX 251 Bubble Memory Multi-Module
iSBX 350 Parallel Port (Centronics-type Printer Interface)
iSBX 351 Serial Communications Port
iSBX 270 CRT Light Pen and Keyboard Interface
SYSTEM 86/300 Family
SYSTEM 286/300 Family

AVAILABLE LITERATURE

The iRMX 86 Documentation Set is comprised of the following four volumes of reference manuals. Order numbers are associated with these four volumes only.

iRMX 86 INTRODUCTION AND OPERATOR'S REFERENCE MANUAL FOR RELEASE 6
Order Number: 146545-001

Introduction to the iRMX 86 Operating System
iRMX 86 Operator's Manual
iRMX 86 Disk Verification Utility Reference Manual

iRMX 86 PROGRAMMERS REFERENCE MANUAL FOR RELEASE 6, PART I
Order Number: 146546-001

iRMX 86 Nucleus Reference Manual
iRMX 86 Basic I/O System Reference Manual
iRMX 86 Extended I/O System Reference Manual

iRMX 86 PROGRAMMERS'S REFERENCE MANUAL FOR RELEASE 6, PART II
Order Number: 146547-001

iRMX 86 Application Loader Reference Manual
iRMX 86 Human Interface Reference Manual
iRMX 86 Universal Development Interface Reference Manual
Guide to Writing Device Drivers for iRMX 86 and iRMX 88 I/O Systems
iRMX 86 Programming Techniques
iRMX 86 Terminal Handler Reference Manual
iRMX 86 Debugger Reference Manual
iRMX 86 System Debugger Reference Manual
iRMX 86 Crash Analyzer Reference Manual
iRMX 86 Bootstrap Loader Reference Manual

iRMX™ 86 OPERATING SYSTEM

iRMX 86 INSTALLATION AND CONFIGURATION GUIDE FOR RELEASE 6
Order Number: 146548-001

iRMX 86 Installation Guide
iRMX 86 Configuration Guide
Master Index for Release 6 of the iRMX 86 Operating System

Application Notes

Ap Note 130 — Using Operating System Processors to Simplify Microcomputer Designs. (Order Number: 230786-001)

Ap Note 174 — Optimizing the iRMX 86 Operating System Performance on System 86/310 and System 86/330 (Order Number: 230990-001)

Training Courses

The iRMX 86 Operating System

Customer Seminars

Contact local Intel Sales Office for details on available video-tape and slide presentations.

ORDERING INFORMATION

The iRMX 86 Operating System is available under a number of different licensing options as noted here. Source listings are available on microfiche. Reconfigurable object libraries are provided on double density ISIS-formatted diskettes or on either double density, single sided iRMX 86-formatted 8″ diskettes, or double density, double sided, 5.25″ diskettes. ISIS-format diskettes may be used on Intel Intellec Development Systems. The iRMX 86-format may be used on any iRMX 86-based system supporting the appropriate compilers and development environment.

The OEM license options listed here allow users to incorporate the iRMX 86 Operating System into their applications. Each use requires payment of an Incorporation Fee.

ORDER CODE	DESCRIPTION
iRMX 86 KIT BRO:	Double density, single-sided 8″ ISIS format OEM license
iRMX 86 KIT ERO:	Double density, single sided 8″ iRMX 86-Format OEM license for use on iRMX 86-based environments.
iRMX 86 KIT JRO:	Double density, double sided 5.25″ iRMX 86-Format OEM license for use on iRMX 86-based environments.

Other licensing options include prepayment of all future incorporation fees, single use rights for a single machine, use at a second development site, one year update service extensions, the right to make copies for additional development systems, and source listing materials.

Each option includes 90 days of support service that provides the quarterly iRMX 86 Technical Report, Software Problem Report Service, and copies of System Updates that occur during this period. Except for source listings, all initial licenses include a complete set of iRMX 86 Documentation.

As with all Intel software, purchase of any of these options requires the execution of a standard Intel Master Software License. The specific rights granted to users depends on the specific option and the License signed.

iRMX™ 286 OPERATING SYSTEM

- Real-time processor management for time-critical iAPX 286 (Native Mode) applications.
- 16 megabytes of memory addressable.
- Hardware traps aid in debugging.
- Call gates provide fast access to system calls and OS extensions.
- On-target system development with Universal Development Interface (UDI).
- Configurable system size and function for diverse application requirements.
- All iRMX™ 286 system code can be (P)ROM'ed to support totally solid state designs.
- Configured system for the iAPX 286 processors in Intel integrated system products (iSYS 286/300).
- Multi-terminal support with multi-user human interface.
- Range of device drivers included for industry standard MULTIBUS® peripheral controllers.
- Complete support of 80287 processor extension.
- Powerful utilities for interactive configuration and debugging.
- Application source code compatible with the iRMX™ 86 Operating System.

The iRMX 286 Operating System is an easy-to-use, real-time, multi-tasking and multi-programming software system designed to manage and extend the resources of iSBC® 286 Single Board Computers, as well as other iAPX 286 (Native Mode) based microcomputers. The iRMX 286 Operating System functions are also fully integrated into the SYSTEM 286/300 family of microcomputer systems. The operating system provides a number of standard interfaces that allow applications to take advantage of industry standard device controllers, hardware components, and software packages developed by Independent Software Vendors (ISVs). With the processing power of the iAPX 286 processor and the 16M byte address space, the utility of iRMX 286 systems extends into applications such as communications networks, transaction processing, and simulation where immediate access to advances in VLSI technology is paramount. These systems deliver real-time performance and explicit control over resources; yet also support applications with multiple users needing to simultaneously access terminals. The configurable layers of the system provide services ranging from interrupt management and standard device drivers for many sophisticated controllers to data file maintenance commands provided by a comprehensive multi-user human interface. By providing access to the standard Universal Development Interface (UDI) for each user terminal, Original Equipment Manufacturers (OEMs) can pass program development and target application customization capabilities to their users. By maintaining application source code compatibility with the iRMX 86 Operating System, users can preserve their software investment.

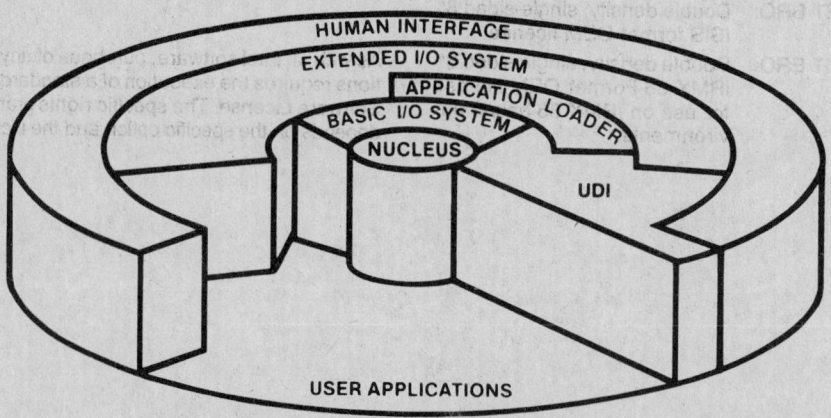

iRMX™ 286 VLSI Operating System

Intel Corporation assumes no responsibility for the use of any circuitry other than circuitry embodied in an Intel product. No other circuit patent licenses are implied. Information contained herein supersedes previously published specifications on these devices from Intel.

© INTEL CORPORATION, 1985

AUGUST, 1985
ORDER NUMBER: 280082-02

iRMX™ 286 OPERATING SYSTEM

OVERVIEW

The iRMX 286 Operating System is a complete set of system software modules that provide the resource management functions needed by computer systems. These management functions allow Original Equipment Manufacturers (OEMs) to best use resources available in microcomputer systems while getting their products to market quickly, saving time and money. Engineers are relieved of writing complex operating system software and can instead concentrate on their application software.

This data sheet describes the major features of the iRMX 286 Operating System. The benefits provided to engineers who write application software and to users who want to take advantage of improving microcomputer price and performance are explained. Compatibility with the iRMX 86 Operating System is discussed. The first section outlines the system resource management functions of the operating system and describes several system calls. The second section gives a detailed overview of iRMX 286 system features aimed at serving both the iRMX 286 system designer and programmer, as well as the end users of the product into which the operating system is incorporated.

Comparison of iRMX™ 86 and iRMX™ 286 Operating Systems

The iRMX 286 Operating System is application source code compatible with the iRMX 86 Operating System to preserve the software investments of the iRMX 86 Operating System users. In several areas there are differences between the two operating systems, to allow the iRMX 286 Operating System to take advantage of some of the iAPX 286 processor features available in the native mode. Some new system calls have been added to support these additional features. The new system call names begin with RQE$. All calls beginning with RQ$ are supported by both operating systems.

New calls have been added in the Nucleus, the EIOS, and the Application Loader to take advantage of the 16M byte addressability of the iRMX 286 Operating System. New calls have been added to the Nucleus to allow the use of descriptor tables, and to allow marking access rights to segments. Call gates rather than software interrupts are used to gain access to system calls, and to implement OS extensions. The 286 OMF is used by the iRMX 286 Operating System, which requires that application source code be recompiled using the iAPX 286 translators and utilities.

FUNCTIONAL DESCRIPTION

To take best advantage of iAPX 286 microprocessors in applications where the computer is required to perform many functions simultaneously, the iRMX 286 Operating System provides a multi-programming environment in which many independent, multi-tasking application programs may run. The flexibility of independent environments allows application programmers to separately manage each application's resources during both the development and test phases.

The resource management functions of the iRMX 286 Operating System are supported by a number of configurable software layers. While many of the functions supplied by the innermost layer, the Nucleus, are required by all systems, all other functions are optional. The I/O systems, for example, may be omitted in systems having no secondary storage requirement. Each layer provides functions that encourage application programmers to use modular design techniques for quick development of easily maintainable programs.

The components of the iRMX 286 Operating System provide both implicit and explicit management of system resources. These resources include processor scheduling, up to sixteen megabytes of system memory, up to 57 independent interrupt sources, all input and output devices, as well as directory and data files contained on mass storage devices and accessed by a number of independent users. Management of these system resources is discussed in the following sections.

Process Management

To implement multi-tasking application systems, programmers require a method of managing the different processes of their application, and for allowing the processes to communicate with each other. The Nucleus layer of the iRMX 286 system provides a number of facilities to efficiently manage these processes, and to effectively communicate between them. These facilities are provided by system calls that manipulate data structures called tasks, jobs, regions, semaphores and mailboxes. The iRMX 286 system refers to these structures as "objects".

Tasks are the basic element of all applications built on the iRMX 286 Operating System. Each task is an entity capable of executing CPU instructions and issuing system calls in order to perform a function. Tasks are characterized by their register values (including those of an optional 80287 Numeric Processor Extension), a priority between 0 and 255, and the resources associated with them.

Each task in the system is scheduled for operation by the iRMX 286 Nucleus. Figure 1 shows the five states in which each task may be placed, and some examples of how a task may move from one state to another. The iRMX 286 Nucleus ensures that each task is placed in the correct state, defined by events in its external environment and by the task issuing system calls. Each task has a priority to indicate its relative importance and need to respond to its environment. The Nucleus guarantees that the highest priority ready-to-run task is the task that runs.

Jobs are used to define the operating environment of a group of tasks. Jobs effectively limit the scope of an application by collecting all of its tasks and other objects into one group. Because the environment for execution of an application is defined by a job, separate applications can be efficiently developed by separate development teams.

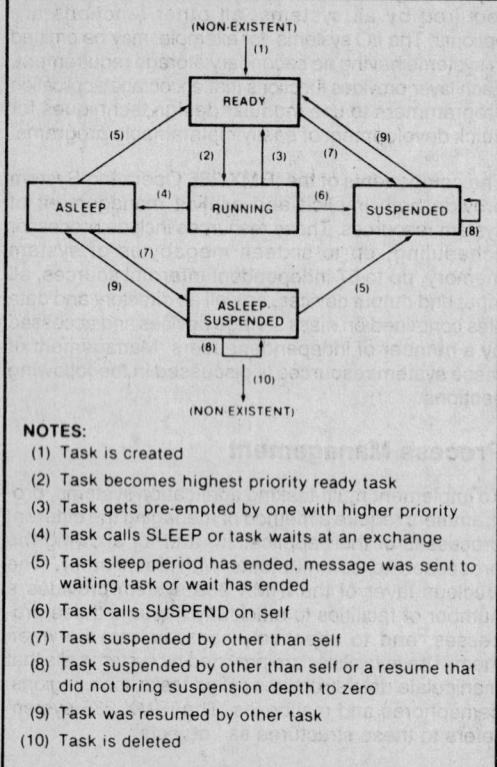

NOTES:
(1) Task is created
(2) Task becomes highest priority ready task
(3) Task gets pre-empted by one with higher priority
(4) Task calls SLEEP or task waits at an exchange
(5) Task sleep period has ended, message was sent to waiting task or wait has ended
(6) Task calls SUSPEND on self
(7) Task suspended by other than self
(8) Task suspended by other than self or a resume that did not bring suspension depth to zero
(9) Task was resumed by other task
(10) Task is deleted

Figure 1. Task State Diagram

The iRMX 286 Operating System provides two primary techniques for real-time event synchronization in multi-task applications: regions and semaphores.

Regions are used to restrict access to critical sections of code and data. Once the iRMX 286 Operating System gives a task access to resources guarded by a region, no other tasks may make use of the resources and the task is given protection against deletion and suspension. Regions are typically used to protect data structures from being simultaneously updated by multiple tasks.

Semaphores are used to provide mutual exclusion between tasks. They contain abstract "units" that are sent between the tasks, and can be used to implement the cooperative sharing of resources.

Multi-tasking applications must communicate information and share system resources among cooperating tasks. The iRMX 286 Operating System assigns a unique 16-bit number, called a token, to each object created in the system. Any task in possession of this token is able to access the object. The iRMX 286 Nucleus allows tasks to gain access to objects, and hence system resources, at run-time with two additional mechanisms: mailboxes and object directories.

Mailboxes are used by tasks wishing to share objects with other tasks. A task may share an object by sending the object token via a mailbox. The receiving task can check to see if a token is there, or can wait at the mailbox until a token is present.

Object directories are also used to make an object available to other tasks. An object is made public by cataloging its token and name in a directory. In this manner, any task can gain access to the object by knowing its name, and job environment that contains the directory.

Two example jobs are shown in Figure 2 to demonstrate how two tasks can share an object that was not known to the programmer at the time the tasks were developed. Both Job 'A' and Job 'B' exist within the environment of the 'Root Job' that forms the foundation of all iRMX 286 systems. Each job possesses a directory in which tasks may catalog the name of an object. Semaphore 'RS', for example, is accessable by all tasks in the system, because its name is cataloged in the directory of the Root Job. Mailbox 'AN' can be used to transfer objects between Tasks 'A2' and 'A3' because its token is accessable in the object directory for Job 'A'. Mailbox 'AN' cannot be used by tasks in Job 'B'.

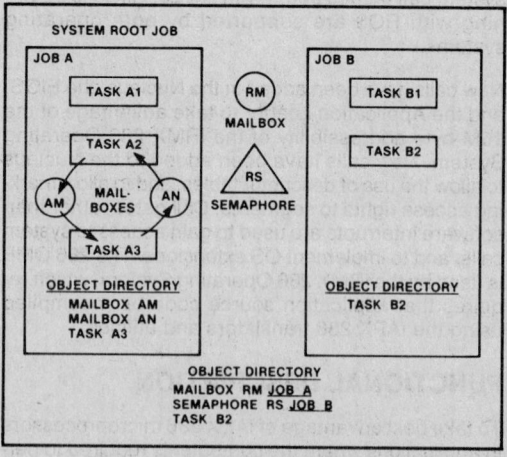

Figure 2. Multiple Jobs Example

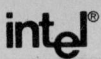

iRMX™ 286 OPERATING SYSTEM

Table 1 lists the major functions of the iRMX 286 Nucleus that manage system processes.

Memory Management

Each job in an iRMX 286 system defines the amount of the 16M bytes of addressable memory to be used by its tasks. All addresses used by the iRMX 286 Operating System are logical addresses. The address is a selector which points to an entry in a descriptor table, and an offset. The iRMX 286 Operating System manages system memory and allows jobs to share this critical resource by providing another object type: segments.

Segments are contiguous pieces of memory up to 64K bytes in length that exist within the environment of the job in which they were created. Segments form the fundamental piece of system memory used for task stacks, data storage, system buffers, loading programs from secondary storage and passing information between tasks.

Segments may be accessed only in the modes (read, write or execute) permitted for them. Segment bound checking and stack overflow are enforced by the hardware. It is estimated that 90% of coding errors will be caught by these hardware traps.

The example in Figure 2 also demonstrates sharing information between Tasks 'A2' and 'A3'; 'A2' only needs to create a segment, put the information in the A2 and memory allocated, and send its token via the Mailbox 'AM' using the RQ$SEND$MESSAGE system call (see Table 1). Task 'A3' would get the message by using the RQ$RECEIVE$MESSAGE system call. The figure also shows how the receiving task could signal the sending task by sending an acknowledgement via the second Mailbox 'AN'.

Each job is created with both maximum and minimum limits set for its memory pool. Memory required by all objects and resources created in the job is taken from this pool. If more memory is required, a job may be allowed to borrow memory from the pool of its containing job (the job from which it was created). In this manner, initial jobs may efficiently allocate memory to jobs they subsequently create without knowing their exact requirements.

The iRMX 286 Operating System supplies other memory managment functions to search specific address ranges for available memory. The system performs this search at system initialization, and can be configured to ignore non-existent memory and addresses reserved for I/O devices and other application requirements.

Table 1. Process Management System Calls

System Call	Function Performed
RQ$CREATE$JOB	Creates an environment with a memory pool of up to 1M byte for a number of tasks and other objects, as well as creating an initial task and its stack.
RQ$DELETE$JOB	Deletes a job and all the objects currently defined within its bounds. All memory used is returned to the job from which the deleted job was created.
RQ$OFFSPRING	Provides a list of all the current jobs created by the specified job.
RQ$CATALOG$OBJECT	Enters a name and token for an object into the object directory of a job.
RQ$UNCATALOG$OBJECT	Removes an object's token and its name from a job's object directory.
RQ$LOOKUP$OBJECT	Returns a token for the object with the specified name found in the object directory of the specified job.
RQGETTYPE	Returns a code for the type of object referred to by the specified token.
RQ$CREATE$MAILBOX	Creates a mailbox with queues for waiting tasks and objects with FIFO or PRIORITY discipline.
RQ$DELETE$MAILBOX	Deletes a mailbox.
RQ$SEND$MESSAGE	Sends an object to a specified mailbox. If a task is waiting, the object is passed to the appropriate task according to the queuing discipline. If no task is waiting, the object is queued at the mailbox.

Table 1. Process Management System Calls (con't.)

System Call	Function Performed
RQ$RECEIVE$MESSAGE	Attempts to receive an object token from a specified mailbox. The calling task may choose to wait for a specified number of system time units if no token is available.
RQ$DISABLE$DELETION	Prevents the deletion of a specified object by increasing its disable count by one.
RQ$ENABLE$DELETION	Reduces the disable count of an object by one, and if zero, enables deletion of that object.
RQ$FORCE$DELETE	Forces the deletion of a specified object if the disable count is either 0 or 1.
RQ$CREATE$TASK	Creates a task with the specified priority and stack area.
RQ$DELETE$TASK	Deletes a task from the system, and removes it from any queues in which it may be waiting.
RQ$SUSPEND$TASK	Suspends the operation of a task. If the task is already suspended, its suspension depth is increased by one.
RQ$RESUME$TASK	Resumes a task. If the task had been suspended multiple times, the suspension depth is reduced by one, and it remains suspended.
RQ$SLEEP	Causes a task to enter the ASLEEP state for a specified number of system time units.
RQGETTASK$TOKENS	Gets the token for the calling task or associated objects within its environment.
RQSETPRIORITY	Dynamically alters the priority of the specified task.
RQGETPRIORITY	Obtains the priority of a specified task.
RQ$CREATE$REGION	Creates a region, with an associated queue of FIFO or PRIORITY ordering discipline.
RQ$DELETE$REGION	Deletes the specified region if it is not currently in use.
RQ$ACCEPT$CONTROL	Gains control of a region only if the region is immediately available.
RQ$RECEIVE$CONTROL	Gains control of a region. The calling task may specify the number of system time units it wishes to wait if the region is not immediately available.
RQ$SEND$CONTROL	Relinquishes control of a region.
RQ$CREATE$SEMAPHORE	Creates a semaphore.
RQ$DELETE$SEMAPHORE	Deletes a semaphore.
RQ$SEND$UNITS	Increases a semaphore counter by the specified number of units.
RQ$RECEIVE$UNITS	Attempts to gain a specified number of units from a semaphore. If the units are not immediately available, the calling task may choose to wait.
RQE$CHANGE$OBJECT$ACCESS	Changes the access byte of an object.
RQEGETOBJECT$ACCESS	Returns the value of an object's access byte.
RQE$CREATE$JOB	Creates an environment with a memory pool of up to 16M bytes for tasks and objects, and creates an initial task and its stack.
RQEGETADDRESS	Returns the physical address of an object.

iRMX™ 286 OPERATING SYSTEM

Code written using the system calls which exist in the iRMX 86 Operating System will run on an iRMX 286 Operating System after recompiling, with few exceptions. The RQSETOS$EXTENSION call is replaced by the new RQESETOS$EXTENSION system call. If more than one megabyte of memory is required in an individual task or job, the new iRMX 286 system calls must be used. Table 2 lists the major system calls used to manage the system memory.

Descriptor Management

Descriptors are used by the iRMX 286 Operating System to make an area of memory addressable. Each descriptor is an entry in a descriptor table and contains the physical address of a segment. Each object is assigned a descriptor when it is created.

There are three types of descriptor tables. The Global Descriptor Table (GDT) is a table containing up to 8000 descriptor entries which contain 24-bit physical addresses used by the system. One Local Descriptor Table (LDT) is reserved for system use. The Interrupt Descriptor Table (IDT) replaces the interrupt vector table used by the iRMX 86 Nucleus. When an interrupt occurs, the processor refers to the IDT to determine the address of the interrupt handling code to be executed.

System calls used in descriptor management are shown in Table 3.

Interrupt Management

Real-time systems, by their nature, must respond to asynchronous and unpredictable events quickly. The iRMX 286 Operating System uses interrupts and the event-driven Nucleus described earlier to give real-time response to events. Use of a preemptive scheduling technique ensures that the servicing of high priority events always takes precedence over other system activities.

The iRMX 286 Operating System gives applications the flexibility to optimize either interrupt response time or interrupt response capability by providing two tiers of interrupt management. These two distinct tiers are managed by interrupt handlers and interrupt tasks.

Interrupt handlers are the first tier of interrupt service. For small simple functions, interrupt handlers are often the most efficient means of responding to an event. They provide faster response than interrupt tasks, but must be kept simple since interrupts (except the iAPX 286 non-maskable interrupt) are masked during their execution. When extended service is required, interrupt handlers "signal" a waiting interrupt task that, in turn, performs more complicated functions.

Interrupt Tasks are distinct tasks whose priority is associated with a hardware interrupt level. They are permitted to make any iRMX 286 system call. While

Table 2. Memory Management System Calls

System Call	Function Performed
RQ$CREATE$SEGMENT	Dynamically allocates a memory segment of the specified size.
RQ$DELETE$SEGMENT	Deletes the specified segment by deallocating the memory.
RQGETPOOL$ATTRIBUTES	Returns attributes such as the minimum and maximum, as well as current size of the memory in the environment of the calling task's job. Attributes have a maximum size of 1M byte.
RQGETSIZE	Returns the size (in bytes) of a segment.
RQSETPOOL$MIN	Dynamically changes the minimum memory requirements of the job environment containing the calling task.
RQEGETPOOL$ATTRIB	Returns minimum, maximum, and current size of memory pools up to 16M bytes. Also returns the amount of memory borrowed and the token of the parent of the target job.

Table 3. Descriptor Management System Calls

System Call	Function
RQE$CREATE$DESCRIPTOR	Returns a segment token for a hardware descriptor.
RQE$CHANGE$DESCRIPTOR	Changes the physical address contained in the GDT to a different physical address or size.
RQE$DELETE$DESCRIPTOR	Removes a descriptor slot from the descriptor table and returns the slot to the free space manager.

iRMX™ 286 OPERATING SYSTEM

an interrupt task is servicing an interrupt, interrupts of lower priority are not allowed to preempt the system.

Table 4 shows the iRMX 286 system calls provided to manage interrupts.

Interrupt Management Example

Figure 3 illustrates how the iRMX 286 interrupt system may be used to output strings of characters to a printer. In the example, a mailbox named 'PRINT' is used by all tasks in the system to queue messages to be printed. Application tasks put the characters in segments that are transmitted to the printer interrupt task via the 'PRINT' mailbox. Once printing is complete, the same interrupt task passes the messages on to another application via the 'FINISHED' mailbox so that an operator message can be displayed.

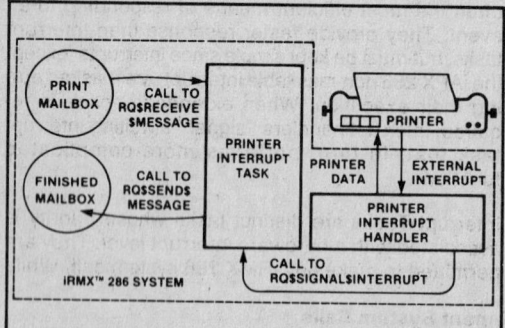

Figure 3. Interrupt Management Example

Hardware Traps

Hardware traps (exception conditions) and their resulting exception codes have been added as a result of the hardware protection features of the iAPX 286 processor. These traps may occur, for example, when a program tries to execute out of its segment bounds, causes a stack overflow, or tries to write in a segment that has been defined as read only.

Basic I/O System

The Basic I/O System (BIOS) provides the direct access to I/O devices needed by real-time applications. The BIOS allows I/O functions to overlap other system functions. In this manner, application tasks make asynchronous calls to the iRMX 286 BIOS, and proceed to perform other activities. When the I/O request must be completed before an application can continue, the task waits at a mailbox for the result of the operation.

The BIOS will check segment boundaries and access rights of segments when system calls are made, which aids in debugging programs. Some system calls provided by the BIOS are listed in Table 5.

The Basic I/O System communicates with peripheral devices through device drivers. These device drivers provide the system with four basic functions needed to control and communicate with devices: Initialize I/O, Finish I/O, Queue I/O, and Cancel I/O. Using the device driver interface, users of non-standard devices may write custom drivers compatible with the I/O system.

The iRMX 286 Operating System includes a number of device drivers to allow applications to use standard USART serial communications devices, multiple CRTs and keyboards, bubble memories, diskettes, disks, a Centronics-type parallel printer, and other Intel iSBC and iSBX device controllers (see Table 12). If an application requires use of a non-standard device, users need only write a device driver to be included with the BIOS, and access it as if it were part of the standard system. For most common random-access devices, this job is further simplified by using

Table 4. Interrupt Management System Calls

System Call	Function Performed
RQSETINTERRUPT	Assigns an interrupt handler and, if desired, an interrupt task to the specified interrupt level. Usually the calling task becomes the interrupt task.
RQ$RESET$INTERRUPT	Disables an interrupt level, and cancels the assignment of the interrupt handler for that level. If an interrupt task was assigned, it is deleted.
RQGETLEVEL	Returns the number of the highest priority interrupt level currently being processed.
RQ$SIGNAL$INTERRUPT	Used by an interrupt handler to signal the associated interrupt task that an interrupt has occurred.
RQ$WAIT$INTERRUPT	Used by an interrupt task to SLEEP until the associated interrupt handler signals the occurrence of an interrupt.
RQ$EXIT$INTERRUPT	Used by an interrupt handler to relinquish control of the System.
RQ$ENABLE	Enables the hardware to accept interrupts from a specified level.
RQ$DISABLE	Disables the hardware from accepting interrupts at a specified level.

iRMX™ 286 OPERATING SYSTEM

Table 5. Key BIOS I/O Management System Calls

System Call	Function Performed
RQAATTACH$FILE	Creates a Connection to an existing file.
RQACHANGE$ACCESS	Changes the types of accesses permitted to the specified user(s) for a specific file.
RQACLOSE	Closes the Connection to the specified file so that it may be used again, or so that the type of access may be changed.
RQACREATE$DIRECTORY	Creates a Named File used to store the names and locations of other Named Files.
RQACREATE$FILE	Creates a data file with the specified access rights.
RQADELETE$CONNECTION	Deletes the Connection to the specified file.
RQAGET$FILE$STATUS	Returns the current status of a specified file.
RQAOPEN	Opens a file for either read, write, or update access.
RQAREAD	Reads a number of bytes from the current position in a specified file.
RQASEEK	Moves the current data pointer of a Named or Physical file.
RQAWRITE	Writes a number of bytes at the current position in a file.
RQ$WAIT$IO	Synchronizes a task with the I/O System by causing it to wait for I/O operation results.

standard routines provided with the system. Use of this technique ensures that applications can remain device independent.

Multi-Terminal Support

The iRMX 286 Terminal Support provides line editing and terminal control capabilities. The Terminal Support communicates with devices through simple drivers that do only character I/O functions. Dynamic terminal reconfiguration is provided so that attributes such as terminal type and line speed may be changed without modifying the application or the iRMX 286 Operating System. Dynamic configuration may be typed in, generated programmatically or stored in a file and copied to a terminal I/O connection.

The iRMX 286 Terminal Support provides automatic translation of control characters to specific control sequences for each terminal. This translation enables applications using standard control characters to function with non-standard terminals. The translation requirements for each terminal can be stored in terminal description files and copied to a connection, as described above.

Random Access Support

Random access devices supported include the iSBC 215G Winchester Disk, iSBX 218A Diskette Controllers and the iSBX 251 Bubble Memory Controller.

Each device driver can be used to interface to a number of separate and, in some cases, different devices (see Figure 4). The iSBC 215G Device Driver, supplied with the system, is capable of supporting the iSBC 215G Winchester Disk Controller and the iSBX 218A Flexible Disk Controller. Each device controller may, in turn, control a number of separate device units. In addition, each driver may control a number of like device controllers. Other device drivers may be added using the random access support code provided in the operating system. This capability allows the use of large storage systems with a minimum of I/O system code to write or maintain.

Extended I/O System

The iRMX 286 Extended I/O System (EIOS) adds a number of I/O management capabilities to simplify access to files. Whereas the BIOS provides users with the basic system calls needed for direct management of I/O resources, many users prefer to have the system perform all the buffering and synchronization of I/O requests automatically. The EIOS allows users to access I/O devices without having to write procedures for buffering data, or to specify particular devices with constant device names.

By performing device buffering automatically, the iRMX 286 EIOS optimizes accesses to disks and other devices. Often, when an application task asks the system to READ a portion of a file, the system is able to respond immediately with the data it has read in advance of the request. Similarly, the EIOS will not delay a task for writing data to a device unless it is specifically told to, or if its output buffers are filled.

Logical file and device names are provided by the EIOS to give applications complete file and device independence. Applications may send data to the 'line printer' (:LP:) without knowing which specific device will be used as the printer. This logical name may, in fact, not be a printer at all, but it could be a disk file that is later scheduled for printing.

iRMX™ 286 OPERATING SYSTEM

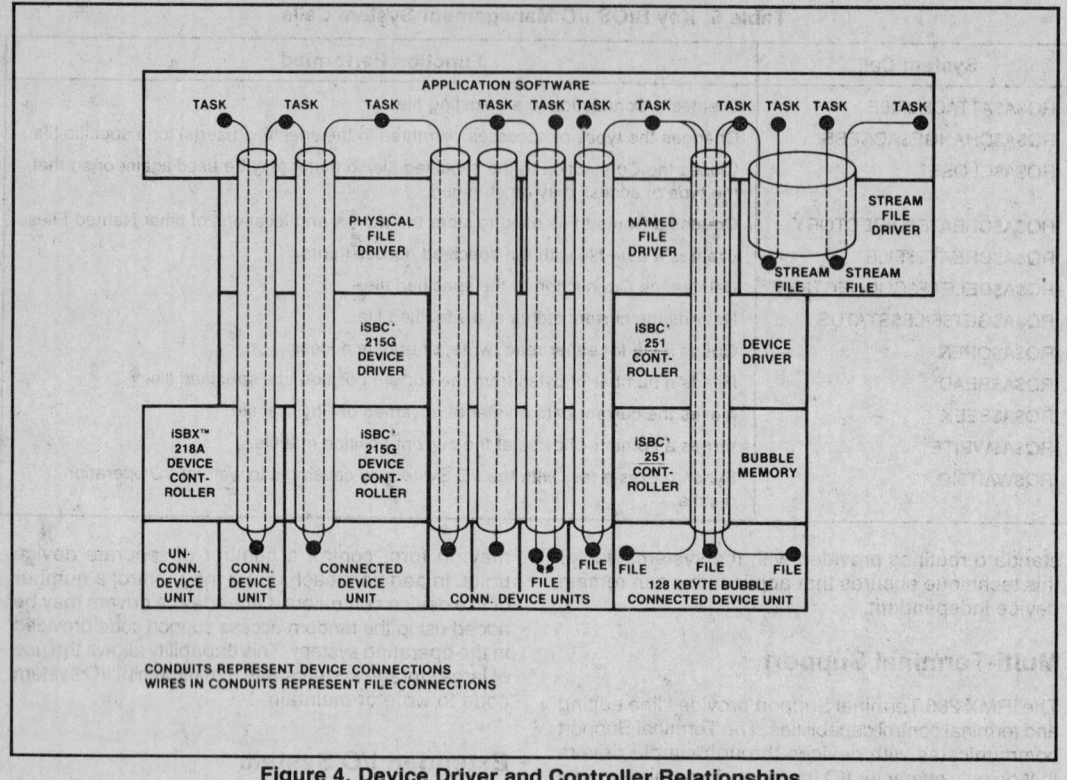

Figure 4. Device Driver and Controller Relationships

The EIOS uses the functions provided by the BIOS to synchronize individual I/O requests with results returned by device drivers. Most EIOS system calls are similar to the BIOS calls, except that they appear to suspend the operation of the calling task until the I/O requests are completed. The RQE$CREATE$IO$JOB system call can be used to allow jobs of up to 16M bytes to be created. I/O jobs can also be created using the RQ$CREATE$IO$JOB system call, which will allow compatibility with existing application code, and has a 1M byte memory limitation.

The EIOS will check segment boundaries and access rights of segments when system calls are made, which aids in debugging programs.

File Management

The iRMX 286 Operating System provides three distinct types of files to ensure efficient management of both program and data files: named files, physical files, and stream files. Each file type provides access to I/O devices through the standard device drivers mentioned earlier. The same device driver is used to access physical and named files for a given device.

NAMED FILES

Named files allow users to access information on secondary storage by referring to a file with its ASCII name. The names of files stored on a device are stored in special files called directories. As directories are themselves named files, the file system allows directories to contain the names of other directories. Figure 5 illustrates the resulting hierarchical file structure. This structure is useful for isolating file names to particular user applications, and for tailoring system data to the requirements of users and applications sharing storage devices. Using different branches on the directory tree, different users do not have to coordinate in naming their files to ensure unique names.

Whenever a request is made involving a file name, the system will search the appropriate directory in order to find the necessary information about the file's size, access rights, and specific location on the storage device.

The iRMX 286 BIOS uses an efficient format for writing the directory and data information into secondary storage. This standard iRMX format is fully compatible with the ISO media standard and other Intel systems such as the iRMX 86 and iRMX 88 Operating Systems.

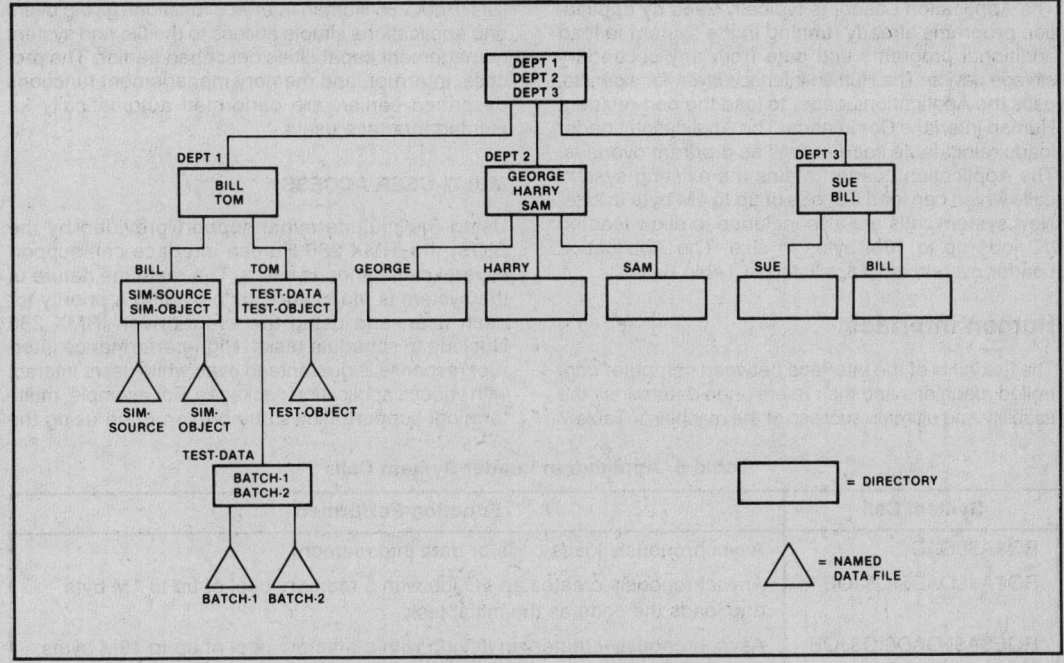

Figure 5. Hierarchical Named File Structure

This structure enables the system to directly access any byte in a file, often without having to do additional I/O to access space allocation information. The maximum size of an individual file is 4.3 billion bytes.

EASE OF ACCESS

The hierarchical file structure is provided to isolate and organize collections of named files. To give operators fast and simple access to any level within the file tree, an ATTACHFILE command is provided. This command allows operators to create a logical name to a point in the tree so that a long sequence of characters need not be typed each time a file is referred to.

ACCESS PROTECTION

Access to each named file is protected by the rights assigned to each user by the owner of the file. Rights to read, append, update, and delete may be selectively granted to other users of the system. In general, users of named files are classified into one of two categories: User and World. Users are specified when certain programmers and programs need to share information stored in a file. The World classification is used when rights are to be granted to all who can use the system.

PHYSICAL FILES

Physical files allow more direct device access than named files. Each physical file occupies an entire device, treated as a single stream of individually accessable bytes. No access control is provided for physical files as they are typically used for such applications as driving a printing device, translating from one device format to another, driving a paper tape device, real-time data acquisition, and controlling analog mechanisms.

STREAM FILES

Stream files provide applications with a method of using iRMX 286 file management methods for data that does not need to go into secondary storage. Stream files act as direct channels, through system memory, from one task to another. These channels are very useful to programs, for example, wishing to preserve file and device independence by allowing data to be sent to a printer one time, to a disk file another time, and to another program on a different occasion.

Bootstrap and Application Loaders

Two utilities are supplied with the iRMX 286 Operating System to load programs and data into system memory from secondary storage devices.

The iRMX 286 Bootstrap Loader is typically used to load the initial system from the system disk into memory, and begin its execution.

iRMX™ 286 OPERATING SYSTEM

The Application Loader is typically used by application programs already running in the system to load additional programs and data from any secondary storage device. The Human Interface layer, for example, uses the Application Loader to load the non-resident Human Interface Commands. The Application Loader loads relocatable code as well as program overlays. The Application Loader retains the existing system calls which can load I/O jobs of up to 1M byte in size. New system calls are also included to allow loading I/O jobs up to 16M bytes in size. The Application Loader system calls are listed in Table 6.

Human Interface

The flexibility of the interface between computer controlled machines and their users often determines the usability and ultimate success of the machines. Table 7 lists iRMX 286 Human Interface functions giving users and applications simple access to the file and system management capabilities described earlier. The process, interrupt, and memory management functions described earlier, are performed automatically for Human Interface users.

MULTI-USER ACCESS

Using the multi-terminal support provided by the BIOS, the iRMX 286 Human Interface can support several simultaneous users. The real-time nature of the system is maintained by providing a priority for each user, and using the event-driven iRMX 286 Nucleus to schedule tasks. High-performance interrupt response is guaranteed even while users interact with various application packages. For example, multi-terminal support allows one person to be using the

Table 6. Application Loader System Calls

System Call	Function Performed
RQALOAD	Asynchronously loads code or data into memory.
RQALOADIOJOB	Asynchronously creates an I/O job with a memory pool of up to 1M byte, and loads the code as the initial task.
RQEALOADIOJOB	Asynchronously creates an I/O job with a memory pool of up to 16M bytes, and loads the code as the initial task.
RQSLOADIOJOB	Synchronously creates an I/O job with a memory pool of up to 1M byte, and loads the code as the initial task.
RQESLOADIOJOB	Synchronously creates an I/O job with a memory pool of up to 16M bytes, and loads the code as the initial task.
RQSOVERLAY	Synchronously loads an overlay into memory.

Table 7. Major Human Interface Utilities

Command	Function
ATTACHDEVICE	Attach a physical device to the system and catalog its logical name.
ATTACHFILE	Give a logical name to a specified location in a file directory tree.
COPY	Copy one or more files to one or more destination files.
CREATEDIR	Create a directory file to store the names of other files.
DIR	List the names, sizes, owners, etc. of the files contained in a directory.
DISKVERIFY	Verify the structure of an iRMX named file volume, and check for possible disk data errors.
PERMIT	Grant or rescind user access to a file.
RENAME	Change the name of a file.
RESTORE	Copy files from a backup volume to a named volume.
SUBMIT	Start the processing of a series of commands stored in a file.
SUPER	Change operator's ID to that of the System Manager with global access rights and privileges.
TIME	Set the system time-of-day clock.

Many real-time systems require high performance operation. To meet this requirement, all of the iRMX 286 Operating System can be put into zero wait-state P(ROM). This approach eliminates the possibility of disk access times slowing down performance, while allowing system designers to take advantage of high performance memory devices.

CONFIGURABILITY

The iRMX 286 Operating System is configurable by system layer, and by system call within each layer. In addition all the I/O port addresses used by the System are configurable by the user. This flexibility gives designers the freedom to choose configurations of hardware and software that best suit their size and functional requirements. Two example configurations are shown in Figure 6. Most configuration options are selected during system design stages. Others may be selected during system operation.

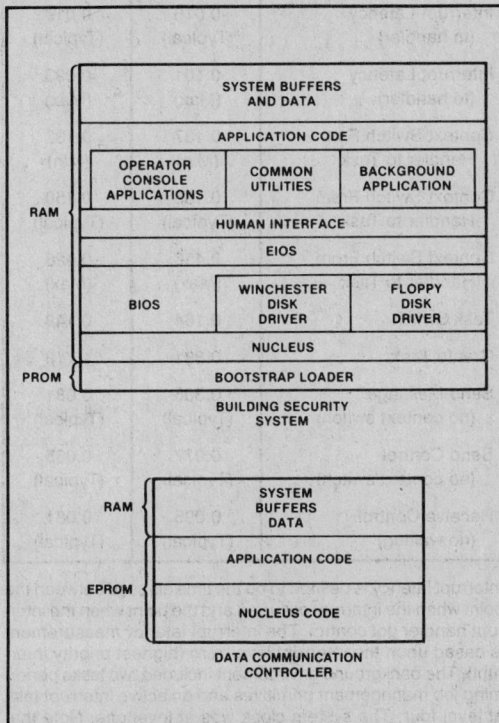

Figure 6. Typical iRMX™ 286 System Configurations

The chart shown in Table 9 indicates the actual memory size required to support these different configurations of the iRMX 286 system. Systems requiring only Nucleus level functions may require no more than 27K bytes for the Operating System. Other applications, needing I/O management functions, may select portions of additional layers that fit their needs and size constraints.

This configurability also applies to the System Debugger. The debugger needs to be included only as a debugging tool (usually only during system development).

Table 9. iRMX™ 286 System Configuration Size Chart

System Layer	Code Size	Data Size
Nucleus	27K	3.5K
BIOS	67K	19.5K
EIOS	16K	16.75K
Application Loader	11K	2K
Human Interface	26K	1K
UDI	9.4K	0.1K
Bootstrap Loader	32K	6K
System Debugger	23K	0.8K
Interactive Configuration Utility		384K

MULTI-USER ACCESS

Many real-time systems must provide a variety of users access to system control functions and collected data.

The iRMX 286 system provides easy-to-use support for applications to access multiple terminals. It also enables multiple and different users to access different applications concurrently.

Figure 7 illustrates a typical iRMX 286 Operating System application simultaneously supporting multi-terminal data collection and real-time environments. Shown is a group of terminals used by machinists on a shop floor to communicate with a job management program, a building security system that constantly monitors energy usage requirements, a system operator console capable of accessing all system functions, and a group of terminals in the production engineering department used to monitor job costs while developing new device control specifications instructions. The iSBC 188/48 Intelligent Terminal Interface supports multiple user terminals without degrading system performance to handle character I/O.

EXTENDABILITY

The iRMX 286 Operating System provides three means of extensions. This extendability is essential for support of OEM and volume end user value added features. This ability is provided by: user-defined operating system calls using OS extensions, user-defined objects (similar to Jobs, Tasks, etc.), and the

iRMX™ 286 OPERATING SYSTEM

AEDIT 286 Editor, while another compiles a PL/M 286 program, while several others load and access applications.

Each terminal attached to the iRMX 286 multi-user Human Interface is automatically associated with a user, a memory pool, and an initial program to run when the terminal is connected. This association is made using a file that may be changed at any time. Changes are effective the next time the system is initialized.

The initial program specified for each terminal can be a special application program, a custom Human Interface, or the standard iRMX 286 Command Line Interpreter (CLI).

Specifying an application program as a terminal's initial program makes the interface between operators and the computer system much simpler. Each operator need only be aware of the function of a particular application; not needing to interact with any unfamiliar functions also available on the application system.

Specifying the standard iRMX 286 Human Interface CLI as the initial program enables users of the terminals to access all iRMX 286 system functions. This CLI makes it easy to manage files, load and execute Intel-supplied and custom programs, and submit command files for execution.

FEATURE OVERVIEW

The iRMX 286 Operating System is well suited to serve the demanding needs of real-time applications executing on complex microprocessor systems. The iRMX 286 system also provides many tools and features needed by real-time system developers and programmers. The following sections describe features useful in both the development and execution environments. The description of each feature outlines the advantages given to hardware and software engineers concerned with overall system cost, expandability with custom and industry standard options, and long-term maintenance of iRMX 286-based systems. The development environment features also describe the ease with which the iRMX 286 Operating System can be incorporated into overall system designs.

Execution Environment Features

REAL-TIME PERFORMANCE

The iRMX 286 Operating System is designed to offer the high performance, multi-tasking functions required by real-time systems. Designers can make use of the latest VLSI devices such as the 80287 Numeric Processor Extension to improve their system cost/performance ratio.

Primitives that create objects will in general take longer in the iRMX 286 Operating System than in the iRMX 86 Operating System because the iAPX 286 has some instructions which take longer to execute in native mode than in real address mode. However, other primitives which manipulate the created objects are in general faster. Typical iRMX 286 system performance characteristics are shown in Table 8.

Table 8. iRMX™ 86 and 286 Real-Time Performance Using iSBC® 286/12 Single Board Computer

Real-Time Function	iRMX™ 86 Execution Time (msec)	iRMX™ 286 Execution Time (msec)
Interrupt Latency (to handler)	0.012 (Min)	0.015 (Min)
Interrupt Latency (to handler)	0.016 (Typical)	0.019 (Typical)
Interrupt Latency (to handler)	0.101 (Max)	0.093 (Max)
Context Switch From Handler to Task	0.137 (Min)	0.132 (Min)
Context Switch From Handler to Task	0.155 (Typical)	0.150 (Typical)
Context Switch From Handler to Task	0.456 (Max)	0.428 (Max)
Task Switch	0.164	0.149
Create Task	0.831	1.718
Send Message (no context switch)	0.308 (Typical)	0.081 (Typical)
Send Control (no context switch)	0.077 (Typical)	0.065 (Typical)
Receive Control (no waiting)	0.095 (Typical)	0.081 (Typical)

Interrupt latency is defined to be the time elapsed between the point when the interrupt occurred and the point when the interrupt handler got control. The interrupt latency measurement is based upon the interrupt level zero (highest priority interrupt). The background environment included two tasks performing job management primitives and an active interrupt task at level four. The system clock was at level one. Note that these times are for a Nucleus only system, and that the latency will probably be higher if an I/O system is used. All memory is contiguous.

Context switch time is defined to be the time elapsed from the signal interrupt until the first instruction of the interrupt task.

The execution times shown in Columns 2 and 3 were measured using an 8MHz iSBC 286/12 Single Board Computer, 1M byte on-board memory, and all program and data stored in on-board memory. All memory was at 0 wait states.

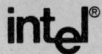

iRMX™ 286 OPERATING SYSTEM

ability to add functions later in the product life cycle. The modular, layered structure of the iRMX 286 system easily facilitates later additions to applications. User-defined objects are supported by the functions listed in Table 10.

Using standard iRMX 286 system calls, users may define custom objects, enabling applications to easily manipulate commonly used structures as if they were part of the original operating system. OS extensions are implemented using call gates rather than software interrupts. This allows OS extensions to have high performance and yet be easy to use.

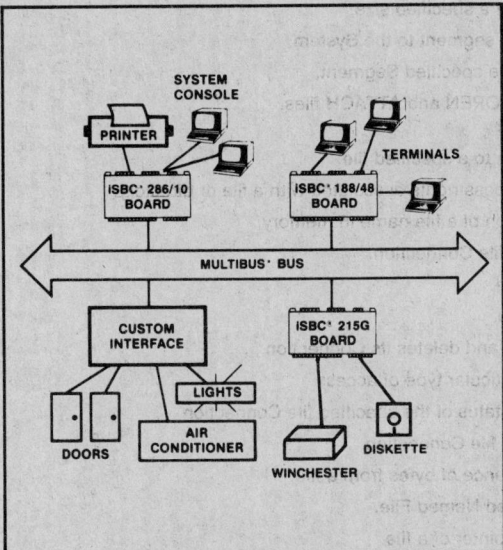

Figure 7. Multi-Terminal and Multi-User Real-Time System

EXCEPTION HANDLING

The system includes predefined exception handlers for typical I/O and parameter error conditions. The error handling mechanism is both configurable and extendable.

SUPPORT OF STANDARDS

The iRMX 286 Operating System supports the many hardware and software standards needed by most application systems to ensure that commonly available hardware and software packages may be interfaced with a minimum of cost and effort. The iRMX 286 system supports the iSBC board family of products built on the Intel MULTIBUS architecture specification (IEEE Standard 796), and a number of standard software interfaces such as the UDI and the common device driver interface (See Figure 8). The procedural interfaces of the UDI are listed in Table 11.

The operating system includes support for the proposed IEEE 80-bit extended real-variable format of the 80287 Numeric Data Processor, and the MULTIBUS hardware interface (IEEE 796).

CPU PERFORMANCE

The iRMX 286 Operating System supports iAPX 80286-based systems. This support enables the user to take advantage of the faster speed and higher performance of Intel's 80286-based microprocessors and the iSBC 286/10, iSBC 286/10A, and iSBC 286/12 Single Board Computers.

COMPONENT LEVEL SUPPORT

The iRMX 286 System may be tailored to support specific hardware configurations. In addition to system

Table 10. User Extension System Calls

System Call	Function Performed
RQ$CREATE$COMPOSITE	Creates a custom object built of previously defined objects.
RQ$DELETE$COMPOSITE	Deletes the custom object, but not the various objects from which it was built.
RQ$INSPECT$COMPOSITE	Returns a list of Token Identifiers for the component objects from which the specified composite object is built.
RQ$ALTER$COMPOSITE	Replaces a component object of a composite object.
RQ$CREATE$EXTENSION	Creates a new type of object and assigns a mailbox used for collecting these objects when they are deleted.
RQ$DELETE$EXTENSION	Deletes an extension definition.
RQESETOS$EXTENSION	Attaches the entry point address of a user written OS extension to a call-gate.
RQ$SIGNAL$EXCEPTION	Used by OS extensions to signal the occurence of an exception.

iRMX™ 286 OPERATING SYSTEM

memory, only an iAPX 286 microprocessor, an 8259A Programmable Interrupt Controller (PIC), an 8255A Programmable Parallel Interface, and either an 8253 or 8254 Programmable Interval Times (PIT) are required.

For systems requiring extended mathematics capability, an 80287 Numeric Data Processor may be added to perform these functions up to 100 times faster than equivalent software. For applications servicing more than 8 interrupt sources, additional 8259A's may be configured as slave controllers.

BOARD LEVEL SUPPORT

The iRMX 286 Operating System includes device drivers to support a range of MULTIBUS architecture

Table 11. UDI System Calls

System Call	Function Performed
Memory Management:	
DQ$ALLOCATE	Creates a Segment of a specified size.
DQ$FREE	Returns the specified segment to the System.
DQGETSIZE*	Returns the size of the specified Segment.
DQ$RESERVE$IO$MEMORY*	Reserves memory to OPEN and ATTACH files.
File Management:	
DQ$ATTACH	Creates a Connection to a specified file.
DQ$CHANGE$ACCESS*	Changes the user access rights associated with a file or directory.
DQ$CHANGE$EXTENSION	Changes the extension of a file name in memory.
DQ$CLOSE	Closes the specified file Connection.
DQ$CREATE	Creates a Named File.
DQ$DELETE	Deletes a Named File.
DQ$DETACH	Closes a Named File and deletes its Connection.
DQ$OPEN	Opens a file for a particular type of access.
DQGETCONNECTION$STATUS*	Returns the current status of the specified file Connection
DQ$FILE$INFO*	Returns data about a file Connection.
DQ$READ	Reads the next sequence of bytes from a file.
DQ$RENAME*	Renames the specified Named File.
DQ$SEEK	Moves the position pointer of a file.
DQ$TRUNCATE	Truncates a file.
DQ$WRITE	Writes a sequence of bytes to a file.
Process Management:	
DQ$EXIT	Exits from the current application job.
DQ$OVERLAY*	Causes the specified overlay to be loaded.
DQ$SPECIAL	Performs special I/O related functions on terminals with special control features.
DQ$TRAP$CC	Captures control when CNTRL/C is typed.
Exception Handling:	
DQGETEXCEPTION$HANDLER	Returns a pointer to the program currently being used to process errors.
DQ$DECODE$EXCEPTION	Returns a short description of the specified error code.
DQ$TRAP$EXCEPTION	Identifies a custom exception processing program for a particular type of error.
Application Assistance:	
DQ$DECODE$TIME	Returns system time and date in binary and ASCII character format.
DQGETARGUMENT*	Returns the next argument from the character string used to invoke the application program.
DQGETSYSTEM$ID*	Returns the name of the underlying operating system supporting the UDI.
DQGETTIME*	Returns the current time of day as kept by the underlying operating system.
DQ$SWITCH$BUFFER	Selects a new buffer from which to process commands.

*Calls available only through the UDI.

iRMX™ 286 OPERATING SYSTEM

device controllers. The particular boards and types of devices supported are listed in Table 12. The device controllers all adhere to industry standard electrical and functional interfaces.

Table 12. Supported Devices

Device Controller	Description
iSBC 215G Board	Standard Winchester Disks
iSBX 218A Board	Single or Double Density, Single or Double Sided, 8″ & 5.25″ Diskette
iSBX 251 Board	Bubble Memory MULTIMODULE™ Board
iSBX 350 Board	1-Channel Parallel Port
iSBX 351 Board	1-Channel Serial Port to CRTs, Modems
iSBC 188/48 Board	8-Channel Serial Ports to CRTs, Modems
8274 Usart	2-Channel Serial Ports to CRTs, Modems
iSBC 286/10 Board Line Printer	Line Printer Port

Development Environment Features

The iRMX 286 Operating System supports the efficient utilization of programming time by providing important tools for program development. Some of the tools necessary to develop and debug real-time systems are included with the operating system. Others, such as language compilers, are available from Intel and from leading independent software vendors.

LANGUAGES

The iRMX 286 Operating System supports 31 standard system calls known as the Universal Development Interface (UDI). Figure 8 shows the iRMX 286 standard interfaces to many compilers and language translators, including the iAPX 286 Macro Assembler and PL/M 286 compilers available from Intel. Also available are other Intel development tools, language translators and utilities available from other vendors. The full set of UDI calls is required to run a compiler.

These standard software interfaces (the UDI) ensure that users of the iRMX 286 Operating System may transport their applications to future releases of the iRMX 286 Operating System and other Intel and independent vendor software products. The calls available in the UDI are shown in Table 11.

The high performance of the iRMX 286 Operating System enhances the throughput of compilers and other development utilities. Table 13 indicates the average performance of typical development environment functions.

TOOLS

Certain tools are necessary for the development of microcomputer applications. The iRMX 286 Human Interface includes many of these tools as non-resident commands. They can be included on the system disk of a application system, and brought into memory when needed to perform functions as listed in Table 7.

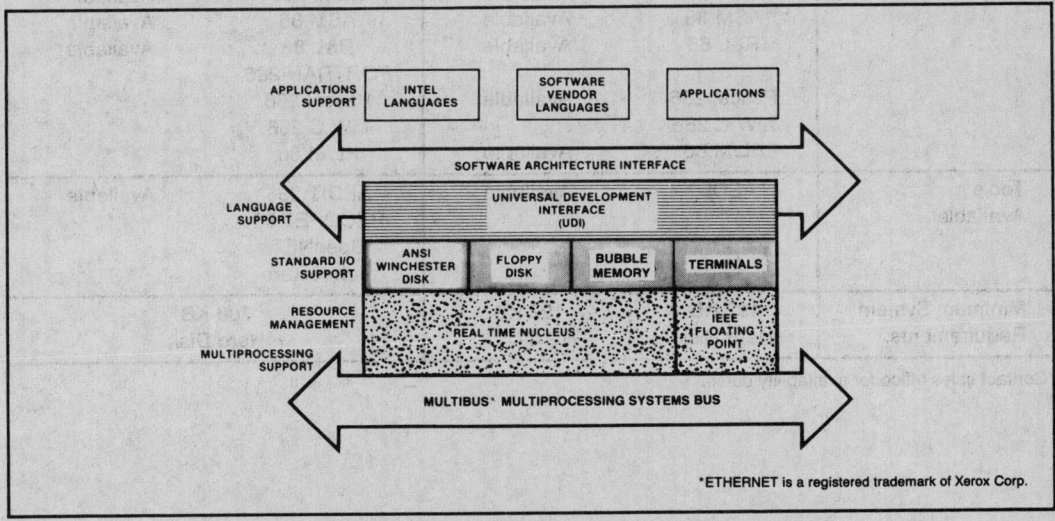

*ETHERNET is a registered trademark of Xerox Corp.

Figure 8. iRMX™ 286 Operating System Standard Interfaces

iRMX™ 286 OPERATING SYSTEM

Table 13. Development Environment Performance

Function	iRMX™ 286 System Execution Time	iRMX™ 86 System Execution Time
Directory command (S format with 79 files)	8.8 sec	9.2 sec
Load the COPY command	0.9 sec	1.5 sec
Copy a 4K byte file (Winchester to Winchester)	2.4 sec	2.6 sec
Copy a 32K byte file	3.7 sec	3.9 sec
Copy a 128K byte file (Winchester to Winchester)	7.9 sec	8.7 sec
Compile PL/M (555 line program)	49 sec 680 lpm	45 sec 740 lpm

INTERACTIVE CONFIGURATION UTILITY

The iRMX 286 Operating System is designed to provide OEMs the ability to configure for specific system hardware and software requirements. The Interactive Configuration Utility (ICU) builds iRMX 286 system configurations by asking appropriate questions and making reasonable assumptions. It runs on either an Intellec® Series III or Series IV development system or iRMX 286 development system that includes a hard disk and the UDI. Table 14 lists the hardware and support software requirements of different development environments for iRMX 286 Operating System-based development.

Figure 9 shows one of the many screens displayed during the process of defining a configuration. It shows the abbreviations for each choice on the left, a more complete description with the range of possible answers in the center, and the current (sometimes default) choice on the right. The bottom of the screen shows a changes made by the operator (lower case lettering), and a request for help on the Exception Mode question. In response to a request for help, the ICU displays an additional screen outlining possible choices and some overall system effects.

Table 14. iRMX™ 286 Development Environments

Order Media Type:	Series III	Series IV	iRMX™ 286 System	
	B (ISIS 8 in)	J (iRMX 5.25 in)	E or (iRMX 8 in)	J (iRMX 5.25 in)
Languages Available:	ASM 286	Available	ASM 286	Available
	R&L 286	Available	R&L 286	Available
	PL/M 286	Available	PL/M 286	Available
	ASM 86	Available	ASM 86	Available
	R&L 86	Available	R&L 86	Available
			FORTRAN 286	*
	Pascal 286	Available	Pascal 286	*
	MW C 286	*	MW C 286	*
	PL/M 86	Available	PL/M 86	*
Tools Available:	AEDIT	Available	AEDIT 286	Available
			PSCOPE 286	*
			OpenNET architecture	*
Minimum System Requirements:	192 KB Hard Disk	192 KB Hard Disk	700 KB Hard Disk	

*Contact sales office for availability dates.

iRMX™ 286 OPERATING SYSTEM

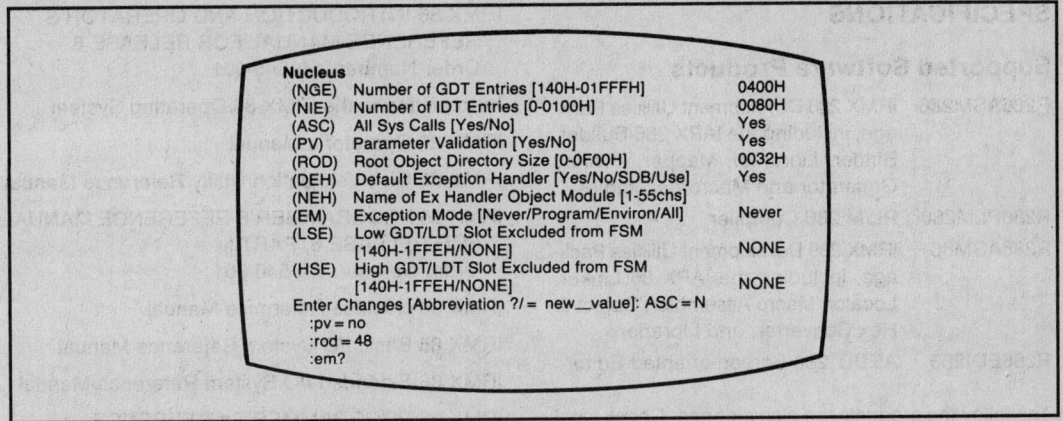

Figure 9. ICU Screen for iRMX™ 286 Nucleus

The ICU requests only information required as a result of previous choices. For example, if no Extended I/O System functions are required, the ICU will not ask any further questions about the EIOS. Once a configuration session is complete, the operator may save all the information in a file. Later when small changes are necessary, this file can be modified. A completely new session is not required.

SYSTEM DEBUGGER

The static debugging aid is the iRMX 286 System Debugger. This debugger is an extension of the iSDM 286 System Debug Monitor. The System Debugger provides static debugging facilities when the system hangs or crashes, when the Nucleus is inadvertently overwritten or destroyed, or when synchronization requirements prevent the debugging of certain tasks. The System Debugger stops the system and allows you to examine the state of the system at that instant, and allows you to:

- Identify and interpret iRMX 286 system calls.
- Display information about iRMX 286 system objects.
- Examine a task's stack to determine system call history.

While the iRMX 286 Operating System does support a multi-user Human Interface, the System Debugger is usually most useful in a single-user environment where modifications made to the system cannot affect other users.

PARAMETER VALIDATION

Some iRMX 286 system calls require parameters that may change during the course of developing iRMX 286 applications. The iRMX 286 Operating System includes an optional set of routines to validate these parameters to ensure that correct numeric values are used and that correct object types are used where the operating system expects to manipulate an object. For systems based only on the iRMX 286 Nucleus, these routines may be removed to improve the performance and code size of the System once the development phase is completed.

START-UP SYSTEMS

A ready-to-run, multi-user start-up system is included in the iRMX 286 Operating System package. This iRMX 286 start-up system is a fully configured, multi-user iRMX 286 Operating System ready to be loaded into memory by the Bootstrap Loader. The start-up system is configured to include all of the system calls for each layer and most of the features provided by the iRMX 286 Operating System. The iRMX 286 start-up system includes UDI support so that users may run languages such as PL/M-286, the AEDIT 286 editor, and software packages from independent vendors.

The start-up system for the iAPX 286 processor is configured for Intel SYSTEM 286/310 or SYSTEM 286/380 with a minimum of 700K bytes of RAM. The System Debugger is included in the start-up system. The following devices are supported:

- iSBC 215G/iSBX 218A disk controllers
- Line Printer for iSBC 286/10 CPU board
- 8274 Terminal Driver

The system will run without hardware or software configuration changes and can be reconfigured on a standard system with at least 700K bytes of RAM.

This start-up system may be used to run the ICU (if a Winchester disk is attached to the system) to develop custom configurations such as those pictured in Figure 6. As shipped, the Human Interface supports two users.

iRMX™ 286 OPERATING SYSTEM

SPECIFICATIONS

Supported Software Products

R286ASM286	iRMX 286 Development Utilities Package, including the iAPX 286 Builder, Binder, Librarian, Mapper, Overlay Generator and Macro Assembler
R286PLM286	PL/M 286 Compiler
R286ASM86	iRMX 286 Development Utilities Package, including the iAPX 86 Linker, Locator, Macro Assembler, Object to Hex Converter, and Librarian
R286EDI286	AEDIT 286 Screen-oriented Editor

The following products are also planned. Check local Intel Sales offices for availability information.

- Mark Williams C 286 Compiler
- FORTRAN 286 Compiler
- Pascal 286 Compiler
- PL/M 86 Compiler

Supported Hardware Products

COMPONENTS

iAPX 286 Microprocessors (Native Mode)
80287 Numeric Data Processor Extension
8253 and 8254 Programmable Interval Timers
8259A Programmable Interrupt Controller
8251A USART Terminal Controller
8255 Programmable Parallel Interface
8274 Terminal Controller

iSBC® MULTIBUS® BOARD AND SYSTEM PRODUCTS

iSBC 286/10 Single Board Computer (Native Mode)
iSBC 286/10A Single Board Computer (Native Mode)
iSBC 286/12 Single Board Computer (Native Mode)
iSBC 215G Winchester Disk Controller
iSBX 218A Flexible Diskette Multi-Module Controller
iSBX 251 Bubble Memory Multi-Module
iSBX 350 Parallel Port (Centronics-type Printer Interface)
iSBX 351 Serial Communications Port
SYSTEM 286/300 Family

AVAILABLE LITERATURE

The iRMX 286 Documentation Set is comprised of the following five volumes of reference manuals. Order numbers are associated with these five volumes only.

iRMX 286 REFERENCE MANUAL FOR RELEASE 1
Order Number: 146693-001

iRMX 86 INTRODUCTION AND OPERATOR'S REFERENCE MANUAL FOR RELEASE 6
Order Number: 146545-001

Introduction to the iRMX 86 Operating System

iRMX 86 Operator's Manual

iRMX 86 Disk Verification Utility Reference Manual

iRMX 86 PROGRAMMER'S REFERENCE MANUAL FOR RELEASE 6, PART I
Order Number: 146546-001

iRMX 86 Nucleus Reference Manual

iRMX 86 Basic I/O System Reference Manual

iRMX 86 Extended I/O System Reference Manual

iRMX 86 PROGRAMMER'S REFERENCE MANUAL FOR RELEASE 6, PART II
Order Number: 146547-001

iRMX 86 Application Loader Reference Manual

iRMX 86 Human Interface Reference Manual

iRMX 86 Universal Development Interface Reference Manual

Guide to Writing Device Drivers for iRMX 86 and iRMX 88 I/O Systems

iRMX 86 Programming Techniques

iRMX 86 Terminal Handler Reference Manual

iRMX 86 Debugger Reference Manual

iRMX 86 System Debugger Reference Manual

iRMX 86 Crash Analyzer Reference Manual

iRMX 86 Bootstrap Loader Reference Manual

iRMX 86 INSTALLATION AND CONFIGURATION GUIDE FOR RELEASE 6
Order Number: 146548-001

iRMX 86 Installation Guide

iRMX 86 Configuration Guide

Master Index for Release 6 of the iRMX 86 Operation System

TRAINING COURSES

Intel offers training workshops related to the iRMX Operating Systems, the PL/M high-level programming language, and other microcomputer topics. An advanced iRMX Application and Debug workshop was announced in Spring 1985.

CUSTOMER SEMINARS

Contact local Intel Sales Office for details on available video-tape and slide presentations.

iRMX™ 286 OPERATING SYSTEM

ORDERING INFORMATION

The iRMX 286 Operating System is available under a number of different licensing options as noted here. Reconfigurable object libraries are provided on double density ISIS-formatted diskettes or on either double density, single sided iRMX-formatted 8″ diskettes, or double density, double sided, iRMX-formatted 5.25″ diskettes. ISIS-format diskettes may be used on Intel Intellec Series III development Systems. The iRMX-format diskettes may be used on any iRMX 286-based system supporting the appropriate compilers and development environment. The 5.25″ iRMX-formatted diskettes may be used on the Intellec Series IV Development System.

The OEM license options listed here allow users to incorporate the iRMX 286 Operating System into their applications. Each use requires payment of an Incorporation Fee.

ORDER CODE	DESCRIPTION
RMX286KITBRO:	Double density 8″ ISIS format OEM license
RMX286KITERO:	Double density, single sided 8″ iRMX-Format OEM license for use on iRMX 286-based environments.
RMX286KITJRO:	Double density, double sided 5.25″ iRMX-Format OEM license for use on iRMX 286-based environments or Intellec Series IV Development Systems.

Other licensing options include prepayment of all future incorporation fees, single use rights for a single machine, use at a second development site and the right to make copies for additional development systems.

Each option includes 90 days of support service that provides the quarterly iRMX 286 Technical Report, Software Problem Report Service, and copies of System Updates that occur during this period. All initial licenses include a complete set of iRMX 286 Documentation. Service after this 90 day period is available through Software Support Contracts.

As with all Intel software, purchase of any of these options requires the execution of a standard Intel Master Software License. The specific rights granted to users depends on the specific option and the License signed.

iSDM™ 86
SYSTEM DEBUG MONITOR

- Supports target system debugging for iSBC®/iAPX 86, 88, 186 and 188-based applications
- Provides interactive debugging commands including single-step code execution and symbolic displays of results
- Supports 8087 Numeric Processor Extension (NPX) for high-speed math applications
- Allows building of custom commands through the Command Extension Interface (CEI)
- Supports application access to ISIS-II files
- Provides program load capability from an Intellec® Development System
- Contains configuration facilities which allow an applications bootstrap from iRMX™ 86 and 88 file compatible peripherals
- Modular to allow use from an Intellec Development System or from a stand-alone terminal

The Intel iSDM™ 86 System Debug Monitor package contains the necessary hardware, software, cables, EPROMs and documentation required to interface, through a serial or parallel connection, an iSBC® 86/05, 86/12A, 86/14, 86/30, 88/25, 88/40, 88/45, 186/03, 186/51, 188/48, or iAPX 86, 88, 186 or 188 target system to an MDS 800, Series II, Series III, or Series IV Intellec® Microcomputer Development System for execution and interactive debugging of applications software on the target system. The Monitor can: load programs into the target system; execute the programs instruction by instruction or at full speed; set breakpoints; and examine/modify CPU registers, memory content, and other crucial environmental details. Additional custom commands can be built using the Command Extension Interface (CEI). The Monitor supports the OEM's choice of the iRMX™ 86 Operating System, the iRMX 88 Real-Time Multi-tasking Executive or a custom system for the target application system. OEM's may utilize any iRMX 86, 88 supported target system peripheral for a bootstrap of the application system or have full access to the ISIS-II files of the Intellect System.

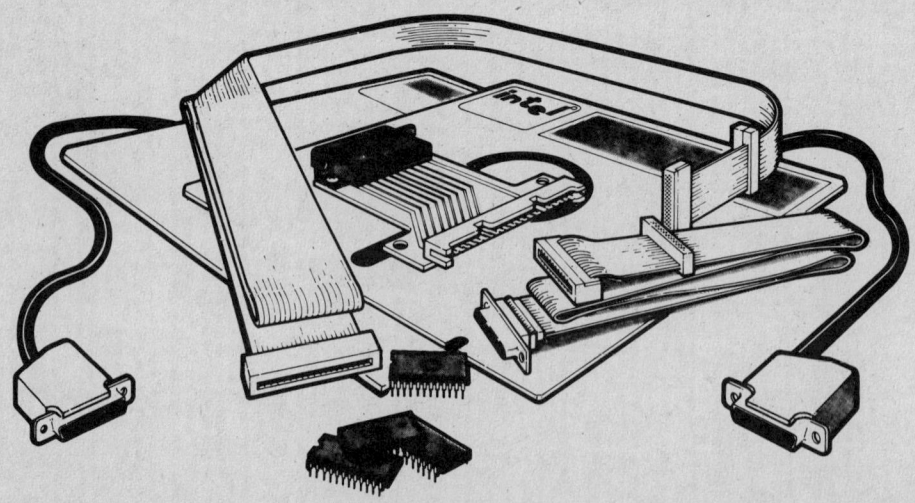

The following are trademarks of Intel Corporation and may be used only to describe Intel products: Intel, ICE, iMMX, iRMX, iSBC, iSBX, iSXM, MULTIBUS, Multichannel and MULTIMODULE. Intel Corporation assumes no responsibility for the use of any circuitry other than circuitry embodied in an Intel product. No other circuit patent licenses are implied. Information contained herein supercedes previously published specifications on these devices from Intel.

© INTEL CORPORATION, 1983

October, 1983
ORDER NUMBER: 230882-002

iSDM™ 86

FUNCTIONAL DESCRIPTION

Overview

The iSDM 86 Monitor extends the software development capabilities of the Intellec system so the user can effectively develop applications to ensure timely product availability.

The iSDM 86 package consists of four parts:

- The loader program
- The iSDM 86 Monitor
- The Command Extension Interface (CEI)
- The ISIS-II Interface

The user can use the ISDM 86 package to load programs into the target system from the development system, execute programs in an instruction-by-instruction manner, and add custom commands through the command extension interface. The user also has the option of using just the iSDM 86 Monitor and the CEI in a stand-alone application, without the use of an Intellec development system.

Powerful Debugging Commands

The iSDM 86 Monitor contains a powerful set of commands to support the debugging process. Some of the features included are: bootstrap of application software; selective execution of program modules based on breakpoints or single stepping requests; examination, modification and movement of memory contents; examination and modification of CPU registers, including NPX registers. All results are displayed in clearly understandable formats. Refer to Table 1 for a more detailed list of the iSDM 86 monitor commands.

Numeric Data Processor Support

Arithmetic applications utilizing the 8087 Numeric Processor Extension (NPX) are fully supported by the iSDM 86 Monitor. In addition to executing applications with the full NPX performance, users may examine and modify the NPX's registers using decimal and real number format.

This feature allows the user to feel confident that correct and meaningful numbers are entered for the application without having to encode and decode complex real, integer, and BCD hexadecimal formats.

Command Extension Interface (CEI)

The Command Extension Interface (CEI) allows the addition of custom commands to the iSDM 86 Monitor commands. The CEI consists of various procedures that can be used to generate custom commands. Up to three custom commands (or sets of commands) can be added

Table 1. Monitor Commands

Command	Function
B	**Bootstrap** application program from target systems peripheral device
C	**Compare** two memory blocks
D	**Display** contents of memory block
E*	**Exit** from loader program to ISIS-II Interface
F	**Find** specified constant in a memory block
G	**Execute** application program
I	**Input** and display data obtained from input port
L*	**Load** absolute Intellec® object file into target system memory
M	**Move** contents of memory block to another location
N	**Display and execute** single instruction
O	**Output** data to output port
P	**Print** values of literals
R*	**Load and execute** absolute Intellec® object file in target system memory
S	**Display and (optionally) modify** contents of memory
T*	**Transfer** block of memory to an Intellec® file
U,V,W	**User** defined custom commands extensions
X	**Examine and (optionally) modify** CPU and NPX registers

* Commands require an attached Series II/Series III.

iSDM™ 86

to the monitor without programming new EPROMs or changing the monitor's source code.

ISIS-II Interface

The ISIS-II interface consists of libraries which contain interfaces to ISIS-II I/O calls. A program running on an iAPX 86, 88, 186 or 188-based system can use the ISIS-II interface and access the individual ISIS-II I/O calls. The interface allows the inclusion of these calls into the program; however, most of the calls require a Series II/Series III system. Table 2 contains a summary of the major I/O calls and parameters.

Program Load Capability

The iSDM 86 loader allows the loading of iAPX 86, 88, 186 or 188-based programs into the target system. It executes on a Intellec Microcomputer Development System and communicates with the target system through a serial or a parallel load interface. If a Series II/Series III/Series IV system containing an Intel I/O expansion board is being used, the board can be used as a fast parallel load interface, freeing up the UPP port for application use.

Configuration Facility

The monitor contains a full set of configuration facilities which allow it to be carefully tailored to the requirements of the target system. Pre-configured EPROM-resident monitors are supplied by Intel for the iSBC 86/05, 86/12A, 86/14, 86/30, 88/45, 186/03, 186/51, and 188/48 boards. The monitor must be configured by the user for the iSBC 88/25, 88/40 boards and for other iAPX 86, 88, 186, 188 applications. iRMX 86 and iRMX 88 system users may use the configuration facilities to include the iAPX 86, 88 Bootstrap Loader (V5.0 or newer) in the monitor.

Variety of Connections Available

The physical interface between the Intellec Microcomputer Development System and the target system can be established in one of three ways. The systems can be connected via a serial link, a parallel link or a fast parallel link. The fast parallel link requires the use of an iSBC 108(A), 116(A), 517 or 519 I/O expansion board in the Intellec system and is only available for connections with the Series II/Series III/Series IV systems. The cabling arrangement is different depending upon the development system being used. Figure 1 displays the cable connections needed between an Intellec Series III system and a target system for a serial interface.

The iSDM 86 Monitor does not require the use of a development system. The monitor can be used by simply attaching a stand-alone terminal to the target system. Figure 1 also displays the cable connections needed for this arrangement.

Table 2. Routines for ISIS-II Services Available to Target System Applications

Routine	Target System Function
ATTRIB	Changes to ISIS-II file **attribute**
CI	Returns a character **input** from the **console**
CO	Transfers a character for **console output**
CLOSE	**Closes** an opened ISIS-II file
DELETE	**Deletes** the specified ISIS-II file
DQ$CFG	Returns information about monitor's communication link and type
ERROR	Displays an **error** message on the Intellec® console
EXIT	**Exits** to the target system monitor
LOAD	**Loads** target system memory with ISIS-II object code file
OPEN	**Opens** an ISIS-II file for access
READ	**Reads** up to 4096 bytes from an ISIS-II file to memory
RENAME	**Renames** an ISIS-II disk file
SEEK	**Seeks** to the specified ISIS-II file location
WRITE	**Writes** up to 4096 bytes from memory to an ISIS-II file

iSDM™ 86

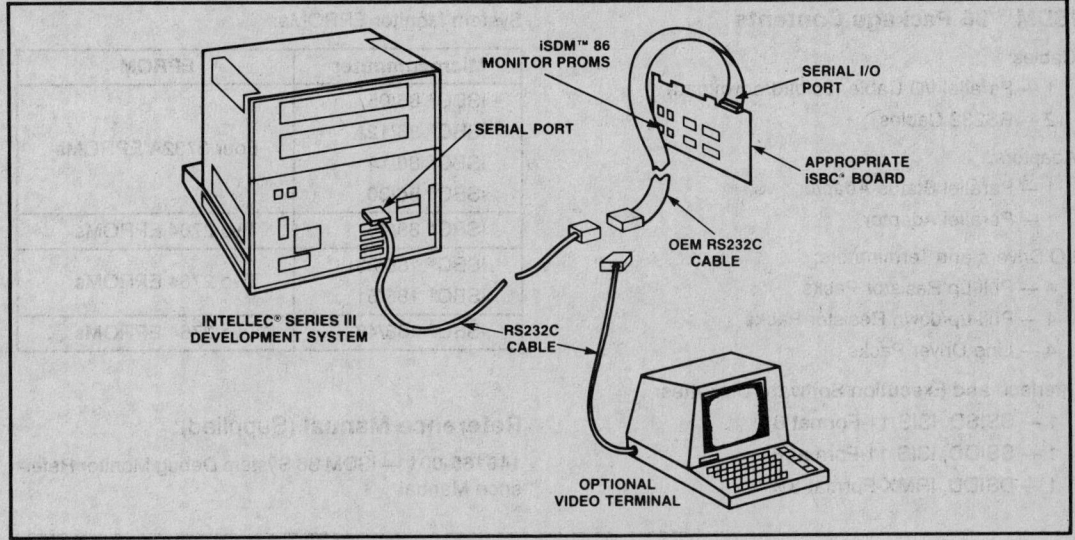

Figure 1. Typical iSDM™ 86 Serial Connection Environment

SPECIFICATIONS

Development System Environment

The Intellec Microcomputer Development System may be utilized for application program development and, if used, requires the following to support the iSDM 86 package:

- 48 Kbytes memory
- Double density or single density diskette subsystem
- ISIS-II Operating System and associated language translators

iAPX 86, 88, 186, 188 TARGET SYSTEM ENVIRONMENT

To support the iSDM 86 package, the target system must contain the following:

- 2K read-write memory beginning at location 0H
- 16K read-only memory beginning at location FC000H
- For Parallel link:
  — 8255A Programmable Peripheral Interface
- For Serial link:
  — 8251A USART or 8274 Multiprotocol Serial Controller, and 8253/4 or 80130 or iAPX 186/188 timer, or
  — 82530 Serial Communications Controller, including 82530 timer

Hardware

- Supported iSBC Microcomputers:

iSBC 86/05	Single Board Computer
iSBC 86/12A	Single Board Computer
iSBC 86/14	Single Board Computer
iSBC 86/30	Single Board Computer
iSBC 88/25	Single Board Computer
iSBC 88/40	Single Board Computer
iSBC 88/45	Single Board Computer
iSBC 186/03	Single Board Computer
iSBC 186/51	Single Board Computer
iSBC 188/48	Single Board Computer

- Supported iSBX MULTIMODULE™ Boards:

  iSBX 350 Parallel I/O MULTIMODULE Board
  iSBX 351 Serial I/O MULTIMODULE Board

iSDM™ 86

iSDM™ 86 Package Contents

Cables:
   1 — Parallel I/O Cable (upload/download)
   2 — RS232 Cables

Adaptors:
   1 — Parallel Status Adaptor
   1 — Parallel Adaptor

I/O Drivers and Terminators:
   4 — Pull-up Resistor Packs
   4 — Pull-up/down Resistor Packs
   4 — Line Driver Packs

Interface and Execution Software Diskettes:
   1 — SSISD, ISIS 11-Format 8″
   1 — SSIDD, ISIS 11-Format 8″
   1 — DSIDD, iRMX-Format 5¼″

System Monitor EPROMs:

Microcomputer	EPROM
iSBC® 86/05	Four 2732A EPROMs
iSBC® 86/12A	
iSBC® 86/14	
iSBC® 86/30	
iSBC® 88/45	Two 2764 EPROMs
iSBC® 186/03	Two 2764 EPROMs
iSBC® 186/51	
iSBC® 188/48	Two 2764 EPROMs

Reference Manual (Supplied):

146165-001 — iSDM 86 System Debug Monitor Reference Manual

ORDERING INFORMATION

Part Number	Description
iSDM 86 RO	Object Software
	Intellec to target system interface and target system monitor, suitable for use on iSBC 86, 88, 186, 188 computers, or other iAPX 86, 88, 186, 188 microcomputers. Package includes cables, EPROMs, software and reference manual.
	The OEM license option listed here allows users to incorporate iSDM 86 into their applications. Each use requires payment of an Incorporation Fee.
	The iSDM 86 package, also includes 90 days of support services that includes Software Program Report Services.
	As with all Intel Software, purchase of any of these options requires execution of a standard Intel Software License Agreement.

iSDM™ 286
iAPX 286 SYSTEM DEBUG MONITOR

- **Development support for iSBC® 286- and iAPX 286-based applications**
- **Real Address Mode (RAM) and Protected Virtual Address Mode (PVAM) support**
- **Support of MULTIBUS® I and MULTIBUS® II environments**
- **Powerful debugging commands, including single step CPU operation**
- **For MULTIBUS® II, software configuration of system boards at start-up and automatic configuration of memory boards**
- **Universal Development Interface (UDI) support via development system connection**
- **Command execution, including program load capability from Intellec® Series III or Series IV Development Systems**
- **Supports 80287 Numeric Processor Extension (NPX) for high-speed math applications**

The Intel iSDM™ 286 System Debug Monitor package contains the necessary software, cables, EPROMs, and documentation required to interface an iSBC® 286 board or iAPX 286 application to an Intellec® Series III or Series IV through a high-speed link. The System Debug Monitor supports an OEM's choice of MULTIBUS® I or MULTIBUS® II environments, and the iRMX™ Real-Time Multitasking Operating System or a custom operating system. The monitor contains debugging tools that examine CPU registers, memory content, CPU descriptor tables, and other crucial environmental details. The Monitor also allows programs to access files on the development system via the internal UDI support and the serial communication link.

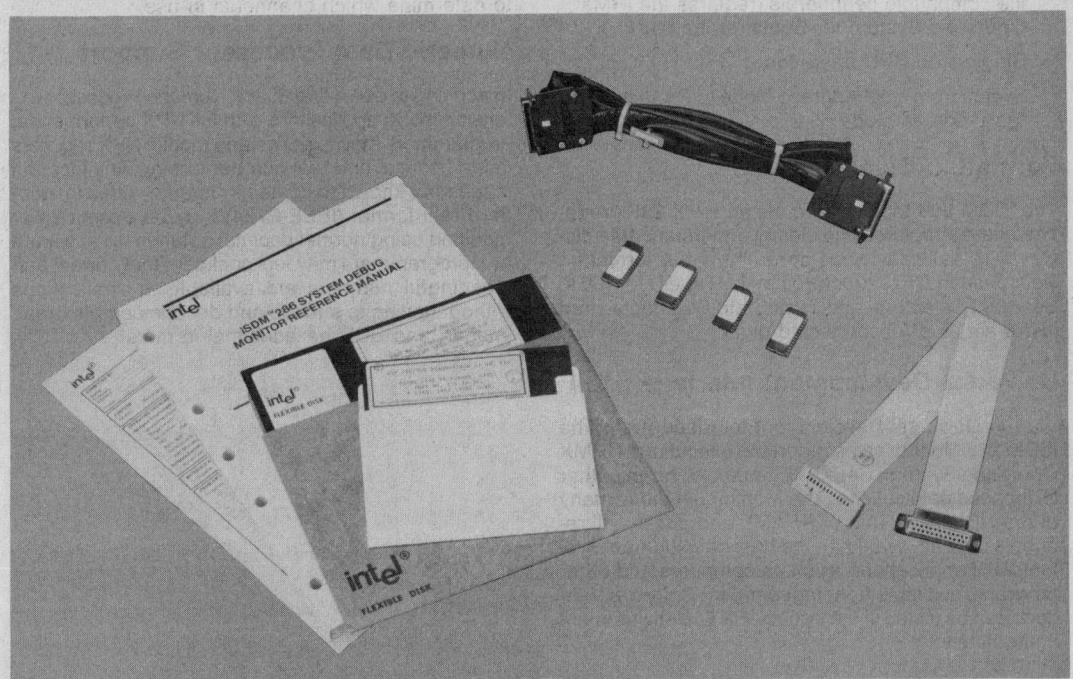

Intel Corporation assumes no responsibility for the use of any circuitry other than circuitry embodied in an Intel product. No other circuit patent licenses are implied. Information contained herein supersedes previously published specifications on these devices from Intel.

© INTEL CORPORATION, 1984

iSDM™286 MONITOR

FUNCTIONAL DESCRIPTION

Overview

The iSDM 286 System Debug Monitor provides programmers of iAPX 286-based applications with the debugging tools needed to test new applications ranging from single-user systems to complex operating systems executing in either a MULTIBUS I or MULTIBUS II environment. Programmers are given direct access to both the Real Address (RAM) and Protected Virtual Address (PVAM) modes of the CPU via a simple terminal interface or via an Intellec Series III or Series IV Development System.

Powerful Debugging Commands

The iSDM 286 Monitor contains a powerful set of user functions, including commands to:

- Examine and modify CPU registers
- Examine, modify, and move memory locations
- Symbolic reference to variable names
- Find and compare memory contents
- Set program breakpoints
- Bootstrap load application software from iRMX file compatible peripherals (requires the iRMX Operating System for Bootstrap Loader)
- Single-step CPU operation
- Switch from Real Address Mode to Protected Virtual Address Mode

Formatted Displays

The iSDM 286 Monitor formats all iAPX 286 predefined data structures into clearly understandable displays. This display gives programmers a formatted view of such CPU structures as LDTs, GDTs, IDTs, Segment Selectors, and Task State Segments—not just a series of unconnected digits.

Universal Development Interface (UDI)

Via the Universal Development Interface (UDI), the iSDM 286 Monitor can support the execution of iRMX Operating System, Series III, Series IV, or any other UDI-based applications. The Monitor emulates many of the UDI calls (RAM or PVAM), and passes all requests for a file system to the host development system. UDI applications, such as compilers and other programs available from Independent Software Vendors, can be tested in the target iAPX 286 environment immediately.

MULTIBUS® II Software Configuration of System Boards

The MULTIBUS II Interconnect Space Registers allow the software to configure boards, eliminating much of the need for jumpers and wire wraps. The iSDM 286 Monitor can initialize these registers at configuration time using user-defined values. The Monitor can also automatically configure memory boards, defining the addresses for each board sequentially in relation to the board's physical placement in the card cage. This feature allows for the swapping, adding, and deleting of memory boards on a dynamic basis.

Command Execution

Commands to the iSDM 286 Monitor are entered interactively via a standalone terminal, an Intellec® Series III or a Series IV Development System. The target application hardware is connected to the terminal or development system via a serial link. Figure 1 shows a typical MULTIBUS I environment and Figure 2 shows a typical MULTIBUS II environment. All control operations and UDI file manipulations occur over the serial link through the cables supplied. More than one channel can be configured for the communication since the Monitor scans all configured channels to determine which channel is in use.

Numeric Data Processor Support

In addition to executing 80287 Numeric Processor Extension (NPX) applications with full NPX performance, programmers may examine and modify NPX registers using decimal and real number format. Any location in memory known to contain numeric values in standard real format (IEEE-P754) may be examined or modified using normal decimal notation. In this manner, programmers may feel confident that correct and meaningful numbers are available to applications without having to encode and decode complex real, integer, and BCD hexadecimal formats.

iSDM™ 286 MONITOR

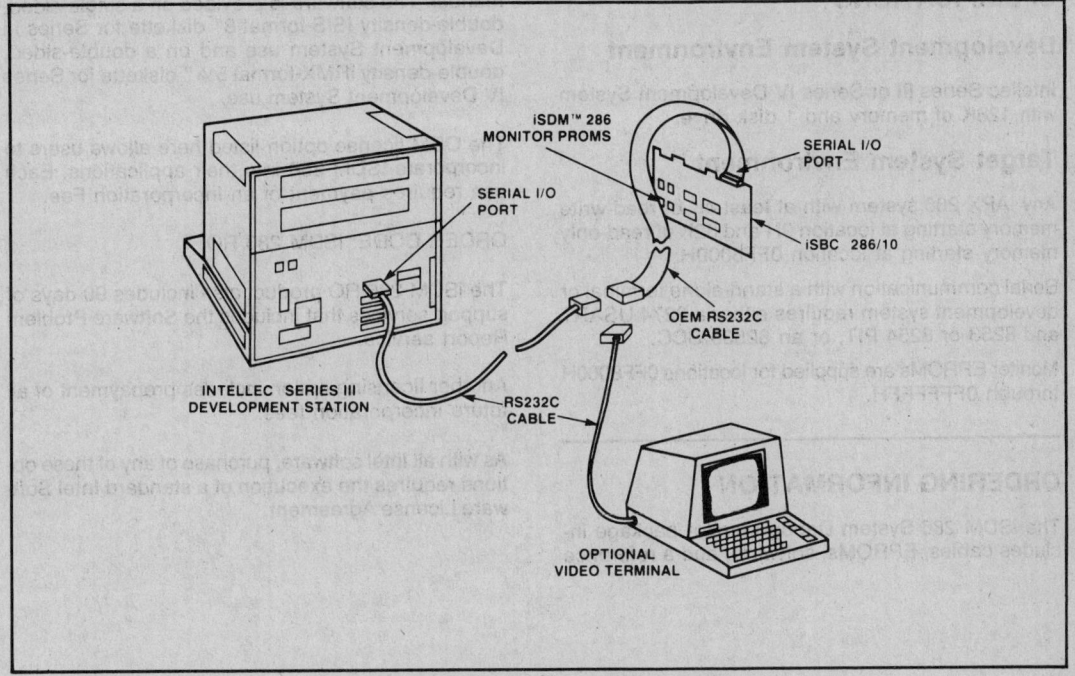

Figure 1. Typical MULTIBUS® I Environment

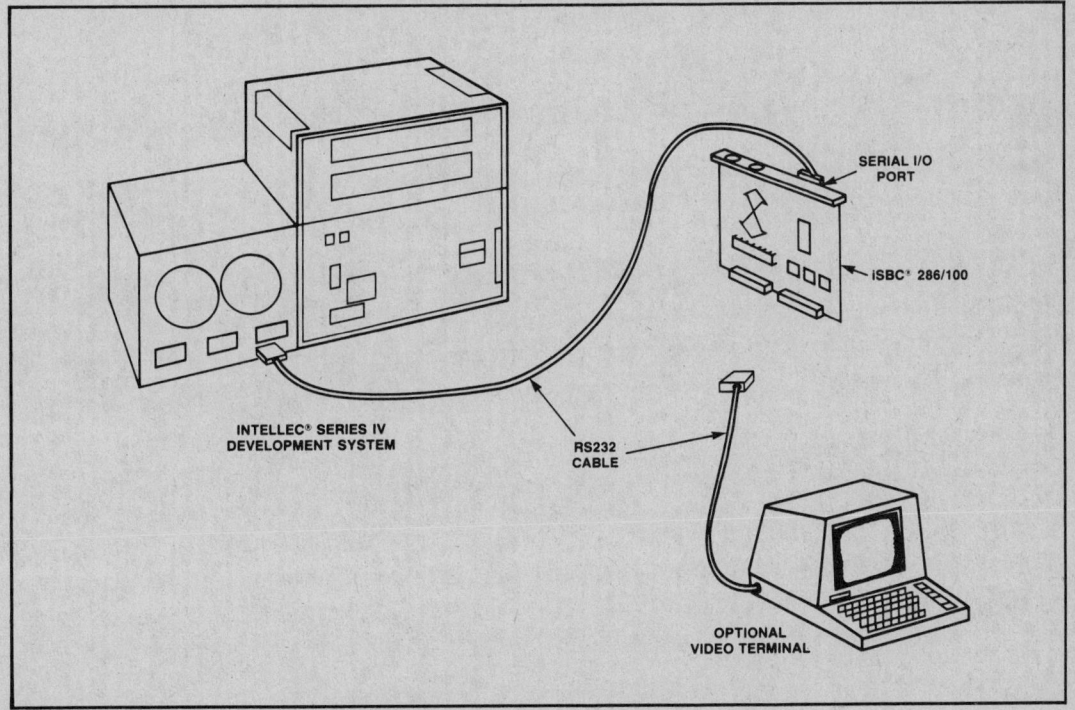

Figure 2. Typical MULTIBUS® II Environment

iSDM™ 286 MONITOR

SPECIFICATIONS

Development System Environment

Intellec Series III or Series IV Development System with 128K of memory and 1 disk drive.

Target System Environment

Any iAPX 286 system with at least 4K of read-write memory starting at location 0H and 32K of read-only memory starting at location 0FF8000H.

Serial communication with a stand-alone terminal or development system requires either a 8274 USART and 8253 or 8254 PIT, or an 82530 SCC.

Monitor EPROMs are supplied for locations 0FF8000H through 0FFFFFFH.

ORDERING INFORMATION

The iSDM 286 System Debug Monitor package includes cables, EPROMs, software, and a reference manual. The software is provided on a single-sided, double-density ISIS-format 8" diskette for Series III Development System use and on a double-sided, double-density iRMX-format 5¼" diskette for Series IV Development System use.

The OEM license option listed here allows users to incorporate iSDM 286 into their applications. Each use requires payment of an Incorporation Fee.

ORDER CODE: iSDM 286 RO.

The iSDM 286 RO product also includes 90 days of support services that includes the Software Problem Report service.

Another licensing option includes prepayment of all future incorporation fees.

As with all Intel software, purchase of any of these options requires the execution of a standard Intel Software License Agreement.

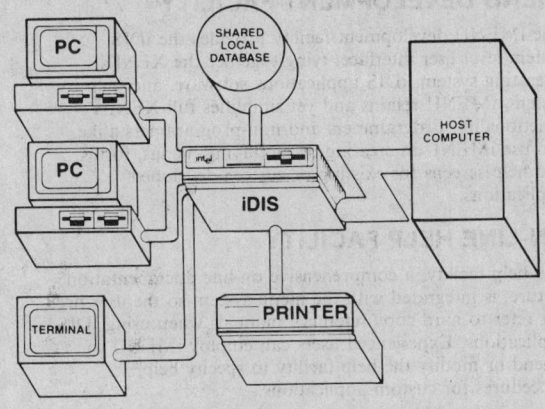

iDIS
DATABASE INFORMATION SYSTEM

- Complete desk-top integrated office productivity software
- Building block for departmental-level applications
- Direct mainframe database extract and file transfer facilities
- Gateway for personal computer and terminal access
- Multiuser XENIX* 3.0 operating system
- Local relational database management and report writer
- Integrated software with on-line help facility
- Word processing, spreadsheet, menu development, and communication options

BUILDING VERTICAL APPLICATIONS

The Intel Database Information System (iDIS) is a fully-integrated multiuser software system. It serves in end-user applications and as a powerful access tool in the connection between a mainframe and the end-user. Data can be maintained by central data processing departments and distributed to departmental users through a network of terminals and PCs. The system can be configured as a gateway in the micro-to-mainframe flow of data or as a stand-alone processor with shared local database capabilities. The iDIS system includes an SQL-compatible, multiuser relational DBMS for shared access to disk storage and features a full range of information processing functions for multiple concurrent users at all levels of technical skill.

iXTRACT HOST DATABASE EXTRACT FACILITIES

The iDIS system offers an interactive, menu-driven mode of database extract. With the Remote File Transfer (RFT) iXTRACT facility, a "flat file" (sequential) data structure can be downloaded from the mainframe and converted into a local relational database. Using host computer utilities to generate the flat file, the RFT facility can download data from virtually any DBMS or file management system. The facility is bidirectional, such that flat files can be transmitted between a mainframe host and an iDIS system with its network of terminals and personal computers.

MICROSOFT XENIX

The iDIS operating system is provided by XENIX 3.0, an enhanced industry-standard version of UNIX.** While the system developer has access to all XENIX functionality, the operating system appears to be transparent to the user who interacts with the iDIS software through its menu system.

iDB-LOCAL RELATIONAL DATABASE MANAGEMENT (DBMS)

The iDIS system offers the iDB DBMS, a full-function relational DBMS that supports an interactive query/update language similar to that of IBM's SQL. Included with iDB is a Report Writer package. This allows users to prepare custom reports quickly from information in iDB without programming knowledge. The iDB DBMS offers the power of a mainframe DBMS at the microsystem level. Multiple iDB users can concurrently access common local databases with confidence in system integrity.

Other features include:
- A user-prompting data entry and update system
- A bulk loading and unloading utility for rapid transfer of data among files and databases
- Extensive on-line help facilities
- Descriptive error and diagnostic messages
- Programmatic interface to the C language and XENIX shell.

INTEGRATED SOFTWARE INTERFACE

The iDIS software family is integrated into a set of productivity tools. Data can be easily transferred among the various iDIS application packages, such that the iWORD processor, iPLAN (Multiplan†) spreadsheet, and iDB DBMS can interchange data and reports. All iDIS decision-support tools can be easily brought to bear on a particular data-analysis problem.

Individually, each package is accessible through a common user interface — a hierarchical menu system serving as a superstructure for the complete iDIS system. A common help facility binds all iDIS software.

iWORD PROCESSOR

Intel iWORD supports a complete office-wide range of document preparation functions. The iWORD user can develop, edit, store, format and print a variety of presentation-quality business documents, including reports, memoranda, technical documents, specifications and manuals. All iWORD commands are in plain English and many can be executed by a single keystroke. The iWORD processor is also sufficiently powerful for the experienced user, offering access to XENIX text processing capabilities including the printer- and typesetter-drivers nroff and troff. An on-line help facility is continuously available.

Major iWORD editing and formatting features include:
- Full-screen editor with on-line display of formatted text
- Embedded commands for global formatting
- Spelling/dictionary module and mail/merge facility
- Right justification, underlining, indentation, centering, footnotes, superscripts and subscripts.

iPLAN (MULTIPLAN) SPREADSHEET

The iDIS system supports 'what if' decision-modeling with iPLAN (Multiplan) Spreadsheet, a multi-purpose tool capable of a wide variety of business and scientific tabulations. The iPLAN user can custom-tailor a versatile two-dimensional matrix for specific analyses, including financial modeling, planning and forecasting. Like the other functions in the iDIS software environment, the iPLAN spreadsheet accepts data four ways: from the keyboard, from the iDB DBMS, from mainframe databases (via the data extract facility), and from formatted XENIX files.

Important iPLAN features include:
- Easy-to-use English commands
- Vertical and horizontal scrolling, multi-window and multi-table display
- Presentation of extra large tables
- Linking and updating multiple interrelated spreadsheets
- Automatic updating of calculations
- Alphanumeric sorting capabilities
- Extensive, on-line help facility.

PERSONAL COMPUTER (iPC) CONNECTION

To complete the Data Pipeline connection, the iDIS system offers a menu-driven file conversion and transfer facility that allows single-user PC files to be accessed in the multiuser XENIX environment. The PC user can use the iDIS system to convert database and spreadsheet files from popular PC file formats (such as dBASE II††, Lotus 1-2-3‡ and Multiplan formats) to iDB file formats. As a result, mainframe files can be downloaded to relational structures within iDB databases and further converted and downloaded to PC-based files for local applications analysis. The PC user can operate in three modes: bidirectional iDIS-to-PC file transfers, terminal emulation, and local PC-DOS control.

iMENU DEVELOPMENT FACILITY

The iMENU development facility provides the iDIS system-level user interface, tying together the XENIX operating system, iDIS applications software, and help system. iMENU retains and yet simplifies full XENIX functionality. Programmers and non-programmers alike can use iMENU in creating or modifying menus, forms, and help screens for existing or custom-developed applications.

ON-LINE HELP FACILITY

The help facility, a comprehensive on-line documentation feature, is integrated with the menu system so the user need not refer to hard copy reference manuals when using iDIS applications. Experienced users can employ iMENU to extend or modify the help facility to specify help procedures for custom applications.

COMMUNICATIONS

The iDIS communications subsystem provides remote job entry (RJE) to mainframe hosts through its emulation of a HASP multileveling workstation or 2780/3780 protocol. TTY passthrough facilities also provide direct access to remote interactive applications, including other iDIS systems and personal computers. Support for 3270 BSC emulation is also available.

BASE SOFTWARE SYSTEM

- XENIX 3.0 operating system
- C programming language
- 'vi' editor
- XENIX utilities (including nroff and troff text processors)
- Electronic mail and calendar
- iDISBASE runtime system menus
- Help facility
- Complete system diagnostics

OPTIONAL SOFTWARE

- iWORD processor
- iPLAN (Multiplan) spreadsheet
- iMENU menu development system
- iDB and Report Writer
- iPC (personal computer link)
- RJE communication support (2780/3780 and/or HASP protocol)
- 3270 BSC emulation

---

iWORD is a version of Horizon Word Processing, a trademark of Horizon Hardware Systems, Inc. iPLAN is a version of Microsoft's Multiplan, a trademark of Microsoft Corporation. iMENU is a version of Schmidt's/menus, a trademark of Schmidt Associates.

*Trademark of Microsoft Corporation
**UNIX is a trademark of AT&T Bell Laboratories.
†Multiplan is a registered trademark of Microsoft Corporation.
††dBASE II is a trademark of Ashton-Tate.
‡Lotus and 1-2-3 are trademarks of Lotus Development Corporation.

iRMX™ LANGUAGES

- Industry-standard languages and utilities for developing applications on iRMX-based systems. Includes FORTRAN, Pascal, C, BASIC, PL/M, Macro assembler, AEDIT text editor
- Complete set of utilities to create and manage object modules
- Mix languages on single application system with UDI standard
- Intel 8087 and 80287 math coprocessor support
- 8086 and 80286 compatibility
- Worldwide post-sales service and support organization

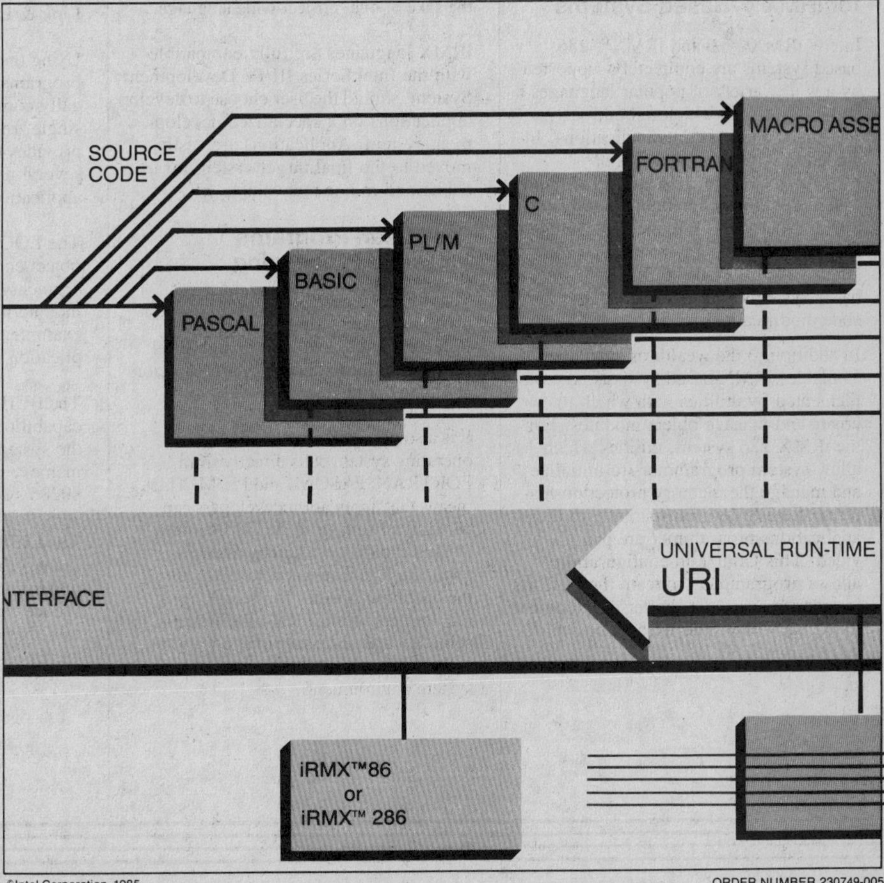

© Intel Corporation, 1985
*XENIX is a trademark of Microsoft Corporation.
†UNIX is a trademark of Bell Laboratories.

ORDER NUMBER 230749-005

Full Language Support for iRMX™-Based Systems

Intel's iRMX™ 86 and iRMX™ 286-based systems are completely supported by a wide variety of popular languages and utilities with which to build fast, real-time, multi-tasking applications. Included are the latest versions of FORTRAN, Pascal, BASIC, PL/M and Macro Assembler for Intel's 8086 and 80286 processors. Previously developed applications using any of these languages port easily to iRMX-based systems with minimal source code modifications.

In addition to the wealth of languages available, iRMX-based systems are complemented by utilities with which to create and manage object modules. For the iRMX 286 system, utilities which allow system programmers to initialize and manage the memory protection features of the 80286 transparently to the applications programmer are provided. This latitude in configurability allows programmers to team their efforts in order to achieve a shorter development time than would otherwise be possible.

Because the high-level languages are actually resident on the iRMX-based system, OEMs can pass application software directly on to end users. End users may then tailor the OEM's system to better meet application needs by writing programs using the same languages.

Language-Independent Application Development

Intel's Universal Development Interface (UDI) and Object Module Format (OMF) enable several users to write different modules of an application, in different languages, then link them together.

The OMF provides users with the ability to mix languages on a single application system, affording the luxury of choosing exactly the right language tools for specific pieces of the application, rather than compromising specialized tasks for the sake of one, project-wide language.

iRMX languages are fully compatible with the Intel Series III/IV Development System, should the user choose to develop applications on a specialized development system. Applications are easily moved to the final target system for test, debug and minor redevelopment.

Fast, Lean Programs for Rapid Processing

The iRMX language products enable programmers to write the smallest, fastest programs available in high-level languages, due to the compiler's superior ability to optimize code.

It is also possible to make iRMX operating system calls directly from FORTRAN, PASCAL and PL/M. This means that application developers can take full advantage of the iRMX multi-tasking capability, whereby multiple applications execute concurrently on the operating system. Multi-tasking, a requirement of most real-time systems, is sometimes as necessary in application software development as in an operating system environment.

Standardized REALMATH Support

All the iRMX languages (except BASIC and C) support the REALMATH floating point standard. This ensures universal consistency in numeric computation results and enables the user to take advantage of the Intel 8087 and 80287 Numeric Data Processor or iSBX™ 337 MULTIMODULE™ boards, which boost performance two to four times over that possible on a mini-computer.

Complete Set of Program Linkage and System Building Utilities

Utilities for iRMX 86 operating systems include Intel's own LINK 86, LOCATE 86 and LIBRARIAN. For iRMX 286, BIND 286 & BUILD 286 replace Link & Locate.

Using the LINK 86 or BIND 286 programs, users may combine individually compiled object modules to form a single, relocatable object module. This provides the ability to merge work from several programmers into one cohesive application system.

The LOCATE 86 utility maps relocatable object code into the processor memory segments, allowing user definition of module/memory type allocation. For example, often-used portions of an application may be mapped to (P)ROM.

The BUILD 286 utility provides the major capabilities of LOCATE 86 plus allows the system programmer to specify the memory protection scheme for the 80286 system.

The LIBRARIAN object code library manager affords easy creation, collection and maintenance of related object code to reduce the overhead of separately maintained modules.

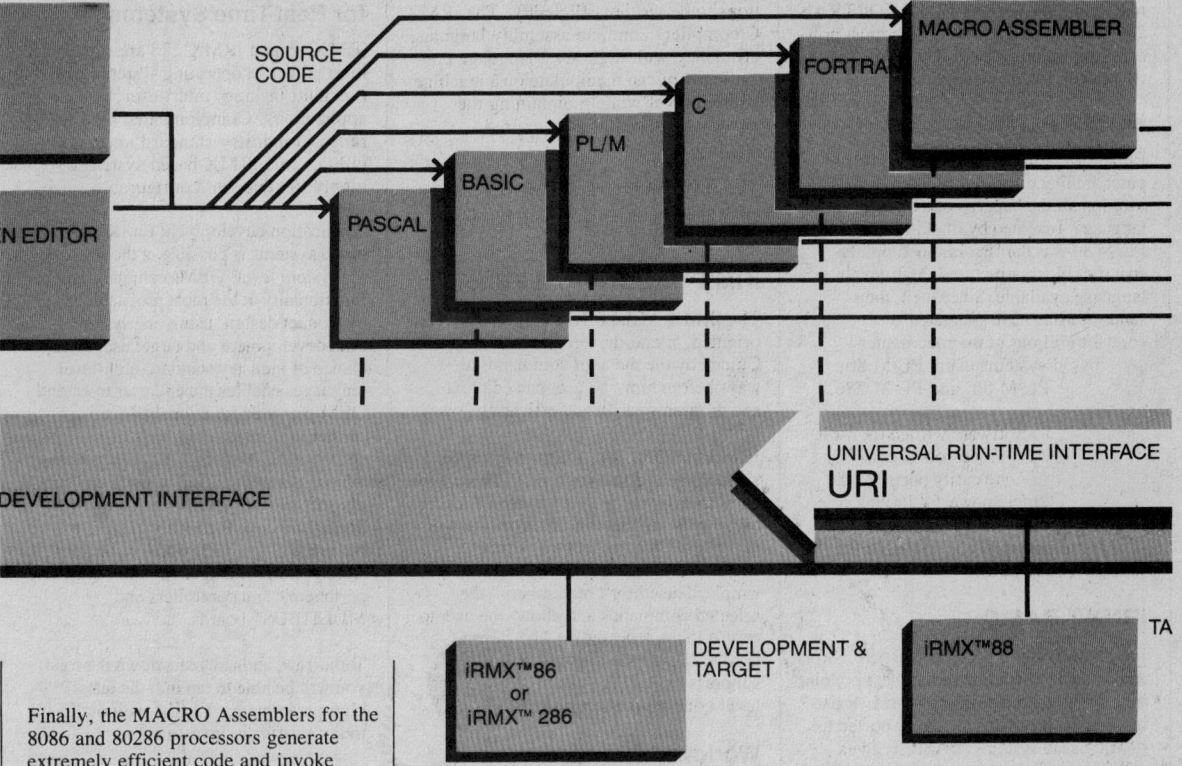

Finally, the MACRO Assemblers for the 8086 and 80286 processors generate extremely efficient code and invoke 8086/8087 or 80286/287 machine instructions.

iRMX™ Pascal

iRMX Pascal meets the proposed ISO language standard and implements several microcomputer extensions. A compile-time option checks conformance to the standard, making it easy to write uniform code. Industry-standard specifications contribute to portability of application programs and provide greater reliability.

iRMX 86 Pascal supports extensions, such as an interrupt-handler and direct port I/O extension, that allow programs to be written specifically for microcomputers. Separate module compilation allows linkage of Pascal modules with modules written in other high-level languages.

iRMX™ FORTRAN

The iRMX FORTRAN compiler provides total compatibility with FORTRAN 66 language standards, plus most new features provided by the FORTRAN 77 language standard including complex numbers. iRMX FORTRAN includes extensions specifically for microcomputer application development. Programming is simplified by relocatable object libraries, which provide run-time support for execution time activities.

iRMX FORTRAN 86 supports the 8087 math coprocessor and iRMX FORTRAN 286 supports the 80287 for the most powerful microcomputer solutions available in number-intensive applications.

iRMX™ PL/M

PL/M offers full access to micro-computer architecture while simultaneously offering all the benefits of a high-level language. Invented by Intel in 1976, PL/M 80 was the first microcomputer-specific, block-structured, high-level language available. Since then, thousands of users have generated code for millions of microcomputer-based systems using PL/M 80, PL/M 86, and PL/M 286.

Software written for 8-bit processors (PL/M 80) are easily ported to the more powerful 16-bit (PL/M 86) environment. The same portability is available for the 80286 (PL/M 286).

iRMX™ BASIC

Intel's offering of Microsoft BASIC 86 is a standardized version of the most popular high-level language in the world. Existing BASIC programs are easily ported to iRMX-based systems. BASIC is an excellent pass-through language by which an OEM can offer customers the ability to write and modify their own applications.

iRMX™ 86 C Compiler

The popular programming language C, is fully supported on iRMX-based systems. iRMX C offers both small and large segmentation models, enabling applications to be written efficiently. The iRMX C compilers combine assembly language efficiency with high-level language convenience; it can manipulate on a machine-address level while maintaining the power and speed of a structured language.

The iRMX 86 C compiler affords easy portability of existing C programs to iRMX-based systems.

iRMX™ AEDIT Text Editor

The iRMX AEDIT Text Editor is screen-oriented, menu-driven and easy to learn. Guided by the menu of commands always before him, the user can edit text and programs easily and efficiently.

iRMX AEDIT Text Editor allows the simultaneous edit of two files. This allows easy transferral of text between files and use of existing material in the creation of new files. Creating macros, strings of frequently-used commands, is also very simple. The editor "remembers" the selected commands and allows the user to re-use them repeatedly. The iRMX 286 version also supports operating system level command execution.

Worldwide Service and Support

All iRMX systems are completely supported by Intel's worldwide staff of trained hardware and software engineers. Support available includes Hotline (telephone) Support, Software Updates, and a Subscription Service.

Complete documentation is provided for all operating system and application software languages, as well as for system hardware components. An Intel system is not a collection of hardware and software pieces as much as a cohesive whole that is supported and serviced as such.

Intel Has Total Solutions for Real-Time Systems

iRMX 86 and iRMX 286 are the fastest, most powerful operating systems available for multi-tasking, multi-user, real-time applications. Complemented by a wide range of industry-standard languages and utilities, the iRMX-based systems are highly flexible and configurable.

Application development for iRMX-based systems is possible at the board or the system level. OEMs can integrate functionality at the most profitable level of product design, using one system for both development and target use. Intel's choice of industry standard high-level languages enables the end user to extend OEM-provided functionality even further, if desired.

Who is better qualified to write and supply software for Intel VLSI than Intel? Today you have the ability to tap into hundreds of available application software packages, languages and utilities, peripherals and controllers and MULTIBUS® boards.

Tomorrow, and ten years down the road, you will be able to tap into the latest, high-performance VLSI—without losing today's software investment.

Specifications

Required Hardware
- Any 8086/286 based or iSBC 86/286 based system including Intel's System 86/300 and 286/300 family. In addition, object code from the 8086 compilers will run on 8088 or 80186 based systems.
- 700KB of memory
- Two iRMX compatible floppy disks or one hard disk
- One 8" single density or 5.25" double-density floppy disk drive for distribution of software
- System console device

Required Software
The iRMX 86 Operating System Release 6 or later including the Nucleus, Basic I/O System, Extended I/O System and Human Interface layers.
— or —
The iRMX 286 Operating System including the Nucleus, Basic I/O System, Extended I/O System and Human Interface.

Purchasing of any iRMX 86-resident language requires signing of Intel's Software License Agreement (SLA). A software license is shipped with each iRMX 286-resident language.

Data Sheets
- 8086 Compilers:
  8086/88/186/188 Software Packages (Intel order number 210689)
- 80286 Compilers:
  80286 Software Development Tools (Intel order number 231665)

Ordering Information

iRMX 86 LANGUAGES		iRMX 286 LANGUAGES	
Language	Order Code	Language	Order Code
ASM 86, Utilities	R86 ASM 86	ASM 286, Utilities	R286 ASM 286
FORTRAN 86	R86 FOR 86	ASM 86, Utilities	R286 ASM 86
PL/M 86	R86 PLM 86	AEDIT Text Editor	R286 EDI 286
AEDIT Text Editor	RMX 864	PL/M 286	R286 PLM 286
BASIC 86	RMX 865		
Pascal 86	R86 PAS 86		
C 86	R86 C 86		

iRMX™ 86 OPERATING SYSTEM

- High-performance, real-time, multi-tasking operating system for Intel's 86/3xx and 286/3xx microcomputer systems
- Highly configurable, modular structure for easy system expansion
- Wealth of design facilities and industry-standard languages to support fast, easy development
- Application software portable to next generation of Intel VLSI
- Supported by Intel's post-sales software support organization

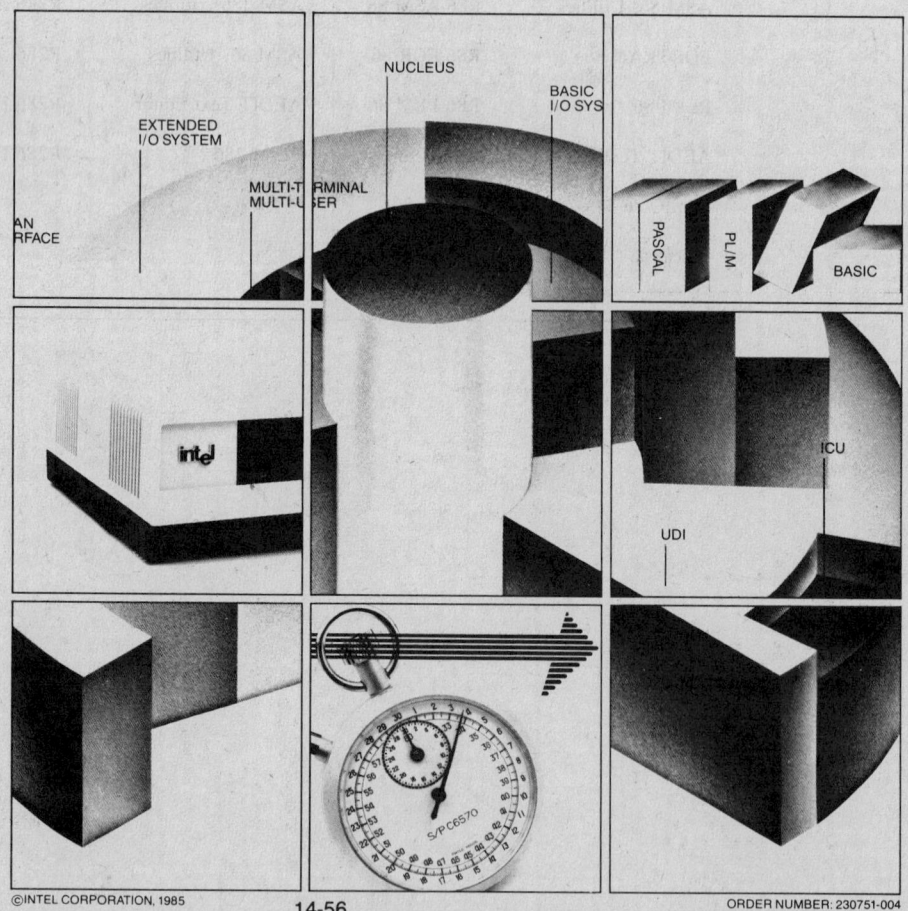

©INTEL CORPORATION, 1985

ORDER NUMBER: 230751-004

The Total Solution for the Real-Time Application OEM

Intel's iRMX™ 86 Operating System is a real-time, multi-tasking, multiuser, multiprogramming operating system designed to support high performance, time-critical applications such as factory automation, industrial control and communications networks. The iRMX 86 operating system serves as an optimized event-driven executive for managing and extending the resources of Intel's System 86/3xx and 286/3xx series microcomputers in real-time applications where high speed and low interrupt latency are required. Added performance for demanding numeric-intensive tasks comes from support of Intel's floating point math coprocessors.

Comprised of modular layers, Intel's iRMX 86 operating system is highly configurable, allowing the OEM to easily customize the system to meet the needs of target applications. In addition, the iRMX 86 operating system provides OEMs with complete development capabilities. It has system debuggers, crash analyzers, screen editors, utilities, and an Interactive Configuration Utility (ICU)—everything the development engineer needs to design and configure efficiently.

To further reduce development time, a complete set of industry-standard languages enables OEMs to take advantage of existing application software. This shaves months off development time and is a key advantage to the competitive OEM.

Speed, the Name of the Real-Time Game

In a real-time system the computer must respond to interrupts instantly; time is always at a premium. Intel's iRMX 86 Operating System delivers superior real-time performance, thanks to ultra-fast context switching, task synchronization and memory-based message passing.

The iRMX 86 Operating System manages the resources of the System 286/3xx series microcomputer in real-address mode. iRMX 86 software makes

possible the utilization of the high-performance capabilities of Intel's iAPX 286 microprocessor for those demanding high-speed applications.

Further accelerating processing power in number-crunching and floating point math applications is the iRMX 86 Operating System's support of Intel's math coprocessors.

Our 8087 numeric data processor in our iRMX 86-based systems can perform floating point operations four times faster than competitive minicomputers with hardware math processors. For even greater performance, OEMs can select the iAPX 286 and the 80287 coprocessor working in tandem in the iRMX 86 system.

The superior price/performance ratio that results from combining Intel's iRMX 86 Operating System and the System 3xx family makes the choice clear: a more competitive Intel micro-based system over a more expensive minicomputer-based system.

Add More Processors for More Power, More Speed

Need still more micro-muscle in your application? In an iRMX-86-based system, additional intelligent boards can be added to enhance system throughput.

Multiprocessing is possible due to the hardware capabilities of Intel's System 3xx MULTIBUS System Bus. Overall system performance and flexibility can be greatly enhanced by off-loading the main CPU with such intelligent I/O boards as Intel's quad serial communication controller, digital controller or Ethernet communications controller.

Modular Software for Versatile, Easy Configuration

The iRMX 86 Operating Systems shipped with Intel's 86/3xx and 286/3xx hardware systems are preconfigured at the factory to support a standard board set; however, the OEM can additionally

configure or extend the operating system to meet specific needs.

Intel's iRMX 86 Operating System is configurable by system layer and by system call within each layer. Such flexibility gives designers the ability to choose software features that best suit their application's size and functional requirements. The iRMX 86 Operating System also includes I/O drivers for many of Intel's MULTIBUS boards

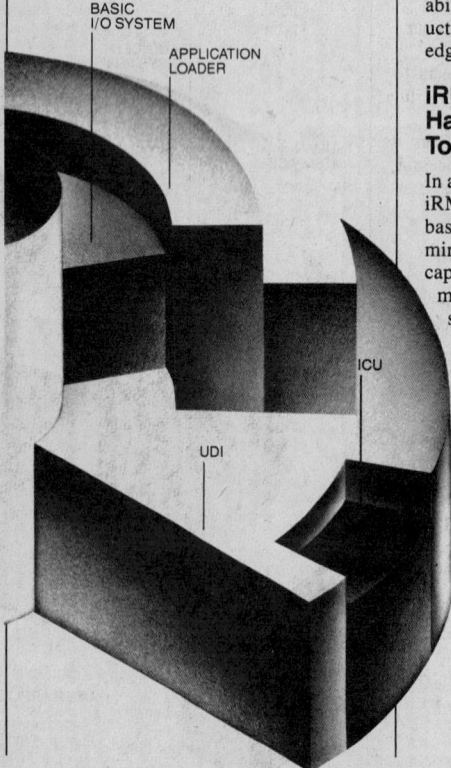

and industry-standard peripherals. You simply select the ones you need.

The Interactive Configuration Utility (ICU) is a built-in facility for assisting the OEM in the configuration process. The ICU prompts the user for system parameters and requirements, then builds a command file to compile, assemble, link, and locate necessary files.

The net results for the OEM: fast, easy system configuration with quick time-to-market benefits.

For customizing and extending your iRMX 86 system, Intel has provided all the "hooks" necessary to make the job easy. The iRMX 86 Operating System contains extendability features that enable the OEM to add custom operating system calls, custom features, and custom functionality to his application—at any time in the appilcation's life. The ability to add functions late in a product's life is key to an OEM's competitive edge in a fast-changing market.

iRMX™ 86 Operating System Has All the Fundamentals, Too!

In addition to multiprocessing, Intel's iRMX 86 Operating System has all the basics you would expect to find in a minicomputer operating system... capabilities such as multitasking, multiprogramming, and multiterminal support.

Multitasking requires a method of managing the different processes of an application and for allowing these processes to communicate with each other. The iRMX 86 Nucleus provides these facilities plus task scheduling. The Basic I/O System provides users with the system calls for direct management of I/O devices needed for real-time applications. The Extended I/O System adds a number of I/O management capabilities to simplify access to files, such as automatic buffering and synchronization of I/O requests.

The Human Interface functions give users and applications simple access to the file and system management capabilities. Using the multiterminal support provided by the Basic I/O system, the Human Interface can suppo several simultaneous users. For example, multi-terminal support allows one person to use the iRMX 86 Editor, while another compiles a FORTRAN or Pascal program, while several others load and access applications.

On-Target Development: One System Does It All

The beauty of Intel systems lies in their flexibility. Engineers developing an iRMX 86-based target system can use the same iRMX 86-based system in the development process; the development and target systems are one in the same. The bottom-line benefit is low entry-level costs for the OEM.

On-target development contributes immeasurably to a shorter development curve and decreased time-to-market, since it isn't necessary to purchase and learn separate development systems. With Intel's iRMX 86-based system, one system does it all.

Tap into a Wide Range of Languages and Utilities

An Intel iRMX 86-based system supports many industry-standard and widely available languages: FORTRAN 77, Pascal (ISO Draft Standard) and PL/M compilers; Intel Assemblers, and popular independent vendor products, such as Microsoft's BASIC and Mark Williams' C compiler.

The iRMX 86 Operating System also has a menu-driven, screen-oriented text editor and a variety of utilities for manipulating object code to facilitate the development process.

Multiple-language support is made possible by a set of systems calls known

as the Universal Development Interface (UDI) which enables the iRMX 86 system to interface with many compilers and language translators. UDI ensures that users will be able to transport applications to future releases of the iRMX 86 Operating System as well as use language and utilities of other software vendors that support UDI. (For more information on Intel iRMX languages, see the iRMX Language Fact Sheet)

As an option, a commercial extension package iCEX is available. It provides such useful utilities as: A Shared I/O System (SIOS) that allows multiple tasks to access mass storage data through shared buffers in main storage; a Re-entrant Program Manager (RPM) that eliminates the need to have multiple copies of the same program in memory to support concurrent applications; a File Printer; Multi-user LOG ON facilities; and many more.

Intel's Open Systems Approach Means Freedom to Grow

At Intel, we believe that systems need to expand in order to meet the needs of a changing market; and that is how we design our products.

Standards are the key to systems that are open to future expansion, future technology and future markets.

Intel's iRMX 86 Operating System is built from the inside-out with industry standards: UDI (Universal Development Interface), RTI (Runtime Interface), MULTIBUS System Bus (IEEE 796), Ethernet (IEEE 802.3), extended math format (IEEE P754), and industry-standard peripheral device interfaces.

An OEM who builds his product around one of Intel's iRMX 86-board systems is assured of multi-vendor hardware/software alternatives and a future upgrade path. In today's highly competitive markets, that is the only kind of system to build.

Today, you'll have the ability to tap into readily available application software packages, languages, and utilities, MULTIBUS boards, and peripherals. Tomorrow, you will be able to tap into the latest, high-performance VLSI without sacrificing today's software investment. Applications written on iRMX 86 will run on Intel's iAPX 86, iAPX 88, iAPX 186, iAPX 188 and iAPX 286 (Real Address Mode) based systems.

Not to be forgotten are the advantages of starting from the systems level to begin with. Intel has invested hundreds of man-years in software and hardware development for its systems products. For the OEM trying to meet a market window, time-to-market is much faster when starting with a system instead of boards or components. It makes good business sense to let Intel provide the "micro-engine", so you can concentrate on your area of expertise and get to market sooner!

Worldwide Service and Support

The iRMX 86 Operating System is a mature proven product with thousands of installations at the component, board and systems levels. Post-sales software support is available to Intel iRMX 86 Operating System OEMs in the form of software updates and routine systems software maintenance. Software support is extendable in one-year increments after the initial 90-day support period. Technical Information Phone Service is available separately to customers needing quick regional software support. All software is completely documented, and users receive monthly technical reports, newsletters and access to the iRMX 86 users group and software libraries.

iRMX 86 users can also take advantage of Intel's worldwide staff of trained hardware and software engineers for application design assistance. We offer complete training for operating system software and associated system hardware, bringing OEM's up to speed and helping get their products to market quickly.

Intel, the Technology Leader ...With the Total Solution

Intel started the microprocessor revolution with the 4004 and has been the market leader with every generation of advanced microprocessor VLSI since. We not only invented the microprocessor but MULTIBUS single board computers, as well.

Intel's technology leadership has, by necessity, extended from microprocessors into operating system software. The iRMX 86 system is recognized as one of the industry's leading real-time VLSI operating systems.

OEMs can enhance their product's marketability by leveraging their value-added on top of the solid foundation of an iRMX 86-based Intel Series 3xx microcomputer system. Intel's solution offers the most price/performance with the least risk to progressive OEMs... because we know the real-time game from the inside out.

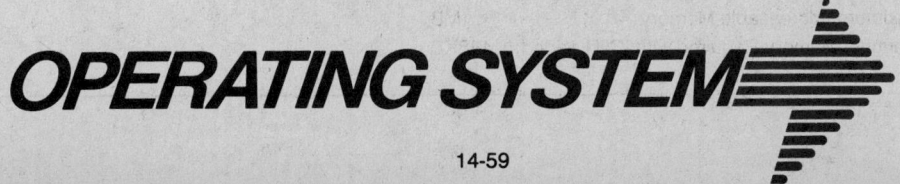

Specifications

Supported Software Products

iRMX 860	iRMX 86 Development Utilities Package including the iAPX 86 and 88 Linker, Locator, Macro Assembler, Librarian, and the iRMX 86 Editor
iRMX 861	Pascal 86/88 Compiler
iRMX 862	FORTRAN 86/88 Compiler
iRMX 863	PL/M 86/88 Compiler
iRMX 864	TX Screen-Oriented Editor
iRMX 865	BASIC Interpreter
iRMX 866	C Compiler
iRMX 868	Commercial Extensions

Supported Hardware Products

iSBC® MULTIBUS® Products

iSBC 86/12A, 86/05, 86/14, 86/30, 86/35, 88/25 and 88/40 Single Board Computers
iSBC 186/03 Single Board Computer
iSBC 186/51 Ethernet Controller
iSBC 188/48 Communications Controller
iSBC 286/10 Single Board Computer (Real Address Mode only)
iSBC 204 Flexible Disk Controller
iSBC 206 Hard Disk Controller
iSBC 208 Flexible Disk Controller
iSBC 215(G) Winchester Disk Controller
iSBC 220 SMD Disk Controller
iSBX 251 Bubble Memory System
iSBC 254 Bubble Memory System
iSBC 534 4-Channel Terminal Interface
iSBC 544 Intelligent 4-Channel Terminal Interface and Controller
iSBX 218(A) Flexible Disk Controller
iSBX 350 Parallel Port (Centronix-type Printer Interface)
iSBX 351 Serial Communications Port
iSBX 270 CRT, Light Pen and Keyboard Interface
System 86/3xx Family
System 286/3xx Family

Available Literature

The iRMX 86 Documentation Set consists of the following four volumes of reference manuals. Order numbers are associated with these four volumes only.

iRMX 86 Introduction and Operator's Reference Manual for Release 6
Order Number: 146545-001

Introduction to the iRMX 86 Operating System

iRMX 86 Operator's Manual

iRMX 86 Disk Verification Utility Reference Manual

iRMX 86 Programmers Reference Manual for Release 6, Part 1
Order Number: 146546-001

iRMX 86 Nucleus Reference Manual

iRMX 86 Basic I/O System Reference Manual

iRMX 86 Extended I/O System Reference Manual

iRMX 86 Programmer's Reference Manual for Release 6, Part II
Order Number 146547-001

iRMX 86 Application Loader Reference Manual

iRMX 86 Human Interface Reference Manual

iRMX 86 Universal Development Interface Reference Manual

Guide to Writing Device Drivers for iRMX 86 and iRMX 88 I/O Systems

iRMX 86 Programming Techniques

iRMX 86 Terminal Handler Reference Manual

iRMX 86 Debugger Reference Manual

iRMX 86 System Debugger Reference Manual

iRMX 86 Crash Analyzer Reference Manual

iRMX 86 Bootstrap Loader Reference Manual

iRMX 86 Installation and Configuration Guide for Release 6
Order Number: 146548-001

iRMX 86 Installation Guide

iRMX 86 Configuration Guide

Master Index for Release 6 of the iRMX 86 Operating System

iRMX™ 86 Configuration Size Chart

System Layer	Min. ROMable Size	Max. Size	Data Size
Bootstrap Loader	1K	1.5K	6K*
Nucleus	10.5K	24K	2K
BIOS	26K	78K	1K
Application Loader	4K	10K	2K
EIOS	10.5K	12.5K	1K
Human Interface	22K	22K	15K
UDI	8K	8K	0
Terminal Handler	3K	3K	0.3K
Debugger	28.5K	28.5K	1K
Human Interface Commands			116K
Interactive Configuration Utility			308K

System 86/300 Memory:	348KB
Maximum Addressable Memory:	1MB
Minimum Memory Required with ICU Loaded:	448KB

*Usable by System after Bootloading.

Ordering Information

Each iRMX operating system includes two startup systems supporting Intel's System 300 standard hardware and Intel processor boards. Intel System customers also receive the iRMX 860 (Assembler, Linker, Locator, Libraries, Editor, Utilities) and iRMX 863 (PL/M Language) products and are entitled to one prepaid incorporation fee. Also included: Software Problem Reporting Service (SPR), and a 90 day System Software Subscription (new s/w release updates). Also includes System Software documentation.

Refer to Intel's OEM price list, OEM Microcomputer System section, for ordering information.

As with all Intel software, purchase of the iRMX 86 Operating System requires the execution of a standard Intel Software License Agreement.

iRMX™ 286/386 Software System

The iRMX™ 286/386 software is an extension of the iRMX 286 Real-Time Operating System designed to manage and extend the resources of iSBC® 386 Single Board Computers and other 80386-based microcomputers. The iRMX 286/386 software is a real-time, multi-tasking and multi-programming software system providing the capability of executing all the configurable layers of the iRMX 286 Operating System on the 80386 microcomputer and the iSBC 386/20 and iSBC 386/100 Single Board Computers. The iRMX 286/386 software functions on MULTIBUS® I architectures and MULTIBUS II architectures, including full message passing support.

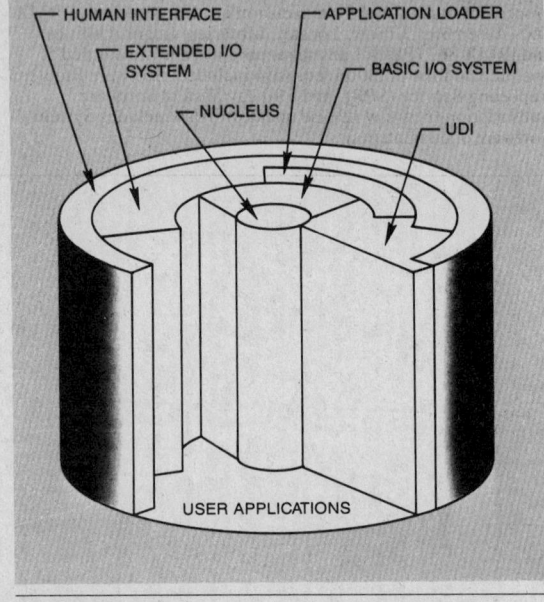

Product Highlights

— Real-time processor management for time critical 80386 applications not requiring use of the extended instruction set
— 16 Megabytes of memory addressable
— Supports 80286-based compilers and tools
— iRMX™ 86 Operating System compatibility
— Supports full Message Passing on industry standard MULTIBUS® II architecture
— Hardware traps aid in debugging
— On-target system development with Universal Develpment Interface (UDI)
— Configurable system size and functions for diverse application requirements
— All iRMX™ 286 code can be (P)ROMmed to support totally solid state designs
— Device drivers included for industry standard MULTIBUS™ peripheral controllers
— Complete support of Numeric Processor Extensions
— Powerful utilities for interactive configuration and debugging

Product Description

The iRMX™ 286/386 software is a real-time, multi-tasking and multi-programming software system providing the capability of executing all the configurable layers of the iRMX 286 Operating System on the 80386 microcomputer and the iSBC® 386/20 and iSBC 386/100 Single Board Computers. With the processing power of the 80386 processor and the ability to address 16 Mbyte of memory, the utility of iRMX 286/386 systems extends into applications where immediate access to the speed and performance advances in VLSI technology is paramount and use of the extended instruction set of the processor is not required.

These iRMX 286/386 systems deliver real-time performance and explicit control over resources; yet also support applications with multiple users needing to simultaneously access terminals. The configurable layers of the system provide services ranging from interrupt management and standard device drivers for many sophisticated controllers to data file maintenance commands provided by a comprehensive multi-user human interface.

By providing access to the standard Universal Development Interface (UDI) for each user terminal,

Original Equipment Manufacturers (OEMs) can pass program development and target application customization capabilities to their users. By maintaining application source code compatibility with the iRMX 86 Operating System, users can preserve their software investment. The system also provides a number of standard interfaces that allow applications to take advantage of industry standard device controllers and hardware components.

The iRMX 286/386 software is a complete set of system software modules that provide the resource management functions needed by computer systems. These management functions allow OEMs to best use resources available in microcomputer systems while getting their products to market quickly, saving time and money. Engineers are relieved of writing complex operating system software and can instead concentrate on their application software.

OpenNET™ PRODUCT FAMILY XENIX* NETWORKING SOFTWARE

- Existing applications distributed without change
- Product family for complete seven layer solution based upon standards
- Network services for XENIX 3.0 industry standard multiuser operating system
- Intel 286/300 Series Supermicro Systems interoperable with IBM personal computers over IEEE 802.3 LAN, "Ethernet"†
- Total system support from Intel's worldwide field and support organization

©INTEL CORPORATION, 1985
*XENIX is a trademark of Microsoft Corp.
†Ethernet is a trademark of Xerox Corp.

SEPTEMBER 1985
ORDER NUMBER: 270055-002

System 286/310AP with 311 Peripheral Subsystem

THE TOTAL LAN SOLUTION FOR MICROCOMPUTER APPLICATIONS

OpenNET is Intel's Open Systems strategy for Local Area Networks (LAN). A LAN is critical for those applications that require dedicated high speed communication within short distances. The OpenNET product family provides all the necessary hardware and software to network multiple Intel 286/300 Series Supermicro Systems together with IBM PCs, XTs, ATs, and their compatibles.

Intel is committed to support and drive standard technology for the microcomputer industry. OpenNET is Intel's strategy for connecting microcomputer systems over local area networks. The OpenNET product family follows the International Standards Organization (ISO) Open Systems Interconnection (OSI) seven layer model. Only integrated products that conform to this model and that are based upon open and public standards will carry the OpenNET name.

The OpenNET LAN solution is comprised of modular layers offered at all levels of integration. Each layer runs with state-of-the-art silicon for the best performance at a low cost. The XENIX Networking software implements layers 5 to 7 of the ISO model by providing a transparent local area network interface for applications. It runs with the industry standard multiuser operating system XENIX 3.0 on 286/300 Series Supermicro Systems sold by Intel. Layers 3 and 4 are implemented by Intel's iNA 961 ISO Transport Software that runs on the 80186-based iSXM™ 552 Ethernet COMMengine which implements layers 1 and 2 with advanced silicon.

STANDARD LAN TECHNOLOGY — CRITICAL FOR SUCCESS

With the proliferation of microcomputers in industry today, high speed communication between these systems is necessary for timely decision making. The most cost efficient method for achieving this communication is through local area networks. Not only do LANs provide direct transfer of information but also the sharing of expensive peripherals. Data can be distributed across the network for better reliability and availability.

LANs provide the capability for easy modular growth. As needs increase more systems can be added to the network at any time. This keeps initial investments low without compromising future growth. Network systems can also be specialized for different applications. OpenNET leads the way by providing the connection of multiuser systems and personal computers, each providing unique user capabilities that are shared across a local area network. With OpenNET based upon standards, the number of different systems that also can connect to the same network will grow.

XENIX NETWORKING — THE TRANSPARENT INTERCONNECT LAN

In combination with the iNA 961 ISO Transport software and the iSXM 552 Ethernet COMMengine, XENIX Networking provides Transparent Remote File Access and additional networking services. The XENIX Networking software runs underneath the XENIX 3.0 operating system. There are no special operating system calls that applications need to do in order to access remote files. Instead, applications make the standard XENIX file access requests to OPEN, CLOSE, READ, and WRITE files across the network. The XENIX operating system determines from the file name if it is on a local storage device or re-

IBM PC

mote across the network. All this implies that since applications can access remote files as if they were local, they do not need to be modified in any way to run across the network!

The OpenNET topology makes networked microcomputer systems look like one large computer system. There is one community of users with a consistent view of the file system. All systems on the OpenNET LAN have an easy to use logical name; a user can LOGON to any system in the network and access files on any remote system simply by using its logical name. The XENIX Networking software keeps track of each system's logical name and where it is on the network (i.e., its Ethernet address), all transparently to the user and application.

The OpenNET LAN is extremely flexible and can be configured to fit the customer's own particular needs of performance and security. Systems can easily be set up to allow all, some, or no systems on the network access to its file system. Once access is granted, the standard XENIX file security is in place for owner, group, and world access.

MAIL, PRINT SPOOLING AND NETWORK SYSTEM BACKUP

The standard XENIX 3.0 mail will operate across the OpenNET LAN allowing XENIX users to communicate with each other. In addition, XENIX users can initiate applications on remote XENIX systems to start at any time using the AT command. This command allows the user to spool print jobs at any system on the network, and all XENIX files can be archived and restored from one tape drive or diskette on the network using the TAR command.

INDUSTRY STANDARD PROTOCOLS

Ethernet is the IEEE 802.3 standard for layers 1 and 2 of the ISO model. It is the physical medium most commonly offered by computer vendors. With over 1,000 possible connections spread over nearly one mile, it provides a high performance solution for both cluster and backbone networks. Intel's iSXM 552 is IEEE 802.3 compatible.

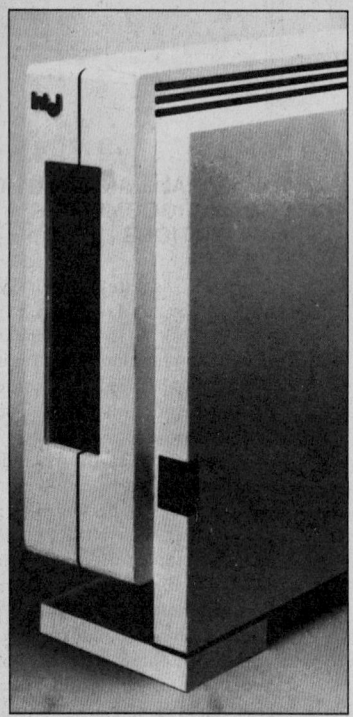
Floorstanding System 286/310AP

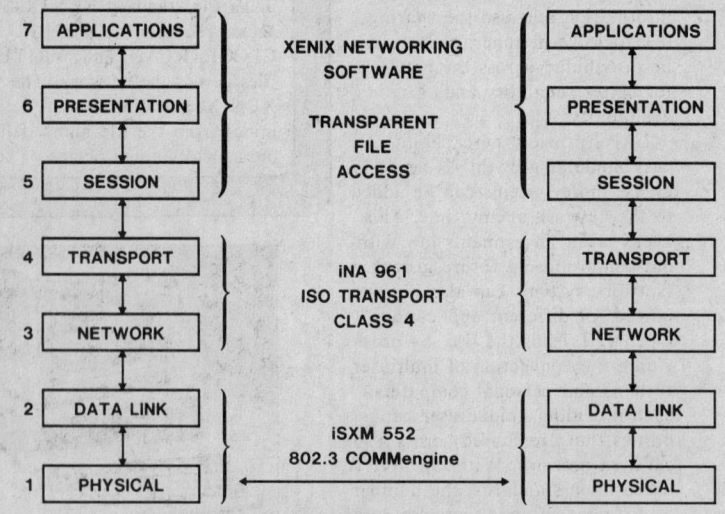

The iNA 961 software was one of the first implementations of the industry standard ISO 8073 Transport Protocol, and it provides a very high transfer rate at the transport layer of over 170 KBytes a second. Intel's iNA 960 is ISO Transport Class 4 compatible.

Layer 7 Network File Access Protocols were jointly developed by Intel, Microsoft, and IBM. The Core Protocols were developed for personal computer operating systems like MS-DOS*. The Extended Protocols add capabilities for multitasking and multiuser operating systems like XENIX and iRMX™. Both of these Network File Access Protocols are publicly available for implementations on other operating systems. XENIX Networking (as well as iRMX

*Trademark of Microsoft Corporation

Networking) is a full implementation of the extended protocols and fully supports the Microsoft Networks implementation for MS-DOS running on IBM Personal Computers and compatibles.

COMPLETE LAN SOLUTION

When the XENIX Networking Kit is ordered with the iSXM 552, it includes all the necessary hardware and software to connect a 286/300 Series system running XENIX 3.0 onto an Ethernet Network. (All Ethernet cable, transceiver, and transceiver cable must be purchased separately.) This solution works equally well with Cheapernet.

The iSXM 552 board is configured strapped for the 286/300 Series and has all the necessary PROMs and RAM included. All that has to be done is to take it out of the box, plug it into the system, and connect the supplied internal cable to the backplane. The iNA 961 Transport Software is preconfigured for the iSXM 552 board and is automatically down loaded onto it by the XENIX Networking software.

The XENIX 3.0 operating system software from Intel already has the special Network File Access hooks built into it and therefore requires no special configuration when the XENIX Networking software is added.

Special utilities are included for creating files that characterize the network to the customer's own particular requirements. These need only be created once and can be dynamically updated.

No software needs to be written for a user to start taking advantage of all the network benefits. Applications that ran before on the stand-alone system will now access files over the network by simply telling it on which network system the files are located. This does not mean that a remote file is brought local and then accessed; rather each RECORD of the remote file is accessed as needed, thus minimizing network activity. The OpenNET transparent file access utilizes a LAN as it is supposed to be used, taking full advantage of a LAN's high bandwidth and low latency to deliver high performance microsystem networks. A network "SYSTEM" can hold conversations with as many as twenty other network systems at the same exact time. The configuration is dynamic and changes automatically to meet the needs of each system such that over 1000 network nodes can be connected.

WORLDWIDE SUPPORT AND SERVICE

The OpenNET Product Family is warranteed for 90 days and includes software updates. Once this warranty expires customers can choose from a variety of support contracts, or they can elect for service on a per-call basis. Additionally, Open Systems service, covering non-Intel portions of the system as well as Intel-supplied parts is available on a negotiated basis.

A factory-resident group offers software service with consulting support, response to problem reports, and a HOT LINE for critical problems that just won't wait. Intel offers complete training on the XENIX Networking software as well as for the entire OpenNET product line.

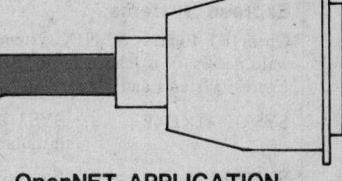

OpenNET APPLICATION SUPPORT

Intel has Field Application Engineers specializing in everything from system software to complex peripherals. These professionals are dedicated to supporting customers in the pre-sales development environment. A separate group, Systems Engineers, is dedicated to post-sales consulting support. Intel's built-in quality, 80-plus worldwide field service locations, and a staff of trained hardware and software application engineers are major advantages for the user or reseller trying to get an application running and, once running, having the systems maintained.

INTEL, THE TECHNOLOGY LEADER ... WITH THE TOTAL LAN SOLUTION — OpenNET

Intel is committed to pushing the frontiers of VLSI design to their ultimate limits. We started the microcomputer revolution with the 4004 and have been the market leader with every generation

System 286/380 with 383 Peripheral Subsystem

of advanced microprocessor VLSI since. Intel not only invented the microprocessor and MULTIBUS single board computer, but also was instrumental in creating the Ethernet standard as well. Systems and system software are a natural for us: who better knows the pieces and how to make them work together over a local area network. No other hardware/software LAN combination offers a faster and more economical path to getting networked systems and applications on the market than the OpenNET product family.

ORDERING INFORMATION

Complete Network-Ready Systems

Complete XENIX OpenNET network-ready systems are available for any of Intel's 286/310 or 286/310AP system configurations. Order one of the 310 or 310AP XENIX systems: SYS310-44X, SYS310-41X, SYS310-50X, SYS310-46X, SYS310AP-44X, SYS310AP-41X, SYS310AP-42X and the XENIX OpenNET Kit: XNX-NET-KIT-NRI.

Express Systems

OpenNET Express XENIX systems are fully preconfigured and staged supermicrosystems with OpenNET capability. All software necessary is loaded on the system Winchester disk. A retrofit OpenNET Express Kit is also available. Also included with Express systems and kits are all necessary hardware and software to fully connect an IBM or compatible PC to OpenNET.

SYS310-41XEXP	SYS310-41X, XENIX-NET, SXM 552, iNA 961, DCM 911-1, MDX 457 (2), NIU, MS-NET, installation and training
SXMXEXP	Equivalent to SYS310-41XEXP without the 310-41X system. Retrofit OpenNET Express kit.

XENIX Networking Software

XNX-NET-961-NSU	XENIX Networking and iNA 961 Object Software (both 8″ and 5¼″ double-sided, double density) plus rights for 8 copies
XNX-NET-KIT-NRI	XENIX Networking and iNA 961 Object Software (both 8″ and 5¼″ double-sided, double density) plus an iSXM 552S Ethernet board for pass-through use
XNX-NET-RO	XENIX Networking Software (both 8″ and 5¼″ double sided, double density) plus license rights
XNX-NET-RF	Software Incorporation Fee for XENIX Networking Software
XNX-NET-SR	Machine readable source code for XENIX Networking Software
iNA-961-RO	iNA 961 Transport Software plus license rights

LAN Hardware

iSXM552	Ethernet COMMengine plus one iNA 961 Software Incorporation Fee
iMDX457	Ethernet Transceiver Cable
iMDX3015	Ethernet Transceiver
iMDX3016-1	Ethernet Cable
iDCM911-1	Intellink

Ethernet Hardware and Software for the IBM Personal Computer is available from Ungermann-Bass, Inc. Contact Jim Langer, 408-496-0111.

SPECIFICATIONS

The XENIX Networking software along with the iNA 961 software and the iSXM 552 are qualified to run on Intel's 286/310, 286/310AP, and 286/380 systems.

XENIX* LANGUAGES

- COBOL, BASIC and FORTRAN support for Xenix-based systems
- Conformation to international standards: ANSI 77 subset FORTRAN, ANSI X3.23 1974 COBOL to Federal High Level and ANSI X3.60—1978 subset BASIC
- Powerful microcomputer extensions to ANSI standards
- Easy porting of mainframe and minicomputer applications to micro environment
- Intel 80287 math coprocessor support in FORTRAN
- Worldwide service and support organization

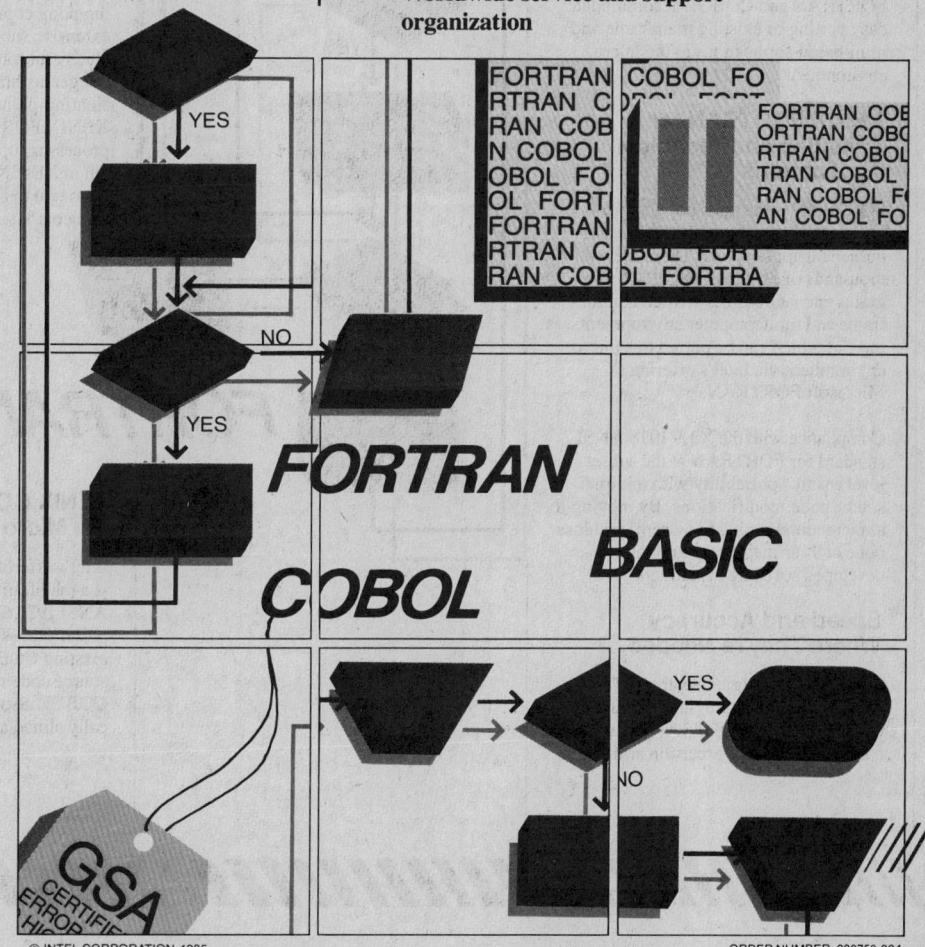

© INTEL CORPORATION, 1985
*XENIX is a trademark of Microsoft Corporation.

ORDER NUMBER: 230750-004

High-level Language Support for XENIX-Based Systems

Intel's XENIX operating system, available for component, board, or system-level integration, is a multi-user operating system well suited for both technical and commercial interactive applications. Typical applications include small business systems, software development/ engineering workstations, distributed data processing and graphics.

For OEM and end-user application development on XENIX, Intel has provided three industry-standard, high-level languages—FORTRAN, COBOL and BASIC—with which to build microcomputer-based solutions for systems products or component and board-level applications. XENIX BASIC, FORTRAN and COBOL accommodate easy porting of existing mainframe and mini-based applications to the micro environment.

XENIX FORTRAN for Scientific and Technical Applications

FORTRAN is the most popular programming language for scientific and numerical applications. There are thousands of existing FORTRAN programs and subroutines written in mainframe and minicomputer environments, most of which can be ported to a micro environment via Intel's offering of Microsoft FORTRAN.

Compliance with the X3.9 1978 ANSI standard for FORTRAN at the subset level ensures portability with minimal source code modifications. By moving to a microcomputer-based system, you lose none of your mainframe and mini-developed software investment.

Speed and Accuracy Where They're Needed

Scientific, math-oriented applications usually require fast, highly accurate processing. XENIX FORTRAN delivers accuracy with double-precision arithmetic

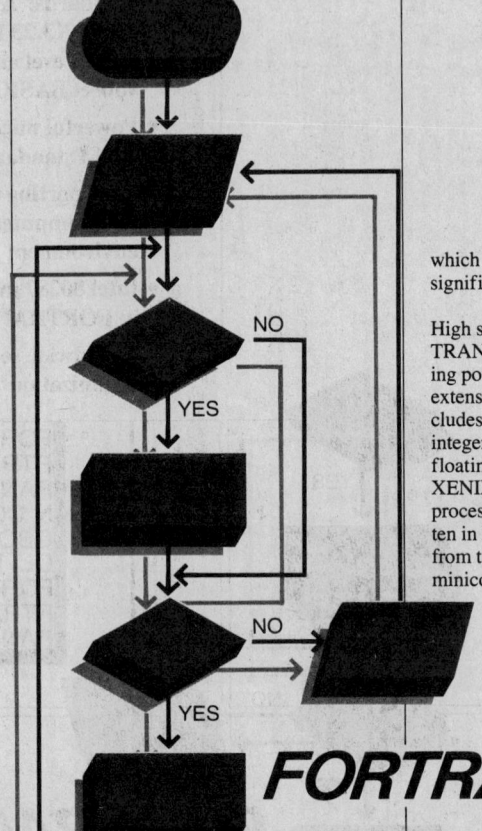
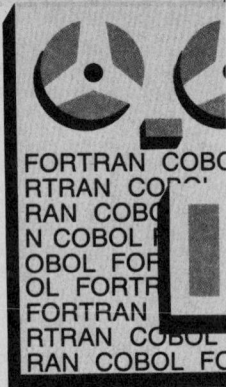

which handles numbers containing 15 significant digits.

High speed results from XENIX FORTRAN support of the Intel 80287 floating point coprocessor, as well as from an extensive subroutine library, which includes subroutines for 16- and 32-bit integer arithmetic and 32- and 64-bit floating-point arithmetic. Because of XENIX FORTRAN's 80287 math coprocessor support, some programs written in XENIX FORTRAN will execute from two to four times faster than their minicomputer counterparts.

XENIX COBOL for the Micro Environment

Intel's offering of Microfocus COBOL is a mainframe-caliber compiler for ANSI 1974 COBOL programs, enabling XENIX-based systems to compile and run existing COBOL programs with minimal source code modification. XENIX COBOL also contains features specifically aimed at facilitating the interactive

*XENIX is a trademark of Microsoft Corporation.

BASIC

program development of new applications in a microcomputer environment.

These features include a facility for dynamically loading sub-programs from disk as required which effectively removes limits on the size of the application code that can be run. XENIX COBOL augments the functionality of the ANSI standard with additional compiler features, such as interactive screen-handling, that further increase convenience and programmer productivity.

Users can license a separate run-time support package. This enables OEMs to pass COBOL applications onto customers at a much lower cost than that involved in transferring full COBOL packages.

XENIX COBOL is one of only eleven COBOL compilers in existence — and the only one for microcomputers — that has been GSA-certified as error-free at the High Level. A special ANSI-defined communications module provides the user with a standard mechanism for program-to-program message-passing in multi-user networks such as those found in an "office of the future" settings.

Forms-2™ Support for Screen-Painting

XENIX COBOL supports FORMS-2, a powerful visual programming tool that speeds the creation of programs involving interactive screen-handling. In an extremely user-friendly environment, the user "paints" a form on the screen, and FORMS-2 generates the COBOL source code to support it. FORMS-2 results in greatly improved programmer productivity in a microcomputer, screen-building environment.

XENIX BASIC for Maximum Flexibility

Intel's offering of Microsoft BASIC opens a whole window of applications to the XENIX user. Since their BASIC is the same as that used on MS-DOS* based machines, most programs written for MS-DOS can now run on XENIX unchanged. When developing your own

COBOL

programs, BASIC is simple and easy for quick prototyping, yet complete enough for total development. Conforming to the ANSI X3.60 1978 subset standard, BASIC also has powerful extensions, 16 significant digit Double Precision floating point arithmetic, and assembly languages routine calling capabilities. From using applications to designing your own programs BASIC is easy, complete, and extremely flexible.

Worldwide Service and Support

All XENIX systems are fully supported by Intel's worldwide staff of trained hardware and software engineers. Complete documentation is provided for all operating systems and application software languages, as well as for system hardware components. The XENIX and XENIX Languages warranty includes Hotline support, Software Updates, and Subscription Service.

Total Solutions for Interactive, Multi-User Applications

Intel's XENIX-based systems offer the most complete solutions for interactive, multi-user applications requiring fast, accurate throughput and a friendly programming environment. XENIX is complemented by industry-standard, high-level languages with which OEMs can create flexible and open end-user systems.

XENIX languages are completely portable — from one level of integration to another (chip to board to system).

Intel is paving the way into the future of VLSI and pioneering VLSI-based systems. We are committed to providing customers with smooth, uninterrupted application development on the latest VLSI-based systems - today and tomorrow.

*MS-DOS is a trademark of Microsoft Inc.

XENIX* LANGUAGES

Specifications

Required Hardware:
- Any iAPX 286 based or iSBC® 286 based system including Intel's 286/300 family and iDIS systems
- 196 KB memory
- Two floppy disks or one hard disk
- One 8" double-density or 5.25" double-density floppy disk drive for distribution of media

Required Software:
- Intel's XENIX 286 Operating System
- Purchase of any Xenix Language requires signing of Intel's Software License Agreement (SLA)

Ordering Information

Language	Order Code	Product Contents	Warranty
COBOL*	XNX 2867	One 8" diskette and one 5.25" diskette Level II COBOL Language Reference Manual—122158 Level II COBOL Operating Guide—122159 Forms II Utility Manual—122160 Level II COBOL Pocket Guide—122161	**90 days:** Software Updates, Subscription Service
	XNX 2868	Incorporation Fee for passing through the COBOL Runtime System	
FORTRAN**	XNX 2862	One 8" diskette and two 5.25" diskettes Fortran Reference Manual Fortran User's Guide	**90 days:** Software Updates, Subscription Service
BASIC*	XNX 2865	One 8" diskette and one 5.25 diskette BASIC Reference Manual BASIC User's Guide	**90 days:** Software Updates, Subscription Service

FORMS-2 is a trademark of Micro Focus.

*Through Q1'85 these language products are available for release 1.0 of Xenix 286. Beginning in Q2'85, compatible versions will begin shipping for Xenix 286 R3.0
**Through Q1'85 this product is available for release 1.0 of Xenix 286. Beginning in Q2'85, an enhanced FORTRAN Compiler will be available for Xenix 286 R3.0 under product code X286 For 286.

XENIX* 3.0 OPERATING SYSTEM

- **XENIX 3.0 Industry Standard Multiuser Operating System**
- **Full binary compatibility with IBM personal computer XENIX**
- **Fully licensed version of the UNIX† operating system optimized for the Intel 80286 processor**
- **Leading edge microprocessor implementation of UNIX, fastest floating point performance on a microprocessor**
- **Important commercial OEM enhancements**
- **Supports multiple levels of integration: components, boards and systems**
- **Supported by Intel's worldwide post-sales service and support organizations**

© INTEL CORPORATION 1985
*XENIX is a trademark of Microsoft Corporation
†UNIX is a trademark of Bell Laboratories.

ORDER NUMBER: 230752-004

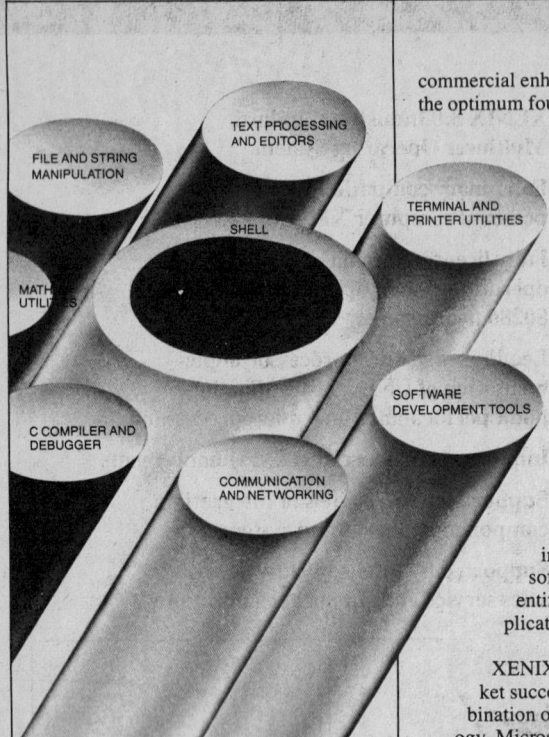

commercial enhancements that make it the optimum foundation for OEM application software solutions.

XENIX: Portable, Flexible, Powerful

XENIX has become the industry-standard microcomputer operating system for interactive, multi-user applications. It has gained wide popularity in applications such as distributed data processing, business data processing, word processing, software development, scientific and engineering applications, and graphics.

XENIX has achieved this market success through a solid combination of UNIX system technology, Microsoft value-added product development, and Intel's experience in microprocessor technology. In the future, XENIX 3.0 will benefit from advances in AT&T UNIX technology, Microsoft software technology and Intel semiconductor and system technology.

XENIX is also an extremely powerful operating system, providing the applications programmer with a wealth of development tools and utilities for bringing OEM products to market quickly.

XENIX 3.0—Industry Standard Multiuser Operating System

Intel's XENIX 3.0 Operating System for the 80286 is a fully-licensed derivation of Bell Laboratories' UNIX System III. XENIX 3.0 includes not only all the functionality of UNIX System III, but also powerful enhancements from Microsoft and Intel that meet the needs of the commercial OEM.

The Best Foundation for Building OEM Solutions

XENIX 3.0 provides the OEM with a complete software base on which to build value-added functionality. It includes the operating system, the C language, text processors, development tools, system accounting and security features, and

XENIX 3.0: Leading Edge UNIX Performance on a Micro

As the first UNIX operating system derivative optimized for the iAPX 286, XENIX 3.0 alone can take full advantage of the 80286's unique features:

On-chip memory management and protection provides two key advantages for XENIX 3.0 over other microprocessor UNIX implementations. First, on-chip memory management and protection drastically reduces the overhead in accessing system memory as compared to the usual separate memory management unit. With this functionality right on the chip, the operating system works more smoothly and efficiently.

Second, on-chip memory management and protection circuitry ensures that each version of XENIX 3.0 will be very compatible with every other version. This heretofore impossible level of compatibility aids OEM, software developers, and end users due to the wider availability of compatible software.

Advanced microprocessor architecture provides pipeline processing, wherein a continual flow of instructions is kept in the CPU queue, results in throughput several times faster than the fastest competing microprocessor.

1.75x	INTEL 286/3
1.5x	CONVERGENT TECHNOLOGY MIN ALTOS 986
1.25x	SUN @ MODEL 100
1.0x	NCR TOWER

Fast floating point processing

is due to XENIX 3.0 support of the Intel iAPX 287 math coprocessor. Floating point processing delivers throughput that is an order of magnitude faster than non-floating point processing. Extra high processing speeds are needed in applications such as data base processing, commercial data reduction and graphics.

*XENIX is a trademark of Microsoft Corporation.

Faster, More Reliable Still When Teamed with Other Intel Systems Components

The throughput enhancements in the XENIX 3.0 software are pushed to even greater speeds by special hardware architecture in Intel's systems and board products.

MULTIBUS® System Architecture is the industry-standard system bus. It accommodates any of the special-purpose Intel iSBC® boards, as well as a multitude of third party Multibus boards and standard peripherals, for easy system expansion.

iLBX™ (Local Bus Exchange) is an Intel hardware innovation that increases the amount of local memory accessible by the operating system to significantly improve system throughput.

Error Correction Circuitry (ECC) automatically detects and corrects soft errors in RAM. This on-board, self-correction facility reduces errors and further underscores data integrity.

XENIX 286 combines UNIX technology from these organizations.

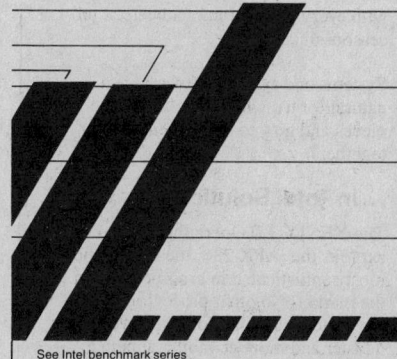

See Intel benchmark series

A Faster Operating System Means Market Leadership

The combination of the industry's most widely accepted operating system for multi-user, interactive applications with the industry's fastest and most advanced microprocessor gives the OEM a far superior price/performance ratio than is available through other options. The result for the OEM: market leadership due to the ability to more attractively price products based on superior performance.

XENIX 3.0: The Best of Everything

The XENIX 3.0 Operating System contains the best of many vendors' UNIX/XENIX development efforts during the last ten years (see Fig. above). We have taken the best features of many UNIX versions—ease of use, flexibility, performance, security, reliability—and added our own enhancements (not the least of which is compatibility with the iAPX 286) to make XENIX 3.0 the optimum software foundation tool for the commercial OEM.

Superior Date Reliability and Integrity

XENIX 3.0 contains enhancements to provide extremely high data reliability and integrity, particularly important to the OEM who is adding value to a system product. The following enhancements in XENIX 3.0 contribute to uniformly reliable data at all stages of application development.

Automatic disk recovery is an improvement of the UNIX file system that allows automatic recovery of the file system in the event of unexpected system shutdown.

Record and file locks arbitrate multiple-access requests to the same record or file, allowing the programmer to extend locks to a single record, group of records or the entire file. This is important in multi-user applications to prevent two or more users accessing and updating the same information simultaneously.

Tools for Easy System Configuration

In addition to increased data reliability measures, XENIX 3.0 has been functionally enhanced for easier system configuration. A configuration utility allows the user to specify device drivers, disk buffers, memory size, etc., making it easy for the OEM to meet unique design requirements. XENIX 3.0 includes over 10 device drivers for highspeed controllers.

Friendlier Interface

The standard UNIX human interface has been enhanced in XENIX 3.0, with the addition of vi, a full-screen editor, for easier and faster application development.

The XENIX C shell augments the capabilities of the standard UNIX shell with the ability to maintain histories of invoked processes and provide the alias feature, saving re-keying of often-used commands. XENIX 3.0 also provides the visual shell, a menu driven command interpreter which makes full use of the screen to display status and environmental information to the user. It has a built-in HELP facility and allows users to add new applications to the menu.

Intel's Open Systems Approach

Intel believes that system components—hardware or software—should be fully compatible with other family members at any level of integration and open to future VLSI advancements. XENIX 3.0 was designed to be part of the Open Systems concept.

Portability from Chip to Board to System

Intel's XENIX 3.0 Operating System is available for and fully compatible across Intel component, board and system designs, something that no other XENIX version offers.

Such portability gives OEMs the flexibility to choose the most appropriate and profitable level of integration for their applications. Component-level integration allows the OEM to meet unique design requirements; board and system-level integration afford reduced time to market.

There is no loss in software development investment as your needs change, since you can port XENIX-based applications from the chip to the system level or even from one Intel processor to another.

Open to Still Greater Configurability through Third-Party Software and Hardware

XENIX 3.0 users can tap into an extensive base of existing third-party languages and application packages for almost endless versatility in system configurability. There are hundreds of such packages available today with many more on the way. To assure the availability and quality of these packages on our systems, we have the Independent Software Vendor Program. Through this activity, software vendors are given Intel systems as well as technical assistance to aid them in porting their packages. The resulting product is thoroughly evaluated by Intel prior to certification for operation on our system products.

Superior Documentation

In line with the OEM orientation of the Intel hardware and software combination, the documentation for Intel's Xenix 286 product provides excellent support for system builders. In addition to the mature UNIX documentation from AT&T and the value-added feature documentation by Microsoft, Intel adds a wealth of publications aimed at helping the OEM to successfully launch XENIX 3.0 based products.

Worldwide Support and Service

XENIX 3.0 customers can take advantage of Intel's worldwide staff of trained hardware and software engineers in contracting for application design assistance. A liberal warranty, including software updates and a technical newsletter, follows the sale. Once the warranty expires customers can choose from a variety of support contracts.

Intel offers complete training on the XENIX 3.0 Operating System as well as the iAPX 286 processor and associated hardware.

Intel, The Technological Leader...

Intel is committed to pushing the frontiers of VLSI design to their ultimate limits. In the process, we move our customers along the technology curve without interruptions in application development or expensive mid-stream architecture changes.

Intel started the micro revolution with the 4004 and has been the market leader with every generation of advanced processors since.

Systems and system software are a natural for us: who better knows the pieces and how to make them work together?

...In Total Solutions

The XENIX 3.0 Operating System fully exploits the iAPX 286, the fastest and most sophisticated microprocessor on the market. No other processor/operating system combination will give OEMs a faster and more economical path to getting systems and applications on the market.

Intel has always been first with the latest and most advanced VLSI and now with system software tailor-made for Intel VLSI. Because we're there first, our customers are first in their respective markets with state-of-the-art OEM and end-user products.

XENIX*3.0

XENIX 3.0 includes support for the following Intel Systems, single board computers and processors.
- System 286/310
- System 286/380

- iSBC® 286/10 Processor Board
  —16mb of addressing
  —On-chip memory protection
- CX Series RAM board
  —ECC (Error Correction Circuitry)
  —iLBX™ (Local Bus Extension)
- iSBC 215 Winchester Controller
- iSBX 218 Floppy Controller
- iSBC 534 Serial I/O Expansion Board
- iSBC 544 Intelligent Serial I/O Expansion Board
- iSBC 188/48 8-channel serial I/O Expansion Board
- iSBC 552 Ethernet Controller Board*
- iSBX 217 Tape Controller Board

- 80286 Central Processor
- 80287 Fast Floating Point Processor

*Available in second quarter '85

Documentation

Documentation Includes:

- Overview of the XENIX 286 Operating System
- XENIX 286 Installation and Configuration Guide
- XENIX 286 System Administrator's Guide
- XENIX 286 Communications Guide
- XENIX 286 Visual Shell User's Guide
- XENIX 286 User's Guide
- XENIX 286 Reference Manual
- XENIX 286 C Library Guide
- XENIX 286 Programmer's Guide
- XENIX 286 Device Driver Guide
- XENIX 286 Text Formatting Guide

Text Books (Available from Bookstores)
The UNIX Book—Banahan & Rutter
The UNIX System—Bourne
The UNIX Operating System—Kaare
Understanding UNIX: A Conceptual Guide—Groff & Weinberg
The UNIX Programming Environment—Kernighan & Pike
Introducing the UNIX System—McGilton & Morgan
A Practical Guide to the UNIX System—Sobell
A User Guide to the UNIX System—Yates & Thomas
A Business Guide to the UNIX System—Yates and Emerson

Ordering Information

SYS 310-17X	System Kit including System 310-17 and XENIX Software
SYS 310-17MX	System Kit including System 310-17, XENIX Software, 6 user support
SYS 310-41X	System Kit including System 310-41 and XENIX Software
SYX 286 RO	License rights extension for system customers
SYX 286 RF	System incorporation fee

XENIX† 286 APPLICATION AND DEVELOPMENT SOFTWARE

- Choice of packages in most application areas
- Choice of application development tools
- Tested by Intel to ensure quality and reliability on Intel Systems
- Major software packages available directly from Intel
- Worldwide support available for many software packages

PRODUCT NAME	VENDOR	AVAILABLE DIRECTLY FROM INTEL
Languages		
Microsoft Basic	Intel	Yes
MicroFocus Cobol	Intel	Yes
FORTRAN	Intel	Yes
cENGLISH	cLINE	Yes
dBase II to cEnglish Converter	cLINE	Yes
Ryan McFarland Cobol	Ryan/McFarland	Yes*
HCR Pascal	Human Computing Resources	
DBL (Dibol)	DISC	
Microsoft FORTRAN	Microsoft	
SMC Basic	SMC	Yes*
Softbol	Omtool	
MX Basic	Perception	
UX Basic	UX Software	
C-LINK (Basic to C)	SMI	
Spreadsheet		
iPLAN (Multiplan)	Intel	Yes
Office Automation		
iWORD (Horizon)	Intel	Yes
iMENU (Schmidt Menus)	Intel	Yes
Q-One	Quadratron	Yes*
Q-Menu	Quadratron	Yes*
Q-Date	Quadratron	Yes*
Q-Mail	Quadratron	Yes*
Q-Note	Quadratron	Yes*
Q-Call	Quadratron	Yes*
Lyrix	SCO	Yes*
Softgram (Telex/TWX)	SofTest	

©INTEL CORPORATION, 1985
† TRADEMARK OF MICROSOFT CORPORATION

OCTOBER, 1985
ORDER NUMBER: 270128-001

XENIX 286 APPLICATION AND DEVELOPMENT SOFTWARE
(Continued)

PRODUCT NAME	VENDOR	AVAILABLE DIRECTLY FROM INTEL
Application Generator		
APGEN	Software Express	
C/Tools	Conetic Systems	
Graphics		
High Tech Business	High Tech Marketing	Yes*
PBG 200	Pacific Basin Graphics	Yes*
GraphHopper	Data Business Vision	
Database		
iDB (Mistress)	Intel	Yes
Informix	RDS	Yes*
File-IT!	RDS	Yes*
C-ISAM	RDS	Yes
Unify	Unify	Yes*
Communications		
i3270BSC (3271/3277)	Intel	Yes
iRBTE (2780/3780 RJE)	Intel	Yes
iHASP	Intel	Yes
iPC	Intel	Yes
3270 SNA	XICOM	Yes*
X.25/29	TITN	
Accounting		
MCBA Accounting	MCBA	Yes*
BACS Accounting	American Business Systems	
Conetic Accounting	Conetic Systems	
Thoroughbred Accounting	SMC Software Systems	
Vertical Applications		
MDX (Medical Accounting)	Clinical Data	
Magazine Circulation	NMI	
Customer Profile	NMI	
ProfitKey Manufacturing	Key Systems	

*Available in the U.S. Only

14-80

MULTIBUS® II Architecture   15

MULTIBUS® II
iLBX™ II Local Bus Extension

- High bus bandwidth —
  — 48 megabytes/sec
- 64 megabyte (26-bit) addressing
- 8-, 16-, 24-, and 32-bit data transfers over a 32-bit path
- Reliable synchronous clocking up to 12 megahertz
- Burst transfers up to 64 kilobytes per transfer
- Primary and secondary bus master exchange capabilities
- Supports up to 6 iLBX™ II compatible devices per bus
- Pipelined protocol for highest performance
- Optional parity protection for address and data

The iLBX™ II Local Bus Extension is one of the family of standard bus structures resident within Intel's MULTIBUS® II Bus Architecture. The iLBX II bus is a dedicated execution bus capable of significantly increasing system performance by removing most processor execution activity from the main iPSB™ Parallel System Bus. It extends the processor board's on-board local bus to off-board resources. Acting in conjunction with the processor board, the iLBX II resources form a multiple board "virtual single board computer". The iLBX II bus preserves advantages in performance and architecture of on-board local memory, while allowing memory configurations larger than those possible on a single board.

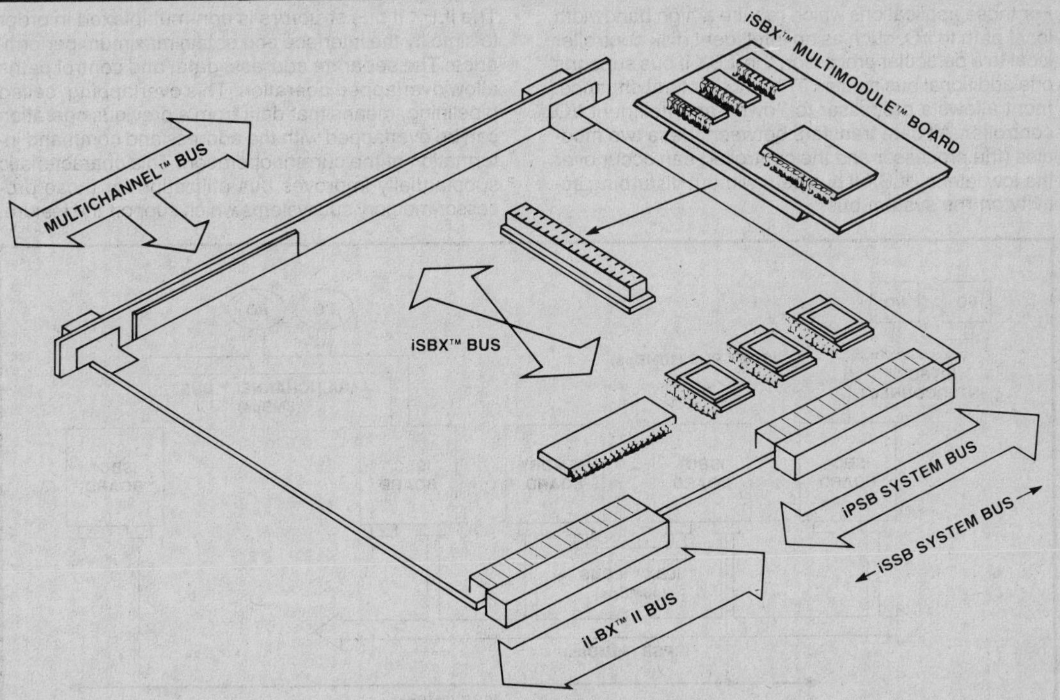

MULTIBUS® II Physical Diagram

MARCH, 1985
ORDER NUMBER: 280055-002

iLBX™ II LOCAL BUS EXTENSION

FUNCTIONAL DESCRIPTION

Architectural Overview

The iLBX II bus is an architectural solution for supporting large amounts of off-board memory with the same performance advantage enjoyed by on-board memory (see Figure 1). It allows the CPU board selection to be decoupled from the on-board memory requirement and still maximizes the processor's performance potential. It eliminates the processor's need to access its off-board memory resources solely over the iPSB system bus. In most systems, the processor is the only master on the iLBX II bus, so no time is required to arbitrate for the bus. This means the processor sees significantly lower memory latency than is possible if it were accessing memory over the multiple master system bus. Lower memory latency translates to higher individual processor performance.

The inclusion of the iLBX II bus in the architecture means not just higher single processor performance but higher system performance as well. The movement of execution traffic from the system bus to the iLBX II execution bus makes that much additional system bus bandwidth available to other system resources such as processors not using an execution bus or I/O devices.

For those applications which require a high bandwidth local path to I/O, such as an intelligent disk controller local to a particular processor, the iLBX II bus supports one additional bus master. This architectural enhancement allows a processor to "own" an intelligent I/O controller. All data transfers between these two modules (the processor and the controller) can occur over the low latency iLBX II bus path without disturbing activity on the system bus.

Structural Features

Overview

The iLBX II bus uses a non-multiplexed, processor independent structure supporting 8-, 16-, and 32-bit processors. It supports 8-, 16-, 24-, and 32-bit data transfers over a 26-bit (64 megabyte) addressing range with a maximum bandwidth of 48 megabytes/sec.

All events performed on the bus are synchronous to a reference bus clock. This is not a fixed frequency clock as in the iPSB bus; the iLBX II bus clock runs at the basic processor bus frequency. In other words, a processor whose bus interface runs at 8 megahertz would drive the iLBX II bus at that frequency. This characteristic helps match the iLBX II bus timing to that of the processor transfer rate for best performance. The maximum iLBX II bus clock frequency is 12 megahertz. (Be careful not to confuse a processor's clock input frequency with its basic bus frequency. Many processors internally divide down their clock input by 2, 3, or 4 to obtain the basic bus frequency. It is this basic bus frequency which defines their transfer rate and which drives the iLBX II bus clock.)

Non-Multiplexed Structure

The iLBX II bus structure is non-multiplexed in order to simplify the interface and obtain maximum performance. The separate address, data, and control paths allow overlapped operation. This overlapping, called pipelining, means that data from a previous operation can be overlapped with the address and command information of the current operation. This characteristic substantially improves bus utilization for those processor-memory subsystems which support the feature.

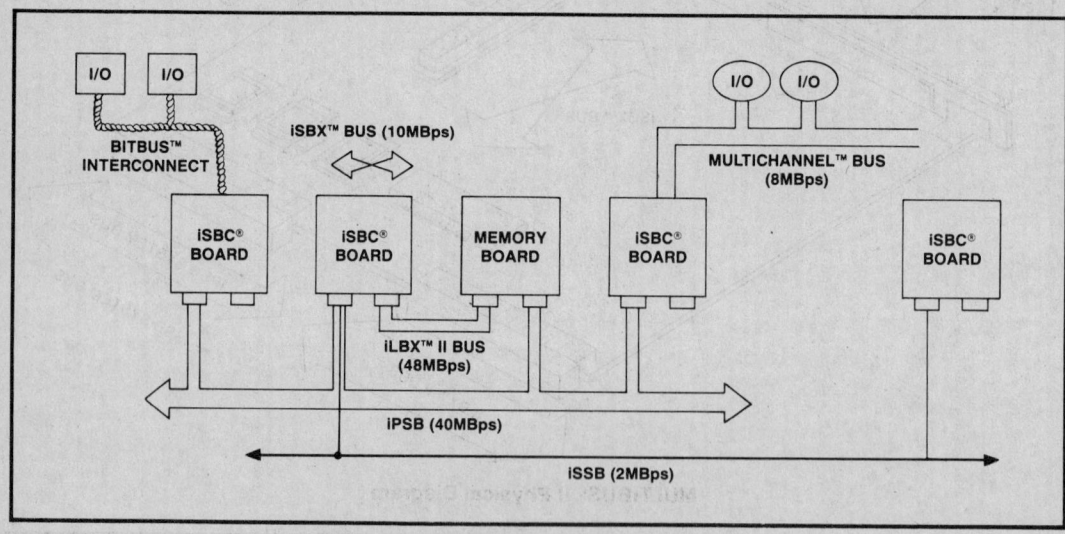

Figure 1. MULTIBUS® II Bus Architecture

iLBX™ II LOCAL BUS EXTENSION

Interconnect Address Space

The iLBX II bus supports the slot-addressing concept of the interconnect address space found in the iPSB bus. Including this facility in the iLBX II bus allows the system to identify and configure iLBX II bus boards even though they may not contain a iPSB bus port. (Please refer to the iPSB bus data sheet for additional information on the Interconnect address space.)

Dual Bus Masters

In order to support a wide range of system configurations, the iLBX II bus defines support for two bus masters. One master is called the Primary master; the other is known as the Secondary master. The Primary master normally "owns" the bus and does not have to spend any time arbitrating for access rights. The Secondary master must ask the Primary master for access rights. The Primary releases the bus at the first opportune time. This hierarchical structure ensures that the Primary master enjoys good memory latency while at the same time gives the Secondary the opportunity to access memory when it needs to.

The iLBX II bus also includes a dedicated interrupt line to facilitate signalling between the two masters for commands and status, and between the memory boards and the Primary master for things such as non-recoverable memory errors.

Bus Cycle Overview

Like the iPSB bus, the iLBX II bus protocol consists of three types of bus cycles: arbitration, transfer, and exception.

Arbitration Cycle

The arbitration cycle ensures that one and only one requesting agent is allowed access to the bus at any given time. When a requesting agent determines the need for a bus operation, it enters the arbitration cycle. For either requesting agent, this cycle lasts until it acquires the right to use the bus. In configurations with only a primary requesting agent, no time is spent for this cycle; the agent always has rights to the bus. In configurations where there are both a primary and secondary agent, the primary agent has to arbitrate for the bus only when the bus is busy under the secondary agent's control. Figure 2 illustrates the arbitration cycle.

Transfer Cycle

The transfer cycle is the event where the request (address and command) and reply (data) information is exchanged between the bus agents. Like the iPSB bus, it consists of a request and a reply phase. During block transfers, the termination of the transfer cycle is controlled by the requesting agent. In non-block transfer cycles, the cycle's termination is implicitly recognized by both agents. Figure 3 shows a transfer cycle example.

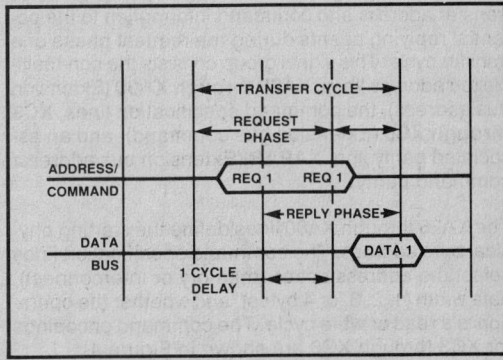

Figure 3. iLBX™ II Transfer Cycle

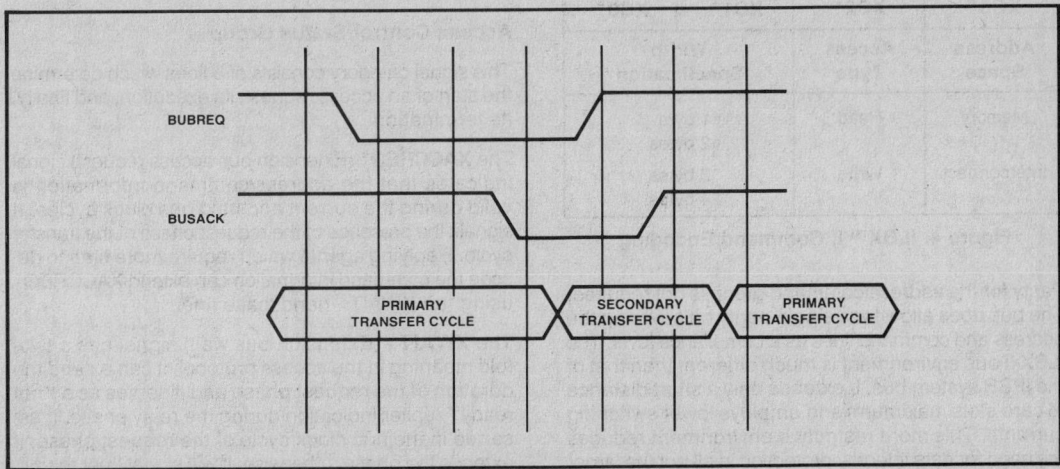

Figure 2. iLBX™ II Bus Arbitration Example

iLBX™ II LOCAL BUS EXTENSION

Exception Cycle

Exception cycles allow the bus agents to signal any detected error or exceptional condition which might arise during a transfer cycle. Typical exceptions are uncorrectable ECC errors, parity errors, or physical boundary overflows.

Signal Groups

Overview

There are five categories of signals used in the iLBX II bus: address/command, data transfer, access control/status, bus control/status, and miscellaneous. An asterisk following the signal name or group indicates that the signal or group use their low electrical state as the active state.

Address/Command

The requesting agent uses this group of signals to transfer address and command information to the potential replying agents during the request phase of a transfer cycle. This signal group consists the non-multiplexed address lines, **XA25 through XA00** (Extension bus address), the command specification lines, **XC3 through XC0** (Extension bus command), and an associated parity line, **XAPAR** (Extension bus address/command parity).

The XA25 through XA00 lines define the starting physical byte address. The command specification lines select the address space (memory or interconnect), data width (1, 2, 3, or 4 bytes), and whether the operation is a read or write cycle. The command encodings for XC3 through XC0 are shown in Figure 4.

XC3*	XC2*	XC1*	XC0*
Address Space	Access Type	Width Specification	
Memory	Read	1 byte	
		2 bytes	
Interconnect	Write	3 bytes	
		4 bytes	

Figure 4. iLBX™ II Command Encoding

Parity for the address/command group is not required. The bus does allow for a single parity bit covering the address and command lines as a compliance level. The iLBX II bus environment is much different than that of the iPSB system bus. It extends only a short distance (6 card slots maximum) and employs lower switching currents. This more restrictive environment reduces the need for data integrity protection in all but the larger systems.

Data Transfer Group

This signal category consists of the 32 bi-directional data lines and their optional parity line. **XD31 through XD0** (Extension bus data) transfer the read or write data between the requesting and replying agents. Each byte in the iLBX II bus memory is mapped to one of the four byte locations of the XD lines. This technique is commonly referred to as "byte lanes" and is illustrated in Figure 5.

Like with the address/command group, the **XDPAR** (Extension bus data parity) line is optional.

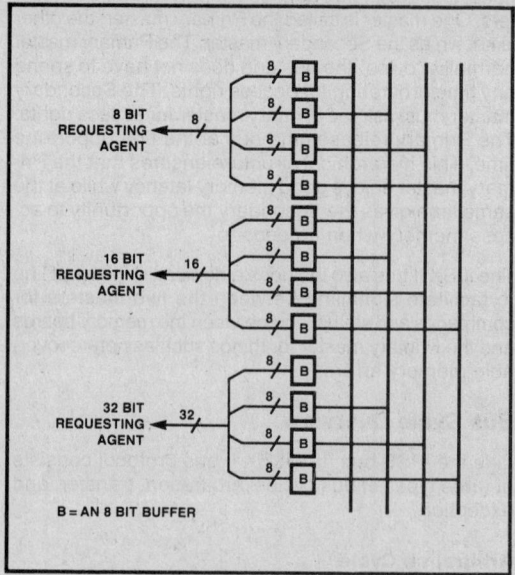

Figure 5. iLBX™ II Data Bus Alignment Interface Requirements

Access Control/Status Group

This signal category consists of 5 lines which determine the start of an access request, its execution, and finally, its termination.

The **XACCREQ*** (Extension bus access request) signal indicates that the address/command information is valid during the current and next bus clock cycles. It signals the presence of the request phase of the transfer cycle. Replying agents which require more time to decode the command information can extend XACCREQ* using the XWAIT* handshake line.

The **XWAIT*** (Extension bus wait) signal has a two-fold meaning in the access protocol: it can extend the duration of the request phase and it serves as a "not ready" replier indication during the reply phase. If asserted in the first clock cycle of the request phase, it extends the phase, otherwise, it will signal "not ready" during the reply phase.

iLBX™ II LOCAL BUS EXTENSION

In many system configurations the iLBX II bus memory boards are dual-ported to both the iLBX II and iPSB buses. This requires a mutual exclusion facility when implementing semaphores and other data structures in this shared memory. The **XLOCK*** (Extension bus lock) signal allows the iLBX II bus requesting agents to lock out the other port while performing indivisible accesses to shared structures.

To perform block transfers on the iLBX II bus, the requesting agent asserts the **XBTCTL*** (Extension bus block transfer control) signal. This line informs the replying agents that two or more data transfer periods will accompany a single request phase. XBTCTL* is de-asserted by the requesting agent to signal the end of the block transfer.

Bus Control/Status Group

The signals in this group control the passing of bus ownership between the primary and secondary requesting agents. When the bus is in use, they also indicate which agent is in control.

The **XBUSREQ*** (Extension bus request) signal is driven by the secondary requesting agent to acquire the bus from the primary agent. Only the primary requesting agent receives this signal. When the primary detects that the secondary is requesting the bus, it replies with the **XBUSACK*** (Extension bus acknowledge) signal to inform the secondary that the bus is now his. This bus exchange occurs at the discretion of the primary.

The secondary owns the bus after asserting XBUSREQ* and receiving XBUSACK* active. The primary can request that the bus be returned at any time by removing XBUSACK*. The secondary must return the bus at the earliest time; typically when it completes its current transfer cycle.

Miscellaneous Control Group

The **XRESET*** (Extension bus reset) is driven by the primary requesting agent to locally initialize its iLBX II bus environment. It is typically asserted after the agent receives a reset indication on the iPSB system bus.

The **XINT*** (Extension bus interrupt) allows the secondary requesting agent and any of the replying agents to signal the primary requesting agent for inter-module communication. Since the secondary agent is usually performing tasks on behalf of the primary agent, this interrupt line removes the need for the primary to continuously poll the secondary for completion of its tasks.

The **XID2* through XID0*** (Extension bus identity) lines are hardwired lines on the backplane to allow any iLBX II bus board to determine its position on the bus. They encode the interconnect space least significant three bits of the slot ID field. (See the iPSB bus data sheet for an explanation of the interconnect address space.)

The final line is the **XBCLK*** (Extension bus clock) line. It provides the reference timing signal for the synchronous bus operations. It is driven by the primary requesting agent at its processor bus frequency.

The iLBX II bus also defines additional +5 volt and ground pins.

Bus Protocol

In the MULTIBUS II specification, both timing diagrams and state-flow diagrams describe the iLBX II bus protocol. The state-flow diagrams present the lowest level and most rigorous definition while the timing diagrams help conceptual understanding. For the purposes of this data sheet, only the timing diagram description is used. The following sections use Figure 6 as an example of the protocol.

Arbitration Cycle

With only two potential requesting agents contending for access rights to the bus, the arbitration cycle is very simple. The figure illustrates the secondary requesting agent requesting the bus from the primary and then running a simple transfer cycle. The secondary requesting agent makes its request by asserting XBUSREQ*. The primary gives up the bus by returning XBUSACK* active. In this example, the secondary uses the bus for only a single transfer cycle so it de-asserts XBUSREQ* when complete. The primary agent responds by withdrawing XBUSACK* to indicate it now owns the bus.

Transfer Cycle

Like in the iPSB bus, the transfer cycle proceeds as a request phase and a reply phase. The requesting agent (either the primary or the secondary depending upon who currently owns the bus) informs the potential replying agents of the request phase by driving valid information on the address/command signal group and asserting XACCREQ*. The request phase normally lasts two clock cycles although the replying agents have the opportunity to extend the phase as long as necessary by asserting XWAIT* during the first clock period of the phase. The phase is extended as long as XWAIT* is active. In the example, the request phase is extended one additional clock.

The reply phase begins when XWAIT* is de-asserted. At this point, the meaning of XWAIT* changes to become a "not ready" indication from the selected replying agent. In the example, the replying agent requires one additional clock period to supply the data so XWAIT* is asserted for one clock. The reply phase terminates on the same clock that data is valid.

Exception Cycle

If transfer integrity checking is implemented on the iLBX II bus, errors are signalled on the clock following the last valid information period. In the example, errors

iLBX™ II LOCAL BUS EXTENSION

detected on the address/command lines during the request phase are signalled on the clock following the removal of valid request information. The same applies to errors detected on the data lines during the reply phase.

Mechanical

The iLBX II bus is defined on the P2 connector of two-connector MULTIBUS II boards. Since the iLBX II bus environment is local to a particular processor board, the iLBX II bus backplane does not extend the entire length of the iPSB bus backplane. This allows for multiple iLBX II bus environments in a given system.

The pin assignment for the iLBX II bus on P2 is shown in iLBX II specification section in the MULTIBUS II Bus Architecture Specification Handbook.

Please refer to Intel's MULTIBUS II Bus Architecture Specification Handbook for more detailed information.

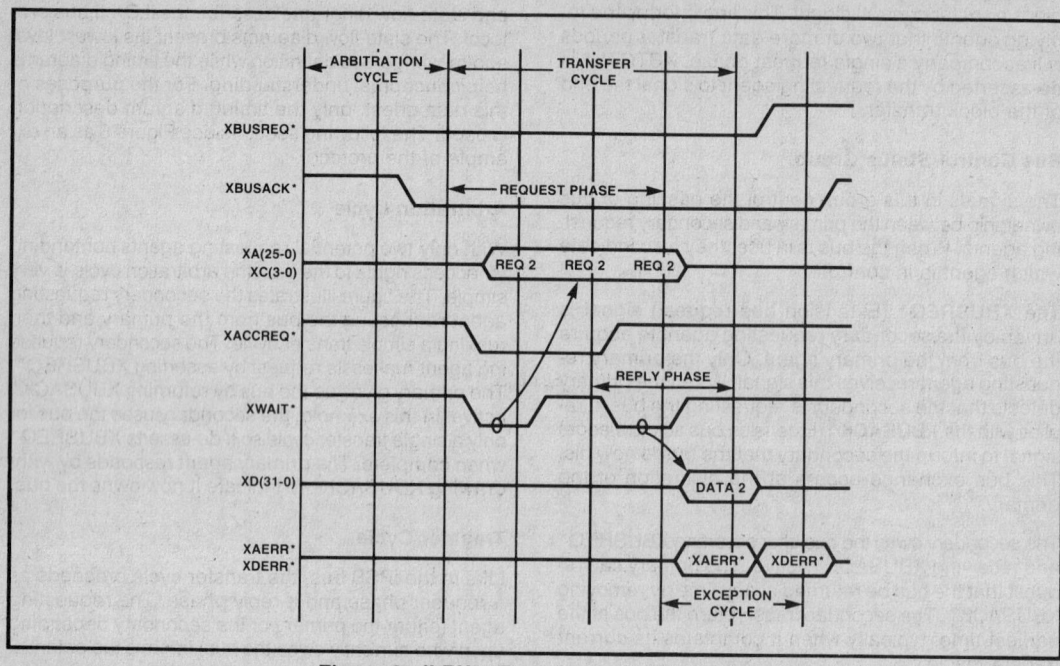

Figure 6. iLBX™ Transfer Cycle Example

MULTIBUS® II
iPSB Parallel System Bus

- **Very high bandwidth —**
  - 40 megabytes/sec using burst transfers
  - 20 megabytes/sec with single cycles
- **4 gigabyte (32-bit) addressing**
- **8-, 16-, 24-, and 32-bit data transfers over a 32-bit path**
- **Pin-efficient multiplexed structure**
- **Reliable synchronous clocking at 10 megahertz with full handshaking for data**
- **Distributed arbitration with up to 20 bus masters**
- **Full parity protection for data transfer integrity**
- **Message passing facility for inter-module communication**
- **Geographic addressing facility for software indentification and configuration of boards**
- **Industry standard Eurocard form factors — 233mm × 220mm and 100mm × 220mm**

The MULTIBUS® II iPSB Parallel System Bus is the foundation of the MULTIBUS II Bus Architecture. It is a general-purpose, processor independent structure which fully supports 8-, 16-, and 32-bit microprocessors. This very high bandwidth structure is defined on a single 96-pin IEC 603-2 (DIN) connector. All data movement functions required in a microcomputer system are defined including such advanced functions as an integrated message passing protocol and a geographic addressing facility which allows software to address a board by its slot position for software-based board identification and configuration.

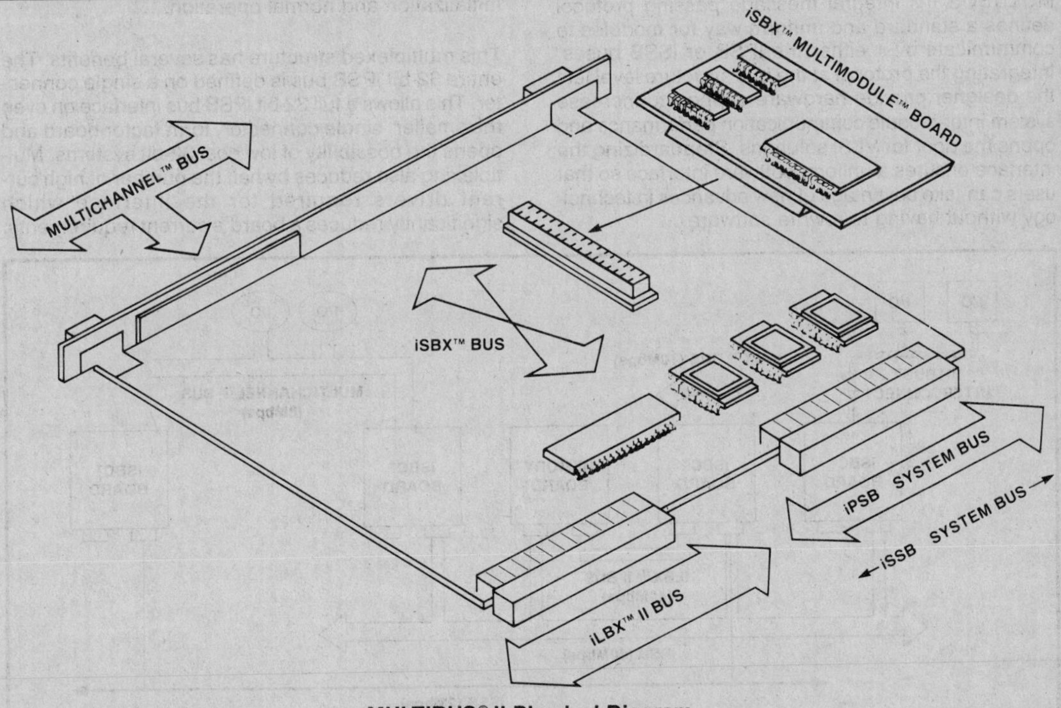

MULTIBUS® II Physical Diagram

MARCH, 1985
ORDER NUMBER: 280055-002

iPSB PARALLEL SYSTEM BUS

FUNCTIONAL DESCRIPTION

Architectural Overview

The MULTIBUS II iPSB Parallel System Bus is the foundation of the MULTIBUS II bus architecture (see Figure 1). As a system bus, it is a very high bandwidth (40 megabytes/sec) bus optimized for inter-module communication; however, it also defines the complete set of basic bus functions required in a microcomputer system: memory accesses for execution or data, accesses to I/O for control of I/O functions, plus inter-module signalling. These basic functions are supplemented with additional functions supporting geographical (by slot) addressing and an integral message passing protocol.

Geographical addressing allows addressing of individual boards via their physical position in the backplane. Software can determine what boards are being used and configure itself appropriately. Software also can configure the hardware characteristics of the board (eg. the starting address of a memory board). This can substantially reduce or even eliminate hardware jumper options and DIP switches for board configuration. Geographical addressing is a function of the interconnect address space.

MULTIBUS II's integral message passing protocol defines a standard and uniform way for modules to communicate over either the iPSB or iSSB buses. Integrating the protocol at the bus structure level lets the designer provide hardware support to increase system inter-module communication performance and opens the door for VLSI solutions. Standardizing the interface ensures a uniform software interface so that users can take advantage of new advances in technology without having to rewrite software.

Structural Features

Overview

The iPSB bus structure is a processor-independent general-purpose bus designed to support 8-, 16-, and 32-bit processors. It is designed to operate at a maximum bandwidth of 40 megabytes/sec while using off-the-shelf components.

Special attention has been given to how the bus structure, both electrically and mechanically, impacts system reliability. Synchronous sampling of all bus signal lines assures good immunity from crosstalk and noise. Full byte parity generation and checking protects all transfers on the bus to ensure that any bus error is detected. Signal quality on the bus is excellent due to the large number of interlaced ground lines. Mechanically, the iPSB bus is defined on a two-piece 96-pin IEC 603-2 connector to ensure good connector reliability.

Multiplexing

The iPSB bus is highly multiplexed. The 32-bit address and data paths are multiplexed and the eight system control lines have different uses depending upon the phase of the transfer cycle. The six arbitration lines also serve dual purposes between system initialization and normal operation.

This multiplexed structure has several benefits. The entire 32-bit iPSB bus is defined on a single connector. This allows a full 32-bit iPSB bus interface on even the smaller, single connector, form factor board and opens the possibility of low cost 32-bit systems. Multiplexing also reduces by half the number of high current drivers required for the interface which significantly reduces a board's current requirements.

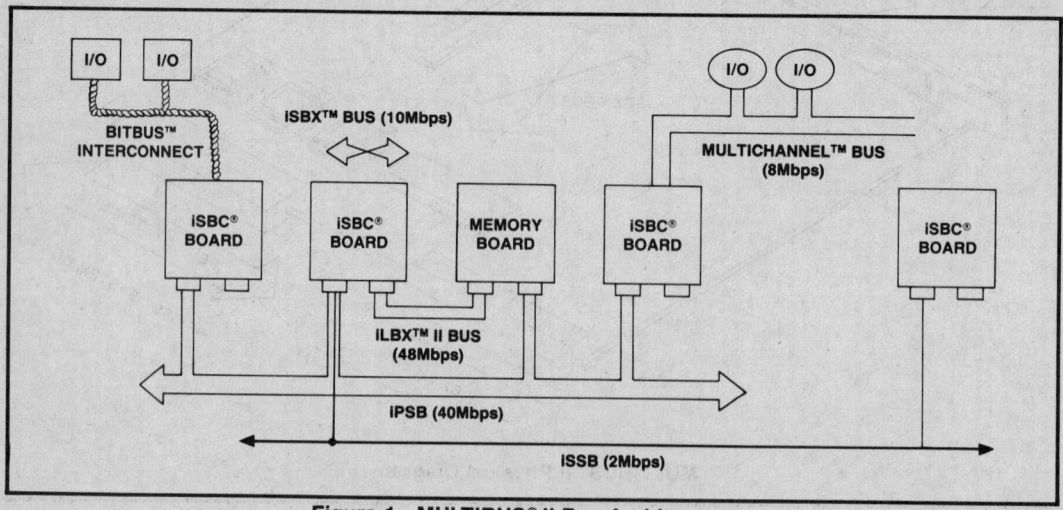

Figure 1. MULTIBUS® II Bus Architecture

iPSB PARALLEL SYSTEM BUS

The routing of signal lines between the bus interface and connector is simplified.

Errors

The iPSB bus defines a complete set of bus error reporting mechanisms. Serious errors, such as a parity error or the failure of a module to complete the data handshake, are flagged on unique bus signal lines and are seen by all modules on the bus. These errors induce a recovery time in which the bus is allowed to stabilize before further transfer cycles may begin.

The iPSB bus also provides mechanisms for signaling less serious operational errors. Operational errors, such as attempting to perform a 32-bit access to a 8-bit device or writing to read-only memory, are signaled as agent errors. These errors may induce retry operations by an intelligent bus interface or may be passed to the on-board processor as errors.

Interconnect Address Space

The ability to address a board by its physical position in the backplane is also supported in the iPSB bus. This facility allows board manufacturers to code such items as their vendor number, board type, board revision number, and serial number on the board. This information is available to the system software. This facility is defined in the iPSB bus interconnect address space.

Aside from this read-only information, the interconnect space allows write operations to support board configuration and diagnostics under software control. This facility can help reduce or eliminate hardware-based jumper options and DIP switches.

Interrupts

The iPSB bus supports up to 255 distinct interrupt sources and 255 interrupt destinations. Rather than the use of the traditional method of dedicated interrupt signal lines on the bus, the iPSB bus defines a special bus cycle to convey interrupt information. This special bus cycle (actually part of the message passing protocol discussed below) redefines the meaning of the address; instead of a byte location in memory for example, 16 of the 32 lines encode 8 bits for the source module generating the interrupt and 8 bits for the destination module to service the interrupt.

This technique overcomes the significant problem of interrupt configuration found in traditional buses. Dedicated lines usually imply that only one particular destination can service one particular interrupt source. If an interrupt source wishes to target some interrupts to one destination and some to a different destination, separate bus interrupt lines are required for each destination. This can quickly consume all dedicated interrupt lines in even a moderate size system.

Using interrupt bus cycles with embedded source and destination module addressing removes the need for dedicated interrupt lines at the same time it allows any interrupt source to signal any interrupt destination.

Message Passing

With the trend in microcomputer systems toward multi-processing, it is important to provide the facilities and mechanisms to lend support for inter-module communication. The iPSB bus includes such mechanisms and defines the protocol for greatly enhanced performance in inter-module communication. This protocol is called MULTIBUS II Message Passing.

Most multiprocessor systems use either a "pass by reference" or a "pass by value" protocol for intermodule communication. In the "pass by reference" case, the two modules share a common memory resource and pass pointers or tokens to extend addressability of a desired data structure to the other module. In "pass by value", the modules exchange a copy of the desired data structure. Each of these protocols has a set of advantages and disadvantages associated with performance, data security, extendability to additional modules, and ease of use.

MULTIBUS II Message Passing takes the best of both methods and lends hardware support. Message passing uses a hardware "pass by value" interface that gives the performance of a "pass by reference" system. It replaces the software module used by the "pass by value" method with a specialized message passing interface. The processor "passes by reference" the reference to the data structure to the message passing co-processor interface. This interface communicates with the destination module's message passing interface to transfer the data without processor intervention. This data transfer is performed in the message address space. This is illustrated in Figure 2. (In many ways, it is helpful to think of the two communication message passing interfaces as a distributed, smart, DMA controller.)

There are several significant benefits to this approach. First of all, the message passing interfaces can take advantage of the full capabilities of the bus (ie, 32-bit data and burst transfer) independent of the type or nature of the controlling processor. Even 8-bit processor or I/O boards can take full advantage of the bus. This means significantly higher inter-module communication performance over a completely software-base method. Another benefit is the elimination of any shared memory. Dual-ported memory structures are no longer needed nor are global memory boards. The other primary benefit is that MULTIBUS II message passing presents a uniform software interface for all modules. Modules can be replaced with new modules containing newer technology (e.g. moving from a single density to a double density disk controller) without any software changes required in the controlling module. This makes it easy for users to integrate new technology without the problem of completely rewriting the driver software.

iPSB PARALLEL SYSTEM BUS

Central Services Module

The iPSB bus specification defines the central system functions as the Central Services Module (CSM). The minimal set of functions are: clock generation, power-down and reset, time-out, and assignment of slot IDs. Collecting these functions in a single module improves overall board area utilization, since the functions are not duplicated on every board and then only used on one. The system designer is free to implement the CSM on a separate board or to include the functions as just one of several modules on another board.

Bus Cycle Overview

The iPSB bus defines three types of bus cycles: arbitration, transfer, and exception cycles. Each cycle is made up of one or more phases. Figure 3 illustrates the relationship among these cycles and phases.

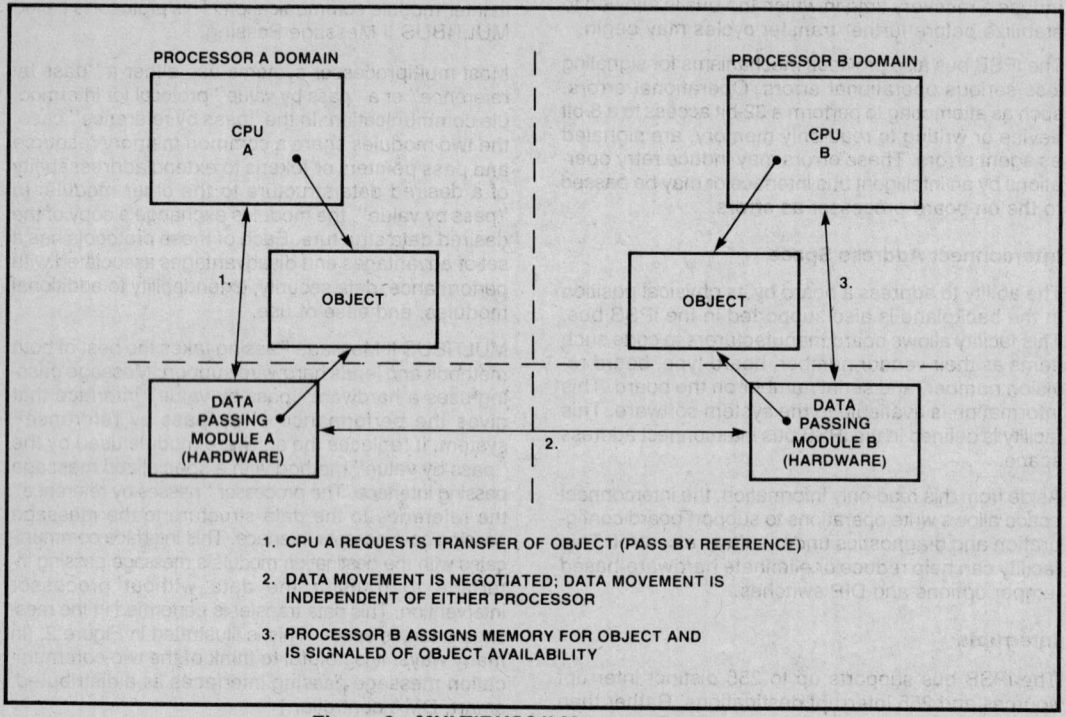

1. CPU A REQUESTS TRANSFER OF OBJECT (PASS BY REFERENCE)
2. DATA MOVEMENT IS NEGOTIATED; DATA MOVEMENT IS INDEPENDENT OF EITHER PROCESSOR
3. PROCESSOR B ASSIGNS MEMORY FOR OBJECT AND IS SIGNALED OF OBJECT AVAILABILITY

Figure 2. MULTIBUS® II Message Passing

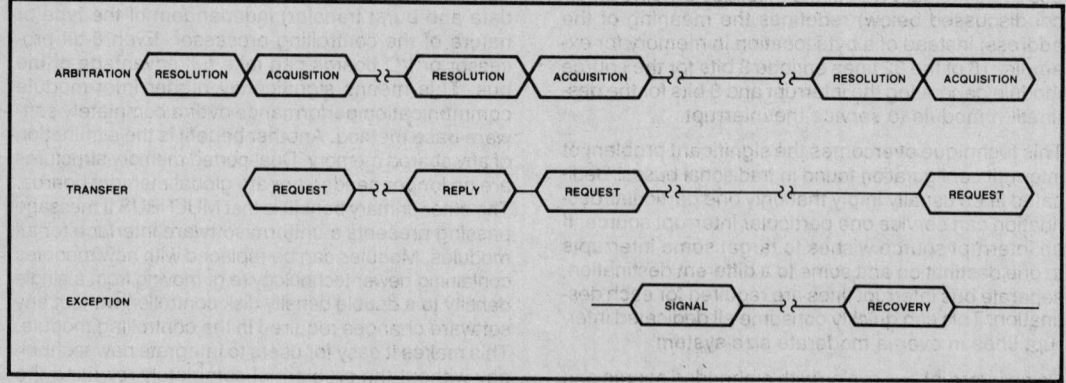

Figure 3. Bus Cycle Relationships

iPSB PARALLEL SYSTEM BUS

Arbitration Cycle

The arbitration cycle is made up of a resolution phase and an acquisition phase. The resolution phase is the time-period in which all requesting agents collectively arbitrate for access rights to the bus. Depending on the arbitration algorithm, the agents decide among themselves which of them is going to control the bus after the current bus owner is done. This arbitration method is referred to self-selecting since the agents decide ownership among themselves.

The agent that wins the arbitration and obtains access rights to the bus begins the acquisition phase; that agent becomes the bus owner. This agent begins its transfer cycle and holds the arbitration logic in the resolution phase (resolving for the next access rights) until the transfer cycle is completed.

Transfer Cycle

Starting the transfer cycle is the request phase. In this phase, the bus owner (requesting agent) places address and command information on the bus. This information defines the replying agent(s), the type of operation, and the type of address space. The request phase lasts one bus clock cycle.

The reply phase starts immediately after the request phase, during this phase, the requesting and replying agents engage in a handshake that synchronizes the data transfer sequence. The reply phase can contain one or more data cycles. The final data transfer is signaled by the requesting agent. During this final transfer, the requesting agent releases ownership of the bus allowing the new bus owner to use the bus immediately. Note how the transfer cycle overlaps the resolution phase of the arbitration cycle to minimize bus dead time.

Exception Cycle

If an agent detects an error during a transfer cycle, it immediately begins an exception cycle. The exception cycle terminates any arbitration cycles and transfer cycles in progress. The exception cycle starts with the signal phase in which the detecting agent activates one of the exception lines. This notifies all agents of the problem causing them to terminate any arbitration or transfer cycles. Next the recovery phase begins. During this phase, all agents idle; this allows the bus a fixed amount of idle-time to stabilize before resuming normal operation.

Signal Groups

Overview

The iPSB bus contains five groups of signals, Figure 4, over which the requesting and replying agents can enact the protocol. An asterisk following the signal name indicates that that particular signal or group of signals are active when at their electrical low.

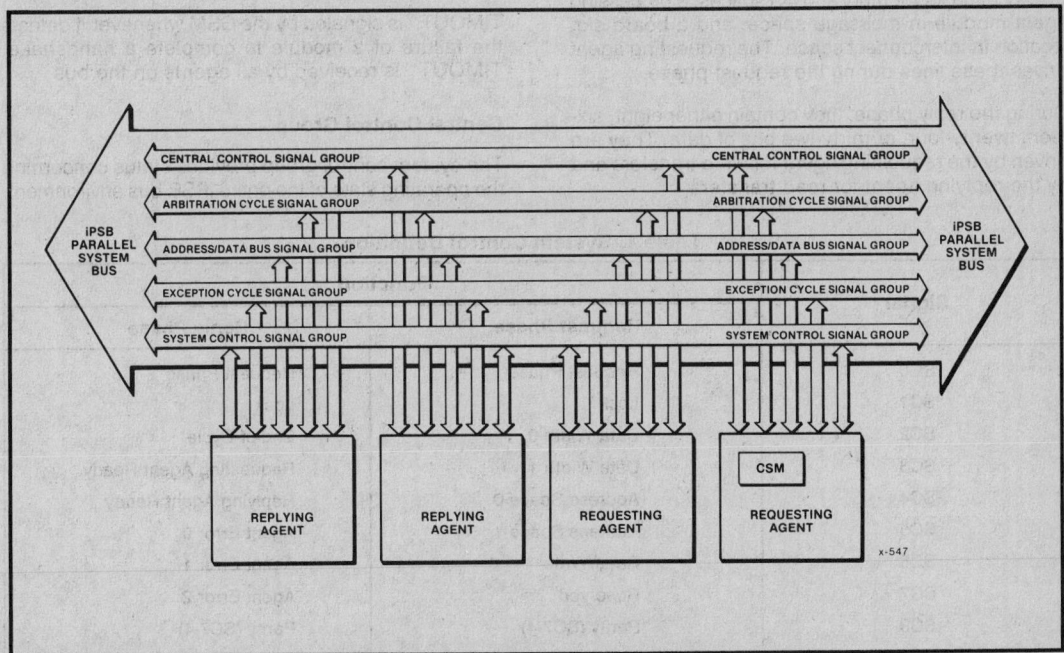

Figure 4. iPSB Bus Signal Groups

iPSB PARALLEL SYSTEM BUS

Arbitration Group

The arbitration signals on the iPSB bus determine which agent gains exclusive access to the bus (which agent is the bus owner). All requesting agents that require access to the bus resources must arbitrate for use of the bus. On being granted bus ownership, an agent begins using the address/data lines to perform a transfer cycle. There are seven signals in the arbitration group: BREQ* and ARB5* through ARB0*.

BREQ* (Bus Request) is an OR-tied signal which is bused on the backplane. All agents that require access to the bus assert the BREQ* signal.

A particular agent's arbitration ID number is coded on lines **ARB4* through ARB0*** (Arbitration). An agent requiring use of the iPSB bus asserts BREQ* and drives its arbitration ID onto the OR-tied ARB lines. The ARB5* line selects one of two arbitration algorithms: fairness or high priority.

Address/Data Bus Group

This signal group contains the lines used to transfer the address and data information plus their respective byte parity lines. The **AD31* through AD0*** (Address/Data) lines are multiplexed and serve a dual purpose depending upon the phase of the transfer cycle.

During the request phase, they contain the address for the ensuing transfer. This address refers to the byte location for memory and I/O spaces, a processing agent module in message space, and a board slot location in interconnect space. The requesting agent drives these lines during the request phase.

During the reply phase, they contain either eight, sixteen, twenty-four, or thirty-two bits of data. They are driven by the requesting agent for write transfers and by the replying agent for read transfers.

The **PAR3* through PAR0*** (Parity) lines are the byte parity lines associated with the respective bytes of the AD lines. They form even parity with their respective address/data byte.

System Control Signal

The transfer signal group consists of ten signals, SC9* through SC0* (System Control). Agents use these signals to define commands or to report status, depending on the phase of the transfer cycle.

During the request phase, the requesting agent drives SC9* through SC0*. The SC lines provide command information to the replying agent(s). During the reply phase, the requesting agent drives SC9* and SC3* through SC0* with its handshake and additional control information. The replying agent drives the remainder with its handshake and status. Table 1 lists the request and reply phase functions for this group.

Exception Signal Group

The iPSB bus provides a group of two signals for passing indications of exception errors to all agents: **BUSERR*** (Bus Error), and **TIMOUT*** (Time-out).

An agent activates BUSERR* to indicate its detection of a data integrity problem during a transfer. Parity errors on the AD or SC lines are typical of errors signaled on BUSERR. Any agent detecting such errors must signal BUSERR* and all agents must receive BUSERR*.

TIMOUT* is signaled by the CSM whenever it detects the failure of a module to complete a handshake. TIMOUT* is received by all agents on the bus.

Central Control Group

The system control group provides status concerning the operating state of the entire iPSB bus environment.

Table 1. System Control Definition

Signal	Function	
	Request Phase	Reply Phase
SC0	Request Phase	Request Phase
SC1	Lock	Lock
SC2	Data Width 0	End-of-Cycle
SC3	Data Width 1	Requesting Agent Ready
SC4	Address Space 0	Replying Agent Ready
SC5	Address Space 1	Agent Error 0
SC6	Read/Write	Agent Error 1
SC7	Reserved	Agent Error 2
SC8	Parity (SC7-4)	Parity (SC7-4)
SC9	Parity (SC3-0)	Parity (SC3-0)

iPSB PARALLEL SYSTEM BUS

It consists of seven signals plus the power and ground lines.

The **RST*** (Reset) signal is a system-level initialization signal sent to all agents by the CSM.

The **RSTNC*** (Reset Not Complete) signal is an OR-tied line driven by any agent whose internal initialization sequence is longer than that provided by the RST* signal itself. Due to its OR-tying, RSTNC* remains active until every agent has completed its initialization sequence. Agents cannot perform bus transfer cycles until RSTNC* is inactive.

The CSM provides a **DCLOW** (DC Power Low) signal to all agents as a warning of an imminent loss of DC power. DCLOW is typically generated from a signal supplied by the system power supply on the loss of AC power. Any agent needing to preserve state information in battery backed-up resources should do so upon receiving an active DCLOW.

Accompanying DCLOW for power-down sequencing is the **PROT*** (Protect) signal. The CSM drives PROT* active a short time after it activates DCLOW to inform all bus interfaces to ignore any transitions on the bus as power is lost.

The **BCLK*** (Bus Clock) and **CCLK*** (Constant Clock) signals are supplied by the CSM to all agents. Agents use the BCLK to drive the arbitration and timing state machines on the iPSB bus. The active going edge of BCLK* provides all system timing references. The CCLK* is an auxiliary clock at twice the frequency of BCLK.

An agent uses its **LACHn*** (ID Latch) signal to save the slot ID it receives from the CSM at reset time via the ARB4* through ARB0* lines. The ID latch signal is called LACHn* where the "n" is the card slot to which the ID is assigned. At each card slot, the LACHn* signal is connected to the AD line of the same number. As an example, card slot 7 has a LACH7* signal that is connected to AD7*.

When RST* is active, the CSM sends successive slot ID's (0 through 19) on the ARB4* through ARB0* lines while activating the corresponding AD line. Agents know when the ARB lines contain the correct slot number when they see their LACHn* line go active.

Power

System power supplied in the iPSB connector includes +5 volts, +12 volts, −12 volts, and facilities for +5 volt battery back-up. Also defined are numerous ground lines some of which are interlaced throughout the connector.

iPSB Bus Protocol

Overview

In the MULTIBUS II specification, both timing diagrams and state-flow diagrams describe the iPSB bus protocol. The state-flow diagrams present the lowest-level and most rigorous definition while the timing diagrams help conceptual understanding. For the purposes of this data book, only the timing diagram description is used.

Arbitration Cycle

An agent that wishes to transfer data on the iPSB bus must begin by performing an arbitration cycle. The cycle performs two functions: first, it gives all agents the opportunity to be granted access to the bus, and second, it eliminates the possibility of more than one agent trying to transfer data on the bus at any one instant. In the case where more than one agent requests access to the bus at the same instant, the arbitration cycle grants access to the agents based upon one of two arbitration algorithms: normal or high priority.

Normal priority mode provides "fairness" or "no starvation", which means each agent has an equal opportunity to grant access to the bus. For example, assume all agents request the bus at the same instant. In the normal priority mode, each agent is granted the bus, one by one, until all requests have been serviced. If an already serviced agent desires to use the bus again before all of the original agents are serviced, it will wait until all of original requesting agents have their requests granted. This "round-robin" granting of access ensures that any agent requesting the bus will eventually get it.

The high priority mode allows an agent with high priority to force its way into the arbitration and be granted the bus before agents with lesser priority. This means that a high priority agent gets access to the bus quickly; however, it can also consume so much of the bus that agents with lesser priority never gaining access; they will "starve".

At reset, the CSM supplies each agent with its slot ID and its arbitration ID. An agent making a normal priority request activates BREQ*, holds ARB5* inactive, and drives its arbitration ID onto ARB4* through ARB0*. If the ARB lines hold its ID after a specified time (3 bus clocks), this agent won the arbitration and can use the bus once any ongoing transfer completes. However, if the ARB lines do not match its ID (after all, other agents might be also requesting the bus and driving the ARB lines), another agent won the arbitration. The losing agent removes its ID and waits for the next resolution phase before trying again.

An agent makes a high priority request by activating BREQ*, holding ARB5* active (ARB5* selects the arbitration mode), and driving its arbitration ID onto the ARB lines. The high priority algorithm requires that

iPSB PARALLEL SYSTEM BUS

when a high priority request enters during an arbitration cycle, the request immediately enters the next resolution phase rather than waiting for the next bus request cycle as do normal priority requests. ARB5* being active causes the other requesting agents to remove their requests guaranteeing the high priority agent access to the bus before any simultaneous normal priority requests. When more than one agent simultaneously makes a high priority request, the agent with the higher priority (lower numerical value) arbitration ID will go first. Figure 5 illustrates the logic required to implement the iPSB bus arbitration. With either priority mode, once an agent owns the bus, it can perform any number of transfer cycles until forced off by arbitration. This characteristic of the arbitration algorithms is called "bus parking".

Transfer Cycle

Transfer cycles consist of two phases: request and reply. For illustration, an example of a access read cycle is shown in Figure 6. During the request phase, the bus owner (requesting agent) uses the transfer cycle signal group (SC lines) to notify the replying agent of the address space (memory, I/O, interconnect, or message), the data width (8-, 16-, 24- or 32-bit), and whether the cycle is read or write. The AD lines contain the desired address for the selected address space. Replying agents know the SC lines contain this request information by the requesting agent activating SC0* (Request Phase). The request phase lasts one clock cycle. All potential replying agents use the request phase to determine whether they contain the addressed resource.

The reply phase starts immediately following the request phase. During this phase the agent with the addressed resource (replying agent) and the requesting agent exchange data and status. Both the requesting and replying agent must agree that the data on the AD lines and the status on the appropriate SC lines are valid via the RQRDY (Requesting agent ready — SC3*)

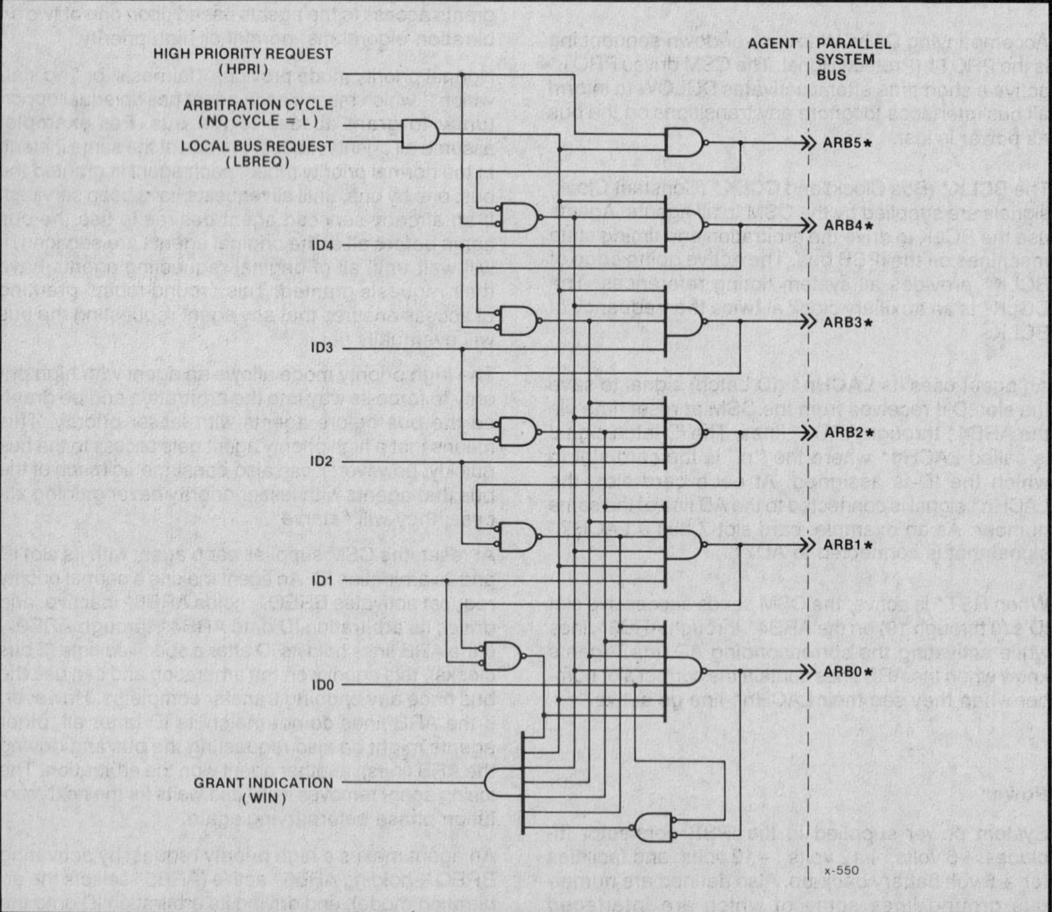

Figure 5. iPSB Bus Arbitration Cycle

iPSB PARALLEL SYSTEM BUS

and RPRDY (Replying agent ready — SC4*) handshake lines. Either agent can hold off the transfer by deactivating its ready line. This handshaking supports any speed requesting or replying agent.

The transfer cycle is complete when the requesting agent signals the last data transfer via the End-Of-Cycle (EOC — SC2*). The last bus clock cycle of the transfer is when EOC, RQRDY, and RPRDY are all active simultaneously.

The replying agent has the opportunity to tell the requesting agent if it does not support the requested operation via the agent error (SC5*, SC6*, and SC7*) lines. These lines encode five types of errors: width violation, continuation error, data error, illegal operation, and negative acknowledgement of a message. Trying to extract 32-bits of data from an 8-bit peripheral is an example of a data width violation. Continuation errors occur when attempting sequential access from an agent which does not support them or running off the ending address of a memory board. Writing to a read-only memory is an example of an illegal operation. A parity or ECC error in a memory board is an example of a data error. A replying agent signals a negative acknowledgement to a message transfer cycle if its destination queue is full (the source must perform source queuing). The transfer cycle is terminated by the requesting agent when it detects that the replier is signalling an agent error. If the bus interface is intelligent, it might retry the operation with a different type that the replying agent can support. Other aspects of transfer cycle include the ability of a requesting agent to LOCK the bus via the SC1* line. SC1* is a non-multiplexed signal which inhibits alternate ports of any multi-ported resource being addressed. By locking the bus, the requesting agent can guarantee itself exclusive access to a multi-ported bus resource and retains bus ownership for more than one transfer cycle.

As noted in the figure, in addition to parity protection on the address/data lines, the SC lines are also protected by parity. The requesting agent is responsible for the SC parity bits (SC8* and SC9*) during the request phase (it drives all SC lines). The reply phase requires two parity bits: one for those lines driven by the requesting agent and one for those driven by the replier. This ensures all aspects of the transfer cycle have parity protection.

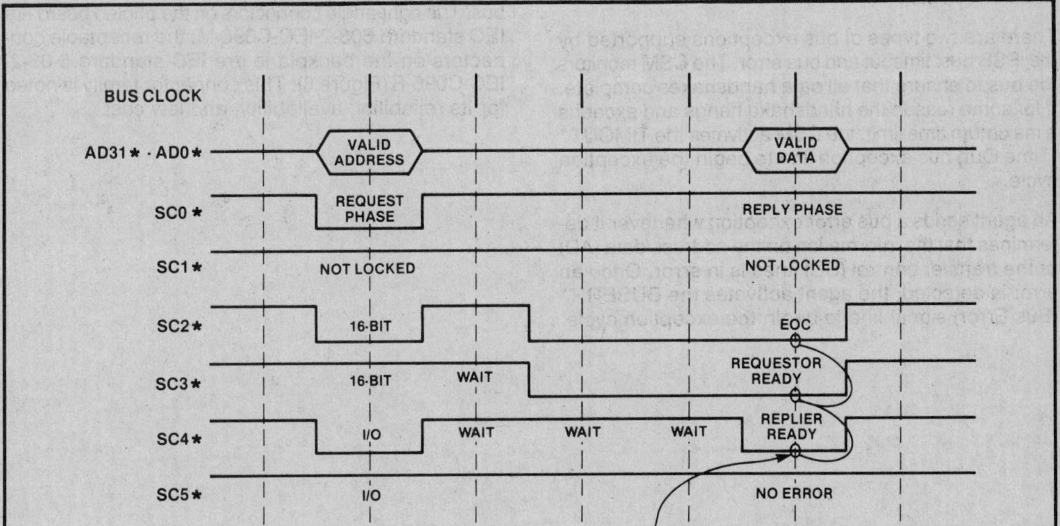

Figure 6. Transfer Cycle Example

iPSB PARALLEL SYSTEM BUS

Exception Cycle

The exception cycle is an error reporting mechanism. An agent or the CSM initiates an exception cycle as a result of sensing an exception. If no exception occurs, no exception cycles occur.

The exception cycle has two purposes in the protocol: first, it provides systematic termination of activity on the iPSB bus and second, it provides a stabilization time before allowing agents to resume operation. These two purposes correspond directly to the two phases of the exception cycle: the signal and recovery phases.

The signal phase begins when an agent or a module senses an exception and activates one of the bus error lines. On receiving a bus error, all agents terminate any transfer or arbitration cycles in progress. The net effect of the signal phase is to terminate all bus activity. The signal phase continues until the error-detecting module deactivates the bus error line.

The recovery phase begins after the bus error line becomes inactive. The recovery phase is a fixed-duration delay (in terms of bus clock cycles) that allows time for the iPSB bus signals to settle before starting more transfer cycles.

There are two types of bus exceptions supported by the iPSB bus: timeout and bus error. The CSM monitors the bus to ensure that all data handshakes complete. If for some reason the handshake hangs and exceeds a maximum time limit, the CSM activates the TIMOUT* (Time Out) bus exception line to begin the exception cycle.

An agent sends a bus error exception whenever it determines that the information on the address/data (AD) or the transfer control (SC) lines is in error. Once an error is detected, the agent activates the BUSERR* (Bus Error) signal line to begin the exception cycle.

Mechanical

The MULTIBUS II boards, board accessories, and backplanes conform to mechanical standards defined by the International Electromechanical Commission (IEC); these standards are commonly referred to as the Eurocard mechanical standards. This mechanical system offers modular board sizes as defined in standard IEC-297-3 and reliable two-piece connectors as defined in IEC-603-2.

Form Factor

The MULTIBUS II specification calls out two modular board form factors: 233 x 220mm and 100 x 220mm (see Figure 7). The iPSB bus and iLBX II bus portions of the MULTIBUS II system architecture are always defined on the P1 and P2 connectors respectively. However, the user can optionally define the use of the P2 connector if the iLBX II bus is not supported. (The iSSB bus is additionally defined on the P1 connector.)

Connector

MULTIBUS II boards and backplanes use two-piece, 96-pin connectors for both the iPSB bus and the iLBX II bus. The right-angle connectors on the printed board are IEC standard 603-2-IEC-C096-M; the receptacle connectors on the backplane are IEC standard 6-03-2-IEC-C096-F (Figure 8). This connector family is noted for its reliability, availability, and low cost.

iPSB PARALLEL SYSTEM BUS

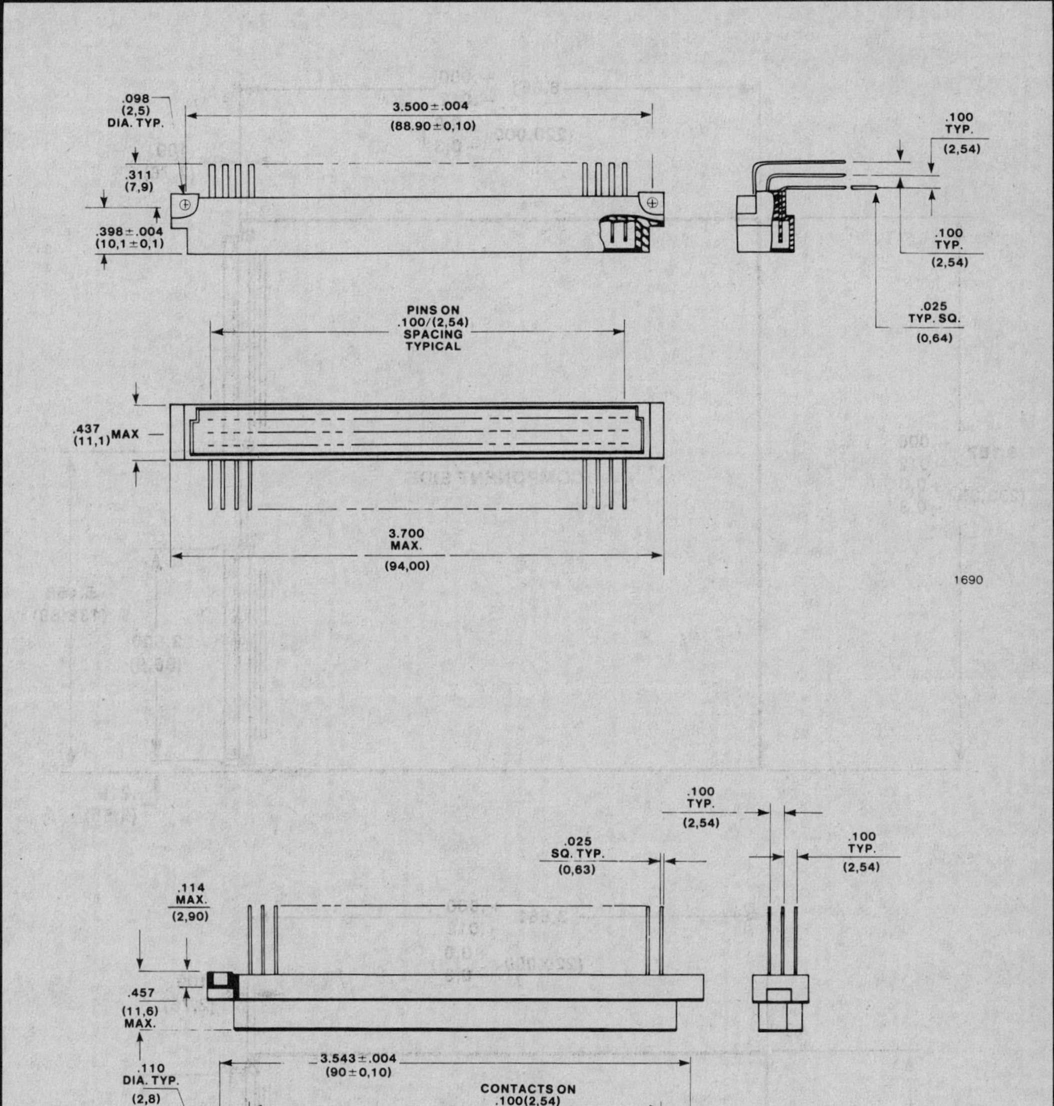

Figure 8. MULTIBUS® II Connectors

iPSB PARALLEL SYSTEM BUS

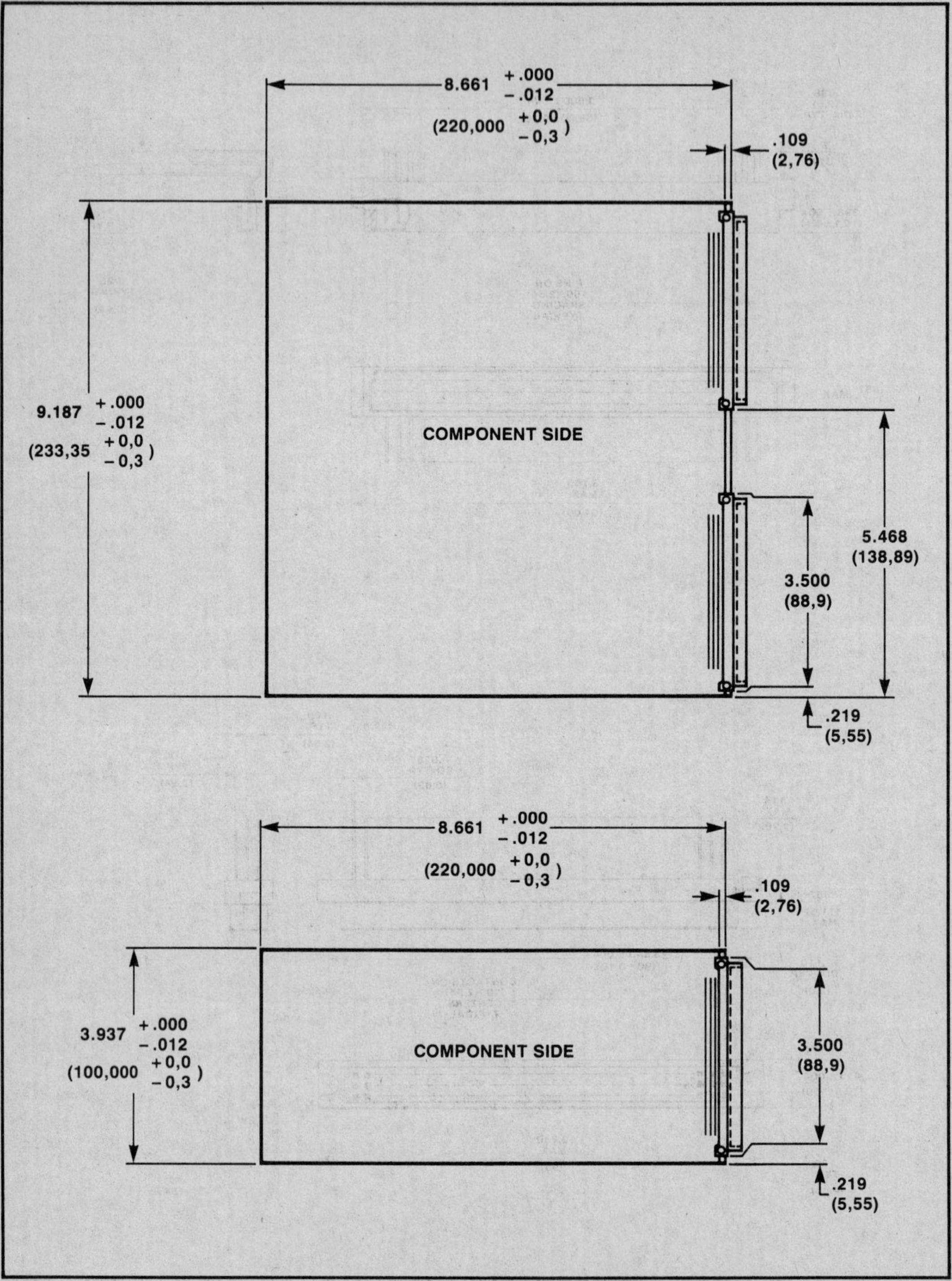

Figure 7. MULTIBUS® II Board Sizes

iPSB PARALLEL SYSTEM BUS

The pin assignment for the iPSB bus on P1 is shown in Table 2.

Please refer to Intel's MULTIBUS II Bus Architecture Specification Handbook for more detailed information.

Table 2. iPSB Bus Pin Assignments

Connector Pin Number	Row A	Row B	Row C
1	0 Volts	PROT*	0 Volts
2	+5 Volts	DCLOW*	+5 Volts
3	+12 Volts	+5 Battery	+12 Volts
4	(Note 2)	SDA (Note 3)	BCLK*
5	TIMOUT*	SDB (Note 3)	0 Volts
6	(Note 1) LACHn	0 Volts	CCLK*
7	AD0*	AD1*	0 Volts
8	AD2*	0 Volts	AD3*
9	AD4*	AD5*	AD6*
10	AD7*	+5 Volts	PAR0*
11	AD8*	AD9*	AD10*
12	AD11*	+5 Volts	AD12*
13	AD13*	AD14*	AD15*
14	PAR1*	0 Volts	AD16*
15	AD17*	AD18*	AD19*
16	AD20*	0 Volts	AD21*
17	AD22*	AD23*	PAR02*
18	AD24*	0 Volts	AD25*
19	AD26*	AD27*	AD28*
20	AD29*	0 Volts	AD30*
21	AD31*	Reserved	PAR3*
22	+5 Volts	+5 Volts	Reserved
23	BUSREQ*	RST*	BUSERR*
24	ARB5*	+5 Volts	ARB4*
25	ARB3*	RSTNC*	ARB2*
26	ARB1*	0 Volts	ARB0*
27	SC9*	SC8*	SC7*
28	SC6*	0 Volts	SC5*
29	SC4*	SC3*	SC2*
30	−12 Volts	+5 Battery	−12 Volts
31	+5 Volts	SC1*	+5 Volts
32	0 Volts	SC0*	0 Volts

NOTES:
1. LACHn* for all agents but the one driving CCLK*; line contains a second CCLK* signal in systems that have more than 12 cardslots.
2. 0 Volts for all agents but the one driving BCLK*; line contains a second BCLK* signal in systems that have more than 12 cardslots.
3. Signal lines SDA and SDB are reserved for the Serial System Bus.

ADVANCE INFORMATION

MULTIBUS® II
iSSB Serial System Bus

- Logical equivalent to the iPSB bus message space
- 2 megabits/sec serial data rate
- Multi-master capability up to 32 nodes
- Physical distribution up to 10 meters
- Deterministic access protocol
- Based upon CSMA/CD (Carrier Sense Multiple Access with Collision Detection)

The iSSB Serial System Bus is a simple, low cost alternative to the iPSB Parallel System Bus message address space. The message passing interface is identical for both buses; this allows easy migration from one bus to the other with no software changes. The iSSB bus serves as a low-cost replacement for the iPSB bus in applications where cost reduction is required and serves as a complement to the iPSB bus where an alternative bus path is needed for interface control, diagnostics, or redundancy changes.

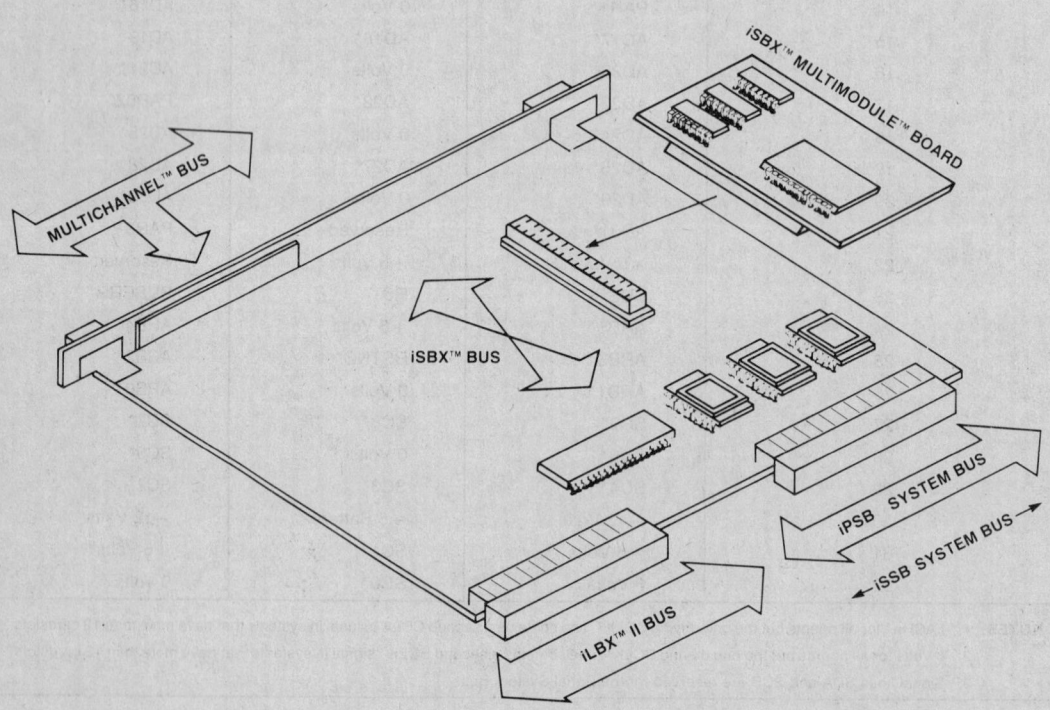

MULTIBUS® II Physical Diagram

15-20

MARCH, 1985
ORDER NUMBER: 280055-002

iSSB SYSTEM BUS

ADVANCE INFORMATION

FUNCTIONAL DESCRIPTION

Architectural Overview

The trend toward a more functional VLSI has driven the cost-functionality vector to allow system designers to pack more and more functionality on a given size board while maintaining approximately constant cost. The iSSB Serial System Bus lets VLSI drive the cost-functionality vector in the other direction; dramatically reduce the cost while maintaining roughly constant functionality. It accomplishes this by reducing the **interconnect cost** and allowing **physical distribution** of modules.

Reduced Interconnect Cost

Most systems today use a parallel interface to interconnect boards within the system. Frequently the cost to provide this interconnect is a significant percentage of the total system cost. Connectors, backplanes and interface logic are all part of this interconnect cost.

The iSSB Serial System Bus dramatically reduces the interconnect cost by replacing the parallel interface's multiple-line connector and backplane with a simple twisted-pair interface using telephone-type connectors. It also reduces the interface logic to a single VLSI component as opposed to the multiple components required in a parallel interface.

Physical Distribution

Being tied to a backplane or bulky ribbon cable limits the system designer's mechanical flexibility in constructing a system from multiple modules. The iSSB bus frees him of these restrictions by letting him physically distribute the system modules up to 10 meters apart.

Structural Features

Physical Characteristics

The iSSB bus consists of a maximum of 32 nodes which can be distributed over a maximum of 10 meters of cable. The nodes may be distributed along an external cable segment or clustered into backplanes as shown in Figure 2. Each backplane may contain up to 20 nodes, the maximum number of cardslots in a iPSB bus backplane.

Clustered systems use repeaters as a connection between backplanes and the iSSB bus cable. The repeaters isolate the cable from the excessive capacitive load on the backplane.

Access Protocol

The iSSB bus employs an access protocol called Carrier-Sense-Multiple-Access with collision detection (CSMA/CD). The CSMA/CD protocol allows agents to transmit data whenever they are ready.

In CSMA/CD operation, an agent with data to transmit looks at the iSSB bus for traffic before beginning a transmission. If the bus is not idle, the agents waits until the line becomes idle and until an interframe space has passed. After both events, the agent begins transmission of the message.

It is possible for more than one agent to initiate a transmission at the same time; in that case, a collision occurs on the bus. The protocol handles collisions on the iSSB bus via a deterministic collision resolution algorithm that uses time slotting.

The deterministic collision algorithm guarantees a time slot during which each agent can transmit without interference from other agents. The resolution guaran-

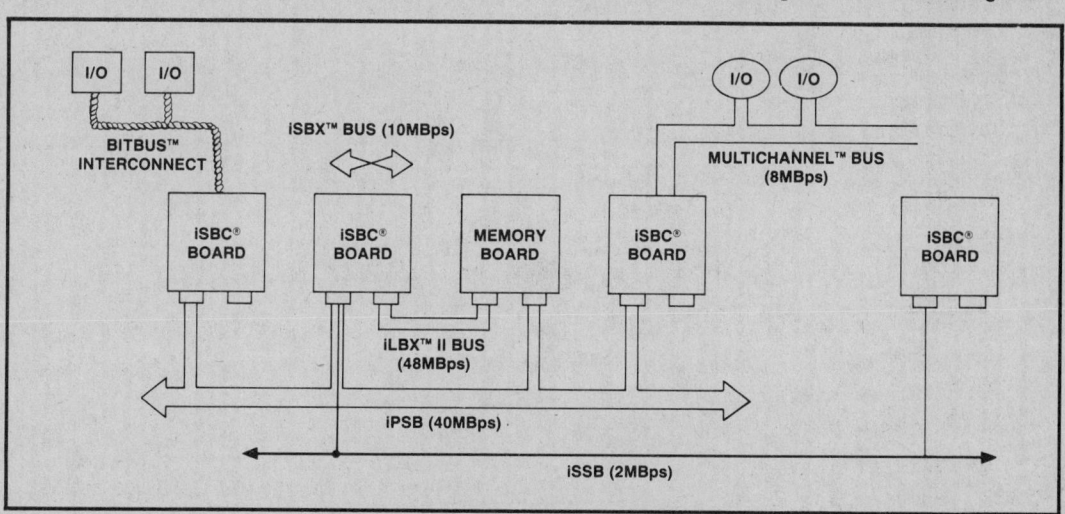

Figure 1. MULTIBUS® II Bus Architecture

iSSB SYSTEM BUS

ADVANCE INFORMATION

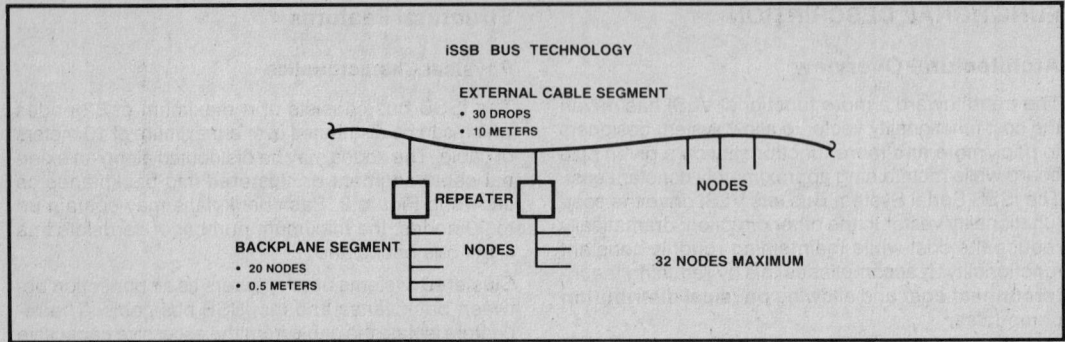

Figure 2. Typical iSSB Bus System Configurations

tees fair access to all agents. This type of collision resolution provides a real-time response that allows agents to resolve collisions in a finite time period.

Error Control

The iSSB bus uses a 16-bit CRC (Cyclic Redundancy Check) in order to provide error detection. Used in conjunction with an intelligent interface, this allows the iSSB to look as reliable as the iPSB bus even though it is up to 10 meters long.

Physical Interface

The physical iSSB bus interface consists of two signal lines (the SDA and SDB lines) that are included as part of the iPSB bus backplane design and may be extended via a 2-wire cable that connects to a repeater, typically located on the CSM. Agents encode data on the complementary, open-collector signal lines as shown in Table 1.

Table 1. iSSB Bus Signal Line Encoding

SDA Line	SDB Line	Line Condition
0	0	collision
0	1	logic 0
1	0	logic 1
1	1	idle

The portion of the signal lines within the backplane is designed to operate in a high-noise environment such as a heavily loaded backplane. Cable extensions to the iSSB bus must adhere to normal transmission line requirements.

To further improve reliability, the bus interface includes receivers that sample the data and filter out noise which may be coupled from the surrounding environment.

Please refer to Intel's MULTIBUS® II Bus Architecture Specification Handbook for more detailed information.

ARTICLE REPRINT

AR-350

October 1984

Message Passing Supports Multiple Processor Design

STEPHEN J. PACKER AND NARJALA BHASKER

Copyright, Computer Design Magazine, June 15, 1984. All rights reserved. Reprinted by permission.

Order Number: 280067-001

AR-350

SPECIAL REPORT ON MICROPROCESSORS/MICROCOMPUTERS PART II

MESSAGE PASSING SUPPORTS MULTIPLE PROCESSOR DESIGN

Enhancing message-passing capabilities on Multibus II allows efficient data transmission among multiple processors.

by Stephen J. Packer and
   Narjala Bhasker

As microcomputer systems have evolved into complex multiple processor designs, they have been very difficult to build. This is because there has been no adequate solution to the problem of interprocessor cooperation. Until recently, the system programmer has been forced to provide software algorithms that are either very complex and slow, or are not extensible to more than two processors. Now, however, the message passing facility of Multibus II provides a hardware solution for interprocessor communication. At the same time, it gives the system programmer a standard software interface well suited for creating a distributed microcomputer-based operating system. Moreover, a special message space pro-

Stephen J. Packer is manager of Multibus II serial architecture at Intel Corp, 5200 NE Elam Young Pkwy, Hillsboro, OR 97123, where he is responsible for Multibus II message passing design and implementation. He holds a BS and an MS in electrical engineering from the University of Washington.

Narjala Bhasker is a software engineer at Intel Corp, Hillsboro, OR, where she is responsible for message passing on the Multibus II serial system bus. He holds a BS in electronic engineering from the Indian Institute of Technology, Madras, India and an MS in computer science from Syracuse University.

vision allows users to name modules with a message address rather than taking up memory address space.

Early microcomputers based on a single microprocessor depended on various support chips for such functions as I/O and memory access. The integration level of these support functions required more than one PC board for use with reasonably sized systems. The Multibus I system architecture allowed separate boards supporting various microcomputer functions to be interconnected. To minimize the cost of the support circuitry needed to interface the local bus to the external bus, the local bus architecture of the chosen processor was extended. Thus, Multibus I supported the memory, I/O address space, and bit transfer width of 8- and 16-bit microprocessors.

The bus I/O space was used to access various I/O devices such as the serial universal asynchronous receiver/transmitter (UART). Even complex I/O boards for disk and tape controllers used the I/O space for control. It soon became apparent, however, that a single processor could not handle the I/O functions required for appropriate performance.

Dividing the system into specialized functions

Intelligent I/O controllers, devised to off-load many complex I/O functions, leave more of the processor bandwidth for the application. This partitioning of the system into specialized functions, usually requiring an entire board, is quite natural. Using shared memory for data exchange between the application processor and the special purpose, functionally partitioned modules is also natural.

In today's microcomputer systems, the system bus that interconnects functional modules is used almost exclusively for data movement between modules rather than for program execution. This data is encapsulated in control structures and is considered an interprocessor message. Memory-mapped control structures of interprocessor messages have variations as numerous as the programmers who program them. Only in those cases where hardware interfaces exist has any controlling standard emerged. The

---

Extending Multibus I into Multibus II

To provide computational power for increasingly complex applications, microcomputer systems have evolved from basic single-processor systems to more intricate multiple processor systems that distribute the total processing load among various hardware modules. Intel's Multibus I system architecture developed a multiple bus structure approach for these complex multiple processor systems. Using a design strategy known as functional partitioning, the Multibus I architecture provided a specialized bus for specific critical functions, thus preserving the bandwidth of the system bus for interprocessor communication and data movement.

The Multibus II system architecture refines this approach and extends its range (see Table). By providing a traditional microprocessor bus for the access of memory and I/O address space via the parallel system bus (the iPSB), Multibus II continues the evolutionary path established by Multibus I. It also prepares the way for future 32-bit microcomputers by providing 32-bit data and address paths to memory. The bus clock frequency of 10 MHz provides a maximum 40-Mbyte/s transfer rate that anticipates performance requirements for future microprocessors.

Like Multibus I, Multibus II permits multiple bus masters capable of requesting and arbitrating for access to the bus. The Multibus II arbitration policy is more involved and allows complex algorithms as well as avoiding access starvation for all modules. In addition, Multibus II provides the centralization of bus functions in a single module. This reduces the cost of multiboard systems, since all boards need not carry the overhead of providing bus-level functions such as clock and timeout.

For designs using large amounts of RAM and executing from this memory with minimal delays (see Figure), the Multibus II specification provides a local bus extension (iLBX II). Multiple iLBX II execution buses can exist in a single Multibus II system that isolates the processors' execution environments from one another and leaves the system bus for data movement between environments.

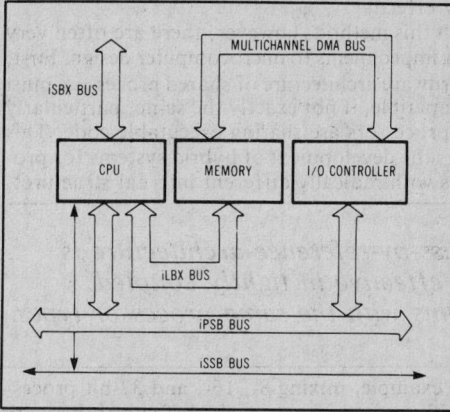

The serial system bus (iSSB) is offered as the lowest cost method of interconnecting functional modules in a system. The processor interface is identical to the message-passing facility in the parallel system bus except for initialization and error management.

Multibus II Specifications in Brief

Parallel system bus (iPSB)	Local bus extension (iLBX II)	Serial system bus (iSSB)
32-bit address and data path width	32-bit memory and 26-bit address path width	bus clock rate of 2 MHz
16-bit I/O address and data width	16-bit I/O address and data width	up to 32 nodes on a maximum of 10 m of cable
synchronous operation with clock rate of 10 MHz	synchronous operation with a clock rate of 12 MHz	up to 20 nodes on one backplane
40-Mbyte/s transfer rate (sequential-transfer)	48-Mbyte/s transfer rate (sequential-transfer)	CSMA/CD access method
up to 20 agents	up to 6 agents (one master and one secondary master)	deterministic collision resolution
support of 8-, 16- and 32-bit processors		16-bit cyclic redundancy check
8-, 16-, 24-, 32-bit transfers	pipelining (overlap of address and data cycles)	System bus extension (iSBX)
no starvation arbitration policy	support of 8-, 16- and 32-bit processors	low cost I/O extension to CPU board
central system functions; clock, timeout, power fail		Multichannel DMA bus
transfer parity, DIN connectors, distributed ground pins	8-, 16-, 32-bit transfers	16-bit address and data path width
interconnect address space (512 eight-bit, one interrupt line registers) for system-level diagnostics and configuration	optional transfer parity, DIN connectors	asynchronous operation with clock rate of 2 MHz
256 interrupt sources	one interrupt line	8-, and 16-bit transfers
message passing		up to 16 nodes on cable of up to 15

purpose of these standard interfaces has been to provide a software-compatible hardware upgrade to earlier products. Hardware available for message passing in an efficient and easy-to-use manner frees the system programmer for more important tasks. Any solution to the interprocessor communication problem comprises one of two options: a pass-by-reference interface, or a pass-by-value interface.

The pass-by-reference approach to interprocessor communication passes pointers between modules without copying the actual data. This requires a shared memory resource accessible by the cooperating processors (Fig 1). In tightly coupled systems having the same types of processors with shared memory and I/O, the pass-by-reference architecture is very effective.

With this method, however, there are often very serious impediments to microcomputer design. First, the hardware architecture of shared processors must be compatible, if not exactly the same, particularly if the processors are sharing executable code. This hinders the development of hybrid systems for processors with radically different internal structures.

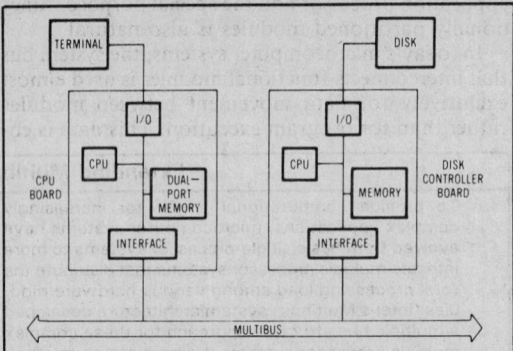

Fig 1 In a pass-by-reference architecture, the CPU board contains a microprocessor such as the Intel 80286, and supports logic, I/O devices, a dual-port RAM array, and a parallel system bus (iPSB) interface logic. The disk controller board has a processor such as the 80188, a parallel I/O interface, and sufficient RAM for sector caching. The disk controller communicates via messages contained in data structures in the dual-port RAM of the CPU board.

A pass-by-reference architecture is very effective in tightly coupled systems with the same processor types.

For example, mixing 8-, 16-, and 32-bit processors with memory is extremely difficult if there are byte-alignment differences among the selected processors. Also, a processor with a wider data path than the accessed memory may be restricted to specific instructions that make only byte-data references. All too often, the software algorithms must be context sensitive to allow processor-independent implementations.

Achieving low cost and high performance execution requires that memory arrays be used on processor boards. For memory-mapped messages, this onboard memory must be dual-ported and accessible from the onboard CPU and the offboard modules via the Multibus interface. This forces the two processors to view the memory by different address ranges (Fig 2). The different addresses by which the processors know the same physical memory location are called aliases. Such "aliasing" results in a loss of performance since one of the processors must recalculate all the pointers to reach the same addresses.

More importantly, the software algorithms for managing shared data structures are not extensible to more than two processors without hardware help. When two-processor algorithms are used in a system with three or more processors, a shared data structure is needed for each communicating pair. Performance suffers in a server module because it must search a list of data structures for each requester. But, the most serious difficulty is configuring such a system when modules are optionally added or deleted.

Almost all memory-mapped, message-passing schemes assume a single-application processor and a dedicated slave processor. In future systems, the functional modules must become servers that will accommodate multiple application processors. In addition, the user must be able to add and remove application modules without disrupting the system. Finally, a pass-by-reference implementation does not lend itself to memory protected systems (like Microsoft's Xenix operating system) that are not object oriented. A failing processor or faulty software can easily compromise a system using shared memory.

Defining the pass-by-value interface

Another choice for a message-passing design is the pass-by-value strategy that copies data, rather than exchanging it, via pointers. This method is usually selected when protection criteria are more important

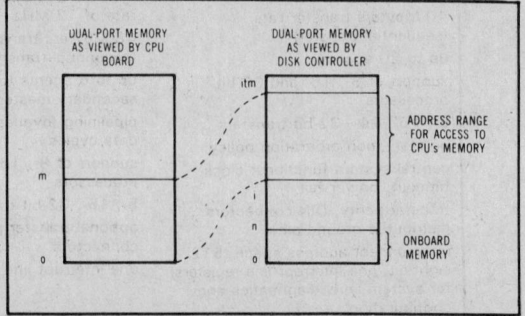

Fig 2 In the pass-by-reference scheme, the disk controller software views the CPU's memory in different address ranges. Aliasing complicates the software and severely reduces performance.

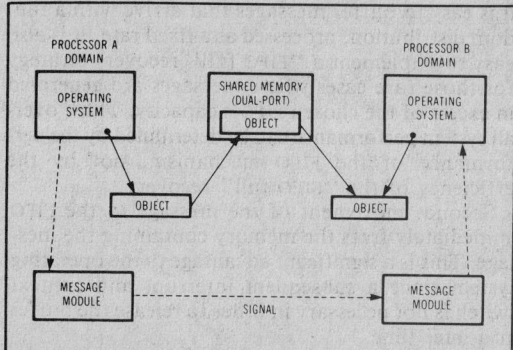

Fig 3 The operating system of processor A in the pass-by-value approach transfers a memory object to the operating system of processor B. It invokes a message-passing module that copies the object from private memory to a shared memory area. As processor B is interrupted, it calls out its message-passing module and copies the data to a private memory area.

than maximum system performance. Given the functional partitions of a distributed microcomputer system, a pass-by-value implementation requires a double copy of the data (Fig 3). The data is copied from application space to some internal system space, where it can be accessed by the second processor. After the first processor interrupts the second, the second can move the data to the memory space of the receiving application.

This process of double-copying the data places a considerable strain on the system's performance and yields a lower level of performance—the most serious disadvantage of the pass-by-value method. Nonetheless, a pass-by-value implementation is easier than a pass-by-reference method because differences in the hardware (eg, memory data width) are confined to the interface software. New modules are easier to develop since internal data structures need not be known to other modules. Finally, existing operating systems such as Xenix can be used without rewriting their internal structures.

An obvious choice for the system programmer is some high performance version of the pass-by-value method. Getting high performance, however, requires an architectural hardware change to augment the software algorithm. A distributed operating system and a distributed application have similar requirements for messages exchanged between modules. This is because both use independent processes that must communicate with other processes.

The messages received by the process providing a service to another process are unsolicited (ie, the receiver cannot predict when a message will occur). These unsolicited messages are used to negotiate the movement of varying and potentially large amounts of data. This partitioning of the kinds of messages expected in a system can be used to define a new model for message passing.

A special Multibus II message space provides a means of naming modules by a message address rather than by using a memory address. This message address space is much smaller than the address space of the supported processors, and the message-passing facility is independent of the physical medium implementation interconnecting the functional modules. This permits a software design that can support a wide range of systems—from those that use the low cost serial bus to the high performance parallel bus. This design will also eventually support the interconnection of single-chip functional modules.

Unsolicited messages can either be requests for service or a reply to a request for service (Fig 4). Thus, messages become the fundamental basis for requester/server implementations of distributed processes. The most important requirement for unsolicited messages is high efficiency and low latency for the movement between functional modules (ie, the cost of sending the message must be a fraction of the task switching time for the operating system). In addition, any delays must be short. Commands can therefore be thought of as processor interrupts with data.

Unsolicited messages generated in a system are usually quite short—usually less than 32 bytes. Nonetheless, they carry the needed control information for such diverse functions as global object management and I/O control. Within a single system, the total system capacity needed to generate unsolicited messages is self-limiting. This is due to a limit on the number of requests that can be sent before a reply is required to continue processing.

These two attributes make unsolicited messages ideally suited for a hardware first in, first out (FIFO) buffer (Fig 5). Messages bounded in size and number can be placed in the output FIFO of the sending module, and then removed by the receiving module. The FIFO implementation has two advantages. First,

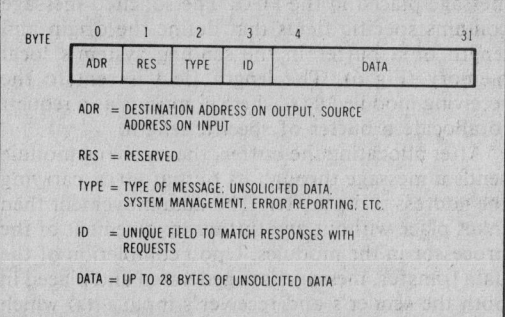

Fig 4 The message in an unsolicited data message format is from 4 to 32 bytes long in increments of 4 bytes. The type field indicates the exact function of the message, which may be an interrupt (with no data); a data message; or a local control message between the processor and the message device. The last category is not transmitted on the bus and hence is not specified in Multibus II.

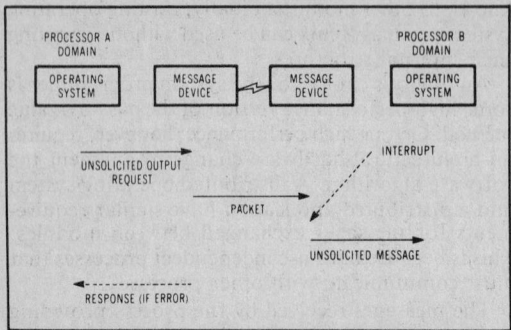

Fig 5 An unsolicited output message is moved into the message module first in, first out (FIFO). This is very efficient for processors with a string move instruction. The message devices cooperate to move a packet containing the unsolicited output message to the receiving module FIFO. The receiving operating system can remove the message from the FIFO on interrupt with a string move or a byte-by-byte read of an I/O port.

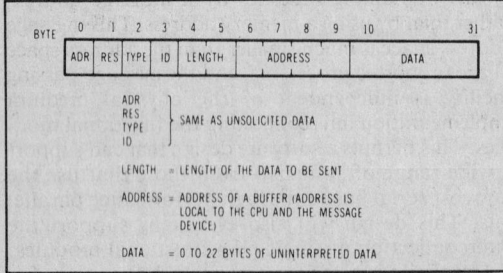

Fig 6 In a solicited output message format, two additional fields appear in the solicited message, indicating the address and the length of the data to be sent. Only the length field is actually transmitted on the bus because the address is local to the processor and its message device.

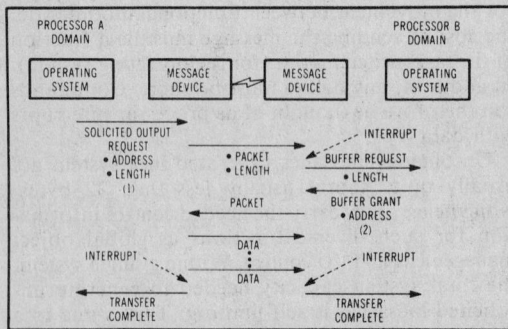

Fig 7 The data address in the solicited message procedure is retained in the sending message device and the length forwarded to the receiving device. On interrupt, the receiving operating system receives the buffer request and replies with a buffer grant message. The message devices move the data, up to 64 Kbytes, without further processor action. On completion, both sender and receiver get a transfer complete message.

it is easy to buffer messages that arrive with a random distribution, processed at a fixed rate. It is also easy to implement a "FIFO full" recovery strategy for those rare cases where messages are generated in excess of the chosen FIFO's capacity. Thus, overall system performance can be determined by the performance of the FIFO mechanism, not by the efficiency of the "FIFO full" recovery.

Second, movement of the message to the FIFO immediately frees the memory containing the message. This is a significant advantage to the operating system since a subsequent interrupt and context switch is not necessary in order to release the buffer at a later time.

When placed in FIFO, unsolicited messages are delivered to the operating system. This expectation is based on the high reliability of a computer bus where errors are very rare, and extraordinary recovery procedures can be tolerated. Thus, the inability to deliver a message is immediately reported to the sender, and the recovery action determined by the appropriate software.

Processing solicited messages

Eventually, the exchange of unsolicited messages results in the need to move a large amount of data. The bulk data movement can be accomplished by many unsolicited messages, but the cost of processing interrupts in the receiving module would bog down the system. Furthermore, such interrupts would no longer arrive randomly and in the limited number originally assumed.

An acceptable alternative is a DMA facility between functional partitions in which each end independently authorizes transfers. This facility must not compromise the low latency required by unsolicited messages. The solicited message facility of Multibus II provides this feature.

Solicited messages are initiated with a special message placed in the FIFO. The solicited message contains specific fields that define the origin and length of a buffer in the sending system's local memory (Fig 6). The length field is sent to the receiving module FIFO, where it appears as a request to allocate a buffer of specific length.

After allocating the buffer, the receiving module sends a message through its output FIFO, carrying the address of its buffer. The data movement then takes place without any further involvement of the processor in the modules. Upon completion of the data transfer, messages are generated and placed in both the sender's and receiver's input FIFO which signals the completion and return status. At this point, ownership of the buffers returns to the modules (Fig 7).

There are several advantages to this method. First, the assignment of buffers is completely under the control of the functional modules that own them. Thus, this facility is compatible with the memory protection features of the operating system. All pointers are used only in their natural address range. Second, the actual data movement can be controlled to optimize the bandwidth of the various buses in the system. This increases overall system performance. The data can be retrieved or stored from the module's memory at the rate of the internal bus on the module.

Pass-by-value message-passing is usually chosen when protection criteria are more important than maximum system performance.

Since the data transfer can be done at the full bandwidth of the interconnect bus, running all three buses at the speed of the slowest bus is not necessary. The module's CPU is not involved in this transfer except for potentially delayed access to its local memory bus during actual transfer.

The data is made into packets to suit the physical medium or to meet realtime needs for low latency access to the interconnect bus. The packets are transferred on the module interconnect bus at the optimum speed, whether serial or parallel, while unused bus bandwidth remains available to other communicating modules.

The design of the Multibus II message-passing facility can be implemented in a single VLSI device. The architecture offers a very simple device that is used only to support interrupts (unsolicited messages with no data). A more complex device is needed to support unsolicited messages with data and solicited messages. This device requires a FIFO controller, a DMA controller, a small amount of RAM for packet buffering, and a logic control unit. The serial system bus device is a derivative of the parallel message device with the replacement of the 32-bit bus interface with a serial interface unit.

While Multibus II-compatible boards do not require custom VLSI, boards designed by Intel will support the message-passing facility of Multibus II when the VLSI devices are fully tested and qualified. These VLSI devices will be available to ensure the rapid acceptance of the Multibus II specification.

ARTICLE REPRINT

AR-356

October 1984

Microprocessor Bus is Ready to Meet 32-Bit Applications of Future

JOHN BEASTON

Multiprocessor bus is ready to meet 32-bit applications of future

Using five buses, Multibus II promises to handle the high speed
and large I/O applications being developed for divergent microprocessors

by John Beaston, *Intel Corp., Hillsboro, Ore.*

☐ Board vendors who want to take advantage of the latest in microprocessor technology no longer have incompatible bus lines and interfaces blocking their paths. Multibus II, which was designed to support systems containing practically any microprocessor, has cleared the way. Moreover, because of its functional partitioned architecture, the latest chips or boards can be easily substituted for their older counterparts without system disruption. In addition, easily expandable inputs and outputs can meet the needs of most applications.

Multibus II's bus architecture takes the multiple-bus structure for microprocessors of Multibus I and expands its available system bandwidth, multiprocessing support, reliability, and cost-performance range, while making the architecture easy to use. Each of its five buses (see "Bus quintet brings networking flexibility," opposite) includes facilities or advanced bus structures that anticipate the needs of processors into the 1990s.

A bus structure consists of the bus's electrical and mechanical characteristics. It includes such things as specifications for the connector pin-out, the control-line protocol, the voltage levels, and current drive. Each bus has slightly different structural characteristics.

The bus architecture, on the other hand, refers to the actual systems that can be built with the bus or buses. A single, simple bus usually means low or moderate performance and limited peripheral expansion. Multiple buses, however, give system designers greater flexibility in meeting the system requirements.

The Multibus II (Fig. 1) has five buses: the parallel system bus (iPSB); the local bus extension (iLBX II); the serial system bus (iSSB); and two buses borrowed from the Multibus I architecture, the iSBX input/output expansion bus and the Multichannel direct-memory-access bus. These buses can be combined in almost any way.

The iPSB is the system's main communication path and provides the complete set of system functions: read/write accesses to memory and I/O, intermodule communication, arbitration between nodes contending for the bus, and central functions such as system reset and power-down. It can support 8-, 16-, and 32-bit processors and both 32-bit address and 8-, 16-, 24-, and 32-bit data transfers. Using 32-bit data-and-burst transfers, a 40-megabyte-a-second transfer rate can be achieved using existing technology for the bus interface.

The iPSB bus is highly multiplexed. The 32-bit address

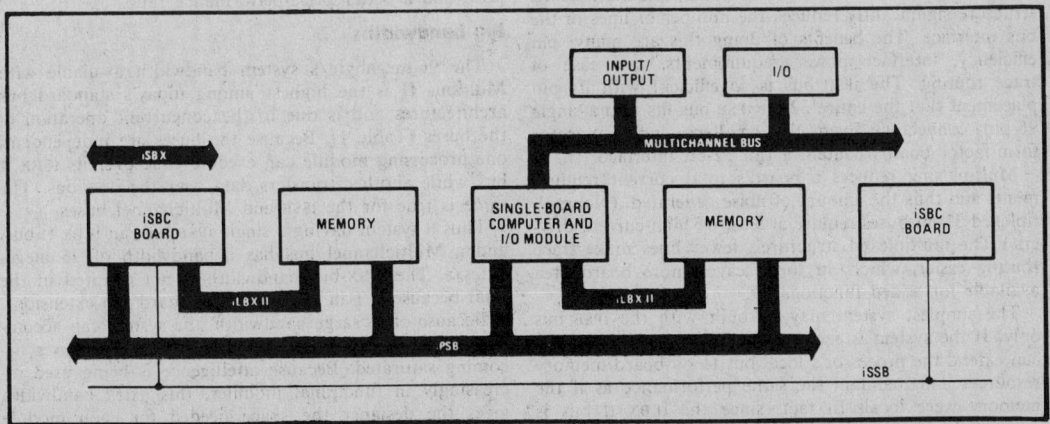

1. Five buses. Multibus II uses five buses: the iSBX input/output expansion bus, the Multichannel DMA bus, the parallel system bus (iPSB), the local bus extension (iLBX II), and the serial system bus (iSSB). With this architecture, boards or chips can be swapped easily.

Bus quintet brings networking flexibility

At the heart of the Multibus II specification lie its five buses, three of which are new. The parallel system bus, the local bus extension, and the serial system bus are the newly created buses; the iSBX input/output expansion bus and the Multichannel direct-memory-access bus are borrowed from Multibus I.

The parallel system bus or the iPSB is a high-performance, general-purpose bus that provides important data-movement and interprocessor-communication functions. It supports arbitration, execution, and I/O data-movement and gives board-configuration support. This bus has four address spaces: a 32-bit-wide memory address space, a 16-bit I/O address space, a 16- or 32-bit message address space, and a 16-bit interconnect address space. Data is clocked at 10 megahertz and can be up to 32 bits wide. In addition, the iPSB's burst-transfer capability yields a maximum sustained bandwidth of 40 megabytes a second.

Multiple processors executing an instruction in shared global memory can easily saturate the system bus and degrade system performance overall. The iLBX II, or local bus extension, can remove the processor's execution functions from the general-purpose system bus and extend local on-board performance to off-board memory resources. The bus provides up to 64 megabytes of arbitration-free local-memory expansion and a 12-MHz clock rate. The iLBX II bus also has a large bandwidth of 48 megabytes/s and advanced features such as pipelining and block transfers.

The iSSB, or serial system bus, is a low-cost serial interconnection that functions as an alternative to the message interface on the iPSB. Whereas the iPSB has 32-bit-wide parallel transfers and runs at 10 MHz, the iSSB is 1 bit wide and runs at 2 MHz. In addition, while the iPSB has 96 pins, the iSSB has only 2. Finally, because of the iSSB's serial structure, it can be extended up to 10 meters, whereas its parallel counterpart must be rigidly packaged.

Carried over from Multibus I, the iSBX I/O bus moves high-speed I/O data to and from physically distributed custom peripherals such as mass-storage devices or graphics-display systems. Block transfers at 8 megabytes/s between peripherals and single-board computers are possible. In addition, the bus provides a standardized I/O interface with full-speed operation at up to 15 meters with a simple asynchronous protocol. The bus supports up to 16 processors, both 8- and 16-bit, and allocates 16 megabytes of memory or register address space to each.

Finally, the iSBX I/O expansion bus is used for incremental on-board system expansion through small iSBX multimodule boards. Currently, iSBX boards add capabilities like parallel I/O, serial I/O, graphics, and advanced mathematical functions. All iSBX boards afford system expansion without the requirement of adding another expansion board. Through this bus, users can customize their single-board computers to individual applications in response to the latest very large-scale-integration technology. Since users are able to buy exactly the capabilities needed, both system cost and size are minimized.

---

and data paths are multiplexed, and the nine system-control lines have different uses depending on the transfer cycle's phase. The six arbitration lines serve the dual purposes of system initialization and normal operation.

Compared with nonmultiplexed buses, this multiplexed structure significantly reduces the number of lines in the bus interface. The benefits of doing this are many: pin efficiency, interface power requirements, and ease of trace routing. The iPSB bus is so efficient with its pin placement that the entire 32-bit iPSB bus fits into a single 96-pin connector. Even the smaller, single-connector form-factor boards contain a full 32-bit interface.

Multiplexing reduces a board's total current requirements and thus the amount of noise generated. (Nonmultiplexed 32-bit buses require at least 64 high-current drivers.) The multiplexed structure's fewer lines make trace routing easier, which, in turn, leaves more board area available for added functionality.

The simplest system may be built with the iPSB bus only. If the system is execution-intensive, an iLBX II bus can extend the processor's local bus to off-board memory resources and maintain the same performance as if the memory were local. In fact, since the iLBX II bus is connected to a given processor, the system might contain as many iLBX II buses as there are processors.

The variety of bus structures in the Multibus II architecture has five significant benefits: increased system bandwidth, improved reliability, reduced service costs and easy configuration, enhanced multiprocessing support, and a better price-performance ratio.

Big bandwidths

The 96-megabyte/s system bandwidth available with Multibus II is the highest among today's standard bus architectures and is due to the concurrent operation of the buses (Table 1). Because the buses are independent, one processing module can execute code over its iLBX II bus while another transfers data over the iPSB bus. The same is true for the iSSB and Multichannel buses.

Thus a system having a single iPSB bus, an iLBX II bus, and a Multichannel bus has a bandwidth of 96 megabytes/s. The iSBX-bus bandwidth is not counted in the total because it is a specialized on-board I/O extension.

Because of its large bandwidth, the system can accommodate many processing modules without the buses becoming saturated. Because intelligence is being used increasingly in functional modules, this extra bandwidth gives the designer the space needed for each module added to improve system performance.

The unusually large bandwidths of the iPSB and iLBX II

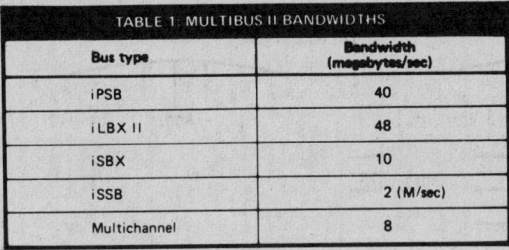

TABLE 1: MULTIBUS II BANDWIDTHS	
Bus type	Bandwidth (megabytes/sec)
iPSB	40
iLBX II	48
iSBX	10
iSSB	2 (M/sec)
Multichannel	8

TABLE 2: iSSB BUS SIGNAL ENCODING		
Line A	Line B	State
0	0	collision
0	1	logic 0
1	0	logic 1
1	1	idle

buses—40 and 48 megabytes/s, respectively—is due to their ability to support sequential or block-mode transfers. The 32-bit data paths are important since advanced 32-bit processors should be readily available soon, and the increased data width doubles the bandwidth over comparable 16-bit buses. Sequential transfers improve bus utilization because only one address is used for multiple data cycles (the replying modules automatically increment the starting address).

The multiple-bus structure increases system reliability by increasing connector reliability, data-transfer integrity, and electrical reliability. Multibus II boards use the popular two-piece DIN (IEC 603-2) connector. This connector is part of the Eurocard mechanical standard. The 96-pin version used by Multibus II is noted for its exceptional reliability and is available from numerous sources.

Another aspect of system reliability concerns detection of errors occurring during data transfers, and each of the new Multibus II buses contain mechanisms to detect such errors. The parallel iPSB and iLBX II buses are parity-protected, while the serial iSSB bus uses cyclic redundancy checks. As a result, every data transfer on these buses is completely protected.

In addition, the buses protect the addresses and commands. The detecting modules signal an error's occurrance on the bus, and the appropriate bus-interface logic notifies the involved modules to correct the problem.

To improve electrical reliability, the parallel buses use synchronous clocking in order to increase immunity from crosstalk and noise. All control, address, and data lines are sampled on a clock edge. Because only one edge of the clock line is important, edges appearing on other lines from noise or crosstalk are ignored, which greatly improves electrical reliability over the more traditional buses that use edge-sensitive asynchronous protocols. Furthermore, synchronous clocking simplifies system design and debugging: the bus interface is easily controlled through state machines, and logic analyzers are easily adapted for debugging.

Configuration ease

Board suppliers tend to produce products that address many diverse needs so the boards are usually loaded with jumper options and switches in dual in-line packages. But cramming all these options on a board can lead to confusion and configuration errors.

However, the iPSB and iLBX II define a mechanism, called geographical addressing, that can eliminate or reduce many of these manual programming options while maintaining flexibility. With it, software can address a board through its physical position in the backplane. Interconnect registers, placed on each board, contain such information as the manufacturer, the board type, and revision level. Software can thus read these registers and identify which boards are in the system and where. It can configure the board by writing into these registers. Changing a memory board's starting address, for example, is as simple as writing to that board's appropriate starting-address register.

The interconnect register opens the door to improved diagnostics performed either locally or remotely. A designer may build in a modem with which service technicians can exercise the system at the customer's site. Technicians can remotely determine the system's exact makeup and either download or trigger the appropriate diagnostic software locally.

The Multibus II's support for multiple processors goes beyond increased system bandwidth. The iPSB bus-arbitration and -interrupt structures are tailored for multiprocessing and, most importantly, the multiprocessing specification includes a message-passing protocol.

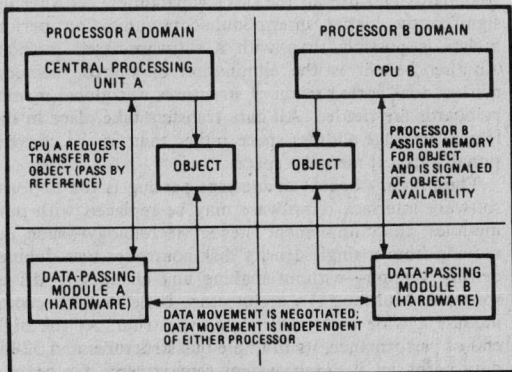

2. Message passing. The message-passing scheme for Multibus II is its strongest attribute and adds significant multiprocessing support. The two communicating message-passing interfaces acts as a distributed intelligent DMA controller.

3. Serial setup. The iSSB serial system bus can have up to 32 external nodes distributed over a 10-meter maximum, or 20 nodes clustered into backplanes connected to the bus cable by repeaters that isolate the bus from the excessive backplane capacitive load.

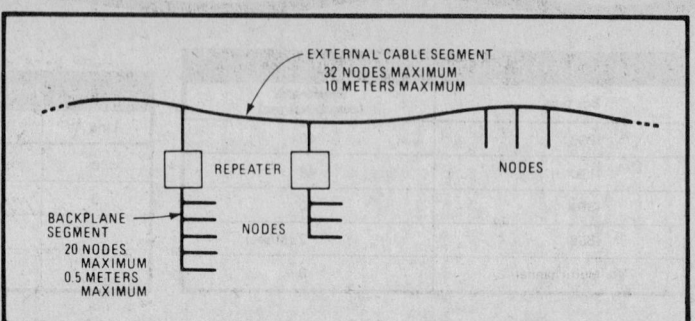

A bus's arbitration structure determines how many master modules can reside simultaneously on the bus. The iPBS allows up to 20 bus masters, whereas standard buses support a handful. In fact, every board in a Multibus II system can be a bus master. Two arbitration algorithms are available: fairness and high priority. The fairness algorithm gives every board a fair chance to access the bus. As a result, no board is forever locked out by a higher-priority master.

On the other hand, the high-priority algorithm can be used to define a priority structure among all the boards in the system. In this case, boards handling real-time events are usually given the highest priority, while less critical boards, such as control panels, get a lower priority. Changing between the two algorithms can be done dynamically; the designer is free to choose one or the other, or both.

Interrupts are usually a source of frustration for the system designer. Large systems contain many interrupt sources, yet most buses provide eight lines or so to handle them. As a result, several sources share a given interrupt line, and either software polling or hardware daisy-chaining is used to decide which source on that line actually generated the interrupt. More interrupt lines are needed, but most buses do not have the extra lines to spare. Using available lines as virtual interrupt lines, the iPSB's interrupt structure supports up to 255 interrupt sources and as many destinations.

Message passing

Each module on the bus is assigned a module message address. Special interrupt bus cycles let any module send an interrupt to any other module by specifying the appropriate source and destination message addresses. Another way to think of this is as memory-mapped interrupts where the source module writes into the destination's message address space to trigger an interrupt. This creates so many virtual lines that the designer does not have to worry about running out of them or having to share lines among modules.

The Multibus II message-passing protocol is probably its most significant contribution to multiprocessing. Most multiple-processor systems use either a pass-by-reference or a pass-by-value intermodule-communication protocol. In the pass-by-reference mode, the communicating modules exchange pointers or tokens so that they may address shared data structures. This method usually performs well, but it is difficult to extend beyond two processors sharing one data structure. It is also not appropriate for memory-protected operating systems, which are more likely to use the pass-by-value-method.

In this method, the modules exchange a copy of the data structure, which prevents the recipient module from corrupting the original data if something goes wrong. The major problem is performance—the processors must execute code to move the data.

Multibus II's message passing combines the best of both methods and gives it hardware support. Message passing uses a hardware pass-by-value interface that gives the performance of a pass-by-reference system. In addition, the software module used by both methods are replaced with a specialized message-passing interface. The processor passes-by-reference the reference to the data structure to the message-passing interface. This interface communicates with the destination module's interface to pass-by-value the data without processor intervention and is performed in the message-address space (Fig. 2). In many ways, it is helpful to think of the two communicating message-passing interfaces as a distributed intelligent DMA controller.

Combining methods has several benefits. First, the message-passing interfaces can take advantage of the bus's full capabilities, independent of the type or nature of the controlling processors. Even 8-bit processors or I/O boards can use all the bus's capabilities. As a result, significantly higher intermodule-communication performance is possible than with a software-based method. Another benefit is the elimination of shared memory: neither dual-ported memory structures nor global memory boards are needed. All data transfers take place in the logical message-address space rather than in the conventional physical-memory space.

The primary benefit of message passing is the uniform software interface. Hardware may be replaced with new modules that implement newer technology—such as moving from a single-density disk controller to a double-density version—without making any changes to driver software. Multibus II's architecture is defined to accommodate a wide cost-performance spectrum. At the high end of performance, its multiple-bus structures and 32-bit data paths let it reach system requirements far beyond those allowed by traditional bus architectures. On the low-cost side, the architecture accommodates the iSSB and a versatile form factor.

The increasing functionality of very large-scale integra-

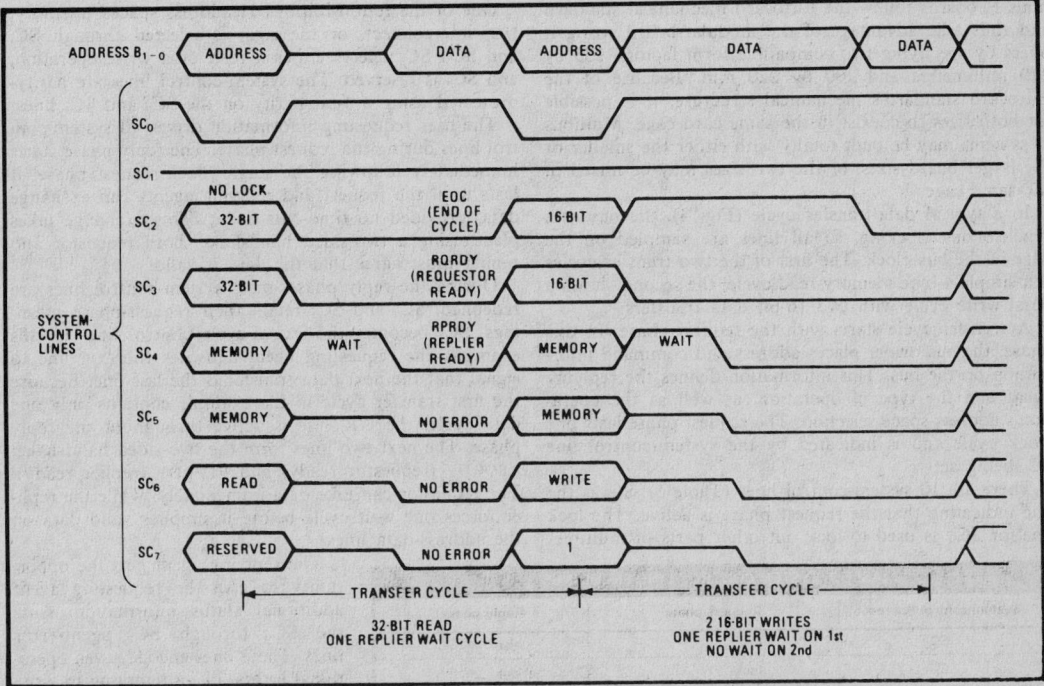

4. Transfer cycle. Synchronous clocking is used in a typical data-transfer cycle; all lines are sampled on the bus clock's edge. The first of the two transfer cycles shown is a 4-byte memory-read cycle; the second is a burst-write cycle with two 16-bit data transfers.

tion has driven the price-performance ratio under 1:1 for a given board size while maintaining constant costs. In addition, the iSSB lets very large-scale integration drive the costs down while maintaining roughly constant functionality. The bus does this by reducing interconnection costs and allowing the physical distribution of modules.

A factor that limits system cost is the module interconnection. Parallel buses, particularly high-performance ones, require relatively expensive backplanes and multiple-line bus interfaces. The iSSB, basically a serial version of the iPSB, defines a message-passing interface identical to that used on the iPSB—yet it requires only a two-line interconnection. It does not need a backplane; a simple twisted pair of wires will do.

The iSSB has a maximum of 32 nodes distributed over a maximum of 10 meters of cable. The nodes may be distributed along an external cable segment or clustered into backplanes (Fig. 3). Each backplane may have 20 nodes, the maximum number of card slots in an iPSB backplane. Cluster nodes use repeaters to connect the backplanes and the iSSB cable. The repeaters isolate the cable from the excessive backplane capacitive load.

The iSSB uses an access protocol based on carrier-sense multiple-access with collision detection and deterministic delivery. When a node has a message to transmit, it looks at the bus for traffic before beginning transmission. If the bus is busy, the node waits until the line becomes idle and until an interface space has passed. Then it begins transmission.

When several nodes simultaneously initiate a transmission, a collision occurs. The CSMA/CD protocol handles these collisions through a deterministic collision-resolution algorithm that uses the principle of time slotting. This algorithm guarantees a time slot for each node during which it can transmit without interference from other nodes. This type of collision resolution guarantees a real-time response so that nodes can resolve collisions in a finite time. The iSSB uses a 16-bit CRC to detect transmission errors. The intelligent message-passing iSSB interface generates and examines the CRCs, making the iSSB as reliable as the iPSB.

The iSSB's physical interface consists of two signal lines that are included as part of the iPSB backplane design. Nodes encode data on the complementary open-collector signal lines (Table 2). The portion of the signal lines within the backplane is designed to operate in a high-noise environment, such as a heavily loaded backplane, relative to a coaxial cable. Cable extensions adhere to standard transmission-line requirements.

The other feature that helps the Multibus II architecture address low-cost applications is its form factor. Multibus II boards follow the Eurocard mechanical standard and thus take advantage of the modular-board sizing it offers by specifying two compatible form factors: 233 by 220 millimeters and 100 by 220 mm. Because of the Eurocard standard's mechanical structure, it is possible for both sizes to coexist in the same card cage. Multibus II systems may be built totally with either the smaller or the larger board sizes, or the two sizes may be mixed in the same cage.

In a typical data-transfer cycle (Fig. 4), the bus uses synchronous clocking, so all lines are sampled on the edge of the bus clock. The first of the two transfer cycles is a simple 4-byte memory-read cycle; the second shows a burst-write cycle with two 16-bit data transfers.

A transfer cycle starts with the request phase. In this phase, the bus owner places address and command information on the bus. This information defines the replying agent and the type of operation, as well as the operation's address-space selection. The request phase lasts one clock cycle and is indicated by the system-control line SC_0 being active.

There are 10 system-control lines (Table 3). SC_0 is the line indicating that the request phase is active. The lock line, or SC_1, is used to lock out other parts of multiple-ported resources during indivisible operations such as test-and-set for semaphores. The next two lines (SC_2 and SC_3) encode the transfer's width.

One of the four Multibus II address spaces (memory, I/O, interconnect, or message) is selected through SC_4 and SC_5. SC_6 selects either a read or a write operation, and SC_7 is reserved. The system-control lines are parity-protected using a 4-bit parity on the SC_8 and SC_9 lines.

The user requesting information drives all system-control lines during the request phase. The reply phase starts immediately following the single clock-request phase; it lasts until the request and replying agents can exchange data, provided no time-outs occur. This exchange takes place using a two-sided handshake: both requestor and replier must agree that the data is valid.

During the reply phase, most system-control lines are redefined. SC_0 and SC_1 retain their request-phase meanings. SC_2 becomes the end-of-cycle control line. In this example, the requesting agent activates the EOC line to signal that the next data transfer is the last one. Because the first transfer cycle in the example contains only one data cycle, the EOC line is active throughout the reply phase. The next two lines form the two-sided handshake: REQRDY (requestor ready) and REPRDY (replier ready). The requestor can take data immediately, while the replier forces one wait cycle before it supplies valid data on the address-data lines.

The replying agent gets the opportunity to give the requesting agent additional status information using the SC_5 through SC_7 agent-error lines. These lines encode seven operational errors, like attempting to write to read-only resources or attempting a 32-bit access from an 8-bit one. These errors may induce retry operations by an intelligent bus interface or may be passed to the offending processor as error interrupts.

The remaining two lines are for the corresponding 4-bit parity. For the reply phase, the requesting agent drives the SC_0 through SC_3 lines and their SC_9 parity bit, while the replying agent drives SC_4 through SC_7 and their SC_8 parity bit. The transfer cycle terminates when EOC, REQRDY, and REPRDY are all active.

The second transfer cycle exhibits a two data-cycle burst write operation to memory. The replying agent injects one wait cycle before accepting the first 16 bits of data, although it takes the second 16 bits on the following clock. A burst transfer may be unlimited in length, although most implementations will restrict it to some maximum—usually 16 to 32 bytes—to ensure that no agent consumes the entire bus bandwidth. □

TABLE 3: SYSTEM CONTROL LINE ENCODINGS

System-control-line no.	Request phase	Reply phase
SC_0	low	high
SC_1	lock	lock
SC_2	data width	EOC
SC_3	data width	REQRDY
SC_4	address space	REPRDY
SC_5	address space	agent error
SC_6	read/write	agent error
SC_7	reserved	agent error
SC_8	parity SC_{4-7}	parity SC_{4-7}
SC_9	parity SC_{0-3}	parity SC_{0-3}

SC_3	SC_2	Data width	SC_5	SC_4	Address space
High	H	8 bits	H	H	memory
H	Low	16 bits	H	L	input/output
L	H	24 bits	L	H	message
L	L	32 bits	L	L	interconnect

SC_7	SC_6	SC_5	Agent error
H	H	H	no error
L	H	H	negative acknowledge (message)
H	L	H	continuation error
L	L	H	reserved
H	H	L	width error
L	H	L	reserved
H	L	L	not understood
L	L	L	reserved

MULTIBUS® II Products 16

iRMX™ 86-MULTIBUS® II SUPPORT PACKAGE

- MULTIBUS® II support for iSBC® 286/100 applications in Real Address Mode, including support for the SCSI peripheral interface and up to 1 megabyte addressability
- Functions in conjunction with the iRMX™ 86 Release 6 Operating System
- Interprocessor Signal Support
- Automatic software configuration of memory boards
- Support for battery backed-up, global time-of-day clock
- Extendable to allow addition of custom device drivers
- Integrated into the iRMX 86 Release 7 Operating System

The iRMX™ 86-MULTIBUS® II Support Package, functioning with the iRMX 86 Release 6 Operating System software, provides the ability to execute all configurable layers of the iRMX 86 software in the MULTIBUS II environment (iRMX 86-MULTIBUS II Operating System). Applications in Real Address Mode are supported for the iSBC® 286/100 board, including support for the SCSI peripheral interface and all iSBX™ boards supported by iRMX 86 Release 6, as well as support for iAPX 286 component applications.

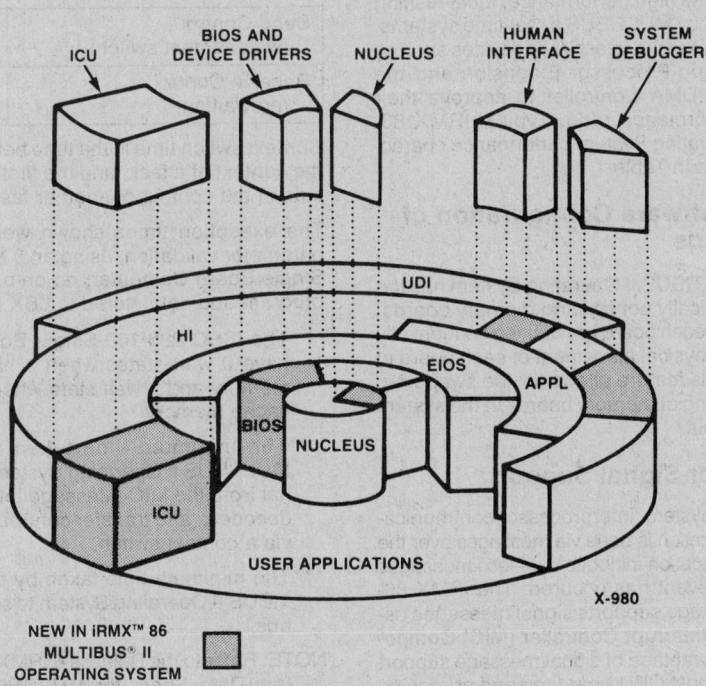

iRMX™ 86 VLSI Operating System

Intel Corporation assumes no responsibility for the use of any circuitry other than circuitry embodied in an Intel product. No other circuit patent licenses are implied. Information contained herein supersedes previously published specifications on these devices from Intel.

© INTEL CORPORATION, 1984

MARCH, 1985
ORDER NUMBER: 280057-002

iRMX™ 86-MULTIBUS® II Support Package

FUNCTIONAL DESCRIPTION

Overview

The iRMX 86-MULTIBUS II Support Package contains system modules that replace portions of the iRMX 86 Release 6 Operating System, allowing the iRMX 86 Operating System to execute in a MULTIBUS II environment. All of the functions in the iRMX 86 Operating System are also available in the iRMX 86-MULTIBUS II Operating System. For a complete description of these functions, please refer to the Release 6 iRMX 86 Operating System Data Sheet (order number 210885-002).

This functional description section describes the performance measurements and new features provided by the iRMX 86-MULTIBUS II Support Package. These new features add the capabilities required for OEMs to execute the iRMX 86 Operating System in a MULTIBUS II environment for iSBC 286/100 or iAPX 286 applications in Real Address Mode.

Real-Time Performance

The iRMX 86-MULTIBUS II Support Package is designed to offer the high performance, multi-tasking functions required by MULTIBUS II real-time systems. Designers can access the latest VLSI devices such as the 80287 Numeric Processor Extension and the 82258 Advanced DMA Controller to improve their system cost/performance ratio. Typical iRMX 86-MULTIBUS II Operating System performance characteristics are shown in Table 1.

Automatic Software Configuration of Memory Boards

The iRMX 86-MULTIBUS II Operating System has the option of automatically configuring memory boards. The addresses for each board are defined sequentially in relation to the physical placement of each board in the card cage. This feature allows for the swapping, adding, and deleting of memory boards in the system on a dynamic basis.

Interprocessor Signal Support

In a MULTIBUS II system, interprocessor communication and synchronization is done via messages over the bus. This communication includes data-less messages to signal that an event has occured. The iRMX 86-MULTIBUS II package supports signal messages using the Message Interrupt Controller (MIC) Component. The major advantage of signal message support is the ability for a host CPU board to send or receive signal messages from up to 254 distinct sources, with the priorities of each message being based on the sending or receiving task's priority. Signal messages are not tied to hardware interrupt levels and priorities as external interrupts were in the MULTIBUS I environment.

**Table 1.
iRMX™ 86-MULTIBUS® II Real-Time Performance Using the iSBC® 286/100 Single Board Computer**

Real-Time Function	iRMX™ 86 MULTIBUS® II iSBC® 286/100 8 MHz* (Times in msec)
Suspend Task	0.53
Interrupt Latency (to handler)	0.10 (max)
Interrupt Latency (to handler)	0.01 (typical)
Receive Signal Time**	0.19
Send Signal Time***	0.11
Context Switch Caused By Interrupt	0.32
Send Message (no context switch)	0.20
Send Message (with context switch)	0.32
Send Control (no context switch)	0.08
Send Control (with context switch)	0.26
Receive Control (no waiting)	0.09

Context switch time is the time between executing in the context of a task, and the first instruction to execute in the context of another task.

The execution times shown were measured with parameter validation, using an 8 MHz iSBC 286/100 Single Board Computer, no on-board RAM, and all program and data stored in LBX RAM.

  *The iSBC 286/100 Single Board Computer will have 0 wait states when a hit occurs in cache memory and 1 wait state when a miss occurs in cache memory.

 **The minimum time taken by the iRMX 86-MULTIBUS II Operating System to extract the signal from the MIC (Message Interrupt Controller), decode it, and transfer control to a receiving task via a context switch.

***The minimum time taken by the iRMX 86-MULTIBUS II Operating System to send a signal on the bus.

NOTE: Refer to the Release 6 iRMX 86 Operating System Data Sheet for MULTIBUS I performance measurements.

Accurate Time-of-Day Clock Support

Resident in every MULTIBUS II system is a Central Services Module (iSBC CSM/001 board). The CSM

iRMX™ 86-MULTIBUS® II Support Package

board contains a battery backed-up, global time-of-day clock. The iRMX 86-MULTIBUS II Operating System uses this clock to automatically initialize the time-of-day clock maintained by the operating system.

Custom Device Driver Support

Like the iRMX 86 Operating System, the iRMX 86-MULTIBUS II Operating System is extendable to support user value-added custom device drivers. This feature allows the system to be more closely tailored to meet a specific application requirement and expands the list of supported hardware products. The user need not purchase iRMX 86 source code to write a custom driver and can configure the driver into the system at configuration time. Custom drivers can use the Message Interrupt Controller (MIC) to pass signal messages.

SPECIFICATIONS

The list of supported products for the iRMX 86-MULTIBUS II Support Package is described below.

Supported Software Products

iRMX 86 Release 6 Operating System

Supported Hardware Products

Components:

iAPX 286 Microprocessor (Real Address Mode only)
80287 Numeric Data Processor Extension
8253 and 8254 Programmable Interval Timers
8259A Programmable Interrupt Controller (PIC)
8255 Programmable Parallel Interface (PPI)
82530 Serial Communications Controller (SCC)
82258 Advanced DMA Controller (ADMA)
Bus Arbiter Controller (BAC)
Message Interrupt Controller (MIC)

iSBC® MULTIBUS® II Board Products:

iSBC 286/100 Single Board Computer (Real Address Mode only)
iSBC CSM/001 Central Services Module
iSBX 218A Flexible Diskette MULTIMODULE Controller
iSBX 270 Alphanumeric Terminal Controller
iSBX 350 Parallel Port (Centronics-type Printer Interface)
iSBX 351 Serial Communications Port
iSBX 354 Serial Communications Port

AVAILABLE LITERATURE

iRMX 86-MULTIBUS II Support Package Reference Manual (order number 147128)

Four manual kits are supplied with the iRMX 86 Release 6 Operating System and are available under the order numbers shown in the iRMX 86 Operating System Data Sheet (order number 210885-002)

ORDERING INFORMATION

The iRMX 86-MULTIBUS II Package is available under a number of different licensing options. Obtaining a license for the iRMX 86 Release 6 Operating System is a prerequisite to licensing the iRMX 86-MULTIBUS II Support Package. Reconfigurable object libraries are provided on: 1) Single-sided, double-density ISIS-format 8″ diskettes; 2) Double-sided, double-density, iRMX format 5.25″ diskettes. ISIS-format diskettes may be used on Series III Development Systems. The iRMX format may be used on Series IV Development Systems (5.25″ diskettes) or any iRMX 86-based system supporting the appropriate disk drivers, compilers and development environment.

The OEM license options listed here allow users to incorporate the iRMX 86-MULTIBUS II package into their applications. Each use requires payment of an Incorporation Fee.

ORDER CODE	DESCRIPTION
RMX 86 BRO:	Single-sided, double-density 8″ ISIS-format, OEM license.
RMX 86 JRO:	Double-sided, double density, 5.25″ iRMX format, OEM license.
RMX 86 KIT BRO:	Includes iRMX 86 Release 6. Single-sided, double-density, 8″ ISIS-format, OEM license.
RMX 86 KIT JRO:	Includes iRMX 86 Release 6. Double-sided, double-density, 5.25″ iRMX format, OEM license.

Other iRMX software licensing options include prepayment of all future incorporation fees and single use rights for a single machine.

Each licensing option includes 90 days of support service that provides Software Problem Report Service and iRMX 86 Operating System Updates that occur during this period.

As with all Intel software, purchase of any of these options requires the execution of a standard Intel Software License Agreement. The specific rights granted to users depend on the specific option and the license signed.

intel

PRELIMINARY

iSBC® 186/224PP MULTIBUS® II
HIGH PERFORMANCE MULTI-PERIPHERAL CONTROLLER

- **Complete Hardware and Software Solution for High Performance Peripheral I/O**
- **Based on the 80186 Microprocessor**
- **On-Board Firmware Provides Concurrency of Operation and Command Queuing**
- **Controls up to Four ST506/412 Winchester Disk Drives, Up to Four SA450/460 Floppy Drives, and four QIC-02 Streaming Tape Drives**
- **128K bytes Of On-Board DRAM Allows Multiple Track Caching for High speed Winchester Data Access**
- **Software Configurability: Geographic Addressing**
- **Real-Time Operating System Support: iRMX™ Drivers Available**
- **Built-in-Self-Test (BIST) Diagnostics On-Board**

The iSBC® 186/224PP High Performance Multi-peripheral Controller Subsystem takes advantage of the MULTIBUS II System Architecture to provide high performance peripheral I/O control for a wide variety of OEM applications. The iSBC 186/224PP controller serves as a complete peripheral I/O subsystem and supports up to four ST506/412 Winchester disks, four SA450/460 Flexible disks, and four QIC-02 compatible streaming tape drives. On-board firmware for the preproduction board provides high performance Winchester disk operation and improved data access through multiple track caching. The hardware/software capability is provided on a single 8.7 x 9.2 inch double-high Eurocard printed circuit board.

Intel Corporation assumes no responsibility for the use of any circuitry other than circuitry embodied in an Intel product. No other circuit patent licenses are implied. Information contained herein supersedes previously published specifications on these devices from Intel. Specifications to change without notice.

© INTEL CORPORATION, 1985

August, 1985
ORDER NUMBER: 280713-001

iSBC® 186/224PP CONTROLLER BOARD

ARCHITECTURE OVERVIEW

Dual-bus Architecture On-Board

The iSBC 186/224PP controller is a pre production version of the iSBC 186/224 board and represents the state of the art in peripheral controller architecture. The board is designed around a dual bus structure and supported by real-time, multitasking firmware. This subsystem also introduces a new Peripheral Communications Interface to take full advantage of the dual-port and message-passing facilities provided in the MULTIBUS II architecture. The iSBC 186/224PP controller supports full request and reply functions as well as unsolicited message interrupts without data as specified in the MULTIBUS II Architecture Handbook. (See Figure 1 for functional block diagram of the 186/224PP board).

The local bus supports the interconnect of the 80186 microprocessor, the EPROM (which contains the multi-tasking executive), the interrupt controller, and the iPSB bus interface. The 80186 component controls the local bus and manages the interface between the iPSB bus and the controller. The CPU is responsible for data transfers between the iSBC 186/224PP subsystem and the host memory. The 80186 component and the real-time multitasking firmware queue the command requests and status outputs.

The I/O Transfer bus supports data transfers between the controller and the various peripheral devices. The Winchester, and flexible disk, and tape interfaces reside on the I/O Transfer bus as do the DMA controller, track cache DRAM and the local bus (through arbitration logic).

The heart of the iSBC 186/224PP data transfer logic is an 8237A-5 DMA controller. This device directly controls four independent DMA channels and provides the capability for performing time-multiplexed, concurrent data transfer operations between the respective device controllers and the local DRAM.

The total of 128K bytes of zero wait state DRAM is provided on-board. This DRAM is local to the I/O Transfer bus. It is accessible to both the CPU and the 8237A-5 DMA controller. The DRAM contains the Peripheral Data Buffers, 80186 stack, 80186 interrupt vectors and 64K bytes of Winchester track cache.

This dual bus system (local bus and I/O Transfer bus) combined with the real-time multitasking firmware and sophisticated PCI command protocol allows the simultaneous transfer of data between the storage devices and the controller and between the controller and the MULTIBUS II Parallel System Bus resulting in improved system level performance.

In addition, the iSBC 186/224PP controller utilizes an intelligent track caching scheme through dynamic allocation of buffer space. This results in reduced access times to the Winchester disk and improved system performance. Sequential data can be supplied directly from the cache without incremental access to the disk.

A small cable scrambler card is supplied with the iSBC 186/224PP board for development purposes. Details and schematics for adding ground pins to the I/O connection are supplied in the iSBC 186/224PP Hardware Reference Manual.

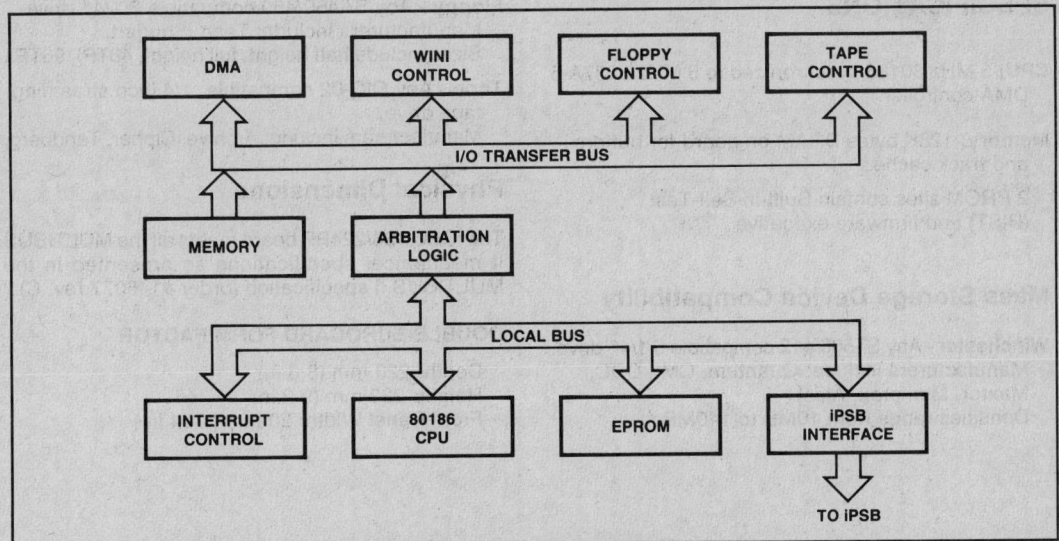

Figure 1. iSBC® 186/224 Board Block Diagram

iSBC® 186/224PP CONTROLLER BOARD

PRELIMINARY

SOFTWARE SUPPORT

PCI Peripheral Communications Interface

PCI is a logical message-based peripheral controller interface designed by Intel to provide a standard software interface on all peripheral I/O boards. This interface protocol provides queues for both commands received and status indicators returned. This allows the 186/224PP board to accept multiple commands and queue them in on-board memory.

iRMX™ 86 Real-Time Operating System Support

The iSBC 186/224PP High Performance Multi-Peripheral Controller is supported by Intel's iRMX 86 Real-Time Multitasking Operating System. The iSBC 186/224PP board basic I/O system driver provides the following features:

— Support for up to four Winchester drives using the ST506/410 Interface

— Support for up to four floppy disk drives using the SA450/460 Interface

— Support for Bad Track information on Winchester disk drives

All communication from the host CPU to the iSBC 186/224PP board is implemented through the peripheral communications Interface.

BACKPLANE BUS INTERFACES

P1 Connector: This is used as the standard MULTIBUS II 32-bit parallel system bus. It contains all signals required to implement the full standard interface.

P2 Connector: The P2 connector is not electrically connected internally on the board.

Winchester Connections: One 50 pin D-type, right angle female, high density connector is provided. The 50 pin connection supplied provides all of the required signals for the control line and the four data lines.

Flexible Disk Connections: The board comes with one 25 pin D-type connection which provides all of the required signals for up to four daisy chained flexible Disks.

QIC-02 Streaming Tape Connections: One 25 pin D-type connection which provides the required signals for up to four daisy-chained tape drives.

I/O Connectors: The I/O connections for each interface are on the front panel. In order to cable to the peripheral devices a mechanism is required which provides additional ground lines to ensure a completely reliable connection.

SPECIFICATIONS

CPU: 5 MHz 80186 synchronized to 5 MHz 8237A-5 DMA controller

Memory: 128K bytes DRAM on-board for buffers and track cache

2 PROM sites contain Built-in-Self-Test (BIST) and firmware executive

Mass Storage Device Compatibility

Winchester - Any ST506/412 compatible 5 1/4" drive.
  Manufacturers include: Quantum, CMI, CDC, Maxtor, Memorex, Atasi.
  Densities range from 10MB to 140MB.

Floppy - Any SA450/460 compatible 5 1/4" drive.
  Manufacturers include: Teac, Shugart.
  Sizes include half height, full height, 48TPI, 96TPI.

Tape - Any QIC-02 compatible, 1/4 inch streaming tape drive.
  Manufacturers include: Archive, Cipher, Tandberg.

Physical Dimensions

The iSBC 186/224PP board meets all the MULTIBUS II mechanical specifications as presented in the MULTIBUS II specification (order #146077 rev. C).

DOUBLE-EUROCARD FORM FACTOR

Depth: 220 mm (8.6 in)
Height: 233 mm (9.2 in)
Front Panel Width: 20 mm (.784 in.)

iSBC® 186/224PP CONTROLLER BOARD

PRELIMINARY

CONNECTORS

Interface	Connector	Part No.
iPSB bus (P1)	96 pin DIN, right angle female	603-2-IEC-C096-F
P2	96 pin DIN, right angle female, not connected internally	603-2-IEC-C096-F
ST506/412 (Winchester)	50 pin D type, right angle female, high density (see note)	
SA450/460 (Floppy)	25 pin D-type, right angle female, (see note)	
QIC-02 (Tape)	25 pin D-type, right angle female, (see note)	

NOTE:
The manufacturers below provide connectors which will plug into the connectors supplied on the iSBC 186/224PP board front-panel.

Connector type	Manufacturer	Pins	Part No.
Flat Ribbon Crimped	T&B Ansley	50	609-50P
	T&B Ansley	25	609-25P
Bulk Cable Solder Cup	Amlan	50	CDS50L
	Amlan	25	CDS25L
	ITT Cannon	50	DD-50P
	ITT Cannon	25	DB-25P
Pin Crimp	AMP	50	206438-1
	AMP	25	205436-1
	ITT Cannon	50	DDC-50P
	ITT Cannon	25	DBC-25P

Reference Manuals

iSBC 186/224PP Board Hardware Reference Manual (order number 136158-001)

Intel MULTIBUS II Bus Architecture Specification (order number 146077)

Manual may be ordered from any Sales Representative, Distribution Office, or from the Intel Literature Department, 3065 Bowers Ave., Santa Clara, CA 95051.

ORDERING INFORMATION

Part Number	Description
iSBC 186/224PP	High Performance Multi-peripheral controller

iSBC® 286/100 MULTIBUS® II SINGLE BOARD COMPUTER

- 8 MHz iAPX 286 Microprocessor
- MULTIBUS® II iPSB (Parallel System Bus) interface for multimaster configurations and multiprocessing system expansion
- MULTIBUS® II iLBX™ II (Local Bus Extension) interface for improved high-speed memory expansion
- MULTIBUS® II interconnect space for software configurability and diagnostics
- Resident firmware to support Built-In-Self-Test (BIST) power-up diagnostics
- Optional 80287 Numeric Data Co-Processor (socket on-board)
- iSBX™ bus interface connector for I/O expansion bus
- Four DMA channels supplied by the 82258 Advanced DMA controller with 8 MBytes/sec. transfer rate
- 16 levels of vectored interrupt control. Up to 255 distinct interrupt sources and 255 interrupt destinations are supported using message-based interrupts
- Two 28-pin JEDEC sites
- 24 programmable I/O lines configurable as SCSI interface, Centronics interface or general purpose I/O
- Two programmable serial interfaces, one RS 232C, the other RS 232C or RS 422A compatible
- Double-high standard Eurocard form factor

The iSBC® 286/100 Single Board Computer takes advantage of the MULTIBUS® II System Architecture for OEM applications. The combination of the iAPX 286 CPU and two new bus structures, the MULTIBUS II Parallel System Bus (iPSB bus) and the Local Bus Extension II (iLBX™ II bus) make the iSBC 286/100 board uniquely suited to high performance, multimaster system applications. The iSBC 286/100 board support of the MULTIBUS II interconnect space provides new software configuration ease and access to Built-In-Self-Test (BIST) power-up diagnostics. The board is a complete microcomputer system on a 8.7 x 9.2 inch double-high Eurocard printed circuit board.

Intel Corporation assumes no responsibility for the use of any circuitry other than circuitry embodied in an Intel product. No other circuit patent licenses are implied. Information contained herein supersedes previously published specifications on these devices from Intel.

©INTEL CORPORATION, 1984

MARCH, 1985
ORDER NUMBER: 280076-002

iSBC® 286/100 Board

FUNCTIONAL DESCRIPTION

Overview

The iSBC 286/100 Single Board Computer utilizes the powerful 8 MHz iAPX 286 CPU within the MULTIBUS II system architecture to provide a high performance multiprocessing solution. Figure 1 shows a typical MULTIBUS II multiprocessing system configuration. Overall system performance is enhanced by the iLBX II bus which allows 0 wait state high speed memory execution.

Architecture

The iSBC 286/100 board supports the new iPSB bus features of interconnect space, Built-In-Self-Test (BIST) diagnostics, and message based interrupts. These new features are described in the following sections. Besides taking advantage of the MULTIBUS II system architecture, the iSBC 286/100 board has complete single board computer capability including iSBX™ bus expansion, 80287 co-processor option, advanced DMA control, JEDEC memory sites and expansion, SCSI configurable parallel interface, serial I/O, and programmable timers. Figure 2 shows the iSBC 286/100 board block diagram.

Central Processing Unit

The central processor for the iSBC 286/100 board board is the 80286 CPU operating at an 8.0 MHz clock rate. The 80286 CPU is upwardly compatible with Intel's iAPX 86 and iAPX 186 CPUs. The 80286 CPU

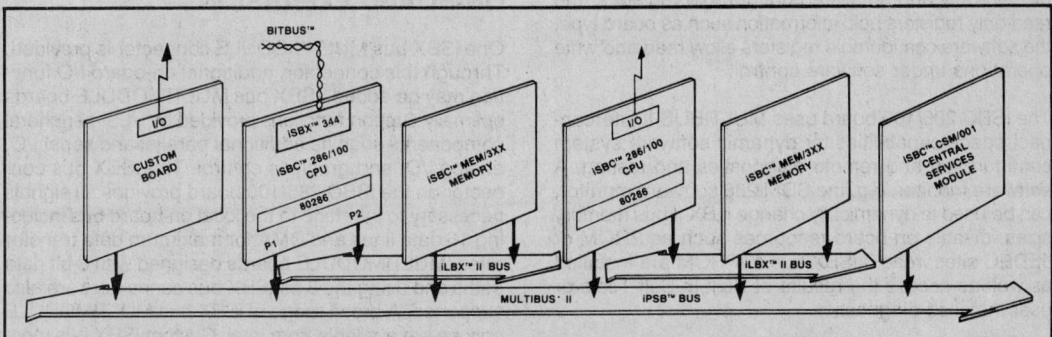

Figure 1. Typical MULTIBUS® II Multiprocessing System Configuration

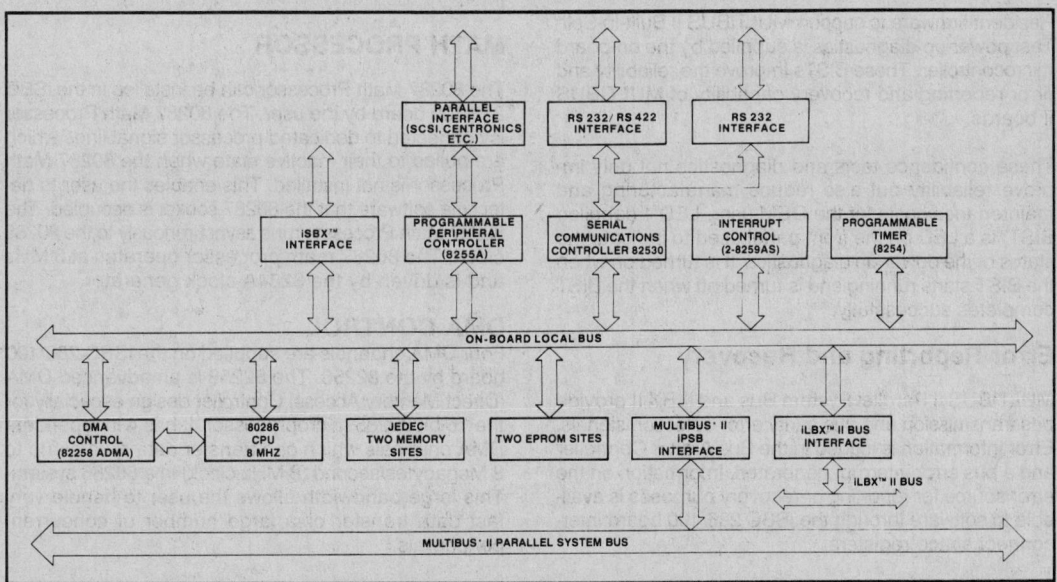

Figure 2. iSBC® 286/100 Board Block Diagram

iSBC® 286/100 Board

runs iAPX 86 and 186 code at substantially higher speeds due to a parallel chip architecture. Numeric processing power may be enhanced with the optional 80287 numeric co-processor. The 80286 CPU operates in two modes: iAPX 86 real address mode and protected virtual address mode. In iAPX 86 real address mode, programs use real address with up to one megabyte of address space. In protected virtual address mode, the 80286 CPU automatically maps 1 gigabyte of virtual address per task into a 16 megabyte real address space. This mode also provides the hardware memory protection for the operating system. The operating mode is selected via CPU instructions.

INTERCONNECT SPACE SUPPORT

MULTIBUS II interconnect space is a standardized set of read-only and software configurable registers; the read-only registers hold information such as board type, the software configurable registers allow read and write operations under software control.

The iSBC 286/100 board uses MULTIBUS II interconnect space capabilities for dynamic software system configuration and remote diagnostics and testing. A software monitor, e.g. the SDM 286 software monitor, can be used to dynamically change iLBX II bus memory sizes, disable on-board resources such as PROM or JEDEC sites, read if iSBX bus or PROM are installed as well as access the results of Built-In-Self-Tests or user installed diagnostics.

BUILT-IN-SELF-TEST (BIST) DIAGNOSTICS

Resident firmware to support MULTIBUS II Built-In-Self-Test power-up diagnostics is supplied by the on-board microcontroller. These BISTs improve the reliability and error reporting and recovery capability of MULTIBUS II boards.

These confidence tests and diagnostics not only improve reliability but also reduce manufacturing and maintenance costs for the OEM user. LED 1 (labelled BIST) is a LED on the front panel used to indicate the status of the power up diagnostics. It is turned on when the BIST starts running and is turned off when the BIST completes successfully.

Error Reporting and Recovery

MULTIBUS II Parallel System Bus and iLBX II provide bus transmission and bus parity error detection signals. Error information is logged in the Bus Arbiter Controller and a bus error interrupt generated. Information on the error source for reporting or recovery purposes is available to software through the iSBC 286/100 board interconnect space registers.

INTERRUPT CONTROL

In a MULTIBUS II system, external interrupts (interrupts originating off the CPU board) are messages over the bus rather than signals on individual lines. Message based interrupts are handled by the Message Interrupt Controller component located on the bus interface MULTIMODULE. This means that 1 interrupt line can handle interrupts from up to 256 sources.

Two on-board 8259A programmable interrupt controllers are used for processing on-board interrupts. One is used as the master and the other as the slave. Table 1 includes a list of devices and functions supported by interrupts.

iSBX® BUS MULTIMODULE™ ON-BOARD EXPANSION

One iSBX bus MULTIMODULE connector is provided. Through this connector, additional on-board I/O function may be added. iSBX bus MULTIMODULE boards optimally support functions provided by VLSI peripheral components such as additional parallel and serial I/O, analog I/O, and graphics control. The iSBX bus connector on the iSBC 286/100 board provides all signals necessary to interface to the local on-board bus including 16 data lines and DMA for maximum data transfer rates. MULTIMODULE boards designed with 8-bit data paths and using the 8-bit iSBX bus connectors are also supported. A broad range of iSBX bus MULTIMODULE options are available from Intel. Custom iSBX bus modules may also be designed. An iSBX bus interface specification and mating connectors are available from Intel.

MATH PROCESSOR

The 80287 Math Processor can be installed in the iSBC 286/100 board by the user. The 80287 Math Processor is connected to dedicated processor signal lines which are pulled to their inactive state when the 80287 Math Processor is not installed. This enables the user to detect via software that the 80287 socket is occupied. The 80287 Math Processor runs asynchronously to the 80286 clock. The 80287 math processor operates at 8 MHz and is driven by the 8284A clock generator.

DMA CONTROL

Four DMA channels are supplied on the iSBC 286/100 board by the 82258. The 82258 is an advanced DMA (Direct Memory Access) Controller design especially for the 16-bit 80286 microprocessor. It has 4 independent DMA channels which can transfer data at rates up to 8 Megabytes/second (8 MHz clock) in a 80286 system. This large bandwidth allows the user to handle very fast data transfer or a large number of concurrent peripherals.

iSBC® 286/100 Board

Table 1. Interrupt Devices and Functions

Device	Function	Number of Interrupts
MULTIBUS® II Interface	Message-based interrupt requests from the iPSB bus via 84120 Message Interrupt Controller.	1 interrupt from up to 256 sources
8751 Interconnect Controller	BIST control functions	1
82530 Serial Controller	Transmit buffer empty, receive buffer full and channel errors	1 interrupt from 10 sources
8254 Timers	Timers 0, 1, 2 outputs; function determined by timer mode	3
8255A Parallel I/O	Parallel port control	2
iLBX™ bus interface	Indicates iLBX™ II bus error condition	3
iPSB bus interface	Indicates transmission error on iPSB bus	1
iSBX® bus connector	Function determined by iSBX® bus MULTIMODULE® board	2
Edge sense out	Converts edge triggered interrupt to a level	1
Bus error	Indicates last iPSB bus operation encountered an error	1
Power-fail	External/Power-Fail interrupts	1

MEMORY CAPABILITIES

The local memory of the iSBC 286/100 board consists of two groups of byte-wide sites. The first group of two sites are reserved for EPROM or ROM and are used for the BIST power-up diagnostic firmware. The second group of two sites support JEDEC standard 28-pin devices.

SCSI PERIPHERAL INTERFACE

The iSBC 286/100 board includes a parallel peripheral interface that consists of three 8-bit parallel ports. As shipped, these ports are configured for general purpose I/O. Programmed PAL (Programmable Array Logic) devices and the octal transceiver 74LS640-1 are provided to make it easy to reconfigure the parallel interface to be compatible with the SCSI (Small Computer System Interconnect) peripheral interface. Alternatively, the parallel interface may be reconfigured as a Centronics compatible line printer interface by adding one PAL and reconfiguring jumpers. Both interfaces may use the 82258 DMA controllers for data transfers.

The SCSI (Small Computer System Interconnect) interface allows multiple mass storage peripherals such as Winchester disk drives, floppy disk drives, and tape drives to be connected directly to the iSBC 286/100 board. A sample SCSI application is shown in Figure 3. The SCSI interface is compatible with SCSI controllers such as: Adaptek 4500, DTC 1410, Iomega Alpha 10, Shugart 1601 and 1610, Vermont Research 8403, and Xebec 1410.

The Centronics interface requires very little software overhead since a user supplied PAL device is used to provide necessary handshake timing. Interrupts are generated for printer fault conditions and a DMA request is issued for every character.

SERIAL I/O

The 82530 Serial Communications Controller (SCC) is used to provide 2 channels of serial I/O. The SCC generates all baudrate clocks and provides loopback capability on both channels. Channel B is RS232C only and is configured as a DCE (may be connected directly to a Display Terminal). Channel A is factory-default configured for DCE RS232C operation. Channel A may be reconfigured by the user for DTE or RS422 operation (or both).

The 82258 ADMA can be programmed to support both channels A and B to perform movement of large bit streams or blocks of data.

iSBC® 286/100 Board

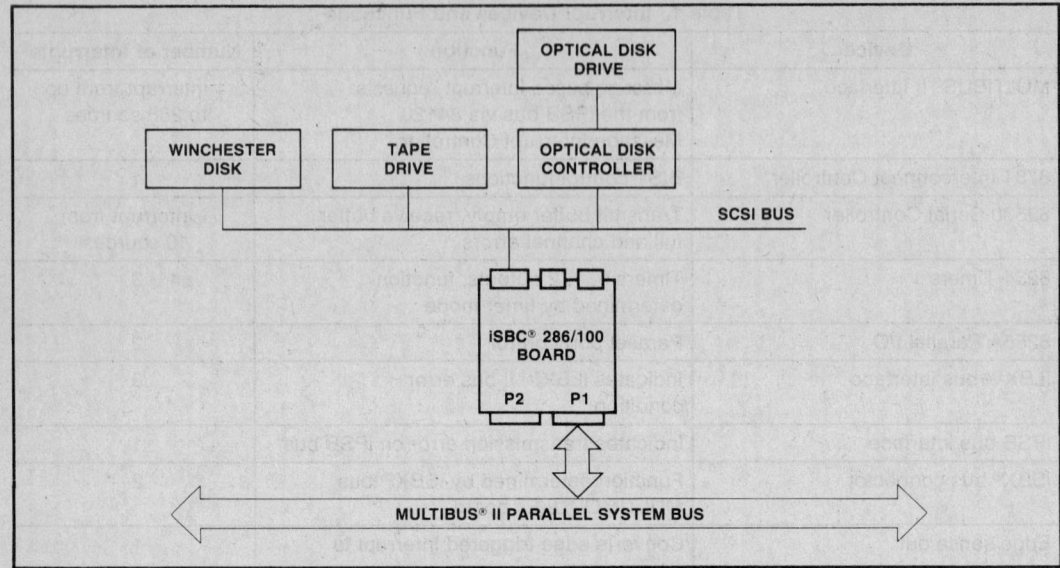

Figure 3. Sample SCSI Applications

PROGRAMMABLE TIMERS

The iSBC 286/100 board provides three independent, fully programmable 16-bit interval timers/event counters utilizing the Intel 8254 Programmable Interval Timer. Each counter is capable of operating in either BCD or binary modes. Three of these timers/counters are available to the systems designer to generate accurate time intervals under software control. The outputs may be independently routed to the 8259A Programmable Interrupt Controller to count external events. The system software configures each timer independently to select the desired function. Seven functions are available as shown in Table 2. The contents of each counter may be read at any time during system operation.

SOFTWARE SUPPORT

The iRMX™ 86 MULTIBUS II Software Support Package, functioning with the iRMX 86 Release 6 Operating System software, provides the ability to execute all configurable layers of the iRMX 86 software in the MULTIBUS II environment. Applications in Real Address Mode are supported for the iSBC 286/100 board, including support for the SCSI peripheral interface and all iSBX bus boards supported by iRMX 86 Release 6 Operating System, as well as support for iAPX 286 component applications.

The iRMX 86 MULTIBUS II package contains system modules that replace portions of the iRMX 86 Release 6 Operating System, allowing iRMX 86 to execute in a MULTIBUS II environment. All the functions available in the iRMX 86 Operating System are available in the iRMX MULTIBUS II Operating System. For a complete description of these functions, their value, and performance, please refer to the Release 6 iRMX 86 Operating System Data Sheet (order number 210885-002).

For on-target MULTIBUS II development, use the iSBX 218A or a SCSI controller and a floppy or winchester drive, or port iRMX application software developed on the System 310, Series II/III, IV to MULTIBUS II hardware.

Language support for the iSBC 286 boards real address mode includes Intel's ASM 86, PL/M 86, PASCAL and FORTRAN as well as many third party 8086 languages. Language support for virtual address mode operation includes ASM 286, PL/M 286, PASCAL and C. Programs developed in these languages can be down loaded from Intel Series III or Series IV Development System to the iSBC 286 board via the iSDM™ 286 System Debug Monitor Release 2. The iSBX 218A can be used to load iRMX software developed on a System 310. The iSDM 286 monitor also provides on-target program debugging support including breakpoint and memory examination features.

The MULTIBUS II Interconnect Space Registers allow the software to configure boards eliminating much of the need for jumpers and wire wraps. The iSDM 286 Monitor can initialize these registers at configuration time using user-defined variables. The monitor can also automatically configure memory boards, defining the addresses for each board sequentially in relation to the board's physical placement in the card cage. This feature allows for the swapping, adding, and deleting of memory boards on a dynamic basis.

iSBC® 286/100 Board

Table 2. Programmable Timer Functions

Function	Operation
Interrupt on terminal count	When terminal count is reached, an interrupt request is generated. This function is extremely useful for generation of real-time clocks.
Programmable one-shot	Output goes low upon request of an external trigger edge or software command and returns high when terminal count is reached. This function is retriggerable.
Rate generator	Divide by N counter. The output will go low for one input clock cycle, and the period from one low going pulse to the next is N times the input clock period.
Square-wave rate generator	Output will remain high until one-half the count has been completed, and go low for the other half of the count.
Software triggered strobe	Output remains high until software loads count (N). N counts after count is loaded, output goes low for one input clock period.
Hardware triggered strobe	Output goes low for one clock period N counts after rising edge counter trigger input. The counter is retriggerable.
Event counter	On a jumper selectable basis, the clock input becomes an input from the external system. CPU may read the number of events occurring after the counter "window" has been enabled or an interrupt may be generated after N events occur in the system.

SPECIFICATIONS

Word Size

Instruction: 8-, 16-, 24-, 32-, or 40-bits
Data: 8- or 16-bits

System Clock

CPU: 8.0 MHz
Numeric Co-Processor: 8.0 MHz

Cycle Time

Basic Instruction: 8.0 MHz - 375 ns; 250 ns (assumes instruction in queue)

NOTE: Basic instruction cycle is defined as the fastest instruction time (i.e., two clock cycles)

Memory Capacity (Maximum)

EPROM: 2732, 8K bytes; 2764, 16K bytes; 27128, 32K bytes; 27256, 64K bytes; 27512, 128K bytes
E²PROM: 2817A, 4KBytes
iRAM: 2186, 16K bytes

NOTES: Two local sites must contain BIST or user-supplied boot-up EPROM.

I/O Capability

Parallel: SCSI, Centronics, or general purpose I/O
Serial: Two programmable channels using one 82530 Serial Communications Controller
Timers: Three programmable timers using one 8254 Programmable Interrupt Controller
Expansion: One 8/16-bit iSBX MULTIMODULE connector

Interrupt Capacity

Potential Interrupt Sources:
255 individual and 1 broadcast

Interrupt Levels:
16 vectored requests using two 8259As and the 80286s NMI line

Serial Communications Characteristics

Asynchronous Modes:

- 5-8-bit character; odd, even, or parity; 1, 1.5, or 2 stop bits

- Independence transmit and receive clocks, 1X, 16X, 32X, or 64X programmable sampling rate

- Error Detection: Framing, Overrun and Parity

- Break detection and generation

iSBC® 286/100 Board

Bit synchronous Modes:

- SDLC/HDLC flag generation and recognition
- Automatic zero bit insertion and detection
- Automatic CRC generation and detection (CRC 16 or CCITT)
- Abort generation and detection
- I-field residue handling
- SDLC loop mode operation
- CCITT X.25 compatible

Byte synchronous Modes:

- Internal or external character synchronization (1 or 2 characters)
- Automatic CRC generation and checking (CRC 16 or CCITT)
- IBM Bisync compatible

Common Baud Rates

Baud Rate	Synchronous (x1 Clock) Time Constant	Asynchronous (x16 Clock) Time Constant
64 K	36	—
48 K	49	—
19.2 K	126	6
9600	254	14
4800	510	30
2400	1022	62
1800	1363	83
1200	2046	126
300	8190	510
110	—	1394

Timers

Input Frequencies:
 1.23 MHz ± 0.1% or 4 MHz ± 0.1%
 (Jumper Selectable)

Output Frequencies/Timing Intervals

	Single Timer/Counter		Dual Timer/Counter (two timers cascaded)	
	Min.	Max.	Min.	Max.
Real-time interrupt	500 ns	53.1 ms	1.00 ms	57.9 min
Programmable one-shot	500 ns	53.1 ms	1.00 ms	57.9 min
Rate generator	18.8 Hz	2 MHz	0.000290 Hz	1 MHz
Square-wave rate generator	18.8 Hz	2 MHz	0.000290 Hz	1 MHz
Software triggered strobe	500 ns	53.1 ms	1.00 ms	57.9 min.
Hardware triggered strobe	500 ns	53.1 ms	1.00 ms	57.9 min.
Event counter	—	5.0 MHz	—	—

INTERFACES

iPSB Bus: All signals TTL compatible

iLBX™ II Bus: All signals TTL compatible

iSBX™ Bus: All signals TTL compatible

SERIAL I/O - Channel A:
 RS232C/RS422 compatible, configurable as a data set or data terminal;

Channel B:
 RS232C compatible, configured as data set

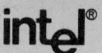

iSBC® 286/100 Board

Timer: All signals TTL compatible

Interrupt Requests: All TTL compatible

CONNECTORS

Location	Function	Part #
P1	iPSB bus	603-2-IEC-C096-F
P2	iLBX™ II Bus	603-2-IEC-C096-F

PHYSICAL DIMENSIONS

The iSBC 286/100 board meets all MULTIBUS II mechanical specifications as presented in the MULTIBUS II specification (#146077).

Double-High Eurocard Form Factor:

Depth: 220mm (8.7 in.)

Height: 233mm (9.2 in.)

Front Panel Width: 20mm (.784 in.)

Weight: 33 oz.

ENVIRONMENTAL REQUIREMENTS

Temperature:
(inlet air) at 200 LFM airflow over boards

Non-operating — −40 to +70°C

Operating — 0 to +55°C

Humidity:

Non-operating — 95% RH @ 55°C

Operating — 90% RH @ 55°C

ELECTRICAL CHARACTERISTICS

The maximum power required per voltage is shown below. These numbers do not include the power required by the optional memory devices, SCSI PALs, or expansion modules.

Voltage (volts)	Max. Current (amps)	Max. Power (watts)
+5	10.3	54
+12	50 mA	.06
−12	50 mA	.06

REFERENCE MANUALS

iSBC 286/100 Board Manual (#146705-001)

Intel MULTIBUS II Bus Architecture Specification (#146077)

Manual may be ordered from any Sales Representative, Distribution Office, or from the Intel Literature Department, 3065 Bowers Ave., Santa Clara, CA 95051

ORDERING INFORMATION

Part Number	Description
SBC 286/100	MULTIBUS II Single Board Computer

intel

PRELIMINARY

iSBC® 386/100PP MULTIBUS® II SINGLE BOARD COMPUTER
iSBC® MEM/201, MEM/202, MEM/204 MULTIBUS® II DRAM MEMORY BOARDS

- High Performance 32-Bit Processor System using the 80386
- MULTIBUS® II iPSB (Parallel System Bus) interface with full message passing capability
- High speed 64K byte static RAM cache on-board providing zero-wait state memory reads
- 8-, 16 Bit iSBX™ Bus IEEE P959 interface connector with DMA for I/O expansion
- 80287 Numeric Data Co-Processor
- Supported by ICE™ 386 emulator and PSCOPE Monitor 386 development tools
- Resident firmware to support built-in-self-test (BIST) power-up diagnostics
- 82258 DMA controller providing 4 high performance DMA channels
- High speed memory interface support for up to 16M byte dual port DRAM
- MULTIBUS II interconnect space for software configurability and diagnostics

The iSBC® 386/100PP Single Board Computer is the highest performance MULTIBUS II CPU board and is the first MULTIBUS II board based on Intel's 80386 high performance 32-bit microprocessor. The 80386 maintains software compatibility with the entire 8086 family while bringing new performance standards to systems using Single Board Computer (iSBC) boards. High speed memory is available to the iSBC 386/100PP board via the iSBC MEM/201, 202 and 204 memory boards. These memory boards have a 32-bit architecture throughout and are specific to the iSBC 386/100PP board. The iSBC 386/100PP board controls access to the iSBC MEM/2XX boards (generally refers to this family of boards) from both the iPSB bus and the local bus.

The iSBC 386/100PP and the iSBC MEM/2XX boards are offered as an early development vehicle allowing board and system designers to quickly assemble an 80386-based system and evaluate the iSBC 386/100PP and 80386 microprocessor in a MULTIBUS II system environment. These boards conform to the MULTIBUS II Specification, using the double high, triple deep Eurocard form factor with pin and socket DIN connectors.

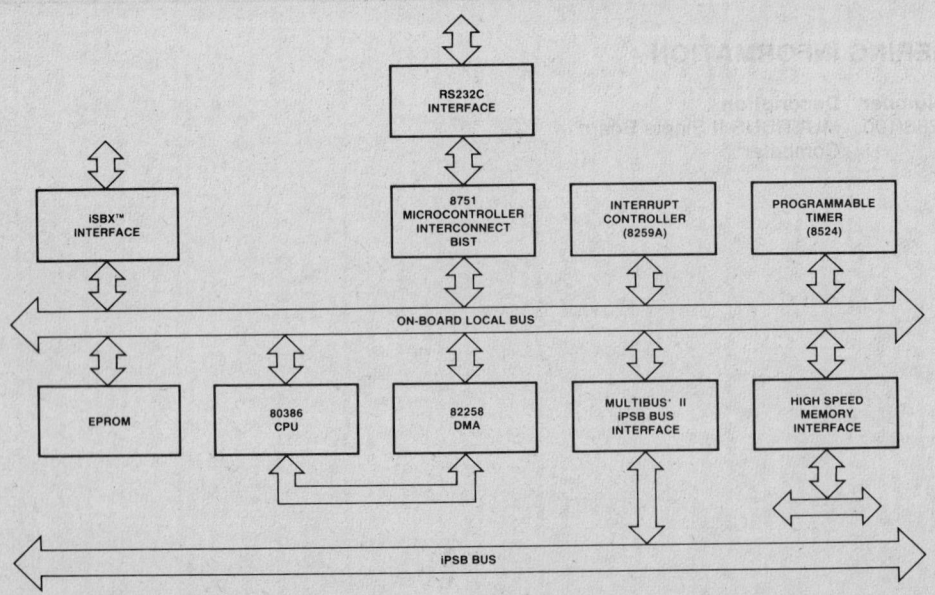

Intel Corporation assumes no responsibility for the use of any circuitry other than circuitry embodied in an Intel product. No other circuit patent licenses are implied. Information contained herein supersedes previously published specifications on these devices from Intel. Specifications to change without notice.

© INTEL CORPORATION, 1985

AUGUST, 1985
ORDER NUMBER: 280162-001

iSBC® 386/100PP SINGLE BOARD COMPUTER

PRELIMINARY

FUNCTIONAL DESCRIPTION

Overview

The iSBC 386/100PP board is the first MULTIBUS II board to utilize the high performance 80386 32-bit microprocessor. The advanced capabilities of the MULTIBUS II architecture coupled with the high performance and compatibility features of the 80386 provide the designer with the most complete and best supported 32-bit solution for multiprocessing systems. By using the MULTIBUS II architecture, multiprocessing systems (multiple processor systems) are now achievable. Advanced features of this architecture embodied in the iSBC 386/100PP board are: distributed arbitration, virtual interrupt capabilities, message passing, iPSB bus parity for higher reliability, and software configurability and diagnostics using interconnect address space. The iPSB bus interface on the iSBC 386/100PP board supports full message passing and dual port architectures and is compatible with iSBC boards using the Bus Arbiter Controller (BAC)/Message Interrupt Controller (MIC) bus interface module.

The iSBC 386/100PP board set includes the P2 backplane for high speed memory execution and on-board monitor software. The monitor software is designed to work with a host system. This software includes host software on diskette in addition to target firmware installed in EPROM on the iSBC 386/100PP board. Five basic functions are provided:

- Read and write to all memory locations and processor registers
- Execute code—Go and Single Step
- Insert software breakpoints
- Disassemble code into 386 assembly language mnemonics
- Download user programs

ARCHITECTURE

The iSBC 386/100PP board supports the full iPSB bus interface functions of solicited and unsolicited message passing, interconnect address space, memory and I/O references. This board supports both requestor and replier functions as described in the MULTIBUS II Architecture Specification (#146077, Rev. C). In addition to supporting the iPSB bus architecture, this board employs functions traditionally found on Intel single board computer boards including iSBX bus expansion, 80287/80387 math coprocessor, advanced DMA control and EPROM/ROM memory sites. The subsystems of this board include the Processor, Memory, I/O, iPSB bus interface and Interconnect Address Space subsystems and are described as follows.

Processor Subsystem

Two functions are performed by the processor subsystem. These functions include 80386 processing and direct memory access (DMA) data movement.

80386 PROCESSOR

The central processor for the iSBC 386/100PP board is the 80386 CPU. This is the first 32-bit member of the 8086 family. The 80386 utilizes concepts such as address pipelining, a high speed execution unit and on-chip memory management/protection to provide the highest level of performance at both CPU and system levels. The 80386 also features an Address Translation Unit that supports up to 64 terabytes of virtual memory and implements a co-processor interface that supports the 80287/80387 numerics co-processor. The 80386 fetches instructions and data from various resources (memory, I/O, iPSB bus). The 386/100PP board supports the 80386 processor in both real or protected modes. This pre-production iSBC 386/100PP board offers math support via a socket containing a 80287 math coprocessor module.

INSTRUCTION SET

The 80386 instruction set includes variable length instruction format (including double operand instructions), 8-, 16-, and 32-bit signed and unsigned arithmetic operators for binary, BCD and unpacked ASCII data, and iterative word and byte string manipulation functions. All existing instructions have been extended to support 32-bit addresses and operands. New bit manipulation and other instructions have been added for extra flexibility in designing complex software.

DIRECT MEMORY ACCESS (DMA) FUNCTION

Four DMA channels are provided by the 82258 DMA component. When a DMA request is received from on-board resources, this component arbitrates among the four requests and performs bus cycles on the local bus to satisfy the request. To perform local bus cycles, the 82258 component must request and be granted ownership of the local bus by the 80386 microprocessor. The four DMA channels on the iSBC 386/100PP board are allocated to the on-board resources in Table 1. The 82258 DMA component and other logic allow the 82258 component to perform 32-bit single-cycle transfers to and from the iPSB bus interface to support full message passing.

Table 1. DMA Channel Allocation

Channel	Function
0	iSBX DMA support
1	iSBX DMA support
2	Solicited Message Transmit
3	Solicited Message Receive

iSBC® 386/100PP SINGLE BOARD COMPUTER

PRELIMINARY

Memory Subsystem

The memory subsystem consists of three subsections: Dynamic RAM, Cache and EPROM memory.

DYNAMIC RAM CAPABILITIES

The iSBC 386/100PP board uses one iSBC MEM/201, MEM 202 or MEM 204 DRAM Memory Boards to provide 1, 2 or 4M bytes of dual ported memory. The high speed 32-bit memory interface supports one iSBC MEM/2XX memory board. The MULTIBUS II form-factor board for these memory boards will migrate to low profile memory modules that plug directly onto the iSBC 386/100 board. These modules will use surface mount technology devices. iSBC 386/100 boards together with high-density 4 and 8M byte memory modules will provide up to 16 Mbytes of system memory. Memory parity is generated and checked via the memory bus interface on the iSBC 386/100PP board. The dual ported DRAM is accessible from both the 80386 or 82258 DMA components on-board and from the iPSB bus. The iSBC 386/100PP board contains all the logic to access the iSBC MEM/2XX boards from on-board resources or from the iPSB bus. The memory boards are automatically configured on power-up via the 8751 microcontroller on the iSBC 386/100PP board.

CACHE MEMORY

The cache memory allows zero wait-state read accesses to memory when the data requested is resident in the cache memory. The 64K byte static RAM cache memory on the iSBC 386/100PP board has 16K, 4-byte entries. Each entry consists of a 32-bit data field. Each 32-bit word in the DRAM array maps to one (and only one) entry in the cache. A tag field is used to determine which actual 4-bytes of memory currently resides in a cache entry. The combination of direct mapped cache array and tag fields ensures data integrity and accurate identification of cache "hits". Data integrity between the DRAM array and corresponding cache entries is maintained for cache "misses" and memory writes through a simple, yet effective replacement algorithm. On a write cycle, data is written to both the cache and the DRAM array. Cache "misses" (memory reads not in the cache) cause the data field of the cache entry corresponding to the addressed memory to be filled from the DRAM array. The cache memory size and effective replacement algorithm were designed to optimize both probability of cache "hits" and local bus utilization.

EPROM MEMORY

Two 28-pin EPROM sites capable of supporting up to 128K bytes of EPROM are supplied on the iSBC 386/100PP board. These sites are reserved for EPROM or ROM only and are used for the BIST power-up diagnostics resident on the iSBC 386/100PP board. This local memory resides at the upper 16M bytes of the 4G-byte 80386 physical memory address space.

I/O Subsystem

The I/O subsystem provides timers, interrupt control and an IEEE P959 iSBX connector for I/O expansion or customization.

PROGRAMMABLE TIMERS AND INTERRUPT CONTROL

The iSBC 386/100PP board has three independent programmable 16-bit interval timers. These may be used by the designer for real time interrupts or time-keeping operations. Outputs from these timers are routed to one of the two 8259A programmable interrupt controllers (PIC) on the iSBC 386/100PP board to provide software programmable time interrupts.

The MULTIBUS II architecture utilizes virtual interrupts. These virtual interrupts (those occurring off-board) are messages over the iPSB bus rather than dedicated interrupt lines. Message based interrupts are queued by the iPSB bus interface logic. This logic interrupts the 80386 microprocessor via an 8259A Programmable Interrupt Controller (PIC) indicating a message has been received.

Two 8259A Programmable Interrupt Controllers on the iSBC 386/100PP board are used in a master-slave configuration for processing on-board interrupts. One of the interrupt lines is used to handle the interrupts received from the iPSB bus. The devices and functions supported are listed in Table 2.

iSBX™ CONNECTOR

One 8/16-bit iSBX connector is provided for I/O expansion. The iSBC 386/100PP board supports both 8-bit and 16-bit iSBX modules through this connector. DMA is also supported to the iSBX connector and can be configured by programming the DMA multiplexor register of the 82258 DMA component. The iSBX connector on the iSBC 386/100PP board supports a wide variety of standard iSBX MULTIMODULE boards available from Intel including BITBUS™ iSBX MULTI-MODULES boards. Custom iSBX bus MULTIMODULE boards designed for MULTIBUS or proprietary bus systems are also supported as long as the IEEE P959 iSBX bus specification is followed.

iPSB Bus Interface Subsystem

This subsystem provides all the logic required to interface to the iPSB bus. Services provided by this subsystem include access to the iPSB by the 80386 processor, full message passing support and dual port memory access to the DRAM boards.

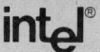

iSBC® 386/100PP SINGLE BOARD COMPUTER

PRELIMINARY

Table 2. iSBC® 386/100PP Board Devices and Functions Supported by Interrupts

Device	Function	Number of Interrupts
iPSB Bus Interface	MINT-Message-based interrupt (unsolicited message) requests from iPSB bus via bus interface logic	Queues up interrupts from up to 255 sources
82258 DMA	Transfer complete	1
8254 Timers	Timers 0, 1, 2 outputs, function determined by timer mode	3
IEEE P959 iSBX Connector	Function determined by iSBX bus MULTIMODULE board	2 to 4
8751 Serial Port	Serial diagnostic port requests	1
iPSB Bus Interface	EINT-Indicates transmission erroron iPSB Bus, MULTIBUS II device has not responded to command within 1 msec	1
Memory Parity Generator/Checker	DERR-Memory Parity Error	1

The iSBC 386/100PP single board computer takes advantage of the full message passing capability as described in the MULTIBUS II Architecture Handbook. Unsolicited and solicited message passing are achieved via the iPSB bus interface logic. This logic also performs all the arbitration, transfer and exception cycle protocols on the iPSB bus. In addition, the bus interface logic is designed to simplify implementation of systems using dual port memory.

Interconnect Subsystem

Interconnect address space is implemented with the 8751 microcontroller and iPSB bus interface logic. Read-only registers are used to hold information such as board type. Software configurable registers are used for auto-software configurability and remote/local diagnostics and testing.

Options on the iSBC 386/100PP board are controlled through interconnect address space. Many of the interconnect registers on this board perform functions traditionally done by jumper stakes. Other interconnect registers provide status information that allows system software to determine configuration status and reconfigure the hardware.

BUILT-IN SELF TEST DIAGNOSTICS

On-board built-in self test (BIST) diagnostics are implemented using the 8751 microcontroller and the 80386 microprocessor. On-board tests include initialization tests on DRAM, AD bus, EPROM, 80386, and power-up tests. These tests are performed by the 80386 microprocessor.

BISTs improve the reliability, error reporting and recover capability of MULTIBUS II boards. In addition these tests and diagnostics reduce manufacturing and maintenance costs for the user. An LED (labeled BIST) on the front panel indicates the status of power-up diagnostics. It is on when BIST diagnostics starts running and is turned off when the BIST is completed successfully.

SERIAL DIAGNOSTIC PORT

The interconnect subsystem provides an RS232C (DTE, ASYNC-only) debug port via the 8751 microcontroller.

Error Handling and Recovery

The MULTIBUS II architecture defines error reporting and recovery protocols using the iPSB bus interface. Bus transmission and bus parity errors on the iPSB bus are detected causing the iSBC 386/100PP board to generate a BUSERR* on the iPSB bus. This signal is asserted until internal operation has been completed to ensure the integrity of on-board operations. The iSBC 386/100PP board also generates agent errors (data, width, NACK, continuation and transfer-not-understood) and implements the reporting mechanism via the iPSB bus interface logic.

Software Support

The iRMX™ 286/386 software is an extension of the iRMX 286 Operating System designed to manage and extend the resources of iSBC single board computers and other 80386 based microcomputers. The iRMX 286/386 software is a real-time multitasking and multi-programming software system capable of executing

iSBC® 386/100PP SINGLE BOARD COMPUTER

PRELIMINARY

all the configurable layers of the iRMX 286 Operating System on the 80386 microprocessor and the iSBC 386/20 and 386/100 single board computers. The iRMX 286/386 software functions on MULTIBUS I architecture and MULTIBUS II architectures and includes full MULTIBUS II message passing support. For multiple user, interactive systems, Intel will offer the XENIX Operating System.

LANGUAGES AND TOOLS

Intel will be offering several languages supported by the iRMX and XENIX* operating systems. For the iRMX 286/386 Software System, this will include ASM 286, Pascal 286, PL/M 286, C 286, and FORTRAN 286. For the XENIX Operating System, languages will include ASM 386, C 386, PL/M 386 and FORTRAN 386. Software development tools will include PSCOPE Monitor 386, PSCOPE 286 Program Debugger, and an ICE 386 In-Circuit Emulator.

SYSTEM COMPATIBILITY

The iSBC 386/100PP Single Board Computer board is complemented by a range of MULTIBUS II hardware and software products. The SYPMB2 Starter System from Intel enables the designer to easily and quickly incorporate the iSBC 386/100PP and iSBC MEM/2XX into a system development environment. Applications which use 16-bit MULTIBUS II Single Board Computer boards (such as Intel's iSBC 286/100 8 MHz, 80286 based board) can be easily ported to the iSBC 386/100PP board. Minor changes to hardware and systems software (for speed and I/O configuration dependent code) may be required.

SPECIFICATIONS

Word Size

Instruction—8-, 16-, 24-, 32-, 40-bit
Data—8-, 16-, 32-bit

System Clock

CPU—12/16 MHz
Numeric Processor—80287 module—8 MHz

Dual-Port Memory

Capacity—One memory expansion board
Maximum Physical Memory—4M Bytes
Compatible DRAM Memory—
  iSBC MEM/201—1M byte DRAM memory board
  iSBC MEM/202—2M byte DRAM memory board
  iSBC MEM/204—4M byte DRAM memory board

Local Memory

Number of Sockets—Two 28-pin EPROM sites—

EPROM	Memory Capacity (maximum) K bytes
2764	16
27128	32
27256	64
27512	128

I/O Capability

Serial: One, asynchronous, DTE-only channel using 8751 microcontroller and DE-9 connector baud rate: 19.2K, 9.6K, 4.8K, 2.4K, 1.2K, 300, 110

Expansion: One 8/16 Bit IEEE P959 iSBX MULTI-MODULE board connector supporting DMA

Interrupt Capability

Potential Interrupt Sources from iPSB Bus—
  255 Individual 1 Broadcast
Interrupt Sources from On-board—
  12 sources (See Table 2)

Timers

Three programmable timers using one 8254 Programmable Interval Timer
Input Frequencies: 5.00 MHz +/± 0.1%

Output Frequencies/ Timing Intervals	Single Timer/Counter	
	Min	Max
Real Time Interrupt	400ns	13.1ms

Interfaces

iPSB Bus: Compliance Level RQA/RPA D32 M32
iSBX Bus: Compliance Level D16/16 DMA
Serial I/O: RS232C compatible, configured DTE only

Connectors

Location	Function	Part #
P1	iPSB	603-2-IEC-C096-F
P2	High Speed Memory Link	603-2-IEC-C096-F

*XENIX is a trademark of Microsoft

iSBC® 386/100PP SINGLE BOARD COMPUTER

PRELIMINARY

Physical Dimensions

The iSBC 386/100PP and iSBC MEM/2XX boards meet all MULTIBUS II mechanical specifications as presented in the MULTIBUS II Architecture Specification Handbook (#146077, Rev. C).

Double-high, triple-deep Eurocard Form Factor—
 Depth—220 mm (8.6 in.)
 Height—233 mm (9.2 in.)
 Front Panel Width—20 mm (.784 in.)

ORDERING INFORMATION

Part Number	Description
386/100PP	MULTIBUS II Single Board Computer
MEM/201	1MByte DRAM Memory Board
MEM/202	2MByte DRAM Memory Board
MEM/204	4MByte DRAM Memory Board

iSBC® MEM/312, 310, 320, 340 CACHE-BASED MULTIBUS® II RAM BOARDS

- iSBC® MEM/3XX MULTIBUS® II memory boards are high-speed cache-based boards with 8 KBytes of cache RAM
- 32-bit MULTIBUS® II Parallel System Bus (iPSB) and Local Bus Extension II (iLBX™ II Bus) interface support
- Zero wait state over iLBX™ II on a cache hit, one wait state for cache misses and writes at 8 MHz
- Dual port memory with four versions available:
  - iSBC® MEM/312   1/2 MBytes
  - iSBC® MEM/310   1 MByte
  - iSBC® MEM/320   2 MBytes
  - iSBC® MEM/340   4 MBytes
- Double-high Eurocard standard form factor, pin and socket DIN connectors
- MULTIBUS® II software interconnect support for dynamic memory configuration and diagnostics with no jumpers necesssary on the board
- Built-In-Self-Test (BIST) diagnostics on-board with both LED indicators and software access to error information
- Automatic memory initialization at power-up and at power-fail recovery
- Byte Parity error detection

The iSBC® MEM/312, 310, 320, 340 cache-based memory boards are the first Intel memory products to implement the MULTIBUS II system architecture. They have 32-bit architecture throughout, supporting 8-, 16-, and 32-bit central processors. The iSBC MEM/3XX (generally refers to this family of boards) memory boards are dual-ported, with access to the interfaces of both the MULTIBUS II Parallel System Bus (iPSB bus) and the iLBX™ II (Local Bus Extension).

In addition to the 32-bit memory transfer, the iSBC MEM/3XX high-speed cache control subsystem, standard on these boards, improves performance by allowing zero wait state read access over the iLBX II when data requested is in the cache memory.

Intel Corporation assumes no responsibility for the use of any circuitry other than circuitry embodied in an Intel product. No other circuit patent licenses are implied. Information contained herein supersedes previously published specifications on these devices from Intel.

©INTEL CORPORATION, 1984

MARCH, 1985
ORDER NUMBER 280071-002

iSBC® MEM/312, 310, 320, 340 BOARD

FUNCTIONAL DESCRIPTION

General

The iSBC® MEM/312, 310, 320, 340 high-speed cache-based memory boards are physically and electrically compatible with the MULTIBUS® II iPSB bus standard and the new iLBX™ II bus (Local Bus Extension) as outlined in the Intel MULTIBUS II specification. Figure 1 illustrates a typical multiprocessing MULTIBUS II system configuration.

Architecture

The four main subsystems of the iSBC MEM/3XX boards are the cache controller subsystem, the cache memory subsystem, the DRAM memory subsystem, and the interconnect space subsystem (see Figure 2). The following sections describe these subsystems and their capabilities in more detail.

Cache Memory Capabilities

The cache memory system is designed around the 32-bit architecture of the main memory system and reduces read access times. The 8 KBytes of 45 nsec SRAM allows zero wait state read accesses over the iLBX II bus when data requested is in the cache memory (cache hit). A cache hit takes only two iLBX II bus clocks (250 nsec at 8 MHz).

Each entry in the 8 KByte cache memory subsystem consists of a data field of 32-bits and a tag field of up to 9-bits (depending on board DRAM size). Each byte in the main memory DRAM array directly maps to one and only one entry on the cache array. This direct mapped cache array along with tag labels ensure data integrity and accurate identification of cache hits. The cache memory size and simple but effective replacement algorithm is designed to optimize both the probability of cache hits and the CPU bus utilization. On any miss or write access, the contents of one cache entry are updated to maintain consistency with the corresponding entry in the DRAM memory array.

Dual Port DRAM Capabilities

The iSBC MEM/312 module contains ½ MByte of read/write memory using 64K dynamic RAM compo-

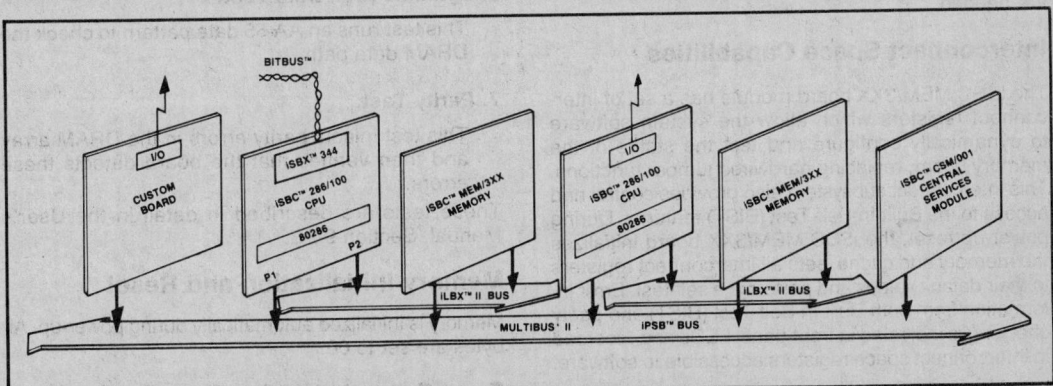

Figure 1. Typical MULTIBUS® II System Configuration

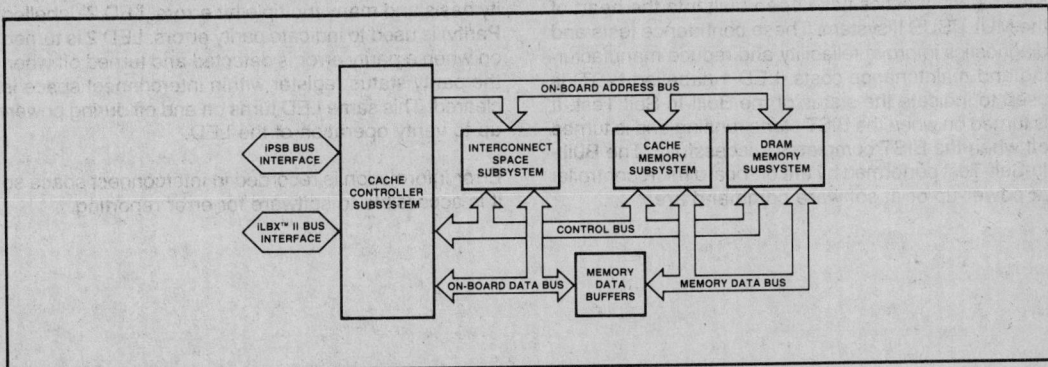

Figure 2. iSBC® MEM/3XX Board Block Diagram

iSBC® MEM/312, 310, 320, 340 BOARD

nents. The iSBC MEM/310, MEM/320 and MEM/340 modules respectively contain 1 MByte, 2 MBytes and 4 MBytes of read/write memory using 256K dynamic RAM components.

The dual port capability of the iSBC MEM/3XX boards allows 32-bit access from either the iPSB bus interface or the iLBX II bus interface (see Figure 1). Due to the simple arbitration nature of the iLBX II bus interface and the cache memory subsystem, the iSBC MEM/3XX family allows optimal access to 20 MBytes of DRAM on the iLBX II bus.

System Memory Size

Using this series of memory boards the maximum system memory capacity based on one CPU board and 19 memory boards is 76 MBytes on the iPSB bus. The memory partitioning is independent for the iPSB bus interface and the iLBX II bus interface.

The start address can be on any 64 KByte boundary on the iPSB bus and any 64 KByte boundary on the iLBX II bus. Software configures the start and ending addresses through the interconnect space. No jumpers are needed.

Interconnect Space Capabilities

The iSBC MEM/3XX board module has a set of interconnect registers which allow the system software to dynamically configure and test the status of the memory board, replacing hardwired jumper functions. This interconnect subsystem also provides control and access to the Built-In-Self-Test (BIST) features. During power-up reset, the iSBC MEM/3XX board initializes the memory and cache, sets all interconnect registers to their default values and performs a self-test. Error information from both Built-In-Self-Test (BIST) and parity checking is indicated in front panel LEDs and recorded in interconnect space registers accessible to software.

Built-In-Self-Test (BIST)

Self-test/diagnostics have been built into the heart of the MULTIBUS II system. These confidence tests and diagnostics improve reliability and reduce manufacturing and maintenance costs. LED 1 (labelled BIST) is used to indicate the status of the Built-In Self Test. It is turned on when the BIST starts running and is turned off when the BIST completes successfully. The Built-In-Self-Test performed by the on-board microcontroller at power-up or at software command are:

1. **EPROM Checksum:**

    This test performs a checksum test on its internal EPROM to check operation of the 8751 microcontroller.

2. **Cache Data Test:**

    The microcontroller performs a sliding ones test on the cache memory in hit-only mode.

3. **Cache Address Test:**

    This test verifies that the cache address path is working properly.

4. **Refresh Check:**

    This test performs RAM test on a small portion of DRAM with an elapsed time between the write operation and the verification of the data.

5. **Dynamic RAM Address Test:**

    This test performs Address Rippled RAM test on the board memory (MISS ONLY operation mode).

6. **Dynamic RAM Data Test:**

    This test runs an AA-55 data pattern to check the DRAM data path.

7. **Parity Test:**

    This test injects parity errors in the DRAM array and then verifies that the board detects these errors.

These tests are described in detail in the User's Manual, Section 9-23.

Memory Initialization and Reset

Memory is initialized automatically during power-up. All bytes are set to 00.

Error Detection Using Byte Parity

Parity will detect all single bit parity errors on a byte parity basis and many multiple bit errors. LED 2 (labelled Parity) is used to indicate parity errors. LED 2 is turned on when a parity error is detected and turned off when the parity status register within interconnect space is cleared. This same LED turns on and off during power-up to verify operation of the LED.

Error information is recorded in interconnect space so it is accessible to software for error reporting.

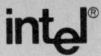

iSBC® MEM/312, 310, 320, 340 BOARD

SPECIFICATIONS

Word Size Supported

8-, 16-, 24-, and 32-bits

Memory Size

1/2 Megabyte (iSBC MEM/312) board
1 Megabyte (iSBC MEM/310) board
2 Megabytes (iSBC MEM/320) board
4 Megabytes (iSBC MEM/340) board

Access Times (All Densities)

MULTIBUS® II Parallel System Bus—iPSB (@10 MHz)

Read	562 ns (avg.)
	775 ns (max.)
Write	662 ns (avg.)
	775 ns (max.)

Note: Average access times assume 80% cache hit rates

iLBX™ II Bus—Local Bus Extension

Read	250 ns (min.)
	275 ns (avg.)
	375 ns (max.)
Write	375 ns (avg.)
	375 ns (max.)

Base Address

iPSB Bus - any 64 KBytes boundary

iLBX II Bus—any 64 KBytes boundary

Power Requirements

Voltage—5V DC ± 5%

PRODUCT	CURRENT
iSBC MEM/312 Board	3.5 A (typ) 6.0 A (max)
iSBC MEM/310 Board	3.5 A (typ) 6.0 A (max)
iSBC MEM/320 Board	3.5 A (typ) 6.0 A (max)
iSBC MEM/340 Board	4.1 A (typ) 6.7 A (max)

ENVIRONMENTAL REQUIREMENTS

Temperature:
(inlet air) at 200 LFM airflow over boards

Non-Operating — −40 to +70°C
Operating — 0 to +55°C

Humidity:
Non-operating — 95% RH @ 55°C
Operating — 90% RH @ 55°C

Physical Dimensions

The iSBC MEM/3XX boards meet all MULTIBUS II mechanical specifications as presented in the MULTIBUS II specification (#146077).

Double High Eurocard Form Factor:

Depth — 220mm (8.6 in.)

Height — 233mm (9.2 in.)

Front Panel Width — 20mm (.784 in.)

Weight:

iSBC MEM/312 board:	6720 gm (24 oz.)
iSBC MEM/310 board:	6160 gm (22 oz.)
iSBC MEM/320 board:	6720 gm (24 oz.)
iSBC MEM/340 board:	10080 gm (36 oz.)

Reference Manuals

iSBC MEM/3XX Board Manual (#146707-001)

Intel MULTIBUS II Bus Architecture Specification (#146077)

Manuals may be ordered from any Intel Sales Representative, Distributor Office, or from the Intel Literature Department. 3065 Bowers Ave., Santa Clara, CA 95051.

Ordering Information

Part Number	Description
iSBC MEM/312	½MByte Cache Based MULTIBUS II RAM Board
iSBC MEM/310	1MByte Cache Based MULTIBUS II RAM Board
iSBC MEM/320	2MByte Cache Based MULTIBUS II RAM Board
iSBC MEM/340	4MByte Cache Based MULTIBUS II RAM Board

iSBC® PKG/606
iSBC® PKG/609
MULTIBUS® II CARDCAGE ASSEMBLIES

- Available in two sizes to hold up to 6 or 9 MULTIBUS® II boards
- Designed to mount inside a chassis or other enclosure
- Uses a 6 layer Parallel System Bus (iPSB) backplane
- All lines fully terminated per the iPSB MULTIBUS® II specification
- Assembly uses aluminum extrusion construction for strength and rigidity
- Accommodates Intel iSBC® PKG/902 and iSBC® PKG/903 2 and 3 slot iLBX™ II backplanes

The iSBC® PKG/606/609 series of cardcages are designed to mount and interconnect up to 6 or 9 MULTIBUS® II boards for small to medium size advanced MULTIBUS II microcomputer systems. The cardcages are compact in size and easily mount in standard or custom enclosures. Extra-wide support extrusions and heavy duty endplates help make the iSBC PKG/606/609 cardcage assemblies especially suited for installation in systems located in high vibration or high shock environments. Installed in the cardcage assembly is a 6 layer iPSB backplane that utilizes separate power and ground planes and fully terminates all signal lines. This layout minimizes system noise and ensures reliable operation even in a fully loaded, multiprocessor-based system.

Intel Corporation assumes no responsibility for the use of any circuitry other than circuitry embodied in an Intel product. No other circuit patent licenses are implied. Information contained herein supersedes previously published specifications on these devices from Intel.

© INTEL CORPORATION, 1984

iSBC® PKG/606 iSBC® PKG/609 Card Cages

FUNCTIONAL DESCRIPTION

Mechanical Features

The cardcages accommodate up to 6 (iSBC PKG/606) or 9 (iSBC PKG/609) MULTIBUS II boards spaced at 0.8 inch centers. The assemblies are designed to hold "double high" (6U) Euro form-factor boards (233.4mm high x 220mm deep) or a mixture of "single high" (3U) and "double high" boards using additional hardware (not supplied). Each installed board is held in place by two screws supplied as part of the board retainer hardware.

The cardcage frame is built using five support extrusions and two aluminum end plates as shown in figure 1. Both cardcages are 10.5" wide and 10.1" deep and vary in height according to model (see specifications section).

The cardcages are designed to mount inside chassis or other enclosures and may be installed so that the MULTIBUS II boards load either horizontally or vertically in the unit. All assembly hardware is countersunk allowing the cardcages to be mounted flush against any internal chassis surface.

A Parallel System Bus (iPSB) backplane is mounted to the P1 side of the assembly, and one or more iLBX™ II backplanes (not supplied) can be mounted to the P2 side.

Electrical Features

The iPSB backplane uses a 6 layer design with separate power and ground layers and a signal routing scheme which minimizes ringing, crosstalk, and capacitive loading on the bus. Mounted on the backplane are 6 or 9, 96-pin, female DIN connectors (depending on model), bus termination resistors, decoupling capacitors, and power terminals. Press-fit technology is used throughout. The PC board is UL recognized for flammability. The card cages themselves are UL recognized components.

Single In-line Package (SIP) style resistors are used to terminate all address, clock, data, and control lines. Each termination consists of two resistors which connects the line to +VCC and ground. Different size resistors are used according to the type of driver connected to the line in an operating system.

The DIN type connectors are female, 96 pins, fully gold plated, and meet IEC standard 603-2-IEC-C096F. The connectors are mounted on 0.8" centers to match Intel's iPSB (Parallel System Bus) MULTIBUS II backplanes and are keyed to ensure proper mating to the MULTIBUS II board. The connector can provide up to 9 amps of current at +5V to each MULTIBUS II board in addition to the current available over the iLBX II backplane.

Screw terminals on the backplane are provided for connection to +5V, ±12V power and ground. In addition, an extra +5V terminal is provided for connection to a backup battery for memory protection during power fail conditions. These terminals, each of which can handle up to 25 amps of current at 55°C, provide a simple and highly reliable connection method to the system power supply.

The first slot position is designed to accept the Central Services Module (CSM) MULTIBUS II board. All other slots can accept any combination of MULTIBUS II boards.

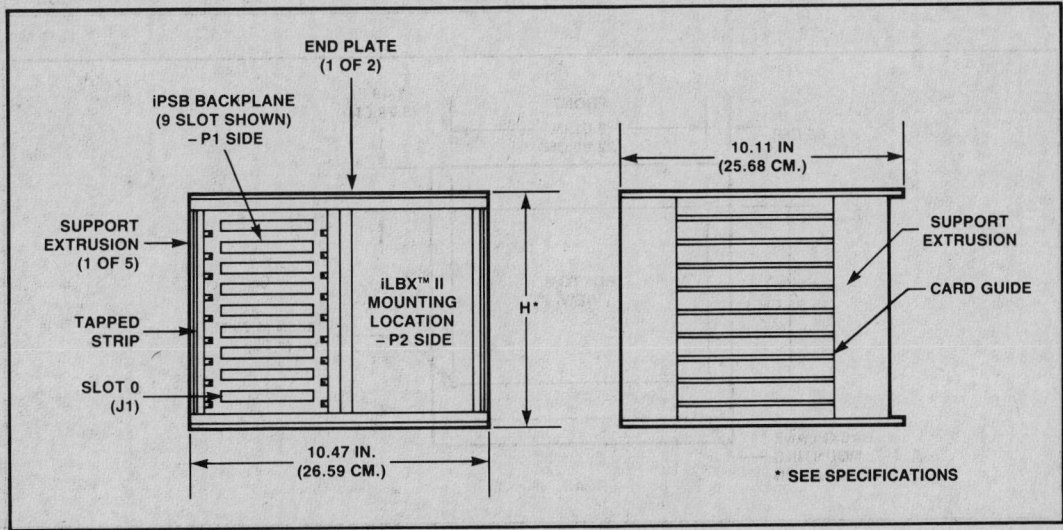

Figure 1. Cardcage Assembly Dimensions (iSBC® PKG/609 shown)

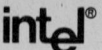

iSBC® PKG/606 iSBC® PKG/609 Card Cages

SPECIFICATIONS
Mechanical

Specification	iSBC® PKG/606 Cardcage	iSBC® PKG/609 Cardcage
Board Capacity	6	9
Dimensions Height	15.20 cm (5.98 in)	21.20 cm (8.38 in)
Width	26.59 cm (10.47 in)	26.59 cm (10.47 in)
Depth	25.93 cm (10.21 in)	25.93 cm (10.21 in)
Weight	4 lbs (1.8 kg)	5 lbs (2.3 kg)
Board Spacing	0.8 in (20.3 cm)	
Mounting Hole Locations	See figure 2	
Construction Materials, Cardcage Frame	Aluminum extrusions and end plates, nylon card guides	
Construction Method iPSB Backplane	Six layer backplane with separate VCC and ground layers; all connectors, power terminals, and resistor/capacitor sockets are press-fit into the backplane	
Connector Type	96 pin "DIN" female, gold plated, meets IEC standard 603-2-IEC-C096-F	

Electrical

iPSB Backplane — Meets Intel MULTIBUS II specification No. 146077 for board dimensions, layout, signal line termination, and transmission characteristics

Power Connections — Type:
  Screw terminal block, AMP P/N 55181-1, Winchester P/N 121-25698-2, or equivalent

Quantity of Power Terminals and Current Rating:

	iSBC® PKG/606 Cardcage		iSBC® PKG/609 Cardcage	
Voltage	Quantity	Current (amps)	Quantity	Current (amps)
+5	3	54	4	81
+12	1	12	1	18
−12	1	12	1	18
+5BB	1	12	1	18
GND	4	78	5	135

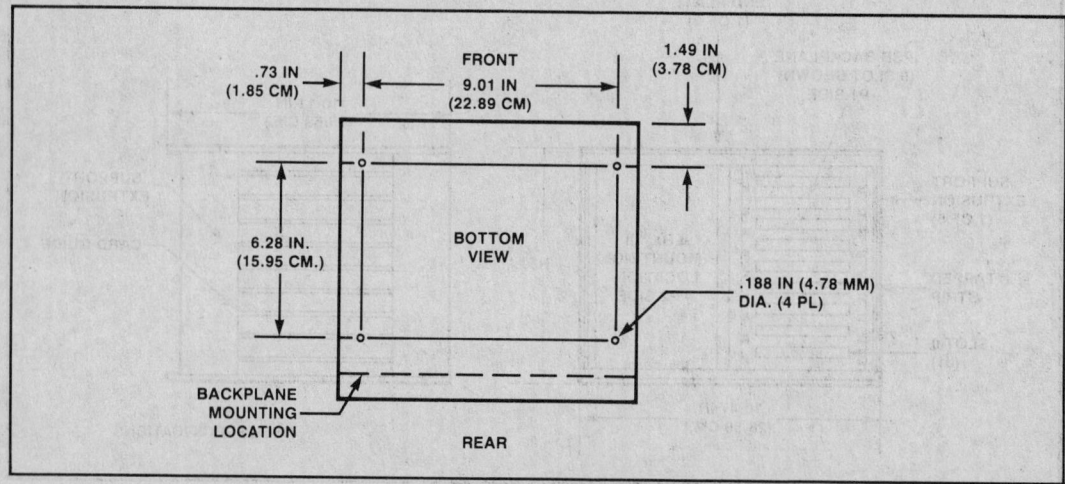

Figure 2. Mounting Hole Locations

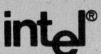

iSBC® PKG/606 iSBC® PKG/609 Card Cages

Mating Connection: No. 6 locking spade or ring tongue lug

Maximum current available per slot:

Voltage	Current
+ 5V	9A
+ 12V	2A
− 12V	2A
+ 5BB	2A

Operating Environment:
0-55°C (at 25 amps per power terminal);
0-70°C (at ≤18 amps per power terminal);
0% to 95% relative humidity, non-condensing;
0-10,000 ft. altitude.

Reference Manual — MULTIBUS II Cardcage Assembly and iLBX II Backplane User's Guide, P/N 146709-001 (supplied).

ORDERING INFORMATION

Part Number	Description
iSBC PKG/606	6 slot MULTIBUS II Cardcage Assembly
iSBC PKG/609	9 slot MULTIBUS II Cardcage Assembly

iSBC® PKG/902
iSBC® PKG/903
MULTIBUS® II iLBX™ II Backplanes

- Provides iLBX™ II interconnect for fastest CPU/memory data transfers
- Designed to mount in MULTIBUS® II carcage assemblies
- Available in 2 slot (iSBC® PKG/902) and 3 slot (iSBC® PKG/903) sizes
- Uses a 6 layer, fully terminated backplane
- Includes a 10 pin connector for BITBUS™ applications
- Meets all electrical and mechanical requirements of the MULTIBUS® II specifications

The iSBC® PKG/902 and iSBC PKG/903 series of iLBX™ II backplanes are designed to mount on the P2 side of Intel's MULTIBUS® II cardcage assembly or other double Euro (6U) cardcage. One or more backplanes may be installed in a system to allow high speed data transfers between the CPU and memory boards installed in the system. The iLBX II backplane uses a 6 layer PCB with separate power and ground planes and full termination on all signal lines. This design minimizes system noise and ensures reliable operation in all applications.

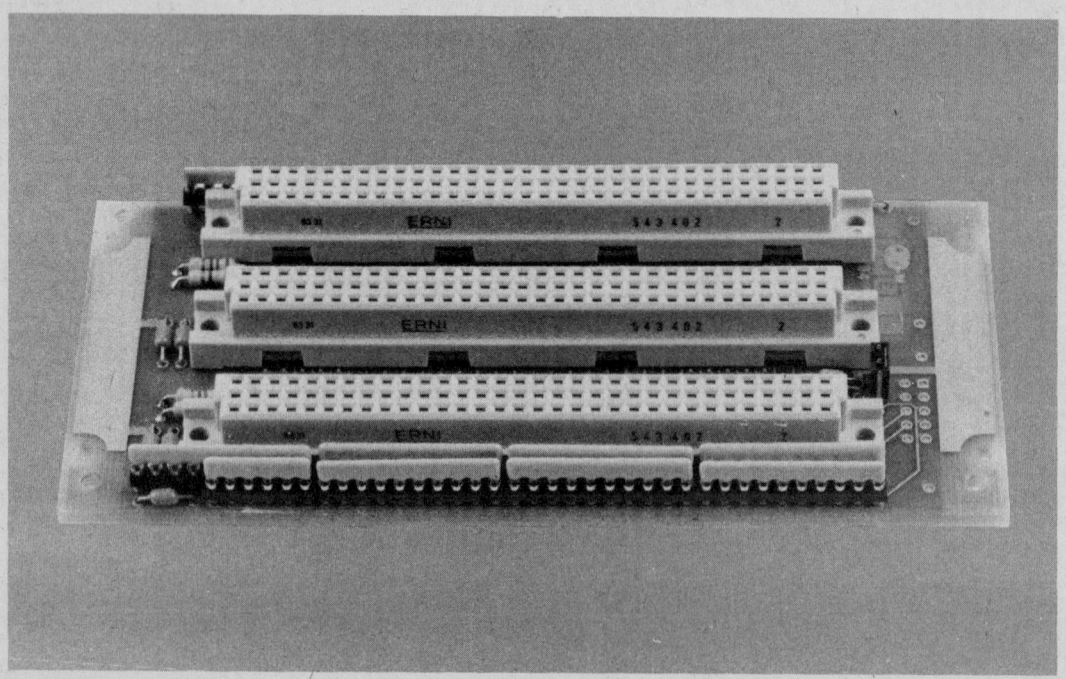

Intel Corporation assumes no responsibility for the use of any circuitry other than circuitry embodied in an Intel product. No other circuit patent licenses are implied. Information contained herein supersedes previously published specifications on these devices from Intel.

© INTEL CORPORATION, 1984

iSBC® PKG/902 iSBC® PKG/903 Backplanes

FEATURES

Mechanical and Electrical

The iSBC® PKG/902 and iSBC® PKG/903 iLBX™ II backplanes use a 6 layer printed circuit board (PCB) with separate power and ground layers and a signal lead routing scheme which minimizes ringing, crosstalk, and capacitive loading on the bus. Mounted on the PCB are two (iSBC PKG/902) or three (iSBC PKG/903) 96 pin DIN connectors, one 10-pin BITBUS™ connector, terminating resistors, decoupling capacitors, and power terminals. The resistors and capacitors are mounted into sockets, and all parts are press-fit into the backplane. The PCB is UL recognized for flammability.

Single In-line Package (SIP) style resistors are used to terminate all address, clock, data, and control lines. Each termination consists of two resistors which connects the line to +VCC and ground. Different size resistors are used according to the type of driver connected to the line in an operating system. The SIP style resistors help make the board compact in size and allows the designer to mount several backplanes directly adjacent to one another in a system without having to skip slots.

Mounted on the rear of the backplane is a 10-pin BITBUS connector. This connector serves as the serial communication interface for any iSBX 344 BITBUS controller boards installed in the system.

The DIN type connectors are female, 96 pins, fully gold plated, and meet IEC standard 603-2-IEC-C096F. The connectors are mounted on 0.8" centers to match Intel's iPSB (Parallel System Bus) MULTIBUS II backplanes and are keyed to ensure proper mating to the MULTIBUS II board. The connector can provide up to 6 amps of current at +5V to each MULTIBUS II board in addition to the current available over the Parallel System Bus backplane.

Screw terminals on the backplane are provided for connection to +5V power and ground. These terminals, each of which can handle up to 25 amps of current, provide a simple and highly reliable connection method to the power supply.

SPECIFICATIONS

Mechanical and Environmental

Connector Spacing — 20.3 cm (0.8 in)
Number of Slots — iSBC PKG/902: 2 slots
  iSBC PKG/903: 3 slots
Board Dimensions — See Figure 1
Weight — iSBC PKG/902 — 0.2kg (8oz)
  iSBC PKG/903 — 0.3kg (12oz)
Connectors:
  DIN — 96-pin female, gold plated, meets IEC standard 603-2-IEC-C096-F
  BITBUS — 10-pin male, gold plated, T&B Ansley 609-1012M, or equivalent
Constructed Method — Six layer backplane with separate VCC and Ground layers
  — All connectors, power terminals, and resistor/capacitor sockets are press-fit into the backplane
Mounting Hole Location — See Figure 1
Operating Environment — 0-70°C ambient temperature; 0% to 90% relative humidity, non-condensing; 0-10,000 ft. altitude

Electrical

Backplane Electrical Characteristics and Line Terminations — Per Intel MULTIBUS II specification 146077, Sec. II, iLBX II

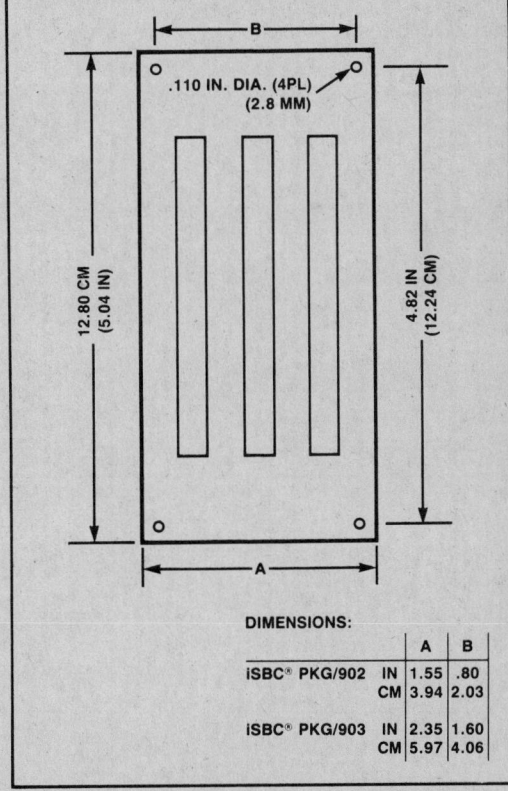

Figure 1. iLBX™ II Board Dimensions (iSBC® PKG/903 Shown)

DIMENSIONS:	A	B
iSBC® PKG/902 IN	1.55	.80
CM	3.94	2.03
iSBC® PKG/903 IN	2.35	1.60
CM	5.97	4.06

iSBC® PKG/902 iSBC® PKG/903 Backplanes

Power Connections
    Type — Screw terminal block: AMP P/N 55181-1; Winchester P/N 121-25698-2; or equivalent
    Mating Connection — No. 6 locking spade or ring tongue lug
    Quantity — 2 (VCC, Ground)
    Current Rating — iSBC PKG/902: 12 amps;
                       iSBC PKG/903: 18 amps
                         (Power and Ground)

Maximum Current — 6 amps (over the iLBX II backplane)
Available Per Slot

REFERENCE MANUAL

MULTIBUS® II Cardcage Assembly and iLBX™ Backplane User's Guide, P/N 146709-001 (not supplied).

ORDERING INFORMATION

Part Number	Description
iSBC PKG/902	2 slot iLBX II Backplane
iSBC PKG/903	3 slot iLBX II Backplane

16-32

280074-002

iSBC® CSM/001
CENTRAL SERVICES MODULE

- iSBC® CSM/001 Central Services Module integrates MULTIBUS® II central system functions on a single board
- MULTIBUS® II Parallel System Bus clock generation for all agents interfaced to the MULTIBUS® II iPSB bus
- System-wide reset signals for power-up, warm start, and power failure/recovery
- System-wide time-out detection and error generation
- Slot I.D. and Arbitration I.D. initialization
- MULTIBUS® II interconnect space for software configurability and diagnostics
- Built-In Self Test (BIST) power-up diagnostics with LED indicator and error reporting accessible to software via interconnect space
- General purpose link interface to other Standard (MULTIBUS® I) or Proprietary Buses
- Time-of-day clock support with battery back-up on board
- Double-high Eurocard standard form factor, pin and socket DIN connectors

The iSBC® CSM/001 Central Services Module is responsible for managing the central system functions of clock generation, power-down and reset, time-out, and assignment of I.D.s defined by the MULTIBUS® II specification. The integration of these central functions in a single module improves overall board area utilization in a multi-board system since these functions do not need to be duplicated on every board. The iSBC CSM/001 module additionally provides a time-of-day clock and the general purpose link interface to the other standard (MULTIBUS I) or proprietary buses.

Intel Corporation assumes no responsibility for the use of any circuitry other than circuitry embodied in an Intel product. No other circuit patent licenses are implied. Information contained herein supersedes previously published specifications on these devices from Intel.

©INTEL CORPORATION, 1984

MARCH, 1985
ORDER NUMBER 280070-002

iSBC® CSM/001 MODULE

FUNCTIONAL DESCRIPTION

Overall

The iSBC® CSM/001 Central Services Module integrates MULTIBUS® II central system functions on a single board. Each MULTIBUS II system requires management of these central system functions as defined in the MULTIBUS II specification. Figure 1 illustrates a typical multiprocessing MULTIBUS II system configuration. To perform its central system functions, the iSBC CSM/001 Central Services Module has a fixed slot I.D. and location in the backplane. The iSBC CSM/001 board additionally provides an interface to the MULTIBUS I Link board and a time-of-day clock.

Architecture

The iSBC CSM/001 board is functionally partitioned into 6 major subsystems. The Centralized System Wide Control subsystem includes MULTIBUS II iPSB bus clock generation and system wide reset signal generation. The Time-Out Control subsystem provides system wide time out detection and error generation. The System Interconnect Space subsystem controls I.D. initialization and software configurable interconnect space. The Link Board interface subsystem provides an interface to the MULTIBUS I Link board or links to other buses. The last two subsystems are the Time-of-Day clock and the iPSB bus interface. These areas are illustrated in Figure 2.

CENTRALIZED SYSTEM-WIDE CONTROL SUBSYSTEM

Parallel System Bus Clock Generation

The CSM generates the Parallel System Bus clocks. The Bus Clock (BCLK*) 10MHz signal and the Constant Clock (CCLK*) 20MHz signal are supplied by the CSM to all boards interfaced to the Parallel System Bus. These boards use the Bus Clock 10 MHz signal for synchronization, system timing, and arbitration functions. The Constant Clock is an auxiliary clock. The frequency of the Bus Clock and Constant Clock can be halved via jumpers for diagnostic purposes.

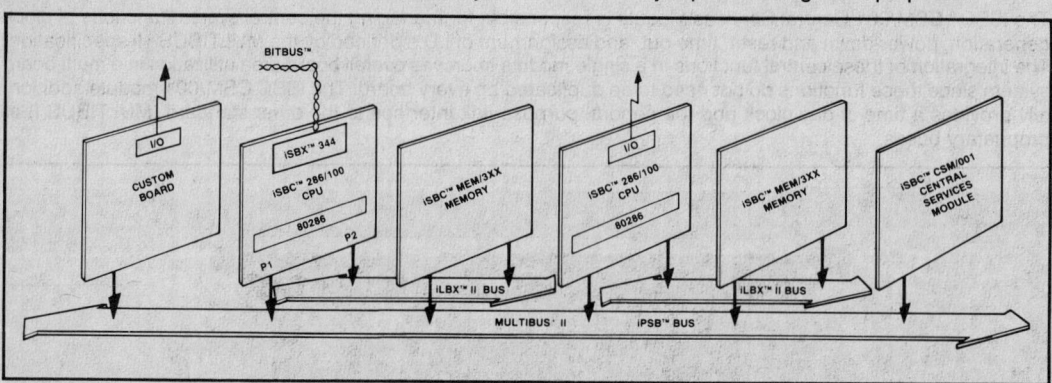

Figure 1. Typical MULTIBUS® II System Configuration

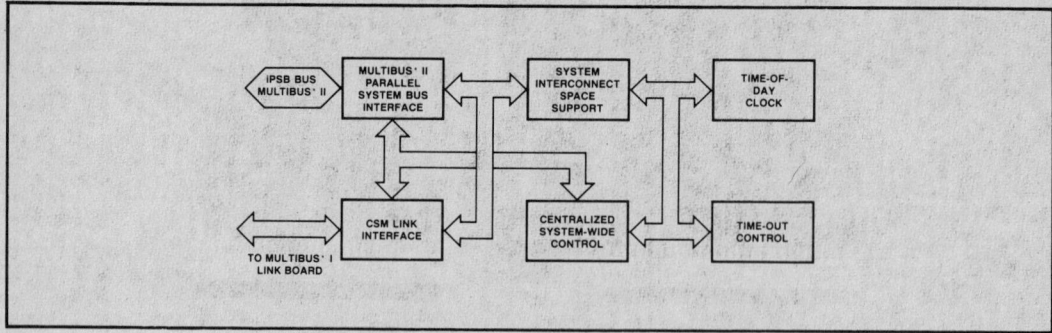

Figure 2. Block Diagram of iSBC® CSM/001 Board

16-34   280070-002

iSBC® CSM/001 MODULE

Reset Control and Power-Fail/Recovery

The CSM sends a system-level reset/initialization signal to all boards interfaced to the Parallel System Bus. The CSM assigns slot I.D. and arbitration I.D. to these boards during this initialization process. It provides this signal upon pressing of the reset switch, restoration of system power or a software request for reset received via the CSM interconnect space. The reset switch may be jumper-configured to cause a power-up or warm reset, with cold reset the default configuration. The reset switch is located on the front panel. Additionally, warm reset and cold reset signals can be input through the P2 connector.

The CSM power supply interface is accomplished via the ACLO input of the P2 connector. ACLO is an open collector input from the power supply which provides advance warning of imminent power fail. If battery back-up is not required, a jumper is provided on the CSM to disable the power fail signal ACLO.

TIME-OUT SUBSYSTEM

The TIMOUT* (Time-out) signal is provided by the CSM whenever it detects the failure of a module to complete a handshake. This TIMOUT* signal is received by all boards interfaced to the iPSB bus and may be disabled via the interconnect space.

INTERCONNECT SUBSYSTEM

The CSM Interconnect subsystem provides arbitration I.D., and slot I.D. initialization, software configurable interconnect space, and on-board diagnostics capability.

At reset, the CSM supplies each board interfaced to the iPSB bus with its slot I.D. and its arbitration I.D. The slot I.D. assignment allows user or system software to address any board by its physical position in the backplane.

The interconnect space has both read-only and software configurable facilities. The read-only registers hold information such as vendor number and board type, so that this information is available to the system software. The CSM software configurable interconnect space allows write operations to support board configuration and diagnostics under software control. The CSM also uses interconnect space for system wide functions such as providing a time/date record (from time-of-day clock), software access to diagnostics and software control of the system wide functions.

BUILT-IN-SELF-TEST (BIST) DIAGNOSTICS

Self-test/diagnostics have been built into the heart of the MULTIBUS II system. These confidence tests and diagnostics improve reliability and reduce manufacturing and maintenance costs. LED 1 (labeled BIST) is used to indicate the status of the Built-In-Self-Test. It is turned on when the BIST starts running and is turned off when the BIST completes successfully. In addition, all error information is recorded in interconnect space so it is accessible to software for error reporting.

The Built-In-Self-Tests performed by the on-board microcontroller at power-up or at software command are:

1. PROM Checksum Test—Verifies the contents of the 8751 microcontroller.

2. RAM Test—Verifies that each RAM location of the 8751 microcontroller may store 0's and 1's by complementing and verifying twice each RAM location.

3. Real Time Clock Chip RAM Test—Verifies that reads and writes to the RAM locations on Real Time Clock Chip are functional

4. Real Time Clock Test—Reads and writes all RAM locations of the RTC chip. Not run at power-up due to destructive nature.

5. Arbitration/Slot I.D. Register Test—Verifies that arbitration and slot I.D.s can be read and written from on-board.

6. 8751 Status Test—Verifies that input pins of the 8751 are at correct level.

7. Clock Frequency Test—Tests accuracy of Real Time Clock to .2% against bus clock.

CSM LINK INTERFACE

The CSM Link Interface and the MULTIBUS I iSBC LNK/001 board provides a bridge between MULTIBUS I and MULTIBUS II systems. Hybrid systems can be built for development or target. The CSM Link Interface uses the P2 connector on the iSBC CSM/001 module for transferring commands and data from MULTIBUS II to a MULTIBUS I Link board. The MULTIBUS I Link board (iSBC LNK/001) is purchased separately from the iSBC CSM/001 board and includes the cable which connects the iSBC CSM/001 board and the MULTIBUS I Link board (see Figure 3).

The CSM Link Interface supports 8 or 16-bit transfers via a 16-bit address/data path. The iSBC LNK/001 board resides in the MULTIBUS I system and provides a memory and I/O access window to MULTIBUS I from the MULTIBUS II Parallel System Bus. Only one iSBC LNK/001 board can be connected to the iSBC CSM/001 module.

TIME-OF-DAY CLOCK SUBSYSTEM

The Time-Of-Day Clock subsystem consists of a clock chip, battery, and interface circuitry. The clock provides time keeping to 0.01% accuracy of fractions of seconds,

iSBC® CSM/001 MODULE

seconds, minutes, hours, day, day of week, month, and year. This information is accessible via the interconnect space. The battery back-up for the clock chip provides 2 years of operation.

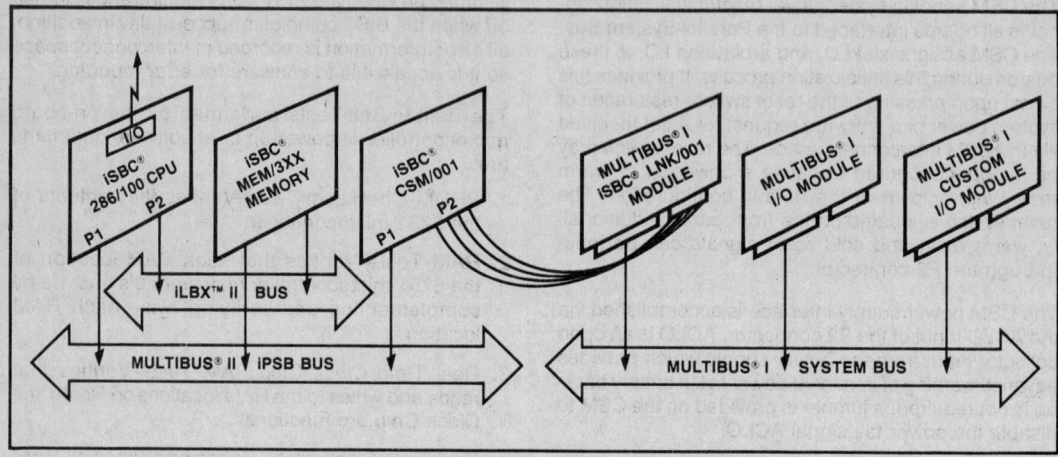

Figure 3. iSBC® CSM/001 Link Interface

SPECIFICATIONS

System Clocks

BCLK* (Bus Clock) 10 MHz
CCLK* (Constant Clock) 20 MHz
LCLK* (Link Clock) 10 MHz

Jumper option available to divide these frequencies in half

Interface Compliance

MULTIBUS II Bus Architecture Specification (#146077)

Link Cable

The Link cable uses a 64 conductor ribbon cable for interconnecting the CSM board to the Link Board. The maximum length for the cable is 1 meter.

Interface Specifications

Location	Function	Part #
P1	iPSB Bus	603-2-IEC-C096-F
P2	Link and Remote Services	603-2-IEC-C064-F

PHYSICAL DIMENSIONS

The iSBC CSM/001 board meets all MULTIBUS II mechanical specifications as presented in the MULTIBUS II specification (#146077).

Double-High Eurocard Form Factor:

Depth—220mm (8.7 in.)

Height—233mm (9.2 in.)

Front Panel Width—20mm (.78 in.)

Weight—4820 gm (16.5 oz.)

ENVIRONMENTAL REQUIREMENTS

Temperature:
(inlet air) at 200 LFM airflow over boards

Non-operating — −40 to +70°C
Operating — 0 to +55°C

Humidity:
Non-operating — 95% RH @ 55°C
Operating — 90% RH @ 55°C

POWER REQUIREMENTS

Voltage (volts)	Current (amps)
+5V	6A (max.)
+5VBB	1A (max.)

BATTERY CHARACTERISTICS

3V nominal voltage; capacity of 160 milliamp hours minimum.

iSBC® CSM/001 MODULE

BATTERY DIMENSIONS

Outside dimension   20mm-23mm

Height   1.6mm-3.2mm

REFERENCE MANUALS

iSBC CSM/001 Board Manual (#146706-001)

Intel MULTIBUS II Bus Architecture Specification (#146077)

Manuals may be ordered from any Sales Representative, Distributor Office, or from the Intel Literature Department, 3065 Bowers Ave., Santa Clara, CA 95051

ORDERING INFORMATION

Part Number	Description
iSBC CSM/001	MULTIBUS II Central Services Module

PRELIMINARY

iSBC® LNK/001 BOARD
MULTIBUS® II to MULTIBUS® I Link Board

- **Development vehicle making MULTIBUS® I iSBC® boards accessible to MULTIBUS® II board designers**
- **On board 128 K Byte Dual Port DRAM Memory**
- **16 M Bytes of MULTIBUS® I memory mapped into MULTIBUS® II memory space configurable from MULTIBUS® II Interconnect space**
- **32 K Bytes of MULTIBUS® I I/O mapped into MULTIBUS® II I/O space configurable from MULTIBUS® II Interconnect space**
- **Conversion of MULTIBUS® I interrupts to MULTIBUS® II interrupt messages**
- **MULTIBUS® I form factor board**
- **Connects to MULTIBUS® II Central Services Module (iSBC CSM/001 board) via a 3 foot flat ribbon cable**

The iSBC LNK/001 board maps MULTIBUS I memory and I/O space into the MULTIBUS II iPSB bus and converts MULTIBUS I interrupts into MULTIBUS II interrupt messages. Up to 16 M Bytes of MULTIBUS I memory and up to 32 K Bytes of MULTIBUS I I/O is addressable from MULTIBUS II through the iSBC LNK/001 board. Additionally, 128 K Bytes of dual port DRAM memory resides on the iSBC LNK/001 board for use by both MULTIBUS I and MULTIBUS II systems. MULTIBUS II OEM product designers can now speed hardware and software development efforts by using the iSBC LNK/001 board to access standard or custom MULTIBUS I products.

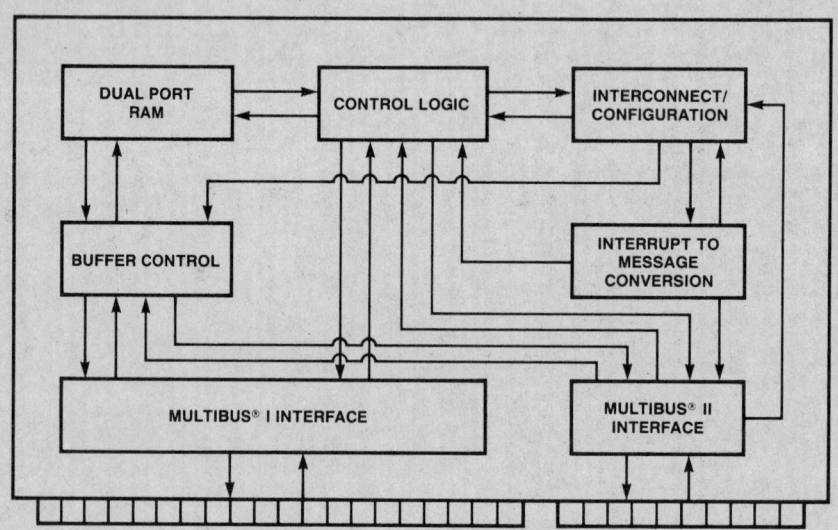

iSBC® LNK/001 Block Diagram

Intel Corporation assumes no responsibility for the use of any circuitry other than circuitry embodied in an Intel product. No other circuit patent licenses are implied. Information contained herein supersedes previously published specifications on these devices from Intel.

© INTEL CORPORATION, 1985

JULY, 1985
ORDER NUMBER: 280135-001

iSBC® LNK/001 BOARD

PRELIMINARY

GENERAL DESCRIPTION

The iSBC LNK/001 board makes MULTIBUS I products accessible to MULTIBUS II designers. The iSBC LNK/001 board resides in the MULTIBUS I system and connects to the Central Services Module (iSBC CSM/001 board) via a 3 foot flat ribbon cable. The ribbon cable connects the P2 connector of the iSBC LNK/001 board to the P2 connector on the Central Services Module. The iSBC LNK/001 board supports:

a. 128 K Bytes of Dual Port DRAM,

b. 16- and 24-bit addressing into 16 M Bytes of MULTIBUS I memory with 8- and 16- bit data paths,

c. 8- and 16-bit addressing into 32 K Bytes of MULTIBUS I I/O with 8- and 16- bit data paths,

d. MULTIBUS I interrupt to MULTIBUS II interrupt message conversions of up to eight levels of non bus-vectored interrupts via an 8259A programmable interrupt controller, and

e. initialization tests and Built-In-Self-Test (BIST) using interconnect address space.

APPLICATIONS

The primary application of the iSBC LNK/001 board is in the design development environment. The iSBC LNK/001 board allows designers to start their development efforts by leveraging existing MULTIBUS I products or to begin modular design efforts and preserve investments in custom products. In either case, the use of leverage with existing MULTIBUS I hardware and software allows designers to begin their MULTIBUS II product designs.

MEMORY AND I/O READ/WRITE SEQUENCE

The iSBC LNK/001 board establishes a master/slave relation between a MULTIBUS II system and a MULTIBUS I system. A MULTIBUS II agent requesting a memory transfer involving the iSBC LNK/001 board is directed through the CSM to the iSBC LNK/001 Dual Port memory or a MULTIBUS I slave. If the access address is within the MULTIBUS II Dual Port window, the transaction is acknowledged by the iSBC LNK/001 board and returned to the MULTIBUS II iPSB through the CSM. In the event the address is outside the MULTIBUS II Dual Port window, the transaction is directed to the MULTIBUS I system. Here the iSBC LNK/001 board enters arbitration for the MULTIBUS I system bus to complete the requested transaction. Once the iSBC LNK/001 board is the owner of the MULTIBUS I system bus, data is transferred to or from the iSBC LNK/001 board/Central Services Module connection. The MULTIBUS I slave acknowledges the transfer and the iSBC LNK/001 board passes the acknowledge on through the Central Services Module to the MULTIBUS II iPSB.

MULTIBUS II I/O operations are always directed to the MULTIBUS I I/O slaves and consequently require arbitration for the MULTIBUS I system bus.

INTERCONNECT MAPPING

The function record of the iSBC LNK/001 board, a function record within the Central Services Module interconnect template, appears as a board within a board (see Table 1). The actual iSBC LNK/001 board configuration is done through unique interconnect registers using the same slot ID as the Central Services Module. The iSBC LNK/001 function record begins at an offset of 256 from the start of the CSM template and the EOT (End Of Template) byte is attached as the last function of the iSBC LNK/001 function record.

Dual Port 128 K Byte DRAM Memory

A dynamic RAM Dual Port, resident on the iSBC LNK/001 board, provides a 128 K Byte media for

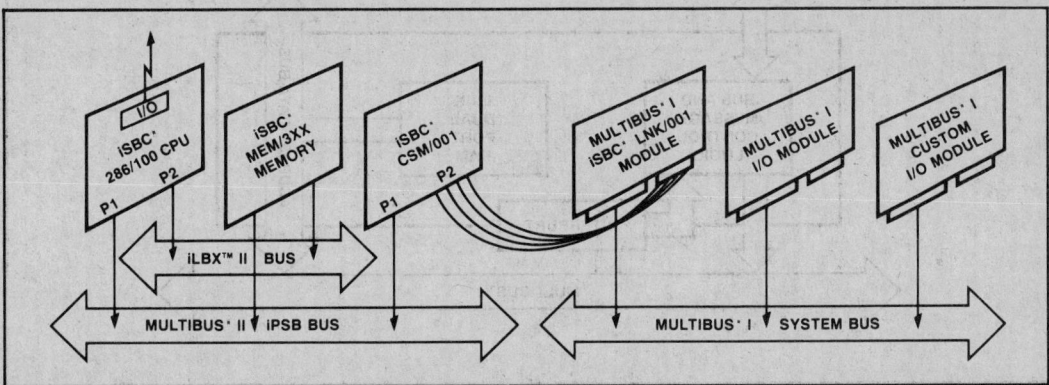

Figure 1. Sequence Diagram

iSBC® LNK/001 BOARD

PRELIMINARY

MULTIBUS I and MULTIBUS II agents to pass data efficiently. With both buses sharing the Dual Port memory the need for the MULTIBUS II system to continuously arbitrate for MULTIBUS I system access is eliminated. Consequently, each bus can continue operating at its respective speed when accessing the iSBC LNK/001 Dual Port memory.

MULTIBUS® I Memory Addressability

The MULTIBUS I system views the iSBC LNK/001 Dual Port as a contiguous 128K Byte memory block mapped into the 16 M Bytes of MULTIBUS I memory address space starting at the Dual Port Start Address register value. This memory block, configurable on

Table 1. Function Record Overview iSBC® LNK/001 Board

OFFSET	DESCRIPTION	OFFSET	DESCRIPTION
0-255	iSBC CSM/001 Header and Function Record	271	MBI Dual Port End Address
		272	MBII Dual Port Start Address
256	Board Specific Record Type	273	MBII Dual Port End Address
257	Record Length	274	MBII Memory Start Address
258	Vendor ID, Low Byte	275	MBII Memory End Address
259	Vendor ID, High Byte	276	I/O 4K Segment Control
260	Link Version Number	277	MBI Interrupt Enable
261	Hardware Revision Test Number	278	Link Interrupt 0 Destination Address
262	Link General Status	279	Link Interrupt 1 Destination Address
263	Link General Control	280	Link Interrupt 2 Destination Address
264	Link BIST Support Level	281	Link Interrupt 3 Destination Address
265	Link BIST Data In	282	Link Interrupt 4 Destination Address
266	Link BIST Data Out	283	Link Interrupt 5 Destination Address
267	Link BIST Slave Status	284	Link Interrupt 6 Destination Address
268	Link BIST Master Status	285	Link Interrupt 7 Destination Address
		286	Interrupt Source Address
269	Link BIST Test ID	287	Link Status Register
270	MBI Dual Port Start Address	288	EOT (End of Template)

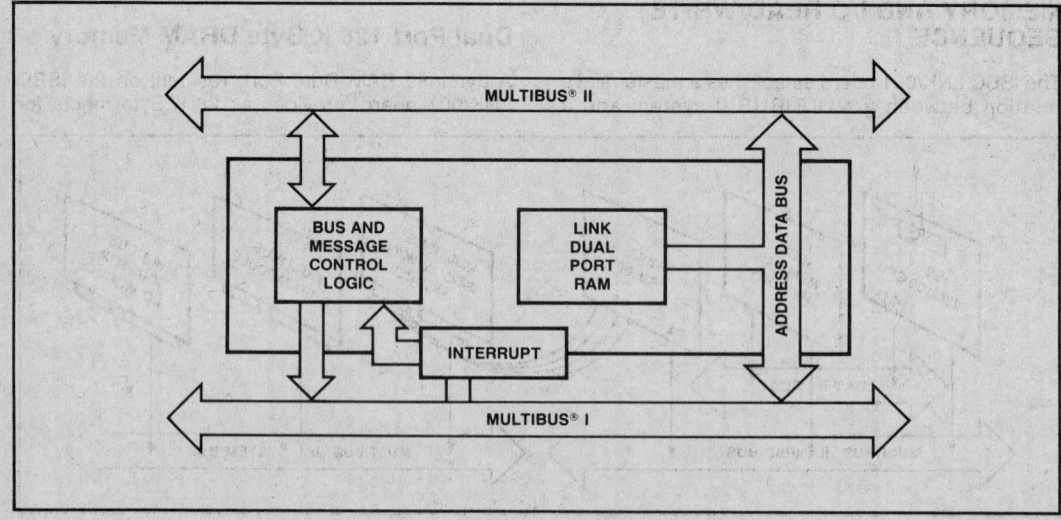

Figure 2. Link Board Dual Port Drawing

any 64 K Byte boundary within the MULTIBUS I memory address space, is set via interconnect accesses to the iSBC LNK/001 function records from the MULTIBUS II system (see Table 1). The first 16 M Bytes of MULTIBUS II memory space can be mapped in the 16 M Bytes of MULTIBUS I memory address space (see Figure 3).

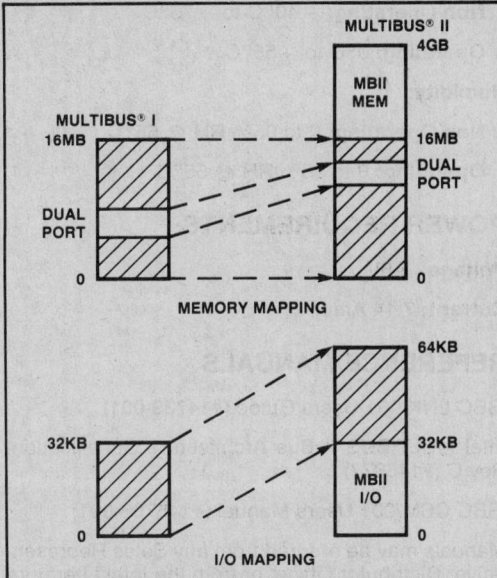

Figure 3. MULTIBUS® I Memory and I/O Mapping Diagram

MULTIBUS® I I/O Addressability

Up to eight 4K Byte blocks of MULTIBUS II I/O space can be mapped into MULTIBUS I I/O space (see Figure 3). MULTIBUS II I/O accesses must be from 32 K Byte to 64 K Byte in order to be mapped into MULTIBUS I I/O address space. These blocks are specified through an interconnect access to the "I/O 4K Segment Control" register (see Table 1). Each bit in the register represents a 4K Byte block of I/O addresses. When a bit (or bits) is set, the 4K Byte block of MULTIBUS II I/O space represented by that bit will be dedicated to MULTIBUS I I/O space.

Interrupt to Message Conversion

As the iSBC LNK/001 board receives non-bus vectored interrupts from the MULTIBUS I system, the onboard 8259A programmable interrupt controller (PIC) prioritizes the MULTIBUS I interrupts and initiates the MULTIBUS II unsolicited interrupt message generation process. Up to 8 levels of non-bus vectored interrupts are supported by the iSBC LNK/001 board.

The iSBC LNK/001 board generates the MULTIBUS II interrupt messages and is the Interrupt Source. The iSBC LNK/001 board is assigned a Source ID through interconnect space when the MULTIBUS II system is powered up or when the user programs the source ID register via interconnect space. The Interrupt Destination is the MULTIBUS II board to which the interrupt message is being sent. Each of the eight MULTIBUS I interrupt lines can be programmed to generate a unique MULTIBUS II destination address. These destination addresses are initialized through interconnect space by programming the iSBC LNK/001 Interrupt Destination Address Registers. The message source address is also configurable via interconnect space by writing to the Interrupt 0 Source Address Register with a base value. Once the base value of source Address 0 is established, Source Address 1 through 7 are set for incrementing values by the 8751A interconnect processor. The iSBC LNK/001 board recognizes MULTIBUS II Negative Acknowledge agent errors ("NACK") and performs an automatic retry algorithm.

Initialization Tests and BIST

Self test and diagnostics have been built into the MULTIBUS II system. The BIST LED is used to indicate the result of the Built-In-Self-Test and turns on when BIST starts running and turns off when it has successfully executed. BIST test failure information is recorded in the interconnect space and is accessible to software for error reporting.

PHYSICAL CHARACTERISTICS

Form Factor

The iSBC LNK/001 board is a MULTIBUS I form factor board residing in a MULTIBUS I system. Physical dimensions are identical to all standard MULTIBUS I boards.

Connection to MULTIBUS® II Bus

The iSBC LNK/001 board connects to the iSBC CSM/001 board in the MULTIBUS II system via a 60 pin conductor flat ribbon cable. The physical connection is made on the P2 connector of both the iSBC LNK/001 board and the iSBC CSM/001 board. The cable termination requirements and DC requirements for the signal drivers and receivers are detailed in the iSBC CSM/001 USERS GUIDE, Section 6.6.4. The maximum length of the cable is 3 feet. The cable and the connectors are shipped unassembled to allow user flexibility.

SOFTWARE SUPPORT

To take advantage of iSBC LNK/001 Dual Port architecture, existing software device drivers may require modification. Device driver changes depend on the specific application and vary in complexity depending upon the device driver.

iSBC® LNK/001 BOARD

PRELIMINARY

SPECIFICATIONS

Word Size

16- and 24-bit Address Paths
8-, and 16-bit Data Paths
Block transfers are not supported

Cable Characteristics

The cable is a 60 pin conductor flat ribbon cable with a maximum length of 3 feet. The P2 connector to the iSBC LNK/001 board is a 30/60 pin board edge connector with 0.100" pin centers, KEL-AM Part Number RF30-2853-5. The connector to the P2 DIN connector on the iSBC CSM/001 board is 3M Part Number 3338-000.

Interface Specifications

Location	Function
P1	MULTIBUS IEEE 796 System Bus
P2	Cable connection to P2 connector of iSBC CSM/001 board

PHYSICAL DIMENSIONS

The iSBC LNK/001 board meets all MULTIBUS I mechanical specifications as presented in the MULTIBUS I specification.

Depth: 17.15 cm (6.75 in.)

Height: 1.27 cm (0.50 in.)

Front Panel Width: 30.48 cm (12.00 in.)

Weight: Estimated 565 g (20 oz.)

ENVIRONMENTAL REQUIREMENTS

Temperature: Inlet air at 200 LFM airflow over boards

   Non Operating: $-40°C$ to $+75°C$

   Operating: $0°C$ to $+55°C$

Humidity:

   Non Operating: 0 to 95% RH @ 55°C

   Operating: 0 to 95% RH @ 55°C

POWER REQUIREMENTS

Voltage: +5V

Current: 7.14 Amps

REFERENCE MANUALS

iSBC LNK/001 Users Guide (#14739-001)

Intel MULTIBUS II Bus Architecture Specification, Rev C (#146077)

iSBC CSM/001 Users Manual (#146706-001)

Manuals may be ordered from any Sales Representative, Distributor Office, or from the Intel Literature Department, 3065 Bowers Ave., Santa Clara, CA. 95051.

ORDERING INFORMATION

Part Number	Description
iSBC LNK/001	MULTIBUS II to MULTIBUS I iSBC LNK/001 Interface Board

SYP/500PP MULTIBUS® II SYSTEM CHASSIS

- Full enclosure MULTIBUS® II design development tool
- 3 full height peripheral bays
- 6 slot MULTIBUS® II cardcage assembly
- 3 slot iLBX™ II backplane
- 270 Watt power supply

ORDER NUMBER: 280153-001

The SYP/500PP System Chassis is a MULTIBUS II design tool enabling product designers to begin work immediately on MULTIBUS II development projects. Two front mounted LEDs indicate "Power On" and "PSB Busy" conditions while a keyswitch provides external "reset" capabilities for the chassis. The voltage selector, power-on switch, and cardcage opening are located in the rear of the chassis. Three peripheral bays, two of which are accessible from the front of the chassis, will accept up to three industry standard full height or six half height peripherals. A six slot cardcage, Parallel System Bus, and iLBX II backplane assembly integrated with a 270 Watt power supply.

FUNCTIONAL DESCRIPTION
Mechanical Features

Intel's SYP/500PP MULTIBUS II Chassis is a full enclosure, off-the-shelf design development tool. The chassis is an ideal vehicle for designers to integrate their MULTIBUS II board set with tape, Wini, or floppy peripherals into a complete system. Three full height 5.25" peripheral bays are built into the SYP/500PP with peripheral power cables, office environment cooling, and peripheral mounting brackets for industry standard full or half-height peripherals are provided with the chassis. Access via the front panel allows two of the bays to be configured with removable media peripherals.

A six slot MULTIBUS II cardcage assembly with 0.8" centers is incorporated in the chassis. The cardcage is made with heavy duty endplates and extra-wide support extrusions to insure adequate support for most applications. Installed in the cardcage assembly is a 6 layer Parallel System Bus backplane that utilizes separate power and ground planes and fully terminates all signal lines. In addition to the cardcage assembly, a three slot iLBX II backplane, providing a high speed CPU to memory bus, is mounted on the P2 side of the cardcage assembly. The iLBX II backplane also has a 10-pin BITBUS connector that serves as a serial interface for any iSBX 344 BITBUS controller boards installed in the system. The cardcage assembly is cabled to the power system and conforms to the published MULTIBUS II specification.

Electrical Features

The power supply in the SYP/500PP chassis is a 270 Watt switching power supply with selectable AC power input of 88-132 VAC at 47-63Hz or 180-264 VAC at 47-63 Hz. The AC input power is externally selectable with a slide switch mounted on the rear of the chassis. A power distribution board is installed in the chassis that allows easy connection to all peripheral bays through a four position plug mounted on the power distribution board. Maximum amperage is 45A at +5V, 4.7A at +12V, 4.7A at −12V with the total power not to exceed 270W.

SPECIFICATIONS:
Electrical Parameters
Maximum Amperage:

Voltage	Current
+5V	45A
+12V	4.7A
−12V	4.7A

Designed to meet: UL 478
CSA C22.2 No. 154
FCC Class A
VDE Level A

Operational Parameters
AC Power Input: 88-132 VAC or 180-264 VAC at 47-63 Hz
Operating Temperature Range: 10°C to 40°C
Storage Temperature: −40°C to 70°C
Operational Humidity: 10% to 85% relative, non-condensing

Physical Parameters
Height: 7.75" (19.38 cm)
Width: 17" (42.50 cm)
Depth: 23" (57.50 cm)
Weight: 50 lbs. (22.50 kg.)

Ordering Information:
MULTIBUS II Chassis: SYP/500PP

MULTIBUS® II STARTER SYSTEM

- Ready-to-Run MULTIBUS® II system based on Intel's 80286
- Supports Industry standard iRMX™ Operating System and languages
- 5.25" 40 MB Winchester disk and 320 KB floppy disk for data storage, backup, and software interchange
- One day of free technical consultation on the customer site
- Total system support from Intel's world-wide field service and support organization

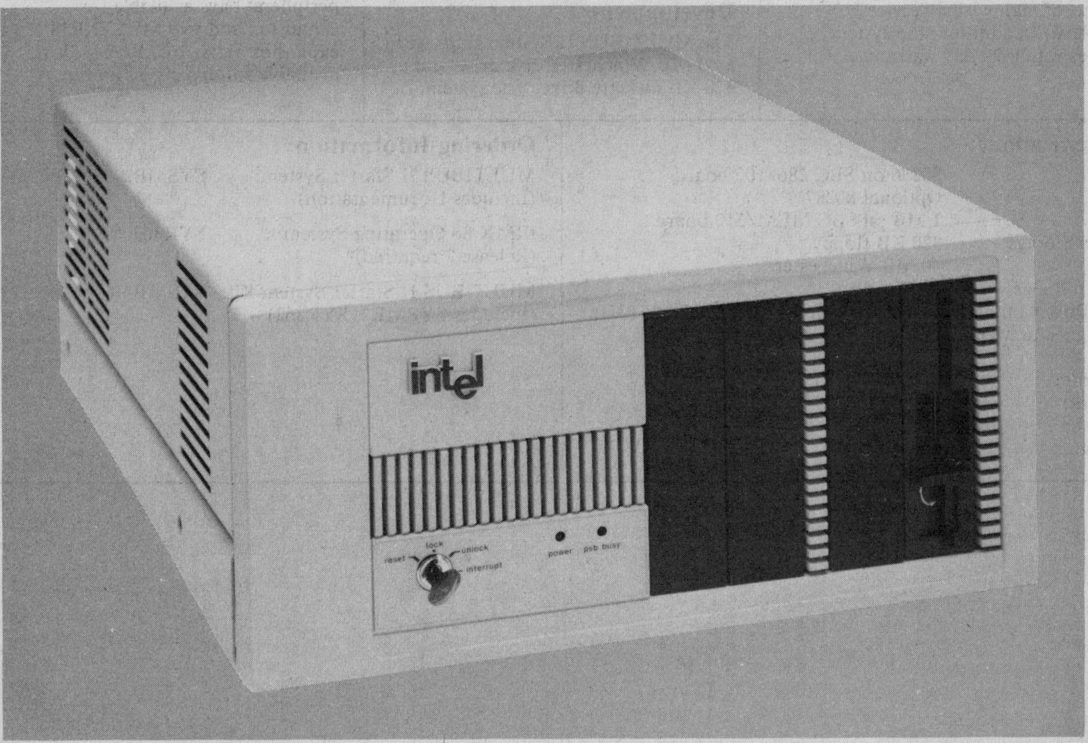

ORDER NUMBER: 280146-002

Ready-to-Run MULTIBUS® II System

Intel's MULTIBUS II System offers OEMs a complete hardware and software MULTIBUS II development environment. Intel has done the integration so you get a ready-to-run system. (The iRMX Operating System must be ordered separately.) Use the system for software development in the iRMX™/MULTIBUS II environment or move existing iRMX applications to the system with no changes needed to the application code. The system also offers an excellent development and test environment for custom MULTIBUS II board design.

Intel is offering one day of free technical consultation on the customer site with the system. Use this valuable resource in any way you wish – for software installation, for orientation to the MULTIBUS II environment, for training on the iRMX Operating System, or for your own unique needs. (Travel expenses not included if beyond a 50 mile radius of major Intel Service Centers.) In addition, the system comes with a 90 day warranty.

MULTIBUS® II Architecture at the Highest Level of Integration

As a fully integrated MULTIBUS II hardware and software environment, the system takes advantage of the new system features of the MULTIBUS II architecture: geographic addressing, bus parity protection, software configurability, message based interrupts, centralized system-wide control, 32 bit transfers, and high reliability physical connections.

The system employs the MULTIBUS II multiple bus architecture to achieve a high performance 80286-based design. These busses are the Parallel System Bus (iPSB), the Local Bus Expansion Bus (iLBX™ II), and the I/O expansion bus (iSBX™). For detailed information on the iPSB, iLBX II, and iSBX busses see the MULTIBUS II Data Book (Order Number: 280055-002).

Ample Storage for Software Development

The MULTIBUS II System ships with a 40 MB Winchester disk drive and a 320 KB diskette drive. The system also includes 1 MB of RAM. This provides more than enough system memory and mass storage for most development environments.

Industry Standard iRMX™ Operating System and Languages

Intel's MULTIBUS II System supports iRMX 86 – the industry standard real-time operating system for Intel microprocessors. The iRMX 86 Operating System is supported by a wide range of development tools and high level languages including PSCOPE 86, ASM 86, C, FORTRAN, Pascal, and BASIC. With the MULTIBUS II system these tools are now available in a MULTIBUS II system environment.

Expansion Capability for Custom Design

The MULTIBUS II System provides both peripheral and board-level expansion capabilities. As shipped, the system has one and a half 5.25″ peripheral bays available for expansion and two MULTIBUS II expansion slots. 16.7A of +5V is available for expansion power.

Specifications:

CPU:	80286 on SBC 286/100 board
	Optional 80287
RAM:	1 MB on SBC MEM/310 board
Mass Storage:	320 KB floppy
	40 MB Winchester
Temp Range:	10°C – 40°C
AC Power Input:	88-132 VAC or 180-264 VAC; 47-63Hz
Designed to Meet:	UL 114; CSA 22.2; FCC Class A; VDE Class A
Height:	7.75″
Width:	17″
Depth:	23″
Weight:	60 lbs.

Ordering Information:

MULTIBUS II Starter System: (Includes Documentation)	SYSMB2
iRMX 86 Operating System: (Release 7 required)	SYR86J
MULTIBUS II Starter System Kit: (Includes SYPMB2, SYR86J)	SYSMB2R

intel

APPLICATION NOTE

AP-256

May 1985

MULTIBUS® II Interfacing Using the BAC And MIC Components

MARK BUDZINSKI
SENIOR TECHNICAL MARKETING ENGINEER

INTEL CORPORATION, 1985

Order Number 280132-001

AP-256

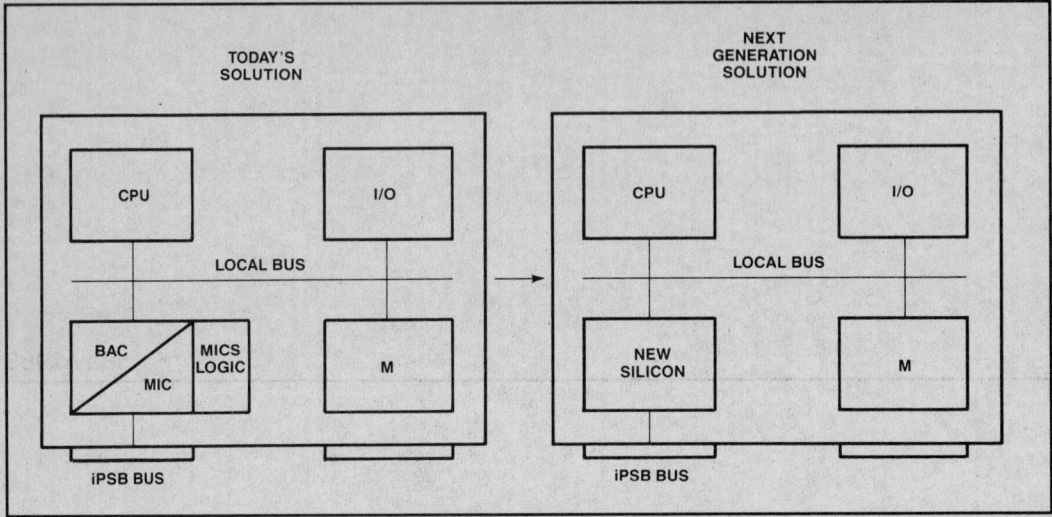

Figure 1. Bus Interface Upgrade Path

INTRODUCTION

The MULTIBUS® II Parallel System Bus (iPSB bus) is specifically designed to take advantage of silicon technology. The multiplexed structure and synchronous protocol will over time, allow migration to a single device which incorporates the bus interface logic. Today, this logic for an intelligent board consists of the Bus Arbiter/Controller (BAC), the Message Interrupt Controller (MIC), and miscellaneous PALs, transceivers, and other logic. Of all the MULTIBUS II architecture's advanced capabilities, full message passing is the only element that is missing from today's solution. The next generation bus interface silicon will support full message passing, as well as integrate all of the functions of today's BAC/MIC solution, except for bus transceivers, into one component.

This application note describes how to design a BAC/MIC bus interface today that has an easy upgrade path to the next generation silicon (see fig. 1). MULTIBUS II board designs can be saved from significant redesign when the full message passing component becomes available. Intel is adopting the upgrade strategy for its own line of MULTIBUS II products (e.g., the iSBC® 286/100 CPU card), and encourages other board designers to do the same.

Physically, the migration strategy defines the bus interface logic to reside on a MULTIMODULE™ daughter board (see fig. 2). This MULTIMODULE board (herein called the Bus Interface MULTIMODULE board) mounts on a baseboard through a predefined socket. By following this strategy, the interface logic is physically separated from the baseboard. Consequently, when the next generation bus interface silicon comes along, the component can be placed on a smaller MULTIMODULE board to fit in the socket of the same baseboard.

This paper begins with background information related to the MULTIBUS II address spaces that the MULTIMODULE board supports. Next, it identifies the requirements for designing an iPSB bus interface. From these requirements, the paper describes in detail the design of Intel's bus interface MULTIMODULE board. The features and functions of the BAC and MIC are discussed, followed by a description of the rest of the logic that is designed into the MULTIMODULE board. Finally, two example scenarios are described, which help tie together the concepts presented throughout the paper.

The reader should be familiar with the MULTIBUS II architecture, iPSB bus functions and protocols, and MULTIBUS II architecture nomenclature. Further information can be found in the MULTIBUS II Architecture Specification Handbook, the MULTIBUS II Message Interrupt/Controller Data sheet, and the MULTIBUS II Bus Arbiter/Controller data sheet. Prior design experience with either MULTIBUS I architecture or MULTIBUS II architecture is not required in order to comprehend this application note.

Background

MULTIBUS II architecture specifies four address spaces:
- Memory Space
- I/O Space
- Interconnect Space
- Message Space

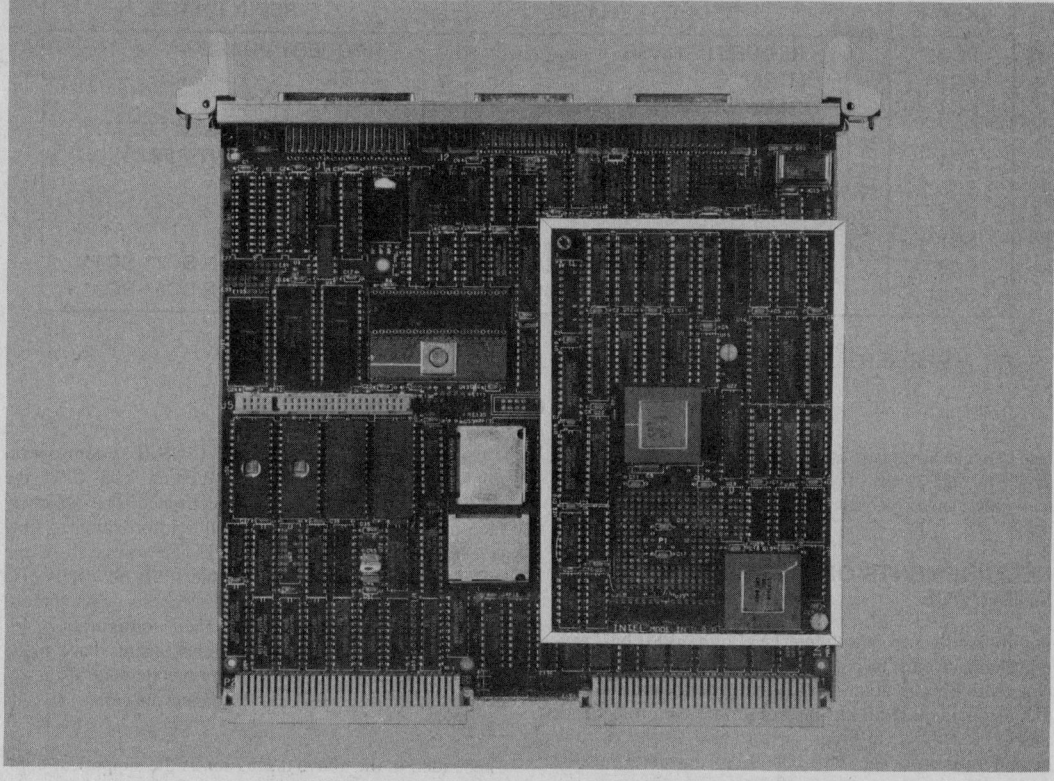

Figure 2. BAC/MIC MULTIMODULE™ Board Mounted on the Mother Board

The interconnect and message spaces are used on the iPSB bus to perform special functions. Since a CPU can only access memory or I/O address space, the interconnect and message spaces are mapped into memory and I/O space.

The memory address space is the most familiar space, used for storing and retrieving both data and program code. Memory space is used by an iSBC board to access memory resources on other boards. It can also be used when microprocessors need to exchange data, typically over traditional buses, where the CPUs share a dual-port RAM area. The I/O address space is also familiar to a traditional bus user, and is used to access peripheral devices (e.g., disk controllers) on the iPSB bus.

The interconnect address space supports an advanced feature of MULTIBUS II architecture called geographic addressing. Simply stated, geographic addressing is the ability to address any board in the system by its slot number. Moreover, configuration registers reside within each board's interconnect space such that system software can identify boards in the system and configure them accordingly. In general, interconnect space is used for software control of board configuration, board self-tests, and diagnostics. This reduces the number of stake pin jumpers and DIP switches since configuration is under software control.

Message address space is a relatively new concept in bus communications. MULTIBUS II architecture defines it to support high performance communications in multiprocessor systems. The trend towards systems with more than one intelligent element stems from the increase in board functionality. Single board computers are handling many of the functional blocks of a system, such that the latest communications controllers, graphics controllers, etc., all contain microprocessors. The requirement for these modules to communicate with each other quickly and reliably motivates the definition of message address space.

Microprocessors are typically very inefficient when trying to communicate over a bus. By assigning this communications function to a dedicated, intelligent bus interface, the processor on each board can perform the jobs it does best. Message passing puts intelligence in the bus interface to perform the communications function on behalf of the processor. The CPU's local bus is effectively decoupled from the iPSB bus. Additionally, the bus inter-

SIGNAL	REQUEST PHASE		REPLY PHASE	
SC0*		REQUEST PHASE		REQUEST PHASE
SC1*		LOCK	RQ	LOCK
SC2*		DATA WIDTH		END-OF-CYCLE
SC3*		DATA WIDTH		REQUESTING AGENT READY
SC4*	REQUESTER	ADDRESS SPACE		REPLYING AGENT READY
SC5*		ADDRESS SPACE	RP	AGENT ERROR
SC6*		READ/WRITE OPERATION		AGENT ERROR
SC7*		RESERVED		AGENT ERROR
SC8*		EVEN PARITY ON SC7*-SC4*		EVEN PARITY ON SC7*-SC4*
SC9*		EVEN PARITY ON SC3*-SC0*	RQ	EVEN PARITY ON SC3*-SC0*

RP = REPLIER   RQ = REQUESTER

Figure 3. System Control Line Summary

face can take advantage of specific iPSB bus features such as 32-bit data and burst transfers, though the processor may only handle 16-bit wide data and no bursts.

REQUIREMENTS OF AN iPSB BUS INTERFACE

For an intelligent agent to interface to the iPSB bus, several elements must be considered. The MULTIBUS II Architecture Specification identifies and defines the signals that make up the iPSB bus, and describes the protocols of iPSB bus activity. In order for an agent to successfully communicate over the iPSB bus, a bus interface must be designed to encompass these protocols at a minimum.

The MULTIBUS II architecture defines iPSB bus activity in three distinct cycles: Arbitration, Transfer, and Exception. The arbitration cycle determines who the next bus owner is to be, and must be supported by the iPSB bus interface logic. Once a board gains bus ownership, it may run transfer cycles. During the request phase of the transfer cycle, address and control information (e.g., read/write, data width, etc.) are driven out onto the bus over the address/data and 10 system control lines. Moreover, during the reply phase of the transfer cycle, handshake information (e.g., Requestor Ready) has to be correctly driven over the same control lines (see fig. 3). In both phases of the transfer cycle, parity must be generated and checked by the appropriate board.

The bus interface must also establish an interface to the local implementation of interconnect address space. Interconnect address space can be implemented as robustly as is desired. For example, Intel uses an 8751 microcontroller which includes Built-in Self Tests for the board in addition to the normal interconnect registers. At the minimum, interconnect space must include two locations to encode the vendor ID of the board. Whatever implementation for interconnect address space is chosen, an interface should be determined and supported by the iPSB bus interface logic.

Throughout the course of MULTIBUS II system operations, information must flow between the local CPU, the iPSB bus, and the local interconnect space. The bus interface must provide the paths for this information to flow (see fig. 4). For example, a CPU can access all of the different address spaces across the iPSB bus. It is also important for a CPU to be able to access its own interconnect space, in order to complete self configuration. Finally, incoming accesses from other agents have to be decoded and routed to the appropriate element of the receiving agent (e.g., CPU, interconnect space).

Embedded in the above discussion is the support of communications through message space. The support can be classified for interrupt messages (virtual interrupts), general unsolicited messages, and solicited messages. The minimum support required is for interrupt messages. The latter two enhance the capability of a MULTIBUS II system, but are not absolutely required.

In summary, an intelligent iPSB bus interface must: (1) support the three cycles of iPSB bus communications, (2) provide the data paths for all address space accesses, both incoming and outgoing to the iPSB bus, and (3) support virtual interrupts.

REQUIREMENTS THAT THE SILICON SATISFIES

The BAC and MIC components satisfy several of the iPSB bus interface requirements. They contribute certain features and functions that make them desirable to use in a iPSB bus interface design. The characteristics of each component are discussed in the next sections to insure an appropriate knowledge level before beginning the design section of this paper. Those that are familiar with the BAC and MIC can proceed directly to the Bus Interface MULTIMODULE board design section.

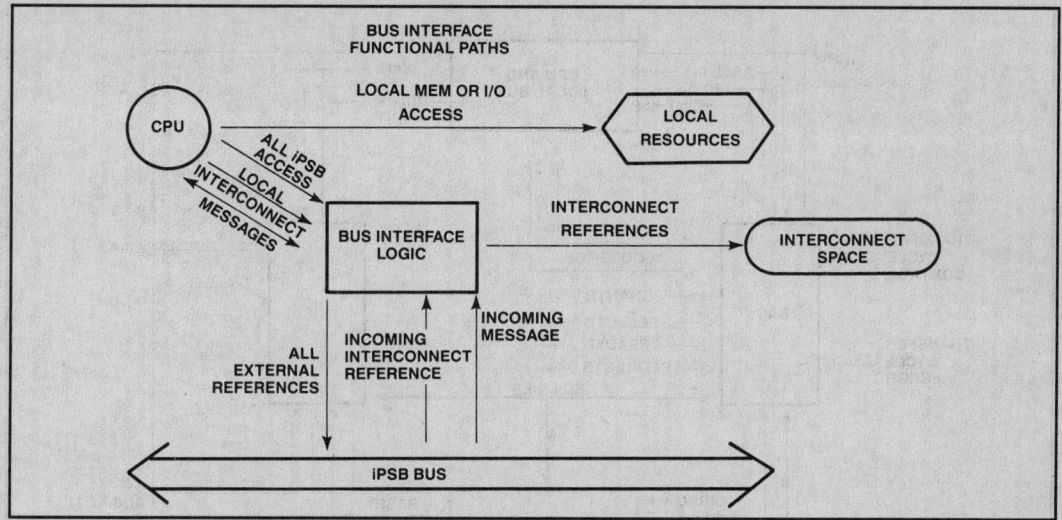

Figure 4. Bus Interface Functional Paths

BAC Purpose and Features

The BAC provides the arbitration and system control logic for an iPSB agent. The agent can function in all of the arbitration cycles, transfer cycles, and exception cycles defined by MULTIBUS II architecture. Furthermore, the BAC supports the agent as either a requestor or replier in the transfer cycle.

The arbitration process that must occur to acquire access to the iPSB bus takes place totally within the BAC component. An agent simply requests bus access via a REQUEST signal, and the BAC executes the arbitration process. The requesting agent, whether it is a MIC device or a CPU, is completely isolated from the arbitration process. When the BAC acquires the iPSB bus, it returns the GRANT signal allowing the transfer to proceed.

Within the transfer cycle, the CPU uses the BAC to coordinate the handshake signals on the iPSB bus. Again, isolation is provided such that the host does not have to directly interface to iPSB bus System Control lines.

The BAC signals can be broken down into three categories (see fig. 5): (1) the iPSB interface, (2) the local bus interface, and (3) a register interface with the CPU.

iPSB BUS INTERFACE SIGNALS

These signals are concerned primarily with arbitration and system control. During the arbitration cycle, the arbitration ID is placed out on the iPSB bus through ARBOUT5-ARBOUT0. These lines are buffered through to the bus ARB lines. The BAC listens to the bus arbitration lines through signals defined as ARBIN4*-ARBIN0*. This is important for both an arbitration cycle and during initialization. The bus request line BREQ is divided into unidirectional signals IBREQ* and OBREQ* in a similar fashion.

The BAC also interfaces to the BUSERR* and TIMOUT* lines defined on the iPSB bus. Since the TIMOUT* signal can only be generated by the Central Services Module in a MULTIBUS II architecture environment, it is an input only signal to the BAC. The BUSERR* condition, though, can be generated as well as accepted by the BAC. Consequently, there are signals defined for each direction (IBUSERR* and OBUSERR).

The System Control (SC) interface from the BAC is bidirectional. Two external 5-bit transceivers are needed to buffer the ten SC lines (SC9*-SC0*). Hence, two transceiver control signals, SCOEH and SCOEL, are included to specify the direction of the signals.

Since the BAC has responsibility for generating Bus Errors, it has to be aware of parity errors detected on the AD lines of the iPSB bus. This byte parity is checked external to the BAC and input via PAR3-PAR0 signals; the BAC qualifies these signals and drives OBUSERR if any error is detected. Rounding out the array of iPSB bus interface signals are RESET, RSTNC*, LACHn, and the CLK signal. Each of these signals is input only, with external inverting provided on all but the RSTNC* line.

LOCAL BUS INTERFACE SIGNALS

Fundamentally, these signals are an isolated version of the System Control lines. That is, the host CPU (or MIC) communicates control information to the BAC so that the SC lines can be driven appropriately. Additionally, the

AP-256

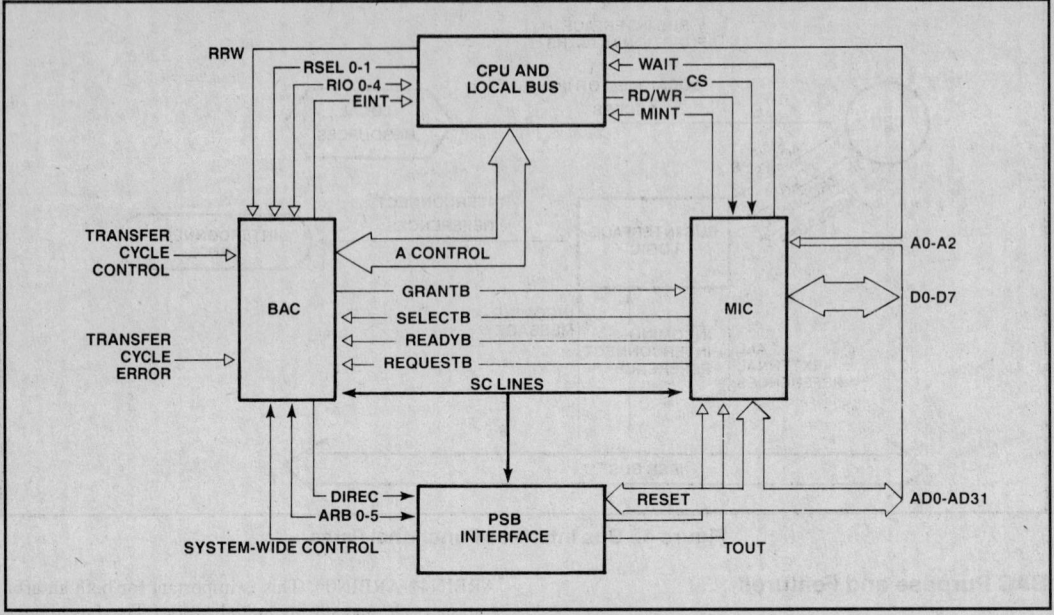

Figure 5. BAC/MIC Interfaces

BAC contains all arbitration logic. Should an agent require access to the iPSB bus (see fig. 6), it generates a REQUESTA(B) signal to the BAC. The BAC then arbitrates for the Bus, and upon acquiring it informs the requesting agent with a GRANTA(B) signal. Should the agent need a high priority request to the Bus, it can activate the PRIORITY line that ultimately ties to the ARB5* signal on the Bus. That is all there is to arbitration!

During the request phase of the transfer cycle, both the data width and address space must be specified by the requestor (see fig. 7). This is done by the CPU driving the encoded WIDTH1* & WIDTH0* lines in addition to the SPACE1* & SPACE0* lines. The WR* signal dictates a read or write transfer. When the information is accurately encoded, the CPU drives the READYA(B) signal. The BAC then, can proceed in driving the pertinent SC lines on the iPSB bus. During the same request phase, the agent at the other end of the transaction must alert its BAC that it has been selected as a replier. This is done simply by activating the SELECTA(B) signal.

During the reply phase, the requesting host must communicate its data across the AD lines. When the information is correctly signaled, the host simply activates the READY line again (see fig 8). When the replying host is ready to process the transaction, it can activate its READY line. Notice that these READY signals simply qualify data so that the BAC can activate the appropriate SC lines.

Further signals allow for block transfers, namely LASTINA and LASTINB. They allow the BAC to encode the SC2* line on the Bus during the reply phase. A LOCK* line is input to the BAC if a bus lock is requested. Also, a delayed SC3* (SC4*) signal is provided as an output to

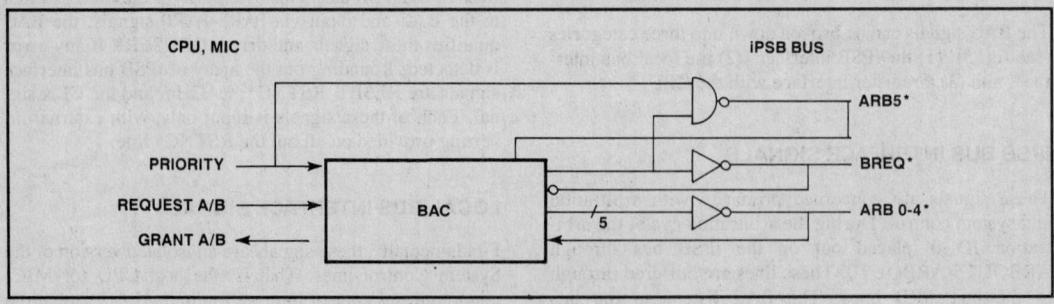

Figure 6. BAC Arbitration

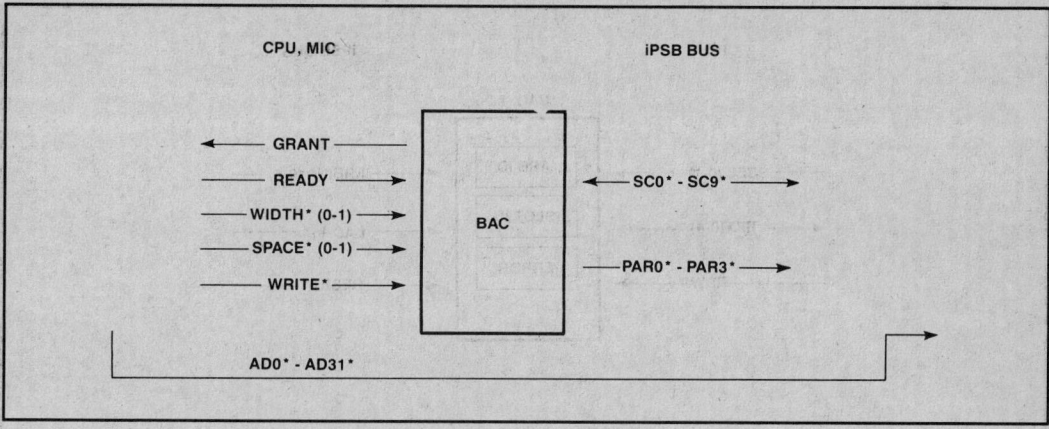

Figure 7. Transfer Cycle — Request Phase

the replying (requesting) agent during the reply phase. This signal is optional, though is does provide additional handshake control within a system.

Agent errors detected by the replier host are encoded into AGERR2-AGERR0 so that SC7*-SC5* can be properly activated during the reply phase. The requesting BAC signals the CPU via EINT if there has been an exception or agent error detected during the transfer.

REGISTER INTERFACE SIGNALS

This final set of signals provides the register interface between the local CPU and the BAC (see fig. 9). There are three registers, namely Arbitration ID, Slot ID, and Error Port. The registers are 5 bits wide so that data is transmitted via a 5-bit bus, RIO4-RIO0. They are addressed through RSEL1-RSEL0, and the direction of the transfer is indicated by the RRW signal. These three registers are accessed by a host to: (1) read slot ID, (2) read/write arbitration ID, and (3) service error conditions.

MIC — Purpose and Features

The MIC provides the interrupt capability to boards interfacing to the iPSB bus. These interrupts are implemented as virtual interrupts in message space. The MIC provides an interface to the local CPU through the local bus such that outgoing messages are buffered from the CPU. To send a message interrupt, the CPU simply writes a four byte message (identifying the source, destination, and type of message) to a port in the MIC. The MIC then insures that the message travels correctly to the destination.

For incoming interrupt messages, the MIC monitors the iPSB bus for its message address. Once detected, the accompanying message gets placed in a four-deep message queue. The MIC interrupts the CPU, whereby the CPU reads the queue contents to identify the source of the message.

The MIC works in close accord with the BAC device (see fig. 10). From the BAC's point of view, the MIC is a

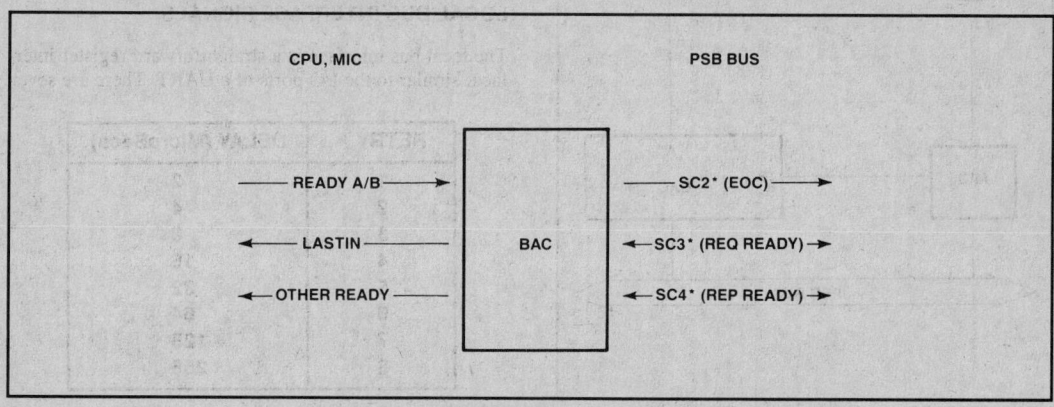

Figure 8. Transfer Cycle — Reply Phase

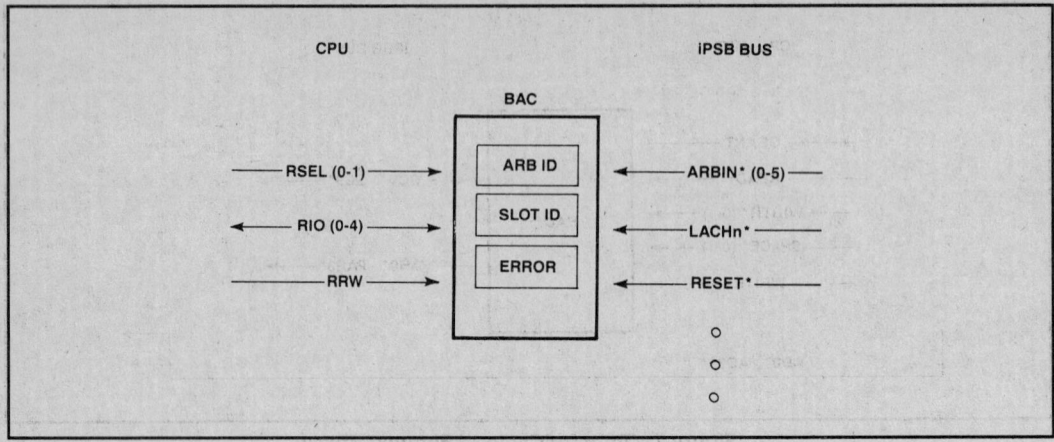

Figure 9. BAC Register Interface

CPU-like agent that it communicates with through the secondary or "B" interface. For example, all arbitration is done by the BAC on the MIC's behalf. Outgoing interrupts are such that the MIC communicates with the BAC to generate the proper control signals (SC7*-SC0*) on the iPSB bus. The actual address/data (AD*) lines are driven by the MIC directly.

The MIC's signals can be broken into basically three interfaces that will be discussed henceforward: (1) iPSB bus interface, (2) the local bus interface, and (3) the BAC interface (see figs. 5 & 10).

iPSB BUS INTERFACE SIGNALS

The iPSB bus interface signals support iPSB bus protocol of both a requesting and replying agent. As a requesting agent, the MIC is responsible for driving the address and data information onto the AD* lines at the appropriate time. If a message is negatively acknowledged (NACKed) by the replying agent, i.e., the queue for incoming messages at the receiving MIC is full, then the sending MIC will try again to send the message (after a time delay). This process continues with a geometric backoff scheme (see fig. 11) up to eight times before finally submitting an error-interrupt to its host processor on the local bus.

As a replying agent on the iPSB bus, the MIC listens to the AD* lines for an interrupt message directed to it. (The destination address matches its host identification). It then replies via BAC and queues the message in its four-deep FIFO. The local CPU can access the message through the register interface of the MIC.

LOCAL BUS INTERFACE SIGNALS

The local bus interface is a straightforward register interface, similar to the I/O ports of a UART. There are seven

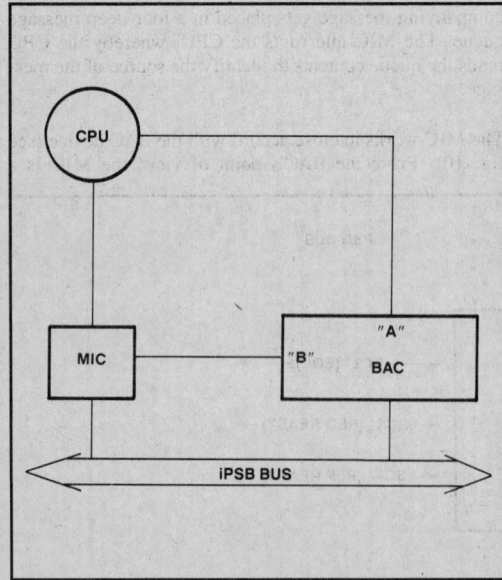

Figure 10. Generic MIC/BAC Interfaces

RETRY #	DELAY (MicroSecs)
1	2
2	4
3	8
4	16
5	32
6	64
7	128
8	256

Figure 11. MIC Retry Algorithm

NAME	READ/WRITE	FUNCTION
Status Register	Read	Used to indicate the status of transmit and receive FIFOs, transmisson error and failure to initialize the MIC after a Reset.
Host ID Register	Read/Write	Contains host CPU unique ID. Written only during initialization, read only during normal operation of the MIC.
Configuration Register	Read/Write	Allows the host CPU to configure static attributes of the MIC. Can be read any time. Written to only during initialization of the MIC.
Control Register	Read/Write	Allows the host CPU software to dynamically control the Interrupt Enables for different sources of interrupt in the MIC.
Command Register	Read/Write	Used for message synchronization between the host CPU and the MIC.
Data Port	Read/Write	Maps to the Message Transmit FIFO when written, and maps to the Message Receive FIFO when read.
Error Port	Read/Write	Host CPU reads this port in response to an interrupt and the ERROR STATUS bit is set in the status register. When written to, clears the ERROR STATUS bit in the status register.

Figure 12. MIC Register Definitions

registers/ports (see fig. 12) that can be addressed via three lines (A2-A0). The contents of the registers is accessed over 8 data lines (D7-D0); RD* and WR* signals simply determine the direction of the transfer. Further signals include a chip select (CS*), WAIT*, and MINT. The WAIT* signal puts the local CPU into wait states until the desired read/write register operation is completed. The message interrupt signal (MINT) signals three events: (1) there is something in the receive FIFO queue, (2) the transmit FIFO is available for use, and (3) there has been a transmit error of some kind. The reason for the interrupt is identified in the Status register.

INTERFACE SIGNALS TO THE BAC

The MIC/BAC interface is implemented through the secondary or "B" BAC agent interface. The MIC is responsible for driving the REQB, READYB, and SELB* lines to the BAC. In turn, the BAC drives the GRANTB signal back to the MIC (See BAC section for a description of these signals).

Further signals include MTOUT, DBERR*, and AGERR2-AGERR0. The MTOUT and DBERR* lines are input to the MIC to alert for exceptions found on the iPSB bus, namely TIMOUT and Bus Error. For incoming messages, the MIC is responsible for detecting an agent error and notifying the BAC through the AGERR lines. The BAC will then encode the iPSB bus System Control lines, alerting the requesting agent of the error.

THE BUS INTERFACE MULTIMODULE™ BOARD

At this point in the discussion, it is appropriate to look at Intel's bus interface MULTIMODULE board in detail. The schematic diagrams found in Appendix 1 are referenced throughout the description, and all PAL equations can be found in Appendix 2. The design (see fig. A-2) is broken into functional blocks: (1) interconnect control, (2) local control, (3) iPSB bus control, (4) interrupt message control, (5) local and interconnect buffering, and (6) iPSB bus buffering. These functional blocks work with each other to provide the total bus interface solution. As described briefly in the requirements section on page 3, this bus interface MULTIMODULE board supports specific activities as follows:

- Memory and I/O references from CPU to the iPSB bus

- Conversion of I/O references to local and iPSB bus interconnect references
- Incoming interconnect references from the iPSB bus
- Sending interrupt messages
- Receiving interrupt messages

Activities that stem from the local CPU, namely references to the iPSB bus, references to local interconnect space, and sending interrupt messages, all go through the local control block of the bus interface MULTIMODULE board. Here, the MULTIMODULE board can determine which of the three reference activities is desired. For references to the iPSB Bus, the local control block works with the iPSB bus control block. For references to local interconnect space, the local control block must work with the interconnect block. Finally, for sending interrupts, the interrupt message control block works with the local control block. Whatever the case, data has to move through internal architecture of the MULTIMODULE board. An internal S-bus (called out as SDATA15*-SDATA0* in fig. A-2) provides the pathway for data to travel between local bus, interconnect bus, and iPSB bus. Each bus interfaces to the S-bus through buffers that reside on the MULTIMODULE board.

Operations in the MULTIMODULE board may occur concurrently as well. Specifically, local references to interconnect space may occur simultaneous with incoming messages from the iPSB bus. Similarly, a CPU may access MULTIMODULE board registers while an incoming interconnect space reference from the iPSB bus is happening.

Local Control

From the CPU's point of view, all references and message operations go through the local control block. This block is implemented in two PALs, one to decode of the local processor signalling and one to control the local and interconnect buffers (see fig. A-3).

The local processor decoding logic determines what the local CPU wants to do. The CPU communicates through several groups of signals as it begins access to the iPSB bus, interconnect space on its own board, etc. Read and write lines, RD* and WR*, define the direction of the desired transaction. The data lines that are valid are determined by the encoded BE1* and BE0* lines. Furthermore, the CPU requests access to a specific address space by activating a series of Select lines. The MEMSEL* signal selects memory space, IOSEL* selects I/O space, and REGSEL* determines whether interconnect space or message space (both register interfaces) is to be accessed. Finally, local bus address lines (A5-A3) and data lines (D15-D14) determine whether interconnect references are local or over the iPSB bus.

The local processor decoding PAL (U20) looks at all of the incoming signals from the host processor in determining the type of transaction that is required. An AND gate (U26) is used to combine the MEMSEL* and IOSEL* lines into one MEMIOS* signal. The PAL then looks at the select lines, byte enable lines, address lines, data lines, and RD* and WR* lines to determine which control signals to activate (see fig. B-10). For example, if the CPU wants to access the MIC's registers (to initiate an interrupt message), it drives the local bus address lines accordingly along with REGSEL*. The MIC's register addresses are defined in a range below 20H (see fig 13), therefore A5 low signals a MIC access request. The control logic responds by sending a MICSEL* signal to the MIC.

Should the CPU want to access interconnect space (anywhere), it writes to two registers, IADRH and IADRL (see fig. 14). They are defined at I/O location 31H and 30H respectively, and encode the slot ID and the interconnect register that the CPU wants to access. The CPU then writes/reads to the data register to complete the interconnect access request. The local processor decoding logic determines whether the access is on board, or must go over the iPSB bus. Slot numbers 0-23 refer to iPSB bus accesses, and 24-31 dictate local (including iLBX II) access. Since the slot number is encoded in D15-D11, D15 and D14 determine where the access is. Local interconnect accesses cause the LICREQ signal to go active, while iPSB bus accesses cause the PSBREQ signal to go active. Additionally, the logic decodes a iPSB bus access request to memory or I/O space and generates the PSBREQ signal. Note that the LICREQ signal connects to the interconnect control block while PSBREQ goes to the iPSB bus control block.

The local processor decoding PAL also determines if the local CPU has to be placed into wait states. For example, when a local interconnect request is desired, the WAIT* signal is driven active until the operation is completed. Should the processor wish to access the MIC's internal register bank, the WAIT* signal is simply an extension of the MIC's wait signal.

The other PAL that provides the local bus control is the Local and Interconnect Buffer Control device (U11). It is solely responsible for generating the buffer control signals to the Local and Interconnect buffers that are described below. It has inputs from the local processor (byte enable lines), the interconnect control block (RIADRH, RIADRL, and RIDATA), iPSB bus control block (PSBRD and PSBDAT), the BAC (LOCGNT), and the other local control PAL (PSBREQ, LICREQ and MICSEL). The idea simply, is to coordinate the S-bus with the local bus and interconnect bus. Data is latched and driven according to the logic operations performed on the listed input signals (refer to figure B-3 for precise logic).

AP-256

PORT ADDRESS	MEANING
30 H	Interconnect Address High
34/31 H*	Interconnect Address High
3C H	Interconnect Data
Note: *To be compatible with new silicon, write to both 34 H and 31 H for high address, followed by 30 H for low address.	

Figure 13. Local Bus I/O Address Map

Interrupt Message Control

The logic that performs the control of interrupt messages is of course the MIC (see fig. A-6). It interfaces with the host CPU directly (e.g., RD* line) and also through the local processor decode logic (e.g., MICSEL*) as mentioned above. The MIC interface to the BAC (within the iPSB bus control block) are exactly the same as was described in the introductory sections of this paper.

Interconnect Control

The Interconnect control portion of the bus interface MULTIMODULE board deals with implementing the Interconnect bus and associated protocols between itself and the microcontroller where the interconnect space implementation resides. Interconnect space requests can come from two sources: the local CPU and the iPSB bus. Should the request come from the CPU, the local control

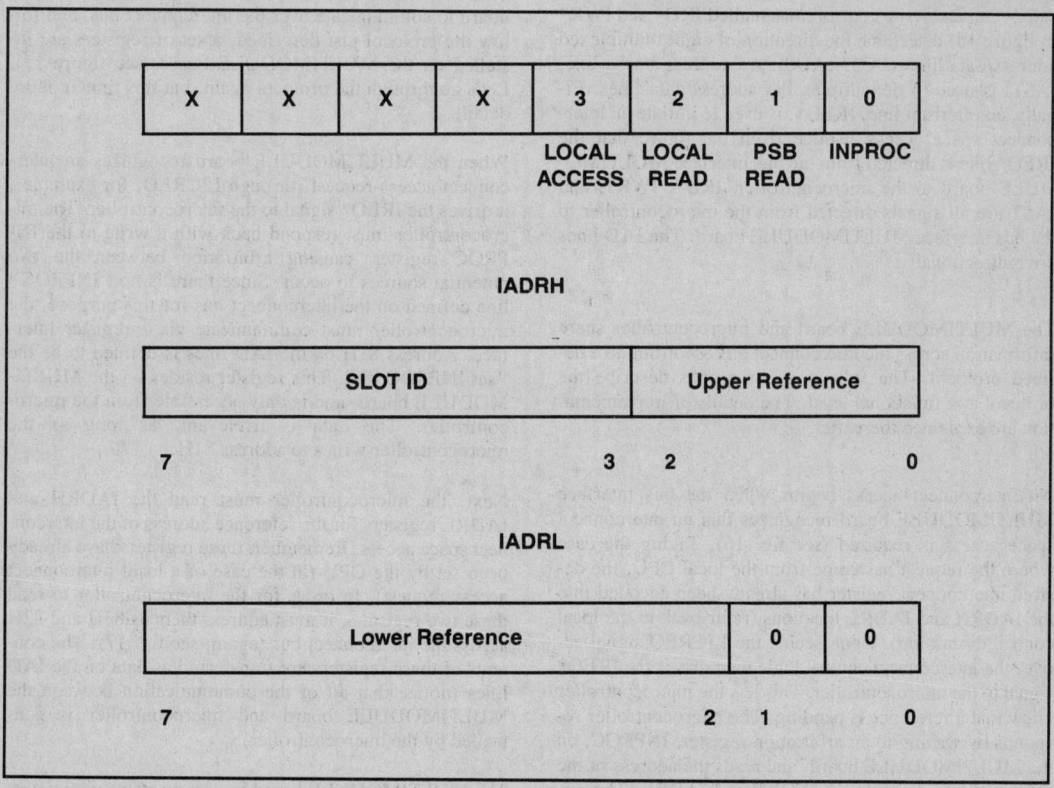

Figure 14. Interconnect Register Breakout

intel AP-256

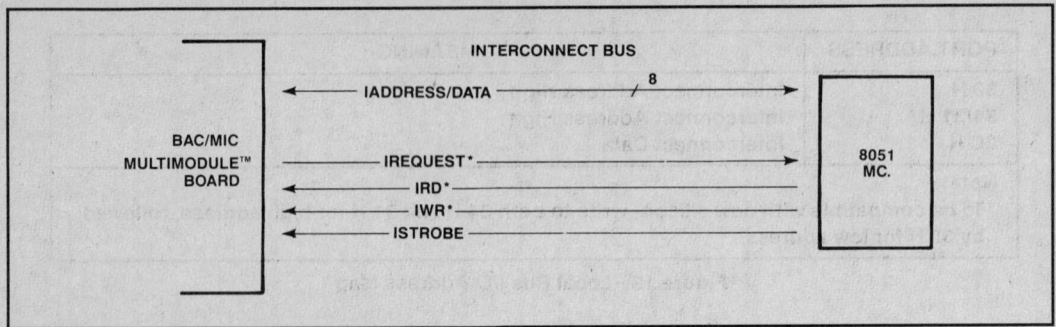

Figure 15. Interconnect Space Implementation

block activates a LICREQ signal. Similarly, a request from the iPSB bus causes the iPSB control block to activate a PICREQ signal. In either case, the interconnect control block causes an access of the interconnect register on the microcontroller via an interconnect bus.

The Interconnect bus consists of just a few signals. Basically, read and write control lines (called IRD* and IWR* in figure 15) determine the direction of eight multiplexed address/data lines (IAD7-IAD0). An address strobe line, IAST, is used to demultiplex the address/data lines. Finally, an interrupt line, IREQ*, is used to initiate an interconnect space access. Notice from the figure that the IREQ* line is directed from the bus interface MULTIMODULE board to the microcontroller. IRD*, IWR*, and IAST are all signals directed from the microcontroller to the bus interface MULTIMODULE board. The IAD lines are bidirectional.

The MULTIMODULE board and microcontroller share information across the interconnect bus according to a defined protocol. The following paragraphs describe the protocol at a functional level. The details of implementation are explained thereafter.

An interconnect access begins when the bus interface MULTIMODULE board recognizes that an interconnect space access is required (see fig. 16). Taking the case where the request has come from the local CPU, the desired interconnect register has already been encoded into the IADRH and IADRL locations (refer back to the local control discussion). Upon seeing the LICREQ signal active, the interconnect control logic then drives the IREQ* signal to the microcontroller. This lets the microcontroller know that a reference is pending. The microcontroller responds by writing to an arbitration register, INPROC, on the MULTIMODULE board, and reads the address of the reference which resides in IADRH and IADRL. The microcontroller then reads status information on the MULTIMODULE board to determine (1) the source of the request and (2) that the reference address is valid.

It becomes the microcontroller's responsibility then to decode the address information and perform the necessary operations to service the request. When the microcontroller has completed the operations, it sends the data to the bus interface MULTIMODULE, and the data is finally carried over the local bus to the CPU.

In order for the microcontroller and MULTIMODULE board to communicate over the interconnect bus, and follow the protocol just described, a set of registers are installed on the MULTIMODULE board (see figure 17). Let's go through the protocol again, but this time in more detail.

When the MULTIMODULE board recognizes an interconnect access request (through LICREQ, for example), it drives the IREQ* signal to the microcontroller. The microcontroller must respond back with a write to the INPROC register, causing arbitration between the two potential sources to occur. Since there is no "INPROC" line defined on the interconnect bus for this purpose, the microcontroller must communicate via a register interface. Address 81H on the IAD lines is defined to be the "set INPROC bit". This register resides on the MULTIMODULE board, and is only accessible from the microcontroller. The data is irrelevant, as long as the microcontroller writes to address 81H.

Next, the microcontroller must read the IADRH and IADRL registers for the reference address of the interconnect space access. Remember, these registers have already been set by the CPU (in the case of a local interconnect access request). In order for the microcontroller to read these two registers, it must address them as 83H and 82H across the interconnect bus (again, see fig. 17). The contents of these registers are transferred as data on the IAD lines (notice that all of the communication between the MULTIMODULE board and microcontroller is controlled by the microcontroller).

The MULTIMODULE board has set up status parameters to indicate (1) if it is a local or iPSB reference (who the source is), (2) whether the desired operation will be read or write, and (3) if the INPROC bit is still set, verifying

16-58

280132-001

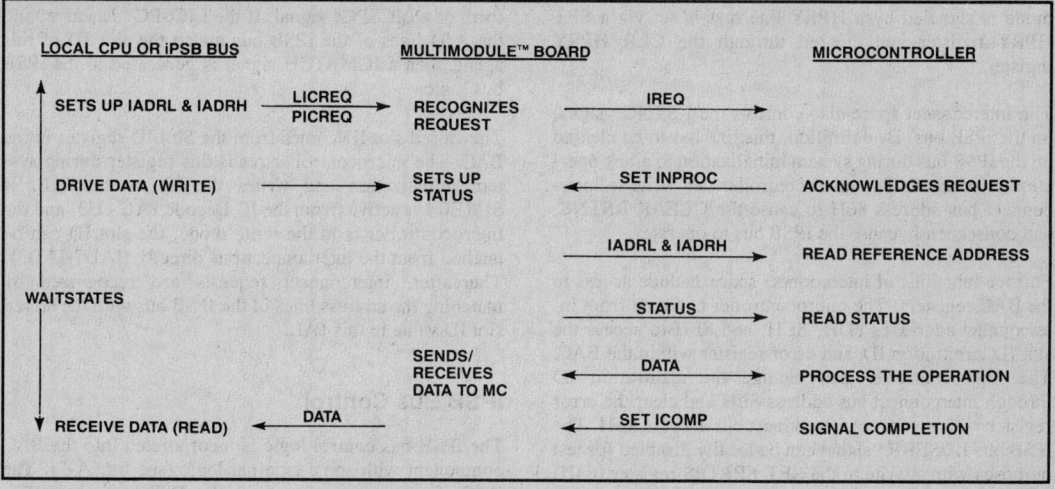

Figure 16. Interconnect Access Protocol

IADRH and IADRL (see figure 14). The interconnect microcontroller can read this status register, RISTAT, through interconnect bus address 80H. If a timeout or bus error has occurred on the bus, the status register will indicate (through lack of INPROC) that the IADRL and IADRH registers contain invalid data and to halt the reference access.

Data is finally transmitted via the DATA register. The microcontroller either reads (RIDATA) or writes (WIDATA) to this register depending on the desired operation. The interconnect bus operation is completed when the microcontroller performs a write to bus address 80H, which sets the ICOMPL bit. In the case of an interconnect request from the local CPU, the WAIT* signal is deactivated and the data is read by the CPU through its local bus address 3CH, the data register. If the data is to go on the iPSB bus, the iPSB control block drives the A/D lines and handshakes with SC4* (replier ready).

There are a few remaining registers concerned with iPSB bus access control that can be addressed over the interconnect bus to implement specific interconnect space functions. For example, the microcontroller can determine if iPSB bus arbitration is to be in high priority mode for that particular bus agent. The high priority access

READ FUNCTION	WRITE FUNCTION	ADDRESS
RISTAT	SET ICOMPL	80H
------	SET INPROC	81H
RIADRL	SET HPRY	82H
RIADRH	CLR HPRY	83H
------	SET ERRDIS	84H
------	CLR ERRDIS	85H
------	CLR RSTNC	86H
------	CSLREG	87H
RIDATA	WIDATA	88H
------	------	89H
------	------	8AH
------	------	8BH
------	------	8CH
SLOT ID	------	8DH
ARB ID	ARB ID	8EH
ERROR REG	ERROR CLEAR	8FH

Figure 17. Interconnect Bus Registers (Accessed by Microcontroller)

mode is signaled by a HPRY line that is set via a SET HPRY register and cleared through the CLR HPRY register.

The interconnect space also controls the RSTNC* signal on the iPSB bus. By definition, this line has to be cleared on the iPSB bus during system initialization to allow operation to proceed. The microcontroller can write to interconnect bus address 86H to cause the CLEAR RSTNC, and consequently cause the iPSB bus to operate.

Further functions of interconnect space include access to the BAC registers. The microcontroller can read from interconnect addresses 8DH, 8EH, and 8FH to access the slot ID, arbitration ID, and error register within the BAC. The microcontroller can change the arbitration ID through interconnect bus address 8EH and clear the error register with a write to interconnect bus address 8FH. The iPSB bus BUSERR* signal can be locally disabled for test purposes with a write to the SET ERRDIS register (84H) and cleared by a write to the CLR ERRDIS register (85H).

All of the aforementioned interconnect control functions are implemented in three PAL devices (16L8s), as shown in figure A-4. The Interconnect Address Latch and Decode PAL (U13) interfaces directly with the interconnect bus and latches the IAD lines when the IAST strobe is active. Furthermore, it implements three register select signals: RIADRL*, RIADRH*, and RISTAT*.

Latched interconnect address lines are decoded in the Interconnect Decode PAL (U3). Here, the ARSTNC, WIDATA*, RIDATA*, and CSLREG* signals are generated. Further decoding is done here to enable communications with the BAC internal registers, namely SLOT ID, ARBITRATION ID, and ERROR register. A cascading signal, WSEL*, enables the Interconnect Control PAL (U2).

The remainder of the interconnect bus registers are implemented in the IC Control PAL. Specifically, the INPROC and ICOMPL bits can be set, and the HPRY and ERRDIS signals can be activated and cleared. The PAL is also responsible for some interconnect control functions. Specifically, it recognizes the PICREQ and LICREQ signals. In both cases, this logic generates the actual interconnect bus request signal, IREQ*, to the microcontroller. Also, interconnect space lock requests coming from both the local bus and iPSB bus are recognized.

The final device that is incorporated within the Interconnect Control section of the bus interface MULTIMODULE board is the Slot ID Latch and Matcher (PAL20L8A in U18). The most important function of this logic device is to listen to the latched address/data lines of the iPSB bus and recognize interconnect requests to its own slot ID. The system control lines of the iPSB bus are decoded elsewhere during the request phase of a transfer cycle. Thus an interconnect space access request comes in from the other logic (the iPSB bus control block) in the form of a LICSPC* signal. If the LICSPC* is active, and the A/D lines of the iPSB bus match the slot ID of this agent, then a ICMATCH signal is generated to the iPSB bus logic.

The stored slot ID comes from the Slot ID register in the BAC. The microcontroller reads this register during system initialization and writes the ID to the PAL. If SLREG* is active (from the IC Decode PAL - U3) and the microcontroller is in the write mode, the slot ID can be latched from the interconnect bus directly (IAD7-IAD3). Thereafter, interconnect requests are recognized by matching the address lines of the iPSB bus with the stored slot ID value in this PAL.

iPSB Bus Control

The iPSB bus control logic is incorporated into the BAC component with some external logic (see fig. A-7). The BAC of course, interfaces with the iPSB bus control signals. It interfaces also with both the MIC component and the local CPU, each being an iPSB bus host. The implementation consists of the BAC with some external logic. Error signals from the MIC are ORed together with errors detected by dual-port memory (if DP memory is installed in your baseboard) and connected to the agent error signals of the BAC. Also, the REGSEL signal is ANDed and inverted with the BAC's local grant signal so that the CPU can drive the reference address of a memory or I/O space access. Note that the bus interface MULTIMODULE board itself does not provide the reference address of such operations.

The BAC interface signals, as they were described in the introductory section, differ in their naming convention on the bus interface MULTIMODULE board. Specifically, the agent interfaces are defined according to where the signals are generated. For example, the register interface of the BAC consists of two RSEL signals, the 5 RIO data lines, and a RRW signal. On the bus interface MULTIMODULE board, the RSEL and RRW signals are tied to the three BACADR lines that are generated in the interconnect control logic discussed in a previous section. The data lines go to the interconnect bus, IADR4-IADR0. The three agent error signals, AGERR2-AGERR0, are tied to the ORed agent error signal from the MIC and host defined above.

The iPSB bus request lines, REQA and REQB, are connected to their respective agent request lines, BACREQ (from the iPSB bus control PALS) and MSGREQ (tied to the MIC request line). Similarly, the SELECT and READY signals are traced to the iPSB bus control and MIC logic devices. When the BAC activates a bus GRANT to the local processor, the signal goes both to the local bus control logic, as well as the iPSB bus control logic. For interconnect operations, the address flows from the local bus, through the S-bus, and finally onto the iPSB bus. For other accesses, the address is driven directly by the CPU. The bus GRANT signal that is relevant to the MIC is sent solely to the MIC, as it has its own direct interface to the iPSB bus (BAD15-BAD0). The LASTIN, LASTOUT, OTHERREADY, and BROADCAST signals are not used in this design.

The rest of the logic that is required to implement the iPSB bus control interface is encoded in three PAL devices. PAL number one (U12) listens to the System Control lines on the iPSB bus to qualify different parameters. For instance, during the request phase of the transfer cycle, the logic activates the PSBDAT buffer control signal upon receipt of the signal from the BAC that the iPSB bus request has been granted (LOCGNT). Data can then move through the S-bus, out onto the iPSB bus.

PAL U12 also controls interconnect accesses from the iPSB bus. An interconnect request signal, PICREQ, is driven if the slot ID matches this agent (ICMATCH), and it is a RD operation. PICREQ is also signaled during a write operation when Requester Ready goes active on the iPSB bus, assuming an ICMATCH. the local processor. Also, note that the PICREQ gets ORed with a memory request, to form a SELECT line to the BAC. This informs the BAC that this agent has been selected to participate in the transfer cycle by another agent, and hence should generate the proper handshake signals over the iPSB bus.

A second PAL (U5) drives the BACREQ and PSBRDY signals. It acts as an asynchronous latch between the local bus and the BAC. BACREQ connects directly to the A-level Request line of the BAC, after being synchronized through a 74F374 (U4). The PSBRDY signal (1) controls the local buffer and (2) deactivates the local WAIT signal during the request phase of a transfer.

The third PAL (U6) generates the RDYA, ENPSB, and ENLCH lines. RDYA is a synchronized control signal that connects to the BAC's READYA pin. The iPSB bus buffer control signal ENLCH, is used to enable the interconnect reference address registers IADRH and IADRL, to be read by the microcontroller during interconnect operations. These registers are latched from the BAD lines of the iPSB bus during the request phase when another agent wants to access interconnect space on this board.

The ENPSB signal controls the 74LS245s that buffer the iPSB bus BAD lines from the internal S-bus. The iPSB buffers are turned towards the iPSB bus when the address access conditions are right. For example, when a memory space access is requested through MEMSEL and the grant signal has been shown, the iPSB bus buffers can be activated through the ENPSB line. The same line is activated in the case of interconnect accesses as well.

Local And Interconnect Buffering

Buffering between the local bus, the interconnect bus, and the internal S bus is provided through the latches shown in figure A-5.

Two 74AS651 latches are used to implement the buffering between the local bus, D15-D0, and the internal S bus, SDATA15*- SDATA0*. Buffer control signals stem from the Local Control logic described above (LGBA*, LGABH, LGABL, LSBA, LSAB, IADRH*, AND IADRL*). In addition, the PSBRDY line generated in the iPSB bus control logic enables the buffers to latch SDATA signals into the AS651 which is in turn driven onto the local bus.

A 74LS240 device is used to buffer the interconnect bus with the high byte of the S-bus, lines SDATA15*-SDATA8*. The buffer enable signal, RIADH*, comes from the interconnect control logic discussed earlier. The interconnect microcontroller reads the high byte of the reference address through this buffer.

The interconnect data is communicated through a 74AS651 latch. The same interconnect bus address/data lines as described above are interfaced to the low order byte of the internal S-bus, SDATA7*-SDATA0*. RIDATA* and WIDATA* signals from the microcontroller (through the interconnect bus registers) are the key control lines to the buffer.

The final device that is included with the Local and Interconnect Buffering portion of the bus interface MULTIMODULE board is a 74LS244. This device implements the status register of the interconnect bus communications protocol. When a RISTAT* signal is detected, the four relevant bits of the register are passed through to the interconnect bus, lines IAD3-IAD0. Specifically, the RD*, LOCACC*, PSBRD*, and INPROC signals are passed as status to the microcontroller during a RISTAT.

iPSB Bus Buffering

The iPSB bus buffering portion of the bus interface design (see fig. A-10) is responsible for (1) detecting and generating parity for the address/data lines of the iPSB bus and (2) latching address/data information onto the internal S-bus depending on System Control handshakes on the iPSB bus.

The parity generators are implemented on four 74F280 devices. All 32 bits of the buffered address/data lines are included in the parity process. Four signals (XPAR3*-XPAR0*) are generated and buffered through a 74LS244, where they are called BPAR3*-BPAR0*.

Parity error detection is done on the lower 16 bits of the buffer A/D lines only in this MULTIMODULE board design. Two 74F280 components generate two parity error signals: PARERR1* and PARERR0*. These signals are transmitted over to the BAC and connect through the lower two bits (PAR0* and PAR1*) of the parity error matrix. Parity checking on the higher 16 bits can be done on the host board. Any parity errors on these bits may be indicated via PARERR2* and PARERR3* which are connected to the BAC (PAR2* and PAR3*). Note that parity checking on the upper 16 bits is only necessary if the agent (1) is 32-bit or (2) replies on the bus in memory space.

Sixteen buffered A/D lines interface to the internal S-bus by two 74LS245s. The direction of the communication is controlled by a directional signal from the BAC. The buffers are enabled by the ENPSB* signal generated by the iPSB bus control logic. The information that is communicated through this interface enables the data path for iPSB bus reference and interconnect operations.

Finally, three PALs are used to interface the buffered System Control lines that determine request phase and replier ready, along with the A/D lines, to the internal S-bus. All PALs are 16R6B latches that are clocked by direct interface to the buffered BCLK signal and are enabled by the ENLCH* signal generated by the iPSB bus control logic.

One PAL (U23) listens to the System Control lines (on the iPSB bus) to define the address space desired during the request phase of the transfer cycle. Should the space be interconnect space, the PAL generates a LICSPC* signal that tells the slot ID matcher logic (in the interconnect control portion of the design) to wake up and determine a match. During the reply phase, the S-bus latches the buffered A/D lines when the replier signals that the data is valid with the SC4* line. This would allow a read transfer cycle to be completed.

Latching is also done for the slot ID matcher in interconnect accesses. The five highest order bits of the word, A/D lines 15 through 11, are buffered into a separate group defined as LSPB15*-LSPB11*. These signals are transmitted to the slot ID matcher within the interconnect control logic to determine the correct interconnect request address and begin the local interconnect communication.

EXAMPLE SCENARIOS

Now that the design of the BAC/MIC MULTIMODULE board has been discussed in detail, two specific examples are now presented. Both are taken from the Intel environment where the MULTIMODULE board resides on the SBC 286/100 CPU card. Example 1 describes the case of the 80286 accessing its own interconnect space. Example 2 then looks at an interrupt message request that must have access to the iPSB bus. The Bus Interface MULTIMODULE board is the primary interface vehicle to accomplish both of these accesses.

Example 1 — Read Your Own Class ID Register In Interconnect Space

The task the host CPU (80286) would like to accomplish is an access of its own interconnect space. Specifically, it would like to look up its class ID, which is encoded in interconnect register 11H within the 8751 microcontroller.

The scenario begins when the CPU generates a local interconnect request (LICREQ) to the MULTIMODULE board (see fig. 18). This is done by addressing the IADRH and IADRL registers across the local bus, and reading the interconnect data register. The slot ID is 31 (11111) and the reference address is 11H. Consequently, the CPU writes a F8H to address 31H and a 44H to address 30H, followed by a read to address 3CH. The CPU is held in wait states until the access is completed. [Note that compatibility with the message passing component can be achieved if one consecutively writes the high byte of the address to both 34H and 31H.]

Next, the MULTIMODULE board activates the interrupt line, IREQ* going to the microcontroller. At this point, all future communication across the interconnect bus is controlled from the microcontroller side.

When the microcontroller recognizes the request, it signals back an INPROC to the MULTIMODULE board. Again, there is no INPROC line that is defined on the bus, so the signal must be encoded in the interconnect register interface (refer back to fig. 16 for register definitions). Specifically, the microcontroller writes to interconnect address 81H (data is "don't care").

Simultaneous with the above, the MULTIMODULE board logic sets up the status information as it arbitrates between the local request and any requests coming over the bus. In this case it establishes that it is a local access and that a read operation is to be performed.

At this point the microcontroller is in control of the communications. It must go access the IADRH and IADRL registers through interconnect addresses 83H and 82H. Next, it reads the status register, address 80H to determine that it is a local read and that INPROC is still set (implying that the IADRH and IADRL just read are valid).

The microcontroller then, must perform a read operation of its register number 11H. When the data (class ID) is available, the microcontroller drives it back through interconnect Data register, 88H where it is latched. The microcontroller signals completion of the operation by writing to interconnect register 80H (ICOMP), causing WAIT* to go inactive. The CPU reads the value over local bus address 3CH.

Example 2 — Generating a Virtual Interrupt to Another Agent

In this example, the goal is for the 80286 to generate an interrupt to another agent across the iPSB bus. Because interrupts are encoded in a message, the protocols for message generation, transmission, and reception at the

	INTERCONNECT BUS	
ACTION	ADR	DATA
1. CPU sets up IADRL & IADRH and generates LICREQ IADRH = 1 1 1 1 1 0 0 0 IADRL = 0 1 0 0 0 1 0 0		
2. MULTIMODULE board generates IREQ to microcontroller		
3. Microcontroller writes to arbitration register (INPROC)	81	—
4. MULTIMODULE board sets Local Access and Local Read bits in Status Register		
5. Microcontroller reads Interconnect Reference address	83 82	IADRH IADRL
6. Microcontroller validates address by reading status	80	STATUS
7. Microcontroller drives data back and sets ICOMP	88 80	CLASS ID —
8. CPU can access data over local bus		

Figure 18. Example Interconnect Access Read Your Own Class ID Register:

other end have to be followed. In other words (see fig. 19), the 80286 must formulate the message and pass it to the message FIFO within its bus interface MULTIMODULE board. Then, the initiating bus interface must converse with the receiving agent's bus interface logic in order to transmit the message. Finally, the receiving agent's bus interface must interrupt its CPU, and pass the actual message through its FIFO interface.

To begin, the sending CPU has to get the interrupt message to its bus interface MULTIMODULE board (see fig. 20). The CPU does this by generating a REGSEL signal that goes through decoding logic to cause a MICSEL to the MIC. This of course causes the MIC to activate its register interface. The CPU writes the message (4 bytes) to its MIC, which enters the sending FIFO. The four bytes characterize the message for the source, destination, message type (00 = interrupt), and a local ID in case there is an error later (see fig. 21A). At this point the sending CPU can go away and do something else. The bus interface will send the interrupt across the iPSB bus, and only report back if the transmission was unsuccessful (see fig. 21C).

The sending MIC now has the message. It must arbitrate for the bus through the REQUEST signal to the BAC. Upon receiving a GRANT, the MIC drives the message out onto the iPSB bus (see fig. 22). The receiving MIC (on the other end) is listening for message space accesses to its address. When the receiving MIC recognizes the message, it stores the message in its FIFO, selects its BAC to handshake back, and finally interrupts its CPU through the MINT signal.

The receiving CPU then looks at the MIC's status register to determine the cause of the interrupt. The CPU then goes to the MIC's receive FIFO and reads out the message, one byte at a time (Note - the first read gives a 4, saying that four bytes are in the message). Assuming that there has been no errors, the operation is complete. If an error has occurred, the sending MIC, and then in turn the sending CPU will be alerted through a MINT interrupt and an encoded ERROR register.

CONCLUSION

The task of designing interface logic for the iPSB bus of MULTIBUS II architecture has been made easier through the introduction of the BAC and MIC components. The silicon manages message based interrupts, arbitration, transfer cycles, and exception cycles as defined by the MULTIBUS II Architecture Specification. Intel has designed a bus interface MULTIMODULE board that incorporates all of these functions, and also implements

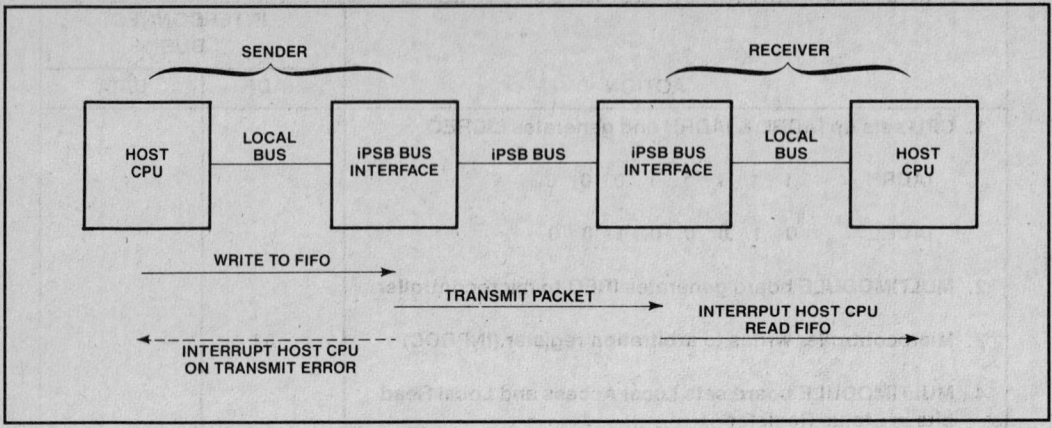

Figure 19. Interrupt Message

interconnect space. A board designer can follow the design described in this paper, and achieve full MULTIBUS II architecture interface capability, with the exception of full message passing.

Intel expects to use the full message passing bus silicon when it is availble. By designing the bus interface on a MULTIMODULE board, the future silicon can be easily integrated into existing board designs through a defined interface. Furthermore, by documenting the design in this paper, Intel is advocating that other board designers follow the same strategy.

Acknowledgements

The author would like to graciously thank Paula Brown, John Beaston, and Pete MacWilliams for their helpful comments in completing this application note.

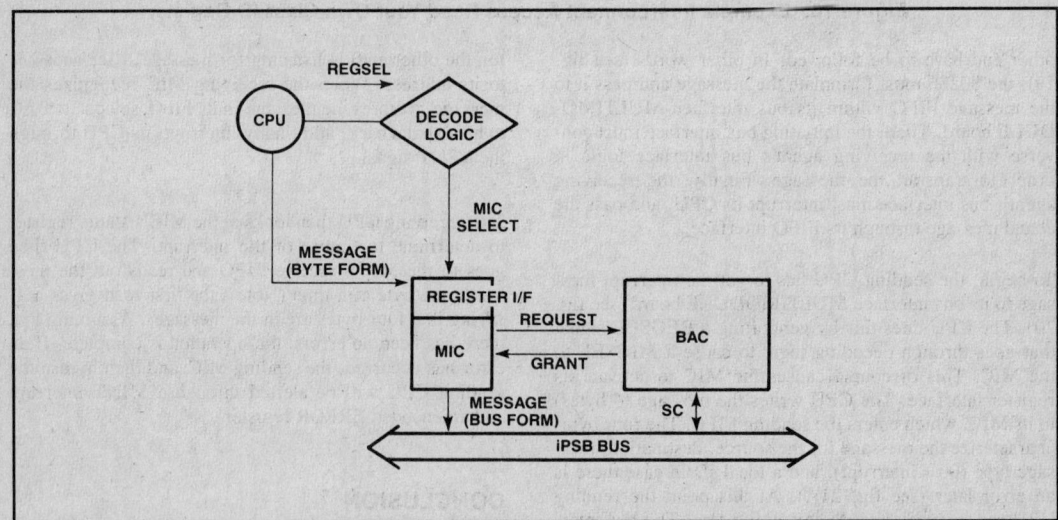

Figure 20. Generating a Virtual Interrupt

(A) Interrupt Byte	(A) Msg. Sent Meaning	(B) Interrupt Byte	(B) Msg. Sent Meaning	(C)*	(C)* Error Packet
1	Dest	1	Dest	1	Dest
2	Source	2	Source	2	Source
3	00 (Message Type)	3	Message Type	3	00 (Message Type)
4	Req ID	4	Reserved	4	Error Code

*NOTE: ERROR CODE = _ _ 0 _ |— REQ ID —|
                    ↑ ↑   ↑
                    Time Bus Retry
                    Out Error Expired

Figure 21. Message Structure (From CPU View)

TRANSFER CYCLE PHASE	AD31-24	AD23-16	AD15-8	AD7-0
Request phase (command)	Invalid	Invalid	Source	Destination
Reply phase (handshake)	Not used but must have valid parity	Not used but must have valid parity	Type specific	Message type (00)

Figure 22. Message to the iPSB Bus

APPENDIX A

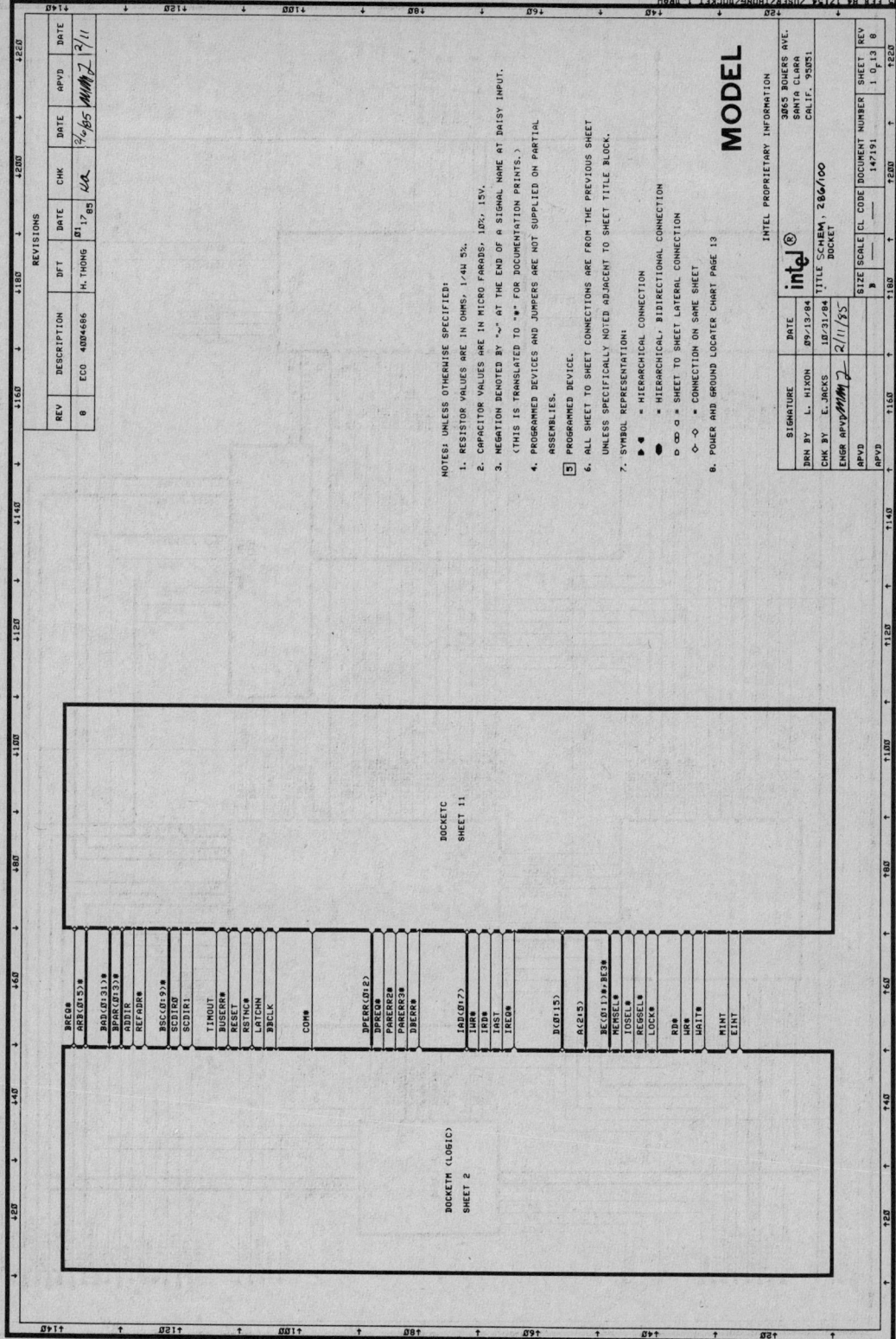

Figure A-1.

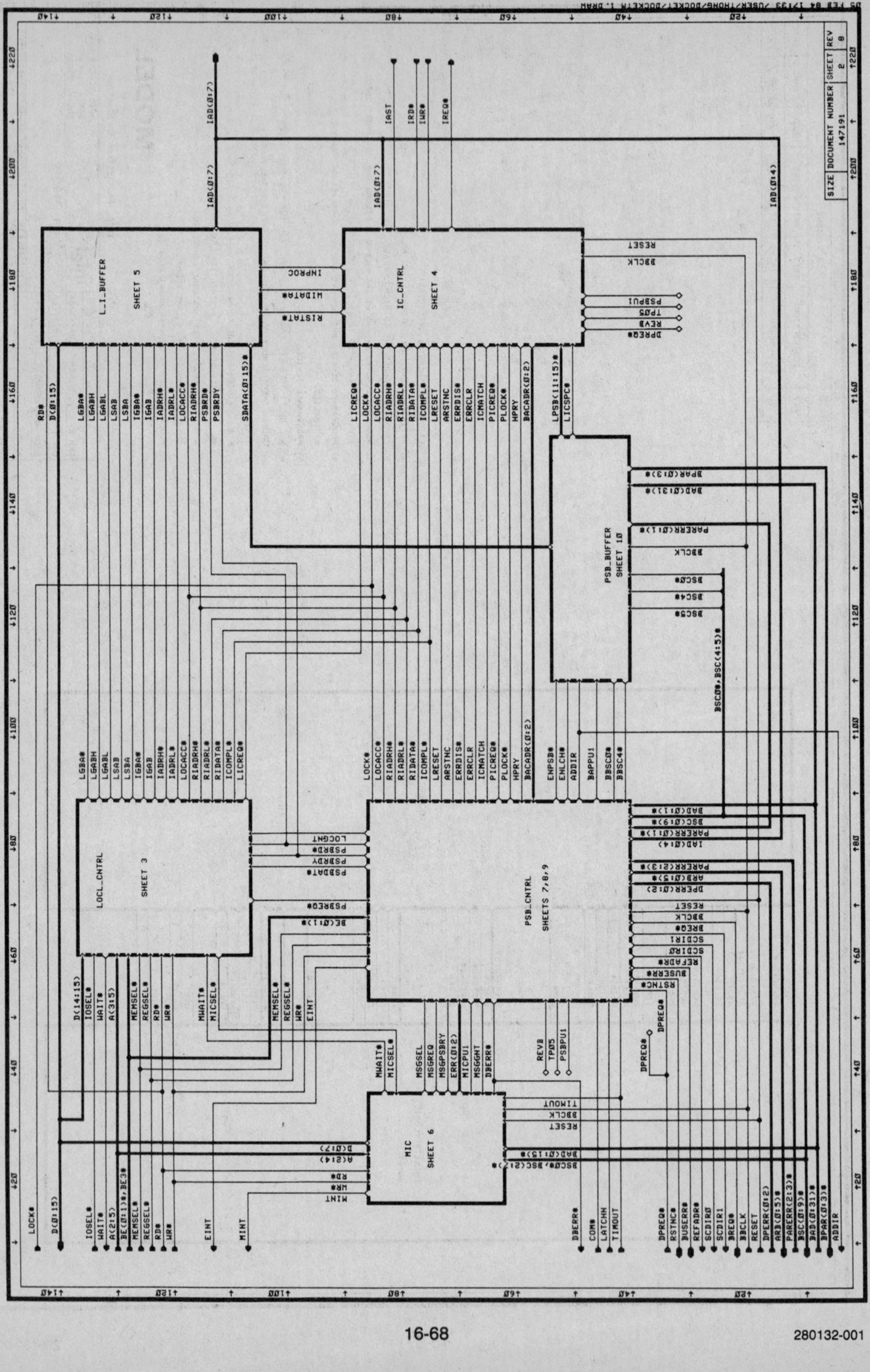
L.I_BUFFER
SHEET 5
IC_CNTRL
SHEET 4
PSB_BUFFER
SHEET 10
LOCL_CNTRL
SHEET 3
PSB_CNTRL
SHEETS 7,8,9
MIC
SHEET 6
SIZE
DOCUMENT NUMBER
147191
SHEET
2
REV
8

Figure A-2.

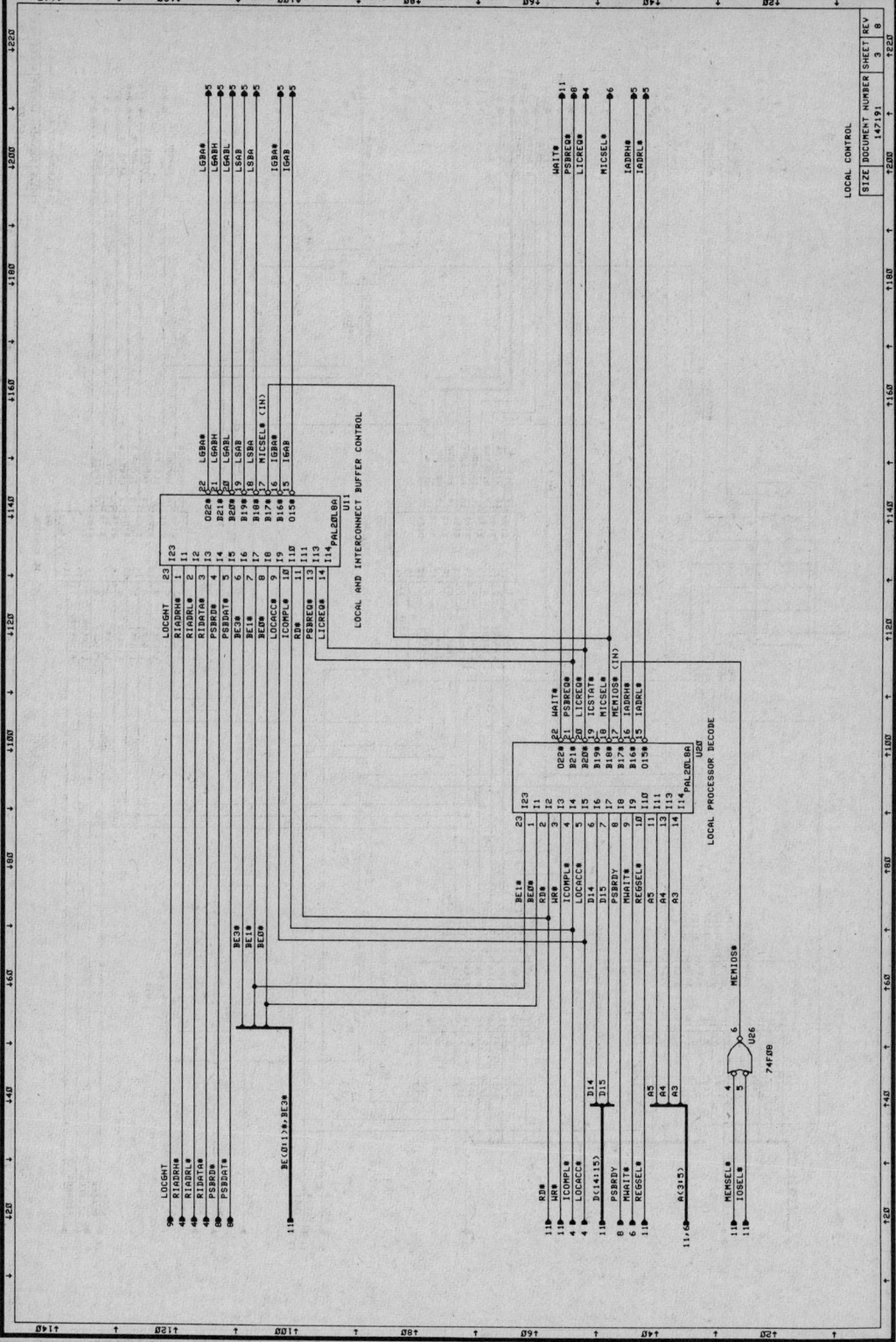

Figure A-3.

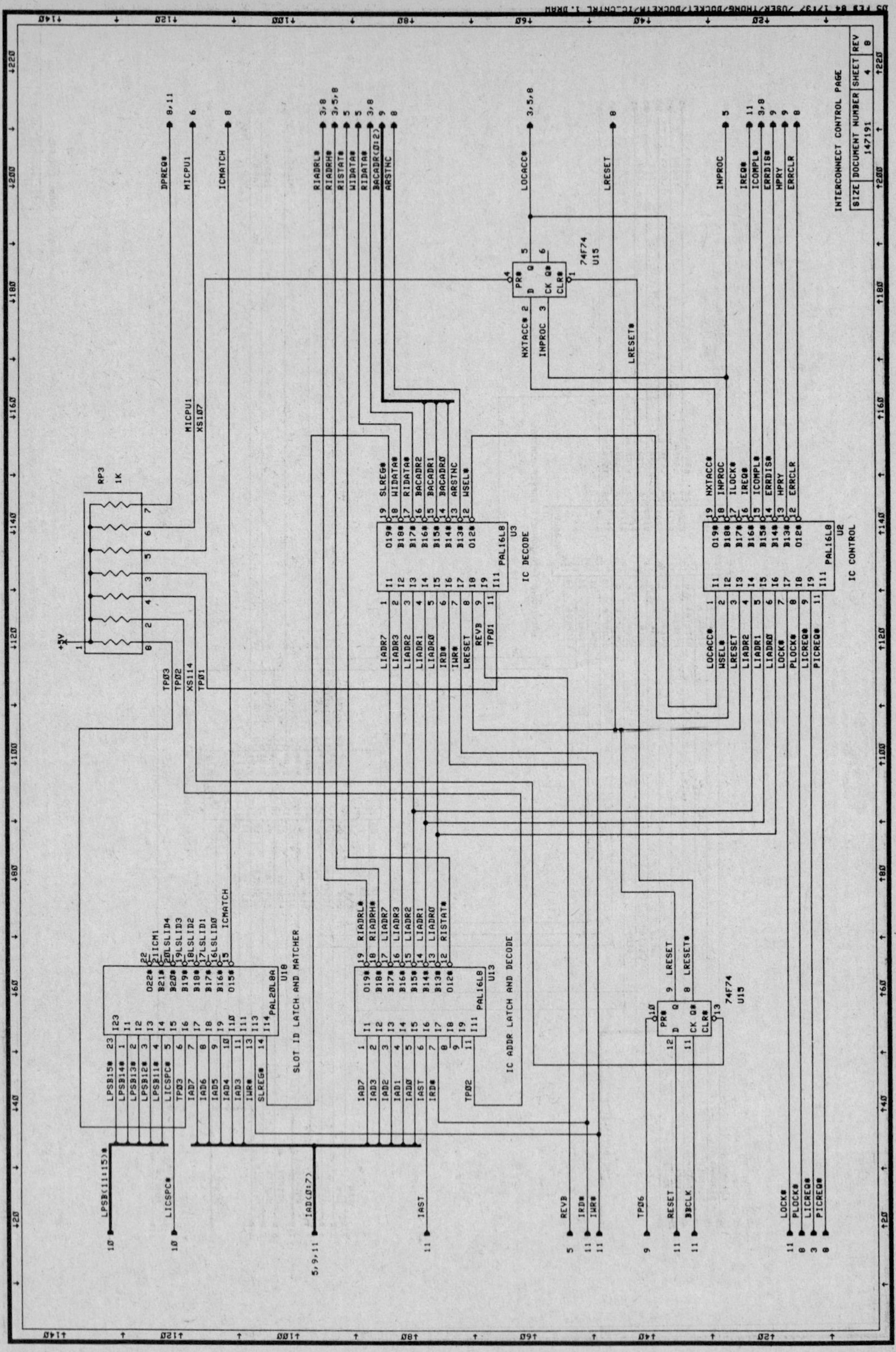
INTERCONNECT CONTROL PAGE
SIZE DOCUMENT NUMBER SHEET REV
147191 4 B
SLOT ID LATCH AND MATCHER
IC ADDR LATCH AND DECODE
IC DECODE
IC CONTROL
74F74
U15

Figure A-4.

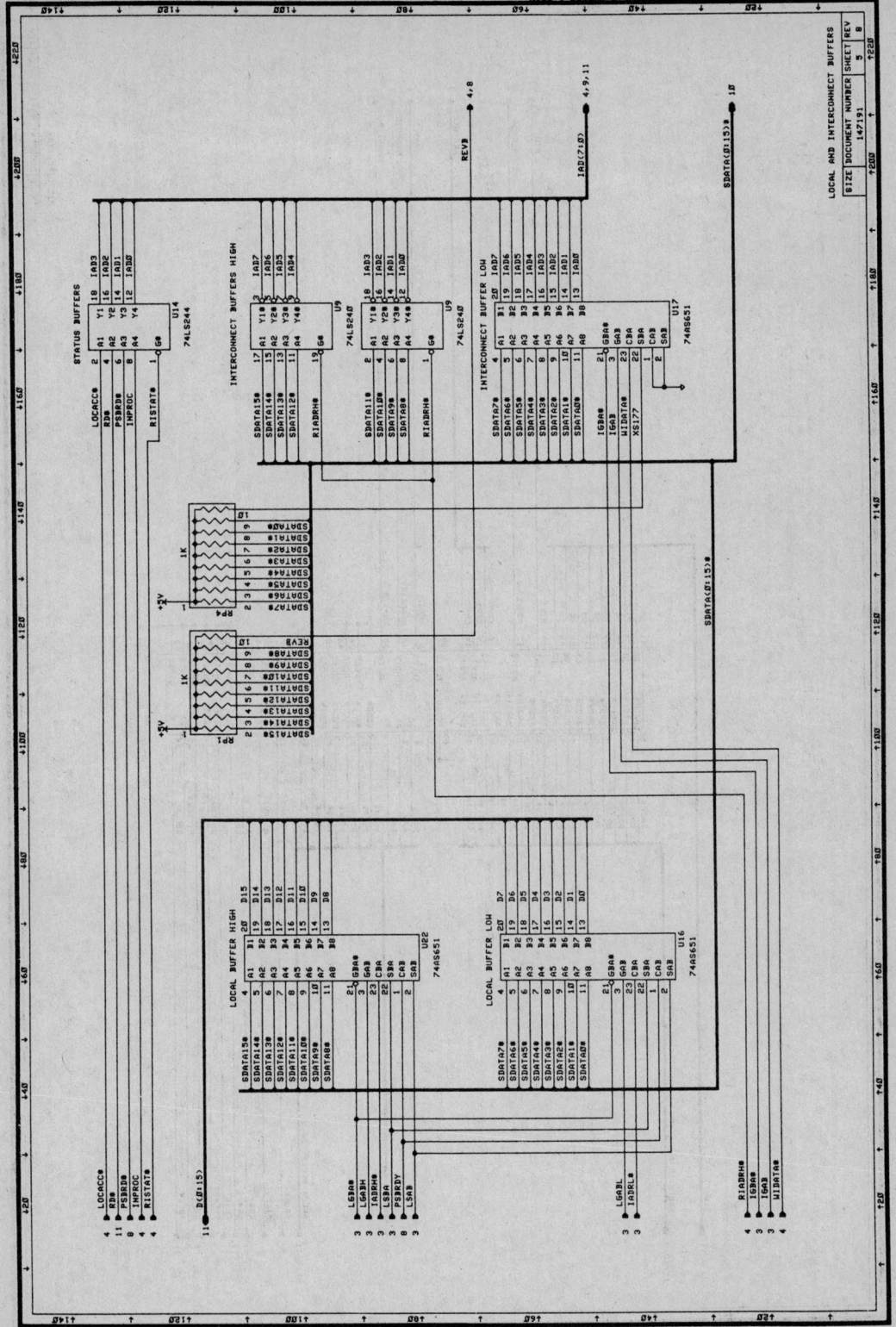

Figure A-5.

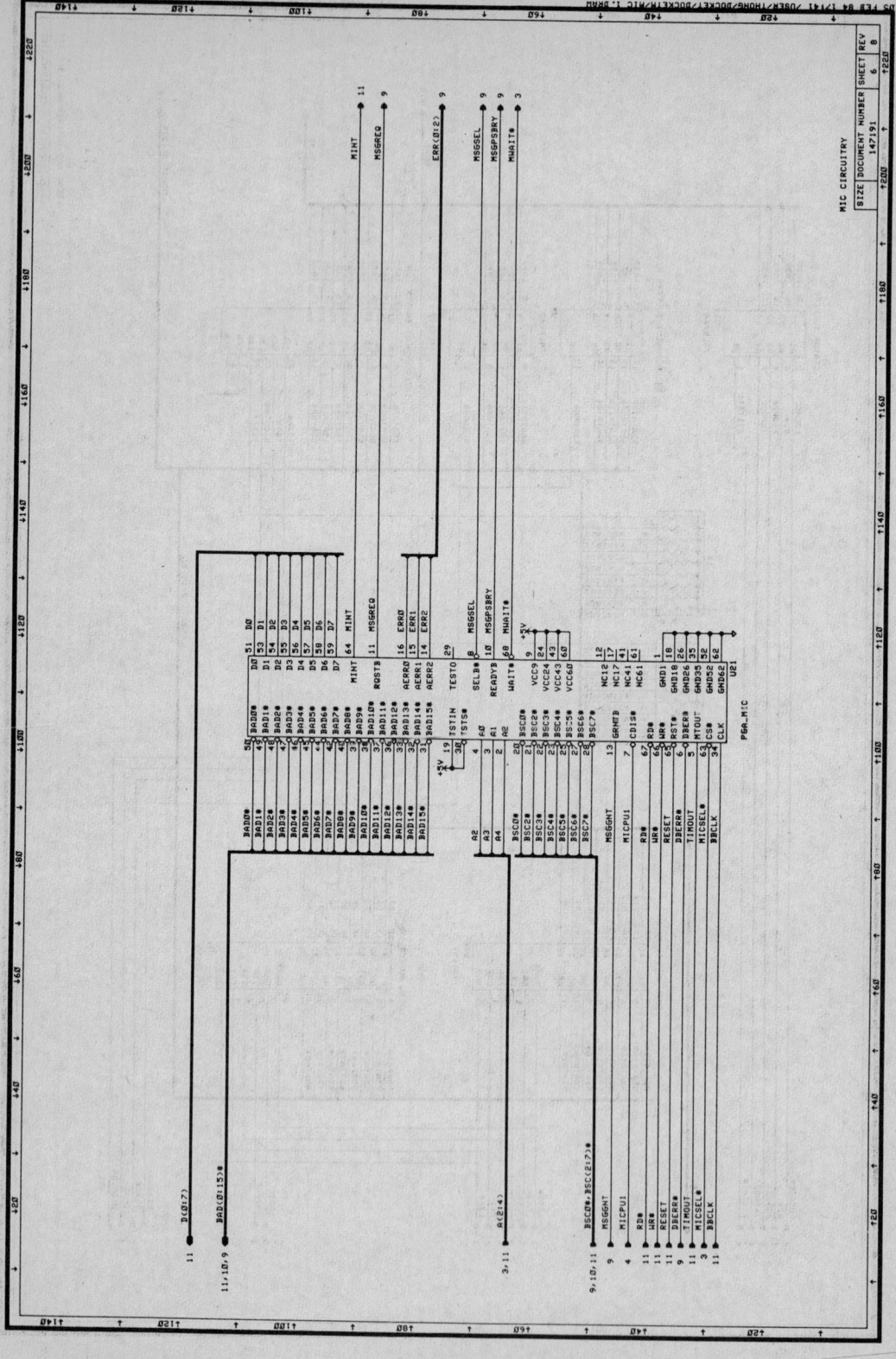

Figure A-6.

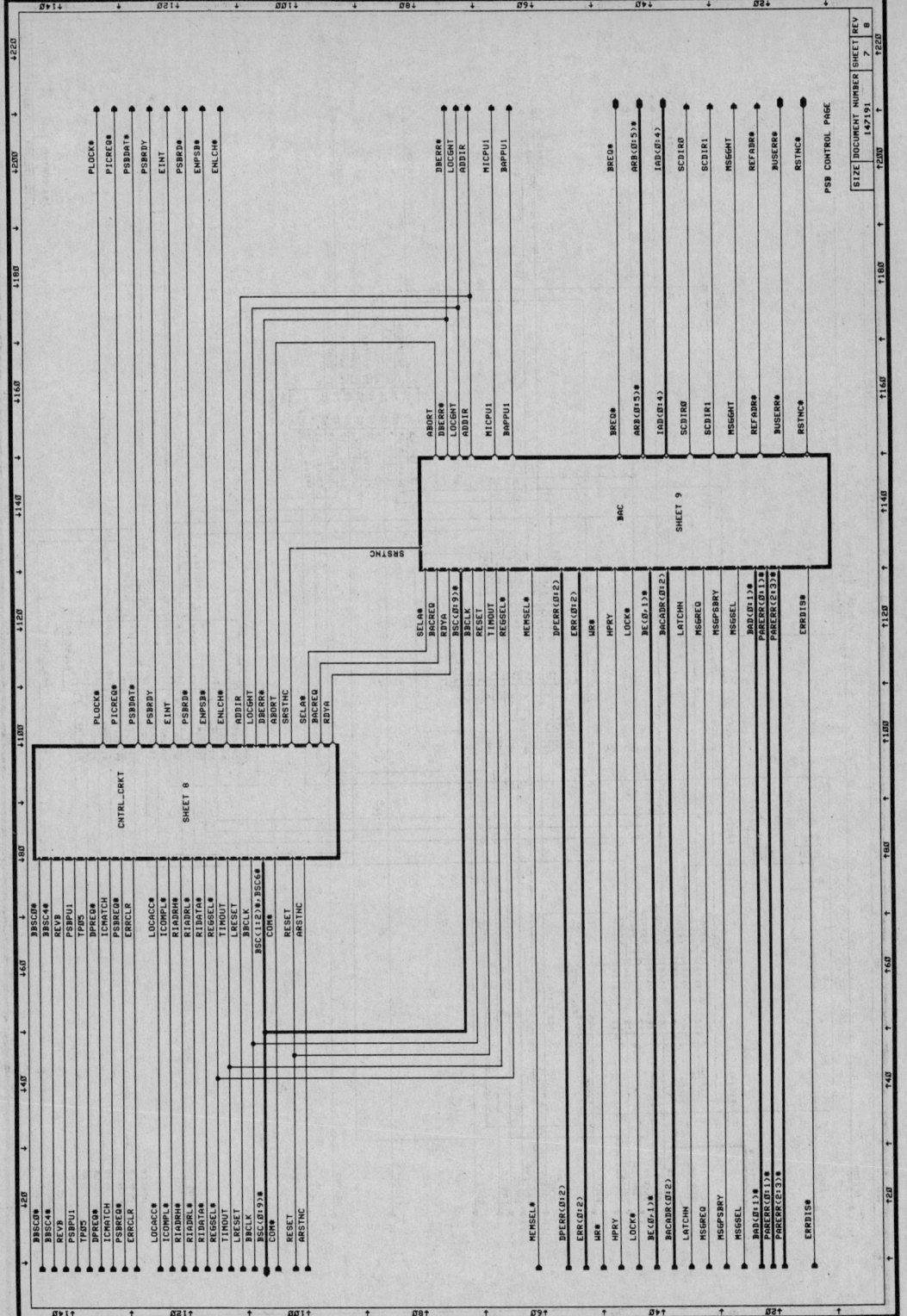

Figure A-7.

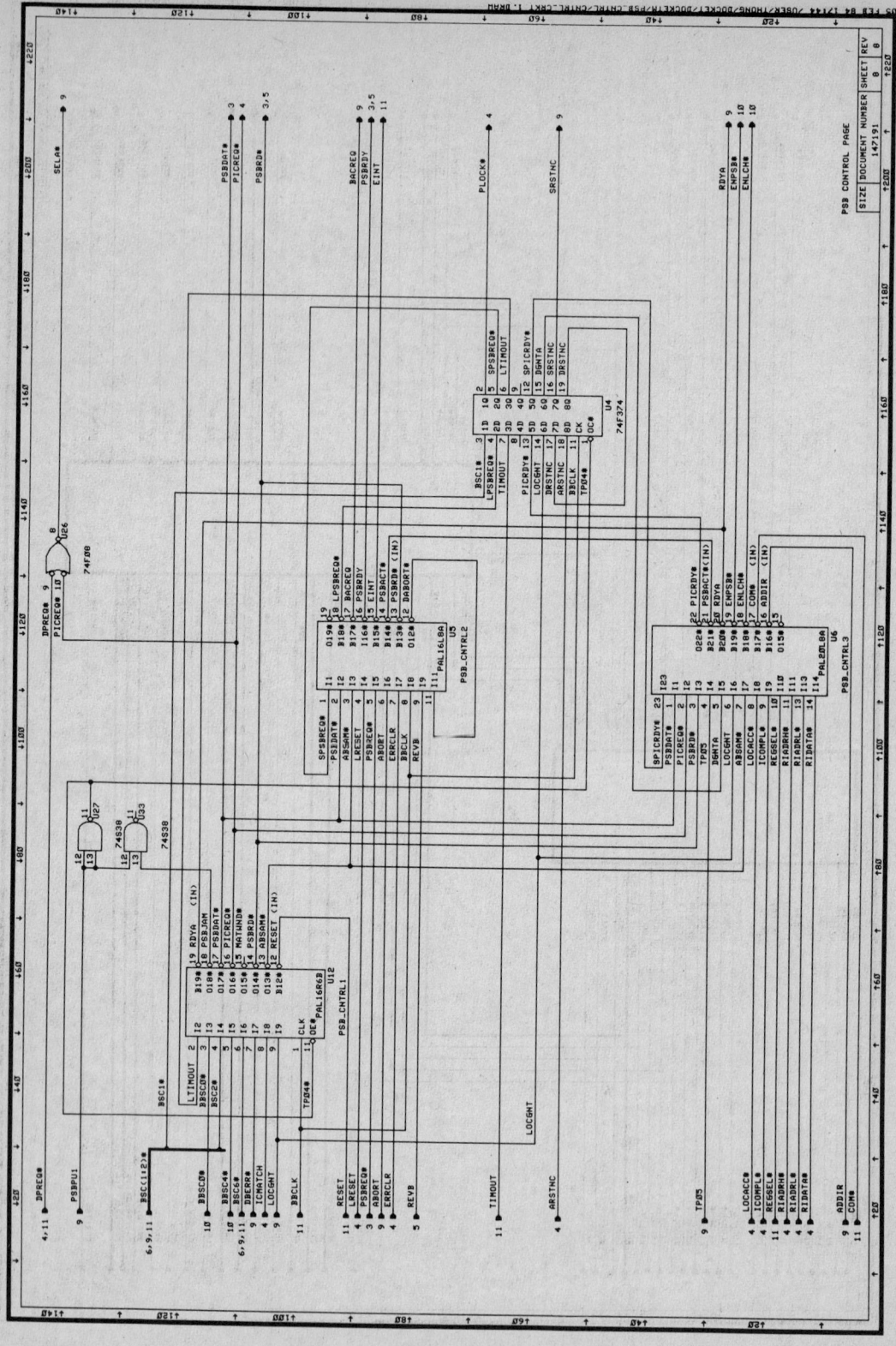

Figure A-8.

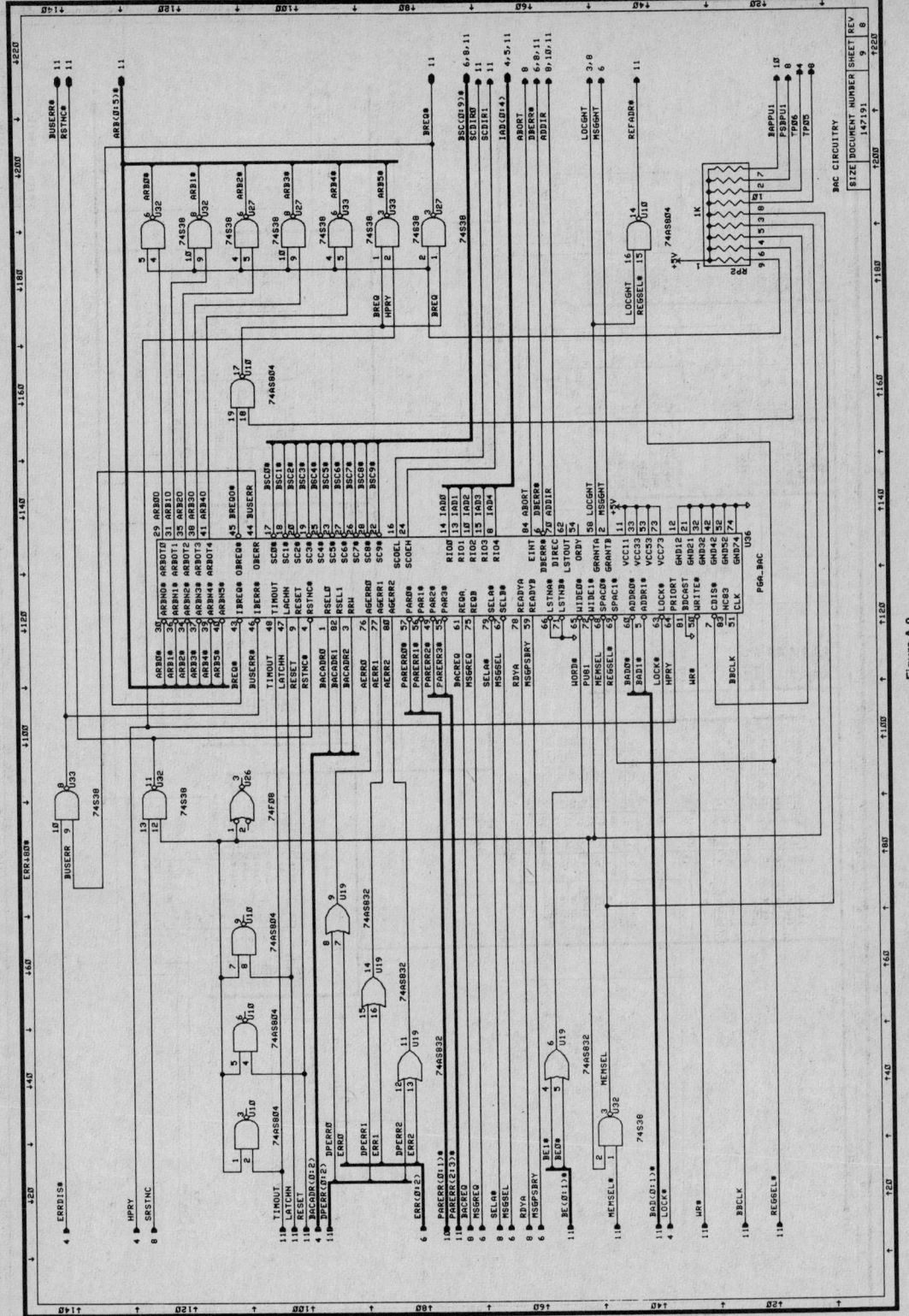

Figure A-9.

BUFFER AND PARITY PAGE
SIZE
DOCUMENT NUMBER
SHEET
REV
147191
10
8
74LS245
74F280
74LS244
PAL16R6B
ADDRESS/DATA LATCH1
ADDRESS/DATA LATCH2
ADDRESS/DATA LATCH3
74AS804
74AS832

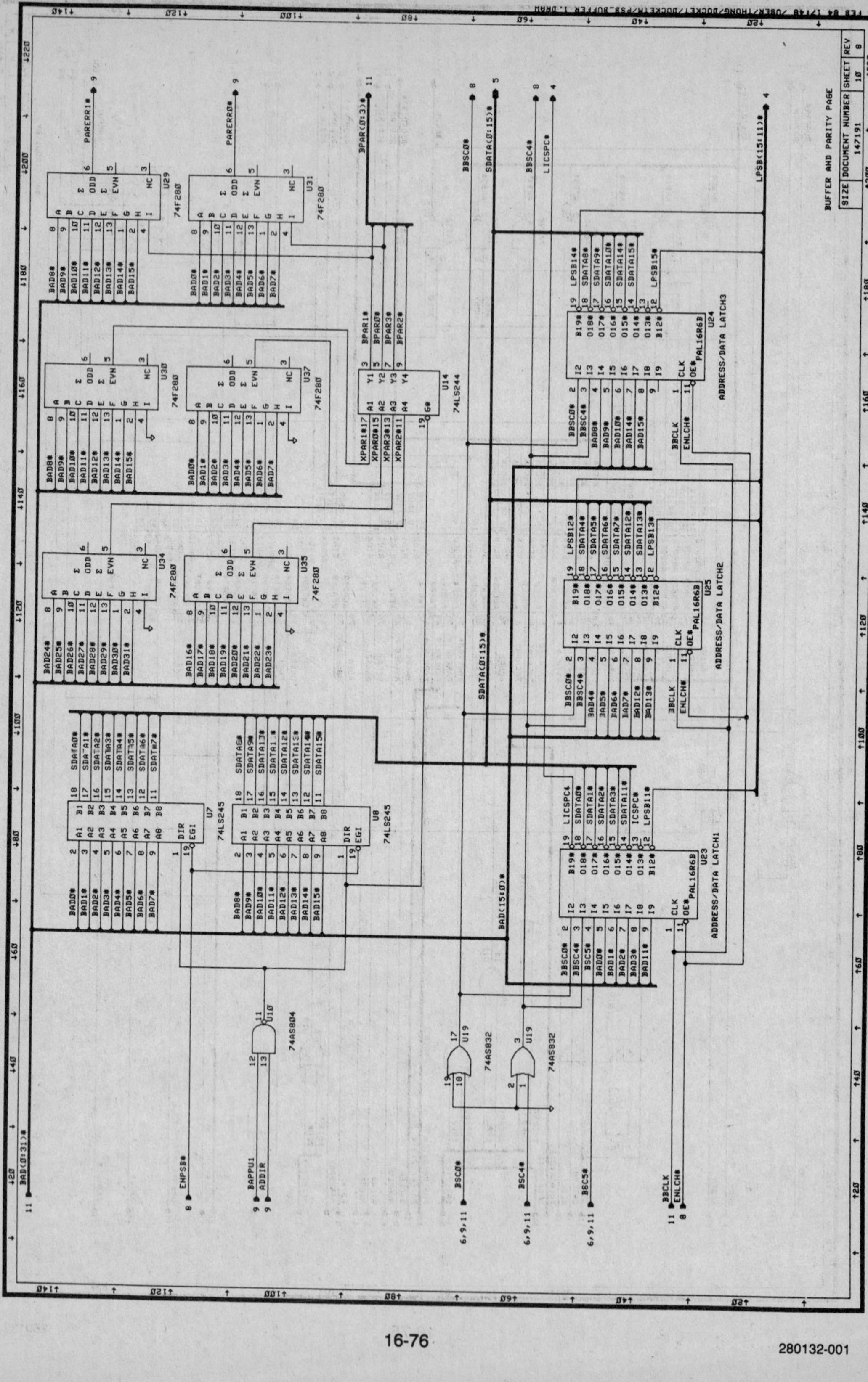

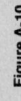

Figure A-10.

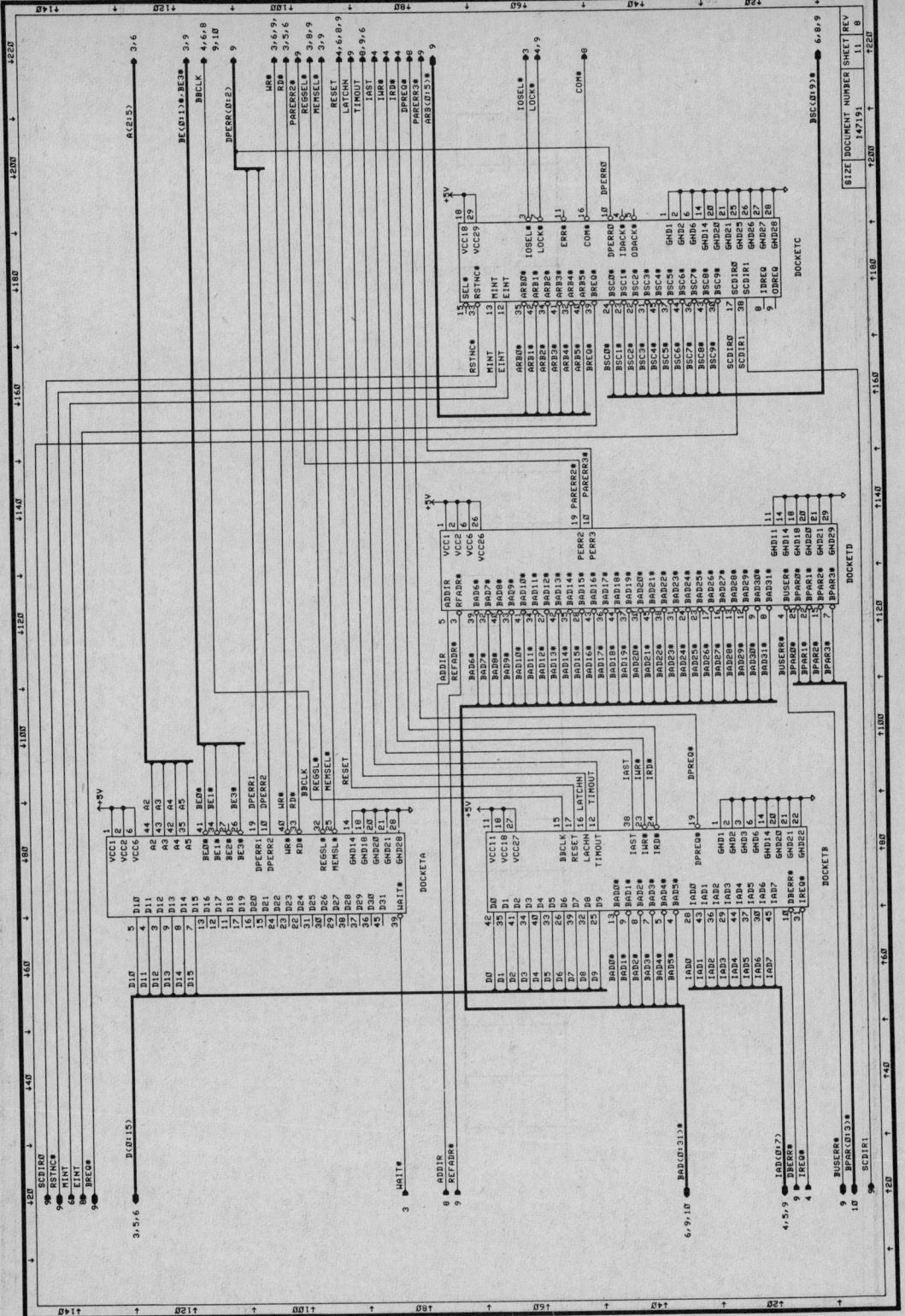

Figure A-11.

SIZE B
DOCUMENT NUMBER 142191
SHEET 12
REV B
+5V
C1 .1Ø
C2 .1Ø
C3 .1Ø
C4 .1Ø
C5 .1Ø
C6 .1Ø
C7 .1Ø
C8 .1Ø
C9 2.2
C1Ø .1Ø
C11 .1Ø
C12 .1Ø
C13 .1Ø
C14 .1Ø
C15 .1Ø
C16 .1Ø
C17 .1Ø
C18 .1Ø
C19 .1Ø
C2Ø .1Ø

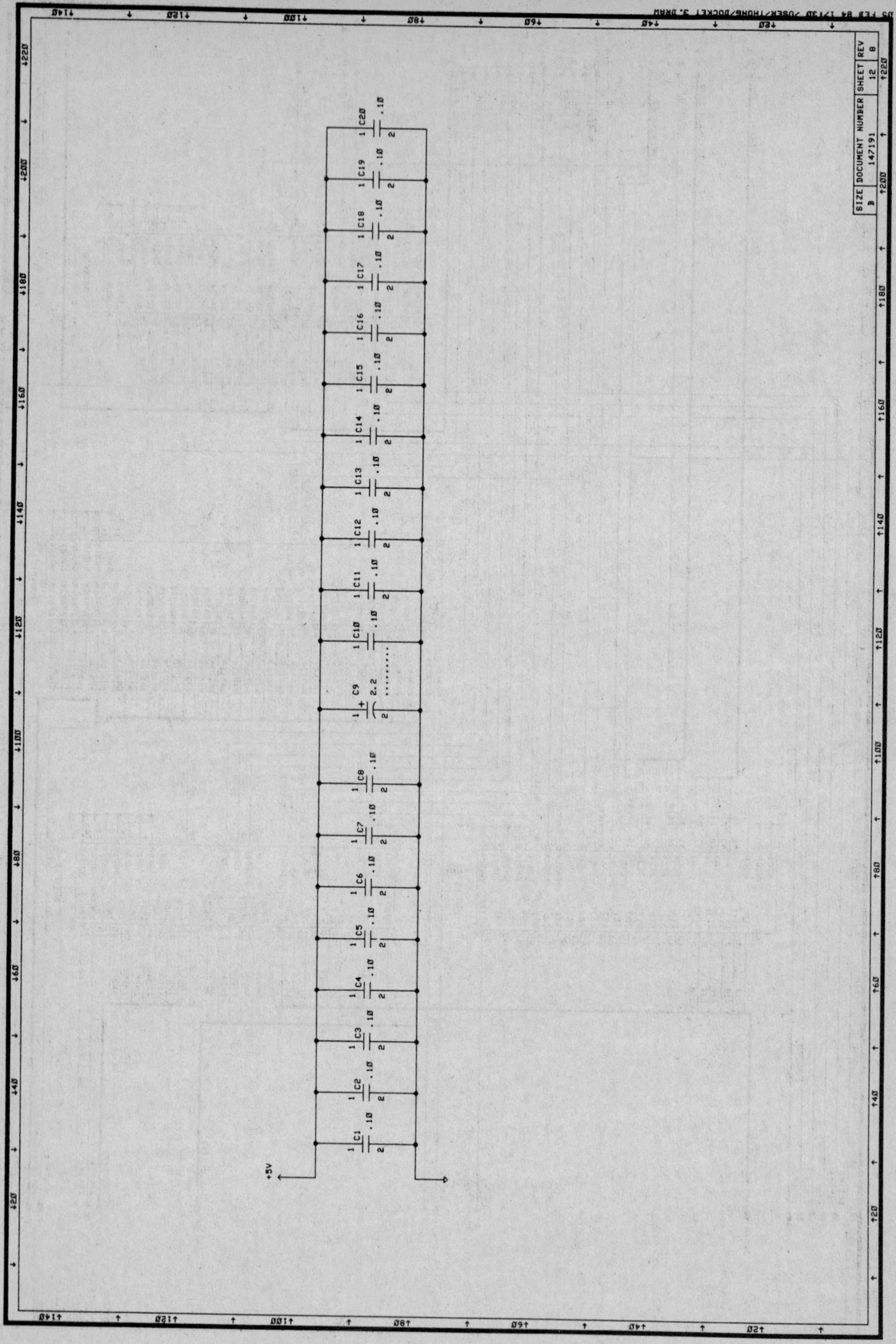

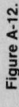

Figure A-12.

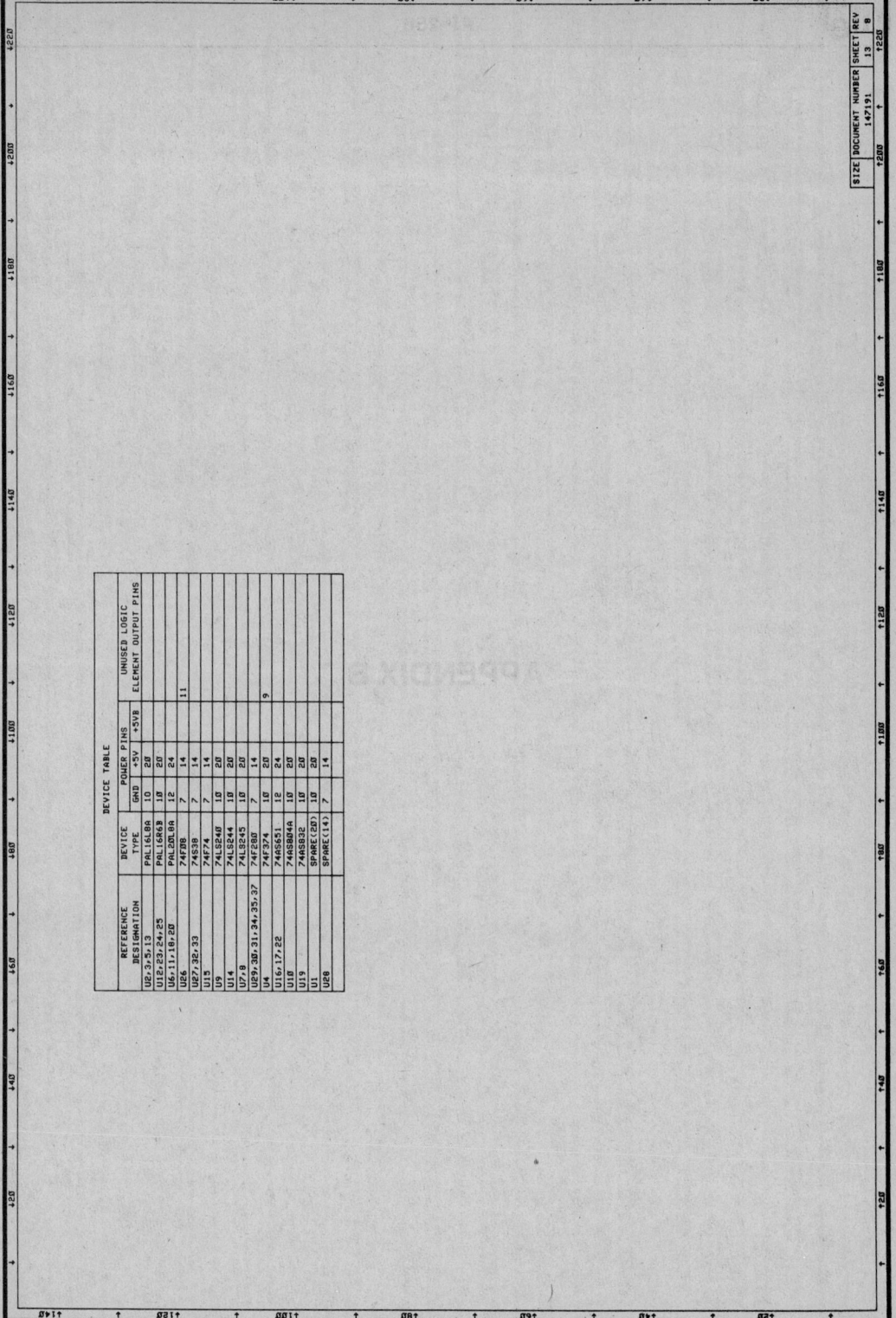

Figure A-13.

APPENDIX B

AP-256

```
PAL16L8A
DU2.003
IC CONTROL
INTEL CORPORATION, HILLSBORO, OREGON
/LOCACC /WSEL LRESET  LIADR2  LIADR1  LIADR0 /LOCK /PLOCK /LICREQ GND
/PICREQ ERRCLR HPRY /ERRDIS /ICOMPL /IREQ /ILOCK INPROC /NXTACC VCC

    IF (VCC) /ERRCLR=            /WSEL
              +                           /LIADR2
              +                                       /LIADR1
              +                                                   /LIADR0

    IF (VCC)  /HPRY = LRESET
              +             WSEL * /LIADR2 * LIADR1 * LIADR0
              +            /WSEL                              * /HPRY
              +                    LIADR2                     * /HPRY
              +                              /LIADR1          * /HPRY
              +                                        LIADR0 * /HPRY

    IF (VCC)  ERRDIS=/LRESET *  WSEL * LIADR2 * /LIADR1 * /LIADR0
              +/LRESET * /WSEL                                 * ERRDIS
              +/LRESET *         /LIADR2                       * ERRDIS
              +/LRESET *                      LIADR1           * ERRDIS
              +/LRESET *                              /LIADR0  * ERRDIS

    IF (VCC)  ICOMPL=/LRESET *  WSEL * /LIADR2 * /LIADR1 * /LIADR0     *IN
              +/LRESET *         LOCACC *  LICREQ * ICOMPL
              +/LRESET *        /LOCACC *  INPROC * ICOMPL

    IF (VCC)  IREQ  =           LOCACC *  LICREQ * /INPROC
              +                /LOCACC *  PICREQ * /INPROC
              +                            LICREQ * /INPROC * /ILOCK
              +                            PICREQ * /INPROC * /ILOCK

    IF (VCC)  ILOCK =       LOCK * LOCACC * /LRESET * ICOMPL
              +            PLOCK * /LOCACC * /LRESET * ICOMPL
              + ILOCK *    LOCK *  LOCACC * /LRESET
              + ILOCK *   PLOCK * /LOCACC * /LRESET

    IF (VCC) /INPROC=         /IREQ *  LOCACC * /LICREQ
              +               /IREQ * /LOCACC * /PICREQ
              +/INPROC * /WSEL
              +/INPROC *  LIADR2
              +/INPROC *  LIADR1
              +/INPROC * /LIADR0
              + LRESET

    IF (VCC)  NXTACC= LOCACC                  *  ILOCK
              +/LOCACC            *  LICREQ * /ILOCK
              + LOCACC            * /PICREQ


;form feed
```

AP-256

DESCRIPTION

```
      LIADR
   7  3  2  1  0   WSEL      Read              Write                   R
   -------------------       ----     -------------     -------------       ---

   0  X  X  X  X             no access         no access

   1  0  0  0  0      X      RISTAT*           set ICOMPL*   (=>0)
   1  0  0  0  1      X      ----              INPROC        (=>1)

   1  0  0  1  0      X      RIADRL*           set HPRY      (=>1)
   1  0  0  1  1      X      RIADRH*           clr HPRY      (=>0)

   1  0  1  0  0      X      ----              set ERRDIS*   (=>0)
   1  0  1  0  1      X      ----              clr ERRDIS*   (=>1)

   1  0  1  1  0             ----              clr ARSTNC    (=>0)
   1  0  1  1  1             ----              SLREG*

   1  1  0  0  0             RIDATA*           WIDATA*
   1  1  0  0  1             ----              ----

   1  1  0  1  0             ----              ----
   1  1  0  1  1             ----              ----

   1  1  1  X  X             BAC               BAC


        BAC addresses             rev a                    rev b
       ------------------       ---R--/---W--          ---R---/--W--
   1  1  1  0  0               no access               no access
   1  1  1  0  1               slot reg                error reg

   1  1  1  1  0      X       arb reg                  arb reg
   1  1  1  1  1      X       error reg/errclr         slot reg/no acce
```

ERRCLR = WSEL*LIADR2*LIADR1*LIADR0

HPRY   = /LRESET*(/WSEL+LIADR2+/LIADR1+/LIADR0)*(WSEL+HPRY)*(/LIADR2+HPRY)
             * (LIADR1+HPRY)*(/LIADR0+HPRY)

INPROC = (/INPROC+LICREQ+ICOMPL+/LOCACC)*(/INPROC+PICREQ+ICOMPL+LOCACC)
             * (INPROC+WSEL)*(INPROC+/LIADR2)*(INPROC+/LIADR1)*(INPROC+IREQ)

;FORM FEED

AP-256

```
PAL16R6B
DU12.004
PSB CONTROL #1
INTEL CORPORATION, HILLSBORO, OREGON
BBCLK LTIMOUT /BBSC0 /BSC2 /BBSC4 /BSC6 /DBERR ICMATCH LOCGNT GND
TP04 RESET /ABSAM /PSBRD /MATWND /PICREQ /PSBDAT PSBJAM RDYA VCC

/PSBJAM:=   RESET
        +                                          /PICREQ
        +                               /PSBJAM * /DBERR    * /LTIMOUT

PSBDAT  := /RESET *  BBSC0 * LOCGNT          * /DBERR  * /LTIMOUT
        +  /RESET * /BSC2           *  PSBDAT * /DBERR  * /LTIMOUT
        +  /RESET * /BBSC4          *  PSBDAT * /DBERR  * /LTIMOUT

PICREQ  := /RESET * /BBSC4 * PSBRD * ICMATCH * MATWND * /DBERR * /LTIMOUT
        +  /RESET * /BBSC4 * BSC2 * /PSBRD * ICMATCH * MATWND * /DBERR * /LT
        +  /RESET * /BSC2                   * /PSBJAM *   PICREQ
        +  /RESET * /BBSC4                  * /PSBJAM *   PICREQ

PSBRD   := /RESET *  BBSC0 * /BSC6
        +  /RESET * /BBSC0          *  PSBRD

MATWND  := /RESET *  BBSC0 * /LOCGNT * /DBERR  * /LTIMOUT
        +  /RESET * /BBSC4 * /BSC2   *  MATWND * /DBERR  * /LTIMOUT * /PSB

ABSAM   := /RESET *  BBSC0 * LOCGNT
        +  /RESET *           ABSAM * PSBDAT
        +  /RESET *  PICREQ * DBERR
        +  /RESET *  PICREQ * LTIMOUT
        +  /RESET *  PICREQ * ABSAM


FUNCTION TABLE
BBCLK LTIMOUT /BBSC0 /BSC2 /BBSC4 /BSC6 /DBERR ICMATCH LOCGNT
TP04 RESET RDYA /ABSAM /PSBRD /MATWND /PICREQ /PSBDAT PSBJAM
-------------------------------------------------------------------

DESCRIPTION

PSBJAM = /RESET*(/PSBJAM+PICREQ)*(PSBJAM+DBERR+LTIMOUT)
;
;   NOTE: BSC2 IN 2ND LINE OF PICREQ AND 2ND LINE OF MATWND S/B BSC3.
;         THIS WILL HAVE NO EFFECT AS LONG AS THERE IS NOT A PROTOCOL
;         VIOLATION. IF THIS HAPPENS THE RESULT WILL BE TIMEOUT INSTEAD
;         OF AGENT ERROR (TRANSFER NOT UNDERSTOOD).
;form feed
```

AP-256

```
PAL16L8A
DU5.004
PSB CONTROL #2
INTEL CORPORATION, HILLSBORO, OREGON
/SPSBREQ /PSBDAT /ABSAM LRESET /PSBREQ ABORT ERRCLR BBCLK REVB GND
/DABIN /DABSAM /PSBRD /PSBACT EINT PSBRDY BACREQ /LPSBREQ NC VCC

IF (VCC)  DABSAM  =  ABSAM                *  /BBCLK
                 +  ABSAM  *  DABIN
                 +            DABIN   *  BBCLK

IF (VCC)  /EINT   =  LRESET
                 +  ERRCLR * /REVB
                 +           /REVB  *  /EINT  *  /DABIN
                 +           /REVB  *  /EINT  *  /ABORT
                 +           /REVB  *  /EINT  *  /PSBACT
                 +           REVB            *  /ABORT

IF (VCC)  /PSBRDY =  LRESET
                 +                  /PSBREQ
                 +                  /PSBRDY *  /PSBACT
                 +                  /PSBRDY *  PSBDAT
                 +                  /PSBRDY *  PSBRD   *  BBCLK

IF (VCC)  PSBACT  =  /LRESET         *  PSBDAT
                 +  /LRESET         *  PSBACT * PSBREQ

IF (VCC)  /BACREQ =                    PSBDAT
                 +                    /SPSBREQ

IF (VCC)  LPSBREQ =                    PSBREQ * /PSBACT * /PSBDAT
```

;form feed

DESCRIPTION

EINT   = /LRESET*(/ERRCLR+REVB)*(REVB+EINT+ABSAM)*(REVB+EINT+/BBCLK)
       * (REVB+EINT+ABORT)*(REVB+EINT+DABIN)*(/REVB+ABORT)

PSBRDY = /LRESET*PSBREQ*(PSBRDY+PSBACT)*(PSBRDY+/PSBDAT)*(PSBRDY+/PSBRD+/B

BACREQ = /LRESET*/PSBDAT*(BACREQ+SPSBREQ)*(BACREQ+/PSBACT)

;form feed

AP-256

```
PAL20L8A
DU6.004
PSB CONTROL #3
INTEL CORPORATION, HILLSBORO, OREGON
/PSBDAT /PICREQ /PSBRD TP05 DGNTA LOCGNT
/ABSAM /LOCACC /ICOMPL /REGSEL /RIADRH GND
/RIADRL /RIDATA NC ADDIR /COM /ENLCH
/ENPSB RDYA /PSBACT /PICRDY /SPICRDY VCC


IF (TP05)   PICRDY =   /LOCACC *  ICOMPL
                   +   PICREQ  *  ABSAM

IF (TP05)   /RDYA  = /SPICRDY * /PSBDAT * /LOCGNT * /COM
                   + /SPICRDY * /PSBDAT *  DGNTA  * /COM

IF (TP05)   ENPSB  =   PSBDAT  * /PSBRD  * /LOCGNT
                   +   REGSEL  *  LOCGNT
                   +   PICREQ  *  PSBRD  *  ADDIR
                   +  /LOCACC  * /PSBRD  *  RIDATA  *  PICREQ * /ABSAM

IF (TP05)   ENLCH  =  /LOCACC  *  RIADRH *  PICREQ
                   +  /LOCACC  *  RIADRL *  PICREQ
                   +   PSBDAT  *  PSBRD
                   +   PSBACT  *  ABSAM  *  PSBRD  * /PICREQ


DESCRIPTION

RDYA   = (SPICRDY+PSBDAT+LOCGNT+COM)*(SPICRDY+PSBDAT+/DGNTA+COM)

;form feed
```

16-85

AP-256

```
PAL16R6B
DU23.001
PSB ADDRESS/DATA LATCH #1
INTEL CORPORATION, HILLSBORO, OREGON
BBCLK /BBSC0 /BBSC4 /BSC5 /BAD0 /BAD1 /BAD2 /BAD3 /BAD11 GND
/ENLCH /LPSB11 /ICSPC /SDATA11 /SDATA3 /SDATA2 /SDATA1 /SDATA0 /LICSPC VCC


IF (VCC) LPSB11 = SDATA11

IF (VCC) LICSPC = ICSPC

            ICSPC   :=  BBSC0  *  BBSC4  *  BSC5
                     + /BBSC0                      *  ICSPC

           SDATA11  :=  BBSC0            *  BAD11
                     +           BBSC4   *  BAD11
                     + /BBSC0 *  /BBSC4             *  SDATA11

            SDATA3  :=  BBSC0            *  BAD3
                     +           BBSC4   *  BAD3
                     + /BBSC0 *  /BBSC4             *  SDATA3

            SDATA2  :=  BBSC0            *  BAD2
                     +           BBSC4   *  BAD2
                     + /BBSC0 *  /BBSC4             *  SDATA2

            SDATA1  :=  BBSC0            *  BAD1
                     +           BBSC4   *  BAD1
                     + /BBSC0 *  /BBSC4             *  SDATA1

            SDATA0  :=  BBSC0            *  BAD0
                     +           BBSC4   *  BAD0
                     + /BBSC0 *  /BBSC4             *  SDATA0

FUNCTION TABLE
BBCLK /BBSC0 /BBSC4 /BSC5 /BAD0 /BAD1 /BAD2 /BAD3 /BAD11
/ENLCH /LPSB11 /ICSPC /SDATA11 /SDATA3 /SDATA2 /SDATA1 /SDATA0 /LICSPC
---------------------------------------------------------------
DESCRIPTION
;form feed
```

```
PAL16R6B
DU25.001
PSB ADDRESS/DATA LATCH #2
INTEL CORPORATION, HILLSBORO, OREGON
BBCLK /BBSC0 /BBSC4 /BAD4 /BAD5 /BAD6 /BAD7 /BAD12 /BAD13 GND
/ENLCH /LPSB13 /SDATA13 /SDATA12 /SDATA7 /SDATA6 /SDATA5 /SDATA4 /LPSB12 V


IF (VCC) LPSB13 = SDATA13

IF (VCC) LPSB12 = SDATA12

        SDATA13 :=  BBSC0           * BAD13
                +           BBSC4 * BAD13
                + /BBSC0 * /BBSC4           * SDATA13

        SDATA12 :=  BBSC0           * BAD12
                +           BBSC4 * BAD12
                + /BBSC0 * /BBSC4           * SDATA12

        SDATA7  :=  BBSC0           * BAD7
                +           BBSC4 * BAD7
                + /BBSC0 * /BBSC4           * SDATA7

        SDATA6  :=  BBSC0           * BAD6
                +           BBSC4 * BAD6
                + /BBSC0 * /BBSC4           * SDATA6

        SDATA5  :=  BBSC0           * BAD5
                +           BBSC4 * BAD5
                + /BBSC0 * /BBSC4 *           SDATA5

        SDATA4  :=  BBSC0           * BAD4
                +           BBSC4 * BAD4
                + /BBSC0 * /BBSC4           * SDATA4

FUNCTION TABLE
BBCLK /BBSC0 /BBSC4 /BAD4 /BAD5 /BAD6 /BAD7 /BAD12 /BAD13
/ENLCH /LPSB13 /SDATA13 /SDATA12 /SDATA7 /SDATA6 /SDATA5 /SDATA4 /LPSB12
-----------------------------------------------------------------

DESCRIPTION
;form feed
```

AP-256

```
PAL16L8A
DU13.001
IC ADDRESS LATCH AND DECODE
INTEL CORPORATION, HILLSBORO, OREGON
IAD7 IAD3 IAD2 IAD1 IAD0 IAST /IRD NC NC GND
TP02 /RISTAT LIADR0 LIADR1 LIADR2 LIADR3 LIADR7 /RIADRH /RIADRL VCC


IF (TP02) RISTAT    =  LIADR7 * /LIADR3 * /LIADR2 * /LIADR1 * /LIADR0 * IR

IF (TP02) RIADRL    =  LIADR7 * /LIADR3 * /LIADR2 *  LIADR1 * /LIADR0 * IR

IF (TP02) RIADRH    =  LIADR7 * /LIADR3 * /LIADR2 *  LIADR1 *  LIADR0 * IR

IF (TP02) /LIADR0   =  /IAD0 *  IAST
                    +          /IAST * /LIADR0
                    +  /IAD0         * /LIADR0

IF (TP02) /LIADR1   =  /IAD1 *  IAST
                    +          /IAST * /LIADR1
                    +  /IAD1         * /LIADR1

IF (TP02) /LIADR2   =  /IAD2 *  IAST
                    +          /IAST * /LIADR2
                    +  /IAD2         * /LIADR2

IF (TP02) /LIADR3   =  /IAD3 *  IAST
                    +          /IAST * /LIADR3
                    +  /IAD3         * /LIADR3

IF (TP02) /LIADR7   =  /IAD7 *  IAST
                    +          /IAST * /LIADR7
                    +  /IAD7         * /LIADR7

;form feed

------------------------------------------------------------

DESCRIPTION

LIADR0 = (IAD0+/IAST)*(IAST+LIADR0)*(IAD0+LIADR0)

LIADR1 = (IAD1+/IAST)*(IAST+LIADR1)*(IAD0+LIADR1)

LIADR2 = (IAD2+/IAST)*(IAST+LIADR2)*(IAD0+LIADR2)

LIADR3 = (IAD3+/IAST)*(IAST+LIADR3)*(IAD0+LIADR3)

LIADR7 = (IAD7+/IAST)*(IAST+LIADR7)*(IAD0+LIADR7)

;form feed
```

AP-256

```
PAL16L8A
DU3.001
IC DECODE
INTEL CORPORATION, HILLSBORO, OREGON
LIADR7 LIADR3 LIADR2 LIADR1 LIADR0 /IRD /IWR LRESET REVB GND
TP01 /WSEL ARSTNC BACADR0 BACADR1 BACADR2 /RIDATA /WIDATA /SLREG VCC


IF (TP01) /ARSTNC =   LIADR7* /LIADR3*  LIADR2*  LIADR1* /LIADR0*   IWR* /LR
                    + /ARSTNC                                          * /LR

IF (TP01)   WSEL  =   LIADR7* /LIADR3* /LIADR2                      *  IWR
                    + LIADR7* /LIADR3*  LIADR2* /LIADR1             *  IWR
                    + LIADR7*  LIADR3*  LIADR2*  LIADR1             *  IWR

IF (TP01) WIDATA  =   LIADR7*  LIADR3* /LIADR2* /LIADR1* /LIADR0*   IWR

IF (TP01) RIDATA  =   LIADR7*  LIADR3* /LIADR2* /LIADR1* /LIADR0*   IRD

IF (TP01)  SLREG  =   LIADR7* /LIADR3*  LIADR2*  LIADR1*  LIADR0

IF (TP01) /BACADR0 =   /LIADR7
                    + /LIADR3
                    + /LIADR2
                    + /LIADR0
                    +                                   /BACADR2 * /IRD

IF (TP01) /BACADR1 =   /LIADR7
                    + /LIADR3
                    + /LIADR2
                    + /LIADR1 * /LIADR0
                    +  LIADR1 *  LIADR0 *  REVB
                    + /LIADR1 *          /REVB
                    +                                   /BACADR2 * /IRD

IF (TP01) /BACADR2 =   /LIADR7
                    + /LIADR3
                    + /LIADR2
                    + /LIADR1 *  LIADR0
                    + /IWR
                    +  LIADR1 *  LIADR0 * /REVB
                    + /LIADR1 *           REVB

;form feed
```

AP-256

DESCRIPTION

```
         LIADR
   7   3  2  1  0     WSEL        Read              Write             R
  ------------------  ----    --------------    --------------       ---

   0   X  X  X  X              no access          no access

   1   0  0  0  0      X        RISTAT*          set ICOMPL*  (=>0)
   1   0  0  0  1      X        ----             INPROC       (=>1)

   1   0  0  1  0      X        RIADRL*          set HPRY     (=>1)
   1   0  0  1  1      X        RIADRH*          clr HPRY     (=>0)

   1   0  1  0  0      X        ----             set ERRDIS*  (=>0)
   1   0  1  0  1      X        ----             clr ERRDIS*  (=>1)

   1   0  1  1  0               ----             clr ARSTNC   (=>0)
   1   0  1  1  1               ----             SLREG*

   1   1  0  0  0               RIDATA*          WIDATA*
   1   1  0  0  1               ----             ----

   1   1  0  1  0               ----             ----
   1   1  0  1  1               ----             ----

   1   1  1  X  X               BAC              BAC


       BAC addresses              rev a                 rev b
       --------------           ---R--/---W--        ---R---/--W--
   1   1  1  0  0               no access            no access
   1   1  1  0  1               slot reg             SLOT /NO ACCE

   1   1  1  1  0      X        arb reg              ARB REG
   1   1  1  1  1      X        error reg/NO ACCESS  ERROR REG
   1   1  1  1  1      X        NO ACCESS/ERRCLR

ERROR := LIADR7.LIADR3.LIADR2.LIADR1.LIADR0
ARB   := LIADR7.LIADR3.LIADR2.LIADR1.LIADR0#
SLOT  := LIADR7.LIADR3.LIADR2.LIADR1#.LIADR0

RRW   := IWT.(ERROR.REVB + SLOT.REVB# + ARB)
RSEL0 := (IRD + RRW).(ERROR + SLOT)
RSEL1 := (IRD + RRW).(ARB + REVB.SLOT + REVB#.ERROR)


ARSTNC = (/LIADR7+LIADR3+/LIADR2+/LIADR1+LIADR0+/IWR+LRESET)*(ARSTNC+LRESE

BACADR0= LIADR7*LIADR3*LIADR2*LIADR0*(BACADR2+IRD)

BACADR1= LIADR7*LIADR3*LIADR2*(LIADR1+LIADR0)*(/LIADR1+/LIADR0+/REVB)
       * (LIADR1+REVB)*(BACADR2+IRD)

BACADR2= LIADR7*LIADR3*LIADR2*(LIADR1+LIADR0)*IWR*(/LIADR1+/LIADR0+REVB)
       * (LIADR1+/REVB)

;FORM FEED
```

AP-256

```
PAL20L8A
DU20.001
LOCAL PROCESSOR DECODE
INTEL CORPORATION, HILLSBORO, OREGON
/BE0 /RD /WR /ICOMPL /LOCACC D14 D15 PSBRDY /MWAIT /REGSEL A5 GND
A4 A3 /IADRL /IADRH /MEMIOS /MICSEL
/ICSTAT /LICREQ /PSBREQ /WAIT /BE1 VCC


IF (VCC) MICSEL= /MEMIOS*  REGSEL* /A5             * /BE1* BE0

IF (VCC) IADRH = /MEMIOS*  REGSEL*  A5*  A4* /A3*  BE1* /BE0*  WR

IF (VCC) IADRL = /MEMIOS*  REGSEL*  A5*  A4* /A3* /BE1*  BE0*  WR

IF (VCC) LICREQ= /MEMIOS*  REGSEL*  A5*  A4*  A3* /BE1*  BE0*  RD*  ICSTAT
               + /MEMIOS*  REGSEL*  A5*  A4*  A3* /BE1*  BE0*  WR*  ICSTAT

IF (VCC) PSBREQ= /MEMIOS*  REGSEL*  A5*  A4*  A3* /BE1*  BE0*  RD* /ICSTAT
               + /MEMIOS*  REGSEL*  A5*  A4*  A3* /BE1*  BE0*  WR* /ICSTAT
               +  MEMIOS* /REGSEL                                *  RD
               +  MEMIOS* /REGSEL                                *  WR

IF (VCC) ICSTAT= D15*  D14*  REGSEL*  A5*  A4* /A3*  BE1* /BE0*  WR
               +              /IADRH                                *  ICSTAT
               + D15*  D14                                          *  ICSTAT
               +                                                /WR*  ICSTAT

IF (VCC) WAIT  = PSBREQ* /PSBRDY
               + LICREQ* /ICOMPL
               +  MWAIT*  MICSEL
               + LICREQ* /LOCACC


;form feed


DESCRIPTION

          Address
     A5 A4 A3   ICSTAT   D14  D15            Activates
     ------------------------------          ---------
      0  X  X      X      X    X                MIC
      1  1  1      0      X    X                PSBREQ
      1  1  1      1      X    X                LICREQ
      1  1  0      X      X    X                IADR
      1  1  0      X      1    1                ICSTAT


;form feed
```

AP-256

```
PAL20L8A
DU11.001
LOCAL AND INTERCONNECT BUFFER CONTROL
INTEL CORPORATION, HILLSBORO, OREGON
/RIADRH /RIADRL /RIDATA /PSBRD /PSBDAT /BE3
/BE1 /BE0 /LOCACC /ICOMPL /RD GND
/PSBREQ /LICREQ IGAB /IGBA /MICSEL LSBA LSAB LGABL LGABH /LGBA LOCGNT VCC


IF (VCC)    LGBA   =     RIADRH   *   LICREQ  *   LOCACC
                   +     RIADRL   *   LICREQ  *   LOCACC
                   +     RIDATA   *   LICREQ  *   LOCACC
                   +     PSBDAT   *   /PSBRD
                   +     LOCGNT

IF (VCC)   /LGABH  =     /RD
                   +      BE3     *   /BE1
                   +      BE3     *    BE1    *    BE0
                   +    /LICREQ   *   /PSBREQ *   /MICSEL

IF (VCC)   /LGABL  =     /RD
                   +      BE3              *   /BE0
                   +    /LICREQ   *   /PSBREQ

IF (VCC)   /LSAB   =     /RD
                   +     LICREQ

IF (VCC)   /LSBA   =  /LOCGNT  *  /RIADRL  *  /RIADRH

IF (VCC)    IGBA   = /RIADRH  *  /RIADRL  *  ICOMPL  *      RD   *  LOCACC
                   + /RIADRH  *  /RIADRL  *  ICOMPL  *    PSBRD  * /LOCACC

IF (VCC)   /IGAB   = /RIADRL * /RIDATA


;form feed



DESCRIPTION

LSLID0 = (IAD3+/SLREG+/IWR)*(SLREG+LSID0)*(LSID0+IWR)*(IAD3+LSLID0)

LSLID1 = (IAD4+/SLREG+/IWR)*(SLREG+LSID1)*(LSID1+IWR)*(IAD4+LSLID1)

LSLID2 = (IAD5+/SLREG+/IWR)*(SLREG+LSID2)*(LSID2+IWR)*(IAD5+LSLID2)

LSLID3 = (IAD6+/SLREG+/IWR)*(SLREG+LSID3)*(LSID3+IWR)*(IAD6+LSLID3)

LSLID4 = (IAD7+/SLREG+/IWR)*(SLREG+LSID4)*(LSID4+IWR)*(IAD7+LSLID4)

;form feed
```

AP-256

```
PAL20L8A
DU18.001
SLOT ID LATCH AND MATCHER
INTEL CORPORATION, HILLSBORO, OREGON
/LPSB14 /LPSB13 /LPSB12 /LPSB11 /LICSPC TP03 IAD7 IAD6 IAD5 IAD4 IAD3 GND
/IWR /SLREG ICMATCH LSLID0 LSLID1 LSLID2
LSLID3 LSLID4 ICM1 NC /LPSB15 VCC


IF (TP03) /LSLID0 = /IAD3 *  SLREG              *   IWR
                  +         /SLREG * /LSLID0
                  +                  /LSLID0 * /IWR
                  + /IAD3          * /LSLID0

IF (TP03) /LSLID1 = /IAD4 *  SLREG              *   IWR
                  +         /SLREG * /LSLID1
                  +                  /LSLID1 * /IWR
                  + /IAD4          * /LSLID1

IF (TP03) /LSLID2 = /IAD5 *  SLREG              *   IWR
                  +         /SLREG * /LSLID2
                  +                  /LSLID2 * /IWR
                  + /IAD5          * /LSLID2

IF (TP03) /LSLID3 = /IAD6 *  SLREG              *   IWR
                  +         /SLREG * /LSLID3
                  +                  /LSLID3 * /IWR
                  + /IAD6          * /LSLID3

IF (TP03) /LSLID4 = /IAD7 *  SLREG              *   IWR
                  +         /SLREG * /LSLID4
                  +                  /LSLID4 * /IWR
                  + /IAD7          * /LSLID4


IF (TP03)/ICMATCH = /LICSPC
                  + /LPSB15 *  LSLID4
                  +  LPSB15 * /LSLID4
                  + /LPSB14 *  LSLID3
                  +  LPSB14 * /LSLID3
                  + /ICM1

IF (TP03)/ICM1    = /LPSB13 *  LSLID2
                  +  LPSB13 * /LSLID2
                  + /LPSB12 *  LSLID1
                  +  LPSB12 * /LSLID1
                  + /LPSB11 *  LSLID0
                  +  LPSB11 * /LSLID0

;form feed

DESCRIPTION

LGABH = RD*(/BE3+BE1)*(/BE3+/BE1+/BE0)*(LICREQ+PSBREQ+MICSEL)

LGABL = RD*(/BE3+BE0)*(LICREQ+PSBREQ)

LSAB  = RD*/LICREQ

LSBA  = LOCGNT+RIADRL+RIADRH

IGAB  = RIADRL+RIDATA

;form feed
```

```
PAL16R6B
DU24.001
PSB ADDRESS/DATA LATCH #3
INTEL CORPORATION, HILLSBORO, OREGON
BBCLK /BBSC0 /BBSC4 /BAD8 /BAD9 /BAD10 /BAD14 /BAD15 9 GND
/ENLCH /LPSB15 13 /SDATA15 /SDATA14 /SDATA10 /SDATA9 /SDATA8 /LPSB14 VCC

IF (VCC) LPSB15 = SDATA15

IF (VCC) LPSB14 = SDATA14

        SDATA15 :=  BBSC0           * BAD15
                  +         BBSC4 * BAD15
                  + /BBSC0 * /BBSC4         * SDATA15

        SDATA14 :=  BBSC0           * BAD14
                  +         BBSC4 * BAD14
                  + /BBSC0 * /BBSC4         * SDATA14

        SDATA10 :=  BBSC0           * BAD10
                  +         BBSC4 * BAD10
                  + /BBSC0 * /BBSC4         * SDATA10

        SDATA9  :=  BBSC0           * BAD9
                  +         BBSC4 * BAD9
                  + /BBSC0 * /BBSC4         * SDATA9

        SDATA8  :=  BBSC0           * BAD8
                  +         BBSC4 * BAD8
                  + /BBSC0 * /BBSC4         * SDATA8

FUNCTION TABLE
BBCLK /BBSC0 /BBSC4 /BAD8 /BAD9 /BAD10 /BAD14 /BAD15
/ENLCH /LPSB15 /SDATA15 /SDATA14 /SDATA10 /SDATA9 /SDATA8 /LPSB14
-------------------------------------------------------------------

DESCRIPTION
;form feed
```

APPENDIX C

Figure C-1. Typical MULTIBUS II Single Board Computer Diagram using the iSBX Bus Interface Component with Dual Port Memory

AP-256

OVERVIEW/NEXT GENERATION

The next generation iPSB Bus Interface Component is a highly integrated CMOS device implementing the full message passing protocol as well as the full functions (arbitration, transfer and exception cycle protocols) of the iPSB bus interface control as defined in the MULTIBUS® II Bus Architecture Handbook Specification.

FUNCTIONAL DESCRIPTION

Introduction

The iPSB Bus Interface Component provides a high integration interface solution for the iPSB bus of the MULTIBUS II bus architecture. This device integrates the logic to supply a full bus interface solution that includes support for message passing and interconnect spaces, as well as, memory and I/O references on the iPSB bus. In addition, this component is designed to simplify implementation of dual port memory functions for those designs which will co-exist with message passing.

Single board computers (SBCs) using this component are hardware and software compatible with SBCs using the Bus Arbiter Controller (BAC) and Message Interrupt Controller (MIC) MULTIMODULE™ board, as described in this application note.

Maximize iPSB Bus And Local On-Board Bus Performance

The message address space in the MULTIBUS II bus architecture has been defined to provide a high performance interprocessor communication mechanism for multiple processor systems. One of the key functions of the iPSB Bus Interface component is to support the message space interface by offloading the local on-board CPU from interprocessor communication tasks, resulting in a decoupling of the local bus activities from the iPSB bus activities. This decoupling eliminates an interface bottleneck present in traditional dual port architectures. The interface bottleneck is a result of dual port architecture requiring a tight coupling between a processor and some shared memory resource.

The advantages gained from using the iPSB Bus Interface component to decouple these resources are as follows. First, resources on the local processor bus and parallel system bus are not held in wait states while arbitration for other resources are occurring. Second, each transfer can occur at the full bandwidth of the associated bus. The benefit is increased overall system performance resulting from processors being able to process other tasks in parallel with message transfers being handled by the iPSB Bus Interface component (parallelism).

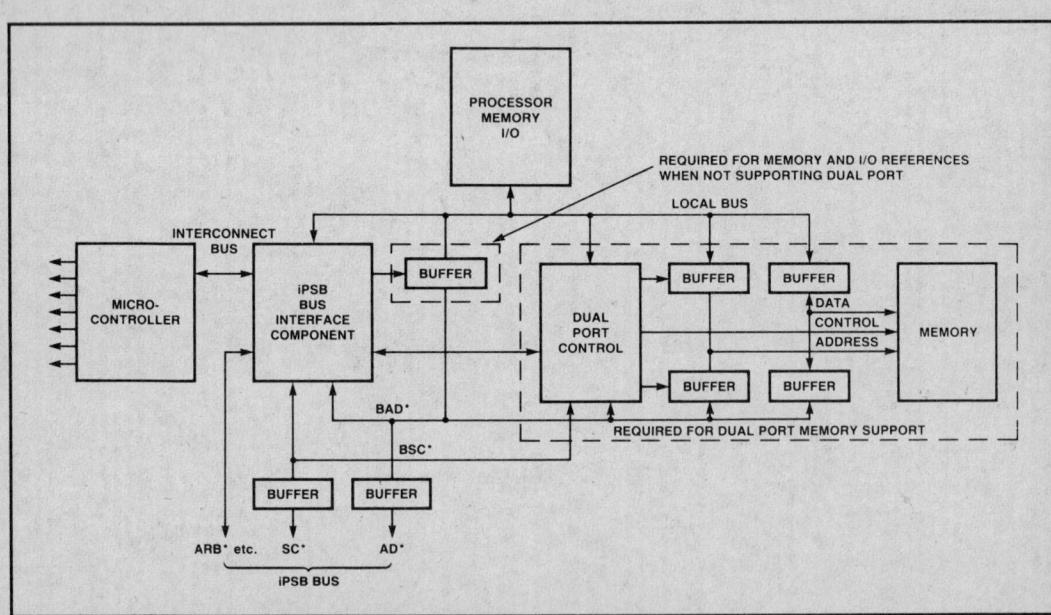

Figure C-1. Typical MULTIBUS® II Single Board Computer Diagram using the iPSB Bus Interface Component with Dual Port Memory

Arbitration, Transfer and Exception Cycle Protocol Support

The iPSB Bus Interface component implements the full arbitration cycle, transfer cycle and exception cycle protocols required to interface to the iPSB bus. Arbitration is supported for both normal fairness mode and high priority mode.

The iPSB Bus Interface component performs the handshake protocols necessary to successfully complete iPSB bus transfer operations. Transfer operations include; access to memory, I/O, message and interconnect address spaces on the iPSB bus. During the transfer cycle, this device generates and checks parity on the System Control lines (SC) and on the Address/Data lines (AD). In addition, the iPSB Bus Interface component recognizes agent errors and bus exceptions and reports these occurrances to the local CPU for recovery action.

INTERFACE DESCRIPTION

This section describes each of four interfaces of iPSB Bus Interface component. These interfaces include; the local bus, the iPSB bus, the interconnect bus and dual port memory.

The Local Bus Interface

The local bus interface is used to provide a processor independent path from the on-board CPU to the iPSB bus. This interface supports direct references (memory, I/O and interconnect address spaces) to the iPSB bus, references to local on-board interconnect space and the full protocol for unsolicited and solicited message operations to/from the on-board CPU. Within the iPSB Bus Interface component, local bus interface support consists of three logical interfaces: register, reference and DMA. The register interface is used for message operations and access to interconnect address registers on-board. These operations are completed fully asynchronous to the bus clock or interconnect bus operations. The reference interface is used to access resources asynchronous to the CPU (local interconnect space and memory, I/O and interconnect address spaces on the iPSB bus). The DMA interface is used to transfer data for solicited message operations. This interface is designed to allow either two cycle or single cycle transfers. Single cycle transfers allow direct transfer of data between the iPSB Bus Interface component and memory. To achieve higher performance via single cycle transfers, the DMA interface is optimized for aligned data structures, however, operation on arbitrary byte strings is also supported.

iPSB Bus Interface

The iPSB bus interface implements a full 32-bit interface to the iPSB bus. This implementation includes arbitration, requestor control, replier control and error handling functions. As a requestor, the iPSB Bus Interface component supports references to memory, I/O, and interconnect spaces, as well as message packet transmission. As a replier the iPSB Bus Interface component supports interconnect space and message packet reception. In addition, this interface provides significant management services for external dual port memory. These services include: address recognition, iPSB bus replier handshake, agent error checking and bus parity generation and checking. Although this device handles the majority of errors, the dual port memory controller is still responsible for generation and check of memory data parity.

Interconnect Bus Support

Simply stated, the interconnect address space provides a physical addressing mechanism (rather than logical) for software initialization and configuration of system parameters (reduces jumper configuration) and system level diagnostics. The interconnect bus provides a simple 8-bit path between the iPSB Bus Interface component and a user defined design for the implementation of interconnect space. All references to interconnect space (either from the local bus or the iPSB bus) are routed through this path for service. In addition, this interconnect bus can be used for non-reference related activities, such as diagnostics and Central Services Module (CSM) functions. An example of a highly functional interconnect space implementation is evidenced by the microcontroller implementation on Intel's iSBC® 286/100 board. Further details of this implementation are available in the iSBC 286/100 Hardware Reference Manual.

Dual Port Memory Support

Although the MULTIBUS II Bus Architecture has defined the message address space for optimized performance of interprocessor communication, more traditional designs can use dual port memory implementations. The iPSB bus interface has been defined to allow a coexistence of dual port memory and message passing architectures, however, it should be noted that the iPSB bus interface is optimized for message passing architectures. The iPSB Bus Interface component is designed to support this coexistence.(See Figure 1) This device can be configured to recognize a range of addresses in memory space and act as an iPSB bus replier when a match is detected. When an address is detected, the iPSB Bus Interface component signals the external dual port memory controller of the request. While the iPSB Bus Interface component provides an error detection and recovery mechanism for most agent errors and bus exceptions in a dual port design, it is still the responsibility of the dual port memory controller to generate and check memory data parity.

AP-256

Single Board Computer Configuration

The iPSB Bus Interface component provides a processor independent iPSB bus interface solution for intelligent SBC boards. Examples include CPU boards, intelligent peripheral controllers, file servers, intelligent data communications controllers and graphics/image processors. This component, like the BAC and MIC components, is optimized for bus master or intelligent slave designs. Figure C-1 below represents a typical CPU-based SBC board with dual port memory support. Using the iPSB Bus Interface component reduces overall board real estate required for the iPSB bus interface. This component actively improves system reliability by performing the error checking and reporting protocols defined in the iPSB bus interface specification.

ARTICLE REPRINT

AR-411

October 1985

MULTIBUS® II Designs Exploit Advanced Bus Concepts

AMY SHUEN
PRODUCT MARKETING ENGINEER
INTEL CORPORATION

JOHN BEASTON
MARKETING MANAGER
INTEL CORPORATION

Copyright 1985. Reprinted by permission from Computer Design February 1985.

Order Number: 280172-001

SYSTEM DESIGN/INTERFACE

MULTIBUS II DESIGNS EXPLOIT ADVANCED BUS CONCEPTS

With several bus architectures available, designers face the problem of choosing one that provides the features and flexibility needed for new multiprocessor designs.

by Amy Shuen and
John Beaston

New bus concepts that provide higher performance and increased reliability are becoming more important in multiprocessor system design. The Multibus II architecture and the products that use it incorporate these bus concepts, including interconnect space, cache-based memory, and message passing.

The family of products incorporating the Multibus II bus architecture ranges from the iSBC 286/100 CPU board to bus interface silicon. At the lowest level of the family are the bus arbiter controller (BAC) and the message interrupt controller (MIC). With their generic local bus interfaces, these CMOS components make it easier to develop boards and systems using any processor family or architecture. Most importantly, standardizing the bus interface portion of a board design ensures that board-level products from multiple vendors can communicate with one another, even with diverse processor or memory technologies.

The BAC and MIC components provide the interface standard for the parallel system bus (iPSB) of the Multibus II architecture. They implement the full data transfer and reliability features of this bus, as well as support for the interrupt message subset of the Multibus II message passing. The BAC performs all the arbitration and system control functions and the MIC transmits and receives interrupt messages.

The first of a family of Multibus II bus interface silicon, BAC and MIC offer the advantages of VLSI. With these components, bus interface real estate requirements are 70 percent less than those of equivalent programmable logic array implementations. The next generation of Multibus II bus interface silicon will integrate this combination of capabilities into one component with full message-passing support.

Bus interface in silicon

The BAC and MIC combination is so flexible that all intelligent Multibus II boards can take advantage of their features. A 286-based CPU board can handle central processing and multiple 186-based boards can perform file serving and other I/O functions in the same backplane. The board designer does not have to worry about mixing and matching bus interface components; the BAC and MIC combination provides a modular, multipurpose standardized interface to the system bus for any intelligent board.

The BAC performs the complete bus arbitration and system control line management for the board. It functions much like a combination of the 82289 bus arbiter and the 82288 system controller Multibus I interface components that has been optimized for the Multibus II specification. When the onboard CPU wishes to access the bus, it activates a bus request input to the BAC. The BAC then performs the appropriate arbitration algorithm (either fairness or priority algorithms are dynamically selectable) and returns a grant signal to the CPU once the bus is

---

Amy Shuen is a product marketing engineer for Multibus II products at Intel (Hillsboro, Ore). She holds an MBA from Harvard University.

John Beaston is marketing manager for Multibus II products at Intel. He holds an MS in electrical engineering from the University of Illinois.

acquired. During the data transfer, the BAC performs all the necessary handshaking and error checking on the system control lines.

The MIC component helps solve the fundamental problem of communicating interrupts among multiple boards. In a multimaster, multiprocessing system, the number of interrupts often exceeds the capacity of the traditional dedicated interrupt lines. Since the onboard MIC sends and receives all interrupt messages, it eliminates the hardware bottleneck. This controller manages up to 255 interrupt sources and destinations.

To send an interrupt message, the CPU simply tells the MIC which module to interrupt and the MIC does the rest. The MIC asks the BAC to gain access to the bus and once that is done, the MIC runs the appropriate message interrupt bus cycle. The CPU and its local bus are free to continue processing rather than waiting for arbitration and access to the system bus. Decoupling the CPU and local bus from the iPSB can dramatically improve CPU utilization.

For receiving interrupt messages, the MIC monitors the bus, looking for interrupt cycles containing its message destination address. When one is received, the message goes in an internal 4-deep first in, first out queue, and the CPU is interrupted. The CPU may then read the message from the queue. The CPU is involved only when a message is received.

The new bus interface components can identify bus parity errors and check for interrupt message accuracy. Any detected errors are registered on the appropriate component and are reported to the onboard CPU. The CPU may then read the error registers to identify the cause and take appropriate action.

The iSBC 286/100 single-board computer takes advantage of the Multibus II system architecture for OEM applications. The combination of the iAPX 286 processor and two new bus structures, the iPSB and the local bus extension II (iLBX II), makes the iSBC 286/100 board uniquely suited to high performance multimaster system application. This board supports the new Multibus II features of interconnect space, built-in-self-test diagnostics, and message-based interrupt.

The board is a complete microcomputer system on an 8.7- x 9.2-in., double-high Eurocard printed circuit board—roughly the same real estate as a Multibus I board. It has the complete functional capability of a single-board computer, including iSBX bus expansion, 80287 numerical coprocessor options, advanced DMA control, JEDEC memory sites and expansion, SCSI configurable parallel interface, serial I/O, and programmable timers.

The ever-increasing performance of CPUs coupled with their larger addressing ranges poses a dilemma to the board designer. The best CPU-to-RAM access performance comes with a high price tag. In addition, the CPU board cannot hold enough RAM to approach the CPU's maximum address size. These constraints have led designers to develop the

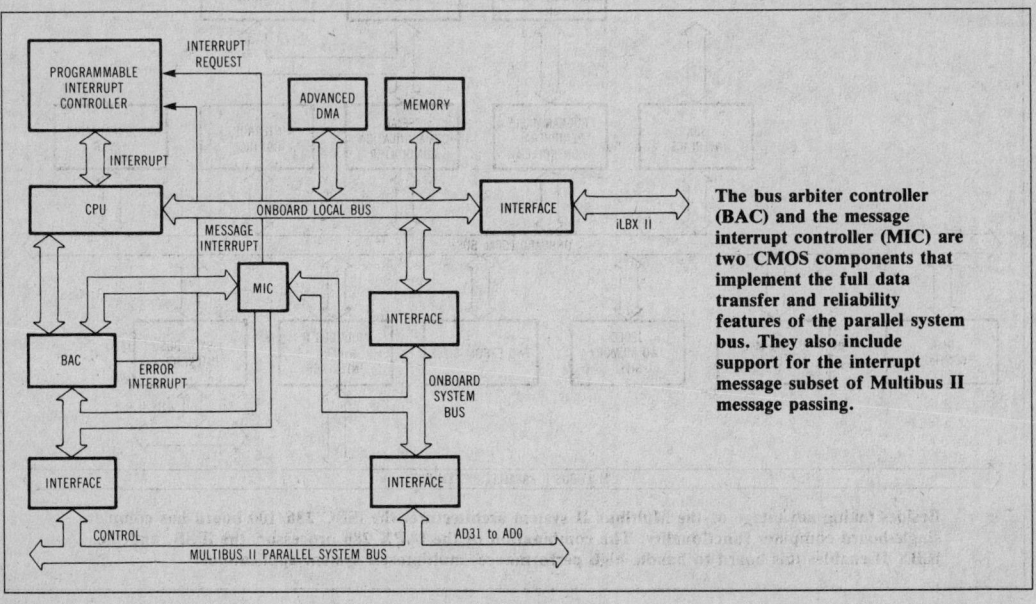

The bus arbiter controller (BAC) and the message interrupt controller (MIC) are two CMOS components that implement the full data transfer and reliability features of the parallel system bus. They also include support for the interrupt message subset of Multibus II message passing.

local extension memory bus concept, such as the iLBX II for the Multibus II.

The iSBC MEM/3xx memory boards in the family are cache-based, 32-bit dynamic RAM boards with dual-port support (iLBX II and iPSB). They provide both the performance and the memory capacity needed. The memory boards, together with the iSBC 286/100 CPU board, give 0 wait-state iLBX II access performance for up to 16 Mbytes of memory.

Cache memory concept

To illustrate the cache concept, imagine a desk drawer and a filing cabinet farther away—both are places to store documents. Frequently used files are in the desk drawer and the less frequently accessed files are in the filing cabinet. Correctly planned, 80 percent of the files needed will be in the drawer, limiting the number of trips to the file cabinet.

The desk drawer is a good analogy for the 8-Kbyte high speed cache memory on the iSBC MEM/3xx memory boards. Data requested by the iSBC 286/100 CPU from the memory board over the iLBX II bus is retrieved with 0 wait-states, if the data is in the cache. Depending upon the application code, 80 percent or more of the time the cache algorithm ensures that the data requested is in the cache. This is called a cache "hit." If the data requested is not in the cache memory, this is called a cache "miss." In the iSBC MEM/3xx and iSBC 286/100 combination, a cache miss takes 1 wait-state. These performance numbers refer to up to 16 Mbytes of iLBX II memory, the full physical addressing range of the 286 CPU. Each memory board added to iLBX II adds an additional 8 Kbytes of cache.

Going back to the desk drawer and file cabinet analogy, a search will go outside the desk drawer less than 20 percent of the time. Some of the unused less current documents from the desk drawer can go into the filing cabinet. The documents needed immediately, as well as some that might be used later, return to the desk. This simple, but effective, algorithm increases the probability that the desk drawer will contain the most useful documents, and that processing time will be used efficiently.

The cache replacement algorithm works in a similar way. On any miss or write access, the contents of one cache entry are updated to maintain consistency with the corresponding entry in the DRAM array. In addition, a full 32 bits, two sequential 16-bit words, are moved each time.

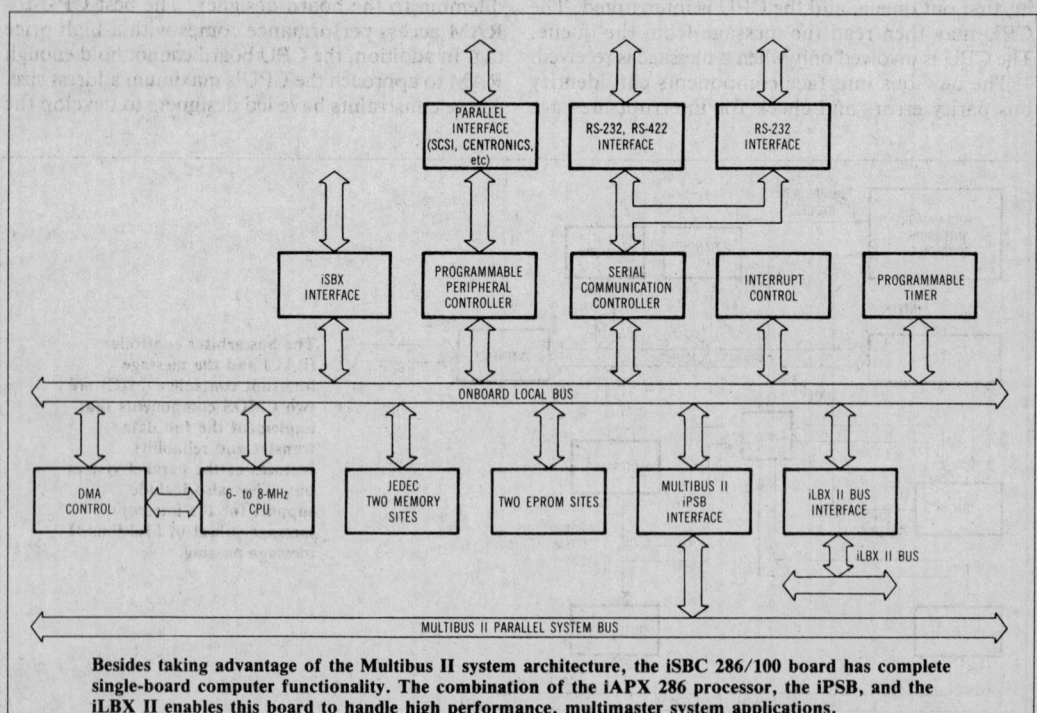

Besides taking advantage of the Multibus II system architecture, the iSBC 286/100 board has complete single-board computer functionality. The combination of the iAPX 286 processor, the iPSB, and the iLBX II enables this board to handle high performance, multimaster system applications.

The cache control and most of the logic required on the iSBC MEM/3xx memory boards are implemented in VLSI. This proprietary cache controller supports the 32-bit architecture of both the iLBX II and iPSB interfaces. A VLSI solution saves real estate for putting large amounts of DRAM (64- or 256-Kbits) on the memory boards along with an 8-Kbyte high speed static RAM. These new cache-based, 32-bit memory boards come in 1/2-, 1-, 2-, or 4-Mbyte sizes.

Software and hardware converge

One of the advanced concepts of the Multibus II architecture is the definition of the interconnect address space, which integrates hardware and software. This integrated approach makes building and dynamically configuring a Multibus II system easier and faster. Multibus II interconnect space is a combination of a standardized set of read-only and software configurable registers on every board and the ability to access them by any bus master.

An integrated approach makes building and dynamically configuring a Multibus II system easier and faster.

The read-only registers hold information, such as board type, revision number, and serial number. This allows board manufacturers to code this information into the hardware so that software can determine what boards are being used in a system, and configure itself automatically. The software configurable registers allow software to write to these registers for board configuration purposes or to access or control diagnostics. This facility can help reduce or completely eliminate hardwired jumpers or DIP switches and gives new flexibility for local and remote diagnostics.

Geographic or by-slot addressing allows the software to address individual boards via their physical position in the backplane. Automatically at power-up, the iSBC CSM/100 assigns slot IDs to the boards located on the iPSB backplane. These IDs are picked up and saved by the onboard BAC. After this assignment, software can identify which boards are in the system and where they are located. This becomes system configuration information.

By using the interconnect address space to perform geographic addressing, the iRMX 86 Multibus II operating system automatically configures all memory boards at power-up. The system software is aware of the hardware characteristics of the memory boards because each of the iSBC MEM/3xx boards has read-only registers in its onboard interconnect space registers. These registers indicate the size of the DRAM array of that particular board.

The iRMX 86 Multibus II operating system identifies which memory boards are in the system and where they are in the iPSB backplane and then assigns the starting and ending address of each board. This assignment is made by the system software writing to the software configurable interconnect registers located on each board. As a result, no hardwired jumpers are necessary on the iSBC MEM/3xx boards. Changing the memory size or swapping memory boards is an easy and straightforward process—simply put new boards in the backplane and power-up the system and the software does the rest.

The central services module also supplies the system clocks and contains front panel reset and interrupt switches. In addition, it provides a battery-powered time-of-day clock so that software can access time/date records and initialize local clocks. It also forms one side of a link to Multibus I systems. Also, it contains an 8751 microcontroller to perform built-in-self-test (BIST) diagnostics.

Every Intel Multibus II board has an 8751 microcontroller onboard and firmware to run these BIST system confidence tests at power-up or at software command to check out each board's vital functions. These confidence tests and diagnostics improve reliability and error reporting capability and reduce manufacturing and maintenance costs for the user.

A microcomputer watchdog

The BIST diagnostics combined with the use of interconnect space provides a powerful diagnostics and development environment. The BISTs provide vital board status and error information at power-up. Because this error information is recorded in each board's interconnect space registers, the information can be accessed from software on a system-wide basis for logging, display, or remote diagnostic purposes. Additionally, during development, modification, or manufacture of a Multibus II system, you can evoke specific BISTs for status information significant to a particular application.

The BIST results are indicated in two ways. First, an LED on the front panel indicates the status of the power-up diagnostics. It is on when the BIST starts running and off when the BIST completes successfully. Second, the diagnostic test results are stored in the onboard interconnect registers accessible to system software.

In a large, complex multiprocessing system it is often difficult to determine the specific hardware source of a system failure. The interconnect space allows software to access board status and diagnostic information. The system software can identify which

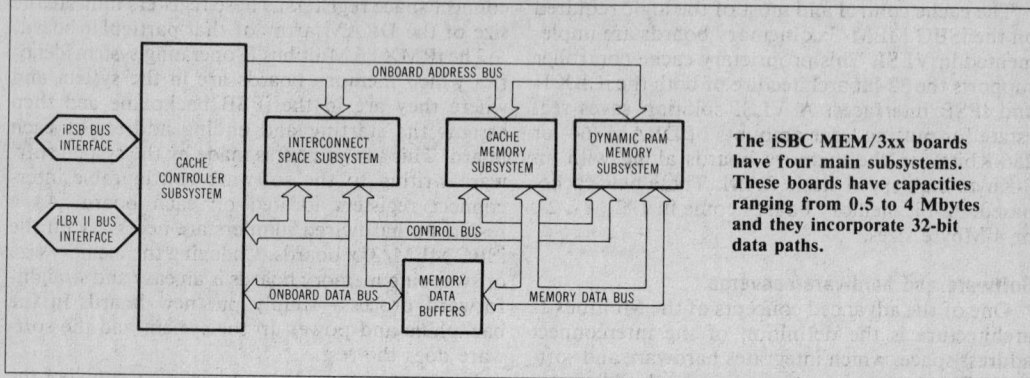

The iSBC MEM/3xx boards have four main subsystems. These boards have capacities ranging from 0.5 to 4 Mbytes and they incorporate 32-bit data paths.

boards in a system passed or failed their power-up diagnostics and by examining the appropriate error register contents determine the possible sources of the failure. The software can then dynamically change the memory size to disable a nonfunctioning memory board. It can also check for correct installation of the iSBX bus or PROM on a remote iSBC 286/100 board. Additionally, the iRMX 86 Multibus II operating system can interrogate the boards in the system for their system-wide go/no go status and thus determine problem boards.

As an example of the BISTs, a memory board will not function properly if the DRAM array, the cache RAM array, or the parity detection are not functioning properly. The BIST performed by the onboard microcontroller checks vital functions; an address ripple RAM test on DRAM array in Miss Only operation mode, a cache RAM test on all the cache memory, a Refresh check on a small portion of DRAM, and a parity test which injects parity errors in the DRAM and verifies that the board detects them accurately.

Until now, system performance enhancements have come primarily from improvements in CPU technology: higher clock speeds and wider data paths. There have been very few similar technology improvements applied to the system architecture. The Multibus II architecture is specifically designed to accommodate CPU improvements while allowing technology to be applied to the system architecture. Enhanced CPUs give raw performance improvements, but the message-passing concept allows similar improvements in system architecture.

Performance improvements lie in the efficient support of multiprocessing. Multiprocessing is not a new concept, however. The problems encountered in implementing it tend to reduce its promised benefits. Many systems contain multiple processors such as a host CPU, an intelligent disk controller, and other intelligent I/O subsystems. The job of communication and data movement among boards has typically been a system software and dual-ported memory task. Multibus II message passing standardizes the communication and data movement functions among the boards. This standardization allows the application of VLSI to the problem. It gives a hardware-based solution to the problem, alleviating the software development burden and giving hardware assistance to data movement.

The message-passing protocol specified by the Multibus II architecture achieves full multiprocessing capability. The next generation of bus interface silicon provides a hardware solution to off-loading the CPU during the interprocessor communication and data movement functions. Very much like a distributed smart DMA controller, this message-passing coprocessor communicates with other intelligent boards to transfer data and information over the system bus. The CPU that initiates this communication is free to continue its computing process until the data is received.

The benefits of this silicon-supported approach are significant. First the message-passing interface can take full advantage of the bus bandwidth—32-bit data and burst transfer mode—independent of the type, word width, or architecture of communicating processors. Hardware transfer rates and I/O system performance is higher than a software-based I/O transfer where the software must copy and check each transfer and CPU intervention is required. Also, since the message-passing interface effectively decouples the local-system-local bus transaction, each portion of the transfer can proceed at the maximum transfer rate of that bus. The communicating boards utilize as little of the all important system bus bandwidth as possible, freeing it for additional communication.

Second, the Multibus II message-passing interface provides a uniform software interface for all boards in the system. Since modules communicate through

Service & Support   17

Service & Support

17

OPEN SYSTEMS MAINTENANCE AGREEMENT SERVICE

- ☐ Gives immediate access to Intel's domestic and international service offerings.
- ☐ Eliminates the need to put an expensive field organization in place.
- ☐ Allows for individually tailored contracts.
- ☐ Provides a comprehensive maintenance program.
- ☐ Combines the technical expertise of factory service and the unified support of third party service in one maintenance offering.

© INTEL CORPORATION, 1984

JANUARY, 1984
ORDER NUMBER: 230940-001

DESCRIPTION

INTEL'S OPEN SYSTEMS MAINTENANCE PROGRAM CAN COVER YOUR ENTIRE SYSTEM, NOT JUST THE INTEL PRODUCTS.

Open Systems Service is Intel's customized Hardware Maintenance Agreement service for systems integrators, OEMs and large volume end-users. The program provides overnight access to an international service organization that will support the entire end-user system, including value-added and other vendor products with full maintenance at the end-user customer site.

The primary difference between an Open Systems Maintenance Agreement and an Intel Standard Hardware Maintenance Agreement (see Standard Hardware Maintenance Agreement Services) is that substantial "pre-product release" interaction occurs between Intel and the System Integrator, OEM or large volume end-user. Usually, the service organization interacts only with an internal engineering organization; not the System Integrator, OEM or large volume end-user. In our Open Systems Maintenance Agreement, the System Integrator, OEM or large volume end-user customer provides the Intel Service organization with the same maintainability items that would have been provided by internal engineering groups had Intel designed the end-product.

FULL SERVICE SUPPORT FOR CUSTOMERS WITH LIMITED SERVICE CAPABILITY.

Open Systems Service is designed for the customer who is developing a custom system composed primarily of Intel product; however, it *can* also include other vendor value-added portions of the system by negotiation.

This service is also ideal for the customer who has limited or no field service capability; or one who has a service organization in place, but lacks the geographic distribution or certain unique technical skills to support the product.

HELPS YOU "ENGINEER IN" SERVICEABILITY.

Timely service planning is key to the successful introduction, installation and ongoing support of your product. Service integrates into every aspect of product planning, from conceptual engineering through production and distribution. Intel's Open Systems Service program helps you to "engineer in" serviceability and "engineer out" costly after-sale support. Your product assumes a position of *quality of design* and *quality of support* in the marketplace.

Typical OEM configuration incorporating an Intel system with other vendor hardware and the customer's application software. Who will provide service and support?

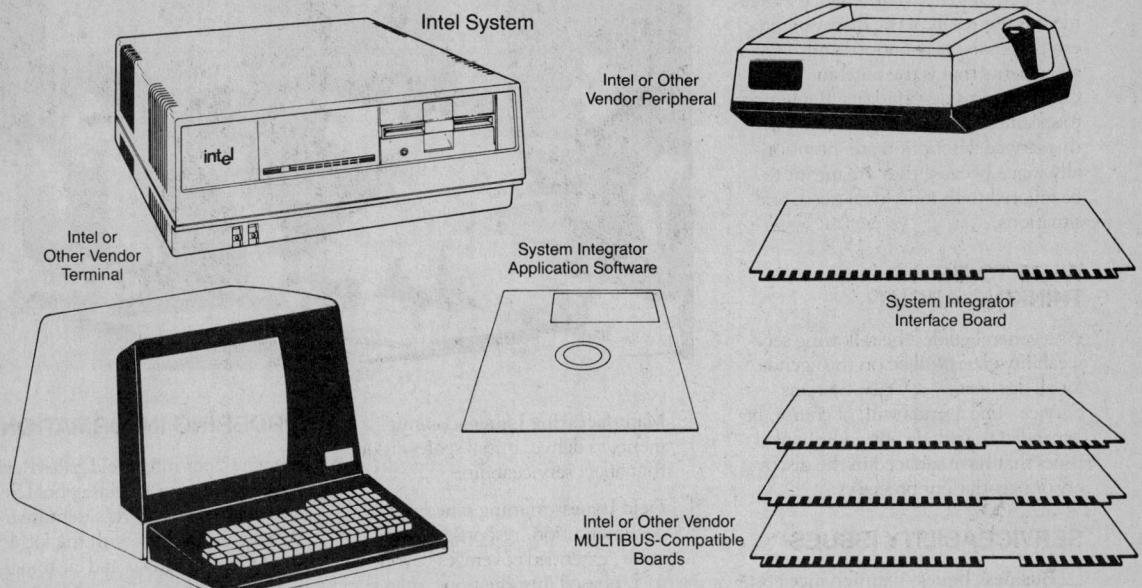

EACH CONTRACT IS INDIVIDUALLY TAILORED BY NEGOTIATION.

Once a need is established by the customer and Intel, a team consisting of the local Intel account salesman, a factory Customer Marketing Engineer and a local field engineering manager will work with you to structure an Open Systems Maintenance Agreement.

After the customer identifies the elements of his systems, a budget planning quote is discussed. An open systems presentation is then given to customer management, and is followed by a discovery meeting, proposals and negotiations. Finally a contract is drawn up, assuring the System Integrator, OEM or volume end-user, that his product will be fully supportable at his end-user customer site, once it is released for sale.

SPECIFICATIONS

DIVISION OF RESPONSIBILITIES

The following chart shows in simplified form, the division of responsibilities between the Systems Integrator, OEM or volume end-user and Intel's service organization.

INTEL

☐ Acts as service agent to end-user customers.

☐ Provides standard system-level parts.

☐ Provides local field management of service organization to ensure a high level of service delivery.

☐ Subcontracts at a base price:
 • unlimited repair service
 • scheduled preventive maintenance.

☐ Subcontracts at an hourly rate:
 • installation/deinstallation
 • equipment relocation
 • engineering change installation
 • service outside contract hours.

SYSTEM INTEGRATOR

☐ Provides spares for all non-Intel system components.

☐ Provides second-level technical back-up for value-added features.

☐ Provides as required:
 • special tools
 • special field test equipment
 • altered diagnostics
 • value-added software/hardware documentation.

☐ Provides equipment and materials for training classes.

☐ Negotiates service outside Intel's established service areas.

THE FINAL CONTRACT DESIGN

An Open Systems Maintenance Agreement is the result of the discovery process, proposals, negotiations and agreements that is the outcome of the Open Systems negotiations. References to specifications of the agreement in this service description are intentionally vague because they are meant to be tailored to fit individual needs and situations.

WHAT TO BE THINKING ABOUT

As a general guide, the following serviceability issues will be on the agenda for all discussions of Open Systems Service. The agenda will, of course, be expanded to include any additional issues that have surfaced in the discovery or negotiations processes.

SERVICEABILITY ISSUES

- ☐ **Business Issues**–maintenance costing, profitability.
- ☐ **Engineering Issues**–serviceability, reliability, diagnostics, manuals, special tools, parts interchangeability, engineering change impact on serviceability.
- ☐ **Logistics Issues**–initial spares demand, spares distribution, failure rates.
- ☐ **Training Issues**–background requirements, how many, how fast, where, what media (i.e., classroom–video–self study) training equipment.
- ☐ **Manufacturing Issues**–commitments to deliver initial spares, issues that affect serviceability.
- ☐ **Field Issues**–training schedules, documentation, response commitment, extended coverages beyond 8 to 5, phased introductions, spares and test equipment in place.
- ☐ **System Issues**–configuration constraints, software support, installation requirements.
- ☐ **The End Result**–enhanced marketability of your product, maximizing it by addressing and solving these significant issues.
- ☐ **Geographic Distribution of Product**

ORDERING INFORMATION

Contact your Intel Field Sales Representative or your Intel Regional Service Manager. A factory representative will be assigned to work with the local Intel representatives and customer personnel.

Following initial discussions, a draft proposal will be prepared. Normal negotiations proceed until a document acceptable to both parties is completed.

Intel Corporation
Customer Support Operations
2402 West Beardsley Road
Phoenix, Arizona 85027

Intel International Ltd.
Customer Support Operations
Pipers Way
Swindon, Wiltshire
England, SN31 RJ

Intel Japan K.K.
IJKK Customer Support Operations
4-15-1 Tsurumaki
Setagaya-Ku, Tokyo 154
Japan

SOFTWARE SUPPORT CONTRACT

- Combines the most commonly requested software support services. Fixed, easy-to-budget monthly fee.
- Customer selects level of support.
  Standard Service: Updates, Subscription Service, and TIP Service
  Basic Service: Updates and Subscription Service

UPDATES

- Diskettes or other media, manuals and documentation for all covered updates as they are released.

SUBSCRIPTION SERVICE

- Product-specific written information service.
- Access to Software Problem Reporting Service.
- Published documentation for the latest identified and validated product problems and their solutions.

TIP SERVICE

- Telephone access to Intel's Software Support Staff.
- Direct, timely product-specific information.
- Technical assistance on operational understanding, usage and documentation; and on suspected product problems or deficiencies.
- On-site customer assistance, at Intel's option.

DESCRIPTION

INTEL'S STANDARD AND BASIC SOFTWARE SUPPORT CONTRACTS PROVIDE THE MOST COMMONLY REQUESTED SUPPORT SERVICES FOR AN EASY-TO-BUDGET MONTHLY CHARGE.

STANDARD SERVICE	
TIP SERVICE	BASIC SERVICE
UPDATES	UPDATES
SUBSCRIPTIONS	SUBSCRIPTIONS

Intel's Software Support Contracts provide: updates, manuals and documentation for covered products as released; Intel's ;COMMENTS technical newsletter; product-specific technical reports; written responses to customer inquiries under our Software Problem Reporting (SPR) Service; and access to TIP Service phone support.

Packaged in a convenient "environment" form, the Standard and Basic Software Contracts cover all supported software products that run in a particular environment.

Additional software products purchased at a later date which run in the covered environment may be added at no extra charge by simply registering the product.

UPDATES INSURE THAT YOU HAVE THE LATEST RELEASED VERSION OF ANY INTEL SOFTWARE.

Under the terms of the contract, Intel will provide manuals, documentation, diskettes or other media of the customer's choice for all covered updates as they are released. The customer must register the products covered in the contract environment. Once the products are registered, the update process is automatic.

UPDATE FLOW CHART
(With Software Support Contract)

```
                    ENTER
                      │
                      ▼
      ┌───────────────────────────────────┐
      │ CUSTOMER CONTRACTS FOR SOFTWARE   │
      │ SUPPORT COVERAGE.                 │
      └───────────────────────────────────┘
                      │
                      ▼
      ┌───────────────────────────────────┐
      │ INTEL SENDS REGISTRATION PACKET   │
      │ TO CUSTOMER DESIGNATED SOFTWARE   │
      │ CONTACT.                          │
      └───────────────────────────────────┘
                      │
          ┌───────────┴───────────┐
          ▼                       ▼
 ┌──────────────────┐   ┌──────────────────┐
 │ CUSTOMER         │   │ INTEL RELEASES   │
 │ DESIGNATED       │   │ NEW SOFTWARE     │
 │ CONTACT          │   │ UPDATE.          │
 │ REGISTERS        │   └──────────────────┘
 │ SOFTWARE         │
 │ PURCHASED UNDER  │
 │ CONTRACT         │
 │ ENVIRONMENT.     │
 └──────────────────┘
          │
          ▼
 ┌───────────────────────────────────────┐
 │ INTEL VERIFIES IF SOFTWARE IS AT      │
 │ CURRENT RELEASE LEVEL.                │
 └───────────────────────────────────────┘
        │                       │
       yes                      no
        ▼                       ▼
 ┌──────────────────┐   ┌───────────────────────────┐
 │ RECORD LEVEL IN  │   │ CHECK FILE AND ORDER      │
 │ CUSTOMER FILE.   │   │ UPDATE IN MEDIA FORMAT    │
 └──────────────────┘   │ SPECIFIED BY CUSTOMER.    │
                        └───────────────────────────┘
                      │
                      ▼
      ┌───────────────────────────────────┐
      │ ASSEMBLE AND MAIL UPDATE,         │
      │ MANUALS, DOCUMENTATION TO         │
      │ CUSTOMER DESIGNATED SOFTWARE      │
      │ CONTACT.                          │
      └───────────────────────────────────┘
```

Updates are released whenever product performance requires it. In the early life of a product, updates will occur quite often. However, as the product matures, update releases will be less frequent, seldom more than quarterly.

INTEL'S SUBSCRIPTION SERVICE HELPS KEEP DESIGN TEAMS UP-TO-DATE AND UP-TO-SPEED.

Intel's Subscription Service is an efficient communications mechanism intended to provide customer engineering personnel with the latest Intel software and system product data, as well as information regarding product and documentation inconsistencies.

It is also a mechanism to enable customers to report suspected product problems to Intel's engineering organization.

Subscription Service consists of two separate information services:

☐ **Information Service** provides product-specific documentation designed to keep design teams up-to-date and productive, with the latest technical information about Intel's software and system products.

Intel's Information Service includes:

☐ **;COMMENTS** - a technical bulletin which contains operational tips, programming techniques and other technical information covering Intel's wide range of software and system products.

☐ **Troubleshooting Guides** - technical information regarding current software problems, interim programming solutions and application articles. Published periodically, by product or product family.

☐ **Software Problem Reporting (SPR) Service** is a written communications vehicle for customers to use to inquire about or to report

SPR FLOW CHART

ENTER

YOU HAVE ENCOUNTERED A PROBLEM WHICH APPEARS TO BE WITH THE INTEL SOFTWARE, OR YOU HAVE A QUESTION ABOUT THE PRODUCT, OR YOU HAVE A SUGGESTION FOR A PRODUCT IMPROVEMENT.

SUBMIT AN SPR

YOU COMPLETE AN SPR AND SUBMIT IT TO INTEL. THE SPR IS LOGGED IN, DATE STAMPED, ASSIGNED AN SPR #, AN ACKNOWLEDGEMENT IS RETURNED (WITHIN 48 HRS.), AND THE SPR IS ASSIGNED TO A MEMBER OF THE INTEL SOFTWARE SUPPORT STAFF FOR ANALYSIS AND RESPONSE. SHOULD ADDITIONAL INFORMATION BE REQUIRED TO GENERATE A RESPONSE, THE ASSIGNED SOFTWARE ENGINEER WILL CONTACT YOU.

PRODUCT DEFICIENCY — yes / no

PERMANENT SOLUTION KNOWN? — yes / no

THE RESPONSE WILL ADVISE ON THE PERMANENT SOLUTION THAT IS AVAILABLE IN THE FORM OF:
☐ AN UPDATE
☐ NEW RELEASE
☐ A PATCH

THE RESPONSE WILL BE A STATEMENT OF INTENT OR ACTION, AS TO WHETHER THE PROBLEM WILL OR WILL NOT BE RESOLVED AND PROVIDE ADVICE ON ANY KNOWN:
☐ INTERIM SOLUTIONS
☐ WORK-AROUNDS
☐ TEMPORARY FIXES
☐ PATCHES

THE RESPONSE WILL PROVIDE AT LEAST ONE OF THE FOLLOWING:
☐ ADVICE ON DOCUMENTATION OR OPERATIONAL PROBLEMS.
☐ SUGGESTONS ON AVOIDING ANY APPLICATION PROBLEMS.
☐ SUGGESTION TO FURTHER ISOLATE AN APPARENT PRODUCT PROBLEM.
☐ A STATEMENT AS TO WHETHER A SUGGESTED IMPROVEMENT WILL BE INCORPORATED INTO THE PRODUCT.

suspected product problems, or to suggest product improvements. All Software Problem Reports (SPRs) are reviewed by a member of the Software Support Staff, and are answered in writing as quickly and completely as possible.

INTEL'S TIP SERVICE PROVIDES TELEPHONE ACCESS TO INTEL'S TRAINED SOFTWARE ENGINEERING STAFF.

TIP Service is a product-specific telephone information service designed to address time-critical product inquiries by providing direct access to Intel's trained Software Engineering Staff. This direct response mechanism will aid in obtaining maximum utilization of your Intel software products. TIP Service provides a timely response to those time-critical product questions that could not be answered by the product documentation, the Software Problem Reporting Service or the regularly published Technical Reports.

SOFTWARE ENGINEERING STAFF HELPS ISOLATE AND SOLVE PROBLEMS.

Intel's Software Engineering Staff is a group specifically established to provide the following services to users of Intel software and system products:

- ☐ Centralized access to Intel's engineering and support resources.
- ☐ The latest technical information on Intel defined and documented product problems and deficiencies, and their associated work-arounds, temporary fixes, patches or other solutions.
- ☐ Technical assistance in isolating the cause or source of a suspected product problem.
- ☐ A central Software Problem Reporting (SPR) Service.

TIP SERVICE FLOW CHART

ENTER

YOU HAVE ENCOUNTERED A SITUATION WHICH APPEARS TO BE A PROBLEM WITH THE INTEL SOFTWARE. NEITHER THE DOCUMENTATION NOR THE LATEST TECHNICAL REPORT ARE OF ANY HELP IN ISOLATING THE PROBLEM OR AVOIDING THE SITUATION.

CALL TIP SERVICE

YOU ARE ASSIGNED AN INCIDENT REPORT NUMBER AND ARE IMMEDIATELY PUT IN CONTACT WITH AN ENGINEER SPECIALLY TRAINED ON INTEL'S SOFTWARE PRODUCTS. THE SOFTWARE ENGINEER WILL, FROM YOUR INPUT AND HIS/HER PRODUCT KNOWLEDGE, ATTEMPT TO ASCERTAIN WHETHER THE SITUATION IS A KNOWN SYMPTOM/PROBLEM.

SYMPTOM/PROBLEM KNOWN?

yes:
THE SOFTWARE ENGINEER WILL, BASED ON THE LATEST KNOWN PRODUCT INFORMATION, SUGGEST:
- ☐ AN UPDATE OR NEW RELEASE
- ☐ A WORK-AROUND
- ☐ A PATCH
- ☐ A TEMPORARY FIX

OR, IF NONE OF THESE ARE AVAILABLE, THE LATEST STATUS OF THE PROBLEM AND ITS RESOLUTION

KNOWN PRODUCT PROBLEM.

NEW PRODUCT DEFICIENCY

SOFTWARE ENGINEER WILL SUBMIT SPR IN YOUR NAME.

no:
THE SOFTWARE ENGINEER WILL WORK WITH YOU PROVIDING PROBLEM ISOLATION TECHNIQUES, GATHERING MORE INFORMATION, ETC., IN AN ATTEMPT TO ASSIST IN ISOLATING THE SOURCE OF THE PROBLEM TO ONE OF THE FOLLOWING:
- ☐ PRODUCT DEFICIENCY
- ☐ OPERATIONAL PROBLEM
- ☐ APPLICATION PROBLEM

RESULTS?

OPERATIONAL/APPLICATION PROBLEM.

THE SOFTWARE ENGINEER WILL DIRECT YOU TO THE APPROPRIATE USER DOCUMENTATION WHICH DESCRIBES THE CORRECT PROCEDURE FOR USING THE PRODUCT.

SPECIFICATIONS

SOFTWARE CONTRACTS

Software contracts are written on "environments," and Intel supported products that run on the environments are covered. All available environments are listed in the current version of the price book.

To select a contract environment, the user should first identify the software products used or planned for use, and then identify the environment or environments that provide the broadest or most complete coverage. To activate support services, the customer must register the products which have been purchased and are included under the environment.

A basic monthly fee is set for the first system covered. All additional systems are covered at a reduced rate per system. Customers are entitled to updates and subscriptions equivalent to the total number of systems covered under the contract. There is a maximum charge on NRM Network Systems.

Standard level service includes TIP phone support, and users are entitled to two callers for each system covered under the contract.

Contracts have a minimum one-year term and continue in force until cancelled with 30 days written notice.

UPDATES

At the time the contract is signed, the customer must provide the name and address of the person who will receive the updates. In addition, the customer must identify the type of media desired. Intel will forward copies of the update, in the specified media, along with associated manuals and documentation, based on the number of system products covered under the contract.

SUBSCRIPTION SERVICE

;COMMENTS Technical Bulletin – ;COMMENTS is published monthly and is provided to all contract customers. ;COMMENTS contains useful application data, operational tips, programming techniques and update notification for all Intel software products.

Troubleshooting Guides – At each release of a software product, an initial Troubleshooting Guide is published. It contains the performance status (known bugs, performance problems and associated interim and permanent solutions, if available) and a description of its differences (problems fixed and enhancements) from the previous release. Addendums to the Technical Reports will be published periodically to provide the latest known technical information.

Software Problem Reporting – TIP Service is the most expeditious form of software support and satisfies the majority of customer inquiries. However, where time is not of the essence and the customer wishes written documentation of the problem, Intel's Software Problem Reporting Service can be used.

To use the service, complete one of the SPR forms provided with the product, attach any listings or documentation needed to clarify the problem, and send it to the address indicated on the form.

Intel will send a receipt acknowledgement, the assigned SPR number for future reference, and a new SPR form. The SPR will be assigned to a member of the Software Support Staff for disposition and a written response will be provided to the customer. Most SPRs are handled in three to four weeks.

Newly identified problems or symptoms and their associated solutions and work-arounds are summarized and published as part of the next Technical Report.

TIP SERVICE

TIP Service will provide telephone assistance for two callers for each system covered under the contract. The callers will have, by phone, direct access to Intel's trained Software Engineering Staff within Intel's Central Customer Support Center during normal working hours (7:00 a.m. MST to 6:00 p.m.). The Software Engineering Staff will provide the latest known information on product problems and their associated work-arounds, temporary fixes, patches or interim solutions.

When the customer calls TIPS, the receptionist will initiate a numbered Incident Report and provide the customer with this assigned number for future reference. At this point, the contact will be able to speak with a member of Intel's Software Engineering Staff. If one is not immediately available, the call will be returned within two hours.

The Intel Software Engineer will provide problem identification; work-around, patch or other solutions when available; or information on existing Software Problem Reports, as shown in the TIP Service flow chart. The Software Engineer will also provide advice on problem isolation techniques to assist in dealing with situations in which a product deficiency has not been confirmed. Upon conclusion of the incident, the Incident Report is closed and permanently logged and filed.

Any new symptom, problem or work-around identified by the customer or the Software Engineer is added to the Software Problem Report (SPR) Service for future reference and incorporated into the appropriate Troubleshooting Guide.

LIMITATIONS AND RESTRICTIONS

Subscription Service is primarily intended to provide known information on product problems.

The SPR System is intended to enable customers to identify product problems to Intel's Engineering departments. Identification and verification of a product problem ensures that it will be inserted into the engineering work schedule. It does not, however, guarantee immediate attention or resolution.

TIP Service is primarily intended to provide known technical information on Intel products and/or advice on techniques for isolating suspected product problems. TIP Service does not promise to provide engineering or consulting time to derive an immediate resolution to a product problem within the customer's environment. Consulting Services are provided for customers whose specific situation requires immediate attention. For a detailed description of this service, please refer to the Consulting Services fact sheet.

Temporary solutions — any workarounds, temporary fixes or patches and interim solutions provided as part of Technical Reports, ;COMMENTS, an SPR response, or made as a result of TIP Service phone recommendations are made only as suggestions, and may have only been partially qualified within the product's standard hardware and operation environment. They are, therefore, not guaranteed to perform within a customer's specific environment.

Permanent solutions to a problem (i.e., updates, new releases and permanent patches) are provided only after they have been qualified and tested to the product's specifications and released by Engineering for incorporation into the product.

New problems — any new suspected product problem or deficiency (i.e., one that is not currently known or documented as an Intel-confirmed product problem) will be submitted through the Software Problem Reporting (SPR) Service.

CUSTOMER RESPONSIBILITIES

Customer education — Intel's Engineering and Software Support staffs concentrate their attention on the current release of Intel software products. Accordingly, to receive the highest level of support, all system hardware, firmware and software should be maintained by the customer at the most current version and release levels. In addition, it is expected that the customer will attend training classes and orientation sessions as appropriate, and will make a reasonable effort to utilize all the product documentation.

Customer contacts — the customer must provide a designated contact and alternate for TIP Service support, a contact for software registration, and proper mailing addresses for updates and documentation. Should these change, it is the customer's responsibility to notify Intel.

Customer documentation — in order to ensure timely and complete response, the customer is encouraged to provide any supportive documentation (including listings, code files, etc.) requested by the Intel Software Engineer for the purpose of identifying and validating a suspected product problem. Any and all customer-specific application documentation received by Intel will be held in strict confidence.

ORDERING INFORMATION

Software support contracts are placed in effect by completing an Intel System Service Agreement. Eligible contract environments are listed in the current Intel price book. Contact your Intel Sales Representative, Field Application Engineer, System Engineer or Customer Engineer through your local Intel Sales or Service office to arrange for contracted coverage.

intel®

Intel Corporation
Customer Support Operations
2402 W. Beardsley Rd.
Phoenix, AZ 85027

Intel International Ltd.
Customer Support Operations
Pipers Way
Swindon, Wiltshire
England, SN31RJ

Intel Japan K.K.
IJKK Customer Support Operations
4-15-1 Tsurumaki
Setagaya-Ku, Tokyo 154
Japan

TRAINING WORKSHOPS

- ☐ Provide in-depth exposure and practical "hands-on" experience with Intel products.
- ☐ Quick and effective microcomputer and systems training.
- ☐ Lab sessions using Intel design equipment and instructional materials including slide/video presentations and reference manuals.
- ☐ Conducted at 18 international Intel Training Center locations, or at Customer sites for on-site project teams.

© INTEL CORPORATION, 1984

SEPTEMBER, 1984
ORDER NUMBER: 230943-002

DESCRIPTION

INTEL'S TRAINING WORKSHOPS PROVIDE HANDS-ON TRAINING, REDUCE DEVELOPMENT TIME.

Intel's comprehensive training workshops are 3 to 9 day training sessions where a limited number of individuals receive detailed technical training and attend hands-on laboratory sessions that enable them to learn to design with Intel products.

The workshops are a proven fast and efficient way to provide training to new design team members who otherwise would spend weeks of self-study to attain optimum productivity. The workshops are an excellent way to get engineers up to speed quickly.

COURSES COVER ALL ASPECTS OF SYSTEMS DESIGN AND IMPLEMENTATION.

A variety of courses is offered regularly. The major course categories include:

- ☐ **Architecture and Assembly Language Workshops.** 8-bit, 16-bit, advance microprocessors — iAPX 86, 88, 186, 286; microcontrollers MCS®-48/49/51 and MCS®-96.

- ☐ **Programming and Operating System Workshops.** iRMX Operating System, PL/M, Pascal, XENIX*, C Language, iDIS.™

- ☐ **Special Products Workshop.** Data Communications, NDs II and I²ICE.™

- ☐ **Commercial Database Systems Workshops.** System 2000® database management workshops.

- ☐ **Introductory Courses on Microprocessors.**

*XENIX is a trademark of Microsoft Corp.

As new products are introduced, additional courses are added to the workshop offerings. Prerequisite workshops or background knowledge are specified for many courses.

Microcomputer Workshops

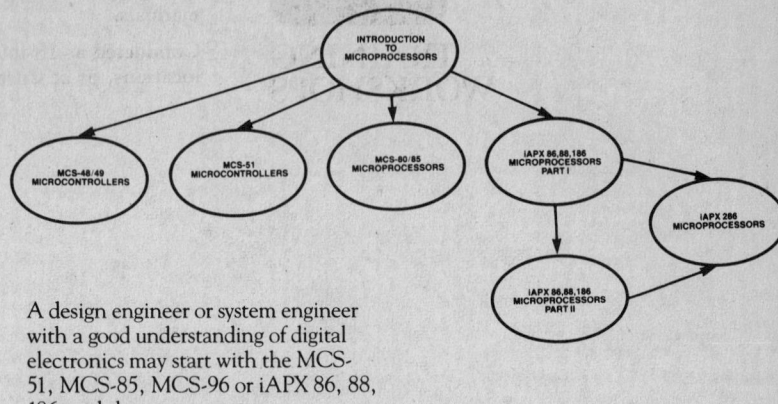

A design engineer or system engineer with a good understanding of digital electronics may start with the MCS-51, MCS-85, MCS-96 or iAPX 86, 88, 186 workshops.

Programming & Operating Systems Workshops

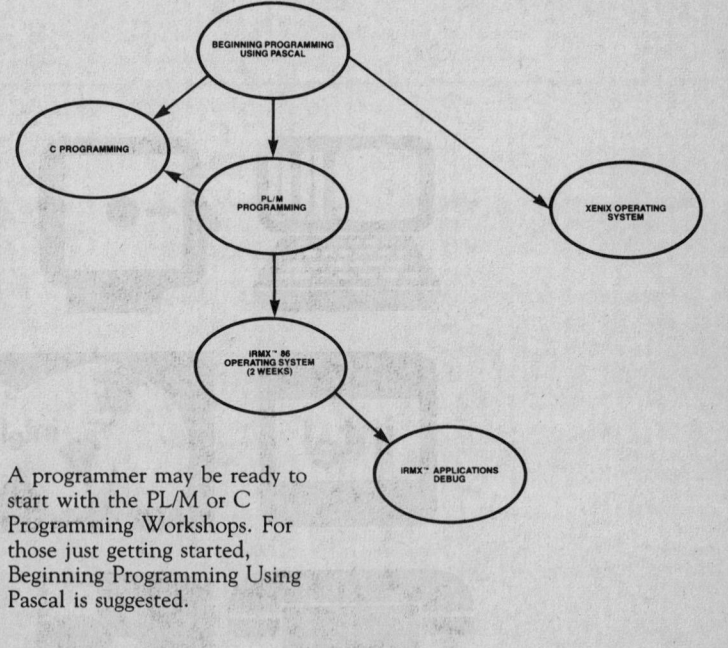

A programmer may be ready to start with the PL/M or C Programming Workshops. For those just getting started, Beginning Programming Using Pascal is suggested.

SPECIFICATIONS

TRAINING LOCATIONS AND DATES

Workshops are offered nearly every week at Intel Training Centers. A Workshop Catalog that details scheduled dates and locations of specific workshops is distributed twice a year. You may obtain your catalog from Intel's Literature Department, your nearest Intel Sales Office, or by calling your Intel Training Center.

CUSTOMER-SITE WORKSHOPS

Training workshops may also be held at the customer's site. All instructional materials and laboratory equipment are brought in by Intel, together with a qualified Intel instructor to conduct the session.

Customer-Site Workshops offer the following benefits:

- ☐ Intensive, personalized training focused on the customer's engineering staff.
- ☐ Adjustments to the courses/sessions to fit the backgrounds and needs of the participants.
- ☐ Improved learning atmosphere as a result of co-workers training together and receiving quality, uniform instruction.
- ☐ Convenience, because the class can be scheduled according to the customer's needs.
- ☐ Cost-effectiveness, because more personnel can be trained at a lower cost per person.

Where is Intel Training?

BOSTON AREA
(617) 256-1374
TWX 710-343-6333

CHICAGO AREA
(312) 981-7250
TWX 910-651-5881

DALLAS
(214) 484-8051
TWX 910-860-5617

LOS ANGELES
Call San Francisco
(415) 940-7800

SAN FRANCISCO BAY AREA
(415) 940-7800
TWX 910-379-5082

WASHINGTON D.C. AREA
(301) 474-2878
TWX 910-997-0428

TORONTO AREA
(416) 675-2105
Telex (389) 69-89278

LONDON AREA
Swindon (0793) 488-388
Telex 444447

MUNICH
(089) 5389-1
Telex 523177

PARIS AREA
Rungis (01) 687-22-21
Telex 270475

STOCKHOLM AREA
Bromma (08) 98.53.85
Telex 12261

MILAN
39-2-8240006
Telex 311271

TOKYO, Shinbashi
03-437-6611

OSAKA
Call Tokyo
03-437-6611

ROTTERDAM
(10) 21.23.77
Telex 22283

COPENHAGEN
(1) 182-000
Telex 19567

ISRAEL
Haifa
(972) 452-4261
Telex 46511

HONG KONG
5-215311/7
Telex 60410 ITLHK HX

WORKSHOP TUITION

Standard Tuition—Includes course notebook, literature, materials (such as the SDK-85 kit for Introduction to Microprocessors Workshop), coffee and any refreshments which may be provided depending on location and specific workshop.

Tuition Discounts—Group rate tuition applies when an organization enrolls three or more individuals in the same course (same date and location) at the same time.

Prepaid Tuition Certificates—Purchased in booklets of 12 (for the price of 10), certificates may be used for enrolling in most workshops. These certificates facilitate workshop attendance without lengthy approval cycles. Orders for the prepaid tuition certificates may be placed through the nearest Intel Training Center or Intel Field Sales Office. Tuition booklets will be sent via registered mail.

ENROLLMENT INFORMATION

To enroll, call the appropriate Intel Training Center between the hours of 8:30 a.m. to 12:00 noon and 1:00 p.m. to 4:30 p.m. and ask for Customer Training.

A confirmation number will be issued upon enrollment to guarantee each registration.

Workshops begin at 8:30 a.m. and end at approximately 5:00 p.m.

SAMPLE COURSE OUTLINE

iAPX 86, 88, 186 Microprocessors

DAY 1
The iAPX Product Family
Introduction to Microprocessors
iAPX 86, 88, 186, 188 Programming Model
Physical Addressing and Segmentation
Data Transfer and I/O Instructions
Overview of Development Process and AEDIT
Lab: Using Tex Editor and Assembler

DAY 2
Arithmetic, Logical, and Conditional Instructions
Defining Data and Addressing Modes
Series III Debugger, ASM Controls, and SUBMIT Files
Minimum and Maximum Mode, Queue Operation, and the CPU Chip Set
Lab: DEBUT-86 and Accessing Data

DAY 3
Procedures and Stack Operations
Programming with Multiple Segments
Interrupts and the 8259A
Memory and I/O Interfacing
Lab: Using Procedures, Multiple Segments and Interrupts

DAY 4
Programming Techniques
Modular Programming using LINK86 and LOC86
Introduction to the iAPX 186, 188 CPU
Optional ICE
Lab: Multiple Module Program and using Programming Techniques

DAY 5
iAPX 186, 188 Hardware Interface
Coprocessors
MULTIBUS® System Interface
The iAPX 286 and the iAPX 386

Intel Corporation
Customer Support Operations
2402 West Beardsley Road
Phoenix, Arizona 85027

Intel International Ltd.
Customer Support Operations
Pipers Way
Swindon, Wiltshire
England, SN31RJ

Intel Japan K.K.
IJKK Customer Support Operations
4-15-1 Tsurumaki
Setagaya-Ku, Tokyo 154
Japan

iMBX 100/110/120/130
MULTIBUS® EXCHANGE
HARDWARE SUBSCRIPTION SERVICE

- **Customized Monthly Update Packages Contain:**
  - Product Histories providing current information on functional changes to Intel products and improvements potentially affecting customer applications
  - Ancillary Notes clarifying and correcting documentation and keeping customers informed of product changes/enhancements
  - Revised Hardware Reference Manuals and Schematics

- **Available for MULTIBUS®, MULTIMODULE™, and BITBUS™ Products**
- **Available for SYP 310**

Intel's MULTIBUS EXCHANGE Hardware Subscription Service is a monthly publication that supports Intel manufactured board and system products. iMBX consists of twelve update packages (sent at the end of each month) containing valuable information that keeps subscribers informed of any changes and/or improvements made to their Intel products. This service allows subscribers to track product changes and, by evaluating or implementing them, to better utilize their Intel products and avoid any potential problems.

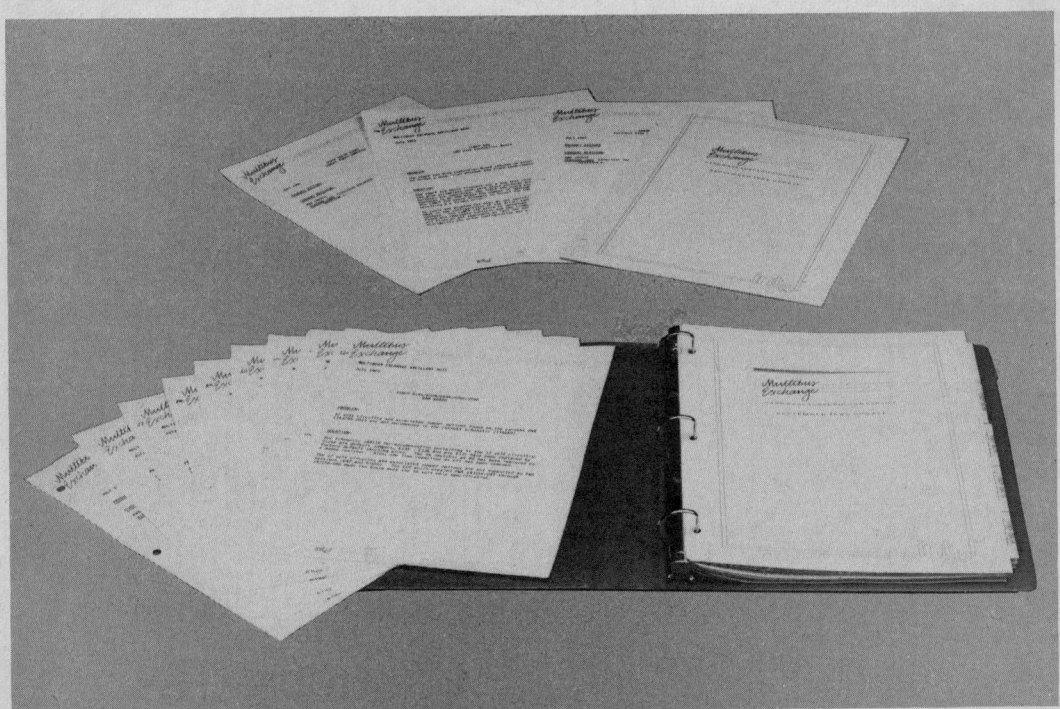

Intel Corporation assumes no responsibility for the use of any circuitry other than circuitry embodied in an Intel product. No other circuit patent licenses are implied. Information contained herein supersedes previously published specifications on these devices from Intel.

©Intel Corporation, 1985

iMBX 100/110/120/130

SUBSCRIPTIONS

MULTIBUS® EXCHANGE customers may subscribe for any combination of over 70 Intel products supported by iMBX. The initial subscription package contains a complete Product History from production release and a notebook in which to file future updates. In addition, iMBX customers receive eleven monthly update packages containing Product Histories, which are written summaries of Engineering Change Orders, and Ancillary notes, which are articles that relate documentation corrections and document suggested changes and/or enhancements to Intel products. The iMBX customers will receive an update package each month even if no changes occurred to their subscription products.

ADDITIONAL MATERIALS

Also included in iMBX monthly update packages are announcements, Dear Customer letters, revised schematics, and new copies of revised Hardware Reference Manuals for the products for which they have subscribed.

ORDERING iMBX

Orders for the MULTIBUS EXCHANGE are a combination of a base order (iMBX 100), plus an order for each product for which they would like to subscribe. MULTIBUS boards, chassis, and backplanes are ordered as iMBX 110, MULTIMODULE and BITBUS boards are ordered as iMBX 120, and the System 310 as iMBX 130.

INSITE™
USER'S PROGRAM LIBRARY

- Program Library Catalog Offering Hundreds of Programs
- Diskettes and Listings Available for Library Programs
- New Program Updates Sent During Subscription Period
- Accepted Program Submittals Entitle You to a Free Membership or Free Program Package
- Free Membership to Software Support Standard Contract Customers
- Free Membership to Warranty Customers
- CP/M 80, ISIS II, iNDX, and iRMX 86™ Operating Systems Supported
- Programs for 8048, 8041, 8051, 8052HB, 8080/8085, 8086/8088, 80286 Processors

Membership. Membership in Insite Library is available on an annual basis. Intel customers may become members through an accepted program contribution or paid membership fee.

Program Submittals. The Insite Library is built on program submittals contributed by users. Customers are encouraged to submit their programs. (Details and forms are available through the Insite Library.) For each accepted program, submittors will receive membership with Insite for one year or a free program package.

Program Library Service. Diskettes, or Source Listings are available for every program in Insite Library. Membership is required to purchase programs.

Insite™ Program Library Catalog. Each member will be sent the Program Library Catalog consisting of an abstract for each program indicating the function of the routine, required hardware and software, and memory requirements.

Insite offices are worldwide, with five locations to serve you:

NORTH AMERICA
Intel Corporation
2402 W. Beardsley Road
Phoenix, Arizona 85027
ATTN: Insite User's Program Library
Telephone: 602-869-3686

THE ORIENT
Intel Japan K.K.
5-6 Tohkohdai, Toyosato-cho,
Tsukuba-gun, Ibaraki, 300-26, Japan
ATTN: Insite User's Program Library
Telephone: 029747-8511

EUROPE
Intel Corporation S.A.R.L.
5 Place de la Balance
Silic 223
94528 Rungis Cedex, France
ATTN: Insite User's Program Library
Telephone: 0687-22-21

Intel Semiconductor GmbH
Seidlstrasse 27
8000 Muenchen 2
West Germany
ATTN: Insite User's Program Library
Telephone: 089-5389-1

Intel Corporation (U.K.) Ltd.
Pipers Way
Swindon SN3 LRJ
Wiltshire, England
ATTN: Insite User's Program Library
Telephone: 0793-488-388

For more information call your local Intel Sales Office or the Phoenix Insite User's Program Library location.

INSITE™ USER'S PROGRAM LIBRARY

- Membership Information

    — Library members have available a variety of programs, Insite catalogs, updates and special discount offers.

    — Annual membership forms may be sent to the local library (see sample form and location list on back page).

    — Membership fee to be covered by check, Purchase Order, or accepted program submittal.

- Ordering Programs

    — Library membership required.

    — Refer to the Insite catalog to determine program needs and order numbers.

    — Program order forms should be sent to the local library (sample form provided on the following page).

    — Telephone orders are accepted, with verbal Purchase Order numbers expediting delivery

    — Program orders are filled within two days, delivery within a week.

    * Call the local Insite library with questions on program orders or technical assistance in program selection.

- Program submittals follow these guidelines:

    — Write in a language capable of compilation/assembly currently supported by Intel.

    — Furnish a well documented source code and listing.

    — Provide a link and locate (or equivalent) listing.

    — Assure validity by inclusion of a demonstration program.

    — Complete submittal form, available in the catalog.

    * Upon the program's technical acceptance to the library, submitter may choose up to three FREE programs (up to $300 value) or a FREE annual membership.

INSITE™ USER'S PROGRAM LIBRARY

Program Order Form

P.O. NO. # _____   AMOUNT ENCLOSED $ _____

ADDRESS: (please print) Membership Information

NAME _____   COMPANY _____

STREET _____   PHONE NO. _____

CITY _____   STATE _____

PLEASE CHECK: ☐ ISIS   ☐ CP/M   ☐ iNDX   ☐ iRMX
               ☐ Double Density ☐ Double Density
               ☐ Single Density ☐ Single Density ☐ Listing
               ☐ iPDS   ☐ iPDS

ORDER NO.	TITLE

INSITE™ USER'S PROGRAM LIBRARY

Membership Form

I WISH TO BECOME A MEMBER OF INSITE. ENCLOSED IS:
- ☐ CHECK/MONEY ORDER
- ☐ PURCHASE ORDER
- ☐ PROGRAM SUBMITTAL

MEMBER NAME: _____

COMPANY: _____

ADDRESS: _____

_____

_____

TELEPHONE: _____

REFER TO THE INSITE PRICE LIST FOR ANNUAL MEMBERSHIP FEE.

RETURN COMPLETED FORM TO THE NEAREST INSITE OFFICE:

NORTH AMERICA

Intel Corporation
2402 W. Beardsley Road
Phoenix, Arizona 85027
ATTN: Insite User's Program Library
Telephone: 602-869-3686

THE ORIENT

Intel Japan K.K.
5-6 Tohkohdai, Toyosato-cho,
Tsukuba-gun, Ibaraki, 300-26, Japan
ATTN: Insite User's Program Library
Telephone: 029747-8511

EUROPE

Intel Corporation S.A.R.L.
5 Place de la Balance
Silic 223
94528 Rungis Cedex, France
ATTN: Insite User's Program Library
Telephone: 0687-22-21

Intel Semiconductor GmbH
Seidlstrasse 27
8000 Muenchen 2
West Germany
ATTN: Insite User's Program Library
Telephone: 089-5389-1

Intel Corporation (U.K.) Ltd.
Pipers Way
Swindon SN3 LRJ
Wiltshire, England
ATTN: Insite User's Program Library
Telephone: 0793-488-388

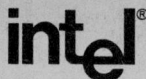

iRUG DESCRIPTION

iRUG is the Intel iRMX™ User's Group. It is a non-profit group chartered to establish a forum for users of the iRMX Operating System and to promote and encourage development of iRMX based software.

iRUG membership is for licensed iRMX Operating System users and their employees. Benefits of membership include: access to the user's library of iRMX software tools and utilities; membership in local and international chapters; access to the group bulletin board; receipt of quarterly international newsletters; synopsis of software problem reports (SPRs) submitted by members; opportunity to present papers and conduct workshops; invitations to seminars devoted to the use of Intel products.

The user's library, maintained by iRUG, contains software programs written and submitted by members and Intel employees. Programs available range from file or directory manipulation commands and terminal attribute selection utilities to dynamic logon, background job facilities and basic communication utilities.

Programs in the library are available through a telephone dial-up service and diskette exchange.

Local and international iRUG chapters provide a forum for members to meet other iRMX Operating System users in an informal setting. At local meetings and the annual international seminar, members can discuss their ideas, share their experiences and techniques, and give feedback to Intel for future improvements and features of the iRMX Operating System. The meetings also showcase new products offered by Intel and other developments in iRMX based software supplied by other companies.

iRUG sponsors a Special Interest Group (SIG) on the CompuServe Information Service. The SIG offers two features, message facilities and an online conference facility. The message facility (bulletin board) allows members to leave and receive messages from other members. These might include problems and solutions regarding the iRMX Operating System or new techniques to be shared. The online conference facility allows users to hold scheduled meetings on any topic. Whatever information a member types at his/her terminal will be displayed at all terminals logged into the conference facility.

"Human Interface" is iRUG's quarterly international newsletter. It serves as a supplement to chapter meetings by providing: library listings, information on the latest releases of products running on the iRMX Operating System; officer messages; member SPRs; release and update plans for the iRMX Operating System; and member articles.

If you are interested in becoming a member of iRUG or desire further information, contact the Intel iRUG Coordinator.
        Catherine R. Moon
        5200 N.E. Elam Young Parkway
        Hillsboro, OR 97123
        Mailstop HF2-57
        (503) 640-7038

DOMESTIC SALES OFFICES

ALABAMA
Intel Corp.
5015 Bradford Drive
Suite 2
Huntsville 35805
Tel: (205) 830-4010

ARIZONA
Intel Corp.
11225 N. 28th Drive
Suite 214D
Phoenix 85029
Tel: (602) 869-4980

Intel Corp.
1161 N. El Dorado Place
Suite 301
Tucson 85715
Tel: (602) 299-6815

CALIFORNIA
Intel Corp.
21515 Vanowen Street
Suite 116
Canoga Park 91303
Tel: (818) 704-8500

Intel Corp.
2250 E. Imperial Highway
Suite 218
El Segundo 90245
Tel: (213) 640-6040

Intel Corp.
1510 Arden Way, Suite 101
Sacramento 95815
Tel: (916) 920-8096

Intel Corp.
4350 Executive Drive
Suite 105
San Diego 92121
(619) 452-5880

Intel Corp.*
2000 East 4th Street
Suite 100
Santa Ana 92705
Tel: (714) 835-9642
TWX: 910-595-1114

Intel Corp.*
1350 Shorebird Way
Mt. View 94043
Tel: (415) 968-8086
TWX: 910-339-9279
910-338-0255

COLORADO
Intel Corp.
3300 Mitchell Lane, Suite 210
Boulder 80301
Tel: (303) 442-8088

Intel Corp.
4445 Northpark Drive
Suite 100
Colorado Springs 80907
Tel: (303) 594-6622

Intel Corp.*
650 S. Cherry Street
Suite 915
Denver 80222
Tel: (303) 321-8086
TWX: 910-931-2289

CONNECTICUT
Intel Corp.
26 Mill Plain Road
Danbury 06810
Tel: (203) 748-3130
TWX: 710-456-1199

EMC Corp.
222 Summer Street
Stamford 06901
Tel: (203) 327-2934

FLORIDA
Intel Corp.
242 N. Westmonte Drive
Suite 105
Altamonte Springs 32714
Tel: (305) 869-5588

Intel Corp.
6363 N.W. 6th Way, Suite 100
Ft. Lauderdale 33309
Tel: (305) 771-0600
TWX: 510-956-9407

FLORIDA (Cont'd)
Intel Corp.
11300 4th Street North
Suite 170
St. Petersburg 33702
Tel: (813) 577-2413

GEORGIA
Intel Corp.
3280 Pointe Parkway
Suite 200
Norcross 30092
Tel: (404) 449-0541

ILLINOIS
Intel Corp.*
300 N. Martingale Road, Suite 400
Schaumburg 60172
Tel: (312) 310-8031

INDIANA
Intel Corp.
8777 Purdue Road
Suite 125
Indianapolis 46268
Tel: (317) 875-0623

IOWA
Intel Corp.
St. Andrews Building
1930 St. Andrews Drive N.E.
Cedar Rapids 52402
Tel: (319) 393-5510

KANSAS
Intel Corp.
8400 W. 110th Street
Suite 170
Overland Park 66210
Tel: (913) 345-2727

LOUISIANA
Industrial Digital Systems Corp.
Tel: (504) 899-1654

MARYLAND
Intel Corp.*
7321 Parkway Drive South
Suite C
Hanover 21076
Tel: (301) 796-7500
TWX: 710-862-1944

Intel Corp.
7833 Walker Drive
Greenbelt 20770
Tel: (301) 441-1020

MASSACHUSETTS
Intel Corp.*
Westford Corp. Center
3 Carlisle Road
Westford 01886
Tel: (617) 629-3222
TWX: 710-343-6333

MICHIGAN
Intel Corp.
7071 Orchard Lake Road
Suite 100
West Bloomfield 48033
Tel: (313) 851-8096

MINNESOTA
Intel Corp.
3500 W. 80th Street
Suite 360
Bloomington 55431
Tel: (612) 835-6722
TWX: 910-576-2867

MISSOURI
Intel Corp.
4203 Earth City Expressway
Suite 131
Earth City 63045
Tel: (314) 291-1990

NEW JERSEY
Intel Corp.
Raritan Plaza III
Raritan Center
Edison 08837
Tel: (201) 225-3000
TWX: 710-480-6238

NEW MEXICO
Intel Corp.
8500 Menual Boulevard N.E.
Suite B 295
Albuquerque 87112
Tel: (505) 292-8086

NEW YORK
Intel Corp.*
300 Vanderbilt Motor Parkway
Hauppauge 11788
Tel: (516) 231-3300
TWX: 510-227-6236

Intel Corp.*
Suite 2B Hollowbrook Park
15 Myers Corners Road
Wappinger Falls 12590
Tel: (914) 297-6161
TWX: 510-248-0060

Intel Corp.*
211 White Spruce Boulevard
Rochester 14623
Tel: (716) 424-1050
TWX: 510-253-7391

T-Squared
6443 Ridings Road
Syracuse 13206
Tel: (315) 463-8592
TWX: 710-541-0554

T-Squared
7353 Pittsford-Victor Road
Victor 14564
Tel: (716) 924-9101
TWX: 510-254-8542

NORTH CAROLINA
Intel Corp.
5700 Executive Center Drive
Suite 213
Charlotte 28212
Tel: (704) 568-8966

Intel Corp.
2700 Wycliff Road
Suite 102
Raleigh 27607
Tel: (919) 781-8022

OHIO
Intel Corp.*
6500 Poe Avenue
Dayton 45414
Tel: (513) 890-5350
TWX: 810-450-2528

Intel Corp.*
Chagrin-Brainard Bldg., No. 300
28001 Chagrin Boulevard
Cleveland 44122
Tel: (216) 464-2736
TWX: 810-427-9298

OKLAHOMA
Intel Corp.
4157 S. Harvard Avenue
Suite 123
Tulsa 74135
Tel: (918) 749-8688

OREGON
Intel Corp.
10700 S.W. Beaverton
Hillsdale Highway
Suite 22
Beaverton 97005
Tel: (503) 641-8086
TWX: 910-467-8741

PENNSYLVANIA
Intel Corp.
1513 Cedar Cliff Drive
Camphill 17011
Tel: (717) 737-5035

Intel Corp.*
455 Pennsylvania Avenue
Fort Washington 19034
Tel: (215) 641-1000
TWX: 510-661-2077

Intel Corp.*
400 Penn Center Boulevard
Suite 610
Pittsburgh 15235
Tel: (412) 823-4970

Q.E.D. Electronics
139 Terwood Road
Box T
Willow Grove 19090
Tel: (215) 657-5600

PUERTO RICO
Intel Microprocessor Corp.
South Industrial Park
Las Piedras 00671
Tel: (809) 733-3030

TEXAS
Intel Corp.
313 E. Anderson Lane
Suite 314
Austin 78752
Tel: (512) 454-3628

Intel Corp.*
12300 Ford Road
Suite 380
Dallas 75234
Tel: (214) 241-8087
TWX: 910-860-5617

Intel Corp.*
7322 S.W. Freeway
Suite 1490
Houston 77074
Tel: (713) 988-8086
TWX: 910-881-2490

Industrial Digital Systems Corp.
5925 Sovereign
Suite 101
Houston 77036
Tel: (713) 988-9421

UTAH
Intel Corp.
5201 Green Street
Suite 290
Murray 84123
Tel: (801) 263-8051

VIRGINIA
Intel Corp.
1603 Santa Rosa Road
Suite 109
Richmond 23288
Tel: (804) 282-5668

WASHINGTON
Intel Corp.
110 110th Avenue N.E.
Suite 510
Bellevue 98004
Tel: (206) 453-8086
TWX: 910-443-3002

Intel Corp.
408 N. Mullan Road
Suite 102
Spokane 99206
Tel: (509) 928-8086

WISCONSIN
Intel Corp.
450 N. Sunnyslope Road
Suite 130
Chancellory Park I
Brookfield 53005
Tel: (414) 784-8087

CANADA

BRITISH COLUMBIA
Intel Semiconductor of Canada, Ltd.
301-2245 W. Broadway
Vancouver V6K 2E4
Tel: (604) 738-6522

ONTARIO
Intel Semiconductor of Canada, Ltd.
2650 Queensview Drive
Suite 250
Ottawa K2B 8H6
Tel: (613) 829-9714
TELEX: 053-4115

Intel Semiconductor of Canada, Ltd.
190 Attwell Drive
Suite 500
Rexdale M9W 6H8
Tel: (416) 675-2105
TELEX: 06983574

QUEBEC
Intel Semiconductor of Canada, Ltd.
620 St. Jean Blvd.
Pointe Claire H9R 3K3
Tel: (514) 694-9130
TWX: 514-694-9234

*Field Application Location

DOMESTIC DISTRIBUTORS

ALABAMA

Arrow Electronics, Inc.
1015 Henderson Road
Huntsville 35805
Tel: (205) 837-6955

†Hamilton/Avnet Electronics
4812 Commercial Drive N.W.
Huntsville 35805
Tel: (205) 837-7210
TWX: 810-726-2162

†Pioneer Electronics
4825 University Square
Huntsville 35805
Tel: (205) 837-9300
TWX: 810-726-2197

ARIZONA

†Hamilton/Avnet Electronics
505 S. Madison Drive
Tempe 85281
Tel: (602) 231-5100
TWX: 910-950-0077

Kierulff Electronics
4134 E. Wood Street
Phoenix 85040
Tel: (602) 437-0750
TWX: 910-951-1550

Wyle Distribution Group
17855 N. Black Canyon Highway
Phoenix 85023
Tel: (602) 866-2888

CALIFORNIA

Arrow Electronics, Inc.
19748 Dearborn Street
Chatsworth 91311
Tel: (818) 701-7500
TWX: 910-493-2086

Arrow Electronics
9511 Ridgehaven Court
San Diego 92123
Tel: (619) 565-4800
TLX: 888064

†Arrow Electronics, Inc.
521 Weddell Drive
Sunnyvale 94086
Tel: (408) 745-6600
TWX: 910-339-9371

Arrow Electronics, Inc.
2961 Dow Avenue
Tustin 92680
Tel: (714) 838-5422
TWX: 910-595-2860

†Avnet Electronics
350 McCormick Avenue
Costa Mesa 92626
Tel: (714) 754-6051
TWX: 910-595-1928

Hamilton/Avnet Electronics
1175 Bordeaux Drive
Sunnyvale 94086
Tel: (408) 743-3300
TWX: 910-339-9332

†Hamilton/Avnet Electronics
4545 Viewridge Avenue
San Diego 92123
Tel: (619) 571-7500
TWX: 910-595-2638

†Hamilton/Avnet Electronics
20501 Plummer Street
Chatsworth 91311
Tel: (818) 700-6271
TWX: 910-494-2207

†Hamilton/Avnet Electronics
4103 Northgate Boulevard
Sacramento 95834
Tel: (916) 920-3150

Hamilton/Avnet Electronics
3002 G Street
Ontario 91311
Tel: (714) 989-9411

Hamilton/Avnet Electronics
19515 So. Vermont Avenue
Torrance 90502
Tel: (213) 615-3909
TWX: 910-349-6263

†Hamilton Electro Sales
10912 W. Washington Boulevard
Culver City 20230
Tel: (213) 558-2458
TWX: 910-340-6364

†Hamilton Electro Sales
3170 Pullman Street
Costa Mesa 92626
Tel: (714) 641-4150
TWX: 910-595-2638

CALIFORNIA (Cont'd)

Hamilton Electro Sales
9650 De Soto Avenue
Chatsworth 91311
Tel: (818) 700-6500

Kierulff Electronics
10824 Hope Street
Cypress 90430
Tel: (714) 220-6300

Kierulff Electronics, Inc.
1180 Murphy Avenue
San Jose 95131
Tel: (408) 947-3471
TWX: 910-379-6430

Kierulff Electronics, Inc.
14101 Franklin Avenue
Tustin 92680
Tel: (714) 731-5711
TWX: 910-595-2599

†Kierulff Electronics, Inc.
5650 Jillson Street
Commerce 90040
Tel: (213) 725-0325
TWX: 910-580-3666

Wyle Distribution Group
26560 Agoura Street
Calabasas 91302
Tel: (818) 880-9000
TWX: 818-372-0232

†Wyle Distribution Group
124 Maryland Street
El Segundo 90245
Tel: (213) 322-8100
TWX: 910-348-7140 or 7111

†Wyle Distribution Group
17872 Cowan Avenue
Irvine 92714
Tel: (714) 843-9953
TWX: 910-595-1572

†Wyle Distribution Group
11151 Sun Center Drive
Rancho Cordova 95670
Tel: (916) 638-5282

†Wyle Distribution Group
9525 Chesapeake Drive
San Diego 92123
Tel: (619) 565-9171
TWX: 910-335-1590

†Wyle Distribution Group
3000 Bowers Avenue
Santa Clara 95051
Tel: (408) 727-2500
TWX: 910-338-0296

Wyle Military
17810 Teller Avenue
Irvine 92750
Tel: (714) 851-9958
TWX: 310-371-9127

Wyle Systems
7382 Lampson Avenue
Garden Grove 92641
Tel: (714) 851-9953
TWX: 910-595-2642

COLORADO

†Wyle Distribution Group
451 E. 124th Avenue
Thornton 80241
Tel: (303) 457-9953
TWX: 910-936-0770

†Hamilton/Avnet Electronics
8765 E. Orchard Road
Suite 708
Englewood 80111
Tel: (303) 740-1017
TWX: 910-935-0787

CONNECTICUT

†Arrow Electronics, Inc.
12 Beaumont Road
Wallingford 06492
Tel: (203) 265-7741
TWX: 710-476-0162

†Hamilton/Avnet Electronics
Commerce Industrial Park
Commerce Drive
Danbury 06810
Tel: (203) 797-2800
TWX: 710-456-9974

†Pioneer Northeast Electronics
112 Main Street
Norwalk 06851
Tel: (203) 853-1515
TWX: 710-468-3373

FLORIDA

†Arrow Electronics, Inc.
350 Fairway Drive
Deerfield Beach 33441
Tel: (305) 429-8200
TWX: 510-955-9456

†Arrow Electronics, Inc.
1001 N.W. 62nd Street
Suite 108
Ft. Lauderdale 33309
Tel: (305) 776-7790
TWX: 510-955-9456

†Arrow Electronics, Inc.
50 Woodlake Drive W., Bldg. B
Palm Bay 32905
Tel: (305) 725-1480
TWX: 510-959-6337

†Hamilton/Avnet Electronics
6801 N.W. 15th Way
Ft. Lauderdale 33309
Tel: (305) 971-2900
TWX: 510-956-3097

†Hamilton/Avnet Electronics
3197 Tech. Drive North
St. Petersburg 33702
Tel: (813) 576-3930
TWX: 810-863-0374

Hamilton/Avnet Electronics
6947 University Boulevard
Winterpark 32792
Tel: (305) 628-3888
TWX: 810-853-0322

†Pioneer Electronics
221 N. Lake Boulevard
Suite 412
Alta Monte Springs 32701
Tel: (305) 834-9090
TWX: 810-853-0284

†Pioneer Electronics
674 S. Military Trail
Deerfield Beach 33442
Tel: (305) 428-8877
TWX: 510-955-9653

GEORGIA

†Arrow Electronics, Inc.
3155 Northwoods Parkway, Suite A
Norcross 30071
Tel: (404) 449-8252
TWX: 810-766-0439

Hamilton/Avnet Electronics
5825 D. Peachtree Corners
Norcross 30092
Tel: (404) 447-7500
TWX: 810-766-0432

Pioneer Electronics
5835B Peachtree Corners E
Norcross 30092
Tel: (404) 448-1711
TWX: 810-766-4515

ILLINOIS

†Arrow Electronics, Inc.
2000 E. Alonquin Street
Schaumburg 60195
Tel: (312) 397-3440
TWX: 910-291-3544

†Hamilton/Avnet Electronics
1130 Thorndale Avenue
Bensenville 60106
Tel: (312) 860-7780
TWX: 910-227-0060

†Pioneer Electronics
1551 Carmen Drive
Elk Grove Village 60007
Tel: (312) 437-9680
TWX: 910-222-1834

INDIANA

†Arrow Electronics, Inc.
2495 Directors Row, Suite H
Indianapolis 46241
(317) 243-9353
TWX: 810-341-3119

Hamilton/Avnet Electronics
485 Gradle Drive
Carmel 46032
Tel: (317) 844-9333
TWX: 810-260-3966

†Pioneer Electronics
6408 Castleplace Drive
Indianapolis 46250
Tel: (317) 849-7300
TWX: 810-260-1794

KANSAS

†Hamilton/Avnet Electronics
9219 Quivera Road
Overland Park 66215
Tel: (913) 888-8900
TWX: 910-743-0005

MARYLAND

Arrow Electronics, Inc.
8300 Guilford Road #H
Rivers Center
Columbia 21046
Tel: (301) 995-0003
TWX: 710-236-9005

†Hamilton/Avnet Electronics
6822 Oak Hall Lane
Columbia 21045
Tel: (301) 995-3500
TWX: 710-862-1861

†Mesa Technology Corporation
16021 Industrial Drive
Gaithersburg 20877
Tel: (301) 948-4350
TWX: 710-828-9702

†Pioneer Electronics
9100 Gaither Road
Gaithersburg 20877
Tel: (301) 948-0710
TWX: 710-828-0545

MASSACHUSETTS

†Arrow Electronics, Inc.
1 Arrow Drive
Woburn 01801
Tel: (617) 933-8130
TWX: 710-393-6770

†Hamilton/Avnet Electronics
50 Tower Office Park
Woburn 01801
Tel: (617) 935-9700
TWX: 710-393-0382

Pioneer Northeast Electronics
44 Hartwell Avenue
Lexington 02173
Tel: (617) 863-1200
TWX: 710-326-6617

MICHIGAN

Arrow Electronics, Inc.
755 Phoenix Drive
Ann Arbor 48104
Tel: (313) 971-8220
TWX: 810-223-6020

†Hamilton/Avnet Electronics
32487 Schoolcraft Road
Livonia 48150
Tel: (313) 522-4700
TWX: 810-242-8775

Hamilton/Avnet Electronics
2215 29th Street S.E.
Space A5
Grand Rapids 49508
Tel: (616) 243-8805
TWX: 810-273-6921

†Pioneer Electronics
13485 Stamford
Livonia 48150
Tel: (313) 525-1800
TWX: 810-242-3271

MINNESOTA

†Arrow Electronics, Inc.
5230 W. 73rd Street
Edina 55435
Tel: (612) 830-1800
TWX: 910-576-3125

Hamilton/Avnet Electronics
10300 Bren Road East
Minnetonka 55343
Tel: (612) 932-0600
TWX: (910) 576-2720

†Pioneer Electronics
10203 Bren Road East
Minnetonka 55343
Tel: (612) 935-5444
TWX: 910-576-2738

MISSOURI

Arrow Electronics, Inc.
2380 Schuetz
St. Louis 63141
Tel: (314) 567-6888
TWX: 910-764-0882

†Hamilton/Avnet Electronics
13743 Shoreline Court
Earth City 63045
Tel: (314) 344-1200
TWX: 910-762-0684

†Microcomputer System Technical Demonstrator Centers

DOMESTIC DISTRIBUTORS

NEW HAMPSHIRE

†Arrow Electronics, Inc.
3 Perimeter Road
Manchester 03103
Tel: (603) 668-6968
TWX: 710-220-1684

Hamilton/Avnet Electronics
444 E. Industrial Drive
Manchester 03104
Tel: (603) 624-9400

NEW JERSEY

†Arrow Electronics, Inc.
6000 Lincoln East
Marlton 08053
Tel: (609) 596-8000
TWX: 710-897-0829

†Arrow Electronics, Inc.
2 Industrial Road
Fairfield 07006
Tel: (201) 575-5300
TWX: 710-998-2206

†Hamilton/Avnet Electronics
1 Keystone Avenue
Bldg. 36
Cherry Hill 08003
Tel: (609) 424-0110
TWX: 710-940-0262

†Hamilton/Avnet Electronics
10 Industrial
Fairfield 07006
Tel: (201) 575-3390
TWX: 710-734-4388

†Pioneer Northeast Electronics
45 Route 46
Pinebrook 07058
Tel: (201) 575-3510
TWX: 710-734-4382

†MTI Systems Sales
383 Route 46 W
Fairfield 07006
Tel: (201) 227-5552

NEW MEXICO

Alliance Electronics Inc.
11030 Cochiti S.E.
Albuquerque 87123
Tel: (505) 292-3360
TWX: 910-989-1151

Hamilton/Avnet Electronics
2524 Baylor Drive S.E.
Albuquerque 87106
Tel: (505) 765-1500
TWX: 910-989-0614

NEW YORK

†Arrow Electronics, Inc.
25 Hub Drive
Melville 11747
Tel: (516) 694-6800
TWX: 510-224-6126

†Arrow Electronics, Inc.
3375 Brighton-Henrietta Townline Road
Rochester 14623
Tel: (716) 427-0300
TWX: 510-253-4766

Arrow Electronics, Inc.
7705 Maltage Drive
Liverpool 13088
Tel: (315) 652-1000
TWX: 710-545-0230

Arrow Electronics, Inc.
20 Oser Avenue
Hauppauge 11788
Tel: (516) 231-1000
TWX: 510-227-6623

Hamilton/Avnet Electronics
333 Metro Park
Rochester 14623
Tel: (716) 475-9130
TWX: 510-253-5470

Hamilton/Avnet Electronics
103 Twin Oaks Drive
Syracuse 13206
Tel: (315) 437-2641
TWX: 710-541-1560

†Hamilton/Avnet Electronics
933 Motor Parkway
Hauppauge 11788
Tel: (516) 231-9800
TWX: 510-224-6166

†Pioneer Northeast Electronics
1806 Vestal Parkway East
Vestal 13850
Tel: (607) 748-8211
TWX: 510-252-0893

NEW YORK (Cont'd)

†Pioneer Northeast Electronics
60 Crossway Park West
Woodbury, Long Island 11797
Tel: (516) 921-8700
TWX: 510-221-2184

Pioneer Northeast Electronics
840 Fairport Park
Fairport 14450
Tel: (716) 381-7070
TWX: 510-253-7001

†MTI Systems Sales
38 Harbor Park Drive
P.O. Box 271
Port Washington 11050
Tel: (516) 621-6200
TWX: 510-223-0846

NORTH CAROLINA

Arrow Electronics, Inc.
5240 Greendairy Road
Raleigh 27604
Tel: (919) 876-3132
TWX: 510-928-1856

†Hamilton/Avnet Electronics
3510 Spring Forest Drive
Raleigh 27604
Tel: (919) 878-0819
TWX: 510-928-1836

Pioneer Electronics
9801 A-Southern Pine Boulevard
Charlotte 28210
Tel: (704) 524-8188
TWX: 810-621-0366

OHIO

Arrow Electronics, Inc.
7620 McEwen Road
Centerville 45459
Tel: (513) 435-5563
TWX: 810-459-1611

†Arrow Electronics, Inc.
6238 Cochran Road
Solon 44139
Tel: (216) 248-3990
TWX: 810-427-9409

†Hamilton/Avnet Electronics
954 Senate Drive
Dayton 45459
Tel: (513) 433-0610
TWX: 810-450-2531

†Hamilton/Avnet Electronics
4588 Emery Industrial Parkway
Warrensville Heights 44128
Tel: (216) 831-3500
TWX: 810-427-9452

†Pioneer Electronics
4433 Interpoint Boulevard
Dayton 45424
Tel: (513) 236-9900
TWX: 810-459-1622

†Pioneer Electronics
4800 E. 131st Street
Cleveland 44105
Tel: (216) 587-3600
TWX: 810-422-2211

OKLAHOMA

Arrow Electronics, Inc.
4719 S. Memorial Drive
Tulsa 74145
Tel: (918) 665-7700

OREGON

†Almac Electronics Corporation
1885 N.W. 169th Place
Beaverton 97006
Tel: (503) 629-8090
TWX: 910-467-8743

Hamilton/Avnet Electronics
6024 S.W. Jean Road
Bldg. C, Suite 10
Lake Oswego 97034
Tel: (503) 635-7848
TWX: 910-455-8179

Wyle Distribution Group
5250 N.E. Elam Young Parkway
Suite 600
Hillsboro 97124
Tel: (503) 640-6000
TWX: 910-460-2203

PENNSYLVANIA

†Arrow Electronics, Inc.
650 Seco Road
Monroeville 15146
Tel: (412) 856-7000

PENNSYLVANIA (Cont'd)

Pioneer Electronics
259 Kappa Drive
Pittsburgh 15238
Tel: (412) 782-2300
TWX: 710-795-3122

†Pioneer Electronics
261 Gibralter Road
Horsham 19044
Tel: (215) 674-4000
TWX: 510-665-6778

TEXAS

†Arrow Electronics, Inc.
3220 Commander Drive
Carrollton 75006
Tel: (214) 380-6464
TWX: 910-860-5377

†Arrow Electronics, Inc.
10899 Kinghurst
Suite 100
Houston 77099
Tel: (713) 530-4700
TWX: 910-880-4439

Arrow Electronics, Inc.
10125 Metropolitan
Austin 78758
Tel: (512) 835-4180
TWX: 910-874-1348

†Hamilton/Avnet Electronics
2401 Rutland
Austin 78757
Tel: (512) 837-8911
TWX: 910-874-1319

†Hamilton/Avnet Electronics
2111 W. Walnut Hill Lane
Irving 75062
Tel: (214) 659-4100
TWX: 910-860-5929

†Hamilton/Avnet Electronics
8750 West Park
Houston 77063
Tel: (713) 780-1771
TWX: 910-881-5523

Pioneer Electronics
9901 Burnet Road
Austin 78758
Tel: (512) 835-4000
TWX: 910-874-1323

Pioneer Electronics
13710 Omega Road
Dallas 75234
Tel: (214) 386-7300
TWX: 910-850-5563

Pioneer Electronics
5853 Point West Drive
Houston 77036
Tel: (713) 988-5555
TWX: 910-881-1606

UTAH

†Hamilton/Avnet Electronics
1585 West 2100 South
Salt Lake City 84119
Tel: (801) 972-2800
TWX: 910-925-4018

Wyle Distribution Group
1959 South 4130 West, Unit B
Salt Lake City 84104
Tel: (801) 974-9953

WASHINGTON

†Almac Electronics Corporation
14360 S.E. Eastgate Way
Bellevue 98007
Tel: (206) 643-9992
TWX: 910-444-2067

Arrow Electronics, Inc.
14320 N.E. 21st Street
Bellevue 98007
Tel: (206) 643-4800
TWX: 910-444-2017

Hamilton/Avnet Electronics
14212 N.E. 21st Street
Bellevue 98005
Tel: (206) 453-5874
TWX: 910-443-2469

WISCONSIN

†Arrow Electronics, Inc.
430 W. Rausson Avenue
Oakcreek 53154
Tel: (414) 764-6600
TWX: 910-262-1193

WISCONSIN (Cont'd)

†Hamilton/Avnet Electronics
2975 Moorland Road
New Berlin 53151
Tel: (414) 784-4510
TWX: 910-262-1182

CANADA

ALBERTA

Hamilton/Avnet Electronics
2816 21st Street N.E.
Calgary T2E 6Z2
Tel: (403) 230-3586
TWX: 03-827-642

Zentronics
Bay No. 1
3300 14th Avenue N.E.
Calgary T2A 6J4
Tel: (403) 272-1021

BRITISH COLUMBIA

Hamilton/Avnet Electronics
105-2550 Boundry Road
Burnaby V5M 323
Tel: (604) 272-4242

Zentronics
108-11400 Bridgeport Road
Richmond V6X 1T2
Tel: (604) 273-5575
TWX: 04-5077-89

MANITOBA

Zentronics
590 Berry Street
Winnipeg R3H OS1
Tel: (204) 775-8661

ONTARIO

Arrow Electronics Inc.
24 Martin Ross Avenue
Downsview M3J 2K9
Tel: (416) 661-0220
TELEX: 06-218213

Arrow Electronics Inc.
148 Colonnade Road
Nepean K2E 7J5
Tel: (613) 226-6903

†Hamilton/Avnet Electronics
6845 Rexwood Road
Units G & H
Mississauga L4V 1R2
Tel: (416) 677-7432
TWX: 610-492-8867

†Hamilton/Avnet Electronics
210 Colonnade Road South
Nepean K2E 7L5
Tel: (613) 226-1700
TWX: 05-349-71

†Zentronics
8 Tilbury Court
Brampton L6T 3T4
Tel: (416) 451-9600
Tel: 06-976-78

Zentronics
564/10 Weber Street North
Waterloo N2L 5C6
Tel: (519) 884-5700

Zentronics
155 Colonnade Road
Unit 17
Nepean K2E 7K1
Tel: (613) 225-8840
TWX: 06-976-78

QUEBEC

Arrow Electronics Inc.
4050 -Jean Talon Quest
Montreal H4P 1W1
Tel: (514) 735-5511
TELEX: 05-25596

Arrow Electronics Inc.
909 Charest Blvd.
Quebec 61N 269
Tel: (418) 687-4231
TLX: 05-13388

Hamilton/Avnet Electronics
2795 Rue Halpern
St. Laurent H4S 1P8
Tel: (514) 335-1000
TWX: 610-421-3731

Zentronics
505 Locke Street
St. Laurent H4T 1X7
Tel: (514) 735-5361
TWX: 05-827-535

†Microcomputer System Technical Demonstrator Centers

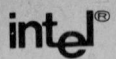

DOMESTIC SERVICE OFFICES

CALIFORNIA
Intel Corp.
21515 Vanowen
Suite 116
Canoga Park 91303
Tel: (818) 704-8500

Intel Corp.
2250 E. Imperial Way
Suite 218
El Segundo 90245
Tel: (213) 640-6040

Intel Corp.
1350 Shorebird Way
Mt. View 94043
Tel: (415) 968-8211
TWX: 910-339-9279
910-338-0255

Intel Corp.
2000 E. 4th Street
Suite 110
Santa Ana 92705
Tel: (714) 835-5577
TWX: 910-595-2475

Intel Corp.
4350 Executive Drive
Suite 150
San Diego 92121
Tel: (619) 452-5880

COLORADO
Intel Corp.
650 South Cherry
Suite 720
Denver 80222
Tel: (303) 321-8086
TWX: 910-931-2289

CONNECTICUT
Intel Corp.
26 Mill Plain Road
Danbury 06811
Tel: (203) 748-3130

FLORIDA
Intel Corp.
1500 N.W. 62nd Street
Suite 104
Ft. Lauderdale 33309
Tel: (305) 771-0600
TWX: 510-956-9407

FLORIDA (Cont'd)
Intel Corp.
242 N. Westmonte
Suite 105
Altamonte Springs 32714
Tel: (305) 869-5588

GEORGIA
Intel Corp.
3280 Pointe Parkway
Suite 200
Norcross 30092
Tel: (404) 441-1171

ILLINOIS
Intel Corp.
300 N. Martingale Rd.
Suite 300
Schaumburg 60194
Tel: (312) 310-8034
Dispatch: (312) 310-1803

KANSAS
Intel Corp.
8400 W. 110th Street
Suite 170
Overland Park 66210
Tel: (913) 642-8080

MARYLAND
Intel Corp.
5th Floor Product Service
7833 Walker Drive
Greenbelt 20770
Tel: (301) 441-1020

MASSACHUSETTS
Intel Corp.
27 Industrial Avenue
Chelmsford 01824
Tel: (617) 256-1800
TWX: 710-343-6333

MICHIGAN
Intel Corp.
7071 Orchard Lake Road
Suite 100
West Bloomfield 48033
Tel: (313) 851-8905

MISSOURI
Intel Corp.
4203 Earth City Expressway
Suite 143
Earth City 63045
Tel: (314) 291-2015

NEW JERSEY
Intel Corp.
385 Sylvan Avenue
Englewood Cliffs 07632
Tel: (201) 567-0820
TWX: 710-991-8593

Intel Corp.
Raritan Plaza III
Raritan Center
Edison 08817
Tel: (201) 225-3000

NORTH CAROLINA
Intel Corp.
2306 W. Meadowview Road
Suite 206
Greensboro 27407
Tel: (919) 294-1541

OHIO
Intel Corp.
Chagrin-Brainard Bldg.
Suite 305
28001 Chagrin Boulevard
Cleveland 44122
Tel: (216) 464-6915
TWX: 810-427-9298

Intel Corp.
6500 Poe
Dayton 45414
Tel: (513) 890-5350

OREGON
Intel Corp.
10700 S.W. Beaverton-Hillsdale
Highway
Suite 22
Beaverton 97005
Tel: (503) 641-8086
TWX: 910-467-8741

OREGON (Cont'd)
Intel Corp.
5200 N.E. Elam Young Parkway
Hillsboro 97123
Tel: (503) 681-8080

PENNSYLVANIA
Intel Corp.
201 Penn Center Boulevard
Suite 301 W
Pittsburgh 15235
Tel: (313) 354-1540

TEXAS
Intel Corp.
313 E. Anderson Lane
Suite 314
Austin 78752
Tel: (512)454-3628
TWX: 910-874-1347

Intel Corp.
12300 Ford Road
Suite 380
Dallas 75234
Tel: (214) 241-8087
TWX: 910-860-5617

WASHINGTON
Intel Corp.
110 110th Avenue N.E.
Suite 510
Bellevue 98004
Tel: 1-800-525-5560
TWX: 910-443-3002

WISCONSIN
Intel Corp.
450 N. Sunnyslope Road
Suite 130
Brookfield 53005
Tel: (414) 784-8087